Social Protest Literature

Social Protest Literature
An Encyclopedia of Works, Characters, Authors, and Themes

Patricia D. Netzley

ABC-CLIO

Santa Barbara, California
Denver, Colorado
Oxford, England

Cover illustration: Bastille Mob Mural (Morton Beebe–S.F./Corbis)

Library of Congress Cataloging-in-Publication Data
Netzley, Patricia D.
    Social protest literature: An encyclopedia of works, characters,
authors, and themes / Patricia D. Netzley.
    p.   cm.
    Includes bibliographical references and index.
    ISBN 0-87436-980-0
    1. Social problems in literature—Encyclopedias. 2. Protest
literature—Encyclopedias. I. Title.
PN56.S65N48   1999
809'.93355—dc21   98-43005
                                                      CIP

05 04 03 02 01 00 99   10 9 8 7 6 5 4 3 2 1

ABC-CLIO, Inc.
130 Cremona Drive, P.O. Box 1911
Santa Barbara, California 93116-1911

This book is printed on acid-free paper ∞ .

Manufactured in the United States of America

CONTENTS

SOCIAL PROTEST LITERATURE

ENTRIES BY CATEGORY

Authors

Abbey, Edward
Abrahams, Peter
Alcaeus
Alegría, Ciro
Aleramo, Sibilla
Allende, Isabel
Anand, Mulk Raj
Angelou, Maya
Aristophanes
Ariyoshi, Sawako
Atwood, Margaret
Baldwin, James
Balzac, Honoré de
Beauvoir, Simone de
Behn, Aphra
Bellamy, Edward
Berger, Thomas
Björnson, Björnstjerne
Boulle, Pierre
Bradbury, Ray
Breytenbach, Breyten
Brown, William Wells
Bryant, William Cullen
Burdick, Eugene
Burgess, Anthony
Burns, Robert
Camus, Albert
Clark, Walter Van Tilburg
Crabbe, George
Crabbe, Jack
Cullen, Countee
Davis, Rebecca Harding
Dickens, Charles
Dostoyevsky, Fyodor

Dreiser, Theodore
Dunbar-Nelson, Alice
Edgeworth, Maria
El Saadawi, Nawal
Ellison, Ralph
Endō, Shūsaku
Farah, Nuruddin
Ferlinghetti, Lawrence
France, Anatole
Franklin, Miles
Fuentes, Carlos
Gaines, Ernest J.
Galsworthy, John
Ginsberg, Allen
Gissing, George
Golding, William
Gorky, Maxim
Greene, Graham
Hansberry, Lorraine
Heller, Joseph
Hellman, Lillian
Hesse, Hermann
Hood, Thomas
Howe, Julia Ward
Hughes, Langston
Hugo, Victor
Hurston, Zora Neale
Huxley, Aldous
Ibsen, Henrik
Jackson, Helen Hunt
Jackson, Shirley
James, Henry
Johnson, James Weldon
Kafka, Franz
Kesey, Ken

Kundera, Milan
Larsen, Nella
Le Guin, Ursula
Lederer, William J.
Lee, Harper
Lessing, Doris
Lewis, Sinclair
London, Jack
Lowell, James Russell
Mann, Thomas
Markham, Edwin
Miller, Arthur
Miller, Henry
Morrison, Arthur
Morrison, Toni
Norris, Frank
northSun, nila
Olsen, Tillie
O'Neill, Eugene
Orwell, George
Paton, Alan
Plevier, Theodor
Rand, Ayn
Sartre, Jean-Paul
Schreiner, Olive
Shaw, George Bernard
Sinclair, Upton
Solzhenitsyn, Aleksandr
Steinbeck, John
Stowe, Harriet Beecher
Swift, Jonathan
Thompson, Eloise Bibb
Toer, Pramoedya Ananta
Tolstoi, Leo
Toomer, Jean

Atkins, Homer
Avery, Shug
Bakha
Beatty, Captain
Bibbett, Billy
Block
Blount, Gil
Breedlove, Cholly and Pauline
Bromden, Chief
Brown, Jonathan
Carlé, Lukas
Carlé, Rolf
Carlson, Georgiana
Castorp, Hans
Castro, Benito
Celie
Chancellor, Olive
Clamence, Jean-Baptiste
Clifton, Tod
Cohen, Joss and Solly
Cosette
Crawford, Janie
Croft, Art
Crowne, Lenina
Cruz, Artemio
Damon, Cross
Davies, Art
De Satigny, Alba Trueba
Deeriye
Del Valle, Clara
Delarue, Mathieu
Doane, Seneca
Dufrenoy, Michel
Erlone, Jan
Everhard, Avis
Ewell, Bob
Falconer, Sharon
Fatheya
Ferreira, Christovao
Finch, Jean Louise ("Scout")
Finchley, Sondra
Finkelberg, Isaac
Galt, John
García, Esteban
García, Pedro Tecero
Green, Horatio
Griffiths, Clyde
Haller, Harry
Holbrook Family
Houston, Ely
Hunt, Alonzo ("Fonny")
Hyer, Aunt Ri'
Imoinda

Javert
Jellyby, Mrs.
Joad Family
Jones, Eric
Joseph K.
Joy, Serena
Jurgis, Arthur
Knecht, Joseph
Knowell, Douglas
Knox, Tom
Kumalo, Stephen
Leete, Edith
MacAlpin, Marian
MacWhite, Gilbert
Mako
Maldonado, Felix
Maqui, Rosendo
Martin, Donald
Marx, Bernard
Maslova, Katusha
McMurphy, Randall Patrick
Mellama, Mauritas
Mellama, Robert
Melvyn, Sybylla
Meredith, Anthony
Merou, Ulysse
Merridew, Jack
Meursault, Monsieur
Milvain, Jasper
Minke
Montag, Guy
Moore, Daniel Vivaldo
Moreno, Señora
Mukhtaar
Mursal
Naranjo, Huberto
Nekhludof, Prince Dmitri
    Ivanovitch
Offred
Old Lodge Skins
Olenska, Countess Ellen
Ontosoroh
Pardiggle, Mrs.
Peace, Sula
Penochkin, Arkady Pavlych
Piggy
Pittman, Jane Brown
Ponderevo, George
Pontmercy, Marius
Proteus, Paul
Quap
Quest, Martha
Quirk, Thady

Radley, Arthur "Boo"
Ralph
Ransom, Basil
Ras the Destroyer
Ratched, Nurse
Reardon, Edwin
Reardon, Hank
Reisling, Paul
Rivers, Clementine ("Tish")
Roberts, David
Rodrigues, Sebastian
Rodríguez, Colonel Tolomeo
Rudkus, Jurgis and Ona
Sarvis, Dr. A. K.
Scott, Ida and Rufus
Sears, Louis
Sereno, Daniel
Sethe
Settembrini, Ludovico
Shallard, Frank
Shatov
Shelby, George
Shukhov, Ivan Denisovich
Smith, Winston
Sorde, Itale
Stark, Joe
Stavrogin, Nikolay
    Vsyevolodovitch
Swartz, Lanny
Tachibana, Akiko
Tachibana, Nobutoshi
Taggert, Dagny
Tarrant, Verena
Tea Cake
Tereza
Tetley, Gerald
Tewce, Ainsley
Thomas, Bigger
Titorelli
Tom, Uncle
Tomas
Trueba, Esteban
Underwood, Andrew
Valjean, Jean
Valtoskar, Piera
Verhovensky, Pyotr
    Stepanovitch
West, Julian
Wright, Nel
Yakovlich, Sofron
Yellow Horse
Yossarian, Captain John
Younger Family

PREFACE

Literature can have a profound influence on human thought. In particular, by challenging old ideas and inspiring new ones, literature has the power to change people's opinions on important social issues and act as the catalyst for reform. For example, the 1852 novel *Uncle Tom's Cabin*, by Harriet Beecher Stowe, furthered the antislavery movement in the United States, and the 1885 novel *Ramona*, by Helen Hunt Jackson, brought about changes in laws regarding Native Americans. Similarly, Upton Sinclair's 1906 novel *The Jungle* helped create new laws related to public health and food handling, and Arthur Morrison's 1896 novel *A Child of the Jago* caused England to change its housing laws.

These works were effective in part because they were social protest novels rather than political documents. When political writers criticize government policies and regimes, readers are presented with arguments that encourage them to think logically, rather than emotionally, about society's problems. In contrast, social protest authors encourage readers to empathize with those who suffer from a particular social problem. For example, Charles Dickens did not rail against poverty. Instead, he encouraged the people of Victorian England to imagine what it would be like to be poor. This is a very effective way of changing the public's attitude toward a particular group of people.

In fact, personalized suffering is an important part of social protest literature, and many of its main characters are innocent victims of social problems. For instance, in the novel *The Twilight Years*, Sawako Ariyoshi protests Japan's nursing care system through the character of Akiko Tachibana, who struggles to care for her senile father-in-law with little help from Japanese society. Similarly, Ciro Alegría protested injustices against Peruvian Indians in the early 1920s by showing the unjust imprisonment of an Indian mayor, Rosendo Maqui.

Ariyoshi and Alegría address problems specific to a particular government and time period. However, in doing so, they deal with the broader issues of ageism and justice. They also concern themselves with universal truths about the human condition. This is another important aspect of social protest literature. As a result, social protest works continue to have meaning long after a particular political era has passed. This is especially true for social protest fiction and poetry, which are the focus of *The Encyclopedia of Social Protest Literature*.

Such literature has appeared in every country in the world from ancient times to the present. For example, Alcaeus protested poverty in ancient Greece, and George Gissing did so in Victorian England. Sibilla Aleramo wrote about injustices against Italian women in the early 1900s, and Nawal El Saadawi wrote about injustices against Egyptian women in the 1970s. Peter Abrahams protested racism in South Africa in the 1940s, and Richard Wright protested racism in the United States in the 1950s. Other broad social issues that have been addressed in social protest literature include anti-Semitism, labor conditions, peace, and individual freedom.

Social protest authors also work in a variety of forms. Native American authors primarily use poetry to address social ills, as did writers from the Beat generation. Memoirs, short stories, and novellas are also common, although they are not as popular as novels. Regarding the latter, authors have used all types of genres to comment on issues. For example, Charles Dickens's *Bleak House* is in essence a mystery, and his *Little Dorrit* is a romance. Theodore Dreiser's *An American Tragedy* is a crime novel. George Orwell's *Animal Farm* is a fantasy, and Kurt Vonnegut's *Player Piano* is science fiction.

But no matter what genre or form a social protest author chooses, his or her intent is to challenge the status quo. Sometimes this entails criticizing a government system or policy. For example, to improve working conditions, writers in capitalist countries have suggested replacing capitalism with socialism. To end racism, South African authors advocated the end of apartheid. As a result of such criticism, many social protest authors have been persecuted for their work, or they have endured government censorship and/or exile from their native countries. For example, Aleksandr Solzhenitzyn and Milan Kundera were expelled from the Soviet Union and Czechoslovakia, respectively, and Pramoedya Ananta Toer has been forbidden to leave his home in Indonesia. American author Tillie Olsen was denied employment during the McCarthy era.

Nonetheless, social protest authors continue to criticize societies and offer solutions to long-standing social problems. *The Encyclopedia of Social Protest Literature* offers entries for recent works that address contemporary concerns such as environmentalism, job satisfaction, and the rights of gays and lesbians and Native Americans in the modern United States. Through extensive cross-referencing, the encyclopedia relates these works to earlier writings on similar issues as well as to other social protest themes.

Exploring *The Encyclopedia of Social Protest Literature* will reveal much about the way authors typically approach important social problems. It will also provide new insights into the human experience. For although writers in North and South America, Africa, Europe, Asia, and other parts of the world, from ancient times to the present, have had different visions of how to solve social problems, they have all wanted the same basic things for humanity: freedom, justice, equality, dignity, and a social system that supports them.

Abbey, Edward

Environmental activist Edward Abbey is the author of more than a dozen fiction and nonfiction books, but he is best known for his novel *The Monkey Wrench Gang*. Published in 1975, this book protested the destruction of wilderness areas by road builders and developers. Its main characters, activists who practice a form of environmental sabotage, or ecotage, called "monkeywrenching," eventually inspired real-life environmentalists to create a similar group called Earth First! As Philip Shabecoff (1993, 123) explains in his book *A Fierce Green Fire: The American Environmental Movement:*

> These radicals . . . choose instead to defend the natural world by direct action, civil disobedience, and the kind of eco-sabotage romanticized by the novelist Edward Abbey as "monkeywrenching." Earth First!ers, some of them remnants of the back-to-the-land movement of the 1960s, have thrown themselves in front of logging trucks, pulled up survey stakes for an oil exploration project, chained themselves to the upper branches of centuries-old trees marked for the chain saw by timber companies, and driven iron spikes into trees to make it dangerous for loggers to cut into the wood.

Dave Foreman, one of the founders of Earth First!, convinced Abbey to join the group and to be present at its first major media event, the "cracking" of the Glen Canyon Dam in 1981. Abbey's *Monkey Wrench Gang* characters had advocated the dam's destruction; Earth First! accomplished it symbolically, unfurling a "crack" of black plastic over the face of the dam. According to Susan Zakin (1993, 150) in her book *Coyotes and Town Dogs,* Abbey watched the event from a nearby bridge, shouting, "Earth First!" and "Free the Colorado!"

For Abbey, radical politics was nothing new. Born on January 29, 1927, in Home, Pennsylvania, he was the son of an avowed anarchist, Paul Revere Abbey, and his wife, Mildred. At age seventeen Edward Abbey hitchhiked west and fell in love with the American desert. That same year he was drafted into the army, and after receiving an honorable discharge in 1946, he actively protested the draft. He also began attending the University of New Mexico, where he received his B.A. in 1951 and M.A. in philosophy in 1956. His thesis was entitled "Anarchism and the Morality of Violence."

While in college he wrote his first novel, the largely autobiographical *Jonathan Troy.* It was published in 1954 but soon went out of print, and Abbey considered it so bad that he refused to allow its republication years later.

Nonetheless, in 1957 Abbey received a writing fellowship to Stanford University in California. By this time he had married one woman, divorced her, and married another; he was to have five wives and several children in his lifetime.

From 1956 to 1971 Abbey spent his summers working for the U.S. National Parks Service, both as a park ranger and a fire watcher, at a succession of desert locations. He also continued to write. His second novel, *The Brave Cowboy,* was published in 1956 and later made into a movie. It focuses on two characters, a cowboy and an intellectual, both of whom are anarchists who suffer government persecution for their political views. According to Zakin, Abbey himself was investigated by the U.S. Federal Bureau of Investigation because of his draft protests. She (303) says:

> The McCarthyesque repression that hammered down on Abbey's fictional [characters] in *The Brave Cowboy* is more dramatic than what Abbey experienced—in Abbey's case, the FBI's busiest period was ten months of scrambling after him while he was working as a clerk-typist for the U.S. Geological Survey in 1952, supporting himself while he finished *Jonathan Troy.* The FBI kept trying to find out if he was a communist but failed to turn up enough evidence to get him fired. . . .The FBI says its investigation of Abbey ended in 1967, when Abbey was working in Death Valley as a school-bus driver.

Abbey's third novel, *Fire on the Mountain* (1962), has political elements, as does his nonfiction book *Desert Solitaire,* published in 1968. *Desert Solitaire* is a first-person account of Abbey's experiences as a ranger at Utah's Arches National Park, and in it he bemoans the negative effects of "industrial tourism" on desert land. He also criticizes the National Park Service. His next book, a novel entitled *Black Sun* (1971), is a love story between a young woman and a park ranger.

With the publication of *The Monkey Wrench Gang* in 1975, Abbey became a cult hero to environmentalists. He not only became involved in Earth First! but also increasingly spoke out against the ravages of technology. He continued to write essays, as well as newspaper columns and letters to the editor, expressing his views on a wide variety of subjects. He died on March 14, 1989, at his home in Tucson, Arizona. (Abbey 1975; McCann 1977; Shabecoff 1993; Zakin 1993)

See also Anarchism; Environmentalism; McCarthyism; *Monkey Wrench Gang, The*

Abolitionist Movement
See Slavery

Abrahams, Peter
Through poetry, short stories, and novels, Peter Henry Abrahams has protested official policies of segregation, or apartheid, in his native country of South Africa. Born on November 19, 1919, in the township of Vrededorp near Johannesburg, he had an Ethiopian father and a mother deemed "coloured," or mixed-race, by the white South African government. Abrahams was therefore also considered coloured, and as such he experienced racial prejudice from an early age.

He first expressed his struggles with racism and segregation in a poem entitled "A Blackman Speaks of Freedom," written in 1938. The following year he left South Africa for good, living first in Great Britain as a merchant seaman and later in Jamaica as a newspaper and radio journalist; however, he never forgot the apartheid of his native land. He used his experiences to write a collection of protest poems, published as *A Blackman Speaks of Freedom!: Poems* (1941); a collection of short stories entitled *Dark Testament* (1942); an autobiography called *Tell Freedom* (1954); and several novels set in South Africa.

His first novel, *Song of the City* (1945), addresses the conflict caused by Afrikaner nationalists who believed that South Africa should become independent from Great Britain and therefore should not enter World War II in England's defense. His second novel, *Mine Boy* (1946), inspired by a 1946 African mine workers' strike, concerns labor issues in a large South African city. His third novel, *The Path of Thunder* (1948), focuses on a coloured man's love for a white woman; it was banned for publication and distribution in South Africa because of that country's prohibitions against interracial marriage, which lasted from 1949 to 1991.

Subsequent novels by Abrahams, who sometimes wrote under the pseudonym Peter Graham, include *Wild Conquest* (1950), which concerns the Great Trek of the Boers in South Africa; *A Wreath for Udomo* (1956), which explores postwar liberalism in West Africa and the issue of independent black nations; and *A Night of Their Own* (1965), which concerns an underground resistance organization for South African Indians. Abrahams's later novels, *This Island Now* (1966) and *The View from Coyaba* (1985), are set in the Caribbean, where the author still lives.

In all of his novels, Abrahams exposes white injustice. However, he does not advocate black hatred for whites. In explaining the reason for this position, he (Ensor 1992, 112–113) says:

> In my fight against the system of South Africa, or against the South African whites, since the two are interlocked at times, I may so change myself that I, too, become diseased by the virus I fight against. That, I hold, is the horror that is active among many Negroes today. . . . In the struggle to be free, many Negroes have arrived at a position where they would counter the white bigot's race-hatred with race-hatred against whites: many who have been humiliated because of their colour, joy openly at the humiliation of a white person because he is white. So many have changed so much that they have lost the magic of the dream that carried them on the uphill journey till "they lifted themselves up by their own bootstrings." Large numbers of Negroes today counterpoise a black humanity against a white humanity.

Abrahams (1975, 113–114) believes that countering "bigotry with more bigotry, prejudice with more prejudice" might result in a disconnection with humanity that would mean "the battle will be lost, though won." (Abrahams 1975; Ensor 1992; Wade 1972)

See also Apartheid; Finkelberg, Isaac; Mako; *Path of Thunder, The*; Racism; Swartz, Lanny

Age of Innocence, The

The Age of Innocence, by Edith Wharton, won the Pulitzer Prize for fiction in 1921. It was first published in four installments in *The Pictorial Review* in 1920 and in book form later the same year. The novel criticizes upper-class social conventions in the United States during the 1870s, particularly in regard to the institution of marriage. Its main character, Newland Archer, is a member of New York high society. A successful attorney, he becomes engaged to May Welland, a socialite who conforms to rigid codes of etiquette. In this regard she is very unlike her cousin, the Countess Ellen Olenska. Ellen is an unconventional woman who does not pay attention to social codes. She wears the "wrong" kind of clothing, lives in the "wrong" neighborhood, and makes friends with the "wrong" people. The wife of a Polish nobleman, she arrives in New York intending to file for divorce. This scandalizes her relatives. They convince Newland to act as her attorney and talk her out of ending the marriage. In the course of doing so, he learns that Ellen's husband is an extremely cruel man. Nonetheless, Newland recommends against a divorce on the grounds that society's concerns are more important than any individual's. He explains, "The individual, in such cases, is nearly always sacrificed to what is supposed to be the collective interest; people cling to any convention that keeps the family together—protects the children, if there are any" (Wharton 1993, 111).

Later Newland regrets this advice, having realized that he has fallen in love with Ellen himself. He wants to ask her to divorce her husband and marry him, but all of his relatives expect him to marry May. He cannot bring himself to cancel his wedding. However,

The Age of Innocence *criticizes nineteenth century upper-class social conventions. This scene from the 1993 film depicts Newland Archer and the Countess Olenska. (Reuters/Archive Photos)*

after the ceremony he continues to long for Ellen. One day he asks her to run away with him as his mistress. She refuses and moves away. Newton is left behind to live out his life with May, conforming to society's expectations for him. Years later, after he is widowed, his son urges him to visit Ellen. The young man has difficulty understanding why his father refuses to do so. Newton reflects on the chasm between the generations, saying, "The difference is that these young people take it for granted that they're going to get whatever they want, and that we almost always took it for granted that we shouldn't" (353).

In discussing the novel in a 1968 introduction to the work, scholar R.W.B. Lewis (xi-xii) describes the theme of *The Age of Innocence* as "the losing struggle between individual aspiration and the silent, forbidding authority of the social tribe." He (xiii) compares this work by Wharton to the novels of Henry James because it shows "the expansive courtesies of the social ceremony which hide the carefully

executed act of destruction." (Howe 1962; Wharton 1993)

> **See also** Class, Social; Feminism; Olenska, Countess Ellen; Wharton, Edith

Age of Reason, The

The Age of Reason was published in French as *L'Âge de raison* in 1945. It is the first and best-known volume in a trilogy of novels entitled *Les Chemins de la liberté* (The Roads to Freedom). The author, Jean-Paul Sartre, intended to write a fourth volume but never finished it, rejecting the novel form to concentrate on plays. The other volumes in the series are *The Reprieve* (Le Sursis), also published in 1945, and *Iron in the Soul* (La Mort dans l'âme; called *Troubled Sleep* in the United States), which was published in 1949.

The Age of Reason emphasizes Sartre's personal philosophy regarding the relationship between freedom and social responsibility. It is the story of Mathieu Delarue, whose mistress, Marcelle Duffet, has just discovered that she is pregnant. A professor of philosophy in Paris, Mathieu is opposed to marriage and speaks often of the importance of freedom. However, he refuses to join any political causes and lives a predictable, ordinary life. Not wanting his routine to change, he decides that Marcelle will have an abortion. For several days he tries to find someone who will loan him the money for the operation, but his friends are either poor or unwilling to help end the pregnancy. Finally Mathieu steals the money from a wealthy acquaintance. When he gives it to Marcelle, she throws him out, saying that she wants to have the child. Shortly thereafter she agrees to marry Mathieu's friend Daniel Sereno, a gay man who longs for the lifestyle that Mathieu has rejected.

The sequels to the novel, *The Reprieve* and *Troubled Sleep,* continue to express Sartre's views on freedom, but they focus more on politics than does *The Age of Reason.* They concern Adolf Hitler's activities in Europe and the fall of France in 1940. (Brustein 1964; Madsen 1977; Sartre 1947)

See also Delarue, Mathieu; Sartre, Jean-Paul; Sereno, Daniel

Ageism

The term *ageism* generally refers to discrimination against the elderly. In social protest literature the concept is most often presented as part of a discussion of poverty and/or working conditions in a particular time and place. For example, in John Steinbeck's *The Grapes of Wrath* the characters of Ma and Pa Joad demonstrate the plight of older migrant farmworkers during the Depression. Similarly, in Upton Sinclair's *The Jungle* the hardships experienced by Jurgis Rudkus's father illustrate the effects of poverty and discrimination on elderly slaughterhouse workers.

Authors use such characters, who are typically good-hearted mothers and fathers, to evoke sympathy from their readers. Their intent is to raise public awareness of problems that affect all age groups. However, a few authors have devoted entire works to the problems of the elderly. The most notable in this regard are French feminist Simone de Beau-

voir, who addressed the issue in both fiction and nonfiction, and Japanese author Sawako Ariyoshi, who made ageism the main theme of her 1972 novel *The Twilight Years.* (Barrow 1979; Copper 1988)

See also Beauvoir, Simone de; *Grapes of Wrath, The; Jungle, The;* Joad Family; Rudkus, Jurgis and Ona; Sinclair, Upton; Steinbeck, John; *Twilight Years, The*

Air-Conditioned Nightmare, The

The Air-Conditioned Nightmare, by Henry Miller, is a work of nonfiction that has fictional elements and includes poetry. Published in 1945, it documents a trip that Miller took through the United States a few years earlier and discusses America's social problems in terms of culture and history. For example, Miller (1970, 28–29) says:

I ought to have an American Indian by my side. . . . Imagine the two of us . . . standing in contemplation before the hideous grandeur of one of those steel mills which dot the railway line. I can almost hear him thinking—"So it was for this that you deprived us of our birthright, took away our slaves, burned our homes, massacred our women and children, poisoned our souls, broke every treaty which you made with us and left us to die." . . . Do you think it would be easy to get him to change places with one of our steady workers? What sort of persuasion would you use? What now could you promise him that would be truly seductive? A used car that he could drive to work in? A slap-board shack that he could, if he were ignorant enough, call a home? An education for his children which would lift them out of vice, ignorance and superstition but keep them in slavery? A clean, healthy life in the midst of poverty, crime, filth, disease and fear? Wages that barely keep your head above water and often not? Radio, telephone, cinema, newspaper, pulp magazine, fountain pen, wrist watch, vacuum cleaner or other gadgets ad infinitum? Are these the baubles that make life worthwhile?

Throughout *The Air-Conditioned Nightmare* Miller argues that the United States is flawed. His words are often harsh. For example, he (20) says:

To call this a society of free peoples is blasphemous. What have we to offer the world beside the superabundant loot which we recklessly plunder from the earth under the maniacal delusion that this insane activity represents progress and enlightenment? The land of opportunity has become the land of senseless sweat and struggle. The goal of all our striving has long been forgotten. We no longer wish to succor the oppressed and homeless; there is no room in this great, empty land for those who, like our forefathers before us, now seek a place of refuge.

Miller continued his criticism in a sequel to *The Air-Conditioned Nightmare* called *Remember to Remember,* which was published in 1947. (Miller 1970; Widmer 1963)

See also Capitalism; Miller, Henry

Alcaeus

The Greek poet Alcaeus lived from approximately 620 B.C. to 580 B.C. in Mytilene on the island of Lesbos. He produced ten books of poetry, including hymns, drinking songs, love poetry, and social and political protest poetry. Only fragments of these works are known today, but the poet is mentioned in the writings of others from the period. For example, the Greek playwright Aristophanes refers to Alcaeus's political odes in his comedy *The Archanians,* which criticizes the circumstances surrounding the Peloponnesian War (431–404 B.C.). (Martin 1972)

See also *Archanians, The;* Aristophanes; "Poverty"; Poverty

Alegría, Ciro

Peruvian novelist Ciro Alegría dedicated his life to protesting the plight of Indians in his native country. Born on November 4, 1909, in Saltimbanca, Peru, he learned the craft of writing from his father, a noted Argentine

novelist, and his teacher, a well-known Peruvian poet. Alegría's social protest inclinations came from his association with a militant pro-Indian organization, the APRA party, which he joined in 1930. Alegría was arrested in 1931 and 1933 for illegal political activities, and in 1934 the Peruvian government exiled him to Chile.

The following year he published his first novel, *La serpiente de oro,* which was published in English as *The Golden Serpent* in 1943. The book portrays the harsh existence of Indians living beside a river in the Huamachuco province, where Alegría grew up. He followed this with *Los perros hambrientos* (The Hungry Dogs) in 1938, which describes the life of Indian sheepherders, and *El mundo es ancho y ajeno* (Broad and Alien Is the World) in 1941, which concerns a group of Indian villagers trying to save their land from white usurpers. *Broad and Alien Is the World* gained him fame in the United States, and he moved there in 1941. In 1948 he was allowed to return to Peru, where he became a politician. He died in Lima, Peru, on February 17, 1967. (Early 1980)

See also *Broad and Alien Is the World;* Exiles

Aleramo, Sibilla

Sibilla Aleramo is the pseudonym for Rina Pierangeli Faccio, author of the feminist novel *Una Donna* (A Woman). Published in Italy in 1906 and as an English translation in 1908, it is the semiautobiographical story of one woman's domination by the men in her life and of her struggles to achieve freedom in a country that regards her as the legal property of her husband.

Aleramo was born in Milan, Italy, in 1876. She moved to southern Italy in 1887 after her father became the manager of a glassworks factory in the town of Porto Civitanova. Shortly thereafter Aleramo began working in his office, and when she was fifteen one of his employees raped her. She was forced to marry the man to preserve her honor. Her new husband proved to be intensely jealous and controlling, and Aleramo became so despondent that she tried to kill herself. Later she assuaged her loneliness by writing short stories about tragic heroines. After she gave birth to a son, her child became the focus of her life.

Then in 1898 Aleramo read a book about feminism and socialism that discussed the typically loveless nature of Italian marriages, and she decided to write her own articles on these issues. By 1899 she had gained national recognition for her work. That same year her husband was fired from his job, and Aleramo convinced him to move to Milan, where she became an editor at a feminist magazine. However, she often quarreled with the magazine's male executive editor, and she resigned her position in January 1900. Her husband then decided to move the family back to Porto Civitanova. By this time Aleramo was having an affair with the poet Guglielmo Felice Damiani and did not want to leave Milan. She begged her husband for a separation; he told her that if she left him, she would lose all contact with her son, who was then six years old. After some indecision Aleramo chose freedom over motherhood.

Aleramo wrote *A Woman* to justify this decision. The novel is a chronicle of her marital unhappiness, although on the advice of her second lover, the poet Giovanni Cena, it omits her affair with Damiani. According to Richard Drake in the introduction to a 1980 edition of the novel, Aleramo regretted this omission. Drake (xv–xvi) explains:

> Cena sensed correctly that the moral force of *A Woman* would be diminished if public attention were distracted by the all-too-familiar device in Italian fiction of an adulterous triangle. He strongly urged her to end the novel on a lofty moral tone, revealing the "naked relentless conscience of a woman facing herself, with a duty toward herself." Aleramo yielded to her lover on this point with extreme reluctance, remembering in 1939 that "by mutilating the truth" she had experienced a sense of committing a sin.

Thirteen years after the publication of *A Woman*, Aleramo corrected her omission in her second novel, *Il passaggio*. Published in 1919, it revisited the memories of *A Woman* but revealed her affair. This novel was a commercial and critical failure. Similarly, her 1924 play *Endimione* was performed only once. Impoverished, Aleramo had to rely on government support. She also continued to write articles about feminist and political issues, as well as poetry. Although none of her writing was ever as well received as *A Woman*, in later years she did regain some of her earlier financial success.

In 1945 she published some of her memoirs as *From My Diary: 1940–1944* (Dal mio diario: 1940–1944), in which she discussed her conversion to Marxism and her love affair with a young poet, Franco Matacotta. During her lifetime she had many affairs with well-known Italian poets, authors, and artists, including Vincenzo Cardarelli, Gabriele D'Annunzio, and Dino Campana. In 1952 she published a collection of her letters to Campana, *Dino Campana-Sibilla Aleramo: Lettere,* and at the end of her life she published the rest of her memoirs as *Diario di una donna: Inediti 1945–1960* (Diary of a Woman: Unedited 1945–1960). She died in Italy on January 11, 1960. (Aleramo 1983)

See also Feminism; Socialism; *Woman, A*

Alessandro

Alessandro is one of the main characters in Helen Hunt Jackson's 1885 novel *Ramona,* which shows the injustices perpetrated against American Indians in California. A Native American, Alessandro is a skilled, hard-working sheepshearer. He is also brave, kind, and handsome, and he is an excellent singer and violinist. Nonetheless, society treats him as an inferior individual. Each time he tries to better himself, white settlers take away his property and his land. Finally he begins to lose his mind. One on occasion he becomes slightly confused and accidentally takes the wrong horse home from the town corral. Its owner tracks Alessandro down and shoots him. (Jackson 1988)

See also Jackson, Helen Hunt; *Ramona*

Allende, Isabel

Born in Lima, Peru, on August 2, 1942, Isabel Allende grew up in Chile, where her Marxist uncle, Salvador Allende Gossens, was president. She worked as a journalist there until 1973. At that time Allende's uncle was assassinated; his government was replaced with a military dictatorship led by General Augusto Pinochet Ugarte, and Allende fled the country for Venezuela. However, her grandfather remained in Chile, and her writings to him eventually became the basis of her first novel, the international bestseller *La casa de los espíritus* (1982). Published in English as *The House of the Spirits* in 1985, it explores interpersonal relationships against a backdrop of political unrest. In 1984 Allende published the novel *De amor y de sombra* (Of Love and Shadows), followed by *Eva Luna* in 1987; both of these novels deal with feminist issues as well as revolutionary politics. Allende moved to the United States in 1988, where she wrote *El plan infinito* (The Infinite Plan) in 1991 and a collection of short stories, *Cuentos de Eva Luna* (The Stories of Eva Luna), in 1990. (Hart 1989; Rojas and Rehbein 1991)

Isabel Allende (Horst Tappe/Archive Photos)

See also *Eva Luna;* Exiles; Feminism; *House of the Spirits, The;* Socialism

Amenabar, Don Alvaro

In Ciro Alegría's 1941 Peruvian novel *Broad and Alien Is the World* Don Alvaro Amenabar is a nonnative rancher who hates Indians and wants to enslave them. He manipulates the government and legal system to falsely imprison anyone who opposes him and arranges for his son Oscar to become a congressman. At one point Don Alvaro says, "I think . . . that these ignorant Indians are no good to the country, and that they should be handed over to men of enterprise, the men who make their countries great" (Alegría 1941, 165). He believes that "Peru needs men of enterprise who will make people work. What's the good of all this cheap humanitarianism? It's work and more work, and so that there will be work there must be men who will make the masses work" (165). Eventually he takes over the Indian village of Rumi and destroys the lives of its inhabitants, either through enslavement, imprisonment, or murder. (Alegría 1941)

See also Alegría, Ciro; *Broad and Alien Is the World;* Castro, Benito; Justice; Maqui, Rosendo

American Tragedy, An

Theodore Dreiser's novel *An American Tragedy* (1925) criticizes the U.S. economic system of the 1920s, which created social divisions based on wealth. Its main character, Clyde Griffiths, is a poor man who struggles but fails to be equal with those who are born rich.

The novel is divided into three parts, Books One, Two, and Three. Book One opens in Kansas City with Clyde as a young boy. His parents are itinerant preachers who force him to participate in street-corner prayer meetings. Embarrassed at their religious fervor, he begins working in a soda shop, and at sixteen he takes a job as a hotel bellhop. His tips are large, and with money he discovers a wild lifestyle. One night he and some friends are out driving in a stolen car when they accidentally hit and kill a little girl. The police spot them and give chase. The car crashes and

Clyde runs off in a panic, leaving Kansas City for Chicago.

Book Two opens in Chicago, where Clyde learns he is wanted by the police. He goes into hiding for almost two years, working at a variety of odd jobs under an assumed name. Finally he decides that the trouble has blown over. He once again uses his real name and gets a job at an exclusive meeting place called the Union League Club, where he eventually encounters his rich uncle, Samuel Griffiths. Griffiths hires Clyde to work at his factory in New York, where Clyde assumes he will receive preferential treatment. However, his cousin Gilbert, whom Clyde greatly resembles, takes an instant dislike to him. Gilbert is in charge of factory assignments, and he gives Clyde a low-level job. Later Clyde's uncle recognizes his son's jealousy and moves Clyde to a better position. However, he himself is not inclined to socialize with his poorer relation.

In the new job as a supervisor Clyde meets Roberta Alden, a young factory worker from a poor background. Company rules forbid him to date an employee. Nonetheless, he asks her out and eventually convinces her to become his mistress. Meanwhile Sondra Finchley, who belongs to Gilbert Griffith's circle of friends, asks Clyde to attend some of their group's parties. Originally she invites him to make Gilbert mad, but when Clyde proves popular, she starts to fall in love with him. Soon the Griffiths are forced to include him in their social invitations.

Clyde envisions a bright future for himself. Then Roberta tells him she is pregnant. He finds her a doctor he believes is an abortionist, but the man refuses to end her pregnancy. Roberta wants Clyde to marry her, but he refuses. Finally she threatens to expose him. Imagining a ruined reputation, he chances upon a newspaper article about a boating accident and decides to drown Roberta. After taking her to a remote resort on the pretense that they will get married there, he coaxes her out on a deserted lake. Once they are on the water, however, he finds himself in turmoil over the thought of killing her. She notices that he is upset and moves toward him, but he pushes her away. In his hand is a camera; it accidentally strikes her in the head, and she falls out of the boat, which then capsizes. Now Roberta is gone, and Clyde swims to shore.

Book Three opens with the discovery of Roberta's body. The police believe that there were two drowning victims, a man and his wife. Then they realize that only the woman was killed. They discover a letter in Roberta's pocket about her impending lakeside marriage, and upon further investigation it leads them to Clyde. He is arrested for the crime, and despite some clever manipulations by his lawyers, he is eventually sentenced to death and executed.

An American Tragedy is based on a real-life murder case. Dreiser had long wanted to do a book related to crime, partly because he admired Fyodor Dostoyevsky's novel *Crime and Punishment* (1866). Dreiser's notes reveal that he tried to develop a novel from several contemporary homicide cases before settling on the 1906 murder of a pregnant factory girl, Grace ("Billy") Brown, by her social-climbing boyfriend, Chester Gillette. He chose the Gillette case specifically because of its relationship to class structure and ambition and incorporated most of its details into his novel. However, he made Clyde far less cold-hearted and sophisticated than Gillette because he wanted *An American Tragedy* to say more about society in general than about the nature of an individual murderer. (Dreiser 1964; Geismar 1953; Kazin and Shapiro 1955; Moers 1969)

See also Class, Social; Dostoyevsky, Fyodor; Dreiser, Theodore; Finchley, Sondra; Griffiths, Clyde; *Possessed, The;* Poverty

Anand, Mulk Raj

Mulk Raj Anand depicted the plight of the lower classes in his native India in novels, short stories, and essays. According to scholar Margaret Berry (1971, 25), his work expresses ideas that "can be found in contemporary movements associated with nationalism, social reform, economic Communism and Socialism, and political democracy." Berry explains that "Anand's attacks on political, as well as social and economic institutions, are carried out mainly on behalf of India's poor, in the effort to destroy forces inimical to their development, and to build a world of freedom and equality where human potential can flourish" (72). Moreover, Anand (1940, 37) himself once said that an author must seek "the real courage to create a literature of protest, which can reveal the insults, humiliations and injustices sought to be perpetrated in our society by the inheritors of privileges who seek everything without offering sacrifices equal to those offered by less privileged people."

Anand was born in Peshawar, a northwest province of India, on December 12, 1905. His mother was a Sikh peasant, and his father was a member of the Thathiar caste (silver- and coppersmiths) who learned English and became the head clerk in a military regiment. Anand was well educated himself. He graduated from the University of Punjab in 1924 and subsequently studied philosophy at University College in London, earning his doctoral degree in 1929.

He continued to live in London for several years, during which he began to write books on Indian culture, including *The Hindu View of Art* in 1933. He also became involved in Indian politics. In one magazine interview, he was quoted as saying that writers should "align themselves with the vanguard of the Indian struggle for political and economic emancipation" (Berry 1971, 30). This attitude led him to write his first novel, *Untouchable,* which depicts life among members of the lowest caste in Hindu society, the Untouchables, who are responsible for cleaning latrines and sweeping dung. *Untouchable* was rejected by 19 publishers before being printed in England in 1935, and it was subsequently banned by the British government in India, as were most of Anand's later works, including *Coolie* (1936), which concerns India's poor, and *Two Leaves and a Bud* (1937), which deals with tea plantations.

Anand wrote several other novels in his career, including *The Village* (1939), *Across the Black Waters* (1940), *The Sword and the Sickle* (1942), *The Big Heart* (1945), and *The Private life of an Indian Prince* (1953). He also worked from 1939 to 1942 as a documentary filmmaker for the British Broadcasting Corporation and Ministry of Information during World War II. In 1945 he returned to India to become a professor at the University of Punjab. He continued his involvement in Indian culture and politics and published several autobiographical novels, including *Seven Summers* (1950), *Morning Face* (1968), *Confession of a Lover* (1972), and *The Bubble* (1988).

In summarizing Anand's career, Berry (1971, 97) says:

What, finally, is the value of Mulk Raj Anand's novels? It is the witness they offer of India's agonizing attempt to break out of massive stagnation and create a society in which men and women are free and equal, in which they can, therefore, live dynamically and creatively. It is the testimony they give of a generation of Indians familiar with the best and the worst of the West and with the best and the worst of India. It is the evidence they afford of the modern educated Indian's struggle to identify himself and his country in the context of modern world society and to find roots that yet live in a mouldering heritage. It is the search they pursue for a center, a principle of unity, which the West, theoretically, has found in the virtue of charity and which Anand knows as *bhakti* [devotion]. The critic can only regret that with such noble matter, Anand's considerable talents and energies should so early and so long have operated in the restrictive climate of a doctrinaire aesthetic.

(Anand 1940; Berry 1971)

See also Bakha; Capitalism; Class, Social; Poverty; Socialism; *Untouchable*

Anarchism

The term *anarchism* means "without a ruler." It refers to an ideology that supports personal freedom and opposes all forms of authority. Proponents of anarchism, called anarchists, advocate the elimination of gov-

Famous U.S. anarchist Emma Goldman (Archive Photos)

ernment and other controlling social and political institutions.

Anarchism as a social movement had its beginnings in the works of William Godwin, an eighteenth-century English political theorist. He argued that because humans are rational beings, they are capable of behaving in an orderly fashion without any government or legal restrictions. During the nineteenth century this concept inspired the formation of anarchist groups throughout Europe, and many poets began advocating anarchism. By the early twentieth century the anarchist movement had become particularly strong in Russia and was given voice through such periodicals as *The Stormy Petrel.* Russian author Maxim Gorky alluded to this periodical in his 1901 poem "Song of the Stormy Petrel." That same year an anarchist assassinated U.S. president William McKinley.

Anarchism was prevalent in U.S. immigrant communities and came to more widespread attention through the lectures of Emma Goldman (1869–1940), a Russian-born activist who was deported from the United States to her native country in 1919. Goldman publicly condemned acts of violence but was involved with an anarchist group that attempted to assassinate millionaire industrialist Henry Clay Frick in 1892.

Goldman and many other anarchists advocated the eventual establishment of a communist society. Anarchism has much in common not only with communism but also with socialism; all three of these ideologies oppose capitalism and class structure. However, only anarchists believe that absolutely no hierarchical structure is necessary to organize society. Anarchists express complete faith in an individual's ability to behave well in the absence of an authority figure. This faith has been criticized in social protest literature, most notably in Eugene O'Neill's 1939 play *The Iceman Cometh* and William Golding's novel *Lord of the Flies. The Iceman Cometh* depicts an anarchist who betrays his own mother, and *Lord of the Flies* shows a society of boys who turn savage when stranded on an island without adults. (Carter 1971; Egbert 1967; Read 1947; Woodcock 1962)

See also Capitalism; Class, Social; Communism; Golding, William; *Iceman Cometh, The; Lord of the Flies;* Marxism; O'Neill, Eugene; Socialism

And Still I Rise

And Still I Rise is a collection of poetry by Maya Angelou. It was first published as a single volume in 1978 and then as part of *The Complete Collected Poems of Maya Angelou* in 1994. The poem that gives the collection its title, "Still I Rise," speaks of racism and sexism from the female African-American perspective, saying, "Out of the huts of history's shame / I rise / Up from a past that's routed in pain / I rise" (Angelou 1994, 164). Similarly, "One More Round" declares, "I was born to work up to my grave / But I was not born / To be a slave" (155), and "My Arkansas" protests the social system of the Old South, where "Old hates and / ante-bellum lace are rent / but not discarded" (143). Other poems illuminate social problems within the African-American community. For example, "A Kind

Maya Angelou reads her poem "On the Pulse of Morning" at President Clinton's inauguration in 1992. (Reuters/ Gary Hershom/Archive Photos)

of Love, Some Say" is in the voice of a battered woman, whereas "Momma Welfare Roll" is from the viewpoint of a welfare recipient, who says, "They don't give me welfare / I take it" (148). Most of the thirty-two poems in the collection deal with some form of oppression, whether economic, racial, or sexual. (Angelou 1994; Elliot 1989; Hagen 1996; McPherson 1990)

See also Angelou, Maya; Feminism; Poverty; Racism

Angelou, Maya

African-American poet Maya Annie Angelou uses images of her painful upbringing in much of her poetry, which often focuses on racial, sexual, or economic oppression in the African-American community. Born Marguerite Johnson on April 4, 1928, in St. Louis, Missouri, and raised by her grand-

mother in Stamps, Arkansas, Angelou was raped at the age of eight by her mother's boyfriend. The trauma caused by this experience, and by the man's trial, conviction, and subsequent lynching, led Angelou to fall mute for five years. After her recovery she moved to California, where at age 16 she bore a son, and then to New York, where she joined the Harlem Writers Guild and began her career as a writer. She also worked as a singer, both in nightclubs and on stage.

During the 1960s Angelou was an activist for civil rights both in the United States and abroad. She spent several years in Ghana, Africa, editing a magazine called *African Review.* At the request of Martin Luther King Jr. she returned to the United States to become the northern coordinator of the Southern Christian Leadership Conference.

In 1970 she published an autobiography, *I*

Know Why the Caged Bird Sings, that focused on her childhood. She wrote about subsequent periods of her life in *Gather Together in My Name* (1974), *The Heart of a Woman* (1981), and *All God's Children Need Traveling Shoes* (1986). She also wrote screenplays and teleplays related to African-American life in the United States, as well as five collections of poetry: *Just Give Me a Cool Drink of Water 'fore I Diiie* (1971); *Oh Pray My Wings Are Gonna Fit Me Well* (1975); *And Still I Rise* (1978); *Shaker, Why Don't You Sing?* (1983); and *I Shall Not Be Moved* (1990). On January 20, 1993, she delivered her poem "On the Pulse of Morning" at the inauguration of President William Jefferson Clinton, and in 1994 she published *Wouldn't Take Nothing for My Journey Now,* a collection of personal essays.

Angelou has received numerous awards and honorary degrees and is on the board of the American Film Institute. In addition, she is currently the Reynolds Professor of American Studies at Wake Forest University in North Carolina. (Elliot 1989; McPherson 1990)

See also *And Still I Rise;* Feminism; Poverty; Racism

Animal Farm

The 1945 novel *Animal Farm* has been called a political tract, but it is also a commentary on human nature and society. Its author, George Orwell, was a British socialist who intended the work to be a cautionary tale against Soviet socialism, which he deplored. On one occasion he (1996, x) wrote: "I understood, more clearly than ever, the negative influence of the Soviet myth upon the western socialist movement. . . . It was of the utmost importance to me that people in western Europe should see the Soviet regime for what it really was."

In *Animal Farm* Orwell depicts the Soviet regime using animal characters. The novel's setting is Manor Farm, where a cruel farmer abuses his animals to excess. One day they rebel and chase him off his land. They then take over management of the farm themselves. At first they are guided by a grand ideology. They create a list of commandments, which

state that anyone on two legs is an enemy and that no animal shall wear clothes, sleep in a bed, drink alcohol, or kill another animal. Their most important principle is that all animals are created equal. After a short time, however, two pigs begin to fight over control of the farm. One of them, Napoleon, quickly takes over and becomes a brutal dictator. He and his loyal assistants, all of whom are pigs, eventually break all of the farm's commandments. They wear clothes, carry whips, walk on two legs, associate with humans, and exploit the other animals, killing those who oppose them or are no longer able to work. In the end their faces become indistinguishable from those of the men who were their former enemies.

Throughout the novel the animals refer to one another as "comrades," just as Soviet communists do. In this way Orwell emphasizes the connection between the animal's farm and the communist system. His work is a pessimistic view of that system's ability to maintain equality and avoid corruption among its leaders. (Crick 1980; Orwell 1996; Williams 1974)

See also Communism; Labor Issues; Orwell, George

Another Country

Published in 1960 when segregation was still prevalent in the United States, *Another Country,* by African-American writer James Baldwin, shows how racism corrupts interpersonal relationships. According to biographer David Leeming (1994, 200), Baldwin once explained that the book's characters "are on desperate searches for the self-knowledge and self-esteem—the identity—without which real love is impossible. Without such love people are unable to learn to see real human beings behind the categories, labels and prejudices created by the loveless, and the horrifying results of such blindness are evident in the history of the twentieth century."

Set in New York City with some minor scenes in Paris, the novel is divided into three parts. Book One, entitled "Easy Rider," introduces all of the book's African-American characters and is primarily concerned with racial prejudice. Book Two, entitled "Any Day Now," contrasts a loving homosexual relationship with a deteriorating white heterosexual one; its themes involve homosexuality and white elitism. Book Three, "Toward Bethlehem," offers a brief conclusion showing how each main character has resolved or succumbed to his or her particular struggles. In all three books the author shifts viewpoints among the novel's eight major characters.

The story begins with Rufus Scott, a young African-American man who was once a jazz drummer but is now out of work and homeless. Rufus feels he has been betrayed by society. Seven months earlier he was in love with a white woman named Leona, but neither blacks nor whites could accept this relationship. The couple continually "encountered the big world when they went out into the Sunday streets. It stared unsympathetically out at them from the eyes of the passing people; and Rufus realized that he had not thought at all about this world and its power to hate and destroy" (Baldwin 1962, 27). Rufus internalized this hatred, and in his anger he began to berate and beat Leona. Eventually she left him. Now she is in a mental institution, and Rufus is wracked with guilt. He commits suicide by jumping off the George Washington Bridge.

Rufus's best friend, an Irish American named Daniel Vivaldo Moore, feels partly responsible for the suicide because he saw Rufus the night before and did not realize how troubled the man was. Daniel tries to help Rufus's family and falls in love with Rufus's sister Ida. But this interracial relationship has its own difficulties, both from without and within. Not only does society frown on the couple, but also Ida herself has problems accepting her love for Vivaldo. She blames all white people for her brother's death.

Ida tells Vivaldo that when Rufus died, "I felt that I'd been robbed . . . by a group of people too cowardly even to know what they had done. And it didn't seem to me that they deserved any better than what they'd given me. I didn't care what happened to them, just

so they suffered" (417). She also explains that she decided not to end up like Rufus, saying, "I was going to get through the world, and get what I needed out of it, no matter how" (417). This attitude leads her to have an affair with an important white man just to further her career as a singer. However, in the end she realizes that this affair is destroying her soul. She confesses everything to Vivaldo, who still loves her.

Similarly, Vivaldo's friend Eric Jones risks destroying his homosexual relationship with a young Parisian named Yves by having an affair with Cass Silenski, a married mother of two. Eric met Yves while living in France and is waiting for him to come to the United States. When Eric becomes involved with Cass, he warns her that he does not love her, but Cass does not care. She admires Eric, an actor who has been asked to play the part of Stavrogin in a movie version of Fyodor Dostoyevsky's novel *The Possessed*. In contrast, she is disappointed in her husband, Richard, who has become famous for writing a popular novel that she considers insignificant. Eventually Richard finds out about the affair and threatens to divorce Cass and keep her away from her children. At the same time Eric ends their affair, partly because Yves is about to arrive and partly because he has just reconnected with his homosexuality by sleeping with Vivaldo. The novel ends with Yves arriving in New York, full of hopeful expectation about the wonders of this new country. (Baldwin 1962; Eckman 1966; Leeming 1994; Macebuh 1973)

See also Baldwin, James; Gay and Lesbian Issues; Jones, Eric; Moore, Daniel Vivaldo; Poverty; Racism; Scott, Ida and Rufus

Anthony, John

John Anthony appears in John Galsworthy's 1928 play *Strife,* which concerns a factory workers' strike at the Trenartha Tin Plate Works. As the founder of the company and the chair of its board of directors, Anthony stubbornly refuses to listen to the workers' demands. He refuses all attempts at compromise and believes that his employees should be treated as inferiors. At one point he says:

It has been said that times have changed; if they have, I have not changed with them. Neither will I. It has been said that masters and men are equal! Cant! There can only be one master in a house! Where two men meet the better man will rule. It has been said that Capital and Labour have the same interests. Cant! Their interests are as wide asunder as the poles. It has been said that the Board is only part of a machine. Cant! We *are* the machine; its brains and sinews, it is for us to lead and to determine what is to be done, and to do it without fear of favour. (Galsworthy 1928, 101)

(Galsworthy 1928)

See also Galsworthy, John; *Strife*

"Antiquity of Freedom, The"

Written by social reformer William Cullen Bryant, the short poem "The Antiquity of Freedom" (1821) depicts freedom as "a bearded man, armed to the teeth" who is "strong from struggling." Even when "Merciless Power" has created a dungeon and chains for him, he is not vanquished. Instead, he rises up out of his imprisonment and calls for nations to help him destroy the "pale oppressor" (Sinclair 1996, 167). (Sinclair 1996; Sturges 1968)

See also Bryant, William Cullen

Anti-Semitism

Anti-Semitism is a term generally used to refer to discrimination against Jewish people, either as a religious group or an ethnic group. This discrimination has taken many forms throughout the centuries. For example, in ancient times Jews were persecuted for refusing to worship pagan gods and were typically denied Roman citizenship. During the fifteenth century they were thrown out of Spain unless they agreed to convert to Christianity, and in the sixteenth century European cities began requiring them to live in walled communities called ghettos, which were locked at night and during Christian festivals.

Most countries had abolished forced segregation of the Jews by the late nineteenth century, although this practice was revived by the Nazis during World War II. However, because of continuing anti-Semitism among Europe's predominantly Christian population, many European Jews continued to live in ghettos even when they were no longer required to do so. Israel Zangwill depicts this type of anti-Semitism in his 1892 novel *Children of the Ghetto,* a work that focuses on the religious differences between Christians and Jews in nineteenth-century London.

Other writers have dealt with anti-Semitism as a form of racism. For example, Yevgeny Yevtushenko's 1961 poem "Babii Yar" concerns a racist Nazi massacre of Ukranian Jews, and Doris Lessing's novels about racism in South Africa include several persecuted Jewish characters. Novelists Jean-Paul Sartre and Émile Zola have protested this type of anti-Semitism in France, as have many political protest writers throughout history. (Flannery 1965; McWilliams 1948; Pulzer 1964)

See also "Babii Yar"; *Children of the Ghetto;* Lessing, Doris; Racism; Sartre, Jean-Paul; Yevtushenko, Yevgeny; Zangwill, Israel; Zola, Émile

Apartheid

The term *apartheid* is derived from an Afrikaans word meaning "apartness." It refers to legal and political policies of racial segregation established in South Africa during the late 1940s. Under apartheid, individuals were classified as white, Bantu (black), or coloured (mixed-race). Later, officials added the classification of Asian. Each race was required to live and do business in certain areas, and a variety of laws sprung up to further segregate one race from another. For example, interracial marriages were forbidden, and nonwhites could not participate in the national government. There were also restrictions regarding what types of jobs each race could hold.

Many authors protested South Africa's social policies. The most notable of these are Alan Paton, Peter Abrahams, Breyten Breytenbach, and Doris Lessing. As the result of such protest, the South African government gradually began relaxing apartheid laws during the 1980s, and official discrimination ended completely in 1994. Nonetheless, the country still struggles against racism in the private sector. (La Guma 1972)

See also Abrahams, Peter; Breytenbach, Breyten; Lessing, Doris; Paton, Alan

Archanians, The

The Archanians, by Aristophanes, is the first in a series of three Greek comedies written during the Peloponnesian War (431–404 B.C.) between the rival Greek city-states of Athens and Sparta. The play's initial performance was in January 426 B.C., when it won first prize at the Lenaean Festival. It was followed by *Peace* in 422 B.C. and *Lysistrata* in 411 B.C.

Aristophanes's goal in writing the series was to criticize the war and the people who perpetuated it. In *The Archanians* an Athenian agriculturist named Dicaeopolis argues for peace in a public forum. When no one listens to him, he sends his representative Amphitheus to negotiate a private peace between himself and the Lacedaemonians of Sparta. Amphitheus returns with three possible treaties, symbolized by three types of wine. Dicaeopolis samples each one and chooses the best tasting: 30 years of peace on land and sea. This displeases the Archanians, a chorus of "old dotards" (Aristophanes 1930, 97) who do not believe Dicaeopolis when he argues that the Lacedaemonians are not responsible for all of Athens's troubles. However, eventually the chorus reports that "convinced by this man's speech, the folk have changed their view and approve him for having concluded peace" (117), and after conducting a series of unusual business deals, Dicaeopolis is invited to a feast. (Aristophanes 1930; Murray 1933)

See also Aristophanes; *Lysistrata; Peace;* Peace

Archer, Newland

A young New York attorney during the 1870s, Newland Archer appears in Edith Wharton's novel *The Age of Innocence* (1986). He struggles with the rigid social codes of his day, often expressing his distaste for conformity, and falls in love with a very unconventional woman. He considers leaving his wife for her, but in the end he succumbs to society's expectations and remains married. He never sees his beloved again. (Wharton, 1986)

See also *Age of Innocence, The*

Aristophanes

Aristophanes was a Greek comedic playwright who lived from approximately 444 to 385 B.C. and wrote more than 40 plays. Only eleven survive today, including *The Archanians* (425 B.C.), *The Knights* (424 B.C.), *The Clouds* (423 B.C.), *The Wasps* (422 B.C.), *Peace* (421 B.C.), and *Lysistrata* (411 B.C.). In these and other comedies, Aristophanes uses humor to criticize the social and political institutions of his time. In particular, he attacks those who threaten traditional democracy in Athens, and he is highly critical of Athens's 27-year war with Sparta. Scholars know very little about Aristophanes's personal life, but they suspect that he was born in Athens and had ties to the island of Aegina. (Aristophanes 1930; Murray 1933)

See also *Archanians, The; Lysistrata; Peace;* Peace

Ariyoshi, Sawako

Born in Wakayama, Japan, on January 20, 1931, Sawako Ariyoshi is noted for her novels describing domestic life in Japan, in which she criticizes certain aspects of modern society. She studied literature and drama at the Tokyo Women's Christian College and began her writing career while working for a publishing company. Her first publications were primarily literary articles and short stories, although she also wrote scripts for radio, movies, television, and stage productions. Her plays are still popular in Japan. In 1959 she published the novel *Kinokawa* (The River Ki), which traces the lives of three generations of Japanese women. Her next novel, *Hanaoka Seishu no tsuma* (The Doctor's Wife), concerns the family of a nineteenth-century Japanese surgeon. It was published in 1967 and translated into French in 1981, becoming a best-seller in France. In 1964 she published the novel *Hishoku* (Without Color), which focused on racism in the United States, followed in 1972 by *Kokotso no hito* (The Twilight Years), which deals with ageism in Japan and sold over a million copies in its first year of publication. Her novel *Fukogo osen* (The Compound Pollution), published in 1975, criticizes environmental pollution. Ariyoshi also wrote a historical novel, *Kazu no miyasama otome* (Her Highness Princess Kazu) in 1978 and a travelogue, *Chugoku repoto* (China Report) in 1979. She died in Tokyo, Japan, on August 30, 1984. (Ariyoshi 1987)

See also Ageism; Feminism; *Twilight Years, The*

Asian-American Literature

Asian Americans have primarily expressed social protest through nonfiction rather than fiction, but not necessarily by choice. As Elaine H. Kim explains in her chapter on Asian-American Literature in the *Columbia Literary History of the United States* (Elliott 1988, 811–812):

> Autobiography has been a popular genre among Asian-American writers, largely because it has been the most marketable. Given the popular image of Asian Americans as perpetual foreigners, some publishers preferred writings with anthropological appeal over fiction. Others encouraged Asian-American writers to present their work as autobiographical even when it was not. Carlos Bulosan was persuaded to write *America Is in the Heart* (1946) as personal history because it seemed likely to sell best that way. Although Maxine Hong Kingston's *The Woman Warrior* (1975) is fiction, it has been classified and sold as autobiography, or more broadly as nonfiction.

In discussing such works, Kim says that early examples, such as Lee Yan Phou's *When I Was a Boy in China* (1887) and New Il-Han's *When I Was a Boy in Korea* (1928), focused on "superficialities of food and dress, or ceremonies and customs, to appeal to the benign curiosity of Western readers" (812). For the most part, these books did not reflect the true problems of the Asian people. According to Kim (812):

These early autobiographical works disclose a marked dissociation between the authors and the common people of both Asia and the West. Even their tentative apologetic pleas for racial tolerance are made primarily for members of the author's own privileged class. Publishers and readers accepted them as representing all Asian Americans, but with few exceptions these works ignored the large numbers of laborers recruited for agricultural and construction work in Hawaii and the American West between 1840 and 1924.

Kim reports that the exception to this lack of realism was *America Is in the Heart*, by migrant farmworker Carlos Bulosan. This semi-autobiographical book describes the lives of Asian-American farmworkers and cannery workers during the 1920s and 1930s; it is not a criticism of American labor institutions but a testament to democracy.

Kim believes that publishers "discouraged or even suppressed writers" who in any way criticized America's treatment of Asians (813). In part, this was because throughout the years, the marketplace continued to support only the most pleasant portrayals of the Asian-American experience. For example, she says: "Both Lin Yutang's *Chinatown Family* (1948) and Chin Yang Lee's *Flower Drum Song* (1957) present euphemistic portraits of Chinatown, and both quickly earned popular and financial success. By contrast, Louis Chu's *Eat a Bowl of Tea* (1961) offers a more realistic insider's view of the daily life, manners, attitudes, and problems of the Chinese American community—and it failed to gain readers or make money" (815).

Moreover, Kim says that Asian Americans' isolation from mainstream culture influenced the nature of their autobiographical material, explaining: "In many stories that portray Asian-American community life, there are no white characters at all simply because segregated existence excluded them. As a result, issues of racism and race relations are submerged" (814). Therefore there are no major social protest novels by Asian Americans.

However, modern Asian-American authors have expressed social protest concerns through a rich body of poetry, much of which has been privately published. Kim cites several examples of Asian-American verse, including "A Homecoming" (1972) by Korean immigrant Kinchung Kim. This work addresses the difficulties of a young Korean returning to his country after ten years in the United States.

Elaine Kim (820) also states that regardless of genre:

> the quest for a place in American life is a recurrent theme in Asian-American literature. Contemporary writers . . . focus not on accommodation or racial self-negation but on the ideal that Carlos Bulosan articulated in the 1940s, of an America of the heart, where it is possible to be both American and nonwhite. Indeed, several contemporary Asian-American writers express kinship with other nonwhite Americans, especially blacks and Native Americans, who frequently appear in their works.

(Elliot 1988)

See also Native American Issues

Atkins, Homer

Homer Atkins appears in the 1958 novel *The Ugly American,* by William Lederer and Eugene Burdick. He is an engineer who travels to Asia as a consultant to the U.S. and French governments on the building of dams and military roads. However, he quickly realizes that the region has more important needs and recommends that the two governments spend their money instead on local projects such as canning and brick factories, which would help make the Asian people self-sufficient. After his opinion is rudely rejected, he decides to help the Asians on his own. He works with an Asian mechanic to invent a water pump that will direct water to hillside crops, and the two men open a factory to mass-produce these machines. They also make their design available to anyone who wants to make his own machine. Atkins therefore represents the authors' position that what is needed in Asia is simple,

basic help. In an epilogue to their novel, Lederer and Burdick (1958, 281–282) say:

> Most American technicians abroad are involved in the planning and execution of "big" projects: dams, highways, irrigation systems. The result is that we often develop huge technical complexes, which some day may pay dividends but which at this moment in Asian development are neither needed nor wanted except by a few local politicians who see such projects as a means to power and wealth. Technicians who want to work on smaller and more manageable projects are not encouraged. The authors of this book gathered statements from native economists of what projects were "most urgently needed" in various Asian countries. These included improvement of chicken and pig breeding, small pumps which did not need expensive replacement parts, knowledge on commercial fishing, canning of food, . . . and the development of small industries. These are the projects which would not only make friends, while costing little, but are also prerequisite to industrialization and economic independence for Asia.

(Lederer and Burdick 1958)

See also Burdick, Eugene; Knox, Tom; Lederer, William J.; *Ugly American, The*

Atlas Shrugged

Atlas Shrugged, by Ayn Rand, presents its author's views on capitalism, government regulation, and individual drive. Published in 1957, the novel depicts an American society that punishes the rich for being rich. The fictional U.S. government passes a series of laws that make it difficult for entrepreneurs to profit from their own efforts, and what money they do make is redirected into the hands of people who are mediocre, shiftless, or manipulative. The worst members of society are feeding off of the best and making the best feel guilty for their success. Of this situation, one character says:

Men who have no courage, pride or self-esteem, men who have no moral sense of their right to their money and are not willing to defend it as they defend their life, men who apologize for being rich—will not remain rich for long. They are the natural bait for the swarms of looters that stay under rocks for centuries, but come crawling out at the first smell of a man who begs to be forgiven for the guilt of owning wealth. They will hasten to relieve him of the guilt—and of his life, as he deserves.

Then you will see the rise of the men of the double standard—the men who live by force, yet count on those who live by trade to crate the value of their looted money—the men who are the hitchhikers of virtue. . . . Money is the barometer of a society's virtue. When you see . . . that in order to produce, you need to obtain permission from men who deal, not in goods, but in favors—when you see that men get richer by graft and by pull than by work, and your laws don't protect you against them, but protect them against you—when you see corruption being rewarded and honesty becoming a self-sacrifice—you may know that your society is doomed. (Rand 1992, 385)

Gradually the most successful industrialists decide that they are no longer willing to live in a society where they represent the mythical figure of Atlas, shouldering the burdens of the world. They "shrug"—or in other words, they go on strike. One by one they destroy or abandon their businesses and disappear, leaving the world without the products they used to produce. But strangely no one can figure out where these industrialists have gone.

Then one person, Dagny Taggert, begins to suspect that there is something sinister involved. Taggert is in charge of her family's railroad line, Taggert Transcontinental, and many of the missing industrialists are her friends. As a dedicated businesswoman she cannot understand how these men could have abandoned their life's work. She beings to investi-

gate the situation and discovers that a mysterious stranger has been leading these men away just when their businesses are the most threatened by government interference.

Taggert wonders whether she will be next. Her railroad is in serious financial trouble, partially because its tracks are in disrepair, and she decides to construct a new line using an untested metal that is cheaper, yet stronger than steel. Government officials insist that this metal will crack, and they publicly accuse Dagny of trying to kill people. They also attack the metal's inventor, Hank Reardon, saying that he is more interested in money than in the people's welfare. Nonetheless, Taggert and Reardon build the railroad, and it proves successful. The two industrialists then begin having an affair.

Later this affair is used against them. The government passes a new law that reads, in part, "All patents and copyrights, pertaining to any devices, inventions, formulas, processes and works of any nature whatsoever, shall be turned over to the nation as a patriotic emergency gift by means of Gift Certificates to be signed voluntarily by the owners of all such patents and copyrights" (499). The authorities want Reardon to sign the Gift Certificate, giving away all of his rights to his special metal, but he refuses. Then they tell him that they know about the affair and will make it public if he refuses to sign. Not wanting Taggert to get hurt, he agrees. But this plan backfires when she finds out about his sacrifice, and during a live radio interview in which she is supposed to express support for the government, she tells the public about the blackmail. The government cuts her microphone, but the damage has already been done. People now realize how corrupt their society has become.

By this time Taggert has learned the whereabouts of the disappearing industrialists. While following a promising young inventor, she discovered a secret valley in the Rocky Mountains of Colorado. All of her missing friends are there, waiting for the time when they can once again profit from their own efforts. Also in the valley is her former lover, Francisco D'Anconia. Head of the largest copper company in the world, he has been gradually destroying the profitability of his copper mines in order to punish those who are planning to take them away. Moreover, D'Anconia was one of the first individuals to join forces with the group's founder, John Galt, a brilliant inventor who walked away from a company that sought to reward other employees for his hard work.

Taggert immediately falls in love with Galt, and he and the other members of the group ask her to stay with them in the valley. She refuses because she is not yet ready to abandon her railroad company. After promising not to reveal their existence or their plans, she returns home, where society has begun to deteriorate. Without the industrialists to work the mines, ship the goods, and create new products, life has become very difficult. Food and heating materials are scarce, and angry mobs are becoming more common. The leaders of the country have begun to fear the public. Nonetheless, they continue to oppress the remaining industrialists, particularly Hank Reardon. Finally he decides to join with Galt's group. Meanwhile Dagny Taggert continues to hope that she will not have to abandon her railroad, but she begins to change her mind after Galt makes a rousing radio speech to the public to reveal his philosophy in full. After this the government tracks him down, captures him, and tortures him to make him support the society. Taggert now decides to abandon her railroad. She helps Galt's group rescue him, and together they go to the valley, where they make plans to rebuild the country.

In discussing this novel, which had an original working title of *The Strike,* Ayn Rand (Rand 1992, 2–3) said: "I start with *the fantastic premise of the prime movers going on strike.* This is the actual heart and center of the novel. A distinction carefully to be observed here; I do not set out to glorify the prime mover. . . . I set out to show how desperately the world needs prime movers, and how viciously it treats them." She intended the work to be a statement of her philosophical principles, which collectively became known as Objectivism and attracted a large

Margaret Atwood, March 22, 1989 (Reuters/Gary Hershom/Archive Photos)

number of followers. (Baker 1987; Rand 1992)

See also Capitalism; Galt, John; Justice; Labor Issues; Rand, Ayn; Reardon, Hank; Taggert, Dagny

Atwood, Margaret

Margaret Eleanor Atwood is the author of several important feminist novels, including *The Edible Woman* (1969) and *The Handmaid's Tale* (1985). Born on November 18, 1939, in Ottawa, Canada, she began her writing career as a poet. Her first poem was published when she was nineteen and her first poetry collection when she was twenty-one. At that time she was attending the University of Toronto, where she received a B.A. in 1961. She received an M.A. from Radcliffe College in Cambridge, Massachusetts, in 1962 and later studied at Harvard University. She has traveled extensively throughout the world.

In 1966 her poetry collection *The Circle Game* was awarded a prestigious national prize, the Canadian Governor General's Award for Poetry. Her novel *The Handmaid's Tale* won the same award for fiction in 1986. Her first novel was *The Edible Woman;* subsequent novels include *Surfacing* (1972), *Bodily Harm* (1981), *Cat's Eye* (1988), and *The Robber Bride* (1993). She has also written short stories, articles, and children's books. (Davidson 1981; Grace 1980; Rosenberg 1984)

See also *Edible Woman, The;* Feminism; *Handmaid's Tale, The*

Autobiography of an Ex-Colored Man, The

The 1912 novel *The Autobiography of an Ex-Colored Man* was first published anonymously in order to make it seem like a true story. Its author, James Weldon Johnson, was a black man who experienced American racism, but unlike his book's unnamed narrator, he did not abandon his heritage. This fictional narrator is so light-skinned that many people mistakenly believe he is a white man. He is also a skilled musician who dreams of becoming a great composer; by so doing, he hopes to prove that blacks are not an inferior race. One day he decides to travel throughout the South listening to black music for inspiration. There he sees a group of white men set a black man on fire, and from that moment on he pretends to be white. Eventually he marries a white woman, who dies giving birth to his second child. He continues to pretend he is white and becomes a prosperous man. However, he concludes, "My love for my children makes me glad that I am what I am and keeps me from desiring to be otherwise; and yet, when I sometimes open a little box in which I still keep my fast yellowing [music] manuscripts, the only tangible remnants of a vanished dream, a dead ambition, a sacrificed talent, I cannot repress the thought that, after all, I have chosen the lesser part, that I have sold my birthright for a mess of pottage" (Johnson 1990, 154).

In writing about the novel in a 1990 introduction to Johnson's work, scholar William Andrews (xxvii) says that this ending does not mean that the narrator's life was meaningless:

> Were the heritage and communal expression of black America to be consigned to this sort of private oblivion, this novel would seem indeed to culminate in tragedy. But through the ex-colored man's acknowledgement of his failure as a composer, Johnson allows him to succeed as a writer. The *Autobiography*'s unprecedented analysis of the social causes and artistic consequences of a black man's denial of the best within himself constitutes perhaps

James Weldon Johnson's greatest service to African-American culture.

But Johnson does not just comment on the black experience. Because his novel's narrator has also lived as a white man, Johnson has the opportunity to discuss the effect that racism has on white society. For example, the narrator says:

> I am sure it would be safe to wager that no group of Southern white men could get together and talk for sixty minutes without bringing up the "race question." If a Northern white man happened to be in the group, the time could be safely cut to thirty minutes. In this respect I consider the conditions of the whites more to be deplored than that of the blacks. Here, a truly great people, a people that produced a majority of the great historic Americans from Washington to Lincoln, now forced to use up its energies in a conflict as lamentable as it is violent. (55)

Johnson also discusses the social protest novel *Uncle Tom's Cabin*. He complains about successful attempts to ban the book in school libraries and calls Harriet Beecher Stowe's novel "a fair and truthful panorama of slavery" (Johnson 1990, 29). (Johnson 1990; Levy 1973; Price and Oliver 1997)

See also Johnson, James Weldon; Racism; Stowe, Harriet Beecher; *Uncle Tom's Cabin*

Autobiography of Miss Jane Pittman, The

Published in 1971, *The Autobiography of Miss Jane Pittman,* by Ernest J. Gaines, protests racism in American society by tracing the life of a fictional black woman during 100 years of history, from the Civil War to the beginning of the civil rights movement. In the novel's introduction a fictional historian explains that in 1962 he interviewed a 110-year-old woman named Jane Pittman and tape-recorded her recollections. The rest of the book is the first-person narration of her life story.

Her narration begins when she is ten or eleven years old. At that time she answers to the name "Ticey." One day she encounters some Yankee soldiers passing through her Louisiana plantation during the Civil War. One of them tells her that Ticey is a slave name. Explaining that she will soon be set free, the soldier renames her "Jane," after his girlfriend in Ohio, and gives her his own last name, "Brown." After the soldiers have left, Jane refuses to answer to the name Ticey anymore. Her owners beat her. A year later the war ends and Jane heads north with several other slaves. Along the way some racist white men kill all of her traveling companions, except for one small boy named Ned. Jane becomes his mother. Together the two try to get to Ohio to find Mr. Brown, but Louisiana is a big state, and they soon give up all hope of leaving it.

Jane finds work on a plantation that has a school for Ned, and for a while life is good. Then a racist takes control of the place. The school is closed and life becomes as bad as it was under slavery. When Ned reaches the age of 17 or 18, he heads north to Kansas. Jane remains in Louisiana and moves in with Joe Pittman, who is an expert at breaking horses. One day he is killed while rounding up a wild stallion. Jane is distraught but goes on with her life. She is delighted when Ned returns to Louisiana to set up a school, but she fears for his life. Racist groups are prevalent in the South. But despite Jane's warnings, Ned refuses to give up his teaching. He believes in its importance, saying: "I want my children to be men. . . . I want my children to fight. Fight for all—not just for a corner. The black man or white man who tell you to stay in a corner want to keep your mind in a corner too. I'm building that school so you'll have a chance to get from out of that corner" (Gaines 1972, 110). Ned is soon murdered for his views, and even though there are several witnesses to the crime, the police make no effort to arrest the killer.

Shortly thereafter Jane moves seven miles north to another plantation, where she lives out the rest of her life. The plantation is owned by Robert Sampson, who has two sons. The oldest, Timmy, is half black and il-

legitimate. The other, Tee Bob, is white and legitimate. Robert treats both boys well, but he is particularly close to Timmy, who acts the most like him. Nonetheless, when Timmy grows too arrogant, Robert sends him away. Later Tee Bob falls in love with a half-black girl. When she refuses to marry him, he kills himself.

By this time the workers on the plantation have become convinced that one of their young people, Jimmy, will become a great man. They want him to be a preacher, but instead he becomes an activist. Jane disagrees with his methods, saying that he is moving too fast. She explains:

> You talk of freedom, Jimmy. Freedom here is able to make a little living and have the white folks say you good. . . . [Your people] want you, Jimmy, but now you here they don't understand nothing you telling them. You see, Jimmy, they want you to cure the ache, but they want you to do it and don't give them pain. And the worse pain, Jimmy, you can inflict is what you doing now—that's trying to make them see they good as the other man. You see, Jimmy, they been told from the cradle they wasn't—that they wasn't much better than the mule. You keep telling them this over and over, for hundreds and hundreds of years, they start thinking that way. (236)

Jane warns him that it could take a long time to change people. Nonetheless, Jimmy organizes a protest in the nearby city of Bayonne, where a black girl has been arrested for drinking from a "whites-only" water fountain. Before the protest can take place, he is killed. Jane then defies Robert Sampson's orders and makes plans to attend the protest with her friends, saying that, although Jimmy is gone, "just a little piece of him is dead. . . . The rest of him is waiting for us in Bayonne" (245).

The Autobiography of Miss Jane Pittman was a powerful statement against racism. However, a television movie based on the novel made Jane Pittman an even stronger advocate of civil rights; it ended with her drinking from the whites-only fountain herself. Televised in 1974, the show earned nine Emmy awards. (Babb 1991; Estes 1994; Gaines 1972)

See also Gaines, Ernest J.; Pittman, Jane Brown; Racism; Slavery

Avery, Shug

Shug Avery appears in Alice Walker's 1982 novel *The Color Purple*. A black singer, she helps the main character, Celie, develop self-respect. Shug encourages her friend to stand up to her oppressive husband, become independent, and start her own clothing business. Eventually Shug also becomes Celie's lover, and the two live together. In turn, Celie teaches Shug to quilt. With their friend Sophia they use quilting to become more deeply connected to one another. *The Color Purple* uses this symbol to show that communal solidarity can enhance personal growth. (Walker 1986)

See also *Color Purple, The;* Walker, Alice

B

Babbitt

Published in 1922, *Babbitt*, by Sinclair Lewis, tells the story of a 46-year-old real estate salesman who leads a successful but unsatisfying life. As the novel progresses, George F. Babbitt's unhappiness grows, and he begins to challenge many of the social conventions he once valued.

The novel begins in April 1920 in the midwestern American town of Zenith. It is a place where people conform in both behavior and thought. Anyone who expresses a different opinion from the masses is suspect. Babbitt himself suspects such nonconformists. For example, he questions the morals of his neighbors, who drink alcohol despite the Prohibition laws then in effect. He also scathingly attacks labor unions that want to change the status quo, saying:

> A good labor union is of value because it keeps out radical unions, which would destroy property. No one ought to be forced to belong to a union, however. All labor agitators who try to force men to join a union should be hanged. In fact, just between ourselves, there oughtn't to be any unions allowed at all; and as it's the best way of fighting the unions, every businessman ought to belong to an employers'- association and to the Chamber of Commerce. In union there is strength. So any selfish hog who doesn't join the Chamber of Commerce ought to be forced to. (Lewis 1950, 44)

Babbitt does not hear the hypocrisy in his words. He parrots his beliefs without seeming to understand them. He also lacks self-awareness. For example, he believes himself to be a reputable businessman, yet many of his real estate practices are unethical, and some border on the illegal. His main goal is to increase his standing in the community.

However, Babbitt begins to experience self-doubt when his best friend and former college roommate, Paul Reisling, goes through a personal crisis. Reisling always wanted to be a violinist, but his artistic career was cut short by marriage. To support his wife, Zilla, he took a job as a roofing salesman, and now he is profoundly unhappy, not only because of his lost dreams but also because Zilla berates him constantly. Babbitt is mildly unhappy at home himself; he feels that his wife, Myra, and children Ted, Verona, and Tinka value him only for his paycheck. Therefore, he suggests that he and Paul go on a fishing trip to Maine to get away from their heavy responsibilities for a while. They have a good time together, but when they return to Zenith, their lives are still the same.

Babbitt finds himself increasingly bored at work. Meanwhile Paul begins having an affair. Eventually he grows so angry with Zilla that he tries to kill her, shooting her in the shoulder. She recovers, but he is sent to prison. This event propels Babbitt into his own personal crisis. He begins to question his values and beliefs and makes some changes in his life. At first these changes are small. For example, he goes to see a movie in the middle of a business day. He expresses admiration for an old college friend, Seneca Doane, who is a hated social reformer, and when a labor strike occurs in town, he expresses sympathy for the strikers and the union leaders. However, eventually Babbitt's nonconformity becomes more extreme. He starts having an affair and spends much of his time drinking with a group of liberal thinkers, particularly when his wife is out of town visiting relatives. His friends and business associates warn him to behave better; when Babbitt does not listen to them, they shun him in public. He bemoans the loss of their respect, yet when they insist he join their newly formed Good Citizen's League, dedicated to preserving conservative thought in Zenith, he stubbornly refuses. Then his wife falls ill. Babbitt watches the townspeople offer her deep emotional support, and he realizes how lonely he has been as a nonconformist. He joins the Good Citizen's League and is once again warmly accepted into the community.

However, he is not quite the same man as he was at the beginning of the novel. When his son Ted tells the family that he and his girlfriend have eloped, and that he is going to leave college and take the job he has always wanted—as an auto mechanic—to support them, Babbitt encourages him to follow his dreams and never let society wear him down. Of this speech, scholar Martin Light (1975, 84) says: "It is impossible . . . to read Babbitt's last speech—his advice to his son to do what he wants to do—without realizing that Lewis had allowed Babbitt to know to a small extent what his experience of rebellion has meant. But George is still very much a Babbitt, frightened,

guilty, and conformist, and both his way of addressing his son and that son's character itself leave little confidence of growth." Babbit's son Ted displays as little self-awareness as Babbit himself.

Soon after the novel was published, the word *Babbittry* came to mean blind support for the status quo, and the character of Babbitt was taken as a symbol for a broader part of society. Scholar Sheldon Grebstein (1962, 82) explains: "By means of this Babbitt, Lewis uses the book as a vehicle for satire and social history, the portrayal of a whole way of life in a representative American city. In this context Lewis gives us . . . [an] account of the conditions of life in an industrial and commercial society, which is dominated by the profit motive and acquiescent to the pressure toward sameness and standardization." Moreover, according to Grebstein (85), the book "summarized every criticism advanced against the middle class in the 1920's, and it rendered a superb account of the devastating effects of a material culture." It therefore engendered much discussion and criticism and as Grebstein reports has often been called "the outstanding social satire of its generation" (85). (Grebstein 1962; Lewis 1950; Schorer 1962)

See also Doane, Seneca; Labor Issues; Lewis, Sinclair; Reisling, Paul; Socialism

"Babii Yar"

"Babii Yar," by Yevgeny Yevtushenko, is the Russian poet's most famous work. This 1961 poem (also spelled "Baby Yar" or "Babi Yar") opens by lamenting the fact that there is no monument at Babii Yar, where thousands of Ukranian Jews were once massacred by the Nazis. It then protests current anti-Semitism in the Soviet Union, saying: "How vile these anti-Semites—without a qualm / they pompously call themselves / 'The Union of the Russian People'!" (Yevtushenko 1989, 147). The poem is extremely direct, a quality that scholar George Reavey believes caused its success. In discussing "Babii Yar" in a 1989 introduction to the work, Reavey (xii) says: "Yevtushenko's direct treatment of the subject [of anti-Semitism] was very forthright and brave. It was this poem more than anything else that gave him such immediate worldwide publicity. 'Babii Yar' . . . was certainly a most effective poem, rousing both emotions and passions, stirring many dovecots and thus demonstrating the potential power of the poetic world." Reavey (xii) adds that the poem therefore was subjected to "a whole barrage of rather savage attacks." Nonetheless, its great popularity abroad made it difficult for the Soviet authorities to punish Yevtushenko for writing the work. (Yevtushenko 1989)

See also Anti-Semitism; Yevtushenko, Yevgeny

Bakha

The main character from Mulk Raj Anand's 1935 novel *Untouchable,* Bakha is a member of India's Untouchables—the lowest caste in Hindu society. As such he is responsible for cleaning latrines and sweeping dung. He bemoans his place in society and agrees with an Indian poet who says that "we must destroy caste, we must destroy the inequalities of birth and unalterable vocations. We must recognise an equality of rights, privileges and opportunities for everyone" (Anand 1940, 155). (Anand 1940)

See also Anand, Mulk Raj; Class, Social; *Untouchable*

Baldwin, James

In novels and essays African-American author James Arthur Baldwin advocated civil rights activism and spoke against racism and sexism. Biographer David Leeming (1994, xiii) explains that Baldwin personally "took the side of those who were made into exiles and outcasts by barriers of race, sex, and class or who turned away from safety and chose the honorable path of tearing down such barriers. [He also] mourned for those who had created the barriers and had unwittingly allowed themselves to be destroyed by them."

Baldwin was born in Harlem, New York City, on August 2, 1924. His mother, Berdis Jones, was unmarried at the time of his birth, but when he was two years old she wed a minister, David Baldwin, who was the son of a

James Baldwin (Walter Daran/Archive Photos)

slave. According to Leeming (3), "illegitimacy and an almost obsessive preoccupation with his stepfather were constant themes in [his] life and work" (3). Baldwin did not respect his stepfather because of the man's "bitter subservience to bill collectors, landlords, and other whites" and considered him "the archetypal black father, one generation removed from slavery, prevented by the ever-present shadow and the frequently present effects of racial discrimination from providing his family with what they needed most—their birthright, their identity as individuals rather than as members of a class or a race" (5). Moreover, as a result of his stepfather's frustration with life, Baldwin's household was filled with "an arbitrary and puritanical discipline and a depressing air of bitter frustration which did nothing to alleviate the pain of poverty and oppression" (5).

Fortunately, the young Baldwin found a mentor in Countee Cullen, a well-known poet who had become a teacher in Harlem. Baldwin considered Cullen "living proof that a black man could be a writer" (22). Nonetheless, upon graduating from junior high school at age 14, Baldwin became not a writer but a minister, preaching in a small evangelical church. There he learned to use language effectively, and the rhythm of his writing would later reflect this experience. After three years in the ministry he left the church and his childhood home in Harlem for Greenwich Village, the bohemian section of New York City, where he became the protégé of Beauford Delany, a black artist. Baldwin also held a series of odd jobs.

Baldwin's writing career began in 1945 when he and a friend started a literary magazine, *This Generation*. At this time Baldwin was working on a novel called *In My Father's House;* he published a portion of it in the magazine as a short story. He also gave readings of *In My Father's House* at writers' gatherings. One of his listeners introduced him to author Richard Wright, then famous for his novel *Native Son,* who shared Baldwin's unfinished manuscript with his editor. As a result, Baldwin received a fellowship and grant money to finish his novel, which was published in 1953 as *Go Tell It on the Mountain.* He also continued to publish short stories and essays. In 1948 he moved to Europe, where he came to terms with his homosexuality. His 1956 novel *Giovanni's Room* reflects this experience.

Baldwin returned to the United States in 1957. By this time, in addition to his first novel, he had published a collection of essays entitled *Notes of a Native Son* (1955). It was followed by two more books of essays, *Nobody Knows My Name* (1961) and *The Fire Next Time* (1963), and the novels *Tell Me How Long the Train's Been Gone* (1968) and *Just Above My Head* (1979). Baldwin also wrote several plays, including *The Amen Corner* (1955), *Blues for Mister Charlie* (1964), and *The Women at the Well* (1972). He died on December 1, 1987, in Saint-Paul, France. (Eckman 1966; Leeming 1994; Macebuh 1973)

See also *Another Country;* Cullen, Countee; Gay and Lesbian Issues; *If Beale Street Could Talk; Native Son;* Poverty; Racism; Wright, Richard

"Ballad of Reading Gaol, The"

"The Ballad of Reading Gaol" is a semiautobiographical poem by Oscar Wilde that draws on his experiences as a prisoner in Reading Gaol, where he served two years for sodomy. Originally published under the pseudonym C.3.3., which was Wilde's cell number, it is the story of a prisoner sentenced to death for murdering his lover. The poem is a lengthy work that not only criticizes society's response to homosexuality but also attacks its legal systems and the hypocrisy of traditional religions. Regarding the latter, for example, the poem says, "That every prison that men build / Is built with bricks of shame, / And bound with bars lest Christ should see / How men their brothers maim" (Sinclair 1996, 115). (Aldington 1946; Ellman 1969; Sinclair 1996)

See also Gay and Lesbian Issues; Prison Reform; Wilde, Oscar

Balzac, Honoré de

Honoré de Balzac is the author of *La Comédie humaine* (The Human Comedy), a series of approximately 90 novels and novellas published in France between 1829 and 1847. Set between 1308 and 1846, these works show the political and social changes that occurred in the country during those years in order to criticize French society and offer insights into the causes and impact of the French Revolution.

Balzac, whose original last name was Balssa, was born on May 20, 1799, in Tours, France. He was educated in the cities of Vendôme and Paris and became a law clerk at age 16. At that time he began writing both plays and novels under a pseudonym. All of his works failed, and for a brief time he became a businessman. This career almost led him to ruin; he amassed many debts that he would struggle to repay for the rest of his life.

However, when Balzac was 30, his luck changed. In 1829, under his own name, he published the novel *Les Chouans* (The Chouans) about a band of peasants who supported the Royalist cause during the French Revolution, as well as the comedy *Les Physiologie du mariage* (The Physiology of Marriage), about marriage and adultery. Both of these books were a success, which scholar Samuel Rogers attributes to a change in

Balzac's politics. Rogers (1953, 15) explains: "Politically . . . his views began to change about his thirtieth year, and . . . he abandoned once and for all the bourgeois liberalism that had been the tradition of his family. Throughout the rest of his life, with minor shifts produced by political events and by new contacts with either people or books, he supported the royalist party and the Catholic Church."

Balzac continued to write novels for the rest of his life. By 1834 he had already decided to group his individual works, both past and future, into *The Human Comedy*. They include *Le Medicine de campagne* (The Country Doctor, 1833), *Le Père Goriot* (Father Goriot, 1835), *La Cousine Bette* (Cousin Bette, 1846), and *Le Cousin Pons* (Cousin Pons, 1847), which was his last novel. He died in Paris, France, on August 18, 1850. (Butler 1983; Marceau 1966; Oliver 1965; Rogers 1953)

See also Class, Social; *Human Comedy, The*

Beat Movement

The term *Beat movement* refers to a literary and social movement that began in the United States during the late 1950s and continued throughout the 1960s. It was led by a group of writers that included Jack Kerouac, William Burroughs, and Gary Snyder, all of whom rejected consumerism and embraced mysticism and drug use. Gary Snyder also became an environmental activist.

Beat writers experimented with literary form and often attempted to recreate the sound of jazz music in their poetry. However, they were largely apolitical and apathetic—or beat, meaning "weary." (Later beat came to refer to these writers' interest in musical beats or in "beatific" or spiritual pursuits.) However, some important social protest works did come out of the movement, most notably Allen Ginsberg's long poem *Howl*. An indictment of many aspects of contemporary society, it contains obscenities and references to homosexuality. It was banned from publication under censorship laws, and its publisher, poet Lawrence Ferlinghetti, was put on trial for distributing it. Ferlinghetti's acquittal in 1957

is considered one of the most important legal rulings on censorship in the United States. (Hickey 1990; Miles 1995)

See also Censorship; Environmentalism; Ferlinghetti, Lawrence; Ginsberg, Allen; *Howl*

Beatty, Captain

As a fire chief in Ray Bradbury's 1953 futuristic novel *Fahrenheit 451*, Captain Beatty's job is to burn books, which are banned in his society. However, Beatty is conflicted about his work. He often quotes from books himself and admits to having read them long ago. He also expresses understanding when another fireman, Guy Montag, questions the morality of their job. After Montag kills Beatty during a conflict over book-burning, Montag wonders whether Beatty *wanted* to be killed.

Although *Fahrenheit 451* never reveals the source of Beatty's unhappiness, its author has suggested a reason. In an afterword to a 1996 edition of the novel Bradbury says that the fire chief was once a scholar and still has a fine book collection. Unable to destroy his books, but wanting to remain within the law, he never reads them. He is therefore a tormented man. (Bradbury 1996)

See also Bradbury, Ray; *Fahrenheit 451*; Montag, Guy

Beauvoir, Simone de

Born on January 9, 1908, in Paris, France, Simone Bertrand de Beauvoir is best known for her nonfiction books. Her most famous works in this regard are *Le Deuxième Sexe* (The Second Sex, 1949), which discusses feminism, and *Old Age* (La Vieillesse, 1970), which discusses ageism. However, she also wrote fiction that reflected her concern with social issues. For example, her 1954 novel *Les Mandarins* (The Mandarins) is the story of a group of intellectuals who begin to engage in political activism. This work is semiautobiographical and includes a character believed to represent the novelist Jean-Paul Sartre.

Beauvoir and Sartre met while studying at the Sorbonne, and in 1945 they founded a monthly magazine, *Les Temps Modernes* (Modern Times). They remained together until

Simone de Beauvoir (UPI/Corbis-Bettmann)

Sartre's death. Beauvoir wrote about their relationship in her memoirs and in a book entitled *La Cérémonie des adieux* (Adieux: A Farewell to Sartre), which was published in 1981. Her other works include philosophy books, travel books, and essay collections. Beauvoir died in Paris on April 14, 1986. (Madsen 1977)

See also Ageism; Feminism; Sartre, Jean-Paul

Behn, Aphra

Aphra Behn is the author of *Oroonoko: or, The Royal Slave,* a book published in 1688. It concerns an African prince named Oroonoko who was captured and made into a slave at the European colony of Surinam in South America. Behn lived in Surinam for a time, and she presented her story as fact. In an introduction to Behn's work, scholar Lore Metzger says that as a result, "during her own time there were rumors that Aphra Behn had had a love affair with the black hero of her story" (Behn 1973, x). Today, however, some scholars consider *Oroonoko* to be a work of fiction.

Much of Behn's own life is also a mystery. She was born in 1640, probably in Kent, England, and as a child she traveled to Surinam, then a colony of England. (Later it was taken over by the Dutch.) At some point she returned to England to marry a merchant named Behn. Some scholars report that this occurred during 1658, others in 1663. She then moved to the Netherlands, where she worked as a spy for England's King Charles II. When she returned to her own country, she was imprisoned for debt and started writing plays to pay her bills. Her first play, *The Forc'd Marriage,* was performed in 1671; a successful comedy, *The Rover,* was published in two parts in 1677 and 1681. In later years she wrote several popular novels, including *Oroonoko,* and was reputed to have had many affairs. However, Metzger suggests that these stories might have been mere rumors, probably the result of the unusual freedom she experienced as a writer. Metzger (ix) says:

The fiction she produced has been supplemented for two and a half centuries by a considerable amount of fiction about her. The facts of her life are so few yet so colorful that they quickly evoked sensational embellishment, insinuation, and speculation about her voyage to [Surinam], her love affairs, and her activities as a spy. The few facts suffice to establish Aphra Behn's opportunities for experience of the world of politics and art as larger and more varied than those open to any woman writer of the eighteenth or nineteenth century.

Aphra Behn died on April 16, 1689 and was buried in Westminster Abbey. (Behn 1973; Goreau 1980; Link 1968)

See also *Oroonoko;* Racism; Slavery

Bellamy, Edward

Author of the novel *Looking Backward, 2000–1887,* Edward Bellamy expresses his ideas for social reform through the character of Julian West, a fictional resident of both the nineteenth and twentieth centuries. West offers harsh comments about the realities of the late 1880s along with a utopian vision of the year 2000, embodying what Robert Shurter (xvii), in his introduction to a 1951 edition of the book, calls Bellamy's "intense hatred of social injustice in any form and his complete sincerity in attempting to strike a blow at the inequities of our social and economic system."

Bellamy had long been interested in social reform issues. The son of a Baptist minister, he was born on March 26, 1850, in Chicopee Falls, Massachusetts, where, according to scholar Cecelia Tichi (9) in her introduction to a 1982 edition, "all the problems involved in late-nineteenth-century industrialization were on view: crowded tenements, unemployment, sickness, strikes, an unstable population of laborers. One newspaper even reported families living in holes dug in the riverbank." Bellamy's social conscience was further heightened during the winter of 1868–1869 when he traveled through Europe with his cousin and began to study German socialism. Of this trip he (1951, xi) later said: "It was in the great cities of Europe and among the hovels of the peasantry that my eyes were first fully opened to the extent and consequences of 'man's inhumanity to man.'"

Upon returning to the United States, Bellamy studied law and opened his own law office, but he quit the profession after his first case, which required him to evict a widow for nonpayment of rent. He then became a newspaper journalist, first as a staff writer for the *New York Evening Post* and later as a book reviewer and editorialist for the *Springfield Daily Union* in Massachusetts. He left the *Union* in 1877 because of poor health and traveled to the Sandwich Islands, subsequently writing two short stories based on his vacation: *Deserted* in 1879 and *A Tale of the South Pacific* in 1880. Between 1878 to 1889 he published a total of 23 short stories in the leading magazines of his time, including *Atlantic Monthly* and *Harper's*. He also continued to write editorials wherein, according to Tichi (Bellamy 1982, 11), he "analyzed the social and economic issues that would dominate the novel *Looking Backward*."

His career as a novelist began with *Six to One: A Nantucket Idyll* in 1878, followed by *The Duke of Stockbridge* in 1879 and *Dr. Heidenhoff's Process* in 1880. In 1882 he married Emma Sanderson and later fathered two children: Paul, who was born in 1884, and Marion, who was born in 1886. His novel *Looking Backward, 2000–1887* was published in 1887. It was a time of great labor unrest in the United States, and Bellamy (1951, xiii) later wrote that his novel had been intended as "a vehicle of a definite scheme of industrial reorganization." In Bellamy's idealized future society all public services have been nationalized.

This concept, called Nationalism, soon became quite popular. By 1890, after approximately 400,000 copies of *Looking Backward* had been sold, there were 162 "Nationalist Clubs," also called "Bellamy Clubs," in the United States dedicated to promoting Bellamy's social reform concepts; club members eventually formed a Nationalist political party. Bellamy himself supported the Nationalist movement through lecture tours and as editor of two periodicals, the monthly *Nationalist* (1889–1891) and the weekly *New Nation* (1891–1894).

In 1897 he published a sequel to *Looking Backward*. Entitled *Equality*, it never achieved the same level of popularity as its predecessor, perhaps because it was more of an essay on economics than a novel. *Equality* was Bellamy's last work, although two collections of essays and letters were published posthumously: *Edward Bellamy Speaks Again!* in 1937 and *Talks on Nationalism* in 1938. The author died of tuberculosis on March 22, 1898.

Without Bellamy's influence, the Nationalism movement ended soon after his death. However, *Looking Backward* continued to influence social reformers for many years. Shurter (Bellamy 1951, xv) explains that in 1935 several independent lists still noted it as one of the most influential books in America, and Tichi (Bellamy 1982, 27) says that "one century after its publication, *Looking Backward* holds its own as a work of contemporary relevance." Shurter (Bellamy 1951, xxi) believes that the novel's endurance is related to Bellamy's character, concluding that Bellamy's "life and his book have lent a dignity to reform movements, for his sincerity cannot be questioned, his high-minded intentions cannot be doubted." (Bellamy 1951, 1982; Bowman 1962, 1979, 1986; Lipow 1982)

See also Capitalism; Labor Issues; *Looking Backward, 2000–1887;* Poverty; Socialism; West, Julian

Beloved

Beloved, by Toni Morrison, is set in Kentucky and Ohio during the late nineteenth century. When the novel was first published in 1987, reviewers compared it to *Uncle Tom's Cabin,* by Harriet Beecher Stowe, because it condemns slavery. Ann Snitow of the *Village Voice* also called it "holocaust writing" because it describes atrocities committed by one race on another (Gates and Appiah 1993c, 26). Morrison based the story on a real-life incident from 1856: upon capture a runaway slave killed her child to protect it from slavery. A similar incident occurs in Aphra Behn's novel *Oroonoko,* which might be based on a true story.

The main character of *Beloved* is Sethe, a former slave, who lives with her daughter Denver in a haunted house. Their ghost is Denver's older sister, who died as a two-year-old baby. One day an old friend, Paul D, comes to stay with them, and he shouts at the ghost to go away. Mysteriously the house becomes quiet.

Later a strange twenty-year-old woman shows up at the door. Her name is Beloved, and she seems in poor health. Sethe takes her in and cares for her. Paul D considers the girl strange and soon finds himself doing things against his will. One day he starts sleeping in the backyard shed, where Beloved comes to seduce him. Meanwhile first Denver and then Sethe realize that Beloved is their ghost, somehow made into flesh, who has taken her name from the only word on her tombstone. They do not reveal Beloved's true identity to Paul D, but Sethe does tell him how her baby daughter died. As a mistreated slave Sethe ran away, and when her white master came for her, she tried to kill her children to keep them safe from his cruelties. Sethe's two boys survived their mother's attack, as did her infant,

Denver. But the two-year-old child died because Sethe had sliced her neck with a handsaw. Sethe was arrested for the crime but later set free.

Paul D cannot handle this truth, and he leaves the house. Beloved immediately takes over, demanding that Sethe wait on her all day long. Happy to have her daughter and guilty over the past, Sethe obliges. Eventually Denver becomes worried about her mother, and she tells another woman about her troubles. That woman tells another and another, and soon thirty women are gathered to drive the ghost from Sethe's house. They arrive to pray there just as a white man drives up in his buggy. Sethe and Beloved are on the doorstep; Beloved is naked and pregnant. Suddenly Sethe flashes back to the time when another white man came to take her child away. She runs toward the man with a knife, but the women stop her. The ghost disappears, and later Paul D returns to comfort a grieving Sethe. When she says that she has lost her "best thing," he responds: "You your best thing, Sethe. You are" (Morrison 1987, 272–273).

Scholar Trudier Harris believes that this ending reflects the novel's main theme, which relates to personal worth. In an essay entitled "Escaping Slavery but Not Its Images," Harris (Gates and Appiah 1993c, 340) says: "Making another human being one's own 'best thing,' then, is ultimately to devolve into a condition worse than slavery. . . . Human freedom, finally, is not about ownership or possession; it is about responsibility, caretaking, and . . . [grace]."

Harris points out that in stressing this theme, *Beloved* uses a great deal of monetary/coin imagery. Moreover,

the ownership-subservience tied to the coinage imagery occurs at important decision-making points in the novel, where characters have the option of moving forward to the future or returning to the past. All of these points presumably occur where human interaction is voluntary rather than forced, yet the characters frequently continue the forced interactions of previous conditions. Thus the question becomes one of how to confront the past, make one's peace with it, and move on into the future. (339–340)

It is therefore interesting to note that, whereas in the past Sethe attacked her children to spare them from the whites, by the end of the novel she is able to attack the white man himself. (Gates and Appiah 1993c; Morrison 1987)

See also Behn, Aphra; Feminism; Morrison, Toni; *Oroonoko;* Racism; Sethe; Slavery

Berger, Thomas

Novelist Thomas Louis Berger uses irony and parody to point out how human thought influences action. As Berger biographer Brooks Landon (1989, 118) explains:

> Berger's novels strongly suggest that many of the problems of human existence stem from . . . verbal constructs and from the consequent confusion of language with the referential world. . . . Consequently, [his] novels focus not so much on ideas or themes (although they swell with both) as on the relationship between language and thought. . . . Again and again, Berger's novels find new ways to suggest that the structures and institutions that order and give meaning to existence are much less important than the ways we talk about them, and that the ways we talk about those organizing beliefs have inevitably been designed by someone to influence the perception and judgment of someone else.

Born in Cincinnati, Ohio, on July 20, 1924, Berger grew up in Lockland, Ohio. He attended two years of college before leaving school to enlist in the army. His tour of duty, which lasted from 1943 to 1946, took him to England, France, and Germany. When he returned to the United States, he finished his education at the University of Cincinnati, receiving his B.A. in 1948. That same year he moved to New York and became a librarian at the Rand School of Social Science. He also attended writers' workshops and began taking graduate classes in English at Columbia University. In 1951 he worked as a staff member of the *New York Times Index,* and in 1952 he became a copy editor for *Popular Science Monthly.* The following year he left his job to become a freelance copy editor and proofreader.

His first novel, entitled *Crazy in Berlin,* was published in 1958. According to Landon (1989, 19), it focuses on a German American named Reinhart who is upset over German atrocities against the Jews during World War II and realizes "that nazism was a human rather than a German phenomenon." A sequel to *Crazy in Berlin,* entitled *Reinhart in Love,* was published in 1962.

Two years later Berger published his most famous work, *Little Big Man,* which concerns the plight of the Plains Indians in the post–Civil War United States. In discussing this novel, which was made into a movie in 1970, Landon (31) quotes scholar L. L. Lee as observing: "This is a most American novel. Not just in its subject, its setting, its story (these are common matters), but in its thematic structures, in its dialectic: savagery and civilization, indeed, but also the virgin land and the city, nature and the machine, individualism and community, democracy and hierarchy, innocence and knowledge, all the divisive and unifying themes of the American experience, or, more precisely, of the American 'myth.'"

Berger's subsequent works include two more sequels to *Crazy in Berlin,* entitled *Vital Parts* (1970) and *Reinhart's Women* (1981), as well as the novels *Killing Time* (1967), about a mass murderer, and *Arthur Rex* (1978), which concerns Arthurian legend. Berger also parodied detective and spy novels, respectively, in *Who Is Teddy Villanova?* (1977) and *Nowhere* (1985). In late 1997 he was reported to be working on a sequel to *Little Big Man.* (Landon 1989)

See also *Little Big Man;* Native American Issues; Racism

Beyond Our Power

The Norwegian play *Over Aevne* (Beyond Our Power), also translated as *Beyond Human Power* or *Beyond Human Might,* was written in two parts, the first in 1883 and the second in 1895. Its author, Björnstjerne Björnson, was a poet, playwright, novelist, and politician who wrote his country's national anthem, "Ja, vi elsker dette landet" (Yes, We Love This Country), in 1859.

According to Björnson translator Edwin Björkman (Björnson 1916, 12), Björnson wrote both parts of *Beyond Our Power* to show, as one of the play's characters says, "that the day will come when mankind must discover that there lies more greatness and poetry in what is natural and possible—however insignificant it may frequently appear—than in the world's whole store of supernaturalism, from the first sun-myth down to the latest sermon preached about it."

The first part of *Beyond Our Power* focuses on the limits of organized religion. Its main characters are Pastor Adolph Sang and his wife, Clara, who does not believe in her husband's ability to perform miracles because he cannot improve her health. However, when his prayers appear to divert a landslide so that it misses his church, she accepts that miracles can happen and is cured. Overcome by the power of what has happened, she and her husband die in each other's arms.

The second part of *Beyond Our Power* is a sequel to the first, but it focuses on Adolph's son and daughter, depicting life in their valley village. According to scholar Harold Larson (1944, 140), the play is a wish for "social peace," that depicts "with stark simplicity the deep social cleavage in the capitalistic world between the slaves of industry living miserably in a sunless valley and the masters of industry dwelling luxuriously upon the sunlit heights." He adds that "arbitration was hinted at in the play by a deputation of workers who spoke of future legislation to provide for the settlement of disputes. But the poet's own program for industrial peace was only visionary socialism, including new inventions to make life more agreeable" (1944, 140).

Björkman (Björnson 1916, 13) believes that *Beyond Our Power, Part Two* "did for social superstition what the earlier play had done for that element in religion which Björnson had come to regard as lying 'beyond the limits of man.' It is one of the most powerful portrayals of the modern struggle between capital and labour which western literature has produced so far." (Björnson 1916; Larson 1944)

See also Björnson, Björnstjerne; Capitalism; Religion

Bibbett, Billy

In Ken Kesey's 1962 novel *One Flew over the Cuckoo's Nest,* 31-year-old Billy Bibbett is a patient in a mental hospital controlled by Nurse Ratched, a friend of his mother's. Both women are emasculating and treat Billy like a child. Consequently, he stutters and is afraid to leave the hospital even though he is sane. When he finally begins to gain strength, flout authority, and express his sexuality, Nurse Ratched ridicules him so severely that he commits suicide. Billy is a victim of a society that requires the suppression of natural urges. (Kesey 1964)

See also Kesey, Ken; *One Flew over the Cuckoo's Nest*; Ratched, Nurse

Biglow Papers, The

The Biglow Papers is a series of satirical poetry by American poet, essayist, and abolitionist James Russell Lowell. The first half of the series was published in the *Boston Courier* newspaper from 1846 to 1848 and in book form in 1849. The second half was published in the *Atlantic Monthly* during the Civil War and in book form in 1867. All of the poems oppose slavery. Therefore, when they appeared in print, they created much controversy, particularly in the South. For example, one critic wrote, "Mr. Lowell is one of the most rabid of the Abolition fanatics; and no Southerner who does not wish to be insulted, and at the same time revolted by a bigotry the most obstinately blind and deaf, should ever touch a volume by this author" (Wortham 1977, xxviii).

Björnstjerne Björnson, the Norwegian poet, novelist, and political leader (Corbis-Bettmann)

Each poem is accompanied by a lengthy, satirical introduction by a fictitious scholar. The verse itself is also written by a fictitious character, the poet Hosea Biglow, in rustic New England dialect. For example, one of these poems says: "Slavery aint o' nary color, / 'Taint the hide thet makes it wus, / All it keers fer in a feller / 'S jest to make him fill its pus" (52). In addition to this antislavery position, *The Biglow Papers* opposes the Mexican War and other forms of U.S. expansionism that would promote the spread of slavery. Another fictitious character, Birdofredum Sawin, reports on the war in several "letters." Lowell also used satire to criticize politicians, editors, and the upper classes. (Duberman 1966; Wortham 1977)

See also Lowell, James Russell; Racism; Slavery

Björnson, Björnstjerne

Poet, playwright, and novelist Björnstjerne Martinius Björnson was born on December 8, 1832, in Kvikne, Norway. He grew up in his country's Romsdal district on the Atlantic coast, but when he was 11, his father, a pastor who valued education, sent him away to school in the nearby town of Molde. At age 18 Björnson began attending a university preparatory school in Christiania (now Oslo), Norway. There he wrote his first play, a historical saga, when he was only 20. The Christiania Theater decided to produce his work; however, feeling that his play was inferior, Björnson asked them not to perform it. Four years later he produced what was, according to scholar and translator Edwin Borkman (Björnson 1916, 4), "his first dramatic work of lasting value," a historical play about the Norwegian civil wars entitled *Between the Battles* (Mellem Slagene), also translated as *Between Blows*.

Björnson would go on to write 20 more plays between 1858 and 1909, including *En handske* (The Gauntlet, 1883), which Borkman (9) calls "one of the main impulses for the Scandinavian feminist movement," and a two-part play entitled *Beyond Our Power* (part one in 1883 and part two in 1895), which criticizes modern spirituality and capitalism, respectively. In addition, he wrote novels critical of certain aspects of Norwegian society; for example, *Det flager i byen og på havnen* (The Heritage of the Kurts, 1884) attacks Christianity, and *På Guds veje* (In God's Way, 1889) focuses on the educational system. In 1903 he won the Nobel Prize in literature.

In addition to writing plays and novels, Björnson worked to revive Norwegian patriotism by encouraging public interest in Norwegian history and legends. As director of the Bergen Theater from 1857 to 1859 and the Christiania Theater from 1863 to 1867, he tried to eliminate Danish influence in Norwegian theater. He was also Norway's national poet, and in 1859 he wrote his country's national anthem, "Ja, vi elsker dette landet" (Yes, We Love This Country). A passionate supporter of Norwegian causes, he wrote articles advocating Norway's political independence from Sweden, with which it had been united since 1814, and according to scholars Eva and Einar Haugen (1978), Björnson was "Norway's most fiery orator and platform personality" (3). The Haugens explain that Björnson "never sought or held office, but throughout his life he was a powerful political force, in the forefront of every fray, opinionated and stubborn, impulsive and generous. The adulation of his admirers and the venom of his opponents left him untouched, as Norway's 'uncrowned king.' Hotly detested and warmly admired, he could not leave anyone indifferent, but in the long run he won respect for his honesty and his unswerving faith in progress and the future of his country" (3). (Björnson 1916; Haugen and Haugen 1978)

> **See also** *Beyond Our Power;* Capitalism; Feminism; Religion

Bleak House

An extremely large and complicated work, *Bleak House,* by British author Charles Dickens, criticizes the law for causing needless suffering in Victorian society. It also depicts social reformers and philanthropists as being more interested in problems in distant lands than in problems in their native England. For example, a minor character, Mrs. Jellyby, is so devoted to African charities that she neglects her own children; Mrs. Pardiggle is a social worker whose children are equally miserable.

The novel was first published in serialized form, appearing in monthly installments in the author's own magazine, *Household Words,* from March 1852 to September 1853. Set around 1850, its story takes place primarily in London, where the High Court of Chancery is hearing an elaborate legal case, *Jarndyce and Jarndyce,* that has dragged on for years. About this case, an omniscient narrator says:

> The parties to it understand it least; but it has been observed that no two Chancery lawyers can talk about it for five minutes, without coming to a total disagreement as to all the premises. . . . Scores of persons have deliriously found themselves made parties in Jarndyce and Jarndyce, without knowing how or why; whole families have inherited legendary hatreds with the suit. The little plaintiff or defendant, who was promised a new rocking-horse when Jarndyce and Jarndyce should be settled, has grown up, possessed himself of a real horse, and trotted away into the other world. Fair wards of court have faded into mothers and grandmothers; a long procession of Chancellors has come and gone out; the legion of bills in the suit have been transformed into mere bills of mortality; there are not three Jarndyces left upon the earth perhaps, since old Tom Jarndyce in despair blew his brains out at a coffee-house in Chancery Lane; but Jarndyce and Jarndyce still drags its dreary length before the Court, perennially hopeless. (Dickens 1987a, 4)

One of the remaining parties in this case is John Jarndyce, who is appointed guardian of Esther Summerson after the death of the aunt who raised her. Esther travels to Jarndyce's home, Bleak House, in the company of his two other wards, Ada Clare and Richard Carstone. They are also parties in the Jarndyce and Jarndyce lawsuit, as is Lady Deadlock, wife of an aristocrat. One day Lady Deadlock receives legal papers related to the case, and she recognizes the handwriting of its copyist as that of a former lover, Captain Hawdon. Lady Deadlock had an illegitimate child with this man before marrying her husband, and no one knows her shame. Without revealing her past, she asks her attorney, Mr. Tulkinghorn, to find the scribe. Tulkinghorn soon discovers that the man, who went by the name Nemo, died penniless and alone. Shortly thereafter Lady Deadlock dresses like her maid and visits a street sweeper, Jo, who knew Nemo. She talks to Jo about her former lover's life among the poor. She also finds Nemo's grave.

Meanwhile Mr. Tulkinghorn, who is a corrupt and evil lawyer, has become suspicious of Lady Deadlock's interest in Nemo. Eventually he discovers Nemo's true identity and threatens to tell Lady Deadlock's husband, Sir Leicester, about her affair. By this time the woman has learned that, although her sister told her otherwise, her illegitimate child survived its birth and is still alive. That child is Esther. Lady Deadlock goes to her daughter and reveals their relationship, telling her to keep it a secret from Sir Leicester. Lady Deadlock is desperate to keep her husband from finding out about the affair. Therefore, when Mr. Tulkinghorn is found dead, the reader suspects Lady Deadlock of killing him. The novel then takes on elements of a classic murder mystery; several minor characters had reason to kill Tulkinghorn.

Afraid that she will be accused of the crime, Lady Deadlock leaves a note for her husband, confessing her past and professing her innocence, and she flees. Upon finding the note, her husband has a stroke. Afterward he hires a detective, Inspector Bucket, to track down his wife and offer her his forgiveness. Esther accompanies Bucket in his search, and eventually they find Lady Deadlock dead on her lover's grave. By this time Bucket has learned that Lady Deadlock was innocent of Tulking-

horn's murder. Instead, the deed was committed by her maid, Hortense, whom Tulkinghorn used to gather information about her mistress's affair.

After discovering her mother's body, Esther falls ill. She is cared for by Allan Woodcourt, a doctor she has known for some time. He asks Esther to marry him, but she refuses, explaining that she has already agreed to marry her guardian, Mr. Jarndyce. Later, however, Jarndyce realizes that Esther would be happier with Allan Woodcourt and releases her from their engagement. Meanwhile, Jarndyce's other two wards, Ada and Richard, have fallen in love and secretly married. Richard is a weak man who has tried several careers but been unable to stick with anything very long. He stakes his future on the Jarndyce and Jarndyce legal case, whose settlement he hopes will bring him a large inheritance. But when the case is finally resolved, Robert discovers that legal fees have exhausted the fortunes of both sides. Already sick from worry, he dies upon hearing this news. Shortly thereafter Ada gives birth to his son.

The novel concludes with Esther's description of her happy life as Allan's wife, seven years later. Throughout *Bleak House* Dickens intersperses his omniscient narration with Esther's first-person accounts of the story. (Dickens 1987a)

See also Dickens, Charles; Jellyby, Mrs.; Justice; Pardiggle, Mrs.; Poverty

Block

A character in Franz Kafka's 1925 novel *Der Prozess* (The Trial), Block is a tradesman who is awaiting trial before a mysterious court that operates outside of the traditional legal system. His case has dragged on for over five years despite his best efforts to end it. As a result, he has lost his business and his life's savings. He lives at the house of his official lawyer, who treats him badly and gives him little hope of success. At the same time Block secretly employs five disreputable, or "pettifogging," lawyers to attempt to influence the court, which is corrupt and unjust. (Kafka 1964)

See also Kafka, Franz; *Trial, The*

Blount, Gil

The character Gil Blount appears in Richard Wright's 1953 novel *The Outsider,* which concerns racism and communism in the United States during the early 1950s. Blount is a white Communist leader who attempts to recruit a black man, Cross Damon. In doing so, Blount demonstrates his misunderstanding of the black race in general and of Damon in particular. He also teaches Damon that the Communist Party is not about ideology but about power. Blount relishes his power and wields it to demoralize others. After watching him, Damon thinks to himself:

This thing of power . . . why had he overlooked it till now? . . . Well, he had not been in those areas of life where power had held forth or reigned openly. Excitement grew in him; he felt that he was beginning to look at the emotional skeleton of man. He understood now the hard Communist insistence on strict obedience in things that had no direct relation to politics proper or to their keeping tight grasp of the reins of power. Once a thorough system of sensual power as a way of life had gotten hold of a man's heart to the extent that it ordered and defined all of his relations, it was bound to codify and arrange all of his life's activities into one organic unity. This systematizing of the sensual impulses of man to be a god must needs be jealous of all rival systems of sensuality, even those found in poetry and music. . . . And now . . . he could understand why the Communists, instead of shooting the capitalists and bankers as they had so ardently sworn that they would do when they came to power, made instead with blood in their eyes straight for the school teachers, priests, writers, artists, poets, musicians, and the deposed bourgeois governmental rulers as the men who held for them the deadliest of threats to their keeping and extending their power. (Wright 1993b, 269)

Blount is a cold-hearted man, and in the end Damon decides to kill him. While Blount is fighting with a racist fascist, Damon clubs them both in the head. (Wright 1993b)

See also Communism; *Outsider, The;* Racism; Wright, Richard

Bluest Eye, The

Published in 1970 and set in 1941, *The Bluest Eye* is the first novel of author Toni Morrison, whose work focuses on black and/or feminist themes. It is the story of a group of black girls growing up in a United States that values white skin and blond hair. The main character, 11-year-old Pecola Breedlove, prays for blue eyes, so that she will be beautiful.

At the same time the story's first-person narrator, a younger girl named Claudia MacTeer, does not accept society's idea of beauty. Whenever someone gives her a traditional white doll, she destroys it, saying: "I had only one desire: to dismember it. To see of what it was made, to discover the dearness, to find the beauty, the desirability that had escaped me, but apparently only me. Adults, older girls, shops, magazines, newspapers, window signs—all the world had agreed that a blue-eyed, yellow-haired, pink-skinned doll was what every girl child treasured" (Morrison 1993, 20–21).

Claudia and her sister, Frieda, like Pecola, but Pecola does not like herself. She believes that she and the rest of her family are too ugly to have value. In fact, many people in the town consider the Breedloves ugly. Claudia explains why:

You looked at them and wondered why they were so ugly; you looked closely and could not find the source. Then you realized that it came from conviction, their conviction. It was as though some mysterious all-knowing master had given each one a cloak of ugliness to wear, and they had each accepted it without question. The master had said, "You are ugly people." They had looked about themselves and saw nothing to contradict the statement; saw, in fact, support for it leaning at them from every billboard, every movie, every glance. "Yes," they had said. "You are right." And they took the ugliness in their hands, threw it as a mantle over them, and went about the world with it. (39)

Pecola's father has let this ugliness destroy his soul. Whereas as a boy he was kind, now he is angry. He drinks heavily and fights with his wife. One day he rapes Pecola. She becomes pregnant, but the baby is born too early and dies. Afterward Pecola goes insane, convinced that her eyes have become blue.

Toni Morrison says that in the early 1960s, when she wrote *The Bluest Eye,* many blacks wanted to look like whites. She explains that her work was an attempt to explore how a child might learn this type of "racial self-loathing" (210). However, in a 1993 afterword to the novel, she reports that her message was poorly received, saying, "With very few exceptions, the initial publication of *The Bluest Eye* was like Pecola's life: dismissed, trivialized, misread" (216). For this reason, scholars often compare *The Bluest Eye* with Zora Neale Hurston's *Their Eyes Were Watching God,* which was similarly dismissed after its 1937 publication. Like Morrison, Hurston depicts black characters who want to appear white. (Gates and Appiah 1993c; Morrison 1993)

See also Breedlove, Cholly and Pauline; Feminism; Morrison, Toni; Racism

Bostonians, The

The Bostonians, by Henry James, concerns the U.S. suffragette movement during the 1870s. The novel criticizes some of the ideas behind the fight for women's rights and questions the motives of its social reformers. The story begins when a Bostonian feminist, Olive Chancellor, meets her Mississippi cousin, Basil Ransom, for the first time. The young woman is unimpressed with her guest, who has been practicing law in New York. Nonetheless, she invites him to a suffragette meeting that evening. He is against the women's rights movement, but he decides to attend as an amusement. Once there, he meets Verena

Tarrant, the daughter of a well-known healer. When Verena is asked to speak at the meeting, both Olive and Basil find themselves physically attracted to the beautiful young woman. After Basil regretfully returns to New York, Olive convinces Verena to become her protégée. She influences Verena's opinions and guides her into becoming a regular speaker for the suffragette movement. She also makes Verena vow never to wed. But despite her friend's vow, Olive fears that Verena might succumb to a man's charms. Her fears intensify during a speaking engagement in New York. Basil Ransom shows up at the meeting, and Olive subsequently learns that he and Verena have been corresponding with each other. In fact, Verena is the one who invited him to the meeting, hoping to convert him to the cause. Shortly after the meeting Basil and Verena go on a date.

During their outing Verena learns Basil's views on the women's movement. Basil not only believes that women are inferior to men, but also suggests that men need to fight against the "feminization" of the world. He says:

The whole generation is womanized; the masculine tone is passing out of the world; it's a feminine, a nervous hysterical, chattering, canting age, an age of hollow phrases and false delicacy and exaggerated solicitudes and coddled sensibilities, which, if we don't soon look out, will usher in the reign of mediocrity, of the feeblest and flattest and the most pretentious that has ever been. The masculine character, the ability to dare and endure, to know and yet not fear reality, to look the world in the face and take it for what it is—a very queer and partly very base mixture—that is what I want to preserve, or rather, as I may say, to recover; and I must tell you that I don't in the least care what becomes of you ladies while I make the attempt! (James 1956, 343)

However, Basil also says: "I don't want to destroy you, any more than I want to save you. There has been far too much talk about you, and I want to leave you alone altogether. My interest is in my own sex; yours evidently can look after itself. That's all I want to save" (342). At the same time he expresses contempt for the "new old maids," such as Olive Chancellor, who have too little to do and must "wander about the world crying out for a vocation" (345). He points out that Verena has been manipulated by Olive, explaining: "You always want to please someone, and now you go lecturing about the country, trying to provoke demonstrations, in order to please Miss Chancellor. . . . It isn't *you*, the least in the world, but an inflated little figure . . . whom you have invented and set on its feet, pulling strings, behind it, to make it move and speak, while you try to conceal and efface yourself there" (346).

Upset over their conversation, Verena leaves Basil and returns to Boston. Later he travels there to see her. He had hoped that his discussion with her in New York might have changed her beliefs. Instead, he finds her rehearsing an important speech for the suffragette movement. Basil asks her to marry him, but she is indecisive because she knows that it will necessitate her abandoning her suffragette work. She goes off by herself to think about the proposal, and no one will tell Basil where she is. On the night of her big speech Basil goes to the auditorium and tries to get backstage to talk to her, but Olive has told the guard not to admit him. Meanwhile Verena has noticed Basil in the auditorium and realizes that she cannot speak in front of him. She refuses to go onstage. The crowd gets angry, and the organizers of the event plead for her to change her mind. Instead, she and Basil slip out of the auditorium, intending to get married. A defeated Olive stays behind to speak in Verena's place. The novel ends with Verena saying, "Ah, now I am glad!" However, at the same time the omniscient narrator notes: "But though she was glad, . . . beneath her hood, she was in tears. It is to be feared that with the union, so far from brilliant, into which she was about to enter, these were not the last she was destined to shed" (464).

The Bostonians was not well received when it was originally published, first as a 1885–1886 serial in *Century Illustrated Magazine* and then as a three-volume book in 1886. Some readers objected to Olive Chancellor's apparent lesbianism, and many Bostonians criticized the novel's portrayal of their city's society. According to scholar Irving Howe (vii), writing in a 1956 introduction to the work, the book's failure "hurt and bewildered James" and "may have hastened his turn from the social novel," which ended "his earlier ambition to become the American Balzac." However, Howe (vii) believes that James made the right decision in abandoning social protest, saying that the author "lacked that passionate absorption in the worlds of business and poetics which a social novelist must have." (Edel 1963; James 1956)

See also Balzac, Honoré de; Chancellor, Olive; Feminism; James, Henry; Ransom, Basil; Tarrant, Verena

Boulle, Pierre

French novelist Pierre Boulle is best known for two works, *Le Pont de la rivière Kwaï* (Bridge over the River Kwai, 1952) and *La Planète des singes* (Planet of the Apes, 1963). The latter is a science fiction novel that comments on human nature and society's shortcomings. Boulle was born on February 20, 1912, in Avignon, France. He spent several years of his adult life in Southeast Asia, where he was a planter and soldier, and wrote several novels based on his experiences there. Boulle died on January 30, 1994, in Paris, France. (Frackman 1996)

See also *Planet of the Apes;* Science Fiction and Fantasy

Bradbury, Ray

Raymond Douglas Bradbury has written articles, essays, and science fiction stories and novels. Some of his fiction contains elements of social protest. For example, his novel *Fahrenheit 451* (1953) depicts a future United States where people are forbidden to read books and individuality is discouraged.

Born in Waukegan, Illinois, on August 22, 1920, Bradbury was 27 when his first book of short stories, entitled *Dark Carnival,* was published. His second collection, *The Martian Chronicles* (1950), is considered a science fiction classic and was made into a movie in 1966. Other story collections include *The Illustrated Man* (1951), *The Machineries of Joy* (1964), and *I Sing the Body Electric!* (1969). He also wrote the screenplay for the movie *Moby Dick,* filmed by John Huston in 1956. Bradbury's other novels include *Dandelion Wine* (1957) and *Something Wicked This Way Comes* (1985). Bradbury currently lives in southern California, where he continues to write both fiction and nonfiction. (Nolan 1975)

See also Censorship; *Fahrenheit 451;* Science Fiction and Fantasy

Brave New World

Published in 1932, *Brave New World,* by Aldous Huxley, is the author's view of the future, based on the misuse of science and a breakdown of morality. The novel opens in the Central London Hatchery and Conditioning Center, where human beings are created in test tubes. In the laboratory fetuses are manipulated to make them fit into a specific intellectual category, from clever Alphas down to dim-witted Epsilons. Laboratory officials also use mind-control techniques and electric shocks to condition people to fit their assigned roles.

One day a center psychologist, Bernard Marx, takes a vacation to a Savage Reservation in New Mexico. He wants to study people who have not been created in test tubes and who live in nature. Bernard's world has become sterile and artificial, and he doesn't feel as though he fits in there. Accompanying Bernard on his trip is Lenina Crowne, a woman who likes modern conveniences and is dependent on soma, a stupor-inducing drug sanctioned by her society. She complains about the reservation's lack of sanitation and is repulsed by its old people, who have wrinkles and missing teeth. One old person, Linda, particularly offends her. When Linda meets the visitors, she rushes up to hug them, and Bernard realizes that she is the former girlfriend of his boss. While touring the reservation with him years ago, she became lost and was left behind. At the time she was pregnant, and because the reservation had no abortion centers she was forced to bear the child, whom she named John.

John is now a charming young man, and Bernard receives permission to bring him and his mother back to his modern world. John is excited, envisioning a "brave new world" with glorious people in it (Huxley 1989, 141). He has read the works of William Shakespeare and has an old-fashioned view of the world. Therefore, he is later shocked to discover that modern people engage in promiscuous sexual behavior, do not quote poetry, and spend most of their time in a haze. His own mother, Linda, uses massive doses of soma to keep herself in a stupor. When she dies from her drug use, John tries to stop people from getting their soma at a local dispensing center. He is brought before an official who tells him that, unlike Shakespeare's time,

> the world's stable now. People are happy; they get what they want, and they never want what they can't get. They're well off; they're safe; they're never ill; they're not afraid of death; they're blissfully ignorant of passion and old age; they're plagued with no mothers or fathers; they've got no wives, or children, or lovers to feel strongly about; they're so conditioned that they practically can't help behaving as they ought to behave. And if anything should go wrong, there's *soma.* Which you go and chuck out of the window in the name of liberty, Mr. Savage. *Liberty!* (226)

Because Bernard was in charge of John, the older man is exiled to Iceland after the young man's outbreak. John goes off to live by himself at an abandoned lighthouse. But the news media have been fascinated with his activities ever since he arrived in the modern world, and they refuse to leave him alone. Eventually John realizes he no longer wants to live in such a cruel, immoral world. He hangs himself in the lighthouse tower.

In writing about this work, Huxley says

that he regrets John's death but believes that after seeing the modern world, he would have been unable to return to the reservation. However, in an introduction to his work, Huxley (ix–x) adds that if he were to rewrite *Brave New World,* he would create a third choice for the young man:

> Between the utopian and the primitive horns of his dilemma would lie the possibility of sanity—a possibility already actualized, to some extent, in a community of exiles and refugees from the Brave New World, living within the borders of the Reservation. In this community economics would be decentralist and . . . cooperative. Science and technology would be used as though, like the Sabbath, they had been made for man, not (as at present and still more so in the Brave New World) as though man were to be adapted and enslaved to them.

Huxley (xi) also explains that the theme of his novel "is not the advancement of science as such; it is the advancement of science as it affects human individuals." He (xi) adds:

> The triumphs of physics, chemistry and engineering are tacitly taken for granted. The only scientific advances to be specifically described are those involving the application to human beings of the results of future research in biology, physiology, and psychology. It is only by means of the sciences of life that the quality of life can be radically changed. The sciences of matter can be applied in such a way that they will destroy life or make the living of it impossibly complex and uncomfortable; but, unless used as instruments by the biologists and psychologists, they can do nothing to modify the natural forms and expressions of life itself. The release of atomic energy marks a great revolution in human history, but not (unless we blow ourselves to bits and so put an end to history) the final and most searching revolution.

For this reason, *Brave New World* has more to say about the moral implications of scientific discovery than about its physical or technological impact. It also contrasts the sterility of the modern world with the passionate emotion that existed in Shakespeare's time. (Atkins 1968; Brander 1970; Huxley 1989; Watts 1969)

See also Censorship; Crowne, Lenina; Huxley, Aldous; Marx, Bernard; Science Fiction and Fantasy

Breedlove, Cholly and Pauline

Cholly and Pauline Breedlove are the parents of 11-year-old Pecola, the main character in Toni Morrison's 1970 novel *The Bluest Eye.* Like their daughter, they are blacks who believe themselves ugly because of their blackness. Pauline Breedlove finds her only joy in the white household where she works as a servant. The place is clean and orderly, and her employers praise her for keeping it that way. Caught up in this world, gradually "she neglected her house, her children, her man— they were like the afterthoughts one has just before sleep, the early-morning and late-evening edges of her day, the dark edges that made the daily life with [her white family] lighter, more delicate, more lovely" (Morrison 1993, 127). But whereas Pauline tries to escape ugliness, Cholly falls deeper into it. He becomes an abusive alcoholic, and one day he rapes his own daughter. He then disappears, leaving his family in ruin. (Gates and Appiah 1993c; Morrison 1993)

See also *Bluest Eye, The;* Morrison, Toni

Breytenbach, Breyten

South African author Breyten Breytenbach expresses antiapartheid views in poems, essays, and nonfiction books written in his native language of Afrikaans. Born on September 16, 1939, when he was 20 he left South Africa and eventually settled in Paris, where he became a painter and poet. He then married a Vietnamese woman, who was labeled "nonwhite" by the South African government. As such, she was not allowed to accompany her husband when he visited Johannesburg,

South Africa, in 1964 to accept a literary award. Breytenbach spoke out against this act of discrimination, turning it into an international incident, and he became involved in antiapartheid politics. In 1972 he again visited South Africa, and this time the government allowed his wife to accompany him, but only for three months.

In 1975 Breytenbach once again traveled to South Africa, this time using a false name and passport. The reason for his visit is unclear. However, the government arrested him for terrorist activities and sentenced him to seven years in prison. This experience led him to write three books: *'n Seisoen in die Paradys* (A Season in Paradise, 1981), about his 1972 visit to South Africa; *Mouroir: Bespieelende notas van 'n roman* (Mouroir: Mirrornotes of a Novel, 1984), which is a collection of essays about freedom; and *The True Confessions of an Albino Terrorist* (1985), about his life in prison. He also published a collection of poems, *In Africa Even the Flies Are Happy: Selected Poems, 1964–77* in 1986, and in 1993 he again discussed apartheid in his book *Return to Paradise.* (Breytenbach 1994; Jolly 1996)

See also Apartheid; Exiles; Racism; *Season in Paradise, A*

Broad and Alien Is the World

Ciro Alegría's novel *El mundo es ancho y ajeno* (Broad and Alien Is the World), published in both Spanish and English editions in 1941, depicts the suffering of Peruvian Indians in the valley village of Rumi between 1912 and 1926. Rumi borders the property of a nonnative landowner, Don Alvaro Amenabar y Roldan, who wants to take over the village so he can enslave its inhabitants on his ranch or at his nearby mining operation. He files a lawsuit falsely claiming that the Indians have built their village on his land, then bribes the judge, the regional governor, and many of Rumi's witnesses so that he wins the case. When the judge orders the Indians to vacate their land, they consider fighting, but they decide to relocate to the neighboring mountainside. Meanwhile they begin the process of appealing their case to Peru's Supreme Court.

However, the mountainside is rocky and steep, and the Indians find life in their new village difficult. Discouraged, many of them leave to find work elsewhere. They quickly become enslaved through debt to cruel nonnative bosses, who rape the women and force the men to gather rubber in the Amazon jungle or pick leaves on coca plantations. Many sicken and die from malaria. Others are bitten by poisonous snakes. But those who remain in the village do not fare much better. Having spent most of their money on legal fees, they have little left to buy supplies. When Don Amenabar steals their cattle, the Indians' well-respected mayor, an old man named Rosendo Maqui, tries to retrieve one of the village bulls and is arrested for cattle theft. Amenabar bribes the newspaper to say that Rosendo is in league with a notorious bandit, Fiero Vasquez, whose wife lives in Rosendo's village. Rosendo therefore has little hope of receiving justice. He has "always despised" the law because he has experienced it "only in the form of abuses and taxes" (Alegría 1941, 326), and he shares the belief of another villager that "as soon as a rich man starts talking about rights that means something crooked is afoot, and if law exists, it is only to do [the Indians] harm" (14).

In fact, Amenabar's attorney delays the case so that Rosendo must spend weeks in prison without a hearing. His living conditions are filthy, and the four walls of his small cell close in on him. Increasingly despondent, he thinks that "no prisoner, however guilty he may be, but feels in the [prison] wall the hardness of the human heart. . . . The sorriest animal, the most insignificant insect, can use his legs or wings freely, while man, who considers himself the superior of all, heartlessly buries his fellow man in a gloomy hole" (326).

Rosendo soon discovers that he is not the only Indian who has been falsely imprisoned. Others offer him their stories of hardship and abuse, and one prisoner, a blacksmith named Jacinto Prieto, argues that the president of the Republic of Peru cannot possibly know about the injustices being perpetrated against his country's poor Indians. Prieto smuggles a letter to the president and receives a polite reply, but the injustices continue. Prieto rails against the government, saying, "There is no justice, there is no country. Where are all the upright men the nation needs? They are all out for what they can get, bootlickers at the orders of the mighty. A rich man can kill and nothing happens to him. A poor man gives someone a stiff punch and they accuse him of attempted homicide. Where is the equality before the law?" (377).

Meanwhile the bandit Vasquez has learned about Amenabar's treachery, and he decides to take revenge on everyone who helped the landowner destroy the village of Rumi. Vasquez's men, some of whom are former villagers, rob the governor and rape his daughter. They also kill a local peddler who was an informant for Amenabar. They attack Amenabar's ranch, but although some of the overseers there are killed, the landowner himself escapes harm. Amenabar calls on the military for help, and eventually Vasquez is captured. He is placed in the same prison cell as Rosendo; the two are to be tried together for crimes against the government. When Vasquez escapes, the prison guards beat Rosendo, who refused to accompany Vasquez. Rosendo dies from the beating.

Shortly thereafter Benito Castro, whom Rosendo raised as his own son, returns to Rumi. Castro has been away in the military for many years and was unaware of Amenabar's treachery. He is outraged to find that his former village has been left in ruins, while its people try to exist on a difficult mountainside. Castro helps the villagers dynamite and drain a mountain lake to create more arable land. He also convinces them to set aside superstition and relocate their houses to a better, yet supposedly haunted site. When some of the villagers accuse him of going against tradition, Castro says that "the only reason he advocated progress was because in his opinion it was only through progress that the Indians could free themselves from slavery and make something of themselves" (418). He argues that the landowners had succeeded specifically because they were not superstitious, adding that "people can be judged by

their beliefs" (419). Eventually the villagers agree with Castro and elect him mayor.

For a while things go well for the villagers. Then the Supreme Court decides not only that Amenabar owns Rumi but also that he owns the land the Indians now occupy on the mountainside. At this news one villager laments that "the Indian is a Christ nailed to the cross of injustice. Oh, that damned cross! Oh, cross, whose hungry arms never tire!" (423). Some want to leave the village, but Castro encourages them to fight. In an impassioned speech he says: "Have no fear of defeat for it is better to die than be a slave. Maybe the government will come to understand that injustice is not good for a country. To justify taking away the communal lands from the Indian, they say they want to develop a sense of private property in him, and they begin by taking away the only thing he's got. We're defending our lives, villagers! We're defending our land!" (425). The villagers are convinced to battle the forces coming to evict them from their land, but in the end most are killed. Castro, who has been mortally wounded, returns to his wife to urge her to leave the village. As he dies, she wonders where she will go. This question was particularly significant to the book's Peruvian author, who wrote his novel while exiled to Chile because of his political activities. (Alegría 1941; Early 1980)

See also Alegría, Ciro; Amenabar, Don Alvaro; Castro, Benito; Exiles; Justice; Maqui, Rosendo; Racism; Slavery

Bromden, Chief

Chief Bromden is the narrator of Ken Kesey's 1962 novel *One Flew over the Cuckoo's Nest*. A Native American from Oregon, he is extremely tall and strong but believes himself to be small and weak. He is a patient in a mental hospital who has endured several years of shock treatments and heavy medication. However, with the encouragement of another patient, Randall Patrick McMurphy, he stops taking his medication and gradually his insanity dissipates. Moreover, McMurphy convinces him that he is growing physically stronger every day. When a sadistic nurse arranges for

McMurphy to have brain surgery that turns him into a vegetable, Bromden kills his friend and throws some heavy equipment through a window so that he can escape the hospital. In the end it is clear that Bromden has recovered his sanity by fighting against social oppression, conformity, and injustice. (Kesey 1964)

See also Kesey, Ken; McMurphy, Randall Patrick; *One Flew over the Cuckoo's Nest*

Brown, Jonathan

A character in the 1958 novel *The Ugly American,* by William Lederer and Eugene Burdick, Jonathan Brown is a U.S. senator who travels to Southeast Asia to assess the strength of U.S. policies there. The U.S. diplomats and military personnel in the region do not want him to learn that they have been losing their fight against communism, so they trick him into believing that things are going well. They incorrectly translate statements from natives who criticize U.S. policy and encourage the senator to spend much of his time at parties and dinners rather than among the Asian people. As a result, Brown returns to the United States with the false impression that democracy is strong in Southeast Asia. (Lederer and Burdick 1958)

See also Communism; *Ugly American, The*

Brown, William Wells

Sometime during the early 1800s William Wells Brown was born a slave near Lexington, Kentucky. Eventually he was sold to a tobacco plantation in St. Louis, Missouri, and on New Year's Day 1834 he gained emancipation by running away to Cincinnati, Ohio. He then gave himself a surname in honor of the Quaker Wells Brown, who had helped him escape.

As a free man Brown was incredibly successful. He became a popular lecturer for antislavery and temperance causes, both in the United States and abroad, and was a delegate to the 1849 World Peace Congress in Paris. He was also the first African American to earn a living as a writer. He wrote 16 books; his first, an autobiography entitled *Narrative of William W. Brown, a Fugitive Slave* (1847), sold 10,000 copies in the first two years alone. His other nonfiction works include *The Black Man*

(1863), *The Negro in the American Rebellion* (1867), and *My Southern Home* (1880). He also wrote the first published novel by an African American, *Clotel* (1853); the first published play by an African American, *The Escape; or, a Leap for Freedom* (1858); and the first published travel memoir by an African American, *Three Years in Europe* (1852). He died on November 6, 1884, in Chelsea, Massachusetts. (Farrison 1969; Gates 1990; Warner 1976)

See also *Clotel;* Racism; Slavery

Bryant, William Cullen

William Cullen Bryant was a social reformer who expressed his views through journalism and poetry. Born on November 3, 1794, in Cummington, Massachusetts, he entered college at the age of 16, eventually leaving to study law on his own. He was admitted to the Massachusetts bar in 1815 and began practicing law. Ten years later he moved to New York City to become an editor for a liberal newspaper, the *New York Evening Post*. He remained in that position for 50 years, eventually becoming editor in chief and part owner of the paper. During that time he promoted many liberal causes, supporting a worker's right to strike and voicing opposition to slavery and political corruption. He died on June 12, 1878, in New York, New York. (Godwin 1967; McLean 1964; Sturges 1968)

See also *Antiquity of Freedom, The;* Slavery

Burdick, Eugene

Eugene Burdick is the author of both nonfiction and fiction books, including the 1962 novel *Fail Safe*, which concerns the Cold War between the United States and the Soviet Union. However, he is best known for his 1958 novel *The Ugly American*. Coauthored by William Lederer, the book criticizes the behavior of Americans living and working in Southeast Asia. (Lederer and Burdick 1958)

See also Lederer, William J.; *Ugly American, The*

Burgess, Anthony

Anthony Burgess is the pseudonym for British author John Anthony Burgess Wilson, who

Anthony Burgess, 1980 (Hulton-Deutsch Collection/-Corbis)

also wrote under the name Joseph Kell. Born in Manchester, England, he became an English teacher in 1946. He also worked for the Ministry of Education in England from 1948 to 1950. From 1954 to 1959 he taught in Malaya and Borneo and began writing novels. He wrote 32 in all, including *The Wanting Seed* (1962), which concerns overpopulation, and *A Clockwork Orange* (1962), about violence in society. He also wrote 16 nonfiction books, primarily biographies, autobiographies, and literary criticism, as well as a volume of poetry, 2 plays, and several musical compositions. He died on November 22, 1993, in London, England. (Burgess 1986; De Vitis 1972)

See also *Clockwork Orange, A;* Science Fiction and Fantasy

Burns, Robert

Scottish poet Robert Burns wrote about life as a common man and supported the rights of the individual. Born on January 25, 1759, in Alloway, Ayrshire, Scotland, he was the son of a poor farmer, and eventually he became a farmer himself. Nonetheless, he received some education and continued to study English literature on his own. He also began writing poems. In 1786 he self-published his first works as *Poems, Chiefly in the Scottish Dialect,* which quickly became a critical success. A national celebrity, Burns spent a few years in the city of Edinburgh before returning to farming. He continued to write verse and songs for the remainder of his life. He also protested conventional eighteenth-century religious and moral beliefs. He died on July 21, 1796, in Dumfries, Dumfriesshire, Scotland. (Daiches 1966)

See also "Man's a Man for a' That, A"

C

Camus, Albert

Algerian author Albert Camus wrote articles, plays, novels, and essays in which he explored the nature of human beings as individuals and as members of society. According to biographer Germaine Brée (1961, 8), Camus's "major preoccupation" was "the daily life of human beings, their freedom and the human justice meted out to them on this earth." This concern brought him the 1957 Nobel Prize in literature, which commended him for "his important literary production, which with clear-sighted earnestness illuminates the problems of the human conscience of our time" (5).

Brée explains that Camus's time was an era when "the age-old questions of the significance of man's odyssey on this earth were being posed anew and no new satisfactory answers were being offered. But for many young Europeans it seemed essential to find an answer to the question Why live? . . . To some the only possible justification for life was participation in some form of social and political action" (26). This was true for Camus. Born in Mondovi, Algiers, on November 7, 1913, he joined the Communist Party at the age of 21. When World War II broke out in 1939, he was a journalist for the radical newspaper *Algier-Republic,* writing about social injustices in Algiers, but he soon became involved in the French underground resistance movement against the Nazis. In 1943 he began to edit and secretly distribute a daily newssheet called *Combat,* dedicated to countering Nazi propaganda, reporting accurate information about the war, and encouraging the hope of an Allied victory.

By this time Camus was already a well-known author. His first novel, *L'Etranger* (The Stranger), had been published in 1942, and it gained immediate recognition. That same year Camus published a philosophical essay, *Le Mythe de Sisyphe* (The Myth of Sisyphus). His previous essays included *L'Envers et l'endroit* (The Wrong Side and the Right Side), published in 1937, and *Noces* (Nuptuals), published in 1938. His second novel, *La Peste* (The Plague), appeared in 1947. Whereas *L'Etranger* concerns one man's isolation from society, *La Peste* shows the isolation of an entire town because of a plague. Brée explains that the plague causes a "stifling oppressiveness" in the town and represents "any force which systematically cuts human beings off from the living breath of life" (128). Camus continued his theme of human isolation in *La Chute* (The Fall), published in 1956. Among his other works are several plays, including *Caligula* (1944), as well as a collection of short stories entitled *L'Exil et le royaume* (The

Exile and the Kingdom, 1957) and a long essay entitled *L'Homme révolté* (The Rebel,
1951). In *L'Homme révolté*, which discusses
political revolution, Camus (237) says, "We
all carry within us our prisons, our crimes, our
destructiveness. But to unleash them in the
world is not our duty. Our duty consists in
fighting them in ourselves and in others." He
maintained this belief until his death in
France on January 4, 1960. (Brée 1961)

See also Clamence, Jean-Baptiste; *Fall, The;*
Justice; Meursault, Monsieur; *Stranger, The*

Cane

Published in 1923, *Cane,* by Jean Toomer, is a
collection of short stories and poems loosely
organized around a central theme. In writing
about that theme, Toomer says that his book
is intended to show the end of an era among
blacks. He (1993, xxii) explains that when he
conceived of the work,

> a family of back-country Negroes had only
> recently moved into a shack not too far
> away. They sang. And this was the first
> time I'd ever heard the folk-songs and
> spirituals. They were very rich and sad and
> joyous and beautiful. But I learned that
> the Negroes of the town objected to them.
> They called them "shouting." They had
> victrolas and player-pianos. So, I realized
> with deep regret, that the spirituals, meet-
> ing ridicule, would be certain to die out.
> With Negroes also the trend was towards
> the small town and then towards the
> city—and industry and commerce and
> machines. The folk-spirit was walking in
> to die on the modern desert. That spirit
> was so beautiful. Its death was so tragic.
> Just this seemed to sum life for me. And
> this was the feeling I put into "Cane."
> "Cane" was a swan-song. It was a song of
> an end.

In describing the passing of an era, *Cane*
addresses issues of social conformity, racism,
and sexism. The work is divided into three
sections. The first, set in Georgia, focuses on
women pressured to conform to society's expectations. The second, set in the cities of
Washington, D.C., and Chicago, shows the
influence of the past on the present as people
struggle to free themselves from childhood
attitudes. The third section is a single story,
"Kabnis." Its main character, Ralph Kabnis,
is a northern-educated black man who has
come to Georgia to teach. Once there he
learns that the state is not as emancipated as
he assumed. He hears stories of whites lynching blacks and fears for his safety. He also
learns that southern blacks do not like northern ones unless they conform to the southern
way of thinking. Sick at heart, he leaves his
teaching position to become apprentice to a
wagonmaker. He begins to drink heavily, engage in immoral behavior, and spend time
with an aged deaf man, waiting for him to
speak. In the end the old man says, "O th sin
th white folks 'mitted when they made th
Bible lie" (115).

Cane is considered one of the most important books to come out the Harlem Renaissance, a literary era in which black writings
flourished. Toomer's work was well received
and made him famous. However, he did not
appreciate praise based on his race. As scholar
Darwin Turner (x) explains in an introduction
to a 1993 edition of the work:

> After *Cane*, Toomer resisted identification
> with any race except the new one—the
> American race—that he envisioned com-
> ing to birth on the North American conti-
> nent. A mixture of several races and na-
> tionalities, an individual who could be
> identified as an Indian or a dark-skinned
> European, Toomer argued that a Black
> label or a white label restricted one's access
> to both groups and limited one's growth.
> As evidence he bitterly cited publishers'
> rejections of his writings after *Cane*. Iden-
> tifying him as a Negro, he argued, they
> expected and desired nothing except a
> duplicate of his earlier work.

Toomer was unable to sell another book manuscript, and eventually he abandoned fiction
altogether to concentrate on poetry, essays,

and autobiographical works. (Benson and Dillard 1980; Toomer 1993)

See also Harlem Renaissance; Racism; Slavery; Toomer, Jean

Capitalism

Capitalism is an economic system of private ownership. In theory, it allows supply and demand to dictate how many goods are produced and at what price they are sold. However, modern capitalism depends on some level of government control to regulate prices. It also depends on the ability of businesses to borrow money, called capital, to finance their endeavors. In capitalistic countries profits dictate the success of a business and economic competition is intense.

Modern capitalism first began in the Middle Ages. At that time the European economy was based on manorialism, a system whereby peasants lived in agricultural communities owned by noblemen. This system was subject to abuse, and peasants eventually began migrating to cities for better opportunities. As populations became more urban, the economy shifted to one based on trade rather than agriculture, and capitalism replaced manorialism.

Eventually, however, there were abuses under the system of capitalism as well. Small business became large corporations, which then tried to eliminate their competition. Some of these corporations joined together into cooperative ventures called trusts to control entire industries by agreeing on certain prices and practices. During the late 1800s trusts developed to control the petroleum industry, the cotton oil industry, the whiskey industry, the sugar industry, the match industry, and the tobacco industry. At the same time American farmers organized into the Grange movement, which protested railroad monopolies that charged usurious rates for transporting grain to market. Frank Norris's 1901 social protest novel *The Octopus* deals with this issue as it relates to the wheat industry.

Because of trusts and other unfair business practices, capitalists have been the subject of much criticism, particularly in social protest literature dealing with poverty and labor issues.

Some examples of such works are *The Jungle,* by Upton Sinclair; *Yonnondio: From the Thirties,* by Tillie Olsen; *Life in the Iron Mills,* by Rebecca Harding Davis; *The Grapes of Wrath,* by John Steinbeck; and *Little Dorrit,* by Charles Dickens. Anticapitalism novels that advocate alternative systems such as socialism or communism include *Babbitt,* by Sinclair Lewis; *The Iron Heel,* by Jack London; and *Looking Backward, 2000–1887,* by Edward Bellamy, the latter of which describes a futuristic utopia. *Tono-Bungay,* by H. G. Wells, is also an indictment of capitalism, as are Theodore Dreiser's *An American Tragedy* and Henry Miller's *The Air-Conditioned Nightmare,* whereas *Atlas Shrugged,* by Ayn Rand, is a defense of it. (Landes 1966; Pruden 1968; Schumpeter 1950)

See also *Air-Conditioned Nightmare, The; American Tragedy, An; Atlas Shrugged; Babbitt;* Bellamy, Edward; Communism; Davis, Rebecca Harding; Dickens, Charles; Dreiser, Theodore; *Grapes of Wrath, The; Iron Heel, The; Jungle, The;* Labor Issues; Lewis, Sinclair; *Life in the Iron Mills; Little Dorrit;* London, Jack; *Looking Backward, 2000–1887;* Manorialism; Miller, Henry; Norris, Frank; *Octopus, The;* Olsen, Tillie; Poverty; Rand, Ayn; Sinclair, Upton; Socialism; Steinbeck, John; *Tono-Bungay;* Wells, H. G.; *Yonnondio: From the Thirties*

Carlé, Lukas

In Isabel Allende's 1987 novel *Eva Luna,* Lukas Carlé is a cruel Nazi from northern Austria. He believes that "man is made for war. History demonstrates that progress is never achieved without violence" (Allende 1988, 35). War had "failed to instill in him any desire for peace; instead, it had etched in his mind the conviction that only gunpowder and blood can produce men capable of steering the foundering ship of humanity to port—abandoning the weak and helpless on the high seas, in accordance with the implacable laws of nature" (35). When he returns from the war, Lukas tortures his wife with sexual sadism and berates his three children, Jochen, Katharina, and Rolf. A schoolmaster, Lukas also torments his students, five of whom eventually hang him during an outing in the woods; the local police quickly deem the death a suicide. (Allende 1988)

See also Allende, Isabel; Carlé, Rolf; *Eva Luna*; Naranjo, Huberto; Rodríguez, Colonel Tolomeo

Carlé, Rolf

Rolf Carlé appears in Isabel Allende's 1987 novel *Eva Luna*. As a child of ten he helped bury concentration-camp dead in his native northern Austria. This experience sensitized him to the cruelties and secrecies of war; as an adult he becomes a news cameraman and documentary filmmaker dedicated to exposing political and social truths. For example, during a South American revolution "he was the only person who dared carry his camera into the Security Force building to record firsthand the piles of dead and wounded, the dismembered agents. . . . He was also at the General's mansion to film the mobs destroying furnishings, slitting paintings, and dragging the First Lady's chinchilla coats and beaded ball gowns into the streets, and he was also present at the Palace when the new Junta composed of rebel officers and prominent citizens were formed" (Allende 1988, 177). (Allende 1988)

See also Allende, Isabel; Carlé, Lukas; *Eva Luna*; Naranjo, Huberto; Rodríguez, Colonel Tolomeo

Carlson, Georgiana

In the 1853 novel *Clotel*, by William Wells Brown, Georgiana Peck Carlson becomes an abolitionist while living on a southern plantation. Her father is a slave owner, and while growing up she argues with him over the morality of owning men and woman. When he dies and she inherits his property, she wants to set her slaves free. However, she realizes that many of them would not be able to get to the free states of the North on their own and would simply end up back in slavery. Therefore, she and her husband devise a plan. They begin paying their slaves a salary, which they put into trust for the future. When a slave has earned enough for passage to the North and a new life there, they give it to him

or her. In this way the freed slaves will have a good chance of staying free. Of Georgiana's eventual death from an illness, the narrator of the story says:

> If true greatness consists in doing good to mankind, then was Georgiana Carlton an ornament to human nature. Who can think of the broken hearts made whole, of sad and dejected countenances now beaming with contentment and joy, of the mother offering her free-born babe to heaven, and of the father whose cup of joy seems overflowing in the presence of his family, where none can molest or make him afraid. Oh, that God may give more such persons to take the whip-scarred Negro by the hand and raise him to a level with our common humanity! (Gates 1990, 170–171)

(Gates 1990)

See also Brown, William Wells; *Clotel*; Slavery

Castle Rackrent

The novella *Castle Rackrent,* by Maria Edgeworth, was first published anonymously in January 1800 when Ireland began its constitutional union with England, but the following year Edgeworth acknowledged authorship, and later editions bore her name. The novel was translated into German in 1802, and in subsequent years it was also published in Dublin, Ireland, and in the United States.

Castle Rackrent offers two distinct voices: that of Thady Quirk, an Irish servant who narrates the story of the Rackrent family, and a fictitious editor, an Englishman who provides the book's preface and glossary. Through this editor's condescending comments about Irish language and customs, Edgeworth demonstrates the lack of understanding between the two cultures. Through Thady, she criticizes Irish landlords and the feudal system, as well as nostalgia and blind loyalty.

The servant is so enamored with the past that he cannot accept the flaws of the feudal system, and he is so loyal to the Rackrents that he cannot talk about them objectively. Scholar Marilyn Butler (12–13), writing in an introduction to a 1992 edition of *Castle Rackrent*, says that Thady "is one of the classic instances of that device so brilliantly handled in eighteenth-century narrative, the unreliable first-person narrator." She compares him to the narrators of Jonathan Swift's *Gulliver's Travels* and *A Modest Proposal*, both of whom are equally unreliable, and calls Edgeworth "Swift's end-of-century counterpart" (13). Moreover, Butler explains that both Swift and Edgeworth use irony and sarcasm to criticize existing social systems, saying that whereas Swift "satirizes modern intellectual innovations, secularization, scientism and self-sufficiency," Edgeworth "satirizes nostalgia, sectarianism, parochialism and blind loyalty" (13).

Thady offers naïve commentary about four successive masters, but despite his reluctance to discuss their faults, it becomes clear that none of them behaves well. The first, Sir Patrick Rackrent, is fond of gambling, parties, and alcohol and dies during a drunken revel. His son, Sir Murtagh, inherits his father's debts but refuses to honor them. He is a stingy man who demands extra money and services from his tenants and spends his spare time filing frivolous lawsuits. When he dies, Castle Rackrent passes to his younger brother, Sir Kit, who raises the rent on its lands, squanders the money on a trip abroad, and is forced to marry for money. He keeps his wife locked in a room and continues to behave as a single man. After he is killed in a duel, Sir Conolly (Condy for short) Rackrent, a distant relative, inherits the estate. Sir Condy is a gambler and spendthrift who accumulates massive debt and eventually sells Castle Rackrent to Thady's son, Jason, a clever attorney. Even though his own son now owns the estate, Thady is upset to see it change hands, and he remains loyal to his master until Sir Condy dies during a drinking contest with another man.

However, some scholars question Thady's loyalty. Butler (8–9) points out that, although many people "agree in finding Thady plain, simple and above all loyal," others have begun to wonder whether he might actually be "a

thieving rogue, the accomplice of his son Jason, who ends up in possession of his master's estate." As an unreliable narrator, Thady would be capable of concealing his own role in Jason's triumph. But perhaps to emphasize his innocence, he concludes his story by saying: "As for all I have here set down from memory and hearsay of the family, there's nothing but truth in it from beginning to end: that you may depend upon; for where's the use of telling lies about the things which every body knows as well as I do?" (121).

Immediately thereafter the editor adds:

The Editor could have readily made the catastrophe of Sir Condy's history more dramatic and more pathetic, if he thought it allowable to varnish the plain round tale of faithful Thady. He lays it before the English reader as a specimen of manners and characters, which are, perhaps, unknown in England. . . . All the features in the foregoing sketch were taken from the life, and they are characteristic of that mixture of quickness, simplicity, cunning, carelessness, dissipation, disinterestedness, shrewdness, and blunder, which, in different forms, and with various success, has been brought upon the state, or delineated in novels. (121)

He then questions whether England's union with Ireland will help the country; however, he says that "the few gentlemen of education, who now reside in [Ireland], will resort to England: they are few, but they are in nothing inferior to men of the same rank in Great Britain. The best that can happen will be the introduction of British manufacturers in their places" (122). (Butler 1972; Edgeworth 1992)

See also Edgeworth, Maria; *Gulliver's Travels;* Manorialism; *Modest Proposal, A;* Quirk, Thady; Swift, Jonathan

Castorp, Hans

Hans Castorp is the main character of Thomas Mann's 1924 novel *Der Zauberberg* (The Magic Mountain). A young man from a middle-class German family, he embarks on a three-week visit to his cousin, Joachim Ziemssen, who is confined to a mountain sanitorium because of tuberculosis. The doctors there soon convince Hans that he is ill, and he decides to put himself under their care. He remains at the sanitorium for seven years, during which he learns about life from patients who represent different social ideologies. For example, Ludovico Settembrini is an Italian humanist and naturalist, Leo Naphta is a rigid Jesuit-trained Catholic converted from Judaism, and Mynheer Peeperkorn is a wealthy hedonist. In discussing Hans's exposure to these various points of view, Mann (1972, 729) explains that the character is "a searcher after the Holy Grail" who is trying to find "the idea of the human being, the conception of a future humanity that has passed through and survived the profoundest knowledge of disease and death." However, before Hans can discover this Grail, World War I breaks out in Europe, and, as Mann explains, he is "snatched downwards from his heights into the European catastrophe" (729). He becomes a soldier, and the novel ends with him on the battlefield, facing an uncertain future. (Mann 1972)

> **See also** *Magic Mountain*, The; Mann, Thomas; Settembrini, Ludovico; Ziemssen, Joachim

Castro, Benito

Benito Castro is a former Peruvian military officer in Ciro Alegría's 1941 novel *El mundo es ancho y ajeno* (Broad and Alien Is the World) who tries to defend his Indian village from nonnative usurpation. Although other villagers consider this a local fight, Castro envisions it as part of a broader social protest movement. He wants to ask all other poor Indians in Peru to join his rebellion against the country's unjust nonnative government. However, during the battle to protect his village, he is mortally wounded, and as he dies, he advises his wife to find another place to live. (Alegría 1941)

> **See also** Alegría, Ciro; Amenabar, Don Alvaro; *Broad and Alien Is the World*; Justice; Maqui, Rosendo

Catch-22

Published in 1961 and set during World War II, *Catch-22*, by Joseph Heller, criticizes many aspects of modern society, particularly the way it conducts its wars. The novel's story is set in two places—Rome and the fictional Italian island of Pianosa, where a U.S. Air Force bombing group is stationed—and is told in a disjointed fashion to reflect the unsettled nature of its main character, Captain John Yossarian. He is a bombadier who tries several tactics to get out of flying his missions. For example, he goes to the hospital complaining of a pain in his liver and remains there while doctors test him for jaundice. He also feigns insanity, engaging in various forms of irrational behavior. Then he learns about Catch-22, a rule that reflects the illogic of the entire military system. Catch-22 states that anyone who flies such dangerous missions must be insane, whereas any flier asking to be relieved of his duties must not be insane. Therefore, there is no way for Yossarian to petition for a medical leave based on insanity.

Consequently, he remains surrounded by death and madness. His superior officers behave irrationally or are corrupt, and when Yossarian goes on leave in Rome, he finds similar insanity and corruption there. The world depicted in *Catch-22* is senselessly violent, and in the end Yossarian decides to escape to neutral Sweden. (Heller 1994; Merrill 1987; Nagel 1984; Seed 1989)

> **See also** Heller, Joseph; Peace; Yossarian, Captain John

Celie

Celie is the main character in Alice Walker's 1982 novel *The Color Purple*, which is presented as a series of her letters. As a girl she is raped by a man she believes to be her father and develops a deep shame. Later she allows her husband to victimize her as well. Then her husband's mistress, Shug Avery, befriends Celie. Shug encourages Celie to become strong. Under her guidance, Celie develops self-respect, starts her own business, and leaves her husband. In the end Celie is a loving and

In this scene from the 1970 movie Catch 22, *Captain John Yossarian protests the illogical military system by refusing to wear his uniform. (Paramount/The Museum of Modern Art Film Stills Archive)*

loved person and no longer anyone's victim. (Walker 1986)

> See also Avery, Shug; *Color Purple, The;* Walker, Alice

Censorship

Censorship is the suppression of information, whether in written, visual, or oral form, by governments, public or private institutions, or individuals. Many works of social protest have been censored by governments wishing to hide social problems. For example, the works of Pramoedya Ananta Toer have been censored in Indonesia, Fyodor Dostoyevsky and Yevgeny Yevtushenko in Russia, and Milan Kundera in Czechoslovakia. In the United States during an era called McCarthyism in the 1950s writers were censored for discussing communism, but more often the reason given for American censorship was obscenity. In this regard Henry Miller's works were banned, Theodore Dreiser was attacked by antiobscenity groups, and Lawrence Ferlinghetti was put on trial for distributing the epic poem *Howl,* by Allen Ginsberg.

In addition, several science fiction novels depict futuristic societies in which books and ideas are censored. Of these, perhaps the most notable are *Fahrenheit 451,* by Ray Bradbury, and *Brave New World,* by Aldous Huxley. (Boyer 1968)

> See also Bradbury, Ray; *Brave New World;* Communism; Dostoyevsky, Fyodor; Dreiser, Theodore; Ferlinghetti, Lawrence; Ginsberg, Allen; *Howl;* Huxley, Aldous; Kundera, Milan; McCarthyism; Toer, Pramoedya Ananta; Yevtushenko, Yevgeny

Chancellor, Olive

Olive Chancellor is a feminist in Henry James's 1886 novel *The Bostonians.* She is one of the first lesbians to appear in American literature but is depicted unflatteringly. An activist in the suffragette movement, Olive vies with a chauvinistic southern gentleman, Basil Ransom, for the affections of a beautiful young woman named Verena Tarrant. Eventually Verena chooses to reject feminism and marry Basil. (James 1956)

> See also *Bostonians, The;* Feminism; Gay and Lesbian Issues; James, Henry; Ransom, Basil; Tarrant, Verena

Child of the Jago, A

Scholars often compare *A Child of the Jago,* by Arthur Morrison, to the works of Charles Dickens because both novelists call attention to problems among the poor in nineteenth-century England. *Jago* depicts life in a British slum called the Jago. Its publication in 1896 brought about changes in government housing laws, and the slum was soon cleared.

The novel is the third-person account of the life of Dicky Perrott, a young boy who grows to manhood in the Jago. Dicky's father, Josh Perrott, is a plasterer by trade but cannot find a job; he steals to support his family. Depressed over their reduced circumstances, his wife, Hannah, takes little interest in their children, Dicky and Dicky's baby sister, Looey, who soon dies from a head injury received when her mother gets into a fistfight with another woman in the street. Fights are constantly breaking out in the Jago, which is dominated by two warring families, the Ranns and the Learys.

Thievery is also common in the Jago, and eventually Dicky begins stealing, too. He fences his stolen goods with a local coffee shop owner, Aaron Weech, who pays Dicky a fraction of what the items are worth. One day a pastor, Reverend Henry Sturt, helps Dicky get a job as a shopkeeper's helper. Dicky is proud of his new job and envisions the day when he will own a shop of his own. But Weech, not wanting to lose one of his best thieves, tells Dicky's employer that the boy is planning to rob him, and Dicky is fired. He goes back to stealing merchandise for Weech. Meanwhile Dicky's father steals a gold watch and takes it to Weech to sell. Weech knows that the watch belongs to a prominent mobster, and wanting to get in the mobster's favor, he turns Josh Perrott in to the police. Perrott is sent to prison for five years.

Now Hannah must struggle to make a living by herself. She gets a job pasting matchboxes together, and Dicky continues to steal.

Children of the Ghetto

By this time he has a new sister, Em, and a brother, Josh Junior, is born while his father is in prison. The family is excited when at last the day comes for Josh Perrott to be released from prison. But as soon as he is released, he goes to Weech's place during the night and murders him. Perrott is arrested and hanged for the crime. Shortly thereafter Dicky is attacked and stabbed by another boy. He dies from his wound, saying he is glad to be out of the Jago. (Morrison 1995)

See also Class, Social; Dickens, Charles; Morrison, Arthur; Poverty

Children of the Ghetto

Children of the Ghetto: A Study of a Peculiar People, by Israel Zangwill, concerns the life of Jewish immigrants in a London ghetto. It was first published in 1892 in two volumes, *Children of the Ghetto* and *Grandchildren of the Ghetto.* The following year a one-volume edition of the works appeared, complete with a glossary of Yiddish words and phrases.

The novels include numerous characters who illustrate different approaches to Jewish immigrant life in a London ghetto. Some of the characters forget their heritage and become assimilated into the Christian culture outside the ghetto. Some observe Jewish traditions only when it is convenient to do so. Others become so rigid in their observance of Jewish rituals that they are more concerned with technicalities than with spirituality. A few become involved in a movement to reestablish a Jewish homeland in Palestine, but when one man travels there, he is disappointed to find it "scarce more than his London Ghetto transplanted, only grown filthier and narrower and more ragged, with cripples for beggars and lepers in lieu of hawkers. The magic of his dream-city was not here" (Zangwill 1895, 221).

Two of the most significant characters in the novel are Hannah Jacobs and Esther Ansell. The daughter of a rabbi, Hannah Jacobs attends a party where the participants are joking about an upcoming marriage. The bridegroom-to-be pretends to go through the marriage ceremony with Hannah instead of with his bride. Later he and Hannah learn that Jewish law does not recognize a joke and that they are truly married in the eyes of God.

Fortunately, no one outside of the family knows what has happened, and Hannah's father arranges for her to get a quiet divorce. Then Hannah meets and falls in love with a young *Cohen,* or Jewish priest. They want to get married, but Hannah's father explains that her divorce means she cannot marry a *Cohen.* Hannah insists that because her marriage was not a real one, her divorce should not be considered real either. She reminds her father that no one knows about the divorce. Nonetheless, the rabbi remains rigid. Finally Hannah and her beloved agree to run away to the United States together to get married. At the last minute, however, Hannah cannot leave her family or religion. She lets the young man go on without her and lives out the rest of her life as a bitter spinster.

Meanwhile Esther Ansell is a child from a poor family who barely has enough to eat. One day she wins a poetry prize and comes to the attention of a wealthy Jewish woman. The woman pays for Esther's family to emigrate to the United States and adopts the little girl as her own. Esther attends the best schools and has fine clothes and good food. Nonetheless, she is pained by the differences she sees between her life and that of her friends in the ghetto. When she becomes a young woman, she writes a book under a male pseudonym criticizing upper- and middle-class Jewish life. No one else knows she has written it, and she has to sit in silence as her adopted family talks about how horrible the book is. One day she realizes that she does not belong with this family, and she runs away to the ghetto. Eventually a young man from her old life seeks her out, having read and admired her book. The editor of a Jewish newspaper, he has been fired for writing articles that do not meet with his sponsors' approval. Soon he realizes that he is in love with Esther, and the two become engaged.

Through these two characters, *Children of the Ghetto* shows the difficulties of maintaining Jewish traditions in a land of modern ideas. The novel also concerns itself with religious hypocrisy and its relationship to social problems. For example, men who need jobs often ignore the Jewish restriction against working on the Sabbath (Saturday), and during a workers' strike they go to a socialist meeting rather than remaining home on a Friday night (the beginning of the Sabbath), which is also required by their religion. Consequently, the third-person omniscient narrator concludes that "ancient piety" cannot withstand "the stress of modern social problems" (241). Similarly, the leader of the meeting is an atheist who keeps his beliefs to himself, knowing that his lack of religion would anger the crowd. Whereas once he used to argue religious issues with everyone he met, the narrator explains that "like so many reformers who have started with blatant atheism, he was beginning to see the insignificance of irreligious dissent as compared with the solution of the social problem" (242). He knows that the best way for him to accomplish change is to appear traditional. Thus, his deception furthers the socialist cause. (Leftwich 1957; Zangwill 1895)

See also Anti-Semitism; Immigrant Communities; Poverty; Religion; Zangwill, Israel

Children of Violence

Children of Violence is a series of five semiautobiographical novels by Doris Lessing: *Martha Quest* (1952), *A Proper Marriage* (1954), *A Ripple from the Storm* (1958), *Landlocked* (1965), and *The Four-Gated City* (1969). Set in Africa and England during the 1930s and 1940s, they trace the political and spiritual awakenings of Martha Quest, a British woman who does not share the racist, anti-Semitic views of other African colonists.

Martha Quest is brought up in a Central African colony. Her father, a weak-willed man, cannot stand up to his racist, anti-Semitic, domineering wife. In contrast, Martha is intelligent and independent, and she and her mother quarrel repeatedly. The household is so filled with tension that when Martha turns 17, her father asks her to leave.

She moves to a nearby city and dreams of becoming a writer, journalist, or political activist of some kind; she believes in equality for the black natives. But the only work she can find is as a secretary, and her dreams soon fade. She falls in with a wild crowd and dates several men. Eventually she marries one of them, Douglas Knowell, simply to conform to society's expectations. Douglas is a narrow-minded, childish man, and Martha immediately knows that she has made a mistake in becoming his wife. She wants a divorce, but her friends and relatives convince her that she is simply experiencing the doubts that all women feel about their husbands. As the years pass, however, her unhappiness grows, particularly after she gives birth to a daughter, Caroline, and realizes that she does not love the girl. Martha simply does she want to be a housewife and mother. When her husband enlists in the war and leaves town, she becomes involved with a Communist group and falls in love with one of its members, an air force officer named William. The two are not lovers, but her husband hears that they are. When Douglas is discharged from the service, he returns home to confront her about the affair. The two quarrel, and she decides to leave him. Douglas begs her to stay. He threatens to kill her or himself if she walks out on him, and he enlists the help of friends and relatives to convince her to keep the marriage intact. Nonetheless, she walks out on Douglas, leaving her daughter behind.

Once free of her marriage, she becomes involved in a Marxist group, exploring various political and social philosophies. Eventually she marries the group's leader, yet she remains unsatisfied and restless. Then she has an affair with a Jewish gardener who has psychic abilities. Through him she learns that she, too, has a psychic gift and begins to explore this inner power. She divorces her husband, and after her lover goes insane, she moves to England, where she experiments with different lifestyles. She lives among dockworkers and then with shopkeepers, finally taking a job as the assistant to a Communist writer and activist. Meanwhile she continues to explore her mental powers.

She also becomes involved with a group of psychics who sense that a nuclear war is coming. The group creates sanctuaries far from major cities, and when the war does happen, they survive to create a new race of people. Unfortunately, Martha is not a part of this new society, having died after exposure to nuclear radiation. (Brewster 1965; Lessing 1964; Lessing 1969; Sprague and Tiger 1986)

See also Anti-Semitism; Feminism; Knowell, Douglas; Lessing, Doris; Quest, Martha; Racism; Socialism

Children's Hour, The

The Children's Hour is a three-act drama by playwright Lillian Hellman. First performed and published in 1934, it depicts prejudice against lesbians. It also shows the destructive nature of malicious gossip, and in this regard is very similar to another drama, The Crucible, by Arthur Miller, which concerns unfair persecution during the Salem witch trials. Both Miller and Hellman were victims of unfair persecution themselves during the era of McCarthyism, an anticommunist "witch-hunt" of the 1950s.

As in The Crucible, the events of The Children's Hour are set into motion by a young girl. Mary Tilford is a student at a New England boarding school, and she hates the school's owners and teachers, Karen Wright and Martha Dobie. After Mary is punished for lying, she retaliates by telling her grandmother, a school sponsor, that the two women are having a lesbian affair. Mrs. Tilford tells the other students' parents, who remove their children from the school. Karen and Martha sue for libel but lose their case. Bankrupt and ashamed, Karen ends her engagement to a man who has stood by her throughout her legal case. Shortly thereafter Martha realizes that she has had feelings of love for Karen, and in despair she kills herself. Mrs. Tilford then arrives to tell Karen she has learned her granddaughter was lying about the affair. (Hellman 1979; Wright 1986)

See also Crucible, The; Hellman, Lillian; McCarthyism; Miller, Arthur

Civil Rights

See Racism

Clamence, Jean-Baptiste

Jean-Baptiste Clamence, the first-person narrator of Albert Camus's 1956 novel La Chute (The Fall), undergoes a shift in self-awareness and tells the story of this shift to an unnamed stranger in an Amsterdam bar. Clamence describes himself as a "judge-penitent" because he has judged his own faults and suffered for them; therefore he feels qualified to judge the faults of others. Years earlier as a lawyer in Paris he let a woman drown rather than trouble himself with rescuing her. This experience and other equally selfish acts eventually led him to reevaluate his life, the life of all human beings, and the structure of his society. (Camus 1958)

See also Camus, Albert; Fall, The; Justice

Clark, Walter Van Tilburg

Author of the novel The Ox-Bow Incident, Walter Van Tilburg Clark used the western genre to write stories critical of human nature. In 1969 scholar Max Westbrook (1969, 138) deemed Clark's work relevant to the civil rights movement; Westbrook compared Clark to prominent African-American author James Baldwin because both men explore the "unspeakable" fears, longings, and prejudices that hide within the human heart.

Clark was born in East Orland, Maine, on August 3, 1909, but from the age of eight he grew up in Reno, Nevada. His father was president of the University of Nevada, and Clark received his B.A. and M.A. degrees there, specializing in both English literature and European and American philosophers. In 1931 he became a teaching assistant in American literature and Greek philosophers at the University of Vermont, and his first publication, a book of poetry entitled Ten Women in Gale's House and Shorter Poems, was published the following year. In October 1933 he married and accepted a teaching position in Cazenovia, New York.

But although he lived in the East, Clark never forgot his childhood in Nevada, and in

1938 he set his first novel, *The Ox-Bow Incident,* in the American West. The book was published two years later. It was a critical success, and in 1943 a major motion picture company, 20th Century Fox, made *The Ox-Bow Incident* into a movie, which was nominated for an Academy Award that same year; Clark did not write the movie script.

In 1945 Clark published his second novel, *The City of Trembling Leaves.* This book was also set in the American West, but according to Westbrook (68), critics considered it "juvenile" in comparison with the "mature craftsmanship" of *The Ox-Bow Incident.* Similarly, Clark's next novel, *The Track of the Cat* (1949), which Westbrook (93) believes "perhaps the finest Western novel written," never received the same level of critical acclaim as *The Ox-Bow Incident,* nor did *The City of Trembling Leaves* when it was republished as *Tim Hazard* in 1951.

By this time Clark had relocated his home to Nevada, but in 1953, three years after publishing his final work, *The Watchful Gods and Other Stories,* he left his teaching position at the University of Nevada after a dispute over administrative policy. He lectured in creative writing, first at the University of Oregon and later at the University of Washington, before becoming an assistant professor of English at the University of Montana in 1954. Two years later he joined the creative writing program at San Francisco State College.

In 1957 Clark testified as a witness for the defense at an important obscenity trial. The case concerned a collection of poetry by Allen Ginsberg entitled *Howl and Other Poems.* *Howl* was a work of social protest that both celebrated and criticized masculinity; its strong language in reference to homosexuality led its publisher, Lawrence Ferlinghetti, to be charged with distributing obscene material. Ferlinghetti's acquittal was considered a landmark decision in regard to First Amendment constitutional rights.

In 1960 Clark became a fellow in English at Wesleyan University in Connecticut, but in 1962 he decided to return to Nevada. He became writer in residence at the University of Nevada and an editor for the University of Nevada Press. He died in 1971 in Reno, Nevada, at the age of 62. (Westbrook 1969)

See also Baldwin, James; Croft, Art; Davies, Art; Ferlinghetti, Lawrence; Ginsberg, Allen; *Howl;* Justice; Martin, Donald; *Ox-Bow Incident, The;* Tetley, Gerald

Class, Social

A social class is a group of people united by economic and/or social commonalities. In some places and time periods a person's class is determined by the amount of money he or she has, whereas in others a person's class is hereditary. In all cases classes are hierarchical, which means that some groups are considered superior to others and have more rights. A great deal of social protest literature concerns the struggle of the lower classes to achieve the same benefits as the upper ones. For example, Theodore Dreiser's novel *An American Tragedy* deals with a middle-class man's desire to better himself by marrying an upper-class woman. *Castle Rackrent,* by Maria Edgeworth, concerns the inferiority of peasants amid the aristocracy in England, and Ivan Turgenev's *A Sportsman's Sketches* addresses the same issue in Russia. The works of Honoré de Balzac, Charles Dickens, John Galsworthy, Victor Hugo, Henry James, Arthur Morrison, George Bernard Shaw, Émile Verhaeren, Edith Wharton, Israel Zangwill, and Émile Zola also depict difficulties between upper and lower economic classes. Some of these authors also include discussions of socialism and/or communism, which do not have the same emphasis on class structure and wealth as capitalism.

As for hereditary class systems, Mulk Raj Anand shows the problems of India's caste system in his novel *Untouchable,* and Pramoedya Ananta Toer shows the inferior social position of concubinage in his Indonesian novel *This Earth of Mankind,* which was banned in his native country. In addition, early feminists typically depicted women as belonging to a separate and inferior social class, regardless of their economic position. (Cole 1976; Crompton 1978; Szymanski 1983)

See also *American Tragedy, An;* Anand, Mulk Raj; Balzac, Honoré de; Capitalism; *Castle Rackrent;* Censorship; Communism; Dickens, Charles; Dreiser, Theodore; Edgeworth, Maria; Feminism; Galsworthy, John; Hugo, Victor; James, Henry; Morrison, Arthur; Poverty; Shaw, George Bernard; Socialism; *Sportsman's Sketches, A; This Earth of Mankind;* Toer, Pramoedya Ananta; Turgenev, Ivan; *Untouchable;* Verhaeren, Émile; Wharton, Edith; Zangwill, Israel; Zola, Émile

Clifton, Tod

A character from Ralph Ellison's 1952 novel *Invisible Man,* Tod Clifton is a confused black man who becomes the pawn of a white-run Communist organization called the Brotherhood. He believes in the Brotherhood, and when the group abandons its support for the black community, he is shattered. He goes into hiding and eventually reappears on a Harlem, New York, street corner selling politically incorrect dancing black dolls. Shortly thereafter he is killed by police, and the Brotherhood refuses to protest his unjust death. (Ellison 1952)

See also Ellison, Ralph; *Invisible Man*

Clockwork Orange, A

A Clockwork Orange, by Anthony Burgess, concerns a person's right to choose whether to be good or evil. Set in the future, the novel depicts a society where youths have become extremely violent and rival gangs roam the streets each night. Its first-person narrator, Alex, is the 15-year-old leader of one such gang. In a unique slang he explains that he and his friends Pete, Georgie, and Dim consider it fun to rob stores and houses, rape women, and brutalize people in their neighborhood. The only nonviolent thing that Alex enjoys is classical music.

One day Georgie decides to fight him over leadership of his group. Alex wins the fight and assumes they are once again friends. But later, while the gang is robbing a house, Georgie attacks him and leaves him for the police to find. Alex is sentenced to many years in prison. To reduce his time he volunteers for a new rehabilitation program in which doctors inject him with a special drug and force him to watch violent movies accompanied by classical music. The drug causes him to become sick at the sight of violence. After a while, even without the drug, he becomes sick at just the thought of violence. Unfortunately, he also becomes sick whenever he hears classical music.

Once Alex's reconditioning is complete, the government displays him to the media and sets him free. He quickly finds it difficult to survive as a pacifist. He is beaten up and brutalized both by his former victims and his former friends, and his parents do not want him to live with them anymore. Eventually he ends up at the house of a government protester and noted author, F. Alexander. He recognizes Alex from his picture in the newspaper. Alex also recognizes Alexander as one of his former victims. Wearing masks, Alex and his gang once broke into the writer's house, beat him, and repeatedly raped his wife, who later died from the attack. They also destroyed one of his manuscripts, *A Clockwork Orange,* which argued that men, like oranges, are natural objects that should not be mechanized.

Fortunately, F. Alexander does not seem to recognize Alex's voice, and he decides to use him to criticize the government. He writes an article using Alex's name, bemoaning his poor treatment in the antiviolence program, and calls in the members of an antigovernment group. This group tells Alex he will soon be a famous public speaker. They leave him at a strange apartment to sleep. When he awakes, classical music is blaring from the walls. He says:

Then it all came over me, the start of the pain and the sickness, and I began to groan deep down in my keeshkas. And then there I was, me who had loved music so much, crawling off the bed and going oh oh oh to myself, and then bang bang banging on the wall creeching: "Stop, stop it, turn it off!" But it went on and it seemed to be like louder. So I crashed at the wall till my knuckles were all red red

A teenage gang terrorizes one of its victims in the 1971 movie A Clockwork Orange. *(Warner/The Museum of Modern Art Film Stills Archive)*

drovvy and torn skin, creeching and creeching but the music did not stop . . . like it was a deliberate torture. (Burgess 1986, 167)

Alex then sees an open window and jumps, intending to kill himself. He wakes up in a government hospital, covered with bandages, and learns that the antigovernment group intended for him to die to promote its cause; F. Alexander did recognize his voice. After his attempted suicide, the newspaper headlines read: "Boy Victim of Criminal Reform Scheme and Government as Murderer" (172).

Now the government wants to make amends. It returns his mind to its former, violent condition and gives him a job upon his release from the hospital. His parents take him back, and his life is as before. However, in a final chapter Alex expresses dissatisfaction at what he has become. He has just turned 19 and meets his former gang-friend Pete, who is married and respectable. Alex starts thinking about the wife and son he'd like to have himself and seems relieved that his childhood is at an end.

When *A Clockwork Orange* was published

in 1962, this last chapter appeared in the British version of the novel but not in the American one. Author Anthony Burgess (Burgess 1986, viii) says his New York publisher omitted it because it "was a sellout. . . . It was bland and it showed . . . [an] unwillingness to accept that a human being could be a model of unregenerable evil." However, Burgess (viii) believes that the last chapter "gives the novel the quality of genuine fiction, an art founded on the principle that human beings change. There is, in fact, not much point in writing a novel unless you can show the possibility of moral transformation, or an increase in wisdom, operating in your chief character or characters." Burgess restored the chapter to the American version of *A Clockwork Orange* in a 1986 reprinting.

In an introduction to that edition, he (ix) discusses the social philosophy behind the plot, saying:

A human being is endowed with free will. He can use this to choose between good and evil. If he can only perform good or only perform evil, then he is a clockwork orange—meaning that he has the appearance of an organism lovely with colour and juice but is in fact only a clockwork toy to be wound up by God or the Devil or (since this is increasingly replacing both) the Almighty State. It is as inhuman to be totally good as it is to be totally evil. The important thing is moral choice.

Therefore, the novel presents government and antigovernment groups in the same negative light, as entities that want to eliminate free choice. (Burgess 1986; De Vitis 1972)

See also Burgess, Anthony; Peace; Science Fiction and Fantasy

Close Sesame

Published in 1983, *Close Sesame* is the final book of a trilogy known as *Variations on the Theme of an African Dictatorship,* which includes the novels *Sweet and Sour Milk* (1979) and *Sardines* (1981). The author of these works, Nuruddin Farah, is from the Republic of Somalia and writes about political and social oppression in that country. In *Close Sesame* Farah depicts the African dictatorship established by Somali natives as being just as corrupt and oppressive as the Italian and British colonial governments that preceded it. The novel's main character is an old man named Deeriye, who is one of the most respected people in the country. As a young man he refused to cooperate with the Italian government and was imprisoned for several years. Now he is a symbol of the liberation movement that established the native-run government. Meanwhile Deeriye's adult son, Mursal, has become involved in a plot to assassinate the general, the country's dictator. One day Mursal's friend Mahad tries to carry out the plot and fails. He is thrown into prison. Later Mahad's uncle, Deeriye's friend Rooble, is arrested after government officials trick him into disobeying a law regarding public assemblies.

Rooble's family is of a different clan from the general's, and the dictator wants the public to believe that the assassination attempt was based on clan rivalries rather than political ideologies. Thus, a campaign of misinfor-

mation begins. Regarding this campaign, the third-person narrator of the story says:

Information, Deeriye was thinking to himself, is the garden the common man in Somalia or anywhere else is not allowed to enter, sit in its shady trees, drink from its streams and eat its delicious fruits; information, or the access to that power and knowledge: power prepared to protect power; keep the populace underinformed so you can rule them; keep them apart by informing them separately; build bars of ignorance around them, imprison them with shackles of uninformedness and they are easy to govern; feed them with the wrong information, give them poisonous bits of what does not count, a piece of gossip here, a rumour there, an unconfirmed report. Keep them waiting; *let them not know;* let them not know what you are up to and where you might spring from again. (Farah 1992, 74)

Because Deeriye has become a symbol for freedom and justice, the government does not want him to become involved in the current situation. Moreover, since Deeriye is not in good health, his family members suggest that he leave the country rather than overtire himself with politics. Nonetheless, Deeriye remains, even after the government begins to harass him, and has long conversations with friends and relatives on various political and social issues in the country. Many of these issues are intertwined. For example, when the father of a young man named Mukhtaar, who was a coconspirator in the assassination attempt, kills his son and gets away with it, Deeriye and Mursal discuss the event's relationship to the traditional customs of the people. Mursal says:

A father can beat his son to madness in full public view and the son is expected not to raise a hand but to receive the beating in total silence. The son is not allowed to question the wisdom of his parent's statements, must never answer back, never raise his voice or head. A daughter is not, of course, expected to refuse or challenge her material worth: she is worth as much dowry as she can obtain for her parents—not more or less than that. As for public justice being confused with private justice, what would happen if Mukhtaar were to receive a fatal blow on the head and die? Nothing. Nothing would happen to avenge Mukhtaar's life and his father would not be submitted to questioning: after all, it is the prerogative of a parent what to do with the life and property of an offspring, in the same way as it is the prerogative of the husband what to do with the life and property of a wife for whom he has paid the necessary dowry. (120–121)

Throughout the novel, private events are related to public ones. Even the assassination attempt has a corresponding event in Deeriye's personal life. On the same day a young neighbor boy who dislikes Deeriye throws a stone at his head and injures him. Deeriye's forgiveness is in sharp contrast to the general's retaliation against his would-be assassins. Every person involved in the plot is eventually killed, including Mursal. When Deeriye hears of his son's death, he decides to kill the general himself. However, at the crucial moment he pulls rosary beads from his pocket instead of a gun and is shot dead by the general's guards. Some believe his act was a mark of insanity, whereas others consider it heroic. (Farah 1992; Wright 1994)

See also Farah, Nuruddin; Justice

Clotel

The 1853 novel *Clotel: or, The President's Daughter* was the first published work of an African American in the United States. Its author, William Wells Brown, was a southern slave who escaped to freedom in the North, and his story concerns the injustice of slavery. The novel's main character is Clotel, the daughter of a slave named Currer and the president of the United States, Thomas Jefferson. Currer was Jefferson's housekeeper in

Virginia, and shortly after he left for Washington, D.C., she was sold at a slave auction, along with Clotel, age 16, and her sister Althesa, age 14. Both girls look white.

At the auction Currer and Althesa are sold to a slave trader, who then sells them to a Methodist minister and a bank teller, respectively, for use as housekeepers. Clotel is sold to Horatio Green, who takes her as his mistress. He and Clotel soon have a daughter, Mary, who is white and beautiful. The three are happy together until Horatio decides to marry into a politically prominent family. His new wife finds out about his mistress and orders her sold south. The woman then takes Mary as her servant—to humiliate the child and punish Horatio.

Clotel eventually ends up in the hands of another man who wants her as his mistress. Before he can take advantage of her, however, she escapes with the help of another slave, William. The two dress Clotel as a white man and pretend that she is William's master; in this way they travel north without suspicion. Once in the North William goes on to Canada, and Clotel heads to Virginia to rescue her daughter Mary. She is soon captured but escapes the jail. As she is about to be caught again, she plunges off a bridge into the Potomac River and dies.

Meanwhile Clotel's sister, Althesa, has married a white man who believes that all slaves should be free. They move to a place where everyone believes Althesa is white, too, and there they have two daughters. The two girls receive the finest education. Then Althesa and her husband both succumb to an illness, and after their death the truth about Althesa's background is revealed. Her two daughters are sold into slavery as part of the estate. They die shortly thereafter, one by killing herself with poison and the other by wasting away from despair.

By this time Clotel's mother, Currer, has died of an illness. However, she was treated well in the last part of her life. Her mistress, Georgiana Peck Carlson, inherited her slaves from her father but wants them set free. She and her husband have devised a plan whereby the slaves work for wages that are credited to an account. When a slave has earned a certain amount, he or she is given the money and sent north to freedom. Georgiana regrets Currer's death because she would have liked to reunite her with her two daughters. No one in the Carlson household knows what became of them.

Currer, Clotel, and Althesa have all died slaves, despite their connection to Jefferson, who has been advocating the abolition of slavery. However, Clotel's daughter Mary does eventually become free. In Horatio Green's household she meets a slave named George and falls in love with him. One day he participates in a slave rebellion, during which he is arrested and sentenced to death. Before his execution Mary visits the jail and changes clothes with him. He then walks out pretending to be her and quickly heads north to Canada. From there he travels to Europe, where he becomes a prosperous businessman. As punishment for helping George escape, Mary is sold south, but while traveling there by boat, she is helped to escape by a young Frenchman. He takes her to Paris and marries her. Sometime later, after her husband has died of an illness, Mary sees George sitting in a park. The two are joyfully reunited. They marry and continue to live in Europe as free human beings. Thus, the novel concludes, "We can but blush for our country's shame when we recall to mind the fact, that while George and Mary Green, and numbers of other fugitives from American slavery, can receive protection from any of the governments of Europe, they cannot return to their native land without becoming slaves" (Gates 1990, 221).

In addition to following the lives of Jefferson's enslaved offspring, *Clotel* offers various anecdotes about other slaves by way of illustrating the injustices of slavery. It also comments on the hypocrisy of American beliefs in regard to freedom. For example, at one point the novel points out that the founders of the country believed in "freedom and liberty for all" and yet instituted slavery almost immediately upon their arrival on American shores.

The narrator says that on the same day in 1620 two very different ships set forth, explaining:

The May-flower brought the seed-wheat of states and empire. . . . Here in this ship are great and good men. Justice, mercy, humanity, respect for the rights of all; each man honoured, as he was useful to himself and others; labour respected, law-abiding men, constitution-making and respecting men; men, whom no tyrant could conquer, or hardship overcome, with the high commission sealed by a Spirit divine, to establish religious and political liberty for all. . . . But look far in the South-east, and you behold on the same day . . . a low rakish ship hastening from the tropics, solitary and alone, to the New World. What is she? She is freighted with the elements of unmixed evil. Hark! Hear those rattling chains, hear that cry of despair and wail of anguish, as they die away in the unpitying distance. Listen to those shocking oaths, the crack of that flesh-cutting whip. Ah! it is the first cargo of slaves on their way to Jamestown, Virginia. (165–166)

The novel includes abolitionist poetry, as well as a concluding chapter that states that the author personally witnessed many of the events in the story. This conclusion gives statistics regarding how many Christians of different sects own slaves and says: "Let no Christian association be maintained with those who traffic in the blood and bones of those whom God has made of one flesh as yourselves" (223). (Farrison 1969; Gates 1990; Warner 1976)

See also Brown, William Wells; Carlson, Georgiana; Green, Horatio; Racism; Slavery

Cohen, Joss and Solly

Joss and Solly Cohen are brothers who appear in Doris Lessing's five-novel series *Children of Violence*. They grow up as the only Jews in a British colony of Central Africa and experience a great deal of prejudice, not only because of their religion but also because of their liberal politics. Their only friend in the community is Martha Quest, with whom they share books on philosophy, sociology, psychology, and politics. Because of their influence, Martha rejects the conservative views of her parents and becomes a Communist. (Lessing 1964)

> See also *Children of Violence;* Lessing, Doris; Quest, Martha

Color

Color was the first collection of poems by noted African-American author Countee (Porter) Cullen. Published in 1925, it presents many aspects of the black experience in the United States, including Cullen's experiences with racism. In one of the most powerful poems in the collection, "The Shroud of Color," Cullen says: "My color shrouds me in, I am as dirt / Beneath my brother's heel; there is a hurt" and later speaks of a racist beating after which "somehow it was borne upon my brain / How being dark, and living through the pain / Of it, is courage more than angels have" (Cullen 1991, 101–102). In another poem, "Heritage," he talks about being disconnected from his African heritage, saying, "What is Africa to me? . . . A book one thumbs / Listlessly, till slumber comes" (104–105). Cullen has inspired many black authors, including Peter Abrahams, who used a line from the Cullen poem "Tableau" as the title of his social protest novel *The Path of Thunder*. In Cullen's work the phrase refers to two young men, one black and one white, who arouse the ire of their communities by daring to walk together; he refers to their walk as creating "a path of thunder" (86). (Cullen 1991)

> See also Abrahams, Peter; Cullen, Countee; *Path of Thunder, The;* Racism

Color Purple, The

The Color Purple, by Alice Walker, concerns the struggle of an African-American woman, Celie, to develop and strengthen her self-respect in a racist, sexist society. The novel was published in 1982, won a Pulitzer Prize in 1983, and became a major motion picture in 1985. The book is written in epistolary form, using Celie's letters to God and her younger sister Nettie, as well as Nettie's letters to Celie, to tell the story. Set in the early twentieth century, it begins when Celie is 14 and living in rural Georgia with her mother and her stepfather, Alphonso. Alphonso repeatedly rapes her, and she bears two of his children, which he takes away. When Celie's mother dies, Alphonso remarries and forces Celie to wed a man named Albert, who really wanted Nettie instead. Albert treats Celie badly and tries to seduce Nettie. Nettie leaves town, and Albert hides her subsequent letters to Celie. Then Albert moves his mistress, Shug Avery, into his house. Shug is a strong individual, and at first she feels contempt for Celie. Eventually, however, the two women become friends and lovers. Shug helps Celie develop self-respect and encourages her to start her own clothing business. Later Celie leaves Albert to move in with Shug. By this time Celie has discovered Nettie's letters. They reveal that Nettie is now living in Africa with the Olinkan tribe, and she has found Celie's lost children, Adam and Olivia, who were adopted by a black missionary named Samuel and his wife, Corinne. When Corinne dies, Nettie marries Samuel.

Meanwhile Alphonso has died, and Celie inherits his home. She moves there with Shug and makes peace with Albert. She has many friends, including Albert's oldest son, Harpo, and his wife, Sofia. A headstrong woman, Sofia once left Harpo because she found him too bossy. However, she soon encountered worse oppression from white men, and she was jailed for refusing to work for the mayor's wife. After her release Sophie reunites with Harpo, and together they join with Celie and Shug to celebrate Nettie's arrival. With her are Olivia, Adam, and Adam's Olinkan bride, Tashi. In the end all of the characters are reunited and reconciled, having matured and discovered their best selves with the help of their friends' support.

Because of the book's black folk dialect and feminist theme, *The Color Purple* has often been compared to the novel *Their Eyes Were Watching God,* by Zora Neale Hurston. This theme is revisited in much of Alice Walker's work, including *The Temple of My Familiar,* which includes some of the same characters as *The Color Purple.* (Gates and Appiah 1993a; Walker 1986; Winchell 1992)

See also Avery, Shug; Celie; Feminism; Gay and Lesbian Issues; Racism; Walker, Alice

Communism

Communism is a political and socioeconomic system related to socialism. Although many of the principles of communism developed in ancient times, the modern Communist movement did not begin until 1848 when German socialist Karl Marx published a work entitled *The Communist Manifesto,* in which he and coauthor Friedrich Engels suggested that socialism would develop from capitalism just as capitalism had developed from manorialism. The authors explained that communism would then develop from socialism after a revolutionary struggle between the upper classes, or bourgeoisie, and working classes, or proletariat.

Marx's ideology soon spread throughout Europe, but during and after the Russian Revolution of 1917 it split into several factions, most notably Marxism and Leninism. Communist groups also appeared in England and the United States, where many writers began advocating communism as an alternative to capitalism. In the 1950s U.S. senator Joseph McCarthy led a crusade against such writers; this crusade became known as McCarthyism.

Authors who discuss communism or depict Communist characters in their works include Isabel Allende, Carlos Fuentes, Graham Greene, Milan Kundera, Doris Lessing, Jack London, Jean-Paul Sartre, and William Lederer and Eugene Burdick. Black American authors Ralph Ellison and Richard Wright depict communism as an unsatisfactory way to combat racism in the United States. (Aaron 1961; Cohen 1962; Ruhle 1969; Williams 1977)

See also Allende, Isabel; Capitalism; Class, Social; Ellison, Ralph; Fuentes, Carlos; Greene, Graham; Kundera, Milan; Lessing, Doris; London, Jack; McCarthyism; Racism; Sartre, Jean-Paul; Socialism; Wright, Richard

Cosette

One of the main characters of Victor Hugo's 1862 novel *Les Misérables,* Cosette is an illegitimate child whose mother leaves her in the care of an innkeeper. Although the innkeeper has been paid to care for the little girl, he keeps her in rags and buys her no toys. When she is five, he makes her into a servant and treats her cruelly. Hugo (1987, 157) uses this incident to discuss the poor treatment of lower-class children throughout France, saying: "Five years old! It will be said that's hard to believe, but it's true; social suffering can begin at any age. Didn't we see recently the trial of Dumollard, an orphan turned bandit, who, from the age of five, say the official documents, being alone in the world, 'worked for his living and stole'!" Eventually, however, Cosette's circumstances improve. She is rescued by a wealthy benefactor, Jean Valjean; grows into a beautiful young woman; and marries a member of the upper classes despite her illegimate past. (Hugo 1987; Swinburne 1970)

See also Hugo, Victor; Justice; *Misérables, Les;* Poverty; Valjean, Jean

Crabbe, George

Born on December 24, 1754, in the small seaside village of Aldeburgh in Suffolk, England, George Crabbe wrote poetry about the plight of the rural poor. He originally worked as a surgeon in Aldeburgh, writing poems as a hobby. Then he decided to stop practicing medicine and become a full-time author. In 1780 he moved to London, where he lived in poverty until he found a wealthy patron, Edmund Burke. He introduced Crabbe to many important men of the time and helped him publish a poem entitled *The Library* in 1781. Now a success, Crabbe decided to study theology. He was ordained as a cleric in 1782 and worked in that capacity for the remainder of his life. He also continued to write poetry. His most famous works are *The Village* (1783), a realistic poem about rural poverty, and *The Parish Register* (1807), in which he traced the life of a rural village through its marriage, birth, and death records. He died on February

3, 1832, in Trowbridge, Wiltshire, England. (Chamberlain 1965)

See also "Parish Workhouse, The"; Poverty

Crabbe, Jack

Jack Crabbe is the 111-year-old first-person narrator of *Little Big Man,* Thomas Berger's 1964 novel about the mistreatment of Native Americans during the 1800s. Although white, Jack spends his childhood among the Cheyenne Indians. As a man he lives in the white world, but eventually he returns to his tribe, where people are more honest and straightforward. Then soldiers from the U.S. Cavalry destroy his village. Vowing revenge on their general, George Armstrong Custer, Jack becomes a civilian employee in his army and is present at the Battle of the Little Big Horn. However, by this time he has realized that killing Custer will not stop the mistreatment of the Indians. (Berger 1964; Landon 1989)

See also Berger, Thomas; *Little Big Man;* Native American Issues; Old Lodge Skins; Racism

Crawford, Janie

The main character of Zora Neale Hurston's 1937 novel *Their Eyes Were Watching God,* Janie Crawford expresses feminist views that are unpopular in her black community. She marries three times, the first to please her grandmother, the second to gain respect, and the third to enjoy life. Her story is about self-awareness and personal empowerment. (Hemenway 1977; Hurston 1990)

See also Hurston, Zora Neale; Stark, Joe; Tea Cake; *Their Eyes Were Watching God*

Croft, Art

The narrator of Walter Van Tilburg Clark's western novel *The Ox-Bow Incident,* Art Croft joins a lynching party out of a misguided sense of loyalty to his fellow cowboys. However, throughout the novel he questions his participation in the group. Scholar Max Westbrook (1969, 60) believes that Art "is moving towards an acceptance of ethical responsibilities" and "wants to think outside himself, to a reality more objective than the personal projects of the romanticized individualist." But despite doubts about the group's validity, both Art and his friend Gil Carter stay with the lynching party, and in the end they discover they have hung three innocent men. (Westbrook 1969)

See also Clark, Walter Van Tilberg; Davies, Art; Justice; Martin, Donald; *Ox-Bow Incident, The;* Tetley, Gerald

Crowne, Lenina

The character Lenina Crowne appears in Aldous Huxley's 1932 novel *Brave New World.* Living in the distant future, she has become completely cut off from nature. In her society women no longer give birth. Children are created in test tubes and raised in large centers, and adults are encouraged to have promiscuous fun. Therefore, when Lenina meets John, a young man from a more primitive world, and finds herself attracted to him, she immediately tries to have sex with him. He is repulsed and becomes violent, whereupon she locks herself in the bathroom. She never understands his response. (Atkins 1968; Brander 1970; Huxley 1989)

See also *Brave New World;* Huxley, Aldous

Crucible, The

The Crucible, by Arthur Miller, is a play about mass hysteria and the persecution of the innocent. Set in Salem, Massachusetts, in 1692, it begins when a girl falls ill after participating in a secret ceremony with her friends, during which they danced and brewed a love potion. Soon the townspeople learn what happened. They condemn it as witchcraft, a practice punishable by death. The girls, to save themselves, insist they did not join the ceremony willingly; agents of the Devil made them do it. They then begin to name these agents: neighbors they dislike. When doubted, the girls twitch and shriek as though tormented by witchcraft, and soon the town leaders believe them. One by one the good people of Salem are arrested, tried, and executed. Only those who confess and repent are spared.

The final victim is John Proctor. He had a brief affair with one of the accusers, a girl named Abigail Williams. At the beginning of the play he has just ended his relationship with Abby and reconciled with his wife. No one in town knows about the affair. However, after Abigail accuses his wife of witchcraft in the hopes of having him to herself, Proctor confesses his shame. He tells the town leaders that Abby has been lying and that there are no witches in Salem. But because he has not been going to church lately, he is immediately accused of being a witch himself. Right before his execution, he considers confessing to save his life. Then he realizes that his honor is more important and that if he confesses, it will imply that his friends are guilty, too. He accepts his fate and dies bravely.

In discussing this conclusion, scholar John Ferres (1972, 8) says, "Miller believes a man must be true to himself and to his fellows, even though being untrue may be the only way to stay alive," adding that this truth is only discovered through "the ordeal of the personal crucible." Similarly, scholar Leonard Moss (1967, 64) identifies the play's theme as having two parts, one of which is "the achievement of moral honesty"; the other, "the generation of hysteria."

Miller wanted to write about mass hysteria because of the historical period in which he lived. *The Crucible* was first performed in New York at the Martin Beck Theater on January 22, 1953. By that time Senator Joseph McCarthy had begun the public persecution of anyone he believed to be a Communist. Called McCarthyism, this witch-hunt destroyed many people's lives, and just as in *The Crucible,* anyone who disagreed with McCarthy was attacked. For example, in 1952 Senator William Benton of Connecticut tried to expel McCarthy from the U.S. Senate; McCarthy then suggested that Benton himself might be a communist and called for an in-depth investigation into his background and lifestyle. In an article called "The Meaning of McCarthyism," Earl Latham (Ferres 1972, 26) writes: "From 1950 to 1954, the activities of Senator McCarthy were an oppressive weight and pain to tens of thousands in government, politics, and the professions specifically, and within the ar-

ticulate and better educated circles of society generally. In America and abroad he became a symbol of mortal danger to liberal values and democratic processes."

Miller believed that McCarthyism was "a kind of personification of [moral] disintegration" (Moss 1967, 59). Moreover, in discussing his decision to write *The Crucible,* Miller (59–60) said: "It was not only the rise of 'McCarthyism' that moved me, but something which seemed much more weird and mysterious. It was the fact that a political, objective, knowledgeable campaign from the far Right was capable of creating not only a terror, but a new subjective reality, a veritable mystique which was gradually assuming even a holy resonance. . . . The terror in these people was being knowingly planned and consciously engineered, and yet all they knew was terror" (Moss 1967). Interestingly, after the play's production Miller himself was accused of being a Communist and had to defend himself before the U.S. Congress. (Corrigan 1969; Ferres 1972; Miller 1954; Moss 1967)

See also Censorship; McCarthyism; Miller, Arthur

Cruz, Artemio

The main character of Carlos Fuentes's 1964 novel *La muerte de Artemio Cruz* (The Death of Artemio Cruz), Artemio Cruz is a wealthy and powerful man who owns land, sulfur mines, hotels, a fish business, and a newspaper in Mexico City. However, he is also extremely dishonest. He frequently bribes government officials, and he uses his newspaper to manipulate public opinion. He has no loyalty to anyone but himself. Artemio Cruz therefore represents human corruption in the Mexican political and economic system. (Fuentes 1964)

See also Fuentes, Carlos; *Hydra Head, The*

Cry for Justice, The

The Cry for Justice is an anthology of social protest literature compiled by Upton Sinclair, whose novel *The Jungle* is itself an important work of social protest. The anthology presents a large body of poems as well as excerpts from longer works, both fiction and nonfiction. It was first published in 1915 and updated by Sinclair in 1963. In a 1915 introduction, Jack London writes that by reading social protest literature, a person learns

> that his fair world so brutally unfair, is not decreed by the will of God nor by any iron law of Nature. He will learn that the world can be fashioned a fair world indeed by the humans who inhabit it, by the very simple, and yet most difficult process of coming to an understanding of the world. Understanding, after all, is merely sympathy in its fine correct sense. And such sympathy, in its genuineness, makes toward unselfishness. Unselfishness inevitably connotes service. And service is the solution of the entire vexatious problem of man. (Sinclair 1996, 9)

(Sinclair 1996)

See also *Jungle, The;* Justice; London, Jack; Sinclair, Upton

Cry, the Beloved Country

Cry, the Beloved Country, by Alan Paton, was published in 1948. Set in South Africa, it depicts the deterioration of black society as its young people forsake rural communities to live in the city. The novel's main character is Stephen Kumalo, a black priest in the tribal village of Ixopo. One day he leaves his home to search for his son, Absalom; his sister, Gertrude; and Gertrude's little boy, who have moved to Johannesburg and never write him anymore. Stephen soon finds Gertrude and her son but is dismayed to learn that she has become a prostitute. It takes him much longer to locate his son, Absalom. Finally, with the help of another priest, Stephen locates the young man in jail, where Absalom has confessed to killing a white man, Arthur Jarvis, during the commission of a robbery. The murder has shocked both blacks and whites in Johannesburg because Jarvis was a social reformer who worked tirelessly to help the black community. Absalom insists that the shooting was an accident. Nonetheless, he

is sentenced to death for the crime, and Stephen leaves Johannesburg with Gertrude's son and Absalom's pregnant wife. Back in Ixopo, he finds it difficult to speak with Arthur Jarvis's father, who lives in the area. Eventually, however, the two come together in grief and concern for the village. Jarvis donates milk to the starving children of Ixopo, starts building a dam to provide needed water to the area, and brings in an agricultural expert to help improve the crops. He also gives Stephen money to build a new church. Jarvis has been reading his son's writings on equal rights and human compassion and has realized how much the black people need and deserve his help. Unfortunately, there are some blacks who do not appreciate Jarvis's efforts, and Stephen recalls the words of another black priest: "I have one great fear in my heart, that one day when they turn to loving they will find we are turned to hating" (Paton 1987, 276).

In a 1987 introduction to *Cry, the Beloved Country,* Edward Callen (xxvi-xxvii) points out that "zealous revolutionaries would scorn the personal actions taken by its characters to restore the village church and the land." However, he says that Alan Paton believed in the importance of such actions. Moreover, the novel portrays the political activism of organized groups as susceptible to corruption. Stephen Kumalo's brother, John, is a leading Johannesburg black activist who is cowardly and dishonest. John also supports violence, and it is his son who leads Absalom into a life of crime.

When *Cry, the Beloved Country* was published, it was not well received in South Africa. Callen (xxiv) reports that the prime minister's wife told its author: "Surely, Mr. Paton, you don't really think things are like that?" Nonetheless, the book was an international best-seller. It was translated into approximately twenty languages, including Zulu and Afrikaans, and was made into a musical, *Lost in the Stars,* and then a movie. (Callan 1982; Paton 1987)

See also Apartheid; Jurgis, Arthur; Kumalo, Stephen; Paton, Alan; Racism

Countee Cullen, circa 1930's–mid 1940's (Corbis-Bettmann)

Cullen, Countee

Countee Porter Cullen was a black American poet whose works expressed pride in his African heritage. Born on May 30, 1903, either in Louisville, Kentucky, or New York, New York, he was raised first by an elderly relative and then by a family friend, Reverend F. A. Cullen. Countee began writing poetry in childhood, winning prizes and publication for his work. As an undergraduate at New York University he received the Witter Bynner Poetry Prize and published his first volume of poetry, *Color* (1925), which was a critical success. He went on to receive a master's degree from Harvard in 1926, and two years later he studied in France under a Guggenheim Fellowship. He also continued to write poetry. His published works include *Copper Sun* (1927), *The Ballad of the Brown Girl* (1928), and *The Black Christ and Other Poems* (1929). In 1934 he became a New York public school teacher, a position he held until his death on January 9, 1946. (Cullen 1991; Ferguson 1966; Shucard 1984)

See also Baldwin, James; *Color;* Harlem Renaissance; *Path of Thunder, The;* Racism

D

Damon, Cross

Cross Damon is the main character in Richard Wright's 1953 novel *The Outsider*, which concerns black alienation within white American society during the early 1950s. Cross is an intellectual who chooses to take a job as a postal worker, and throughout the novel he is continually denying various aspects of his past and his identity. He is a perpetual outsider, a role he discusses with a white district attorney, Ely Houston, who is interested in understanding the black experience. In talking about racism, Damon says:

> After many of the restraints have been lifted from the Negro's movements, and after certain psychological inhibitions have been overcome on his part, then the problem of the Negro in America really starts, not only for whites who will have to become acquainted with Negroes, but mainly for Negroes themselves. Perhaps not many Negroes, even, are aware of this today. But time will make them increasingly conscious of it. Once the Negro has won his so-called rights, he is going to be confronted with a truly knotty problem. . . . Will he be able to settle down and live the normal, vulgar, day-to-day life of the average white American? Or will he still cling to his sense of outsidedness? (Wright 1993b, 164–165)

In the end Damon cannot lose his own outsidedness. He becomes the ultimate outsider—a lawless murderer without a reasonable motive—and is eventually murdered himself. (Wright 1993b)

See also Houston, Ely; *Outsider, The;* Racism; Wright, Richard

Davies, Art

In the 1940 western novel *The Ox-Bow Incident,* by Walter Van Tilburg Clark, Art Davies tries to persuade a lynching party not to hang three men suspected of murder and cattle rustling. He believes in the legal system and tells the narrator of the story, cowboy Art Croft, that mob justice can "weaken the conscience of the nation" by committing a "sin against society" (Clark 1960, 48). However, scholar Max Westbrook (1969, 57) points out that Davies and another character who objects to the lynching, Gerald Tetley, "are repeatedly associated—both in language and action— with a degrading femininity" and are therefore not taken seriously. Davies also displays weakness by emotionally collapsing after he discovers that the hanging victims were innocent men. (Clark 1960; Westbrook 1969)

See also Clark, Walter Van Tilburg; Croft, Art; Justice; Martin, Donald; *Ox-Bow Incident, The;* Tetley, Gerald

Davis, Rebecca Harding

Born in 1831, novelist Rebecca Harding Davis was the author of several works of social protest. They include *Waiting for the Verdict* (1868), which concerns racism, and *John Andross* (1874), which is about political corruption. However, Davis's most famous work is the 1861 novella *Life in the Iron Mills.* Originally serialized in the *Atlantic Monthly* magazine, the novella heightened public awareness of working-class problems. It is based on Davis's experiences in the mill town of Wheeling, Virginia, where she moved when she was five years old. The book received critical acclaim and brought Davis to the attention of journalist Lemuel Clark Davis, who married her in 1863. Shortly thereafter Davis began raising a family but continued to write novels. She also worked on the editorial staff of the *New York Tribune* from 1869 to the mid-1870s. Davis died in 1910. (Harris 1991; Rose 1993; Wagner-Martin and Davidson 1995)

See also Labor Issues; *Life in the Iron Mills*

Days to Come

First performed in December 1936, the three-act drama *Days to Come,* by American playwright Lillian Hellman, concerns a factory strike in a small Ohio town where everyone gets along well. The factory owner, Andrew Rodman, wants to cut his workers' salaries because he is going bankrupt. Unable to survive on less money, his employees strike, and after they have been off the job for three weeks, Rodman pays for strikebreakers to come in. Rodman believes the strikebreakers will take his workers' place at the machines. Instead, they try to start a fight with the strikers, so that the law can be called in to end the strike forcibly. Eventually violence erupts, and an innocent girl is shot. The strikers decide to go back to work. However, now they hate their employer, and Rodman is afraid to walk through the town he once loved. (Hellman 1979)

See also Hellman, Lillian; Labor Issues

De Satigny, Alba Trueba

One of the narrators of Isabel Allende's 1982 novel *La casa de los espíritus* (The House of the Spirits), Alba Trueba de Satigny is the daughter of Blanca Trueba and her lover, socialist activist Pedro Tecero García. However, for many years Alba believes that her father is Count Jean de Satigny, whom Blanca was forced to marry to make Alba legitimate. Like Pedro Tecero, both Blanca and Alba are involved in socialist causes; like her mother, Alba takes a revolutionary, Miguel, as a lover. Eventually Alba is arrested for her political activities. While in prison she is tortured and raped, but she refuses to become bitter, even after she learns she is pregnant. At the end of the novel she says: "I want to think that my task is life and that my mission is not to prolong hatred but simply to fill these pages while I wait for Miguel, . . . while I wait for better times to come, while I carry this child in my womb, the daughter of so many rapes or perhaps of Miguel, but above all, my own daughter" (Allende 1985, 368). (Allende 1985)

See also Allende, Isabel; Del Valle, Clara; Feminism; García, Esteban; García, Pedro Tecero; *House of the Spirits, The;* Socialism; Trueba, Esteban

Death of Artemio Cruz, The

First published in Spanish in 1962, *La muerte de Artemio Cruz* (The Death of Artemio Cruz), by Carlos Fuentes, shows the transformation of a poor but honest boy into a wealthy but dishonest man. Its main character is 71-year-old Artemio Cruz, who controls a newspaper in Mexico City. After Cruz becomes bedridden with a fatal illness, he begins to flash back to important dates in his personal history. The novel alternates among these memories, which are written in the third person; Cruz's thoughts about the people surrounding his deathbed, which are written in the first person; and his speculations on what will be or might have been, which are written in the second person. Through all three techniques, Fuentes uses Cruz's life to comment on Mexican political issues and government corruption.

Cruz was born on April 9, 1889, as a result of his mother's rape by a wealthy landowner. Raised by a poor tobacco picker, he does not know the identity of his father, and he accidentally kills his paternal uncle. Ten years later while fighting on the side of the Rebels in the Mexican Revolution, he flees an important battle but is mistakenly labeled a hero. At the same time he learns that his lover, Regina, has been killed by his enemies, the Federals. He becomes crazed with revenge and fights heroically in the next battle.

Eventually he is captured by the Federals and is condemned to die. He shares a cell with a young lawyer named Gonzalo Bernal, who has also been condemned. Gonzalo tells him about his sister, Catalina Bernal, and his father, Don Gamaliel Bernal, an aristocratic landowner. The next morning Gonzalo is executed while Cruz is bargaining for his freedom with his captors. He agrees to give them information in exchange for his freedom. The information is false, but before the Federals can discover this, the Rebels defeat them and the war ends.

Cruz immediately seeks out Gonzalo's father and sister. He portrays himself as a friend of his former cellmate. Through clever tactics he takes over the management of Don Bernal's land and frightens away Catalina's boyfriend. He then marries Catalina himself, and they have two children, a boy named Lorenzo and a girl named Teresa. However, Catalina does not love Cruz and makes his life miserable, even as he is becoming more powerful and more corrupt. Teresa also does not love him, and at Cruz's deathbed she makes disparaging comments about him. Both women blame Cruz for the death of Lorenzo, who decided to fight in World War II and was killed by Italian bombers in Spain. Cruz believes that Lorenzo's life is the one he was meant to live. Instead, he is left to die of a gangrenous intestine, surrounded by people who are interested only in his last will and testament. (Fuentes 1964)

See also Cruz, Artemio; Fuentes, Carlos; Justice

Deeriye

Deeriye is the main character in Nuruddin Farah's 1983 Somalian novel *Close Sesame*. Once imprisoned for fighting against his country's oppression by colonial Italians and British, he has become a symbol of Somali freedom fighting. However, he eventually realizes that the new native government run by his people is as corrupt and oppressive as the colonial government once was. He attempts to assassinate the dictator of Somali and is killed. Later his daughter envisions that his epitaph will read, "Here lies dead a hero whose vision and faith in Africa remained unshaken" (Farah 1992, 237). (Farah 1992)

See also *Close Sesame*; Farah, Nuruddin; Justice

Del Valle, Clara

Clara del Valle is a clairvoyant whose journals allow her granddaughter to narrate the story of her life in Isabel Allende's 1982 novel *La casa de los espíritus* (The House of the Spirits). Clara's mother, Nívea del Valle, was an early supporter of women's rights in South America, and Clara encourages her own children to think for themselves. As a result, all three Trueba youngsters grow up to become active in socialist politics and charity work. Meanwhile as Clara ages, she becomes less involved in the world. She pursues the occult and speaks to the spirits until finally she decides she has lived long enough. She soon dies; according to her doctors, her death was due to her own will rather than an illness. (Allende 1985)

See also Allende, Isabel; De Satigny, Alba Trueba; Feminism; García, Esteban; García, Pedro Tecero; *House of the Spirits, The*; Socialism; Trueba, Esteban

Delarue, Mathieu

Mathieu Delarue is the main character in Jean-Paul Sartre's novel *L'Âge de raison* (The Age of Reason). A professor of philosophy, he advocates living a life of freedom and shuns the conventionality of marriage. Therefore, when his mistress tells him she is pregnant, he decides to pay for her to have an illegal abortion. But this decision troubles him. He is not as free of his conscience or upbringing as he would like to be. In fact, in all areas of his life he has difficulty reconciling his philosophy with his actions. As his brother Jacques points out to him during an argument:

> I should myself have thought . . . that freedom consisted in frankly confronting situations into which one has deliberately entered, and accepting all one's responsibilities. But that, no doubt, is not your view: you condemn capitalist society, and yet you are an official in that society; you display an abstract sympathy with Communists, but you take care not to commit yourself, you have never voted. You despise the bourgeois class, and yet you are a bourgeois, son and brother of a bourgeois, and you live like a bourgeois. (Sartre 1947, 138)

Mathieu is a symbol of hypocrisy. (Sartre 1947)

See also *Age of Reason, The;* Communism; Sartre, Jean-Paul

Dickens, Charles

Charles John Huffam Dickens was born February 7, 1812, in Portsmouth, Hampshire, England, but spent his early childhood in Chatham, England. His father, a navy clerk who often squandered his money, went to debtor's prison in 1824. By this time the family was living in London, and Dickens was forced to leave school to take a factory job there. He remained at work until his father's release from prison, whereupon he returned to school. At age 15, however, Dickens again left his studies, this time to become a law clerk. He later worked as a newspaper reporter, becoming involved in the liberal politics of his day. In 1833 he had several stories and essays published in various periodicals; in 1836 they were reprinted in a collection, *Sketches by "Boz."* Dickens also used the Boz pseudonym to publish installments of a serialized novel, *Pickwick Papers,* during 1836 and 1837. This work was extremely popular and appeared in book form in 1837. Dickens followed it with

Oliver Twist (1838), *Nicholas Nickelby* (1839), *The Old Curiosity Shop* (1841), and *Barnaby Rudge* (1841). All were published first in installments and then in book form. During this time Dickens also became a magazine editor, married, and started a family. He was to have nine children in all, but eventually he left his wife for another woman.

Dickens's later works include *A Christmas Carol* (1843), *Martin Chuzzlewit* (1844), *David Copperfield* (1850), and *A Tale of Two Cities* (1859). All of his novels contain elements of social protest. However, five books are particularly critical of Victorian society: *Bleak House* (1853), *Hard Times* (1854), *Little Dorrit* (1857), *Great Expectations* (1861), and *Our Mutual Friend* (1865). In addition to novels, Dickens wrote plays, poetry, essays, and articles. He also enjoyed giving public readings of his work. His performances were extremely popular, but unfortunately they strained his health. Dickens died on June 9, 1870, after falling ill during one of these tours. He left behind one unfinished novel, *Edwin Drood.* (Cruikshank 1949; Fielding 1958; Gissing 1924; Hibbert 1967)

See also *Bleak House;* Class, Social; *Great Expectations; Hard Times; Little Dorrit;* Poverty

Doane, Seneca

A minor character in the 1922 novel *Babbitt,* by Sinclair Lewis, Seneca Doane represents the author's own views about the value of nonconformity in American society. Doane is a highly intelligent, logical lawyer working as a social reformer. He persistently fights against government corruption, supports labor unions and their strikes, and openly advocates freedom of speech. When he was in college, Doane's goal was to be a rich man; in later years he came to view the enrichment of humanity as more important. Conversely, in college the novel's main character, George F. Babbitt, wanted to be a lawyer and help the poor; instead he became an unethical real estate salesman concerned with wealth and social standing. (Grebstein 1962; Lewis 1950)

See also *Babbitt;* Labor Issues; Lewis, Sinclair; Reisling, Paul

Doll's House, A

The 1879 three-act play *A Doll's House*, originally published in Norwegian as *Et dukkehjem* by Henrik Ibsen, concerns the emancipation of a housewife, Nora Helmer, whose husband treats her like a child. Years earlier, Nora's husband Torvald fell ill and required a vacation to a warmer climate. However, the couple was poor at the time, so Nora forged her father's name on a document in order to obtain a private loan. (Women were not allowed to conduct business transactions on their own.) Now the man who loaned her the money is using the document to blackmail her; he works for Torvald and wants Nora to convince her husband not to fire him. Meanwhile, Nora considers a variety of ways to keep Torvald from discovering the truth, and it becomes clear that the two have a highly dysfunctional marriage. Torvald treats Nora as though she were incompetent, while Nora submerges her own intellect in order to make him happy. Their life is built on illusions. When Torvald finally discovers Nora's deceit, he behaves badly and she realizes that he is not the man she thought him to be. She also realizes that she is not the woman she ought to be. She says (Ibsen 1978, 85–87):

> When I was at home with papa, he told me his opinion about everything, and so I had the same opinions; and if I differed from him I concealed the fact, because he would not have liked it. He called me his doll-child, and he played with me just as I used to play with my dolls. And when I came to live with you . . . I was simply transferred from papa's hands into yours. You arranged everything according to your own taste, and so I got the same tastes as you—or else I pretended to, I am really not quite sure which . . . [Now] I must try and educate myself—you are not the man to help me in that. I must do that for myself. And that is why I am going to leave you now.

Despite the fact that society will frown on her decision to leave her husband and chil-

dren, Nora walks out on Torvald. When he begs her to remember her responsibilities, saying "before all else, you are a wife and a mother," she replies (88): "I don't believe that any longer. I believe that before all else I am a reasonable human being, just as you are—or, at all events, that I must try and become one. I know quite well, Torvald, that most people would think you right, and that views of that kind are to be found in books, but I can no longer content myself with what most people say, or with what is found in books. I must think over things for myself and get to understand them."

Because of its strong feminist statement, *A Doll's House* engendered much controversy when it was first produced. The work was also misunderstood. According to H. L. Mencken, writing in an introduction to the work (x), "the German middle classes mistook *A Doll's House* for a revolutionary document against monogamy." In other words, they saw it as an indictment of *all* marriage, rather than an indictment of a particular *type* of marriage. (Ibsen 1978)

See also Feminism; Ibsen, Henrik

Dostoyevsky, Fyodor

Russian author Fyodor Mikhaylovich Dostoyevsky wrote novels about human behavior and beliefs, many of which criticized Russian society. His most famous works are *Prestuplenie i nakazanie* (Crime and Punishment, 1866), *The Idiot* (1868), *Besy* (The Possessed, 1871–1872), and *Bratya Karamazovy* (Brothers Karamazov, 1880).

Dostoyevsky was born in Moscow, Russia, on November 11, 1821. His mother died when he was 16, and two years later his widowed father, a physician, was murdered by serfs. Dostoyevsky then went to St. Petersburg, where he studied at the Military Engineering College. He graduated in 1843 as an officer but soon began to write. His first published short story, "Bednye Lyudi" (Poor Folk), appeared in 1846 and gained him critical acclaim.

In 1849, however, he was arrested for his membership in the Petrashevsky Circle, an underground political organization. At first he was condemned to death, but later his sentence was commuted to confinement in a Siberian prison. He remained there until 1854. After his release he wrote *Zapiski iz myortvovo doma* (1861–1862), which later appeared in English as *Buried Alive; or, Ten Years of Penal Servitude in Siberia* (1881). In 1867 he married Anna Grigorievna Snitkina, and the two lived abroad until 1871, when Dostoyevsky returned to Russia to become a journal editor. He also continued to write novels. He died on February 9, 1881 in St. Petersburg, Russia. (Dostoyevsky 1936; Dostoyevsky 1968)

See also Censorship; *Possessed, The;* Verhovensky, Pyotr Stepanovitch

Dreiser, Theodore

American novelist Theodore Dreiser was lauded as a social reformer after the publication of his novel *An American Tragedy* in 1925. Because the book criticizes a society that bases class divisions on economics, some people believed that Dreiser intended it as an argument in favor of communism. However, this was not the case. Biographer Ellen Moers (1969, 240) explains:

> Soon after the publication of *An American Tragedy,* the Russian critic Sergei Dinamov wrote to its author to say that he had noted Dreiser's bitter criticism of the inequities and hypocrisies of American capitalism and to inquire what system the novelist believed should take its place. Dreiser wrote in reply that he had "no theories about life, or the solution of economic and political problems. Life, as I see it, is an organized process about which we can do nothing in the final analysis." He wished the Russian experiment well, but he thought there was no plan, from the Christian to the Communist, "that can be more than a theory. And dealing with man is a practical thing—not a theoretical one. Nothing can alter his emotions, his primitive and animal reactions to life."

Dreiser's interest in economic inequity originated not in his politics but in his upbringing. He was born in Terre Haute, Indiana, on August 27, 1871, as the eleventh of twelve children. Because his German-immigrant parents were extremely poor, he could not afford a good education. However, a high school teacher decided to help him, paying one year's tuition at Indiana University. When her support ran out, he left college to become a journalist.

Dreiser worked for newspapers in several major cities before settling in New York, where he eventually became a magazine editor-in-chief. In 1900 he wrote his first novel, *Sister Carrie,* about a woman who attains economic success in life by becoming a mistress. At the time this was not a popular topic; the novel appeared in print only because Frank Norris, a prominent social protest author, urged his publisher to support the project. Nonetheless, the book was not a commercial success, and so Dreiser continued working as an editor. In 1910 he was forced to resign his position because of a scandal involving an office romance. He then became a freelance writer, publishing collections of short stories, essays, and plays as well as autobiographical works. He also continued to write novels, including *The Financier* (1912) and *The Titan* (1914), which are the fictionalized story of a real-life American businessman. In 1915 he published the semiautobiographical *The 'Genius,'* which describes the love affairs of an immoral man. This book was censured by the New York Society for the Suppression of Vice, but the ban was lifted a year later after it was protested by many other prominent authors. Dreiser's next novel, *An American Tragedy,* appeared ten years later and was his most famous work. When he died on December 28, 1945, in Hollywood, California, he was working on a sequel to *The Titan* entitled *The Stoic,* which was published posthumously. (Geismar 1953; Gerber 1964; Kazin and Shapiro 1955; Moers 1969)

See also *American Tragedy, An;* Censorship; Norris, Frank

Dufrenoy, Michel

The main character in Jules Verne's 1863 novel *Paris au XXe Siècle* (Paris in the Twentieth Century). Michel Dufrenoy is a poet struggling to earn a living in a society that values only science and technology. In the end he falls into poverty and despair, collapsing in the snow of a Paris cemetery. (Verne 1996)

See also *Paris in the Twentieth Century;* Science Fiction and Fantasy; Verne, Jules

Dunbar-Nelson, Alice

Alice Dunbar-Nelson was an African-American author who wrote short stories and articles about racial prejudice. Born Alice Ruth Moore in 1875, she attended the University of Pennsylvania and Cornell University and married black poet Paul Laurence Dunbar, who was the son of slaves. The couple eventually divorced. In 1916 Alice Dunbar married publisher Robert John Nelson and became a high school teacher in Wilmington, Delaware. She was fired from this position in 1920 because of her political views. Dunbar-Nelson was involved with the National Association of Colored Women and later the American Interracial Peace Committee. She also worked toward the establishment of a school for troubled black girls. After losing her teaching position, she became a magazine editor and newspaper columnist. Her diary was published in 1984 and a collection of her works in 1988. Dunbar-Nelson died in 1935. (Roses and Randolph 1996)

See also Harlem Renaissance; "Hope Deferred"

E

Edgeworth, Maria

Maria Edgeworth was born January 1, 1767, in Oxfordshire, England. She was the oldest daughter of an Irish inventor and landowner, Richard Lovell Edgeworth. Schooled in England, she began living on her father's estate in Edgeworthtown, Ireland, at the age of 15, where she became governess to his 21 other children from four successive marriages. Her first published work, a collection of stories called *The Parent's Assistant* (1796), was based on her experiences with her half brothers and half sisters.

Castle Rackrent, written in 1800, was her first novel. It criticizes the Irish feudal system and highlights the differences between Irish and English culture. Edgeworth originally published it anonymously in England, but the following year she acknowledged authorship, and subsequent editions bore her name. It garnered the praise of both King George III and his prime minister, as well as such authors as Sir Walter Scott, who credited its influence on his own novel, *Waverly*. Similarly, Edgeworth's next novel, *Belinda* (1801), was praised by author Jane Austen.

Following *Belinda,* Edgeworth published a six-volume novel series entitled *Tales of Fashionable Life* (1809–1812). This series included *The Absentee* (1812), which criticizes absentee English landlords. She followed her series with three more novels. All of these, like their predecessors, were edited by her father, who maintained a great deal of influence over her life. She died on May 22, 1849. (Butler 1972; Edgeworth 1992)

See also *Castle Rackrent;* Class, Social

Edible Woman, The

The Edible Woman, by Margaret Atwood, was written in 1964 at the beginning of second-wave feminism but was not published until 1969. At that time reviewers did not appreciate the novel, but today it is considered an important work of feminist literature. Its theme concerns the struggle for self-identity in a depersonalized world; its main character is a woman who gradually subjugates herself to her boyfriend. This subjugation is expressed through extended metaphors and literary allusions, most of which relate to food consumption.

At the beginning of the novel Marian MacAlpin narrates her story in the first person. She tells of her work at a product test-marketing company, where she designs research questionnaires on food preferences, and offers mundane details about her life. Marian lunches every day with three coworkers, virgins named Emmy, Lucy, and Millie, and develops a friendship with one of her research subjects, Duncan, a painfully thin and neurotic graduate student. Marian also has a roommate, Ainsley Tewce, who is her exact opposite. Whereas Marian is staid and conventional, Ainsley is promiscuous and liberated.

One day Ainsley decides that she wants to have a baby. As she makes plans to trick Marian's friend Len Slank into having sex with her at the appropriate time, Marian grows angry but says little. She also does not warn Len of Ainsley's upcoming trickery. In fact, Marian increasingly finds herself unable to express her own views, particularly around her boyfriend, Peter. On one occasion when she and Peter are visiting with Len and Ainsley, Marian feels so insignificant that she hides under the bed, literally making herself invisible to the others. It takes her friends a while to notice she is missing. This upsets her and she runs away. When Peter finds her, he asks her to marry him, and she agrees without much feeling. She begins to plan her wedding, and the novel changes abruptly from first person to third, so that Marian no longer narrates her own story.

At the same time Marian begins to have a problem with food. Whenever she realizes that something was once alive, she cannot eat it. In the beginning only foods that look like animal parts disturb her: hunks of cow or pig, for example. Later she cannot stand the sight of ground meats. Eventually she also stops eating eggs, because they remind her of embryonic chickens, and vegetables, because they were once alive and growing. When she tastes a piece of cake and realizes that it is "spongy and ceullar against her tongue, like the bursting of thousands of tiny lungs," she cannot eat that either (Atwood 1996, 227).

By this time Peter has completely consumed her life, and during their engagement party she realizes she has to escape their future together. She sneaks away from the party and spends the night with Duncan, who refuses to help her solve her problems. The next morning Marian decides to end her engagement. She invites Peter over, and while waiting, she bakes him an elaborate cake shaped and decorated to look like a woman. When he arrives, she serves it to him, saying: "You've been trying to destroy me, haven't you. . . . You've been trying to assimilate me. But I've made you a substitute, something you'll like much better. This is what you really wanted all along, isn't it?" (299–300). Embarrassed, Peter leaves, and suddenly Marian is starving. She begins eating the cake, and after she severs its head, the novel's narration returns to the first person. Marian then finishes her story, telling of Ainsley's decision to marry a strange man just to give her baby a father and of Duncan visiting her house and sharing the rest of the cake with her. She is pleased by his obvious enjoyment of the cake, yet discomfitted by the determination with which he consumes it.

Because of this ending, scholars typically discuss *The Edible Woman* in terms of its obvious feminism. However, Robert Lecker, in his article "Janus Through the Looking Glass: Atwood's First Three Novels," points out that the novel has a significant message for men. He (Davidson and Davidson 1981, 186) says that *The Edible Woman* is a "comedy of manners which comments tragically on a contemporary world in which even the semblance of identity has disappeared and men (and women) are seen only as faceless nonentities in a zombified crowd. In such a world, the hope that one can find one's 'true identity' can only lead to the 'sinking feeling' which plagues Marian at the end of *The Edible Woman*." Atwood's male characters are as unhappy as her female ones. Peter doubts whether he will make a good husband, Len does not want to be a father, and Duncan questions his purpose as a graduate student. Defined by roles rather than individual traits, these people all struggle against society's expectations for them. (Atwood 1996; Davidson and Davidson 1981)

See also Atwood, Margaret; Feminism; MacAlpin, Marian; Tewce, Ainsley

El Saadawi, Nawal

A noted feminist, Nawal El Saadawi was born on October 27, 1931, in Kafr Tahia, Egypt, and received a medical degree at Cairo University in 1955. In 1966 she received a master's degree in public health from Columbia University in New York City. As a physician at Cairo University, she became the editor of *Health* magazine, and eventually she was named Egypt's director of public health. However, in 1972 she was dismissed from that position after writing a nonfiction book called *Woman and Sex*, in which she expressed a feminist viewpoint. Undeterred, she wrote several novels that argued against the oppression of women, including *Mawt al-rajul al-wahid 'ala 'l-ard* (God Dies by the Nile, 1974), *Imra'ah 'ind nuqtat al-sifr* (Women at Point Zero, 1975), *Al-wajh al-'ārī lil-mar'ah al-'Arabiyyah* (The Hidden Face of Eve, 1977), and *Jannât wa-Iblîs* (The Innocence of the Devil, 1992). In 1981 the Egyptian government, led by Anwar Sadat, imprisoned El Saadawi for two months as punishment for her feminist beliefs. (El Saadawi 1990; Malti-Douglas 1995)

See also Feminism; *God Dies by the Nile*

Ellison, Ralph

Ralph Waldo Ellison is the author of *Invisible Man*, published in 1952. The novel examines the role of black men in American society during the late 1940s. Born in Oklahoma City, Oklahoma, on March 1, 1914, Ellison originally wanted to be a musician, and in 1933 he began studying music at Alabama's Tuskegee Institute. Then he decided to pursue a career in writing. In 1936 he left Tuskegee to join the Federal Writer's Project in New York City, New York, where he met novelist Richard Wright. With Wright's encouragement, Ellison began contributing short stories and articles to a variety of magazines, and after a stint of service in the merchant marine during World War II, he started writing *Invisible Man*. Upon its publication in 1952, it was an immediate success, winning the National Book Award in 1953. Ellison then became a university lecturer on writing and American black culture. His subsequent books were two essay collections, *Shadow and Act* (1964) and *Going to the Territory* (1986), and a collection of short stories, *Flying Home: And Other Stories*

Ralph Ellison (right) presenting the Howells Medal for Fiction to John Cheever, May 19, 1965. (UPI/Corbis-Bettmann)

(1994), published posthumously. At the time of his death on April 16, 1994, he was working on a second novel. (Hersey 1974)

See also *Invisible Man;* Racism; Wright, Richard

Elmer Gantry

Elmer Gantry (1927), by Sinclair Lewis, is an attack on religious institutions and beliefs in the early twentieth century. Its main character, Elmer Gantry, is a minister who engages in immoral behavior, and its most moral character, a fellow minister named Frank Shallard, is secretly an atheist.

The novel begins in the year 1902. Elmer Gantry is a 22-year-old student at a Baptist college in Kansas. However, he is more interested in drinking, fighting, and having sex than he is in studying. But very quickly Elmer's life changes. One day in town he sees a theology student being heckled while trying to preach, and Elmer defends the man's right to speak. Believing that Elmer has been inspired by God, religious leaders at the college try to convince him to join the Baptist Church and become a minister. Meanwhile his best friend, Jim, an avowed atheist, argues against it. After some internal struggle Elmer is caught up with emotion during a prayer session and does indeed become a convert to the Baptist faith. Afterward he gives a moving speech about the power of love; no one but Jim knows that he has plagiarized it from the works of a great social reformer of the time, Robert G. Ingersoll.

Elmer then begins studying for the ministry. In addition to biblical facts, he learns various techniques for increasing church donations and improving his public speaking skills. At the same time he secretly continues to drink and smoke, and when he is sent to preach at a nearby church, he seduces a young Sunday school teacher. Her father finds out and complains to the college; as a result, Elmer is forced to propose to the girl. But just before the marriage, he tricks her father into believing she is seeing another man, and the engagement is broken. Elmer is sent to another town to preach, but along the way he gets drunk and is kicked out of the ministry.

After a brief time as a salesman, he realizes he misses the adulation of the crowd that he used to feel when he preached. He becomes the assistant to a woman evangelist, Sharon Falconer, and travels the country with her preaching. He also becomes her lover, and together they engage in various immoral behaviors. Elmer soon learns that much about Sharon is false, even her name. However, when a fire breaks out while she is preaching, she tests her faith in God by remaining inside to lead people through the flames while Elmer runs out through a back door. He survives; Sharon dies.

Elmer tries to continue alone as an evangelist, but he fails to attract crowds. He then learns enough Hindu beliefs to promote mysticism, but he finds it does not pay well enough. He ingratiates himself with a bishop in the Methodist Church, converts, and becomes a Methodist minister. When he learns that he will get a better church appointment if married, he chooses a wife whom he believes will reflect well on his position. He does not love her.

He advances quickly as a minister, moving to larger and larger towns. At last he is sent to head the Methodist Church in the town of Zenith, which has a population of 400,000. There he vows to clean up sin and corruption, staging several "vice raids" and gaining a great deal of publicity. His church thrives. At the same time, to better his own position, he accuses a former friend and fellow minister, Frank Shallard, of being an atheist. This accusation is true. Frank does have doubts about God, but he is otherwise an outstanding minister, helping the sick and guiding his parishioners to make wise, moral decisions in life. Nonetheless, he loses his job. Meanwhile Elmer has two affairs, one with his former fiancée, who is now married. At the end of the novel a third mistress publicizes his infidelity, and for a brief time his parishioners suspect his true nature. But when Elmer has the woman's private life investigated and threatens to ruin her, she recants her story, and the townspeople reaffirm their faith in their minister.

Elmer remains unchanged at the end of the novel, as does the view of religion offered by author Sinclair Lewis. Throughout *Elmer Gantry* churchmen are depicted as hypocritical people more interested in commerce than in spirituality. The two characters with the highest morals, Jim Lefferts and Frank Shallard, are atheists. Moreover, when Sharon the evangelist rises above her hypocrisy and expresses her faith in God, He fails her.

Many scholars believe that the character of Sharon was modeled after a real-life evangelist of the time, Aimee Semple McPherson. They also note similarities between Elmer Gantry and real-life preacher Billy Sunday. Sunday, like Gantry, plagiarized one of his speeches from social reformer Robert Ingersoll. In addition, according to Sheldon Grebstein (1962, 100–101), "the boisterous activities of Sharon's evangelist troupe are based on 1915 court proceedings in which a Philadelphia landlord sued Sunday for the damage caused to his house by Sunday's party of assistants." Grebstein (105) adds: "We must . . . remember, in judging *Elmer Gantry*, that Lewis was writing in the most hotly charged religious atmosphere in America since the Salem witch burnings." It was a time when people were debating whether the science of evolution, instead of or in addition to biblical creationism, should be taught in the public schools. The publication of *Elmer Gantry* was perceived as yet one more attack on the Christian religion. Grebstein (106) reports:

> The novel sold over two hundred thousand copies in the first ten weeks after publication, and it provoked dozens of incidents as well. . . . A well-known Los Angeles minister invited Lewis to visit the city, promising he would personally lead a lynching party in the novelist's honor; at the same time another clergyman started proceedings in New Hampshire to jail Lewis for writing *Elmer Gantry.* . . . For a time it seemed that Lewis's prediction that he would be thrown out of the country for *Elmer Gantry* might be coming true. But at least he had calculated correctly on one point. He had wanted the book to make the nation take notice, and he was not disappointed. With all its faults, *Elmer Gantry* continues to remind us of the bitterness of the struggle in Lewis's generation between religious liberalism and literalism, modernism and fundamentalism; and it remains to this day one of the two or three best American novels centered upon religion.

(Grebstein 1962; Lewis 1970; Schorer 1962)

See also Falconer, Sharon; Lewis, Sinclair; Religion; Shallard, Frank

Endō, Shūsaku

Shūsaku Endō is noted for writing novels that examine the differences between Japanese and Western cultures and morality. He was born in Tokyo, Japan, on March 27, 1923. His family urged him to become a Roman Catholic when he was 11 years old. He never became completely comfortable with this religion and consequently explored his sense of conflict through his work. His first fiction was published in 1955 as two short-story collections: *Shiroi hito* (White Man) and *Kiiroi hito* (Yellow Man). His most internationally well-

Shūsaku Endō, 13 December 1993 (AP Photo/Masahiro Yokota)

known novel, *Chimmoku* (Silence), was published in 1966; it concerns the persecution of Japanese Christians in seventeenth-century Japan. Shūsaku Endō's other novels include *Umi to dokuyaku* (The Sea and Poison, 1957) and *Samurai* (1980). He has also written essays, plays, and a biography. (Endō 1980)

See also Religion; *Silence*

Environmentalism

Environmentalism is a concern for the health of the earth, and it is expressed in a large body of environmental literature, most of it nonfiction. However, a few novelists and poets have addressed environmental issues. In fact, one of the most famous works of environmental literature is the novel *The Monkey Wrench Gang,* by Edward Abbey. The poets of the Beat movement also criticized attitudes in American society that contributed to environmental destruction. In addition, many works of science fiction depict a future of severe pollution, thereby protesting antienvironmental practices of the present.

See also Abbey, Edward; Beat Movement; *Monkey Wrench Gang, The;* Science Fiction and Fantasy

Erlone, Jan

The character of Jan Erlone appears in Richard Wright's 1940 novel *Native Son,* which concerns American racism. He is a Communist who believes that all men deserve respect. He treats the novel's main character, a black man named Bigger Thomas, as an equal and does not understand why this makes the man hate him. After Bigger kills Jan's girlfriend and tries unsuccessfully to blame Jan for the crime, Jan is angry. Then he realizes he has not understood the full depth of the black experience. He visits Bigger in jail and says:

> Though this thing hurt me, I got something out of it. . . . It taught me that it's your right to hate me, Bigger. I see now that you couldn't do anything else but that; it was all you had.. . . . I'm not trying to make up to you, Bigger. I didn't come here to feel sorry for you. . . . I'm here because I'm trying to live up to this thing as I see it. . . . I was . . . grieving for Mary and then I thought of all the black men who've been killed, the black men who had to grieve when their people were snatched from them in slavery and since slavery. I thought that if they could stand it, then I ought to. (Wright 1993, 332)

Jan helps Bigger get an attorney and fight for white justice. Unfortunately, his efforts fail and Bigger is condemned to death. (Wright 1993)

See also Communism; *Native Son;* Racism; Thomas, Bigger

Eva Luna

Published in Spain in 1987 and the United States in 1988, *Eva Luna,* by Isabel Allende, is set against a background of political unrest in an unnamed South American country where the government is moving from dictatorship to democracy. As guerrilla forces try to turn the people toward socialism, the novel's first-person narrator, Eva Luna, eventually realizes that for the revolutionaries, "the people" are "composed exclusively of men; we women should contribute to the struggle but were excluded from decision-making and power" (Allende 1988, 233).

Eva is a strong woman at a time when feminism is virtually unknown in her country. She lives with her friend Mimi, a beautiful actress who began life as a transsexual named Melesio. Mimi encourages Eva to become a writer and helps her sell a telenovela series, or soap opera, to the director of national television. In the series Eva uses her fiction to expose many of her country's real problems and political events, causing one military leader, Colonel Tolomeo Rodríguez, to warn her that revealing such truths to the public can be dangerous. Eva has been getting her political information from two people: a guerrilla leader named Huberto Naranjo, who is also her lover, and a filmmaker named Rolf Carlé, who at the end of the novel becomes her husband.

Throughout *Eva Luna* Eva tells Rolf's life story along with her own. Born in northern Austria, he grows up with a cruel father, Lukas Carlé, a schoolteacher who so torments his students that they hang him during a school outing. After his father's death Rolf goes to live with his aunt and uncle in South America, where he eventually becomes a famous cameraman and documentary filmmaker. He meets Eva while filming a guerrilla revolutionary group led by Naranjo.

Eva first meets Naranjo while roaming the streets of the city. Her mother died when she was six, and she has spent the seven years since then working as a servant in a series of homes. Naranjo arranges for her to stay in a house of prostitution, where she lives sheltered from all sexual activities until the house is raided by the police. She escapes the raid and goes to work for Riad Halabí, a Turkish shopkeeper. Riad loves his adopted country because, whereas in Turkey "there are many castes and many codes [and a] man dies right where he is born," in South America there is "a single class, a single people. Everyone thinks he's king of the mountain, free of social ranks and rules—no one better than anyone else either by birth or money" (211).

When Riad's wife, Zulema, commits suicide, Eva is arrested for the murder and is beaten by police. Riad bribes them to set her free, and Eva returns to the city, where she encounters Mimi and begins a career as a writer. Eva also runs into Naranjo, who has become the famous guerrilla leader Comandante Rogelio. Mimi warns Eva not to become Naranjo's lover, telling Eva that his guerrilla revolution will fail, but that even if Naranjo "wins his revolution, . . . in a very short time he would be acting with the arrogance of every man who attains power" (267). Mimi argues that all men "operate on the same principal: authority, competitiveness, greed, repression—it's always the same" (268). Nonetheless, Eva helps Naranjo liberate a group of political prisoners from a guarded fortress before leaving the city with Rolf, who has filmed the prison raid. (Allende 1988)

See also Allende, Isabel; Carlé, Lukas; Carlé, Rolf; Naranjo, Huberto; Rodríguez, Colonel Tolomeo; Socialism

Everhard, Avis

Avis Everhard is the wife of revolutionary activist Ernest Everhard in Jack London's 1908 novel *The Iron Heel.* As the first-person narrator of his life story, she recounts his socialist speeches and describes his attempts to fight an oppressive American oligarchy called the Iron Heel. She is a strong woman and eventually becomes a spy to help her husband's cause. In an introduction to her manuscript a fictional scholar of the future, Anthony Meredith, tells of her fate:

It is quite clear that she intended the Manuscript for immediate publication, as soon as the Iron Heel was overthrown, so that her husband . . . should receive full credit for all that he had ventured and accomplished. Then came the frightful crushing of the Second Revolt, and it is probable that in the moment of danger, ere she fled or was captured by the Mercenaries, she hid the Manuscript. . . . Of

Avis Everhard there is no further record. Undoubtedly she was executed . . . and, as is well known, no record of such executions was kept by the Iron Heel. (London 1924, xi-xii)

(London 1924)

See also *Iron Heel, The;* London, Jack; Meredith, Anthony; Socialism

Ewell, Bob

In Harper Lee's 1960 novel *To Kill a Mockingbird,* Bob Ewell is a coward and bully who hates African Americans. He falsely accuses a black man of raping his daughter and threatens the lawyer who defends the man. Eventually he tries to kill the lawyer's children and is himself killed during the attack. (Lee 1993)

See also Lee, Harper; *To Kill a Mockingbird*

Exiles

An exile is a person who has been banished from his or her native country. The term also refers to those who have left their country voluntarily after a period of persecution, oppression, and/or censorship. Several social protest authors have been exiled, either forcibly or voluntarily, because of their work and beliefs. These include Ciro Alegría, Isabel Allende, Breyten Breytenbach, Nuruddin Farah, Anatole France, Maxim Gorky, Milan Kundera, and Aleksandr Solzhenitsyn.

Physical or emotional exiles are common characters in social protest literature. For example, in Aldous Huxley's *Brave New World* Bernard Marx is banished to an island for social misfits, and in Ayn Rand's *Atlas Shrugged* a group of revolutionaries exile themselves to a secret mountain community. In the works of Ralph Ellison and Richard Wright black men are depicted as exiles from white society, as are Native Americans in Helen Hunt Jackson's *Ramona.* In Edith Wharton's novel *The Age of Innocence* Countess Ellen Olenska escapes her husband's brutality by leaving Poland for the United States, where she finds herself not only physically but also emotionally exiled because of her failure to fit in with high society. Fictional revolutionaries, criminals, time-travelers, and explorers, such as Avis Everhard, Lemuel Gulliver, Jean Valjean, and Julian West, are shown to be exiles from their societies. (Tabori 1972)

See also *Age of Innocence, The;* Alegría, Ciro; Allende, Isabel; *Atlas Shrugged; Brave New World;* Breytenbach, Breyten; Ellison, Ralph; Everhard, Avis; Farah, Nuruddin; France, Anatole; Gorky, Maxim; *Gulliver's Travels;* Huxley, Aldous; Jackson, Helen Hunt; Kundera, Milan; Olenska, Countess Ellen; *Ramona;* Rand, Ayn; Solzhenitsyn, Aleksandr; Valjean, Jean; West, Julian; Wharton, Edith; Wright, Richard

F

Fahrenheit 451

First published in 1950 as a short story entitled "The Fire Man," the title of the 1953 novel *Fahrenheit 451,* by Ray Bradbury, refers to the temperature at which paper burns. The story is set in a future United States where it is a crime to own or read books. Independent thought is discouraged, and people spend most of their time watching television or speeding nowhere along fast highways. They lead uncaring lives in fireproof metal homes, and it is the job of firemen such as Guy Montag to burn books.

Montag enjoys this job until he meets a young neighbor who questions his decision to become a fireman. He starts reevaluating his life, and when he encounters a woman who would rather burn to death than leave her books, he wonders why they could be so important. He secretly steals several books for himself. His fire chief, Beatty, becomes suspicious, warning him that if he does have any books, he has 24 hours to turn them in. Beatty then tells Montag how book-burning came about. He says that at first it was individuals, not the government, who wanted books destroyed, explaining:

You must understand that our civilization is so vast that we can't have our minorities upset and stirred. Ask yourself, What do we want in this country, above all? People want to be happy, isn't that right? . . . That's what we live for, isn't it? . . . Colored people don't like *Little Black Sambo.* Burn it. White people don't feel good about *Uncle Tom's Cabin.* Burn it. Someone's written a book on tobacco and cancer of the lungs? The cigarette people are weeping? Burn the book. Serenity, Montag. Peace, Montag. Take your fight outside. Better yet, into the incinerator. (Bradbury 1996, 59)

Later Montag considers turning the books in, but first he wants to read them. His wife, Mildred, is horrified. She doesn't want to know about books. She only wants to watch television. Disgusted with her, Montag goes to visit a man, Faber, he once suspected of owning books. He asks Faber to help him make copies of his books, and the two discuss ways to end book-burning in the United States. They also discuss the news that the country might soon be at war.

When Montag returns home, he discovers that Mildred has invited some friends over to watch her favorite television program. Montag begins reading them poetry instead. They leave upset, and Mildred soon follows. Later

The book burners raid a house in this scene from the 1966 movie Fahrenheit 451. *(Rank/The Museum of Modern Art Film Stills Archive)*

she turns him in to the fire department, and Captain Beatty tells Montag he must burn his own house. Montag refuses and burns Captain Beatty instead. Now wanted for murder, he runs to Faber's house, and with his friend's help he escapes the city to join up with a group of book-loving hobos. Montag soon learns that each one has memorized a different part of a book. As one man explains:

> It wasn't planned, at first. Each man had a book he wanted to remember, and did. Then, over a period of twenty years or so, we met each other, traveling, and got the loose network together and set out a plan. . . . We're nothing more than dust jackets for books, of no significance otherwise. Some of us live in small towns. Chapter One of Thoreau's *Walden* in Green River, Chapter Two in Willow Farm, Maine. . . . And when the war's

over, someday, some year, the books can be written again, the people will be called in, one by one, to recite what they know and we'll set it up in type until another Dark Age, when we might have to do the whole damn thing over again. (153)

Montag remembers what he has read and agrees to join the group as the Book of Ecclesiastes from the Bible. Together with his new friends he sits on a hillside and watches as bombs strike and destroy the city.

In discussing *Fahrenheit 451* in a 1996 edition of the work, Bradbury argues that, although the novel was written in 1951, it is still an important work of social protest for today's society. He (176–178) states that special-interest groups continue to threaten books, saying:

> There is more than one way to burn a

book. And the world is full of people running around with lit matches. Every minority, be it Baptist/Unitarian, Irish/Italian/Octogenarian /Zen Buddhist, Zionist/ Seventh-day Adventist, Women's Lib/Republican/Mattachine/FourSquare Gospel feels it has the will, the right, the duty to douse the kerosene and light the fuse. . . . Fire-Captain Beatty . . . described how the books were burned first by minorities, each ripping a page or a paragraph from this book, then that, until the day came when the books were empty and the minds shut and the libraries closed forever. . . . [And today] it is a mad world and it will get madder if we allow the minorities, be they dwarf or giant, orangutan or dolphin, nuclear-head or water-conservationist, pro-computerologist or Neo-Luddite, simpleton or sage, to interfere with aesthetics. The real world is the playing ground for each and every group, to make or unmake laws. But the tip of the nose of my book or stories or poems is where their rights end and my territorial imperatives begin, run and rule. If Mormons do not like my plays let them write their own. . . . If the Chicano intellectuals wish to re-cut my "Wonderful Ice Cream Suit" so it shapes "Zoot," may the belt unravel and the pants fall.

(Bradbury 1996; Nolan 1975)

See also Beatty, Captain; Bradbury, Ray; Censorship; Montag, Guy; Science Fiction and Fantasy; *Uncle Tom's Cabin*

Falconer, Sharon

Sharon Falconer, a secondary character in the novel *Elmer Gantry*, by Sinclair Lewis, represents religious hypocrisy. She is a woman evangelist and was most likely modeled after Aimee Semple McPherson, a real-life evangelist of the 1920s. McPherson, who died of a drug overdose in 1944, lived a questionable lifestyle and was involved in several scandals. Similarly, Sharon Falconer indulges in wild parties and sexual adventures while professing her deep spirituality. She claims to be from an

old, upstanding Virginia family, but her real name is Katie Jonas and her father is a simple bricklayer. She tells one follower: "Perhaps I'm a prophetess, a little bit, but I'm also a good liar. I picked out the name Sharon Falconer while I was a stenographer. . . . And yet I'm not a liar! . . . I *am* Sharon Falconer now! I've made her—by prayer and by having a right to be her!" (Lewis 1970, 182). She believes that her faith will sustain her, and when a fire breaks out at one of her spiritual gatherings, she tells people that together she and God will lead them through the flames. She dies both despite and because of her religion. (Lewis 1970)

See also *Elmer Gantry;* Religion

Fall, The

The 1956 novel *The Fall,* written in French by Algerian author Albert Camus and published in that language as *La Chute,* addresses a wide variety of human failings, but it particularly criticizes those who are self-serving and consider themselves superior to other human beings. The novel expresses this theme through former lawyer Jean-Baptiste Clamence, who relates the story of his life in a one-sided dialogue with an unnamed stranger, whom he calls a "cultured bourgeois" (Camus 1958, 9).

The two men first meet in an Amsterdam bar, and for the next five days Clamence confesses his past faults. Clamence explains that at one time "my popularity was great and my successes in society innumerable" (27). He lived in Paris, where he was particularly noted for his charitable acts. However, he performed these acts not because he wanted to help others but because he needed to feel superior. He says, "I was always bursting with vanity. I, I, I is the refrain of my whole life, which could be heard in everything I said. I could never talk without boasting" (48).

Because Clamence craved public recognition, he did not perform a good deed unless someone was there to notice it. When he heard a woman jump off a deserted bridge into the Seine River late one night, he did nothing to save her from drowning. "I have forgotten what I thought then," he says. "'Too late, too far . . .' or something of the sort" (70). This event and others eventually led Clamence to question his nature. "I had the suspicion that maybe I wasn't so admirable," he says (77).

Once Clamence judged himself to be flawed, he began to believe that others were judging him with equal harshness. He explains, "In my eyes my fellows ceased to be the respectful public to which I was accustomed. . . . The moment I grasped that there was something to judge in me, I realized that there was in them an irresistible vocation for judgment" (78). As a result of this attitude, Clamence started expressing uncharitable or otherwise outrageous opinions in public. He abused alcohol and indulged in immoral behavior; his career as a lawyer suffered.

Then one day while on an ocean liner he momentarily glimpsed a black speck on the sea. "I was on the point of shouting, of stupidly calling for help," he explains, "when I saw it again. It was one of those bits of refuse that ships leave behind them. Yet I had not been able to endure watching it; for I had thought at once of a drowning person" (108). At that point Clamence realized that the cry of the drowning woman he had failed to save would never leave him, and he admitted his guilt (109).

But this guilt is not Clamence's alone. He explains, "The more I accuse myself, the more I have a right to judge you. Even better, I provoke you into judging yourself, and this relieves me of that much of the burden" (140). Clamence calls himself a "judge-penitent" and points out flaws in both individuals and society as a whole, saying, "The portrait I hold out to my contemporaries becomes a mirror" (140).

In the end he encourages the stranger to talk about his own transgressions, saying that "we are odd, wretched creatures, and if we merely look back over our lives, there's no lack of occasions to amaze and horrify ourselves. Just try" (140). Clamence is sure that the stranger has encountered his own woman on the bridge and that he, too, has longed for a second chance to save her—while at the same time feeling fortunate that such a second chance is impossible because, after all, "the water's so cold!" (147). In this way *The Fall* suggests that all people experience a conflict between their desire to better humanity and their desire to remain selfish; the work is therefore a generalized criticism of human society rather than a specific call for social reform. (Camus 1958)

See also Camus, Albert; Clamence, Jean-Baptiste; Justice

Farah, Nuruddin

Born in 1945 in what is now the Republic of Somalia, novelist Nuruddin Farah is credited as being the first published novelist and first English-language author from his country. His works are political in nature. For example, his first novel, *From a Crooked Rib* (1970), deals with sexism, and his trilogy, comprising *Sweet and Sour Milk* (1979), *Sardines* (1981), and *Close Sesame* (1983), shows the oppression of an African dictatorship.

Although Farah is Somali, he has spent much of his time elsewhere. He attended schools in Ethiopia and India and has lived in several different countries for fear of persecution in his own. He received a German fellowship in 1990 and the Swedish Tucholsky Literary Award, which is awarded to exiles, in 1991. (Farah 1992; Wright 1994)

See also *Close Sesame;* Exiles

Fascism

Fascism is a form of totalitarian dictatorship that first appeared in the twentieth century. The term was coined in 1919 by Italian politician Benito Mussolini, who was referring to an ancient Roman power symbol called the fasces. Mussolini believed in the government's right to control and punish its citizens at will. When he seized the Italian government in 1922, he banned all political parties except the Fascist Party and eliminated labor unions and the right to strike.

From 1919 to 1945 fascism spread throughout Europe. Different countries embraced different types of fascism, but all forms had certain things in common. For example, fascists opposed individual freedom, capitalism, feminism, and the women's rights movement. Most were also racist and supported military action, domination, oppression, and censorship. Consequently, many authors, including Lillian Hellman, Sinclair Lewis, Upton Sinclair, and Richard Wright, spoke out against fascism. Others did not specifically criticize the fascist movement but attacked the attitudes that encouraged it. For example, Walter Van Tilburg Clark's *The Ox-Bow Incident,* which concerns an American lynching, is often interpreted as an antifascist novel. (Cohen 1962)

> See also Clark, Walter Van Tilburg; Hellman, Lillian; Lewis, Sinclair; *Ox-Bow Incident, The;* Sinclair, Upton; Wright, Richard

Fatheya

Fatheya appears in the 1974 Egyptian feminist novel *Mawt al-rajul al-wahid 'ala 'l-ard* (God Dies by the Nile), by Nawal El Saadawi. Her husband is the religious leader of the village, yet when he finds an illegitimate child on their doorstep, he wants to leave it to die. Fatheya insists that they keep the baby, even after the villagers decide it is bringing the town bad luck. When a mob comes to kill the boy, she tries to defend him with her own life, dying with his body in her arms. (El Saadawi 1990)

> See also El Saadawi, Nawal; *God Dies by the Nile*

Feminism

The term *feminism* refers to the belief that women should be treated as equals to men, not only politically but also economically and socially. A great deal of feminist literature is therefore also social protest literature. In nonfiction, such works include English author Mary Wollstonecraft's 1792 treatise *A Vindication of the Rights of Woman,* American author Betty Friedan's 1963 book *The Feminine Mystique,* and the speeches and writings of such notable early feminists as Susan B. Anthony, Elizabeth Cady Stanton, Julia Ward Howe, and Sojourner Truth. In fiction, feminist authors include Sibilla Aleramo, Isabel Allende, Maya Angelou, Sawako Ariyoshi, Margaret Atwood, Nawal El Saadawi, Miles Franklin, Zora Neale Hurston, Nella Larsen, Toni Morrison, Tillie Olsen, and Alice Walker. Many male social protest authors also deal with feminist issues in their work. For example, Henry James's novel *The Bostonians* concerns the women's rights movement in the United States, and Pramoedya Ananta Toer's novel *This Earth of Mankind* depicts the oppression of women in Indonesia. (Jenness 1972; Ramelson 1967; Schneir 1972)

> See also Aleramo, Sibilla; Allende, Isabel; Angelou, Maya; Ariyoshi, Sawako; Atwood, Margaret; *Bostonians, The;* El Saadawi, Nawal; Franklin, Miles; Howe, Julia Ward; Hurston, Zora Neale; James, Henry; Larsen, Nella; Morrison, Toni; Olsen, Tillie; *This Earth of Mankind;* Toer, Pramoedya Ananta; Walker, Alice

Ferlinghetti, Lawrence

Born on March 24, 1919 or 1920, in Yonkers, New York, Lawrence Ferlinghetti is a poet best known for fighting against censorship in the United States. He also founded a San Francisco bookstore, City Lights, where many writers of the Beat movement congregated, and he started his own publishing company, City Lights Books, to disseminate many of their works. The first publication of City Lights Books was Ferlinghetti's first book of poems, *Pictures of the Gone World* (1955). His second book, *A Coney Island of the Mind* (1958), is his most famous and has several short social protest poems. His subsequent works include *Landscapes of Living and Dying* (1979), *Wild Dreams of a New Beginning* (1988), and *These Are My Rivers, 1950–1993* (1993). (Cherkovski 1979; Ferlinghetti 1958)

> See also Beat Movement; Censorship

Ferreira, Christovao

Christovao Ferreira is one of the main characters in Shūsaku Endō's 1966 novel *Chimmoku* (Silence). A Portuguese priest sent to gain converts to Christianity in Japan, he is arrested by Japanese authorities who want to end the religion's spread. When Ferreira refuses to renounce his religion, he is cut and left to bleed to death, hung upside down in a pit with other dying men. In the end he rejects Christianity not to save himself but to save his fellow sufferers, believing that Jesus Christ would have done this, too. Nonetheless, after he is released from the pit and word of his actions reaches Portugal, he becomes an object of scorn there, and over time he becomes a dispirited man. He spends the rest of his life in Japan, living as a Japanese, writing anti-Christianity materials, and helping the authorities identify Christians for persecution. (Endō 1980)

See also Endō, Shūsaku; *Silence*

Finch, Jean Louise ("Scout")

Jean Louise Finch, nicknamed "Scout," is the first-person narrator of *To Kill a Mockingbird* (1960), by Harper Lee. She describes a series of events during her childhood that teach her about morals, courage, and prejudice. In her town of Maycomb, Alabama, she observes that most people associate only with those from their own social class and that whites discriminate against blacks. Her father, however, is different; he treats everyone with respect regardless of class or race. Eventually Scout learns to do this herself. (Lee 1993)

See also Lee, Harper; *To Kill a Mockingbird*

Finchley, Sondra

In Theodore Dreiser's 1925 novel *An American Tragedy,* Sondra Finchley is a rich girl who falls in love with Clyde Griffiths, a man of poor background. She originally begins dating him on a lark, but she later falls in love and wants to marry him despite her family's objections. However, when Clyde is arrested for killing a mistress whom he has impregnated, Sondra allows her parents to keep her away from him. The Finchleys fear for their reputation in the community, and Sondra is as much a prisoner of her social status as Clyde. (Dreiser 1964; Moers 1969)

See also *American Tragedy, An;* Dreiser, Theodore; Griffiths, Clyde

Finkelberg, Isaac

Son of a Jewish shopkeeper and a character from the 1948 South African novel *The Path of Thunder,* by Peter Abrahams, Isaac Finkelberg is an intellectual who discusses his country's racial policies with his friends, Mako and Lanny. Lanny is a mixed-race, or "coloured," man, whereas Mako is a Zulu native who tells Isaac that the situation of the Jewish people is similar to that of the coloureds because both live "in lands of other nations" and have "no independent nationality" (Abrahams 1975, 89). Isaac's father disagrees, saying that a man can be a Jew or a Zulu no matter where he lives and tells Isaac that he is a fool to associate with Mako and Lanny because the Dutch who control the area will persecute him for this association. Consequently, father and son quarrel, and Isaac concludes that the old man "seemed to have forgotten how to strike a blow for his own freedom and independence" (72). In fact, Isaac believes that all Jews have become "too civilized. Too humane. They were known for the peaceful arts. The creative arts. Scholarship. They were too . . . deeply steeped in the peaceful, commercial, and creatively gentle art of living. They knew how to build but they had forgotten how to destroy. And the foundations were rotten" (72). (Abrahams 1975; Ensor 1992)

See also Abrahams, Peter; Mako; *Path of Thunder, The;* Racism; Swartz, Lanny

France, Anatole

Anatole France was born Jacques-Anatole-François Thibault on April 16, 1844, in Paris, France. He wrote novels, plays, poems, essays, and literary criticism and commentary, including an introduction to Jack London's social protest novel *The Iron Heel.* France also dealt with social issues in some of his own works. For example, his 1903 three-act comedy *Crainquebille* depicts some of the beliefs that led France to embrace socialism, and his 1908 novel *L'Île des Pingouins* (Penguin Island) shows the development of civilization, industrialization, and pollution on an island of humanlike penguins.

France was also known for his involvement in the Dreyfus Affair. In 1894 Captain Alfred Dreyfus was falsely accused of treason, court-martialed by the military, and sent to prison on Devil's Island. His conviction was based not on evidence but on the fact that he was Jewish. Consequently, France and many other writers, including Émile Zola, began demanding Dreyfus's release, and in 1906 a civilian court finally declared Dreyfus innocent. France deals with this issue in his satirical novel *Monsieur Bergeret a Paris* (1901), which is the last volume in a trilogy known as *L'Histoire contemporaine* (1897–1901).

France was elected to the Academie Française in 1896 and received a Nobel Prize in literature in 1921. He died on October 12, 1924, in Saint-Cyr-sur-Loire, France. (May 1970; Vertanen 1968)

See also Anti-Semitism; Exiles; *Iron Heel, The;* London, Jack; Socialism; Zola, Émile

Franklin, Miles

Australian author Stella Maria Sarah Miles Franklin is known for her feminist novels, which include *My Brilliant Career* (1901) and its sequel, *My Career Goes Bung.* The latter was considered too controversial for publication until 1946. She also wrote under the pseudonyms Brent of Bin Bin and Mrs. Ogniblat l'Artsau. Born on October 14, 1879, in Talbingo, New South Wales, Australia, Franklin was raised in remote bush country. In 1906 she moved to the United States, where she worked as an editor, and nine years later to England. In 1927 she returned to Australia to write historical fiction set in her native country. These works include *Up the Country* (1929), *Prelude to Waking* (1950), and *Gentlemen at Gyang Gynag* (1956), all published under the name Brent of Bin Bin. This pseudonym was not recognized as hers until after her death on September 19, 1954, in Sydney, New South Wales. Additional works under her own name include *Some Everyday Folk and Dawn* (1909) and *All That Swagger* (1936). (Barnard 1967; Franklin 1965; Roderick 1982)

See also Feminism; *My Brilliant Career*

Fuentes, Carlos

Mexican writer Carlos Fuentes is best known for his novels exploring Mexican culture and politics in the twentieth century. However, he has also written short stories, plays, essays, and a television series entitled *El espejo enterrado* (The Buried Mirror), which concerns Mexican history and culture and was published in book form in English and Spanish in 1992.

Fuentes was born on November 11, 1928, in Mexico City, where he studied to be a lawyer. Eventually he became a diplomat, as was his father. He held several important posts, including cultural attaché at the Mexican Embassy in Geneva, Switzerland, from 1950 to 1952 and Mexican ambassador to France from 1975 to 1977.

His first published work appeared in 1954; it was a collection of short stories entitled *Los días enmascarados* (The Masked Days). His first novel, *La región transparente* (Where the Air Is Clear) was published in Spanish in 1958 and in English in 1960. It criticized many aspects of Mexican society and gained Fuentes recognition in his own country, as did

Carlos Fuentes, 21 April 1988 (Reuters/High Peralton/ Archive Photos)

his second and third novels, *Las buenas con-ciencias* (The Good Conscience, 1959) and *Aura* (1962). However, his third novel, *La muerte de Artemio Cruz* (The Death of Artemio Cruz), gained him international recognition. Published in Spanish in 1962 and in English in 1964, it, too, criticizes Mexican society as it presents the memories of a wealthy man on his deathbed.

Fuentes is the author of several more nov-els, including *La cabeza de la hidra* (The Hydra Head, 1978), a spy thriller about Mexican backroom politics, and *Una familia lejana* (Distant Relations, 1980), an experimental novel about alternate realities. He also wrote a work of literary criticism entitled *La nueva novela hispanoamericana* (The New Hispano-American Novel, 1969). (Faris 1983)

See also *Death of Artemio Cruz, The; Hydra Head, The*

G

Gaines, Ernest J.

African-American author Ernest James Gaines is best known for writing *The Autobiography of Miss Jane Pittman,* a novel about slavery and the civil rights movement. Published in 1971, the book was made into an award-winning television special in 1974.

Gaines was born on a plantation in Oscar, Louisiana, on January 15, 1933. As a boy he worked in the fields for 50 cents a day. When he was 15, he moved to California, where he graduated from San Francisco State College in 1957. He later received a writing fellowship at Stanford University. His first novel, *Catherine Carmier* (1964), won a prestigious award, the Joseph Henry Jackson Literary Prize. His other works include *In My Father's House* (1978), *A Gathering of Old Men* (1983), and *A Lesson before Dying* (1993). (Babb 1991; Estes 1994; Gaines 1972)

> See also *Autobiography of Miss Jane Pittman, The;* Racism; Slavery

Galsworthy, John

English author John Galsworthy is best known for a series of novels entitled *The Forsyte Saga,* published together in 1922 and later made into a television drama. However, he also wrote important social protest plays, including *Strife* (1909), which deals with a la-bor strike, and *Justice* (1910), which led to prison reform in England.

Galsworthy was born in Kingston Hill, Surrey, England, on August 14, 1867. He grew up in a wealthy family and was educated at Harrow and New College, Oxford. In 1890 he became a lawyer, but he soon grew dissatisfied with the profession. He began to write, and in 1898 he self-published a collection of short stories and a novel, entitled *Jocelyn,* under the pseudonym John Sinjohn. It was not until 1904 that he published a novel, *The Island Pharisees,* under his own name. His other novels include *The Man of Property* (1906), *Chancery* (1920), and *To Let* (1921), which were later published collectively as *The Forsyte Saga,* as well as several sequels to the saga: *The White Monkey* (1924), *The Silver Spoon* (1926), *Swan Song* (1928), which were published collectively as *A Modern Comedy* in 1929, and *End of the Chapter* (1931–1932). Galsworthy died on January 31, 1933, in Grove Lodge, Hamstead, England. (Barker 1969)

> See also Labor Issues; Prison Reform; *Strife*

Galt, John

Throughout Ayn Rand's novel *Atlas Shrugged* characters use the slang phrase "Who is John Galt?" to mean "Who knows?" There are various theories regarding the expression's origin, but eventually the truth is revealed. John Galt is an inventor who once worked for a motorcar company. One day the company decided that extra effort, creativity, and merit would no longer be rewarded. Every worker was to be treated equally, so that the industrious would actually be subsidizing the mediocre. Galt quickly realized that this approach was going to spread throughout the United States. He quit his job and announced that he would stop the motor of the world. He created a secret society that is fighting to preserve capitalism. By the end of the novel he has succeeded in destroying the government and is ready to lead a new society based on profit and individual effort. (Rand 1992)

See also *Atlas Shrugged;* Rand, Ayn

García, Esteban

In Isabel Allende's 1982 South American novel *La casa de los espíritus* (The House of the Spirits) Esteban García is a cruel policeman who enjoys torturing innocent people. The illegitimate grandson of wealthy conservative senator Esteban Trueba, he feels betrayed out of his rightful inheritance and seeks his revenge by punishing Trueba's granddaughter, Alba. After a military coup he arrests Alba for political crimes and subjects her to rapes, beatings, and electric shock treatments. (Allende 1985)

See also Allende, Isabel; De Satigny, Alba Trueba; Del Valle, Clara; García, Pedro Tecero; *House of the Spirits, The;* Trueba, Esteban

García, Pedro Tecero

In Isabel Allende's 1982 novel *La casa de los espíritus* (The House of the Spirits), Pedro Tecero García is a revolutionary who supports socialism in his South American homeland by handing out pamphlets and singing social protest songs. He works to overturn the conservative government, but the new socialist regime is short-lived. A military coup soon occurs, ushering in a dictatorship, and Pedro Tecero and his lover, Blanca Trueba, must escape the country with the help of her father, a disillusioned conservative politician. (Allende 1985)

See also Allende, Isabel; De Satigny, Alba Trueba; Del Valle, Clara; García, Esteban; *House of the Spirits, The;* Socialism; Trueba, Esteban

Gay and Lesbian Issues

Homosexuality involves a sexual relationship between members of the same sex. Gays and lesbians have been persecuted to varying degrees throughout history, and many authors have protested this persecution. They have also encouraged an understanding of gay and lesbian issues and lifestyle. For example, Jean-Paul Sartre and James Baldwin depict men struggling to accept their homosexuality in their novels *The Age of Reason* and *Another Country,* respectively, and Alice Walker shows a woman exploring lesbianism in her novel *The Color Purple.* Lillian Hellman examines the persecution of lesbians in her play *The Children's Hour,* and Allen Ginsberg provoked censorship for his mention of homosexuality in his poem *Howl.* (Galloway and Sabish 1982)

See also *Age of Reason, The; Another Country;* Baldwin, James; Censorship; *Children's Hour, The; Color Purple, The;* Ginsberg, Allen; Hellman, Lillian; *Howl;* Sartre, Jean-Paul; Walker, Alice

Ginsberg, Allen

American poet Allen Ginsberg was the author of the epic poem *Howl,* which protests society's suppression of individuality and personal exploration. Published in 1956, it created immediate controversy for its raw language, and its publisher was arrested for distributing obscenity. The American Civil Liberties Union defended the book and its publisher in the resulting obscenity trial, eventually winning the case.

Ginsberg was born on June 3, 1926, in Newark, New Jersey. His mother was a Russian immigrant, his father a poet and schoolteacher. At age 17 he began attending Columbia University, but he was expelled in 1945 for bad behavior. He then worked at a variety of odd jobs, including dishwasher, night porter, copy boy, and literary agent, before being readmitted to Columbia in 1948. He graduated

Allen Ginsberg (Russell Reif/Archive Photos)

that same year with a bachelor of arts degree and entered into graduate study. In 1949 he spent two months in a state hospital for psychiatric problems. He also began experimenting with drugs.

In 1954 he moved to San Francisco, where he wrote *Howl and Other Poems* and became involved in the Beat movement, a counterculture social and literary movement that took place in the United States during the late 1950s and early 1960s. He published a great deal of poetry during this period, including *Kaddish and Other Poems* (1961) and *Reality Sandwiches* (1963). His recent works include *Cosmopolitan Greetings: Poems 1986–1992* (1994) and *Journals Mid-Fifties, 1954–1958* (1995). He died on April 5, 1997, in New York City. (Merrill 1969; Miles 1995)

See also Beat Movement; Censorship; *Howl*

Gissing, George

Born in 1857, English novelist George Robert Gissing was one of the most productive authors of his time. He published 19 novels, many of them written in three volumes. Perhaps the most famous of these was *New Grub*

Street (1891). Named for the literary district of London, it presents the desperation of the poor in Victorian England.

In his early years as a writer Gissing himself lived in poverty. The son of a pharmacist, he fell in love with a woman suspected of being a prostitute while he was away at college. To support her, he stole money from coat pockets. He was soon expelled, and his family disowned him. Later he married the woman, and despite his prolific writing career, he remained relatively poor until her death in 1888, when he was able to live more economically. However, although Gissing discusses the economic disadvantages of marriage in *New Grub Street,* the year it was published he married another lower-class woman. The two eventually separated, and he lived in France with a mistress until his death in 1903. Two of Gissing's books, *Commonplace Book* (1962) and *The Diary of George Gissing, Novelist* (1982), were published posthumously. (Gissing 1926; Goode 1979; Selig 1983)

See also Class, Social; *New Grub Street;* Poverty

Glass Bead Game, The

Published as *Magister Ludi* in a 1949 English translation, the 1943 novel *Das Glasperlenspiel* (The Glass Bead Game), by Hermann Hesse, examines the compartmentalization of society and the conflict that occurs within people who do not lead a balanced life. It is the fictional biography of Joseph Knecht, a man of the twenty-third century, as told by a twenty-fifty-century scholar. As a young boy Knecht is identified as a talented musician and asked to join an elite order of intellectuals. This order is supported by the government and segregated from the rest of society. Its members are not allowed to marry or participate in worldly activities, and although they learn meditation, they do not practice a religion. They also do not study history or politics, believing them to be too worldly and common. Knecht has mixed feelings about joining this order, but eventually becomes one of its leaders, or Magisters, and is placed in charge of the Glass Bead Game. The game is an important mental exercise for those in the order. The narrator's description of it is vague, but it appears to be a meditative pursuit in which players use music, mathematics, and other intellectual disciplines to make complex mental connections between various objects and concepts. Constantly evolving and changing, the game's many variations and strategies are recorded in a great archive in the province of Castalia, which is overseen by Knecht in his position as Magister Ludi.

This position is the pinnacle of success in the order, but after several years Knecht becomes dissatisfied with it. He realizes that if he remains isolated from the rest of his society, he will never learn or grow as an individual. Moreover, after studying history and politics, he decides that the outside world will eventually stop supporting the order unless it makes some fundamental changes. When its governing board refuses to heed his warnings, Knecht resigns his position and becomes a tutor for a young man from a politically powerful family. Knecht believes that his influence on this man will ultimately benefit society, and he is full of hope for the future. Unfortunately, he drowns in a swimming accident shortly after meeting his new pupil. Nonetheless, the young man's perception of the world and his role in it have been altered by his contact with Joseph Knecht.

Although set in the future, *The Glass Bead Game* is actually a statement on contemporary society. As scholar Theodore Ziolkowsky (xv) points out in a 1986 introduction to the novel, Knecht's order "has more than a little in common with the intellectual and cultural institutions of the sixties, to the extent that they have become autonomous empires cut off from the social needs of mankind and cultivating their own Glass Bead Games in glorious isolation." The novel portrays not only the order but also the world outside the order as being dysfunctional, suggesting that both halves of society suffer from the separation of intellectual and nonintellectual pursuits. (Hesse 1986; Ziolkowski 1965)

See also Hesse, Hermann; Knecht, Joseph

God Dies by the Nile

The novel *God Dies by the Nile,* which first appeared in Arabic in 1974 as *Mawt al-rajul al-wahid 'ala 'l-ard,* concerns the oppression of women in modern-day Egypt. Its author, Nawal El Saadawi, is a noted Egyptian feminist.

The story is set in Kafr El Teen, a small town beside the Nile River, where the mayor completely controls the lives of the peasants. On a whim he taxes people until they forfeit their land or arrests them on contrived charges. He uses three men as his spies and henchmen: Sheikh Zaran, who is chief of the Village Guard; Sheikh Hamzawi, who is in charge of prayer at the mosque; and Haj Ismail, who is the village barber. These three help the mayor obtain peasant girls for his personal pleasure.

One day the mayor decides that he must have the beautiful young Nefissa. Haj Ismail convinces her father, Kafrawi, to force her to work as a servant in the mayor's house. Kafrawi is a poor widower who lives with his widowed sister, Zakeya. Neither he nor the other peasants suspect that the mayor, who is married, will rape Nefissa. In fact, even after she becomes pregnant and leaves the village, they believe the mayor is blameless. They do, however, think that Nefissa's baby is evil simply because it is illegitimate. When Sheikh Hamzawi finds the baby on his doorstep, they urge him to get rid of the child, and they are angry when his childless wife, Fatheya, takes the little one as her own.

By this time the mayor has decided that he wants Nefissa's younger sister, Zeinab. She refuses to come to his house, so he spreads the rumor that a peasant named Elwau fathered Nefissa's baby, then arranges Elwau's murder and frames Kafrawi for the crime. With her father in jail, Zeinab is left alone to care for her Aunt Zakeya, who has gone crazy with grief. Zeinab begs Sheikh Hamzawi to help her cure her aunt. He sends the two women to a great mosque in a nearby city, where a holy man gives them a message from God: to cure her aunt's mental illness, Zeinab must work in the house of the mayor. The two women return home, and Zeinab becomes the mayor's servant and mistress. No one in the village knows of her shame.

Meanwhile the town's crops have started to fail. The people blame Nefissa's illegitimate son for their bad fortune. They kill both the baby and Fatheya, who is trying to protect him. Shortly thereafter Zakeya's son, Galal, a soldier, returns home from a war on the Sinai Peninsula. He marries Zeinab, and she stops working as a servant girl. Angry that Zeinab no longer comes to his house, the mayor plants a bag of silver in Galal's home and has him arrested for theft. Zeinab goes to visit him at the jail and is kidnapped by a strange man. She is never seen again.

Now Zakeya realizes that the mayor must have told the holy man to send Zeinab to him. Alone and angry, she sees him coming out of his house. She takes a hoe and hammers him to death. After she is arrested, she tells another prisoner that God has now been buried on the banks of the Nile.

Zakeya's retribution brings the death of a tyrant. But although his destruction is the act of an individual, the novel makes it clear that that eventually the other peasants would have risen up against him. Near the end of *God Dies by the Nile* the chief of the Village Guard says: "People have changed. . . . The people who at one time could not look me in the eye, now look at me straight in the face, and no longer bow their heads to the ground when I pass by. Just yesterday, one of the villagers refused to pay his taxes and shouted, 'We work all the year round and all we end up with are debts to the government.' I never used to hear this kind of talk from any of them before" (El Saadawi 1990, 126–127). (El Saadawi 1990; Malti-Douglas 1995)

See also El Saadawi, Nawal; Fatheya; Feminism; Justice; Zakeya; Zeinab

Golding, William

English novelist Sir William Gerald Golding wrote primarily about human violence. His first and most famous work, *Lord of the Flies* (1954), concerns a group of schoolboys stranded on an island who quickly turn savage. His second novel, *The Inheritors* (1955), is set in prehistoric times among brutal Neanderthals. Subsequent novels include *Free Fall* (1959), *The Spire* (1964), *Rites of Passage* (1980), and *Fire Down Below* (1989).

Golding was born on September 19, 1911, near Newquay in Cornwall, England. The son of a teacher, he graduated from Brasenose College in Oxford in 1935 and became a teacher himself, working at Bishop Wordsworth's School in Salisbury. During World War II he joined the Royal Navy, and in 1941 he was present during the military campaign that sunk the German battleship *Bismarck*. After the war he returned to his teaching job, a position he held until 1961. In 1983 he won the Nobel Prize for Literature, and in 1988 he was knighted. He died on June 19, 1993, in Perranarworthal, Cornwall, England. (Baker 1965; Dick 1967; Hynes 1964)

See also *Lord of the Flies*

Gorky, Maxim

Maxim Gorky is the pseudonym for Russian novelist, short-story writer, and poet Aleksey Maksimovich Peshkov. The word *gorky* in Russian means "bitter one," and the author chose it to represent his difficult upbringing. Born in March 1868 in Nizhny Novgorod, Russia, Gorky grew up in his grandfather's home, his father having died when he was only five. When Gorky turned eight, his grandfather made him begin working at odd jobs, which continued into his adulthood. At various times he was an errand boy, a dishwasher, a bakery shop worker, a fisherman, a railroad worker, a clerk, a dockworker, and a night watchman. His life was so harsh that he once tried to commit suicide, and eventually he ended up a vagabond.

From his experiences as a tramp came several ideas for stories, sketches, and articles. His first published fiction appeared in 1892 in local newspapers, whereupon he attracted the attention of author and journalist Vladimir Korolenko. Korolenko helped Gorky get his work published in important journals, and Gorky quickly became famous. He went on to write plays and novels, the latter of which included *Ispoved* (A Confession, 1908) and *Mat* (Mother, 1906). He also established his own publishing house.

Gorky was a Marxist and used much of his income to support the Social Democratic Party and the Marxist movement. This made him unpopular with government officials. In 1901 he was arrested for writing a revolutionary poem, "Pesnya o burevestnike" (Song of the Stormy Petrel), and although he was soon released, he continued to have trouble with the government. In 1906 he was again arrested for his involvement with the Russian Revolution of the previous year. However, his international notoriety made it difficult for the government to keep him in jail, and once more his confinement was brief. After his release he toured the United States and then went into a self-imposed political exile on Italy's island of Capri.

In 1913 Gorky ended his exile and went back to Russia, where he protested some of Vladimir I. Lenin's policies. Lenin then censored Gorky's writings, and eventually Gorky ended his protests. Except for a period in Italy from 1921 to 1928, he lived the rest of his life in Russia. He wrote several more novels, including an autobiography in three volumes, and in 1934 he founded the Soviet Writers' Union. His later work addressed the decline of the merchant families and the intelligentsia in Russia. He died suddenly and mysteriously in 1936, and many scholars suspect that Gorky's death was actually a murder ordered by Joseph Stalin. (Levin 1965)

See also Exiles; "Song of the Stormy Petrel"

Grapes of Wrath, The

The Grapes of Wrath, by John Steinbeck, is the story of a poor farm family struggling for survival amid the harsh economic conditions of the 1930s. However, it is also a timeless protest against oppression and injustice in American society. Its title refers to a phrase from the lyrics of "The Battle Hymn of the Republic," written in 1862 by social reformist Julia Ward Howe.

The novel created a great deal of controversy when it was published in 1939. Some readers believed that Steinbeck was a revolutionary who exaggerated the plight of working-class families in order to promote his political views. Others recognized that the novel realistically portrays the hardships of migrant farmworkers during the period. The author lived among such people while doing research for his work, and reporters later confirmed that he accurately depicted these lives. *The Grapes of Wrath* was awarded the Pulitzer Prize in 1940 and was made into a movie the same year.

The novel alternates omniscient discussions about the plight of migrant farmworkers in general with a narrative about the Joad family of Oklahoma in particular. At the beginning of the narrative Tom Joad Jr. has just been released from prison, where he served four years for killing a man in self-defense. On his way home Tom meets Jim Casy, who was once his preacher but has lost his faith and left the church. Together the two travel to Tom's family farm through land wasted by drought. The Joads have been tenants on the farm for a long time, but when the two men reach it, they find the farm deserted. Another farmer tells them that the Joads are at a relative's house getting ready to leave for California. Because of the drought, tenant farming throughout the Midwest has become unprofitable, and the landowners have decided to either sell their property or turn to mechanized farming. The tenant farmers, or sharecroppers, are therefore being forced to move, but not before selling their furniture and equipment at reduced prices and buying used cars at inflated ones.

Tom and Jim find the Joads at an uncle's house. The family includes Pa and Ma Joad; their sons Noah and Al; their pregnant teenage daughter Rose of Sharon (referred to as Rosasharn) and her husband Connie Rivers; the Joads' two youngest children, Ruthie and Winfield; and Granma and Grampa Joad. Glad to see Tom, they tell him about a handbill advertising for farmworkers in California. They have bought an old truck to carry them there and ask Jim to accompany them. He gladly agrees. But the trip across the country is hard, and along the way Grampa dies of a stroke. The family buries him by the side of the road. Later the truck breaks down

Tom Joad kneels to check on the family truck in a scene from the 1940 movie The Grapes of Wrath. *(Library of Congress/Corbis)*

and must be repaired. Finally the family crosses the California border. The Joads camp by a river where some other migrant families are gathered and learn that work in California is hard to find. They also discover that migrants are not treated well in California. One person tells them that Californians "hate you 'cause they're scairt. They know a hungry fella gonna get food even if he got to take it" (Steinbeck 1972, 225). This man then explains that all migrant workers are called "Okies," saying: "Okie use' ta mean you was from Oklahoma. Now it means you're . . . scum. Don't mean nothing itself, it's the way they say it. But I can't tell you nothin'. You got to go there. I hear there's three hunderd thousan' of our people there—an' livin' like hogs, 'cause ever'thing in California is owned. They ain't nothin' left. An' them people that owns it is gonna hang onto it if they got ta kill ever'-body in the worl' to do it" (225–226).

Later the omniscient narrator also discusses the fears of the owners, saying:

And the great owners, who must lose their land in an upheaval, the great owners with access to history, with eyes to real history and to know the great fact; when property accumulates in too few hands it is taken away. And that companion fact: when a majority of the people are hungry and cold they will take by force what they need. And the little screaming fact that sounds through all history: repression works only to strengthen and knit the repressed. The great owners ignored the three cries of history. The land fell into fewer hands, the number of the dispossessed increased, and every effort of the great owners was directed at repression. The money was spent for arms, for gas to protect the great holdings, and spies were sent to catch the murmuring of revolt so that it might be stamped out. The changing economy was ignored, plans for the change ignored; and only means to destroy revolt were considered, while the causes of revolt went on. (262)

The Joads are warned several times that they might starve in California, but they know they cannot return to Oklahoma. While they rest at the river camp, they plan their journey across the desert to the fertile land around Bakersfield. Suddenly Noah decides that he will not continue with the group. He tells Tom that he plans to stay by the river and eat fish, then disappears. Shortly thereafter a policeman arrives and orders the family to move on. The Joads head west, and Granma dies in the desert. The family leaves her body with the coroner in Bakersfield and heads to a migrant camp on the outskirts of town. There Tom gets into a fight with a cruel police deputy who is harassing an innocent man. Jim knocks the deputy out and tells Tom to hide. He reminds Tom that as a newly released convict, he was supposed to have stayed in Oklahoma, has therefore violated his parole, and will undoubtedly be sent back to prison. Tom runs away, and when the rest of the police arrive, Jim takes full blame for the incident. He is arrested and taken to jail.

When Tom returns, he discovers that Connie, who has been complaining about their harsh living conditions, has deserted his family. The Joads decide to relocate to a government-run camp, where no deputies will bother them. There they are pleased to find that the camp has good sanitary conditions and is governed with fairness by a committee of its residents. Then Tom learns that the townspeople have a plan to shut down the camp. They intend to start a fight at a camp dance, so that deputies can come in and clear the place out. Tom warns the other residents, and the troublemakers are stopped before they can do any damage. The camp remains open.

Unfortunately, the Joads cannot find enough work in the area, so they head north to a large farm that needs peach pickers. They must enter the gate with a police escort, past an angry mob protesting the farm's unfair wages. Once inside, the Joads spend all day picking peaches for five cents a box; even though every member of the family is working, they earn only enough money for one meal. Not only are wages low, but also the goods at the company store are overpriced. That night Tom goes for a walk, crawls under the fence, and encounters the protesters. To his surprise, he discovers that Jim Casy is among them. Jim explains that the protesters are former employees of the farm who went on strike when their wages were cut from a dollar and a half per box of peaches picked to two and a half cents a box. Jim asks Tom to convince the strikebreakers to join their protest. While the two are talking, some strangers attack them. Jim is killed, and Tom kills one of the attackers. He returns to the farm and asks his family to hide him until he can escape.

But Ma Joad is unwilling to let him leave them. Instead, she decides that the entire family will move on, hiding Tom under a mattress in the truck as they drive away. Her plan works. Eventually they come upon a group of migrants camped in some abandoned boxcars. They make camp and get jobs picking cotton. Tom remains in hiding. Then Ruthie tells another girl about him, and Ma Joad realizes that Tom is now in danger of being caught. She tells him to leave. He agrees, vowing to spend his life fighting against injustice. He says: "Wherever they's a fight so hungry people can eat, I'll be there. Wherever they's a cop beatin' up a guy, I'll be there. . . . I'll be in the way guys yell when they're made an'—I'll be in the way kids laugh when they're hungry an' they know supper's ready. An' when our folks eat the stuff they raise an' live in the houses they build—why, I'll be there" (463).

After Tom is gone, a heavy rainstorm causes a stream to overflow and flood the camp, despite the migrants' efforts to prevent it. At the same time Rose of Sharon delivers a stillborn baby. Eventually the waters rise so high that the Joads' car will not work, and the family must flee on foot. They find a barn, where a

Man in a soup kitchen, New York City, 1938 (Library of Congress)

man is starving to death. Rose of Sharon feeds him with her breast milk. In this way the poor nourish their own and life goes on.

Throughout the novel those in power either neglect or mistreat the downtrodden. Police, bank managers, and landowners are depicted as either cruel or easily intimidated by those with more power. For example, one landowner does not want to reduce his farmworkers' pay; however, the bank has threatened to foreclose on his loan if he refuses to do so. Similarly, some townspeople want to destroy the government-run migrant camps, which provide toilets and hot water. One man says that the migrants do not deserve hot water, adding: "We ain't gonna have no peace till we wipe them camps out. They'll be wantin' clean sheets, first thing we know" (417). Faced with such discrimination, the Joads develop a social conscience. At the beginning of the novel they are highly individualistic. However, as the story progresses, they begin to show concern for other migrants and to recognize that their problems are everyone's problems. This concern for the greater good is also shared by the former preacher, Jim Casy. Having lost his faith in traditional religion, he discovers a new religious fervor through his fight for justice among the farmworkers. He dies protesting their mistreatment. (Moore 1968; Steinbeck 1972)

See also Great Depression; Immigrant Communities; Joad Family; Poverty; Steinbeck, John

Great Depression

The Great Depression was a time of economic hardship that developed during the 1930s throughout the world. In the United States one in every four workers lost his or her job. Stocks decreased in value, businesses failed, and many affluent people were thrown into poverty. At the same time farmers in the Dust Bowl region of the country, which includes the Oklahoma and Texas panhandles and parts of Colorado, Kansas, and New Mexico, experienced a drought and began migrating to other areas looking for work. In major cities they competed with immigrants from other countries who had come to the United States hoping for an end to their poverty. One of the most famous American social protest novels, *The Grapes of Wrath,* by John Steinbeck, was inspired by this situation. Another significant social protest novel of the period was *Yonnondio: From the Thirties,* by Tillie Olsen. (Shannon 1960; Swados 1966)

See also *Grapes of Wrath, The;* Olsen, Tillie; Poverty; Steinbeck, John; *Yonnondio: From the Thirties*

Great Expectations

Great Expectations, by Charles Dickens, was first published in serialized form in a weekly periodical, *All the Year Round,* from 1860 to 1861. The novel was published in book form in 1861. It is the first-person narrative of Phillip Pirrip, known as Pip. As a child Pip is orphaned and raised by his sister, who is cruel, and her husband, Joe, who is kind. One day the boy meets an escaped prisoner who asks him for food. Pip brings him a pork pie and a file to cut the chain from his leg. The man promises he will repay Pip someday for his kindness.

Meanwhile Pip's sister makes him visit an old woman, Miss Haversham, each day. Miss Haversham is bitter because her fiancé disappeared on her wedding day, and she is teaching her young ward, Estella, to be cruel to men. Consequently, Estella often teases Pip. Nonetheless, when a lawyer approaches Pip and tells him that a benefactor has arranged for him to go to London, the young man assumes that Miss Haversham is behind his good fortune. He assumes that she wants him to become a gentleman, so that he can marry Estella. Later Miss Haversham encourages this belief.

While in London Pip moves among the upper classes and becomes conceited. Consequently, when Estella visits London and he falls in love with her, she rejects him for another man. Then Pip discovers that his benefactor was not Miss Haversham but Abel Magwitch, the convict he once helped. Shortly after Pip rescued him from hunger, Magwitch was recaptured and exiled to New South Wales, where he made a fortune as a sheep farmer. He returned to England specifically to help Pip, even though this was against the law.

Pip confronts Miss Haversham with her deceit and learns that Estella is about to be married. Later he visits Miss Haversham again and discovers that her house is on fire. He tries to save the old woman but fails. By this time he knows that Magwitch's long-standing enemy, Arthur Compeyson, is plotting to kill the former convict and that Compeyson is the man who once jilted Miss Haversham. Pip has also discovered that Magwitch is Estella's father. The young man tries to get his benefactor out of England to safety. During the escape Compeyson attacks Magwitch and Magwitch kills him. The old man is captured and sent to prison, where he dies before his trial. Pip now reunites with a widowed Joe, loses the last of his conceit, and goes into business with a pleasant young man named Herbert Pocket. Eleven years later he also reunites with Estella, whose husband has died.

The story of *Great Expectations* is primarily a romance and a mystery, but there are elements of social protest in Pip's rise through the social classes. Pip's moral corruption as he gains wealth reflects Dickens's view of the upper classes in general. This theme appears in many of his works and is particularly prominent in *Little Dorrit.* (Dickens 1963; Fielding 1958; Hibbert 1967)

See also Class, Social; Dickens, Charles; *Little Dorrit;* Poverty

Green, Horatio

Horatio Green is a character in the 1853 novel *Clotel,* by William Wells Brown, which concerns slavery in the United States during the 1800s. He falls in love with a young slave, Clotel, and takes her to be his mistress. They live together as man and wife and have a beautiful young daughter. Nonetheless, society does not recognize Clotel as anything but Horatio's slave. Moreover, when Horatio decides that he wants to become politically powerful, he finds it easy to abandon his love for Clotel and marry a white woman from a well-connected family. He allows his new wife to sell

Clotel and make her daughter a house slave, and he lives out the rest of his life as an unhappy man. (Gates 1990)

See also *Clotel*

Greene, Graham

The works of English novelist Henry Graham Greene deal with human corruption and decay in contemporary political settings. Many of his novels are set in countries with unstable governments. For example, *The Quiet American* (1956) takes place in Vietnam during the 1950s; *Our Man in Havana* (1958) in Cuba just prior to the Communist revolution. One of his most famous novels, *The Power and the Glory* (1940), concerns religious persecution in Mexico under a revolutionary government. Graham's other novels include *Stamboul Train*, also titled *Orient Express* (1932), *Brighton Rock* (1938), *The Heart of the Matter* (1948), *A Burnt-Out Case* (1961), *The Comedians* (1966), and *The Tenth Man* (1985). He also wrote several collections of short stories, as well as plays, essays, and memoirs.

Greene was born in Berkhamsted, Hertfordshire, England, on October 2, 1904. The son of a teacher, he ran away from school and was later sent to live with a psychoanalyst in London. He attended Balliol College in Oxford and became a Roman Catholic in 1926. The following year he moved back to London and became a copy editor for *The Times* newspaper. His first published novel, *The Man Within,* appeared in 1929, and because of its success, he quit his job to become a film critic and literary editor for *The Spectator,* a position he held until 1940. He died on April 3, 1991, in Vevey, Switzerland. (De Vitis 1964; Pryce-Jones 1968)

See also Exiles; Justice; *Power and the Glory, The;* Religion

Griffiths, Clyde

As the main character of Theodore Dreiser's 1925 novel *An American Tragedy,* Clyde Griffiths is more concerned with social climbing than morality. He was raised in poverty but wants to be a rich man. Therefore, he is over-joyed when a girl from a prominent New York family becomes romantically interested in him. There is just once problem: he already has a girlfriend, Roberta Alden. When Roberta tells Clyde she is pregnant and threatens to expose him as a cad unless he marries her, he decides to murder her. At the last minute he changes his mind but accidentally kills her anyway. This is not the first accident in Clyde's life; he is often the victim of chance or circumstance because Dreiser wanted to show human beings as victims of their backgrounds, social roles, and passions. Nonetheless, Clyde receives full punishment for Roberta's death from a legal system that considers outcome more important than intent. Eventually he is executed for murder. (Dreiser 1964; Moers 1969)

See also *American Tragedy, An;* Dreiser, Theodore; Finchley, Sondra

Gulliver's Travels

Gulliver's Travels, by Jonathan Swift, was published in 1726 as *Travels into Several Remote Nations of the World, by Lemuel Gulliver.* A satirical novel, it criticizes various aspects of British society in particular and human nature in general. The story takes place from 1699 to 1713. During this time the main character, Lemuel Gulliver, journeys to four different lands: Lilliput, Brobdingnag, Laputa, and Houyhnhnmland. In each place he compares and contrasts various social and political institutions with those in his native England.

Gulliver's adventure begins when he signs on as a ship's doctor. After setting sail for the South Seas, the vessel encounters a storm and is wrecked. Gulliver then swims to the nearest shore and collapses with exhaustion. When he wakes up, he finds himself tied with tiny ropes and learns that he is in a world ruled by six-inch-tall people. His captors, the Lilliputians, make him their prisoner, but when Gulliver behaves well and learns their language, he is set free. Later he helps them fight and defeat their enemies, the Blefuscudians. The Blefuscudians were once Lilliputians but fled to the nearby island of Blefuscu over a matter of principle: Lilliputian law declares that they must break eggs on the small end before eating them, whereas Blefuscudian tradition is to break eggs on the large end.

After Gulliver captures the Blefuscudian fleet, the Lilliputians' emperor wants to make the Blefuscudians into slaves. Gulliver convinces the Lilliputian Parliament to oppose the emperor. This makes Gulliver unpopular with the royal court but popular in Blefuscu. Later the emperor of Blefuscu alerts Gulliver to a plot against him. Gulliver escapes to Blefuscu and discovers a wrecked ship of his size there. The people of Blefuscu help him repair it, and he sails home.

Gulliver then embarks on a ship to India. The vessel is blown off course, and its sailors go ashore in a strange land to find food. Gulliver accompanies them but becomes separated from the group. He is captured by a giant farmer and becomes the pet of the man's nine-year-old daughter, who is 40 feet tall. Later the farmer displays Gulliver in the city, where the queen buys him. Gulliver and the king discuss the social, political, and philosophical differences between the giant land, Brobdingnag, and Great Britain. In addition, Gulliver experiences many dangers because of his small size. For example, he has to fight off giant rats and wasps. One day a giant bird picks up his tiny home and drops it in the sea, where a ship finds him.

Gulliver is soon back in England. Once again he signs up as a ship's doctor, and this time his vessel is attacked by pirates. He is set adrift, alone in a small boat, and lands on yet another strange shore. Shortly thereafter he notices a flying island hovering above the land. He receives permission to climb up to it and meets the people of Laputa. The Laputans are unrealistic, absentminded intellectuals, and Gulliver quickly grows tired of them. The Laputans lower him down to the continent of Balnibarbi, where he visits an academy where men work on impractical projects and inventions. From Balnibarbi Gulliver travels to the island of Glubbdubdrib, where many sorcerers live. They contact the spirit world and bring forth historical figures for Gulliver to question. He learns that

he has been harboring many misconceptions about these people and says:

> I was chiefly disgusted with modern history. For having strictly examined all the persons of greatest name in the courts of princes for an hundred years past, I found how the world had been misled by prostitute writers, to ascribe the greatest exploits in war to cowards, the wisest counsel to fools, sincerity to flatterers, Roman virtue to betrayers of their country, piety to atheists, chastity to sodomites, truth to informers. How many innocent and excellent persons had been condemned to death or banishment, by the practising of great ministers upon the corruption of judges, and the malice of factions. How many villains had been exalted to the highest places of trust, power, dignity, and profit; how great a share in the motions and events of courts, councils, and senates might be challenged by bawds, whores, pimps, parasites, and buffoons. How low an opinion I had of human wisdom and integrity, when I was truly informed of the springs and motives of great enterprises and revolutions in the world, and of the contemptible accidents to which they owned their success. (Swift 1960, 216)

Gulliver soon sails from Glubbdubdrib to the land of Luggnagg, where he meets a race of immortals, the struldbrugs. These people lose their legal rights and estates at age 80 and their teeth and hair at age 90. They are ugly, melancholy people with extremely poor memories, and their society does not want them around. In fact, their situation is so hideous that Gulliver thinks "no tyrant could invent a death into which I would not run with pleasure from such a life" (232). However, he agrees with the struldbrugs' legal oppression, saying, "Otherwise, as avarice is the necessary consequent of old age, those immortals would in time become proprietors of the whole nation and engross the civil power, which, for want of abilities to manage, must end in the ruin of the public" (232).

In this illustration from Gulliver's Travels, *Lemuel Gulliver finds himself in the land of Lilliput after surviving a shipwreck (Archive Photos).* Gulliver's Travels *critiques British society by comparing it to several imaginary cultures.*

From Luggnagg Gulliver travels to Japan and then to England. After a brief time there, he again boards a ship for the South Seas, this time as its captain. En route the crew mutinies and Gulliver is set adrift. He lands in a world of rational horses, called Houyhnhnm, and irrational apelike men, called Yahoos. He lives with the Houyhnhnms and tells them about England. They are horrified to learn about its wars, legal system, and other cruel customs.

Eventually they tell Gulliver that he must either live among the Yahoos or leave. He builds a boat, sets sail, and is picked up by a Portuguese ship. Back in England, he finds himself unable to stand his fellow man. He spends most of his time among his horses.

Gulliver's Travels expresses a great deal of hatred for humankind, and upon the book's publication some people pronounced its author mentally ill. Indeed, Swift was repulsed by the uncleanness of the human body and bathed frequently. But in an introduction to the work, scholar Marcus Cunliffe (xviii–xx) argues that this does not mean the man was insane:

> While certainly an unusual man, Swift was far from being a monster. He was *not* mentally unbalanced, although he did become senile toward the end of his long life. . . . The man himself . . . is not particularly gross or grotesque. Nor is the lesson imparted by *Gulliver's Travels*. Not all mankind is portrayed as worthless and bestial. Swift has no fault to find, for example, with the Portuguese sea captain whom Gulliver meets after leaving the Yahoos. Swift may be an ironist but he is not a cynic: he cares too deeply. . . . Men are fallible: they have also made things steadily worse for themselves. In other words, Swift assumes that in a former, yeoman order men had the dignity of simplicity. This has been spoiled by kings and tyrants, courts, pride, wealth. To the curse of original sin has been added the subordinate curse of sophistication.

(Swift 1960)

See also Science Fiction and Fantasy; Swift, Jonathan

H

Haller, Harry

The main character of Hermann Hesse's 1927 novel *Steppenwolf,* Harry Haller has trouble fitting in with bourgeois society. He thinks of his personality as being split in two, into a human part and a wolf part. As the novel progresses, he struggles to suppress his natural urges and eventually learns how important it is to release them. However, he also learns that when this release is uncontrolled, it results in chaos, both for the individual and for society. (Hesse 1963)

See also Hesse, Hermann; *Steppenwolf*

Handmaid's Tale, The

Published in 1985, *The Handmaid's Tale,* by feminist Margaret Atwood, is a futuristic story about the suppression of women. It is set in the late twentieth century in the United States, where religious fundamentalists have created their own country, the Republic of Gilead.

In Gilead women have no rights. Men have divided them into different classes, each with its own designated clothing color and societal role. For example, the Marthas, who wear green, are household servants. The Unwomen, who dress in gray, are political rebels whose punishment is to work in the pollution-plagued colonies outside of Gilead. The Aunts, all in brown, indoctrinate the red-clad Handmaids in their duties as sexual surrogates for the blue-clad Wives, who are the spouses of Gilead's leaders, the Commanders.

Environmental pollution and unusual viruses have made most women sterile. Since procreation is vital for the survival of the government, the Commanders have designated all fertile women as Handmaids. This idea was taken from the biblical story of Rachel, who cannot have a child but tells her husband, Jacob: "Behold my maid Bilhah, go into her; and she shall bear upon my knees, that I may also have children by her" (Genesis 30:1–3). Each Commander can therefore have both a Handmaid and a Wife, who is sterile. However, the two women are treated differently. Wives are highly esteemed in the community; Handmaids are considered vital but unworthy of respect. Moreover, once a baby is born, it becomes the Wife's child, and when the infant is three months old and weaned, the Handmaid is sent to another household.

The first-person narrator of *The Handmaid's Tale* has been forced to become a Handmaid against her will. Taken from her husband and daughter during the revolution that created Gilead, she is trained as a Handmaid and sent first to one Commander's home and then another. Like all Handmaids, she is given a name representative of the Commander to whom she belongs. The story begins with her as Offred, the new Handmaid of Commander Fred.

The Commander's Wife is a former television evangelist named Serena Joy. Serena hates Offred but suffers her presence because she desperately wants the status that comes with having a child. Serena also breaks some of Gilead's rules to try increasing Offred's chances of becoming pregnant. For example, a Handmaid's couplings with a Commander are supposed to take place only during a particular biblical ritual, with the Wife lying with the Handmaid on the bed. However, Serena encourages Offred and the Commander to meet more frequently in private. During these meetings the Commander offers Offred forbidden items, such as old magazines and scented soaps, and tells her that he wants her life to be bearable because her predecessor hanged herself. Offred believes that the Commander really wants an intimacy that she cannot give.

As time passes and Offred fails to get pregnant, Serena secretly arranges for her to have sex with the Commander's chauffeur, Nick. Offred and Nick develop a close relationship, and later they sneak off to meet on their own. In addition, the Commander smuggles Offred into a brothel to try exciting her. There she meets a former friend, Moira, who is now a prostitute. Moira talks about escaping Gilead. By this time Offred has discovered that another Handmaid, Ofglen, is a member of an underground antigovernment group called Mayday. One day she hears that Ofglen's activities have been discovered and that she has killed herself rather than be arrested. Offred falls into despair. Then some men in a government van come to arrest her. She is frightened until Nick whispers that they are actually members of Mayday, as is he, and have come to help her escape. She leaves hoping he is telling her the truth.

The novel ends with a section entitled "Historical Notes," which is "a partial transcript of the proceedings of the Twelfth Symposium on Gileadean Studies," dated June 25, 2195 (Atwood 1986, 299). In it keynote speaker James Pieixoto of Cambridge University reports that *The Handmaid's Tale* was transcribed from some ancient tapes discovered in a buried footlocker. Pieixoto then discusses Gilead as a historical era, comparing it to the restrictive regime of Iran during the same time period, and explains that an Underground Femaleroad helped women escape from Gilead into Canada. During this discussion he makes derogatory jokes about women, and his male audience laughs appropriately.

The Handmaid's Tale does not tell Offred's ultimate fate, nor does it say what became of Offred's husband when she became a Handmaid. At one point in the novel she says that she wants to believe he escaped capture. However, she fears that he was executed along with others who oppose Gilead's brutal theocracy. The novel makes it clear that in this new society men are as oppressed and unhappy as women; even Commander Fred wonders whether his elite group made the right decisions in creating Gilead.

The Handmaid's Tale also serves as a cautionary tale regarding the cashless, paperless society of the United States. The revolution that created Gilead succeeded largely because it took over the country's computers, including Compubank. One of the first actions of the new leaders was to cut off people's access to their savings accounts, making them dependent on their government for food and other necessities. Offred says: "If there had still been portable money, it would have been more difficult" (174). This kind of government control also appears in the novel *1984*, by George Orwell, another political novel set in the future, to which scholars often compare *The Handmaid's Tale*. (Atwood 1986; Grace 1980; McCombs 1988)

See also Atwood, Margaret; Feminism; Joy, Serena; *1984;* Offred; Orwell, George

Hansberry, Lorraine

Lorraine Hansberry wrote the first play by a black woman ever performed on Broadway. Entitled *A Raisin in the Sun,* it won numerous awards for its portrayal of a black working-class family rediscovering pride in its African heritage.

Hansberry was born on May 19, 1930, in Chicago, Illinois. Her father was a real estate agent who decided to take a stand against racist housing laws by moving the family into an all-white neighborhood. He eventually won a lawsuit to keep them there, but the struggle soured him on living in the United States, and he relocated the family to Mexico. Hansberry studied art there as well as in the United States. She also spent two years at the University of Wisconsin. In 1950 she settled in New York, where she began to write while working at a variety of odd jobs. With the production of *A Raisin in the Sun,* her success seemed assured; she was only 29, the youngest professional playwright in the United States. But while her second play, *The Sign in Sidney Brustein's Window,* was appearing on Broadway, she developed cancer. She died in New York on January 12, 1965, at the age of 35. (Cheney 1984; Hansberry 1994)

See also Racism; *Raisin in the Sun, A*

Hard Times

Hard Times (1854), by Charles Dickens, protests unfair living conditions among the working classes in nineteenth-century England. It also depicts narrow-mindedness among the aristocracy and middle class and shows how this type of thinking leads to unhappiness. The novel's main character, Thomas Gradgrind, runs a school in Coketown, England, that teaches nothing but facts. He abhors flights of fancy and is appalled to discover two of his children, Tom Jr. and Louisa, spying on some circus people. When this happens, he wonders what his friend Mr. Bounderby would think. Bounderby, a wealthy factory owner and banker, is very opinionated. He tells Gradgrind that the children's interest in the circus is the fault of their playmate, Sissy Jupe, whose father is a clown. After Sissy's father deserts her in order to give her a chance at a better life, Gradgrind takes the girl into his own household in hopes of reforming her.

Meanwhile Stephen Blackpool, a powerloom weaver at Bounderby's mill, is leading a miserable life. Dickens's portrait of Blackpool's oppression is an indictment of laws he believed unfair to the labor class. These laws result not only in harsh working conditions but also in difficult social problems. For example, although Blackpool's wife is a drunk, he does not have enough money to divorce her, and if he were to leave her, he would be judged too immoral to deserve a job. This situation makes Blackpool so desperate that for a brief moment he considers giving his wife poison.

Hard Times then jumps several years into the future. Tom Jr. is an employee at Bounderby's bank, and Bounderby has convinced Louisa to marry him. Shortly thereafter social unrest spreads through the town. A labor-union agitator, Slackbridge, tries to lead the workers, but he is just as corrupt as their employers. Blackpool is the only one who realizes this. Therefore, when he refuses to join the union, his fellow workers shun him. Blackpool is then summoned before Bounderby, who questions him about Slackbridge's activities. Blackpool tells him about the workers' problems, saying:

> Look round town—so rich as 'tis—and see the numbers o' people as has been broughten into bein heer, fur to weave, an' to card, an' to piece out a livin', aw the same one way, somehows, 'twixt their cradles and their graves. Look how we live, an' wheer we live, an' in what numbers, an' by what chances, and wi' what sameness; and look how the mills is awlus a goin, and how they never works us no nigher to onny dis'ant object—ceptin awlus, Death. Look how you considers of us, and writes of us, and talks of us, and goes up wi' yor deputations to Secretaries o' State 'bout us, and how you are awlus right, and how we are awlus wrong, and never had'n no reason in us sin ever we were born. Look how this ha' growen an' growen, Sir, bigger an' bigger, broader an' broader, harder and harder fro year to year, fro generation unto generation. Who can look on 't, Sir, and fairly tell a man 'tis not a muddle? (Dickens 1966, 114)

Bounderby's response is to say that he will have all agitators arrested. He then fires Blackpool for complaining about working conditions and labor politics.

After Blackpool leaves, Louisa, who has heard his conversation with her husband, goes to his house. Tom Jr. accompanies her. Louisa has never been among the poor before, and she has always thought of them as objects. Now she sees them as real people. Horrified by Blackpool's suffering, she gives him money. Then Tom Jr. pulls Blackpool aside and tells him he might be able to get the young man a bank job. Tom tells Blackpool to wait outside the bank each evening to be ready for his chance. Later the bank is robbed, and Stephen is suspected of the crime. Unfortunately, he cannot be found.

Meanwhile Louisa has met a young man, James Harthouse, who tries to woo her. He makes her realize how sterile her life with Mr. Bounderby really is. Upset, she goes to her father's house and asks Sissy to talk to Mr. Harthouse for her. Sissy convinces the man to leave Louisa alone, and he leaves town. Bounderby thinks that Louisa has left with him, and when he finds her at her father's house, he is angry. He tells her that their marriage will be over if she does not return home immediately. She remains with her father.

Now a bachelor again, Bounderby puts all his effort into finding the bank robber. He offers a reward for Blackpool's arrest. Eventually the young man is found lying at the bottom of an abandoned mine shaft. He has fallen in and been trapped there for several days. The townspeople pull him out, but it is clear he is dying. He professes his innocence, tells about Tom's request that he wait outside the bank, expresses his love for humankind, and dies. When Gradgrind hears about Tom's plot, he is disappointed in his son and the educational system that produced him. He finds Tom hiding at the circus and says he is going to send him away. A young man, Blitzer, interferes. Blitzer intends to take Tom back to Bounderby, not because he believes in justice but because it will earn him a promotion. Blitzer tells Gradgrind: "I am sure you know that the whole social system is a question of self-interest" (218). Nonetheless, the circus people help Tom escape. A final chapter forecasts the future of the characters, predicting a lonely death for Tom, a happy marriage for Sissy, and a life of social concern for Louisa.

When *Hard Times* was published, critics disagreed on its merit and significance. In a critical edition of the work, scholars George Ford and Sylvere Monod (330) report: "About none of [Dickens's] novels has there been less agreement. Some writers who generally admire Dickens, such as . . . [George Bernard] Shaw, have found *Hard Times* to be one of his most successful works; others, such as George Gissing, consider it a sorry failure. In one of his books on Dickens, Gissing remarks: 'Of *Hard Times*, I have said nothing; it is practically a forgotten book, and little in it demands attention.' This verdict, published in 1898, has been shared by many otherwise enthusiastic Dickensians" (330).

But in 1912 George Bernard Shaw wrote that *Hard Times* is far superior to another of Dickens's social protest novels, *Bleak House*, because it demonstrates a better understanding of Victorian social problems and the possible solutions for them. About these solutions, and Dickens's view of them, Shaw (334) writes:

> Whereas formerly men said to the victim of society who ventured to complain, "Go and reform yourself before you pretend to reform Society," it now has to admit that until Society is reformed, no man can reform himself except in the most insignificantly small ways. He may cease picking your pocket of half crowns; but he cannot cease taking a quarter of a million a year from the community for nothing at one end of the scale, or living under conditions in which health, decency, and gentleness are impossible at the other, if he happens to be born to such a lot.

In addition, Shaw refers to the "mercilessly faithful and penetrating exposures of English social, industrial, and political life" in *Hard*

Times and *Bleak House* (335). He says that Dickens assaults "the conscience of the governing class," adding, "*Hard Times* was written to make you uncomfortable" (335). (Cruikshank 1949; Dickens 1966; Fielding 1958; Gissing 1924; Hibbert 1967)

> See also *Bleak House;* Dickens, Charles; Gissing, George; Labor Issues; Poverty; Shaw, George Bernard

"Harlem, Montana: Just Off the Reservation"

The poem "Harlem, Montana: Just Off the Reservation," by Native American author James Welch, first appeared in his 1971 poetry collection *Riding the Earthboy 40.* It depicts the life of Native Americans in a town near a reservation, showing the prevalence of alcoholism, discrimination, and hopelessness. In Harlem "money is free if you're poor enough," and "booze is law" (Velie 1991, 238). (Velie 1991)

> See also Native American Issues; Welch, James

Harlem Renaissance

The term *Harlem Renaissance* refers to a period in American literary history from the 1920s to the early 1930s. At that time African-American authors, most of whom lived in the Harlem district of New York City, began writing about life in the United States from the black perspective, exploring issues of white racism and black pride. These authors include Countee Cullen, Alice Dunbar-Nelson, Lorraine Hansberry, Langston Hughes, Zora Neale Hurston, Nella Larsen, James Weldon Johnson, Eloise Bibb Thompson, and Jean Toomer. Their works were initially published by black magazines, but eventually they were supported by major publishing houses as well. Unfortunately, the economic hardships of the Great Depression decreased sales of black literature, effectively ending the Harlem Renaissance. (Huggins 1971)

> See also Cullen, Countee; Dunbar-Nelson, Alice; Great Depression; Hansberry, Lorraine; Hughes, Langston; Hurston, Zora Neale; Johnson, James Weldon; Larsen, Nella; Thompson, Eloise Bibb; Toomer, Jean

Heller, Joseph

Joseph Heller is the author of *Catch-22* (1961), a satirical antiwar novel set during World War II. He participated in this war himself as a bombardier for the U.S. Air Force. Born on May 1, 1923, in Brooklyn, New York, he received a master's degree at Columbia University in 1949 and studied at Oxford University as a Fulbright scholar from 1949 to 1950. He then taught for two years at Pennsylvania State University. Shortly thereafter he began writing advertisements for magazines. With the publication of *Catch-22* he became a freelance author. His subsequent works include the novels *Something Happened* (1974), *Good as Gold* (1979), and *God Knows* (1984), as well as the play *We Bombed in New Haven* (1968). In 1998 he published his memoirs entitled *Now and Then: From Coney Island to Here.* (Merrill 1987; Seed 1989)

> See also *Catch-22;* Peace

Hellman, Lillian

Lillian Hellman was a playwright and screenwriter who often used her work to protest prejudice and injustice in American society. Born on June 20, 1905, in New Orleans, Louisiana, she was married to playwright Arthur Kober from 1925 to 1932, but she divorced him because of her involvement with writer Dashiell Hammett, who became famous for his detective novels. Hellman first became famous herself for *The Children's Hour* (1934), a play concerning society's prejudice against lesbians. It was made into a movie in both 1936 and 1962. Hellman's subsequent social protest plays, which include *Days to Come* (1936), *The Little Foxes* (1939), and *Watch on the Rhine* (1941; film 1943), were also extremely popular. In addition to plays, Hellman edited story and letter collections and wrote several memoirs. One of these, *Scoundrel Time* (1976), tells of the persecution that she and other writers experienced during the McCarthy era. Hellman died on June 30, 1984, at Martha's Vineyard, Massachusetts. (Lederer 1979; Rollyson 1988; Wright 1986)

> See also *Children's Hour, The; Days to Come;* McCarthyism; *Watch on the Rhine*

Lillian Hellman receiving the Gold Medal of The National Institute of Arts and Letters, May 20, 1964 (Archive Photos)

Hesse, Hermann

German-Swiss author Hermann Hesse primarily wrote about the relationship between the individual and society. In doing so, he criticized many aspects of modern life. Born on July 2, 1877, in Calw, Germany, Hesse entered a seminary as a young man but left there to become a factory apprentice. Later he began working in a bookstore. In 1904 he became a freelance author and published his first novel, *Peter Camenzind.* His subsequent novels include *Unterm Rad* (Beneath the Wheel, 1906), *Demian* (1919), and *Siddhartha* (1922). During World War II Hesse moved to Switzerland, where he wrote essays and articles protesting German ideology and arguing for peace. In 1923 he became a naturalized citizen of Switzerland. After the publication of *Das Glaperlenspiel* (The Glass Bead Game) in 1943, Hesse abandoned long fiction and began writing essays, letters, poems, and short stories instead, and in 1946 he won the Nobel Prize in literature. He died on August 9, 1962, in Montagnola, Switzerland. (Hesse 1986; Ziolkowski 1965)

See also *Glass Bead Game, The;* Peace

Holbrook Family

An American pre-Depression-era family in Tillie Olsen's novel *Yonnondio: From the Thirties* (1974), the Holbrooks must deal with poverty on a daily basis. Jim, the head of the household, holds a series of jobs that place him in difficult working conditions, yet offer little income. His wife, Anna, suffers from poor health and despair. His daughter, Mazie, and sons, Will, Ben, Jim Junior, and Bess, have little hope for the future. There is barely enough money to feed them; their clothes are ragged, and they cannot afford an education. Moreover, Jim and Anna teach their children the common view of their time regarding sexual stereotypes: men and woman have different roles in life. As Deborah Rosenfelt says in her essay "From the Thirties: Tillie Olsen and the Radical Tradition" (Nelson and Huse 1994, 84–85):

> The conditioning of children to accept limiting sex roles is an important theme in *Yonnondio.* . . . Anna, full of her own repressed longings, imparts the lessons of sex

roles to her children. "Boys get to do that," she tells Benjy wistfully, talking of travel by trains and boats, "not girls" (113). And when Mazie asks her, "Why is it always me that has to help? How come Will gets to play?" Anna can only answer, "Willie's a boy" (142). Olsen, then, suggests throughout *Yonnondio* that both women and men are circumstanced to certain social roles, and that these roles, while placing impossible burdens of responsibility on working-class men, constrict the lives of women in particularly damaging ways.

(Nelson and Huse 1994; Olsen 1980)

See also Feminism; Great Depression; Labor Issues; Olsen, Tillie; *Yonnondio: From the Thirties*

Hood, Thomas

English poet Thomas Hood is the author of two of the most famous social protest poems ever written, "The Song of the Shirt" and "The Lay of the Labourer" (both 1825), which concern labor abuses and unemployment. Born in London, England, on May 23, 1799, Hood worked as a book engraver and then as a magazine editor before publishing his first volume of poetry, *The Plea of the Midsummer Fairies,* in 1827. His subsequent works include the humorous *Odes and Addresses to Great People* (1825). He died in London on May 3, 1845. (Walter 1968)

See also Labor Issues; Poverty; "Song of the Shirt, The"

"Hope Deferred"

The short story "Hope Deferred," by African-American author Alice Dunbar-Nelson, was originally published in the magazine *Source: The Crisis* in September 1914. Its main character is Louis Edwards, a civil engineer. Unable to find work because he is black, he becomes a waiter and endures abuse from the people he waits on. One day he loses his temper and attacks a man. He is arrested and sent to a county workhouse. Meanwhile the restaurant puts up a sign: "Waiters Wanted.

None but White Men Need Apply" (Roses and Randolph 1996, 90). "Hope Deferred" is representative of the author's work, which sought to depict racial prejudice and injustice in the United States. (Roses and Randolph 1996)

See also Dunbar-Nelson, Alice; Harlem Renaissance; Racism

House of the Spirits, The

The House of the Spirits, by Chilean author Isabel Allende, was originally published in Spain as *La casa de los espíritus* in 1982. Reprinted in the United States in 1985, the novel follows the lives of several members of the Trueba family, who live during a time of political turmoil in an unnamed South American country. The story is narrated by two characters: Esteban Trueba, who writes in the first person, and his granddaughter, who offers a third-person narrative based on the journals of her deceased grandmother, Esteban's wife, Clara.

Clara, daughter of politician Severo del Valle and his suffragette wife, Nívea, is a clairvoyant who can predict the future, speak with spirits, and make objects float into the air. She falls mute after witnessing the autopsy of her older sister, Rosa, who was killed by drinking poisoned wine meant for her father. Clara remains silent for nine years, until the day she announces that she is destined to marry Rosa's former fiancé, Esteban Trueba.

In the years since Rosa's death, Esteban, who grew up in poverty, has inherited an abandoned family ranch, Tres Marías, and turned it into a profitable enterprise. He spends much of his time raping young peasant women, including Pancha, the sister of his foreman, Pedro Segundo García. When Pancha becomes pregnant, Esteban becomes uninterested in her and decides to take a wife from his own social class. Returning to his hometown, he meets and marries Clara. Esteban and Clara have three children: Jaime, Nicolás, and Blanca. Esteban does not get along well with any of them, particularly after he becomes a senator from the Conservative Party, because they are involved in socialist activities. When

Jaime becomes a doctor for the poor, Esteban calls him a "hopeless loser" who has "no sense of reality" and has "put [his] faith in utopian values that don't even exist" (Allende 1985, 252). When Nicolás forms his own religious group and begins holding protests for religious freedom and civil rights, Esteban makes him leave the country. When Blanca becomes pregnant by socialist singer Pedro Tecero García, the son of her father's foreman, Esteban becomes enraged and attacks Pedro Tecero, cutting off three of the young man's fingers. He also beats Blanca and forces her to marry a French count, Jean de Satigny, but the marriage breaks up before Blanca's daughter, Alba, is born.

Alba does not learn the identity of her real father until she is a young woman. By this time she has become involved in socialist activities herself. Esteban, who is now a widower, ignores these activities because he loves his granddaughter dearly. However, he continues to be a vocal opponent of socialism, and when the Liberal Party defeats his Conservative Party in a major election, he works secretly to encourage a military coup. He believes that the military leaders will seize the government and return it to the conservative politicians. During the coup Esteban realizes he was wrong and that "this was not the best way to overthrow Marxism" (320). The military leaders prove themselves cruel and power-hungry; they assassinate the president and kill Esteban's son Jaime, who had become the president's friend and doctor. They also take Alba away for questioning because she has become the girlfriend of a socialist leader. Alba's interrogation is handled by Esteban García, the grandson of Pancha García and Esteban Trueba, who is angry that Alba has taken his place as Esteban Trueba's acknowledged grandchild. Esteban García therefore tortures Alba unnecessarily. He and his men continually rape and abuse her until her grandfather finally arranges for her release. Now pregnant, she returns to live with Esteban Trueba, who dies shortly after writing his life story in the presence of his wife's spirit. Alba is alone because her mother has left the country with Pedro Tecero García,

yet she is comforted by reading her grandmother's journals. She begins to recite her story, and the last line of *The House of the Spirits* is therefore the same as the first.

Although the novel primarily focuses on family relationships, there are social protest elements throughout. Clara's suffragette mother, who would "chain herself with other ladies to the gates of Congress and the Supreme Court" (58), is a vocal supporter of women's rights. Clara's husband opposes such activities, considering them "a degrading spectacle that made all their husbands look ridiculous" (58). Esteban also criticizes socialism, communism, and Marxism, which he calls a "cancer" that must be stopped (260). In addition, he argues that the poor do not deserve charity because "those people don't even try. It's very easy to stretch out your hand and beg for alms!" He says he believes only "in effort and reward" (117).

Moreover, when Esteban discovers that Pedro Tecero García has been handing out pamphlets to the peasants of Tres Marías advocating "Sundays off, a minimum wage, retirement and health plans, maternity leave for women, elections without coercion, and . . . a peasant organization that would confront the owners," he whips him (133). But Pedro Tecero will not stop distributing his socialist literature. By this time World War II is under way, and Pedro tells Blanca "about what was going on the rest of the world and in the country, about the distant war that had sent half of humanity into a hail of shrapnel, and an agony of concentration camps, and produced a flood of widows and orphans. He spoke of the workers of Europe and the United States, whose rights were respected because the slaughter of organizers and Socialists of the preceding decades has led to laws that were more just and republics that were governed properly" (147).

The novel's most powerful social protest passages come after the socialists gain power and are destroyed by the conservative-supported military coup. At that time "the upper middle class and the economic right, who had favored the coup, were euphoric. . . . They thought the loss of democratic freedom would be temporary and that it was possible to go without individual or collective rights for a while so long as the regime respected the tenets of free enterprise" (326). However, they soon realized that the military regime wanted to remain in power forever and had no concern for human rights. In the concluding chapters, entitled "The Terror" and "The Hour of Truth," and the "Epilogue," *The House of the Spirits* offers vivid descriptions of military cruelty, torture, and murder. (Allende 1985; Hart 1989; Rojas and Rehbein, 1991)

See also Allende, Isabel; Communism; De Satigny, Alba Trueba; Del Valle, Clara; Feminism; García, Esteban; García, Pedro Tecero; Socialism; Trueba, Esteban

Houston, Ely

The character Ely Houston appears in Richard Wright's 1953 novel *The Outsider*. A white district attorney in New York, he is trying to understand racism and the black experience. He questions a black intellectual, Cross Damon, about this, and the two have many interesting discussions. For example, Houston says:

The way Negroes were transported to this country and sold into slavery, then stripped of their tribal culture and held in bondage; and then allowed, so teasingly and over so long a period of time, to be sucked into our way of life is something which resembles the rise of all men from whatever it was we all came from. . . . We are not now keeping the Negro on such a short chain and they are slowly entering into our cultures. But that is not the end of this problem. It is the beginning. . . . Negroes, as they enter our culture, are going to inherit the problems we have, but with a difference. They are outsiders and they are going to *know* that they have these problems. They are going to be self-conscious; they are going to be gifted with a double vision, for, being Negroes, they are going to be both *inside* and *outside* of our culture at the same time. Every emo-

tional and cultural convulsion that ever shook the heart and soul of Western man will shake them. Negroes will develop unique and specially defined psychological types. They will become psychological men, like the Jews. . . . They will not only be Americans or Negroes; they will be centers of *knowing*, so to speak. (Wright 1993b, 164–165)

Houston remains fascinated by Cross Damon throughout the novel, and when he learns that Damon is a murderer, he is even more fascinated by what has become of this intellectual outsider. As Damon is dying of a bullet wound, Houston continues to quiz him about the nature of his experience. (Wright 1993b)

See also Damon, Cross; *Outsider, The;* Wright, Richard

Howe, Julia Ward

Julia Ward Howe was a poet and social reformer best known for writing "The Battle Hymn of the Republic." This hymn, which was adopted as a marching song for the North during the U.S. Civil War, was first published

Julia Ward Howe, mid-nineteenth century (Photo by J. E. Purdy/Library of Congress)

in the magazine *Atlantic Monthly* in February 1862. Howe was born in New York City on May 27, 1819. She and her husband, Samuel Grinley Howe, edited a Boston newspaper, *Commonwealth,* that advocated the end of slavery. Howe was also dedicated to promoting women's rights. In this regard she served as president of both the New England Woman Suffrage Association and the Association for the Advancement of Women. In her later years she became an activist for prison reform and world peace. In addition to her lectures and essays on social reform issues, she continued to write poetry and was the first woman elected to the American Academy of Arts and Letters. She died on October 17, 1910, in Newport, Rhode Island. (Clifford 1979)

See also Feminism; Slavery

Howl

Published in 1956, *Howl* is American poet Allen Ginsberg's outcry against society's suppression of individuality and personal exploration. The poem is divided into three parts, the first of which is a listing of the different ways that people look for excitement and meaning through sex, drugs, music, and religion. Its second part, which Ginsberg admits he wrote while under the influence of drugs, is an indictment of a society that makes people feel insane for wanting to satisfy their natural urges. Its third section is an expression of unity with an individual, Carl Solomon, driven mad by society and confined to a mental institution.

In a letter discussing this work, Ginsberg (Miles 1995, 152) writes that, contrary to many people's opinions, *Howl* is not a "negative howl of protest." He explains:

> The title notwithstanding, the poem itself is an act of sympathy, not rejection. In it I am leaping *out* of a preconceived notion of social "values," following my own heart's instincts—*allowing* myself to follow my own heart's instincts, overturning any notion of propriety, moral "value," superficial "maturity," . . . and exposing my true feelings—of sympathy and identification

with the rejected, mystical, individual even "mad."

> I am saying that what seems "mad" in America is our expression of natural ecstasy . . . which suppressed, finds no social form organization background frame of reference or rapport or validation from the outside and so the "patient" gets confused thinks he is mad and really goes off rocker. I am paying homage to mystical mysteries in the forms in which they actually occur here in the U.S. in our environment.

> I have taken a leap of detachment from the Artificial preoccupations and preconceptions of what is acceptable and normal and given my yea to the specific types of madness listed in the [first part of the poem].

Ginsberg catalogs this madness in passionate, raw language—language that led to the arrest of the poem's publisher, Lawrence Ferlinghetti, on charges of distributing obscenity. During Ferlinghetti's trial lawyers from the American Civil Liberties Union defended the poem's literary value, and eventually it was judged not to be an obscene work; Ferlinghetti was found not guilty. (Merrill 1969; Miles 1995)

See also Beat Movement; Censorship; Ferlinghetti, Lawrence; Ginsberg, Allen

Hughes, Langston

James Mercer Langston Hughes was an African-American poet who protested racism in much of his work. Born on February 1, 1902, in Joplin, Missouri, he was raised by his mother and lived in several different cities. He graduated from a Cleveland, Ohio, high school in 1921, the same year his first poem, "The Negro Speaks of Rivers," was published in the magazine *Crisis.* Hughes then began attending New York's Columbia University, but he left there after only one year to become a ship's steward. After traveling to Africa and back, he became a busboy in Washington, D.C. One day he left some of his poems at the table of American poet Vachel Lindsay, and the next morning the newspapers were report-

Langston Hughes (Archive Photos)

ing Lindsay's praise for Hughes's work. As a result, Hughes received a scholarship to Lincoln University in Pennsylvania. He graduated in 1929, by which time he had already published two books of verse, *The Weary Blues* (1926) and *Fine Clothes to the Jew* (1927). In 1930 he published his first prose work, *Not without Laughter* (1930), and in 1931 he coauthored a play, *Mule Bone,* with Zora Neale Hurston. He published a collection of short stories, *The Ways of White Folks,* in 1934 and an autobiography in 1940.

In later years he not only continued to write poetry, stories, and plays, but also authored essays, anthology collections, poetry translations, song lyrics, a history book, and a newspaper column. Hughes traveled extensively throughout the world, and in 1937 he reported on the Spanish Civil War as a newspaper correspondent. His most famous work, however, was the poem "Harlem," published in 1951 as part of a poetry collection entitled *Montage of a Dream Deferred.* This collection addresses various aspects of life in the black community of Harlem, New York. Despite his travels, Hughes remained very attached to this community throughout his life. He died in New York, New York, on May 22, 1967. (Emanuel 1967; Hughes 1958; Muller 1986; O'Daniel 1971)

   See also Harlem Renaissance; Hurston, Zora Neale; *Montage of a Dream Deferred;* Racism

Hugo, Victor

Born on February 26, 1802, in Besançon, France, Victor Hugo originally intended to be a lawyer. He attended law school in Paris but had a difficult time with his studies. In 1819 he founded a literary review, *Conservateur Litteraire,* and began contributing essays and articles to it. He published a book of poetry in 1822. It expressed his royalist views and therefore earned the praise of King Louis XVIII, who awarded Hugo a pension.

In 1823 Hugo began publishing novels as well as poems and plays. His best-known novels are *Notre-Dame de Paris* (The Hunchback of Notre-Dame, 1831) and *Les Misérables* (1862), but the amount of creative work he produced during his lifetime is extremely large. He was also a politician and political writer who protested many aspects of French society, including censorship and capital punishment. In 1841 he was elected to the French Academy, but ten years later he fled France when the government changed hands. He lived first in Brussels and then on the island of Jersey in the English Channel. Later he moved to the neighboring island of Guernsey.

Hugo returned to Paris in 1871 when the French Third Republic began, having added considerably to his body of work while in exile. His writings during this time include a great deal of poetry, much of it political in nature. In Paris he had become a national hero, and he was elected senator. However, his personal life was marked by tragedies. While a young man, he had married and had five children; one died in 1843, another in 1871, and another in 1873. His wife died in 1868 and his mistress in 1885. Hugo himself died in 1885 after suffering from cerebral palsy for seven years. He was buried in the Pantheon during a national funeral. (Houston 1975; Richardson 1976; Swinburne 1970)

See also *Misérables, Les*

Human Comedy, The

Published in France as *La Comédie humaine* between 1829 and 1847, *The Human Comedy,* by Honoré de Balzac, is a collection of approximately 90 novels and novellas that take place between 1308 and 1846. In writing them, Balzac wanted to trace the social and political history of France and show how the French Revolution affected the life of the country rather than the lives of individuals. He therefore set his stories among many types of people. According to scholar Felicien Marceau (1966, 12), Balzac used 2,472 characters to "depict the whole of society, town and country, Court and commerce, the world of high finance and the world of the press, of the law courts, of the moneylenders, of the drapers and of the tarts."

The individual novels of *The Human Comedy* can be read in any order. As Marceau (6) explains: "To Balzac, each one of his novels had its own separate meaning and internal unity. In each one of them, we are always provided with all the indispensable data necessary to understand it." However, characters do recur, and sometimes secondary characters in one novel become main characters in another. Therefore, Marceau (7) says that each novel "is a novel with windows onto a larger world—a novel with avenues, prospects, paths continually leading out of it if we choose to take them."

Balzac himself said that his novels fall into three general categories: *études analytiques* (analytic studies), which deal with the principles of human society; *études philosophiques* (philosophical studies), which deal with the reasons behind human activities; and *études de moeurs* (studies of manners), which show the results of human activities. In each of these categories Balzac criticizes social conventions. Scholar Samuel Rogers (1953, ix) explains that Balzac "lived through and described an exceptionally crowded and interesting period. The air was full of social and political, religious and aesthetic ideas and systems, merging into each other or struggling against each other. There is hardly one of these that is not reflected in *La Comédie humaine.*"

Balzac's novels protest many aspects of the social system prevalent in postrevolutionary France. For example, Balzac particularly objected to the demise of the aristocracy, believing that only through wealth could intellectualism and great art thrive. Many of his novels therefore present ambitious, yet poor men who find it difficult to succeed in an increasingly materialistic world. (Butler 1983; Marceau 1966; Rogers 1953)

See also Balzac, Honoré de; Class, Social

Hunt, Alonzo ("Fonny")

A 22-year-old black man in James Baldwin's 1974 novel *If Beale Street Could Talk,* Fonny Hunt has been falsely imprisoned for a crime he did not commit. While in prison awaiting trial, he gains strength from the love of his

19-year-old pregnant fiancée, Clementine "Tish" Rivers. According to Baldwin biographer David Leeming (1994, 122), Fonny represents "victims who have nonetheless found some reason for remaining alive in the social prison in which they find themselves." In addition, Leeming compares Fonny, who is a gifted sculptor, to Tish's unborn child, saying, "The baby in Tish's womb is a prisoner yearning to be free as surely as her lover is a man in bondage longing to become himself through his love and his art" (325). (Baldwin 1988; Leeming 1994)

See also Baldwin, James; *If Beale Street Could Talk;* Racism; Rivers, Clementine ("Tish")

Hurston, Zora Neale

Zora Neale Hurston is the author of what many scholars consider to be the first African-American feminist novel. She was born in Eatonville, Florida, on January 7 sometime between 1898 and 1903. (Records are unclear, and Hurston herself refused to reveal her true age.) Her mother died when she was 9, and her father, a carpenter and Baptist preacher, quickly remarried. Hurston hated her stepmother and began living with other relatives. At 16 she joined a Gilbert and Sullivan traveling theater group as a wardrobe girl. She left the troupe 18 months later, in Baltimore, when she decided she needed an education. In 1920 she received an associate degree from Howard University. The following year, while continuing her education, she published her first short story, "John Redding Goes to Sea," in a campus literary magazine. She then began submitting stories to *Opportunity: A Journal of Negro Life,* which was published by the National Urban League. Her work was not only published but also won her awards in the magazine's literary contest.

In 1925 Hurston decided to become a full-time writer and moved to New York, the home of many prominent black literary figures. She also became a student at Barnard College on a full scholarship. Always before Hurston had struggled to pay for her tuition, working as a manicurist, waitress, or secretary. Now she could completely devote herself to her education. She quickly became fascinated with the social sciences and chose to perform research studies for anthropologist Franz Boas. She began to collect black folklore not only in New York but also in the South. Meanwhile, she continued to publish many more short stories, as well as articles about black history. In 1930 she collaborated on a play, *Mule Bone,* with noted black author Langston Hughes; however, the two quarreled and the play was left unfinished until after their deaths.

Hurston's first novel, *Jonah's Gourd Vine,* was published in 1934, followed by a collection of folktales, *Of Mules and Men,* in 1935. She then went to Haiti to study Haitian folklore and voodoo. While there she wrote her most famous novel, *Their Eyes Were Watching God,* which was published after her return to the United States in 1937. Over the next several years Hurston wrote more novels, short stories, and plays. She worked as a college drama teacher in 1939 and as a story consultant for Paramount Pictures in 1941. She also became involved in race-related politics. In 1942 she published her autobiography, *Dust Tracks on a Road,* which received the Anisfield-Wolf Book Award in Race Relations. But despite her success, Hurston was experiencing financial difficulties and remained poor even after the publication of a new novel, *Seraph on the Suwanee* (1948). She started working as a maid, then a librarian, than a substitute teacher. In 1959 after suffering a stroke, she was forced to enter a welfare home in Florida, and after she died there on January 28, 1960, she was buried in an unmarked grave. In 1973 author Alice Walker searched for the grave and provided it with a headstone, subsequently publishing an article in *Ms.* magazine entitled "In Search of Zora Neale Hurston" (1975), which revived interest in Hurston's work. (Hemenway 1977; Hurston 1990; Lyons 1990)

See also Feminism; Hughes, Langston; Racism; *Their Eyes Were Watching God;* Walker, Alice

Huxley, Aldous

English novelist Aldous Leonard Huxley is best known for his science fiction novel *Brave*

New World (1932), about a distant time when people are scientifically engineered to fulfill predetermined roles. By suggesting a dark future, the novel criticizes politics and technology in the twentieth century.

Huxley was born on July 26, 1894, in Godalming, Surrey, England. His grandfather was a noted biologist, his father a prominent biographer. In 1916 Aldous graduated from Balliol College in Oxford and began writing for the journal *Athenaeum*. He became a freelance writer in 1921. His first novel, *Chrome Yellow,* was published the same year. Subsequent works include *Antic Hay* (1923), *Eyeless in Gaza* (1936), and *The Devils of Loudun* (1952). He died on November 22, 1963, in Los Angeles, California. (Atkins 1968; Brander 1970; Watts 1969)

See also *Brave New World*

Hydra Head, The

Set in Mexico City, *La cabeza de la hidra* (The Hydra Head), by Carlos Fuentes, is a 1978 spy thriller that criticizes the backroom politics of Mexico and the Israeli-Palestinian conflict in the Middle East during the 1970s. Much of the intrigue in the novel revolves around Israel's desire to reclaim its ancient lands in Palestine. The atrocities that Israeli agents commit against the Palestinians is likened to those that Adolf Hitler committed against the Jewish people when he took over Germany.

The main character of *The Hydra Head* is Felix Maldonado, a Mexican convert to Judaism. Felix works as the chief of the Bureau of Cost Analysis for Mexico's Ministry of Economic Development and is an expert on the country's nationalized oil industry. One day a powerful government official, the director general of Mexico, tells him that his name will be used in conjunction with a crime. In exchange for his name, Felix will get a new identity and passport for himself and his wife, Ruth, as well as a great deal of money. Felix does not want to cooperate with the director general, but it is not clear whether he has a choice in the matter.

At the same time Felix is preparing to attend an important government function, an awards ceremony for the National Prizes in Arts and Sciences, where the president of Mexico will honor Felix's former economics professor, Professor Bernstein. The director general's henchman, an Arab named Simon Ayub, tells Felix not to go to the ceremony. Felix's wife, Ruth, asks him not to go because Sara Klein is going to be there. Felix was once in love with Sara, but he lost touch with her when she moved to Palestine to become a teacher. Felix is upset to learn that Sara is now Bernstein's lover.

Felix was also once sexually involved with a woman named Mary, who is now married to a wealthy man named Abie Benjamin. All of the people closest to Felix—Ruth, Mary, Sara, Abie, Professor Bernstein—are part of Mexico's Jewish community. It is Felix's connection to this community that caused the director general to want his identity. The director general has arranged for a sharpshooter to assassinate the president of Mexico at the precise moment that Felix steps forward to shake the man's hand during the awards ceremony. In the ensuing confusion someone from the crowd will put a gun in Felix's hand, and he will be accused of being an Israeli agent. He will then "die" in prison. The director general believes that this event will cause Mexico to cut all ties with the Israelis, who are battling with the Arabs over who should possess Palestine and that Mexico will then join the Organization of Petroleum Exporting Countries, which regulates oil production. Only a few years earlier, in 1973, scientists discovered a huge oil reserve in Mexico.

The director general's plan fails when Felix faints before reaching the president. No assassination occurs, but the director general still uses the incident to his advantage. He shows the president Felix's gun and tells him that the Israelis are trying to kill him. The still-unconscious Felix is taken to jail, where he is switched with a dead man of similar appearance and subjected to plastic surgery to change his face. When he awakes, he finds that his family and friends think him dead and have already attended his funeral.

Felix escapes from the hospital and learns that Sara Klein has been killed. Shortly thereafter he contacts a mysterious friend named Timon, who is the head of a new spy agency that operates in Mexico but is independent of the Mexican government. At this point the novel begins to use the first person, as Timon reveals that he is the one who provided the preceding third-person narration of Felix's predicament.

Felix is actually an agent working for Timon. In that capacity he proceeds to unravel the mystery surrounding Sarah's death and his own loss of identity. He learns that Professor Bernstein is working as a spy for the Israelis and has uncovered very detailed information about the Mexican oil fields. This information has been placed holographically in the large stone of Bernstein's ring, so that it can be delivered to spies in the United States. With this information, if the Arabs shut off oil to Israel and the United States, the United States would know where to find oil in Mexico. Professor Bernstein believes that with enough economic incentive, Mexico could be convinced to denationalize its oil industry, so that private industry could harvest this reserve.

Through some very complicated maneuvers that result in several deaths, Felix manages to retrieve the ring and get it to Timon. He also learns that Mary and Abie Benjamin, as well as his own wife, Ruth, are Israeli agents and were responsible for Sara Klein's death. Sara had learned that the Israelis were committing atrocities against the Palestinians, and she was planning to expose Bernstein's in-

volvement in them. Sara had become intimate with the professor just to gather information. Her real boyfriend was a young Palestinian who was helping her in her efforts. He was killed and buried in Felix's grave.

Without friends and family Felix takes a new name and once again begins working as an economist at the Ministry of Economic Development. The director general believes that Felix will be acting as a spy for him, whereas Timon is convinced that Felix will continue to work as a spy for his independent agency. At the end of the novel Felix, now Diego Vasquez, is at a public ceremony, walking toward the president to shake his hand. (Faris 1983; Fuentes 1978)

See also Fuentes, Carlos; Justice; Maldonado, Felix

Hyer, Aunt Ri'

The character of Aunt Ri' Hyer appears in Helen Hunt Jackson's 1885 novel *Ramona*, which concerns the plight of California's Native Americans during the late 1880s. A settler from Tennessee, Aunt Ri' is prejudiced against all Indians, believing them to be lazy and ignorant. Then she meets Alessandro and Ramona, a young Indian couple who are good, hard-working, intelligent people. Slowly her perceptions begin to change. She becomes their friend and later visits an Indian village. Afterward she complains to an agent from the U.S. government that Native Americans deserve better treatment. (Jackson 1988)

See also Jackson, Helen Hunt; *Ramona*

I

Ibsen, Henrik

Norwegian playwright Henrik Ibsen criticized human nature and social conventions during the nineteenth century. His best-known work is *En dukkehjem* (A Doll's House, 1879), in which a wife keeps secrets from her husband meant to protect him and then leaves him when he castigates her for doing so. At the time the play was produced, this woman's declaration of independence shocked theater audiences.

Ibsen was born on March 20, 1828, in Skien, Norway. His father, once a prosperous merchant, went bankrupt in 1836. Seven years later the 15-year-old Ibsen left home to become apprentice to an apothecary. In 1850 he entered the university in Christiania (now Oslo) and became involved in its theater. The following year he was appointed the director and playwright for a theater in Bergen, Norway, and from 1857 to 1862 he took the same position at the Christiania Theater. (Roberts 1974; Rose 1973)

See also *Doll's House, A;* Feminism

Henrik Ibsen, c. 1895 (Corbis-Bettmann)

Iceman Cometh, The

The Iceman Cometh is a four-act tragedy by Eugene O'Neill. Written in 1939, it was first produced and published in 1946. The play's main theme is that human beings need to deceive themselves about their lives and their natures; otherwise they will succumb to despair and self-destructive acts. However, in presenting this theme, *The Iceman Cometh* depicts an anarchist who acts not out of political convictions but for emotional reasons rooted in his childhood. This character is Don Parritt, whose mother has been involved with the anarchist movement since before he was born. One day his mother is arrested for participating in an anarchist bombing. Parritt, who says he is being sought by police himself, moves into a rooming house connected to a New York saloon. In the bar he encounters a group of friends who have gathered for a birthday party. One of these men, Theodore Hickman, confronts each party guest individually and forces all of them to see the reality of their lives. When Parritt is confronted, he admits that he turned in the bombing group to the law. He says:

> I want you to understand the reason. You see, I began studying American history. I got to admiring Washington and Jefferson and Jackson and Lincoln. I began to feel patriotic and love this country. I saw it was the best government in the world, where everybody was equal and had a chance. I saw that all the ideas behind the Movement came from a lot of Russians . . . and were meant for Europe, but we didn't need them here in a democracy where we were free already. I didn't want this country to be destroyed for a damned foreign pipe dream. After all, I'm from old American pioneer stock. I began to feel I was a traitor for helping a lot of cranks and bums and free women plot to overthrow our government. (O'Neill 1967, 686)

At the same time Parritt insists that he never thought his mother would be arrested, too, and that he feels terrible about it. Hickman does not accept this explanation, and Parritt soon changes his story. Now he says that he turned informant for money. Nevertheless, Hickman remains skeptical. In the end Parritt confesses that he became an informant specifically so his mother would get arrested. He has hated her all his life. Once this truth is revealed, he decides to commit suicide, saying: "I can see now it's the only possible way I can ever get free from her. I guess I've really known that all my life. . . . It ought

to comfort Mother a little, too. It'll give her the chance to play the great incorruptible Mother of the Revolution, whose only child is the Proletariat. She'll be able to say: 'Justice is done! So may all traitors die!' She'll be able to say: 'I am glad he's dead! Long live the Revolution!'" (751).

Parritt then hangs himself, and in so doing, he shows the weakness of any social or political movement: its members are flawed, emotional human beings with self-serving motives. Meanwhile Hickman reveals that he, too, is flawed, having just come from killing his own wife. (Clark 1947; O'Neill 1967)

See also Anarchism; O'Neill, Eugene

If Beale Street Could Talk

Written in 1974 by African-American author James Baldwin, *If Beale Street Could Talk* deals with racism and false imprisonment in Harlem, New York. According to biographer David Leeming (1994, 325), the novel was "Baldwin's answer in this period of his career to the deficiency in the protest novel, his attempt to 'make this tradition articulate. . . . For a tradition expresses . . . nothing more than the long and painful experience of a people; it comes out of the battle waged to maintain their integrity or . . . out of their struggle to survive.'"

In addition, Leeming (323) explains that Baldwin used prison as a metaphor: "Prisoners were those who were deprived of their birthright in the unfeeling and unseeing prison that was racism in America." Therefore, *If Beale Street Could Talk* was "the natural illustration and culmination of [Baldwin's] long meditation on psychological, emotional, and intellectual imprisonment" (323).

The novel's first-person narrator is Clementine "Tish" Rivers, a pregnant 19-year-old black woman whose 22-year-old fiancé, Alonzo "Fonny" Hunt, has been arrested for a crime he did not commit. Prior to his arrest, Fonny and Tish were being harassed by a racist white policeman, Officer Bell, who later insisted that he saw Fonny running away from the scene of a rape. Bell also convinced the victim that Fonny was her attacker, even though Fonny was not in the neighborhood when the crime occurred.

While Fonny is in prison awaiting trial, Tish and her family work to help with his defense. Tish visits him in prison every day, promising him that he will be free by the time their child is born, and Tish's sister, Ernestine, engages a young white lawyer, Mr. Hayward, to represent him. Tish's father, Joseph, and Fonny's father, Frank, both begin stealing to pay for Fonny's legal expenses. They keep their activities a secret from Fonny's mother and two sisters, who hate Fonny and undermine his case by telling the district attorney's office that he has always been a bad person.

As the trial approaches, Ernestine investigates Officer Bell's background. When she learns that he was transferred to Harlem from Manhattan because he had killed a 12-year-old black boy there, she believes that this information can be used to discredit him as a witness. At the same time Hayward asks Tish's mother, Sharon, to visit the victim, who is living in Puerto Rico until the trial. Sharon goes there but cannot convince the woman to change her story. However, under Sharon's pressure the woman suffers a miscarriage, goes insane, and disappears. Hayward therefore asks the district attorney to drop the case. He refuses, merely postponing the trial until the woman can be found; however, the judge does grant Hayward's request that Fonny be released on bail. Joseph, Frank, and Ernestine struggle to raise the bail money, but Frank is caught stealing and loses his job. Ashamed, he commits suicide as Tish goes into labor.

Fonny's dysfunctional father, mother, and sisters contrast harshly with Tish's family, who, according to Leeming (347), "through their African-American identity have achieved genuine strength in the face of the harsh realities of their life." In this regard the Rivers "represent community, the only possibility of survival in a hostile white world that cannot see humanity in blackness. . . . Never the sweet-talking victims exuding humility . . . they are angry, determined, hard-talking . . . people who . . . 'endure' . . . actively, by fighting back from the fortress of their self-respect

and their love for each other" (324). Leeming (325) concludes that they are "representative of Baldwin's private hopes and of the hope of all those strangers in the 'house of bondage.'" (Baldwin 1988; Leeming 1994)

See also Baldwin, James; Hunt, Alonzo ("Fonny"); Racism; Rivers, Clementine ("Tish")

Immigrant Communities

Throughout history residents of immigrant communities have had to struggle against poverty and racial discrimination. These struggles have been depicted in two important works of social protest, *The Jungle,* by Upton Sinclair, and *Children of the Ghetto,* by Israel Zangwill. John Steinbeck showed similar difficulties among migrant farmworkers in his novel *The Grapes of Wrath.*

See also Anti-Semitism; *Children of the Ghetto; Grapes of Wrath, The; Jungle, The;* Poverty; Racism; Sinclair, Upton; Steinbeck, John

Imoinda

Imoinda is the black heroine of the 1688 novel *Oroonoko* by Aphra Behn. She is beautiful, kind, and highly moral. One day an African prince, Oroonoko, asks her to marry him and she agrees. But before the ceremony can take place, Oroonoko's grandfather, the king, forces Imoinda to marry him instead. The king then sells her into slavery when he discovers she has given herself to Prince Oroonoko.

Later Oroonoko is also enslaved. At a South American slave colony he discovers Imoinda, called Clemene by her white masters, and marries her. Imoinda soon becomes pregnant, but she is unhappy that her child will not be born free. She and Prince Oroonoko run away from the colony. When the Europeans find them, Imoinda fights bravely beside her husband. Nonetheless, they are recaptured, and Imoinda allows her husband to kill her, so that their child will not be born a slave. (Behn 1973)

See also Behn, Aphra; *Oroonoko;* Racism

Indian Reservations

See Native American Issues

Intimation of Things Distant, An

An Intimation of Things Distant is a 1992 collection of short stories by Nella Larsen, who wrote about black women and racism at the time of the Harlem Renaissance. This collection contains two of her novellas, *Quicksand* and *Passing*, which were first published in 1928 and 1929, respectively. *Quicksand* is the story of Helga Crane, a mixed-race woman hated by her family because of her black skin. Throughout the novella Helga struggles with issues of self-acceptance and racism. *Passing* concerns a mixed-race woman, Clare Kendry, who cannot accept her color. She passes herself off as a white woman to gain acceptance in society.

An Intimation of Things Distant also includes the short stories "The Wrong Man" and "Freedom," which were first published in *Young's Magazine* in 1926. Neither of these concerns racism. However, another story, "Sanctuary," is the story of a black man, Jim Hammer, who asks a friend's mother, Annie Poole, to hide him from the police. She does so, and when the police arrive, she learns that they believe Jim has just murdered her son. Jim expects Annie to turn him in. Instead, she keeps his location a secret, and once the police have gone, she tells him to "nevah stop thankin' yo' Jesus he done gib you dat black face" (Roses and Randolph 1996, 14). Annie recognizes the need for racial solidarity regardless of its personal cost, and she has learned that a black man cannot be assumed guilty just because white lawmen are chasing him.

"Sanctuary" initially appeared in *Forum* magazine in 1931, but its publication brought Larsen a great deal of trouble. She was accused of plagiarizing the work and had to defend herself. Although she was eventually exonerated, none of her later stories was ever published. (Larsen 1992; Roses and Randolph 1996)

See also Feminism; Larsen, Nella; Racism

Invisible Man

Ralph Ellison's 1952 novel *Invisible Man* depicts the identity crisis of American blacks at the beginning of the civil rights movement. Set in Harlem, New York, during the late 1940s and early 1950s, it offers the first-person narrative of an unnamed small-town southern black whose idealism is gradually destroyed by the reality of big-city politics.

The novel opens with a prologue in which the narrator explains that he is literally invisible, not because of some "biochemical accident to [his] epidermis" but because his true self is unknown and therefore unrecognized by a predominantly white society (Ellison 1952, 3). He lives alone and friendless in a dark basement illuminated by 1,369 light bulbs, stealing his electricity through illegal wiring. For him these lights illuminate the truth.

The narrator then flashes back to the time of his high school graduation. A naïve young man in a small southern town, he gives a speech extolling humility and social responsibility to a group of racist local businessmen, who award him a scholarship to the State College for Negroes. There he gets into trouble by driving a white trustee past some lower-class black homes, even though the white man requested it. The college president, Mr. Bledsoe, believes that blacks should present a false image to whites, and he berates the narrator for showing the trustee a less-than-idealized version of black society. Moreover, he tells the young man that he is too honest and that "the only way to please a white man is to tell him a lie" (107).

Bledsoe then lies to the young man, telling him that he must leave the school but can return in the fall; actually, the narrator has been permanently expelled. Bledsoe sends him to Harlem with sealed letters that are supposed to help him get an executive job. However, after delivering the letters to several offices, the narrator discovers that Bledsoe is really warning employers not to hire him.

Nearly penniless, the young man is forced to take a menial job at a paint factory, where a boiler explodes and injures him. The factory doctors subject him to experimental shock treatments before firing him and paying him off. While out of work, he passes the site of an eviction, where he makes an impromptu speech that rallies a crowd to riot in protest. Consequently, a Communist organization, the Brotherhood, hires him as one of its speakers.

The leaders of the Brotherhood, all of whom are white, immediately insist that the narrator's speeches focus on Communist issues rather than black ones. They do not want to help blacks unless it benefits their own cause. As a result, the Brotherhood's support in the black community is tenuous, and the group's members are often physically attacked by the members of an all-black organization led by Ras the Destroyer. Ras is proud of his African heritage and does not understand why blacks would want to work with whites.

Nonetheless, the narrator continues to do whatever the Brotherhood wants him to do, until a former member, Tod Clifton, is shot by police. Clifton was selling black dancing dolls on a street corner when the police accosted him. Because these dolls are politically incorrect, the Brotherhood does not want any of its members to speak at Clifton's funeral, nor will they join the black protest against his death. When the narrator defies their wishes, the leaders of the Brotherhood reprimand him. At the same time they use Clifton's death to incite a race riot in the community. The narrator rushes to stop the riot, telling Ras that the white Communists "want this to happen. They planned it. They want the mobs to come uptown with machine guns and rifles. They want the streets to flow with blood; your blood, black blood and white blood, so that they can turn your death and sorrow and defeat into propaganda" (421). But Ras does not listen and tries to kill the narrator, who in turn kills him.

After the riot the narrator realizes that he has been suffering from a sickness, one that "came upon [him] slowly, like that strange disease that affects those black men whom you see turning slowly from black to albino, their pigment disappearing as under the radiation of some cruel, invisible ray" (434). He

traces his path from "being 'for' society and then 'against' it" (435) and decides that the only way to stay healthy is to stay entirely separate from society. It is for this reason that he has retreated to his basement hole, "because up above there's an increasing passion to make men conform to a pattern" (435). He bemoans this "passion toward conformity," saying that conformity would

> end up by forcing me, an invisible man, to become white, which is not a color but the lack of one. Must I strive toward colorlessness? But seriously, and without snobbery, think of what the world would lose if that should happen. America is woven of many strands. . . . Our fate is to become one, and yet many—This is not prophesy, but description. Thus one of the greatest jokes in the world is the spectacle of the whites busy escaping blackness and becoming blacker every day, and the blacks striving toward whiteness, becoming quite dull and gray. None of us seems to know who he is or where he's going. (435–436)

All at once he realizes that it is a "social crime" for him to stay in his hole too long because "there's a possibility that even an invisible man has a socially responsible role to play," and he decides to go out into the world again (439).

Eventually the narrator himself becomes disillusioned with the Brotherhood. He realizes that the group does not really care about blacks as people, saying, "What did they know of us, except that we numbered so many, worked on certain jobs, offered so many votes, and provided so many marchers for some protest parade of theirs?" (383).

The narrator's search for identity as a black man in a white society has led many scholars to compare *Invisible Man* to the novels of James Baldwin and Richard Wright, who wrote during the same period. In fact, Wright was Ellison's friend and encouraged him in his work. (Ellison 1952; Hersey 1974)

See also Baldwin, James; Communism; Ellison, Ralph; Racism; Wright, Richard

Iron Heel, The

The Iron Heel, by Jack London, traces the rise of a fictional oligarchy, the Iron Heel, in the United States during the years 1912–1917. Published in 1908, the novel is presented as a manuscript written by Avis Everhard, who offers a first-person narration of her life with her husband, Ernest, a famous revolutionary. This manuscript includes scholarly footnotes, written by a fictional historian approximately seven centuries in the future, to explain various terms and concepts, which are also clever commentaries on society's ills. For example, to explain the term *watchman,* the footnote says:

> In those days thievery was incredibly prevalent. Everybody stole property from everybody else. The lords of society stole legally or else legalized their stealing, while the poorer classes stole illegally. Nothing was safe unless guarded. Enormous numbers of men were employed as watchmen to protect property. The houses of the well-to-do were a combination of safe deposit vault and fortress. The appropriation of the personal belongings of others by our own children of to-day is looked upon as rudimentary survival of the theft-characteristic that in those early times was universal. (London 1924, 43–44)

The plot begins with Ernest and Avis's first meeting, at a dinner given by her father, John Cunningham, who is a respected scientist and professor at a university in Berkeley, California. During this meeting Ernest expounds on his socialist theories, argues that the ruling classes have too much power, and suggests that one day a revolution will take place. At subsequent speaking engagements throughout the city Ernest develops his ideas still further. He explains that the capitalists and trusts are a ruling oligarchy, which he calls the Iron Heel, and warns that this heel will eventually crush everyone beneath it. He suggests that the owners of small businesses join with the working classes before the Iron Heel stamps out not only their livelihoods but also their lives. Although many of these business owners

think that Ernest's opinions regarding socialism make sense, most will not accept his concept of the Iron Heel, and they refuse to believe that his predictions of a future working-class revolution will come true.

At first Avis also resists Ernest's views. Then he challenges her to investigate the case of a workman who lost his arm in an industrial accident and then was persecuted for it. She tracks down everyone involved in the incident, and learns that, even though the accident was not the man's fault, the company blamed him for it and refused to pay him any monetary compensation for his injury. The man's life was ruined. In addition, Avis learns that many other working-class people are not being treated fairly because of the oppression of the Iron Heel. She tries to get the newspapers to report on these injustices, but she soon discovers that the Iron Heel controls the media. She now believes in Ernest's philosophy.

Ernest makes another convert out of Bishop Morehouse by challenging this idealistic minister to study working-class life. Morehouse soon discovers that society is more cruel than he imagined. The minister tells Ernest that he will give a speech to his fellow clergymen, rousing them to do more to help the downtrodden. Ernest warns him against it, saying that he will be attacked for going against the best interests of the capitalistic class to which he belongs. Nonetheless, the minister follows through with his plans, preaching:

> Let each one of you who is prosperous take into his house some thief and treat him as his brother, some unfortunate and treat her as his sister, and San Francisco will need no police force and no magistrates; the prisons will be turned into hospitals, and the criminal will disappear with his crime. We must give ourselves and not our money alone. . . . You have hardened your hearts. You have closed your ears to the voices that are crying in the land—the voices of pain and sorrow that you will not hear but that some day will be heard. (115–116)

After his speech the minister is deemed insane and sentenced to a mental asylum. He pretends to "get well," is released, and secretly begins selling his property. When he has enough money, he changes his identity and disappears to work among the poor. The Iron Heel eventually finds him again, and he ends up back in a mental institution.

When Ernest and Avis get engaged, Ernest warns John Cunningham that he, too, will be persecuted for associating with revolutionary ideas. He urges his future father-in-law to leave the country. Cunningham decides to stay, and the Iron Heel pressures the university to give him a leave of absence from his job. The authorities then make up a false mortgage on his home, although he owns it free and clear, and foreclose on it. Cunningham loses everything, and like the Bishop, he goes to live among the working classes.

By this time Avis and Ernest are married, and she has become involved in his revolutionary activities. She participates in a general strike and a failed revolution, during which she pretends to be working for the government. Later Ernest is falsely accused of planting a bomb while giving a speech to Congress. Powerful members of the oligarchy have set him up, and they use the incident to accuse any congressman who opposes them of being a revolutionary. Over 30 men, including Ernest, are sent to prison. Meanwhile Avis goes into hiding, changes her identity, and awaits her husband's escape. The two are part of a large, growing underground organization seeking to overthrow the oligarchy. Eventually the couple is reunited to participate in a final action against the Iron Heel. The manuscript ends in midsentence, with a footnote remarking how unfortunate it is that the book was not completed because then it "would have cleared away the mystery that has shrouded for seven centuries the execution of Ernest Everhard" (354).

In writing about this novel in 1924, social protest author Anatole France argues that London's warning of socialism's demise is justified. France believes that if the powerful want socialism to disappear, then it will, saying: "There is no reason to believe that . . . be it sooner or later, Socialism will be crushed beneath the Heel of Iron and be drowned in blood" (xv). In this France disagrees with the prevailing view when the novel was published. He (xv–xvi) reports: "In 1907 Jack London was shouted at as a frightful pessimist. Even sincere socialists blamed him for casting terror into the party ranks. They were wrong; those who have the precious and rare gift of foreseeing the future are bound to reveal the dangers it presents." At the same time France agrees with London that, even if socialism is crushed, the oligarchy will not last forever. France (xvi–xvii) insists that the working classes will prevail, saying: "Already, in its very strength we can perceive signs of its ruin. It will perish because all caste government is vowed to death. It will perish because it is unjust. It will perish swollen with pride and at the height of its power, just as slavery and serfdom have perished. Even now if one observes it attentively one can see that it is decrepit." (London 1924; O'Conner 1964)

See also France, Anatole; London, Jack; Socialism

J

Jackson, Helen Hunt

Born on October 15, 1830, in Amherst, Massachusetts, Helen Hunt Jackson was a poet, novelist, and children's book writer who advocated better treatment for Native Americans, particularly those in California. She began writing in 1863 after the deaths of her husband and two sons, and her poetry received much acclaim. In 1875 she remarried and moved to Colorado, where she wrote *A Century of Dishonor* (1881). The book criticized government policies in regard to Native Americans, and its publication led to Hunt's appointment to a federal commission investigating the treatment of California's Mission Indians. This experience led Hunt to write her most famous work, *Ramona* (1885). The novel was extremely popular and aroused public sympathy for the plight of Native Americans everywhere. Hunt died on August 12, 1885, in San Francisco, California. (Banning 1973; Mathes 1990)

See also Native American Issues; Racism; *Ramona*

Jackson, Shirley

Novelist Shirley Hardie Jackson is best known for her short story "The Lottery" (1948), which depicts a town that holds a yearly lottery to select a sacrificial victim. Some schol-

ars have interpreted the work as a protest against unexamined traditions. Jackson wrote several other short stories, as well as Gothic novels and fictionalized memoirs.

Born on December 14, 1916, in San Francisco, California, she attended Syracuse University in New York. After her graduation in 1940, she married literary critic Stanley Edgar Hyman, and in 1945 the couple moved to Bennington, Vermont. Jackson died there on August 8, 1965. (Friedman 1975)

See also "Lottery, The"

James, Henry

Novelist Henry James wrote primarily about the societal differences between Europeans and Americans. He was born on April 15, 1843, in New York, New York, into a family of prominent philosophers. As a child he and his brother had private tutors and traveled with their parents throughout Europe, intermittently returning to the eastern United States. In 1862 James began attending Harvard Law School. He also studied literature and wrote stories. His first story was published anonymously in 1864 in a New York magazine, the *Continental Monthly*. Shortly thereafter he became a regular contributor to the *Atlantic Monthly*. He also wrote book reviews for the *North American Review*.

Henry James (Archive Photos)

In 1875 James moved to Paris, France, where he published his first novel, *Roderick Hudson.* He also befriended the Russian social protest novelist Ivan Turgenev, whose work he admired, but James left Paris after a year to move to London, England. There he produced his most important novels, including *Daisy Miller* (1879), *The Portrait of a Lady* (1881), and two works concerning social and political reform, *The Bostonians* (1886) and *The Princess Casamassima* (1886), respectively. During his career James wrote a total of 20 novels, 12 plays, and over 100 stories. He also wrote articles, essays, criticisms, and travel literature. In 1915 he became an English citizen, and a year later, on February 28, 1916, he died in London, England. (McElderry 1965)

See also *Bostonians, The*

Javert

A police inspector in Victor Hugo's 1862 novel *Les Misérables,* Monsieur Javert is a narrow-minded man incapable of mercy. He pursues an escaped convict, Jean Valjean, for years, even though the man has reformed and does not deserve to be jailed. One day during a civil uprising Valjean saves Javert's life, and the police inspector realizes that he cannot arrest the man. Distraught over his failure to do his duty, Javert drowns himself in the Seine River. (Hugo 1987)

See also Hugo, Victor; *Misérables, Les;* Valjean, Jean

Jellyby, Mrs.

Mrs. Jellyby is a character in Charles Dickens's novel *Bleak House,* which first appeared in serialized form between 1852 and 1853. She is introduced in a chapter entitled "Telescopic Philanthropy" and described as a woman obsessed with philanthropic efforts. One of her friends explains: "Mrs. Jellyby . . . is a lady of very remarkable strength of character, who devotes herself entirely to the public. She has devoted herself to an extensive variety of public subjects, at various times, and is at present (until something else attracts her) devoted to the subject of Africa; with a view to the general cultivation of the coffee berry—*and* the natives—and the happy settlement, on the banks of the African rivers, of our superabundant home population" (Dickens 1987, 34).

However, it soon becomes apparent that Mrs. Jellyby is a bit too involved in her social reform efforts. One observer reports:

> Mrs. Jellyby had very good hair, but was too much occupied with her African duties to brush it. . . . The room, which was strewn with papers and nearly filled by a great writing-table covered with similar litter, was, I must say, not only very untidy, but very dirty. . . . But what principally struck us was a jaded and unhealthy-looking . . . girl, at the writing-table, who sat biting the feather of her pen, and staring at us. I suppose nobody ever was in such a state of ink. And, from her tumbled hair to her pretty feet, which were disfigured with frayed and broken satin slippers trodden down at heel, she really seemed to have no article of dress upon her, from a pin upwards, that was in its proper condition or its right place. (37)

Mrs. Jellyby neglects her children and husband at home in order to participate in causes that will benefit people abroad. The term *telescopic* in the chapter's title means "distant." Charles Dickens often criticized activists for overlooking the suffering children in their own neighborhoods to concentrate on problems elsewhere. (Dickens 1987a)

See also *Bleak House;* Dickens, Charles

Joad Family

The Joad family is featured in John Steinbeck's 1939 novel *The Grapes of Wrath.* Composed of three generations, its members include Tom Joad Jr. and his siblings Rose of Sharon, Noah, Al, Ruthie, and Winfield; Tom's parents Tom Joad Sr. and Ma Joad; and Tom's grandparents Granma and Grampa Joad. They represent the thousands of tenant farmers in the American Midwest who were forced from their land during the 1930s. Like most other Oklahomans, they migrate to California expecting to find a better life. Instead, they find prejudice, injustice, and unfair working conditions. The family, which was once strong and unified, begins to break apart. Some members die; some drift away. Tom Joad Jr. commits a murder in self-defense and becomes a wanted man, but he vows to continue fighting for justice while on the run. Tom Joad Sr. works with a group of migrants to prevent a river from overflowing and learns that people must join together for the greater good. Meanwhile Ma Joad comes to view her family not as an individual unit but as a part of a whole. She sees life as "all one flow, like a stream, little eddies, little waterfalls" and says that, despite difficulties, "the river, it goes right on," adding: "We ain't gonna die out. People is goin' on—changin' a little, maybe, but goin' right on" (Steinbeck 1972, 467). The Joads's story suggests that the poor and downtrodden will always exist and will do what they have to do in order to survive. (Steinbeck 1972)

See also *Grapes of Wrath, The;* Great Depression; Immigrant Communities; Steinbeck, John

Johnson, James Weldon

James Weldon Johnson is best known today for his novel *The Autobiography of an Ex-Colored Man,* which he first published anonymously in 1912. The work did not appear under his own name until 1927, the same year he published a collection of poetry entitled *God's Trombones: Seven Negro Spirituals in Verse.*

Born June 17, 1871, in Jacksonville, Florida, Johnson attended Atlanta University before studying law at New York's Columbia University. He was the first black man admitted to the Florida bar. Nonetheless, in 1901 he and his brother became composers for the New York stage, and together they wrote over 200 songs for Broadway productions. In 1906 he accepted a diplomatic position, serving as a U.S. consul in Venezuela and Nicaragua. His diplomatic career ended in 1914, and shortly thereafter he began teaching creative writing at Fisk University in Tennessee. He also helped found the National Association for the Advancement of Colored People and acted as its secretary from 1916 to 1930. His other works include a poetry collection, *Fifty Years and Other Poems* (1917); an anthology, *Book of American Negro Poetry* (1922); and an autobiography, *Along This Way* (1933). Johnson died on June 26, 1938, in Wiscasset, Maine. (Levy 1973)

See also *Autobiography of an Ex-Colored Man;* Harlem Renaissance; Racism

Jones, Eric

Eric Jones appears in James Baldwin's 1960 novel *Another Country.* After a series of homosexual relationships, he has an affair with a married woman. He begins the affair in part because she is an old friend, but mostly because it would be easier for him to be heterosexual. However, in the end he realizes that, even though "the life you think you *should* want . . . is always the life that looks safest," in actuality "you've got to be truthful about the life you *have*" (Baldwin 1962, 336). He ends the affair and returns to homosexuality. (Baldwin 1962)

See also *Another Country;* Baldwin, James; Gay and Lesbian Issues; Moore, Daniel Vivaldo; Scott, Ida and Rufus

Joseph K.

Joseph K. is the main character in Franz Kafka's 1925 novel *Der Prozess* (The Trial). An ordinary bank clerk, he is accused of a crime by a mysterious court but allowed to remain free until his trial. Yet no one will tell him what he has done wrong, and although he struggles to obtain more information, he cannot find out much about the court or its officers. A year after his arrest two officers of the court execute him in a deserted field near a stone quarry. (Kafka 1964)

See also Kafka, Franz; *Trial, The*

Joy, Serena

The character Serena Joy appears in the futuristic novel *The Handmaid's Tale* (1985), by Margaret Atwood. A former television evangelist, Serena supported a rebellion that created Gilead, a country run by religious fundamentalists. Under this theocracy her assigned role as Wife of a Commander is to run the household, maintain the garden, and socialize with other Wives. She has great power over women in lesser roles, but she is ultimately powerless in a regime controlled by men. Moreover, as a barren woman who longs for a child, she is powerless in a more personal sense. Serena Joy is Atwood's caution to women of religious movements who are too eager to give away their power as individuals. (Atwood 1986; McCombs 1988)

See also Atwood, Margaret; Feminism; *Handmaid's Tale, The*; Offred

Jungle, The

Upton Sinclair's 1906 novel *The Jungle* exposes injustice and corruption in the U.S. meatpacking industry during the early twentieth century. Because of the book's emphasis on slavelike working conditions within the industry, in 1905 reviewer Jack London (Sinclair 1972, vii) compared it to the antislavery novel *Uncle Tom's Cabin* and called it an important socialist work, saying: "It will be read by every workingman. It will open countless ears that have been deaf to Socialism. It will plough the soil for the seed of our propaganda. It will make thousands of converts to our cause."

However, the public largely ignored the human injustices portrayed in the story, preferring instead to focus on what the book revealed about the unsanitary practices of food processing. As Sinclair (viii) himself explains: "I aimed at the public's heart and by accident I hit it in the stomach." As a result, President Theodore Roosevelt launched an investigation into the sanitation of meatpacking factories. This led to the enactment of new health laws, including the Pure Food and Drug Act.

Other laws to address poor working conditions were slower to arrive. In a 1946 introduction to the work Sinclair Lewis (viii) wrote:

> Forty years have passed [since *The Jungle* was published], and the workers throughout America have fought a bitter war for a share of control over their own destinies. . . . The labor of slaughtering animals is still hard and often dangerous; it is ill-paid and uncertain, as all labor must be so long as it is carried on under the profit system; but it is not so bad as it was forty years ago, and that much comfort can be offered to present-day readers of *The Jungle*.

The novel's story of social injustice is shown through the struggles of its main character, Jurgis Rudkus, and his family, which includes Jurgis's father, Antanas; Jurgis's fiancée, Ona; Ona's cousin Marija; Ona's stepmother, Elzbieta; Elzbieta's brother, Jonas; and Elzbieta's six children. Jurgis is a big, muscular Lithuanian peasant who does not understand English. Nonetheless, he takes his family to the United States, where he believes that people can make good money as laborers in the stockyards of Chicago. There he gets a job sweeping cattle entrails into a trap in the floor, and he is able to save up enough money to pay for his wedding. Meanwhile Marija finds work painting labels on cans of smoked beef.

The family lives in a crowded, dirty boardinghouse but soon decides to purchase a brand-new house. However, after the deed is signed, the Rudkuses learn that they have been cheated. The house is not new at all, only freshly painted, and in addition to regular payments they will be charged interest as well as additional sums for insurance and other expenses. Consequently, other members of the family are forced to find jobs. Antanas mops floors around vats of chemically treated beef, but because he is old, he must work for little money. Ona sews covers on hams, and Elzbieta's oldest son, 14-year-old Stanislovas, places cans on a lard-canning machine. His younger brothers sell newspapers on street corners.

In every case working conditions are unusually hard and business practices are unsanitary. Diseased hogs and cattle are slaughtered along with healthy ones, and spoiled food is doctored with colorants and chemicals to make it look edible. Employees are expected to work as quickly as possible until they drop. Under such conditions Antanas falls ill and dies. Shortly thereafter Marija's canning factory shuts down because of overproduction, and in the winter Jurgis's work hours are reduced. The family slips deeper into poverty. Ona, Jurgis, and Stanislaus can no longer afford to ride a streetcar to work; instead they must walk two miles each way through the snow. They also cannot afford much coal, and the house grows cold.

In the spring things seem to improve. Marija finds work as a beef trimmer, and Ona gives birth to a boy she names Antanas. However, she cannot take time off from work to recuperate from the birth, and her health deteriorates. Then Jurgis injures his ankle on the job and must go home to recuperate without pay. Although his injury heals, he is no longer as strong as before. He loses his job and has difficulty finding another. Finally he agrees to work in the fertilizer department, where conditions are so toxic that most workers are not expected to survive more than five years. Despondent, he begins to drink.

One day he discovers that Ona, who is pregnant again, has been forced to become her boss's mistress in order to save her job. Jurgis rushes to the factory, beats the man up, and is sentenced to 30 days in jail. Stanislaus visits him and reveals that Marija was injured at work and has lost her job. Ona is also out of work, as is Stanislaus, because of what Jurgis did to the factory boss. The family is starving to death.

When Jurgis is released from jail, he learns that his family has been evicted. Everyone is back at the old boardinghouse, where a severely malnourished Ona has gone into premature labor. She and the child both die. Shortly thereafter baby Antanas drowns in a mucky street. Disgusted with the city, Jurgis hops a train to the country, where he becomes a hobo and occasional farmworker. Unfortunately he can find no work or shelter for the winter and he decides to return to Chicago, where he finds a job as a tunnel digger. When a runaway underground train engine injures his shoulder, he must become a beggar and a thief in order to survive. He begins to make friends among his fellow thieves, and eventually a corrupt politician gets him a job at his old factory, so that he can influence voters there. When the employees go out on strike, Jurgis keeps working and is promoted to foreman. One day he encounters the man who seduced Ona, beats him up again, and is arrested. While out on bail he leaves the district and again becomes a beggar. On the streets he learns that Marija has become a prostitute. He visits her, and she encourages him rejoin the family, now living near the house of prostitution. On the way to see them Jurgis attends a political meeting to get warm and hears an impassioned speech about socialism. He becomes involved in the socialist cause and begins working as a porter for a socialist hotel owner. His spirit is uplifted, and he anticipates converting many more workers to the cause.

The novel ends with a socialist speaker arguing that when the Democrats do not deliver on their election promises, they will lose power:

> We shall have the sham reformers self-stultified and self-convicted; we shall have the radical Democracy left without a lie with which to cover its nakedness! And then will begin the rush that will never be

checked, the tide that will never turn till it has reached its flood—that will be irresistible, overwhelming—the rallying of the outraged workingmen of Chicago to our standard! And we shall organize them, we shall drill them, we shall marshal them for the victory! We shall bear down the opposition, we shall sweep it before us—and Chicago will be ours! (Sinclair 1972, 342–343)

In discussing this speech, Sinclair Lewis explains that he heard similar orations during his own activities in support of the socialist cause and is surprised that more people have not been inspired by such words. He questions whether he has "placed far too high an estimate upon the intelligence of the human race, and its moral qualities." However, he is encouraged by the fact that the novel did bring about some reforms in both industry and politics and hopes that more will come in the future (Sinclair 1972, viii). (Bloodworth 1977; Mookerjee 1988; Sinclair 1972)

See also Labor Issues; London, Jack; Rudkus, Jurgis and Ona; Socialism; *Uncle Tom's Cabin*

Jurgis, Arthur

Arthur Jurgis is a character in Alan Paton's 1948 South African novel *Cry, the Beloved Country*. He does not appear in life; however, his writings feature prominently in the story after his death. Murdered by a black man during a burglary, Jurgis was a white activist who worked for black equality and often quoted Abraham Lincoln. After his funeral his grieving father studies his son's work and decides to help the blacks in his rural village. (Paton 1987)

See also *Cry, the Beloved Country;* Paton, Alan

Justice

Justice is a major concern of social protest authors. For example, Albert Camus, Charles Dickens, Victor Hugo, Franz Kafka, and Harper Lee criticize injustice in their countries' legal systems. Nuruddin Farah, Carlos Fuentes, and Milan Kundera protest political injustice. Ciro Alegría's novel *Broad and Alien Is the World* depicts both political and legal corruption, whereas Walter Van Tilburg Clark's *The Ox-Bow Incident* concerns the injustice of a lynch mob. Writers who deal with issues of apartheid, feminism, racism, homosexuality, anti-Semitism, Native American rights, and other forms of discrimination, particularly those involving labor issues and class structure, are also concerned with injustice.

See also Alegría, Ciro; Anti-Semitism; Apartheid; *Broad and Alien Is the World;* Camus, Albert; Clark, Walter Van Tilburg; Class, Social; Dickens, Charles; Farah, Nuruddin; Feminism; Fuentes, Carlos; Gay and Lesbian Issues; Hugo, Victor; Kafka, Franz; Kundera, Milan; Labor Issues; Lee, Harper; Native American Issues; *Ox-Bow Incident, The; Racism*

K

Kafka, Franz

Born on July 3, 1883, in Prague, Bohemia, Austria-Hungary (now part of the Czech Republic), Franz Kafka wrote fiction that concerned the modern person's alienation from society. This theme was inspired in part by his own alienation from society. As a Jewish man living in an anti-Semitic Germanic community, he had difficulty both fitting in and honoring his heritage. Eventually he broke off all connections to his past by becoming a socialist and an atheist. In 1906 Kafka received a doctorate, and from 1906 to 1922 he worked in the insurance industry. He left the business in 1923 to devote himself entirely to his writing. A year later, on June 3, 1924, he died of tuberculosis in a town near Vienna, Austria. Most of his writings were published posthumously, by his friend and promoter Max Brod, despite Kafka's expressed wish that they be destroyed. These works include the novels *Der Prozess* (The Trial, 1925) and *Der Schloss* (The Castle, 1926). Of the works published during Kafka's lifetime, the stories *Die Verwandlung* (The Metamorphosis 1915) and *In der Strafkolonie* (In the Penal Colony, 1919) are perhaps the best known. (Hamalian 1974; Spann 1976)

  See also *Trial, The*

Franz Kafka, c. 1890's–1910's (Corbis-Bettmann)

Kesey, Ken

As a member of the 1960s Beat Movement in the United States, Ken Kesey wrote fiction and nonfiction critical of American culture.

His most significant novel in this regard was *One Flew over the Cuckoo's Nest*, published in 1962. The book was based in part on Kesey's experience testing psychedelic drugs as a paid volunteer at a veterans' hospital, where he later worked as an aide.

Born on September 17, 1935, in La Junta, Colorado, Kesey attended both the University of Oregon and Stanford University. He continues to write, although his works appear irregularly. His most recent books are *The Further Inquiry* (1990) and *Sailor Song* (1992).

See also Beat Movement; *One Flew Over the Cuckoo's Nest*

Knecht, Joseph

Joseph Knecht is the subject of Hermann Hesse's 1943 fictional biography *Das Glasperlenspiel* (The Glass Bead Game), also entitled *Magister Ludi*. He is a member of an elite intellectual order but gradually realizes that his isolation from nonintellectuals is hindering his personal growth. He resigns from his order to become a tutor to a young man from a politically powerful family, hoping to help change society. However, before Knecht can realize his goal he drowns in a swimming accident. (Hesse 1986)

See also *Glass Bead Game, The;* Hesse, Hermann

Knowell, Douglas

Douglas Knowell appears in Doris Lessing's five-novel series *Children of Violence*. Married to the main character, Martha Quest, he tries to prevent her from becoming involved in political activism, believing that women should be wives and mothers and little else. He also submerges his own political views, choosing to abandon his interest in communism to take a job in the civil service. He is an alcoholic, and when Martha tells him she wants a divorce, he threatens to kill either her or himself. (Lessing 1964)

See also *Children of Violence;* Lessing, Doris

Knox, Tom

A character in the 1958 novel *The Ugly American,* by William J. Lederer and Eugene Burdick, Tom Knox is an expert on poultry who travels to Asia as part of a group called the American Aid Mission. During a conference of American agricultural experts, he recommends that funds be allotted to buy chickens and sugarcane processing machines for local communities. But his superiors want to spend the money on a new canal and a large mechanized farm, which are far more impressive projects, and they ridicule Knox for his suggestions. As a result, he leaves for the United States, intending to protest their decision. However, his return trip has been arranged by Asian officials who will profit from the mechanized farm, and as he travels, they subtly convince him to abandon his complaints. Once home he forgets all about the problems of the Asian people. (Lederer and Burdick 1958)

See also *Ugly American, The*

Kumalo, Stephen

The main character of Alan Paton's 1948 South African novel *Cry, the Beloved Country,* Stephen Kumalo is a black priest from a rural village. His son, Absalom, moves to the city of Johannesburg; falls in with a bad crowd; and commits several crimes, including murder. When Absalom ends up in jail, he blames everyone else for his fate, but Stephen insists that his son take responsibility for his actions. At the same time the old priest recognizes that it is difficult for his people to maintain their morality when they become separated from their families and ancient customs. He works to improve life in his village, so that young people will not want to leave it. (Paton 1987)

See also *Cry, the Beloved Country;* Paton, Alan

Kundera, Milan

Czechoslovakian author Milan Kundera writes novels, short stories, plays, and poems, many of which include political and social criticism. Born on April 1, 1929, in the city of Brno, his first poetry collections were condemned by the Czechoslovakian government. After 1969 the government banned the publication of all of his work, including his internationally famous novel *Nesnesitelná lehkost bytí* (The Unbearable Lightness of Being,

1984). Most of his works therefore appeared first in translation.

Kundera was politically active in his country and participated in a liberalization movement during 1967–1968, which led authorities to fire him from his teaching positions and oust him from the Communist Party. In 1975 he left Czechoslovakia for France and took a teaching position at the University of Rennes. Four years later the Czech government revoked his citizenship, and his works remained banned in the Czech Republic until 1989. Kundera continues to live and write in France today. (Aji 1992; Kundera 1984)

See also Censorship; Communism; Exiles; *Unbearable Lightness of Being, The*

L

Labor Issues

Social protest authors have written about a wide variety of labor issues. For example, the works of Rebecca Harding Davis, Charles Dickens, and Tillie Olsen express concern for the poor quality of life among factory workers. Dickens's novels also protest child labor. Upton Sinclair and John Steinbeck expose unfair labor practices in the meatpacking and agricultural industries, respectively, in their novels *The Jungle* and *The Grapes of Wrath*. John Galsworthy and Lillian Hellman depict labor strikes in their respective plays *Strife* and *Days to Come*. Jack London's novel *The Iron Heel*, Ayn Rand's novel *Atlas Shrugged*, and H. G. Wells's novel *Tono-Bungay* examine labor issues as they relate to the differences between socialism and capitalism. Job satisfaction is the subject of Sinclair Lewis's novel *Babbitt* and is also a common subject for science fiction novels, including Edward Bellamy's *Looking Backward, 2000–1887;* Aldous Huxley's *Brave New World;* George Orwell's *1984;* Jules Verne's *Paris in the Twentieth Century;* and Kurt Vonnegut's *Player Piano*. In addition, writers who depict racism or other types of prejudice, such as anti-Semitism or antifeminism, often deal with discrimination in the workplace. (Wortman 1969)

See also Anti-Semitism; *Atlas Shrugged; Babbitt;* Bellamy, Edward; *Brave New World;* Capitalism; Davis, Rebecca Harding; *Days to Come;* Dickens, Charles; Feminism; Galsworthy, John; *Grapes of Wrath, The;* Hellman, Lillian; Huxley, Aldous; *Iron Heel, The; Jungle, The;* Lewis, Sinclair; London, Jack; *Looking Backward, 2000–1887; 1984;* Olsen, Tillie; Orwell, George; *Paris in the Twentieth Century; Player Piano;* Poverty; Racism; Rand, Ayn; Sinclair, Upton; Socialism; Steinbeck, John; *Strife; Tono-Bungay;* Verne, Jules; Vonnegut, Kurt; Wells, H. G.

Larsen, Nella

Born in 1891, probably in either Chicago, Illinois, or New York, New York, Nella Larsen wrote novels and short stories that drew on her own experiences with racism in the United States. She was of mixed race, having a mother who was Danish and a father who was a black West Indian. Although she gave different versions of her childhood, biographers believe that as a girl she was expelled from her family because of her color. In 1912 she began attending a nursing school in New York City, graduating in 1915. She worked as a nurse until 1921, when she took a job as a librarian and started writing fiction. By this time she lived in the Harlem district of New

York City. Her first publications were stories in black magazines. Her first novella, *Quicksand*, was published in 1928, and her second, *Passing*, in 1929. In 1992 these works and some of her short stories were republished in a collection entitled *An Intimation of Things Distant.*

In 1930 Larsen became the first black woman to win a Guggenheim fellowship. Unfortunately, she experienced personal difficulties soon afterward, and her writing suffered. None of her later works was ever published. Eventually she returned to nursing in New York City, where she died on March 30, 1964. (Davis 1994; Larson 1993)

See also Feminism; *Intimation of Things Distant, An;* Racism

Le Guin, Ursula

Science fiction and fantasy writer Ursula Le Guin often uses fictional worlds to comment on the failings of the real world. Born on October 21, 1929, in Berkeley, California, she attended Radcliffe College and Columbia University in New York. Her first novel was the first in a trilogy involving an alien society on the planet Hain, which established human life on Earth. She followed this trilogy with the first in a series of four children's books known as the Earthsea Quartet. At the same time she published several novels for adults, including *The Left Hand of Darkness* (1969), which comments on human sexuality and morality; *The Dispossessed* (1974), which depicts both an anarchist world and a world of capitalists and Communists; and *Malafrena* (1979), which concerns political and social oppression in a fictional nineteenth-century European country. Le Guin continues to write fiction, as well as essays on fiction, feminism, and other topics. (Spivack 1984)

See also Anarchism; *Malafrena;* Science Fiction and Fantasy

Lederer, William J.

William Julius Lederer is the author of several fiction and nonfiction books, but his best-known work is the novel *The Ugly American,* which he coauthored with Eugene Burdick. Published in 1958, the novel protests U.S. policies in Southeast Asia, as well as the behavior of U.S. and French military and diplomatic leaders in the region. (Lederer and Burdick 1958)

See also Burdick, Eugene; Justice; *Ugly American, The*

Lee, Harper

Nelle Harper Lee is the author of *To Kill a Mockingbird* (1960), a novel that protested racism in the southern United States. Born in Monroeville, Alabama, on April 28, 1926, she wanted to become a lawyer like her father. However, although she studied law at the University of Alabama from 1945 to 1949, she became an airline clerk instead. *To Kill a Mockingbird* was her only work. (Lee 1993)

See also *To Kill a Mockingbird*

Leete, Edith

Edith Leete, a character in the 1887 novel *Looking Backward, 2000–1887,* embodies author Edward Bellamy's vision of a twentieth-century woman. Writing from the perspective of the late 1880s, Bellamy made Edith not only compassionate, kind, and beautiful, but also rational, intelligent, and straightforward. In her society women are supposedly equal to men in every way. As Edith's father, Dr. Leete, explains, "No woman is heard nowadays wishing she were a man, nor parents desiring boy rather than girl children. Our girls are as full of ambition for their careers as our boys. Marriage, when it comes, does not mean incarceration for them, nor does it separate them in any way from the later interests of society" (Bellamy 1951, 212). However, scholar Cecelia Tichi (25), writing in an introduction to a 1982 edition, believes that "beneath the surface of Bellamy's feminist program . . . lies the sexual segregation of separate and unequal women's lives. The women's industrial army, which mirrors that of men, exists only through *noblesse oblige,* as Dr. Leete reveals when he says of women, 'We have given them a world of their own.'" Moreover, Edith "has

Actor Gregory Peck and novelist Harper Lee on the set of the Universal Pictures movie To Kill a Mockingbird, *1962 (UPI/Corbis-Bettmann)*

no discernible occupation apart from shopping and nurturing Julian West" (25) a visitor who was born in 1857 but, through an accident of hypnosis, slept for 113 years. At the end of the novel the two become engaged. (Bellamy 1951, 1982)

> See also Bellamy, Edward; Feminism; *Looking Backward, 2000–1887;* West, Julian

Legal Issues
See Justice

Lessing, Doris
Doris Lessing writes novels and short stories that primarily concern characters trying to deal with social and political change. She was born Doris May Taylor in Persia (now Iran) on October 22, 1919, but was brought up on a farm in southern Rhodesia (now Zimbabwe). In 1949 she moved to England, and a year later she published her first book, *The Grass Is Singing,* which is set in Africa. She has written many more novels in her career. Some scholars believe that her most important work is a five-novel series entitled *Children of Violence* (1952–1969), which concerns the issues of racism, feminism, socialism, and anti-Semitism, both in Africa and in England. Lessing's other works include *The Golden Notebook* (1962), *The Good Terrorist* (1986), and *The Fifth Child* (1988), as well as nonfiction books, essays, and science fiction stories. In 1995 she received an honorary degree from Harvard University and published the first volume of her autobiography, *Under My Skin.* The second volume, *Walking in the Shade,* appeared in 1997. (Brewster 1965; Sprague and Tiger 1986)

> See also Anti-Semitism; *Children of Violence;* Feminism; Racism; Science Fiction and Fantasy; Socialism

Doris Lessing, 13 October 1992 (Reuters/Peter Morgan/ Archive Photos)

Lewis, Sinclair

Harry Sinclair Lewis wrote several novels criticizing conventional middle-class beliefs regarding business, religion, and politics in the United States of the 1920s. His most famous work is *Babbitt* (1922), whose main character is a successful, yet dissatisfied real estate salesman. After the novel's publication the word *Babbittry* entered the vernacular, meaning mindless conformity to middle-class values.

Lewis was born on February 7, 1885, in Sauk Center, Minnesota. From 1901 to 1903 he worked as a typesetter for local newspapers, and in 1903 he moved to New Haven, Connecticut, to attend Yale University, where he edited the campus literary magazine. He graduated in 1908 and began traveling throughout the United States as a freelance editor and journalist. He also sold story ideas to fiction writer Jack London.

In 1910 Lewis returned to New York to work at a variety of publishing-related jobs and began writing novels in his spare time. His first novel, an adventure story for children called *Hike and the Aeroplane,* was published in 1912 under the pseudonym Tom Graham. Under his own name he published two novels for adult readers, *Our Mr. Wrenn* (1914) and *The Trail of the Hawk* (1915). In 1915 he became a full-time freelance writer. Over the next five years he wrote several short stories, a play, and three more novels, entitled *The Job*

(1917), *The Innocents* (1917), and *Free Air* (1919). However, these books did not attract much attention; it was his seventh novel that brought Lewis recognition.

Entitled *Main Street* (1920), it examines life in an American small town, where bigotry and ignorance are commonplace. Lewis's subsequent work, *Babbitt,* is set in a medium-sized town with the same faults. Both books were commercial successes. However, they were also severely criticized for their unflattering portrait of American middle-class culture.

Lewis went on to write 14 more novels, including *Elmer Gantry* (1927) and *It Can't Happen Here* (1935). *Elmer Gantry* concerns religious hypocrisy, whereas *It Can't Happen Here* is a cautionary tale about the spread of fascism. In 1926 Lewis was awarded the Pulitzer Prize for another novel, *Arrowsmith* (1925), which focuses on the problems of a medical researcher working within a materialistic society. However, Lewis refused the award, believing he should have won it for *Main Street* or *Babbitt* instead. In 1930 he did accept the Nobel Prize in literature as the first American so honored. By this time he had divorced his first wife to marry a well-known journalist, Dorothy Thompson, whom he divorced in 1942.

After receiving the Nobel Prize, Lewis continued to write novels, but none was as well received as his earlier works. In fact, Sheldon Norman Grebstein (1962, 7) says that "no writer has ever risen higher in our critical esteem and then dropped more precipitately. In 1930 he was by far the most famous and among the two or three most respected American novelists. By the time of his death twenty years later, despite two best-sellers published just a few years before, the critics had written him off."

Nonetheless, Lewis was active in the theater, not just as a playwright but as a director, producer, and actor, and he lectured about writing at several universities. According to Martin Light, Lewis often spoke about the influence other writers had on his work. He particularly praised novelists Honoré de Balzac and Charles Dickens, who "led him to understand that it was possible to be realistic in descriptions of . . . common people" (Light 1975, 20), as well as Theodore Dreiser, whom Lewis lauded in his Nobel Prize acceptance speech. Lewis also said that the social protest novel *Tono-Bungay* was perhaps the greatest book he had ever read; its author, H. G. Wells, was Lewis's friend and mentor.

Lewis spent the last years of his life traveling, and in 1951 he died in Rome, Italy, of heart disease. His final work, *World So Wide*, was published posthumously. (Grebstein 1962; Schorer 1962)

See also *Babbitt;* Balzac, Honoré de; Dreiser, Theodore; *Elmer Gantry; Tono-Bungay;* Wells, H. G.

Life in the Iron Mills

Rebecca Harding Davis's novella *Life in the Iron Mills* was originally published in the April 1861 issue of the magazine *Atlantic Monthly.* It garnered much acclaim and was published in book form that same year. Set in Virginia and told by an unnamed first-person narrator of indeterminate gender, the story concerns the fate of Hugh Wolfe, a young Welsh furnace-tender at an iron-rolling mill. One day he encounters a group of upper-class men inspecting the mill. They notice a beautiful carved statue of a woman, and Hugh admits that he carved it himself. The men praise the work, and one of them, a physician named Doctor May, tells Hugh: "Do you know, boy, that you have it in you to be a great sculptor, a great man? . . . A man may make himself anything he chooses. God has given you stronger powers than many men,— me, for instance" (Wagner-Martin and Davidson 1995, 212). Hugh then asks May for help in accomplishing this goal. The doctor replies that he does not have enough money to educate the young man. The other men agree that it takes a lot of money to achieve goals in the United States. They toss Hugh a few coins and leave.

Hugh's cousin Deborah has witnessed this event, and later she brings Hugh a wallet she pickpocketed from one of the men. It is filled with money, and Deborah tells Hugh it is his right to keep it, to make a great man of himself. Hugh is tempted, but in the end he decides to return the money to its rightful owner. Before he can do so, he is arrested for theft, tried, and sentenced to 19 years of hard labor. Deborah is sentenced to 3 years as his accomplice. Shortly after his sentencing Hugh uses a scrap of tin to slit his wrists. A Quaker woman arrives at the jail to tend to his body, speaks with Deborah, and invites the young woman to live with her after her prison sentence has been served. Deborah accepts the offer and spends the rest of her life in a good home. The narrator concludes the story by admitting to be the current owner of Hugh's statue, "through which the spirit of the dead [sculptor] looks out, with its thwarted life, its mighty hunger, its unfinished work" (228). (Harris 1991; Rose 1993; Wagner-Martin and Davidson 1995)

See also Davis, Rebecca Harding; Labor Issues

Little Big Man

The 1964 novel *Little Big Man,* by Thomas Berger, depicts the social injustices perpetrated against Native Americans during the 1800s. Nonetheless, the author (Landon 1989, 30) himself once said: "I did not write *Little Big Man* as an exercise in social criticism. It was not intended as an indictment of the white man. I wrote it for the same motive that informs all my fiction: to amuse myself."

The novel opens with a foreword by a fictional journalist, Ralph Fielding Snell, who reports that during 1952 and 1953 he conducted a series of interviews with Jack Crabbe, an 111-year-old man in a nursing home. Jack claims to have been with General George Armstrong Custer at the Battle of the Little Big Horn. The rest of the novel is Jack's account of his life among both whites and Native Americans.

His story begins in 1852 when he is ten years old. While traveling west across the American plains to California, his family meets a group of Cheyenne Indians. Jack's father gives them whiskey and is killed in the ensuing drunken brawl. Because of a misunderstanding, Jack and his sister, Caroline, believe

Jack Crabbe and Old Lodge Skins ride together in a scene from the 1970 movie Little Big Man *(The Museum of Modern Art Film Stills Archive). The story depicts the conflicts between white and Native American people during the era of the American Indian Wars.*

they are now the Cheyenne's prisoners. Caroline later escapes her captors, but Jack remains with them throughout his childhood, living in the lodge of their chief, Old Lodge Skins.

When Jack is 15, he joins a Cheyenne raid on a Crow Indian camp. The Crow and the Cheyenne are always stealing ponies from each other. During this raid Jack is forced to kill a Crow to defend a fellow Cheyenne, Younger Bear. This shames Younger Bear but earns Jack full membership in the tribe and a Cheyenne name: Little Big Man. Old Lodge Skins chooses this name because Jack is short but has a big heart and because Little Big Man was a great warrior.

A brief while later Jack participates in a battle against the U.S. Cavalry. He is nearly killed before he convinces the soldiers that he is white. They take him to their fort, where he is adopted by the Reverend Silas Pendrake, an older man, and his beautiful young wife. Jack becomes infatuated with Mrs. Pendrake and tries to follow her teachings about morality. However, he soon discovers that she has been having affairs and lying to him. Disillusioned, he leaves town, but he cannot return to the Cheyenne because "being primitive ain't the easiest thing in the world to get used to if you know better. You get showed a more regular manner of obtaining your grub, for example, and it's pretty hard to return to a method that ain't guaranteed" (Berger 1964, 143).

He therefore takes on a series of roles in the white man's world: trader, mule skinner, buffalo hunter, drunkard, gunfighter, gambler, Indian scout. As a trader he marries a Swedish woman, Olga, and has a son, both of whom are later captured by Indians. As a drunkard he meets his sister, Caroline, who teaches him to shoot a gun. He also meets many famous people of his day, including Wild Bill Hickock, Wyatt Earp, and Calamity Jane.

Eventually Jack returns to the Cheyenne. He again lives with Old Lodge Skins's tribe and takes a woman named Sunshine as his wife. Later he discovers that Olga is with his old enemy, Younger Bear, and has become an ugly nag; she no longer recognizes Jack, and he is glad. Younger Bear also has another "wife," Yellow Horse, a homosexual. Jack explains that the Cheyenne do not stigmatize people according to their sexual preference, just as they do not consider a white man evil just because he is white. In this and many other ways he shows the Cheyenne to be fair and accepting people.

Meanwhile the whites are incredibly brutal. They decide to exterminate the Indians, and during one attack they kill many of Jack's friends and destroy their village. Afterward Sunshine is missing, and Jack vows revenge on the leader of the attack, George Armstrong Custer. After finding the general's encampment, however, he realizes that killing Custer will not stop the slaughter of the Indians. He therefore decides to act as a spy. He gets a job handling pack animals for Custer's troops and becomes an unwilling participant at the Battle of the Little Big Horn, where he is rescued by Younger Bear, who says: "You and I are even at last, and the next time we fight, I can kill you without becoming an evil person" (415). Jack then sees Old Lodge Skins again, and the two discuss the relationship between the whites and the Indians. Afterward Old Lodge Skins decides that he is old and has seen enough of life. Saying "It is a good day to die," he does (436). Journalist Snell then reports that Jack Crabbe himself died soon after telling this story, adding that the old man "was either the most neglected hero in the history of this country or a liar of insane proportions" (440). (Berger 1964; Landon 1989)

See also Berger, Thomas; Crabbe, Jack; Native American Issues; Old Lodge Skins; Racism

Little Dorrit

Little Dorrit, by Charles Dickens, was first published in serial form from 1855 to 1857 and in book form in 1857. The novel concerns the life of Amy Dorrit, whom everyone calls Little Dorrit. Her father was imprisoned for debt right before her birth, and Little Dorrit was born in a debtor's prison. After her mother dies, she begins taking care of her father. Her older brother and sister are selfish and do little to help. As a young woman Little Dorrit begins to earn money as a seamstress, and it is in this capacity that she meets Arthur Clennam. Arthur's mother has given Little Dorrit work, but he suspects there is a deeper connection between the two women. When his father died, the man seemed to refer to some wrong that he or his wife had committed. Arthur believes that Little Dorrit has something to do with this. Therefore, he begins giving Little Dorrit and her family money. However, after an investigator discovers that Little Dorrit's father is the heir to a wealthy estate, the woman's father, brother, and sister want nothing more to do with Arthur. They are ashamed of their background.

Released from prison, the Dorrit family begins traveling throughout Europe. Meanwhile Arthur makes a bad investment and loses his fortune. Now he is in debtor's prison, and Little Dorrit comes to stay with him. He refuses her help, saying that because he loves her, he cannot take her money. However, she reveals that she, too, lost her fortune in the same bad investment. Then it is revealed that Arthur's mother is not really his mother; his father had an affair with a young woman who was a friend of Little Dorrit's uncle. Moreover, in his will Arthur's father left a substantial sum of money to Arthur and Little Dorrit, but Mrs. Clennam concealed the document. Now Arthur and Little Dorrit both have fortunes, and they soon get married.

Little Dorrit is therefore both a romance and a mystery, but it also has many elements of social protest. In fact, playwright George Bernard Shaw credited the novel with converting him to socialism. The story not only offers a harsh portrayal of debtor's prisons but also severely criticizes the wealthy for ignoring the needs of the poor. Its characters include a seemingly philanthropic landowner who encourages his rent collector to harass his tenants and an apparently rich man who intentionally defrauds investors. Moreover, as Little Dorrit's father moves up in social class, he loses any endearing qualities he once had and becomes an unhappy man. At the end of his life he loses touch with reality and believes himself back in debtor's prison. (Dickens 1987b; Fielding 1958; Gissing 1924)

See also Class, Social; Dickens, Charles; Shaw, George Bernard

London, Jack

American writer Jack London is best known for his adventure stories and novels, which include *The Call of the Wild* (1903) and *White*

Jack London, American adventurer and writer (Archive Photos)

Fang (1906). However, he also wrote works of social protest. These include *The Iron Heel* (1907), which concerns a socialist revolution, and *The Valley of the Moon* (1913), which criticizes urbanization. London was born John Griffith Chaney on January 12, 1876, in San Francisco, California. As a boy he had a series of jobs related to the fishing industry, and at the age of 17 he became a sailor on a sealing schooner. A year later he became a hobo, traveling across the United States by rail. In 1893 he was arrested for being a vagrant and subsequently became a socialist. When he was 19, he decided to acquire an education. He became an avid reader and completed a four year high-school course in one year. He then briefly attended the University of California at Berkeley before going to the Klondike during the gold rush of 1897. During this time he began writing about his experiences. His first story, "To the Man on the Trail," was published in the *Overland Monthly* in 1899. His first book, a collection of stories entitled *The Son of the Wolf,* was published in 1900. He eventually published over 50 books, both fiction and nonfiction, and continued to live an adventurous life, sailing a ketch to the South Pacific and indulging in alcohol. He died of a drug overdose on November 22, 1916, in Glen Ellen, California. (O'Connor 1964)

See also *Iron Heel, The;* Socialism

Looking Backward, 2000–1887

Although published in 1887, *Looking Backward, 2000–1887* begins with a preface dated December 26, 2000. In it the book's author, Edward Bellamy, speaks as though he were a resident of the twentieth century. He explains that the object of *Looking Backward* is to help people "gain a more definite idea of the social contrasts between the nineteenth and twentieth centuries" (Bellamy 1951, xxv-xxvi). He then offers as fact the first-person narrative of a fictional character, Julian West, whom he says has lived in both time periods.

West was born on December 26, 1857. At the age of 30 he is a wealthy Bostonian engaged to a socially prominent young woman named Edith Bartlett, and the only difficulty in his life is his insomnia. West has so much trouble sleeping that he has constructed a special sleep chamber under the foundation of his house. In this subterranean room he meets regularly with Dr. Pillsbury, a "mesmerist" who hypnotizes him into sleep. No one else knows about the room except West's servant Sawyer, who has learned how to revive him.

But on May 30, 1887, something goes wrong. Dr. Pillsbury hypnotizes West into sleep, but Sawyer does not awaken him. Instead, when West regains consciousness, he finds himself in the company of Dr. and Mrs. Leete and their daughter, Edith, who reminds him of his fiancée. Dr. Leete tells West that they discovered him during an excavation of their garden. His subterranean room is all that remains of his house, which burned down the very night he fell asleep. That was 113 years ago; it is now 2000.

West reports that it feels as though he were asleep far longer because the differences between the nineteenth and twentieth centuries are so extreme. For example, there are no politicians and no lawyers, and the U.S. government is now run as "one great business corporation" (Bellamy 1951, 41). It manufactures and provides all goods through a national distribution system, and a sample of every available product is displayed in identical regional shops.

Citizens purchase these products not with money, which no longer exists, but with credits equal to each person's share of the annual gross national product. In return, after receiving an excellent education, every individual must work until retirement in a job for which the government has determined he or she is best suited. Young women can choose to leave their careers to have children, but anyone else who refuses to work is jailed.

Under this system all occupations are considered equally important. For example, as Dr. Leete tells West, "no difference is recognized between a waiter's functions and those of any other worker" because "the individual is never regarded, nor regards himself, as the servant of those he serves" (Bellamy 1951, 126). Instead, "it is always the nation which he is serving" (126). Therefore, there are no class distinctions and no labor disputes.

West contrasts this to the situation in 1887, when "the working classes had quite suddenly and very generally become infected with a profound discontent with their condition, and an idea that it could be greatly bettered if they only knew how to go about it. On every side, with one accord, they preferred demands for higher pay, shorter hours, better dwellings, better educational advantages, and a share in the refinements and luxuries of life" (8).

When he was living in the nineteenth century, West believed that these demands were unrealistic because the relationship between the rich and the poor was like "a prodigious coach which the masses of humanity were harnessed to and dragged toilsomely along a very hilly slope" while the rich sat on top of the coach in seats that were "very breezy and comfortable" (3). The coach's driver "was hunger, and permitted no lagging, though the pace was necessarily very slow" (3). Consequently, no one on top of the coach willingly gave up his or her seat, although they would occasionally "call down encouragingly to the toilers of the rope, exhorting them to patience, and holding out hopes of possible compensation in another world for the hardness of their lot, while others contributed to buy salves and liniments for the crippled and injured" (4).

West is relieved that this attitude no longer exists in the year 2000, and he is therefore extremely upset when, during a dream, he believes himself back in 1887. In the dream he berates the citizens of the nineteenth century in general and his fiancée and her family in particular for their treatment of the poor, saying, "Do you not know that close to your doors a great multitude of men and women, flesh of your flesh, live lives that are one agony from birth to death?" (267). He now knows that the solution to the nation's problems is to regulate the labor force "for the common good" (270).

When West reawakens in the year 2000 he is doubly grateful to have left his old life behind. By this time the government has already offered him a career as a historian specializing in the nineteenth century, a job for which it has deemed him perfectly suited. In addition, he is engaged to marry Edith Leete, whom he has learned is coincidentally the great-granddaughter of his former fiancée. Now he finds her in her garden, where he professes love for both her and the twentieth century.

West's relationship with Edith led Edward Bellamy, in a postscript to the 1889 edition of *Looking Backward,* to call the form of his novel "a fanciful romance." However, the author explains that the book's deeper intent is "as a forecast, in accordance with the principles of evolution, of the next stage in the industrial and social development of humanity" (273). Because this forecast is idyllic, scholars have designated *Looking Backward* a utopian novel.

However, Robert L. Shurter (vi) points out in an introduction to the 1951 edition of the book that *Looking Backward* is more importantly "a sincere attempt to chart a course for a better society." He explains that the book, which appeared at a time of great unemployment and labor unrest, "included most of the reform ideas of Bellamy's generation, expressed in a form so attractive and with a social system so seemingly capable of attainment that the book immediately became the focal point of innumerable idealistic schemes" (vii).

The book's publication resulted in a short-lived "Nationalist" movement dedicated to making Bellamy's national labor system a reality. According to Sylvia Bowman, members of this movement did not realize that Nationalism was similar to socialism; she believes that this is the reason for the success of *Looking Backward,* of which 400,000 copies were sold between 1888 and 1897. Bowman (1962, 32–33) explains that, "although *Looking Backward* appealed to its readers because of its graphic explanation of complex principles and because of its constructive, hopeful, and sincere message, its sale would probably have been greatly curtailed had . . . Bellamy not called his form of government Nationalism rather than socialism" because at the time "the ideas of socialists and philosophical anarchists were an anathema."

However, the book did generate some criticism, as did its 1897 sequel, *Equality*, which was more an economic treatise than a novel. Bowman (1979, 306) reports that Bellamy appreciated these attacks, believing that "all reformers would have to welcome opposition, since this would keep the issue before the public and open the way for discussion and debate." In fact, *Looking Backward* continued to generate discussion for many years after its publication, and Bellamy's ideas had a significant impact on social reformers of his era. Shurter (Bellamy 1951, vi-vii) therefore believes that "*Looking Backward* deserves to rank along with *Uncle Tom's Cabin* and *Ramona* as one of the most timely books ever to appear in America." (Bellamy 1951; Bowman, 1962, 1979, 1986)

See also Anarchism; Bellamy, Edward; Capitalism; Leete, Edith; *Ramona;* Socialism; *Uncle Tom's Cabin;* West, Julian

Piggy and Ralph consult on survival strategies in this scene from the 1963 movie Lord of the Flies. *(Allen-Hogden Productions/The Museum of Modern Art Film Stills Archive)*

Lord of the Flies

Lord of the Flies, by William Golding, suggests that human beings are inherently barbaric. The novel, which was published in 1954, concerns a group of British schoolboys whose plane is shot down during wartime. Stranded on a deserted island with no adults present, they establish their own system of rules and elect a leader, Ralph, a 12-year-old who is more charismatic than clever. Ralph relies on the advice of an intelligent, overweight, unpopular boy known as "Piggy," while another boy, Jack Merridew, takes charge of a group of hunters.

At first things go well. The children begin building shelters and maintain a signal fire to attract passing ships. But their enthusiasm for work does not last long, and most of the shelters are left unfinished. Meanwhile Jack becomes obsessed with killing pigs. He turns into a bloodthirsty savage, painting his face and leading his hunters in chants and rituals. One day the boys convince themselves that there is a beast on the island. When they disagree on how to handle the danger, Jack uses this as an opportunity to challenge Ralph's authority. He talks most of Ralph's followers into joining his group and establishes a new camp on the other side of the island. Shortly thereafter Jack's hunters mistake a member of Ralph's group for the beast and kill him.

The murderers feel no remorse. In fact, they grow even wilder, attacking Piggy and stealing his glasses, so that they can start their own fire. When Piggy tries to get the glasses back, they kill him and force Ralph's remaining followers to join their group. Jack then orders his group to hunt Ralph like a pig. They plan to kill him and put his head on a stake, but before they can catch him, they encounter a naval officer who has just landed on the beach. When the man sees Ralph being chased by boys in war paint, he assumes that the children are playing a game and is embarrassed when they all burst into tears.

In describing the meaning of his novel, Golding (1954, 204) writes:

The theme is an attempt to trace the defects of society back to the defects of human nature. The moral is that the shape of a society must depend on the ethical nature of the individual and not on any political system however apparently logical or respectable. The whole book is symbolic in nature except the rescue in the end where adult life appears, dignified and capable, but in reality enmeshed in the same evil as the symbolic life of the children on the island. The officer, having interrupted a man-hunt, prepares to take the children off the island in a cruiser which will presently be hunting its enemy in the same implacable way. And who will rescue the adult and his cruiser?

However, in an essay on the novel's symbolism published in the 1954 edition of the work, scholar E. L. Epstein says that this description is too simplistic. He suggests that each of the main characters represents a different aspect of the British political system. Ralph symbolizes "civilization with its parliaments and his brain trust (Piggy, the intellectual whose shattering spectacles mark the progressive decay of rational influence as the story progresses)," and Jack is "the leader of the forces of anarchy" (206). The struggle between the two boys symbolizes "the struggle in modern society between those same forces translated on a worldwide scale" (206). Epstein also discusses the central image of the book, the "lord of the flies." A pig's head on a stick, it is Jack's ritual offering to the imaginary beast. But Epstein notes that "lord of the flies" is a translation of *Ba'alzevuv* in Hebrew and *Beelzebub* in Greek, another name for the Devil. He believes that "this pungent and suggestive name for the Devil, a devil whose name suggests that he is devoted to decay, destruction, demoralization, hysteria and panic . . . fits in very well with Golding's theme" (205). (Golding 1954)

See also Anarchism; Golding, William; Merridew, Jack; Peace; Piggy; Ralph

"Lottery, The"

A short story by Shirley Jackson, "The Lottery" was first published in 1948 in *The New Yorker* magazine and was part of a 1949 short story collection called *The Lottery: or, The Adventures of James Harris*. It deals with social pressures and human sacrifice in a small New England town. Every year the town holds a lottery, a festive tradition that has been going on for generations. However, the reader does not learn the winner's reward until the end of the story. When Tessie Hutchinson draws the honor, she is stoned to death despite her protests. In discussing "The Lottery," scholars have provided various interpretations of the story's meaning. Among these is the suggestion that the work protests unexamined social customs and traditions. (Friedman 1975)

See also Jackson, Shirley

Lowell, James Russell

American poet and essayist James Russell Lowell was an abolitionist during the Civil War, and many of his works reflect his political position. Born on February 22, 1819, in Cambridge, Massachusetts, he graduated from Harvard University in Boston in 1838. In 1840 he received a law degree. Instead of becoming a lawyer, however, he became a writer. In 1841 he published a collection of poems, *A Year's Life*. He also began writing critical essays, particularly on the subject of slavery. In 1844 he married a noted abolitionist, the poet Maria White, and from 1845 to 1850 he wrote approximately 50 antislavery articles. He also began publishing one of his best-known works, an antislavery poetry series called *The Biglow Papers*. After his wife died in 1853, Lowell turned his attention to literary subjects, writing not only about literature and language but also about authors. He became a professor at Harvard University and a newspaper editor, first for the *Atlantic Monthly* and then for the *North American Review*. From 1877 to 1880 he was the U.S. ambassador to Spain and from 1880 to 1885 the ambassador to Great Britain. He died in Cambridge, Massachusetts, on August 12, 1891. (Duberman 1966; Wortham 1977)

See also *Biglow Papers, The*; Slavery

Lysistrata

Lysistrata, by Aristophanes, is the third play in a series of three comedies about the Peloponnesian War (431–404 B.C.) between the rival

Greek city-states of Athens and Sparta. First performed in 411 B.C., the play's predecessors were The *Archanians* (426 B.C.) and *Peace* (422 B.C.). *Lysistrata* is the most bawdy of the three; it concerns the decision of women throughout Greece to refuse sexual favors to their men until peace is declared. Led by an Athenian named Lysistrata, they ceremonially vow to resist temptation and, if forced to yield, to "be cold as ice, and never stir a limb . . . [or] aid him in any way," so that the men take no pleasure in their actions (Aristophanes 1930, 241). At the same time a group of older women takes over the Acropolis and its state treasury. Faced with such widespread insubordination, the frustrated men eventually agree to sign peace agreements. They then prepare for a celebration banquet marking the end of Grecian celibacy. (Aristophanes 1930; Murray 1933)

See also *Archanians, The;* Aristophanes; *Peace;* Peace

M

MacAlpin, Marian

Marian MacAlpin is the main character in Margaret Atwood's 1969 feminist novel *The Edible Woman.* Over the course of the story she subjugates herself to her fiancé, allowing him to control her life. At the same time she develops an eating disorder and cannot eat anything that was once alive and growing. In the end she refuses to allow him to consume her. She bakes him a cake shaped like a woman and tells him he should eat that instead. (Atwood 1996)

> See also Atwood, Margaret; *Edible Woman, The;* Feminism

MacWhite, Gilbert

Gilbert MacWhite is a character in the 1958 novel *The Ugly American,* by William J. Lederer and Eugene Burdick. After he is appointed U.S. ambassador to a small Asian country, he attempts to learn more about Asian culture and beliefs. Eventually he develops a deep understanding of the region's problems and tries to convince his superiors that a new approach to Asian politics is necessary. His suggestions are rejected, and the U.S. government removes him from his post. (Lederer and Burdick 1958)

> See also Burdick, Eugene; Lederer, William J.; *Ugly American, The*

Magic Mountain, The

Published in German in 1924 and English in 1927, *Der Zauberberg* (The Magic Mountain), by Thomas Mann, is set in a Swiss sanitorium during the early 1900s. Its main character, Hans Castorp, travels there to spend three weeks with his cousin, Joachim Ziemssen, who is being treated for tuberculosis. However, before his visit ends, Hans contracts a cold and a doctor convinces him that he also has tuberculosis. Hans therefore cancels his plans to leave the sanitorium, even though he has just taken a job as a ship engineer, and begins to revel in his illness. He also becomes fascinated with death. He studies science texts and arranges to visit the bedsides of the dying. At the same time he engages in deep philosophical discussions with various members of the sanitorium, each of whom represents a different ideology and approach to European life. For example, Ludovico Settembrini is an optimistic Italian humanist, Leo Naphta is a pessimistic Catholic convert, Mynheer Peeperkorn is a wealthy hedonist, and Ellen Brand is a spiritual medium. Hans learns from all of these people and eventually forms his own opinions about the world. He remains at the sanitorium even after his cousin's departure, subsequent return, and death, until seven years have passed. Then war breaks out in Europe, and Hans decides to leave the mountain and become a soldier. The novel ends with him on the battlefield facing a future as uncertain as Europe's.

The Magic Mountain examines the society of pre–World War I Europe, presenting its various ideologies and problems through somewhat one-dimensional characters at the sanitorium. It also illustrates the flaws inherent in any isolated and idle society. Various individuals react differently to their confinement, and Hans himself goes through a series of reactions to his situation, from resistance to acceptance to boredom to restlessness. In addition, on a more superficial level the novel criticizes the need for sanitoriums, which were prevalent when Mann began writing *The Magic Mountain* in 1912. As he (1972, 721) explains:

> You will have got from my book an idea of the narrowness of this charmed circle of isolation and invalidism. It is a sort of substitute existence, and it can, in a relatively short time, wholly wean a young person from actual and active life. Everything there, including the conception of time, is thought of on a luxurious scale. The cure is always a matter of several months, often of several years. But after the first six months the young person has not a single idea left save flirtation and the thermometer under his tongue. . . . Such institutions . . . were a typical prewar phenomenon. They were only possible in a capitalistic economy that was still functioning well and normally. Only under such a system was it possible for patients to remain there year after year at the family's expense. *The Magic Mountain* became the swan song of that form of existence.

Mann had firsthand knowledge of this existence, having spent three weeks at a sanitorium in Davos, Switzerland, when his wife was being treated there. As with Hans, the doctors tried to convince Mann that he was also ill and should remain under their care. He says: "If I had followed his advice, who knows, I might still be there! I wrote *The Magic Mountain* instead" (721). (Cleugh 1968; Hatfield 1964; Mann 1972)

See also Castorp, Hans; Mann, Thomas; Settembrini, Ludovico; Ziemssen Joachim

Major Barbara

A three-act play by Irish author George Bernard Shaw, *Major Barbara* is a satire involving religious hypocrisy and society's attitudes toward the poor. It was first performed in 1905 and published in 1907. Its title refers to one of its main characters, Barbara Undershaft, who is a major in the Salvation Army. She tries to save the souls of working-class men but finds many of them unreceptive to her words because they are out of work and more interested in food than religion.

Barbara is engaged to a young man named Adolphus Cusins, who is pretending to be a Salvationist in order to woo her. He is a poor scholar and can offer her little money. Therefore, Barbara's mother sends for her estranged husband, Andrew Undershaft, and asks him to give his daughter money. Shortly after Andrew arrives, he and Barbara's mother begin rehashing an old quarrel over the inheritance of their three children: Barbara; her sister, Sarah; and her brother, Stephen. Andrew is a wealthy manufacturer of armory and ammunition. A foundling, he received the business from a stranger who adopted him. This is a long-standing tradition in the munitions factory; each owner must choose a foundling as his successor, regardless of whether or not he has a son of his own. Andrew intends to uphold the tradition. His wife opposes it.

When Andrew is reunited with his children, whom he has not seen in years, he becomes fascinated with Barbara. The two debate various issues, and Barbara professes disgust for her father's profession. She says that no one of good moral character could make money from war. She vows to convert him to Salvationism, and in return Andrew vows to convert his daughter into a supporter of his munitions factory. He goes to the Salvation Army shelter where she works and easily convinces her superiors to accept a £5,000 donation of money from him. Disillusioned, Barbara quits her position. She then accompanies her father to his factory and its surrounding town and sees that the people there are well treated, happy, productive, and spiritual. When she asks him how he keeps such order without being oppressive, Andrew explains:

> Practically, every man of them keeps the man just below him in his place. I never meddle with them. I never bully them. . . . I say that certain things are to be done; but I don't order anybody to do them. I don't say, mind you, that there is no ordering about and snubbing and even bullying. The men snub the boys and order them about; the carmen snub the sweepers; the artisans snub the unskilled laborers; the foremen drive and bully both the laborers and the artisans; the assistant engineers find fault with the foremen; the chief engineers drop on the assistants; the departmental managers worry the chiefs; and the clerks have tall hats and hymnbooks and keep up the social tone by refusing to associate on equal terms with anybody. The result is a colossal profit, which comes to me. (Shaw 1962, 419)

But Barbara sees that much of that money has been spent on the workers. The factory workers' town is clean and well appointed, and their church is thriving. She now realizes that Andrew Undershaft has done more to uplift the lower classes than the Salvation Army ever did. This proves his earlier arguments concerning the importance of alleviating poverty, during which he explained:

> Food, clothing, firing, rent, taxes, respectability and children. Nothing can lift those seven millstones from Man's neck but money; and the spirit cannot soar until the millstones are lifted. . . . [Poverty is] the worst of crimes. All other crimes are virtues beside it. . . . Poverty blights whole cities; spreads horrible pestilences; strikes dead the very souls of all who come

within sight, sound or smell of it. What you call crime is nothing: a murder here and a theft there. . . . But there are millions of poor people, abject people, dirty people, ill fed, ill clothed people. They poison us morally and physically: they kill the happiness of society: they force us to do away with our own liberties and to organize unnatural cruelties for fear they should rise against us and drag us down into their abyss. Only fools fear crime: we all fear poverty. (434)

Adolphus is impressed with Andrew's arguments. In turn, Andrew is impressed with his future son-in-law. When he learns that the young man is a foundling, he announces that he will leave the business to Adolphus. Adolphus accepts the offer, explaining to Barbara that he has no problem making money from manufacturing weapons because they help the common man fight his oppressors. He says: "I love the common people. I want to arm them against the lawyers, the doctors, the priests, the literary men, the professors, the artists, and the politicians, who, once in authority, are more disastrous and tyrannical than all the fools, rascals, and impostors. I want a power simple enough for common men to use, yet strong enough to force the intellectual oligarchy to use its genius for the general good" (442). In the end Barbara rejoices over Adolphus's new role in society, having realized that she can do more good for the people using her father's methods than the Salvation Army's.

Shaw (305–306) discusses this aspect of *Major Barbara* in a preface to the work:

> In the millionaire Undershaft I have represented a man who has become intellectually and spiritually as well as practically conscious of the irresistible natural truth which we all abhor and repudiate: to wit, that the greatest of our evils, and the worst of our crimes is poverty, and that our first duty, to which every other consideration should be sacrificed, is not to be poor. . . . Security, the chief pretence of civilization, cannot exist where the worst of dangers,

the danger of poverty, hangs over everyone's head, and where the alleged protection of our persons from violence is only an accidental result of the existence of a police force whose real business is to force the poor man to see his children starve whilst idle people overfeed pet dogs with the money that might feed and clothe them.

Shaw also criticizes class distinctions and snobbery in his preface, as well as the Salvation Army in particular and religion in general. He concludes that because of hypocrisy, "at present there is not a single credible established religion in the world" (339). Shaw criticizes religion in other writings as well. For example, in the preface to his play *Heartbreak House,* he calls the church "that stuffy, uncomfortable place of penance in which we suffer so much inconvenience on the slenderest chance of gaining a scrap of food for our starving souls" (482). As a socialist Shaw was a harsh critic of British society. In addition to his numerous plays, he wrote antiwar speeches and other political essays and tracts. (Hill 1978; McCabe 1974; Shaw 1962)

See also Poverty; Religion; Shaw, George Bernard; Undershaft, Andrew

Mako

This well-educated Zulu man from Peter Abrahams's 1948 novel *The Path of Thunder* believes in black nationalism. Mako criticizes South Africa's foreign rulers, who control all education and force native people "to assimilate many of their ways to survive" (Abrahams 1975, 91). He does not believe in interracial marriage if it is done as an attempt of the blacks to become more like the whites. However, if it is a union born out of true love, he supports it, saying that such intermarriage "is a mirror to the nationalism on a higher plane. There are those who say the world will not be free and happy—and I agree—until nations stop fighting the other nations and nations stop oppressing other nations. The national intermarriage, whether it is between white and black or between pink and red, is a mirror of this highest form of world nationalism

when man will really be free" (93). (Abrahams 1975; Ensor 1992)

See also Abrahams, Peter; Finkelberg, Isaac; *Path of Thunder, The;* Racism; Swartz, Lanny

Malafrena

Published in 1979, *Malafrena,* by Ursula Le Guin, concerns political and social oppression. The novel is set in the early nineteenth century in the fictional country of Orsinia, which is under the control of Austria. Its two main characters are Piera Valtoskar and Itale Sorde, who live in the Malafrena Valley. At the beginning of the story Piera is a young woman whose only thoughts are of falling in love. She is attracted to Itale, but when he shows no interest in her, she secretly becomes engaged to another man, then breaks off her engagement to become betrothed to someone else. Eventually, however, she breaks that engagement to take over the management of her ailing father's estate. No woman in Malafrena has ever done such a thing, but Piera proves herself as competent at the job as any man.

Meanwhile Itale has been examining his own role in society. He is heir to a large estate, and his father expects him to manage it. However, Itale is passionate about his political beliefs and moves to a nearby city, Krasnoy, to take part in revolutionary activities. He also has a secret affair with Baroness Luisa Paludeskar, a lady-in-waiting to the Grand Duchess. Eventually Itale is arrested by the Austrian police for his political activities, and Luisa uses her influence to have him freed. But after two years in prison he is not the same man. His health is poor, and he has lost his passion for revolution. Luisa realizes she is no longer attracted to him and ends their affair. Shortly thereafter Itale learns that the French have overthrown their king. His political passion returns, and he participates in a revolution against the Orsinian government. When the battle is lost, he flees to Malafrena, where he plans to live in exile. There he meets Piera Valtoskar. They express their friendship and go rowing together. (Le Guin 1979)

See also Le Guin, Ursula; Science Fiction and Fantasy; Sorde, Itale; Valtoskar, Piera

Maldonado, Felix

The main character of Carlos Fuentes's 1978 novel *La cabeza de la hidra* (The Hydra Head), Felix Maldonado is an agent of an independent Mexican spy organization that wants that country's oil industry to remain nationalized. Felix's father worked in the industry when it was still controlled by private corporations, and he considers it a terrible time in Mexico's history. Felix tells a friend that whenever his father went to talk to his British boss, "he never saw his face. Each time my father entered, this Englishman was sitting with his back to him. That was the custom; you received Mexican employees with your back turned, to make them feel they were inferior, like the Hindu employees of the British Raj" (Fuentes 1978, 218). However, after the oil companies were nationalized, there were "no more White Guards, the company's private army, stealing land and cutting off the ears of rural schoolteachers. And most important of all, people looked one another in the face" (218). Because of his emotions regarding Mexico's oil industry, Felix becomes involved in an intricate plot involving a large oil reserve whose existence is important to both the Israelis and the Arabs. Caught between these two factions, Felix eventually loses his identity and everyone he loves. (Fuentes 1978)

See also Fuentes, Carlos; *Hydra Head, The*

"Man with the Hoe, The"

Written in 1899 by American poet Edwin Markham, the poem "The Man with the Hoe" concerns the plight of the farmer, upon whose back rests "the burden of the world." Overworked, he is a "monstrous thing distorted and soul-quenched," and the poet calls upon the "masters, lords and rulers in all lands" to "straighten up this shape" and "rebuild in it the music and the dream," or fear the day "when whirlwinds of rebellion shake the world" (Sinclair 1996, 29–30). (Sinclair 1996)

See also Labor Issues; Markham, Edwin

Mann, Thomas

German novelist and essayist Thomas Mann often addressed political and social issues in his work, examining the nature of Western culture and its relationship to the human spirit. His novels include *Tristan* (1903), *Der Tod in Venedig* (Death in Venice, 1912), *Der Zauberberg* (The Magic Mountain, 1924), and *Doktor Faustus* (Doctor Faustus, 1947). Born on June 6, 1875, in Lübeck, Germany, Mann moved to Munich after his father's death in 1891. He remained there until 1933, working first in an insurance office and later as an editor on a weekly magazine. While at the magazine he began writing stories. His first novel, *Buddenbrooks*, was published in 1901. Many other novels followed, and in 1929 he won the Nobel Prize for Literature. In 1930 he began speaking out against Nazi policies in Germany. Three years later, while he was on vacation in Switzerland, family members warned him not to return home, fearing for his safety. He remained in Switzerland until 1938 when, after making several visits to the United States, he decided to move to America. He spent two years on the east coast before settling in southern California. By this time his native country had stripped him of his German citizenship, and in 1944 he became an American citizen. During the tumultuous period after leaving Germany, he wrote a series of novels based on the biblical story of Joseph, collectively called *Joseph und seine Brüder* (Joseph and His Brothers): *Die Geschichten Jaakobs* (The Tales of Jacob in the United Kingdom, Joseph and His Brothers in the United States, 1933), *Der junge Joseph* (Young Joseph, 1934), *Joseph in Ägypten* (Joseph in Egypt, 1936), and *Joseph der Ernährer* (Joseph the Provider, 1943). Four years later he published *Doktor Faustus*, which relates the personal tragedy of a German composer to the destruction of Germany during World War II. Mann's last novel was a humorous work, *Die Bekenntnisse des Hochstaplers Felix Krull* (The Confessions of Felix Krull, Confidence Man, 1954). It was left unfinished at his death on August 12, 1955, near Zurich, Switzerland.

See also *Magic Mountain, The*

Manorialism

Manorialism was an economic and social system whereby members of the nobility allowed peasants to farm their land in exchange for money, goods, and services. It began in the fourth century, became widespread during the Middle Ages, and remained the prevalent economic system until the end of the sixteenth century, when it was largely replaced by capitalism. In Austria, however, manorialism remained until the eighteenth century, and in Russia it lasted until the revolution of 1917. In all countries injustices against peasants laboring under manorialism were rampant. Consequently, many authors called attention to the unfairness of the system, including Maria Edgeworth, Leo Tolstoi, and Ivan Turgenev. (Herlihy 1970)

> See also Capitalism; Edgeworth, Maria; Tolstoi, Leo; Turgenev, Ivan

"Man's a Man for a' That, A"

Written in Scottish dialect by poet Robert Burns, the poem "A Man's a Man for a' That" (1786) expresses the view that all men, however poor, are still human beings and that a person should be defined by his character rather than his income or social position. Burns (Sinclair, 1996, 163) writes: "The honest man, though e'er sae puir [ever so poor],/ Is king o' men for a' that." Conversely, a lord "what struts, and stares, and a' that" is not worthy of much respect (163).

> See also Burns, Robert; Class, Social; Poverty

Maqui, Rosendo

Mayor of the Indian village of Rumi in Ciro Alegría's 1941 novel *El mundo es ancho y ajeno* (Broad and Alien Is the World), Rosendo Maqui is an old man who has long been respected for his wisdom and his kindness. Nonetheless, as a result of the trickery of non-native rancher Don Alvaro Amenabar, he is labeled a thief and thrown into prison, where he is beaten to death by the guards. However, government officials declare that he has died of a heart attack and bury his body in secret. (Alegría 1941)

> See also Alegría, Ciro; Amenabar, Don Alvaro; *Broad and Alien Is the World;* Castro, Benito; Justice

Markham, Edwin

Edwin Markham (originally Charles Edward Anson Markham) is best known for his 1899 social protest poem "The Man with the Hoe," which was his first published work. His poetry collections include *The Man with the Hoe and Other Poems* (1899), *Lincoln and Other Poems* (1901), and *Shoes of Happiness* (1915). Markham was born in Oregon City, Oregon, on April 23, 1852, and grew up in California. He died on March 7, 1940, in New York, New York. (Sinclair 1996)

> See also "Man with the Hoe, The"

Martin, Donald

Donald Martin is the innocent victim of a lynching in Walter Van Tilburg Clark's 1940 western novel *The Ox-Bow Incident*. After struggling to convince the lynching party that it is about to hang the wrong man, Martin accepts his fate with courageous resignation. He writes a loving farewell note to his wife and arranges for someone to help provide for her after his death. In an analysis of the novel's main characters, scholar Max Westbrook (1969, 67) calls Martin "an innocent, naïve in the affairs of the manly world, the natural prey of the mob-beast." (Westbrook 1969)

> See also Clark, Walter Van Tilberg; Croft, Art; Davies, Art; Justice; *Ox-Bow Incident, The;* Tetley, Gerald

Marx, Bernard

Bernard Marx is one of the main characters in Aldous Huxley's 1932 futuristic novel *Brave New World*. He lives in a society where people are created in test tubes and chemically altered to have different intellects and personalities. They are labeled from Alpha down to Epsilon according to their traits; Alphas have superior intellects, whereas Epsilons are drone workers. After being created as an Alpha fetus, Bernard is accidentally given a solution meant for a Beta. This makes him slightly different from others in his classification, and he does not feel comfortable among them. One day he goes on vacation to the Savage Reservation in New Mexico and discovers a misfit in its primitive culture. The young man, John, is the son of a woman from Bernard's society who got lost while visiting the reservation. When Bernard brings John home with him, he finally feels popular and important. He brags about his role as John's guardian and ignores the young man's unhappiness. But Bernard's position in his society is still tenuous, and when John speaks out against his new world, Bernard is blamed for the resulting trouble and exiled to an island of misfits. (Huxley 1989)

See also *Brave New World;* Exiles; Huxley, Aldous

Marxism

See Communism; Socialism

"Masks, a Story"

"Masks, a Story" is a short story by Eloise Bibb Thompson, an African American who often wrote about racism in the United States. Originally published in *Opportunity* magazine in October 1927, the story tells of a black man, Aristile Blanchard, who believes that the way for black men to achieve greatness is to appear to be white. He begins making white masks, and after his death his granddaughter Julie takes over his work. She quickly realizes that no mask would be as realistic as natural skin, and she therefore decides that breeding is the only way for black people to appear white. She marries a black man who looks white, and when she becomes pregnant, she is certain that the baby will look white, too. When the child is born dark, Julie looks at her and dies. The epitaph on her tombstone reads, "Because she saw with the eyes of her grandfather, she died at the sight of her babe's face" (Roses and Randolph 1996, 38). This story is representative of much of Thompson's work, which concerns feelings of self-worth and pride. (Roses and Randolph 1996)

See also Harlem Renaissance; Racism; Thompson, Eloise Bibb

Maslova, Katusha

In Leo Tolstoi's 1899 novel *Voskreseniye* (Resurrection), Katusha Maslova is an innocent peasant girl who becomes pregnant by a Russian nobleman. Her child dies en route to an orphanage, and she becomes a prostitute. Later she is sentenced to prison for murder, even though she is clearly innocent. One of the jurors at her trial is the same nobleman who seduced her, Prince Dmitri Ivanovitch Nekhludof. Feeling guilty for his sin, he works for her release and offers to marry her. She refuses, choosing instead to marry a member of her own social class. At the same time, through Nekhludof's attentions and her association with political prisoners who expose her to high ideals, Maslova regains her self-respect. (Tolstoy 1911)

See also Nekhludof, Prince Dmitri Ivanovitch; *Resurrection;* Tolstoi, Leo

Materialism

See Capitalism

McCarthyism

The term *McCarthyism* refers to the anticommunist attitudes that existed during a period in U.S. history known as the McCarthy era. In 1950 Senator Joseph McCarthy began a campaign to expose Communists in the government, whom he believed were evil subversives. His accusations soon spread to include writers, artists, actors, and other prominent figures. Anyone suspected of being a Communist was attacked, and many lost their jobs as McCarthy's anticommunism hysteria spread throughout the country.

Social protest authors were particularly susceptible to charges of being subversives. Many of them, such as Tillie Olsen, belonged to the Communist Party or had attended its meetings. This automatically made them targets for persecution. In addition, when Arthur Miller protested the injustice of McCarthyism in his play *The Crucible,* he, too, was attacked for being a Communist sympathizer. Another playwright who experienced McCarthyism was Lillian Hellman, who depicted unfair persecution in her play *The*

Senator Joseph McCarthy with his two investigators, Roy Cohn and David Schine, during the House Un-American investigation (Archive Photos)

Children's Hour. The McCarthy era ended in 1954 after televised hearings exposed McCarthy as being irrational in his accusations. (Schrecker 1994, 1998)

> **See also** Censorship; *Children's Hour, The;* Communism; *Crucible, The;* Hellman, Lillian; Miller, Arthur; Olsen, Tillie

McMurphy, Randall Patrick

Randall Patrick McMurphy is one of the main characters in Ken Kesey's 1962 novel *One Flew over the Cuckoo's Nest.* A gambler, a swindler, and a fighter, McMurphy feigns insanity to gain transfer from a prison work camp to a mental hospital, where he believes that life will be easier. However, he soon finds himself in a battle of wills with the head nurse, Nurse Ratched, a domineering woman who in some ways is less sane than her charges. McMurphy challenges her authority with humor and wit, and gradually the other patients come to share his strength of character. Then McMurphy learns that his six-month sentence, of which he had already served two months, is now an indefinite one; he cannot leave the hospital without Nurse Ratched's approval. He begins to conform to her demands, but when the other patients quickly slip back into submission and insanity, he decides to sacrifice himself for the group. He escalates his opposition to Nurse Ratched's rules and in a fit of frustration and anger attacks her. This act helps the patients regain their sanity but ultimately brings about McMurphy's death. In this regard the novel uses Christ imagery to emphasize McMurphy's martyrdom. (Kesey 1964)

> **See also** Kesey, Ken; *One Flew over the Cuckoo's Nest*

Mellama, Mauritas

In the 1980 novel *Bumi manusia* (This Earth of Mankind), by Pramoedya Ananta Toer, the character of Mauritas Mellama represents the arrogance of the Dutch rulers of Indonesia, who are prejudiced against native Javanese. Mauritas is the son of a Dutch colonialist, Herman Mellama, who abandoned his wife to move to the island of Java. Mauritas was raised by his mother in the Netherlands. As an adult he travels to Java on business and discovers that his father is living there with his concubine, Ontosoroh. He confronts Herman and castigates him for associating with native women. When Ontosoroh tries to defend her master, Mauritas does not even acknowledge her existence. Later, when Herman dies, he takes over the estate and throws the woman off the farm. He also separates her from her daughter, Annalies, whom he considers more European than native. He then dissolves Annelies's marriage to a native man and sends her to school in the Netherlands. (Toer 1996)

See also Ontosoroh; *This Earth of Mankind;* Toer, Pramoedya Ananta

Mellama, Robert

Robert Mellama appears in *Bumi manusia* (This Earth of Mankind) (1980), by Pramoedya Ananta Toer, which concerns the prejudice that Europeans have against native Javanese in Indonesia. Robert is the child of a native concubine and her Dutch master. However, he pretends to be fully European. He expresses hatred for all natives and threatens to kill his sister's native lover, Minke. He is consumed by anger, and on one occasion he rapes his own sister. When his father is poisoned, he disappears and is suspected of the crime. He visits his sister on her wedding day and tells her he is going to Europe, where he hopes to erase his past. (Toer 1996)

See also Minke; *This Earth of Mankind;* Toer, Pramoedya Ananta

Melvyn, Sybylla

First-person narrator of Miles Franklin's 1901 Australian novel *My Brilliant Career,* Sybylla Melvyn is a feminist at a time when women are encouraged to subjugate themselves in marriage. She often finds herself frustrated by her male relatives' patronizing treatment of women. Moreover, although she is poor, she breaks off her engagement to a wealthy, kind man because he does not view women as equal to men. (Franklin 1965)

See also Feminism; Franklin, Miles; *My Brilliant Career*

Meredith, Anthony

Anthony Meredith is the fictional scholar who provides the footnotes for Jack London's 1907 novel *The Iron Heel.* Meredith lives seven centuries in the future, after a series of revolts have created a truly socialistic American society, and he makes it clear that his world is far better than previous ones. For example, the society of the future has no theft, no bloodshed, and no poverty. Meredith's footnotes therefore allow London to comment on the problems within contemporary American society. (London 1924)

See also *Iron Heel, The;* London, Jack

Merou, Ulysse

Ulysse Merou is the first-person narrator of Pierre Boulle's 1963 science fiction novel *La Planète de singes* (Planet of the Apes). After traveling from Earth to a distant planet, he encounters a world where humans behave like apes and apes like humans. His observations on the prejudices and faulty reasoning within ape society are Boulle's way of commenting on the flaws within human society. (Boulle 1963)

See also Boulle, Pierre; *Planet of the Apes;* Science Fiction and Fantasy

Merridew, Jack

In William Golding's 1954 novel *Lord of the Flies,* the character of Jack Merridew symbolizes violence as a threat to civilization. He is one of several British schoolboys stranded on an island without adult supervision. As time passes, he becomes a cruel, primitive savage who enjoys hunting and killing pigs. Eventually he challenges the established order of the group and tries to kill its elected leader, Ralph. (Golding 1954)

See also Golding, William; *Lord of the Flies;* Ralph

Meursault, Monsieur

Narrator of Albert Camus's 1942 novel *L'Etranger* (The Stranger), Monsieur Meursault is a man who shows no outward emotion, even at his mother's funeral. When he kills a man in a moment of panic, the prosecutor condemns him for this lack of grief and accuses Meursault of displaying no remorse. Meursault admits: "I have never been able to truly feel remorse for anything. My mind was always on what was coming next, today or to-morrow" (Camus 1989, 100). According to Camus biographer Germaine Brée (1961, 112), Meursault is "a man content just to live and who asks no questions," and ultimately it is his apathy toward life that causes his death. (Bree 1961; Camus 1989)

See also Camus, Albert; Justice; *Stranger, The*

Mexican-American Literature

Although Mexican Americans have histori-cally experienced racism and social injustices similar to other nonwhite ethnic groups in the United States, they have not created a large body of book-length fiction to protest their circumstances. As Raymond A. Paredes ex-plains in a chapter on Mexican-American lit-erature in the *Columbia Literary History of the United States* (Elliott 1988, 800–801):

In the second half of the nineteenth cen-tury, when a distinctly Mexican-American literature began to emerge, it followed a line of development common among frontier cultures. Historical and personal narratives predominated, many of them apologetic in tone. . . . Mexican Ameri-cans also produced a considerable volume of verse. . . . Oddly enough, so far as we now know, little sustained fiction was produced, perhaps because the harsh envi-ronment of the Southwestern frontier dis-couraged prolonged periods of creativity.

However, Paredes also reports that Mexi-can-American creativity did find one impor-tant outlet for expression: oral verse, most no-tably a type of ballad called the *corrido*. These *corridos* spoke of "economic struggle, legends of the [Mexican] revolution, and . . . the pain of immigration and acculturation" (803).

During the 1940s and 1950s Mexican-American authors also increasingly expressed themselves through written personal narra-tives and short stories. Once again, their liter-ature primarily dealt with acculturation into white society. But in the 1960s a new form of expression began to develop—the social protest drama. According to Paredes, a group

called the Teatro Campesino sprang up during the 1960s to support César Chávez's farm-workers' union and began to produce plays, or *actos*. Paredes (806) reports:

Performed in open fields as well as univer-sity halls and theaters, the Teatro's *actos* at-tacked greedy farmers, dishonest labor con-tractors, brutal policemen—in short, all the enemies of the farmworkers' union—with deadly wit. More than any other develop-ment of the time, the Teatro Campesino demonstrated to Mexican Americans the manifold potential of literary expression.

Consequently, Mexican-American writing began to flourish, and new publishing compa-nies sprang up to produce Spanish-language books and magazines. Paredes (806–807) writes of one, Quinto Sol Publications, which was established in 1967:

Quinto Sol Publications opened its doors in Berkeley [California] for the sole pur-posed of issuing Mexican-American writ-ing. Although diverse, the authors associ-ated with Quinto Sol shared certain assumptions and goals. They wanted to create a body of work that remained free of stereotypes while remaining faithful to their Mexican folk and belletristic tradi-tions; they wanted to find forms and tech-niques compatible with the social, politi-cal, and cultural needs of their people; and they wanted, like their predecessors, to confront the language issue and the questions of voice. In addition, however, they displayed new pride in their Indian heritage by evoking Aztec thought and culture. The notion of Aztlan, the ances-tral home of the Aztecs believed to be lo-cated in the American Southwest, became a controlling metaphor for many writers. Aztlan freed Mexican Americans from the onus of being recent, displaced immi-grants and provided them with a sense of place and continuity. With the concept of Aztlan, the Southwest became theirs again.

The most notable Mexican-American writers discovered by Quinto Sol Publications, according to Paredes, were Roland Hinojosa-Smith, who wrote sketches about Mexican Americans in Texas; Rudolfo Anaya, who wrote short stories about ethnic and economic issues; and Tomas Rivera, who wrote stories and sketches about Mexican-American farmworkers during the 1970s. Of these, only Anaya published in English, and as with earlier authors, they all preferred short forms.

Although Quinto Sol Publications no longer exists, short-form Mexican-American literature continues to thrive via Spanish-language magazines and newspapers. However, Paredes points out that the nature of this literature has changed. He (809) says: "Mexican-American writers no longer feel bound to the program of cultural preservation and political activism of the 1960s and early 1970s. Richard Rodriguez's autobiographical *Hunger of Memory* (1981), which accepts as inevitable—and deems ultimately desirable—the process of assimilation, makes this clear."

Paredes believes that modern Mexican-American authors are more concerned with "self-examination" (809), which they express primarily through poetry. Their protest literature increasingly concerns itself with problems within the Mexican-American community, such as poverty and violence, as opposed to struggles between Anglo and Mexican cultures. (Elliott 1988)

Miller, Arthur

Playwright Arthur Miller is the author of several dramas that criticize American society. His most famous works are *Death of a Salesman* (1949) and *The Crucible* (1953), for which he was persecuted by the U.S. government.

Born on October 17, 1915, in New York, New York, Miller grew up in a comfortable home as the son of a coat manufacturer. However, when he was 13, his father lost his business, and the family was forced to move into a poorer neighborhood in Brooklyn, New York. Miller graduated from high school there in 1932 and went to work in an auto parts warehouse. Each week he set aside part of his

salary for college tuition; in 1934 he enrolled at the University of Michigan as a journalism student. Eighteen months later he started writing plays, and his first drama, *Honors at Dawn,* won a prestigious drama award. The following year another of his dramas, *No Villain,* won the same award.

After graduating from college in 1938, Miller worked at a variety of odd jobs, including delivery boy, dishwasher, waiter, and warehouse clerk. At the same time he wrote dramas for the Federal Theater Project and radio scripts for both the Columbia Workshop (CBS) and the Cavalcade of America (NBC). Although Miller appreciated the income from these scripts, he disliked the censorship he encountered among radio executives. He (Moss 1967, 25) later said: "There is so much you can't say on the radio that for a serious writer it presents a blank wall. . . . Radio today is in the hands of people most of whom have no taste, no will, no nothing but the primitive ability to spot a script that does not conform to the format."

With the onset of World War II, he began visiting army camps to collect material for a movie screenplay, *The Story of GI Joe.* He was exempt from serving in the military himself because of an old injury. In 1944 he published a journal of his experiences at the camps, entitled *Situation Normal,* and wrote more award-winning plays, as well as a novel, *Focus* (1945), about anti-Semitism. However, his work did not become widely known until 1947 when his drama *All My Sons* received the New York Drama Critics Award. Two years later his drama *Death of a Salesman* received several prestigious awards, including the Pulitzer Prize.

However, these awards did not protect him from attack after the publication of his play *The Crucible* in 1953. Set in 1692, the drama concerns witch-hunts in Salem, Massachusetts, but critics correctly interpreted it as being an attack on the anticommunist "witch-hunts" that were taking place at the time of the play's production. Miller was immediately labeled a Communist sympathizer, and on those grounds he was denied a passport to attend the play's

Belgian premiere in 1954. Two years later, in June 1956, he was called to testify before the House Committee on Un-American Activities, the anticommunist witch-hunting agency of the U.S. Congress. Forced to defend himself as a loyal American, he said that, although he once attended a few Communist-sponsored meetings for writers, he was no longer involved with such things. However, he refused to name the other writers at the meeting and was therefore indicted for contempt of court. He stood trial and on May 31, 1957, was found guilty and fined $500. The following year the U.S. Court of Appeals for the District of Columbia reversed the decision, clearing Miller's name.

During the period of his persecution and trial, Miller wrote little. Afterward, however, he returned to his work. His later plays include *After the Fall* (1964), *The Price* (1968), *The Archbishop's Ceiling* (1977), *The Ride Down Mount Morgan* (1991), and *The Last Yankee* (1991). He also wrote the screenplay for *The Misfits* (1961), which starred his second wife, actress Marilyn Monroe, as well as a collection of short stories, *I Don't Need You Any More* (1967), and an autobiography, *Timebends* (1987). Miller currently lives in the Connecticut countryside. (Moss 1967)

See also Censorship; *Crucible, The;* McCarthyism

Miller, Henry

The novels of American author Henry Miller were banned in the United States until the 1960s because of their sexual explicitness. He therefore became a symbol in the fight against censorship. He was also a social critic, and his 1945 nonfiction book *The Air-Conditioned Nightmare,* which includes poetry, is a harsh commentary on modern American life. Many of his works are a mixture of poetic fiction and autobiographical material.

Miller was born on December 26, 1891, in New York, New York. He grew up in Brooklyn but traveled to France in 1930. His most famous novel, *Tropic of Cancer,* is based on his experiences there. It was published in France in 1934 and the United States in 1961. *Tropic of Capricorn,* published in France in 1939 and the United States in 1961, concerns Miller's earlier experiences in New York. Both books were the subject of a protracted court case; in 1964 the U.S. Supreme Court reversed a ruling that they were obscene. His other works include the novels *Black Spring* (1936) and *The Colossus of Maroussi* (1941) and the essay collections *The Cosmological Eye* (1939) and *The Wisdom of the Heart* (1941). In later years Miller lived in Big Sur, California. He died in Pacific Palisades, California, on June 7, 1980. (Widmer 1963)

See also *Air-Conditioned Nightmare, The;* Censorship

Milvain, Jasper

A character in George Gissing's 1891 novel *New Grub Street,* Jasper Milvain is a writer who does not care about his work's artistic merit. He writes strictly for money, saying: "I maintain that we people of brains are justified in supplying the mob with the food it likes. . . . If only I had the skill, I would produce novels out-trashing the trashiest that ever sold fifty thousand copies" (Gissing 1926, 10). But since he is unable to write novels, Milvain instead writes articles for newspapers and magazines, and eventually he becomes moderately successful. Then he breaks off his engagement to a poor woman to marry a rich one because he believes that "to have money is becoming of more and more importance in a literary career; principally because to have money is to have friends" (27). To Jasper Milvain, poverty "is the root of all social ills; its existence accounts even for the ills that arise from wealth. The poor man is a man labouring in fetters" (30). (Gissing 1926)

See also Gissing, George; *New Grub Street;* Reardon, Edwin

Minke

Minke is the main character in Pramoedya Ananta Toer's 1980 novel *This Earth of Mankind,* which concerns social and political injustices on the island of Java. A native, he attends a Dutch-run school and experiences a great deal of prejudice because of his race.

Students tease him for having no last name, which is what separates the natives from the Europeans. However, at a school assembly a teacher honors Minke by saying: "Students, having a family name is just a custom. Before Napoleon Bonaparte appeared on the stage of European history, not even our ancestors— not one of them—used family names. . . . It was through contact with other peoples that Europeans learned the importance of family names" (Toer 1996, 215). Moreover, she attacks racism by saying: "Europeans who feel themselves to be a hundred percent pure do not really know how much Asian blood flows in their veins. From your study of history, you will all know that hundreds of years ago, many different Asian armies attacked Europe, and left descendants" (215).

For raising such points, the teacher is fired. However, Minke continues to spread her views in his writings. He is an accomplished author and becomes a regular contributor to an Indonesian newspaper, addressing many important social and political issues. At the same time he becomes embroiled in a personal scandal that threatens to end his education and his writing career. When his lover's father is murdered, rumors spread regarding Minke's relationship to the girl and her family. He writes a passionate defense, and in the end many people rally to his side. He has shown his ability to influence public opinion and will undoubtedly be influential in Indonesia's political future. (Toer 1996)

See also *This Earth of Mankind;* Toer, Pramoedya Ananta

Misérables, Les

Les Misérables, by Victor Hugo, was published both in French and in English in 1862. The novel, which covers a period of approximately 18 years, comments on French politics, war, and history, discussing such events as the fall of Napoleon, the restoration of the monarchy, and the revolution of 1830. One of its most famous passages describes and analyzes the Battle of Waterloo. More importantly, however, the novel offers a portrait of French society and examines various aspects of human nature. For this reason, the book is often compared to the works of Charles Dickens and Fyodor Dostoyevsky, which portray English and Russian society, respectively.

The plot of *Les Misérables* centers around the life of Jean Valjean, who arrives at the home of Monsieur Charles-François-Bienvenu Myriel, the bishop of Digne, one evening in 1815. Valjean has just been released from prison, where he served 5 years for stealing a loaf of bread and 14 more for trying to escape. He explains to the bishop that the inns have all refused him lodging because of his criminal past, which is revealed through his specially marked passport, and the bishop does not hesitate to take him in. But despite the bishop's kindness, during the night Valjean steals his silver table settings and flees. When the police catch him with the silver, they bring him to the bishop, who insists that he gave his dishes to the man as a gift. The bishop then tells Valjean: "Do not forget, ever, that you have promised me to use this silver to become an honest man. . . . You no longer belong to evil but to good. It is your soul I am buying for you. I withdraw it from dark thoughts and from the spirit of perdition, and I give it to God!" (Hugo 1987, 106). Valjean leaves town with the silver, and shortly thereafter he steals a small boy's coin. Remembering the bishop's words, his conscience is troubled, and he realizes the depths to which he has sunk. He vows to reform.

Meanwhile a young Parisian girl named Fantine has been abandoned by her lover, with whom she has had a child, Cosette. Shortly thereafter she leaves her three-year-old daughter with the Thénardier family and sets off to the nearby city of Montreuil-sur-mer to find a job. Soon she is working at the factory of the mayor, Monsieur Madeleine, who has a mysterious past. Madeleine arrived in town as a stranger, but because he saved the lives of two little girls during a fire, he was immediately accepted into the community. He became rich after inventing a new manufacturing process, opened his factory, and began donating much of his profits to the poor. For his kindness the government awarded him the

Legion of Honor, but out of modesty he refused to accept it.

Fantine is pleased to be working at Madeleine's factory, but soon the overseer learns that she had a child out of wedlock and fires her. Now she has difficulty paying the Thénardiers for Cosette's upkeep, yet they continue to ask for more and more money. Fantine quickly descends into poverty, prostitution, and illness, blaming Madeleine for her fate. Her only comfort is that she believes her daughter is living a better life. She is unaware that the Thénardiers have turned Cosette into their slave even though the girl is only five years old; as the story's omniscient narrator points out, "social suffering can begin at any age" (157).

When Madeleine learns of Fantine's suffering, he takes her home, summons a doctor, and sends for Cosette. Meanwhile the town's police inspector, Javert, informs Madeleine that he once suspected Madeleine of being Jean Valjean, a convict who stole money from a little boy and was never caught. Javert then offers apologies and says that the real Jean Valjean has just been arrested for the crime. Madeleine wrestles with his conscience and finally interrupts the man's trial to announce that he is really Jean Valjean. He then goes home to await his arrest. Javert finds him in Fantine's sickroom and berates him, whereupon a shocked Fantine dies.

After Jean Valjean's arrest everyone in town forgets about his good deeds and excellent reputation. They condemn him as a convict and are glad to be rid of him. However, his former servants remain loyal to him, and when he escapes from jail, they help him leave town. He withdraws a large sum of money from the bank and hides it before being arrested again. He is sent to work on board a ship, where he saves a sailor's life, then falls into the sea and is believed drowned.

Shortly thereafter he rescues eight-year-old Cosette from the Thénardiers and takes her to Paris, where Javert discovers him and gives chase. Valjean escapes with the little girl to a convent, where he becomes the gardener's assistant under an assumed name. Cosette attends the convent school as his granddaughter. After she graduates, Valjean decides that she should see something of the world and takes her from the convent. He believes that no one will recognize him after so many years.

The two live together in a small house in Paris, where Valjean becomes involved in charitable causes. One day he answers the plea of a man named Monsieur Jondrette, who has written him for aid. When Valjean and Cosette bring them clothes and blankets, Jondrette recognizes them; he is actually Monsieur Thénardier, but Valjean and Cosette do not realize this. Meanwhile a young man is observing the scene through a crack in the wall. He is Jondrette's neighbor, Marius Pontmercy. Marius was raised by his maternal grandfather, Monsieur Gillenormand, who kept the young man from knowing his father because of the elder Pontmercy's political views. Upon his father's death Marius expressed support for those same views, and Gillenormand threw him out of the house. Marius then became a lawyer and a member of a revolutionary group.

Now Marius recognizes Cosette and Valjean as well, but not for the same reason. He has been in love with Cosette for some time, having seen her in the park from a distance. Shortly after they leave Jondrette's room, he overhears Jondrette telling his wife that when Valjean returns, he will ask the man for a lot of money and perhaps kill him. Marius reports this to Inspector Javert, who tells him to hide in his room and fire a pistol when the crime has begun, so that his officers will know when to rush in. Marius returns home, and soon Valjean arrives.

When Jondrette tells Valjean that he is Thénardier, Marius is shocked. In his last request before death his father had asked him to find Thénardier, who once saved his life in a battle, and honor him. As Thénardier talks, Marius realizes it is the same man, and he does not fire the pistol at the appropriate time. Nonetheless, the police arrive, and during the ensuing scuffle Valjean escapes through a window. Marius disappears, too, not willing to testify against Thénardier, and begins searching for Cosette. One day he finds her again, and the two fall in love.

Meanwhile Valjean has decided that he is no longer safe in France and decides to take Cosette to England. She tells Marius of their travel plans and asks him to accompany them, but Marius cannot afford to do so. He goes to his grandfather for help but finds none. Now certain that he will never marry Cosette, Marius joins his revolutionary friends in a riot. He sends Cosette a note to this effect, and when Valjean intercepts it, he rushes to keep the young man from harm. In the process he rescues Javert from revolutionaries who intend to kill him and carries a wounded, unconscious Marius to safety through the sewers of Paris. He then encounters Javert once more, and the two men take Marius to his grandfather's house. Afterward Javert lets Valjean go home to say good-bye to Cosette and realizes that he cannot arrest someone who saved his life. Feeling himself a failure as a police officer, he drowns himself in the Seine River.

When Marius recovers from his wounds, his grandfather tells him that he may marry Cosette. The day after the wedding Valjean confesses to Marius that he is a former convict. Marius is horrified and does not want Valjean in his home. For a time Valjean visits Cosette when Marius is away, but eventually he stops visiting altogether. Knowing nothing of what he has told Marius, she does not understand why he is staying away. Meanwhile Marius investigates Valjean's past and learns that the convict murdered a factory owner named Madeleine and stole his money and later killed Inspector Javert. Eventually he discovers that that these facts are wrong and that Valjean was the one who saved his life during the revolt. With Cosette, he rushes to Valjean's home and professes his love for the man. Valjean is happy, but he is also ill, and he dies shortly after the young couple's arrival. He is buried under a stone with no name.

In discussing his work, Hugo emphasizes its religious aspects, presenting the tale as the struggle between good and evil within each individual's soul. However, the novel also makes it clear that people are a product of their environment, influenced by society and experience. Valjean commits his first theft because his family is starving; he is redeemed by the kind treatment of a stranger, the bishop. However, Hugo recognizes that under some circumstances no act of charity can change a man's nature. For this reason, despite Valjean's generosity, Thénardier remains a thief and a murderer. (Hugo 1987; Swinburne 1970)

See also Cosette; Dickens, Charles; Dostoyevsky, Fyodor; Hugo, Victor; Javert; Pontmercy, Marius; Valjean, Jean

Modest Proposal, A

Written by Jonathan Swift, *A Modest Proposal* is a satirical pamphlet published in October 1729. It outlines a plan to reduce the number of Irish poor by allowing them to sell their children as food. In this way, according to Swift (Van Doren 1977, 555–556),

> the poorer tenants will have something valuable of their own. . . . It would increase the care and tenderness of mothers toward their children. . . . We should see an honest emulation among the married women, which of them could bring the fattest child to the market, men would become as fond of their wives, during the time of their pregnancy, as they are now of their mares in foal, their cows in calf, or sows when they are ready to farrow, nor offer to beat or kick them (as it is too frequent a practice) for fear of a miscarriage.

(Van Doren 1977)

See also Poverty; Swift, Jonathan

Monkey Wrench Gang, The

The Monkey Wrench Gang is a novel by environmental activist Edward Abbey. Published in 1975, it concerns the escapades of a band of activists who use ecological sabotage, or ecotage, to fight against development in the deserts of the American Southwest. The book inspired the environmental group Earth First! to adopt similar tactics in real life. Today these tactics, which include damaging roads, bridges, and industrial equipment, are called monkeywrenching.

The Monkey Wrench Gang begins with a fictional act of ecotage: the dynamiting of a new bridge across Glen Canyon, intended to connect Utah and Arizona. The novel then flashes back to an earlier episode: Dr. A. K. Sarvis and his assistant, Bonnie Abzzug, setting fire to billboards along a desert highway. Sarvis considers it one of his "nighttime highway beautification projects" (Abbey 1975, 47). Shortly thereafter Sarvis and Abzzug go on a river-rafting trip. Their guides are Joseph Fielding "Seldom Seen" Smith and his new assistant, a Vietnam veteran and former Green Beret named George Washington Hayduke. Both Smith and Hayduke believe that the government is destroying the desert. After Smith tells Sarvis and Abbzug that the Glen Canyon Dam has diminished the power of the Colorado River and ought to be dynamited, the group begins to discuss environmental activism. By the time the four of them leave the river, the Monkey Wrench Gang has been born.

Their first act of ecotage is against some bulldozers clearing a forest. After nightfall gang members use a variety of methods to damage the bulldozers' engines and succeed in delaying the clear-cutting project. Emboldened by this success, they undertake more difficult acts of ecotage. They move surveying stakes for a government road project, damage power lines and geological sensor devices, and blow up an electric train at a coal company, leaving behind clues that suggest a Native American activist group is responsible for the damage. Eventually, however, a local Mormon bishop named Love begins to suspect that Smith is involved in these activities. Bishop Love is the leader of a desert Search and Rescue Team, and after Hayduke and Smith drive an untended bulldozer off a cliff in broad daylight, he and his team chase them. The two monkeywrenchers escape, but afterward Love continues to look for them.

Pursued by Bishop Love and law enforcement officials, the gang temporarily splits up. Sarvis returns to work, Smith stays out of sight, and Hayduke and Abzzug head for a forest near the Grand Canyon to destroy clear-cutting equipment. Abzzug was once Sarvis's lover, but now she is in love with Hayduke. At the Grand Canyon the couple encounters another ecoteur, a masked horseman whom Hayduke calls the Lone Ranger. The man helps them destroy some bulldozers and rides off without telling them his name. Hayduke and Abzzug return to the desert, where they commit another act of ecotage, but two helicopter pilots catch Abzzug in the act. Hayduke rescues her and sets the helicopter on fire. Now Bishop Love increases his efforts to find the monkeywrenchers, and one night he discovers all four trying to blow up a bridge. He and his posse chase the gang into a desert wilderness area. The terrain is difficult, and the monkeywrenchers have little water. Nevertheless, they keep hiking until Bishop Love falls ill and his team calls on Dr. Sarvis for help. Unable to let Love die, Sarvis and Abzzug turn themselves in, but Hayduke and Smith keep going. Eventually the two men split up. Smith is captured when he tries to steal food from some campers. Hayduke is cornered at the edge of a cliff, and law enforcement officials shoot his body to pieces. Later Sarvis's lawyers manage to keep Sarvis, Abzzug, and Smith from serving time in prison.

The group settles along the Colorado River and appears to lead a quiet life. Then Hayduke and the Lone Ranger show up, and Hayduke explains that he fooled the lawmen by putting a dummy in his place. Hayduke accuses the monkeywrenchers of being responsible for blowing up the new bridge across Glen Canyon, but the book ends without the monkeywrenchers admitting their involvement.

Inspired by *The Monkey Wrench Gang*, Earth First! decided to stage its first major act of ecotage at the Glen Canyon Dam. Earth First!ers snuck on top of the dam and unfurled a plastic "crack" across its face, symbolically destroying the concrete. Abbey was present during the event. (Abbey 1975; McCann 1977)

See also Abbey, Edward; Environmentalism; Sarvis, Dr. A. K.

Montag, Guy

Guy Montag is the main character of Ray Bradbury's 1953 novel *Fahrenheit 451*. Montag lives in a future society where owning books is a crime, and as a fireman it is his job to burn them. One day he begins to wonder what is inside the books he burns. He steals some and reads them. After that he can no longer destroy them. He becomes a fugitive from society and lives among a hobo band of fellow book lovers, each of whom has memorized a different section of a text. Someday they hope to rewrite what has been lost. (Bradbury 1996)

> See also Beatty, Captain; Bradbury, Ray; Censorship; *Fahrenheit 451*

Montage of a Dream Deferred

Montage of a Dream Deferred, by American poet Langston Hughes, is a collection of poetry devoted to the black experience in Harlem. In writing his verse, the author intends to imitate a cycle of jazz music or, as he once explained in a speech, to "put jazz into words" (Hughes 1958, 494). Published in 1951, *Montage* is organized into six sections and subtitles to address all aspects of Harlem life. Many of the poems also protest racism and the inequalities in American society. For example, "Children's Rhymes" points out that "what's written down / for white folks / ain't for us a-tall" (91) and notes that black children cannot hope to grow up to be president, and "Not a Movie" talks about a black man who is beaten for trying to vote in a southern election (91). The most famous poem in the collection, "Harlem," suggests that if a dream is deferred, it will either "dry up like a raisin in the sun," fester, and sicken or eventually explode (123). Author Lorraine Hansberry was inspired by Hughes in writing her social protest play *A Raisin in the Sun*. (Hughes 1958; Muller 1986; O'Daniel 1971)

> See also Hansberry, Lorraine; Harlem Renaissance; Hughes, Langston; *Raisin in the Sun, A*

Moore, Daniel Vivaldo

Daniel Vivaldo Moore appears in James Baldwin's 1960 novel *Another Country*. Called Vivaldo by his friends, he is an Irish American who prefers the company of African Americans at a time when racism is prevalent in the United States. His best friend, Rufus Scott, is a black jazz drummer from Harlem, and his girlfriend is Scott's sister, Ida. When Rufus commits suicide, Vivaldo blames himself for not being friend enough to prevent it. But when Ida blames Vivaldo for being white, and therefore part of the reason for Rufus's suffering, Vivaldo says, "Suffering doesn't *have* a color" (Baldwin 1962, 417). He accuses her of being just as racist as the people she condemns, arguing: "What I've never understood is that you always accuse me of making a thing about your color, of penalizing you. But you do the same thing. You always make me feel white" (414). (Baldwin 1962)

> See also *Another Country;* Baldwin, James; Jones, Eric; Racism; Scott, Ida and Rufus

Moreno, Señora

In Helen Hunt Jackson's 1885 novel *Ramona*, Señora Moreno is a wealthy Mexican woman living in Southern California during the late 1880s. She is extremely prejudiced against Native Americans, even though her adopted daughter, Ramona, is half Indian. Señora Moreno does not tell the girl of her heritage and refuses to let Ramona marry a full Indian named Alessandro. Moreover, Señora Moreno lies and tells the girl that her mother's will gave her the power to decide whom Ramona would wed. Distraught, Ramona and Alessandro run away to a life of poverty and hardship. Meanwhile Señora Moreno keeps the girl's dowry of precious jewels locked away, intending to give them to her church. She dies without repenting her lies and theft, whereupon her son finds the jewels and eventually returns them to Ramona. (Jackson 1988)

> See also Alessandro; Jackson, Helen Hunt; *Ramona*

Morrison, Arthur

British author Arthur Morrison wrote novels that called attention to the plight of the poor in England's slums. As a result of his work, the

British government changed its housing laws to improve living conditions there.

The son of an engine fitter, Morrison was born in Popular, Kent, England, on November 1, 1863. He worked first as a clerk and then as a journalist, writing stories for several London journals, including the *National Observer*. His first book was a collection of these stories, *Tales of Mean Streets* (1894). His most important work was a novel, *A Child of the Jago*. Published in 1896, it depicted the desperate plight of the poor in a London slum called the Jago and eventually led to the area's cleanup. Morrison also wrote a novel entitled *A Hole in the Wall* (1902), a series of detective stories, and a book about Japanese art entitled *Painters of Japan* (1911). He died on December 4, 1945, in Chalfont St. Peter, Buckinghamshire, England. (Morrison 1995)

See also *Child of the Jago, A;* Poverty

Morrison, Toni

American author Toni Morrison writes novels from a black feminist perspective. In 1988 she received the Pulitzer Prize for her novel *Beloved*, which concerns black slavery during the Civil War, and in 1993 she was awarded the Nobel Prize in literature.

Morrison was born Chloe Anthony Wofford on February 18, 1931, in Lorain, Ohio, and attended both Howard University and Cornell University. After graduation she became a university professor, teaching first at Texas Southern University, then at Howard University, and finally at the State University of New York, where in 1965 she also began working as a senior editor at Random House, a large publishing company. Her first novel, *The Bluest Eye*, appeared in 1970, and her second, *Sula*, in 1973. Both novels deal with black issues from a woman's perspective. She continues to write novels today. Her other works include *The Song of Solomon* (1977), *Tar Baby* (1981), and *Jazz* (1992). In addition, she has written several critical essays and articles. (Gates and Appiah 1993c; McKay 1988; Samuels 1990)

See also *Beloved; Bluest Eye, The;* Feminism; Racism; *Sula*

Mukhtaar

Mukhtaar is a character in Nuruddin Farah's 1983 novel *Close Sesame*, which protests certain social and political practices in modern Somalia. After he attempts to assassinate the leader of the country, his father beats him to death. Later the incident is deemed a suicide because Mukhtaar's father is a member of the ruling clan. However, even if Mukhtaar's death had been judged a murder, his murderer would not have stood trial. As another character in the novel explains: "A father can beat his son to madness in full public view and the son is expected not to raise a hand but to receive the beating in total silence. The son is not allowed to question the wisdom of his parent's statements, must never answer back, never raise his voice or head. . . . Nothing would happen to avenge Mukhtaar's life and his father would not be submitted to questioning: after all, it is the prerogative of a parent what to do with the life and property of an offspring" (Farah 1992, 120–121). (Farah 1992)

See also *Close Sesame;* Farah, Nuruddin

Toni Morrison, 1994 (Horst Tappe/Archive Photos)

Mursal

Mursal is a character in Nuruddin Farah's 1983 novel *Close Sesame*. Opposed to the corrupt, oppressive dictatorship of his native country of Somalia, he becomes involved in a plot to assassinate the ruling general. The plot fails, and one by one each of the four men who helped plan the assassination are murdered. Mursal is last on the list, and before he can be arrested, he tries to blow up the general. Mursal fails and is later killed. After his death his widow tries to decide whether to stay in the country. She was born in the United States and does not understand the Somali language or culture very well. (Farah 1992)

See also *Close Sesame;* Farah, Nuruddin

My Brilliant Career

The 1901 novel *My Brilliant Career,* by Miles Franklin, concerns an educated but tomboyish Australian girl, Sybylla Melvyn, who has been reduced to poverty through her father's alcoholism and bad investments. While visiting wealthy relatives, she meets a rich landowner, and he falls in love with her. He is a good man, and they become secretly engaged. However, she soon realizes that as his wife she would always be under his control; he is the kind of man who would never consider a woman to be his equal. Therefore, she breaks off their engagement and determines to make her own way in life. Sybylla's decision reflects the feminism of the author, who was a journalist active in the women's rights movement. (Franklin 1965)

See also Feminism; Franklin, Miles

N

Naranjo, Huberto

A guerrilla fighter in Isabel Allende's 1987 novel *Eva Luna,* Huberto Naranjo leads a revolutionary group in the mountains of South America. Also known as Comandante Rogelio, he moves people not by persuasive oration but "by the force of his courage" (Allende 1988, 182). He instills great loyalty in his men and succeeds in freeing political prisoners from a supposedly impenetrable prison. (Allende 1988)

> **See also** Allende, Isabel; Carle, Lukas; Carle, Rolf; *Eva Luna;* Rodríguez, Colonel Tolomeo

Native American Issues

The first social protest literature to deal with Native American issues was written by non-Native Americans. Perhaps the most famous of these is Helen Hunt Jackson's 1885 novel *Ramona,* which deals with prejudice against Native Americans in California. This work influenced public opinion and helped create new government policies toward Indian management.

Another novel that raised public awareness of Native American issues was Thomas Berger's novel *Little Big Man.* It was published in 1964 at a time when Native Americans were beginning to become active politically. Therefore, although *Little Big Man* depicts in-justices that were perpetrated against Native Americans during the 1800s, the book did much to further the modern Native American rights movement of the 1960s and 1970s.

Little Big Man shows the forced relocation of Native Americans to Indian reservations owned and controlled by the U.S. government. The first reservations were established in 1815, and they still exist today. However, they are now owned by the Native Americans themselves. During the transition from government to tribal ownership, many reservations fell into poverty and alcoholism rose among their residents. These problems continue to be a part of modern reservation life, and they are the main concern of Native American social protest authors, including James Welch and nila northSun. Such authors also depict the difficulties experienced by Native Americans who leave the reservation to live in large cities. However, like Asian-American and Mexican-American authors, their primary means of expression is through poetry or nonfiction, and much of their work is ignored by major publishers. (Grossman 1996)

> **See also** Asian-American Literature; Berger, Thomas; Jackson, Helen Hunt; *Little Big Man;* Mexican-American Literature; northSun, nila; *Ramona;* Welch, James

First and second graders during their singing lesson at the Carlisle Indian School, 1901 (Cumberland County Historical Society)

Native Son

The 1940 novel *Native Son*, by Richard Wright, addresses the problem of racism in the United States by showing both the injustice of oppression and the anger of the oppressed. In writing about the novel, Wright (1993a, 523) categorizes its main character, a 20-year-old black man named Bigger Thomas, as "resentful toward whites, sullen, angry, ignorant, emotionally unstable, depressed and unaccountably elated at times, and unable even, because of his own lack of inner organization which American oppression has fostered in him, to unite with the members of his own race." He reports that he hesitated to write about such an angry, bitter character for fear that it would upset blacks and whites alike. However, he had met people like Bigger and felt it was important to acknowledge their existence in American society.

According to scholar Arnold Rampersad (xi), writing in a 1993 introduction to *Native Son*, Wright wanted to dispel misperceptions about blacks and whites and their relationship with each other:

Wright believed that few Americans, black or white, were prepared to face squarely and honestly the most profound consequences of more than two centuries of the enslavement and segregation of blacks in North America. . . . Wright knew, black and whites alike continued to cling to a range of fantasies about the true nature of the relationship between the two races even as the nation lurched inexorably toward a possible collapse over the fundamental question of justice for the despised African American minority.

Moreover, Rampersad (xii) believes that Wright was concerned with showing black men's "sometimes unconscious but powerful identification of violence against other human beings as the most appropriate response to the disastrous conditions of their lives. Within the confines of the black world, this violence was easily directed at fellow blacks; but increasingly, Wright warned his readers, this violence would be aimed at whites.

At first Bigger Thomas takes out his anger on other blacks, bullying and robbing them at will. He does not dare rob a white store because he and his friends believe that such an act "would be a violation of ultimate taboo; it would be a trespassing into territory where the full wrath of an alien white world would be turned loose upon them; in short, it would be a symbolic challenge of the white world's rule over them; a challenge which they yearned to make, but were afraid to" (14). Bigger also avoids contact with the white world. Then he is offered a job as a chauffeur to a white millionaire, Mr. Dalton, who is a prominent citizen in Chicago. Bigger decides to take the job because

> his mother had always told him that rich white people liked Negroes better than they did poor whites. He felt that if he were a poor white and did not get his share of the money, then he would deserve to be kicked. Poor white people were stupid. It was the rich white people who were smart and knew how to treat people. He remembered hearing somebody tell a story of a Negro chauffeur who had married a rich white girl and the girl's family had shipped the couple out of the country and had supplied them with money. (37)

When around Mr. Dalton, Bigger immediately falls into a subservient role and hates himself for doing so. He also hates Mr. Dalton's daughter, Mary, whom he has heard is a Communist. His first night on the job, Bigger is ordered to drive Mary to a university lecture. However, once they are in the car, she asks Bigger to pick up her radical boyfriend, Jan Erlone, and take them to a black restaurant, making him promise not to tell her father about it later. Bigger is uncomfortable with the situation. Moreover, he is angry at the couple for treating him as an equal. He

does not want to go into the restaurant with the two of them, but they insist.

Once inside, all of Bigger's friends stare at him. Meanwhile Jan and Mary tell him about communism. They also have a lot to drink, and by the time Bigger gets Mary home, she can barely walk. He helps her to her room, but after he puts her into bed, her mother walks in. Mrs. Dalton is blind but has sharp ears. When Mary starts to mumble, Bigger is afraid she will give his presence away, and he is frightened at what will happen if he is found in a white girl's bedroom. He covers Mary's face with a pillow until Mrs. Dalton leaves. To his horror, he then discovers that he has inadvertently killed the young woman. Bigger knows he must cover up his crime. He puts the body in a trunk, carries it to the furnace, and burns it. Later he thinks about his intent when he killed Mary and realizes that,

> though he had killed by accident, not once did he feel the need to tell himself that it had been an accident. He was black and he had been alone in a room where a white girl had been killed; therefore he had killed her. That was what everybody would say anyhow, no matter what he said. And in a certain sense he knew that the girl's death had not been accidental. He had killed many times before, only on those other times there had been no handy victim or circumstance to make visible or dramatic his will to kill. His crime seemed natural; he felt that all of his life had been leading to something like this. It was no longer a matter of dumb wonder as to what would happen to him and his black skin; he knew now. The hidden meaning of his life—a meaning which others did not see and which he had always tried to hide—had spilled out. No; it was no accident, and he would never say that it was. There was in him a kind of terrified pride in feeling and thinking that some day he would be able to say publicly that he had done it. It was as though he had an obscure but deep debt to fulfil to himself in accepting the deed. (119)

In this scene from the 1950 movie Native Son, *Bigger Thomas (played by author Richard Wright) appeals to his girlfriend, Bessie Mears, for help. (The Museum of Modern Art Film Stills Archive)*

At first Bigger thinks he is going to get away with his crime. Mary's parents think she has just run off. But later they begin to suspect foul play and hire a private investigator. This man questions Bigger, who intentionally casts suspicion on Jan. Later Jan asks Bigger what he has done to deserve the young man's accusations. Bigger grows frightened and pulls a gun on him, and Jan runs away. Suddenly Bigger decides to take an action that he has long been considering. He writes a ransom note that makes it seem as though Mary has been kidnapped by the Communist Party, demanding payment of $10,000 for her release. The Daltons take the note seriously, while Jan believes that Mr. Dalton has set up a fake kidnapping to increase public opposition to the Communist Party. Then someone finds one of Mary's bones and an earring in the Dalton's furnace ashes. Bigger sneaks away from the house and goes to his girlfriend, Bessie, for help. But after he confesses his crime, he realizes that he cannot let her live. He kills her and runs.

On the streets he sees newspaper headlines that suggest he not only killed Mary but also raped her. The public is incensed. Violent acts against innocent blacks increase, and many are fired from their jobs without cause. A massive manhunt takes place, and eventually Bigger is caught. He refuses to speak. Then Jan visits him in jail and tells him that he understands why Bigger hates white people and that he wants to help Bigger with his defense. Jan brings in an attorney, Max, who works for the Communist Party. After some resistance Bigger realizes that Jan and Max are his friends. Later, when police try to get him to say that the Communists were involved in Mary's death, Bigger refuses to comply. Instead, he dictates an honest confession, explaining that Mary's death was an accident. Shortly thereafter the court holds an inquest to determine whether Bigger should stand trial for the crime, and it quickly becomes apparent that the coroner and prosecutor are racist and anticommunist.

Max fights back by exposing Mr. Dalton, who is involved in black charities, as a hypocrite; the millionaire owns many rental properties and charges blacks an exorbitant rate to live in them. But the inquest turns sensational when Bessie's battered body is displayed for all to see. Now Max realizes that no jury will view Mary's death as accidental. He decides to change Bigger's plea from not guilty to guilty, so that the sentence will be determined by a judge. Max hopes that the judge will recognize Bigger's innocence and give him a merciful sentence. The lawyer offers an eloquent argument in this regard, discussing slavery, racism, and black anger and fear. Nonetheless, Bigger is sentenced to death in the electric chair. He awaits his execution with a bitter smile.

Native Son is a powerful novel, and it became a best-seller shortly after its publication. It was also nominated for several major literary awards. However, according to scholar Kenneth Kinnamon in his essay "How *Native Son* Was Born" (Gates and Appiah 1993b, 126), "literary America was not yet ready to award a black writer a major prize in fiction," and the novel was passed over for the Pulitzer Prize. Kinnamon adds that aside from its literary merits, *Native Son* had an immediate impact on American society. He (126–127) says:

> Several journalists and sociologists cited *Native Son* in discussions of poor housing in Chicago and elsewhere. Others drew parallels between Bigger Thomas and actual living individuals. A writer in the denominational organ of the Disciples of Christ suggested that *Native Son* "would be a good book for all judges, police officers, and prosecutors who have to do with a Negro to read." Irving Howe once wrote that "the day *Native Son* appeared, American culture was changed forever." The change was not basic or profound, but it was real. The several hundred thousand readers of the work could no longer see racial issues in quite the same way. *Native Son* did not start a war, as Lincoln claimed *Uncle Tom's Cabin* did, or directly bring about legislation, as *The Jungle* did, but it

did alter the social as well as literary sensibilities of many of its readers.

(Gates and Appiah 1993b; Wright 1993a)

See also Communism; Erlone, Jan; *Jungle, The;* Racism; Thomas, Bigger; *Uncle Tom's Cabin;* Wright, Richard

Nekhludof, Prince Dmitri Ivanovitch

Prince Dmitri Ivanovitch Nekhludof is one of the main characters in *Voskreseniye* (Resurrection, 1899), by Leo Tolstoi. A member of the Russian nobility, the prince begins the novel as an arrogant spendthrift who seduces a young girl without concern for her feelings. Later he discovers that this seduction ruined her life; she became pregnant, descended into prostitution, and ended up in prison for murder even though she was innocent of the crime. Feeling guilty for his sin, Nekhludof works for her release. He also asks her to marry him, but she refuses. Nonetheless, he visits her often in prison, where he learns that many other innocent people have been jailed. He begins to question the justice of the Russian prison system and to consider the causes of crime among the lower classes. Consequently, he visits the peasants who farm his estate and for the first time sees their poverty. He gives them his land, vowing to live more modestly himself. In addition, he studies the Bible and decides that oppression, imprisonment, and capital punishment are against its teachings. He condemns the Russian church for supporting such activities. (Tolstoy 1911)

See also *Resurrection;* Tolstoi, Leo

New Grub Street

Published in 1891, *New Grub Street,* by George Gissing, concerns the London literary scene. Its plot centers on the lives of two authors: Edwin Reardon, who writes for artistic reasons, and Jasper Milvain, who writes for money. The former soon finds himself penniless, whereas the latter becomes extremely successful. After Reardon's wife begs him to write something more commercial and he fails, he decides to abandon the writing trade, and she leaves him. He dies alone, and a few months later she marries Milvain.

New Grub Street criticizes many aspects of the literary establishment, including book reviewers who base their comments on whether they like a writer's personality. But the novel also offers broader social protest commentary on the plight of the poor. Gissing (1926, 251) depicts a London of uncaring rich, describing one character as a woman who "would shed tears over a pitiful story of want, and without shadow of hypocrisy. It was hard, it was cruel; such things oughtn't to be allowed in a world where there were so many rich people. The next day she would argue with her charwoman about halfpence, and end by paying the poor creature what she knew was inadequate and unjust." Through Reardon, the author bemoans a world that "has no pity on a man who can't do or produce something it thinks worth money. You may be a divine poet, and if some good fellow doesn't take pity on you you will starve by the roadside. Society is as blind and brutal as fate" (209). (Coustillas 1968; Gissing 1926; Goode 1979)

See also Gissing, George; Milvain, Jasper; Poverty; Reardon, Edwin

1984

Published in 1949, George Orwell's novel *1984* is the author's antiutopian vision of the future. It is set in the aftermath of a global war in a society where people's thoughts and actions are under the complete control of their government. Orwell wrote the novel as a commentary on the totalitarian dictatorships of his time, but he also intended it to be a cautionary tale, fearing that one day his vision would become a reality. The book's tone is pessimistic and was written while the author was dying of a fatal illness.

The novel's main character is 39-year-old Winston Smith. Separated from his wife, he lives in Oceania and works at the Ministry of Truth. His job is to rewrite historical records, making it seem as though the government's predictions are always accurate and its stated goals always met. One day while on his lunch break he unconsciously doodles a slogan

Winston Smith fears the watchful eye of Big Brother in this scene from the 1956 film 1984. *(Hulton Deutsch Collection/Corbis)*

against Big Brother, the symbol of the all-watching party that controls the government. Big Brother keeps an eye on the citizens of Oceania through two-way telescreens and other means. The government also uses telescreens during a daily two-minute hate period, showing a picture of one of its enemies and rousing the viewers to hate him.

As Winston goes about his daily routine, he notices that a young woman is often nearby. He becomes afraid that she is a member of the thought police. He considers killing her, until she leaves him a note saying she loves him. Consequently, the two begin having an affair, and Winston rents a room over an antique shop where they can meet in privacy. The room appears to have no telescreen; however, Winston and Julia eventually discover a hidden one. By this time they have become involved with a man named O'Brien, who purports to be part of a conspiracy to overthrow the government. He gives Winston and Julia a book about the conspiracy. While the couple is reading it aloud in the room, police rush into the room to arrest both of them. Winston realizes that the owner of the antique shop is a member of the thought police. Later he learns that O'Brien is actually working for the government, too, and that the book was created by the government to catch would-be conspirators. Because he has fallen into O'Brien's trap, Winston is severely tortured for several days. Eventually he says whatever they want him to say. The narrator explains:

> His sole concern was to find out what they wanted him to confess, and then confess it quickly, before the bullying started anew. He confessed to the assassination of eminent party members, the distribution of seditious pamphlets, embezzlement of public funds, sale of military secrets, sabotage of every kind. . . . He confessed that he was a religious believer, an admirer of capitalism, and a sexual pervert. . . . He confessed that for years he had been . . . a member of an underground organization which had included almost every human being he had ever known. It was easier to confess everything and implicate everybody. (Orwell 1961, 200)

Eventually Winston's torturers break his spirit, and he renounces his love for Julia. He is released from jail and returns to an ordinary life. On one occasion he meets Julia, and she confirms what Winston's captors once told him: under torture she, too, betrayed their love. Their relationship is over, and Winston has no one to love. In the end he begins to love Big Brother because there is nothing else. (Orwell 1961; Williams 1974)

See also Orwell, George; Science Fiction and Fantasy; Smith, Winston

Norris, Frank

Frank Norris is the author of one of the most famous social protest novels ever written. En-titled *The Octopus* and published in 1901, it concerns political corruption and immoral business practices as they relate to the wheat industry in the United States.

Norris was born Benjamin Franklin Norris in Chicago, Illinois, on March 5, 1870. He originally planned to be an artist, but he later decided on a career in journalism, working as a newspaper reporter for the San Francisco *Chronicle* from 1895 to 1896. His first novel was published in 1899. Entitled *McTeague,* it concerns the destructive force of materialism, which eventually leads a man to murder his wife over money and jealousy. Norris's subsequent novel, *The Octopus,* was the first in a trilogy collectively called *The Epic of the Wheat.* Its second volume is *The Pit* (1903), but its third remained unfinished upon Norris's death in San Francisco on October 25, 1902. At that time another of his novels, *Vandover and the Brute,* was still unpublished. It was then lost during the 1906 San Francisco earthquake but rediscovered and published in 1914. (Dillingham 1969; Graham 1978; McElrath 1992; Norris 1901; Pizer 1966)

See also Labor Issues; *Octopus, The*

northSun, nila

Born in Nevada in 1951, nila northSun is a Native American poet who uses her work to comment on the social and economic hardships of her people. Her mother is Shoshone, and her father is Chippewa. northSun's poetry collections include *Small Bones, Little Eyes* (1982), which was written with Jim Sagel, and *A Snake in Her Mouth: Poems 1974–96* (1997). (Velie 1991)

See also Native American Issues; "up & out"

O

Octopus, The

Set in the San Joaquin Valley of Central California, the 1901 novel *The Octopus,* by Frank Norris, focuses on moral corruption within the wheat and railroad industries. Its title refers to the railroad engine, a Cyclopean monster "with tentacles of steel clutching into the soil" (Norris 1901, 48).

Norris intended *The Octopus* to be the first volume of a trilogy entitled *The Epic of the Wheat.* In 1889 he (Pizer 1966, 113) wrote, "My Idea is to write three novels around the one subject of Wheat. First, a study of California (the producer), second, a study of Chicago (the distributor), third, a study of Europe (the consumer) and in each to keep to the idea of this huge, Niagara of wheat rolling from West to East." The trilogy's second volume, *The Pit,* was published posthumously in 1903, but Norris died before writing his third volume, *The Wolf.*

The Octopus, subtitled *The Story of California* and divided into Books 1 and 2, has three central characters: Presley, Annixter, and Vanamee. Each of these young men struggles with a particular obsession. Vanamee, a rootless shepherd, cannot forget his deceased girlfriend; he tries to use psychic powers to bring her back from the grave. Annixter, a wealthy rancher, is in love with his milkmaid, but to marry her, he must replace self-absorption with altruism. Presley, an idealistic poet, is fixated on writing the perfect epic. He rejects this idea once he develops a social protest conscience.

At the beginning of the novel Presley is a guest of the Derrick family at its vast wheat ranch, El Rancho de los Muertos, where he admires the beauty of the wheat but has little concern for those who steward it. When Hooven, a German tenant on Los Muertos, begs Presley to ask the Derricks not to evict their tenants, Presley refuses to help. He does not want to get involved because "these uncouth brutes of farmhands and petty ranchers, grimed with the soil they worked upon, [are] odious to him beyond words. Never could he feel in sympathy with them, nor with their lives, their ways, their marriages, deaths, bickerings, and all the monotonous round of their sordid existence" (Norris 1901, 3).

But Presley soon finds himself drawn into a dispute between the wheat ranchers and the railroad executives. The railroad, through its local representative, S. Behrman, has raised the freight rate for wheat, leaving the ranchers with little possibility of making a profit on their harvest. Behrman later hikes the price for freighting hops when a hops farmer, Dyke, boasts that he will actually profit from his crop. Financially ruined, Dyke turns to crime and eventually ends up in prison.

When Presley learns of such unjust tariffs, he is "roused to a pitch of exaltation . . . [and] a mighty spirit of revolt heaved tumultuous within him" (85). He abandons his idea for a romantic epic and instead writes a poem of social protest called "The Toilers." His friend Vanamee urges him to publish it in the daily press rather than in a literary magazine because the poem "must be read *by* the Toilers. It *must* be common; it must be vulgarized. You must not stand upon your dignity with the People if you are to reach them" (91). Vanamee warns Presley not to be as insincere as "the social reformer [who] writes a book on the iniquity of the possession of land, and out of the proceeds, buys a corner lot. The economist who laments the hardships of the poor, [but] allows himself to grow rich upon the sale of his book" (91).

Presley does publish his poem in the daily press, and it brings him some measure of fame, but it does not bring about social reform. In fact, the situation in the valley grows worse. The railroad industry, which owns most of the land there, has reneged on a promise to sell it at a reasonable price. The wheat growers had settled on the land and improved it based on its previously advertised price, and when the amount is raised, they are incensed. They take legal action against the railroad and in the process become as morally corrupt as the railroad men themselves.

When the wheat growers lose their legal battle, a group of railroad representatives arrives to evict them from their land. A gunfight breaks out, and several men are killed, including Annixter, Hooven, and a member of the Derrick family. Now destitute, Hooven's wife travels to San Francisco, where she and her youngest daughter starve to death in the streets outside a lavish railroad-sponsored charity banquet.

Meanwhile grief-stricken by Annixter's death, Presley throws a bomb into Behrman's home. Behrman survives the blast, and Presley realizes that he cannot embrace violence as a means of social protest. He leaves the valley and arranges passage on a ship that carries wheat to the starving poor in India. Ironically, Behrman visits the ship before it sails and accidentally falls into the hold of wheat. There he drowns beneath waves of grain and remains unnoticed.

The Octopus ends with a reminder that "greed, cruelty, selfishness, and inhumanity are short-lived; the individual suffers, but the race goes on. Annixter dies, but in a far-distant corner of the world a thousand lives are saved. The larger view always and through all shams, all wickednesses, discovers the Truth that will, in the end, prevail, and all things, surely, inevitably, resistlessly work together for good" (361).

Frank Norris's preoccupation with truth and realism has led some scholars to compare him with author Émile Zola, whose writings Norris often discussed. In creating *The Octopus,* Norris

> drew upon Zola for such matters as the metaphor of the railroad engine as an animal. . . . He also borrowed an entire plot from Zola, that of the symbolic conquest of the grave by the "return" of a girl many years after her death. . . . Most important of all, however, Norris derived from *Germinal* and *La Terre,* Zola's most successful panoramic novels, two of the unifying structural devices of *The Octopus. Germinal,* which deals with a dispute between miners and their employers, suggested to Norris the technique (also used in *La Terre* to a lesser degree) of introducing an outsider into an economic struggle and of using his innocence as a means both for exposition and for the gradual crystallization of an attitude towards the dispute. (126)

Norris was also influenced by historical events. The climactic gun battle of *The Octopus* was based on the Mussel Slough massacre of 1880, which broke out when agents of the Southern Pacific Railroad attempted to evict wheat growers from their land. Other events in the novel were also drawn from real life, in particular the 1894 Mid-Winter Fair in San

Francisco and the 1897 famine in India. Similarly, the characters of Presley, Annixter, and Vanamee were loosely based on Norris and his friends Seymour Waterhouse and Bruce Porter. Presley's poem "The Toiler" was a reference to Edwin Markham's poem "The Man with the Hoe," which was published in the *San Francisco Examiner* on January 15, 1899.

As for Norris's own views regarding social protest, some scholars believe that he was not really interested in reform; he merely used social protest issues as a literary device. Others believe Norris did seek social reform. They call *The Octopus* "an early, prime example of Progressive Era muckraking art" that uniquely depicts immorality on *both* sides of a conflict (McElrath 1992, 92).

Donald Pizer (1966, 120), in discussing the issue of Norris's social consciousness, acknowledges that Norris did indeed use the Mussel Slough massacre "less [for] the opportunity it offered for the depiction of social injustice than [for] its literary usefulness." But he argues that Norris was nonetheless interested in social reform and intended to protest a larger target than just the railroad trusts.

Pizer (152) believes that Norris's goal was to use *The Octopus* to portray "some of the principal social problems and injustices caused by the growth of corporate wealth and power." The novel is therefore still relevant to modern society because, "although trusts no longer plague us as they once did, many of our social problems still arise out of the relationship between the individual and vast corporate and state powers which seem inexorably to control his life" (153). (Dillingham 1969; Graham 1978; McElrath 1992; Norris 1901; Pizer 1966)

See also Capitalism; Justice; Labor Issues; "Man with the Hoe, The"; Markham, Edwin; Norris, Frank; Poverty; Zola, Émile

Offred

The narrator of Margaret Atwood's futuristic novel *The Handmaid's Tale* (1985), Offred tells the story of her life under the regime of Gilead, run by religious fundamentalists. Gilead's government assigns women to specific roles within society. For example, women who work as household servants are called Marthas and must wear brown, whereas Wives of government leaders wear blue and spend most of their time socializing with other Wives. Offred is a Handmaid and must wear red. As a fertile woman her job is to bear children for the Wives, who are sterile. She performs this duty against her will, struggling to maintain her sanity while remembering the way life used to be when she was free. Her story serves as a cautionary tale for women who take their own freedoms for granted. (Atwood 1986; McCombs 1988)

See also Atwood, Margaret; Feminism; *Handmaid's Tale, The;* Joy, Serena

Old Lodge Skins

In *Little Big Man,* Thomas Berger's 1964 novel about the mistreatment of Native Americans during the 1800s, Old Lodge Skins is peace chief of a Cheyenne tribe. According to the story's narrator, Jack Crabbe, this means that he advises his people on daily matters but does not lead them into battle. Fighting is the duty of the war chief. Old Lodge Skins is a wise and thoughtful man. His people do not call themselves Cheyenne, which is a white man's term, but rather Tsistsistas, which means "the human beings." However, white soldiers do not consider them human beings and want to exterminate them. They systematically set out to destroy their villages and put them in compounds with other Native Americans. Eventually the tribal leaders fight back, slaughtering General George Armstrong Custer's troops at the Battle of the Little Big Horn.

After the battle Old Lodge Skins, who is nearly blind, sees a great deal, and he realizes that his people and white men have different philosophies regarding battles. He says that for the Cheyenne, who enjoy a good fight, after the Little Big Horn

it would now be the turn of the other side to try to whip *us.* We would fight as hard as ever, and perhaps win again, but they would definitely start with an advantage, because that is the *right* way. There is no permanent winning or losing when things move, as they should, in a circle. For is not life continuous? And though I shall die, shall I not also continue to live in everything that *is*? . . . But white men, who live in straight lines and squares, do not believe as I do. With them it is rather everything or nothing. . . . And because of their strange beliefs, they are very persistent. They will even fight at night or in bad weather. But they hate the fighting itself. Winning is all they care about, and if they can do that by scratching a pen across paper or saying something into the wind, they are much happier. . . . For killing is a part of living, but they hate life. They hate war. (Berger 1964, 433–434)

Old Lodge Skins then decides that he has lived too long. He prays and gives thanks to the Everywhere Spirit who made all people, sings a death song, and dies. (Berger 1964)

> **See also** Berger, Thomas; Crabbe, Jack; *Little Big Man;* Racism

Olenska, Countess Ellen

In Edith Wharton's 1920 novel *The Age of Innocence,* Countess Ellen Olenska is an unconventional woman who lives in a conventional age. During the 1870s she leaves her Polish husband and moves in with her relatives in New York, where she discovers a rigid set of social codes. She has difficulty fitting into this society; her untraditional clothing, friends, and behavior bring her much criticism. She also finds herself attracted to her cousin's husband, and when he asks her to run away with him, she realizes that he would be unhappy living outside of his society. In the end she leaves him and moves to Paris, where she believes that her bohemian lifestyle will be more acceptable. (Wharton 1993)

> **See also** *Age of Innocence, The;* Exiles; Feminism; Wharton, Edith

Olsen, Tillie

A political activist during the Great Depression, Tillie Olsen is the author of the unfinished novel *Yonnondio: From the Thirties* (1974). She was born January 14, 1913, on a Nebraska tenant farm. Her parents, Samuel and Ida Lerner, were socialist Russian Jews who emigrated to the United States after the failed 1905 revolution in their homeland. In 1917 they took their six children to Omaha, Nebraska, where Olsen's father found work at the local meatpacking house. This setting features prominently in *Yonnondio,* which is partly autobiographical.

In Omaha Olsen was exposed to many socialist ideas. Her father was active in the Socialist Party and had many guests in his home, including workers who wanted to organize themselves and fight unfair labor practices. During her high school years, Olsen herself became a worker, shelling almonds at a local processing plant. She also joined the Young People's Socialist League.

In 1929 when the Depression began, Olsen quit high school and took a series of low-paying jobs. Over the next four years she moved several times, from Nebraska to California, then to the Kansas-Missouri area, Minnesota, and back to California again. She also started writing both poetry and novels and became involved in the Communist Party. While in the Kansas-Missouri area, she was arrested briefly for passing out leaflets to packing house workers. While in Minnesota, her first daughter was born.

In 1934 she settled in San Francisco, California, where she became romantically involved with a leader of the Young Communist League, Jack Olsen. He had a job in a waterfront warehouse and encouraged Tillie to help him organize the workers there. She wrote and passed out leaflets and was consequently arrested during a general strike. Shortly thereafter she published several poems and short pieces in support of workers' rights, as well as the short story "The Iron Throat," which was actually the first chapter of her novel *Yonnondio.*

Over the next several years she continued to be involved in workers' rights. In 1939 she joined the Congress of Industrial Organizations and soon became its California director.

By this time her second daughter had been born, and, in 1943, after giving birth to a third, she married Jack Olsen. The following year she worked to establish San Francisco's first child care center. Her fourth daughter was born in 1948, whereupon Tillie became involved in bettering public schools and libraries. She was also an antinuclear activist. However, the pressure of raising four children and working odd jobs to help support the family kept her from producing fiction.

In the 1950s, however, she once again began to write. During this period Senator Joseph McCarthy was persecuting American members of the Communist Party, and Olsen and her husband were labeled subversives. Forced to quit job after job, Olsen enrolled in a creative writing course, and in 1955 she published a short story, "I Stand Here Ironing." The following year she received a Stanford University Creative Writing Center Fellowship. In 1960, her novella "Tell Me a Riddle" won the O. Henry Award for Best Story of the Year. In 1964 this novella was published along with three short stories as a book entitled *Tell Me a Riddle*. Her novel *Yonnondio,* although unfinished, was published in 1974.

Olsen received a great deal of public recognition for both books. She became a writing professor, and over the next two decades she taught at several prominent universities, including Stanford University, Amherst College, Radcliffe, the University of Massachusetts in Boston, and the University of California at Los Angeles. She also received many prestigious writing awards and honorary degrees. In 1979 she published a nonfiction book about creativity entitled *Silences*. During the 1980s she wrote several essays, and today she continues to lecture about writing at various conferences throughout the United States, including the 1998 Festival of Books at the University of California at Los Angeles. (Nelson and Huse 1994; Olsen 1980; Pearlman and Werlock 1991)

See also Feminism; Labor Issues; *Yonnondio: From the Thirties*

One Day in the Life of Ivan Denisovich

The novel *Odin den iz zhizni Ivana Denisovicha* (One Day in the Life of Ivan Denisovich) was written by Aleksandr Solzhenitsyn, who opposed the prison camps that existed in the Soviet Union under Stalin's regime. Published in Russian in 1962 and in English in 1963, the novel presents a day in the life of a prisoner, Ivan Denisovich Shukhov, who was once a carpenter in a small village. During World War II he was captured by the Germans and escaped. His government then sent him to a forced-labor camp for having associated with the enemy. Now it is 1951 and Shukhov doubts he will ever be set free. Nonetheless, he does not submit to despair. As one of the best workers in the camp, he takes pride in his job skills and in his ability to stay alive under difficult living conditions. However, as he struggles to stay warm and get enough to eat, he reflects that he still has 3,655 days left to his sentence.

One Day in the Life of Ivan Denisovich was based on Solzhenitsyn's own experiences in Soviet labor camps; he spent eight years in forced labor for criticizing Joseph Stalin's policies. Its 1962 publication, initially in an issue of a Soviet magazine, was personally approved by Soviet president Nikita Khrushchev, who saw it only as a condemnation of an earlier era. Other people, however, quickly realized that that the novel was intended to criticize problems in Soviet society. In a 1963 introduction to the book, scholars Max Hayward and Leopold Labedz (ix) explain:

> Solzhenitsyn goes far beyond the bounds of what had hitherto been permissible in public discussions about the past. He shows that the camps were not an isolated feature in an otherwise admirable society—the unfortunate result of a temporary "infringement of socialist legality"—but that they were, in fact, microcosms of that society as a whole. The novel draws an implicit parallel between life "inside" and "outside" the camp: A day in the life of an ordinary Soviet citizen had much in common with that of his unfortunate fellow

countrymen behind barbed wire. We now see that on both sides of the fence it was the same story of material and spiritual squalor, corruption, frustration, and terror.

As a result of his honesty, Solzhenitsyn eventually got into more trouble with government authorities, and his subsequent works were not published in the Soviet Union. However, he continued to campaign for human rights, and in 1974 he was officially exiled from the country. (Carter 1977; Solzhenitsyn 1972)

See also Exiles; Prison Reform; Shukhov, Ivan Denisovich; Solzhenitsyn, Aleksandr

One Flew over the Cuckoo's Nest

One Flew over the Cuckoo's Nest (1962), by Ken Kesey, concerns conformity to social norms and questions society's definitions of insanity. Its narrator, Chief Bromden, is an inmate at an Oregon mental hospital. A Native American from a tribe on the Columbia River, he is an extremely tall, strong man but has been made to feel weak by white society. As a boy he became used to having his opinions ignored; now he pretends to be a deaf-mute and endures verbal abuse without complaint. Moreover, because he has been given medication and shock treatments to control his behavior, he sometimes imagines himself in a thick fog and believes that the hospital is part of a mechanized combine that uses mysterious technological devices to control people. In discussing the head nurse, Nurse Ratched, he says:

Practice has steadied and strengthened her until now she wields a sure power that extends in all directions on hairlike wires too small for anybody's eye but mine; I see her sit in the center of this web of wires like a watchful robot, tend her network with mechanical insect skill, know every second which wire runs where and just what current to send up to get the results she wants. . . . What she dreams of there in the center of those wires is a world of precision efficiency and tidiness like a pocket watch with a glass back, a place where the schedule is unbreakable and all the patients who aren't . . . obedient under her beam . . . [sit in wheelchairs] with catheter tubes run direct from every pant-leg to the sewer under the floor. (Kesey 1964, 26–27)

For several years Nurse Ratched has had complete control over every person on her ward, patient or staff member. But at the opening of the novel a new inmate, Randall Patrick McMurphy, arrives to threaten her dominance. McMurphy feigned insanity to get himself transferred out of a prison work camp. He is a powerful, charismatic leader who brags about his sexual conquests, and the other inmates are immediately in awe of him. A gambler and a hustler with a strong sense of humor, he immediately begins challenging Nurse Ratched's rules through manipulative teasing and joking rather than violent confrontation. He convinces the ward's attending physician, Dr. Spivey, to allow the patients to use a spare room for card games and Monopoly and tries to gain permission to watch the World Series. When Nurse Ratched blocks his attempts to see the baseball game, McMurphy sits in front of the blank television screen and pretends he is watching anyway. The other inmates soon join him. Under McMurphy's spell, they have begun to share his strength of character and disrespect for authority, and Bromden believes that McMurphy has the power to make them all stronger not just in an emotional sense but in a physical sense as well. After McMurphy touches his hand, Bromden says: "I remember the fingers were thick and strong closing over mine, and my hand commenced to feel peculiar and went to swelling up out there on my stick of an arm, like he was transmitting his own blood into it. It rang with blood and power. It blowed up near as big as his, I remember" (23–24).

But one day McMurphy learns that because he was involuntarily committed to the hospital, Nurse Ratched holds the power to keep him there forever, whereas most of the other patients were self-committed and are therefore

In this scene from the 1975 movie One Flew over the Cuckoo's Nest, *new inmate Randall Patrick McMurphy challenges the authority of Nurse Ratched. (United Artists/The Museum of Modern Art Film Stills Archive)*

free to leave at any time. He feels betrayed and decides to cooperate with the nurse, who quickly reestablishes her dictatorial control. When she closes the card-playing room and no one complains, McMurphy realizes that the others will not learn to stand up to her without his help. He "accidentally" puts his fist through her glass window and again becomes her opponent. Nurse Ratched quickly appears to accept defeat, but Bromden knows that she is only waiting for a chance to bring McMurphy down. Her chance arrives after McMurphy arranges for several of the patients to go on a fishing trip with Dr. Spivey. During the trip the patients grow much stronger, while McMurphy seems to be growing weaker and more tired. When they return home, an orderly goads McMurphy into getting into a fistfight with him, and he loses control. After Chief Bromden joins the fight, both inmates are taken away for shock treatment.

This is the turning point for Bromden.

Whereas before he allowed the treatments to propel him further into madness, this time he struggles toward sanity. When he returns to the ward, he is able to talk to the other men with confidence. McMurphy seems unchanged, but several of the inmates realize that their friend is not the same. They help him plan an escape, which will take place after a secret, middle-of-the-night party designed to help Billy Bibbett lose his virginity. McMurphy smuggles in a prostitute for Billy and himself, and the women bring alcohol. Everyone gets drunk and falls asleep, and McMurphy fails to make his escape. In the morning Nurse Ratched discovers what has happened, and she ridicules Billy Bibbett so cruelly that he later slits his throat. When the nurse blames McMurphy for this death, McMurphy loses control and attacks her. He is sent to another floor to have a lobotomy.

Meanwhile most of the other patients realize that they are no less sane than their keepers and check themselves out of the hospital. Shortly thereafter McMurphy returns to the ward as a "vegetable" on a gurney. That night Bromden kills McMurphy by smothering him with a pillow, then throws a heavy control panel through a window and escapes. He hitches a ride north toward his former home, clearly competent to face life in the outside world.

In analyzing *One Flew over the Cuckoo's Nest*, many scholars believe that Chief Bromden is the protagonist of the story because he has taken an almost mythic journey from insanity to sanity. Others, however, argue that the protagonist is actually McMurphy, an archetypal hero battling against an oppressive society as represented by Nurse Ratched. Bromden often comments on this society and on its ability to pressure people into submitting to conformity. For example, after seeing a train disgorge its passengers, "a string of full-grown men in mirrored suits and machined hats . . . a hatch of identical insects," he notes that they enter "five thousand houses punched out identical by a machine and strung across the hills outside of town," and he says:

> All that five thousand kids lived in those five thousand houses, owned by those guys that got off the train. The houses looked so much alike that, time and again, the kids went home by mistake to different houses and different families. Nobody ever noticed. They ate and went to bed. The only one they noticed was the little kid at the end of the whip. He'd always be so scuffed and bruised that he'd show up out of place wherever he went. He wasn't able to open up and laugh either. It's a hard thing to laugh if you can feel the pressure of those beams coming from every new car that passes, or every new house you pass. (227–228)

The novel suggests that in fighting this conformity, McMurphy is a Christ figure who redeems men while sacrificing himself. There is a great deal of Christ imagery in the novel.

For example, when McMurphy is being prepared for shock treatment on a "crucifix-shaped table" he says, "Do I get a crown of thorns?" (270). His death gives Bromden a clear mind that allows him to break free of oppression.

However, despite the novel's strong social protest message and the fact that its narrator is a Native American, *One Flew over the Cuckoo's Nest* has been criticized for being a racist and sexist novel. Nurse Ratched and most other female characters in the book are depicted as evil emasculators, and the orderlies, all of whom are African American, as lazy, cruel, and cowardly. But Bromden's narration suggests that these traits do not apply to society as a whole because Nurse Ratched has skewed her staff in accordance with her own view of the world. He says:

> Year by year she accumulates her ideal staff. . . . Her three daytime black boys she acquires after more years of testing and rejecting thousands. They come at her in a long black row of sulky, big-nosed masks, hating her and her chalk doll whiteness from the first look they get. She appraises them and their hate for a month or so, then lets them go because they don't hate enough. When she finally gets the three she wants . . . she's damn positive they hate enough to be capable. (27–28)

Moreover, the novel was published in 1962, when African Americans were typically relegated to menial jobs such as orderly or janitor and women who held positions of power were often seen as threatening. The 1960s were also a time when struggles against authority figures were becoming more common. Therefore, the book was very successful, as was a film version of the novel. Released in 1975, it was the first movie in 41 years to win all five top Academy Awards: Best Picture, Best Director, Best Screenplay, Best Actor, and Best Actress. (Kesey 1964)

See also Bibbett, Billy; Bromden, Chief; Kesey, Ken; McMurphy, Randall Patrick; Ratched, Nurse

O'Neill, Eugene

Eugene O'Neill was an American playwright who won the Nobel Prize in literature in 1936. He was deeply interested in the family relationships, and many of his plays concern broader social issues as well. Born on October 16, 1888, in New York, New York, O'Neill was the son of Irish immigrants. His father moved from poverty to wealth by becoming a famous actor. Consequently, O'Neill attended a Catholic boarding school, and in 1906 he enrolled in Princeton University. He was suspended a year later for bad behavior. After a series of odd jobs he shipped off to sea, but in 1912 he returned to New York and became an alcoholic vagrant. Shortly thereafter he tried to commit suicide. He then briefly held a job as a reporter, but in 1913 he was diagnosed as having tuberculosis and went to the Gaylord Farm Sanatorium in Wallingford, Connecticut. There he began to write plays. Between 1920 and 1943 he produced more than 20 works, only one of which, *Ah Wilderness!* (1933), was a comedy. His first major success was a play called *Beyond the Horizon;* it won the Pulitzer Prize and was produced on the Broadway stage in 1920. He also won Pulitzer Prizes for *Anna Christie* (1921), *Strange Interlude* (1928), and *Long Day's Journey into Night* (1956). However, many critics consider *The Iceman Cometh* to be his best work. Written in 1939 and published and performed in 1946, this four-act drama deals with self-deception and questions the motives of a social reformer. During the late 1940s O'Neill developed serious health problems. No longer able to write, he became a recluse. He died in Boston, Massachusetts, on November 27, 1953. (Clark 1947)

See also *Iceman Cometh, The*

Ontosoroh

The character of Ontosoroh appears in Pramoedya Ananta Toer's 1980 Javanese novel *Bumi manusia* (This Earth of Mankind). As a girl, Ontosoroh's native father gives her to a Dutch colonialist in exchange for a better job. She becomes the man's concubine and bears two children. In the beginning her husband, Herman Mellama, treats her well. He teaches her to read, write, and speak Dutch and trains her to run the family farm. She becomes a shrewd businesswoman. Then Herman is visited by his oldest son, Mauritas Mellama, whose mother lives in the Netherlands. The young man scorns his father for associating with natives and makes him feel ashamed. Consequently, Herman becomes a drunkard and begins associating with prostitutes at a nearby pleasure palace. Now Ontosoroh must run the farm by herself. She does a good job, but after Herman dies, Mauritas takes it over and throws her out. He also becomes guardian of Ontosoroh's half-European daughter, and the law recognizes Mauritas's right to separate Ontosoroh from her child. Nonetheless, she plans to continue fighting for her rights. (Toer 1996)

See also Mellama, Mauritas; *This Earth of Mankind;* Toer, Pramoedya Ananta

Oroonoko

Oroonoko: or, The Royal Slave, by Aphra Behn, criticizes the treatment of blacks by whites during the seventeenth century. Published as a novel in 1688 and presented as a play in 1694, it tells the story of Oroonoko, an African prince who always behaves honorably and is incapable of lying. As a young man he is tutored in French and English, and he proves himself a great soldier in battle.

One day he falls in love with a beautiful woman named Imoinda and asks her to marry him. She agrees, but before the wedding the king, Oroonoko's grandfather, hears of Imoinda's many virtues and forces her to become his wife instead. Oroonoko is upset but is determined not to go against his king. However, when he visits Imoinda at the palace, his passion overtakes him. Discovering that her marriage has not yet been consummated, he makes love to her. Later the king hears about this and sells Imoinda into slavery, but he tells Oroonoko she is dead.

Oroonoko grieves deeply for his lost bride. Then he and some of his friends are invited to a sumptuous dinner on a European ship. They become drunk, and the captain imprisons them before setting sail for Surinam, a

European colony in South America. Oroonoko rails against such trickery; among his own people, slaves are only those who have been captured nobly in battle. He therefore resolves to starve himself to death. However, the captain apologizes for what has happened and tells him that he will set him free at the next land they come to. He releases Oroonoko from his bonds on the promise that the prince will eat and behave well while on board. Despite this promise, Oroonoko is chained and sold as a slave as soon as they reach Surinam, where his regal bearing earns him the respect and admiration of everyone at the colony, including his master, Trefry.

Trefry has bought Oroonoko in the name of Surinam's lord-governor, who is off on a voyage, but Trefry promises that he will do everything possible to return the prince to Africa as soon as possible. Meanwhile Oroonoko, who has been renamed Caesar, discovers that Imoinda, now named Clemene, is at the colony. The two marry and she immediately becomes pregnant. Wanting his child to be born free, Oroonoko becomes even more eager to return to Africa.

> He was every day treating with Trefry for his and Clemene's Liberty, and offer'd either Gold, or a vast quantity of Slaves, which should be paid before they let him go, provided he could have any Security that he should go when his Ransom was paid. They fed him from day to day with Promises, and delay'd him till the Lord-Governour should come; so that he began to suspect them of Falshood, and that they would delay him till the time of his Wife's Delivery, and make a Slave of that too: for all the Breed is theirs to whom the Parents belong. (Behn 1973, 45)

Consequently, Oroonoko goes to the other slaves and entreats them to rise up against their masters, saying:

> And why . . . should we be Slaves to an unknown People? Have they vanquished us nobly in Fight? Have they won us in Honourable Battle? And are we by the Chance of War become their Slaves? This wou'd not anger a noble Heart; this would not animate a Soldier's Soul: no, but we are bought and sold like Apes or Monkeys, to be the sport of Women, Fools and Cowards; and the Support of Rogues and Runagades, that have abandoned their own Countries. . . . And shall we render Obedience to such a degenerate Race, who have no one human Vertue left, to distinguish them from the vilest Creatures? (61)

The slaves follow him into the jungle, and when their escape is discovered, they are pursued by the Europeans. There is a fierce battle, during which the other slaves desert Oroonoko. He continues to fight until Trefry convinces him to surrender on the promise that he and his wife will be returned to Africa. Afterward, however, the governor orders him whipped and tortured. When he recovers from his wounds, he vows to revenge himself on his captors. But first, afraid that Imoinda will be tortured for his deeds, he kills her and their unborn child. This act causes him such grief that he collapses and is unable to attack his captors. When they discover Imoinda's body, they try to arrest Oroonoko; he slices his own stomach in an attempt to kill himself. They chain him, heal him, and then publicly dismember him while he is still alive, hoping to make him an example to other rebellious slaves.

Author Aphra Behn points out that Oroonoko's behavior is more honorable than that of his Christian captors. She had an opportunity to witness such cruelties firsthand. *Oroonoko* was written while she was living in Surinam, and she introduces the novel as though it were a true story. (Behn 1973)

See also Behn, Aphra; Imoinda; Racism; Slavery

Orwell, George

George Orwell is the pseudonym of Eric Arthur Blair, an English novelist and essayist who often wrote against political and social oppression in his work. Born in India in

1903, Orwell attended Eton School in England. After graduation he traveled to Burma (now Myanmar), where he became a member of the Indian Imperial Police. He stayed in that position for five years. Eventually, however, he grew discouraged over the race and class distinctions in Burma. In 1927 he decided to travel through England and live among the poor. He dressed as a beggar to discover what it was like to be a social outcast and subsequently published a book about his experiences entitled *Down and Out in Paris and London* (1933). His first novel, *Burmese Days,* was published the next year. It, too, addressed the issue of social oppression, and there were elements of social protest in the two comic novels that followed it. Orwell began to identify himself as an independent socialist, and in 1937 he published a political treatise, *The Road to Wigan Pier,* to express some of his views. He also traveled to Spain to become involved in the Spanish Civil War, first as a reporter and then as a volunteer for Republican militia. In 1938 he published a book about his experiences, *Homage to Catalonia* (1938). It expressed his opposition to Communist oppression and totalitarian governments, a theme that would recur in his subsequent works. Orwell also worked as a journalist during World War II, and in 1945 he published the novel *Animal Farm,* which brought him international fame. His equally popular novel *1984* was published in 1949. Orwell died on January 21, 1950, in London, England. (Crick 1980)

   See also *Animal Farm; 1984;* Science Fiction and Fantasy

Outsider, The

First published in 1953, *The Outsider,* by Richard Wright, examines racism in terms of the personal identity of blacks in the United States. Many scholars have compared it to Ralph Ellison's *Invisible Man* because both novels concern black men who try to use communism to become a part of the white world, but remain outsiders nonetheless.

The main character of *The Outsider* is a black man named Cross Damon, an intellec-tual who works as a postal clerk in Chicago. Unhappy with his life, he drinks heavily and abandons his wife and three children. When his underaged girlfriend becomes pregnant, she threatens to sue him for rape unless he marries her. Unfortunately, his wife not only refuses to give Damon a divorce, but also tells him that unless he pays her $800, she will turn him in to the authorities herself. Damon reluctantly takes out a loan from his employers. On the way home he is in a subway wreck, and the police mistakenly identify him as one of the dead. Now free of his past, he changes his name and makes plans to leave town. However, before he can escape, he runs into an old friend, who is shocked to see him alive. Damon kills the man.

Damon then takes a train to New York. En route he meets Ely Houston, the district attorney of New York City. Houston is curious about the black race, and the two men talk about the psychology of what Houston calls "excluded people" (Wright 1993b, 162). Houston is impressed with Damon's intelligence. Meanwhile Damon is feeling guilty and nervous about his fake identity. Shortly after Damon reaches New York, he realizes that he will need a birth certificate in order to get a job. He goes to a black cemetery and chooses yet another new name, this time of someone only three days dead. Damon knows that it will take far longer for officials in the Office of Public Records to learn of the man's death, and indeed he easily obtains a duplicate of "his" birth certificate. Damon is now Lionel Lane.

As Lionel he tracks down a black man he met on the train and through him meets Gilbert Blount, a white man who is in the upper levels of the Communist Party. Gilbert and his wife, Eva, are impressed with Damon. They mistakenly believe that he is in hiding from a crime against white injustice and view him as sympathetic to their cause. They ask him to come live with them, so that he can study communism. As Damon considers their offer, the story's third-person narrator explains: "He had no desire whatsoever to join the Communist Party, but he knew that he would feel somewhat at home with Communists, for they, like he, were outsiders. Would not Communism be the best temporary camouflage behind which he could hide from the law? Would not his secret past make the Communists think that he was anxious for their help? To be with them was not at all a bad way of ending his isolation and loneliness" (223).

Damon goes to live with the Blounts. When he arrives, they explain that they have invited him in order to make a political point. Their landlord, Herndon, is a racist fascist, and the Blounts know that the man will object to Damon living in his building. However, Damon's being there is legal. The Blounts hope to provoke some kind of incident with Herndon in order to make a point about racism in the United States. Unfortunately, this plan soon turns disastrous. Herndon demands to see Gil, and the two get into a horrible fight in the fascist's apartment. Damon walks in to find both of them bloody and battered. He grabs a table leg and smashes both of their heads, making it look as though they killed each other. He then goes out and makes the door lock behind him. When the police arrive, they believe as Damon had hoped. For a moment, however, Damon is afraid that the district attorney, whom he met earlier on the train, will realize that his name has changed. But Houston only recalls their pleasant conversation and treats Damon as a friend.

Meanwhile the Communist Party, in the person of a man named Hilton, is trying to use Gil's death to advantage. The Communists want Damon to say that he saw Herndon kill Gill before dying of his own wounds. Damon has admitted being in the apartment but says he was chased outside by Herndon before the two men died. In trying to convince Damon to support the Communist position, Hilton says:

> You are a Negro and you've an instinct for this sort of thing. I don't mean a racial instinct; it's a socially conditioned instinct for dissimulation which white Americans have bred in you, and you've had to practice it in order to survive. Watching and

coping with the racially charged behavior of white Americans are a part of your learning how to live in this country. Look, every day in this land some white man is cussing out some defenseless Negro. But that white bastard is too stupid in intelligence and deficient in imagination to realize that his actions are being duplicated a million times in a million other spots by other whites who feel hatred for Negroes just like he does; therefore, he is too blind to see that this daily wave of a million tiny assaults acts to build up a vast reservoir of resentment in Negroes. At night at home Negroes discuss this bitterly. But the next morning, smiling, they show up on their jobs, swearing that they love white people. . . . Why? You know the answer. They have to live, eat, have a roof over their heads. . . . So they collaborate with people who they feel are their sworn enemies. . . . White America has built upon something in you that can help the Party now. . . . If you are honest in your heart, you cannot deny the Party. (330–331)

Once again Damon does not accept the party's position, but he decides to cooperate nonetheless. Later he learns that Hilton has discovered evidence that Damon killed Gil and is planning to use it to control him. Damon then kills Hilton, too. Now the party is suspicious of Damon. Their members investigate his background, uncover his true name, and turn it over to the police. When Gil's wife, Eva, learns of Damon's deception, she kills herself; by this time she has fallen in love with him. Houston quickly realizes that Damon is a murderer but does not have enough evidence to arrest him. The two men talk, discussing lawlessness, racism, and the nature of outsiders. Finally Houston says:

> I'm pretty certain you're finished with this killing phase. . . . So, I'm going to let you go. . . . I'm going to let you keep this in your heart 'til the end of your days! Sleep with it, eat with it, brood over it, make love with it. . . . You are going to punish

yourself, see? You are your own law, so you'll be your own judge. . . . I wouldn't *help* you by taking you to jail. . . . I've very little concrete evidence. . . . And I'll not give you the satisfaction of sitting in a court of law with those tight lips of yours and gloating at me or any jury while we try to prove the impossible. . . . I'll not give you the chance to make that kind of fool out of me, Damon! (571–572)

But once Damon is out on the street, he realizes how alone he is. When a party member sneaks up on him and shoots him, he is almost glad to die. With his last breaths, he tells Houston: "I wish I had some way to give the meaning of my life to others . . . to make a bridge from man to man. . . . Starting from scratch every time is . . . is no good. Tell them not to come down this road. . . . Men hate themselves and it makes them hate others. . . . We must find some way of being good to ourselves. . . . Man is all we've got. . . . I wish I could ask men to meet themselves. . . . We're different from what we seem . . . maybe worse, maybe better . . . but certainly different. . . . We're strangers to ourselves" (585).

Earlier Cross's mother told him that he was named for Jesus' death on the cross. Therefore, according to scholar Maryemma Graham in a 1993 introduction to the work (xxviii), "because of the death-rebirth symbolism and the moral tone which Cross adopts, many critics have chosen to read this story as Wright's attempt to reinscribe a politically corrupt world with a moral message. Just as Cross Damon, himself demonic, is born again, so too must the ideas of humankind be grounded in morality." However, Graham believes that more emphasis should be placed on the work as "a cautionary tale about the excesses of individuality and the dangers of human alienation" (xxviii). She adds: "By demonstrating the consequences of human alienation—irrational, irresponsible murder and death—in a racist society, Wright highlights the inadequacy of interpretations which privilege individualism, even at the risk of being self-critical. Cross's fatal flaw is ultimately

his individualism. When carried to its logical conclusion, he has nothing left" (xxviii-xxix). (Gates and Appiah 1993b; Webb 1968; Wright 1993b)

See also Blount, Gil; Communism; Damon, Cross; Ellison, Ralph; Houston, Ely; *Invisible Man;* Racism; Wright, Richard

Ox-Bow Incident, The

The western novel *The Ox-Bow Incident,* by Walter Van Tilburg Clark, is about an American lynching. However, when it was published in 1940, many people believed its deeper meaning concerned the fascism of Nazi Germany, even though, as scholar Max Westbrook (1969, 11) points out, the Nazi parallel "ignores the fact that no one in the novel uses Nazi techniques, believes in Nazi values, or works for Nazi aims."

In an afterword to a 1960 edition of *The Ox-bow Incident,* Walter Prescott Webb (223) quotes author Clark as explaining: "The book was written in 1937 and '38, when the whole world was getting increasingly worried about Hitler and the Nazis. . . . A number of the reviewers . . . saw it as something approaching an allegory of the unscrupulous and brutal Nazi methods, and as a warning against the dangers of temporizing and of hoping to oppose such a force with reason, argument, and the democratic approach." But Clark (224) says that it was actually "a kind of American Naziism that I was talking about. I had the parallel in mind, all right, but what I was most afraid of was not the German Nazis . . . but that ever-present element in any society which can always be led to act the same way, to use authoritarian methods to oppose authoritarian methods."

Westbrook (1969, 67) believes that the book can be interpreted even more broadly, as an "archetypal ethic" representing the reality that "man does not achieve his real self in idea or office or emotion, but as an individual part of a larger whole. Man's only hope is to act from a sense of the integrity of that larger entity, and his most shocking failure is to murder innocent men on behalf of his own dedication to a severed piece of man called the

The cowboys prepare for a lynching in this scene from the 1943 movie The Ox-Bow Incident, *which depicts how mob mentality can lead to violence. (Twentieth Century Fox/Archive Photos)*

male ego." Westbrook (67) concludes that "the subject of *The Ox-Bow Incident* is not a plea for legal procedure. The subject is man's mutilation of himself, man's sometimes trivial, sometimes large failures to get beyond the narrow images of his own ego."

On the surface the novel is the first-person narrative of Art Croft, a cowboy who rides into the town of Bridger's Wells with his partner, Gil Carter. The two men have just spent a winter together on the range. Extremely irritable, they decide to get drunk at Canby's saloon, where they hear some disturbing news: someone has been rustling cattle from the valley, and everyone is a suspect, including Art and Gil. Therefore, the atmosphere in the bar is tense. When Art and Gil join a poker game, another cowboy, Farnley, implies that Gil is cheating. A fight breaks out between the two men; Canby ends it by hitting Gil over the head with a bottle.

After Gil recovers, a young cowboy, Greene, rushes in to report that the rustlers have killed Farnley's friend Kinkaid and stolen his cattle. Farnley declares that he is going to hunt the killers down. Other cowboys agree to go with him, declaring they will hang the rustlers as soon as they are found. Osgood, a minister, and Davies, who owns the town's only store, try to convince them to let the sheriff handle the situation. However, an old rancher, Bartlett, delivers a powerful speech convincing the group to take action. Bartlett criticizes the legal system, saying: "They don't wait for that kind of justice in Texas anymore, do they? No, they don't. They know they can pick a rustler as quick as any fee-gouging lawyer that ever took his time in any courtroom. They go and get the man, and they string him up" (Clark 1960, 35). While the men rush to find a rope, Davies asks Art to find the sheriff. Art discovers that the sheriff has gone out of town for the day and has left his deputy, Mapes, in charge. Mapes is eager to join the lynching party, as is Major Tetley, a prominent rancher.

After much discussion and argument, a posse of 28 men finally rides out after the killers. This group includes Davies and Sparks, a former minister, who want to convince everyone to return home; Sparks is the town's only African American, and he once saw his own brother lynched because of racism. Another reluctant participant is Tetley's son Gerald. Gerald tells Art that his father made him come along, explaining, "I'm here because I'm weak and my father's not" (106). Gerald believes that most of the other members of the group do not really want to be there either. He compares the men of the lynching party to a pack of wolves or coyotes and says: "We're doing it because we're afraid not to be in the pack. We don't dare show our pack weakness; we don't dare resist the pack" (106). Gerald then offers a scathing criticism of human nature, and Art becomes uncomfortable at his outburst. Art knows that he and Gil have joined the posse not because they believe it to be right but because they want to fit in with the other cowboys. As Westbrook (1969, 59) explains: "Both give in to society's divisive value system which associates virtue with a willingness to join the he-man lynch mob. Repeatedly, Art and Gil show themselves ready to fight with fists or with guns in order to show their allegiance to a cause in which they do not believe."

The two men often question their decision to be a part of the posse. Nonetheless, they continue forward. Along the way, tracks and witnesses reveal that three men and a herd of cattle are heading for the Ox-Bow, a small valley between high peaks. The posse follows their trail, even after heavy snow and darkness begin to fall. Finally it is so dark that the men do not see an approaching stagecoach until it almost runs them down. They yell, and the stagecoach drivers, thinking they are bandits, fire several shots into the crowd before stopping the coach. Art is hit in the shoulder but refuses to take the stagecoach back to town, partly because its passengers include Gil's girlfriend, Rose Mapen, and Rose's new husband,

who treats Gil badly. Art endures the painful bandaging of his wound and remounts his horse.

Finally the posse comes across three sleeping men: a cowboy named Donald Martin and his employees, a confused old man and a Mexican who at first pretends to speak no English. The Mexican has Kinkaid's gun, and nearby is a herd of cattle, marked with the brand of a local rancher named Drew. The posse concludes that the cattle are stolen and that these men killed Kinkaid. Martin insists that he bought the cattle from Drew, who let him take them without a receipt, and that the Mexican found the gun on the road. He says he is taking the herd to his new ranch in nearby Pike's Hole, where his wife and small children are waiting for him. The posse does not believe him. Major Tetley, who is now in charge, tells Martin that he and his friends must hang.

Martin begs the men to send someone to check out his story with Drew. No one is willing to do this, and after much arguing Martin finally resigns himself to his fate. He writes a farewell letter to his wife and gives it to Davies, who reads it and realizes that Martin is innocent. Davies tries to convince the posse not to go through with the lynching, but Major Tetley orders the hangings to proceed. Gerald does not want to participate because he finds lynching morally repugnant. Earlier he confessed to Art: "I tell you I won't go on living and remembering I saw a thing like this; was part of it myself. I couldn't. I'd go really crazy" (107). Major Tetley scorns his son's feelings and places him in charge of Martin's hanging. Gerald botches the job, so that Martin does not die. Major Tetley orders Farnley to shoot the dangling, choking man.

With the lynching over, the posse rides back to town. On the way the men encounter Drew, the sheriff, and Kinkaid, who had not been murdered after all. Now they know that Martin was telling the truth; the posse killed three innocent men. This mistake troubles everyone involved, particularly Gerald, Major Tetley, and Davies. Gerald tries to kill himself on the way back to town, and later he hangs himself in his barn. Shortly afterward his father commits suicide in his library. Davies is also tortured by guilt. He tells Art that he knew Martin was innocent and that he should have shot Major Tetley because it would have stopped the hangings. Art agrees that this would have been the only solution. Davies berates himself for lacking the courage to shoot, and it is clear that he will never forgive himself. In the end Art and Gil are glad to leave town and return to their range. (Clark 1960; Westbrook 1969)

See also Clark, Walter Van Tilburg; Croft, Art; Davies, Art; Fascism; Justice; Martin, Donald; Tetley, Gerald

P

Pardiggle, Mrs.

The character Mrs. Pardiggle appears in Charles Dickens's novel *Bleak House,* which was first published in serialized form between 1852 and 1853. She is a social worker whose own children are extremely unhappy and resent her activities. Moreover, she offers the poor her opinions but does nothing to ease their miseries. When she barges into one house to ask its owner questions and preach cleanliness, he says:

> I wants a end of these liberties took with my place. I wants a end of being drawed like a badger. Now you're a-going to poll-pry and question according to custom—I know what you're a-going to be up to. Well! You haven't got no occasion to be up to it. I'll save you the trouble. Is my daughter a-washin? Yes, she *is* a-washin. Look at the water. Smell it! That's wot we drinks. How do you like it, and what do you think of gin, instead! An't my place dirty? Yes, it is dirty—it's nat'rally dirty, and it's nat'rally onwholesome; and we've had five dirty and onwholesome children, as is all dead infants, and so much the better for them, and for us besides. Have I read the little book wot you left? No, I an't read the little book wot you left. There an't nobody here as knows how to read it; and if there wos, it wouldn't be suitable to me. It's a book fit for a babby, and I'm not a babby. If you was to leave me a doll, I shouldn't nuss it. How have I been conducting of myself? Why, I've been drunk for three days; and I'd a been drunk four, if I'd a had the money. Don't I never mean for to go to church? No, I don't never mean for to go to church. I shouldn't be expected there, if I did; the beadle's too gen-teel for me. And how did my wife get that black eye? Why, I giv' it her; and if she says I didn't, she's a Lie! (Dickens 1987a, 107)

Mrs. Pardiggle's response is to pull out a religious tract and begin reading it to him. She completely misunderstands the poor and seems to have become a charity worker for her own self-aggrandizement rather than for the good of the downtrodden. (Dickens 1987a)

See also *Bleak House;* Dickens, Charles; Poverty; Religion

Paris in the Twentieth Century

The novel *Paris au XXe Siècle* (Paris in the Twentieth Century) was written in 1863 by French science fiction author Jules Verne, but it was not published in France until 1994; an

English version first appeared in 1996. The original manuscript had been rejected for publication and was tucked away in a household safe. It was rediscovered by the author's great-grandson upon the sale of the Verne family home in 1989.

Set in the future (specifically, 1960), the novel concerns a young classical poet, Michel Dufrenoy, who cannot practice his art because society has become completely dedicated to science and technology. The only poets who succeed are ones who write about the glories of industrialism; people are uninterested in literature from earlier times. They also do not care for classical music, preferring a chaotic modern form that represents the dissonance of machinery. In this world Michel struggles to earn a living. He works at a bank until he is fired and then tries his hand at writing drama. However, dramatic works are written in collaborative groups according to a prescribed format, and Michel finds he cannot work this way. He values originality too much. He therefore decides to quit his job and write a book of poetry, but after much effort he realizes he will never get it published. Meanwhile he has fallen in love with the daughter of a classics professor who loses his job. One day in deep winter Michel goes to visit her and discovers that she and her father have been evicted. He cannot find them and believes that they will freeze to death on the cold Paris streets. In despair he goes to a graveyard and collapses on the snow.

Scholar Eugen Weber, in a 1996 introduction to the novel, explains that Michel's plight reflects the difference between this book and the other works of Jules Verne. Weber (xii) says: "In classic Jules Verne adventures the environment is there to be mastered; in twentieth century Paris it can only be suffered, and the narrative offers less entertaining description than cultural criticism." In discussing this criticism, Weber compares the novel to Aldous Huxley's *Brave New World* and George Orwell's *1984,* both of which depict a bleak future of conformity and government control. He also likens one character in *Paris in the Twentieth Century,* a man who is trying to save great literature of the past, to the book-savers in Ray Bradbury's *Fahrenheit 451.*

Interestingly, Weber also points out that Verne predicted many of today's modern conveniences long before they were invented. For example, the novel mentions automobiles, elevated railways and subways, electric musical instruments, the electric chair, fax machines, copy machines, and calculators. It also mentions many social problems that did not yet exist, such as the corruption of the French language by American phrases, the weakening of marriage as an institution, and the increasing acceptability of illegitimate births. Nonetheless, Verne's publisher, Pierre-Jules Hetzel, rejected the manuscript as implausible, saying, "No one today will believe your prophecy" (xxv). (Verne 1996)

See also Bradbury, Ray; *Brave New World;* Dufrenoy, Michel; *Fahrenheit 451;* Huxley, Aldous; *1984;* Orwell, George; Science Fiction and Fantasy; Verne, Jules

"Parish Workhouse, The"

The 1807 poem "The Parish Workhouse," by George Crabbe, concerns itself with a poorhouse housing children and their parents, along with widows, unmarried women, the handicapped, the insane, and the chronically ill. It is a place of grief and toil, in sharp contrast to life among the rich. The poet criticizes those more fortunate who complain of imaginary pains, lying on a "downy couch" and asking their doctor "to name the nameless evernew disease" when there is real suffering in the world (Sinclair 1996, 99). He asks such complainers: "How would ye bear in real pain to lie, / Despised, neglected, left alone to die?" (99). (Sinclair 1996)

See also Crabbe, George; Poverty

Path of Thunder, The

Written by South African author Peter Abrahams, this novel addresses the issue of interracial marriage in South Africa. It was published in the United States in 1948, just one year prior to South Africa's passage of the Prohibition of Mixed Marriages Act, which made such unions illegal. *The Path of Thunder* was therefore banned for publication and distribution in Abrahams's native country.

In the novel Abrahams (1975, 29) explains that there are three classes of people in South Africa: whites, blacks, and coloureds, who are "neither white nor black; neither Europeans nor native Africans but a blending of the two that was at once different from both white and black, and lived neither in the one world nor in the other, but precariously between the two." These three races exist on a "colour bar" that ranks racial superiority, with whites at the top, coloureds in the middle, and blacks at the bottom. Therefore, the novel's main character, a coloured teacher named Lanny Swartz, thinks himself better than Mako, the Zulu teacher from a neighboring black village.

Lanny has returned to his hometown, Stilleveld, after earning his teacher's certificate and arts degree in Capetown, South Africa. Now that he is an educated man, Lanny finds himself emotionally distant from his people. The only person he can talk to about his feelings is Isaac Finkelberg, the well-educated son of a Jewish shopkeeper. He and Isaac have long conversations that often include Isaac's friend Mako. He believes in black nationalism and criticizes the coloureds for feeling superior because they have white blood in them. He says that "they try to grade toward the white man because he has power. They accept the inferior position and try to escape it by trying to become white themselves. You see, it is a slavery of the mind and that is even worse than the slavery of the body" (91). He also applies this attitude toward interracial marriages, arguing: "If it is compensation for not being white then I will fight it with all my strength. If it is the business of a man and a woman who love and have stepped above and beyond color then it is their business" (91).

Nonetheless, when Lanny falls in love with Sarie Villier, a young white woman from a prominent family, Mako tries to convince him to give up the affair. Sarie is related by adoption to a prominent white landowner, Gert Villier, and Mako knows that this will bring Lanny trouble. He tells Lanny:

If our country were a free country where people lived freely and not like slaves it would be only your business and her business. In a world that is sane I would wish you luck, and you two, coloured boy and white girl, would be married and would be happy. But it is not so. Here the black people are like slaves. The white people here fear the very idea of equality between you and that girl and when they find out, there will be trouble for you, you know that, and there will be trouble for her too. It will lead only to unhappiness and pain. (232)

Lanny refuses to listen, even after he learns that another villager, a crippled, mentally disturbed person called "Mad Sam," once a normal young man named Sam Du Plessis, was in love with a white woman related to Gert Villier. When this love was discovered, Gert beat Sam nearly to death, and soon thereafter the young woman died under mysterious circumstances. Now Sam works for Gert. According to scholar Robert Ensor (1992, 174), Sam symbolizes "alienated manhood, deformed and literally rendered impotent by white male dominance."

Similarly, Gert tries to emasculate Lanny. When the teacher first comes to Capetown, the white man threatens him, saying: "You are proud. You feel as good as any man. . . . You have forgotten your place! . . . *We* don't like that sort of spirit here" (63). Gert expresses nothing but hatred for Lanny, who eventually discovers that he and Gert are actually half brothers. This relationship means nothing to Gert. When he finds out that Lanny and Sarie are planning to run away together to Portuguese East Africa, where interracial mingling is allowed, Gert lies in wait for Lanny. He beats the young man until Mad Sam intervenes. Sam and Gert struggle, and in the end both die of knife wounds. Lanny then flees to Sarie's house, and the two try to hold off Gert's friends. A gunfight breaks out, and the next day the newspaper reports that "a young coloured teacher . . . had run amok, killed a prominent farmer, Mr. Gert Villier, and then been chased into the house of Mr. Villier. Alone in the house was Miss Sarie Villier. He had found a gun, shot her, and then turned the gun on his pursuers. In the ensuing battle three other people had been killed before Swartz had finally been shot down" (279).

Ensor (1992, 128) reports that Lanny and Sarie's "unity in death is not in itself a conclusion to the struggle for equality as it does not penetrate into the consciousness of the dominant white community." However, he (128) adds that "their short-lived relationship . . . serves as an example, pointing ahead to a future liberation and opens up the possibility of interracial love." In fact, at one point in *The Path of Thunder* Mako suggests that Lanny think more about the future than the present, saying that he should not only give up Sarie but "go away from here, live in another place and fight till your people are no longer slaves so that one day in the future if another coloured man loves another white woman they will be free to love openly and it will not be a crime. That is a good thing to do for your people. And in the fight you will find forgetfulness and your pain will be less. . . . For [our generation] there is no time for love. There is only the fight to live and be men instead of slaves" (Abrahams 1975, 232). However, Mad Sam disagrees with this position. He argues that "love is the only thing that can kill hate, nothing else. You see, hate destroys and that's why love is stronger. It builds. There is hope for all the coloured people in this country while one white woman can love one coloured man" (177).

Abrahams relates Lanny and Sarie's love to a relationship expressed in the poem "Tableau," by Countee Cullen, which he quotes in the novel. This poem describes a moment when "the black boy and the white" can walk together "locked arm in arm" along a "path of thunder," despite the censure of their communities (241). Cullen was a black American poet and one of the leaders of a black literary movement called the Harlem Renaissance. According to Ensor, Abrahams's work was heavily influenced by this movement, as well as by the work of social protest author Richard Wright. Ensor compares the

structure of *The Path of Thunder*, which is divided into three sections entitled "Home," "Love," and "Hate," to the structure of Wright's novel *Native Son*, which is divided into three sections entitled "Fear," "Flight," and "Fate." (Abrahams 1975; Ensor 1992)

See also Abrahams, Peter; Apartheid; Cullen, Countee; Finkelberg, Isaac; Mako; *Native Son;* Racism; Swartz, Lanny; Wright, Richard

Paton, Alan

Alan Stewart Paton was a prominent South African writer whose novel *Cry, the Beloved Country* (1948) brought international attention to his country's policies regarding racial discrimination and segregation. Born January 11, 1903, in Pietermaritzburg, Natal, South Africa, he attended the University of Natal and became a teacher and then a principal. He worked for reforms at his school, and in 1953 he helped form the Liberal Party of South Africa, which sought to end apartheid. That same year he published the novel *Too Late the Phalarope.* He subsequently wrote a short story collection and two collections of articles and speeches, as well as novels, biographies, memoirs, and a newspaper column. He died on April 12, 1988, near Natal. (Callan 1982)

See also Apartheid; *Cry, the Beloved Country;* Racism

Peace

Peace, by Aristophanes, is the second play in a series of three comedies about the Peloponnesian War (431–404 B.C.) between the rival Greek city-states of Athens and Sparta. First performed in 422 B.C., it was preceded by *The Archanians* in 426 B.C. and followed by *Lysistrata* in 411 B.C. It concerns a patriot named Trygaeus who trains a dung-beetle to fly him to the home of the god Zeus on Mount Olympus. Trygaeus wants to convince Zeus to end the war, but at Olympus he finds that Zeus has given his house to the god War and that the goddess Peace is now War's prisoner in a distant pit. After some difficulty Trygaeus frees Peace and restores her to her honored place on earth. (Aristophanes 1930; Murray 1933)

See also *Archanians, The;* Aristophanes; *Lysistrata;* Peace

Peace

Peace appears as the main theme in many works of social protest. One early example is the play *Peace,* by Aristophanes. Later examples include the antiwar novels *Stalingrad,* by Theodor Plevier, and *Catch-22,* by Joseph Heller. Science fiction novels such as *Brave New World,* by Aldous Huxley; *Looking Backward, 2000–1887,* by Edward Bellamy; *1984,* by George Orwell; *Planet of the Apes,* by Pierre Boulle; and *Player Piano,* by Kurt Vonnegut deal with the issue of peace by showing how futuristic societies deal with conflict. Works that discuss socialist revolutions and fascism also talk about conflict; however, they often advocate war rather than peace. (Cohen 1962; Hook 1959)

See also Aristophanes; Bellamy, Edward; Boulle, Pierre; *Brave New World; Catch-22;* Fascism; Heller, Joseph; Huxley, Aldous; *Looking Backward, 2000–1887; 1984;* Orwell, George; *Peace; Planet of the Apes; Player Piano;* Plevier, Theodor; Socialism; *Stalingrad;* Vonnegut, Kurt

Peace, Sula

Sula Peace is the main character of Toni Morrison's 1973 novel *Sula.* Restless because she has no outlet for her creative energies, she behaves contrary to the morals of her black community. Her neighbors therefore ostracize her. After her death, however, her former best friend, Nel Wright, recognizes the value of Sula's individuality and vitality. (Gates and Appiah 1993c; Morrison 1974)

See also Feminism; Morrison, Toni; *Sula;* Wright, Nel

Penochkin, Arkady Pavlych

Russian landowner Arkady Pavlych Penochkin appears in the short story "Bailiff," which is part of an 1852 collection entitled *Zapiski okhotnika* (A Sportsman's Sketches). Written by Ivan Turgenev, this collection emphasizes the unfair treatment of the peasants by the landed gentry, and "Bailiff" is perhaps

its harshest story. In it, Penochkin treats his peasants poorly and feeds them very little, a fact that causes the first-person narrator of the story to say:

> A strange kind of unease seizes hold of you in his house; even the comforts of it evoke no pleasure, and each evening, when the frizzle-haired lackey appears before you . . . and proceeds deferentially to pull off your boots, you feel that if only in place of his lean and hungry figure there were suddenly presented to you . . . a strapping lad just brought in from the plough by the master of house . . . you would be indescribably pleased and would willingly submit to the danger of losing, along with your boot, the whole of your leg right up to the thigh. (Turgenev 1983, 101–102)

(Lloyd 1972; Turgenev 1983)

See also *Sportsman's Sketches, A;* Turgenev, Ivan

Piggy

In the microcosm of society represented in William Golding's 1954 novel *Lord of the Flies,* the character "Piggy" has the role of scapegoat. He is a bright but overweight child stranded on an island with a group of British schoolboys. With no adults present, Piggy endures teasing, yet continues to make suggestions that help the boys survive. He is an important member of the group, and his eyeglasses are the only way the children can light fires. Nonetheless, his intelligence separates him from the rest of his society. In fact, one of the boys, Jack Merridew, hates Piggy so much that he convinces the rest to steal his glasses, which by then are cracked, and kill him. (Golding 1954)

See also Golding, William; *Lord of the Flies;* Merridew, Jack

Pittman, Jane Brown

Jane Brown Pittman is the first-person narrator of Ernest J. Gaines's 1971 novel *The Autobiography of Miss Jane Pittman.* An African-American woman over 100 years old, she describes her life in Louisiana from the time of the Civil War to the beginning of the civil rights movement. She is an intelligent, perceptive, strong-willed character who represents an indomitable spirit in the fight against racism. (Gaines 1971)

See also *Autobiography of Miss Jane Pittman, The;* Gaines, Ernest J.

Planet of the Apes

Published in 1963, the science fiction novel *La Planète des singes* (Planet of the Apes), by Pierre Boulle, depicts racism and rigid thinking in a simian society on the planet Soror. Its first-person narrator, a French journalist named Ulysse Merou, travels there from Earth in the year 2500 in the company of a brilliant scientist, Professor Antelle, and his protégé, Arthur Levain. The three men take a small craft from their spaceship to the planet's surface, where they encounter a primitive tribe of humans who attack them simply to destroy their clothes and equipment. Merou notes that these people are apparently unintelligent and unable to smile or talk. He finds one young woman, whom he names Nova, particularly attractive.

The scientists spend the night in the humans' camp, and the next morning they are awakened by shouts and gunshots. They flee the sounds with the rest of the humans, but Professor Antelle cannot keep up and is left behind. Meanwhile Merou and Levain soon find themselves surrounded by hunters. To Merou's horror, these hunters are not humans but gorillas. He is astonished to see them wearing clothes, firing guns, and shouting orders to their assistants, who are chimpanzees. Merou hides in the brush, but Arthur Levain panics and bursts into the clearing, where he is shot dead. While his killer is reloading, Merou runs away but is snared in a net. He is then taken to a research laboratory, where he speaks to his guards. They are astonished by his vocalizations but do not understand his language. They call one of the scientists, a female chimpanzee named Zira, who suspects that Merou might have some form of intelligence. She reports this to her superior, an

orangutan named Zaius, but he refuses to listen, believing that Merou was once an ape's pet who has been taught some simple tricks. He continues to treat Merou as an ignorant animal and gives him Nova, who has also been captured, as a mate.

Meanwhile Zira meets with Merou in secret to teach him her language. In return, he teaches her French. Together the two discuss his journey from Earth and the differences between Earth and Soror. Zira introduces Merou to her fiancé, Cornelius, who arranges for the man to appear at a scientific gathering. The assembled guests believe that Merou is there to do some tricks. Instead, he delivers a speech about his journey from Earth and the wonders of technology he can show them.

The apes decide to release him to work with Cornelius. One day the two travel to an archaeological dig, where they discover evidence that an advanced human culture existed on the planet over 10,000 years ago. Back at the laboratory, Cornelius manipulates human brains to extract collective memories of the race and discovers that humans were once masters over apes. Gradually the apes learned to mimic their oppressors and took over the planet. The humans then descended into a primitive state. Cornelius has proof that men can easily revert to a savage state; a few weeks earlier Merou discovered Professor Antelle in the zoo, and the scientist had forgotten how to talk or behave in a civilized manner. Despite Merou's efforts to rehabilitate him, Antelle remains savage and stupid.

Cornelius's discoveries about ape evolution are revolutionary, and he is afraid to reveal them to his superiors. At the same time the government has decided that Merou is a threat to the ape way of life. Nova has given birth to his child, and the boy has demonstrated intelligence and an ability for speech. Fearing that the family could create a new race of clever humans, government officials plot to kill Merou and Nova and imprison their baby in a research institution. Before this can happen, Zira and Cornelius switch the family with three humans who are to be sent into space on an experimental satellite. Merou then pilots the satellite to his spaceship and takes off for Earth. When he arrives there, he discovers that gorillas are running the airport. He takes off again, planning to find a safe planet somewhere. Meanwhile he places his story in a sealed bottle and jettisons it into space.

The main plot of *Planet of the Apes* is framed by the discovery of the bottle by a young couple, Phyllis and Jinn, who are taking a holiday in space. They are not from Earth, but because Jinn once went to school there, he can read the manuscript. At the end of the novel they express disbelief over Merou's story, and the reader learns that they are chimpanzees.

Planet of the Apes blames the deterioration of the human race on its loss of interest in mental pursuits. In the section describing the collective memory of the race, Merou quotes one woman as saying: "What is happening could have been foreseen. A cerebral laziness has taken hold of us. No more books; even detective novels have now become too great an intellectual effort. No more games; at the most a hand or two of cards. Even the childish motion picture does not tempt us any more. Meanwhile the apes are meditating in silence. Their brain is developing in solitary reflection" (Boulle 1963, 116).

Similarly, in discussing how easy it was for apes to take over human activities, Merou says:

What is it that characterizes a civilization? . . . Let us concede that it is principally the arts, and first and foremost, literature. Is the latter really beyond the reach of our higher apes, if it is admitted that they are capable of stringing words together? Of what is our literature made? Masterpieces? . . . But once an original book has been written—and no more than one or two appear in a century—men of letters *imitate* it, in other words, they copy it so that hundreds of thousands of books are published on exactly the same theme, with slightly different titles and modified phraseology. This should be able to be achieved by apes, who are essentially imi-

tators, provided, of course, that they are able to make use of language. (100)

In fact, the orangutans in Soror's ape society are prolific authors, writing countless derivative works. They are rigid thinkers incapable of seeing reason. They are given control of the scientific community, even though the chimpanzees make most of the scientific and technical discoveries. Meanwhile the gorillas are masters at exploiting those discoveries and making them profitable. In this way each type of ape fulfills a designated role in society, exhibiting racism toward those unlike itself.

By showing the flaws in this fictional ape society, *Planet of the Apes* is actually criticizing real-life human society. However, many aspects of this criticism were missing from a movie version of the novel released in 1968. The movie attributed humanity's downfall not to a loss of intellectualism but to a nuclear war. The film is set entirely on Earth, although this is not revealed until the end of the story. (Boulle 1963; Frackman 1996)

See also Boulle, Pierre; Merou, Ulysse; Science Fiction and Fantasy; Zaius

Player Piano

The 1952 science fiction novel *Player Piano,* which was reissued as *Utopia 14* in 1954, is author Kurt Vonnegut's vision of a future where people are oppressed because of technology. A modern industrial revolution has occurred in the United States, and machines have replaced a large percentage of the nation's workers. Engineers, scientists, and managers who can care for machines have become an elite class. Meanwhile those people whose jobs have been replaced by machines must join either the army or the Reconstruction and Reclamation Corps, which performs menial jobs such as road repair.

The novel's main character, Dr. Paul Proteus, is a member of the elite class. He is in charge of the machines in Ilium, New York, but his wife hopes he will be promoted to the Pittsburgh division. Paul, however, is not seeking a promotion and is vaguely unhappy with his current job. He has been visiting the nonelite section of town and has realized that machines have increased unemployment, which in turn has increased a variety of social ills. In discussing the dispossessed workers, he tells his wife: "In order to get what we've got, . . . we have, in effect, traded these people out of what was the most important thing on earth to them—the feeling of being needed and useful, the foundation of self-respect" (Vonnegut 1980, 151).

Paul's friend Ed Finnerty has come to the same conclusion. One day he quits his job as an act of rebellion. Later he becomes involved in a revolutionary group, the Ghost Shirts, which intends to smash the machines and overturn the government. Because of Paul's continuing friendship with Ed, Paul's superiors pretend to fire him, so that he can join the Ghost Shirts as a spy. What they do not understand is that Paul shares the philosophy of the revolutionaries and soon becomes a true member of their group. He is arrested and put on trial, but he escapes when the Ghost Shirts begin their nationwide revolution. It is a failure everywhere but Ilium. However, after the machines are smashed, the working-class people begin fixing them again. Paul and his associates realize that human nature will not allow an end to technology, and they surrender to authorities.

Player Piano alternates Paul's story with chapters concerning a Middle Eastern shah who is visiting the United States. The shah's guide, an American diplomat named Ewing J. Halyard, keeps referring to the American people as "citizens." The shah insists on using the word *slave*. The shah is an astute judge of the nation's flaws, and Ewing's defense of U.S. society is weak. By the end of the novel Ewing has lost his job because of a technicality, and he realizes that the work policies of the United States are unjust. (Schatt 1976; Vonnegut 1980)

> See also Proteus, Paul; Science Fiction and Fantasy; Vonnegut, Kurt

Plevier, Theodor

German novelist Theodor Plevier, who also used the pseudonym Plivier, protested Nazi political and social policies in his work. The German government banned his books in 1933 and expelled him from the country in 1934. Born in Berlin, Germany, on February 12, 1892, Plevier served in his country's navy during World War I. In 1918 while the government was discussing the terms of its surrender, he participated in a mutiny of the German fleet in Kiel, Germany. Afterward he became a Communist and was involved in liberal causes. He began writing articles and novels to express his views. His best-known work is a trilogy of novels concerning World War II, *Stalingrad* (1945), *Moskau* (Moscow, 1952), and *Berlin* (1954). Plevier died in Avegno, Switzerland, on March 12, 1955. (Plevier 1948)

> See also Peace; *Stalingrad*

Ponderevo, George

George Ponderevo is the first-person narrator of *Tono-Bungay* (1908), by H. G. Wells. A successful British boat builder, Ponderevo reflects on a time in his life when he made money through less honest means. His uncle Edward, a chemist, created a worthless medicine called Tono-Bungay, and the two men used clever advertising to promote it. Soon they were rich, but George's conscience was troubled. Meanwhile his uncle squandered their fortune, turned to forgery, and died a ruined man. George now realizes how easily greed can corrupt people's morals. He also criticizes British society for creating the conditions under which greed can spread. (Wells 1935)

> See also Quap; *Tono-Bungay*; Wells, H. G.

Pontmercy, Marius

Marius Pontmercy is a French revolutionary in Victor Hugo's 1862 novel *Les Misérables*. He was raised by his grandfather, a royalist, but becomes estranged from him when he expresses his support for the politics of his deceased father, who was one of Napoleon's soldiers. After leaving his grandfather's house, Marius becomes involved with a revolutionary group and participates in a citizen uprising in June 1832, during which he is seriously wounded. When he recovers, he reconciles with his grandfather and marries a beautiful young woman named Cosette. (Hugo 1987)

See also Cosette; Hugo, Victor; *Misérables, Les*

Possessed, The

Published in two volumes between 1870 and 1872, the novel *Besy* (The Possessed), by Fyodor Dostoyevsky, concerns social and political turmoil in Russia during the 1860s. At that time Russian liberalism was being supplanted by Russian radicalism, which sought to overthrow governments and undermine spiritual and moral beliefs. *The Possessed* criticizes this revolutionary movement, portraying its leaders as godless men who do not care about individual worth.

In a foreword to a 1936 edition of the book, scholar Avrahm Yarmolinsky (v) says that "Dostoyevsky's avowed intention in writing it was to drive home certain convictions of his, regardless of whether or not he met the requirements of the art of fiction. He wanted to deal a body blow to the rebels who threatened what he considered to be the foundations of Russian life." Consequently, the novel is "a tangled skein of many threads" with an intricate plot that presents the author's beliefs on a wide variety of political and social issues (vii). In particular, it highlights Dostoyevsky's belief that only through Christianity can humanity better itself. The novel's two main characters, Pyotr Stepanovitch Verhovensky and Nikolay Vsyevolodovitch Stavrogin, are both atheists who use people to their own advantage, Verhovensky on a political level and Stavrogin on a personal one.

Verhovensky is the son of eccentric writer and professor Stepan Trofimovich Verhovensky, whose friend, Mr. G—v, narrates the story. Stepan Verhovensky's patroness, Vavara Petrovna Stavrogin, is a member of the wealthy elite, and Pyotr Verhovensky uses this connection to Vavara to gain stature in the community for himself. At the same time he forms a small, secret revolutionary group whose intention is to sow discord throughout the area, "to bring about the downfall of everything—both the government and its moral standards" (617). To this aim, Verhovensky

Fyodor Dostoyevsky (Popperfoto/Archive Photos)

exhorts his followers to "organize to control public opinion; it's shameful not to snatch at anything that lies idle and gaping at us" (617). He has them print manifestos, which he then secretly distributes throughout the town in hope of inciting riots.

Verhovensky's ultimate plan is to use Vavara's son, Nikolay Vsyevolodovitch Stavrogin, to help him gain power once the government is overthrown. Verhovensky believes that Stavrogin, because he is nobly born, will be accepted as the new ruler of postrevolutionary Russia and that through Stavrogin Verhovensky's group will control the government. However, Stavrogin does not want to participate in the plan. He is a man troubled by guilt and a desire for self-punishment. The reason for Stavrogin's guilt is explained in a chapter entitled "At Tihon's," which the novel's original editor refused to print and which remained unknown until its publication in 1927. In it Stavrogin confesses to a monk named Tihon that he once sexually abused a 12-year-old girl, who then committed suicide.

This act has led Stavrogin to want to believe in the Devil, although he professes not to believe in God; therefore he is struggling with the issue of religious faith.

Because of this struggle, Avrahm Yarmolinsky (vii) calls Stavrogin "the real protagonist of the tale." He explains that Dostoyevsky originally planned to write a novel concerning the "Life of a Great Sinner" and that he incorporated parts of that work into *The Possessed*. Stavrogin represents Dostoyevsky's sinner, a man "unable to distinguish between good and evil, or to give himself in love, without attachment to his people and so without religious faith" and therefore "beyond the pale of the living" (viii).

Stavrogin becomes involved with several women during the course of *The Possessed*, and because he is incapable of love, he ultimately ruins them all. But he feels particularly guilty over the death of Marya Timofyevna, a mentally imbalanced girl whom he married out of his desire for self-punishment. Verhovensky ordered a convict named Fedka to kill the girl because she was not a suitable wife for Stavrogin and therefore would have interfered with his image of the new ruler of Russia. At the same time Fedka murdered Marya's brother, Captain Lebyadkin, for threatening to expose the secret organization.

But while Stavrogin's conscience is tortured by these deaths, Verhovensky feels no remorse over them. He is an atheist who does not believe in a punishing God, and he remains confident that his revolutionary group will succeed in taking over the government. When his followers start to doubt him, he falsely tells them that he is connected to hundreds of similar groups throughout Russia, implying that their organization is powerful. Nonetheless, Verhovensky's control over his group soon weakens. He argues with Fedka and later kills him. He also kills Shatov, who announced he was planning to leave the organization, and dumps the body in a remote lake.

Shatov's murder is actually based on a true event. In 1869 a Russian revolutionary group led by Sergey Nechayev killed one of its members and abandoned his body in a pond at the Moscow Agricultural Academy. According to Yarmolinsky, Dostoyevsky based *The Possessed* on this event, much in the way Theodore Dreiser based his social protest novel, *An American Tragedy*, on a real murder. However, Yarmolinsky also notes that, whereas Nechayev was born of peasants, Dostoyevsky chose to make Verhovensky the son of a professor and gentleman, a European sophisticate. Yarmolinsky says Dostoyevsky made this choice because he "hated the liberals who would Europeanize Russia, and considered them the begetters of revolution" (vi).

Moreover, in the end Verhovensky proves himself to be an ineffectual revolutionary. He convinces a troubled man, Kirillov, to confess to the murders in writing and then kill himself. Once Kirillov is dead, Verhovensky leaves town and disappears. Shortly thereafter the members of his group begin informing on one another. At the same time Stavrogin's guilt overwhelms him, and he hangs himself. Verhovensky's father also dies after an illness caused by disillusionment and grief; just before his death he questions his own atheism and begins to accept God. (Dostoyevsky 1936; Dostoyevsky 1968)

See also *American Tragedy, An;* Dostoyevsky, Fyodor; Dreiser, Theodore; Religion; Shatov; Stavrogin, Nikolay Vsyevolodovitch; Verhovensky, Pyotr Stepanovitch

"Poverty"

The short social protest poem "Poverty" is one of the few surviving works of the Greek poet Alcaeus, who lived from approximately 620 to 580 B.C. Published in the second century B.C., it was included in one of ten books of Alcaeus's poetry, along with other social and political protest poems, hymns, drinking songs, and love poetry. Describing a society where "wealth makes the man," it calls penury "the worst of ills" (Sinclair 1996, 283) and speaks of the desolation of the poor. (Sinclair 1996)

See also Alcaeus; Poverty

Poverty

Poverty is perhaps the most common problem depicted in social protest literature throughout the world. It appears in ancient writings, such as the poems of Alcaeus, as well as in modern novels, such as Kurt Vonnegut's *Player Piano.* Times of economic hardship inspire the largest amount of antipoverty literature. For example, George Crabbe, Charles Dickens, and Arthur Morrison wrote about poverty during the Industrial Revolution, and Rebecca Harding Davis, Tillie Olsen, Upton Sinclair, and John Steinbeck addressed the issue during the Depression. Poverty also appears in literature that addresses labor issues, socialism, capitalism, and a rigid class structure. In many works, such as Theodore Dreiser's *An American Tragedy,* George Gissing's *New Grub Street,* and Frank Norris's *The Octopus,* a desire for wealth leads to moral corruption, and the poor are depicted as more honorable than the rich. (Marris and Rein 1967)

> **See also** Alcaeus; *American Tragedy, An;* Capitalism; Class, Social; Crabbe, George; Davis, Rebecca Harding; Dickens, Charles; Dreiser, Theodore; Gissing, George; Great Depression; Labor Issues; Morrison, Arthur; *New Grub Street;* Norris, Frank; *Octopus, The;* Olsen, Tillie; *Player Piano;* Sinclair, Upton; Socialism; Steinbeck, John; Vonnegut, Kurt

Power and the Glory, The

Published in 1940, *The Power and the Glory,* by Graham Greene, concerns religious persecution in Mexico during the late 1930s. The novel is set in the state of Tabasco, where Catholic priests are forbidden to practice their faith. In fact, unless a priest openly forsakes his religious beliefs by getting married, he is executed. As a result, at the beginning of the novel only one practicing priest still lives in the area.

The Power and the Glory traces this man's attempts to avoid capture while he continues to perform his duties. It also depicts his struggles to come to terms with his sins. He is an alcoholic who once fathered a child out of wedlock and therefore does not believe himself worthy of the priesthood. Nonetheless, he perseveres under deplorable conditions. He has little to eat and must run from one village to another to escape the police. His main pur-

suer, a police lieutenant, is a good man who is as passionate about communism as the priest is about Catholicism.

Finally the priest decides to leave Tabasco. He is almost to safety when someone comes to tell him that a dying man has requested his services. The priest recognizes the messenger as a police informant but still decides to go with him. Consequently, the priest is caught and sentenced to die. Just before his execution he becomes reconciled to his sins, and the day of his death another priest arrives in town to take his place.

Of the work Greene (1962, xiii) says, "I think *The Power and the Glory* is the only novel I have written to a thesis," which is that the power of the Catholic Church will remain despite human corruption and persecution. However, Greene's other novels are also set in oppressive world regions, including Cuba, Haiti, Czechoslovakia, Poland, Indo-China, Africa. (Greene 1962)

> **See also** Greene, Graham; Religion

Prison Reform

Social protest authors often raise public awareness of prison conditions, and sometimes this has led to prison reforms. For example, John Galsworthy's play *Justice* brought about changes in England's prison system, and Charles Dickens's depiction of debtor's prison in *Little Dorrit* hastened its already impending demise. Leo Tolstoi and Aleksandr Solzhenitsyn called attention to problems within the Russian prison system. Authors Julia Ward Howe and Oscar Wilde were prison-reform activists, and writers concerned with the issue of justice, such as Victor Hugo and Ursula Le Guin, often discussed prisons in their work.

> **See also** Dickens, Charles; Galsworthy, John; Howe, Julia Ward; Hugo, Victor; Justice; Le Guin, Ursula; *Little Dorrit;* Solzhenitsyn, Aleksandr; Tolstoi, Leo; Wilde, Oscar

Proteus, Paul

Dr. Paul Proteus is the main character in Kurt Vonnegut's 1940 science fiction novel *Player Piano.* Proteus's father was one of the leaders of an industrial revolution that made an American society almost completely dependent on machines. As a result of this revolution, many workers became unemployed, and society's middle class descended into poverty and dissatisfaction. Paul gradually realizes that mechanization is killing men's souls. He joins a revolutionary group, the Ghost Shirts, dedicated to destroying technology and overturn-ing the government. In the process he loses his job, his wife, and his privileged status in society. At the same time he inspires others to revolt against society. But in the end the revolution fails, and Vonnegut suggests that this was inevitable because it is human nature to love machines. (Vonnegut 1980)

See also *Player Piano;* Vonnegut, Kurt

Q

Quap

A fictional radioactive substance, Quap appears in H. G. Wells's 1908 novel *Tono-Bungay* as a symbol of moral decay. It is part of a get-rich-quick scheme; the novel's main character, George Ponderevo, intends to steal the quap from an African island and sell it in England. Unfortunately, his journey is a failure. Everyone who handles the quap breaks out in sores, and George ends up shooting a native to keep the man from reporting the theft. In fact, George admits, "I hated all humanity during the time that the quap was near me" (Wells 1935, 339). When the crime is discovered, George barely escapes from the island. However, while at sea the quap destroys the cargo hold of his ship, and the vessel sinks. (Wells 1935)

See also Ponderevo, George; *Tono-Bungay;* Wells, H. G.

Quest, Martha

Martha Quest is the main character in Doris Lessing's five-novel series *Children of Violence.* The series explores her awakening to various social problems, including racism and anti-Semitism, as well as her interest in socialism and her struggle against a society that wants to see her as a wife and mother rather than an individual. In the end she discovers that she has psychic abilities and that the power to change society resides within herself. (Lessing 1964)

See also *Children of Violence;* Lessing, Doris

Quirk, Thady

First-person narrator of Maria Edgeworth's 1800 novel *Castle Rackrent,* Thady Quirk is an Irish servant devoted to the Rackrent family. In fact, he is so devoted that he excuses all of the Rackrents' faults, which are many. For example, when one of his masters, a drunkard, goes into debt by throwing lavish parties, Thady praises the man for being so merry and generous. He is therefore considered an unreliable narrator, and as such he is a device for Edgeworth's ironic criticisms of the Irish feudal system. (Edgeworth 1992)

See also *Castle Rackrent;* Edgeworth, Maria

R

Racism

The term *racism* refers to any prejudice against a person based on her or his inherited ethnic group or race. This prejudice is often based on an easily identified physical characteristic, such as skin color, or a behavior, such as a religious practice.

Racism against blacks in the United States is addressed in the works of James Baldwin, Ralph Ellison, Alice Walker, Richard Wright, and the authors of the Harlem Renaissance. It is also the subject of antislavery literature such as Harriet Beecher Stowe's novel *Uncle Tom's Cabin.* Racism in South Africa is the focus of antiapartheid writings such as Alan Paton's *Cry, the Beloved Country.* Racism against Jews, or anti-Semitism, is featured prominently in the novel *Children of the Ghetto* by Israel Zangwill.

Other groups have also experienced racism. For example, in *This Earth of Mankind,* Ananta Pramaodya Toer protests racism against native Javanese; in *Broad and Alien Is the World,* Ciro Alegría shows the persecution of Peruvian Indians; and in *Untouchable,* Mulk Raj Anand deals with the racism inherent in India's caste system. However, the most widely read and influential of works depicting racism against Native Americans, such as Thomas Berger's *Little Big Man* and Helen

Hunt Jackson's *Ramona,* have been written not by Native Americans, but by whites; Native American authors more often protest racism through nonfiction or poetry. (Feldstein 1972; Frederickson 1997; Moss 1978; Witt and Steiner 1972)

See also Alegría, Ciro; Anand, Mulk Raj; Apartheid; Baldwin, James; Berger, Thomas; *Broad and Alien Is the World; Children of the Ghetto; Cry, the Beloved Country;* Ellison, Ralph; Harlem Renaissance; Jackson, Helen Hunt; *Little Big Man;* Native American Issues; Paton, Alan; *Ramona;* Stowe, Harriet Beecher; *This Earth of Mankind;* Toer, Ananta Pramaodya; *Uncle Tom's Cabin; Untouchable;* Walker, Alice; Wright, Richard; Zangwill, Israel

Radley, Arthur ("Boo")

The character Arthur "Boo" Radley appears in *To Kill a Mockingbird,* by Harper Lee (1960). He never leaves his house and is rumored to be crazy and dangerous. One day he saves the life of a little girl, proving himself to be a kind, compassionate man. Through this act the girl, who is also the narrator of the story, learns not to judge people by outward appearances or rumors. (Lee 1993)

See also Lee, Harper; *To Kill a Mockingbird*

Raisin in the Sun, A

The three-act play *A Raisin in the Sun,* by Lorraine Hansberry, was produced in 1959. It is credited with being the first drama by a black woman ever performed on Broadway, and is considered important for its statements on racism and a black family's pride in its African heritage.

However, audiences of the time were eager to dismiss the black pride elements of the story, remarking on how much the central characters, the Youngers, resembled white people. In an article about the play, one of its actors, Ossie Davis, explains:

> One of the biggest selling points about *Raisin*—filling the grapevine, . . . laying the foundation for its wide, wide acceptance—was how much the Younger family was just like any other American family. Some people were ecstatic to find that "it didn't really have to be about Negroes at all!" It was, rather, a walking, talking, living demonstration of our mythic conviction that, underneath, all of us Americans, *color-ain't-got-nothing-to-do-with-it,* are pretty much alike. People are just people, whoever they are; and all they want is a chance to be like other people. This uncritical assumption . . . made any other questions about the Youngers, and what living in the slums of Southside Chicago had done to them, not only irrelevant and impertinent, but also disloyal . . . because everybody who walked into the theater saw in Lena Younger . . . his own great American Mama. (Hansberry 1988, 9)

Lena is the head of her household, which includes her daughter, Beneatha; her son, Walter; his wife, Ruth; and his son, Travis. The family lives in a cramped ghetto apartment. At the beginning of the play Lena is awaiting the arrival of a check for $10,000, the insurance payment on the death of her husband. Walter wants to use the money to start a liquor business because he hates his current job as a white man's chauffeur. Meanwhile Beneatha argues that the money should

be used to send her to college. She is interested in her black heritage and wants to become a doctor, perhaps in Africa.

Lena decides to pay for Beneatha's schooling, but she refuses to let Walter buy his business. As a result, he becomes despondent, and his mood darkens further when Ruth tells him she's pregnant. The two discuss abortion, and when Lena finds out, she is horrified. Wanting to give her family hope for the future, she uses part of her money as down payment on a new home in an all-white neighborhood. This upsets Walter so much that he refuses to go to work anymore.

Finally Lena gives her son what is left of her money, telling him to spend part of it on the liquor business and put the rest in the bank for Beneatha. Instead, he gives all of it to his business partner, who promptly disappears. Now his dreams as well as Beneatha's have been destroyed, and when the white home owners' committee offers to pay the family not to move into the neighborhood, he considers taking the offer. Then he realizes that his pride and self-respect are more important than money. He turns down the offer just as the moving van arrives.

With this resolution, *A Raisin in the Sun* emphasizes the importance of dreams and hope. It also does this through its title, which was taken from the poem "Harlem," by black poet Langston Hughes. Hughes suggests that "a dream deferred" can "dry up / like a raisin in the sun" (Hansberry 1988, 3). (Cheney 1984; Hansberry 1994)

See also Hughes, Langston; Racism; *Raisin in the Sun, A;* Younger Family

Ralph

In William Golding's 1954 novel *Lord of the Flies,* Ralph symbolizes authority and civilized society. He is the elected leader of a group of British schoolboys stranded on an island without adults. Although he establishes rules and tries to maintain order, he eventually loses control of the group, and the boys begin to follow Jack, a primitive savage. Eventually Jack convinces his tribe to hunt and kill Ralph. Before they can catch him, however, he is rescued by the arrival of a British naval officer, the representative of an even stronger civilization. (Golding 1954)

See also Golding, William; *Lord of the Flies;* Merridew, Jack

Ramona

Published in 1885, *Ramona,* by Helen Hunt Jackson, changed public opinion about the American Indian. In a 1988 introduction to the work, Native American author Michael Dorris points out that it was Jackson's portrayal of her characters, as well as her criticisms about oppressive society policy, that made the work so effective. He explains: "By peopling these communities with [Native American] characters who exemplified the highest American attitudes and behaviors, Mrs. Jackson invited her readers to empathize with Native Americans whom the public had been educated—by a century of U.S. dishonor and conquest—to disdain. According to *Ramona . . .* [they] were paragons of industry, gentle creatures who were hard-working, law-abiding, and devout" (Jackson 1988, xvii).

For this reason, Dorris calls the novel propaganda and reports that it helped bring about the passage of the Dawes Act in 1887. This piece of legislation was intended to promote Indian homesteading by decreeing that tribal lands be divided into individual land grants. In actuality, however, the Dawes Act made it easier for white settlers to move into Indian Territory.

The year after the novel's publication, the *North American Review* compared *Ramona* with Harriet Beecher Stowe's 1852 novel *Uncle Tom's Cabin,* which created sympathy for black slaves and furthered the antislavery, or abolitionist, movement. According to Dorris (v), the magazine classified the two works as the greatest "ethical novels" of the century. But *Ramona* is also a love story. Set in California, its main character, Ramona, is the daughter of an Irish man and a Native American woman. She has blue eyes and does not look Indian. As an infant she is given to a wealthy but childless Mexican landowner to raise, and when the woman dies, her sister,

Señora Moreno, takes Ramona in. The girl does not know her ancestry, but because Señora Moreno knows Ramona's race, she cannot love her. Consequently, she treats the girl far worse than her own son, Señor Felipe.

One day Ramona falls in love with an Indian named Alessandro, and the two plan to be married. When Señora Moreno finds out, she is furious. She refuses to let Ramona marry an Indian and threatens to send her to a convent. Felipe, who loves Ramona himself, tries to convince his mother to change her mind. He wants Ramona to be happy. But although Señora Moreno agrees not to send the young woman away, she still refuses to sanction the marriage. As a result, Ramona and Alessandro are forced to run away together.

By this time Alessandro's people have been driven from their village by greedy white men, and the young couple must travel south to San Diego to find work. Eventually he earns enough money to start his own farm. When some white homesteaders take it away, the young couple must again travel to another town to start over. Along the way Ramona and Alessandro meet a kindly white woman, Aunt Ri' Hyer, who becomes like a mother to Ramona. Nevertheless, the hardships continue. Their firstborn child falls ill, and when Alessandro goes to a government doctor for help, the man refuses to see the little girl. Instead, he gives Alessandro some medication to take home. The tonic proves fatal. Saddened and hearing rumors that whites want to take over the new town, Alessandro and Ramona decide to move up into the mountains, where Ramona gives birth to another child. All goes well until Alessandro accidentally takes the wrong horse home from a nearby village. Before he can return it, the owner finds him and shoots him for horse thieving. Grief-stricken, Ramona falls unconscious and is too ill to testify at the man's trial. He is found innocent.

Meanwhile Señora Moreno has died and Felipe has been searching for Ramona. He finds her right after the trial and helps nurse her back to health. He also threatens to kill Alessandro's murderer, and the man flees the country. When Ramona recovers, Felipe takes her and her daughter home. Eventually he marries her, and the family moves to Mexico. Greedy Americans have begun taking away the land of the Mexicans in California, and Felipe knows he will not find justice there. (Jackson 1988; Mathes 1990)

See also Alessandro; Hyer, Aunt Ri'; Jackson, Helen Hunt; Moreno, Señora; Native American Issues; Racism; Slavery

Rand, Ayn

American novelist Ayn Rand, in her writings, promotes selfishness, extols the virtues of capitalism, and opposes the oppressive nature of governments. She was born in St. Petersburg, Russia, as Alice or Alissa Rosenbaum on February 2, 1905. In 1926 she moved to the United States, where she worked as a Hollywood screenwriter. Her first novel, *We the Living* (1936), concerns a Russian career woman who struggles against government oppression. She followed it with *The Fountainhead* (1943), which addresses issues of creativity and nonconformity, and *Atlas Shrugged* (1957), which emphasizes the benefits of capitalism in furthering the interests of the individual. Rand also wrote nonfiction books and journals related to her views. They include *The Virtue of Selfishness* (1964), *Capitalism: The Unknown Ideal* (1967), and *The Ayn Rand Letter* (1971–1976). She died on March 6, 1982, in New York, New York. (Baker 1987)

See also *Atlas Shrugged;* Capitalism

Ayn Rand, 1957 (The New York Times Company/ Archive Photos)

Ransom, Basil

Basil Ransom is one of the main characters in Henry James's 1886 novel *The Bostonians.* A chauvinistic southern gentleman who practices law in New York, he falls in love with a speaker for the suffragette movement, Verena Tarrant. Throughout the course of the novel he tries to convince Verena that her feminist views are foolish. He expresses his own convictions with passion, and in the end he convinces her to marry him and abandon her cause. (James 1956)

See also *Bostonians, The;* James, Henry; Tarrant, Verena

Ras the Destroyer

A character from Ralph Ellison's 1952 novel *Invisible Man,* Ras the Destroyer proselytizes black separatism on street corners in Harlem, New York, during the late 1940s. He berates blacks who join a Communist organization called the Brotherhood because the group is run by white men. He is eventually killed during a race riot incited by the Brotherhood. (Ellison 1952)

See also Communism; Ellison, Ralph; *Invisible Man*

Ratched, Nurse

Nurse Ratched is the antagonist in Ken Kesey's 1962 novel *One Flew over the Cuckoo's Nest.* The head nurse in a mental hospital, she represents social conformity, rigid control, and the suppression of sexuality. She cannot stand to have her authority challenged or her femininity pointed out, and as she tries to emasculate the men in her care, she becomes increasingly cruel. This behavior calls into question society's definition of sanity. (Kesey 1964)

See also Kesey, Ken; *One Flew over the Cuckoo's Nest*

Reardon, Edwin

Edwin Reardon is a character in George Gissing's 1891 novel *New Grub Street* who dies in poverty despite a once-promising career as a novelist. Marriage was his undoing; whereas he was able to support himself by writing books, he could not bring in enough income to provide for his wife and newborn son. Another character, Jasper Milvain, points out that Edwin Reardon could have maintained his literary career if only he had remained single, saying: "As a bachelor, he might possibly have got into the right circles. . . . But as a married man, without means, the situation was hopeless. Once married, you must live up to the standard of the society you frequent; you can't be entertained without entertaining in return" (Gissing 1926, 28). Milvain believes that Reardon should have at least married a rich woman, as he himself did. (Gissing 1926)

See also Gissing, George; Milvain, Jasper; *New Grub Street*

Reardon, Hank

In Ayn Rand's 1957 novel *Atlas Shrugged*, Hank Reardon is an industrialist who invents a new kind of metal. The material proves incredibly profitable, but Reardon's family makes him feel guilty for the wealth it brings him. Moreover, the government wants to take away his exclusive rights to manufacture the material. The novel presents a United States that takes from the rich and gives to the poor. It punishes Reardon for his inventiveness, and in the end he decides to join a group dedicated to ending the current regime. (Rand 1992)

See also *Atlas Shrugged;* Rand, Ayn

Reisling, Paul

A character in the 1922 novel *Babbitt*, by Sinclair Lewis, Paul Reisling struggles to conform to the expectations of American middle-class society but fails in the attempt. In his youth he wants to be a violinist, but after marrying he must become a roofing salesman to support his wife, Zilla. She proves to be a terrible nag, making him feel like a failure in life. He hates his job and grows despondent. Eventu-

ally he begins having an affair, but this only increases his misery. One day, in response to his wife's nagging, he shoots her. She recovers from her injury, but he is sent to prison. (Grebstein 1962; Lewis 1950)

See also *Babbitt;* Doane, Seneca; Lewis, Sinclair

Religion

When social protest authors criticize religion, they often do so on the basis of hypocrisy, arguing that a church's members often do not adhere to its rules. For example, in *Elmer Gantry* Sinclair Lewis exposes the transgressions of Protestant ministers. In *Major Barbara*, George Bernard Shaw shows how greed corrupts Salvation Army Christians.

In other cases social protest authors question theology and examine issues of faith. For example, Björnstjerne Björnson's play *Beyond Our Power* considers religious superstition. Graham Greene's *The Power and The Glory* deals with religious persecution in Mexico and the subsequent loss of faith among its Catholic priests. Shūsaku Endō examines the difficulties of adapting Catholicism to the Japanese way of thinking in the novel *Silence*, which also depicts religious persecution. (Commons 1967)

See also *Beyond Our Power;* Björnson, Björnstjerne Martinius; *Elmer Gantry;* Endō, Shūsaku; Greene, Graham; Lewis, Sinclair; *Major Barbara; Power and the Glory, The;* Shaw, George Bernard; *Silence*

Resurrection

The novel *Voskreseniye* (Resurrection), by Leo Tolstoi, protests the Russian prison system and questions whether capital punishment is an effective deterrent to crime. Published in 1899, the novel concerns a domestic servant, Katusha Maslova, who becomes pregnant by a member of the Russian nobility, Prince Dmitri Ivanovitch Nekhludof. The young man does not learn of Maslova's predicament until years later when, while serving on a jury, he recognizes her as the defendant. She is now a prostitute and has been accused of helping someone else poison and rob one of her clients. She insists that she is innocent, having believed that the poison was actually a harmless sleeping poison.

Nekhludof is convinced that she is innocent of the crime. The other jury members concur. However, they fill out the verdict form incorrectly, and as a result she is sentenced to several years of hard labor in Siberia. Nekhludof protests the decision, but the judge says he can do nothing to remedy the situation. Nekhludof hires a lawyer to begin an appeal. The prince visits Maslova in jail to atone for his sins. He tells her that he will marry her and follow her to Siberia. She refuses his offer, hating him for ruining her life, but he continues to visit her. Gradually he becomes aware of injustices within the prison system. He asks himself:

> What right have some men to imprison, torture, exile, flog, and kill other men, when they themselves are just like those they torture, flog, and kill? And he was answered by discussions as to whether man has a free will or not? Whether a man can be proved a criminal by the measurements of his skull, etc.? What part does heredity play in crime? Is there such a thing as natural depravity? What is morality? What is insanity? What is degeneration? What is temperament? How do climate, food, ignorance, imitativeness, hypnotism, and passions affect crime? What is society? What are its duties, etc.? (Tolstoi 1911, 117)

Eventually Nekhludof begins to reexamine his own role in the oppression of others. He decides that he has no right to own land, believing that much of the peasants' misfortunes were due to their enslaving by landowners. In discussing Nekhludof's reasoning, the omniscient narrator says:

> Nobody could deny that infants and old people died for want of milk; the reason they had no milk was because they had no pastures for their cattle, no land for raising bread-stuffs, no hay-fields. It is perfectly

plain that all the people's misery, or at least the greater part of it, arises from the fact that they do not own the land which ought to support them, this same land being in the hands of men who take advantage of their ownership to exact the utmost amount of labor from the tillers of the soil. The peasants, reduced to the depths of poverty, actually dying for want of enough land to support them, go on toiling in order that the landowners may have crops to sell in foreign lands, and buy all the hats and canes, carriages and bronzes, that their hearts desire. (274–275)

After much thought, Nekhludof realizes why the peasants do not protest this arrangement. The narrator says:

> At this moment everything seemed so clear to him that he could never cease wondering why others couldn't see it, too. . . . The people are dying out; and they have really become so accustomed to the perishing process, that they have unconsciously come to accept as inevitable the untimely deaths of the children, the overwork of the women, and the insufficient nourishment, particularly for the old people. And this state of affairs has been of a growth so gradual, that the peasants have not realized the full horror of it, neither have they lifted up their voices to complain. (274)

Consequently, Nekhludof decides that "the only sure remedy for the uplifting of the masses . . . is to return to them the land which has been taken from them and which they so much need" (275). He gives his land to local peasants, not as individual plots but as a single estate whose profits will be shared by all. He also donates cash to the poorest of the villagers. Then he follows Maslova to Siberia while continuing to use his political contacts to obtain her release. During this process he learns that many other prisoners besides Maslova are actually innocent. He realizes that

Russian officials have a backward approach to justice: "In this way not only was that rule neglected which enjoins forgiveness of ten guilty men sooner than one innocent man should suffer, but quite the contrary. . . . They removed ten innocent persons in order to get rid of one guilty person" (101). Therefore, he wonders whether "all this talk about God, justice, religion, kindness, and the law, were only words that concealed the most brutal cupidity and cruelty" (102).

Nekhludof is a harsh critic of the Russian church, believing it to be hypocritical. When he witnesses a prison church service, the narrator says:

And not one among those who were present . . . seemed to be aware that this same Jesus whom the priest had lauded . . . had expressly forbidden all that had been going on here; not only the senseless volubility and the blasphemous incantations of the priest over the wine and the bread, but had most positively forbidden one man to call another master, had forbidden all worship in temples, commanding every man to pray in solitude, had forbidden the very temples themselves . . . but above all the rest, he had forbidden human judgments and the imprisonment of men, or their subjection to the shame, torture, or death which was visited on them in this place. He had forbidden violence in all its forms and had proclaimed that he set the captive free. (171)

In the final chapter of the novel Nekhludof reads the Bible and decides that the church has distorted its message. He vows to begin a new life using its tenets as his guide. By this time his efforts have led to Maslova's release from prison, and she has decided to marry a man in her own social class even though she now loves Nekhludof. She and Nekhludof both recognize that Russian society would never accept their union.

Because of the novel's denunciation of the church, its author was excommunicated in 1901. *Resurrection* was his last full-length

novel. He contributed much of his profits from the work to the Dukhobors, a peasant religious sect that rejected both church and government authority. The group emigrated to western Canada in 1898. Tolstoi remained in Russia, where he continued to criticize his society. (Tolstoi 1911)

See also Class, Social; Maslova, Katusha; Nekhludof, Prince Dmitri Ivanovitch; Poverty; Prison Reform; Tolstoi, Leo

Rivers, Clementine ("Tish")

Tish Rivers is the first-person narrator of James Baldwin's 1974 novel *If Beale Street Could Talk*. A pregnant, 19-year-old black woman, she is engaged to Alonzo "Fonny" Hunt, a 22-year-old sculptor who is awaiting trial for a crime he did not commit. Tish's love for Fonny is strong, and according to Baldwin biographer David Leeming (1994, 325), "when Tish cries for Fonny and longs for his freedom, she is the Baldwin voice expressing his life's search for a lover free of the bondage of society's taboos." (Baldwin 1988; Leeming 1994)

See also Baldwin, James; Hunt, Alonzo ("Fonny"); *If Beale Street Could Talk;* Racism

Roberts, David

David Roberts appears in the three-act play *Strife* (1909), by John Galsworthy. Roberts represents the factory workers in a labor dispute, encouraging them to remain out on strike despite severe hardships. When the labor union tries to get the men to accept a compromise position, he fights against it. In this respect he is just as rigid as his opposition. However, whereas the people who control the factory are wealthy and can weather a strike, Roberts and his men truly suffer for their beliefs. In fact, Roberts's wife falls ill and dies because her home lacks heat and good food. (Galsworthy 1928)

See also Galsworthy, John; *Strife*

Rodrigues, Sebastian

Sebastian Rodrigues appears in the 1969 novel *Chimmoku* (Silence), by Shūsaku Endō. A Portuguese priest, Sebastian goes to Japan trying to find his mentor, Father Christovao Ferreira, whom he has heard renounced his faith. In Japan Rodrigues is forced to hide from the Japanese authorities, who have been torturing and killing Christians in order to stamp out the religion. Eventually he is captured, and during his imprisonment he meets often with officials to discuss and defend Christianity. In the end, however, he, too, recants his faith, having been convinced by his mentor Ferreira that the lives he will save through his sacrifice are ultimately more important than his religious convictions. (Endō 1980)

See also Endō, Shūsaku; Ferreira, Christovao; *Silence*

Rodríguez, Colonel Tolomeo

A South American military leader in Isabel Allende's 1987 novel *Eva Luna,* Colonel Tolomeo Rodríguez is feared by everyone but the novel's main character, Eva Luna. When the colonel asks her to become his mistress, Eva refuses, believing it would be dangerous for her. Tolomeo respects her refusal; however, he also warns her that her relationship with guerrilla leader Huberto Naranjo is dangerous. (Allende 1988)

See also Allende, Isabel; Carlé, Lukas; Carlé, Rolf; *Eva Luna;* Naranjo, Huberto

Rougon-Macquart Cycle

The *Rougon-Macquart cycle* is a term used for a series of 20 novels by the French author Émile Zola. The first title in the series, *La Fortune des Rougon* (The Fortune of the Rougons) was published in 1871, and the last, *Le Docteur Pascal* (Doctor Pascal) was published in 1893. Collectively, these works are subtitled *The Natural and Social History of a Family under the Second Empire.* They depict several generations of a family that has split into two branches: the Rougons, who are legitimate, and the Macquarts, who are illegitimate and lower class. Through their lives, Zola comments on many aspects of French society. For example, the 1877 novel *L'Assommoir* (The Drunkard) deals with alcoholism among working-class people, the 1885 novel *Germinal* shows the struggle of laborers in a mining community, and the 1887 novel *La Terre* (The Earth) concerns peasants who want to own land. (Grant 1966)

See also Zola, Émile

Rudkus, Jurgis and Ona

Jurgis Rudkus is the main character of Upton Sinclair's 1906 novel *The Jungle,* which exposes injustices and unsanitary conditions in the U.S. meatpacking industry during the early twentieth century. A Lithuanian immigrant, Jurgis and his fiancée, Ona, come to Chicago hoping to make their fortune working in a stockyard factory. At first things go well, and they save enough to afford a festive wedding. Later, however, Jurgis is injured and loses his job. Meanwhile Ona's boss forces her to become his mistress in order to save her job. Jurgis finds out, attacks the boss, and is jailed. Without her husband's income and love, Ona falls into malnourishment and despair; she eventually dies in childbirth. Jurgis then works at a series of jobs, but while living as a beggar and thief, he discovers socialism. A socialist hotel keeper gives him a job, and he experiences much better treatment in life. In the end he believes that socialism will save others as well. (Sinclair 1972)

See also *Jungle, The;* Sinclair, Upton; Socialism

S

Sartre, Jean-Paul

French philosopher and author Jean-Paul Sartre believed that with freedom comes social responsibility. He expressed this view in many of his novels, plays, and essays. Born in Paris, France, on June 2, 1905, he graduated from the École Normale Supérieure in 1929 and became a teacher, working at various schools from 1931 to 1945. He also spent a year in Germany studying philosophy. His first published works were articles on literature, and his first novel, *Le Nausée* (Nausea), appeared in 1938. The following year he joined the French army to fight in World War II, only to be taken captive by the Germans in 1940. After nine months of imprisonment he escaped and went to Paris to join an underground Resistance movement. His play *Les Mouches* (The Flies, 1943) was written during this period to express his views on freedom, responsibility, and resistance to oppression.

Sartre produced many plays during his career, including *Le Diable et le bon dieu* (The Devil and the Lord, 1951), which concerns political activism, and *Les Séquestrés d'Altona* (The Condemned of Altona, 1959), which deals with a Nazi obsessed with his past crimes. He also edited a monthly review with writer Simone de Beauvoir, with whom he had a lifelong romantic relationship. His es-

Jean-Paul Sartre, October 23, 1964 (Archive France/Archive Photos)

says from this period were later included in a collection entitled *Situations*, a ten-volume series published from 1947 to 1972. Of his novels, perhaps his most widely read is *L'Âge de raison* (The Age of Reason), which was published in 1945. Part of a trilogy known as *Les Chemins de la liberté* (The Roads to Freedom), it depicts a philosopher who has trouble putting his beliefs into practice. Sartre also wrote biographies, memoirs, and other non-fiction books. He received the Nobel Prize in literature in 1964 but declined it, believing that no honor was necessary for his work. His last work, the third volume of a biography of Gustave Flaubert, was published in 1972. He subsequently went blind and was unable to write anymore. He died on April 15, 1980, in Paris, France. (Brustein 1964; Madsen 1977)

See also *Age of Reason, The;* Beauvoir, Simone de

Sarvis, Dr. A. K.

In Edward Abbey's 1975 novel *The Monkey Wrench Gang*, Dr. A. K. Sarvis is a wealthy surgeon who funds an environmental group that engages in acts of ecological sabotage. Its members destroy bulldozers and other equipment used by road builders and developers. Sarvis's motives for participating in such activities concern the public health. The narrator remarks:

> The Southwest had once been the place where Eastern physicians sent their more serious respiratory cases. No more; the developers—bankers, industrialists, subdividers, freeway builders and public utility chiefs—had succeeded with less than thirty years' effort in bringing the air of Southwestern cities "up to the standard," that is, as foul as any other.
>
> Doc thought he knew where the poison came from that had attacked the boy's lungs, the same poison eating into the mucous membranes of several million other citizens including himself. From poor visibility to eye irritation, from allergies to asthma to emphysema to general asthenia, the path lay straight ahead, pathogenic all the way. They were already having afternoons right here in Albuquerque when schoolchildren were forbidden to play outside in the "open" air, heavy breathing being more dangerous than child molesters. (Abbey 1975, 203)

An older man, Sarvis himself is physically weak, and Abbey uses him to show why all people should be involved in environmental activism. (Abbey 1975)

See also Abbey, Edward; Environmentalism; *Monkey Wrench Gang, The*

Schreiner, Olive

An ardent feminist, Olive Schreiner was a nineteenth-century novelist who wrote about women's rights at a time when men considered themselves superior to women. She was born in South Africa in 1855, the daughter of a German Methodist missionary and his English wife. Schreiner's first novel, *The Story of an African Farm,* was based on her childhood experiences; it was published when she was only 28 years old under the pseudonym Ralph Irons. Her subsequent works include *Women and Labour* (1911), a sociological study that advocated equality between men and women; *Trooper Peter Halkett of Mashonaland* (1897), an allegorical discussion of British politics in South Africa; and the feminist novels *From Man to Man* (1927) and *Undine* (1929), both published posthumously. In *From Man to Man,* Schreiner writes about a feminist who marries, bears a child, and becomes an unhappy housewife; Schreiner herself did not marry until the age of 39, and she was, according to scholar Dan Jacobson in a 1970 essay accompanying the work (Schreiner 1970, 18), a "desperately unhappy woman." She insisted that her husband, S. P. Cronwright, change his last name to Cronwright-Schreiner. In 1924, four years after her death, he published a biography of his wife entitled *The Life of Olive Schreiner.* (Clayton 1997; Schreiner 1970)

See also Feminism; *Story of an African Farm, The*

Science Fiction and Fantasy

The science fiction and fantasy genre offers authors an opportunity to criticize contemporary society by showing how problems might evolve or be resolved in the future. Anthony Burgess, Ursula Le Guin, Jack London, George Orwell, Jules Verne, Kurt Vonnegut, and H. G. Wells have all taken advantage of this opportunity. Their novels depict fictional societies that highlight flaws in the real world. (Ketterer 1974)

See also Burgess, Anthony; Le Guin, Ursula; London, Jack; Orwell, George; Verne, Jules; Vonnegut, Kurt; Wells, H. G.

Scott, Ida and Rufus

Sister and brother, Ida and Rufus Scott are two African-American characters from James Baldwin's 1960 novel *Another Country*. Both encounter racism when they begin dating white people. Both also become angry at their situations and take that anger out on their loving partners. Rufus beats and berates his girlfriend, Leona; Ida cheats on her boyfriend, Vivaldo.

Eventually Rufus feels ashamed of his cruelty. According to Baldwin biographer David Leeming (1994, 201), Rufus represents someone who is "too broken to accept love or to give it. Society has taken away his freedom to find *his* individual identity and in so doing has removed the self-respect and respect for human life that, for Baldwin, make love possible. Rufus can only assume the worst even of those who mean well." Isolated from society, he commits suicide by jumping off New York City's George Washington Bridge.

Rufus's death increases Ida's own sense of isolation. She tells a white woman, "*You* don't know, and there's no way in the world for you to find out, what it's like to be a black girl in this world" (Baldwin 1962, 347). Moreover, her brother's suicide increases her anger at society and at Vivaldo. According to Leeming (1994, 201), "Ida's love for Vivaldo is marred by a deep need to avenge what she considers her brother's murder at the hands of white racism." At one point she says, "Some days, honey, I wish I could turn myself into one big fist and grind this miserable country to powder. Some days, I don't believe it has a right to exist" (Baldwin 1962, 351).

Leeming (1994, 201) quotes author Baldwin as explaining that the main action in *Another Country* was "the journey of Ida and Vivaldo toward some kind of coherence." At the book's conclusion Ida sets aside her anger, ends her affair, and confesses her infidelity to

Vivaldo, who still loves her. (Baldwin 1962; Leeming 1994)

See also *Another Country;* Baldwin, James; Jones, Eric; Moore, Daniel Vivaldo; Poverty; Racism

Sears, Louis

Louis Sears is a character in *The Ugly American* (1958), by William J. Lederer and Eugene Burdick. At the beginning of the novel Sears is the U.S. ambassador in Sarkhan, a small country in Southeast Asia. He has little interest in his job, having taken the position merely to improve his chances of being appointed a U.S. judge. He spends a great deal of his time at diplomatic parties and is appallingly ignorant of Asian culture. In an epilogue to the novel the authors explain that, even though Sears is a fictional character, he is based on his real-life counterparts. Lederer and Burdick (1958, 272) say: "Ambassador Sears . . . does not exist. But there have been more than one of him in Asia during recent years. He is portrayed as a political warhorse, comfortably stabled by his party while he awaits a judgeship. . . . The roster of our ambassadors throughout the world bears out the fact that too often personal wealth, political loyalty, and the ability to stay out of trouble are qualities which outweigh training in the selection of ambassadors." (Lederer and Burdick 1958)

See also Burdick, Eugene; Lederer, William J.; *Ugly American, The*

Season in Paradise, A

The book *'n Seisoen in die Paradys* (A Season in Paradise), by poet Breyten Breytenbach, chronicles a visit he made to South Africa after being exiled from that country for his antiapartheid stance. Published in 1980, it is primarily a work of nonfiction, but it includes some of the author's social protest poetry translated from Afrikaans. Of this writing Breytenbach (1980, 160) says:

> To write is to communicate, to eat together, to have intercourse, a communion, all of our blood, all of our flesh. We are

men, writing for men about men, and therefore about relationships between men.. . . . I want to write for *here,* for *now.* I want to come as close as I can in my work to the temporal—not the infinite; that has always been around. . . . I think that by taking cognizance of the nature of the struggle we are involved in and share, by making that struggle clearer—and even more: by taking a stand based on this knowledge—we expand our humanity and our language.

Breytenbach uses his poetry to comment on the injustices perpetrated against his country and his people and argues that a writer has a "social responsibility" to speak out for the freedom of all people (155). (Breytenbach 1994; Jolly 1996)

See also Apartheid; Breytenbach, Breyten; Exiles

Sereno, Daniel

Daniel Sereno appears in Jean-Paul Sartre's 1945 novel *L'Âge de raison* (The Age of Reason). A homosexual filled with self-loathing, he hides his lifestyle from all of his friends. When he learns that an acquaintance has become pregnant by a man who will not marry her, he decides to marry her himself. He does not love her, but he desperately wants to live an "acceptable" life as a husband and father. (Sartre 1947)

See also *Age of Reason, The;* Sartre, Jean-Paul

Sethe

The main character of Toni Morrison's 1987 novel *Beloved,* Sethe must come to terms with a difficult past. Before the Civil War she was a black slave who ran away from a cruel master. Upon recapture she killed her child to save her from being enslaved, too. The novel begins 18 years later. The ghost of Sethe's daughter, now a 21-year-old woman, arrives in the flesh to haunt her, and in the end, with the help of friends, Sethe must free herself from her torment. (Gates and Appiah 1993c; Morrison 1987)

See also *Beloved;* Morrison, Toni

Settembrini, Ludovico

The character Ludovico Settembrini appears in Thomas Mann's 1924 novel *Der Zauberberg* (The Magic Mountain). An Italian humanist and nationalist, he tries to convince the main character, Hans Castorp, to share his point of view on various philosophical, social, and political issues. He is opposed in these discussions by a converted Catholic, Leo Naphta, who defends a rigid spiritual, authoritarian, medieval approach to life. The two men quarrel passionately over their beliefs and eventually decide to duel with pistols. But when the moment comes, Settembrini refuses to shoot the Jesuit. Naphta then cannot honorably shoot the Italian, but he also cannot forget their quarrel; he shoots himself instead. Naphta's death troubles Settembrini, who descends deeper into his illness. At the same time he begins to question his beliefs, especially after war breaks out in Europe. As the novel explains, in Settembrini "the boldness of the eagle was gradually outbidding the mildness of the dove" (Mann 1972, 710). (Mann 1972)

See also Castorp, Hans; *Magic Mountain, The;* Mann, Thomas

Sexism
See Feminism

Shallard, Frank

Frank Shallard, a character in the novel *Elmer Gantry* (1927), reflects author Sinclair Lewis's opposition to organized religion. Frank becomes a minister because his father wants him to be one, yet he is an atheist. He is also the most moral character in Lewis's novel. Shallard lives an otherwise ethical life and helps his parishioners in many important ways. Yet when church leaders discover that he is not a true believer, they force him to leave the pulpit in disgrace. Meanwhile the novel's main character, the highly immoral Elmer Gantry, is lauded as an exemplary man of God. (Lewis 1970)

See also *Elmer Gantry;* Lewis, Sinclair

Shatov

Shatov is the member of a Russian revolutionary organization in Fyodor Dostoyevsky's novel *Besy* (The Possessed) published in two volumes between 1871 and 1872. Shatov struggles with his religious and political beliefs and eventually decides to leave the radical group. He believes that "socialism is . . . an atheistic organization of society . . . [that] intends to establish itself exclusively on the elements of science and reason" and that as such it cannot succeed because "there never has been a nation without a religion, that is, without an idea of good and evil. . . . Reason has never had the power to define good and evil, or even to distinguish between good and evil. . . . It has always mixed them up in a disgraceful and pitiful way" (Dostoyevsky 1936, 253–254). But the leader of the group, Pyotr Stepanovitch Verhovensky, does not want Shatov to leave because he fears the man might become a police informant. Verhovensky therefore lures Shatov to a dark, secluded place and murders him. Shatov's death is modeled after a real-life incident, the murder of a young revolutionary in Russia in November 1869. (Dostoyevsky 1936; Wasiolek 1964)

See also Dostoyevsky, Fyodor; *Possessed, The;* Stavrogin, Nikolay Vsyevolodovitch; Verhovensky, Pyotr Stepanovitch

Shaw, George Bernard

Born on July 26, 1856, in Dublin, Ireland, George Bernard Shaw wrote five unsuccessful socialist novels before becoming a book, art, music, and theater critic in 1885. He then decided to try promoting his socialist views through plays. Unfortunately, he could find no one willing to produce his first works, some of which had been banned by government censors. In 1898 he published them in a collection entitled *Plays Pleasant and Unpleasant.* The book includes a lengthy preface for each play, a practice Shaw was to continue in later collections of his work. As a result of this publication, Shaw's works began to be performed in the United States and Europe. However, they did not appear in England until 1907 when a play about Irish-English conflict, *John Bull's Other Island* (1904), was performed in London. That same year Shaw published his play *Major Barbara,* an important work that criticizes English attitudes toward poverty and religion. In subsequent years he published the plays *The Doctor's Dilemma* (1911), *Pygmalion* (1914), *Androcles and the Lion* (1916), and *Heartbreak House* (1919), all of which deal with social issues. He also began to become involved in politics, helping to found a socialist group called the Fabian Society in 1883. In addition, he wrote political essays, antiwar speeches and pamphlets, and a political tract entitled *The Intelligent Woman's Guide to Socialism and Capitalism* (1928). He died on November 2, 1950, in Ayot St. Lawrence, Hertfordshire, England. (Hill 1978; McCabe 1974)

See also *Major Barbara;* Socialism

Shelby, George

George Shelby is the son of a plantation owner in Harriet Beecher Stowe's 1852 novel *Uncle Tom's Cabin.* When Shelby's father sells one of his trusted slaves, Uncle Tom, the young George vows that one day he will buy him back. Eventually he is ready to fulfill his promise, but he discovers that Tom has been beaten to death by a cruel owner. George helps two other slaves escape the man's plantation and returns home to free his own slaves after his father's death. (Stowe 1960)

See also Stowe, Harriet Beecher; Tom, Uncle; *Uncle Tom's Cabin*

Shukhov, Ivan Denisovich

Ivan Denisovich Shukhov is the main character in Aleksandr Solzhenitsyn's 1962 novel *Odin den iz zhizni Ivana Denisovicha* (One Day in the Life of Ivan Denisovich). Ivan has been unjustly sentenced to several years in a forced-labor camp, and it is a struggle for him to survive. The camp is bitterly cold, his clothing and food are inadequate, he is seriously overworked, and some of the other prisoners are dangerous. Nonetheless, he wonders whether life outside the camp would be just as bad. (Solzhenitsyn 1972)

See also *One Day in the Life of Ivan Denisovich;* Solzhenitsyn, Aleksandr

Silence

Chimmoku (Silence), by Japanese writer Shūsaku Endō, is a historical novel concerning the persecution of Japanese Christians during the late 1500s and early 1600s. However, when it was published in Japan in 1969, it was received as a criticism of contemporary anti-Christian sentiments in that country. Scholar William Johnson (xiv–xv) points this out in a 1980 introduction to the work, adding that "one is left with the impression that the novel is in some way the expression of a conflict between [the author's] Japanese sensibility and the Hellenistic Christianity that has been given to him." The novel's theme concerns whether Christianity is a suitable religion for the Japanese people. In this regard Johnson (xviii) explains that *Silence* has been controversial with both non-Christian and Christian Japanese and suggests that this indicates the country is "not indifferent to Christianity but looking for that form of Christianity that will suit its national character."

The novel's main character is a Portuguese priest, Sebastian Rodrigues, who decides to travel to Japan to find his missing mentor, Father Christovao Ferreira. Portuguese authorities have heard that Ferreira renounced his faith, or apostatized, after being tortured by the Japanese. Rodrigues cannot believe that such a pious man would ever abandon his faith. The first four chapters of the novel are letters from Rodrigues to Portugal concerning his travel to Japan and attempts to remain hidden from authorities there. Japan has banned Catholicism and has a policy of killing all known Catholics unless they are willing to apostatize. Eventually Rodrigues is captured, too, and his letters end.

The rest of the novel relates his experiences at the hands of his Japanese persecutors. The Japanese want him to step on a picture of Jesus Christ and renounce him. When Rodrigues refuses, he is forced to watch the torture and execution of innocent people. At first he remains firm in his resolve to honor his faith. Then the authorities bring Ferreira to talk to him. Ferreira is now living as a Japanese, having indeed apostatized in order to save lives. He convinces Rodrigues that Jesus Christ would have done the same thing because He would have considered a man's life more important than a mere ritual. Ferreira urges Rodrigues to step on the picture as a formality, without changing what is in his heart. Rodrigues does so, but he realizes that his heart is changed nonetheless. He is no longer a Christian. He and Ferreira live out the rest of their lives as Japanese, dying of old age on foreign soil.

Interestingly, throughout the novel various characters discuss the relationship of Christianity to the Japanese in terms of a soil metaphor. Christianity is called a tree that has been transplanted in Japan only to wither and die. Rodrigues believes that the tree's death has been caused by a lack of nurturing, by not having fertilizer applied. In other words, Japanese authorities have not encouraged it to grow, and so it has not. But other characters, such as Ferreira and a Japanese official, argue that the tree has died because it is not suited to the climate or soil of the foreign country. They believe that no nurturing can change its suitability, and therefore it should be left to die.

According to Johnson, when the novel was published, some Japanese Christians pointed out that the people who died as martyrs when Rodrigues refused to apostatize do indeed prove that Christianity can exist in Japan even without nurturing. He (xvii–xviii) quotes one of them as saying: "Obviously the belief of Ferreira . . . that Japan is a swamp which cannot absorb Christianity is not a reason for apostasy. It was because he lost his faith that Ferreira began to think in this way. . . . In that Christian era there were many Japanese who sincerely believed in Christ, and there are many who do so today. No Christian will believe that Christianity cannot take root in Japan."

Because *Silence* had engendered so much discussion regarding the nature of Christianity and its appropriateness in a particular society, Johnson compares the work to the writing of Graham Greene. Greene wrote not only about Christianity but also about religious persecution, and his novel *The Power and the Glory* has many similarities to *Silence*. (Endō 1980)

See also Endō, Shūsaku; Ferreira, Christovao; Greene, Graham; *Power and the Glory, The;* Religion; Rodrigues, Sebastian

Sinclair, Upton

Born on September 20, 1878, in Baltimore Maryland, Upton Beall Sinclair is perhaps best known for his best-selling social protest novel *The Jungle,* which brought public attention to poor working and sanitary conditions at slaughterhouses. Its publication in 1906 led Congress to pass the Pure Food and Drug Act that same year. The novel was originally printed at Sinclair's expense after several publishers rejected the manuscript. At the time he was working as a journalist and had investigated the meatpacking industry as part of a newspaper assignment. After *The Jungle* became a success, however, he left journalism to write more novels, including *Oil!* (1927) and *Boston* (1928). The former was based on the Teapot Dome Scandal of the 1920s and the latter on the case of Sacco and Vanzetti, whom many people believe were tried and executed for murder not because they were guilty but because they were avowed anarchists.

As a socialist Sinclair often wrote about social and political issues. He also edited a collection of social protest literature entitled *Cry for Justice* (1915). In addition, he was politically active. With the money he received from sales of *The Jungle,* he founded a short-lived cooperative housing project, the Helicon Home Colony, in Englewood, New Jersey. He then moved to California, where he organized a socialist reform group called End Poverty in California (EPIC). In 1934 he ran for governor of California using the EPIC platform and nearly won the election. In later years he became increasingly interested in international politics, and his writings reflect this interest. Starting in 1940, he wrote a series of 11 novels featuring an antifascist who fights against injustice and tyranny. He also wrote nonfiction books and an autobiography. Sinclair died on November 25, 1968, in Bound Brook, New Jersey. (Bloodworth 1977)

See also Anarchism; Fascism; *Jungle, The;* Labor Issues; Socialism

Slavery

Slavery is the ownership and exploitation of one human being by another. It has occurred throughout the world from ancient times, and writers have always protested the practice. The most extensive antislavery literature, however, concerns black slavery in the United States, which began when the country was founded and lasted until 1865. During this period an antislavery activist, or abolitionist, named Harriet Beecher Stowe produced one of the most influential works of literature in history, *Uncle Tom's Cabin.* This novel increased antislavery sentiment in the United States, and some scholars credit it with hastening slavery's demise. *The Biglow Papers,* by abolitionist James Russell Lowell, similarly furthered the abolitionist cause, as did *Oroonoko,* by Aphra Behn. American slavery is also an issue in modern works concerning racism against blacks, such as the novel *Sula,* by Toni Morrison. (Filler 1960; Mathews 1972; Thomas 1965)

See also Behn, Aphra; *Biglow Papers, The;* Lowell, James Russell; Morrison, Toni; *Oroonoko;* Racism; Stowe, Harriet Beecher; *Sula; Uncle Tom's Cabin*

Smith, Winston

The main character of George Orwell's 1949 novel *1984,* Winston Smith lives in a society of the future where the government controls people's thoughts and actions. He tries to obey its wishes but finds himself disobeying several rules. He keeps a secret journal, has an affair with a woman even though he is married, and is eventually drawn into a revolutionary group. The group proves to be a government trap, and Winston is arrested. He is then tortured for his crimes and betrays his mistress. Their love destroyed, he later gives his love to the government. (Orwell 1961)

See also *1984;* Orwell, George

Socialism

Socialism is an ideology that advocates equality and the abolition of class structure and capitalism. Socialists believe that the people, in the form of the state, should control all property and production of goods. Many forms of modern socialism have developed since the concept originated in the late eighteenth century. Two of these, Marxism and Leninism, are the foundation of communism.

During the nineteenth century the socialist movement became powerful throughout Europe and England, where playwright George Bernard Shaw helped create the Fabian Society. The Fabian Society promoted a more democratic version of socialism, arguing that men of science and wisdom, rather than the state, should control property and production. During the twentieth century the differences between British and Soviet socialism grew more pronounced, and in 1945 British author George Orwell offered an unflattering portrayal of Soviet socialism in his novel *Animal Farm.*

Socialism never gained much credence in the United States. However, a few authors, such as Edward Bellamy, Jack London, and Upton Sinclair, did promote its doctrines. Authors in other parts of the world also examined socialist issues in their work. These include Doris Lessing in South Africa, Sibilla Aleramo in Italy, and Mulk Raj Anand in India. (Cohen 1962; Egbert 1967; Shaw 1984)

> **See also** Aleramo, Sibilla; Anand, Mulk Raj; *Animal Farm;* Bellamy, Edward; Lessing, Doris; London, Jack; Orwell, George; Shaw, George Bernard; Sinclair, Upton

Solzhenitsyn, Aleksandr

Russian novelist and historian Aleksandr Tsayevich Solzhenitsyn protested social and political policies in the Soviet Union. He was expelled from his country in 1974. Born on December 11, 1918, in Kislovodsk, Russia, he was awarded a degree in mathematics from the University of Rostov-na-Donu. He then joined the military but was arrested after criticizing Joseph Stalin. Solzhenitsyn was imprisoned and worked in forced-labor camps before being released as rehabilitated in 1956. His first novel, *Odin den iz zhizni Ivana*

Soviet author Aleksandr Solzhenitsyn takes notes at Stanford University Library. (UPI/Corbis-Bettmann)

Denisovicha (One Day in the Life of Ivan Denisovich, 1962), was based on his experiences as a prisoner. It was very successful and led to the appearance of several short stories in a Soviet magazine followed by a collection of short stories published in 1963.

These stories displeased the Soviet government, however, and his subsequent works were banned for publication in his own country. He was also ousted from the Soviet Writers Union for his efforts to oppose censorship. Nonetheless, Solzhenitsyn had several novels, including *Rakovy Korpus* (Cancer Ward, 1968) and *Avgust 1914* (August 1914, 1971), published abroad, and in 1970 he was awarded the Nobel Prize in literature. By this time his relationship with the government was extremely poor, and in 1973 he was arrested for writing *Arkhipelag Gulag* (The Gulag Archipelago), which criticized many aspects of Soviet history and policy. Solzhenitsyn was subsequently convicted of treason and forced into exile. He eventually settled in the United States, in Cavendish, Vermont, and wrote several more books. In 1989 the Soviet Union finally began publishing Solzhenitsyn's work, including *The Gulag Archipelago,* and in 1990 the government restored the author's citizenship. He returned to his country in 1994 to live in Moscow, where he recently completed a collection of essays that have not yet been published. (Moody 1975)

See also Exiles; *One Day in the Life of Ivan Denisovich;* Prison Reform

"Song of the Shirt, The"

Published in 1825, the poem "The Song of the Shirt," by English author Thomas Hood, is considered one of the most important social protest poems ever written. It brought attention to the plight of poor women who labor at piecemeal work, sewing shirts "till the brain begins to swim . . . till the eyes are heavy and dim" (Sinclair 1996, 46) in exchange for meager wages and deplorable living conditions. (Sinclair 1996)

See also Hood, Thomas; Labor Issues; Poverty

"Song of the Stormy Petrel"

"Pesnya o burevestnike" (Song of the Stormy Petrel) is a revolutionary poem by Russian novelist, short-story writer, and poet Maxim Gorky. Its publication in 1901 led to the author's arrest. The phrase "Stormy Petrel" refers both to the *Stormy Petrel,* a Russian anarchist periodical, and to a type of bird, the storm petrel. The storm-petrel always flies ahead of a storm, thereby warning of its approach. (Levin 1965)

See also Anarchism; Gorky, Maxim

Sorde, Itale

Itale Sorde is one of the main characters in Ursula Le Guin's 1979 novel *Malafrena*. The heir to a large estate in the Austrian-controlled country of Orsinia, Sorde values his political beliefs more than his family responsibilities. He leaves home, becomes involved in a revolutionary group, and gains prominence for his political writings and speeches. He is eventually arrested by the Austrian police and spends two years in prison, an experience that damages both his health and his spirit. However, he soon recovers his passion for revolution and continues the fight for his country's freedom from oppression. (Le Guin 1979)

See also Le Guin, Ursula; *Malafrena*

South Africans
See Apartheid

Sportsman's Sketches, A

The collection of stories *Zapiski okhotnika* (A Sportsman's Sketches), by Russian author Ivan Turgenev, was first published in the Russian journal *The Contemporary* between 1847 and 1851. Their 1852 appearance in book form, in a collection of the same name, led to their author's arrest and exile. During this time Turgenev continued to write new stories; he eventually produced a total of 25. Collections in English have been published in varying numbers under different titles, including *Sketches from a Hunter's Album, A Sportsman's Notebook,* and, simply, *Sketches.*

Turgenev's stories primarily concern the relationship between Russian peasants and the landed gentry prior to the 1861 emancipation of the serfs. Their fictional first-person narrator is a member of the nobility who expresses sympathy for the peasants he encounters during his hunting trips. He also expresses contempt for those who exploit the serfs or treat them cruelly. Perhaps the harshest story in this regard is "Bailiff," which concerns a young landowner, Arkady Pavlych Penochkin, and the overseer of his estate, Sofron Yakovlich. Penochkin tells the narrator that the way to deal with peasants is to "treat them like children" (Turgenev 1983, 100). When an extremely poor peasant approaches him to protest Yakovlich's cruelty and injustice, Penochkin shouts: "Be quiet, I'm telling you! Be quiet! Oh, my God, this is quite simply rebellion. No, my friend, I don't advise you to try being rebellious on my property" (115). Later the narrator learns from another peasant that the overseer will surely punish the protester for his temerity. The peasant says that Yakovlich is "just that kind of a cur, a dog . . . that he knows who to get his teeth into. The old men what are richer and with bigger families, them he doesn't touch" (117). Because of such portraits, Turgenev's work increased public awareness of the harsh realities of peasant life, thereby fueling the movement to emancipate Russia's serfs. (Lloyd 1972; Turgenev 1983)

See also Class, Social; Penochkin, Arkady Pavlych; Poverty; Turgenev, Ivan; Yakovlich, Sofron

Stalingrad

The 1948 novel *Stalingrad,* by Theodor Plevier, is primarily a war story, but it has elements of social protest. In portraying the battle between the German and Red Armies near Stalingrad, Russia, the book not only exposes the difficulties that soldiers must endure in the field but also shows the attitudes that cause these difficulties. For example, in discussing why the dying soldiers do not receive more compassion, one German soldier says: "The strong eat up the weak; the weak fall; the sick lie and are left behind. It's all logical. If a man is sick and can no longer crawl to the feed trough, it shows poor breeding, inferior racial stock. But those who steal from others and fill their own bellies will live a few minutes longer and are therefore of superior stock" (Plevier 1948, 122).

The novel also criticizes Germany's war policies and, like all of the author's works, was banned from that country. Plevier was exiled from his native Germany in 1934 for criticizing the government's social and political policies. (Plevier 1948)

See also Peace; Plevier, Theodor

Stark, Joe

Joe Stark appears in the 1937 black feminist novel *Their Eyes Were Watching God,* by Zora Neale Hurston. After Joe marries the story's main character, Janie Crawford, he tries to make her into his ideal wife. Conscious of his social standing in the community, he tells her how to dress, where to go, what to do, and whom to talk to. At the same time he does not allow Janie to criticize his own behavior. Eventually he falls ill, and on his deathbed his wife scolds him for treating her so badly when they could have had a wonderful life together. (Hemenway 1977; Hurston 1990)

See also Crawford, Janie; Hurston, Zora Neale; *Their Eyes Were Watching God*

Stavrogin, Nikolay Vsyevolodovitch

Son of a Russian nobleman in Fyodor Dostoyevsky's novel *Besy* (The Possessed), which was published in two volumes between 1871 and 1872, Nikolay Vsyevolodovitch Stavrogin is an atheist who is incapable of loving anyone, even himself. He damages every woman with whom he comes in contact. He enjoys perverse sexual behavior until his abuse of a 12-year-old girl causes her to commit suicide, at which point he begins to feel guilt. Eventually this guilt expands to include other misdeeds in his life, and he commits suicide. In struggling with his lack of religious faith, Stavrogin represents Dostoyevsky's belief that without God, humanity is doomed. (Dostoyevsky 1936; Dostoyevsky 1968)

See also Dostoyevsky, Fyodor; *Possessed, The;* Shatov; Verhovensky, Pyotr Stepanovitch

Steinbeck, John

American novelist John Steinbeck received the Nobel Prize in literature in 1962. He is perhaps best known for his social protest novel *The Grapes of Wrath* (1939), about the struggle of a poor Oklahoma farm family against harsh environmental and economic conditions.

Steinbeck was born in Salinas, California, on February 27, 1902. In 1920 he enrolled at Stanford University as an English major, but his attendance was sporadic, and he left in 1925 without his degree. He then began working for a New York newspaper called the *American*. In 1929 he published his first novel, *Cup of Gold*. It was unsuccessful, as were his next two novels, *The Pastures of Heaven* (1932) and *To a God Unknown* (1933). His third novel, *Tortilla Flats* (1935), and a collection of stories entitled *The Red Pony* (1937) were more popular. However, it was not until the 1937 publication of the novel *Of Mice and Men* that Steinbeck became truly successful. *Of Mice and Men* earned him many prestigious awards, both as a novel and as a play adaptation, and two years later he received the Pulitzer Prize and the National Book Award for *The Grapes of Wrath,* which was the top best-seller of 1939.

Shortly thereafter Steinbeck became interested in documentary films. He traveled to Mexico to do a movie on its mountain villages, and during World War II he wrote propaganda films and literature for the U.S. government. The most significant of this work is a novel entitled *The Moon Is Down* (1942), about Nazi oppression in Norway. After the war he continued writing best-selling novels, including *Cannery Row* (1945), *The Pearl* (1947), and *East of Eden* (1952), as well as movie adaptations of his work. He also wrote nonfiction books, such as *Travels with Charley in Search of America* (1962), which documents a three-month trip through the United States with his poodle Charley. Steinbeck died on December 20, 1968, in New York, New York. (Fontenrose 1964; French 1975; Lisca 1958)

See also *Grapes of Wrath, The;* Great Depression

Steppenwolf

Steppenwolf (1927), by Hermann Hesse, depicts a man struggling to repress his natural human urges in order to fit in with modern society. The novel's main character, Harry Haller, considers himself half man, half wolf, although he has been told that this view of himself as a duality is too simplistic. As he goes about his daily life, the "wolf" side of him frequently breaks through his civilized veneer, and at first he despairs of ever being able to control its cruelty. In fact, he sees all of life's efforts as futile, saying:

Just as I dress and go out to visit the professor and exchange a few more or less insincere compliments with him, without really wanting to at all, so it is with the majority of men day by day and hour by hour in their daily lives and affairs. Without really wanting to at all, they pay calls and carry on conversations, sit out their hours at desks and on office chairs; and it is all compulsory, mechanical and against the grain, and it could all be done or left undone just as well by machines; and indeed it is this never-ceasing machinery that prevents their being, like me, the critics of their own lives and recognising the stupidity and shallowness, the hopeless tragedy and waste of the lives they lead, and the awful ambiguity grinning over it all. (Hesse 1963, 86)

Eventually Harry rejects this sense of hopelessness and allows himself to enjoy sensory experiences, such as dancing and making love. However, when he discovers happiness, he grows uneasy, saying: "My happiness fills me with content and I can bear it for a long while yet. But sometimes when happiness leaves a moment's leisure to look about me and long for things, the longing I have is not to keep this happiness forever, but to suffer once again, only more beautifully and less meanly than before. I long for the sufferings that make me ready and willing to die" (168).

Later he attends a mysterious performance called The Magic Theater, which leads him to an alternate reality in which chaos reigns. After watching and participating in several strange events, he meets the German composer Mozart, who tells him: "You are to live and to learn to laugh. You are to listen to life's radio music and to reverence the spirit behind it and to laugh at the bim-bim in it" (244). In the end Harry realizes that life is a game he has been taking too seriously. Like Hesse's other works, *Steppenwolf* relies heavily on symbolism to tell the story of a man's inner conflicts and personal growth. It also includes criticism of those who support a political position without understanding or questioning it. (Hesse 1963; Ziolkowski 1965)

See also Haller, Harry; Hesse, Hermann

Story of an African Farm, The

The Story of an African Farm, by Olive Schreiner, was first published in 1883 under the pseudonym Ralph Iron. According to scholar Dan Jacobson in his introduction to a 1970 edition of the book, it was the first work of fiction ever set in colonial South Africa. However, he (21) points out that the novel is "far from being the novel of 'race relations' which many people have come to expect every South African novel to be," because the story concerns "the white people on the farm, not the black. . . . The black people in it are merely extras, supernumeraries, part of the background."

Therefore, *The Story of an African Farm* does not concern itself with racism. Instead, it deals with feminist issues at a time when British and Dutch white males considered themselves superior to other members of their society. Its main character, Lyndall, is a young Englishwoman who values her independence and decides to live with a man rather than marry him. The novel's editors tried to convince its author to change this aspect of the plot, so that Lyndall marries her lover, but Schreiner refused.

The story begins with Lyndall's childhood. She is the orphaned cousin of a girl named Em, with whom she lives on an African farm. Em's parents are also dead; the girls are both under the care of Em's stepmother, an un-

pleasant Boer woman named 'Tant Sannie who treats them badly. In a separate building on the farm lives the overseer, a kindly German man, and his son, Waldo. He is much like Lyndall; both yearn for knowledge and want to leave the farm someday.

Into this setting comes an unscrupulous drifter named Bonaparte Blenkins. He convinces 'Tant Sannie that he is related to nobility and will someday inherit a small fortune. After he gains her trust, he tells her that her overseer has been stealing sheep from her. She throws the old man out, but the morning he is to leave the farm, they find that he has died in his sleep. Blenkins now takes over his possessions and his job. He treats Waldo cruelly, ridiculing and beating him. On one occasion, after Em gives Waldo one of her late father's books, Blenkins berates the boy, then calls the book evil and burns it. The narrator says that Blenkins's philosophy was "whenever you come into contact with any book, person, or opinion of which you absolutely comprehend nothing, declare that book, person, or opinion to be immoral. Bespatter it, vituperate against it, strongly insist that any man or woman harbouring it is a fool or a knave, or both. Carefully abstain from studying it. Do all that in you lies to annihilate that book, person, or opinion" (Schreiner 1970, 112).

Eventually, however, 'Tant Sannie discovers that Bonaparte Blenkins is a rogue and throws him out of the house. By that time, however, Lyndall has gone away to school. She returns when Em writes that she is planning to be married to a farmer named Gregory Rose. Em has followed the traditional path for a woman, becoming a dutiful housekeeper and striving for nothing more than a husband. But Lyndall says, "I am not in so great a hurry to put my neck beneath any man's foot; and I do not so greatly admire the crying of babies" (184). She then enters into a long discussion with Em about the role of women in a society that values their beauty more than their intelligence. Lyndall is far more beautiful than Em; therefore it does not surprise either of them when Gregory Rose decides he would rather marry Lyndall.

Lyndall rejects Gregory, but he becomes obsessed with her, even after she runs off with a secret lover. Gregory follows her, and after a long search he discovers that she gave birth to a child who lived only three days, then fell ill and sent her lover away. Now she is alone on her deathbed. Gregory disguises himself as a nurse and tends to her needs until she dies. Then he returns to the farm to marry Em. Meanwhile Waldo has left the farm to travel. He comes back shortly after Lyndall's death, and Em offers him money to go away to school. Waldo refuses it, saying that he no longer wants to learn about the world. He leaves her to sit and contemplate the pleasures of the farm, and apparently drifts into death.

Jacobson (20) notes the similarity between the fates of Lyndall and Waldo, saying, "Those who seek and strive are killed off; the others survive." He explains that this has relevancy to Schreiner's own life. Her novel was semiautobiographical; she grew up in South Africa as a missionary's daughter, was jilted by a lover when she was 16, and ended up in an unsatisfying job as a governess. After marrying at age 39, she became, according to Jacobson (18), a "desperately unhappy woman" who suffered from a variety of psychosomatic ailments. A devout feminist, she wrote in favor of women's rights, and during World War I she also advocated pacifism. Schreiner died on December 11, 1920, in Cape Town, South Africa. (Clayton 1997; Schreiner 1986)

See also Feminism; Schreiner, Olive

Stowe, Harriet Beecher

Harriet Beecher Stowe is best known for writing *Uncle Tom's Cabin,* an 1852 novel that protested American slavery. Born on June 14, 1811, in Litchfield, Connecticut, she was the daughter of a famous clergyman, Lyman Beecher. In 1824 she began attending the Connecticut Female Seminary at Hartford, and eight years later she started working as a schoolteacher in Cincinnati, Ohio, where she sometimes encountered slaves who had escaped across the Ohio River. She would later incorporate this knowledge into *Uncle Tom's*

Harriet Beecher Stowe (Library of Congress)

Cabin. Meanwhile Stowe wrote stories for local publications, and in 1834 she won a short story competition with a work entitled *A New England Sketch.* That same year she published her first book, entitled *The Mayflower; or, Sketches of Scenes and Characters among the Descendants of the Pilgrims.*

In 1836 Stowe married a theological professor, and in 1850 the couple settled in Brunswick, Maine. After the appearance of *Uncle Tom's Cabin* in 1852, Stowe became famous and went on a European tour. She continued to write articles and novels for the rest of her life, although none of them brought her the same acclaim as *Uncle Tom's Cabin* did. Her novels include *Dred: A Tale of the Great Dismal Swamp* (1856), which also concerns slavery; *The Minister's Wooing* (1859), which deals with religion; and a series based on her husband's New England childhood that includes the books *The Pearl of Orr's Island* (1862), *Old-Town Folks* (1869), and *Poganuc People* (1878). She is also noted for her series of articles on the English poet Lord Byron (1869). Stowe died on July 1, 1896, in Hartford, Connecticut. (Stowe 1960)

See also Slavery; *Uncle Tom's Cabin*

Stranger, The

The Stranger was originally published in 1942 in French as *L'Etranger* and in English as *The Outsider*. Written by Algerian author Albert Camus, it offers the first-person narrative of Monsieur Meursault, who is ultimately condemned to death for not conforming to society's expectations of how a loving son should behave.

The Stranger opens with Meursault traveling to attend his mother's funeral at an old person's home near Algiers. He does not know the exact day she died, or her correct age, and he displays no emotion over her death. Of the funeral he says, "Everything happened so fast, so deliberately, so naturally that I don't remember any of it anymore" (Camus 1989, 17). When he returns home, he sleeps for 12 hours, then goes for a swim at the beach, where he runs into Marie Cardona, a former coworker. The two of them go to the movies, and Marie stays overnight with Meursault. Shortly thereafter the two become engaged.

Meursault begins to spend time with his neighbor Raymond Sintes, whose girlfriend has been cheating on him. Sintes asks Meursault to write a letter to her, "one with a punch and also some things in it to make her sorry for what she's done" (32). Meursault obliges, and consequently the woman shows up at Sintes's apartment. Sintes beats her until the police arrive, and afterward he asks Meursault to be a witness at his trial.

Meursault also spends time with another neighbor, Salamano, who is distraught because his dog has run away. The old man says that Meursault must be sad about the death of his mother, adding that many people think he was wrong to send her to the old people's home. Meursault replies simply that he did not have enough money to care for her in his apartment anymore and that she was bored living with him. He does not say that he is saddened by her death.

One day Meursault, Marie, and Sintes take the bus to a friend's beach house. Meursault has already testified on Sintes's behalf regarding the beating, and the two men notice that the victim's brother is following them. At the beach they encounter the man and a group of his friends. A fight breaks out, and Sintes is slightly wounded. After a doctor attends to the injury, Meursault and Sintes, who now has a gun, return to the beach. This time the man appears unarmed; Meursault convinces Sintes to give him the gun to make the fight fair. But the man does not want to fight, so Meursault and Sintes return to the beach house.

Minutes later Meursault decides to go for a walk alone, and once more he sees the man. This time Meursault panics. He pulls out Sintes's gun and shoots the man five times. He is arrested for murder, and at his trial the prosecutor portrays him as a ruthless killer without a soul, emphasizing that Meursault went on a date the day after his mother's death. Witnesses confirm that Meursault did not grieve properly for his mother, and in the end the jury sentences him to the guillotine.

Meursault cannot believe that "men who change their underwear" can actually order someone to die (109). He wants to "reform the penal code" (111) so that a condemned man has a one in ten chance to escape his fate. What bothers him is that "it was an open-and-shut case, a fixed arrangement, a tacit agreement that there was no question of going back on" (111). He rails against the unfairness of society but finally realizes that nothing matters because all people are condemned to death. He accepts "the gentle indifference of the world," which reminds him of his own indifference toward life (122).

Meursault's plight shows, as scholar René Girard (Bloom 1989, 88) explains, that *The Stranger* "was not written for pure art's sake, nor was it written to vindicate the victims of persecution everywhere. Camus set out to prove that the hero . . . will necessarily be persecuted by society. He set out to prove, in other words, that 'the judges are always in the wrong.'" Girard (80) points out that Camus also depicts judges as flawed in his subsequent novel, *La Chute* (The Fall), wherein the main character, a lawyer, seeks "not to save his clients but to prove his moral superiority by discrediting the judges." These judges are, according to Girard (102), "the middle class who [are Camus's] sole potential readers." Camus's ultimate intent is not just to criticize the legal system but to criticize the judgmental nature of his society and to explore the relationship between that society and the individual.

However, Girard (102) reports that "instead of rejecting the book as the author had half hoped, half feared, [his] bourgeois readers showered it with praise. The 'judges,' obviously, did not recognize their portrait when they saw it. They, too, cursed the iniquitous judges and howled for clemency. They, too, identified with the innocent victim." (Bloom 1989; Camus 1958, 1989)

See also Camus, Albert; *Fall, The;* Meursault, Monsieur

Strife

A three-act drama, by John Galsworthy, *Strife* concerns a strike at the Trenartha Tin Plate Works factory around the turn of the century. The play was written in 1909. When it opens, it is February, and the workers have been off the job since October. The company's board of directors is ready to settle the strike, but the chair of the board, John Anthony, is firmly against it. He believes that the workers will return to their jobs once their wives and children begin to starve to death. Moreover, he thinks that giving in to strikers is bad for the country. He says: "I have been accused of being a domineering tyrant, thinking only of my pride—I am thinking of the future of this country, threatened with the black waters of confusion, threatened with mob government, threatened with what I cannot see. If by any conduct of mine I help to bring this on us, I shall be ashamed to look my fellows in the face" (Galsworthy 1928, 101–102).

Meanwhile the leader of the workers' committee, an engineer and inventor named David Roberts, believes that the strike is "the fight o' the country's body and blood against a blood-sucker. The fight of those that spend themselves with every blow they strike and every breath they draw, against a thing that fattens on them . . . a thing that buys the sweat o' men's brows and the tortures o' their brains, at its own price" (92). Roberts is sup-

porting the men with his own savings and refuses to compromise the workers' demands, even when his men ask him to. Soon it becomes clear that the battle between the two groups is really a personal struggle between Anthony and Roberts.

In the middle of these two men is trade union official Simon Harness. He has been suggesting a compromise position since the beginning of the strike. The union believes that the men's demands are excessive and will not support them; at the same time the union believes that the company's directors are being unfair. Also caught in the middle is Anthony's daughter, Enid Underwood. Her former maid, Annie, is Robert's wife. Enid knows that Annie is ill and needs money for medical care, heat, and good food. However, the Roberts will not accept her charity, so Enid tries to convince David Roberts to end the strike. He refuses. Later while at a workers' meeting he receives word that his wife has died. He rushes from the room, and in his absence the workers vote to accept the union's compromise position. The company's board then votes to accept it, too, and an infuriated Anthony resigns. In the end both men have lost everything, and the workers have gained very little of what they were asking for.

Strife shows the difficulties inherent in reaching a compromise on labor issues, but it also expresses some hope for future generations. Anthony's son, Edgar, is a very different man from his father. During discussions of the strike he suggests that employers need to take more responsibility for the suffering of their employees, and after Annie Roberts dies, he accuses the company of murdering her. Ultimately even Anthony acknowledges that things are changing, but he criticizes the new sensibility, saying: "There is only one way of treating 'men'—with *the iron hand.* This half and half business, the half and half manners of this generation has brought all this upon us. Sentiment and softness, and what this young man, no doubt, would call his social policy. You can't eat cake and have it! This middle-class sentiment, or socialism, or whatever it may be, is rotten. Masters are masters, men are men! Yield one demand, and they will make it six" (101). Anthony's position is unyielding, as is Robert's. This rigidity of thinking makes them obsolete in a world of change and compromise. (Barker 1969; Galsworthy 1928)

See also Anthony, John; Galsworthy, John; Labor Issues; Roberts, David

Suffragist Movement
See Feminism

Sula

Written in 1973, *Sula,* by Toni Morrison, is the story of two women, Sula Peace and Nel Wright, who grow up together in a black neighborhood called the Bottom on the outskirts of Medallion, Ohio. The novel begins in 1920, when Nel is ten years old. Both she and Sula come from fatherless homes, but their personalities are very different. Nel is well mannered and conservative, whereas Sula is rebellious and promiscuous. Nonetheless, their friendship remains strong until Nel's wedding day, when Sula leaves town. She returns ten years later and soon seduces Nel's husband. Later she tells Nel that she did not see anything wrong with sharing a man with her friend.

Sula often fails to follow the moral guidelines of her community. For example, when her mother's skirt catches fire, Sula watches her burn to death rather than run for help, and when her grandmother accuses her of behaving badly, Sula sends her to a nursing home noted for its poor management. Her neighbors also accuse her of what they consider to be the ultimate sin—sleeping with white men. As their dislike of Sula grows, they begin to shun her. They call her a witch or a devil and keep their children away from her. In fact, their hatred of Sula unifies the community. When she dies of a prolonged illness, people consider it God's punishment and no one mourns her death. However, the community loses its unity and strength, and some time later Nel realizes that Sula's passing was a terrible loss. She begins to mourn her friend's death.

In discussing *Sula,* scholar Roberta Rubenstein says that the community is one of the main characters of the novel. In her essay "Pariahs and the Community," she (Gates and Appiah 1993c, 148) explains that it is "a kind of collective conscience that arbitrates the social and moral norms of its members. Functioning as a life-sustaining structure for its members, it tolerates certain kinds of eccentricity. . . . Yet it is also punitive to those who step absolutely outside the boundaries of the communally acceptable." She (148) quotes Morrison as saying: "In the black community where I grew up, there were eccentricity and freedom, less conformity in individual habits—but close conformity in terms of the survival of the village, of the tribe." Through the lives of Nel and Sula, the novel shows both the positive and negative aspects of such conformity.

Sula also presents the idea that every woman should have a purpose in life. In "A Hateful Passion, a Lost Love," scholar Hortense J. Spillers (Gates and Appiah 1993c, 212–213) explains that it is a feminist novel in which the main character's faults "are directly traceable to the absence of a discursive/imaginative project—some *thing* to do, some object-subject relationship which establishes the identify in time and space. We do not see Sula in relationship to an 'oppressor,' a 'whitey,' a male, a dominant and dominating being outside the self. . . . Instead, Sula emerges as an embodiment of a metaphysical chaos in pursuit of an activity both proper and sufficient to herself." When Sula's grandmother suggests that having a baby will settle her down, Sula replies: "I don't want to make somebody else. I want to make myself" (Morrison 1974, 92). And in describing the source of Sula's unhappiness and rebellion, the narrator remarks: "Had she paints, or clay, or knew the discipline of the dance, or strings; had she anything to engage her tremendous curiosity and her gift for metaphor, she might have exchanged the restlessness and preoccupation with whim for an activity that provided her with all she yearned for. And like any artist with no art form, she became dangerous" (121).

Morrison's work is therefore similar to another feminist novel, *A Woman,* by Sibilla

Aleramo, in which the main character must express her creativity or go insane. Many scholars have also compared *Sula* to Zora Neale Hurston's novel *Their Eyes Were Watching God* and to Jean Toomer's novel *Cane*, both of which are set within the black community and show characters ostracized by their neighbors. (Gates and Appiah 1993c; McKay 1988; Morrison 1974; Samuels 1990)

See also *Cane;* Feminism; Hurston, Zora Neale; Morrison, Toni; Peace, Sula; Racism; *Their Eyes Were Watching God;* Toomer, Jean; Wright, Nel

"Surviving"

"Surviving" is a poem by Native American author James Welch. Originally published in a 1971 collection entitled *Riding the Earthboy 40,* it depicts a group of Native Americans huddled around a stove on a cold day. They tell stories of better times and bemoan all they have lost because "to stay alive this way, it's hard" (Turner 1974, 597). (Turner 1974)

See also Native American Issues; Poverty; Welch, James

Swartz, Lanny

As the main character in Peter Abrahams's 1948 novel *The Path of Thunder,* Lanny is a South African coloured man who returns to his rural village after receiving a good education in the nearby city of Capetown. He opens a school and, according to scholar Robert Ensor (1992, 273), "sets an example of essential equality, self-respect and assertiveness for the community." Ensor (237) sees Lanny as "the black representative of a European-based liberal humanism" who only wants to "liberate and educate" his people. However, before Lanny can accomplish these goals, he falls in love with a white woman named Sarie Villiers. Since intermingling of the races is forbidden in South Africa, Lanny and Sarie try to flee to the more liberal Portuguese East Africa. Before they can escape, white landowners kill them both. (Abrahams 1975; Ensor 1992)

See also Abrahams, Peter; Finkelberg, Isaac; Mako; *Path of Thunder, The;* Racism

Swift, Jonathan

Born on November 30, 1667, Jonathan Swift is best known for two works, an essay entitled *A Modest Proposal* (1729) and a novel entitled *Gulliver's Travels* (1726). Both of them use satire to criticize English society. Swift's parents were English, but they lived in Dublin, Ireland, and Swift attended Trinity College there. In 1689, amid anti-Catholic sentiment in his country, he left for England as secretary to a retired politician. He soon became interested in politics himself and considered becoming a politician. However, in 1694 during a visit to Ireland Swift was ordained a minister, and his first published work, *Tale of a Tub* (1794), is a satire of religious extremists. Swift continued writing essays about religion and politics, and in 1710 he became editor of a journal, the *Examiner,* that was the voice of the Tory political party. He remained in this position until the Tories lost control of the government in 1714. At this point Swift became dean of Saint Patrick's Cathedral in Dublin. He soon began to write about the poor treatment of the Irish people by the English and produced his two greatest works. A national hero, Swift died in Dublin on October 19, 1745. (Murry 1967)

See also *Gulliver's Travels; Modest Proposal, A*

T

Tachibana, Akiko

One of the main characters of Sawako Ariyoshi's novel *The Twilight Years*, Akiko Tachibana must care for her senile father-in-law with almost no help from her husband. A modern, working woman, she nonetheless accepts the traditional Japanese role of wife and mother at home. She worries over what to cook for her family, which dislikes easy-to-prepare frozen foods, and is obsessed with keeping her house immaculate. Given the extra responsibility of her father-in-law's care, she quickly becomes overwhelmed. She is angry at her husband for making her deal with the situation alone, yet she has trouble expressing that anger. Even when she does tell him how she feels, he appears to ignore her, and she wonders how their life together will be when they grow old. (Ariyoshi 1987)

See also Ageism; Ariyoshi, Sawako; Feminism; Tachibana, Nobutoshi; *Twilight Years, The*

Tachibana, Nobutoshi

This character from Sawako Ariyoshi's 1972 novel *Kokotso no hito* (The Twilight Years) represents the traditional Japanese male in his fifties. He refuses to help his working wife, Akiko, with any household chores or with the care of his own father, who has become senile. He views Akiko's pleas for help as nagging and does not consider her work outside the home important. As the narrator explains: "The younger generation probably had different views about the role of women, but the feudalistic attitude among men of Nobutoshi's age could not easily be brushed aside. Men of his generation did not acknowledge the fact that a family's financial situation was vastly improved when the wife worked. They gave the impression that they were simply letting their wives do as they pleased and put up with their neglect of their household duties with tolerance and patience" (Ariyoshi 1987, 69). (Ariyoshi 1987)

See also Ariyoshi, Sawako; Feminism; *Twilight Years, The*

Taggert, Dagny

Dagny Taggert is the main character in Ayn Rand's 1957 novel *Atlas Shrugged*. In charge of a railroad company, Taggert Transcontinental, Taggert embodies capitalism. She is intelligent, creative, strong-willed, and beautiful, yet masculine. When the government tries to destroy her business through a variety of socialistic laws, she fights back and tries to save it. In the end, however, she is forced to walk away from her company in order to save society instead. (Rand 1992)

See also *Atlas Shrugged;* Rand, Ayn

Tarrant, Verena

Verena Tarrant is a speaker for the suffragette movement in Henry James's 1886 novel *The Bostonians*. Although she has a powerful speaking voice, she is a weak-willed woman easily swayed by others' opinions. At first she is ruled by her parents. Then she falls under the control of a feminist named Olive Chancellor and gradually accepts Olive's ideas as her own. Later, however, Verena is wooed by a chauvinistic southern gentleman, Basil Ransom, who convinces her not to listen to the opinions of Olive or her parents. Instead, he talks her into leaving the suffragette cause to marry him. Verena therefore represents a social reformer who lacks conviction. (James 1956)

See also *Bostonians, The;* Chancellor, Olive; Feminism; James, Henry; Ransom, Basil

Tea Cake

Tea Cake appears in Zora Neale Hurston's black feminist novel *Their Eyes Were Watching God* (1937). After he marries Janie Crawford, he teaches her to enjoy life, not just as a woman but as a human being. Tea Cake does not worry about social conformity; he values Janie's individuality. Moreover, he ultimately sacrifices his own life to save hers by protecting her from a rabid dog. After he contracts rabies and goes mad, Janie is forced to shoot him. (Hemenway 1977; Hurston 1990)

See also Crawford, Janie; Hurston, Zora Neale; *Their Eyes Were Watching God*

Temple of My Familiar, The

Published in 1989, *The Temple of My Familiar,* by Alice Walker, includes some of the characters from the author's best-known novel, *The Color Purple*. Both books address issues of racism and oppression, particularly as they relate to women. *The Temple of My Familiar* primarily concerns the lives of two women, a South American native named Zede and a black woman named Lizzie, and all of the people who are important to them. Some of these people existed thousands of years ago because Lizzie has been reincarnated many times and can remember all of her past lives. She has experienced human life in all its forms and was once even a lion.

As an old woman Lizzie tells her stories to a young man named Suwelo, who in return tells her of his problematic marriage with Fanny Nzingha. Fanny is the daughter of Olivia, who appeared in *The Color Purple*. One day she and her mother decide to go to Africa so that Fanny can meet her father, a political activist known as Ola. During the trip Fanny and her parents discuss the history of racism against their people. For example, on one occasion her mother says:

[The white man] was all-powerful. In fear and dread we watched him from our compounds the world over. Some of us were greedy. We believed, as he seemed to, that he was bringing something better than we had. This *never* happened. Always, we were left poorer, with a lowered opinion of ourselves. He blocked the view between us and our ancestors, us and our ways; not all of them good ways, but needing to be changed according to our own light. He needed to keep us terrorized and desperately poor, in order to feel powerful. No one who was secure in himself as a person would put such emphasis on the nonpersonhood and unworthiness of another. (Walker 1990, 307)

Other characters in the novel also discuss racism and share tales of historical figures, both real and fictional, who have suffered from oppression in Africa and the Americas. In addition, characters refer to the work of black feminist social protest authors such as Zora Neale Hurston and Nella Larsen. After Ola dies, Fanny decides to become a protest author, writing plays with her half sister Nzingha in memory of her father's political activism. At the same time Fanny decides to return to the United States to work things out with Suwelo.

Suwelo has become involved with Zeda's daughter, Carlotta, but when Fanny returns he drops Carlotta. Then the two women become friends, and they begin talking about their mothers with Suwelo and Carlotta's husband, Arveyda, who is a musician and somewhat of a mystic. Zeda was a teacher in South America when the government arrested her for being too progressive. Later she escaped to the United States, where she raised Carlotta and had an affair with her daughter's husband. Zeda and Arveyda then went to South America together. He eventually returned to live with Carlotta, while Zeda remained behind to find her own mother. Zeda was successful, and the two women now live in Mexico. After hearing this story, Suwelo reveals that both of his parents were killed in a car accident. Suwelo's father often drove drunk and forced his wife to sit beside him. Suwelo now realizes the fear his mother must have experienced.

By this point Lizzie has died and left Suwelo a tape recording about her life as a lion. He goes to share it with her friend, a man who never understood all of what Lizzie was. Meanwhile Arveyda and Fanny make love and pronounce themselves of one spirit and one flesh. (Walker 1990)

See also Feminism; Hurston, Zora Neale; Larsen, Nella; Racism; Walker, Alice

Tereza

A character in the 1984 novel *Nesnesitelna lehkost byti* (The Unbearable Lightness of Being), by Milan Kundera, Tereza documents political oppression through photography. Of her work, the unnamed narrator of the story says:

All previous crimes of the Russian empire had been committed under the cover of a discreet shadow. . . . Sooner or later they will therefore be proclaimed as fabrications. Not so the 1968 invasion of Czechoslovakia, of which both stills and motion pictures are stored in archives throughout the world. Czech photographers and cameramen were acutely aware that they were the ones who could best do the only thing left to do: preserve the face of violence for the distant future. . . . Seven days in a row, Tereza roamed the streets, photographing Russian soldiers and officers in compromising situations. . . . Many of her photographs turned up in the Western press. They were pictures of tanks, of threatening fists, of houses destroyed, of corpses covered with bloodstained red-white-and-blue Czech flags. (Kundera 1984, 67)

But despite the importance of her work, Tereza abandons it to concentrate on her lover, who eventually becomes her husband. Other characters in the novel make choices between personal relationships and political awareness and/or activism. In Tereza's case, she justifies her decision by convincing herself that her photographs actually advanced the Soviet cause by providing the Communists with pictures of rebels. (Kundera 1984)

See also Communism; Kundera, Milan; *Unbearable Lightness of Being, The*

Tetley, Gerald

Gerald Tetley participates in a lynching party in Walter Van Tilburg Clark's western novel *The Ox-bow Incident* (1940). He is only a part of the group because he is afraid to oppose its leader: his father, Major Tetley. To other people, Gerald voices his disgust for the mob's actions. Scholar Max Westbrook (1969, 56) has therefore called him an "articulate spokesman for morality." But Westbrook (56) also points out that Gerald's arguments against lynching, which are made in an overly emotional manner, make him appear "so weak that he is disgusting to Art Croft, the narrator." Moreover, after the lynching takes place and the men discover they have killed three innocent men, this weak nature leads Gerald to suffer such guilt that he hangs himself in the family barn. His father commits suicide shortly thereafter. (Clark 1960; Westbrook 1969)

See also Clark, Walter Van Tilberg; Croft, Art; Davies, Art; Justice; Martin, Donald; *Ox-Bow Incident, The*

Tewce, Ainsley

A character in Margaret Atwood's 1969 novel *The Edible Woman*, Ainsley Tewce professes to be a feminist, yet cannot shake off conventionality. Feeling unfulfilled, she decides to get pregnant and looks for a suitable sperm donor. She has no intention of marrying, believing it will be easy to raise the child on her own. But during her pregnancy, after she reads an article on the importance of fathers in a child's upbringing, she asks her baby's father to marry her. When he refuses, she convinces another man to marry her instead. (Atwood 1996)

See also Atwood, Margaret; *Edible Woman, The;* Feminism

Their Eyes Were Watching God

Their Eyes Were Watching God, by Zora Neale Hurston, is the story of a black woman's search for independence and love in a black community where men have all the power. In an afterword to the novel, scholar Henry Louis Gates Jr. (187) calls it a "bold feminist novel, the first to be explicitly so in the Afro-American tradition."

However, when the novel was published in 1937, it was criticized by both white and black reviewers. Scholar Mary Helen Washington reports that white men had difficulty believing black people could have so much power, whereas black men did not think the novel was an accurate depiction of life in the rural American South. In a foreword to the novel, Washington (viii) explains that Hurston was chastised for not following the "protest tradition" among black writers, which required a harsh portrayal of racism, and adds:

> The most damaging critique of all came from the most well-known and influential black writer of the day, Richard Wright. Writing for the leftist magazine *New Masses,* Wright excoriated *Their Eyes* as a novel that did for literature what the minstrel shows did for theater, that is, make white folks laugh. The novel, he said, "carries no theme, no message, no thought," but exploited those "quaint" aspects of Negro life that satisfied the tastes of a white audience. By the end of the forties, a decade dominated by Wright and by the stormy fiction of social realism, the quieter voice of a woman searching for self-realization could not, or would not, be heard.

As a result of such criticism, the book went out of print and remained so for almost 30 years. Hurston herself died in poverty in 1960. Shortly thereafter the American feminist movement began, and used copies of *Their Eyes Were Watching God* became popular among women everywhere. The book was reissued in a limited quantity, and university professors such as noted author Alice Walker began featuring the novel in their literature classes. Nonetheless, *Their Eyes* was often out of print until 1978, when scholars finally encouraged publishers to make it permanently available.

Today *Their Eyes Were Watching God* is considered one of the most important feminist works in African-American literature. Its significance lies in the voice of its main character, Janie Crawford, who tells the story of her three marriages to her best friend, Pheoby. Janie's first husband, Logan Killicks, is chosen for her by her grandmother. Janie does not love Logan, but her grandmother tells her to serve him nonetheless, saying: "Honey, de white man is de ruler of everything as fur as Ah been able tuh find out. . . . So de white man throw down de load and tell de nigger man tuh pick it up. He pick it up because he have to, but he don't tote it. He hand it to his womenfolks. De nigger woman is de mule uh de world so fur as Ah can see" (14).

But Janie has trouble obeying Logan, and one day she runs off with Joe Stark, an older man who is on his way to a black-run town in Florida. She imagines a life with him of love and freedom. But after Joe becomes the town mayor and builds his own general store, he becomes as controlling as Janie's first husband. He tells her what to do and does not allow her to socialize with most of the townspeople, who call her "Mrs. Mayor Stark." She quickly loses her own identity, and when Joe contracts a fatal illness, she tells him: "You gointuh listen tuh me one time befo' you die. . . . Ah run off tuh keep house with you in uh wonderful way. But you wasn't satisfied wid me de way Ah was. Naw! Mah own mind had tuh be squeezed and crowded out tuh make room for yours in me. . . . All dis bowin' down, all dis obedience under yo' voice—dat ain't whut Ah rushed off down de road tuh find out about you" (82).

After Joe's death she meets Tea Cake, a younger man who encourages her to enjoy life. He takes her hunting, fishing, and picnicking. The townspeople believe she is making a fool of herself; only Pheoby believes that

Janie can make her own decisions. Eventually Tea Cake marries her, and the two leave town to take a job picking beans on a plantation. Their love remains strong, and Janie is finally her own person. Her only aggravation is a local black woman, Mrs. Turner, who believes that light-skinned blacks like Janie are superior to dark-skinned ones like Tea Cake.

Then one day a violent hurricane hits the plantation. While Janie and Tea Cake are running for higher ground, a mad dog bites Tea Cake in the face. He contracts rabies, goes mad, and attacks Janie, who is forced to shoot him. The white townspeople put her on trial for murder. After she testifies, she is acquitted and returns to her former home to tell Pheoby her story.

Interestingly, the novel does not offer Janie's speech to the white jury. Mary Helen Washington reports that this aspect of *Their Eyes* has engendered much debate among scholars. She (xi) says that in 1979 Robert Stepto of Yale University first "raised the issue that has become one of the most highly controversial aspects of the novel: whether or not Janie is able to achieve her voice." She (xi-xii) explains:

What concerned Stepto was the courtroom scene in which Janie is called on not only to preserve her own life and liberty but also to make the jury, as well as all of us who hear her tale, understand the meaning of her life with Tea Cake. Stepto found Janie curiously silent in this scene, with Hurston telling the story in omniscient third person so that we do not hear Janie speak—at least not in her own first-person voice. Stepto was quite convinced . . . that the frame story in which Janie speaks to Pheoby creates only the illusion that Janie has found her voice. . . . [However,] Alice Walker . . . [insists] passionately that women did not have to speak when men thought they should, that they would choose when and where they wish to speak because while many women *had* found their own voices, they also knew when it was better not to use it.

Washington (xii) believes that this argument reflects "the earliest feminist reading of voice in *Their Eyes*." The novel has many references to oral tradition, perhaps because Hurston was not only a novelist but also a folklorist. In addition, Gates (187) believes that it powerfully shows "language as an instrument of injury and salvation, of selfhood and empowerment." (Hemenway 1977; Hurston 1990)

See also Crawford, Janie; Feminism; Hurston, Zora Neale; Racism; Stark, Joe; Tea Cake; Walker, Alice; Wright, Richard

This Earth of Mankind

The book *Bumi Manusia* (This Earth of Mankind), by Javanese author Pramoedya Ananta Toer, concerns racism and sexism on the Dutch-controlled island of Java. Written while Toer was in prison for his political writings, it was published in 1980, a year after his release. He followed this book with three sequels, *Anak semua bangsa* (Child of All Nations), *Jejak langkah* (Footsteps), and *Ruma kaca* (House of Glass), also composed while he was in prison. Together these books are known as the Buru Quartet. All of them have been banned in Indonesia.

This Earth of Mankind begins in 1898, when its main character, Minke, is 18. He is one of the few natives in Java to attend a prestigious Dutch-run school there. An excellent student gifted in several languages, he is expected to become a government official. However, he would rather be a journalist. He writes articles and stories for local publications about his people and their culture, and these are well received by the public. Meanwhile, the leaders of the Dutch school are unhappy that he, a native, has proved himself to be superior to the European students there, and no one applauds when he is recognized as the institution's top scholar.

One day a friend takes him to visit a beautiful young woman, Annalies Mellema. Annalies is the daughter of a European's concubine, or *nyai*, named Ontosoroh. Although native women are usually uneducated, Ontosoroh is intelligent and has taught herself to read well. Her Dutch master, Herman Mellama, is a drunkard who cannot manage their farm, so she successfully runs it herself. Minke is drawn to her and her half-European daughter. However, he is frightened by Annalies's brother, Robert Mellema, who pretends to be a full European and hates all natives. After Minke accepts Ontosoroh's invitation to move in with the family, Robert threatens his life. Nonetheless, Minke becomes romantically involved with Annalies, who grows ill every time he leaves her side.

Rumors about Minke's relationship with the girl and her mother spread throughout the town. They grow worse after Annalies's father is poisoned while in a pleasure palace. During the investigation into his death authorities uncover the fact that Minke has been sleeping with Annalies, and he is expelled from school. However, because he has become an influential writer, many people rise to his defense, and he is reinstated. Meanwhile Robert Mellama has disappeared, so the court delays its verdict on the death until his capture.

Shortly thereafter Minke marries Annalies to quell the rumors. His marriage does not last. With Herman Mellama dead, the estate passes into the hands of Annalies's half brother, Mauritas Mellama. The son of Herman Mellama and his lawful Dutch wife, Mauritas becomes Annalies's legal guardian and convinces a European court to annul the marriage because she is underage and did not have her father's permission to wed. Minke and Ontosoroh try to fight the court's decision. Several religious groups come to their aid, saying that under Islamic law the marriage cannot be annulled. Nonetheless, Mauritas eventually takes custody of Annalies and sends her to the Netherlands. Minke is dejected over his defeat, but Ontosoroh reminds him that at least they tried to fight their oppressors.

This Earth of Mankind emphasizes the importance of struggling against injustice. Many characters stand up for their rights, typically with success. For example, Minke defends himself in print against ugly rumors and is reinstated in school. Ontosoroh stands up to her drunken husband and expels him from her house. Minke's friends frighten away a

man sent to kill Minke. Annalies fights off her brother Robert while he is raping her and fires a gun at him as he flees.

The novel also compares the unfairness of racism with that of sexism. Throughout the story Minke is persecuted for being a native, but Ontosoroh is persecuted far worse for being a native woman. Minke is allowed to attend school, and when he distinguishes himself through his writing, he is considered an important person. Ontosoroh, who became a concubine against her will, cannot attend school, and when she becomes an accomplished businesswoman, her farm is taken away, as is her daughter. European law does not even honor her role as a mother. *This Earth of Mankind* harshly criticizes European law and Dutch colonialism. In addition, it provides enough information about Javanese history to show that, even though the Dutch have modernized the island, they have also destroyed many important aspects of Javanese culture. (Toer 1996)

See also Censorship; Class, Social; Feminism; Mellama, Mauritas; Mellama, Robert; Minke; Ontosoroh; Racism; Toer, Pramoedya Ananta

Thomas, Bigger

Bigger Thomas is the main character of the 1940 novel *Native Son*, by Richard Wright. An angry black man emasculated by white society, he commits acts of violence against other blacks. Then he accidentally kills a white woman and experiences the full wrath of the white community. Despite the best efforts of his Communist lawyer, he is tried and sentenced to death without receiving true justice.

In writing about Bigger Thomas, Richard Wright relates him to angry victims of oppression in other parts of the world. He (1993a, 519) says that before writing the novel, "I read every account of the Fascist movement in Germany I could lay my hands on, and from page to page I encountered and recognized familiar emotional patterns." Eventually he (521–522) came to a conclusion:

I felt that Bigger, an American product, a native son of this land, carried within him the potentialities of either Communism or

Fascism. I don't mean to say that the Negro boy I depicted in *Native Son* is either a Communist or a Fascist. He is not either. But he is a product of a dislocated society; he is a dispossessed and disinherited man; he is all of this, and he lives amid the greatest possible plenty on earth and he is looking and feeling for a way out. Whether he'll follow some gaudy, hysterical leader who'll promise rashly to fill the void in him, or whether he'll come to an understanding with the millions of his kindred fellow workers under trade-union or revolutionary guidance depends upon the future drift of events in America. But, granting the emotional state, the tensity, the fear, the hate, the impatience, the sense of exclusion, the ache for violent action, the emotional and cultural hunger, Bigger Thomas, conditioned as his organism is, will not become an ardent, or even a lukewarm, supporter of the *status quo.*

(Wright 1993a)

See also Communism; Fascism; *Native Son;* Wright, Richard

Thompson, Eloise Bibb

Born in 1878, Eloise Bibb Thompson was a black poet, playwright, and short story author who wrote about racism and black pride. Her first book, *Poems,* appeared in 1895. She attended Howard University in Washington, D.C., and graduated from its Teacher's College in 1908. Shortly thereafter she moved to Los Angeles, where she began writing for newspapers. Many of her short stories were published in a magazine called *Opportunity,* but her plays were largely unpublished. One 1915 drama, however, did attract a great deal of attention. Entitled *A Reply to the Clansman,* it was a criticism of a racist group called the Ku Klux Klan. But although the rights to make it into a movie were bought by two noted filmmakers, Cecil B. DeMille and D. W. Griffith, the play was never produced. Thompson died in 1928. (Roses and Randolph 1996)

See also Harlem Renaissance; *Masks, a Story*

Titorelli

Titorelli appears in Franz Kafka's 1925 novel *Der Prozess* (The Trial). He is a portrait painter for a mysterious court that operates outside the traditional legal system. Titorelli inherited his position from his father, and he must adhere to strict rules regarding the poses and settings he uses in his paintings. However, his close connection with the court also provides him with a chance to influence its judges. When an accused man, Joseph K., comes to ask for his help, Titorelli explains the types of verdicts the man can expect and offers to prolong his trial indefinitely, explaining that no one is ever deemed innocent. In return, Joseph K. is expected to buy Titorelli's landscapes, which all depict the same bleak scene. (Kafka 1964)

See also Joseph K.; Kafka, Franz; *Trial, The*

To Kill a Mockingbird

To Kill a Mockingbird was published in 1960, a time of racial segregation in the southeastern United States. The novel depicts racial prejudice and moral courage in Alabama during the 1930s. The book's author, Harper Lee, won a Pulitzer Prize for the novel, which is narrated in the first-person by Jean Louise "Scout" Finch, a woman recalling the events of her childhood from ages six to nine. Scout lives in the fictional town of Maycomb, Alabama, with her brother, Jem; black housekeeper, Calpurnia; and widowed father, Atticus, an attorney. Scout's story begins when she meets six-year-old Charles Barker "Dill" Harris, who dares Scout and Jem to run up and touch Arthur "Boo" Radley's house. Boo developed psychological problems as a boy, and rather than send him to a mental institution, his family has kept him cloistered at home for years. The children have never seen him but imagine that he is a monster.

After Jem suppresses his fear of Boo and takes the dare, he becomes fascinated with the Radley house. He tries to leave Boo a note asking him to come out, but his father catches him and tells him never to bother Boo again. Jem finds it hard to obey, and in a nearby tree he sometimes finds little gifts, such as chewing gum or a coin, that he believes have been left there by Boo.

Atticus Finch defends Tom Robinson in this courtroom scene from the 1962 movie To Kill a Mockingbird, *which depicts racial injustice in the segregated southern United States. (United Artists/The Museum of Modern Art Film Stills Archive)*

Time passes, and Scout describes other, seemingly minor events in her life. These incidents reveal a great deal about the moral character of the town. Some of the people of Maycomb are good and courageous, whereas others are evil and cowardly, but most are a mixture of both good and bad. Scout learns this more fully when Atticus is appointed to defend Tom Robinson, a black man accused of battering and raping a white woman, Mayell Ewell. The night before the trial, a group of men show up at the jail to lynch Tom. Atticus tries to stop them, and soon it appears that they will hurt him, too. Then Scout recognizes the father of one of her friends in the crowd. She calls out to him, asks him about his boy, and tries to carry on a pleasant conversation with him. Reminded of his child and his humanity, the man grows embarrassed and leaves; the crowd disperses.

At the trial the next day Atticus proves that Tom could not have committed the crime. The assailant was clearly left-handed, and

Tom's left hand was crippled when he was a boy. Atticus points out that Mayell's father, Bob Ewell, is left-handed, and it soon becomes clear that the man beat up his daughter when he saw her with a black man. However, because the members of the jury are racially prejudiced, they convict Tom despite the facts. He is sentenced to death and is later shot while trying to escape from prison. Scout overhears talk of racial tension in the town, and she and Jem cannot understand why all people are not treated the same.

Meanwhile Bob Ewell has vowed revenge on Atticus for the way he defended Tom. Ewell is too cowardly to attack Atticus directly, so one night he follows Scout and Jem home from a school pageant and attacks them with a knife. Boo Radley saves the children's lives, killing Bob Ewell during the struggle. There are no witnesses to the crime, and the sheriff decides that Ewell killed himself by falling on his own knife. He does not want to expose the sheltered Boo to fame. It would be like killing a mockingbird, a creature that harms no one, or like causing the death of an innocent man.

By the end of the novel, Scout's view of the world has broadened. As scholar Timothy Healy (304) explains in a 1993 afterword to the book:

> Scout's understanding of life gradually widens as the story progresses. She begins with the street, the neighbor's houses, the small world of people who live within sight of her front porch. . . . As the trial begins, Scout enters the larger world of Maycomb itself. She learns about juries, the kind of people who make them up, and about the larger issues of justice and prejudice. In the last part of the book, though it is only hinted at, Scout discovers the world beyond Maycomb and Alabama. There are discussions of national events . . . and the bad times that make people unable to pay their taxes. Finally the whole wide world itself breaks into the schoolroom as . . . the children talk about Adolf Hitler and his racial hatred.

This discussion relates Hitler's persecution of the Jews to racial prejudice in the United States and is perhaps the most powerful passage of social protest in the book. Scout's teacher says that she cannot understand why Hitler does not like the Jews because "they contribute to every society they live in, and most of all, they are a deeply religious people," adding that their story is horrible because they "have been persecuted since the beginning of history, even driven out of their own country" (259). The comparison with African Americans is obvious. Yet Scout observes that her teacher is one of the most racially prejudiced people in town.

Because of such passages, when *To Kill a Mockingbird* was published, some people criticized it for being more of a sermon than a story. Nonetheless, the book was a best-seller and was made into a successful motion picture in 1962. Both the book and the movie increased awareness of racial issues at a time when the civil rights movement in the United States was just beginning to come to public awareness. (Lee 1993)

See also Ewell, Bob; Finch, Jean Louise ("Scout"); Justice; Lee, Harper; Racism; Radley, Arthur ("Boo")

Toer, Pramoedya Ananta

Born on the island of Java in 1925, Pramoedya Ananta Toer has written about racism, sexism, and colonialism in Indonesia. His father was the headmaster of a nationalist school in Blora, Java, and a prominent political figure. However, the young Toer was a poor scholar and took ten years to complete a seven-year elementary school course at his father's school. Afterward, using money he earned from trading rice, he went to the city of Surabaya to attend the Dutch-run Radio-vakschool (Radio Vocational School). The Dutch had been in control of Indonesia for hundreds of years, and Toer was soon forced to join the radiotelegraph section of the Stadswacht (City Civil Defense). He fled the city and returned home, where he remained until his mother's death. He then moved to Jakarta, became a newspaper editor, and joined a movement to make Indonesia independent. In 1947 he was arrested by the Dutch Colonial Army for his activities. He spent two years in prison, where he wrote a short story collection, *Percikan Revolusi,* and a novel, *Perburuan.* After his release he started teaching history and journalism. In 1949 Indonesia at last became independent. Toer became active in political and social reform groups and often spoke in favor of social protest writing. He severely criticized novels that ignored his country's problems.

In 1965 he was again arrested. The Communists had attempted to take over the government, and in the aftermath the anticommunist rulers arrested anyone involved in a left-wing political group. An estimated 500,000 people were killed during this purge, and Toer was imprisoned on Buru Island from 1965 to 1979. During this time he told stories to the other prisoners, and after eight years he was allowed to use paper to write them down. After his release this material was published as four novels, *Bumi manusia* (This Earth of Mankind), *anak semua bangsa* (Child of All

Nations), *Jejak langkah* (Footsteps), and *Rumah kaca* (House of Glass). They are collectively known as the Buru Quartet. All of Toer's works have been banned in Indonesia, and Toer himself cannot leave Jakarta to travel overseas. Moreover, the translator of the Buru Quartet, a secretary in the Australian Embassy in Jakarta, was forced to leave the city in 1981 because of his work on the novels.

In 1988 Toer was awarded the PEN Freedom-to-Write Award and in 1995 the Raymond Magsaysay Award. In 1996 he filed suit to have his home returned to him; it had been confiscated by the Indonesian government in 1966, and all of his books, papers, and manuscripts had been burned. However, the court refused to return Toer's property, and the verdict is currently being appealed. (Toer 1996)

See also Censorship; Racism; *This Earth of Mankind*

Leo Tolstoi (Corbis-Bettmann)

Tolstoi, Leo

Leo Tolstoi is considered one of the world's greatest novelists. His works criticize various aspects of Russian society and human nature. The son of a nobleman, Tolstoi was born on September 9, 1828, just south of Moscow, in Yasnaya Polyana, Tula province, Russia. His mother died when he was a year old, and when he was nine his father died as well. He and his three brothers were subsequently raised by their aunts. In 1844 Tolstoi enrolled in the University of Kazan, but he was unhappy there and returned home in 1847. In 1851 he traveled to the Caucasus Mountains, where he joined the army and fought in several battles.

The next year he published the first part of an autobiographical trilogy. Entitled *Detstvo* (Childhood), it was followed by Otrochestvo (Boyhood) in 1854 and *Yunost* (Youth) in 1857, and depicted life on Tolstoi's estate. In 1854 during the Crimean War the army transferred him to the city of Sevastopol, and Tolstoi wrote several stories there. Three of them, known collectively as *Sevastopolskiye rasskazy* (Sevastopol Sketches) and published between 1855 and 1856, brought him recognition as a short story writer.

Tolstoi's first novel, *Kazaki* (The Cossacks),

was published in 1863, but it was two subsequent novels, *Voyna i mir* (War and Peace, 1865–1869) and *Anna Karenina* (1875–1877), that made him famous as a novelist. *War and Peace* concerns Napoleon's invasion of Russia in 1812, and *Anna Karenina* is the story of an adulterous affair with tragic consequences. Tolstoi's later works, which include short stories, plays, novels, and essays, show his increasing concern for social and moral problems. For example, *Voskreseniye* (Resurrection, 1899) depicts a young nobleman's awakening to the need for social reform. Tolstoi himself was a social reformer. He was involved in a variety of causes and publicly condemned capitalism, private property laws, and the labor system. In November 1910 he decided to retire to a monastery, but he died at a train station along the way. (Tolstoy 1911)

See also Capitalism; Labor Issues; *Resurrection*

Tom, Uncle

The main character in Harriet Beecher Stowe's 1852 novel *Uncle Tom's Cabin*, Uncle Tom is an African-American slave whose owner, Mr. Shelby, describes him as a "good, steady, sensible, pious fellow," adding: "I've trusted him . . . with everything I have,—

money, house, horses,—and let him come and go round the country; and I always found him true and square in everything" (Stowe 1960, 14). Nonetheless, when Shelby falls into debt, he sells Tom to a slave trader. Eventually Tom becomes the property of an evil plantation owner, Simon Legree, who beats him to death. (Stowe 1960)

See also Stowe, Harriet Beecher; *Uncle Tom's Cabin*

Tomas

One of the main characters in Milan Kundera's 1984 novel *Nesnesitelná lehkost byti* (The Unbearable Lightness of Being), Tomas is a Czechoslovakian physician with several mistresses; even after he marries, he continues to see other women. Then he writes a political essay and his life changes. The government asks him to write a retraction to the essay, but he refuses and eventually loses his job. He becomes a window washer and later a farmer, gives up his mistresses, and eventually attains happiness. However, his wife notes that in doing so, he has given up his power, and she dreams that he has turned into a rabbit pursued by hunters from the government. Shortly thereafter Tomas and his wife are reported to have died in a car crash. (Kundera 1984)

See also Kundera, Milan; Tereza; *Unbearable Lightness of Being, The*

Tono-Bungay

The 1908 novel *Tono-Bungay* was first published in serialized form in the *English Review*. Written by H. G. Wells, it criticizes British society for clinging to outmoded traditions and class distinctions. The novel also suggests that people are too easily duped by clever marketing strategies. The first-person narrator of the story, George Ponderevo, is the son of a housekeeper. He goes to college to better himself, but his studies are difficult and he is impatient. When his uncle Edward, a chemist, invents a "miracle medicine" called Tono-Bungay, George leaves school to help him sell it. In actuality, Tono-Bungay is worthless, but through a clever advertising campaign the Ponderevos convince the public that it can cure almost any ailment. Edward and George

soon become wealthy. Edward spends his money freely, buying his way into the upper classes.

Meanwhile George longs to give society something of value. He studies aerodynamics and experiments with gliders and hot-air balloons in an attempt to invent an airplane. At the same time he falls in love with Beatrice Normandy, the mistress of a wealthy man. Then George learns that Edward has mismanaged their company's finances. In an attempt to save his fortune, George sails for Africa to acquire a rare, valuable, highly radioactive substance called quap. But before he can return it to England for trade, it eats away at the wood in his ship and the vessel sinks. When George is rescued, he discovers that he and Edward are bankrupt. Moreover, Edward is wanted for forgery. George helps him escape to France in a hot-air balloon, but the journey makes the old man ill.

After Edward dies, George returns to England and asks Beatrice to marry him despite his poverty. She refuses, explaining that she has been spoiled by money and that "people can be ruined by wealth just as much as by poverty" (Wells 1935, 388). After she returns to her lover, George becomes a boat builder and develops a new perception of England. He sees it as a place of "greedy trade, base profit-seeking, [and] bold advertisement" and says that despite its ruling classes, "kingship and chivalry . . . are dead" (394).

Wells uses the metaphor of quap to show the destructive power of greed. The radioactive substance eats away at the ship and at the hands of the men who handle it, and George becomes sick in his soul during his journey to find it. He even shoots a man in the back rather than have him interfere with the success of the adventure. Similarly, as Edward becomes rich, the quality of his once-loving marriage deteriorates. He becomes estranged from his wife and his health suffers.

Meanwhile George criticizes the institutions of marriage and religion and tries to find something to replace them. An atheist, he considers joining a socialist group but decides that its members are not his sort of people. However, he continues to believe in socialism as a theory. When he sees the ruin of the mansion his uncle was constructing before his death, George says, "For this the armies drilled, for this the Law was administered and the prisons did their duty, for this the millions toiled and perished in suffering, in order that a few of us should build palaces we never finished, . . . run imbecile walls round irrational estates, scorch about the world in motor-cars, devise flying-machines, play golf and a dozen such foolish games of ball, crowd into chattering dinner parties, gamble and make our lives one vast, dismal spectacle of witless waste!" (356).

In the end, however, George realizes that all things change and suggests that England's "feudal scheme" will eventually crumble (296). He builds a destroyer, which he considers a symbol of progress, and sails it down the Thames River, reflecting on England as it passes by. (Wells 1935)

See also Capitalism; Ponderevo, George; Quap; Wells, H. G.

Toomer, Jean

Nathan Eugene Toomer is the author of *Cane*, a collection of short stories and poems about the black experience in the United States during the 1920s. Born on December 26, 1894, Toomer was a mixed-race child: his paternal grandfather was a wealthy white plantation owner, and his maternal grandfather was a prominent black politician and activist. Toomer identified with both races. He spent his childhood with his mother's family in Washington, D.C., his father having disappeared shortly after his birth. In 1914 Toomer enrolled in the University of Wisconsin as an agricultural student. He was unhappy there and soon left to enroll in the American College of Physical Training in Chicago, where he planned to become a gym teacher. Then he decided to change careers. In 1916 he enrolled in the University of Chicago as a biology major, intending to become a doctor. Shortly thereafter he began studying socialism and decided to become a scholar. In 1917 he enrolled in New York University as a sociology major, but soon changed course again, studying history and psychology at the City College of New York. Finally he quit school altogether.

After a short period as a salesman, he began teaching physical education. Meanwhile he continued to study literature on his own time. In 1920 he decided to become a writer himself. He began producing stories and poems, and in 1923 his famous collection, *Cane,* was published. All of his subsequent books were rejected for publication, and Toomer grew frustrated. Even though his stories had been published in magazines, eventually he abandoned fiction writing entirely. However, he continued to write poetry, essays, and autobiographical works, and in 1931 he self-published a book of sayings entitled *Essentials.* In addition, he lectured on writing and on a meditational philosophy that he learned in France. In his later years he experimented with communal living and various Eastern religions. Toomer died on March 30, 1967.

(Benson and Dillard 1980)

See also *Cane;* Harlem Renaissance

Trial, The

The Trial, by Franz Kafka, was published in German as *Der Prozess* in 1925, a year after the Austrian author's death. Some of its chapters were left unfinished, and it was Kafka's last wish that the entire manuscript be destroyed, but the executor of his will refused to honor this request. The novel was translated into English in 1937 and was one of the most widely read books of the period.

Written in the third person, the story is told from the point of view of Joseph K., who is placed under arrest on the morning of his thirtieth birthday. The two arresting officers represent a mysterious court that operates outside of the traditional legal system. They will not tell him why he is under arrest, nor will they provide him with any information about court procedures. However, they say that he can continue his daily routine as a bank clerk until the matter is settled. At first Joseph considers his arrest a practical joke and refuses to take it seriously, but eventually he decides it is real. He complies with a summons to attend a court interrogation in a seedy tenement, where he finds an evasive, hostile crowd that leaves him more confused than before. He gives an indignant speech to the assembly and walks out. The next day he returns to the tenement to try to learn more about the court. When his efforts prove useless, he decides to take his uncle's advice and hire a lawyer who specializes in such cases. But the lawyer does little and tells him nothing, and finally Joseph decides to handle his own defense. When he goes to the lawyer's house to fire him, he meets another of the man's clients, a tradesman named Block. His case has been ongoing for over five years, and he paints a bleak picture of Joseph's future.

Shortly thereafter Joseph hears about a portrait painter, Titorelli, who is known for influencing the court's decisions. He visits the man and learns that the judges are corrupt, vain, and loath to admit that anyone can be innocent. Titorelli gives Joseph little hope of being acquitted but says that he might be able to postpone the case indefinitely. Joseph cannot decide what to do. Then he encounters the court chaplain, who implies that Joseph's conviction is certain. In the end Joseph does nothing to advance his case, and on the night before his thirty-first birthday two men arrive to escort him from the city. At a distant site they plunge a knife into Joseph's heart.

Scholars have long debated the meaning of Kafka's story. Some believe that the mysterious court represents a totalitarian regime. Others suggest that it symbolizes religious oppression. However, the novel offers no certainties. Its readers remain as confused as Joseph K., who accepts his fate without understanding it. (Kafka 1964)

See also Block; Joseph K.; Kafka, Franz; Titorelli

Trueba, Esteban

In Isabel Allende's 1982 novel *La casa de los espíritus* (The House of the Spirits), Esteban Trueba is a senator from the Conservative Party in an unnamed South American country who vocally opposes communism, Marxism, and socialism. He believes that the poor are incapable of governing themselves because "they need someone to do their thinking for them, someone around to make decisions"

(Allende 1985, 241). He criticizes his wife, Clare; his children, Jaime, Nicolás, and Blanca; and his granddaughter, Alba, for supporting charitable causes because "charity, like Socialism, is an invention of the weak to exploit the strong and bring them to their knees" (252). However, after he encourages a military dictatorship that brings about Nicolás's death and Alba's arrest and torture, Esteban realizes the error of his beliefs. (Allende 1985)

See also Allende, Isabel; Capitalism; De Satigny, Alba Trueba; Del Valle, Clara; Garcia, Esteban; Garcia, Pedro Tecero; *House of the Spirits, The;* Socialism

Turgenev, Ivan

Born on November 9, 1818, in Orel province, Russia, Ivan Turgenev wrote about the relationship between peasants and nobility in his native country. His collection of short stories, *Zapiski okhotnika* (A Sportsman's Sketches, 1847–1852), is credited with hastening Russia's emancipation of the serfs, which occurred in 1861. Turgenev graduated from the University of St. Petersburg and subsequently studied at the University of Berlin in Germany. There he became involved with a group of Russian students who discussed philosophical and political issues. When he returned to Russia in 1841, he sought out similar friends. He also obtained a job in the civil service. In 1843 he met the woman who was to be his life-long lover, a married singer named Pauline Viardot-Garcia. He wrote part of *A Sportsman's Sketches* while visiting her estate.

In 1850 Turgenev inherited his family's wealth, and he was able to begin writing full-time. He associated with many of the most important authors of his time, including Fyodor Dostoyevsky and Leo Tolstoi, and wrote several more novels. These works include *Nakanune* (On the Eve, 1860), whose main character fights against social injustice, and *Ottsy i deti* (Fathers and Sons, 1862), which depicts conflict between aristocrats and a new generation of intelligentsia. The latter provoked so much criticism that Turgenev decided to leave Russia. He lived first in Germany, then London, and then Paris. However, he continued to write about his native country; his last novel,

Nov (Virgin Soil, 1877), concerns Russian revolutionaries. In his later years Turgenev developed cancer of the spine and began making short visits to Russia. He died in France on August 23, 1883. (Lloyd 1972; Turgenev 1973)

See also Dostoyevsky, Fyodor; *Sportsman's Sketches, A;* Tolstoi, Leo

Twilight Years, The

Published in 1972, *Kokotso no hito* (The Twilight Years), by Sawako Ariyoshi, focuses on the problem of ageism in Japan. The novel's main character, Akiko Tachibana, is forced to deal with the advancing senility of her father-in-law, Shigezō, when her mother-in-law dies suddenly. Akiko's husband, Nobutoshi, is a traditional Japanese man who does not offer any help in the household, despite the fact that his wife works full-time as a secretary in a law firm and Akiko's son, Satoshi, is busy studying for his college entrance exams. In addition to doing the cooking, the cleaning, and the laundry, Akiko must take care of her father-in-law herself.

At first things go fairly well. Akiko and Nobutoshi move Shigezō into their home, and a neighbor takes him to a senior citizen's center each day; Satoshi picks him up at night. But soon Shigezō's mental condition grows worse. He becomes less communicative, has trouble recognizing people, and wakes the family up every night to insist there are burglars in the house. He also occasionally runs away from home, and the police have to bring him back. Finally Akiko decides to put him in a nursing home; however, when she speaks to a government social worker, she learns that Shigezō does not qualify for nursing home care. The only facility that will accept him is a mental institution. Moreover, the social worker explains that there is a long waiting list for all types of elderly care in Japan. When Nobutoshi researches the subject himself, he learns that "the percentage of senior citizens had increased dramatically in Japan in recent years, and that very few measures had been taken to deal with the aged even in the advanced countries of the West. The more he investigated, the more he appreciated the gravity of each aspect of the problem—the psychological as well as the medical" (Ariyoshi 1987, 166).

As Nobutoshi and Akiko watch Shigezō deteriorate both physically and mentally, they begin to confront their own fears about aging. They talk to friends, family, colleagues, and geriatric experts about the problems associated with old age and with a society that "by about the year 2000" will have "more than 30 million people over sixty" and therefore be a "nation of senior citizens" (167). Several people tell them that "the young are no longer taught to respect the elderly" (118), even though the aged have great wisdom to share. At the same time Akiko and Nobutoshi are concerned about student unrest at the universities and worry that their own son might become involved in such "defiance" (193).

Nonetheless, they hire two of the student protesters, a young married couple, to look after Shigezō during the day. The arrangement allows Akiko to continue working three days a week. By now Shigezō is behaving like an infant. He must wear diapers, and when Akiko leaves him alone in the bath, he almost drowns. Finally he becomes ill, and he dies peacefully at home. Akiko handles the funeral arrangements calmly and expertly, having learned the traditional customs for burying the dead when her mother-in-law passed away. At that time she marveled about the high cost of funerals and "wondered how a family with only one breadwinner could make ends meet in these times of rampant inflation. Since both she and her husband worked, they had somehow managed up till now, but their end-of-year bonuses had been used up on the funeral expenses" of Nobutoshi's mother (48). Such criticisms of Japan's economy as it relates to the elderly and their health care appear frequently throughout *The Twilight Years.* (Ariyoshi 1987)

See also Ageism; Ariyoshi, Sawako; Tachibana, Akiko; Tachibana, Nobutoshi

U

Ugly American, The

The Ugly American, by William J. Lederer and Eugene Burdick, concerns the spread of communism in Southeastern Asia during the 1950s. Published in 1958 and set primarily in the fictional country of Sarkhan near Vietnam, the novel has little plot. Instead, it presents several characters and shows their successes or failures in dealing with the Asian people. In this regard, the novel depicts most of the American and French politicians and military leaders as appallingly ignorant of Asian customs and beliefs, whereas the Russians know much about the Asian culture. Moreover, whereas the Americans refuse to learn Sarkhanese, the Russians are fluent in Asian languages. Lederer and Burdick (1958, 275) discuss this difference in an epilogue to their novel, saying: "Think, for a moment, what it costs us whenever an official American representative demands that the native speak English, or not be heard. The Russians make no such mistake. The sign on the Russian Embassy in Ceylon, for example, identified it in Sinhalese, Tamil, English, and Russian. The American Embassy is identified only in English." The authors (275–276) also quote an American politician, John Foster Dulles, who says: "Interpreters are no substitute. It is not possible to understand what is in the minds of other people without understanding their language, and without understanding their language it is impossible to be sure that they understand what is on our minds."

Many characters in *The Ugly American* cause diplomatic problems because of their inability to understand Sarkhanese. They also behave in ways that offend the Asians, throwing lavish parties and refusing to socialize with the natives. These characters do not understand the needs of the lower classes or recognize the appeal of communism among the poor. The few Americans who are knowledgeable about such things are treated badly by the U.S. government. For example, when an engineer brought to Asia to help plan the construction of dams and military roads recommends that the money be spent instead on local projects such as brick factories and canning plants, the U.S. and French governments dismiss his advice as worthless. Similarly, an agricultural expert is ridiculed for suggesting that money be spent on chickens instead of a new canal. According to Lederer and Burdick (281), these characters were created "to point out the fact that we spend billions on the wrong aid projects while overlooking the almost costless and far more helpful ones."

In fact, *The Ugly American* illustrated so many deficiencies in the way the U.S. government was dealing with the Asians that the book created an uproar among the American

Tomas with his wife, Tereza, in a scene from the 1987 movie The Unbearable Lightness of Being, *which explores political and moral corruption. (Technicolor/The Museum of Modern Art Film Stills Archive)*

public. Eventually this led Congress to review its policies and change some of its practices regarding foreign aid. In addition, the term *ugly American* passed into the common language; it refers to Americans abroad who display insensitivity and ignorance regarding other cultures. (Lederer and Burdick 1958)

> **See also** Atkins, Homer; Brown, Jonathan; Burdick, Eugene; Communism; Lederer, William J.; MacWhite, Gilbert; Sears, Louis; *Ugly American, The*

Unbearable Lightness of Being, The

The Unbearable Lightness of Being, by Czechoslovakian author Milan Kundera, was published in English and French in 1984 and in its original language as *Nesnesitelná lehkost bytí* in 1985, but it was banned in Czechoslovakia until 1989. The novel primarily concerns love and personal choices, but it is set against a background of political unrest and has elements of social protest. The main character, Tomas, is a Czechoslovakian physician who becomes involved in one love affair after another while remaining detached from his

country's political troubles. One day in 1968, however, he writes a letter to a newspaper criticizing those who do nothing to stop Communist abuses of power. For him, ignorance is no excuse. He believes that "whether they knew or didn't know is not the main issue; the main issue is whether a man is innocent because he didn't know. . . . When Tomas heard Communists shouting in defense of their inner purity, he said to himself, As a result of your 'not knowing,' this country has lost its freedom, lost it for centuries, perhaps, and you shout that you feel no guilt? How can you stand the sight of what you've done? How is it you aren't horrified?" (Kundera 1984, 177).

The government pressures Tomas to retract his letter, and when he refuses, he is forced out of his job. Eventually he becomes a window washer. Meanwhile his wife, Tereza, worries that government agents have been spying on her. She was once a photographer who took pictures of political unrest to document her people's struggles for freedom, but she allowed her love for Tomas to pull her away from her work. At her urging Tomas abandons his many mistresses, and the couple moves to the country. Shortly thereafter both are reported killed in a car crash. (Kundera 1984)

See also Censorship; Kundera, Milan; Tereza; Tomas

Uncle Tom's Cabin

Uncle Tom's Cabin: Or, Life Among the Lowly, by Harriet Beecher Stowe, was published in serialized form in the *National Era,* a Washington, D.C., antislavery newspaper, from 1851 to 1852 and as a book in 1852. The novel offers a powerful protest of the institution of slavery, humanizing its African-American characters and presenting them in a positive light. As a result, many scholars believe that the book's publication and subsequent popularity hastened the onset of the U.S. Civil War.

The story's protagonist is an African-American man named Uncle Tom, who is owned by a white man named Mr. Shelby. Shelby treats his slaves well and does not want to sell any of them. However, when he falls into debt, he changes his mind. Despite protests from his wife and son George, he sells Tom and a young boy, Harry, to a slave dealer named Haley. Before the dealer can take him away, Harry's mother, Eliza, hears of this and escapes with her child across the Ohio River. Haley sends two slave catchers in pursuit. They encounter her in a Quaker settlement, but they are unable to capture her because by this time Eliza's husband, George, has also escaped and is there to defend her. George fights with the slave catchers; one of them is wounded, and the other flees.

Meanwhile Haley has shackled Tom and taken him on a boat bound for New Orleans. On route Tom saves the life of a young girl, Eva St. Clare, and her grateful father buys him. Tom becomes head coachman for the St. Clare family. For a while he is happy, but when Eva dies of an illness and her father is accidentally killed during a knife fight, Tom is sent to the slave market. This time he is bought by a cruel plantation owner named Simon Legree. Tom tries to please his new master, but when he is ordered to whip a woman

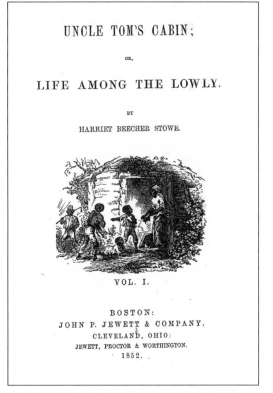

Frontispiece from the first edition of Uncle Tom's Cabin *by Harriet Beecher Stowe, 1852 (Library of Congress/ Rare Book Division)*

who did nothing wrong, he refuses and is himself flogged. Later he is flogged again when two female slaves turn up missing and Legree decides that Tom knows where they are. This beating is extremely harsh, and two days later Tom dies from his wounds. Just before his death George Shelby, the son of Tom's former owner, arrives to buy him back.

Seeing what has happened to Tom, George threatens to have Legree tried for murder, and when Legree laughs, George hits him. George then finds the two missing slaves, who have been hiding in an attic, and helps them escape the plantation. The two women eventually go to Canada, where Eliza and her husband, George, are now living with their son, Harry. Back on the plantation, George Shelby's father dies, and the young man frees all of his father's slaves in the name of Uncle Tom.

At the end of the novel its author offers a chapter of concluding remarks concerning her abolitionist views. Stowe (1960, 511) explains that her novel "has given only a faint shadow, a dim picture, of the anguish and despair that are, at this very moment, riving thousands of hearts, shattering thousands of families, and driving a helpless and sensitive race to frenzy and despair." She calls for an end to slavery, reminding her audience of their Christian beliefs, and she argues that the newly freed slaves should not be returned to Africa. Instead, she suggests that the United States has the obligation to provide former slaves with an education and chance to improve their lives in the United States. (Stowe 1960)

> See also Shelby, George; Slavery; Stowe, Harriet Beecher; Tom, Uncle

Undershaft, Andrew

Andrew Undershaft is one of the main characters in George Bernard Shaw's 1904 play *Major Barbara*. A wealthy munitions manufacturer, Undershaft is called immoral for making weapons of war. He counters his critics by pointing out that he is also providing the common people with a way to fight their oppressors and better themselves. At one point he says:

> I hate poverty and slavery worse than any other crimes whatsoever. And let me tell you this. Poverty and slavery have stood up for centuries to your sermons and . . . articles: they will not stand up to my machine guns. . . . Killing . . . is the final test of conviction, the only lever strong enough to overturn a social system, the only way of saying Must. . . . Whatever can blow men up can blow society up. The history of the world is the history of those who had courage enough to embrace this truth. (Shaw 1962, 436)

In the end the other characters in the play are persuaded to accept Undershaft's point of view. (Shaw 1962)

> See also *Major Barbara;* Shaw, George Bernard

Untouchable

Indian author Mulk Raj Anand wrote *Untouchable* in 1935 to publish the plight of the Untouchables in his native country. Responsible for cleaning latrines and sweeping dung, the Untouchables are the lowest caste in Hindu society. As such, they are forbidden to touch other human beings, and anything else they touch, such as a doorstep or a coin, must be ritually washed before anyone else can handle it.

According to Anand, as quoted by scholar Margaret Berry (1971, 40), his novel derives its conflict from "the anal-erotic complex of the puritan upper caste Hindus against whom [an Untouchable] is constrained to say: 'They think we are dung, because we clean their dung.' [This Untouchable] can't put it like a Professor of Psychology, but he says it in his own naïve manner. And his insights about the joy of the upper castes in seeing the outcasts condemned to do the business of cleaning at the same time as they express disgust against the untouchable reflects the paradox of the puritan temperament, unified for generations into ritualistic orthodoxy."

Berry (47–48) explains that "Anand's depiction of caste shows . . . that no one is ever so low that someone else is not lower, that snobbery flourishes everywhere. Among the untouchables, washermen hold themselves higher than leatherworkers; leatherworkers insist on preceding the sweepers." Moreover, the novel's main character, an Untouchable 18-year-old named Bakha who chafes at his restraints and longs for a classless society, "himself despises the beggars, a congeries of many castes" (48).

Untouchable depicts one day in Bakha's life. It begins well, with Bakha cheerfully going about his duties, cleaning latrines and streets, and playing field hockey with neighbor boys who ignore the fact that he is an Untouchable. However, when his father sends him on an errand and Bakha accidentally touches an adult, he is berated by an angry mob. From that moment on nothing seems the same to him. He is despondent about his position in life and is drawn to the temple, but as an Untouchable he is not allowed inside. He creeps up the steps anyway, and once again he finds himself berated by an angry mob. After several smaller indignities he returns home dejected and quarrels with his father.

Running away to sulk, Bakha comes upon a Salvation Army missionary who tries to convert him to Christianity. Bakha does not understand the man's teachings, so he goes instead to hear Mahatma Gandhi speak. Gandhi says that India's attitude toward the Untouchables is "the greatest blot on Hinduism" because "while we are asking for freedom from the grip of [the British], we have ourselves, for centuries, trampled underfoot millions of human beings without feeling the slightest remorse for our iniquity" (Anand 1940, 146). Gandhi believes that the Untouchables should no longer be oppressed.

This cheers Bakha, but he is more interested in a remark heard after Gandhi's speech, when a noted poet comments that "caste is now mainly governed by profession. When the sweepers change their profession, they will no longer remain Untouchables. And they can do that soon, for the first thing we will do . . . will be to introduce the machine which clears dung without anyone having to handle it—the flush system. Then the sweepers can be free from the stigma of untouchability and assume the dignity of status that is their right as useful members of a casteless and classless society" (155). Bakha is intrigued by the idea of such a machine and thinks about it all the way home.

Author E. M. Forster (vii-viii), writing in an introduction to the novel, finds this solution "prosaic, straightforward, and considered in the light of what has gone before in the book, it is very convincing. No god is needed to rescue the Untouchables, no vows of self-sacrifice and abnegation on the part of more fortunate Indians, but simply and solely—the flush system. Introduce water-closets and main-drainage throughout India, and all this wicked rubbish about untouchability will disappear." However, Berry (1971, 63) points out that the novel also deals with broader issues; it promotes socialism and "calls for a casteless and classless society." (Anand 1940; Berry 1971)

See also Anand, Mulk Raj; Bakha; Class, Social; Poverty; Socialism

"up & out"

The poem "up & out" first appeared in a collection entitled *Small Bones, Little Eyes*, by Native American poet nila northSun. It is typical of her work, which protests the social and economic hardships endured by her people. The poem speaks of Native Americans who try to better themselves by moving off the reservation and into cities, where they can make more money. But although they get good jobs, they soon discover that their cost of living is higher. The poem explains: "We made better money but it / got sucked up" (Velie 1991, 291). Therefore, they feel poorer than ever before. (Velie 1991)

See also Native American Issues; northSun, nila

V

Valjean, Jean

Jean Valjean is the main character in Victor Hugo's 1862 novel *Les Misérables*, which concerns poverty, morality, and injustice. Sentenced to 5 years in prison for stealing a loaf of bread for his sister's starving family, Valjean serves 19 because of several escape attempts. This experience hardens him. After his release he steals a bishop's silver and a small boy's coin, but his conscience is troubled, and he decides to change his life. He takes a new name, moves to a small town, and eventually becomes a man of good standing in the community. Highly respected by all, he donates large sums of money to the poor. Nonetheless, when his true identity is uncovered, he is sentenced to life in prison for theft. Later he escapes and, under another assumed name, again lives a good and charitable life. But because he is afraid of capture, he does not truly live a free life. (Hugo 1987)

See also Hugo, Victor; *Misérables, Les*

Valtoskar, Piera

One of the main characters in Ursula Le Guin's 1979 novel *Malafrena,* Piera Valtoskar lives in Europe during the early nineteenth century. As a young girl she is concerned about nothing but marriage, but as she matures, she realizes that other things in life are more important. She breaks tradition and takes over the management of her father's estate when he becomes ill, proving herself as competent as any man. In the end she doubts whether she will ever take a husband, saying: "I don't understand what love is, or what it's supposed to be. Why is it supposed to be my whole life?" (Le Guin 1979, 268). (Le Guin 1979)

See also Le Guin, Ursula; *Malafrena*

Verhaeren, Émile

Born on May 21, 1855, in Saint Amand lez-Puers, Belgium, Émile Verhaeren was a poet who often wrote about social problems. His most well-known works in this regard are "Les Villages illusoires" (The Illusory Villages) and "Les Villes tentaculaires" (The Tentacled Cities). Both poems were published in 1895 and concern the decline of peasant life. Verhaeren believed in socialism and bemoaned the loss of rural communities. As a young man he studied law but became involved in a Brussels literary group and decided to write. His first book was published in 1883. A collection of poems entitled *Les Flamandes,* it praised peasant life and was very popular. Verhaeren produced more than 30 volumes of poetry over the ensuing years. His works include *Les Moines* (The Monks, 1886), *Les Campagnes hallucinées* (The Moonstruck

Jean Valjean attempts to defend himself in an illustration from Les Misérables, *which explores the conditions that led to the French Revolution of 1830. (North Wind Picture Archive)*

Countryside, 1893), and a trilogy of love poems to his wife entitled *Les Heures claires* (The Sunlit Hours, 1896), *Les Heures d'apres-midi* (The Afternoon Hours, 1905), and *Les Heures du soir* (The Evening Hours, 1918). He also wrote short stories, plays, and books on art. Verhaeren died on November 27, 1916, in Rouen, France.

See also Class, Social; Poverty

Verhovensky, Pyotr Stepanovitch

Leader of a Russian revolutionary group in Dostoyevsky's novel *Besy* (The Possessed), which was published in two volumes between 1871 and 1872, Pyotr Verhovensky manipulates people to gain social and political advantage. An avowed atheist, he has no conscience. He hires a convict named Fedka to kill two people because they threaten the secrecy of his group, and after the murders, when Fedka argues with him, Verhovensky decides to kill him, too. Verhovensky also kills a member of his group, Shatov, who wants to leave the organization, and he encourages another man, Kirillov, to take the blame for the murder and commit suicide. In the end Verhovensky escapes to Petersburg, leaving his followers to suffer for his crimes. (Dostoyevsky 1936; Dostoyevsky 1968)

See also Dostoyevsky, Fyodor; *Possessed, The;* Shatov; Stavrogin, Nikolay Vsyevolodovitch

Verne, Jules

Jules Verne is the author of several famous science fiction novels. One of them, the futuristic *Paris au XXe Siècle* (Paris in the Twentieth Century), is an important work of social protest, but the manuscript was rejected for publication in Verne's time and did not resurface until 1994. Verne was born on February 8, 1828, in Nantes, France. He studied law but later chose to become a playwright. His first success in this regard was *Les Pailles rompues* (The Broken Straws), which was produced at the Theatre Historique in 1850. He worked as a secretary for that theater from 1852 to 1854. He subsequently became a stockbroker but continued to write.

His first novel, *Voyages extraordinaires— Cinq semaines en ballon* (Five Weeks in a Balloon), was published in 1863, followed by *Le Voyage au centre de la Terre* (Journey to the Center of the Earth) in 1864, *De la Terre à la Lune* (From the Earth to the Moon) in 1865, *Vingt Mille Lieus sous les mer* (Twenty Thousand Leagues under the Sea) in 1869, *Le Tour du mond en quatre-vingt jour* (Around the World in Eighty Days) in 1873, and *L'Île mystérieuse* (The Mysterious Island) in 1874. All of Verne's works were extremely popular, and they uncannily predicted many future inventions. Verne died on March 24, 1905, in Amiens, France. (Quackenbush 1985)

See also *Paris in the Twentieth Century;* Science Fiction and Fantasy

Vonnegut, Kurt

Kurt Vonnegut is a novelist who uses science fiction and satire to criticize various aspects of modern society. Born on November 11, 1922, in Indianapolis, Indiana, he worked for an electric company until 1950, when he became a freelance writer and began selling his short stories to science fiction magazines. His first novel was published in 1952. Entitled *Player Piano*, it depicts a futuristic United States in which the workers have been replaced by machines and society is beginning to crumble. Vonnegut's best-known novels are *Cat's Cradle* (1963) and *Slaughterhouse Five* (1969), which concern war and global destruction. He continues to write novels, plays, short stories, articles, and autobiographical works. His most recent novels include *Galapagos* (1985), *Bluebeard* (1987), and *Hocus Pocus* (1990). (Schatt 1976)

See also *Player Piano;* Science Fiction and Fantasy

W

Walker, Alice

Alice Walker writes primarily about black feminist issues in the United States. Born on February 9, 1944, in Eatonton, Georgia, she participated in the civil rights movement in the 1960s, and her first published writings were poetry collections. They include *Once* (1968) and *Revolutionary Petunias* (1973). Her first novel was *The Third Life of Grange Copeland* (1970), which concerns racism among black sharecroppers. She has written several more novels, poems, and short stories dealing with issues of racism and feminism but is perhaps best known for *The Color Purple.* This 1982 novel received the Pulitzer Prize and was made into a highly successful motion picture in 1985. In 1989 Walker published a sequel to the work, *The Temple of My Familiar,* which includes some of the same characters but addresses new themes. Her most recent works include the novels *Possessing the Secret of Joy* (1992), *Everyday Use* (1994), and *By the Light of My Father's Smile* (1998), a collection of essays entitled *In Search of Our Mother's Gardens* (1983), and the nonfiction book *Warrior Marks: Female Genital Mutilation and the Sexual Blinding of Women* (1993). (Gates and Appiah 1993a; Winchell 1992)

See also *Color Purple, The;* Feminism; Racism; *Temple of My Familiar, The*

Alice Walker, 1991 (F. Capri/Saga/Archive Photos)

Watch on the Rhine

The three-act drama *Watch on the Rhine,* by American playwright Lillian Hellman, was first performed in April 1941. It concerns an antifascist freedom fighter, Kurt Muller, who eventually commits murder to protect his family. Muller is visiting his wife's relatives in the United States when another houseguest, Teck de Brancovis, discovers his true identity and antifascist activities. Brancovis threatens to turn Muller in to his enemies, so Muller murders him and makes plans to return to Europe. Before he leaves, he compares his situation to that of a character in a novel, saying:

> Do you remember when we read "*Les Misérables*"? . . . Well, he stole bread. The world is out of shape we said, when there are hungry men. And until it gets in shape, men will steal and lie and— . . . kill. But for whatever reason it is done, and whoever does it—you understand me—it is all bad. I want you to remember that. Whoever does it, it is bad. . . . But you will live to see the day when it will not have to be. All over the world, in every place and every town, there are men who are going to make sure it will not have to be. They want what I want: a childhood for every child. For my children, and I for theirs. . . . In every town and every village and every mud hut in the world, there is always a man who loves children and will fight to make a good world for them. (Hellman 1979, 299)

(Hellman 1979)

See also Fascism; Hellman, Lillian; *Misérables, Les*

Welch, James

Born in 1940 in Browning, Montana, James Welch is a Native American poet and novelist who writes about the history and experiences of his people. He grew up on reservations and attended the University of Montana. A collection of his poetry entitled *Riding the Earthboy 40* was published in 1971. Its poems, which include "Surviving" and "Harlem, Montana: Just Off the Reservation," depict reservation life, as does his first novel, *Winter in the Blood,* which was published in 1974. His other novels include *The Death of Jim Loney* (1979),

Fools Crow (1986), and *The Indian Lawyer* (1990). (Velie 1991)

See also "Harlem, Montana: Just Off the Reservation"; Native American Issues; "Surviving"

Wells, H. G.

Writing in the late nineteenth and early twentieth centuries, English novelist Herbert George Wells correctly predicted many future inventions. At one point he believed that science would solve humanity's problems, but later he decided that society's overdependence on technology would eventually destroy it. He also used his works to criticize various aspects of capitalism and class structure.

Wells was born on September 21, 1866, in Bromley, Kent, England. The son of a maid and a shopkeeper, he received a scholarship to the Normal School of Science in London, and after graduation he attended London University on a grant. The university awarded him a degree in biology in 1890. Shortly thereafter he decided to become a freelance writer.

At first he wrote articles and short stories, but later he turned to novels. His first book, *The Time Machine,* was published 1895 to immediate success. It is considered one of the first works of science fiction but is also a commentary on the class structure, depicting a futuristic London society that has split into two races: the materialistic, flighty Eloi and the laboring Moloch who care for them in order to eat them.

Wells's subsequent works include *The Invisible Man* (1897), *The War of the Worlds* (1898), and *Tono-Bungay* (1908), which criticizes many aspects of London society. He also wrote a nonfiction work on social issues, *Anticipations* (1901). Shortly thereafter he joined a socialist group called the Fabian Society, whose founders include George Bernard Shaw, but Wells left over a philosophical disagreement. Throughout his life he continued to write nonfiction books outlining his position on social problems. These include *A Modern Utopia* (1906), *New Worlds for Old* (1908), *The Shape of Things to Come* (1933), and *The Work, Wealth, and Happiness of*

Mankind (1931), which he coauthored. Wells also wrote a one-volume history of humanity entitled *Outline of History,* which was published in 1920 and revised in 1931. He died in London, England, on August 13, 1946. (Scheick and Cox 1988)

See also Science Fiction and Fantasy; Shaw, George Bernard; Socialism; *Tono-Bungay*

West, Julian

Julian West is the fictional narrator of Edward Bellamy's 1887 novel *Looking Backward, 2000–1887.* Born in Boston on December 26, 1857, by the age of 30 West has developed terrible insomnia, and after a hypnotist helps him fall asleep, he accidentally wakes up 113 years later, in the year 2000. Subsequently, from his perspective as an inhabitant of two very different societies, West reports on the contrasts between the nineteenth century, with its labor struggles and poverty, and the twentieth century, which he views as a utopia of equality and justice. He eventually becomes a historian and marries Edith Leete, who is the great-granddaughter of a woman he loved in his previous life. (Bellamy 1982)

See also Bellamy, Edward; Capitalism; Leete, Edith; *Looking Backward, 2000–1887;* Poverty; Socialism

Wharton, Edith

Edith Wharton was born Edith Jones on January 24, 1862, in New York, New York, and married Boston banker Edward Wharton in 1885. A member of upper-class society, she wrote about her world and criticized its rigid attitudes and customs. Her work has often been compared to that of another critic of social norms, Henry James, with whom she was acquainted. Wharton's first successful writing was a book entitled *The Decoration of Houses* (1897), an attack on upper-class interior decorating. Later she incorporated her interest in decorating and architecture in her fiction, using detailed settings and commenting on the order or disorder in her characters' homes and lives.

Wharton's first story collection was *The Greater Inclination* (1899) and her first novel

The Valley of Decision (1902). Her first successful book was *The House of Mirth* (1905), the story of a woman who descends from the upper classes into poverty. Two years after its publication Wharton began having an affair, and six years after that she divorced her husband. She moved to France and remained there for the rest of her life, receiving the French Legion of Honor award in 1916 for her volunteer work with war refugees during World War I. In addition to this work, she continued to write. Her novels include *Ethan Frome* (1911), *The Reef* (1912), *The Custom of the Country* (1913), and *The Age of Innocence* (1920), which won her the Pulitzer Prize in 1921. She was the first woman to receive this honor. Wharton also wrote short stories, poetry, an autobiography, and several nonfiction books, including *The Writing of Fiction* (1925). Her last novel, *The Buccaneers* (1938), was published posthumously. Wharton died on August 11, 1937, in St.-Brice-sous-Foret, France. (Howe 1962)

See also *Age of Innocence, The;* Feminism; James, Henry

Wilde, Oscar

Oscar Wilde is considered one of Ireland's greatest writers. He wrote poetry, plays, essays, and a novel, *The Picture of Dorian Gray* (1891). Several of his plays, including *The Importance of Being Earnest* (1895), reveal flaws within Victorian society, and his most important poem, "The Ballad of Reading Gaol" (1898), protests inhumane prison conditions.

Wilde was born on October 16, 1854, in Dublin, Ireland, and attended Trinity College there. In 1881 he published his first volume of poetry, and he toured the United States and Canada in 1882 to lecture on writing. In 1884 he married and had two children, but in 1891 he became romantically involved with Lord Alfred Douglas. Because of his relationship with this man, Wilde was eventually sentenced to two years of hard labor. It was this experience that prompted him to write "The Ballad of Reading Gaol." After his release Wilde found himself bankrupt. He moved to

Paris, France, where he died on November 30, 1900. (Aldington 1946; Ellman 1969)

See also "Ballad of Reading Gaol, The"; Prison Reform

Woman, A

Published in Italy as *Una Donna* in 1906, *A Woman,* by Sibilla Aleramo, concerns the plight of Italian women during the early 1900s. At that time they were under the complete control of their fathers and husbands, with no rights under the law. Therefore, the novel's publication engendered great controversy, particularly after it was translated into English in 1908, and it has since been hailed as one of the most important feminist works in world literature.

Written in the first person, *A Woman* is largely autobiographical, describing Aleramo's own struggles to free herself from an abusive husband. Like Aleramo, the narrator of the story was raped at the age of 15 and forced to marry her rapist to maintain her honor. Despite her husband's brutal nature, she tries to be a dutiful wife and, later, a good mother to her son. Nonetheless, her life is miserable, and eventually she tries to commit suicide. After her attempt fails, she begins to write to maintain her sanity. Her articles appear in many Italian magazines, and she is offered an editing job in Rome. When her husband loses his job, he allows her to accept the position, and they move to the city.

Now the narrator experiences a new sense of freedom and begins fighting with her husband. When he decides to move back to his small town, she asks him for a separation. After some argument he agrees, but he tells her she will never see her son again. She remains in Rome thinking that the law will help her gain custody of her child. However, she soon finds she has no rights in that regard. Left with no way to tell her son why she left him, she writes a novel for him to read when he is older.

In addition to offering this story, *A Woman* comments on the role of women in Italian society. For example, the narrator speaks of the way mothers sacrifice their identities for their children, saying: "Who gave us this inhuman idea that mothers should negate their own wishes and desires? The acceptance of servitude has been handed down from mother to daughter for so many centuries that it is now a monstrous chain which fetters them. . . . What if mothers refused to deny their womanhood and gave their children instead an example of a life lived according to the needs of self-respect?"(Aleramo 1983, 193–194).

The narrator also criticizes poets who praise only women who are "unattainable," yet fail to mention "the women they lived with, who bore their children! They idolised one set of women in verse, while the prosaic reality of their lives was that even if they married them they turned the women they lived with into domestic servants" (156). She speaks often of women as slaves, as mere sexual objects whose sole duty is to satisfy their husbands or be beaten for their defiance. In addition, the narrator mentions the beginnings of socialism in Italy, expressing her desire to see all people live decent lives. In fact, at the end of *A Woman* the narrator satisfies her longing for her own child by helping other children at a clinic for the poor. (Aleramo 1983)

See also Aleramo, Sibilla; Feminism

Women's Rights
See Feminism

Working Conditions
See Labor Issues

Wright, Nel
Nel Wright is the childhood friend of Sula Peace, the main character in Toni Morrison's 1973 novel *Sula.* Whereas Sula is rebellious and promiscuous, Nel conforms to the expectations of the black community in which she lives. She marries but separates from her husband when he and Sula have an affair. At this point Nel ends her friendship with Sula. Afterward her life is colorless, and when Sula dies, Nel realizes how much she missed by losing her friend. (Gates and Appiah 1993c; Morrison 1974)

See also Feminism; Morrison, Toni; Peace, Sula; *Sula*

Wright, Richard

Richard Wright has written novels and short stories protesting racism in the United States during the 1940s and 50s. Born near Natchez, Mississippi, on September 4, 1908, he was the grandson of southern slaves and grew up in poverty. He held a variety of jobs before joining the Federal Writers' Project during the Depression, first in Chicago and then in New York. In 1932 he joined the Communist Party and began writing for Communist publications. He became the Harlem editor of the *Daily Worker* in 1937. The following year he gained recognition with the publication of *Uncle Tom's Children*, a volume of novellas. His first novel, *Native Son* (1940), only increased his fame. It was extremely popular and triggered a great deal of discussion about the nature and causes of racism in the United States.

In subsequent works Wright continued to write about racism, and eventually he decided that American society would never consider blacks equal to whites. Consequently, in 1945 he moved to Paris, France. By this time he had become dissatisfied with the Communist Party and broken his ties to it. His novel *The Outsider* (1953) reflects this dissatisfaction. Wright's other works include an autobiograph-

Richard Wright, 1950 (Archive Photos)

ical novel, *Black Boy* (1945), a nonfiction book entitled *Black Power* (1954), and a posthumously published collection of short stories, *Eight Men* (1961). Wright died on November 28, 1960, in Paris, France. (Webb 1968)

See also *Native Son; Outsider, The;* Racism

Y

Yakovlich, Sofron

Sofron Yakovlich is a cruel overseer in the short story "Bailiff," from a collection by Ivan Turgenev entitled *Zapiski okhotnika* (A Sportsman's Sketches). Yakovlich exploits the serfs under his control, manipulating the serf system in order to make himself rich at the peasants' expense. When they protest, he makes their situation worse or beats them into compliance. In describing Yakovlich, one peasant says: "Clever, awful clever he is, and rich, too, the varmint! What's bad about him is—he's always knocking someone about. A wild beast, not a man. I tell you he's a dog, a cur, a real cur if ever there was one" (Turgenev 1983, 116). (Turgenev 1983)

See also *Sportsman's Sketches, A;* Turgenev, Ivan

Yellow Horse

In *Little Big Man,* Thomas Berger's 1964 novel about the mistreatment of Native Americans during the 1800s, Yellow Horse is a gay man whose Cheyenne tribe not only tolerates him but also appreciates him. The narrator of the story explains: "If a Cheyenne don't believe he can stand a man's life, he ain't forced to. He can become a heemaneh, which is to say half-man, half-woman. There are uses for these fellows and everybody likes them. They are sometimes chemists, specializing in the making of love-potions, and generally good entertainers. They wear women's clothes and can get married to another man, if such be his taste" (Berger 1964, 76–77). Throughout the novel the Cheyenne are shown to be loving, accepting people, in contrast to the whites, who have many prejudices. (Berger 1964; Landon 1989)

See also Berger, Thomas; Crabbe, Jack; Gay and Lesbian Issues; *Little Big Man;* Old Lodge Skins; Racism

Yevtushenko, Yevgeny

During the 1950s and 1960s Russian poet Yevgeny Aleksandrovich Yevtushenko (also spelled Evgenii Evtushenko) was an outspoken critic of the way the Soviet government sought to limit artistic freedom. A gifted speaker, he was popular with the public and spread his message through poetry readings in Europe, the United States, and Australia. Born on July 18, 1933, Yevtushenko was a descendent of Ukrainians exiled to Siberia. He studied at the Gorky Institute of World Literature in Moscow and produced a large body of work during his lifetime. He is perhaps best known for the 1961 poem "Babii Yar" (also spelled "Baby Yar" or "Babi Yar"), which criticizes anti-Semitism in the Soviet Union. In 1963 he published his *A Precocious Autobiog-*

271

raphy in English without prior approval of Soviet censors. This led the Soviet government to recall him from one of his reading tours and revoke many of his privileges. Eventually his rights were restored, and for a time he continued to live and write in Russia. His later works include a novel, *Yagodnyye mesta* (Wild Berries, 1981), and *The Collected Poems, 1952–1990* (1991). In writing about his work, Yevtushenko (1989) once said that he intended his poems to promote "liberation from the tyranny of censorship, from the tyranny of the observing eye of Orwell's Big Brother." Today Yevtushenko lives in the United States. In 1996 he was appointed a professor of Russian literature at Queen's College in New York, where in 1966 he gave his first American poetry reading. (Yevtushenko 1989)

See also Anti-Semitism; "Babii Yar"; Censorship; Orwell, George

Yonnondio: From the Thirties

The title of this unfinished novel, *Yonnondio*, is a Native American word meaning "lament for the lost." Its story focuses on the hardships of working-class Americans during the 1920s. Although the novel was not published until 1974, the first chapter of *Yonnondio* appeared as a short story, "The Iron Throat," in a 1934 issue of the radical journal the *Partisan Review*. During the Great Depression, author Tillie Olsen was a political activist involved in labor and feminist issues.

Yonnondio follows two and a half years in the life of the Holbrook family: Jim Holbrook; his wife, Anna; and his children, Mazie, Will, Ben, Jim Junior, and Bess, who is born during the course of the story. At first Jim is a miner in a Wyoming mining town. Every day he risks lung damage from mine dust or death from a cave-in, while his wife and children endure poor living conditions and have little hope of bettering themselves. Finally he decides to become a tenant farmer, and the family travels to the Dakotas, where the children have good food and start going to school. However, at the end of the year Jim discovers that he is in debt to his landlord and must give up his livestock and some of his possessions.

The family leaves the farm and moves to a rental house in a midwestern city. Jim is soon hired to dig sewer ditches, but in this job, too, he finds it difficult to get ahead. Eventually he quits and gets a position at the local meat-packing house. There his pay is better, but the working conditions are horrible. The packing house bosses want the employees to work as quickly as possible and to take few breaks. During a heat wave, temperatures inside the packing house reach 108 degrees, but workers are still not allowed to slow down. As a result, one suffers a heart attack, and others are scalded when a steam pipe breaks.

Tillie Olsen knew about such labor abuses firsthand. Shortly before beginning to write *Yonnondio,* she was jailed for helping to organize workers in the Kansas City meatpacking industry. Later, in 1934, she became involved in a longshoreman's strike and various other forms of union activity. She was particularly concerned with the plight of female workers, whom she believed were doubly oppressed because of their gender. A feminist, Olsen uses the characters of Anna and her daughter Mazie to show how society conditions women to accept a subservient role.

It is Jim, not Anna, who makes the decisions in the family. Although he appears to love her, he ignores her opinions about where they should live and what they should do. Moreover, he treats many of her concerns as foolish, and on one occasion when she refuses to make love to him, he rapes her. But Anna does not teach her daughter to expect better, and when Mazie expresses an interest in male activities, Anna tells her that girls do not do such things.

Anna eventually suffers for her oppression. She has a miscarriage, becomes ill, and begins to lose touch with reality. Had Olsen finished the novel, Anna's fate was to have been far worse. Deborah Rosenfelt, who studied Olsen's papers and notes, says in her essay "From the Thirties: Tillie Olsen and the Radical Tradition" (Nelson and Huse 1994, 72):

What we have today is only the beginning of the novel that was to have been. In

Olsen's initial plan, Jim Holbrook was to have become involved in a strike in the packing houses, a strike that would draw out the inner strength and courage of his wife Anna, politicize the older children as well, and involve some of the women in the packing plant as strike leaders in the essential collective action. Embittered by the length of the strike and its lack of clear initial success, humiliated by his inability to support his family, Jim Holbrook was finally to have abandoned them. Anna was to die trying to give herself an abortion. Will and Mazie were to go West to the Imperial Valley in California, where they would themselves become organizers. Mazie was to grow up to become an artist, a writer who could tell the experiences of her people, her mother especially living in her memory.

Many scholars have noted that the character of Mazie is partly autobiographical. Olsen experienced many of the same events as Mazie, including her family's move to the meatpacking town of Omaha. In addition, her father was a member of the Socialist Party who actively supported the unionization of American workers. (Nelson and Huse 1994; Olsen 1980)

See also Feminism; Holbrook Family; Labor Issues; Olsen, Tillie

Yossarian, Captain John

As the main character in Joseph Heller's 1961 novel *Catch-22,* Captain John Yossarian points out the absurdities of war. He is a bombardier stationed in Italy during World War II who feigns insanity to try to get out of flying. However, because the air force considers the desire to avoid warfare sane, Yossarian is judged fit for service. Tired of the death and corruption he sees all around him, he eventually escapes to neutral Sweden. (Heller 1994)

See also *Catch-22;* Heller, Joseph

Younger Family

The Youngers are the main characters in Lorraine Hansberry's three-act play *A Raisin in the Sun* (1959). Lena Younger, the head of the household, is a strong-willed matriarch who works as a domestic servant. Her daughter-in-law, Ruth, also cleans white people's houses, and her son, Walter, is a white man's chauffeur. Lena's daughter, Beneatha, is in school and wants to become a doctor. Her grandson, Travis, does not know what he wants to become, but he says he would be happy driving a bus. This makes his father mad.

The family lives together in a roach-infested ghetto apartment, sharing the bathroom with another family. The Youngers are discouraged but gain strength from one another and from pride in their African heritage. At the end of the play they are in the process of moving to a new home in an all-white neighborhood, where they will clearly not be welcome. (Hansberry 1994)

See also Hansberry, Lorraine; Racism; *Raisin in the Sun, A*

Z

Zaius

Zaius is an orangutan who appears in the 1963 science fiction novel *La Planète des singes* (Planet of the Apes), by Pierre Boulle. Zaius lives on a planet where apes behave like humans and humans like apes. A leading scientist, he is extremely narrow-minded, refusing to accept facts that counter his opinions. In fact, when he is presented with a human who acts like an ape, he wants to destroy him. (Boulle 1963)

See also Boulle, Pierre; *Planet of the Apes*

Zakeya

Zakeya is the main character in the 1974 Egyptian feminist novel *Mawt al-rajul al-wahid 'ala 'l-ard* (God Dies by the Nile), by Nawal El Saadawi. At the beginning of the novel Zakeya is hoeing crops and trying to forget her hard life. Then her brother, Kafrawi, comes to tell her that his daughter Nefissa has run away. Nefissa had been a servant in the house of the village mayor, who is a cruel tyrant. Now the mayor wants her younger sister, Zeinab, to take over the job. When she refuses, the mayor contrives to have Kafrawi arrested for a crime he did not commit. Shortly thereafter Zeinab marries Galal, and the mayor arranges for him to be arrested, too. Zeinab runs away, and Zakeya realizes that the mayor raped both of her nieces. She takes up her hoe and bludgeons him to death. (El Saadawi 1990)

See also El Saadawi, Nawal; Feminism; *God Dies by the Nile*

Zangwill, Israel

Novelist and playwright Israel Zangwill wrote about the lives of Jewish immigrants in London ghettos. Born on February 14, 1864, in London, England, he was himself the son of immigrants and eventually became a Zionist leader. His best-known work is the novel *Children of the Ghetto* (1892), which shows the struggles of Jews trying to maintain their spirituality in a Christian culture. Zangwill wrote not only novels but also plays on immigrant culture, as well as a collection of essays on famous Jews. He died on August 1, 1926, in Midhurst, West Sussex, England. (Leftwich 1957)

See also Anti-Semitism; *Children of the Ghetto;* Poverty

Zeinab

Zeinab is a young peasant woman in Nawal El Saadawi's 1974 feminist novel *Mawt al-rajul al-wahid 'ala 'l-ard* (God Dies by the Nile). Beautiful and kind, she is the object of the village mayor's lust. He forces her to be his mistress, and when she marries and refuses to see him anymore, he has her husband arrested on a false charge. Nonetheless, Zeinab remains firm in rejecting the mayor. She leaves the village to visit her husband in jail but is waylaid by a man who wants her sexual favors. She is never seen again. (El Saadawi 1990)

See also El Saadawi, Nawal; *God Dies by the Nile*

Ziemssen, Joachim

A character in Thomas Mann's 1924 novel *Der Zauberberg* (The Magic Mountain), Joachim Ziemssen is a single-minded, practical soldier. He is therefore very unlike his cousin, Hans Castorp, an intellectual who allows other people to influence his decisions. Both men live in a mountain sanitorium, but whereas Hans revels in his illness and remains under a doctor's care even after he is pronounced well, Joachim denies his illness and leaves the sanitorium to further his military career. He spends several enjoyable months reveling in life, then returns to the sanitorium to die. (Mann 1972)

See also Castorp, Hans; *Magic Mountain, The;* Mann, Thomas

Zola, Émile

French novelist Émile Zola often wrote about the relationship between social conditions and evil. In this regard he created a sequence of 20 novels known collectively as the Rougon-Macquart Cycle (1871–1893), which depict such social ills as alcoholism among the labor classes and covetousness among peasants. Zola was born in Paris, France, on April 2, 1840. After failing his university examinations, he was unemployed for two years. Then he became a clerk in a shipping company and later worked for a publishing company. There he was encouraged to write, and in 1864 his first work, a collection of short stories entitled

Émile Zola (Library of Congress/Corbis)

Contes à Ninon, was published. His other works include *La Confession de Claude* (1865) and *Thérèse Raquin* (1867).

In later years Zola became involved in a famous court case involving anti-Semitism. He and many other French writers, including Anatole France, protested the unfair conviction of a Jewish army officer accused of treason. To bring the case to public attention, Zola wrote a letter, "J'Accuse" (I Accuse), which accused the French military of being prejudiced and deceitful. This letter was published in the January 13, 1898, edition of the newspaper *L'Aurore,* and the following month Zola was convicted of libel, fined 3,000 francs, and sentenced to one year in prison. He fled to London, where he remained until he was pardoned in 1899. He died in Paris, France, on September 28, 1902. (Grant 1966)

See also France, Anatole; Rougon-Macquart Cycle

REFERENCES

Aaron, Daniel. 1961. *Writers on the Left: Episodes in American Literary Communism*. New York: Harcourt, Brace and World.

Abbey Edward. 1975. *The Monkey Wrench Gang*. Philadelphia: Lippincott.

Abrahams, Peter. 1975. *The Path of Thunder*. Chatham, NJ: Chatham Bookseller.

Aji, Aron (ed.). 1992. *Milan Kundera and the Art of Fiction: Critical Essays*. New York: Garland.

Aldington, Richard (ed.). 1946. *The Portable Oscar Wilde*. New York: Viking Press.

Alegría, Ciro. 1941. *Broad and Alien Is the World*. New York: Farrar and Rinehart.

Aleramo, Sibilla. 1983. *A Woman*. Berkeley and Los Angeles: University of California Press.

Allende, Isabel. 1985. *The House of the Spirits*. New York: Knopf.

———. 1988. *Eva Luna*. New York: Bantam Books.

Anand, Mulk Raj. 1940. *Untouchable*. New York: Penguin Books.

Angelou, Maya. 1994. *The Complete Collected Poems of Maya Angelou*. New York: Random House.

Aristophanes. 1930. *Aristophanes: The Eleven Comedies*. New York: Horace Liveright.

Ariyoshi, Sawako. 1987. *The Twilight Years*. Trans. Mildred Tahara. New York: Kodansha America.

Atkins, John. 1968. *Aldous Huxley: A Literary Study*. New York: Orion Press.

Atwood, Margaret. 1986. *The Handmaid's Tale*. Boston: Houghton Mifflin.

———. 1996. *The Edible Woman*. New York: Bantam Books.

Babb, Valerie Melissa. 1991. *Ernest Gaines*. Boston: Twayne.

Baker, James R. 1965. *William Golding: A Critical Study*. New York: St. Martin's Press.

Baker, James Thomas. 1987. *Ayn Rand*. Boston: Twayne.

Baldwin, James. 1962. *Another Country*. New York: Dial Press.

———. 1988. *If Beale Street Could Talk*. New York: Dell.

Banning, Evelyn I. 1973. *Helen Hunt Jackson*. New York: Vanguard Press.

Barker, Dudley. 1969. *The Man of Principle: A Biography of John Galsworthy*. New York: Stein and Day.

Barnard, Marjorie Faith. 1967. *Miles Franklin*. New York: Twayne.

Barrow, Georgia M. 1979. *Ageing, Ageism, and Society*. St. Paul, MN: West.

Behn, Aphra. 1973. *Oroonoko: or, The Royal Slave*. New York: Norton.

Bellamy, Edward. 1951. *Looking Backward, 2000–1887*. Introduction by Robert Shurter. New York: Modern Library.

———. 1982. *Looking Backward, 2000–1887*. Introduction by Cecelia Tichi. New York: Penguin Books.

Benson, Brian Joseph, and Mabel Mayle Dillard. 1980. *Jean Toomer*. Boston: Twayne.

Berger, Thomas. 1964. *Little Big Man*. New York: Dial Press.

Berry, Margaret. 1971. *Mulk Raj Anand: The Man and the Novelist.* Amsterdam: Oriental Press.

Björnson, Björnstjerne. 1916. *Plays by Björnson Björnstjerne.* Trans. Edwin Björkman. New York: Scribner's.

Bloodworth, William A. 1977. *Upton Sinclair.* Boston: Twayne.

Bloom, Harold (ed.). 1989. *Modern Critical Views: Albert Camus.* New York: Chelsea House.

Boulle, Pierre. 1963. *Planet of the Apes.* New York: Signet.

Bowman, Sylvia. 1962. *Edward Bellamy Abroad: An American Prophet's Influence.* New York: Twayne.

———. 1979. *The Year 2000: A Critical Biography of Edward Bellamy.* New York: Octagon Books.

———. 1986. *Edward Bellamy.* Boston: Twayne.

Boyer, Paul S. 1968. *Purity in Print: The Vice-Society Movement and Book Censorship in America.* New York: Scribner's.

Bradbury, Ray. 1996. *Fahrenheit 451.* New York: Ballantine Books.

Brander, Lawrence. 1970. *Aldous Huxley: A Critical Study.* London: Hart-Davis.

Brée, Germaine. 1961. *Camus.* New Brunswick, NJ: Rutgers University Press.

Brewster, Dorothy. 1965. *Doris Lessing.* New York: Twayne.

Breytenbach, Breyten. 1994. *A Season in Paradise.* San Diego: Harcourt, Brace.

Brustein, Robert. 1964. *The Theatre of Revolt.* Boston: Little, Brown.

Burgess, Anthony. 1986. *A Clockwork Orange.* New York: Norton.

Butler, Marilyn. 1972. *Maria Edgeworth: A Literary Biography.* Oxford: Clarendon Press.

Butler, Ronnie. 1983. *Balzac and the French Revolution.* Totowa, NJ: Barnes and Noble Books.

Callan, Edward. 1982. *Alan Paton.* Boston: Twayne.

Camus, Albert. 1958. *The Fall.* Trans. Justin O'Brien. New York: Knopf.

———. 1989. *The Stranger.* Trans. Matthew Ward. New York: Vintage Books.

Carter, April. 1971. *The Political Theory of Anarchism.* New York: Harper and Row.

Carter, Stephen. 1977. *The Politics of Solzhenitsyn.* New York: Holmes & Meier.

Chamberlain, Robert Lyall. 1965. *George Crabbe.* New York: Twayne.

Cheney, Anne. 1984. *Lorraine Hansberry.* Boston: Twayne.

Cherkovski, Neeli. 1979. *Ferlinghetti: A Biography.* Garden City, NY: Doubleday.

Clark, Barrett Harper. 1947. *Eugene O'Neill: The Man and His Plays.* New York: Dover.

Clark, Walter Van Tilburg. 1960. *The Ox-Bow Incident.* New York: Penguin Books.

Clayton, Cherry. 1997. *Olive Schreiner.* New York: Twayne.

Cleugh, James. 1968. *Thomas Mann: A Study.* New York: Russell and Russell.

Clifford, Deborah Pickman. 1979. *Mine Eyes Have Seen the Glory: A Biography of Julia Ward Howe.* Boston: Little, Brown.

Cohen, Carl. 1962. *Communism, Fascism, and Democracy: The Theoretical Foundations.* New York: Random House.

Cole, George Douglas Howard. 1976. *Studies in Class Structure.* Westport, CT: Greenwood Press.

Commons, John Rogers. 1967. *Social Reform and the Church.* New York: Kelley.

Copper, Baba. 1988. *Over the Hill: Reflections on Ageism between Women.* Freedom, CA: Crossing Press.

Corrigan, Robert Willoughby (ed.). 1969. *Arthur Miller: A Collection of Critical Essays.* Englewood Cliffs, NJ: Prentice-Hall.

Coustillas, Pierre (comp.). 1968. *Collected Articles on George Gissing.* New York: Barnes and Noble Books.

Crick, Bernard R. 1980. *George Orwell: A Life.* Boston: Little, Brown.

Crompton, Rosemary, and Jon Gubbay. 1978. *Economy and Class Structure.* New York: St. Martin's Press.

Cruikshank, Robert James. 1949. *Charles Dickens and Early Victorian England.* London: Pitman.

Cullen, Countee. 1991. *My Soul's High Song: The Collected Writings of Countee Cullen.* New York: Doubleday.

Daiches, David. 1966. *Robert Burns.* New York: Macmillan.

Davidson, Arnold E., and Cathy N. Davidson (eds.). 1981. *The Art of Margaret Atwood: Essays in Criticism.* Toronto: Anansi Press.

Davis, Thadious M. 1994. *Nella Larsen, Novelist of the Harlem Renaissance: A Woman's Life Unveiled.* Baton Rouge: Louisiana State University Press.

De Vitis, A. A. 1964. *Graham Greene.* New York: Twayne.

———. 1972. *Anthony Burgess.* New York: Twayne.

Dick, Bernard F. 1967. *William Golding.* New York: Twayne.

Dickens, Charles. 1963. *Great Expectations.* New York: Signet Books.

———. 1966. *Hard Times.* New York: Norton.

———. 1987a. *Bleak House.* Oxford: Oxford University Press.

———. 1987b. *Little Dorrit.* Introduction by Lionel Trilling. Oxford: Oxford University Press.

Dillingham, William B. 1969. *Frank Norris: Instinct and Art.* Lincoln: University of Nebraska Press.

Dostoyevsky, Fyodor. 1936. *The Possessed.* New York: Modern Library.

———. 1968. *The Notebooks for The Possessed.* Ed. by Edward Wasiolek. Chicago: University of Chicago Press.

Dreiser, Theodore. 1964. *An American Tragedy.* New York: Signet Books.

Duberman, Martin B. 1966. *James Russell Lowell.* Boston: Houghton Mifflin.

Early, Eileen. 1980. *Joy in Exile: Ciro Alegria's Narrative Art.* Washington, DC: University Press of America.

Eckman, Fern Marja. 1966. *The Furious Passage of James Baldwin.* New York: Evans.

Edel, Leon. 1963. *Henry James: A Collection of Critical Essays.* Englewood Cliff, NJ: Prentice-Hall.

Edgeworth, Maria. 1992. *Castle Rackrent and Ennui.* New York: Penguin Books.

Egbert, Donald Drew. 1967. *Socialism and American Art in the Light of European Utopianism, Marxism, and Anarchism.* Princeton, NJ: Princeton University Press.

El Saadawi, Nawal. 1990. *God Dies By the Nile.* London: Zed Books Ltd.

Elliot, Jeffrey M. (ed.). 1989. *Conversations with Maya Angelou.* Jackson: University Press of Mississippi.

Elliott, Emory (ed.). 1988. *Columbia Literary History of the United States.* New York: Columbia University Press.

Ellison, Ralph. 1952. *Invisible Man.* New York: Random House.

Ellman, Richard (ed.). 1969. *Oscar Wilde: A Collection of Critical Essays.* Englewood Cliffs, NJ: Prentice-Hall.

Emanuel, James A. 1967. *Langston Hughes.* New York: Twayne.

Endō, Shūsaku. 1980. *Silence.* New York: Taplinger.

Ensor, Robert. 1992. *The Novels of Peter Abrahams and the Rise of Nationalism in Africa.* Essen, Germany: Verlag die Blaue Eule.

Estes, David C. (ed.). 1994. *Critical Reflections of the Fiction of Ernest Gaines.* Athens: University of Georgia Press.

Farah, Nuruddin. 1992. *Close Sesame.* St. Paul, MN: Graywolf Press.

Faris, Wendy B. 1983. *Carlos Fuentes.* New York: Ungar.

Farrison, William Edward. 1969. *William Wells Brown: Author and Reformer.* Chicago: University of Chicago Press.

Feldstein, Stanley. 1972. *The Poisoned Tongue: A Documentary History of American Racism and Prejudice.* New York: Morrow.

Ferguson, Blanche F. 1966. *Countee Cullen and the Negro Renaissance.* New York: Dodd, Mead.

Ferlinghetti, Lawrence. 1958. *A Coney Island of the Mind.* New York: New Directions.

Ferres, John H. (ed.). 1972. *Twentieth-Century Interpretations of* The Crucible. Englewood Cliffs, NJ: Prentice-Hall.

Fielding, K. J. 1958. *Charles Dickens: A Critical Introduction.* London: Longmans, Green.

Filler, Louis. 1960. *The Crusade against Slavery.* New York: Harper.

Flannery, Edward H. 1965. *The Anguish of the Jews: Twenty-Three Centuries of Anti-Semitism.* New York: Macmillan.

Fontenrose, Joseph Eddy. 1964. *John Steinbeck: An Introduction and Interpretation.* New York: Barnes and Noble Books.

Frackman, Lucille. 1996. *Pierre Boulle.* New York: Twayne.

Franklin, Miles. 1965. *My Brilliant Career.* Sydney: Angus and Robertson.

Fredrickson, George M. 1997. *The Comparative Imagination: On the History of Racism, Nationalism, and Social Movements.* Berkeley and Los Angeles: University of California Press.

French, Warren G. 1975. *John Steinbeck.* Boston: Twayne.

Friedman, Lenemaja. 1975. *Shirley Jackson.* Boston: Twayne.

Fuentes, Carlos. 1964. *The Death of Artemio Cruz.* Trans. Sam Hileman. New York: Farrar, Straus.

———. 1978. *The Hydra Head.* Trans. Margaret Sayers Peden. New York: Farrar Straus Giroux.

Gaines, Ernest J. 1972. *The Autobiography of Miss Jane Pittman.* New York: Bantam Books.

Galloway, David, and Christian Sabish (eds.). 1982. *Calamus: Male Homosexuality in*

Twentieth-Century Literature—An International Anthology. New York: Morrow.

Galsworthy, John. 1928. *Plays by John Galsworthy.* New York: Scribner's.

Gates, Henry Louis, Jr. (ed.). 1990. *Three Classic African-American Novels.* New York: Vintage Books.

Gates, Henry Louis, Jr., and K. A. Appiah (eds.). 1993a. *Alice Walker: Critical Perspectives Past and Present.* New York: Amistad.

Gates, Henry Louis, Jr., and K. A. Appiah (eds.). 1993b. *Richard Wright: Critical Perspectives Past and Present.* New York: Amistad.

Gates, Henry Louis, Jr., and K. A. Appiah (eds.). 1993c. *Toni Morrison: Critical Perspectives Past and Present.* New York: Amistad.

Geismar, Maxwell David. 1953. *Rebels and Ancestors: The American Novel 1890–1915: Frank Norris, Stephen Crane, Jack London, Ellen Glasgow, Theodore Dreiser.* Boston: Houghton Mifflin.

Gerber, Philip L. 1964. *Theodore Dreiser.* New York: Twayne.

Gissing, George. 1924. *Critical Studies of the Works of Charles Dickens.* New York: Greenberg.

———. 1926. *New Grub Street.* New York: Modern Library.

Godwin, Parke. 1967. *A Biography of William Cullen Bryant, with Extracts from His Private Correspondence.* New York: Russell and Russell.

Golding, William. 1954. *Lord of the Flies.* New York: Perigee Books.

Goode, John. 1979. *George Gissing: Ideology and Fiction.* New York: Barnes and Noble Books.

Goreau, Angeline. 1980. *Reconstructing Aphra: A Biography of Aphra Behn.* New York: Dial Press.

Grace, Sherrill. 1980. *Violent Duality: A Study of Margaret Atwood.* Montreal: Vehicule Press.

Graham, Don. 1978. *The Fiction of Frank Norris: The Aesthetic Context.* Columbia: University of Missouri Press.

Grant, Eliott M. 1966. *Emile Zola.* New York: Twayne.

Grebstein, Sheldon Norman. 1962. *Sinclair Lewis.* New York: Twayne.

Greene, Graham. 1962. *The Power and the Glory.* New York: Time.

Grossman, Mark. 1996. *The ABC-CLIO Companion to the Native American Rights Movement.* Santa Barbara, CA: ABC-CLIO.

Hagen, Lyman B. 1996. *Heart of a Woman, Mind of a Writer, and Soul of a Poet: A Critical Analysis of the Writings of Maya Angelou.* Lanham, MD: University Press of America.

Hamalian, Leo (comp.). 1974. *Franz Kafka: A Collection of Criticism.* New York: McGraw-Hill.

Hansberry, Lorraine. 1994. *A Raisin in the Sun.* New York: Vintage Books.

Harris, Sharon M. 1991. *Rebecca Harding Davis and American Realism.* Philadelphia: University of Pennsylvania Press.

Hart, Patricia. 1989. *Narrative Magic in the Fiction of Isabel Allende.* Rutherford, NJ: Fairleigh Dickinson University Press.

Hatfield, Henry Caraway (ed.). 1964. *Thomas Mann: A Collection of Critical Essays.* Englewood Cliffs, NJ: Prentice-Hall.

Haugen, Eva Lund, and Einar Haugen (eds.). 1978. *Land of the Free: Björnstjerne Björnson's American Letters, 1880–1881.* Northfield, MN: Norwegian-American Historical Association.

Heller, Joseph. 1994. *Catch-22.* New York: Simon and Schuster.

Hellman, Lillian. 1979. *Six Plays by Lillian Hellman.* New York: Vintage Books.

Hemenway, Robert E. 1977. *Zora Neale Hurston: A Literary Biography.* Chicago: University of Illinois Press.

Herlihy, David (comp.). 1970. *The History of Feudalism.* New York: Harper and Row.

Hersey, John (ed.). 1974. *Ralph Ellison: A Collection of Critical Essays.* Englewood Cliffs, NJ: Prentice-Hall.

Hesse, Hermann. 1963. *Steppenwolf.* New York: Modern Library.

———. 1986. *Magister Ludi.* New York: Bantam Books.

Hibbert, Christopher. 1967. *The Making of Charles Dickens.* New York: Harper and Row.

Hickey, Morgen. 1990. *The Bohemian Register: An Annotated Bibliography of the Beat Literary Movement.* Metuchen, NJ: Scarecrow Press.

Hill, Eldon C. 1978. *George Bernard Shaw.* Boston: Twayne.

Hook, Sidney. 1959. *Political Power and Personal Freedom: Critical Studies in Democracy, Communism, and Civil Rights.* New York: Criterion Books.

Houston, John Porter. 1975. *Victor Hugo.* New York: Twayne.

Howe, Irving (ed.). 1962. *Edith Wharton: A Collection of Critical Essays.* Englewood Cliffs, NJ: Prentice-Hall.

Huggins, Irvin. 1971. *Harlem Renaissance.* New York: Oxford University Press.

Hughes, Langston. 1958. *The Langston Hughes Reader.* New York: Braziller.

Hugo, Victor. 1987. *Les Misérables.* New York: Signet Classic.

Hurston, Zora Neale. 1990. *Their Eyes Were Watching God.* New York: HarperPerennial.

Huxley, Aldous. 1989. *Brave New World.* New York: HarperPerennial.

Hynes, Samuel Lynn. 1964. *William Golding.* New York: Columbia University Press.

Ibsen, Henrik. 1978. *Eleven Plays of Henrick Ibsen.* Ed. by H. L. Mencken. New York: Modern Library/Random House.

Jackson, Helen Hunt. 1988. *Ramona.* New York: Signet Books.

James, Henry. 1956. *The Bostonians.* New York: Modern Library.

Jenness, Linda (ed.). 1972. *Feminism and Socialism.* New York: Pathfinder Press.

Johnson, James Weldon. 1990. *The Autobiography of an Ex-Colored Man.* New York: Penguin Books.

Jolly, Rosemary Jane. 1996. *Colonization, Violence, and Narration in South African Writing: Andre Brink, Breyten Bretenbach, and J. M. Coetzee.* Athens: Ohio University Press.

Kafka, Franz. 1964. *The Trial.* New York: Modern Library.

Kazin, Alfred, and Charles Shapiro (eds.). 1955. *The Stature of Theodore Dreiser: A Critical Survey of the Man and His Work.* Bloomington: Indiana University Press.

Kesey, Ken. 1964. *One Flew over the Cuckoo's Nest.* New York: Viking Press.

Ketterer, David. 1974. *New Worlds for Old: The Apocalyptic Imagination, Science Fiction, and American Literature.* Garden City, NY: Anchor Books.

Kundera, Milan. 1984. *The Unbearable Lightness of Being.* New York: Harper and Row.

La Guma, Alex. 1972. *Apartheid: A Collection of Writings on South African Racism by South Africans.* London: Lawrence and Wishart.

Landes, David S. (ed.). 1966. *The Rise of Capitalism.* New York: Macmillan.

Landon, Brooks. 1989. *Thomas Berger.* Boston: Twayne.

Larsen, Nella. 1992. *An Intimation of Things Distant.* New York: Anchor Books.

Larson, Charles R. 1993. *Invisible Darkness: Jean Toomer and Nella Larsen.* Iowa City: University of Iowa Press.

Larson, Harold. 1944. *Björnstjerne Björnson: A Study in Norwegian Nationalism.* New York: King's Crown Press.

Le Guin, Ursula. 1979. *Malafrena.* New York: Putnam's.

Lederer, Katherine. 1979. *Lillian Hellman.* Boston: Twayne.

Lederer, William J., and Eugene Burdick. 1958. *The Ugly American.* New York: Norton.

Lee, Harper. 1993. *To Kill a Mockingbird.* Pleasantville, NY: Reader's Digest.

Leeming, David. 1994. *James Baldwin: A Biography.* New York: Knopf.

Leftwich, Joseph. 1957. *Israel Zangwill.* New York: Yoseloff.

Lessing, Doris. 1964. *Children of Violence.* Vols. 1 and 2. New York: Simon and Schuster.

———. 1969. *The Four-Gated City.* New York: Knopf.

Levin, Dan. 1965. *Stormy Petrel: The Life and Work of Maxim Gorky.* New York: Appleton-Century.

Levy, Eugene D. 1973. *James Weldon Johnson: Black Leader, Black Voice.* Chicago: University of Chicago Press.

Lewis, Sinclair. 1950. *Babbitt.* New York: Harcourt, Brace, and World.

———. 1970. *Elmer Gantry.* New York: Signet Books.

Light, Martin. 1975. *The Quixotic Vision of Sinclair Lewis.* West Lafayette, IN: Purdue University Press.

Link, Frederick M. 1968. *Aphra Behn.* New York: Twayne.

Lipow, Arthur. 1982. *Authoritarian Socialism in America: Edward Bellamy and the Nationalist Movement.* Berkeley and Los Angeles: University of California Press.

Lisca, Peter. 1958. *The Wide World of John Steinbeck.* New Brunswick, NJ: Rutgers University Press.

Lloyd, John Arthur Thomas. 1972. *Ivan Turgenev.* Port Washington, NY: Kennikat Press.

London, Jack. 1924. *The Iron Heel.* New York: McKinlay, Stone, and MacKenzie.

Lyons, Mary E. 1990. *Sorrow's Kitchen: The Life and Folklore of Zora Neale Hurston.* New York: Scribner's.

Macebuh, Stanley. 1973. *James Baldwin: A Critical Study.* New York: Third Press.

Madsen, Axel. 1977. *Hearts and Minds: The Common Journey of Simone de Beauvoir and Jean-Paul Sartre.* New York: Morrow.

Malti-Douglas, Fedwa. 1995. *Men, Women, and God(s): Nawal El Saadawi and Arab Feminist*

Poetics. Berkeley and Los Angeles: University of California Press.

Mann, Thomas. 1972. *The Magic Mountain.* New York: Knopf.

Marceau, Felicien. 1966. *Balzac and His World.* Trans. Derek Coltman. New York: Orion Press.

Marris, Peter, and Martin Rein. 1967. *Dilemmas of Social Reform: Poverty and Community Action in the United States.* London: Routledge.

Martin, Hubert. 1972. *Alcaeus.* New York: Twayne.

Mathes, Valerie Sherer. 1990. *Helen Hunt Jackson and Her Indian Reform Legacy.* Austin: University of Texas Press.

Mathews, Donald G. (ed.). 1972. *Agitation for Freedom: The Abolitionist Movement.* New York: Wiley.

May, J. Lewis. 1970. *Anatole France: The Man and His Work.* Port Washington, NY: Kennikat Press.

McCabe, Joseph. 1974. *George Bernard Shaw: A Critical Study.* New York: Haskell House.

McCann, Garth. 1977. *Edward Abbey.* Boise, ID: Boise State University.

McCombs, Judith (ed.). 1988. *Critical Essays on Margaret Atwood.* Boston: Hall.

McElderry, Bruce R., Jr. 1965. *Henry James.* New York: Twayne.

McElrath, Joseph R., Jr. 1992. *Frank Norris Revisited.* New York: Twayne.

McKay, Nellie Y. (ed.). 1988. *Critical Essays on Toni Morrison.* Boston: Hall.

McLean, Albert, Jr. 1964. *William Cullen Bryant.* New York: Twayne.

McPherson, Dolly Aimee. 1990. *Order Out of Chaos: The Autobiographical Works of Maya Angelou.* New York: Lang.

McWilliams, Carey. 1948. *A Mask for Privilege: Anti-Semitism in America.* Boston: Little, Brown.

Merrill, Robert. 1987. *Joseph Heller.* Boston: Twayne.

Merrill, Thomas F. 1969. *Allen Ginsberg.* New York: Twayne.

Miles, Barry (ed.). 1995. *Allen Ginsberg: Howl.* New York: HarperPerennial.

Miller, Arthur. 1954. *The Crucible.* New York: Viking Press.

Miller, Henry. 1970. *The Air-Conditioned Nightmare.* Vol. 1. New York: New Directions Books.

Moers, Ellen. 1969. *Two Dreisers.* New York: Viking Press.

Moody, Christopher. 1975. *Solzhenitsyn.* New York: Harper and Row.

Mookerjee, Rabindra Nath. 1988. *Art for Social Justice: The Major Novels of Upton Sinclair.* Metuchen, NJ: Scarecrow Press.

Moore, Harry Thornton. 1968. *The Novels of John Steinbeck: A First Critical Study.* Port Washington, NY: Kennikat Press.

Morrison, Arthur. 1995. *A Child of the Jago.* Chicago: Academy Publications.

Morrison, Toni. 1974. *Sula.* New York: Knopf.

———. 1987. *Beloved.* New York: Knopf.

———. 1993. *The Bluest Eye.* New York: Plume.

Moss, George L. 1978. *Toward the Final Solution: A History of European Racism.* New York: Fertig.

Moss, Leonard. 1967. *Arthur Miller.* Boston: Twayne.

Muller, Edward J. (ed.). 1986. *Critical Essays on Langston Hughes.* Boston: Hall.

Murray, Gilbert. 1933. *Aristophanes: A Study.* Oxford: Clarendon Press.

Murry, John Middleton. 1967. *Jonathan Swift: A Critical Biography.* New York: Farrar, Straus and Giroux.

Nagel, James (ed.). 1984. *Critical Essays on Joseph Heller.* Boston: Hall.

Nelson, Kay Hoyle, and Nancy Huse (eds.). 1994. *The Critical Response to Tillie Olsen.* Westport, CT: Greenwood Press.

Nolan, William F. 1975. *The Ray Bradbury Companion.* Detroit: Gale Research.

Norris, Frank. 1901. *The Octopus.* New York: Doubleday.

O'Connor, Richard. 1964. *Jack London: A Biography.* Boston: Little, Brown.

O'Daniel, Therman B. (ed.). 1971. *Langston Hughes, Black Genius: A Critical Evaluation.* New York: Morrow.

Oliver, Edward James. 1965. *Honoré de Balzac.* London: Weidenfeld and Nicholson.

Olsen, Tillie. 1980. *Yonnondio: From the Thirties.* London: Virago.

O'Neill, Eugene. 1967. *Selected Plays of Eugene O'Neill.* New York: Random House.

Orwell, George. 1961. *1984.* New York: Signet Books.

———. 1996. *Animal Farm.* New York: Signet Books.

Paton, Alan. 1987. *Cry, the Beloved Country.* New York: Collier Books.

Pearlman, Mickey, and Abby H.P. Werlock. 1991. *Tillie Olsen.* Boston: Twayne.

Pizer, Donald (ed.). 1966. *The Novels of Frank Norris.* Bloomington: Indiana University Press.

Plevier, Theodor. 1948. *Stalingrad.* Trans. Richard

and Clara Winston. New York: Appleton-Century-Crofts.

Price, Kenneth M., and Lawrence J. Oliver (eds.). 1997. *Critical Essays on James Weldon Johnson.* New York: Hall.

Pruden, Durward. 1968. *Democracy, Capitalism, and Communism.* New York: Oxford Book Company.

Pryce-Jones, David. 1968. *Graham Greene.* New York: Barnes and Noble Books.

Pulzer, Peter G.J. 1964. *The Rise of Political Anti-Semitism in Germany and Austria.* New York: Wiley.

Quackenbush, Robert M. 1985. *Who Said There's No Man on the Moon?: A Story of Jules Verne.* Englewood Cliffs, NJ: Prentice-Hall.

Ramelson, Marian. 1967. *The Petticoat Rebellion: A Century of Struggle for Women's Rights.* London: Lawrence and Wishart.

Rand, Ayn. 1992. *Atlas Shrugged.* New York: Signet Books.

Read, Herbert Edward. 1947. *Poetry and Anarchism.* London: Freedom Press.

Richardson, Joanna. 1976. *Victor Hugo.* New York: St. Martin's Press.

Roberts, R. Ellis. 1974. *Henrik Ibsen: A Critical Study.* New York: Haskell House.

Roderick, Colin Arthur. 1982. *Miles Franklin: Her Brilliant Career.* Adelaide, Australia: Rigby.

Rogers, Samuel. 1953. *Balzac and the Novel.* Madison: University of Wisconsin Press.

Rojas, Sonia Riquelme, and Edna Aguirre Rehbein (eds.). 1991. *Critical Approaches to Isabel Allende's Novels.* New York: Lang.

Rollyson, Carl E. 1988. *Lillian Hellman: Her Legend and Legacy.* New York: St. Martin's Press.

Rose, Henry. 1973. *Henrik Ibsen: Poet, Mystic, and Moralist.* New York: Haskell House.

Rose, Jane Atteridge. 1993. *Rebecca Harding Davis.* New York: Twayne.

Rosenberg, Jerome H. 1984. *Margaret Atwood.* Boston: Twayne.

Roses, Lorraine Elena, and Ruth Elizabeth Randolph (eds.). 1996. *Harlem's Glory: Black Women Writing, 1900–1950.* Cambridge, MA: Harvard University Press.

Ruhle, Jurgen. 1969. *Literature and Revolution: A Critical Study of the Writer and Communism in the Twentieth Century.* New York: Praeger.

Samuels, Wilfred D. 1990. *Toni Morrison.* Boston: Twayne.

Sartre, Jean-Paul. 1947. *The Age of Reason.* New York: Knopf.

Schatt, Stanley. 1976. *Kurt Vonnegut Jr.* Boston: Twayne.

Scheick, William J., and J. Randolph Cox. 1988. *H. G. Wells: A Reference Guide.* Boston: Hall.

Schneir, Miriam (ed.). 1972. *Feminism: The Essential Historical Writings.* New York: Random House.

Schorer, Mark (ed.). 1962. *Sinclair Lewis: A Collection of Critical Essays.* Englewood Cliffs, NJ: Prentice-Hall.

Schrecker, Ellen. 1994. *The Age of McCarthyism: A Brief History with Documents.* Boston: Bedford Books.

———. 1998. *Many Are the Crimes: McCarthyism in America.* Boston: Little, Brown.

Schreiner, Olive. 1986. *The Story of an African Farm.* New York: Penguin Books.

Schumpeter, Joseph Alois. 1950. *Capitalism, Socialism, and Democracy.* New York: Harper.

Seed, David. 1989. *The Fiction of Joseph Heller.* New York: St. Martin's Press.

Selig, Robert L. 1983. *George Gissing.* Boston: Twayne.

Shabecoff, Philip. 1993. *A Fierce Green Fire.* New York: Hill & Wang.

Shannon, David A. (ed.). 1960. *The Great Depression.* Englewood Cliffs, NJ: Prentice-Hall.

Shaw, George Bernard. 1962. *George Bernard Shaw: Complete Plays with Prefaces.* New York: Dodd, Mead.

———. 1984. *The Fabian Society: Its Early History.* London: The Fabian Society.

Shucard, Alan R. 1984. *Countee Cullen.* Boston: Twayne.

Sinclair, Upton. 1972. *The Jungle.* Cambridge, MA: Bentley.

——— (ed.). 1996. *The Cry for Justice: An Anthology of the Great Social Protest Literature of All Time.* New York: Barricade Books.

Solzhenitsyn, Aleksandr. 1972. *One Day in the Life of Ivan Denisovich.* New York: Praeger.

Spann, Meno. 1976. *Franz Kafka.* Boston: Twayne.

Spivack, Charlotte. 1984. *Ursula K. Le Guin.* Boston: Twayne.

Sprague, Claire, and Virginia Tiger (eds.). 1986. *Critical Essays on Doris Lessing.* Boston: Hall.

Steinbeck, John. 1972. *The Grapes of Wrath.* New York: Bantam Books.

Stowe, Harriet Beecher. 1960. *Uncle Tom's Cabin.* Garden City, NY: Dolphin Books.

Sturges, Henry C. 1968. *Chronologies of the Life and Writings of William Cullen Bryant.* New York: Franklin.

Swados, Harvey (ed.). 1966. *The American Writer and the Great Depression.* Indianapolis: Bobbs-Merrill.

Swift, Jonathan. 1960. *Gulliver's Travels.* New York: Signet Books.

Swinburne, Algernon Charles. 1970. *A Study of Victor Hugo.* Port Washington, NY: Kennikat Press.

Szymanski, Albert. 1983. *Class Structure: A Critical Perspective.* New York: Praeger.

Tabori, Paul. 1972. *The Anatomy of Exile: A Semantic and Historical Study.* London: Harrap.

Thomas, John R. (ed.). 1965. *Slavery Attacked: The Abolitionist Crusade.* Englewood Cliffs, NJ: Prentice-Hall.

Toer, Pramoedya Ananta. 1996. *This Earth of Mankind.* New York: Penguin Books.

Tolstoy, Leo. 1911. *Resurrection.* New York: Crowell.

Toomer, Jean. 1993. *Cane.* New York: Liveright.

Turgenev, Ivan. 1973. *On the Eve.* London: Heinemann.

———. 1983. *Sketches from a Hunter's Album.* New York: Penguin Books.

Turner, Frederick W. (ed.). 1974. *The Portable North American Reader.* New York: Viking Press.

Van Doren, Carl (ed.). 1977. *The Portable Swift.* New York: Penguin Books.

Velie, Alan R. (ed.). 1991. *American Indian Literature: An Anthology.* Norman: University of Oklahoma Press.

Verne, Jules. 1996. *Paris in the Twentieth Century.* Trans. Richard Howard. New York: Random House.

Virtanen, Reino. 1968. *Anatole France.* New York: Twayne.

Vonnegut, Kurt. 1980. *Player Piano.* New York: Laurel Books.

Wade, Michael. 1972. *Peter Abrahams.* London: Evans Brothers.

Wagner-Martin, Linda, and Cathy N. Davidson (eds.). 1995. *The Oxford Book of Women's Writing in the United States.* Oxford: Oxford University Press.

Walker, Alice. 1986. *The Color Purple.* Boston: Hall.

———. 1990. *The Temple of My Familiar.* New York: Pocket Books.

Walter, Jerrold. 1968. *Thomas Hood: His Life and Times.* New York: Haskell House.

Warner, Lucile Schulberg. 1976. *From Slave to Abolitionist: The Life of William Wells Brown.* New York: Dial Press.

Watts, Harold H. 1969. *Aldous Huxley.* New York: Twayne.

Webb, Constance. 1968. *Richard Wright: A Biography.* New York: Putnam's.

Wells, H. G. 1935. *Tono-Bungay.* New York: Modern Library.

Westbrook, Max. 1969. *Walter Van Tilburg Clark.* New York: Twayne.

Wharton, Edith. 1993. *The Age of Innocence.* New York: Collier Books.

Widmer, Kingsley. 1963. *Henry Miller.* New York: Twayne.

———. 1965. *The Literary Rebel.* Carbondale: Southern Illinois University Press.

Williams, Raymond. 1977. *Marxism and Literature.* Oxford: Oxford University Press.

——— (comp.). 1974. *George Orwell: A Collection of Critical Essays.* Englewood Cliffs, NJ: Prentice-Hall.

Winchell, Donna Haisty. 1992. *Alice Walker.* New York: Twayne.

Witt, Shirley, and Stan Steiner (eds.). 1972. *The Way: An Anthology of American Indian Literature.* New York: Vintage Books.

Woodcock, George. 1962. *Anarchism: A History of Libertarian Ideas and Movements.* Cleveland: Meridian Books.

Wortham, Thomas. 1977. *James Russell Lowell's The Biglow Papers.* DeKalb: Northern Illinois University Press.

Wortman, Max S., Jr. 1969. *Critical Issues in Labor.* New York: Macmillan.

Wright, Derek. 1994. *The Novels of Nuruddin Farah.* Bayreuth, Germany: Bayreuth University Press.

Wright, Richard. 1993a. *Native Son.* New York: HarperPerennial.

———. 1993b. *The Outsider.* New York: HarperPerennial.

Wright, William. 1986. *Lillian Hellman: The Image, the Woman.* New York: Simon and Schuster.

Yevtushenko, Yevgeny. 1989. *Early Poems.* Trans. George Reavey. London: Marion Boyars.

Zakin, Susan. 1993. *Coyotes and Town Dogs: Earth First! and the Environmental Movement.* New York: Penguin Books.

Zangwill, Israel. 1895. *Children of the Ghetto: A Study of a Peculiar People.* New York: Macmillan.

Ziolkowski, Theodore. 1965. *The Novels of Hermann Hesse: A Study in Theme and Structure.* Princeton, NJ: Princeton University Press.

INDEX

deleted

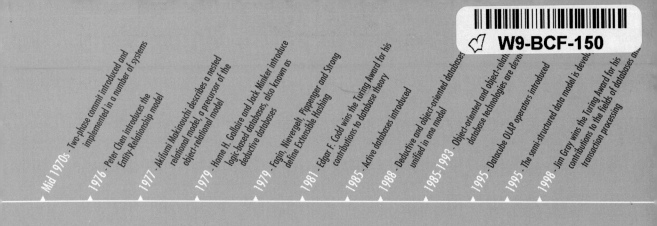

The timeline across the top reads:

- Mid 1970s - Two-phase commit introduced and implemented in a number of systems
- 1976 - Peter Chen introduces the Entity-Relationship model
- 1977 - Akifumi Makinouchi describes a nested relational model, a precursor of the object-relational model
- 1979 - Herve H. Gallaire and Jack Minker introduce logic-based databases, also known as deductive databases
- 1979 - Fagin, Nievergelt, Pippenger and Strong define Extensible Hashing
- 1981 - Edgar F. Codd wins the Turing Award for his contributions to database theory
- 1985 - Active databases introduced
- 1988 - Deductive and object-oriented databases unified in one model
- 1985-1993 - Object-oriented and object-oriented databases, database technologies are developed
- 1995 - Datacube OLAP operators introduced
- 1995 - The semi-structured data model is developed
- 1998 - Jim Gray wins the Turing Award for his contributions to the fields of databases and transaction processing

For Students

- Selected solutions to problems for students
- Addison-Wesley's automated database tutorials, allowing for additional practice online:

SQL (SQL Tutor):

SQL Tutor provides nearly 200 problems to practice writing SQL queries. It provides ten complete databases and six different levels of feedback for students (depending on their skill level) and keeps track of student progress.

Normalization (NormIT):

With NormIT, students practice database normalization. NormIT supports data normalization, including the relational synthesis algorithm.

Modeling (ER Tutor):

The ER Tutor allows students to practice conceptual database design using the Entity-Relationship (ER) data model. The tutor contains 50 predefined problems that students solve by drawing ER diagrams. The tutor checks solutions and provides feedback.

Student supplements are available at www.aw-bc.com/kifer.

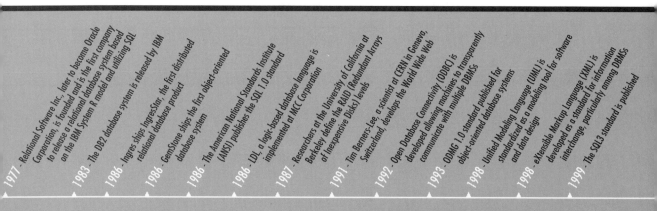

The timeline across the bottom reads:

- 1977 - Relational Software Inc., later to become Oracle Corporation, is founded and is the first company to release a relational database system based on the IBM System R model and utilizing SQL
- 1983 - The DB2 database system is released by IBM
- 1986 - Ingres ships IngresStar, the first distributed relational database product
- 1986 - GemStone ships the first object-oriented database system
- 1986 - The American National Standards Institute (ANSI) publishes the SQL 1.0 standard
- 1986 - LDL, a logic-based database language is implemented at MCC Corporation
- 1987 - Researchers at the University of California at Berkeley define the RAID (Redundant Arrays of Inexpensive Disks) levels
- 1991 - Tim Berners-Lee, a scientist at CERN in Geneva, Switzerland, develops the World Wide Web
- 1992 - Open Database Connectivity (ODBC) is developed, allowing machines to transparently communicate with multiple DBMSs
- 1993 - ODMG 1.0 standard published for object-oriented database systems
- 1998 - Unified Modeling Language (UML) is standardized as a modeling tool for software and data design
- 1998 - eXtensible Markup Language (XML) is developed as a standard for information interchange, particularly among DBMSs
- 1999 - The SQL3 standard is published

Online Access for *Database Systems*!

Thank you for purchasing a new copy of *Database Systems: An Application-Oriented Approach*, Second Edition. Your textbook includes six months of prepaid access to the book's Companion Website. This prepaid subscription provides you with full access to all student support areas, including:

- Interactive tutorial environments for writing SQL queries, practicing normalization problems and working with the Entity-Relationship data model.
- Automatically graded practice questions in the areas of normalization, SQL, database modeling, relational algebra, and more, to help you assess your basic understanding of the material.
- An interlinked, online glossary.

To access the *Database Systems: An Application-Oriented Approach* Companion Website for the first time:

You will need to register online using a computer with an Internet connection and a Web browser. The process takes just a couple of minutes and only needs to be completed once.

1. Go to **http://www.aw-bc.com/kifer**.
2. Click the **Register** button.
3. Use a coin to scratch off the gray coating below and reveal your student access code.* Do not use a knife or other sharp object, which can damage the code.

4. On the registration page, enter your student access code. Do not type the dashes. You can use lowercase or uppercase letters.
5. Follow the on-screen instructions. If you need help at any time during the online registration process, simply click the **Need Help?** icon.
6. Once your personal Login Name and Password are confirmed, you can begin using the *Database Systems: An Application-Oriented Approach* Companion Website!

To log in to this Website after you've registered:

You only need to register for this Companion Website once. After that, you can access the site by going to http://www.aw-bc.com/kifer and providing your Login Name and Password when prompted.

*IMPORTANT: The access code on this page can only be used once to establish a subscription to the *Database Systems: An Application-Oriented Approach* Companion Website. This subscription is valid for six months upon activation and is not transferable. If this access code has already been scratched off, it may no longer be valid. If this is the case, you can purchase a subscription by going to http://www.aw-bc.com/kifer and clicking "Register."

Database Systems

An Application-Oriented Approach

SECOND EDITION

Database Systems

An Application-Oriented Approach

SECOND EDITION

Michael Kifer   Arthur Bernstein   Philip M. Lewis

STATE UNIVERSITY OF NEW YORK, STONY BROOK

PEARSON

Addison
Wesley

Boston San Francisco New York
London Toronto Sydney Tokyo Singapore Madrid
Mexico City Munich Paris Cape Town Hong Kong Montreal

Executive Editor	Susan Hartman Sullivan
Acquisitions Editor	Matt Goldstein
Project Editor	Maite Suarez-Rivas
Marketing Manager	Nathan Schultz
Senior Marketing Coordinator	Lesly Hershman
Senior Production Supervisor	Jeffrey Holcomb
Project Management	Windfall Software
Copyeditor	Elisabeth Beller
Proofreader	Jennifer McClain
Composition	Windfall Software, using ZzTEX
Text Designer	Sandra Rigney
Cover Designer	Joyce Cosentino Wells
Cover Photo	© 2004 Digital Vision
Prepress and Manufacturing	Caroline Fell

Access the latest information about Addison-Wesley titles from our World Wide Web site:
http://www.aw-bc.com/computing

Many of the designations used by manufacturers and sellers to distinguish their products are claimed as trademarks. Where those designations appear in this book, and Addison-Wesley was aware of a trademark claim, the designations have been printed in initial caps or all caps.

The programs and applications presented in this book have been included for their instructional value. They have been tested with care, but are not guaranteed for any particular purpose. The publisher does not offer any warranties or representations, nor does it accept any liabilities with respect to the programs or applications.

Library of Congress Cataloging-in-Publication Data

Kifer, M. (Michael), 1954–
    Database systems : an application-oriented approach / Michael Kifer, Arthur Bernstein,
    Philip M. Lewis.—Introductory version, 2nd ed.
        p. cm.
    Lewis's name appears first on the earlier edition.
    Rev. ed. of: Databases and transaction processing / Philip M. Lewis. 2002.
    ISBN 0-321-22838-3 (hardcover)
    1. Database management. 2. Transaction systems (Computer systems) I. Bernstein, Arthur J.
    II. Lewis, Philip M., 1931– Databases and transaction processing. III. Title.

QA76.9.D3K4965 2004
005.74—dc22   2003068925

ISBN 0-321-22838-3
1 2 3 4 5 6 7 8 9 10—CRW—08 07 06 05

In memory of my late parents, Luba and Isaac;
and to my wife, Lora, and my children. M.K.

To my wife, Edie, my children, and my grandchildren. A.J.B.

To my wife, Rhoda, my children, and my grandchildren. P.M.L.

Contents

Preface

We are publishing the second edition of our textbook in two versions:

- This version, which consists of introductory material, is appropriate for a first undergraduate or graduate course in databases.
- The second version, which is the complete book, is appropriate for three courses:
  - An introductory undergraduate or graduate course in databases
  - An undergraduate or graduate course in transaction processing for students who have had an introductory course in databases
  - An advanced undergraduate or a first graduate course in databases for students who have had an introductory course in databases

One of our goals was to reduce the size and make this introductory version more affordable to students. Another was to capitalize on our experience in using the first edition of the book to make an even better introductory text.

The chapters in this book are not just a subset of those in the complete book. We believe that instructors of an introductory database course should have the option of enriching an introductory course by including material on object databases and XML—topics that are covered in great detail in several chapters in the complete book. Therefore we have added to the introductory book two new chapters, Chapter 16, Introduction to Object Databases, and Chapter 17, Introduction to XML and Web Data, which contain an appropriately chosen subset of the material in the full version of this book.

To keep the book up-to-date with the rapidly changing technology, we have added a substantial amount of material on UML to a number of chapters and have included a new chapter on Database Tuning, Chapter 12, in both the introductory and complete books.

As with the first edition, our focus is on how to build applications using databases rather than on how to build the database management system itself. We believe that many more students will be implementing applications than will be building DBMSs. Thus, we include substantial material describing the languages and APIs used by transactions to access a database, such as embedded SQL, ODBC, and JDBC.

Although we cover many practical aspects of database and transaction processing applications, we are primarily concerned with the concepts that underlie these topics rather than with the details of particular commercial systems or applications.

Thus we concentrate on the concepts behind the relational and object data models. These concepts will remain the foundation of database processing long after SQL is obsolete.

To enhance students' understanding of the technical material, we have included a case study of a transaction processing application, the Student Registration System, which is carried through the book. While a student registration system can hardly be considered glamorous, it has the unique advantage that all students have interacted with such a system as users. More importantly, it turns out to be a surprisingly rich application, so we can use it to illustrate many of the issues in database design, query processing, and transaction processing.

A unique aspect of the book is a presentation of the software engineering concepts required to implement transaction processing applications, using the Student Registration System as an example. Since the implementations of many information systems fail because of poor project management and inadequate software engineering, we feel that these topics should be an important part of the student's education. Our treatment of software engineering issues is brief, since many students will take a separate course in this subject. However, we believe that they will be better able to understand and apply that material when they see it presented in the context of an information system implementation. Since the courses that use this text at Stony Brook are not software engineering courses, we do not cover this material in class. Instead, we ask the students to read it and require that they use good software engineering practice in their class projects. We do cover in class those aspects of the Student Registration System that illustrate important issues in databases and transaction processing.

Changes in the Second Edition

The technology underlying database and transaction processing systems is changing so rapidly that we have made a large number of changes and additions to the material of the first edition. One rapidly advancing technology is the Unified Modeling Language, UML. We added substantial amount of material on UML in Chapter 4 on database design, in addition to the material on E-R diagrams that was already there. We also added UML to the material on software engineering in Chapters 2, 14, and 15.

A new chapter on Database Tuning, Chapter 12, was added because so much effort in the real world is spent increasing the throughput of database and transaction processing applications.

In addition, material has been added and updated in almost all the chapters. Significant examples of this are the coverage of SQL/XML and RAID technology.

One important area that is *not* included in this volume is Web Services. Since this is a rapidly developing and interesting application-oriented subject we have significantly revised the compete version of this text to include material on this topic. In addition to strengthening the book on the subject of XML Technology by updating the chapter on XML and Web Data and adding a section on SQL/XML, we have added a new chapter on Web Services that contains material on SOAP,

WSDL, BPEL, UDDI, and XML-based transaction processing using WS-Coordination and WS-Transaction. In the chapter on Security and Internet Commerce, we added a section on XML-based encryption, using XML-Encryption, XML-Signature, WS-Security, and SAML. And in the chapter on Architecture of Transaction Processing Systems, we added material on Web Application Servers and J2EE, which are used to implement the back-end of many Web services.

Organization of the Book

Chapters 1 through 7 should be taught in the order in which they appear in the book. Chapter 8 contains much of the information that students need in order to put the knowledge they acquired in the preceding chapters into practice. However, subsequent chapters do not significantly depend on Chapter 8. Chapters 9 through 12 in Part 3 should be taught sequentially. Chapter 13 in the same part is largely independent. The software engineering chapters in Part 4 utilize the material of the chapters in Parts 2 and 3, but the software engineering chapters can be read in parallel with the database material. Chapters 16 and 17 in the advanced part of the book depend on the first seven chapters in Part 2.

Finally we note that the sections in this book that are marked with an asterisk ($\star$) are optional and can be omitted, if the instructor prefers to do so. Sections marked with the ⓒⓢ icon in the table of contents deal with the case study. Also, exercises that are marked with an asterisk are slightly harder than the rest, and exercises that are marked with two asterisks are even harder.

Supplements

In addition to the text, the following supplementary materials are available to assist instructors:

- Online PowerPoint presentations for all chapters
- Online PowerPoint slides of all figures
- An online solution manual containing solutions for the exercises
- Additional references, notes, errata, homeworks, and exams.

For more information on obtaining these supplements, please visit this book's Companion Website at *www.aw-bc.com/kifer*. The solutions manual and PowerPoint presentations are available only to instructors through your Addison-Wesley sales representative. To contact your representative, please visit *www.aw.com*.

Acknowledgments

We would like to thank the reviewers, whose comments and suggestions significantly improved the second edition of the book:

Tran Cao Son, New Mexico State University

Frantisek Franek, McMaster University

Junping Sun, Nova Southeastern University

Philip Cannata, Sun Microsystems

Dehu Qi, Lamar University

Nematollah Shiri, Concordia University

Jian Pei, State University of New York at Buffalo

Jack Wileden, University of Massachusetts Amherst

Sibel Adali, Rensselaer Polytechnic Institute

Roger King, University of Colorado at Boulder

Markus Schneider, University of Florida

Yaron Y. Goland, BEA

Dennis Shasha, New York University

Christelle Scharff, Pace University

Zhiwei Wang, Graduate Programs in Software Engineering, IT, and IS University of St. Thomas.

We would also like to thank the reviewers of the first edition of the book:

Suad Alagic, Wichita University

Catriel Beeri, The Hebrew University

Rick Cattel, Sun Microsystems

Jan Chomicki, SUNY Buffalo

Henry A. Etlinger, Rochester Institute of Technology

Leonidas Fegaras, University of Texas at Arlington

Alan Fekete, University of Sidney

Johannes Gehrke, Cornell University

Hershel Gottesman, Consultant

Jiawei Han, Simon Fraser University

Peter Honeyman, University of Michigan

Vijay Kumar, University of Missouri–Kansas City

Jonathan Lazar, Towson University

Dennis McLeod, University of Southern California

Rokia Missaoui, University of Quebec in Montreal

Clifford Neuman, University of Southern California

Fabian Pascal, Consultant

Sudha Ram, University of Arizona

Krithi Ramamritham, University of Massachusetts–Amherst, and IIT Bombay

Andreas Reuter, International University in Germany, Bruchsal

Arijit Sengupta, Georgia State University

Munindar P. Singh, North Carolina State University

Greg Speegle, Baylor University

Junping Sun, Nova Southeastern University

Joe Trubisz, Consultant

Vassilis J. Tsotras, University of California, Riverside

Emilia E. Villarreal, California Polytechnic State University

We would also like to thank the following people who were kind enough to provide us with additional information and answers to our questions: Don Chamberlin, Daniela Florescu, Jim Gray, Pankaj Gupta, Rob Kelly, and C. Mohan.

Two people taught out of beta versions of the book and made useful comments and suggestions: David S. Warren and Radu Grosu. Joe Trubicz served not only as a reviewer when the manuscript was complete, but provided critical comments on early versions of many of the chapters.

A number of students were very helpful in reading and checking the correctness of various parts of the book: Ziyang Duan, Shiyong Lu, Swapnil Patil, Guizhen Yang, and Yan Zhang.

Many thanks to the staff of the Computer Science Department at Stony Brook, and in particular Kathy Germana, who helped make things happen at work.

We would particularly like to thank Matt Goldstein and Maite Suarez-Rivas, our editors at Addison-Wesley, who played an important role in shaping the contents and approach of the book in its early stages and throughout the time we were writing it. We would also like to thank the various staff members of Addison-Wesley and Windfall Software, who did an excellent job of editing and producing the book: Jeffrey Holcomb, Paul Anagnostopoulos, Elisabeth Beller, Jennifer McClain, and Joe Snowden.

Last, but not least, we would like to thank our wives, Lora, Edie, and Rhoda, who provided much needed support and encouragement while we were writing the book.

PART ONE

Introduction

THE INTRODUCTORY PART of the book consists of two chapters.

In Chapter 1, we will try to get you excited about the fields of databases and transaction processing by giving you some idea of what the book is all about.

In Chapter 2, we will introduce many of the technical concepts underlying the fields of databases and transaction processing, including the SQL language and the ACID properties of transactions. We will expand on these concepts in the rest of the book.

1

Overview of Databases and Transactions

1.1 What Are Databases and Transactions?

During your vacation, you stand at the checkout counter of a department store in Tokyo, hand the clerk your credit card, and wait anxiously for your purchases to be approved. In the few seconds you have to wait, messages are sent around the world to one or more banks and clearinghouses, accessing and updating a number of databases until finally the system approves your purchase. Over 100 million such credit card transactions are processed each day from over 10 million merchants through more than 20 thousand banks. Billions of dollars are involved, and the only record of what happens is stored in the databases on the network. The accuracy, security, and availability of these databases and the correctness and performance characteristics of the transactions that access them are critical to the entire credit card business.

What is a database?   A **database** is a collection of data items related to some enterprise—for example, the depositor account information in a bank. A database might be stored on cards in a Rolodex or on paper in a file cabinet, but we are particularly interested in databases stored as bits and bytes in a computer. Such a database can be **centralized** on one computer or **distributed** over several, perhaps widely separated geographically.

An increasing number of enterprises depend on such databases for their very existence. No paper records exist within the enterprise; the only up-to-date record of its current status—for example, the balance of each bank customer's checking account—is stored in its databases. Many enterprises view their databases as their most important asset.

For example, the database of the company that manufactured the airplane on which you flew to Tokyo contains the only record of information about the engineering design, manufacturing processes, and subassembly suppliers involved in producing that plane 10 years ago, together with every test made on it over its lifetime. If, at some time in the future, a test shows that a turbine blade on one of the plane's jet engines has failed, the company can determine from its database which subcontractor supplied that particular engine, and the subcontractor can determine from its database the date on which that turbine blade was manufactured, the machines and people involved, the source of the materials from which the blade was fabricated, and the results of quality assurance tests made while the blade was being manufactured. In this way it can determine the cause of the failure and increase the quality of future planes. The existence of these detailed historical databases, as well as the ability to search them for information about the fabrication of a specific turbine blade in a specific jet engine on a specific airplane manufactured 10 years ago, gives the airplane manufacturer a significant strategic advantage over any other manufacturer that does not maintain such databases.

In some cases, a database is the major asset of an enterprise—for example, the database of the credit history company that your credit card company consulted when you applied for your card. In other cases, the accuracy of the information in the database is critical for human life—for example, the database in the air traffic control system at the Tokyo airport.

What is a database management system? To make access to them convenient, databases are generally encapsulated within a **database management system** (**DBMS**). The DBMS supports a high-level language in which the application programmer describes the database access it wishes to perform. Typically, all database access is classified into two broad categories: **queries** and **updates**. A query is a request to retrieve data, and an update is a request to insert, delete, or modify existing data items. The most commonly used data access language, and the one we study the most in this text, is the Structured Query Language (**SQL**). Although it is called a *query* language, updates are also done through SQL. The beauty of SQL lies in its declarative nature: the application programmer need only state what is to be done; the DBMS figures out how to do it efficiently. The DBMS interprets each SQL statement and performs the action it describes. The application programmer need not know the details of how the database is stored, need not formulate the algorithm for performing the access, and need not be concerned about many other aspects of managing the database. Compare this to the regular file systems where the programmer not only has to know the details of the file structure but also provide the algorithms to search the files to retrieve the desired information.

What is a transaction? Databases frequently store information that describes the current state of an enterprise. For example, a bank's database stores the current balance in each depositor's account. When an event happens in the real world that changes the state of the enterprise, a corresponding change must be made to the information stored in the database. With online DBMSs, these changes are made in real time by programs called **transactions**, which execute when the real-world event occurs. For example, when a customer deposits money in a bank (an event in the real world), a deposit transaction is executed. Each transaction must be designed so that it maintains the correctness of the relationship between the database state and the real-world enterprise it is modeling. In addition to changing the state of the database, the transaction itself might initiate some events in the real world. For example, a withdraw transaction at an automated teller machine (ATM) initiates the event of dispensing cash, and a transaction that establishes a connection for a telephone call requires the allocation of resources (bandwidth on a long-distance link) in the telephone company's infrastructure.

Credit card approval is only one example of a transaction that you executed on your vacation in Tokyo. Your flight arrangements involved a transaction with the airline's reservation database, your passage through passport control at the airport involved a transaction with the immigration services database, and your check-in at the hotel involved a transaction with the hotel reservation database. Even the phone call you made from your hotel room to tell your family you had arrived safely involved transactions with the hotel billing database and with a long-distance carrier to arrange billing and to establish the call.

Other examples of transactions you probably execute regularly involve ATM systems, supermarket scanning systems, and university registration and billing systems. Increasingly, these transactions entail access to **distributed databases**: multiple databases managed by different DBMSs stored at different geographical locations. Your phone call transaction at the Tokyo hotel is an example.

What is a transaction processing system?   A **transaction processing system (TPS)** includes one or more databases that store the state of an enterprise, the software for managing the transactions that manipulate that state, and the transactions themselves that constitute the application code. In its simplest form the TPS involves a single DBMS that contains the software for managing transactions. More complex systems involve several DBMSs. In this case, transaction management is handled both within the DBMSs and without, by additional code called a **TP monitor** that coordinates transactions across multiple sites (see Figure 1.1).

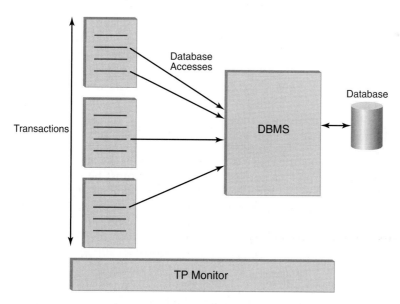

FIGURE 1.1 The structure of a transaction processing system.

The database is at the heart of a transaction processing system because it persists beyond the lifetime of any particular transaction. An increasing number of enterprises depend on such systems for their business. For example, one might say that the credit card transaction processing system *is* the credit card business.

Our concern in this book is with the technical aspects of databases and the transaction processing systems that use them. Specifically, we are interested in the design and implementation of applications, including the organization of the application database, but we are not concerned with the algorithms and data structures used to implement the underlying DBMS and transaction processing system modules. Nevertheless, we must learn enough about these underlying systems so that we can use them intelligently in an application.

1.2 Features of Modern Database and Transaction Processing Systems

Modern computer and communication technology has led to significant advances in the architecture, design, and use of database and transaction processing systems. Their enhanced functionality has lead to important new business opportunities for the enterprises that deploy them and, in turn, implies a number of additional requirements on their operation:

- *High availability.* Because the system is online, it must be operational at all times when the enterprise is open for business. In some enterprises, this means that the system must always be available. For example, an airline reservation system might be required to accept requests for flight reservations from ticket offices spread over a large number of time zones, so the system is never shut down. With online systems, failures can result in a disruption of business—if the computer in an airline reservation system is down, reservations cannot be made. The ability to tolerate failures depends on the nature of the enterprise. Clearly a flight control system has considerably less tolerance for failures than a flight reservation system has. VISA claimed in 2002 that its system had been down a total of eight minutes in the previous five years (an uptime of greater than 99.9999%). Highly available systems generally involve replication of hardware and software.

- *High reliability.* The system must accurately reflect the results of all transactions. This implies not only that transactions must be correctly programmed but also that errors must not be introduced because of concurrent execution of (correctly programmed) transactions or intercommunication of modules while the transaction is executing. Furthermore, large, distributed transaction processing systems include thousands of hardware and software modules, and it is unlikely that all are working correctly. The system must not forget the results of any transaction that has completed despite all but the most catastrophic forms of failure. For example, the database in a banking system must accurately reflect the effect of all the deposits and withdrawals that have completed and cannot lose the results of any such transactions should it subsequently crash.

■ *High throughput.* Because the enterprise has many customers who must use the transaction processing system, the system must be capable of performing many transactions per second. For example, a credit card approval system might perform thousands of transactions per second during its busiest periods. As we shall see, this requirement implies that individual transactions cannot be executed sequentially but must be executed concurrently—thus significantly complicating the design of the system.

■ *Low response time.* Because customers might be waiting for a response from it, the system must respond quickly. Response requirements may differ depending on the application. Whereas you might be willing to wait fifteen seconds for an ATM to output cash, you expect a telephone connection to be made in no more than one or two seconds. Furthermore, in some applications, if the response does not occur within a fixed period of time, the transaction will not perform properly. For example, in a factory automation system the transaction might be required to actuate a device before some unit passes a particular position on the conveyor belt. Applications of this type are said to have **hard real-time** constraints.

■ *Long lifetime.* Transaction processing systems are complex and not easily replaced. They must be designed in such a way that individual hardware or software modules can be replaced with newer versions (that perform better or have additional functionality) without necessitating major changes to the surrounding system.

■ *Security.* Many transaction processing systems contain information about the private concerns of individuals (e.g., the items they purchase, their credit card number, the videos they view, and their health and financial records). Because these systems can be accessed by a large number of people from a large number of places (perhaps over the Internet), security is important. Individual users must be authenticated (are they who they claim to be?), users must be allowed to execute only those transactions they are authorized to execute (only a bank teller can execute a transaction to generate a certified check), the information in the database must not be corrupted or read by an attacker, and the information transmitted between the user and the system must not be altered or overheard by an eavesdropper.

1.3 Major Players in the Implementation and Support of Database and Transaction Processing Systems

A transaction processing system, together with its associated databases, can be an immensely complex assemblage of hardware and software, with which many different types of people interact in various roles. Examining these roles is a useful way of understanding what a transaction processing system is. First consider the people involved in the design and implementation of a transaction processing system:

- *System analyst.* The system analyst works with the customer of a proposed application system to develop formal requirements and specifications for it. He or she must understand both the business rules of the enterprise for which the application is being implemented and the database and transaction processing technology underlying the implementation so that the application will meet the customer's needs and execute efficiently. The specifications developed by the system analyst are then refined into the design of the database formats and the individual transactions that will access the database.

- *Database designer.* The database designer specifies the structure of the database appropriate for an application. The database contains the information that describes the current state of the real-world application. The structure must support the accesses required by the transactions and allow those accesses to be performed in a timely manner.

- *Application programmer.* The application programmer implements the graphical user interface and the individual transactions in the system. He or she must ensure that the transactions maintain the correspondence between the state of the real-world application and the state of the database. Together with the database designer, the application programmer must ensure that the rules governing the workings of the enterprise are enforced. For example, in the Student Registration System, to be discussed in Section 2.1, the number of students enrolled in a course should not exceed the number of seats in the room assigned to the course.

- *Project manager.* The project manager is responsible for the successful completion of the implementation project. He or she prepares schedules and budgets, assigns people to tasks, and monitors day-to-day project operation. Project management is surprisingly difficult. According to a widely quoted report of the Standish Group, an Information Technology (IT) consulting group, of the more than eight thousand IT projects the group surveyed, only 16% completed successfully—on time and on budget [Standish 2000]. The primary reason for the failures was almost always poor project management.[1]

The people interacting with (as opposed to building) an operational transaction processing system include the following:

- *User.* The user causes the execution of individual transactions, usually by interacting through some graphical user interface. The user interface must be

---

[1] For large companies, the success rate dropped to 9%. For projects that completed late or over budget, the average completion time was 222% of the scheduled time and the average cost was 189% of the budgeted cost. An astonishing 31% of the projects were canceled before they were completed. At the time this book was written, information about this study, called Chaos, could be found in [Standish 2000].

appropriate to the capabilities of the intended class of users. As an example, the user interface presented by an ATM is simple enough that an average person can use the system to perform bank deposit and withdraw transactions without any training or instructions except those presented on the screen. By contrast, the interface to an airline reservation system, which is used by reservation clerks or travel agents, requires advanced training. In both cases, however, most of the complexities of the system are hidden from the user.

- *Database administrator.* The database administrator is responsible for supporting the database while the system is running. Among his or her concerns are allocating storage space for the database, monitoring and optimizing database performance, and monitoring and controlling database security. In addition, the database administrator might modify the structure of the database to accommodate changes in the enterprise or to handle performance bottlenecks.

- *System administrator.* The system administrator is responsible for supporting the system as a whole while it is running. Among the things he or she must keep track of are

  - *System architecture.* What hardware and software modules are connected to the system at any instant, and how are they interconnected?
  - *Configuration management.* What version of each software module exists on each machine?
  - *System status.* What is the health of the system? Which systems and communication links are operational or congested, and what is being done to repair the situation? How is the system currently performing?

Our main interest in this book lies at the application level. Thus, we are particularly concerned with the roles of the system analyst, the application programmer, and the database designer. However, in order for someone working at the application level to take full advantage of the capabilities of the underlying system, he or she must be knowledgeable about the other roles as well.

1.4 Decision Support Systems—OLAP and OLTP

Transaction processing is not the only application domain in which databases play a key role. Another such domain is **decision support**. While transaction processing is concerned with using a database to maintain an accurate model of some real-world situation, decision support is concerned with using the information in a database to guide management decisions. To illustrate the differences between these two domains, we discuss the roles they might play in the operation of a national supermarket chain.

Transaction processing. Each local supermarket in a chain maintains a database of the prices and current inventory of all the items it sells. It uses that database (together with a bar code scanner) as part of a transaction processing system at the checkout counters. One transaction in this system might be, "Three cans of Campbell soup and one box of Ritz crackers were purchased; compute the price, print out a receipt, update the balance in the cash drawer, and subtract these items from the store's inventory." The customer expects this transaction to complete in a few seconds.

The main goal of such a transaction processing system is to maintain the correspondence between the database and the real-world situation it is modeling as events occur in the real world. In this case, the event is the customer's purchase, and the real-world situation is the store's inventory and the amount of cash in the cash drawer.

Decision support. The managers of the supermarket chain might want to analyze the data stored in the databases in each store to help them make decisions for the chain as a whole. Such decision support applications are becoming increasingly important as enterprises attempt to turn the *data* in their databases into *information* they can use to advance their long-term strategic goals.

Decision support applications involve queries to one or more databases, possibly followed by some mathematical analysis of the information returned by the queries. Decision support applications are sometimes called **online analytic processing (OLAP)**, in contrast with the **online transaction processing (OLTP)** applications we have been discussing.

In some decision support applications, the queries are so simple they can be implemented as transactions in the same local database used for OLTP applications—for example, "Print out a report of the weekly produce sales in Store 27 for the past six months."

In many applications, however, the queries are quite complex and cannot be efficiently executed against the local databases. They take too long to execute (because the database has been optimized for OLTP transactions) and cause the local transactions—for example, the checkout transactions—to execute too slowly. The supermarket chain therefore maintains a separate database specifically for such complex OLAP queries. The database contains historical information about sales and inventory from all its branches for the past 10 years. This information is extracted from the individual store databases at various times and updated once a day. Such a database is called a **data warehouse**.

A manager can enter a complex query about the data in the data warehouse—for example, "During the winter months of the last five years, what is the percentage of customers in northeast urban supermarkets who bought crackers at the same time they bought soup?" (Perhaps these items should be placed near each other on the shelves.)

Data warehouses can contain terabytes (10^{12} bytes) of data and require special hardware to maintain that data. An OLAP query might be quite difficult to formulate and might require query language concepts more powerful than those needed for OLTP queries. OLAP queries usually do not have severe constraints on execution time and might take several hours to execute. The warehouse database might have been structured to speed up the execution of such queries. The database need be updated only periodically because minute-by-minute correctness is not needed for the types of queries it supports—satisfactory responses might be obtained even if the database is less than 100% accurate.

Data mining. A manager might also be interested in making a much less structured query about the data in the warehouse database—for example, "Are there *any* interesting combinations of items bought by customers?" Such queries are called **data mining**. In contrast with OLAP, in which requests are made to obtain specific information, data mining can be viewed as knowledge discovery—an attempt to extract new knowledge from the data stored in the database.

Data mining queries can be extremely difficult to formulate and might require sophisticated mathematics or techniques from the field of artificial intelligence. A query might require many hours to execute and might involve several interactions with the manager for obtaining additional information or reformulating parts of the query.

One widely repeated but perhaps apocryphal success story of data mining is that a convenience store chain used the above query ("Are there *any* interesting combinations . . . ") and found an unexpected correlation. In the early evenings, a high percentage of male customers who bought diapers also bought beer—presumably these customers were fathers who were going to stay home that night with their babies.

2

The Big Picture

2.1 Case Study: A Student Registration System

Your university is interested in implementing a student registration system so that students can register for courses from their home PCs. You have been asked to build a prototype of that system as a project in this course. The registrar has prepared the following preliminary **Statement of Objectives** for the system.

> The objectives of the Student Registration System are to allow students and faculty (as appropriate) to
>
> 1. Authenticate themselves as users of the system
> 2. Register and deregister for courses (offered for the next semester)
> 3. Obtain reports on a particular student's status
> 4. Maintain information about students and courses
> 5. Enter final grades for courses that a student has completed

This brief description is typical of what might be supplied as a starting point for a system implementation project, but it is not specific or detailed enough to serve as the basis for the project's design and coding phases. We will be developing the student registration scenario throughout this book and will be using it to illustrate the various concepts in databases and transaction processing.

Our next step is to meet with the registrar, faculty, and students to expand this brief description into a formal Requirements Document for the system. We will discuss the Requirements Document in Chapter 14, which we expect you to read at appropriate times as you proceed through the rest of the book. In this chapter, we will take a closer look at some of the underlying concepts of databases and transaction processing that are needed for that system.

The following sections provide a brief overview of these concepts. Although we will revisit these concepts in a more detailed fashion in subsequent chapters, an overview will help you see the big picture and will set the stage for better understanding of the following chapters.

2.2 Introduction to Relational Databases

A database is at the heart of most transaction processing systems. At every instant of time, the database must contain an accurate description—often the only one—of the real-world enterprise the transaction processing system is modeling. For example, in the Student Registration System the database is the only source of information about which students have registered for each course.

Relations and tuples. We are particularly interested in databases that use the **relational model** [Codd 1970, 1990], in which data is stored in **tables**. The Student Registration System, for example, might include the STUDENT table, shown in Figure 2.1. A table contains a set of **rows**. In the figure, each row contains information about one student. Each **column** of the table describes the student in a particular way. In the example, the columns are Id, Name, Address, and Status. Each column has an associated type, called its **domain**, from which the value in a particular row for that column is drawn. For example, the domain for Id is integer and the domain for Name is string.

This database model is called "relational" because it is based on the mathematical concept of a relation. A **mathematical relation** captures the notion that elements of different sets are related to one another. For example, John Doe, an element of the set of all humans, is related to 123 Main St., an element of the set of all addresses, and to 111111111, an element of the set of all Ids. A relation is a set of **tuples**. Following the example of the table STUDENT, we might define a relation called STUDENT containing the tuple ⟨111111111, John Doe, 123 Main St., Freshman⟩. The STUDENT relation presumably contains a tuple describing every student.

We can view a relation as a predicate. A **predicate** is a declarative statement that is either true or false depending on the values of its arguments—for example, the predicate "It rained in Detroit on date X" is either true or false depending on the value chosen for the argument X. When we view a relation as a predicate, the arguments of the predicate correspond to the elements of a tuple, and the predicate is defined to be true for arguments $a_1, \ldots, a_n$ exactly when the tuple $(a_1, \ldots, a_n)$ is in the relation. For instance, we might define the predicate STUDENT

Id	Name	Address	Status
111111111	John Doe	123 Main St.	Freshman
666666666	Joseph Public	666 Hollow Rd.	Sophomore
111223344	Mary Smith	1 Lake St.	Freshman
987654321	Bart Simpson	Fox 5 TV	Senior
023456789	Homer Simpson	Fox 5 TV	Senior
123454321	Joe Blow	6 Yard Ct.	Junior

FIGURE 2.1 The table STUDENT. Each row describes a single student.

with arguments Id, Name, Address, and Status. Then we can say that the predicate STUDENT ⟨111111111, John Doe, 123 Main St., Freshman⟩ is true, because the tuple ⟨111111111, John Doe, 123 Main St., Freshman⟩ is in the table STUDENT shown in Figure 2.1.

The correspondence between tables and relations should now be clear: the tuples of a relation correspond to the rows of a table, and the column names of a table are the names of the **attributes** of the relation. Thus, the rows of the STUDENT table can be viewed as enumerating the set of all 4-tuples (tuples with four attributes of the appropriate types) that satisfy the STUDENT relation (i.e., the Id, Name, Address, and Status of a student).

Operations on tables are mathematically defined. In real applications, tables can become quite large—a STUDENT table for our university would contain over 15 thousand rows, and each row would likely contain much more information about each student than is shown here. In addition to the STUDENT table, the complete database for the Student Registration System at our university would contain a number of other tables, each with a large number of rows, containing information about other aspects of student registration. For example, a TRANSCRIPT table might contain a row for each course that every student has ever taken. Hence, the databases for most applications contain a large amount of information and are generally held in mass storage.

In most applications, the database is under the control of a database management system (DBMS), which is supplied by a commercial vendor. When an application wants to perform an operation on the database, it does so by making a request to the DBMS. A typical operation might extract some information from the rows of one or more tables, modify some rows, or add or delete rows. For example, when a new student is admitted to the university, a row is added to the STUDENT table.

In addition to the fact that tables in the database can be modeled by mathematical relations, operations on the tables can also be modeled as mathematical operations on the corresponding relations. Thus, a particular unary operation might take a table, T, as an argument and produce a result table containing a subset of the rows of T. For example, an instructor might want to display the roster of students registered for a course. Such a request might involve scanning the TRANSCRIPT table, locating the rows corresponding to the course, and returning them to the application. A particular binary operation might take two tables as arguments and construct a new table containing the union of the rows of the argument tables. A complex query against a database might be equivalent to an expression involving many such relational operations involving many tables.

Because of this mathematical description, relational operations can be precisely defined and their mathematical properties, such as commutativity and associativity, can be proven. As we shall see, this mathematical description has important practical implications. Commercial DBMSs contain a **query optimizer** module that converts queries into expressions involving relational operations and then uses these mathematical properties to simplify those expressions and thus optimize query execution.

SQL: Basic SELECT statement.   An application describes the access that it wants the DBMS to perform on its behalf in a language supported by the DBMS. We are particularly interested in SQL, the most commonly used database language, which provides facilities for accessing a relational database and is supported by almost all commercial DBMSs.

The basic structure of the SQL statements for manipulating data is straightforward and easy to understand. Each statement takes one or more tables as arguments and produces a table as a result. For example, to find the name of the student whose Id is 987654321, we might use the statement

```
SELECT   Name
FROM     STUDENT
WHERE    Id = '987654321'
```
2.1

More precisely, this statement asks the DBMS to extract from the table named in the FROM clause—that is, the table STUDENT—all rows satisfying the condition in the WHERE clause—that is, all rows whose Id column has value 987654321—and then from each such row to delete all columns except those named in the SELECT clause—that is, Name. The resulting rows are placed in a result table produced by the statement. In this case, because Ids are unique, at most one row of STUDENT can satisfy the condition, and so the result of the statement is a table with one column and at most one row.

Thus, the FROM clause identifies the table to be used as input, the WHERE clause identifies the rows of that table from which the answer is to be generated, and the SELECT clause identifies the columns of those rows that are to be output in the result table.

The result table generated by this example contains only one column and at most one row. As a somewhat more complex example, the statement

```
SELECT   Id, Name
FROM     STUDENT
WHERE    Status = 'senior'
```
2.2

returns a result table (shown in Figure 2.2) containing two columns and multiple rows: the Ids and names of all seniors. If we want to produce a table containing all the columns of STUDENT but describing only seniors, we use the statement

```
SELECT   *
FROM     STUDENT
WHERE    Status = 'senior'
```

Id	Name
987654321	Bart Simpson
023456789	Homer Simpson

FIGURE 2.2 The database table returned by the SQL SELECT statement (2.2).

The asterisk is simply shorthand that allows us to avoid listing the names of all the columns of STUDENT.

In some situations the user is interested not in outputting a result table but in information *about* the result table. An example is the statement

```
SELECT   COUNT(*)
FROM     STUDENT
WHERE    Status = 'senior'
```

which returns the number of rows in the result table (i.e., the number of seniors). COUNT is referred to as an **aggregate** function because it produces a value that is a function of all the rows in the result table. Note that when an aggregate is used, the SELECT statement produces a single value instead of a table.

The WHERE clause is the most interesting component of the SELECT statement; it contains a general condition that is evaluated over each row of the table named in the FROM clause. Column values from the row are substituted into the condition, yielding an expression that has either a true or a false value. If the condition evaluates to true, the row is retained for processing by the SELECT clause and then stored in the result table. Hence, the WHERE clause acts as a filter.

Conditions can be much more complex than we have seen so far: A condition can be a Boolean combination of terms. If we want the result table to contain information describing seniors whose Ids are in a particular range, for example, we might use

```
WHERE   Status = 'senior' AND Id > '888888888'
```

OR and NOT can also be used. Furthermore, a number of predicates are provided in the language for expressing particular relationships. For example, the IN predicate tests set membership.

```
WHERE   Status IN ('freshman', 'sophomore')
```

Additional aggregates and predicates and the full complexity of the WHERE clause are discussed in Chapter 5.

Multi-table SELECT statements. The result table can contain information extracted from several base tables. Thus, if we have a table TRANSCRIPT with columns StudId, CrsCode, Semester, and Grade, the statement

```
SELECT    Name, CrsCode, Grade
FROM      STUDENT, TRANSCRIPT
WHERE     StudId = Id AND Status = 'senior'
```

can be used to form a result table in which each row contains the name of a senior, a particular course she took, and the grade she received.

The first thing to note is that the attribute values in the result table come from different base tables: Name comes from STUDENT; CrsCode and Grade come from TRANSCRIPT. As in the previous examples, the FROM clause produces a table whose rows are input to the WHERE clause. In this case the table is the Cartesian product of the tables listed in the FROM clause: a row of this table is the concatenation of a row of STUDENT and a row of TRANSCRIPT. Many of these rows make no sense. For example, Bart Simpson's row in STUDENT is not related to a row in TRANSCRIPT describing a course that Bart did not take. The first conjunct of the WHERE clause ensures that the rows of TRANSCRIPT for a particular student are associated with the appropriate row of STUDENT by matching the Id values of the rows of the two tables. For example, if TRANSCRIPT has a row ⟨987654321, CS305, F1995, C⟩, it will match only Bart Simpson's row in STUDENT, producing the row ⟨Bart Simpson, CS305, C⟩ in the result table.

Query optimization. One very important feature of SQL is that the programmer does not have to specify the algorithm the DBMS should use to satisfy a particular query. For example, tables are frequently defined to include auxiliary data structures, called **indices**, which make it possible to locate particular rows without using lengthy searches through the entire table. Thus, an index on the Id column of the STUDENT table might contain a list of pairs ⟨*Id, pointer*⟩ where the pointer points to the row of the table containing the corresponding Id. If such an index were present, the DBMS would automatically use it to find the row that satisfies the query (2.1). If the table also had an index on the column Status, the DBMS would use that index to find the rows that satisfy the query (2.2). If this second index did not exist, the DBMS would automatically use some other method to satisfy (2.2)—for example, it might look at every row in the table in order to locate all rows having the value senior in the Status column. The programmer does not specify what method to use—just the condition the desired result table must satisfy.

In addition to selecting appropriate indices to use, the query optimizer uses the properties of the relational operations to further improve the efficiency with which a query can be processed—again, without any intervention by the programmer. Nevertheless, programmers should have some understanding of the strategies the DBMS uses to satisfy queries so they can design the database tables, indices, and

SQL statements in such a way that they will be executed in an efficient manner consistent with the requirements of the application.

Changing the contents of tables. The following examples illustrate the SQL statements for modifying the contents of a table. The statement

```
UPDATE    STUDENT
SET       Status = 'sophomore'
WHERE     Id = '111111111'
```

updates the STUDENT table to make John Doe a sophomore. The statement

```
INSERT
INTO      STUDENT (Id, Name, Address, Status)
VALUES    ('999999999', 'Winston Churchill', '10 Downing St',
          'senior')
```

inserts a new row for Winston Churchill in the STUDENT table. The statement

```
DELETE
FROM      STUDENT
WHERE     Id = '111111111'
```

deletes the row for John Doe from the STUDENT table. Again, the details of how these operations are to be performed need not be specified by the programmer.

Creating tables and specifying constraints. Before you can store data in a table, the table structure must be created. For instance, the STUDENT table could have been created with the SQL statement

```
CREATE TABLE  STUDENT(
Id            INTEGER,
Name          CHAR(20),
Address       CHAR(50),
Status        CHAR(10),
PRIMARY KEY(Id) )
```

2.3

where we have declared the name of each column and the domain (type) of the data that can be stored in that column. We have also declared the Id column to be a **primary key** to the table, which means that each row of the table must have a unique value in that column and the DBMS will (most probably) automatically construct an index on that column. The DBMS will enforce this uniqueness constraint by not allowing any INSERT or UPDATE statement to produce a row with a value in the Id column that duplicates a value of Id in another row. This requirement is an example of an **integrity constraint** (sometimes called a **consistency constraint**)—an application-based restriction on the values that can appear as entries in the database. We discuss integrity constraints in more detail in the next section.

We have given simple examples of each statement type to highlight the conceptual simplicity of the basic ideas underlying SQL, but be aware that the complete language has many subtleties. Each statement type has a large number of options that allow very complex queries and updates. For this reason, mastery of SQL requires significant effort. We continue our discussion of relational databases and SQL in Chapter 3.

2.3 What Makes a Program a Transaction— The ACID Properties

In many applications, a database is used to model the state of some real-world enterprise. In such applications, a transaction is a program that interacts with that database so as to maintain the correspondence between the state of the enterprise and the state of the database. In particular, a transaction might update the database to reflect the occurrence of a real-world event that affects the enterprise state. An example is a deposit transaction at a bank. The event is that the customer gives the teller the cash and a deposit slip. The transaction updates the customer's account information in the database to reflect the deposit.

Transactions, however, are not just ordinary programs. Requirements are placed on them, particularly on the way they are executed, that go beyond what is normally expected of regular programs. These requirements are enforced by the DBMS and the TP monitor.

Consistency.   A transaction must access and update the database in such a way that it preserves all database integrity constraints. Every real-world enterprise is organized in accordance with certain rules that restrict the possible states of the enterprise. For example, the number of students registered for a course cannot exceed the number of seats in the room assigned to the course. When such a rule exists, the possible states of the database are similarly restricted.

The restrictions are stated as integrity constraints. The integrity constraint corresponding to the above rule asserts that the value of the database item that records the number of course registrants must not exceed the value of the item that records the room size. Thus, when the registration transaction completes, the database must satisfy this integrity constraint (assuming that the constraint was satisfied when the transaction started).

Although we have not yet designed the database for the Student Registration System, we can make some assumptions about the data that will be stored and postulate some additional integrity constraints:

- *IC0.* The database contains the Id of each student. These Ids must be unique.
- *IC1.* The database contains a list of prerequisites for each course and, for each student, a list of completed courses. A student cannot register for a course without having taken all prerequisite courses.

- ***IC2.*** The database contains the maximum number of students allowed to take each course and the number of students who are currently registered for each course. The number of students registered for each course cannot be greater than the maximum number allowed for that course.

- ***IC3.*** It might be possible to determine the number of students registered for (or enrolled in) a particular course from the database in two ways: the number is stored as a count in the information describing the course, and it can be calculated from the information describing each student by counting the number of student records that indicate that the student is registered for (or enrolled in) the course. These two determinations must yield the same result.

In addition to maintaining the integrity constraints, each transaction must update the database in such a way that the new database state reflects the state of the real-world enterprise that it models. If John Doe registers for CS305, but the registration transaction records Mary Smith as the new student in the class, the integrity constraints will be satisfied but the new state will be incorrect. Hence, consistency has two dimensions.

> ***Consistency.*** The transaction designer can assume that when execution of the transaction is initiated, the database is in a state in which all integrity constraints are satisfied and, in addition, the database correctly models the current state of the enterprise. The designer has the responsibility of ensuring that when execution has completed, the database is once again in a state in which all integrity constraints are satisfied and, in addition, that the new state reflects the transformation described in the transaction's specification (in other words, that the database still correctly models the state of the enterprise).

SQL provides some support for the transaction designer in maintaining consistency. When the database is being designed, the database designer can specify certain types of integrity constraints and include them within the statements that declare the format of the various tables in the database. The primary key constraint of the SQL statement (2.3) is an example of this. Later, as each transaction is executed, the DBMS automatically checks that each specified constraint is not violated and prevents completion of any transaction that would cause a constraint violation.

Atomicity. In addition to the transaction designer's responsibility for consistency, the TP monitor must provide certain guarantees concerning the manner in which transactions are executed. One such condition is atomicity.

> ***Atomicity.*** The system must ensure that the transaction either runs to completion or, if it does not complete, has no effect at all (as if it had never been started).

In the Student Registration System, either a student has registered for a course or he has not registered for a course. Partial registration makes no sense and might leave the database in an inconsistent state. For example, as indicated by constraint IC3, two items of information in the database must be updated when a student registers.

If a registration transaction were to have a partial execution in which one update completed but the system crashed before the second update could be executed, the resulting database would be inconsistent.

When a transaction has successfully completed, we say that it has **committed**. If the transaction does not successfully complete, we say that it has **aborted** and the TP monitor has the responsibility of ensuring that whatever partial changes the transaction has made to the database are undone, or **rolled back. Atomic execution** means that every transaction either commits or aborts.

Notice that ordinary programs do not necessarily have the property of atomicity. For example, if the system were to crash while a program that was updating a file was executing, the file could be left in a partially updated state when the system recovered.

Durability.   A second requirement of the transaction processing system is that it does not lose information.

> *Durability.* The system must ensure that once the transaction commits, its effects remain in the database even if the computer, or the medium on which the database is stored, subsequently crashes.

For example, if you successfully register for a course, you expect the system to remember that you are registered even if it later crashes. Notice that ordinary programs do not necessarily have the property of durability either. For example, if a media failure occurs after a program that has updated a file has completed, the file might be restored to a state that does not include the update.

Isolation.   In discussing consistency, we concentrated on the effect of a single transaction. We next examine the effect of executing a set of transactions. We say that a set of transactions is executed sequentially, or **serially**, if one transaction in the set is executed to completion before another is started. The good news about serial execution is that if all transactions are consistent and the database is initially in a consistent state, serial execution maintains consistency. When the first transaction in the set starts, the database is in a consistent state and, since the transaction is consistent, the database will be consistent when the transaction completes. Because the database is consistent when the second transaction starts, it too will perform correctly and the argument will repeat.

Serial execution is adequate for applications that have modest performance requirements. However, many applications have strict requirements on response time and throughput, and often the only way to meet the requirements is to process transactions concurrently. Modern computing systems are capable of servicing more than one transaction simultaneously, and we refer to this mode of execution as **concurrent**. Concurrent execution is appropriate in a transaction processing system serving many users. In this case, there will be many active, partially completed transactions at any given time.

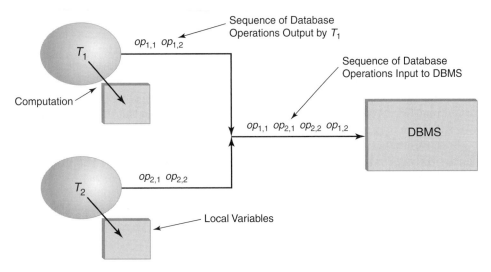

FIGURE 2.3 The database operations output by two transactions in a concurrent schedule might be interleaved in time. (Note that the figure should be interpreted as meaning that $op_{1,1}$ arrives first at the DBMS, followed by $op_{2,1}$, etc.)

In concurrent execution, the database operations of different transactions are effectively interleaved in time, a situation shown in Figure 2.3. Transaction T_1 alternately computes using its local variables and sends requests to the database system to transfer data between the database and its local variables. The requests are made in the sequence $op_{1,1}$, $op_{1,2}$. We refer to that sequence as a **transaction schedule**. T_2 performs its computation in a similar way. Because the execution of the two transactions is not synchronized, the sequence of operations arriving at the database, called a **schedule**, is an arbitrary merge of the two transaction schedules. The schedule in the figure is $op_{1,1}$, $op_{2,1}$, $op_{2,2}$, $op_{1,2}$.

When transactions are executed concurrently, the consistency of each transaction is not sufficient to guarantee that the database that exists after both have completed correctly reflects the state of the enterprise. For example, suppose that T_1 and T_2 are two instances of the registration transaction invoked by two students who want to register for the same course. A possible schedule of these transactions is shown in Figure 2.4, where time progresses from left to right and the notation $r(cur\_reg : n)$ means that a transaction has read the database object cur_reg, which

FIGURE 2.4 A schedule in which two registration transactions are not isolated from each other.

T_1: $r(cur\_reg$: 29) $w(cur\_reg$: 30)

T_2: $r(cur\_reg$: 29) $w(cur\_reg$: 30)

records the number of current registrants, and the value n has been returned. A similar notation is used for $w(cur\_reg : n)$. The figure shows only the accesses[1] to cur_reg.

Assume that the maximum number of students allowed to register is 30 and the current number is 29. In its first step, each of the two transactions will read this value and store it in its local variable, and both will decide that there is room in the course. In its second step, each will increment its private copy of the number of current registrants; hence, both will calculate the value 30. In their write operations, both will write that same value, 30, into cur_reg.

Both transactions complete successfully, but the number of current registrants is incorrectly recorded as 30 when it is actually 31 (even though the maximum allowable number is 30). This is an example of what is often referred to as a **lost update** because one of the increments has been lost. The resulting database does not reflect the real-world state, and integrity constraint IC2 has been violated. By contrast, if the transactions had executed sequentially, T_1 would have completed before T_2 was allowed to start. Hence, T_2 would find the course full and would not register the student.

As this example demonstrates, we must specify some restriction on concurrent execution that is guaranteed to maintain the consistency of the database and the correspondence between the enterprise state and the database state. One such restriction that is obviously sufficient follows.

> *Isolation.* Even though transactions are executed concurrently, the overall effect of the schedule must be the same as if the transactions had executed serially in some order.

It should be evident that if the transactions are consistent and if the overall effect of a concurrent schedule is the same as that of some serial schedule, the concurrent schedule will maintain consistency. Concurrent schedules that satisfy this condition are called **serializable**.

As was the case with atomicity and durability, ordinary programs do not necessarily have the property of isolation. For example, if programs that update a common set of files are executed concurrently, updates might be interleaved and produce an outcome that is quite different from that obtained if they had been executed in any serial order. That result might be totally unacceptable.

ACID properties. The features that distinguish transactions from ordinary programs are frequently referred to by the acronym **ACID** [Haerder and Reuter 1983]:

- *Atomic.* Each transaction is executed completely or not at all.
- *Consistent.* Each transaction maintains database consistency.
- *Isolated.* The concurrent execution of a set of transactions has the same effect as some serial execution of that set.

---

[1] In a relational database, r and w represent SELECT and UPDATE statements.

■ *Durable.* The effects of committed transactions are permanently recorded in the database.

When a transaction processing system supports the ACID properties, the database maintains a consistent and up-to-date model of the real world and the transactions supply responses to users that are always correct and up to date.

BIBLIOGRAPHIC NOTES

The relational model for databases was introduced in [Codd 1970, 1990]. The SQL language is described by the various SQL standards, such as [SQL 1992]. The term "ACID" was coined by [Haerder and Reuter 1983], but the individual components of ACID were introduced in earlier papers—for example, [Gray et al. 1976] and [Eswaran et al. 1976].

EXERCISES

2.1 Given the relation MARRIED that consists of tuples of the form $\langle a, b \rangle$, where a is the husband and b is the wife, the relation BROTHER that has tuples of the form $\langle c, d \rangle$, where c is the brother of d, and the relation SIBLING, which has tuples of the form $\langle e, f \rangle$, where e and f are siblings, describe how you would define the relation BROTHER-IN-LAW, where tuples have the form $\langle x, y \rangle$ with x being the brother-in-law of y.

2.2 Design the following two tables (in addition to that in Figure 2.1) that might be used in the Student Registration System. Note that the same student Id might appear in many rows of each of these tables.

    a. A table implementing the relation COURSESREGISTEREDFOR, relating a student's Id and the identifying numbers of the courses for which she is registered

    b. A table implementing the relation COURSESTAKEN, relating a student's Id, the identifying numbers of the courses he has taken, and the grade received in each course

Specify the predicate corresponding to each of these tables.

2.3 Write an SQL statement that

    a. Returns the Ids of all seniors in the table STUDENT

    b. Deletes all seniors from STUDENT

    c. Promotes all juniors in the table STUDENT to seniors

2.4 Write an SQL statement that creates the TRANSCRIPT table.

2.5 Using the TRANSCRIPT table, write an SQL statement that

    a. Deregisters the student with Id = 123456789 from the course CS305 for the fall of 2001

    b. Changes to an A the grade assigned to the student with Id = 123456789 for the course CS305 taken in the fall of 2000

    c. Returns the Id of all students who took CS305 in the fall of 2000

2.6   Write an SQL statement that returns the names (not the Ids) of all students who received an A in CS305 in the fall of 2000.

2.7   State whether or not each of the following statements could be an integrity constraint of a checking account database for a banking application. Give reasons for your answers.

  a. The value stored in the `balance` column of an account is greater than or equal to $0.
  b. The value stored in the `balance` column of an account is greater than it was last week at this time.
  c. The value stored in the `balance` column of an account is $128.32.
  d. The value stored in the `balance` column of an account is a decimal number with two digits following the decimal point.
  e. The `social_security_number` column of an account is defined and contains a nine-digit number.
  f. The value stored in the `check_credit_in_use` column of an account is less than or equal to the value stored in the `total_approved_check_credit` column. (These columns have their obvious meanings.)

2.8   State five integrity constraints, other than those given in the text, for the database in the Student Registration System.

2.9   Give an example in the Student Registration System where the database satisfies the integrity constraints IC0–IC3 but its state does not reflect the state of the real world.

2.10   State five (possible) integrity constraints for the database in an airline reservation system.

2.11   A reservation transaction in an airline reservation system makes a reservation on a flight, reserves a seat on the plane, issues a ticket, and debits the appropriate credit card account. Assume that one of the integrity constraints of the reservation database is that the number of reservations on each flight does not exceed the number of seats on the plane. (Of course, many airlines purposely over-book and so do not use this integrity constraint.) Explain how transactions running on this system might violate

  a. Atomicity
  b. Consistency
  c. Isolation
  d. Durability

2.12   Describe informally in what ways the following events differ from or are similar to transactions with respect to atomicity and durability.

  a. A telephone call from a pay phone (Consider line busy, no answer, and wrong number situations. When does this transaction "commit?")
  b. A wedding ceremony (Suppose that the groom refuses to say "I do." When does this transaction "commit?")
  c. The purchase of a house (Suppose that, after a purchase agreement is signed, the buyer is unable to obtain a mortgage. Suppose that the buyer backs out during the closing. Suppose that two years later the buyer does not make the mortgage payments and the bank forecloses.)
  d. A baseball game (Suppose that it rains.)

2.13 Assume that, in addition to storing the grade a student has received in every course he has completed, the system stores the student's cumulative GPA. Describe an integrity constraint that relates this information. Describe how the constraint would be violated if the transaction that records a new grade were not atomic.

2.14 Explain how a lost update could occur if, under the circumstances of the previous problem, two transactions that were recording grades for a particular student (in different courses) were run concurrently.

PART TWO
Database Management

Now we are ready to begin a more in-depth study of databases.

In Chapter 3, we will discuss how data items are specified in modern database management systems and how they appear to the transactions that use them. In other words, we will learn a few things about data models and data definition languages.

In Chapter 4, we will study conceptual database design, which includes methodologies for organizing data around a set of high-level concepts.

In Chapter 5, we will discuss how transactions access and modify data in a DBMS using data manipulation and query languages—in particular, SQL.

In Chapter 6, we will resume the design theme and will talk about the Relational Normalization Theory. This theory provides algorithms and objective measures for improving the quality of database design.

Chapter 7 introduces the mechanism of triggers—a powerful device for maintaining the consistency of databases and for enabling databases to react to external events.

Chapter 8 concludes this part of the book with a discussion of how SQL statements can be executed from within a host language, such as C or Java.

3

The Relational Data Model

This chapter is an introduction to the relational data model. First we define its main abstract concepts, and then we show how these concepts are embodied in the concrete syntax of SQL. Specifically, this chapter covers the data definition subset of SQL, which is used to specify data structures, constraints, and authorization policies in databases.

3.1 What Is a Data Model?

Data independence. Ultimately, all data is recorded as bytes on a disk. However, as a programmer you know that working with data at this low level of abstraction is quite tedious. Few people are interested in how sectors, tracks, and cylinders are allocated for storing information. Most programmers much prefer to work with data stored in *files*, which is a more reasonable abstraction for many applications.

From a course on file structures, you might be familiar with a variety of methods for storing data in files. **Sequential** files are best for applications that access records in the order in which they are stored. **Direct access** (or **random access**) files are best when records are accessed in a more or less unpredictable order. Files might have **indices**, which are auxiliary data structures that enable applications to retrieve records based on the value of a **search key**. We will discuss various index types in Chapter 9. Files might also consist of fixed-length records or records that have variable lengths.

The details of how data is stored in files belong to the **physical level** of data modeling. This level is specified using a **physical schema**, which in the field of databases refers to the syntax that describes the structure of files and indices.

Early data-intensive applications worked directly with the physical schema instead of the higher levels of abstraction provided by a modern DBMS. This choice was made for a number of reasons. First, commercial database systems were rare and costly. Second, computers were slow, and working directly with the file system offered a performance advantage. Third, most early applications were primitive by today's standards, and building a level of abstraction between those programs and the file system did not seem justified.

A serious drawback of this approach is that changes to the file format at the physical level could have costly repercussions for software maintenance. The "year 2000 problem" was a good example of such repercussions. In the 1960s and 1970s, it was common to write programs in which the data item representing the calendar year was hard-coded as a two-digit number. The rationale was that these programs would be replaced within fifteen to twenty years, so using four digits (or using a data abstraction for the DATE data type) was a waste of precious disk space. The result was that every routine that worked with dates expected to find the year in the two-digit format. Hence, any change to that format implied finding and changing code throughout the application. The consequence of these past decisions was the multibillion-dollar bill presented to the industry in the late 1990s for fixing outdated software.

If a data abstraction, DATE, had been used in those programs, the whole problem could have been avoided. Applications would have viewed years as four-digit numbers, even though they had been physically stored in the database as two-digit numbers. To adjust to the change of millennium, designers could have changed the underlying physical representation of years in the database to four-digit numbers by (1) building a simple program that converted the database by adding "1900" to every existing year field and (2) correspondingly changing the implementations of the appropriate functions within the DATE data type to access the new physical representation. None of the existing applications would have had to be modified because they could still use the same DATE data abstraction.

When the underlying data structures are subject to change (even infrequently), basing the design of data-intensive applications on a bare file system becomes problematic. Even trivial changes, such as adding or deleting a field in a file, imply that every application that uses this file must be manually updated, recompiled, and retested. Less trivial changes, such as merging two fields or splitting a field into two, might impact the existing applications quite significantly. Accommodating such changes can be labor intensive and error prone. In addition, the data in the original file needs to be converted to the new representation, and without the appropriate tools such conversion can be costly.

Also, the file system offers too low a level of abstraction to support the development of an application that requires frequent and rapid implementation of new queries. For such applications, the **conceptual level** of data modeling becomes appropriate.

The conceptual model hides the details of the physical data representation and instead describes data in terms of higher-level concepts that are closer to the way humans view it. For instance, the **conceptual schema**—the syntax used to describe the data at the conceptual level—could represent some of the information about students as

STUDENT (Id: INT, Name: STRING, Address: STRING, Status: STRING)

While this schema might look similar to the way file records are represented, the important point is that the different pieces of information it describes might be *physically* stored in a different way than that described in the schema. Indeed, these pieces of information might not even reside in the same file (perhaps not even on the same computer!).

The possibility of having separate schemas at the physical and conceptual levels leads to the simple, yet powerful, idea of **physical data independence**. Instead of working directly with the file system, applications see only the conceptual schema. The DBMS maps data between the conceptual and physical levels *automatically*. If the physical representation changes, all that needs to be done is to change the mapping between the levels, and *all* applications that deal exclusively with the conceptual schema will continue to work with the new physical data structures.

The conceptual schema is not the last word in the game of data abstraction. The third level of abstraction is called the **external schema** (also known as the **user** or **view** abstraction level). The external schema is used to customize the conceptual schema to the needs of various classes of users, and it also plays a role in database security (as we will see later).

The external schema looks and feels like a conceptual schema, and both are defined in essentially the same way in modern DBMSs. However, while there is a single conceptual schema per database, there might be several external schemas (i.e., views on the conceptual schema), usually one per user category. For example, to generate proper student billing information, the bursar's office might need to know each student's GPA and status and the total number of credits the student has taken, but not the names of the courses and the grades received. Even though the GPA and total number of credits might not be stored in the database explicitly, the bursar's office can be presented with a view in which these items appear as regular fields (whose values are calculated at run time when the field is accessed), and all fields and relations that are irrelevant to billing are omitted. Similarly, an academic advisor does not need to know anything about billing, so much of this information can be omitted from the advisor's view of the registration system.

These ideas lead to the principle of **conceptual data independence**: Applications tailored to the needs of specific user groups can be designed to use the external schemas appropriate for these groups. The mapping between the external and conceptual schemas is the responsibility of the DBMS, so applications are insulated from changes in the conceptual schema *as well as* from changes in the physical schema. The overall picture is shown in Figure 3.1.

Data model. A **data model** consists of a set of concepts and languages for describing

1. **Conceptual and external schemas**. A schema specifies the structure of the data stored in the database. Schemas are described using a **data definition language (DDL)**.

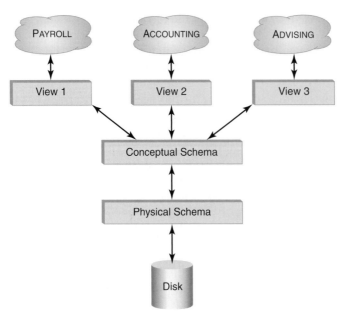

FIGURE 3.1 Levels of data independence.

2. **Constraints.** A constraint specifies a condition that the data items in the database must satisfy. A constraint specification sublanguage is usually part of the DDL.

3. **Operations on data.** Operations on database items are described using a **data manipulation language (DML)**. The DML is usually the most important and interesting part of any data model because it is the set of operations that ultimately gives us the high-level data abstraction.

   In addition, all commercial systems provide some kind of **storage definition language (SDL)**, which allows the database designer to *influence* the physical schema (although most systems reserve the final say). The SDL is usually tightly integrated with the DDL. Changes in the physical schema that might occur if the database administrator introduces new SDL statements into a database do not affect the semantics of the applications because physical data independence shields the application from changes at the storage level. Hence, although the performance of an application might change, the results it produces do not.

   In Sections 3.2 and 3.3, we describe the mother of all data models used by commercial DBMSs, the *relational model*, and the *lingua franca* these DBMS speak, **Structured Query Language (SQL)**. Be aware, however, that despite its name SQL is not *just* a query language; it is an amalgamation of a DML, a DDL, and an SDL—three for the price of one!

3.2 The Relational Model

The *relational data model* was proposed in 1970 by E. F. Codd and was considered a major breakthrough at the time. In fact, database research and development in the 1970s and 1980s was largely shaped by the ideas presented in Codd's original work [Codd 1970, 1990]. Even today, most commercial DBMSs are based on the relational model, although they are beginning to acquire object-oriented features, especially due to the increased use of XML-based data.

The main attraction of the relational model is that it is built around a simple and natural mathematical structure—the *relation* (or table). Relations have a set of powerful, high-level operators, and data manipulation languages are deeply rooted in mathematical logic. This solid mathematical background means that relational expressions (i.e., queries) can be analyzed. Hence, any expression can potentially be transformed (by the DBMS itself) into another, *equivalent,* expression that can be executed more efficiently, in a process called *query optimization*. Thus, application programmers need not study the nitty-gritty details of the internals of each database and need not be aware of how query evaluators work. The application programmer can formulate a query in a simple and natural way and leave it to the query optimizer to find an equivalent query that is more efficient to execute.

Nevertheless, query optimizers have limitations that can result in performance penalties for certain classes of complex queries. It is therefore important for both programmers and database designers to understand the heuristics they use. With this knowledge, programmers can formulate queries that the DBMS can optimize more easily, and database designers can speed up the evaluation of important queries by adding appropriate indices and using other design techniques.

3.2.1 Basic Concepts

The central construct in the relational model is the **relation**. A relation is two things in one: a **schema** and an **instance** of that schema.

Relation instance. A **relation instance** is nothing more than a table with rows and named columns. When no confusion arises, we refer to relation instances as just "relations." The rows in a relation are called *tuples*; they are similar to *records* in a file, but unlike file records all tuples have the same number of columns (this number is called the **arity** of the relation), and no two tuples in a relation instance can be the same. In other words, a relational instance is a *set* of unique tuples. The **cardinality** of a relation instance is the number of tuples in it.

Figure 3.2 shows one possible instance for the Student relation. The columns in this relation are named, which is the usual convention in the relational model. These named columns are also known as **attributes**. Because relations are sets of tuples, the order of these tuples is considered immaterial. Similarly, because columns are named, their order in a table is of no importance either. The relations in Figures 3.2 and 3.3 are thus considered to be the same relation.

STUDENT	Id	Name	Address	Status
	111111111	John Doe	123 Main St.	Freshman
	666666666	Joseph Public	666 Hollow Rd.	Sophomore
	111223344	Mary Smith	1 Lake St.	Freshman
	987654321	Bart Simpson	Fox 5 TV	Senior
	023456789	Homer Simpson	Fox 5 TV	Senior
	123454321	Joe Blow	6 Yard Ct.	Junior

FIGURE 3.2 Instance of the STUDENT relation.

STUDENT	Id	Name	Status	Address
	111223344	Mary Smith	Freshman	1 Lake St.
	987654321	Bart Simpson	Senior	Fox 5 TV
	111111111	John Doe	Freshman	123 Main St.
	023456789	Homer Simpson	Senior	Fox 5 TV
	666666666	Joseph Public	Sophomore	666 Hollow Rd.
	123454321	Joe Blow	Junior	6 Yard Ct.

FIGURE 3.3 STUDENT relation with different order of columns and tuples.

We should note that the terms "tuple," "attribute," and "relation" are preferred in relational database theory, while "row," "column," and "table" are the terms used in SQL. However, it is common to use these terms interchangeably.

The value of a particular attribute in any row of a relation is drawn from a set called the **attribute domain**—for example, the Address attribute of the STUDENT relation has as its domain the set of all strings. One important requirement placed on the values in a domain is **data atomicity**.[1] Data atomicity does not mean that these values are not decomposable. After all, we have seen that the values can be strings of characters, which means that they *are* decomposable. Rather, data atomicity means that the relational model does not specify any means for looking into the internal structure of the values, so that the values appear indivisible to the relational operators.

This atomicity restriction is sometimes seen as a shortcoming of the relational model, and most commercial systems relax it in various ways. Some remove it altogether, which leads to a breed of data models known as *object-relational*. We will return to the object-relational model in Chapter 16.

---

[1] The notion of *data atomicity* should not be confused with the unrelated notion of *transaction atomicity*, which we discussed in Section 2.3.

Brain Teaser: Can a relation have zero attributes?

Relation schema. A **relation schema** consists of

1. The **name** of the relation. Relation names must be unique across the database.
2. The names of the *attributes* in the relation along with their associated *domain names*. An **attribute** is simply the name given to a column in a relation instance. All columns in a relation must be named, and no two columns in the same relation can have the same name. A **domain name** is just a name given to some well-defined set of values. In programming languages, domain names are usually called *types*. Examples are INTEGER, REAL, and STRING.
3. The *integrity constraints* (*IC*). **Integrity constraints** are restrictions on the relational instances of this schema (i.e., restrictions on which tuples can appear in an instance of the relation). An instance of a schema is said to be **legal** if it satisfies all ICs associated with the schema.

To illustrate, let us revisit the schema that was mentioned before:

STUDENT(Id:INTEGER, Name:STRING, Address:STRING, Status:STRING)

This schema states that STUDENT relations must have exactly four attributes: Id, Name, Address, and Status with associated domains INTEGER and STRING. As seen from this example, different attributes in the same schema must have distinct names but can share domains.

The domains specify that in STUDENT relations all values in the column Id must belong to the domain INTEGER, while the values in all other columns must belong to the domain STRING. Naturally, we assume that the domain INTEGER consists of all integers and that the domain STRING consists of all character strings. However, schemas can also have *user-defined* domains, such as SSN or STATUS, that can be constrained to contain precisely the values appropriate for the attributes at hand. For instance, the domain STATUS can be defined to consist just of the symbols "freshman," "sophomore," and so forth, and the domain SSN can be defined to contain all (and only) nine-digit positive numbers. The point of this discussion is that relation schemas impose so-called type constraints.

A **type constraint** is a requirement that if S is a relation schema and s is a relation instance, then s must satisfy the following two conditions:

1. *Column naming.* Each column in s must correspond to an attribute in S (and vice versa), and the column names must be the same as the names of the corresponding attributes.
2. *Domain constraints.* For each attribute-domain pair, attr:DOM, in S, the values that appear in the column attr in s must belong to the domain DOM.

FIGURE **3.4** Fragment of the Student Registration database schema.

STUDENT (Id:INTEGER, Name:STRING, Address:STRING, Status:STRING)
PROFESSOR (Id:INTEGER, Name:STRING, DeptId:STRING)
COURSE (DeptId:STRING, CrsCode:STRING, CrsName:STRING, Descr:STRING)
TRANSCRIPT (StudId:INTEGER, CrsCode:STRING, Semester:STRING, Grade:STRING)
TEACHING (ProfId:INTEGER, CrsCode:STRING, Semester:STRING)

As we shall see, typing is just one of the several classes of constraints associated with relation schemas. To be legal, a schema instance must therefore satisfy typing as well as those additional constraints.

Relational database.   A **relational database** is a finite set of relations. Because a relation is two things in one, a database is also two things: a set of relation schemas (and other entities that we will describe shortly)—called a **database schema**— and a set of corresponding relation instances—called a **database instance**. When confusion does not arise, it is common to use the term "database" to refer to database instances only. Figure 3.4 depicts one possible fragment of a database schema for our Student Registration System. Figure 3.5 gives examples of instances corresponding to these relation schemas. Observe that each relation satisfies the type constraint specified by the corresponding schema.

> *Brain Teaser:* If you solved the previous teaser, what are the tuples of a 0-ary relation? How many tuples can such a relation have?

3.2.2 Integrity Constraints

We discussed the role that integrity constraints play in an application in Section 2.2. Now we have to fit these constraints into the database schema that supports that application. An **integrity constraint** (IC) is a statement about all *legal instances* of a database. That is, to be qualified as a legal instance a set of relations must satisfy all ICs associated with the database schema. We have already seen the type and domain constraints, and we will discuss several other kinds of constraints later.

Some integrity constraints are based on the business rules of the enterprise. The statement "No employee can earn more than his boss" is one example. Such constraints are often listed in the Requirements Document of the application. Other constraints, such as type and domain constraints, are based on the schema design and are specified by the database designer.

Since ICs are part of the database schema, they are usually specified in the original schema design. It is also possible to add or remove ICs later, after the database has been created and populated with data. Once constraints have been specified in the schema, it is the responsibility of the DBMS to make sure that they are not violated by the execution of any transactions.

PROFESSOR	Id	Name	DeptId
	101202303	John Smyth	CS
	783432188	Adrian Jones	MGT
	121232343	David Jones	EE
	864297531	Qi Chen	MAT
	555666777	Mary Doe	CS
	009406321	Jacob Taylor	MGT
	900120450	Ann White	MAT

COURSE	CrsCode	DeptId	CrsName	Descr
	CS305	CS	Database Systems	On the road to high-paying job
	CS315	CS	Transaction Processing	Recover from your worst crashes
	MGT123	MGT	Market Analysis	Get rich quick
	EE101	EE	Electronic Circuits	Build your own computer
	MAT123	MAT	Algebra	The world where $2 * 2 \neq 4$

TRANSCRIPT	StudId	CrsCode	Semester	Grade
	666666666	MGT123	F1994	A
	666666666	EE101	S1991	B
	666666666	MAT123	F1997	B
	987654321	CS305	F1995	C
	987654321	MGT123	F1994	B
	123454321	CS315	S1997	A
	123454321	CS305	S1996	A
	123454321	MAT123	S1996	C
	023456789	EE101	F1995	B
	023456789	CS305	S1996	A
	111111111	EE101	F1997	A
	111111111	MAT123	F1997	B
	111111111	MGT123	F1997	B

FIGURE 3.5 Examples of database instances.

TEACHING	ProfId	CrsCode	Semester
	009406321	MGT123	F1994
	121232343	EE101	S1991
	555666777	CS305	F1995
	864297531	MGT123	F1994
	101202303	CS315	S1997
	900120450	MAT123	S1996
	121232343	EE101	F1995
	101202303	CS305	S1996
	900120450	MAT123	F1997
	783432188	MGT123	F1997
	009406321	MGT123	F1997

FIGURE 3.5 (continued)

An IC can be **intrarelational**, meaning that it involves only one relation, or it can be **interrelational**, meaning that it involves more than one relation. The type constraint is an example of an intrarelational constraint; another example is a constraint that states that the value of the Id attribute in all rows of an instance of the STUDENT table must be unique. The latter is called a *key constraint* (discussed later). The constraint that asserts that the value of the attribute Id of each professor shown as teaching a course must appear as the value of the Id attribute of some row of the table PROFESSOR is an example of an interrelational constraint called a *foreign-key constraint* (discussed later). It expresses the requirement that each faculty member teaching a course must be described by some row of the table that describes all faculty members. The constraint that no employee can earn more than the boss[2] can be intrarelational or interrelational, depending on whether the salary information and the management structure information are stored in the same or different relations. This constraint belongs to the class of **semantic constraints**, which we will discuss later in this section.

The constraints up to this point were **static ICs. Dynamic ICs** are different: instead of restricting the legal instances of a database, they restrict the evolution of legal instances. This type of constraint is particularly useful for representing the business rules of an enterprise. An example is a rule that salaries must not increase or decrease by more than 5% per transaction. Another example is a rule that the marital status of a person cannot change from single to divorced. A bank might have a rule that if an overdraft has been made, it must be covered by the end of the next business day through a transfer of funds from the line-of-credit account.

---

[2] Let us not worry about such subtleties as how this constraint applies to the company president, who has no boss.

Unfortunately, the mainstream data manipulation languages (such as SQL) and commercial DBMSs provide little support for automatic enforcement of dynamic constraints. Therefore, application designers must provide code that enforces such constraints within the transactions that update the database. Because there is no easy way to verify that the transactions actually obey those rules, the integrity of such databases depends on the competence of the design, coding, and quality assurance groups that implement the transactions.

The situation with static ICs is much more satisfactory. Such constraints are both easier to specify and—in most cases—easier to enforce than dynamic ICs. In this section, we discuss the most common static integrity constraints. Section 3.3 shows how they are specified in SQL.

Key constraints.   We have already seen one example of a key constraint: values of the Id attribute in an instance of the STUDENT table must be unique. For a more complex example, consider the TRANSCRIPT relation. Because it seems reasonable to assume that a student can get only one (final) grade for any course in any given semester, we can specify that {StudId, CrsCode, Semester} is a key. This specification ensures that for any given value for StudId, CrsCode, and Semester, there is *at most* one transcript record with these values. If such a tuple actually exists, it specifies the one and only grade that a given student got for a given course in a given semester.

With this intuition in mind, we can give a more precise definition of a key constraint. A **key constraint**, $key(\overline{K})$, associated with a relation schema, **S**, consists of a subset, $\overline{K}$ (called a **key**), of attributes in **S** with the following **minimality property**: if $\overline{L}$ is a proper subset of $\overline{K}$ then $key(\overline{L})$ cannot be specified as a key constraint in the same schema **S**. A relation instance, **s**, of the schema **S** **satisfies** the constraint $key(\overline{K})$ if it has the following **uniqueness property**: **s** does not contain a pair of distinct tuples whose values agree on *all* of the attributes in $\overline{K}$.

Therefore, it is an error to specify, for example, both key(A) and key(A,B) as key constraints in the same relation schema. Also, if {A,B} is a key, then at most one tuple can have a given pair of values, *a* and *b*, in attributes A and B, respectively. However, it is possible for two different tuples to have the same value in the attribute A but not in B, and vice versa.

Example 3.2.1 (Key Constraint).   The TRANSCRIPT relation of Figure 3.5 satisfies the uniqueness property for the constraint key(StudId,CrsCode,Semester) since there are no distinct tuples whose values agree on each of these three attributes. On the other hand, this relation does not satisfy the constraint key(StudId,CrsCode) because, for example, tuples 1 and 3 are distinct and yet their values over StudId and CrsCode are the same. Similarly, the constraint key(StudId,Semester) is not satisfied because of, say, the last two tuples.

Note that some particular instance of TRANSCRIPT *could* satisfy the uniqueness property for, say, key(StudId,CrsCode). However, since this is not a reasonable constraint (since it implies that students are not allowed to re-take courses), it is unlikely to appear as one of the constraints for the Student Registration System. Note also that if this *were* specified as a constraint after all, then key(StudId,CrsCode,

Semester) could not have been a constraint at the same time, due to the minimality property.

Thus, if we decided to adopt the constraint key(StudId,CrsCode,Semester) for our system, then it would be allowed to have different tuples that record the same course taken by the same student, provided that this course was taken in different semesters (this would correspond to re-taking the course). It would also be allowed for any student to take several different courses during the same semester. However, it would not be possible for a student to get two different grades for the same course in the same semester. ■

The following points are important for understanding the notion of a key:

1. *Superset of a key has key-like properties.* If key($\overline{K}$) is a key constraint in schema **S**, and $\overline{L}$ is a set of attributes in **S** that *contains* $\overline{K}$, then legal instances of **S** cannot have *distinct* tuples that agree on every attribute in $\overline{L}$. Indeed, if t and s are tuples that have the same values for each attribute in $\overline{L}$, then they must have the same values for each attribute in $\overline{K}$. But because key($\overline{K}$) is a key constraint, it must have the uniqueness property, and thus t and s must be the same tuple.

    These ideas lead to the following notion: a set of attributes in **S** that contains a key is called a **superkey** of **S**. Thus, every key is also a superkey. The converse is not always true. For instance, in our TRANSCRIPT example, {StudId, CrsCode, Semester, Grade} is a superkey but not a key (because {StudId, CrsCode, Semester} is said to be a key, and they both cannot be keys at the same time, due to the minimality property). In other words, a superkey is like a key but without the minimality condition.

2. *Every relation has a key (and hence a superkey).* Indeed, the set of all attributes in a schema, **S**, is always a superkey because if a legal instance of **S** has a pair of tuples that agree on all attributes in **S**, then these must be identical tuples: since relations are sets, they cannot have identical elements. Now, if the set of all attributes in **S** is not a minimal superkey, there must be a superkey that is a strict subset of **S**. If that superkey is not a minimal superkey, there must be an even smaller superkey. As the number of attributes in a relation is finite, we will eventually hit the minimal superkey, which must then be a key, by definition.

3. *A schema can have several different keys.* For instance, in the COURSE relation, CrsCode can be one key. But because it is unlikely that the same department will offer two different courses with the same name, we can specify that {DeptId, CrsName} is also a key in the same relation.

    If a relation has several keys, they are referred to as **candidate keys**. However, one key is often designated as the **primary key**. A primary key might or might not have any particular semantic significance in the application (often a primary key is just the first among equals). However, commercial DBMSs treat primary keys as hints for optimizing the storage structures to enable efficient access to data whenever the value of a primary key is given. Thus, the choice of a primary key affects the physical schema and may affect performance.

FIGURE **3.6** Fragment of the Student Registration database with key constraints.

> STUDENT(Id:INTEGER, Name:STRING, Address:STRING, Status:STRING)
>   Key: {Id}
> PROFESSOR(Id:INTEGER, Name:STRING, DeptId:STRING)
>   Key: {Id}
> COURSE(CrsCode:STRING, DeptId:STRING, CrsName:STRING, Descr:STRING)
>   Keys: {CrsCode}, {DeptId,CrsName}
> TRANSCRIPT(StudId:INTEGER, CrsCode:STRING, Semester:STRING, Grade:STRING)
>   Key: {StudId,CrsCode,Semester}
> TEACHING(ProfId:INTEGER, CrsCode:STRING, Semester:STRING)
>   Key: {CrsCode,Semester}

Our fragment of the student registration database schema, with all of the key constraints included, is summarized in Figure 3.6. Note that the relation COURSE has two keys.

Referential integrity. In relational databases, it is common for tuples in one relation to reference tuples in the same or other relations. For instance, the value 009406321 of ProfId in the first tuple in TEACHING (Figure 3.5) refers to Professor Jacob Taylor, whose tuple in the table PROFESSOR has the same value in the Id field. Likewise, the value MGT123 in the first tuple of TEACHING references the Market Analysis course described by a tuple in the COURSE table.

In many situations, it is a violation of data integrity if the referenced tuple does not exist in the appropriate relation. For instance, it makes little sense to have a TEACHING tuple ⟨009406321, MGT123, F1994⟩ and not have the tuple describing MGT123 in the COURSE relation: otherwise, which course is Jacob Taylor teaching? Likewise, if the PROFESSOR relation has no tuple with Id 009406321, who is said to be teaching Market Analysis?

The requirement that the referenced tuples must exist (when the semantics of the data so requires) is called **referential integrity**. One important type of referential integrity is the *foreign-key constraint*.

Suppose that S and T are relation schemas, $\overline{F}$ is a list of attributes in S, and key$(\overline{K})$ is a key constraint in T. Suppose further that there is a known 1-1 correspondence between the attributes of $\overline{F}$ and $\overline{K}$ (but the names of the attributes in $\overline{F}$ and $\overline{K}$ need not be the same). We say that relation instances s and t (over schemas S and T, respectively) satisfy the **foreign-key constraint** "$S(\overline{F})$ references $T(\overline{K})$" and that $\overline{F}$ is a **foreign key** if and only if, for every tuple $s \in s$, there is a tuple $t \in t$ that has the same values over the attributes in $\overline{K}$ as does s over the corresponding attributes in $\overline{F}$.

The concept of a foreign-key constraint is illustrated in Figure 3.7, where attribute D in table T_1 has been declared a foreign key that refers to attribute E in table T_2. E must be a candidate (or primary) key of T_2, but note that the names of the referring and referenced attributes (D and E) in the two tables need not be the same. Note also that, although each row of T_1 must reference exactly one row of T_2, not all

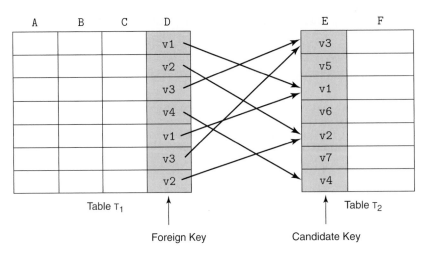

FIGURE 3.7 Attribute D in Table T_1 is a foreign key that refers to the candidate key, attribute E, in Table T_2.

rows of T_2 need be referenced, and two or more rows in T_1 can reference the same row in T_2.

In Section 3.3, we will show how foreign-key constraints are specified in SQL and will discuss the precise semantics of such constraints (which are slightly more permissive than the definition we have just given).

In a foreign-key constraint, the referring and the referenced relations need not be distinct. For instance, in the schema

EMPLOYEE(Id:INTEGER, Name:STRING, MngrId:INTEGER)

with the key {Id} the supervisor is also an employee. Thus, we have the constraint "EMPLOYEE (MngrId) references EMPLOYEE(Id)." This constraint implies that in every tuple of the EMPLOYEE relation—for example, ⟨....., ..., 998877665⟩—the MngrId value 998877665 must occur in the Id field in this or some other tuple of the same relation.

Example 3.2.2 (Foreign Keys for the Student Registration System). The following is a set of foreign-key constraints that is appropriate for the schema of the fragment of our Student Registration System shown in Figure 3.6.

TRANSCRIPT(StudId) references STUDENT(Id)
TRANSCRIPT(CrsCode) references COURSE(CrsCode)
TEACHING(ProfId) references PROFESSOR(Id)
TEACHING(CrsCode) references COURSE(CrsCode)
TRANSCRIPT(CrsCode,Semester) references TEACHING(CrsCode,Semester)

These constraints illustrate several important points. First, the attributes used to cross-reference relations need not have the same name. For instance, the attribute StudId of TRANSCRIPT references a STUDENT attribute named Id, not StudId. The foreign-key constraint in the EMPLOYEE relation above is another example of the same phenomenon.

Second, a foreign key can consist of more than one attribute, as in the last constraint. In plain English, this constraint says that if a student took a course in a particular semester, there must be a professor who taught that course in that semester. ■

Not all referential constraints are foreign-key constraints. Indeed, contrary to a popular belief, professors do not teach empty classes—at least at some universities. In other words,

TEACHING(CrsCode,Semester)
        <u>references</u> TRANSCRIPT(CrsCode,Semester)   **3.1**

appears to be an appropriate constraint for our database: at least one student must have taken (or be taking) the course named in each tuple of TEACHING. Hence, (3.1) is a referential integrity constraint, but is it a foreign-key constraint? The definition of foreign keys requires that the set of the *referenced* attributes must be a candidate key in the referenced relation.

The set ⟨CrsCode, Semester⟩ is not a candidate key of TRANSCRIPT because, naturally, we must allow several students to take the same course in any given semester. Thus, (3.1) is a referential integrity constraint, but not a foreign-key constraint.

The above constraint is known as an **inclusion dependency** in the database theory. A foreign-key constraint is just a special kind of inclusion dependency, one where the referenced attribute set is a key. Unfortunately, because of the complexity of automatic enforcement of general inclusion dependencies, such dependencies are not part of SQL's DDL. However, they can be expressed using SQL's assertion mechanism. This is illustrated later in this chapter: the CREATE ASSERTION statement (3.4) is one possible representation of constraint (3.1).

Semantic constraints. Type, domain, key, and foreign-key constraints deal with the structure of the data. Other types of constraints might have little to do with structure but rather implement a business rule or convention in a particular enterprise. Such constraints are *semantic* because they are derived from the particular application domain being modeled by the database.

Some semantic constraints were mentioned earlier: the number of students registered for a course must not exceed the capacity of the classroom where the course is scheduled to meet; a student registered for a course must meet all the prerequisites for the course; no employee can earn more than the boss; and so forth.

As we will see later, SQL provides support for specifying a wide range of semantic constraints.

3.3 SQL—Data Definition Sublanguage

Having familiarized ourselves with the basic concepts of the relational model—tables and constraints—we are now ready to look at how these concepts are specified in the "real world"—the data definition sublanguage of SQL. We base our discussion on the SQL-92 standard, but be aware that most database vendors do not fully support this standard. Because most SQL manuals are hundreds of pages long (and the actual standard has several thousand pages), we discuss only the most salient points of the language. You will need a vendor-specific reference manual if you plan to undertake serious SQL projects.

Still, SQL-92 belongs to the past, while we are planning for the future. So, to prepare for the things to come, we will also be peeking into the new standards, SQL:1999 and SQL:2003. We will discuss other parts of SQL:1999 and SQL:2003 later in the book. The most significant of those are triggers in Section 7.3 and object-relational databases in Section 16.3. Some vendors are beginning to support parts of this standard in their latest releases.

Schemas are specified using the CREATE TABLE statement of SQL. This statement has a rich syntax, which we will introduce gradually. As a bare minimum, CREATE TABLE specifies the typing constraint: the name of a relation and the names of the attributes with their associated domains. However, the same statement can also specify primary and candidate keys, foreign-key constraints, and even certain semantic constraints.

3.3.1 Specifying the Relation Type

The type for the STUDENT relation is defined as follows.

```
CREATE TABLE  STUDENT (
    Id           INTEGER,
    Name         CHAR(20),
    Address      CHAR(50),
    Status       CHAR(10) )
```

You should have no difficulty relating this SQL schema to earlier examples. Note that SQL allows the same symbolic name to be used for the name of a relation, an attribute, or even an attribute domain. Therefore, to distinguish the different parts of an SQL clause, we will be using different fonts for different syntactic categories.

3.3.2 The System Catalog

A DBMS must use information describing the structure of the database when it translates a statement of the DML into an executable program. It finds this information

Columns	AttrName	RelName	Position	Format
	AttrName	Columns	1	CHAR(255)
	RelName	Columns	2	CHAR(255)
	Position	Columns	3	CHAR(255)
	Format	Columns	4	CHAR(255)
	CrsCode	Course	1	CHAR(6)
	DeptId	Course	2	CHAR(4)
	CrsName	Course	3	CHAR(20)
	Descr	Course	4	CHAR(100)
	Id	Student	1	INTEGER
	Name	Student	2	CHAR(20)
	Address	Student	3	CHAR(50)
	Status	Student	4	CHAR(10)
	...	...	...	...

FIGURE 3.8 Catalog relation.

in the **system catalog**. Therefore, while conceptually the purpose of the CREATE TABLE clause is to define a schema, technically this means inserting rows that describe the schema of a created table into the catalog. The catalog is a collection of special relations with their own schema. Figure 3.8 shows a table, called Columns, which could be part of a catalog. Each row of Columns contains information about a column in some database table, and all columns in all database tables are described in this way. The four columns of the table Course, for example, are described by four rows in the middle of the Columns table.

Because Columns is a table itself, its description must also be recorded. Rather than creating special machinery for this purpose, it is convenient to describe Columns (and the other tables of the catalog) as a set of tuples in the catalog itself! Thus, the first few rows of Columns describe the schema of that very relation. For example, the first row says that the first column of Columns has the attribute name AttrName and the domain CHAR (255).

How then does all this referential complexity get bootstrapped? The catalog schema of a DBMS is designed by the vendor, and an instance of the catalog is created automatically whenever a new database is created by the database administrator.

3.3.3 Key Constraints

Primary keys and candidate keys are specified in SQL using two separate statements: PRIMARY KEY and UNIQUE. For instance, the schema of the table Course might look like this:

```
CREATE TABLE  COURSE   (
     CrsCode        CHAR(6),
     DeptId         CHAR(4),
     CrsName        CHAR(20),
     Descr          CHAR(100),
     PRIMARY KEY    (CrsCode),
     UNIQUE         (DeptId,CrsName) )
```

3.3.4 Dealing with Missing Information

Relations, as we have defined them, consist of tuples, which in turn are sequences of *known* values. For instance, in tuple ⟨111111111, Doe John, 123 Main St., freshman⟩, we have known values for Id, Name, Address, and so forth. In practice, the values of certain attributes might not be known. For example, when John Doe initially registers as a student we might not know his address. We might ask him to supply it as soon as possible, but we do not want to keep him out of our database until he complies. Instead, we use a placeholder, called NULL, and store it in place of the address until more information becomes available. Similarly, a tuple is entered in the TRANSCRIPT relation when a student registers for a course, but the Grade attribute for that tuple has no value until the semester completes.

The NULL placeholder is commonly referred to as a **null value**, but this is somewhat misleading because NULL is not a value—it indicates the *absence* of a "normal" value. In database theory and practice, NULL is treated as a special value that is a member of every attribute domain but is different from any other value in any domain. In fact, as we will see in Chapter 5, NULL is not even considered to be equal to itself!

In our example, null values arise because of a lack of information. In other situations, they arise by design. For instance, the attribute MaidenName is applicable to females but not to males. A database designer might decide that the schema

EMPLOYEE(Id:INT, Name:STRING, MaidenName:STRING)

is an appropriate description of a company's employees. If such a relation includes tuples for male employees, those tuples will not and cannot have any value for the MaidenName attribute. Again, we can use NULL here.

As we will show later, null values often introduce additional problems, especially in query processing. For these reasons and others, it is sometimes desirable not to allow null values in certain sensitive places, such as the primary key. Indeed, how can we interpret a row of STUDENT of the form ⟨NULL, Doe John, 123 Main St., freshman⟩? What if John Doe is sharing a room with a friend, also John Doe, who attends the same university and is a freshman? In this case, we might end up having two identical tuples in the same relation (each representing a different John Doe) and yet not being able to tell which John is represented by which tuple.

To preclude the above semantic difficulty, it is necessary to ensure that there is at least one key in each relation where null values are prohibited, and the primary key is the logical choice for this. Thus, the SQL standard does not permit any attribute of a primary key to have a null value. In addition to the primary key, there may be other places where NULL is inappropriate. For instance, while it might be acceptable to temporarily allow NULL in the address field, a missing student name would certainly be a problem.

Although null values are not allowed in primary keys, they are allowed in other candidate keys (unless the database designer explicitly prohibits this). Note that a null in a candidate key does not violate the definition of a key. Indeed, as mentioned earlier, NULL is not equal to itself. Therefore, if a null value occurs in a candidate key of a tuple, t, no other tuple can agree with t on that candidate key.

In summary, database designers can deal with the null value problem by not allowing nulls in attributes that are deemed crucial to the semantic integrity of the database. We can, for instance, banish the nulls from the Name field as follows.

```
CREATE TABLE  STUDENT   (
     Id              INTEGER,
     Name            CHAR(20)  NOT NULL,
     Address         CHAR(50),
     Status          CHAR(10) DEFAULT 'freshman',
     PRIMARY KEY (Id) )
```

In this example, null values are not allowed in the primary key, Id (which we do *not* need to specify explicitly), or in Name (which we *do* need to specify). One additional feature to note: The user can specify a *default* value for an attribute. This value will be automatically assigned to the attribute of a tuple should the tuple be inserted without this attribute being given a specific value.

3.3.5 Semantic Constraints

Semantic constraints are specified using the CHECK clause, whose basic syntax is

```
CHECK ( conditional expression )
```

The conditional expression can be any predicate or Boolean combination of predicates that can appear in the WHERE clause of an SQL statement. The integrity constraint is said to be violated if the conditional expression evaluates to false.

The CHECK clause is not used as a stand-alone statement: it is either attached to a CREATE TABLE statement, in which case it serves as an *intra*relational constraint on that particular relation, or it can be attached to a CREATE ASSERTION statement, in which case it is an *inter*relational constraint.

CHECK constraints in table definitions. CHECK constraints attached to CREATE TABLE statements are generally used to impose conditions on the content of individual relations. The following example illustrates how the CHECK clause can limit the range of an attribute.

```
CREATE TABLE  TRANSCRIPT  (
    StudId    INTEGER,
    CrsCode   CHAR(6),
    Semester  CHAR(6),
    Grade     CHAR(1),
    CHECK ( Grade IN ('A', 'B', 'C', 'D', 'F') ),
    CHECK ( StudId > 0 AND StudId < 1000000000 )   )
```

3.2

Restricting the applicable range of attributes is not the only use of the CHECK constraint in the above context. Using the somewhat contrived relation schema below, we can express the constraint that managers must always earn more than their subordinates.

```
CREATE TABLE  EMPLOYEE  (
    Id           INTEGER,
    Name         CHAR(20),
    Salary       INTEGER,
    MngrSalary   INTEGER,
    CHECK ( MngrSalary > Salary )  )
```

The semantics of the CHECK clause inside the CREATE TABLE statement requires that *every tuple* in the corresponding relation satisfy all of the conditional expressions associated with all CHECK clauses in the corresponding CREATE TABLE statement.

One important consequence of this semantics is that the *empty relation*—a relation that contains no tuples—*always satisfies all* CHECK *constraints* as there are no tuples to check. This can lead to certain unexpected results. Consider the following syntactically correct schema definition.

```
CREATE TABLE  EMPLOYEE  (
    Id           INTEGER,
    Name         CHAR(20),
    Salary       INTEGER,
    DepartmentId CHAR(4),
    MngrId       INTEGER,
    CHECK ( 0 < (SELECT COUNT(*) FROM EMPLOYEE) ),
    CHECK ( (SELECT COUNT(*) FROM MANAGER)
              < (SELECT COUNT(*) FROM EMPLOYEE) ) )
```

3.3

Both CHECK clauses involve SELECT statements that count the number of rows in the named relation. Hence, the first CHECK clause presumably says that the EMPLOYEE relation cannot be empty. However natural this constraint may seem to be, it *does not* achieve its intended goal. Indeed, as we have remarked, this condition is supposed to be satisfied by *every tuple* in the EMPLOYEE relation, *not* by the relation itself. Therefore, if the relation is empty, it satisfies every CHECK constraint, even the one that supposedly says that the relation must not be empty!

The second CHECK clause in (3.3) shows that in principle nothing stops us from trying to (mis)use this facility for interrelational constraints. We have assumed that there is a relation, MANAGER, that has a tuple for each manager in the company. The constraint presumably says that there must be more employees than managers, which it in fact does, but only if the EMPLOYEE relation is not empty.

General constraints: ASSERTIONS. Apart from the subtle bug, the second constraint in (3.3) looks particularly unintuitive because it is symmetric by nature and yet it is asymmetrically hardwired into the table definition of just one of the two relations involved. To overcome this problem, SQL provides one more way to use the CHECK clause—inside the CREATE ASSERTION statement. An assertion is a component of the database schema, like a table, so incorporating the CHECK clause within it puts the constraint in a symmetric relationship with the two tables. Thus, the two constraints can be restated as follows (and this time correctly!):

```
CREATE ASSERTION   ThouShaltNotFireEveryone
    CHECK ( 0 < (SELECT COUNT(*) FROM Employee) )
CREATE ASSERTION   WatchAdminCosts
    CHECK ( (SELECT COUNT(*) FROM Manager)
                < (SELECT COUNT(*) FROM Employee) ) )
```

Unlike the CHECK conditions that appear inside a table definition, those in the CREATE ASSERTION statement must be satisfied by the contents of the entire database rather than by individual tuples of a host table. Thus, a database satisfies the first assertion (above) if and only if the number of tuples in the EMPLOYEE relation is greater than zero. Likewise, the second assertion is satisfied whenever the MANAGER relation has fewer tuples than the EMPLOYEE relation has.

For another example of the use of assertions, suppose that the salary information about managers and employees is kept in different relations. We can then state our rule about who should earn more using the following assertion, which literally says that there must not exist an employee who has a boss who earns less. For the sake of this example, we assume that the MANAGER relation has the attributes Id and Salary.

```
CREATE ASSERTION   ThouShaltNotOutearnYourBoss
    CHECK ( NOT EXISTS
              (SELECT * FROM Employee, Manager
               WHERE Employee.Salary > Manager.Salary
                  AND Employee.MngrId = Manager.Id ))
```

An interesting question now is, what if, at the time of specifying the constraint THOUSHALTNOTFIREEVERYONE, the EMPLOYEE relation is empty? And what if, at the time of specifying THOUSHALTNOTOUTEARNYOURBOSS, there already is an employee who earns more than the boss? The SQL standard states that if a new constraint is defined and the existing database does not satisfy it, the constraint is *rejected*. The database designer then has to find out the cause of constraint violation and either amend the constraint or rectify the database.

Our last example is a little more complex.[3] It shows how assertions can be used to specify inclusion dependencies that are not foreign-key constraints. More specifically, we express the inclusion dependency (3.1) on page 45 using the assertion statement of SQL.

```
CREATE ASSERTION   CoursesShallNotBeEmpty
    CHECK (NOT EXISTS (
        SELECT * FROM Teaching
        WHERE NOT EXISTS (                                    3.4
            SELECT * FROM Transcript
            WHERE Teaching.CrsCode = Transcript.CrsCode
                AND Teaching.Semester = Transcript.Semester)))
```

The CHECK constraint here verifies that there is no tuple in the TEACHING relation (the outer NOT EXISTS statement) for which no matching class exists in the TRANSCRIPT relation (the inner NOT EXISTS statement). A tuple in the TEACHING relation refers to the same class as does a tuple in the TRANSCRIPT relation if in both tuples the CrsCode and Semester components are equal. This test is performed in the innermost WHERE clause.

Different assertions have different maintenance costs (the time required for the DBMS to check that the assertion is satisfied). Generally, intrarelational constraints come cheaper than do interrelational constraints. Among the interrelational constraints, those that are based on keys are easier to enforce than those that are not. Thus, for instance, foreign-key constraints come cheaper than do general inclusion dependencies, such as (3.4).

The automatic checking of integrity constraints by a DBMS is one of the more powerful features of SQL. It not only protects the database from errors that might be introduced by untrustworthy users (or sloppy application programmers) but can simplify access to the database as well. For example, a primary key constraint ensures that at most one tuple containing a particular primary key value exists in a table. If a DBMS did not automatically check this constraint, an application program attempting to insert a new tuple or to update the key attributes of an existing tuple would have to scan the table first to ensure that the primary key constraint is maintained.

---

[3] It involves the use of a nested, correlated subquery. If you do not understand (3.4), plan to come back here after reading Chapter 5.

3.3.6 User-Defined Domains

We have already seen how the CHECK clause lets us limit the range of the attributes in a table. SQL provides an alternative way to enforce such constraints by allowing the user to define appropriate ranges of values, give them domain names, and then use these names in various table definitions. This approach makes the design more modular. We could, for example, create the domain GRADES and use it in the TRANSCRIPT relation instead of using the CHECK constraint directly in the definition of that relation.

```
CREATE DOMAIN  GRADES CHAR(1)
    CHECK ( VALUE IN ('A', 'B', 'C', 'D', 'F', 'I') )
```

The only difference between this and the previous constraint (3.2) on page 50, which was directly imposed on the table STUDENT, is that here we use a special keyword, VALUE, instead of the attribute name—we cannot use attribute names here, because the domain is not attached to any particular table. Now we can add

```
Grade GRADES
```

to the definition of STUDENT. The overall effect is the same, but we can use this predefined domain name in several tables without having to repeat the definition. At a later time, if we need to change this domain definition, the change will automatically propagate to all the tables that use that domain. A domain is a component of the database schema, like a table or an assertion.

Note that, as with assertions, we can use complex queries to define fairly nontrivial domains.

```
CREATE DOMAIN  UpperDivisionStudent INTEGER
    CHECK ( VALUE  IN  (SELECT Id FROM Student
                         WHERE Status IN ('senior', 'junior')
                         AND  VALUE IS NOT NULL ) )
```

The domain UpperDivisionStudent consists of student Ids that belong to students whose status is either senior or junior. In addition, the last clause excludes NULL from that domain. Observe that, in order to verify that the constraint imposed by this domain is satisfied, a query against the database is run. Since such queries might be quite expensive, not every vendor supports the creation of such "virtual" domains.

3.3.7 Foreign-Key Constraints

SQL provides a simple and natural way of specifying foreign keys. The following statement makes CrsCode a foreign key referencing COURSE and makes ProfId a foreign key referencing the PROFESSOR relation.

```
CREATE TABLE Teaching (
     ProfId    INTEGER,
     CrsCode   CHAR(6),
     Semester CHAR(6),
     PRIMARY KEY (CrsCode, Semester),
     FOREIGN KEY (CrsCode) REFERENCES Course,
     FOREIGN KEY (ProfId) REFERENCES Professor (Id)   )
```

If the names of the referring and the referenced attributes are the same, the referenced attribute can be omitted. The attribute CrsCode above is an example of this situation. If the referenced attribute has a different name than that of the referring attribute, both attributes must be specified. The term Professor (Id) in the second FOREIGN KEY clause shows how this is done.

It should be noted that, although the SQL standard does not require that the referenced attributes form a *primary* key (they can form *any candidate* key), some database vendors impose the primary key restriction.

In the above example, whenever a Teaching tuple has a course code in it, the actual course record with this course code must exist in the Course relation. Similarly, the professor's Id in a Teaching tuple must reference an existing tuple in the Professor relation. The DBMS is expected to enforce these constraints automatically once they are specified. Thus, as part of the procedure for deleting a tuple in the Professor relation, a check is made to ensure that there is no corresponding tuple in the Teaching relation.

Foreign keys and nulls. What if, in a particular tuple, the value of an attribute in a foreign key is NULL? Should we insist that there be a corresponding tuple in the referenced relation with a null value in a key attribute? Not a good idea, especially if the referenced key is a primary key. Therefore, SQL *relaxes the foreign-key constraint* by letting foreign keys have null values. In this case there need not be a corresponding tuple in the referenced relation.

Chicken-and-egg problems. Foreign-key constraints raise other subtle issues too. Consider the table Employee defined in (3.3). Suppose that we also have a table that describes departments.

```
CREATE TABLE   Department   (
     DeptId    CHAR(4),
     Name      CHAR(40)
     Budget    INTEGER,
     MngrId    INTEGER,
     FOREIGN KEY (MngrId) REFERENCES Employee (Id) )
```

Now, if we look back at the DepartmentId attribute of the EMPLOYEE table, it is clear that this attribute is intended to represent valid department Ids (i.e., Ids of the departments stored in the DEPARTMENT relation). In other words, the constraint

FOREIGN KEY (DepartmentId) REFERENCES DEPARTMENT (DeptId)

is in order as part of the CREATE TABLE EMPLOYEE statement.

The problem is that either EMPLOYEE or DEPARTMENT has to be defined first. If EMPLOYEE comes first, we cannot have the above foreign-key constraint in the CREATE TABLE EMPLOYEE statement because it refers to the yet-to-be-defined table DEPARTMENT. If DEPARTMENT is defined before EMPLOYEE, the DBMS will issue an error trying to process the foreign-key constraint in the CREATE TABLE DEPARTMENT statement because this constraint references the yet-to-be-defined table EMPLOYEE. We are facing a chicken-and-egg problem.

The solution is to *postpone* the introduction of the foreign-key constraint in the first table. That is, if CREATE TABLE EMPLOYEE is executed first, we should not have the FOREIGN KEY clause in it. However, after CREATE TABLE DEPARTMENT has been processed, we can *add* the desired constraint to EMPLOYEE using the ALTER TABLE directive. This directive will be described in detail later in this section. Here we give only the final result.

ALTER TABLE   EMPLOYEE
    ADD CONSTRAINT EMPDEPTCONSTR
        FOREIGN KEY (DepartmentId) REFERENCES DEPARTMENT (DeptId)

If, after settling this circular reference problem, we now want to start populating the database, we are in for another surprise. Suppose that we want to put the first tuple, ⟨000000007, James Bond, 7000000, B007, 000000000⟩, into the EMPLOYEE relation. Since at this moment the DEPARTMENT table is empty, the foreign-key constraint that prescribes that B007 must refer to a valid tuple in the DEPARTMENT relation is violated.

One solution is to initially replace the DepartmentId component in all tuples in the EMPLOYEE relation with NULL. Then, when DEPARTMENT is populated with appropriate tuples, we can scan the EMPLOYEE relation and replace the null values with valid department Ids. However, this solution is awkward and error-prone. A better solution is to use a transaction and deferred checking of integrity constraints.

In Chapter 2, we pointed out that the intermediate states of the database produced by a transaction might be inconsistent—they might temporarily violate integrity constraints. The only important thing is that constraints must be preserved when the transaction commits. To accommodate the possibility of temporary constraint violations, SQL allows the programmer to specify the mode of a particular integrity constraint to be either IMMEDIATE, in which case a check is made after each SQL statement that changes the database, or DEFERRED, in which case a check is made only when a transaction commits. Then, to deal with the circular reference problem just described, we can

1. Declare the foreign-key constraints in the two tables, EMPLOYEE and DEPART-MENT, as INITIALLY DEFERRED to set the initial mode of constraint checking.
2. Make the updates that populate these tables part of the same transaction. This will allow the intermediate states to be temporarily inconsistent.
3. Make sure that when all updates are done, the foreign-key constraints are satisfied. Otherwise, the transaction will be aborted when it terminates.

The full details of how transactions are defined in SQL and how they interact with constraints will be discussed in Chapter 8.

3.3.8 Reactive Constraints

When a constraint is violated, the corresponding transaction is typically aborted. However, in some cases, other remedial actions are more appropriate. Foreign-key constraints are one example of this situation.

Suppose that a tuple ⟨007007007, MGT123, F1994⟩ is inserted into the TEACH-ING relation. Because the table PROFESSOR does not have a professor with the Id 007007007, this insertion violates the foreign-key constraint that requires all non-NULL values in the ProfId field of TEACHING to reference existing professors. In such a case, the semantics of SQL is very simple: the insertion is rejected.

When constraint violation occurs because of deletion of a referenced tuple, SQL offers more choices. Consider the tuple $t = $ ⟨009406321, MGT123, F1994⟩ in the table TEACHING. According to Figure 3.5, t references Professor Taylor in the PROFESSOR relation, and the course Market Analysis in the COURSE relation. Suppose that Professor Taylor leaves the university. What should happen to t? One solution is to temporarily set the value of ProfId in t to NULL until a replacement lecturer is found. Another solution is to have the attempt to delete Professor Taylor's tuple from the PROFESSOR relation fail, which might reflect the policy that professors are not allowed to leave in the middle of a semester. Finally, if Professor Taylor is the only faculty member capable of teaching the course, we might remove MGT123 from the curriculum altogether. By deleting the referencing tuple, t, the violation of referential integrity is resolved.

These possibilities can be rephrased as **reactive constraints**. A reactive constraint is a static constraint coupled with a specification of *what to do* if a certain event happens. For instance, the first alternative above is a constraint that requires that whenever a PROFESSOR tuple is deleted, the field ProfId of all the referencing tuples in TEACHING must be set to NULL. The second alternative is a constraint that asserts that if a referencing tuple exists it cannot be deleted. The third alternative asserts that all referencing tuples are deleted when the referenced tuple is deleted.

We can specify the appropriate response to an event using **triggers**, which are statements of the form

WHENEVER *event* DO *action*

Triggers attached to foreign-key constraints. SQL supports a special kind of triggers, which are attached to foreign-key constraints. These triggers are specified as part of the FOREIGN KEY clause using the options ON DELETE and ON UPDATE, which indicate what to do if a referenced tuple is deleted or updated. To illustrate, let us revisit the definition of TEACHING.

```
CREATE TABLE  TEACHING   (
     ProfId    INTEGER,
     CrsCode   CHAR(6),
     Semester CHAR(6),
     PRIMARY KEY (CrsCode, Semester),
     FOREIGN KEY (ProfId) REFERENCES PROFESSOR(Id)
          ON DELETE NO ACTION
          ON UPDATE CASCADE,
     FOREIGN KEY (CrsCode) REFERENCES COURSE (CrsCode)
          ON DELETE SET NULL
          ON UPDATE CASCADE  )
```

Here we have specified four triggers. One is **fired** (i.e., executed) whenever a PROFESSOR tuple is deleted, one whenever a PROFESSOR tuple is modified, one when a COURSE tuple is deleted, and one when a COURSE tuple is modified. The clause ON DELETE NO ACTION means that any attempt to remove a PROFESSOR tuple must be rejected outright if the professor is referenced by a TEACHING tuple. NO ACTION is the default situation when an ON DELETE or ON UPDATE clause is not specified. The clause ON UPDATE CASCADE means that if the Id number of a PROFESSOR tuple is changed, the change must be propagated to all referencing TEACHING tuples (i.e., the new Id must be stored in the referencing tuples). Hence, the same professor is recorded as teaching the course. (Similarly, a specification ON DELETE CASCADE causes the referencing tuple to be deleted.) ON DELETE SET NULL tells the DBMS that if a COURSE tuple is removed and there is a referencing TEACHING tuple, the referencing attribute, CrsCode, in that tuple must be set to NULL. Alternatively, the designer can specify SET DEFAULT (instead of SET NULL): if CrsCode was defined with a DEFAULT option (e.g., the Status attribute in the STUDENT relation), then it will be reset to its default value if the referenced tuple is deleted; otherwise, it will be set to NULL (which is the default value for the DEFAULT option).

Any combination of DELETE or UPDATE triggers with NO ACTION, CASCADE, or SET NULL/DEFAULT options is allowed in foreign-key triggers. The action taken to repair a foreign-key violation in one table, T_2, in response to a change in another table, T_1, (e.g., delete a row in T_2 if a row is deleted in T_1) might cause a violation of a foreign-key constraint in T_3 that refers to T_2. The action specified in T_3 controls how that violation is handled. If the entire chain of violations cannot be resolved (e.g., the action specified in T_3 is NO ACTION), the initial deletion from T_1 is rejected.

General triggers. The ON DELETE/UPDATE triggers are simple and powerful, but they are not powerful enough to capture a wide variety of constraint violations that arise in database applications and are not due to foreign keys. For instance, the referential integrity constraint (3.1) on page 45 is *not* a foreign-key constraint and yet the same problems arise here when tuples of the TRANSCRIPT relation are modified or deleted. More importantly, foreign-key triggers cannot even begin to address common needs such as preventing salaries from changing by more than 5% in the same transaction.

To handle these needs, all major database vendors took destiny into their own hands and retrofitted their products with trigger mechanisms. Interestingly, the original design of SQL—before there was an SQL-92 standard—did have relatively powerful triggers. Triggers reappeared in SQL with the SQL:1999 standard, but some vendors are yet to align their offerings with the new standard. We will briefly describe the general trigger mechanism here and leave the details to Chapter 7.

The basic idea behind triggers is simple: whenever a specified *event* occurs, execute some specified *action*. Consider the following simple trigger defined using the syntax of SQL:1999. The trigger fires whenever CrsCode or Semester is changed in a tuple in the TRANSCRIPT relation. When the trigger fires and the grade recorded for the course is not NULL, an exception is raised and the changes made by the transaction are rolled back. Otherwise (if the grade *is* NULL), we interpret the change as a student dropping one course in favor of another, so the trigger does nothing and the change is allowed to take hold. This trigger is created with the statement

```
CREATE TRIGGER   CrsChangeTrigger
        AFTER UPDATE OF  CrsCode, Semester   ON Transcript
        WHEN    ( Grade IS NOT NULL )
            ROLLBACK
```

This definition is self-explanatory except, perhaps, for the WHEN clause, which acts as a guard, that is, as a precondition that must be satisfied in order for the trigger to fire. If the precondition is true, the statements following WHEN are executed. In our case, the statement aborts the transaction.

In general, many more details might need to be specified in order to define a trigger. For instance, should the action be executed just before the triggering update is applied to the database or after it? Should this action be executed immediately after the event or at some later time? Can a triggered action trigger another action? Moreover, to specify the guard in the WHEN clause, we might need to refer to both the *old* and the *new* values of the modified tuples (e.g., to check that salaries have not been changed by more than 5%). We postpone the discussion of these issues until Chapter 7, where many more examples of triggers will be given. In particular, we will discuss how general triggers can be used to maintain inclusion dependencies in the presence of updates (analogous to how ON DELETE and ON UPDATE triggers are used to maintain foreign-key constraints).

3.3.9 Database Views

In Section 3.1, we discussed the three levels of abstraction in databases: the physical level, the conceptual level, and the external level. We have already shown how the conceptual layer is defined in SQL. We now discuss the external (or view) layer of SQL. The physical layer will be discussed in detail in Chapter 9.

In SQL, the external schema is defined using the CREATE VIEW statement. In many respects, a view is like an ordinary table: you can query it, modify it, or control access to it. However, in several important ways a view is not a table. For one thing, the rows of a view are derived from tables (and other views) of the database. Thus, in reality a view repackages information stored elsewhere. Furthermore, the contents of a view do not physically exist in the database. Instead, a recipe for *constructing* the contents on the fly from other database tables is stored in the system catalog. As will be seen shortly, the view definition is a hybrid of the CREATE TABLE statement and the SELECT statement introduced in Chapter 2. Because of this, views are often called **virtual tables**.

To illustrate, consider the following view, which tells which professors have taught which students (a professor is said to have taught a student if the student took a course in the semester in which the professor offered it).

```
CREATE VIEW     PROFSTUD (Prof, Stud)   AS
SELECT TEACHING.ProfId, TRANSCRIPT.StudId
FROM TRANSCRIPT, TEACHING                              3.5
WHERE TRANSCRIPT.CrsCode = TEACHING.CrsCode
        AND TRANSCRIPT.Semester = TEACHING.Semester
```

The first line defines the name of the view and its attributes. The rest is just an SQL query that tells how to obtain the contents of the view. These contents, with respect to the database instance of Figure 3.5, are shown in Figure 3.9. To help you understand where the tuples in the view come from, each tuple is annotated with a "justification." (A justification for a tuple $\langle p, s \rangle$ is a course code together with the semester in which student s took that course from professor p.)

The view PROFSTUD might be part of the external schema that helps the university keep in touch with its alumni since establishing the relationship between students and professors through courses might be an important and frequent operation in such an application. So, instead of this relationship being reinvented by every single application, it can be defined once and for all in the form of a view. Once it is defined, all applications can refer to the view as if it were an ordinary table. The rows of the view are constructed at the time it is accessed, so the contents change as the underlying relations are updated by transactions.

PROFSTUD	Prof	Stud	Justification
	009406321	666666666	MGT123,F1994
	121232343	666666666	EE101,S1991
	900120450	666666666	MAT123,F1997
	555666777	987654321	CS305,F1995
	009406321	987654321	MGT123,F1994
	101202303	123454321	CS315,S1997; CS305,S1996
	900120450	123454321	MAT123,S1996
	121232343	023456789	EE101,F1995
	101202303	023456789	CS305,S1996
	900120450	111111111	MAT123,F1997
	009406321	111111111	MGT123,F1997
	783432188	111111111	MGT123,F1997

FIGURE 3.9 Contents of the view defined by SQL statement (3.5).

In Chapter 5, we will expand our discussion of the view mechanism and show how views can be used to modularize the construction of complex queries. The authorization mechanism is another important use of views. In Section 3.3.12, we will see that views can be treated as ordinary tables for the purpose of granting selective access rights to the information stored in the database.

3.3.10 Modifying Existing Definitions

Although database schemas are not supposed to change frequently, they do evolve. Occasionally, new fields are added to relations or existing fields are dropped; new constraints and domains are created, or old ones become invalid (perhaps because business rules change). Of course, we can always copy the old contents of a relation to a temporary space, erase the old relation and its schema, and then create a new relation schema with the old name. However, this process is tedious and error-prone. To simplify schema maintenance, SQL provides the ALTER statement, which in its simplest form looks like this.

```
ALTER TABLE   STUDENT
      ADD COLUMN Gpa  INTEGER DEFAULT 0
```

This command adds a new field to the STUDENT relation and initializes the field's value in each tuple to 0. You can also use DROP COLUMN to remove a column from a relation and add or drop constraints. For instance,

```
ALTER TABLE  STUDENT
    ADD CONSTRAINT GPARANGE CHECK (Gpa >= 0 AND Gpa <= 4)
ALTER TABLE  TEACHING
    ADD CONSTRAINT TEACHKEY UNIQUE(ProfId, Semester, Time)
```

If the current instance of STUDENT violates the new constraint GPARANGE, or if TEACHING violates TEACHKEY, the newly added constraints are rejected.

In order for a constraint to be "droppable" from a table definition, the constraint must be named at the time when it is defined—an option we have not used until now. We make up for this by naming every constraint in a revised definition of TRANSCRIPT.

```
CREATE TABLE  TRANSCRIPT  (
    StudId      INTEGER,
    CrsCode     CHAR(6),
    Semester    CHAR(6),
    Grade       GRADES,
    CONSTRAINT TRKEY PRIMARY KEY (StudId, CrsCode, Semester),
    CONSTRAINT STUDFK FOREIGN KEY (StudId) REFERENCES STUDENT,
    CONSTRAINT CRSFK FOREIGN KEY (CrsCode) REFERENCES COURSE,
    CONSTRAINT IDRANGE CHECK ( StudId > 0 AND
                                StudId < 1000000000 ))
```

Now we can alter the above definition by dropping any one of the specified integrity constraints. For example,

```
ALTER TABLE  TRANSCRIPT DROP CONSTRAINT TRKEY
```

When a table is no longer needed, its definition can be erased from the catalog. In this case, the schema of the table and its instance are *both* lost. Previously defined assertions and domains can also be dropped. For example,

```
DROP TABLE  EMPLOYEE  RESTRICT
DROP ASSERTION THOUSHALTNOTFIREEVERYONE
DROP DOMAIN GRADES
```

> *Brain Teaser:* What should happen to the foreign key CrsCode in TRANSCRIPT if we drop COURSE?

The **DROP TABLE** command has two options: RESTRICT and CASCADE. With the RESTRICT option, the DROP statement would refuse to delete a table if it is used in some other definition, such as integrity constraint. For instance, the constraint

THOUSHALTNOTFIREEVERYONE would prevent deletion of EMPLOYEE in the above case. The CASCADE option, in contrast, deletes a table definition along with any other definition that uses this table. So, for example, if we used CASCADE in the above DROP TABLE command, the assertion THOUSHALTNOTFIREEVERYONE would be deleted along with the EMPLOYEE table (and with the constraint WATCHADMIN-COSTS). In this case, the above DROP ASSERTION statement would be redundant.

The DROP DOMAIN command has its own quirks. For instance, deleting the domain GRADES above will *not* leave the attribute Grade of TRANSCRIPT in limbo. Instead, the CHECK clause that defines GRADES is copied over and is attached to all tables where this domain is used. Only after the orphaned attributes are taken care of will the GRADE domain be erased from the system catalog.

> *Brain Teaser:* Can a relation instance become invalid after execution of an ADD CONSTRAINT statement? What about DROP CONSTRAINT? DROP DOMAIN?

3.3.11 SQL-Schemas

The structure of a database is described in the system catalog. A catalog is SQL's version of a directory, in which elements are schema objects, such as tables and domains. Thus, for example, Figure 3.8 on page 47 is a simplified version of a part of the catalog for the Student Registration System. SQL partitions the catalog into SQL-schemas. An **SQL-schema**[4] is a description of a portion of a database that is under the control of a single user who has the authorization to create and access the objects within it. For example,

CREATE SCHEMA SRS_STUDINFO AUTHORIZATION JohnDoe

creates the SQL-schema SRS_STUDINFO describing the part of the Student Registration System database that contains information about students. The AUTHORIZATION clause specifies the user (JohnDoe in our case) who controls the permissions for accessing tables and other objects defined in that SQL-schema.

The naming mechanism used in conjunction with SQL-schemas is similar to that used for directories in operating systems. For example, if JohnDoe wants to create a STUDENT table in the SRS_STUDINFO SQL-schema, he refers to it as SRS_STUDINFO.STUDENT. To refer to the STUDFK constraint, he uses SRS_STUDINFO.STUDFK. Thus, an SQL-schema also serves as a kind of namespace mechanism that allows use of the same name for different relations (domains, constraints, etc.) by putting them under the scope of different schemas.

As with every CREATE statement, there is a matching DROP SCHEMA statement. For instance, JohnDoe can delete the above schema (and the entire portion of the database under it) using the following statement:

---

[4] Note that this use of the word "schema" is different than our previous use to describe a relation schema or database schema. We use the term "SQL-schema" to refer to the SQL usage.

```
DROP SCHEMA  SRS_STUDINFO
```

SQL does not specify the format in which the information in an SQL-schema must be stored, but it does require that each system catalog contains one particular schema, named INFORMATION_SCHEMA, whose contents are precisely specified. INFORMATION_SCHEMA contains a set of SQL tables that repeat, in a precisely defined way, all the definitions from all other SQL-schemas in the catalog. The information in INFORMATION_SCHEMA can be accessed by any authorized user.

Finally, we note that SQL defines a **cluster** as a set of catalogs. A cluster describes the set of databases that can be accessed by a single SQL program. Thus, our university might define a cluster describing all of the databases it maintains that can be accessed by a single transaction.

3.3.12 Access Control

Databases often contain sensitive information. Therefore, the system must ensure that only those authenticated users who are authorized to access the database are allowed to and that they are only allowed to access information that has been specifically made available to them. Many transaction processing systems provide extensive authentication and authorization mechanisms. Authentication occurs prior to access. It might be the result of providing a password to the DBMS, or it can be a more elaborate scheme involving a separate security server. In any case, once authentication has been completed, the user is assumed to be (correctly) associated with an *authorization Id* and access to the database can begin. In SQL, **authorization Ids** are tokens that denote sets of privileges. Several database users can have the same authorization Id, in which case they would all have the same privileges.

The creator of a table or other object is assumed to own that object and has all privileges with respect to it. The owner can grant other users certain specific privileges with respect to that object by using the GRANT statement

```
GRANT  { privilege-list  |  All PRIVILEGES }
          ON  object
          TO  { user-list  |  PUBLIC }  [ WITH GRANT OPTION ]
```

where WITH GRANT OPTION means that the recipient can subsequently grant to others the privileges she has been granted.

If the object is a table or a view, *privilege-list* can include

```
SELECT
DELETE
INSERT    [(column-comma-list)]
UPDATE    [(column-comma-list)]
REFERENCES    [(column-comma-list)]
```

The first four options grant the privilege of performing the specified statement. The options that include (*column-comma-list*) grant the privilege only for the specified columns. For example, if the INSERT privilege has been granted, only the values of the attributes named in *comma-list* can be specified in the inserted tuple. All *comma-lists* are optional, as indicated by the square brackets.

REFERENCES grants the privilege of referring to the table or column using a foreign key. It might seem strange to control this type of access, but security is not complete if foreign-key constraints are not controlled. Two problems arise if foreign-key constraints can be set up arbitrarily. Suppose that a student is permitted to create the table

```
CREATE TABLE  DontDismissMe  (
    Id    INTEGER,
    FOREIGN KEY (Id) REFERENCES Student)
```

If she inserts a single row in DontDismissMe containing her Id, the registrar will not be able to dismiss the student—that is, delete the student's row from Student—because a deletion would cause a violation of referential integrity and hence be rejected by the DBMS.

Unrestricted access to foreign keys can also create certain information leaks. Suppose that, in the interest of protecting student information, SELECT access to Student is granted only to university employees in the registrar's office. If however, an intruder were allowed to create the above table (perhaps with the name ProbeProtectedInfo), this restriction could be circumvented. If the intruder inserted the Id of a particular individual in the table and the insertion were permitted by the DBMS, the intruder could conclude that a row for that individual existed in Student (since referential integrity would otherwise be violated). Similarly, if the insertion were denied, the intruder could conclude that the individual was not a student. Hence, even though the intruder did not have permission to access the table through a SELECT statement, he was able to extract some information.

Example 3.3.1 (Grant Statement).   The following GRANT statement gives John Smyth and Mary Doe the permission to read a row and to update the ProfId column of the Teaching relation.

```
GRANT SELECT, UPDATE (ProfId) ON StudRegSystem.Teaching
      TO JohnSmyth, MaryDoe WITH GRANT OPTION
```

It also gives them permission to pass on the same privileges to other users. Note, however, that these users are not allowed to delete tuples from that relation. Nor can they change other columns. However, they can see the information stored in all columns of the relation.   ∎

Example 3.3.2 (Authorization through Views).   SQL allows control of not only direct access to databases but also indirect access through views. For instance, the following statement gives all users who are classified as alumni unrestricted query access to the PROFSTUD view defined in statement (3.5) on page 59.

    GRANT SELECT ON PROFSTUD TO Alumnus

However, this **GRANT** statement does not permit the alumni to pass their query rights to others, and they cannot update the view. What is more interesting is that these users do not even have the rights to access TRANSCRIPT and TEACHING—the two relations that supply the contents for the PROFSTUD view. Their access is *indirect* and only to the parts of these relations that are visible through the view. ■

It would have been convenient to use views to selectively grant UPDATE, INSERT, or DELETE privileges. For example, one might want to grant prof_smith the right to update the Grade column of the TRANSCRIPT table, but only on the rows corresponding to courses he has taught. Unfortunately, not every view is updatable, and so it is not always possible to use views in this way. Chapter 5 will have further discussion on this subject.

Privileges can also be granted for objects other than tables (for example, domains). We omit the details.

Privileges, or the grant option for privileges, can be revoked using the REVOKE statement.

    REVOKE [GRANT OPTION FOR] *privilege-list*
        ON *object*
        FROM *user-list* {CASCADE | RESTRICT}

CASCADE means that if some user, U_1, whose user name appears on the list *user-list*, has granted those privileges to another user, U_2, the privileges granted to U_2 are also revoked. If U_2 has granted those privileges to still another user, those privileges are revoked as well, and so on. The option RESTRICT means that if any such dependent privileges exist, the REVOKE statement is rejected.

In many applications, granting privileges at the level of database operations, such as SELECT or UPDATE, is not adequate. For example, only a depositor can deposit in a bank account and only a bank official can add interest to the account, but both the deposit and interest transactions might use the same UPDATE statement. For such applications, it is more appropriate to grant privileges at the level of subroutines or transactions. Many transaction processing systems control access at this level.

BIBLIOGRAPHIC NOTES

The relational data model was introduced in [Codd 1970, 1990]. Later on [Codd 1979] proposed various extensions to the original model in order to capture more semantic information.

These ideas were extended and implemented in the two pioneering relational systems: System R [Astrahan et al. 1981] and INGRES [Stonebraker 1986]. Eventually, System R became DB2, a commercial product from IBM, and INGRES became a commercial product under the same name (currently sold by Computer Associates, Intl.).

A rich body of theory has been developed for relational databases, much of which found its way into research prototypes and commercial products. More in-depth discussion as well as additional topics not covered in this book can be found in [Maier 1983; Atzeni and Antonellis 1993; Abiteboul et al. 1995].

EXERCISES

3.1   Define data atomicity as it relates to the definition of relational databases. Contrast data atomicity with transaction atomicity as used in a transaction processing system.

3.2   Prove that every relation has a key.

3.3   Define the following concepts:

   a. Key
   b. Candidate key
   c. Primary key
   d. Superkey

3.4   Define

   a. Integrity constraint
   b. Static, as compared with dynamic, integrity constraint
   c. Referential integrity
   d. Reactive constraint
   e. Inclusion dependency
   f. Foreign-key constraint

3.5   Looking at the data that happens to be stored in the tables for a particular application at some particular time, explain whether or not you can tell

   a. What the key constraints for the tables are
   b. Whether or not a particular attribute forms a key for a particular table
   c. What the integrity constraints for the application are
   d. Whether or not a particular set of integrity constraints is satisfied

3.6   We state in the book that once constraints have been specified in the schema, it is the responsibility of the DBMS to make sure that they are not violated by the execution of any transactions. SQL allows the application to control when each constraint is checked. If a constraint is in *immediate mode*, it is checked immediately after the execution of any SQL statement in a transaction that might make it false. If it is in *deferred mode*, it is not checked until the transaction requests to commit. Give an example where it is necessary for a constraint to be in deferred mode.

3.7   Suppose we do not require that all attributes in the primary key are non-null and instead request that, in every tuple, at least one key (primary or candidate) does not have nulls in it. (Tuples can have nulls in other places and the non-null key can be different for different tuples.) Give an example of a relational instance that has two distinct tuples that *might* become one once the values for all nulls become known (that is, are replaced with real values). Explain why this is not possible when one key (such as the primary key) is designated to be non-null for all tuples in the relation.

3.8 Use SQL DDL to specify the schema of the Student Registration System fragment shown in Figure 3.4, including the constraints in Figure 3.6 and Example 3.2.2. Specify SQL domains for attributes with small numbers of values, such as `DeptId` and `Grade`.

3.9 Consider a database schema with four relations: SUPPLIER, PRODUCT, CUSTOMER, and CONTRACTS. Both the SUPPLIER and the CUSTOMER relations have the attributes Id, Name, and Address. An Id is a nine-digit number. PRODUCT has PartNumber (an integer between 1 and 999999) and Name. Each tuple in the CONTRACTS relation corresponds to a contract between a supplier and a customer for a specific product in a certain quantity for a given price.

    a. Use SQL DDL to specify the schema of these relations, including the appropriate integrity constraints (primary, candidate, and foreign key) and SQL domains.

    b. Specify the following constraint as an SQL assertion: *there must be more contracts than suppliers*.

3.10 You have been hired by a video store to create a database for tracking DVDs and videocassettes, customers, and who rented what. The database includes these relations: RENTALITEM, CUSTOMER, and RENTALS. Use SQL DDL to specify the schema for this database, including all the applicable constraints. You are free to choose reasonable attributes for the first two relations. The relation RENTALS is intended to describe who rented what and should have these attributes: `CustomerId`, `ItemId`, `RentedFrom`, `RentedUntil`, and `DateReturned`.

3.11 You are in a real estate business renting apartments to customers. Your job is to define an appropriate schema using SQL DDL. The relations are PROPERTY(Id, Address, NumberOfUnits), UNIT(ApartmentNumber, PropertyId, RentalPrice, Size), CUSTOMER (choose appropriate attributes), RENTALS (choose attributes; this relation should describe who rents what, since when, and until when), and PAYMENTS (should describe who paid for which unit, how much, and when). Assume that a customer can rent more than one unit (in the same or different properties) and that the same unit can be co-rented by several customers.

3.12 You love movies and decided to create a personal database to help you with trivia questions. You chose to have the following relations: ACTOR, STUDIO, MOVIE, and PLAYEDIN (which actor played in which movie). The attributes of MOVIE are Name, Year, Studio, and Budget. The attributes of PLAYEDIN are Movie and Actor. You are free to choose the attributes for the other relations as appropriate. Use SQL DDL to design the schema and all the applicable constraints.

3.13 You want to get rich by operating an auction Web site, similar to eBay, at which students can register used textbooks that they want to sell and other students can bid on purchasing those books. The site is to use the same proxy bidding system used by eBay (*http://www.ebay.com*).

Design a schema for the database required for the site. In the initial version of the system, the database must contain the following information:

1. For each book being auctioned: name, authors, edition, ISBN number, bookId (unique), condition, initial offering price, current bid, current maximum bid, auction start date and time, auction end date and time, userId of the seller, userId of the current high bidder, and an indication that the auction is either currently active or complete

2. For each registered user: name, userId (unique), password, and e-mail address

3.14 You want to design a room-scheduling system that can be used by the faculty and staff of your department to schedule rooms for events, meetings, classes, etc. Design a schema for the database required for the system. The database must contain the following information:

1. For each registered user: name, userId (unique), password, and e-mail address

2. For each room: room number, start date of the event, start time of the event, duration of the event, repetition of the event (once, daily, weekly, monthly, mon-wed-fri, or tues-thurs), and end date of repetitive event

3.15 Design the schema for a library system. The following data should either be contained directly in the system or it should be possible to calculate it from stored information:

1. About each patron: name, password, address, Id, unpaid fines, identity of each book the patron has currently withdrawn, and each book's due date

2. About each book: ISBN number, title, author(s), year of publication, shelfId, publisher, and status (on-shelf, on-loan, on-hold, or on-loan-and-on-hold). For books on-loan the database shall contain the Id of the patron involved and the due date. For books on hold the database shall contain a list of Ids of patrons who have requested the book.

3. About each shelf: shelfId and capacity (in number of books)

4. About each author: year of birth

The system should enforce the following integrity constraints. You should decide whether a particular constraint will be embedded in the schema, and, if so, show how this is done or will be enforced in the code of a transaction.

1. The number of books on a shelf cannot exceed its capacity.

2. A patron cannot withdraw more than two books at a time.

3. A patron cannot withdraw a book if his/her unpaid fines exceed $5. Assume that a book becomes overdue after two weeks and that it accumulates a fine at the rate of $.10 a day.

3.16 Suppose that the fragment of the Student Registration System shown in Figure 3.4 has two user accounts: Student and Administrator. Specify the permissions appropriate for these user categories using the SQL GRANT statement.

3.17 Suppose that the video store of Exercise 3.10 has the following accounts: Owner, Employee, and User. Specify GRANT statements appropriate for each account.

3.18 Explain why the REFERENCES privilege is necessary. Give an example of how it is possible to obtain partial information about the contents of a relation by creating foreign-key constraints referencing that relation.

4

Conceptual Modeling of Databases with Entity-Relationship Diagrams and the Unified Modeling Language

We have interviewed the users of the proposed Student Registration System, understood the requirements, and prepared a detailed Specification Document. That document has been approved by the university registrar, and we are ready to begin designing the database portion of the system. Ultimately this means coming up with a set of appropriate CREATE statements that declare the database schema—tables, indices, domains, assertions, and so forth.

The main issue in database design is to provide an accurate model of a large enterprise in the form of a relational database that can be efficiently accessed by concurrently executing transactions. As in other engineering disciplines, the complexity of the task requires that the design process be performed according to a well-defined methodology and be evaluated according to a set of objective criteria.

In this chapter, we present two design methodologies for relational databases: the *entity-relationship (E-R) approach* [Chen 1976] and *UML class diagrams* [Booch et al. 1999]. While the E-R approach is the more established of the two, UML is quickly gaining in popularity due to its rich feature set and because—unlike the many E-R notations—it has been standardized by the Object Management Group (*http://www.omg.org/*).

Database design is typically a two-stage process. The initial phase is based on the E-R or UML methodology, which we will learn about in this chapter. The result of this phase is then refined using the *relational normalization theory*, which provides objective criteria for evaluating alternative designs. This theory is discussed in Chapter 6.

A typical database design involves many dozens of relations, hundreds of attributes, and dozens of constraints—a task of daunting complexity. The good news is that many of the mechanisms underlying the E-R approach, UML, and the relational normalization theory have been captured in design software, which relieves humans of the most arduous, routine work. Still, database design requires a good deal of creativity, experience, technical expertise, and understanding of the fundamental principles. You will make significant headway toward the last two requirements by the time you finish reading this chapter.

4.1 Conceptual Modeling with the E-R Approach

First, keep in mind that the E-R approach is *not* a relative, a derivative, or a generalization of the relational data model. In fact, it is not a data model at all but a *design methodology*, which can be applied (but is not limited) to the relational model. The term "relationship" refers to one of the two main components of the methodology rather than to the relational data model.

The two main components of the E-R approach are the concepts of *entity* and *relationship*. Entities model the objects that are involved in an enterprise—for example, the students, professors, and courses in a university. Relationships model the connections among the entities—for example, professors *teach* courses. In addition, *integrity constraints* on the entities and relationships form an important part of an E-R specification, much as they do in the relational model. For example, a professor can teach only one course at a given time on a given day.

An **entity-relationship (E-R) diagram** (peek ahead at Figure 4.1, page 72, and Figure 4.2, page 74) is a graphical representation of the entities, relationships, and constraints that make up a given design. As in other visually oriented design methodologies, it provides a graphical summary of the database structure, which is extremely useful to the designer—not only in validating the correctness of the design but also in discussing it with colleagues and in explaining it to the programmers who will be using it. Unfortunately, there is no standard drawing convention for E-R diagrams, and hence there is a good deal of variation among database texts in many aspects of this approach.

Once the enterprise is represented by a set of E-R diagrams, there are standard ways of converting the diagrams into sets of CREATE TABLE statements. Unfortunately, not all aspects of an E-R diagram can be adequately captured with CREATE statements. These and related issues will be discussed in Section 4.5.

The creative part of the E-R methodology consists in deciding what entities, relationships, and constraints to use in modeling the enterprise. Some examples included in this and other texts might make these decisions look easy, but in practice designers must combine a detailed understanding of the workings of the enterprise with a considerable amount of technical knowledge and experience.

An important advantage of the methodology is that the designer can focus on complete and accurate modeling of the enterprise, without (initially) worrying about efficiently executing the required queries and updates against the final database. Later, when the E-R diagrams are to be converted to CREATE TABLE statements, the designer can add efficiency considerations to the final table designs using the normalization theory (Chapter 6) and tuning techniques to be discussed in Chapter 10.

4.2 Entities and Entity Types

The first step in the E-R approach is to select the entities that will be used to model the enterprise. An **entity** (or **entity instance**) is quite similar to an *object*, except that an entity does not have methods, that is, operations that take arguments and either return values or change the entity in some way. An entity can be a concrete object in the real world, such as John Doe, the Cadillac parked at 123 Main Street, or the

Empire State Building. Or it might be an abstract object, such as the Citibank account 123456789, the database course CS305, or the Computer Science Department at Stony Brook.

Similar entities are aggregated into **entity types**. For instance, John Doe, Mary Doe, Joe Blow, and Ann White might be aggregated into the entity type PERSON based on the fact that these entities represent humans. John Doe and Joe Blow might also belong to the entity type STUDENT because in our sample database of Chapter 3 these objects represented students. Similarly, Mary Doe and Ann White might be classified as members of the entity type PROFESSOR.

Other examples of entity types include

- CS305, MGT315, and EE101—entities of type COURSE
- Alf and E.T.—entities of type SPACEALIEN
- CIA, FBI, and IRS—entities of type GOVERNMENTAGENCY

Attributes. Like relations and objects, entities are described using attributes. Every attribute of an entity specifies a particular property of that entity. For instance, the Name attribute of a PERSON entity normally specifies a string of characters that denotes the real-world name of the person represented by that database entity. Similarly, the Age attribute specifies the number of times the earth had circled around the sun since the moment that a particular person was born. As in the relational model, the **domain** of an attribute specifies the set from which its values are drawn.

In principle, it is possible for two different entities of the same type to have identical values in all of their attributes. This is one important difference with tuples in the relational model. However, in practice it is not advisable to introduce entity types that can have entities that cannot be distinguished by their attributes.

In all of our examples, each particular entity type included only semantically related entities. Indeed, it is usually pointless to classify people, cars, and paper clips in one entity type because they have little in common in a typical enterprise. It is more useful to classify semantically similar entities in one entity type, since they are likely to have common attributes that describe them. For example, in any enterprise, people have many common attributes, such as Name, Age, and Address. Classification into entity types allows us to associate these attributes with the entity type instead of with the individual entities.

Of course, different entity types will generally have different sets of attributes. For instance, the PAPERCLIP entity type might have attributes Size and Price, while COURSE might have attributes CrsName, CrsCode, Credits, and Description.

> *Brain Teaser:* Is it possible for an entity type not to have attributes?

Unlike the relational model, E-R attributes can be **set-valued**. This means that the value of an attribute can be a set of values from the corresponding domain rather than a single value. For example, an entity type PERSON might have set-valued attributes ChildrenNames and Hobbies.

The inability to express set-valued attributes conveniently was one of the major criticisms of the relational data model that motivated the development of the object-oriented data model. However, the use of set-valued attributes in the E-R model is just a matter of convenience. Relations (as defined in Chapter 3) can be used to model entities with set-valued attributes with some extra effort.

Keys. As with the relational model, it is useful to introduce key constraints associated with entity types. A **key constraint** on an entity type, S, is a set of attributes, $\overline{A}$, of S such that

1. No two entities in S have the same value for each of the attributes in $\overline{A}$ (for instance, two different COMPANY entities cannot have the same value in both the Name and the Address attributes).
2. No proper subset of the attributes in $\overline{A}$ has property 1 (i.e., the set $\overline{A}$ is *minimal* with respect to property 1).

Brain Teaser: Does an entity type necessarily have to have a key?

Entity keys are analogous to candidate keys in the relational model. One subtle difference is that attributes in the E-R approach can be set-valued and such an attribute can be part of a key. However, in practice set-valued attributes that occur in keys are not very natural and are often indicative of poor design.

Schema. As in the relational model, we define the **schema** of an entity type to consist of the name of the type, the collection of its attributes (with their associated domains and the indicator of whether each attribute is set-valued or single-valued), and the key constraints.

E-R diagram representation. Entity types are represented in E-R diagrams as rectangles, and their attributes are represented as ovals. Set-valued attributes are represented as double ovals. Underlined attributes are keys. Figure 4.1 depicts one possible representation of the PERSON entity type.

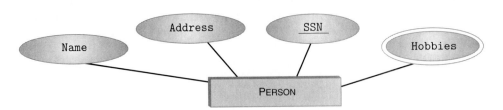

FIGURE 4.1 Fragment of the E-R diagram for the entity type PERSON. Here Hobbies is a set-valued attribute, and SSN is underlined to indicate that it is a key.

4.3 **Relationships and Relationship Types**

The E-R approach makes sharp distinction between the entities themselves and the mechanism that relates them to each other. This mechanism is called **relationship** (or **relationship instance**). Just as entities are classified into entity types, relationships that relate the same types of entities and that have the same meaning are grouped into **relationship types**.

For instance, STUDENT entities are related to PROGRAM entities via relationships of type MAJORSIN. Thus two instances of MAJORSIN might be the relationships between John Doe and computer science and Joe Blow and economics. Likewise, PROFESSOR entities are related to the departments they work for via relationships of type WORKSIN.

The concept of a *relationship* in the E-R approach is distinct from the concept of a *relation* (i.e., table) in the relational data model. Along with entities, relationships are modeling primitives in the arsenal of the E-R approach, and they are not tied to a particular data model. For instance, in a relational DBMS, both entity and relationship types are typically represented as relations. In an object-oriented database, they are typically modeled as classes. We will see, however, that in some cases relationship types are represented not as tables or classes, but rather as attributes and constraints.

Attributes and roles.   Like entities, relationships can have attributes. For instance, the relationship MAJORSIN might have an attribute Since, which indicates the date the student was admitted into the corresponding major. The WORKSIN relationship might have the attribute Since to indicate the start date of employment.

Attributes do not provide a complete description of relationships. Consider the entity type EMPLOYEE and the relationship REPORTSTO, which relates employees to other employees. The first type of employee is the subordinate while the second is the boss. Thus, if we just say that ⟨John, Bill⟩ is a relationship, of type REPORTSTO, we still do not know who reports to whom.

Splitting the EMPLOYEE entity type into SUBORDINATE and SUPERVISOR does not help, because REPORTSTO might represent the entire chain of reporting in a corporate hierarchy, making some employees subordinates and supervisors at the same time.

The solution is to recognize that the various entity types participating in a relationship type play different roles in that relationship. For each entity type participating in a relationship type we define a **role** and give that role a name. For example, Subordinate and Supervisor are two roles that connect a relationship instance of REPORTSTO to the two entity instances that it relates in EMPLOYEE. Thus, a role is similar to an attribute, but instead of specifying some property of a relationship, it specifies in what way an entity type participates in the relationship. Both roles and attributes are part of the schema of the relationship type.

For example, the relationship type WORKSIN has two roles, Professor and Department. The Professor role identifies the PROFESSOR entity involved in a WORKSIN relationship, and the Department role identifies the corresponding

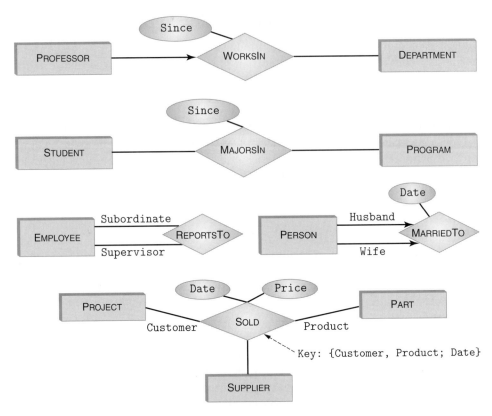

FIGURE 4.2 E-R diagrams for several relationship types.

DEPARTMENT entity in the relationship. Similarly, the relationship type MAJORSIN has two roles, Student and Program.

When all of the entities involved in a relationship belong to distinct entity types (as in WORKSIN and MAJORSIN), it is not necessary to explicitly indicate the roles, because we can always adopt some convention, such as naming the roles after the corresponding entity types (which is typical in practice).[1] Thus, the roles of WORKSIN are Professor and Department. This simplifying convention is not possible when some of the entities involved are drawn from the same entity type, as is the case with the REPORTSTO relationship. Here, we have to explicitly indicate the roles, Subordinate and Supervisor. In other situations (e.g., the relationship SOLD), naming the roles explicitly can help understand the intent behind the particular entity type. Figure 4.2 shows several examples of relationships, including those where roles are named explicitly.

---

[1] When confusion might arise, we will use different fonts to distinguish entity types from the roles they play in various relationships.

To summarize, the **schema of a relationship type** includes

- A list of attributes along with their corresponding domains. An attribute can be single-valued or set-valued.

- A list of roles along with their corresponding entity types. Unlike attributes, roles are always single-valued.

- A set of constraints. In Figure 4.2, some constraints are represented as arrows. This will be explained later.

The number of roles engaged in a relationship type is called the **degree** of the type.

We can now define the concept of a relationship more precisely. A relationship type **R** of degree n is defined by its attributes $A_1, \ldots, A_k$ and roles $R_1, \ldots, R_n$. The relationships populating **R** are defined to be tuples of the form

$$\langle \mathbf{e}_1, \mathbf{e}_2, \ldots, \mathbf{e}_n; a_1, a_2, \ldots, a_k \rangle$$

where $\mathbf{e}_1, \ldots, \mathbf{e}_n$ are entities involved in the relationship in roles $R_1, \ldots, R_n$, respectively, and $a_1, a_2, \ldots, a_k$ are values of the attributes $A_1, \ldots, A_k$, respectively. We assume that all of the values of the attributes in the relationship are in their respective domains, as defined in the relationship type, and all of the entities are of the correct entity types, as defined in their respective roles.

For instance, the relationship type MAJORSIN can have the schema

$$\langle \texttt{Student, Program; Since} \rangle$$

where `Student` and `Program` are roles and `Since` is an attribute. One instance in this relationship type might be

$$\langle \texttt{'Homer Simpson', EE; 1994} \rangle$$

This relationship states that the entity `Homer Simpson` is a student who has been enrolled since 1994 in the program represented by the entity `EE`. The first two components in the tuple are entities; the last is a constant from the domain of years.

> *Brain Teaser:* Is it possible for a relationship type not to have attributes? Roles?

E-R diagram representation. In E-R diagrams, relationship types are represented as diamonds and roles are represented as edges that connect relationship types with the appropriate entity types. If a role must be named explicitly, the name is included in the diagram. Figure 4.2 shows the E-R diagram for several of the relationships we have been discussing (we omitted the attributes of all entities to reduce clutter). The first three relationships in the figure are **binary** because they each relate two entity types. The last relationship is **ternary** because it relates three entity types. This last diagram also illustrates the point that sometimes the semantics of a diagram can be easier to convey if default role names, such as `Project` and `Part` are renamed into something more appropriate, such as `Customer` and `Product`, respectively.

Keys. The key of a relationship enables the designer to express many constraints naturally and uniformly. In the case of the entity types, a key is just a set of attributes that uniquely identifies each entity. However, attributes alone do not fully characterize relationships. Roles must also be taken into account, so we define the **key of a relationship type**, **R**, to be a minimal set of roles and attributes of **R** whose values uniquely identify the relationship instances in that relationship type.

In other words, let $R_1, \ldots, R_k$ be a subset of the set of all roles of **R**, and $A_1, \ldots, A_s$ be a subset of the attributes of **R**. Then the set $\{R_1, \ldots, R_k; A_1, \ldots, A_s\}$ is a key of **R** if the following holds:

1. *Uniqueness.* **R** does not have a pair of distinct relationship instances that have the same values for every role and attribute in $\{R_1, \ldots, R_k; A_1, \ldots, A_s\}$.

2. *Minimality.* No subset of $\{R_1, \ldots, R_k; A_1, \ldots, A_s\}$ has property 1.

In some cases, the key of a relationship takes a special form. Consider the relationship WORKSIN between entities of type PROFESSOR and type DEPARTMENT. It is reasonable to assume that each department has several professors but that each professor works for at most one department. Because any given PROFESSOR entity can occur in at most one relationship of type WORKSIN, the role Professor is a key of WORKSIN. While there is no universally accepted representation for relationship keys in E-R diagrams, a relationship key that consists of just one role (a **single-role key**) can be conveniently expressed by drawing this role as an arrow pointing in the direction of the relationship's diamond. Observe that there can be several roles each of which forms a key, and so an E-R diagram can have several arrows pointing toward the same diamond. For instance, in Figure 4.2 both {Husband} and {Wife} are keys of the relationship type MARRIEDTO, so each of these roles is represented as an arrow.

Keys that consist of more than one role or attribute are usually represented textually, next to the diamonds that represent the corresponding relationship type. When representing such keys, we first list the roles and then the attributes. For example, in the last diagram of Figure 4.2 one key could be {Customer, Product; Date}. If such a key is declared, it would signify that there can be at most one sales transaction involving a given customer entity and a given product entity on a given date.

In many situations, however, the relationship has only one key that is the set of all roles. In such a case, we do not specify the key in the diagram.

> *Brain Teaser:* Is it possible to have two distinct relationships of the same type that relate the same entities in the same roles and have the same values of attributes?

Cardinality constraints.   Single-role key constraints, which are drawn as arrows, can be generalized using the notion of a *cardinality constraint*.

Let **C** be an entity type and **A** be a relationship type that is connected to **C** via a role, *R*. A **cardinality constraint** on the role *R* is a statement of the form min..max attached to *R*; it restricts the number of relationship instances of type **A** in which

FIGURE **4.3** Cardinality
in the E-R model.

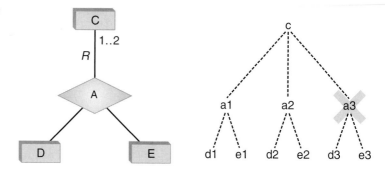

a single entity of type **C** can participate in role R to be a number in the interval
`min..max` (with end points included).

Figure 4.3 shows a diagram with a cardinality constraint on role R. On the right
side it shows a valid instance of this diagram where the entity **c** participates in two
relationships of type **A**. The relationship **a3** is crossed out because it would violate
the cardinality bounds 1..2 on the role R.

More generally, the E-R model supports cardinality constraints of the form
`min..max`, where `min` is a number greater than or equal to 0, `max` is a number greater
than 0, and `min` ≤ `max`. In addition, `max` can be the * symbol, which represents
infinity. Thus, a constraint of the form `3..*` on a role R that connects an entity type,
C, with a relationship type, **A**, means that every entity of type **C** *must* participate in
role R in *at least* three relationships of type **A** (with no upper limit). A constraint of
the form `1..3` means that every such entity must participate in at least one but no
more than three relationships. A constraint of the form `0..2` means that an entity
does not have to participate in any relationship of type **A** in role R. However, if it
does, then it must not participate in more than two relationships. Finally, we note
that cardinality constraints of the form `N..N` (where `min` = `max`) are often abbreviated
to just `N`, and that * stands for `0..*`.

> *Brain Teaser:* What does the constraint `0..*` mean?

Cardinality constraints generalize the notion of a single-role key, which we
earlier represented using arrows. Indeed, representing a role, R, using an arrow is tan-
tamount to giving it a cardinality constraint `0..1`, as shown in Figure 4.4. Database
designers also find it useful to talk about one-to-one, many-to-one, one-to-many,
and many-to-many correspondences. These concepts refer to the correspondences
between pairs of entity types *implied* by relationships of higher degree. Figure 4.5
illustrates these notions using a relationship type, **B**, of degree 4. The type of the
relationship is determined by the cardinality constraints on the roles of the relationship. For instance, the relationship **B** implies a **one-to-one** correspondence between
the entity types **C** and **D**. This means that an entity of type **C** can be associated

FIGURE 4.4 Two ways to represent single-role key constraints.

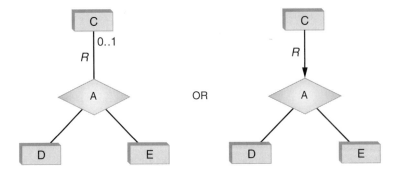

FIGURE 4.5 Many-to-one, one-to-one, and many-to-many correspondences.

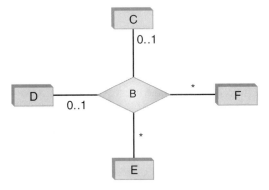

with at most one entity of type **D**, and vice versa. At the same time, **B** implies **one-to-many** correspondences of **E** to **C** and **D** (and of **F** to **C** and **D**). This means that an entity of type **E** can be associated with any number (including zero) of entities of types **C** and **D**, but, for example, an entity of type **C** can be associated with at most one **E**-entity. Note that the one-to-many correspondence is not symmetric; the inverse correspondence (for example, the correspondence of **C** to **E**) is called **many-to-one**. Finally, the correspondence between **E** and **F** is said to be **many-to-many**, meaning that an **E**-entity can be associated with any number of **F**-entities, and vice versa.

4.4 Advanced Features in Conceptual Data Modeling

In this section we introduce a number of more advanced modeling concepts, such as type hierarchies, participation constraints, and the part-of relationship.

4.4.1 Entity Type Hierarchies

When modeling an enterprise with the E-R approach, you may find that some entity types are subtypes of others. For instance, every entity of type STUDENT is also a member of the type PERSON. Therefore, all of the attributes of the PERSON type are applicable to student entities. Students can also have attributes that are not applicable to a typical PERSON entity (e.g., Major, StartDate, GPA). In this case, we say that the entity type STUDENT is a subtype of the entity type PERSON.

Formally, a statement that an entity type **R** is a **subtype** of the entity type **R**′ is a constraint with the following meaning:

1. Every entity instance in **R** is also an entity instance in **R**′.
2. Every attribute in **R**′ is also an attribute in **R**.

One important consequence of this definition is that any key of a supertype is also a key of all of its subtypes.

Subtyping is not only a constraint but also a relationship between the supertype and its subtype with roles Sub(type) and Super(type). It is often called the IsA **relationship**. For instance, in the IsA relationship type that relates STUDENT and PERSON, the role Sub refers to STUDENT and the role Super refers to PERSON. A particular instance of this relationship type could be ⟨Homer Simpson, Homer Simpson⟩, which states that Homer Simpson is an element of both STUDENT *and* PERSON. Note that the two entities involved in an IsA relationship are always identical (although the entity types are different), and the names of the roles are fixed.

So what is so special about the IsA relationship? The answer lies in the fact that subtype constraints introduce a **classification hierarchy** in the conceptual model. For instance, FRESHMAN is a subtype of STUDENT, which in turn is a subtype of PERSON. This property is *transitive*, which means that FRESHMAN is also a subtype of PERSON. The transitive property gives us a way to draw diagrams in a more concise and readable manner. Because of property 2 of subtyping, every attribute of PERSON is also an attribute of STUDENT and, by transitivity, is also an attribute of FRESHMAN. This phenomenon is often expressed by saying that STUDENT **inherits** attributes from PERSON and that FRESHMAN inherits attributes from both PERSON and STUDENT.

Note that the inherited attributes (SSN, Name, etc.) are not shown explicitly in Figure 4.6 for the entity types STUDENT and FRESHMAN, and yet they are considered valid attributes because of the IsA relationship. In addition to the inherited attributes, STUDENT and FRESHMAN might have attributes of their own, which their corresponding supertypes might not have. Figure 4.6 illustrates this idea. As STUDENT is a subtype of PERSON, this entity type inherits all of the attributes specified for PERSON, and so there is no need to repeat the attributes Name and D.O.B. (date of birth) for the STUDENT type. Similarly, FRESHMAN, SOPHOMORE, and so forth, are subtypes of STUDENT, and so we do not need to copy the attributes of STUDENT and PERSON over to these subtypes. The EMPLOYEE branch of the IsA tree provides another example of attribute inheritance. Every EMPLOYEE entity has attributes Department and Salary. The relationship EMPLOYEE IsA PERSON says that, in addition, every EMPLOYEE entity is also a PERSON entity and, as such, has the attributes Name, SSN, and so forth.

Note that each IsA triangle in Figure 4.6 represents several relationship types. For instance, the upper triangle represents the relationship types STUDENT IsA PERSON

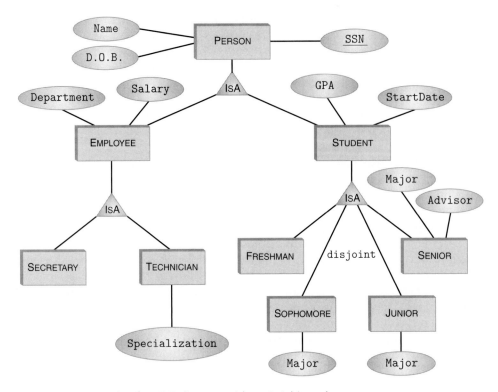

FIGURE 4.6 Example of an E-R diagram with an IsA hierarchy.

and EMPLOYEE ISA PERSON. Although this notation makes the representation of the IsA relationship different from the representation of other kinds of relationships, it is used because there are a number of constraints associated with entity type hierarchies that can be naturally expressed using such notation.

For instance, the union of the entities that belong to the entity types FRESHMAN, SOPHOMORE, JUNIOR, and SENIOR might be equal to the set of entities of type STUDENT (for example, in a four-year college). This constraint, called the *covering constraint*, can be associated with the lower right IsA triangle. In addition, these entity types might always be disjoint (they are in most American universities), and such a *disjointness constraint* can also be associated with the lower right triangle. There is no universally accepted way of representing covering and disjointness constraints in the E-R diagrams—the most straightforward way is to write the word "disjoint" directly on the diagram.

Formally, a group of IsA relationships, C_1 IsA C; . . . ; C_k IsA C, satisfies the **disjointness constraint** if the sets of entity instances of $C_1, \ldots, C_k$ are disjoint. This group satisfies the **covering constraint** if the union of the sets of instances of $C_1, \ldots, C_k$ equals the set of instances of C.

FIGURE 4.7 Using IsA for data partitioning.

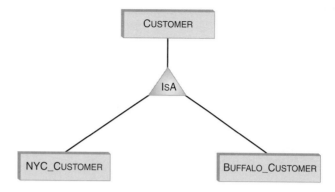

Entity type hierarchies and data partitioning. While discussing the IsA relationship, we have been focusing on conceptual organization and attribute inheritance. However, these hierarchies are also a good way to approach the issue of physical **data partitioning**. The need for data partitioning often arises in distributed environments, where multiple geographically diverse entities must access a common database. Banking is a typical example because banks often have many branches in different cities.

The problem that arises in such distributed enterprises is that of network delay: accessing a database in New York City from a bank branch in Buffalo can be prohibitive for frequently running transactions. However, the bulk of the data needed by a local bank branch is likely to be of mostly local interest, and it might be a good idea to distribute fragments of such information among databases maintained at the individual branches. This approach is taken in distributed databases.

To see how data partitioning can be addressed at the database design stage, consider an entity type, CUSTOMER, which represents the information about all customers of a bank. For each branch, we can create subtypes, such as NYC_CUSTOMER or BUFFALO_CUSTOMER, that are related to CUSTOMER as described in Figure 4.7.

Observe that the constraints associated with type hierarchies provide considerable expressive power in specifying how data might be partitioned. For instance, Figure 4.7 could be interpreted as a requirement that the New York City and Buffalo data must be stored locally. It does not say that the New York City database and the Buffalo customer database must be disjoint, but this can be specified using the disjointness constraint introduced earlier. In addition, we can add the covering constraint to specify that the combined customer information at the branches includes all customers.

4.4.2 Participation Constraints

Suppose that while developing an E-R diagram for your university you have introduced a relationship type, WORKSIN, between the entity types PROFESSOR and DEPARTMENT. Each department has several professors but each professor is a member of a single department, so the role `Professor` is a key of WORKSIN.

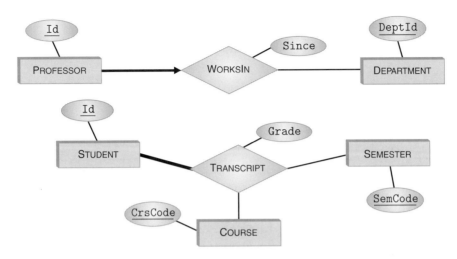

FIGURE 4.8 Participation constraints.

This key constraint ensures that no professor can occur in more than one relationship of type WORKSIN. However, it does not guarantee that each professor occurs in *some* relationship of this type. In other words, the key constraint does not rule out professors who do not work for any department (and possibly get away without teaching any courses!). To close this loophole, the designer can use *participation constraints*.

Given an entity type, E, a relationship type, R, and a role, *R*, a **participation constraint** of E in R in role *R* states that for every entity instance **e** in E, there is a relationship **r** in R such that **e** participates in **r** in role *R*.

Clearly, requiring that the entity type PROFESSOR participates in the relationship type WORKSIN in role Professor ensures that every professor works in some department.

For another example, we may want to ensure that every student takes at least one course. To this end, we can assume that there is a ternary relationship type, TRANSCRIPT, which relates STUDENT, COURSE, and SEMESTER. Our goal can be achieved by imposing a participation constraint on the Student role that connects the STUDENT entity type to the relationship TRANSCRIPT.

One common way of representing participation constraints in an E-R diagram is to draw a thick line for the role that connects the participating entity with the corresponding relationship, as in Figure 4.8. The thick arrow connecting PROFESSOR to WORKSIN indicates both that each professor participates in at least one relationship (denoted by the thick line) and that each professor can participate in at most one relationship (denoted by the arrow). Hence, a one-to-one mapping between PROFESSOR entities and WORKSIN relationships exists.

Alternatively, participation constraints can be represented using cardinality constraints. Participation of an entity type, E, in a relationship type, R, in role *R*

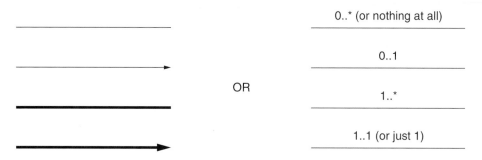

FIGURE 4.9 Line-based representation vs. cardinality constraints.

can be represented using the constraint of the form 1..* placed on the role *R*. A participation constraint combined with the single-role key (represented using a thick arrow) can be expressed as a cardinality constraint of the form $1..1$ (or simply 1). Figure 4.9 summarizes the correspondence between the two representations.

4.4.3 The Part-of Relationship

The collective experience of database design suggests that, alongside the IsA, **part-of** is a useful kind of relationship. For example, a wheel entity can be part of an automobile entity.

There are two kinds of part-of relationships. In one, the subpart of the whole can exist independently even if the whole is destroyed. This type of part-of relationship is **non-exclusive**. A good example of a non-exclusive part-of relationship is the relationship between an automobile entity and the entities representing its parts. When it is no longer feasible to keep repairing an automobile, it might be brought to a junk yard and taken apart. The automobile no longer exists, but its wheels, transmission, and camshaft may continue their independent existence and even find new life as part of another automobile. In certain cases, the same entity can even be part of several other objects. For instance, the same course may be an integral part of two or more programs of study in a university curriculum.

Another kind of part-of relationship is when the subpart has no existence outside of the whole: when the whole object is destroyed, the subpart goes as well. It is usually further assumed that the subpart cannot be shared, that is, it can belong to *exactly one* whole. For instance, PROGRAM of study (biology, physics, etc.) is part of UNIVERSITY. If a university is dissolved, its programs no longer exist. Similarly, in a payroll database, DEPENDENT can be part of the information associated with the EMPLOYEE entity type. When an employee leaves, the information about his dependents is also erased. This type of part-of relationship is **exclusive**.

Non-exclusive part-of relationships do not have special representation in the E-R model. They are treated as regular relationships, and cardinality constraints are used to state whatever is appropriate in each particular situation. In a non-exclusive relationship, a subpart (e.g., an automobile wheel) can exist without

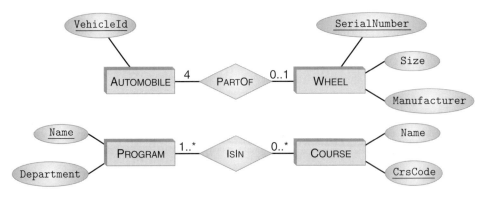

FIGURE 4.10 Non-exclusive part-of relationship in E-R.

being part of a concrete automobile. Therefore, there need not be a participation constraint between subparts and parts. Likewise, there need not be a many-to-one correspondence between the subpart entity type and the type of the whole part, because the same subpart (e.g., course) can be part of several different wholes (e.g., programs of study). Figure 4.10 shows examples of E-R diagrams representing non-exclusive part-of relationships. This is indicated by the minimum cardinality of 0 for entity types WHEEL and COURSE.

In contrast to non-exclusive part-of relationships, the exclusive ones are represented within the E-R approach using the special machinery of **weak entity types** and **identifying relationships**. Weak entities represent subparts and identifying relationships are the corresponding exclusive part-of relationships. In our examples, PROGRAM and DEPENDENT are weak entity types that are related through identifying relationships to their *master* entity types (which represent whole entities), UNIVERSITY and EMPLOYEE. In E-R diagrams, weak entities and their identifying relationships are represented using double boxes and double diamonds, respectively.

Observe that weak entities always participate in their identifying relationships and that each such entity is related to a single master object. Thus, there is always a thick arrow going from a weak entity to its identifying relationship, as shown in Figure 4.11.

Sometimes designers choose to strip weak entity types of their key attributes and have the entities identified through their relationship with the master entity. For example, the DEPENDENT entity might have the Name attribute, but not the SSN attribute. To find a dependent entity, one would have to first find the corresponding master (an EMPLOYEE entity) and then follow the identifying relationship.

Note that the identifying relationship is not the only kind of relationship in which a weak entity can take part. For instance, PROGRAM in Figure 4.11 can be related to another entity type, EMPLOYEE, via the relationship PROGRAMDIRECTOR. This relationship would not be identifying for PROGRAM (since a program might not have a director), and thus it would be represented using a single diamond. It is also conceivable (although not common) that a weak entity type can participate

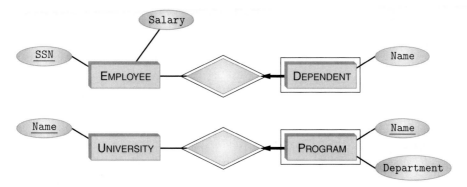

FIGURE 4.11 Exclusive part-of relationship in E-R: weak entities.

in a *ternary* (or higher-degree) relationship type with several master entity types. For instance, certain educational programs might be jointly run by universities and companies. In this case, PROGRAM takes part in a ternary identifying relationship with entities of the types UNIVERSITY and COMPANY, and destruction of either of these entities implies the destruction of the program entity.

Figure 4.12 summarizes the notation used in E-R diagrams.

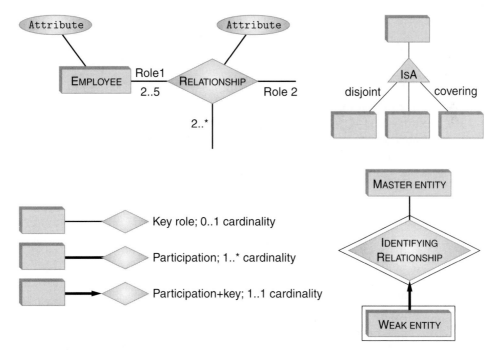

FIGURE 4.12 Summary of the E-R notation.

4.5 From E-R Diagrams to Relational Database Schemas

Conceptual design is only a means to an end: producing a relational schema and, ultimately, SQL's CREATE statements that can be used to build an actual database. In this section, we will retrace our steps through the entity-relationship approach and show how the various mechanisms discussed so far affect the translation into the relational model and SQL.

4.5.1 Representation of Entities

The correspondence between entities in the E-R model and relations in the relational model is straightforward. Each entity type is converted into a relation, and each of its attributes is converted into an attribute of the relation.

This simple set of rules might seem suspicious in view of the fact that entities can have set-valued attributes while relations cannot. How can a set-valued attribute of an entity be turned into a single-valued attribute of the corresponding relation without violating the property of data atomicity (defined in Section 3.2) of the relational model?

The answer is that, although each set-valued attribute of an entity type is represented as a single-valued attribute in the resulting relation, each entity instance is represented in the translation by a *set* of tuples—one for each member in the set of the attribute's values. To illustrate, suppose that the entity type PERSON of Figure 4.1 is populated by the following entities:

⟨111111111, John Doe, 123 Main St., {Stamps, Coins}⟩
⟨555666777, Mary Doe, 7 Lake Dr., {Hiking, Skating}⟩
⟨987654321, Bart Simpson, Fox 5 TV, {Acting}⟩

In translation, we obtain the relation depicted in Figure 4.13.

The next question is, What are the candidate keys of the relation obtained by the above translation? If the entity type does not have set-valued attributes, the answer is simple. Each key (which is a set of attributes) of the entity type becomes a key of the corresponding relation schema. However, if one of the entity attributes is

PERSON	SSN	Name	Address	Hobby
	111111111	John Doe	123 Main St.	Stamps
	111111111	John Doe	123 Main St.	Coins
	555666777	Mary Doe	7 Lake Dr.	Hiking
	555666777	Mary Doe	7 Lake Dr.	Skating
	987654321	Bart Simpson	Fox 5 TV	Acting

FIGURE 4.13 Translation of entity type PERSON into a relation.

set-valued, determining the keys is a bit more involved. In the entity type PERSON, the attribute SSN is a key because no two PERSON entities can have the same Social Security number. However, in the PERSON relation of Figure 4.13, both John Doe and Mary Doe are represented by a pair of tuples, and their Social Security numbers occur twice. Therefore, SSN is not a key of that relation. What is the problem here?

Clearly, the set-valued attribute Hobby is the troublemaker: to obtain a key of the relation in question, we must include this attribute. Thus, the key of the PERSON relation in Figure 4.13 is {SSN, Hobby}.

The following CREATE TABLE statement defines the schema for the PERSON relation.

```
CREATE TABLE  PERSON  (
    SSN       INTEGER,
    Name      CHAR(20),
    Address   CHAR(50),
    Hobby     CHAR(10),
    PRIMARY KEY (SSN, Hobby) )
```
4.1

Even though we have identified a key, a careful examination of the above table leaves us uneasy. It does not seem right that the Hobby attribute should have anything to do with identifying tuples in the PERSON relation. Furthermore, in the original entity type PERSON, any concrete value of SSN is known to uniquely identify the value of Name and Address. In the translation of Figure 4.13, we see that this property still holds, but it is not captured by the primary-key constraint, which states that in order to uniquely determine a tuple, we must specify the value of *both* SSN and Hobby. In contrast, in the entity type PERSON the value of Hobby is not required to determine the value of Name and Address. This important constraint has been lost in the translation!

The preceding example is the first indication that the E-R approach alone does not guarantee good relational design. Chapter 6 will provide a host of objective criteria that can help database designers evaluate the relational schema obtained by converting E-R diagrams into relations. In particular, the problem with the relation in Figure 4.13 is that it is not in a certain *normal form*. Chapter 6 proceeds to develop algorithms that can automatically rectify the problem by splitting the offending relations into smaller relations that are in a desired normal form. For instance, in our case, the PERSON relation would be split into two: one with the attributes SSN, Name, and Address, and another with the attributes SSN and Hobby.

Algorithm for converting entities into relations. We can now summarize the algorithm for translating entity types into the relational schema:

- Each entity type becomes a relation.
- Each attribute of the entity becomes an attribute of that relation.

- If attributes $K_1, K_2, \ldots, K_n$ form a key of the entity, then the attributes $K_1, K_2, \ldots,$ $K_n, S_1, \ldots, S_k$ form a candidate key of the relation. Here $S_1, \ldots, S_k$ is a list of all set-valued attributes of the entity.

4.5.2 Representation of Relationships

The algorithm that maps relationship types into relation schemas can be summarized as follows:

1. Determine the attributes of the relation schema for the relationship type.
2. Determine the candidate keys of the schema.
3. Determine the foreign-key constraints.

We discuss each step of the algorithm in turn.

1. *Attributes of the relation schema derived from a relationship type* **R**. The attributes of the relation schema are

   (a) The attributes of **R** itself.
   (b) For each role in **R**, the primary key of the associated entity type. These attributes will become foreign keys referencing the corresponding entity types (as explained below).
   (c) Each attribute in these primary keys must be declared as NOT NULL unless this is already implied by the PRIMARY KEY constraint.

   Note that in (b) we use the primary key of the entity type—not the primary key of the relation schema constructed out of that entity type—because the goal is to uniquely identify the entity involved in the relationship. Thus, for example, in the case of a role associated with the entity type PERSON we use SSN and omit Hobby.

   Also, spend a moment to contemplate the reason for the NOT NULL requirement in step (c): By definition, a relationship, for example, of degree four must have exactly four entities involved and none of them can be missing—otherwise, it will not be a relationship of degree four. Therefore, a relationship must provide references to all of its participating entities, and none of the corresponding attributes can be NULL.

   While this sounds simple enough, there are two small problems: the primary keys of different roles can have identically named attributes that mean different things or different attributes that mean the same thing. For example, in the MARRIAGE relationship, the primary key of each of the roles, Husband and Wife, could be ⟨FirstName, FamilyName⟩. Assuming that couples use the same family name, the relation schema derived from this relationship will have two pairs of identically named attributes. In the first pair, the two occurrences of FirstName mean different things and must be renamed (e.g., to HusbandFirstName and WifeFirstName). In the second pair, the two occurrences of FamilyName mean the same thing—the family name of a married couple. In this case we can simply delete the second occurrence. We can also imagine situations where the keys can have differently named attributes that mean the same thing. In this case we can also delete duplicate occurrences of such attributes.

2. *Candidate keys of the relation schema.* In most cases, the keys of the relation schema are obtained by direct translation from the keys of **R** itself. That is, if a role, R, of **R** belongs to the key of **R**, then the attributes of the primary key, $\mathcal{K}$, of the entity type associated with R must belong to the candidate key of the relation schema derived from **R**.

   A slight problem arises when **R** has set-valued attributes. In that case, we resort to an earlier trick that was used for converting entity keys into relation keys: all set-valued attributes must be included in the candidate key of the relation (see the PERSON entity-to-relation translation in (4.1)). Note that roles are always single-valued, so this special treatment of set-valued attributes does not apply to roles.

3. *Foreign-key constraints of the relation schema.* Because, in the E-R model, a role always refers to some entity (which is mapped to a relation), roles translate into foreign-key constraints. The foreign keys of the relation schema derived from **R** are constructed as follows.

> Let R be a role in **R** that connects **R** to an entity type, **E**. We use `rel(R)` and `rel(E)` to denote the relational schemas derived from **R** and **E**, respectively.
>
> For each such role, the primary key, $\mathcal{K}$, of **E** (which, by construction, is included among the attributes of `rel(R)`) becomes a foreign key of the schema `rel(R)` that references `rel(E)`, *provided that* $\mathcal{K}$ *is also the primary key of* `rel(E)`.

The reason for the caveat in this definition is that, as we have seen, the primary key of an entity type need not be the primary key of the corresponding relational schema. For instance, in the case of the PERSON entity type, SSN is the primary key of the entity type, but not of the corresponding relation schema (which has {SSN, Hobby} as its primary key). This type of problem is eliminated by the relational normalization theory, to be discussed in Chapter 6.

Figure 4.14 shows the CREATE TABLE commands that define the schemas corresponding to some of the relationships in Figure 4.2 on page 74. Observe that, in the MARRIEDTO relation, we did not define the foreign-key constraint: although SSNhusband and SSNwife clearly reference the SSN attribute of the PERSON relation, SSN is not a candidate key for that relation, as explained earlier. The UNIQUE constraint in the schema guarantees that SSNwife is a candidate key. The NOT NULL constraints in WORKSIN and MARRIEDTO comes from step 1(c) of the above algorithm: it ensures that each relationship has both of its entities present.

Note that when E-R diagrams are translated into tables, some of these tables describe entities and others describe relationships. Thus, the first E-R diagram of Figure 4.2 would translate into three tables: one to describe the entity type PROFESSOR, one to describe the entity type DEPARTMENT, and one to describe the relationship type that links professors to departments.

FIGURE **4.14** Translations of some relationships.

```
CREATE TABLE   WORKSIN   (
     Since         DATE,
     ProfId        INTEGER,
     DeptId        CHAR(4) NOT NULL,
     PRIMARY KEY (ProfId),
     FOREIGN KEY (ProfId) REFERENCES PROFESSOR (Id),
     FOREIGN KEY (DeptId) REFERENCES DEPARTMENT )
CREATE TABLE   MARRIEDTO   (
     Date          DATE,
     SSNhusband    INTEGER,
     SSNwife       INTEGER NOT NULL,
     PRIMARY KEY (SSNhusband),
     UNIQUE (SSNwife) )
CREATE TABLE   SOLD   (
     Price         INTEGER,
     Date          DATE,
     ProjId        INTEGER,
     SupplierId    INTEGER,
     PartNumber    INTEGER,
     PRIMARY KEY (ProjId, SupplierId, PartNumber, Date),
     FOREIGN KEY (ProjId) REFERENCES PROJECT,
     FOREIGN KEY (SupplierId) REFERENCES SUPPLIER (Id),
     FOREIGN KEY (PartNumber) REFERENCES PART (Number) )
```

4.5.3 Representing IsA Hierarchies in the Relational Model

There are several ways to represent the IsA relationship using relational tables. First we present a general way of dealing with IsA in the relational model, and then we show two other techniques, which may have advantages in certain situations.

1. *General representation.* Choose a candidate key for all entity types related by the IsA hierarchy. Add the attributes of this key to each entity type in the hierarchy, and then convert the resulting entities into relations, as discussed in Section 4.5.1. The choice of such a key is possible because, as was observed in Section 4.4.1, a key of a supertype is also a key of each subtype. Therefore, the required key is the key of the top entity type in the hierarchy.

   For instance, in Figure 4.6 we can choose {SSN} as the common key of all entity types in the hierarchy, so SSN will be added to STUDENT, EMPLOYEE, etc. The next step in the translation process will yield the following relation schemas.

   PERSON(SSN, Name, D.O.B.)
   STUDENT(SSN, StartDate, GPA)
   FRESHMAN(SSN)
   SOPHOMORE(SSN, Major)
   JUNIOR(SSN, Major)

Senior(SSN, Major, Advisor)
Employee(SSN, Department, Salary)
Secretary(SSN)
Technician(SSN, Specialization)

In addition, inclusion dependencies pointing from sub-entity types to parent entity types are needed. This ensures that every entity in a subtype also belongs to the supertype. In our particular case, since SSN is a key in the super-types, the inclusion dependencies can be specified as foreign-key constraints. For instance, the relations Student and Employee will have the constraint

FOREIGN KEY (SSN) REFERENCES Person

Similarly, the relations corresponding to the sub-entity types Freshman, ... , Senior will have the constraint

FOREIGN KEY (SSN) REFERENCES Student

Finally, the relations Secretary and Technician will have the constraint

FOREIGN KEY (SSN) REFERENCES Employee

2. *Representation for disjoint* IsA *relationships.* If a group of IsA relationships, C_1 IsA C; ... ; C_k IsA C, satisfies the disjointness constraint, then the following representation can be used. All entities that participate in the relationship are stored in a single relation whose attribute set is the union of the attribute sets of all entity types involved (i.e., attributes(C) $\cup_{i=1}^{k}$ attributes(C_i)). One extra attribute is added to indicate the original entity type of each tuple in the relation. We should also add the common key inherited from the top type in the IsA hierarchy, as in the general translation algorithm discussed earlier. Tuples that come from the entity types that do not have certain attributes are padded with NULLs over such attributes. (For instance, tuples from C that are not in any of the C_is are likely to have such NULLs.)

As an example, consider the part of the hierarchy below the Student entity type. We can create a single relation schema with the attributes SSN, GPA, StartDate, Major, Advisor (SSN is the key attribute inherited from the supertype Person) plus the new attribute Status with the domain {Freshman, Sophomore, Junior, Senior}. This attribute is used to indicate the original entity type of every tuple. For instance, a Freshman entity will be represented by a tuple that has normal values in the attributes SSN, GPA, StartDate, and Status, and NULL in the attributes Major and Advisor. A student who does not belong to any of the four subtypes of Student will have a NULL also in the Status attribute.

> *Brain Teaser:* Name one advantage and one disadvantage of this representation compared to the general representation for the IsA relationship.

3. *Representation for covering* IsA *relationships*. If a group of IsA relationships, C_1 IsA C; . . . ; C_k IsA C, satisfies the covering constraint, we can use the following translation: create one relation schema per each subtype of the IsA relationship. The attribute set of the relation associated with a subtype, C_i, is the union of the attribute sets for the subtype and the supertype (i.e., attributes(C_i) ∪ attributes(C)) plus the key inherited from the top entity in the hierarchy, which was used in all previous translations.

For instance, assuming that the only people described in our database are employees and students, the IsA relationship that connects EMPLOYEE and STUDENT to their supertype PERSON satisfies the covering constraint and can be represented by the following pair of relation schemes:

```
EMPLREL(SSN,Name,D.O.B.,Department,Salary)
STUDREL(SSN,Name,D.O.B.,GPA,StartDate)
```

An advantage of this representation over the general one is that attributes such as Name and Salary are in the same relation and thus queries of the form "What is John's salary?" can be answered more efficiently. On the other hand, this representation causes redundant information to be stored if, for example, John is both an employee and a student. In that case, John's name, date of birth, and SSN will be stored both in the tuple that represents John in the EMPLREL relation and in the tuple for John in STUDREL.

4.5.4 Representation of Participation Constraints

Conceptually, representing participation constraints in the relational model is easy. We have already seen, in Figure 4.14 on page 90, the CREATE TABLE statement for the WORKSIN relationship. So all it takes to enforce the participation constraint of PROFESSORS in WORKSIN is to specify an inclusion dependency (refer back to Section 3.2.2 for the definition) that states

```
PROFESSOR(Id) references WORKSIN(ProfId)
```

Since Id is a foreign key (because ProfId is a key of WORKSIN), we can state the participation constraint in SQL by simply declaring the Id attribute of PROFESSOR as a foreign key.

```
CREATE TABLE   PROFESSOR   (
     Id        INTEGER,
     Name      CHAR(20),
     PRIMARY KEY (Id),
     FOREIGN KEY (Id) REFERENCES WORKSIN (ProfId) )
```

Note that the foreign-key constraint does not rule out the possibility that Id can be NULL, which means that in general a NOT NULL constraint for Id would be in order. However, in our case, Id is declared as a primary key of PROFESSOR, so the NOT NULL constraint is implicit. Also observe that the DeptId attribute is missing (in contrast to Figure 3.5). It was not included because the above schema for PROFESSOR was derived from the E-R diagram in Figure 4.8, and DeptId is not one of the attributes of the PROFESSOR entity type there. Instead, the connection between professors and departments is represented by the WORKSIN relation.

We can do a better translation by noticing that Id is a key of PROFESSOR and also of WORKSIN (indirectly, through the foreign-key constraint). Thus, we can merge the attributes of WORKSIN into the PROFESSOR relation and identify the attribute ProfId with Id. This is possible because the common key of these tables guarantees that each PROFESSOR tuple has *exactly* one corresponding WORKSIN tuple, so no redundancy is created by concatenating such related tuples. This yields the table PROFESSORMERGEDWITHWORKSIN.

```
CREATE TABLE   PROFESSORMERGEDWITHWORKSIN   (
       Id        INTEGER,
       Name      CHAR(20),
       DeptId    CHAR(4) NOT NULL,
       Since     DATE,
       PRIMARY KEY (Id)
       FOREIGN KEY DeptId REFERENCES DEPARTMENT )
```

Note one subtle point about this merge—the NOT NULL clause in the DeptId attribute. One might conjecture that DeptId simply inherited NOT NULL from the WORKSIN relation during the merge. However, this is not a sufficient reason, for if professors could exist in the database without working for any department, then the DeptId attribute in PROFESSORMERGEDWITHWORKSIN should be allowed to accept a null value. In reality, the NOT NULL specification follows from two facts: the NOT NULL clause in the DeptId attribute on WORKSIN *and* the participation constraint by PROFESSOR in WORKSIN, which ensures that professors cannot exist outside of a department.

Although conceptually the representation of participation constraints in the relational model amounts to nothing more than specifying an inclusion dependency, the actual representation in SQL is not always as simple as the previous examples might suggest. The reason is that not all inclusion dependencies are foreign-key constraints (see Section 3.2.2), and expressing such constraints in SQL requires the heavier machinery of assertions or triggers, which can negatively affect the performance.

An example of this situation is the constraint on the participation of STUDENT entity type in the TRANSCRIPT relationship, depicted in Figure 4.8. The translation of TRANSCRIPT to SQL is

```
CREATE TABLE   TRANSCRIPT   (
       StudId    INTEGER,
       CrsCode   CHAR(6),
       Semester  CHAR(6),
       Grade     CHAR(1),
```

```
PRIMARY KEY (StudId, CrsCode, Semester),
FOREIGN KEY (StudId) REFERENCES STUDENT (Id),
FOREIGN KEY (CrsCode) REFERENCES COURSE (CrsCode),
FOREIGN KEY (Semester) REFERENCES SEMESTERS (SemCode))
```

As before, the foreign-key constraints specified for the TRANSCRIPT table do not guarantee that every student takes a course. To ensure that every student participates in some TRANSCRIPT relationship, the STUDENT relation must have an inclusion dependency of the form

STUDENT(Id) <u>references</u> TRANSCRIPT(StudId)

However, since StudId is not a candidate key in TRANSCRIPT, this inclusion dependency is not a foreign-key constraint. In Chapter 3, we illustrated how inclusion dependencies can be defined using the CREATE ASSERTION statement (see (3.4) on page 52).

Unfortunately, verifying general assertions is often significantly more costly than verifying foreign-key constraints, so the use of constraints such as (3.4) should be carefully weighed against the potential overhead. For instance, if it is determined that including such an assertion slows down crucial database operations, the designer might opt for checking the inclusion dependency as part of a separate, periodically run transaction and forgo the real-time check.

4.5.5 Representation of the Part-of Relationship

We distinguish three cases: two deal with various forms of non-exclusive part-of relationships and one with the exclusive case.

■ *Non-exclusive part-of: subpart can exist independently and be shared between different wholes.* In this case, translation into the relational model is done as if part-of were a regular relationship with no special properties, that is, it translates into a separate relation.

■ *Non-exclusive part-of: subpart can exist independently but can be part of at most one whole.* This type of relationship would be represented by a diagram that has a thin arrow leading from the subpart entity to the part-of relationship (or an edge adorned with a cardinality constraint 0..1). Since every subpart can participate in at most one part-of relationship, we can represent both the subpart type and the relationship type using a single relation similarly to the merge of the relations PROFESSOR and WORKSIN into PROFESSORMERGEDWITHWORKSIN on page 93. A foreign key in the merged relation will reference the whole entity that contains the subpart and, in this way, the relationship between the subpart and the whole will be preserved.

Since subparts do not need to be part of a whole, those that do not will have a null value in the fields of that foreign key. Therefore, the NOT NULL clause should *not* be attached to the attributes of that foreign key. For example, if AUTOMOBILE has {VehicleId} as its key and WHEEL has the attributes

SerialNumber, Size, and Manufacturer, then both the WHEEL entity type and the PARTOF relationship (see Figure 4.10) can be represented as

```
CREATE TABLE   WHEELMERGEDWITHPARTOF   (
       SerialNumber  INTEGER,
       Size          CHAR(10),
       Manufacturer  CHAR(20),
       VehicleId     CHAR(20)
       PRIMARY KEY (SerialNumber),
       FOREIGN KEY (VehicleId) REFERENCES AUTOMOBILE )
```

In line with the previous discussion, we did *not* declare VehicleId to be NOT NULL. So, if the car is disembodied and the wheel is sold separately, then VehicleId can be set to NULL.

- *Exclusive part-of.* In this case, the subpart is a weak entity and the part-of relationship is its identifying relationship. A weak entity participates in one and only one identifying relationship, and a thick arrow must exist between the subpart and the relationship. Therefore, this case is translated according to the rules for participation and key constraints. The main difference with respect to the previous case is that now the attributes of the foreign key that point to the master entity must have NOT NULL attached to them. An example of this kind of translation was given before (see PROFESSOR, WORKSIN, and PROFESSORMERGEDWITHWORKSIN).

4.6 UML: A New Kid on the Block *

Unified Modeling Language (UML) [Booch et al. 1999] is a culmination of a long process, which led to unifying and generalizing a number of methodologies in software engineering, business modeling and management, database design, and others. The E-R approach was just one of the many inputs that have influenced the final product. Because UML designers tried to capture every known aspect of the design activity, the approach ended up with every complication a modeling language can possibly have. Nevertheless, perhaps actually *due* to its Swiss Army knife model, UML is gaining in popularity in many areas of design, including database design. In this section, we will introduce UML *class diagrams*—a subset of UML that is suitable for conceptual modeling of databases.

We should mention that other parts of UML are also useful for modeling various aspects of database applications. Thus, in Chapter 14 we employ UML **use case diagrams** to describe user interactions with the Student Registration System and UML **sequence diagrams** to model the dynamic aspects of those use cases. In Chapter 15, we use UML **state diagrams** to describe the behavior of various objects in that system. In addition UML **activity diagrams** can be used to show how activities are coordinated, and **collaboration diagrams** can be used to describe interactions (i.e., message exchange) among the different objects that comprise a complex system. And then there are **component diagrams, deployment diagrams,** and more.

OPTIONAL

```
┌─────────────────────────────────┐   ┌─────────────────────────────────────┐
│            PERSON               │   │              STUDENT                │
├─────────────────────────────────┤   ├─────────────────────────────────────┤
│ Name:       CHAR(20)            │   │ Name:       CHAR(20)                │
│ SSN:        INTEGER  <<PK>>     │   │ Id:         INTEGER   <<PK>>        │
│ Address:    CHAR(50)            │   │ Address:    CHAR(50)                │
│ Hobbies[0..*]: CHAR(10)         │   │ GPA:        DEC(2,1)                │
│                                 │   │ StartDate:  DATE                    │
├─────────────────────────────────┤   ├─────────────────────────────────────┤
│ ChangeAddr(NewAddr: CHAR(50))   │   │ ChangeAddr(NewAddr: CHAR(50))       │
│ AddHobby(Hobby: CHAR(10))       │   │ SetStartDate(Date: DATE)            │
│ ...    ...    ...               │   │ ...    ...    ...                   │
│                                 │   │ <<Invariant>> self.GPA > 2.0        │
└─────────────────────────────────┘   └─────────────────────────────────────┘
```

FIGURE 4.15 Examples of UML classes.

4.6.1 Representing Entities in UML

UML is an object-oriented modeling language, and, not surprisingly, entities are called **classes** there. Classes are depicted as boxes—as in the E-R case—and appear in UML **class diagrams**. The main visual difference between class diagrams and E-R diagrams is that entity attributes in E-R diagrams are shown inside ovals attached to the box, while in class diagrams attributes appear directly inside the box. UML classes corresponding to the entities PERSON and STUDENT are shown in Figure 4.15. Note that class attributes in UML can be set-valued, as in the E-R model. This is specified by means of a *multiplicity constraint* on the corresponding attribute. In the figure, the attribute Hobbies has the multiplicity [0..*], meaning that it can have any number of values (including none). Other multiplicities, such as [0..3] or [5..*], are also possible.

UML classes extend E-R entities in several ways. First, UML classes can include methods that operate on the objects (i.e., entities) that belong to these classes. Some methods that operate on STUDENT objects and on PEOPLE objects are shown in the bottom portion of Figure 4.15. The inclusion of methods allows the designer to specify operations that can be performed on entities that populate each class. This has a particular advantage for object-oriented databases (where the main building blocks are objects rather than relations), but even in relational databases we can use methods to represent transactions that are deemed to be closely associated with particular tables.

Second, UML 2.0 will include the **Object Constraint Language** (or OCL), which can be used to specify certain kinds of constraints directly in the UML diagrams. These constraints can impose restrictions on a single class or on several classes at once, and in this way they are analogous to CHECK and ASSERTION constraints of SQL.

Third, UML has extensibility mechanisms, which can be used to add additional features to the language and make it more suitable for database design. Unfortunately, database-specific extensions are not quite there yet. UML was designed to model software, not data, and it shows. For instance, while OCL is quite a complex language, it does not have the expressive power of assertions in SQL and thus it is lacking an important functionality required for data modeling. We therefore do not discuss OCL here and instead just show an example of a simple OCL constraint in Figure 4.15. This constraint, indicated with the <<Invariant>> flag, requires that all members of the STUDENT class have a grade point average higher than 2.

At present, UML is lacking even such basic data modeling features as standard ways for specifying primary keys. Not everything is lost, however, since the designers of UML provided for a way to extend the language with new features using *stereotypes*. A **stereotype** is a symbol enclosed in double-angled brackets, such as <<PK>> and <<Invariant>>—see Figure 4.15. Stereotypes have no set meaning within UML. Instead, their meaning is defined by conventions. For example, you and your coworkers may agree that expressions tagged with the stereotype <<Invariant>> represent constraints. Database designers, as a community, may agree that attributes tagged with the stereotype <<PK>> form a primary key of a class. Such sets of conventions within an organization or a community are called **UML profiles**. Clearly, a great deal of data semantics can be specified using stereotypes because one can put any phrase inside the double-angled brackets and then develop a set of conventions around the new stereotype. However, no universally agreed-upon data modeling profile has been adopted by the database community so far. (However, Rational Software [*http://www.rational.com/*], now a division of IBM, has put forward one proposal for a UML data modeling profile.)

4.6.2 Representing Relationships in UML

In UML, relationships are called **associations**, and relationship types are known as **association types**. In general, UML diagrams attach more semantics to associations than is normally found in E-R diagrams, and we will examine some of these mechanisms later in this and the next section.

Associations without attributes. As in the E-R approach, objects (i.e., entities) that are related to each other by associations (i.e., relationships) may play different roles in those associations. When ambiguity can arise or when greater clarity is desired, the roles can be given explicit names. For binary association types, UML simply uses a line to connect the classes involved in the association. When more than two classes are involved, UML uses a diamond, as in the E-R approach. Figure 4.16 shows the UML version of some of the relationship types previously depicted in Figure 4.2 using the E-R approach.

Association classes. Note that the relationships WORKSIN and SOLD have attributes, but the corresponding associations in Figure 4.16 do not, because UML does not offer this facility. Can a designer represent the information contained in those attributes? The answer is provided by **association classes**. An association class is like a regular class, but it is attached to an association in a special way (using a dashed line), which is intended to say that the attributes of the class are intended

OPTIONAL

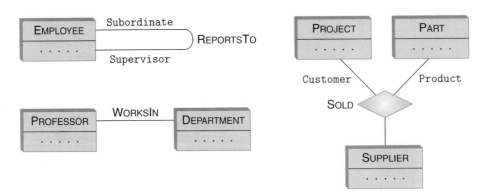

FIGURE 4.16 UML associations.

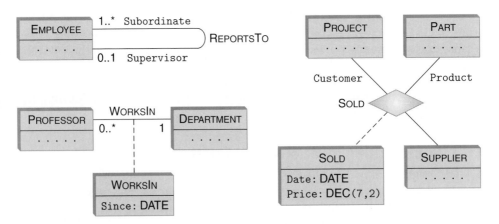

FIGURE 4.17 UML associations with association classes.

to describe the association. The relationships WORKSIN and SOLD with attached association classes are depicted in Figure 4.17.

Multiplicity constraints on roles. Recall that relationship keys can be specified in the E-R diagrams by drawing arrows (see Figure 4.2) or by explicitly writing down the attributes and roles that comprise those keys. In UML, arrows (and even more general constraints) are represented using *multiplicity constraints*.

A **multiplicity constraint** on a role, R, that connects an association type, A, with a class, C, is a range specification of the form n..m attached to R, where n $\geq$ 0 is a nonnegative integer and m is either the * symbol or an integer $\geq n$. The range gives the lower and upper bounds on the number of objects of class **C** that can be connected by means of an association of type **A** to any given set of objects that are attached to the other ends of the association (one object for each end).

OPTIONAL

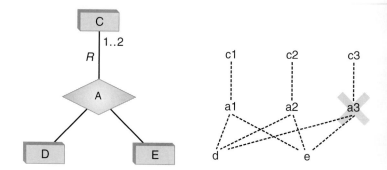

FIGURE 4.18 The meaning of the multiplicity constraint in UML.

To better understand this concept, take a look at Figure 4.18. In the picture, the class **C** is connected via the role R to the association type **A**, and other roles connect the association to classes **D** and **E**. The multiplicity constraint on R is 1..2. Therefore, each pair of objects, $d \in D$ and $e \in E$, must be connected by associations of type **A** to at least one and at most two objects of class **C**. In the figure, having just two associations, a1 and a2, is legitimate. Adding a3 would violate the upper bound of the multiplicity constraint because this would allow three objects of type **C** to be connected to a particular pair of objects (d and e) of classes **D** and **E**, respectively. Likewise, it would be a violation of the lower bound of the constraint if d and e were not connected to *any* object of class **C** by an association of type **A**.

According to this semantics, the range 5..* attached to a role, R, which connects the association type **A** to class **C**, means that at least five C-objects (* means no upper limit) must participate in role R in associations of type **A** with each distinct set of objects attached to the other roles of these associations. The range * means 0..* and the range 3 means 3..3 (i.e., exactly 3). Figure 4.17 shows several uses of the multiplicity constraint in UML. The EMPLOYEE/REPORTSTO example illustrates the assignment of ranges to each role of an association. In this case each range is interpreted separately. The range on the Supervisor role says that an employee can have zero or one supervisor; the range on the Subordinate role says that a supervisor can supervise several employees (but at least one). The ranges in the PROFESSOR/WORKSIN example say that every professor works in exactly one department, but a department can have any number of professors including none.

UML multiplicity vs. E-R cardinality constraints.   On the surface, the notion of multiplicity appears to be similar to cardinality constraints in the E-R approach. However, they are quite different. To see this, compare Figure 4.3 on page 77 with Figure 4.18. In these figures, the diagrams on the left are identical, but their interpretations are different. The valid instance of the UML diagram (on the right side of Figure 4.18) is nothing like the valid instance of the E-R diagram (on the right side of Figure 4.3).

In fact, it can be gleaned from Figures 4.18 and 4.3 that the multiplicity constraint in UML has, in a way, the opposite meaning to that of the cardinality

FIGURE 4.19 Cardinal-
ity vs. multiplicity.

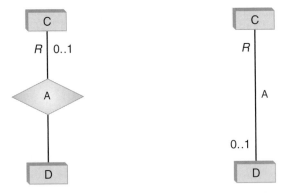

Cardinality constraint in E-R   Equivalent multiplicity constraint in UML

FIGURE 4.20 Cardinal-
ity constraints in E-R
that cannot be repre-
sented using multiplicity
in UML.

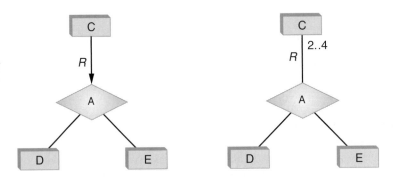

constraint in E-R. This is certainly true in the case of binary relationships and associations: Figure 4.19 shows an E-R diagram with a cardinality constraint on a binary
relationship and an equivalent UML diagram with the corresponding multiplicity
constraint. In both cases, the diagrams say that each entity of type **C** can be associated with at most one entity of type **D**. We see that the range specification in UML
and E-R appear on the opposite ends of the association/relationship.

For binary relationships, multiplicity and cardinality constraints have equivalent expressive power, although their interpretations are exactly the opposite of each
other. For ternary and higher-degree relationships, the difference is greater: the two
types of constraints have different, incomparable expressive power. For instance, it
is unclear how one can use multiplicity to express the constraints shown in the E-R
diagrams in Figure 4.20.

The apparent similarity and the not-so-apparent differences between the notions
of cardinality and multiplicity can be an endless source of confusion.

Key constraints in associations.   Recall that in the E-R model, an arrow that leads
from an entity type, **C**, to a relationship type, **A**, specifies a key constraint. It says

that an element of **C** can participate in at most one relationship, and this implies that the primary key of the entity type is also a candidate key of the relationship. In UML, for *binary associations* the same constraint can be specified using multiplicity. If **A** is an association type connecting classes **C** and **D**, then placing the range 0..1 on the role that connects **A** with **D** enforces the same constraint: it says that each instance of **C** can be associated with at most one instance of **D**. This is illustrated in Figure 4.19. Figure 4.17 shows more examples of the use of multiplicity constraints to specify keys in association types.

As mentioned earlier, multiplicity cannot imitate certain constraints in ternary (and higher-degree) relationships, such as the ones in the E-R diagrams of Figure 4.20. General key constraints cannot be expressed using multiplicity constraints either. For example, a constraint on an association **A** relating classes **C**, **D**, and **E** that asserts that a particular pair of elements from **C** and **D** can participate in at most one association of type **A** cannot be expressed. However, UML allows just about any text to be placed inside curly braces on the diagram. Such text is intended to be understood as a UML constraint, but of course, it is up to the designer to interpret the meaning of such annotations. For instance, in Figure 4.21 we have annotated the association SOLD with the constraint {Key: Customer,Product; Date}. By itself, this notation means nothing in UML, but the design team and the programming team might adopt internal conventions, which would make such notation meaningful.

Foreign-key constraints. As with primary keys, UML does not have a standard way of representing foreign keys. Typically, database designers use the stereotype <<FK>> for that purpose. Figure 4.21 shows examples of the use of this stereotype. This technique, although very common, requires that related attributes in different classes have the same name. Otherwise, it would not be possible to determine which primary keys are referred to by the foreign keys. To overcome this limitation, more expressive stereotypes are needed. For instance, if the identity of a professor is established via the Id attribute (as it has been in all previous examples), then the following stereotype (modeled after SQL) could be used in the WORKSIN association class: <<FK PROFESSOR(Id)>> ProfId: INT. This means that the attribute ProfId in WORKSIN refers to the Id attribute of PROFESSOR.

4.6.3 Advanced Modeling Concepts in UML

We will now discuss the UML representation of the advanced modeling concepts, which were studied in Section 4.4 in the context of the E-R approach.

Class hierarchies. In UML, the IsA relationship is called **generalization**. It is represented as a solid arrow with a large hollow head leading from a subclass to a superclass. An example of a generalization is shown in Figure 4.22.

As in E-R diagrams, several IsA/generalization relationships can be combined, as depicted on the right side of the figure. Covering and disjointness constraints

FIGURE 4.21 Foreign
keys in UML.

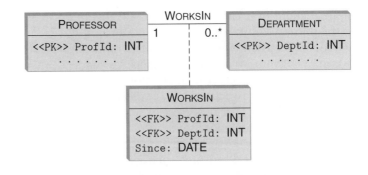

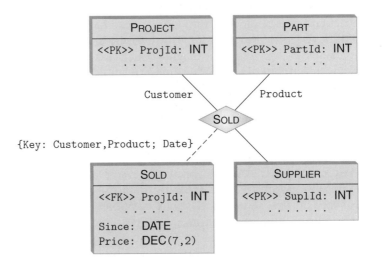

are noted directly on the UML diagrams. In the figure, the covering constraint
(which says that any student must belong to one of the four categories: FRESHMAN,
SOPHOMORE, etc.) is indicated with the keyword "complete," and the disjointness
constraint with the keyword "disjoint." They are written inside curly braces, as
required by the UML conventions for constraints.

Participation constraints. It might seem natural to try to model participation
constraints using multiplicity. However, it turns out that the problem is not so
simple. Participation in binary association types can, indeed, be modeled using
multiplicity constraints, but this cannot be done for associations of higher degree.

Recall the duality principle for binary relationships in E-R and UML shown in
Figure 4.19. It says that any cardinality constraint, expressed as a range $n..m$ on role R
of the relationship A in E-R can be equivalently represented in UML by imposing the
same range on the opposite end of the association A. Since participation constraints
in E-R can be specified using the range $1..*$, as discussed earlier, expressing the same

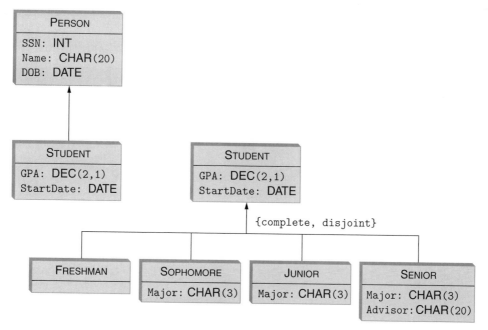

FIGURE 4.22 IsA (or generalization) hierarchies in UML.

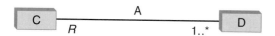

FIGURE 4.23 UML representation of the participation constraint for class **C** in binary association type **A**.

constraints in UML should be obvious. Figure 4.23 shows a UML diagram where class **C** participates in a binary association **A**.

For ternary and other associations, the issue is more involved. One might think that the duality principle can work here as well, and it should be possible to represent the participation constraint in E-R in Figure 4.24(a) using the multiplicity constraint in the UML diagram in Figure 4.24(b). However, the two constraints are not the same. The E-R participation constraint says: "For every entity c in **C** there are entities $d \in$ **D** and $e \in$ **E** that participate in a relationship $a \in$ **A** with c." In contrast, the (UML) multiplicity constraint says: "For every pair of objects $c \in$ **C** *and* $e \in$ **E** there is at least one object $d \in$ **D** that participates in a relationship $a \in$ **A** with c and e." The multiplicity constraint is stronger in some respects and weaker in others. Indeed, unless class **C** is empty, the multiplicity constraint implies that *every* **E**-object should be related to at least one **D** object. The participation constraint does not require this. On the other hand, if class **E** is empty, the multiplicity constraint is vacuously

FIGURE 4.24 Participation constraints for ternary relationships.

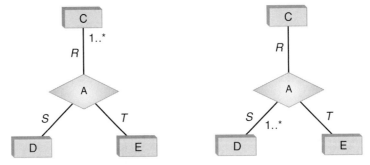

(a) Participation in a ternary relationship in E-R   (b) Partial simulation of the same in UML

FIGURE 4.25 Aggregation: non-exclusive part-of association in UML.

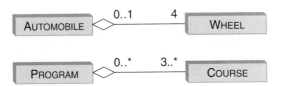

satisfied, while the corresponding E-R diagram does not permit either class **D** or **E** to be empty.

Of course, since UML allows any constraint to be specified inside braces, one can simply attach the annotation {participates} to the role *R* in the UML diagram. However, this type of annotation requires that all parties to the design understand what this means since this annotation does not have any built-in semantics in UML.

Part-of relationship. In UML, the non-exclusive part-of relationship (where sub-parts can have independent existence) is called **aggregation**. UML aggregation has special notation—a line with a hollow diamond—as shown in Figure 4.25. (Recall that E-R does not use special notation for this kind of relationship.) Aggregation in UML is often accompanied by appropriate multiplicity constraints. For instance, the multiplicity constraints in Figure 4.25 indicate that each automobile must have four wheels and that a wheel can be part of at most one automobile. Similarly, the multiplicity constraints between programs in a university and courses indicate that a course can be associated with any number of programs (including none) but any particular program must include at least three courses.

The exclusive part-of relationship is called **composition** in UML; it is viewed as a special kind of aggregation. Compositions are represented using lines with filled diamonds at one end; Figure 4.26 shows two examples of composition analogous to

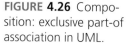

FIGURE **4.26** Composition: exclusive part-of association in UML.

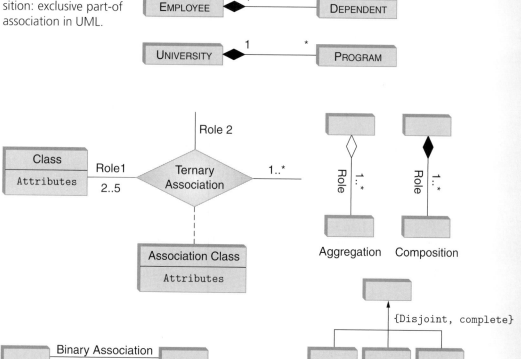

FIGURE **4.27** Summary of the UML notation.

the examples of Figure 4.11 on page 85 for the E-R model. As in those examples, we assume that a PROGRAM object is destroyed if its master object of type UNIVERSITY is destroyed and that a DEPENDENT object is destroyed upon the destruction of the corresponding EMPLOYEE object.

Figure 4.27 summarizes the notation used in the UML diagrams.

4.6.4 Translation to SQL

Due to the close correspondence between the basic components of the E-R model and those of UML, translation of UML class diagrams into the relational model is done the same way as in the E-R case. The main problem is how to adequately translate the constraints that might exist in the diagram. In general, this is a complicated matter, which requires the use of CHECK and ASSERTION constraints. The following sections illustrate some of these issues.

4.7 A Brokerage Firm Example

So far we have been using the Student Registration System to illustrate the various issues in database conceptual modeling. In this section, we use a different example to illustrate design problems that are not found in the Student Registration System enterprise.

The Pie-in-the-Sky Securities Corporation (PSSC) is a brokerage firm that buys and sells stocks for its clients. Thus, the main actors are *brokers* and *clients*. PSSC has offices in different cities, and each broker works in one of these offices. A broker can also be an office manager (for the office she works in).

Clients own accounts, and any account can have more than one owner. Each account is also managed by at most one broker. A client can have several accounts and a broker can manage several accounts, but a client cannot have more than one account in a given office.

The requirement is to design a database for maintaining the above information as well as information about the trades performed in each account. We will first show two alternative designs using the E-R model and then discuss what is different in the UML representation.

4.7.1 An Entity-Relationship Design

The information about brokers and clients is shown with the diagrams in Figures 4.28 and Figure 4.29. Here we make additional assumptions that a broker can manage at most one office and that each office has at most one manager. Notice that we did not specify a participation constraint for OFFICE in the relationship MANAGEDBY, so it is possible that an office might not have a manager (e.g., if the manager quits and the position remains vacant). Since each account must be maintained in exactly one office and by at most one broker, Figure 4.29 shows a participation constraint of entity ACCOUNT in the relationship ISHANDLEDBY by the thick arrow leading

FIGURE 4.28 The IsA hierarchy of the PSSC enterprise.

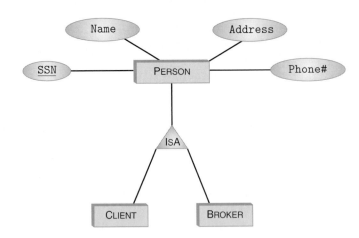

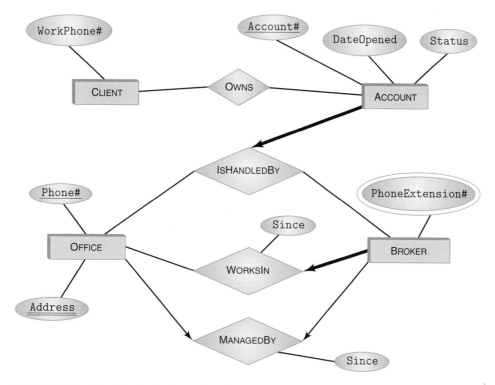

FIGURE 4.29 Client/broker information: first attempt.

from ACCOUNT to ISHANDLEDBY. Thus, {Account} is a key of ISHANDLEDBY. Notice that the attributes that form keys of entity types are underlined and different keys are underlined differently. Thus, for instance, OFFICE has two keys: {Phone#} and {Address}.

Unfortunately, the E-R diagram in Figure 4.29 has problems. First, it requires every account to have a broker. This was not part of our requirements. Second, the requirement that a client cannot have two separate accounts in the same office is not represented in the diagram.

We might try to rectify these problems using the diagram depicted in Figure 4.30. Here we take a slightly different approach and introduce a ternary relation HAS-ACCOUNT with {Client, Office} as a key. Since BROKER is not involved in this relationship, it does not require that an account have a broker. The participation constraint on ACCOUNT says that each account has to be associated with at least one client-office pair and the key of HASACCOUNT guarantees that a client can have at most one account in a given office. In addition, we modify the relationship ISHANDLEDBY so that it involves accounts and brokers only; it does not require that every account has a broker.

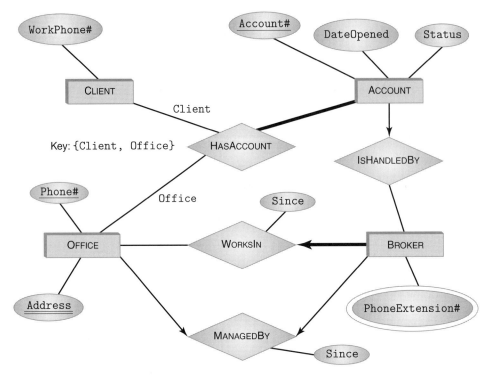

FIGURE 4.30 Client/broker information: second try.

Unfortunately, even this diagram has problems. First, notice that the edge that connects ACCOUNT and HASACCOUNT does not have an arrow. Such an arrow would have made the role Account a key of the relationship HASACCOUNT, which contradicts the requirement that an account can have multiple owners. However, our new design introduces a different problem: the constraint that each account is assigned to exactly one office is no longer represented in the diagram. The participation constraint of ACCOUNT in HASACCOUNT says that each account must be assigned to at least one office (and at least one customer), but nothing here says that such an office must be unique. Furthermore, we cannot solve this problem by adding an arrow to this participation constraint because this would imply that each account has at most one owner.

There is one more problem with our new design (which, in fact, was also present in our original design in Figure 4.29). Suppose that we have the following relationships:

⟨Client1, Acct1, Office1⟩ ∈ HASACCOUNT

⟨Acct1, Broker1⟩ ∈ ISHANDLEDBY

⟨Broker1, Office2⟩ ∈ WORKSIN

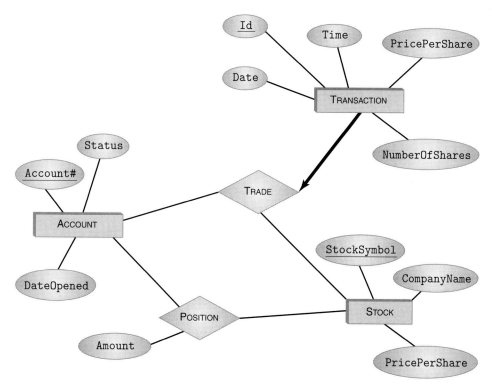

FIGURE 4.31 Trading information in the PSSC enterprise.

What is there to ensure that Office1 and Office2 are the same (i.e., Account1's office is the same as that of the broker who manages Account1)? This last problem is known as a **navigation trap**: starting with a given entity, Office1, and moving along the triangle formed by the three relationships HASACCOUNT, ISHANDLEDBY, and WORKSIN, we might end up with a different entity, Office2, of the same type. Navigation traps of this kind are particularly difficult to avoid in the E-R model because doing so requires the use of participation constraints in combination with *functional dependencies* (introduced in Section 6.3), but these constraints are supported by the E-R model only in a very limited way: as keys and participation constraints.

Note that we can avoid the navigation trap by removing the relationship HAS-ACCOUNT completely and reintroducing the OWNS relationship between clients and accounts. However, this brings back the problem that the constraint that a client cannot have more than one account in any given office is no longer represented.

After these vain attempts to achieve a perfect design for this part of the database, we now turn our attention to the part that deals with stock trading. On a bigger canvas, Figures 4.30 and 4.31 would be connected through the entity type ACCOUNT.

Trading information is specified using three entities: ACCOUNT, STOCK, and TRANSACTION. These entities are linked through the relationship POSITION, which relates stocks with the accounts they are held in, and the relationship TRADE, which represents the actual buying and selling of stocks. This information is depicted in Figure 4.31.

Notice that the role Transaction is a key of the relationship TRADE and that every transaction must be involved in some TRADE relationship. These constraints are expressed using a thick arrow, which states that there is a one-to-one correspondence between TRANSACTION entities and TRADE relationships.

4.7.2 A UML Design*

The UML diagram for the part of the PSSC enterprise shown in Figure 4.30 is given in Figure 4.32. Let us first acknowledge some obvious differences. Attributes are shown inside the boxes that describe classes, primary and candidate keys are represented using the stereotypes <<PK>> and <<UNIQUE>>, arrows and thick lines are represented by multiplicity constraints, and attributes attached to relationships (such as Since in the relationships WORKSIN and MANAGEDBY) now require separate association classes, which are attached with dotted lines.

Focusing on the multiplicity constraints, the UML diagram specifies, among other things, that there is no limit on the number of clients that can be associated with a particular account and office, that each account is handled by exactly one broker, and that an arbitrary number of brokers can work in each office. The multiplicity constraint assigned to the Account role of HASACCOUNT asserts that a particular client-office pair can be associated with an arbitrary number of accounts, but this problem is redeemed by the key attached to the association, which guarantees that any given client-office pair can be associated with at most one account through the HASACCOUNT association.

Recall that the E-R representation in Figure 4.30 did not capture the intended semantics completely because the constraint that an account can be associated with exactly one office did not follow from that diagram. Instead, this constraint is approximated in Figure 4.30 by the participation constraint of ACCOUNT in HASACCOUNT, which says only that an account can be maintained in at least one office. Since, as we know, participation constraints on ternary relationships cannot be captured in UML, Figure 4.32 approximates the above participation constraint as suggested in Figure 4.24. Interestingly, this approximation brings us closer to expressing the original constraint (that each account is associated with exactly one office) than the participation constraint. Indeed, the multiplicity constraint on the Office role of HASACCOUNT now says that any account object *together* with a client object uniquely determines the office. This constraint is weaker than what is required, because it allows the same account to be associated with different offices for different clients. However, the E-R diagram in Figure 4.30 does not capture even this much.

OPTIONAL

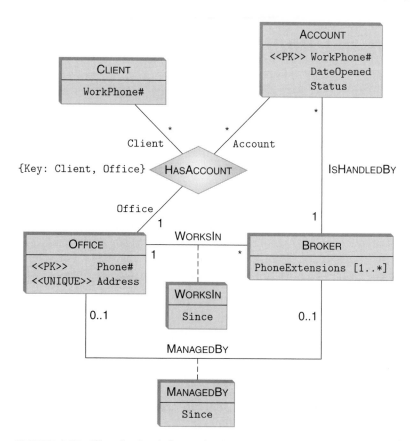

FIGURE 4.32 Client/broker information in UML.

4.8 Case Study: A Database Design for the Student Registration System

In this section, we carry out a conceptual design for the database part of the Student Registration System. The outcome of this design—an E-R or a UML diagram and a set of definitions for tables and constraints—is typically included in the Design Document for the entire application. The Design Document itself will be discussed in more detail in Section 15.1.

Before we can start designing an application, we need to write down *precisely* what the system is supposed to do so that we know what it is that we want to design. The document that contains this description is called the **Requirements Document**. In this section, we are interested only in the conceptual design of the database part of our application, so we will focus on only the relevant parts of the Requirements Document for the Student Registration System: namely, the data items to be included in the database and the associated constraints. The complete Requirements Document will be given in Section 14.2.

4.8.1 The Database Part of the Requirements Document

I. Information to be contained in the system. The information to be stored in the system includes four major categories of data: personal information about students and faculty members, academic records of students, information about courses and course offerings, and teaching records of faculty members. Information about classrooms and other auxiliary data is also stored in the system.

A. *Personal records.* The system shall contain a name, an Id number, and a password for each student and faculty member allowed to use the system. The password and the Id authenticates users. Id numbers are unique. It is assumed that at least one faculty member has been initialized as a valid user at startup time.

B. *Academic records.* The system shall contain the academic record of each student.

  1. Each course the student has completed, the semester the student took the course, and the grade the student received (all grades are in the set {A, B, C, D, F, I}).
  2. Each course for which the student is enrolled this semester.
  3. Each course for which the student has registered for next semester.

C. *Course information.* The system shall contain information about the courses offered, and for each course the system shall contain

  1. The course name, the course number (must be unique), the department offering the course, the textbook, and the credit hours.
  2. Whether the course is offered in spring, fall, or both.
  3. The prerequisite courses (there can be an arbitrary number of prerequisites for each course).
  4. The maximum allowed enrollment, the number of students who are enrolled (unspecified if the course is not offered this semester), and the number of students who have registered (unspecified if the course is not offered next semester).
  5. If the course is offered this semester, the days and times at which it is offered; if the course is offered next semester, the days and times at which it will be offered. The possible values shall be selected from a fixed list of weekly slots (e.g., MWF10).
  6. The Id of the instructor teaching the course this semester and next semester (Id unspecified if the course is not offered in the specified semester; it must be specified before the start of the semester in which the course is offered).
  7. The classroom assignment of the course for this semester and next semester (classroom assignment unspecified if the course is not offered in the speci-

fied semester; it must be specified before the start of the semester in which the course is offered).

D.   *Teaching information.* The system shall contain a record of all courses that have been taught previously or are being taught currently, including the semester in which they were taught and the Id of the instructor.

E.   *Classroom information.* The system shall contain a list of classroom identifiers and the corresponding number of seats. A classroom identifier is a unique three-digit integer.

F.   *Auxiliary information.* The system shall contain the identity of the current semester and the next semester (e.g., F1997, S1998).

II. Integrity constraints.   The database shall satisfy the following integrity constraints.

A.   Id numbers are unique.

B.   If in item I.B.2 (or I.B.3), a student is listed as enrolled (registered) for a course, that course must be indicated in item I.C.2 as offered this semester (or next semester).

C.   In item I.C.4, the number of students registered or enrolled in a course cannot be larger than the maximum enrollment.

D.   The count of students enrolled (registered) in a course in item I.B.2 (or I.B.3) must equal the current enrollment (registration) indicated in item I.C.4.

E.   An instructor cannot be assigned to two courses taught at the same time in the same semester.

F.   Two courses cannot be taught in the same room at the same time in a given semester.

G.   If a student is enrolled in a course, the corresponding record must indicate that the student has completed all prerequisite courses with a grade of at least C.

H.   A student cannot be registered (enrolled) in two courses taught at the same hour.

I.   A student cannot be registered for more than 20 credits in a given semester.

J.   The room assigned to a course must have at least as many seats as the maximum allowed enrollment for the course.

K.   Once a letter grade of A, B, C, D, or F has been assigned for a course, that grade cannot later be changed to an I.

4.8.2 The Database Design

We will now present the conceptual design of the database and the corresponding relational representation.

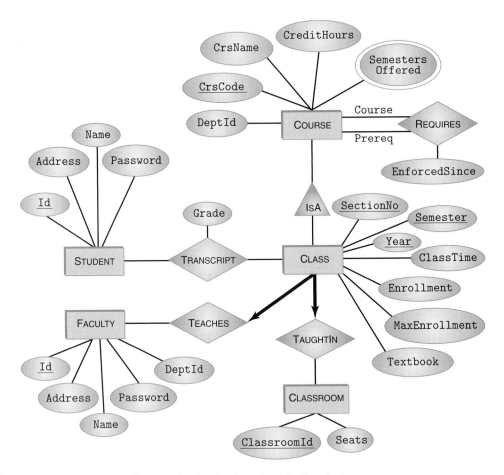

FIGURE 4.33 An E-R diagram for the Student Registration System.

A conceptual design diagram. The first step in the design process is to construct a diagram using the E-R approach or UML. The E-R diagram is shown in Figure 4.33. It is a model of the student registration enterprise as described in the sections of the Requirements Document that we just discussed. Note from the diagram that

- STUDENT is related to CLASS through TRANSCRIPT, which signifies that a student is registered, is enrolled, or has completed a class in some semester.

- FACULTY is related to CLASS through TEACHES, meaning that a faculty member teaches a class in some semester and every class is taught by exactly one faculty member.

- COURSE is related to itself through the relationship REQUIRES; that is, a course can be a prerequisite for another course in some semester. The attribute EnforcedSince specifies the date when the prerequisite was established.

- CLASS is related to CLASSROOM through TAUGHTIN; that is, a class is taught in a classroom in some semester.

- A class (i.e., a particular offering of a course) can use at most one textbook since the attribute Textbook is single-valued in the entity type CLASS.

UML representation. * As far as UML is concerned, the Student Registration System does not introduce any new or interesting issues beyond what was shown in the E-R diagram. (Exercise 4.13 involves redrawing Figure 4.33 using UML conventions.)

Relational representation. On the basis of this E-R diagram and the list of integrity constraints given in the Requirements Document, the next step is to produce the schema shown in Figures 4.34 and 4.35. The translation was done in a straight-forward manner using the techniques described in this chapter. Note that we did not create tables for the TEACHES and TAUGHTIN relationships: because of the participation and key constraints involving these relationships (i.e., a CLASS entity participates in exactly one TEACHES and one TAUGHTIN relationship), their corresponding tables can *both* be merged with the table for the entity CLASS, as explained in Section 4.5.2. The result of the merge is that the schema of the CLASS table includes the attributes ClassroomId, which identifies the room where the class is taught, and InstructorId of the faculty member who teaches it—see the corresponding CREATE TABLE statement in Figure 4.35.

Note that the simpler integrity constraints among those that are specified in the Requirements Document can and are defined within CREATE TABLE statements with the help of the CHECK clause (specifically the constraints that involve a single relation, such as constraints A, C, E, and F). In the complete schema design, other integrity constraints are defined as separate CREATE ASSERTION statements plus one trigger. However, this part of the design requires SQL constructs that we have not yet discussed, and so we will complete the schema design in Section 15.7 after we cover these constructs.

We selected this particular design for inclusion in the book because it is straight-forward. In practice, such a design might be a starting point for a number of enhancements whose goal is to capture more features and increase the efficiency of the final implementation.

Alternatives. Let us consider a few possible enhancements and alternatives. Consider course dependencies. One obvious omission in our schema is the *co-requisite* relationship and all of the constraints entailed by it. More subtly, university curricula change all the time: new courses are introduced, old courses are removed, and prerequisite dependencies between courses evolve in time. Thus, the REQUIRES relationship in Figure 4.33 might need two additional attributes, Start and End, to designate the period when the prerequisite relationship is effective. Even more interesting is the possibility that a particular prerequisite relationship might exist at different times. For instance, course A might be a prerequisite for course B between 1985 and 1990 and again between 1999 and the present. (Modeling this situation is left to Exercise 4.11.)

FIGURE 4.34 A schema for the Student Registration System—Part 1.

CASE STUDY

```
CREATE TABLE STUDENT  (
       Id              CHAR(9),
       Name            CHAR(20) NOT NULL,
       Password        CHAR(10) NOT NULL,
       Address         CHAR(50),
       PRIMARY KEY (Id) )

CREATE TABLE FACULTY  (
       Id              CHAR(9),
       Name            CHAR(20) NOT NULL,
       DeptId          CHAR(4) NOT NULL,
       Password        CHAR(10) NOT NULL,
       Address         CHAR(50),
       PRIMARY KEY (Id) )

CREATE TABLE COURSE (
       CrsCode         CHAR(6),
       DeptId          CHAR(4) NOT NULL,
       CrsName         CHAR(20) NOT NULL,
       CreditHours     INTEGER NOT NULL,
       PRIMARY KEY (CrsCode),
       UNIQUE (DeptId, CrsName) )

CREATE TABLE WHENOFFERED (
       CrsCode         CHAR(6),
       Semester        CHAR(6),
       PRIMARY KEY (CrsCode, Semester),
       CHECK (Semester IN ('Spring','Fall') ) )

CREATE TABLE CLASSROOM  (
       ClassroomId   CHAR(3),
       Seats           INTEGER NOT NULL,
       PRIMARY KEY (ClassroomId) )
```

Another interesting enhancement is to account for the possibility that certain highly popular courses might be restricted to certain majors only. In this situation, the E-R diagram and the schema have to include information about the subjects in which each student is majoring, the majors allowed in a particular course (both are set-valued attributes), and a constraint to ensure that the restriction is enforced. (This enhancement is left to Exercise 4.12.)

Enhancements to express more complex requirements are one source of modifications to the proposed design. Another source is the vast range of possible alter-

FIGURE 4.35 A schema for the Student Registration System—Part 2.

```
CREATE TABLE   REQUIRES    (
    CrsCode       CHAR(6),
    PrereqCrsCode CHAR(6),
    EnforcedSince DATE      NOT NULL,
    PRIMARY KEY (CrsCode, PrereqCrsCode),
    FOREIGN KEY (CrsCode) REFERENCES COURSE(CrsCode),
    FOREIGN KEY (PrereqCrsCode) REFERENCES COURSE(CrsCode)  )

CREATE TABLE    CLASS   (
    CrsCode       CHAR(6),
    SectionNo     INTEGER,
    Semester      CHAR(6),
    Year          INTEGER,
    Textbook      CHAR(50),
    ClassTime     CHAR(5),
    Enrollment    INTEGER,
    MaxEnrollment INTEGER,
    ClassroomId   CHAR(3),      -- from TAUGHTIN
    InstructorId  CHAR(9),      -- from TEACHES
    PRIMARY KEY (CrsCode,SectionNo,Semester,Year),
    CONSTRAINT TIMECONFLICT
        UNIQUE (InstructorId,Semester,Year,ClassTime),
    CONSTRAINT CLASSROOMCONFLICT
        UNIQUE (ClassroomId,Semester,Year,ClassTime),
    CONSTRAINT ENROLLMENT
        CHECK (Enrollment <= MaxEnrollment AND Enrollment >= 0),
    FOREIGN KEY (CrsCode) REFERENCES COURSE(CrsCode),
    FOREIGN KEY (ClassroomId) REFERENCES CLASSROOM(ClassroomId),
    FOREIGN KEY (CrsCode, Semester)
        REFERENCES WHENOFFERED(CrsCode, Semester),
    FOREIGN KEY (InstructorId) REFERENCES FACULTY(Id)  )

CREATE TABLE   TRANSCRIPT    (
    StudId        CHAR(9),
    CrsCode       CHAR(6),
    SectionNo     INTEGER,
    Semester      CHAR(6),
    Year          INTEGER,
    Grade         CHAR(1),
    PRIMARY KEY (StudId,CrsCode,SectionNo,Semester,Year),
    FOREIGN KEY (StudId) REFERENCES STUDENT(Id),
    FOREIGN KEY (CrsCode,SectionNo,Semester,Year)
        REFERENCES CLASS(CrsCode,SectionNo,Semester,Year),
    CHECK (Grade IN ('A','B','C','D','F','I') ),
    CHECK (Semester IN ('Spring','Fall') )  )
```

native designs, which might have implications for the overall performance of the system. We discuss one such alternative and its implications.

Consider the attribute `SemestersOffered` of entity Course in Figure 4.33. Because it is a set-valued attribute, we translate it using a separate table, WhenOffered. We chose this particular design because it makes it easy to express the constraint that the semester in which any particular class is taught must be one of the allowable semesters. For instance, it should not be possible for course CS305 to be offered only in spring semesters but for a certain class of this course to be taught in fall 2004. However, this should be allowed if CS305 is offered in both spring and fall semesters.

In our design, this requirement is expressed as a foreign-key constraint attached to table Class.

```
FOREIGN KEY (CrsCode, Semester)
            REFERENCES WhenOffered(CrsCode, Semester)
```

This constraint says that if a class of a course with code abc is offered during a semester, sem, then ⟨abc, sem⟩ should be a tuple in the relation WhenOffered; that is, sem must be one of the allowed semesters for the course.

Despite the simplicity of this design, one might feel that creating a separate relation for such a trivial purpose is unacceptable overhead. A separate relation requires an extra operation for certain queries and additional storage.[2] An alternative is to define a new SQL domain with three values in it:

```
CREATE DOMAIN  Semesters CHAR(6)
     CHECK ( VALUE IN ('Spring', 'Fall', 'Both') )
```

The set-valued attribute `SemestersOffered` of the entity Course is now single-valued, but it ranges over the domain Semesters. The advantage is that the translation into the relational model is more straightforward and there is no need for the extra relation WhenOffered. However, it is now more difficult to specify the constraint that a class can be taught only in the semesters when the corresponding course is offered. (Details are left to Exercise 4.14.)

Finally, let us consider the possible alternatives for representing the current and the next semesters, as required in item I.F. In fact, our design has no obvious place for this information. One simple way to tell which semester is current or next is to create a separate relation to store this information. However, this entails that any reference to the current or the next semester would require a database query—an expensive way to obtain such simple information. The right way to do this type of thing is to use the function CURRENT_DATE provided by SQL and the function EXTRACT to extract particular fields from that date. For instance, the following calls

---

[2] In our particular case, none of these disadvantages seems to apply: in all likelihood, the relation WhenOffered will be used to verify the above foreign-key constraint, and having a separate relation for course-semester pairs provides efficient support for such verification.

EXTRACT(YEAR FROM CURRENT_DATE)
EXTRACT(MONTHS FROM CURRENT_DATE)

return the numeric values of the current year and month. This should be sufficient to determine whether any given semester is current or next.

4.9 **Limitations of Data Modeling Methodologies**

We have now seen two case studies where the entity-relationship model and UML were used for conceptual database design. If conceptual design still is not completely clear to you, do not despair. Although we have discussed several concepts that might provide general guidance in organizing enterprise data, applying these concepts in any concrete situation requires a great deal of experience, intuition, and some black magic. There is considerable freedom in deciding whether a particular datum should be an entity (or class), a relationship (or association), or an attribute. Furthermore, even after these issues are settled, the various relationships that exist among entities can be expressed in different ways. This section discusses some of the dilemmas that are often faced by database designers. For concreteness, we use the E-R model in our examples, but the discussion equally applies to UML.

Entity or attribute?   In Figure 4.8 on page 82, semesters are represented as entities. However, we could as well make TRANSCRIPT into a binary relation and turn SEMESTER into one of its attributes. The obvious question is which representation is best (and in which case).

To some extent, the decision about whether a particular datum should be represented as an entity or an attribute is a matter of taste. Beyond that, the representation might depend on whether the datum has an internal structure of its own. If the datum has no internal data structure, keeping it as a separate entity makes the E-R diagram more complex and, more important, adds an extra relation to your database schema when you convert the diagram into the relational model. On the other hand, if the datum has attributes of its own, it is possible that these attributes cannot be represented if the datum itself is demoted to the status of an attribute.

For instance, in Figure 4.8 the entity type SEMESTER does not have descriptive attributes apart from the identifying semester code, so representing the semester information as an entity appears to be an overkill. However, it is entirely possible that the Requirements Document might state that the following additional information must be available for each semester: Start_date, End_date, Holidays, Enrollment (which represents total enrollment in all courses during the semester). In such a case, the semester information cannot be an attribute of the TRANSCRIPT relationship as there would then be no place to specify the information about the key dates and the enrollment associated with semesters (e.g., the total enrollment in the university during a semester is not an attribute of any particular transcript relationship).

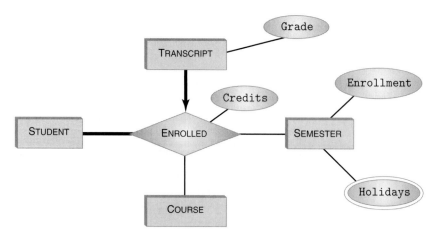

FIGURE 4.36 An alternative representation of the transcript information.

Entity or relationship? Consider once again the diagram in Figure 4.8 on page 82, where we treat transcript records as relationships between STUDENT, COURSE, and SEMESTER entities. An alternative to this design is to represent transcript records as entities and use a new relationship type, ENROLLED, to connect them. This alternative is shown in Figure 4.36. Here we incorporate some of the attributes for the entity SEMESTER, as discussed earlier. We also add an extra attribute, Credits, to the relationship ENROLLED, which means that the same course (e.g., thesis research) can be taken for a variable number of credits. Clearly, the two diagrams represent the same information (except for the extra attributes added to Figure 4.36), but which one is better?

As with the "entity vs. attribute" dilemma, the choice largely depends on your taste. However, a number of points are worth considering. For instance, it is a good idea to keep the total number of entities and relations as small as possible because it is directly related to the number of relations that will result when the E-R diagram is converted to the relational model. Generally, it is not too serious a problem if two relations are lumped together at this stage because the relational design theory presented in Chapter 6 will help identify the relation schemas that must be split. On the other hand, it is much harder to spot the opposite problem: needless decomposition of one relation into two or more.

Coming back to Figure 4.36, we notice that there is a participation constraint for the entity TRANSCRIPT in the relationship type ENROLLED. Moreover, the arrow leading from TRANSCRIPT to ENROLLED indicates that the Transcript role forms a key of the ENROLLED relationship. Therefore, there is a one-to-one correspondence between the relationships of type ENROLLED and the entities of type TRANSCRIPT. This means that relationships of type ENROLLED can be viewed as superfluous because TRANSCRIPT entities can be used instead to relate the entities of types STUDENT, COURSE, and SEMESTER. All that is required (in order not to lose information) is to

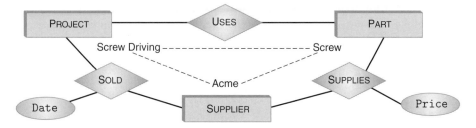

FIGURE 4.37 Replacing the ternary relationship SOLD of Figure 4.2 with three binary relationships.

transfer the descriptive attributes of ENROLLED to TRANSCRIPT after converting the latter into a relationship.

This discussion leads to the following rule:

> Consider a relationship type, R, that relates the entity types $E_1, \ldots, E_n$, and suppose that E_1 is attached to R via a role that (by itself) forms a key of R, and that a participation constraint exists between E_1 and R. Then it might be possible to collapse E_1 and R into a new relationship type that relates the entity types $E_2, \ldots, E_n$.

Note that this rule is only an indication that E_1 can be collapsed into R, not a guarantee that this is possible or natural. For instance, E_1 might be involved in some other relationship, R'. In that case, collapsing E_1 into R leaves an edge that connects two relationship types, R and R', which is not allowed by the construction rules for E-R diagrams. Such is the situation of the BROKER and ACCOUNT entities in Figure 4.30: The above rule suggests that BROKER can be collapsed into WORKSIN, and ACCOUNT can be collapsed into ISHANDLEDBY. However, both BROKER and ACCOUNT are involved in two different relationships, and each such collapse leaves us with a diagram where two relationships, WORKSIN and ISHANDLEDBY or HASACCOUNT and ISHANDLEDBY, are directly connected by an edge. On the other hand, the TRANSACTION entity type in Figure 4.31 *can* be collapsed into the TRADE relationship type.

Information loss. We have seen examples where the degree of a relationship might change by demoting an entity to an attribute or by collapsing an entity into a relationship. In all of these cases, however, the transformations obviously preserve the information content of the diagrams. Now we are going to discuss some typical situations where seemingly innocuous transformations cause **information loss**; that is, they lead to diagrams with subtly changed information content.

Consider the PART/SUPPLIER/PROJECT diagram of Figure 4.2, page 74. Some designers do not like ternary relationships, preferring to deal with multiple binary relationships instead. Such a decision might lead to the diagram shown in Figure 4.37.

Although superficially the new diagram seems equivalent to the original, there are several subtle differences. First, the new design introduces a navigation trap of the kind we saw in the stock-trading example: It is possible that a supplier, Acme, sells "Screw" and that Acme has sold something to project "Screw Driving." It is even possible that the screw-driving project uses screws of the kind Acme sells. However, from the relationships represented in the diagram it is not possible to conclude that it was Acme who sold these screws to the project. All we can tell is that Acme *might* have done so. In other words, we have introduced a navigation trap—a problem that we have already seen in Section 4.7.

The other problem with the new design is that the price attribute is now associated with the relationship SUPPLIES. This implies that a supplier has a fixed price for each item regardless of the project to which that item is sold. In contrast, the original design in Figure 4.2 supports different pricing for different projects. Similarly, the new design allows only one transaction between a particular supplier and project on any given day because each sale is represented as a triple ⟨project, supplier; date⟩ in the SOLD relationship. So there is no way to represent different transactions between the same parties on the same day. The original design, on the other hand, allows several such deals, provided that different parts were involved.

Having realized the problem posed by navigation traps, one might become inclined to use higher-degree relationships whenever possible. For instance, in Figure 4.30 we might want to try eliminating the navigation trap caused by the relationships HASACCOUNT, WORKSIN, and ISHANDLEDBY by collapsing these three relationships into one. However, this transformation introduces more problems than it solves. For instance, if this transformation keeps the arrow that connects BROKER and WORKSIN, we unwittingly introduce the constraint that a broker can have at most one account and at most one client. If we do not keep this arrow, we lose the constraint that each broker is assigned to exactly one office. This transformation also makes it impossible to have brokers who have no accounts and accounts that have no brokers.

Conceptual design and object databases.   Although we will not discuss object databases until Chapter 16, we briefly mention here that some of the difficult issues involved in translating the conceptual design diagrams into schemas become easier for object databases.

- In Section 4.2, we discussed the issues involved in representing entities with set-valued attributes in a relational database. The objects stored in an object database can have set-valued attributes, so the representation of such entities in the schema of the object database is considerably easier.

- In Section 4.4, we discussed the issues involved in representing the IsA relationship in a relational database. Object databases allow a direct representation of the IsA relationship within the schema, so, again, representation of such relationships is considerably easier.

- UML class diagrams allow methods to be specified along with attributes. These methods can be directly translated into the methods supported by object-oriented databases.

From these examples, it should be apparent that not only is it generally easier to go from conceptual design to object-oriented schemas, but for many applications, object databases support a much more intuitive model of the enterprise than do relational databases.

BIBLIOGRAPHIC NOTES

The entity-relationship approach was introduced in [Chen 1976]. Since then it has received considerable attention and various extensions have been proposed (see, for example, research papers in [Spaccapietra 1987]). Conceptual design using the E-R model has also been advanced significantly. The reader is referred to [Teorey 1999; Batini et al. 1992; Thalheim 1992] for comprehensive coverage.

The Unified Modeling Language [Booch et al. 1999] was a product of a long line of research on object-oriented modeling and design. Precursors of UML include OMT [Rumbaugh et al. 1991], the methods developed in [Booch 1994], and the methodology for modeling software through use cases [Jacobson 1992]. While UML was primarily motivated by the needs of software engineering, it borrows many ideas from the E-R model and extends it in the direction of object-oriented modeling. In particular, it provides means to model not only the structure of the data but also the behavioral aspects of programs and how large applications are to be deployed in complex computing environments. A succinct introduction to UML can be found in [Fowler and Scott 2003].

A number of tools exist to help the database designer with E-R and UML modeling. These tools guide the user through the process of specifying the diagrams, attributes, constraints, and so forth. When all is done, they map the conceptual model into relational tables. Such tools include *ERwin* from Computer Associates, *ER/Studio* from Embarcadero Technologies, and *Rational Rose* from Rational Software. In addition, DBMS vendors provide their own design tools, such as *Oracle Designer* from Oracle Corporation and *PowerDesigner* from Sybase.

EXERCISES

4.1 Suppose that you decide to convert IsA hierarchies into the relational model by adding a new attribute (such as `Status` in the case of STUDENT entities, as described on page 91—the second option for representing IsA hierarchies). What kind of problems exist if subentities are not disjoint (e.g., if a secretary can also be a technician)? What problems exist if the covering constraint does not hold (e.g., if some employees are not classified as either secretary or technician)?

4.2 Construct your own example of an E-R or UML diagram whose direct translation into the relational model has an anomaly similar to that of the PERSON entity (see the discussion regarding Figure 4.13 on page 86).

4.3 Represent the IsA hierarchy in Figure 4.6, page 80, in the relational model. For each IsA relationship discuss your choice of the representation technique Discuss the circumstances in which an alternative representation (to the one you have chosen) would be better.

4.4 Suppose, in Figure 4.8, the PROFESSOR entity did not participate in the relationship WORKSIN, but the arrow between them was still present. Would it make sense to merge PROFESSOR with WORKSIN during translation into the relational model? What kind of problems can arise here? Are they serious problems?

4.5 Translate the brokerage example of Section 4.7 into an SQL schema. Use the necessary SQL machinery to express all constraints specified in the E-R model.

4.6 Identify the navigation traps present in the diagram of Figure 4.29, page 107.

4.7 Consider the following database schema:

- SUPPLIER(SName, ItemName, Price)—supplier SName sells item ItemName at Price
- CUSTOMER(CName, Address)—customer CName lives at Address.
- ORDER(CName, SName, ItemName, Qty)—customer CName has ordered Qty of item ItemName from supplier SName.
- ITEM(ItemName, Description)—information about items.
  (a) Draw the E-R diagram from which the above schema might have been derived. Specify the keys.
  (b) Suppose now that you want to add the following constraint to this diagram: *Every item is supplied by some supplier*. Modify the diagram to accommodate this constraint. Also show how this new diagram can be translated back to the relational model.
  (c) Repeat parts (a) and (b) in UML.

4.8 Perform conceptual design of the operations of your local community library. The library has books, CDs, tapes, and so forth, which are lent to library patrons. The latter have accounts, addresses, and so forth. If a loaned item is overdue, it accumulates penalty. Some patrons are minors, so they must have sponsoring patrons who are responsible for paying penalties (or replacing a book in case of a loss).

a. Use the E-R approach.
b. Use UML.

4.9 A real estate firm keeps track of the houses for sale and customers looking to buy houses. A house for sale can be *listed* with this firm or with a different one. Being "listed" with a firm means that the house owner has a contract with an agent who works for that firm. Each house on the market has price, address, owner, and a list of features, such as the number of bedrooms, bathrooms, type of heating, appliances, size of garage, and the like. This list can be different for different houses, and some features can be present in some houses but missing in others. Likewise, each customer has preferences that are expressed in the same terms (the number of bedrooms, bathrooms, etc.). Apart from these preferences, customers specify the price range of houses they are interested in. Perform conceptual design for this enterprise.

a. Use the E-R approach.
b. Use UML.

4.10 A supermarket chain is interested in building a decision support system with which they can analyze the sales of different products in different supermarkets at different times. Each supermarket is in a city, which is in a state, which is in a region. Time can be measured in days, months, quarters, and years. Products have names and categories (produce, canned goods, etc.).

a. Design an E-R diagram for this application.
b. Do the same in UML.

4.11   Modify the E-R diagram for the Student Registration System in Figure 4.33 on page 114 to include co-requisite and prerequisite relationships that exist over multiple periods of time. Each period begins in a certain semester and year and ends in a certain semester and year, or it continues into the present. Modify the translation into the relational model appropriately.

4.12   Modify the E-R diagram for the Student Registration System in Figure 4.33 on page 114 to include information about the student majors and the majors allowed in courses. A student can have several majors (which are codes of the various programs in the university, such as CSE, ISE, MUS, ECO). A course can also have several admissible majors, or the list of admissible majors can be empty. In the latter case, anyone is admitted into the course. Express the constraint that says that a course with restrictions on majors can have only those students who hold one of the allowed majors.

Alas, in full generality this constraint can be expressed only as an SQL assertion (introduced in Section 3.3) that uses features of Section 5.2 (which we have yet to study). However, it is possible to express this constraint under the following simplifying assumption: when a student registers for a course, she must declare the major toward which the course is going to be taken, and this declared major is checked against the admissible majors.

Modify the relation schema in Figures 4.34 and 4.35 to reflect this simplifying assumption and then express the aforesaid integrity constraint.

4.13   Redo the E-R diagram of the Student Registration System (Figure 4.33) in UML.

4.14   Make the necessary modifications to the schema of the Student Registration System to reflect the design that uses the SQL domain SEMESTERS, as discussed at the end of Section 4.8. Express the constraint that a class can be taught only during the semesters in which the corresponding course is offered. For instance, if the value of the attribute SemestersOffered for the course CS305 is Both, then the corresponding classes can be taught in the spring and the fall semesters. However, if the value of that attribute is Spring then these classes can be taught only in the spring.

4.15   Design an E-R model for the following enterprise. Various organizations make business deals with various other organizations. (For simplicity, let us assume that there are only two parties to each deal.) When negotiating (and signing) a deal, each organization is represented by a lawyer. The same organization can have deals with many other organizations, and it might use different lawyers in each case. Lawyers and organizations have various attributes, like address and name. They also have their own unique attributes, such as specialization and fee, in the case of a lawyer, and budget, in the case of an organization.

Show how information loss can occur if a relationship of degree higher than two is split into a binary relationship. Discuss the assumption under which such a split does not lead to a loss of information.

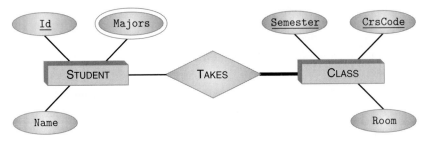

FIGURE 4.38 E-R diagram for Exercise 4.17.

4.16 Design an E-R model for the library system described in Exercise 3.15. Do the same with UML.

4.17 Consider the E-R diagram depicted in Figure 4.38. Write down the corresponding relational schema using SQL. Include all keys and other applicable constraints.

4.18 Consider the partial translation of an E-R participation constraint into UML (shown in Figure 4.24). Show that this is, indeed, an imprecise translation in that there are instances of the database (i.e., collections of objects and associations) that comply with the E-R constraint in Figure 4.24(b) such that it does not satisfy the multiplicity constraint in UML.

5

Relational Algebra and SQL

Now that we know how to create a database, the next step is to learn how to query it to retrieve the information needed for some particular application. Before relational databases, database querying was a dreadful task. To pose even a simple query (by today's standards), one would use a conventional programming language to write a program that could include multiple nested loops, error handling, and boundary condition checking. In addition, the programmer would deal with numerous details of the internal physical schema—in those days, data independence was only on the wish list.

A **database query language** is a special-purpose programming language designed for retrieving information stored in a database. The relational query language in which we are most interested is SQL (Structured Query Language). It is quite different from conventional programming languages. In SQL, you specify the properties of the information to be retrieved but not the detailed algorithm required for retrieval. For example, a query in the Student Registration System might specify retrieval of the names and Ids of all professors who have taught a particular course in a particular semester, but it would not provide a detailed procedure (involving while loops, if statements, pointer variables, etc.) to traverse the various database tables and retrieve the specified names. Thus, SQL is said to be *declarative*, as its queries "declare" what information the answer should contain, not how to compute it. Contrast this to conventional programming languages (e.g., C or Java), which are said to be *procedural* because programs written in them describe the exact actions to be performed to compute the answer.

As with other computer languages, a programmer can design simple queries after only a brief introduction to SQL, but the design of the complex queries needed in real applications requires a more detailed knowledge of the language and its semantics. Therefore, before we introduce SQL we study the *relational algebra*, which is another relational query language that is used by the DBMS as an intermediate language into which SQL statements are translated before they are optimized.

5.1 Relational Algebra: Under the Hood of SQL

Relational algebra is called an algebra because it is based on a small number of **operators**, which operate on relations (tables). Each operator operates on one or more relations and produces another relation as a result. A query is just an expression involving these operators. The result of the expression is a relation, which is the answer to the query.

While SQL is a declarative language, meaning that it does not specify the algorithm used to process queries, relational algebra is procedural. A relational expression can be viewed as a specification of such an algorithm (although at a much higher level than the algorithms specified using traditional programming languages).

Thus, even when programmers use SQL to specify their queries, DBMSs use relational algebra as an intermediate language for specifying query evaluation algorithms. The DBMS parses the SQL query and translates it into an expression in relational algebra, which usually leads to a rather simplistic, inefficient algorithm. The **query optimizer** then converts this algebraic expression into one that is *equivalent* but that (hopefully) takes less time to execute.[1] On the basis of the optimized algebraic expression it produced, the query optimizer prepares a **query execution plan**, which is then transformed into executable code by the code generator within the DBMS. Because algebraic expressions have precise mathematical semantics, the system can verify that the resulting "optimized" expression is equivalent to the original. The semantics also makes it possible to compare different proposed query evaluation plans. A schematic view of query processing is shown in Figure 5.1.

The relational algebra is the key to understanding the inner workings of a relational DBMS, which in turn is essential in designing SQL queries that can be processed efficiently.

5.1.1 Basic Operators

Relational algebra is based on five basic operators:

1. *Select*
2. *Project*
3. *Union*
4. *Set difference*
5. *Cartesian product* (also known as *cross product*)

each of which we consider in turn. In addition, there are three *derived* operators (i.e., they can be represented as expressions involving the basic operators): *intersection*, *division*, and *join*. We also discuss the *renaming* operator, which is useful in conjunction with Cartesian products and joins.

---

[1] Query optimizers do not really "optimize" (in the sense of producing the *most efficient* query evaluation algorithm) because this is generally an impossible task. Instead, they use heuristics known to produce equivalent expressions that are generally cheaper to evaluate.

FIGURE **5.1** Schematic view of query processing.

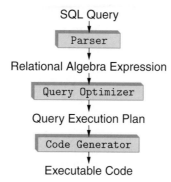

SQL Query

Parser

Relational Algebra Expression

Query Optimizer

Query Execution Plan

Code Generator

Executable Code

Select operator. One of the most frequent operations performed on relations is **selection** of a subset of tuples (i.e., selection of some subset of the rows in a table). For instance, you might want a list of the professors in the CS department. Surely they are all listed in the PROFESSOR relation, but this relation might be large and a manual scan for the tuples of interest might be difficult. Using the select operator, this query can be expressed as

$$\sigma_{\text{DeptId}\,=\,\text{'CS'}}\,(\text{PROFESSOR})$$

The query reads as "Select all tuples from the PROFESSOR relation that satisfy the condition DeptId = 'CS'."

The general syntax of the select operator is

$$\sigma_{selection\text{-}condition}\,(relation\text{-}name)$$

We will see later that the argument of the select operator can be more general than simply a name that identifies a relation. It can also be an expression that evaluates to a relation.

The selection condition can have one of the following forms:

- *simple-selection-condition* (explained below)
- *selection-condition* AND *selection-condition*
- *selection-condition* OR *selection-condition*
- NOT (*selection-condition*)

A simple selection condition can be any one of the following:

- *relation-attribute* oper *constant*
- *relation-attribute* oper *relation-attribute*

where oper can be any one of the following comparison operators: $=, \neq, >, \geq, <,$ and $\leq$. Each attribute that occurs in a comparison must be one of the attributes in the *relation-name* argument of the selection operator.

It is important to realize that the above syntactic rules *must be followed*, in the same way that you follow the rules of syntax in any other programming language. For instance, a common syntax error is to write a query such as

$$\sigma_{\text{ProfId=Professor.Id AND Professor.DeptId='CS'}} (\text{Teaching})$$

to list all courses taught by computer science professors. However natural this expression might seem, it is *syntactically incorrect* because the selection condition uses attributes of the PROFESSOR relation whereas the syntax rules permit only the attributes of the TEACHING relation—the relation specified in the argument of the selection.

By itself, the expression $\sigma_{selection\text{-}condition}(\mathbf{R})$ is meaningless—it is just a string of characters. However, in a concrete database it can have a *value*, which represents the *meaning* of the expression in the context of that database. Thus, we always assume that we are working in the context of some concrete database, which associates a concrete relation instance with each relation name.

Suppose that $\mathbf{r}$ is such a relation instance associated with relation schema $\mathbf{R}$. We define the *value* of the above expression with respect to $\mathbf{r}$, denoted $\sigma_{selection\text{-}condition}(\mathbf{r})$, to be the relation that consists of the set of all tuples in $\mathbf{r}$ that satisfy *selection-condition*. Thus, the value of the select operator applied to a relation is another relation with the same set of attributes as the original.

For instance, the value of $\sigma_{\text{DeptId = 'CS'}}$ (PROFESSOR) with respect to the database of Figure 3.5 on page 39 is the relation CSPROF.

CSPROF	Id	Name	DeptId
	101202303	Smyth, John	CS
	555666777	Doe, Mary	CS

It should be clear what it means for a tuple in $\mathbf{r}$ to satisfy a selection condition. For instance, if the condition is $A > c$, where A is an attribute and c is a constant, a tuple, t, satisfies the condition if (and only if) the value of attribute A in t is greater than c.[2] When the selection condition is more complex (e.g., $cond_1$ AND $cond_2$), satisfaction is defined recursively. It is satisfied by t if and only if t satisfies both $cond_1$ and $cond_2$. The condition $cond_1$ OR $cond_2$ is similar, except that t needs to satisfy only one of the subconditions. Analogously, t satisfies NOT($cond$) if t violates $cond$.

For instance, tuple 2 in the relation CSPROF satisfies the complex condition Id > 111222333 AND NOT (DeptId = 'EE') because it satisfies both of the following:

- Id > 111222333, since 555666777 > 111222333.
- NOT (DeptId = 'EE'), since 'CS' ≠ 'EE' and thus the tuple violates the condition DeptId = 'EE'.

---

[2] We assume the existence of some ordering on the domain of A. In the case of numeric domains, the order is clear; in the case of domains of strings, we assume lexicographic order.

In contrast, tuple 1 in that relation violates the above complex condition because it violates the first term, Id > 111222333, of that condition (since 101202303 ≯ 111222333).

Here is a more complex selection:

$$\sigma_{\text{StudId}\neq 111111111 \text{ AND (Semester='S1991' OR Grade}<'B')}(\text{Transcript})$$

where the comparison among strings (Grade < 'B') assumes lexicographic order in which 'A' < 'B', etc. The value of this expression in the context of the database of Figure 3.5 is the relation

SUBTRANSCRIPT	StudId	CrsCode	Semester	Grade
	666666666	MGT123	F1994	A
	666666666	EE101	S1991	B
	123454321	CS315	S1997	A
	123454321	CS305	S1996	A
	023456789	CS305	S1996	A

One obvious generalization of the selection condition is to allow conditions of the form *expression*$_1$ oper *expression*$_2$, where *expression* can be either an arithmetic expression that involves attributes (which act as variables) and constants, or a string expression (e.g., pattern matching, string concatenation).

Examples of such expressions are EmplSalary > (MngrSalary * 2) and (DeptId + CrsNumber) LIKE CrsCode (here + denotes string concatenation and LIKE denotes pattern matching). The utility of such extended selections is obvious, and they are extensively used in database languages.

Project operator. When discussing selection, we often refer to values of certain attributes in a tuple. In relational algebra, such references are very common, so we introduce special notation for them. Let A denote an attribute of a relation, $\mathbf{r}$, and let t be a tuple in $\mathbf{r}$. Then $t.A$ denotes the component of tuple t that corresponds to the attribute A. For instance, if t denotes tuple 1 in relation SUBTRANSCRIPT, then t.CrsCode is MGT123.

Also, we often need to extract a *subtuple* from a tuple. A **subtuple**, t, is a sequence of values extracted from t in accordance with some list of attributes. It is denoted as

$$t.\{A_1, \ldots, A_n\}$$

where $A_1, \ldots, A_n$ are attributes.

For instance, if t is tuple 1 in SUBTRANSCRIPT, then $t.\{\text{Semester, CrsCode}\}$ is the tuple ⟨ F1994, MGT123 ⟩. Note that the order of attributes here does not

(and need not) follow the order in which these attributes are listed in the relation
SUBTRANSCRIPT. Moreover, sometimes it is convenient to allow duplicate attributes
in the list. Thus, $t.\{$Semester, CrsCode, Semester$\}$ is $\langle$F1994, MGT123, F1994$\rangle$.

Now we are ready to define the **projection operator**, whose general syntax is

$$\pi_{attribute\text{-}list} \ (relation\text{-}name)$$

For example, if **R** is a relation name and $A_1, \ldots, A_n$ are *some* (or all) of the attributes
in **R**, then $\pi_{A_1,\ldots,A_n}(\mathbf{R})$ is called the **projection** of **R** on attributes $A_1, \ldots, A_n$. In
other words, projection picks some subset of the columns in a table. (Sometimes it
is convenient to view $A_1, \ldots, A_n$ as a list with possible repetition of attributes, but
we will not need this generality here.)

As in the case of selection, the above expression can be assigned a value in the
context of a concrete database. Suppose that **r** is a relation instance corresponding
to **R** in such a database. Then the *value* of $\pi_{A_1,\ldots,A_n}(\mathbf{R})$, denoted $\pi_{A_1,\ldots,A_n}(\mathbf{r})$, is the
set of *all* tuples of the form $t.\{A_1, \ldots, A_n\}$, where t ranges over all tuples in **r**.

For instance, $\pi_{\text{CrsCode,Semester}}$ (TEACHING) is the relation

OFFERINGS	CrsCode	Semester
	MGT123	F1994
	EE101	S1991
	CS305	F1995
	CS315	S1997
	MAT123	S1996
	EE101	F1995
	CS305	S1996
	MAT123	F1997
	MGT123	F1997

Observe that the original TEACHING relation of Figure 3.5 (page 40) has 11 tuples,
while OFFERINGS has only 9. What happened to the other tuples? The answer
becomes apparent if we examine the original relation more closely. It is easy to
see that tuples 1 and 4 are identical in their CrsCode and Semester attributes. The
only difference between them is in the value of the ProfId attribute. The same is
true of tuples 10 and 11. Applying the projection operator to tuples 1 and 4 (and to
tuples 10 and 11) yields identical tuples because the attribute ProfId is eliminated.
Relations are sets and so do not allow duplicates; thus, only one copy in each group
of identical tuples is kept.

The purpose of the projection operator is to help us focus on the relationships
of interest and ignore the attributes that are irrelevant to a particular query. For instance, suppose that we wish to know which courses are offered in which semesters.

The OFFERINGS relation shows this information clearly without diluting the answer with data that we did not ask for (i.e., ProfId). Projection also eliminates duplicates, which can save us time on analyzing the answer.

Now that we have seen two relational operators, we can construct **relational expressions** out of them. This is not just an abstract mathematical exercise. Expressions are a general way of constructing queries in relational databases. For instance, the relation CSPROF, which contains the tuples corresponding to computer science professors, is the result of applying the selection operator to PROFESSOR. We could further request just the names of those professors using the projection operator: π_{Name} (CSPROF). The advantage of the algebra is that operators can be combined just as in high-school algebra, so we write

$$\pi_{\text{Name}} (\sigma_{\text{DeptId = 'CS'}} (\text{PROFESSOR}))$$

without specifying the intermediate result, CSPROF, and without creating a temporary relation.

Set operations.   The next two operators are the familiar set operators **union** and **set difference**. Clearly, since relations are sets, set operators are applicable to relations. The syntax is $R \cup S$ and $R - S$. If r and s are the relations corresponding to R and S, then

- The **value** of $R \cup S$ is $r \cup s$, the set of all tuples that belong to either r or s.
- The **value** of $R - S$ is $r - s$, the set of all tuples in r that *do not* belong to s.

We can also use the **intersection** operator, $R \cap S$ (whose value on r and s is, naturally, $r \cap s$), but this operator is not independent of the rest. It can be represented as an expression built out of the basic five operators mentioned at the beginning of this section.

Unfortunately, we are not done yet. While the union of two sets is always a set, we cannot say the same about arbitrary relations. Consider the union of PROFESSOR with TRANSCRIPT. One problem is that relations are *tables* where all rows have the same number of items. However, the tuples in the PROFESSOR relation have three items each, while the tuples in the TRANSCRIPT relation have four. Since they have different arities, the collection of all of these tuples is a set (all right), but it does not constitute a relation.

Even when the arities are the same, in order for the union to be meaningful all items in the corresponding columns must belong to the same domain. Consider the set-theoretic union of PROFESSOR and TEACHING. If we match the columns, then Id, Name, and DeptId in PROFESSOR will correspond to ProfId, CrsCode, and Semester. In the union, the values in the first column are members of the same domain, so no problem there. However, the second and the third columns clearly do not belong to the same domain (e.g., people's names and course codes). Again, the union does not make sense.

CrsCode	Semester
CS305	F1995

$$\pi_{\text{CrsCode},\text{Semester}}(\sigma_{\text{Grade}=\text{'C'}}(\text{TRANSCRIPT}))$$
$$-\pi_{\text{CrsCode},\text{Semester}}(\sigma_{\text{CrsCode}=\text{'MAT123'}}(\text{TEACHING}))$$

CrsCode	Semester
CS305	F1995
MAT123	S1996
MAT123	F1997

$$\pi_{\text{CrsCode},\text{Semester}}(\sigma_{\text{Grade}=\text{'C'}}(\text{TRANSCRIPT}))$$
$$\cup \; \pi_{\text{CrsCode},\text{Semester}}(\sigma_{\text{CrsCode}=\text{'MAT123'}}(\text{TEACHING}))$$

CrsCode	Semester
MAT123	S1996

$$\pi_{\text{CrsCode},\text{Semester}}(\sigma_{\text{Grade}=\text{'C'}}(\text{TRANSCRIPT}))$$
$$\cap \; \pi_{\text{CrsCode},\text{Semester}}(\sigma_{\text{CrsCode}=\text{'MAT123'}}(\text{TEACHING}))$$

FIGURE 5.2 Examples of relational expressions that involve set operators.

To overcome these problems, we limit the scope of the union operator and apply it only to *union-compatible* relations. Relations are **union-compatible** if their schemas satisfy the following rules:

■ Both relations have the same number of columns.

■ The names of the attributes are the same in both relations.

■ Attributes with the same name in both relations have the same domain.

We also require union-compatibility for the difference and intersection operators.

Example 5.1.1 (Complex Relational Expressions). Figure 5.2 illustrates some nontrivial uses of set operators combined with select and project operators. The first query retrieves all course offerings *other than* MAT123, where some student received the grade C. The second query is a bit contrived but is a good illustration; it yields all course offerings where either somebody got a C or the offered course was MAT123. The third query lists all offerings of MAT123 where somebody got a C.

One interesting aspect of these examples is that the original relations, TRANSCRIPT and TEACHING, are not union-compatible. However, they become compatible after the incompatible attributes are projected out. All expressions in this figure are evaluated in the context of our running example of Figure 3.5 on page 39. ■

Id	Name
111223344	Smith, Mary
023456789	Simpson, Homer
987654321	Simpson, Bart

A subset of $\pi_{\text{Id}, \text{Name}}$(STUDENT)

Id	DeptId
555666777	CS
101202303	CS

A subset of $\pi_{\text{Id}, \text{DeptId}}$(PROFESSOR)

STUDENT.Id	Name	PROFESSOR.Id	DeptId
111223344	Smith, Mary	555666777	CS
111223344	Smith, Mary	101202303	CS
023456789	Simpson, Homer	555666777	CS
023456789	Simpson, Homer	101202303	CS
987654321	Simpson, Bart	555666777	CS
987654321	Simpson, Bart	101202303	CS

Their Cartesian product

FIGURE 5.3 Two relations and their Cartesian product.

The Cartesian product and renaming. The **Cartesian product** (also known as **cross product**), **R** × **S**, is close to the cross product operation on sets. If **r** and **s** are relational instances corresponding to **R** and **S**, respectively, the *value* of this expression, denoted **r** × **s**, is the set of all tuples, t, that can be obtained by concatenation of a tuple $r \in \mathbf{r}$ and a tuple $s \in \mathbf{s}$.[3]

Figure 5.3 shows a Cartesian product of a subset of $\pi_{\text{Id}, \text{Name}}$(STUDENT) and a subset of $\pi_{\text{Id}, \text{DeptId}}$(PROFESSOR). To make it clear which parts of each tuple in the product come from which relation, we have marked the boundary between the parts with a double line.

Brain Teaser: What is **r** × **s** when **s** is an empty relation?

---

[3] A slight difference between the usual set-theoretic cross product operation on relations and the relational cross product operation defined above is that in the former the result is a set of pairs of tuples of the form ($< a, b >, < c, d >$) while in the latter it is a set of concatenated tuples (i.e., $< a, b, c, d >$).

We are now forced to address the problem of attribute naming in the results of the relational expressions, which so far we have conveniently ignored. The relations that are arguments to the algebraic expressions have their schema defined in the system catalog, so the names of their attributes are known. In contrast, the relations produced by evaluating the expressions are created on the fly, and their schema is not explicitly defined. For some operations, such as σ and π (when projection list does not include repeated attributes), this does not present a problem as we can simply reuse the schema of the argument relation. For $\cup$, $\cap$, and $-$, we do not have a naming problem either because the relations involved in these operations are union-compatible and so have the same schema, which, again, can be reused for the query answer.

The Cartesian product is the first time we must deal with the naming problem. Observe how some attributes in the product relation in Figure 5.3 have mysteriously changed names. This is because the relations involved in the operation, $\pi_{\text{Id,Name}}$ (STUDENT) and $\pi_{\text{Id,DeptId}}$ (PROFESSOR) have an identically named attribute, Id, which would otherwise appear twice in the product. The relational model does not allow different columns to have the same name within the same schema. To overcome this problem, we rename the attributes by prefixing them with the relation of their origin.

In this Cartesian product example, the problem of attribute name clashes was conveniently solved through a simple renaming convention, which we will continue to use in the future whenever possible. Unfortunately, this convention does not always work—for instance, it breaks down in the case of a cross product of two instances of the same PROFESSOR relation. Rather than trying to invent increasingly complex renaming schemes, we will place the burden on the programmer, who now becomes responsible for the renaming. To this end, we introduce the **renaming operator**, which does not belong to the core of the algebra and has no standard notation. We choose the following simple notation:

$$expression[A_1, \ldots, A_n]$$

where *expression* is an expression in relational algebra and $A_1, \ldots, A_n$ is a list of names to be used for the attributes in the result of that expression.

We assume that n represents the number of columns in the result of the expression. Moreover, we assume that there is some standard order of columns in the relation produced by evaluating the expression. For example, in the results of π, σ, $\cup$, $\cap$, and $-$, the order is the same as that in which the attributes are listed in the schema of the argument relations. For $\mathbf{R} \times \mathbf{S}$, the attributes should be listed as in Figure 5.3. The attributes of $\mathbf{R}$ followed by the attributes of $\mathbf{S}$. For instance,

$$(\pi_{\text{Id,Name}}(\text{STUDENT}) \times \pi_{\text{Id,DeptId}}(\text{PROFESSOR}))[\text{StudId,StudName,ProfId,}$$
$$\text{ProfDept}]$$

renames the attributes of the product relation in Figure 5.3 to StudId, StudName, ProfId, ProfDept from left to right. In particular, the two occurrences of Id are renamed StudId and ProfId, respectively.

The renaming operator can also be applied to subexpressions. The following example is similar to the previous one except that we renamed the attributes of the PROFESSOR relation before applying other operators.

$$\pi_{\text{Id,Name}}(\text{STUDENT}) \times \pi_{\text{ProfId,ProfDept}}(\text{PROFESSOR } [\text{ProfId,ProfName,}$$
$$\text{ProfDept}])$$

The result is the same as before, but the names of the attributes (from left to right) are now Id, Name, ProfId, ProfDept. Also note that we had to change the attributes in the rightmost π operator because the attributes in the argument relation were changed as a result of the renaming.

The Cartesian product holds the distinction of being the most computationally expensive operator in the whole of relational algebra. Consider $\mathbf{R} \times \mathbf{S}$, and suppose that $\mathbf{R}$ has n tuples and $\mathbf{S}$ has m tuples. The Cartesian product has $n \times m$ tuples. In addition, each tuple in the product is larger in size. For concreteness, let both $\mathbf{R}$ and $\mathbf{S}$ have 1,000 tuples with 100 bytes per tuple. Then $\mathbf{R} \times \mathbf{S}$ has 1,000,000 tuples with 200 bytes per tuple. Thus, while the total size of the original relations is 200 kilobytes, the product has 200 megabytes. The cost of just writing out such a relation on disk can be prohibitive. This is just a small example. We will soon see that it is not uncommon for a query to involve three or more relations. Even in the case of four tiny relations of 100 tuples with 100 bytes per tuple, the Cartesian product has 100,000,000 tuples with 400 bytes per tuple—40 gigabytes of data!

In a course on analysis of algorithms, you might have been taught that algorithms with polynomial time complexity are acceptable as long as the degree of the polynomial is not too high. As you can see from the above example, in query processing even quadratic algorithms can be unacceptably expensive if they operate on large volumes of data. Because of the potentially huge costs, query optimizers attempt to avoid cross products if at all possible.

5.1.2 Derived Operators

Joins. A **join** of two relations, $\mathbf{R}$ and $\mathbf{S}$, is an expression of the form

$$\mathbf{R} \bowtie_{\text{join-condition}} \mathbf{S}$$

The *join condition* is a restricted form of the already familiar selection condition used in the σ operator:

$$\mathbf{R}.A_1 \; oper_1 \; \mathbf{S}.B_1 \text{ AND } \mathbf{R}.A_2 \; oper_2 \; \mathbf{S}.B_2 \text{ AND } \dots \text{ AND } \mathbf{R}.A_n \; oper_n \; \mathbf{S}.B_n \qquad \textbf{5.1}$$

Here the list $A_1, \dots, A_n$ is a subset of the attributes of $\mathbf{R}$, and $B_1, \dots, B_n$ is a subset of the attributes of $\mathbf{S}$. Finally, $oper_1, \dots, oper_n$ are the comparison operators $=, \neq, >$, and so forth.

These restrictions imply that join conditions can have only the AND connective (no ORs or NOTs) and that comparisons between attributes and constants are not allowed.

STUDENT.Id	Name	PROFESSOR.Id	DeptId
111223344	Smith, Mary	555666777	CS
023456789	Simpson, Homer	555666777	CS
023456789	Simpson, Homer	101202303	CS

$$\pi_{\texttt{Id,Name}}(\text{STUDENT}) \bowtie_{\texttt{Id}<\texttt{Id}} \pi_{\texttt{Id,DeptId}}(\text{PROFESSOR})$$

FIGURE 5.4 Join of relations in Figure 5.3.

Even though we use a new symbol to represent it, join is not a radically new operator. *By definition*, the above join is equivalent to

$$\sigma_{join\text{-}condition'}(\mathbf{R} \times \mathbf{S})$$

However, as joins occur frequently in database queries, they have earned the privilege of having their own symbol.

Notice one subtlety: we use *join-condition'* in $\sigma_{join\text{-}condition'}$ above rather than *join-condition*, which was used in $\bowtie_{join\text{-}condition}$ in the definition of the join. This is because **R** and **S** might have identically named attributes, which must be renamed as part of the Cartesian product operation. Thus, *join-condition'* is like *join-condition*, except that it uses the actual renamed attributes of $\mathbf{R} \times \mathbf{S}$ rather than the qualified attribute names in (5.1) above.

Example 5.1.2 (Join). Figure 5.4 is an example of a join of two relations. Note the simplified join condition Id < Id, which we use instead of STUDENT.Id < PROFESSOR.Id. It means that in order to qualify for the join, the value of the Id attribute in the STUDENT tuple must be less than the value of the Id attribute in the PROFESSOR tuple. We will continue to use such simplified join conditions when it is clear which attributes come from which relations. ■

Note that the definition of a join involves a Cartesian product as an intermediate step. Therefore, a join is a potentially expensive operation. However, the silver lining is that the Cartesian product is hidden inside the join. In fact, Cartesian products rarely occur on their own in typical database queries. Thus, even though the intermediate result (the product) can potentially be very large, the final result can be manageable, as only a small number of tuples in the product might satisfy the join condition.

For example, the result of the join in Figure 5.4 is half the size of the Cartesian product in Figure 5.3. It is not uncommon for the size of a join to be just a tiny fraction of the size of the corresponding cross product. The tricky part is to compute a join without having to compute the intermediate Cartesian product! This might sound like magic, but there are several ways to accomplish this feat, and query optimizers do so routinely. This subject is discussed in Chapter 10.

The general joins described above are sometimes called **theta-joins** because in antiquity the Greek letter θ was used to denote join conditions. While theta-joins are certainly common in query processing (the query *List all employees who earn more than their managers* involves a theta-join), the more common kind is one where all comparisons are equalities:

$$R.A_1 = S.B_1 \text{ AND } \ldots \text{ AND } R.A_n = S.B_n$$

Joins that utilize such conditions are called **equi-joins**.

Equi-joins are essentially what gives relational databases their "intelligence" because they tie together pieces of disparate information scattered throughout the database. Using equi-joins, programmers can uncover complex relationships hidden in the data with just a few lines of SQL code.

Example 5.1.3 (More Joins). Here is how one can find the names of professors who taught a course in the fall of 1994:

$$\pi_{\text{Name}} \; (\text{PROFESSOR} \bowtie_{\text{Id=ProfId}} \sigma_{\text{Semester='F1994'}} (\text{TEACHING}))$$

The inner join lines up the tuples in PROFESSOR against the tuples in TEACHING that describe courses taught by the respective professors in fall 1994. The final projection cuts off the uninteresting attributes. Finding the names of courses and the professors who taught them in the fall of 1995 is almost as easy:

$$\pi_{\text{CrsName,Name}} \; (\; (\text{PROFESSOR} \bowtie_{\text{Id=ProfId}} \sigma_{\text{Semester='F1995'}} (\text{TEACHING})) \bowtie_{\text{CrsCode=CrsCode}} \text{COURSE} \;)$$

The second query in the above example involves two joins. We placed parentheses around the first join to indicate the order in which the joins are to be computed. However, this was not really necessary because join happens to be an *associative* operation, as can be proved using its definition:

$$R \bowtie_{\text{cond}_1} (S \bowtie_{\text{cond}_2} T)$$
$$= \sigma_{\text{cond}_1}(R \times \sigma_{\text{cond}_2}(S \times T)) \quad \text{by definition of } \bowtie$$
$$= \sigma_{\text{cond}_1}(\sigma_{\text{cond}_2}(R \times (S \times T))) \quad \text{because } \sigma \text{ and } \times \text{ commute (check!)}$$
$$= \sigma_{\text{cond}_2}(\sigma_{\text{cond}_1}(R \times (S \times T))) \quad \text{because two } \sigma\text{'s commute (check!)}$$
$$= \sigma_{\text{cond}_2}(\sigma_{\text{cond}_1}((R \times S) \times T)) \quad \text{by associativity of } \times \text{ (check!)}$$
$$= (R \bowtie_{\text{cond}_1} S) \bowtie_{\text{cond}_2} T \quad \text{by definition of } \bowtie$$

The double-join query of Example 5.1.3 illustrates one additional point. Join conditions such as TEACHING.CrsCode = COURSE.CrsCode, which test for equality of attributes with the same name (but in different relations) are quite common. The main reason for this is that it is considered a good design practice to assign the same name to attributes that denote the same thing but belong to different relations. For instance, the semantics of CrsCode in COURSE, TEACHING, and TRANSCRIPT are the same (which is why we used the same name in all three cases!). Because finding hidden connections in the data often amounts to comparing similar attributes in different relations, the above design practice leads to equi-join conditions that equate identically named attributes.[4]

In fact, this design practice in which the join condition equates *only* identically named attributes yields equi-joins of a special variety. In recognition of their importance, such joins received their very own name: the **natural join**. A natural join actually is a little more than that. First, the join condition equates *all* identically named attributes in the two relations being joined. Second, as the equated attributes really denote the same thing in both relations (as indicated by the identity of their names), there is no reason to keep both of the columns. Thus, one copy is always projected out. In sum, the *natural join* of **R** and **S**, denoted **R** ⋈ **S**, is defined by the following relational expression:

$$\pi_{attr\text{-}list}(\sigma_{join\text{-}cond}(\mathbf{R} \times \mathbf{S}))$$

where

1. *attr-list* = *attributes*(**R**) ∪ *attributes*(**S**); that is, the attribute list used in the project operator contains all the attributes in the union of the argument relations *with duplicate attribute names removed*. Since duplicate attributes are deleted, there is no need to perform attribute renaming.

2. The join condition, *join-cond*, has the form

   $$\mathbf{R}.A_1 = \mathbf{S}.A_1 \text{ AND } \dots \text{ AND } \mathbf{R}.A_n = \mathbf{S}.A_n$$
   ------

   where $\{A_1, \dots, A_n\}$ = *attributes*(**R**) ∩ *attributes*(**S**). That is, it is the list of all attributes that **R** and **S** have in common.

Note that the notation for natural joins *omits the join condition* because the condition is implicitly (and uniquely) determined by the names assigned to the attributes of the relations in the join.

A typical example of the use of natural joins is the following query:

$$\pi_{\text{StudId,ProfId}} (\text{TRANSCRIPT} \bowtie \text{TEACHING})$$
------

[4] A natural question is, Why have we used different names for the Id attributes in STUDENT (Id) and TRANSCRIPT (StudId)—in clear violation of the design rule previously mentioned? We did it so that we could squeeze more examples out of a reasonably sized schema. In a well-designed database schema, StudId would be used in both places; likewise, ProfId would be used in both PROFESSOR and TEACHING; or, perhaps, Id would be used in all four places.

which lists all Ids of students who ever took a course along with the Ids of professors who taught them.

To further illustrate the difference between the natural join and the equi-join, it is instructive to compare the following two expressions:

$$\text{TRANSCRIPT} \bowtie \text{TEACHING}$$
$$\text{TRANSCRIPT} \bowtie_{\text{Cond}} \text{TEACHING}$$

where the equi-join condition Cond is TRANSCRIPT.CrsCode=TEACHING.CrsCode AND TRANSCRIPT.Semester=TEACHING.Semester. Both expressions are equi-joins, and both use the same join conditions (the natural join uses it implicitly). However, the resulting relations have different sets of attributes.

Natural join:
> StudId, CrsCode, Semester, Grade, ProfId

Equi-join:
> StudId, TRANSCRIPT.CrsCode, TEACHING.CrsCode,
> > TRANSCRIPT.Semester, TEACHING.Semester, Grade, ProfId

The two expressions represent essentially the same information. However, the schema of the equi-join has two extra attributes (which are duplicates of other attributes), and the natural join benefits from a simpler attribute-naming convention.

Apart from finding hidden connections in the data, joins can be used for certain counting tasks. Here is how we can find all students who took at least two different courses:

$$\pi_{\text{StudId}} \, ($$
$$\quad \sigma_{\text{CrsCode}\neq\text{CrsCode2}} \, ($$
$$\qquad \text{TRANSCRIPT} \bowtie$$
$$\qquad \text{TRANSCRIPT}[\text{StudId},\text{CrsCode2},\text{Semester2},\text{Grade2}]$$
$$\quad))$$

One obvious limitation of this technique is that if we want students who had taken fifteen courses, we have to join TRANSCRIPT with itself fifteen times. A better way is to extend the relational algebra with so-called *aggregate* functions, which include the counting operator. We do not pursue this possibility here, but we will return to aggregate functions in the context of SQL in Section 5.2.

The discussion of joins cannot be complete without mentioning that—rather unexpectedly—the intersection operator is a special case of a natural join. Suppose that **R** and **S** are union-compatible. It then follows directly from the definitions that $R \cap S = R \bowtie S$.

> *Brain Teaser:* What is $R \bowtie S$, if **R** and **S** have not even one common attribute?

Outer joins.   When two relations are joined, tuples that do not match fall by the wayside. The operators *outer join, left outer join,* and *right outer join* were introduced for the situations where this particular feature of joins is not wanted.

   An **outer join** of two relations **r** and **s** with join condition *cond*, denoted $r \bowtie_{cond}^{outer} s$, is defined as follows. As before, it is a relation over the schema that contains the union of the (possibly renamed) attributes in **R** (the schema of **r**) and **S** (the schema of **s**). However, the tuples in $r \bowtie_{cond}^{outer} s$ consist of three categories:

1.   The tuples that appear in the regular join of **r** and **s**, $r \bowtie_{cond} s$.

2.   The tuples of **r** that do not join with any tuple in **s**. Since these tuples do not have values for the attributes that come from **S**, they are padded with NULL over these attributes.

3.   The tuples of **s** that do not join with any tuple in **r**. Again, these tuples are padded with NULL over the attributes of **R**.

   The outer join is sometimes also called **full outer join**. The **left outer join**, $r \bowtie_{cond}^{left} s$, is like the full outer join, except it does not include the third category of tuples (the tuples from **S** that are padded with NULL over **R**). The **right outer join**, $r \bowtie_{cond}^{right} s$, is like the full outer join, except that the second type of tuple is missing. Figure 5.5 illustrates these notions.

   Note that the outer joins are not independent operators: they can be expressed using the other relational operators (see Exercise 5.9).

Example 5.1.4 (Left Outer Join).   Outer joins are useful when the NULL-padded tuples still carry useful information for the task at hand. Suppose we need to compute the average grade for every student (let us assume, for the sake of this example, that the grades are numeric). We could join the STUDENT relation of Figure 3.3 on page 36 with the TRANSCRIPT relation of Figure 3.5 on page 39. Then we could group tuples corresponding to each student Id and compute the average (the relational algebra can be extended with operators that support such computation—see Exercise 5.11).

   However, it is easy to see that the student with Id 111223344 has no TRANSCRIPT records. Therefore, we will have no information about the average grade of that student (which is 0). To rectify this problem, we could compute the left outer join instead of the regular join:

$$\text{STUDENT} \bowtie_{\text{Id=StudId}}^{left} \text{TRANSCRIPT}$$

SupplName	PartNumber
Acme Inc.	P120
Main St. Hardware	N30
Electronics 2000	RM130

SUPPLIER relation

PartNumber	PartName
N30	10'' screw
KCL12	2lb hammer
P120	10-ohm resistor

PARTS relation

SupplName	PartNumber	PartNumber2	PartName
Acme Inc.	P120	P120	10-ohm resistor
Main St. Hardware	N30	N30	10'' screw
Electronics 2000	RM130	NULL	NULL
NULL	NULL	KCL12	2lb hammer

Full outer join SUPPLIER $\bowtie^{outer}_{PartNumber=PartNumber}$ PARTS

SupplName	PartNumber	PartNumber2	PartName
Acme Inc.	P120	P120	10-ohm resistor
Main St. Hardware	N30	N30	10'' screw
Electronics 2000	RM130	NULL	NULL

Left outer join SUPPLIER $\bowtie^{left}_{PartNumber=PartNumber}$ PARTS

SupplName	PartNumber	PartNumber2	PartName
Acme Inc.	P120	P120	10-ohm resistor
Main St. Hardware	N30	N30	10'' screw
NULL	NULL	KCL12	2lb hammer

Right outer join SUPPLIER $\bowtie^{right}_{PartNumber=PartNumber}$ PARTS

FIGURE 5.5 Outer joins.

Now the tuple with Id 111223344 is part of the result and can take part in the computation of the average grade. In fact, we will see that, in practical languages like SQL, nulls are ignored during the computation of the average, which will give us the desired average grade for our student. ∎

Division operator. While the join operator brings intelligence to query answering, the division operator holds the distinction of being the most difficult to understand and use correctly.

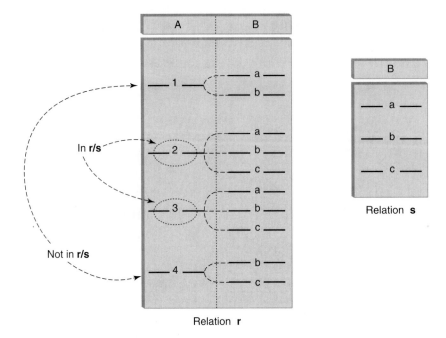

FIGURE 5.6 Division operator.

The **division operator** becomes useful when you feel the urge to find out *which professors taught* all *courses offered by the Computer Science Department* or *which students took a class from* every *professor in the Electrical Engineering Department*. The key here is that we are looking for tuples in one relation that match *all* tuples in another relation.

Here is a precise definition. Let **R** be a relation schema with attributes $A_1, \ldots, A_n, B_1, \ldots, B_m$ and let **S** be a relation schema with attributes $B_1, \ldots, B_m$. In other words, the set of attributes of **S** is a subset of the attributes of **R**. The **division** of **R** by **S** is an expression of the form **R/S**. If **r** and **s** are relation instances corresponding to **R** and **S** in our database, the **value** of **R/S**, denoted **r/s**, is a relation over the attributes $A_1, \ldots, A_n$ that consists of all tuples $\langle a \rangle$ such that, *for every* tuple $\langle b \rangle$ in **s**, the concatenated tuple $\langle a, b \rangle$ is in **r**. A schematic view of this definition is depicted in Figure 5.6.

An equivalent way to define division is

$$\langle a \rangle \in \mathbf{r/s} \text{ if and only if } \{\langle a \rangle\} \times \mathbf{s} \subseteq \mathbf{r}$$

Here $\{\langle a \rangle\}$ denotes a relation that contains a single tuple, $\langle a \rangle$. Note that, if we view $\times$ as multiplication, we can view division as multiplication's inverse, which explains the name for this operation.

Brain Teaser: What is **r/s**, if **s** is empty?

Example 5.1.5 (Division).   Consider the query *List all courses that have been taught by every computer science professor*. Here, by "every professor," we mean "every professor recorded in the database." That is, it is assumed that the database describes all we know about the situation. Not only does every tuple in the database assert a fact about the real-world enterprise being modeled, but there are no additional known facts that could be represented as tuples in the database relations. This is known as the **closed-world assumption** and is implicit in relational query processing.

Figure 5.7 shows three relations. The relation

$$\text{PROFCS} = \pi_{\texttt{Id}}(\sigma_{\texttt{DeptId='CS'}}(\text{PROFESSOR}))$$

contains the Ids of all known computer science professors. The relation

$$\text{PROFCOURSES} = (\pi_{\texttt{ProfId,CrsCode}}(\text{TEACHING}))[\texttt{Id,CrsCode}]$$

is a relationship between courses and professors who have taught them (at any time); it contains all known relationships of this kind. (Note that we have applied the renaming operator to make sure that the first attribute of PROFCOURSES has the same name as that of the attribute of PROFCS.) The third relation shows PROF-COURSES/PROFCS, the answer to the query.   ∎

Observe that before applying the division operator in the above example we carefully projected out some attributes (and renamed some others) to make the division operator applicable. The situation when projection must be applied to the operands of the division operator in order to make the division possible is quite typical. Here is another example.

Example 5.1.6 (Another Division).   Consider the following query: *Retrieve all students who took a course from every professor who ever taught a course*. In the numerator we need a relation that associates students with professors who instructed them in some course. We can get this by taking the natural join of TRANSCRIPT and TEACHING:

$$\text{STUDPROF} = \text{TRANSCRIPT} \bowtie \text{TEACHING}$$

STUDPROF has attributes StudId, CrsCode, Semester, Grade, ProfId, which is more information than we want, so we eliminate unwanted columns using projection to get the numerator: $\pi_{\texttt{StudId,ProfId}}(\text{STUDPROF})$.

Because we are interested in students who took a course with *every professor*, we need a relation in the denominator that has a tuple for every professor. Professors

PROFCS	Id
	101202303
	555666777

All computer science professors: $\pi_{\text{Id}}(\sigma_{\text{DeptId}='\text{CS}'}(\text{PROFESSOR}))$

PROFCOURSES	Id	CrsCode
	783432188	MGT123
	009406321	MGT123
	121232343	EE101
	555666777	CS305
	101202303	CS315
	900120450	MAT123
	101202303	CS305

Who taught what: $(\pi_{\text{ProfId},\text{CrsCode}}(\text{TEACHING}))[\text{Id},\text{CrsCode}]$

CrsCode
CS305

The answer: `ProfCourses/ProfCS`

FIGURE 5.7 The anatomy of a query: *Courses taught by every computer science professor.*

who have taught a course have their Ids inside the tuples of the TEACHING relation. (We do not want to use PROFESSOR here as this would include tuples for professors who have not done any teaching.) Hence, the denominator is $\pi_{\text{ProfId}}(\text{TEACHING})$, and the answer to our query is

$$\pi_{\text{StudId},\text{ProfId}}(\text{STUDPROF}) \ / \ \pi_{\text{ProfId}}(\text{TEACHING}) \qquad \textbf{5.2}$$

∎

Example 5.1.7 (Complex Division). *Find all students who took all courses that were taught by all computer science professors.* Here we need double division:

$$(\pi_{\text{Id},\text{Name}}(\text{STUDENT}))[\text{StudId},\text{Name}] \bowtie$$
$$(\pi_{\text{StudId},\text{CrsCode}}(\text{TRANSCRIPT}) \ /$$
$$((\pi_{\text{ProfId},\text{CrsCode}}(\text{TEACHING}))[\text{Id},\text{CrsCode}] \ / \qquad \textbf{5.3}$$
$$\pi_{\text{Id}}(\sigma_{\text{DeptId}='\text{CS}'}(\text{PROFESSOR}))) \ )$$

The second division above is our friend from Figure 5.7, which yields all courses taught by every computer science professor. Therefore, the last three lines in the expression define the Ids of all students who took all such courses. The natural join in the first line is then used to obtain the names of these students. We had to rename the attributes of the STUDENT relation before taking the join. ∎

We conclude by showing how the division operator can be expressed using other relational operators: projection, set difference, and cross product. Let **R** be a relation with attributes A and B, and let **S** be a relation over a single attribute B. (The construction, below, works even if A and B are disjoint lists of attributes.) The expression **R/S** can then be computed without the use of division as follows:

$T_1 = \pi_A(\mathbf{R}) \times \mathbf{S}$ All possible associations between A-values in **R** and B-values in **S**.

$T_2 = \pi_A(T_1 - \mathbf{R})$ All those A-values in **R** that are **not** associated in **R** with every B-value in **S**. These are precisely those A-values that should **not** be in the answer.

$T_3 = \pi_A(\mathbf{R}) - T_2$ *The answer:* All those A-values in **R** that are associated in **R** with all B-values in **S**.

5.4

5.2 The Query Sublanguage of SQL

SQL is the most widely used relational database language. An initial version was proposed in 1974, and it has been evolving ever since. A widely used version, generally referred to as SQL-92, is a standard of the American National Standards Institute (ANSI). The language continues to evolve and recently SQL:1999 and SQL:2003 have been completed. Like any rapidly changing language whose form is influenced by its many users, SQL has become surprisingly complex. The purpose of this section and the next is to introduce you to some of the complexity of the data manipulation sublanguage of SQL. However, you should be aware that a full treatment of this subject is well worth a book of its own. For example, [Melton and Simon 1992, Date and Darwen 1997] are more complete references to SQL-92; [Gulutzan and Pelzer 1999] describes SQL:1999. The unfortunate reality, however, is that commercial databases do not always adhere to the standards, and a vendor-specific reference is almost always a must for serious application development.

SQL can be used interactively by submitting an SQL statement directly to the DBMS from a terminal. However, particularly in transaction processing systems, SQL statements are usually embedded in a larger program that submits the statements to the DBMS at run time and processes the results. The special considerations that relate to such embedding will be discussed in Chapter 8.

5.2.1 Simple SQL Queries

Simple SQL queries are easy to design. Need a list of all professors in the Electrical Engineering (EE) Department? Happy to oblige:

```
SELECT   P.Name
FROM     PROFESSOR P
WHERE    P.DeptId = 'EE'
```

5.5

Note the symbol P here, which is called a **tuple variable**. It ranges over the tuples of the relation PROFESSOR.[5] The tuple variable is actually unnecessary in this statement, and, if you recall, we tried to avoid its use in our brief introduction to SQL in Chapter 2. In simple queries, such as above, we could have referred to the attributes simply as `Name` and `DeptId` instead of `P.Name` and `P.DeptId`, since there is no ambiguity as to which relation the attributes come from. In some multi-table queries, we could have used PROFESSOR.Name and PROFESSOR.DeptId in case of ambiguity.

However, as we shall see shortly, in some situations the use of tuple variables is essential. In fact, *not* using tuple variables in SELECT statements is considered poor programming practice, which often leads to subtle mistakes. Therefore, from now on we will be pedantically declaring all tuple variables.

Although this statement is rather simple, it is important to understand operationally how a SELECT statement might be evaluated. SELECT statements can become very complex, and following an operational flow through the statement is often the only way to figure out what is going on. Of course, different DBMSs might adopt different strategies for evaluating the same statement, but since they all produce the same result it is useful to describe a particularly simple strategy.

An evaluation strategy for simple queries. The basic algorithm for evaluating SQL queries can be stated as follows:

Step 1. *The* FROM *clause is evaluated.* It produces a table that is the Cartesian product of the tables listed as its arguments. If a table occurs more than once in the FROM clause, as in query (5.11) on page 151, then this table occurs as many times in the product.

Step 2. *The* WHERE *clause is evaluated.* It takes the table produced in step 1 and processes each row individually. Attribute values from the row are substituted for the attribute names in the condition, and the condition is evaluated. The table produced by the WHERE clause contains exactly those rows for which the condition evaluates to true.

---

[5] Mastering SQL often means stuffing one's head with redundant terminology. For instance, SQL variables are also known as *table aliases*.

Step 3. *The* SELECT *clause is evaluated.* It takes the table produced in step 2 and retains only those columns that are listed as arguments. The resulting table is output by the SELECT statement.

As we discuss new features of the language, we will be adding additional steps to this strategy, but the basic idea remains the same. Each clause produces a table, which is the input to the next clause to be evaluated. Certain steps need not be present in a particular evaluation. For example, step 2 might not have to be evaluated because a SELECT statement does not have to have a WHERE clause. Other steps might be trivial. For example, although every SELECT statement must have a FROM clause, if the clause names only a single relation, the Cartesian product is not required and that relation is simply passed on to step 2.

In view of the above algorithm, the relational algebra equivalent of the SQL query (5.5) is

$$\pi_{\text{Name}}(\sigma_{\text{DeptId='EE'}}(\text{PROFESSOR}))$$

Join queries.   Queries that express a join between two relations follow the same pattern as above. The following query, which returns the list of all professors who taught in fall 1994, involves a join.

```
SELECT   P.Name
FROM     PROFESSOR P, TEACHING T                        5.6
WHERE    P.Id = T.ProfId  AND  T.Semester = 'F1994'
```

Note that the tuple variables in this example clarify the meaning of the statement because they identify the table from which each attribute is drawn. In this particular case, however, there is no ambiguity as to where the attributes are coming from and so the use of these variables is just a matter of good practice. If, on the other hand, the Id attribute of PROFESSOR were called ProfId, then we would *have* to use tuple variables to distinguish the two references to Id.

Evaluation of the above statement follows the steps outlined above. In this example, in contrast to query (5.5), processing the FROM clause involves taking a Cartesian product. Take the time to convince yourself that query (5.6) is equivalent to the relational algebra expression

$$\pi_{\text{Name}}(\text{PROFESSOR} \bowtie_{\text{Id=ProfId}} \sigma_{\text{Semester='F1994'}}(\text{TEACHING}))$$ **5.7**

where we split the condition in the WHERE clause into a *join condition* and a *selection condition*. The join condition, Id = ProfId, ensures that related tuples in the two tables are combined. It makes no sense to combine a tuple from PROFESSOR that describes a particular professor with a tuple from TEACHING that describes a course taught by a different professor. Hence, the join condition eliminates garbage. The selection condition `Semester ='F1994'`, on the other hand, eliminates tuples that are not relevant to the query.

The relationship between SQL and relational algebra. The relational algebra expression

$$\pi_{\text{Name}}(\sigma_{\text{Id=ProfId AND Semester='F1994'}}(\text{PROFESSOR} \times \text{TEACHING}))$$

is equivalent to the expression (5.7) and to the SQL query (5.6). Although this expression leads to one of the least efficient ways of evaluating query (5.6), it is simple, uniform, and, from the syntactic point of view, reflects more closely the corresponding SQL statement. More generally, the query template

SELECT	*TargetList*	
FROM	$\text{REL}_1 \; V_1, \ldots, \text{REL}_n \; V_n$	**5.8**
WHERE	*Condition*	

is roughly equivalent to the algebraic expression

$$\pi_{TargetList}\sigma_{Condition}(\text{REL}_1 \times \ldots \times \text{REL}_n) \qquad \textbf{5.9}$$

"Roughly" means that we have to transform *Condition* into a relational algebra form. To be more concrete, consider the query *Find the names of the courses taught in fall 1995 together with the names of the professors who taught those courses.* In SQL we get

SELECT	`C.CrsName, P.Name`	
FROM	PROFESSOR `P`, TEACHING `T`, COURSE `C`	
WHERE	`T.Semester = 'F1995' AND`	**5.10**
	`P.Id = T.ProfId AND T.CrsCode = C.CrsCode`	

The corresponding algebraic expression in the inefficient, but uniform, form described above is

$$\pi_{\text{CrsName,Name}}(\sigma_{Condition}(\text{PROFESSOR} \times \text{TEACHING} \times \text{COURSE}))$$

where *Condition* denotes the contents of the WHERE clause (modified to suit relational algebra):

```
Id = ProfId AND TEACHING.CrsCode = COURSE.CrsCode AND
    Semester = 'F1995'
```

Self-join queries. Let us return to the query that we considered earlier, *Find all students who took at least two courses.* We expressed this in relational algebra as

$$\pi_{\text{StudId}} \, ($$
$$\sigma_{\text{CrsCode} \neq \text{CrsCode2}} \, ($$
$$\text{TRANSCRIPT} \bowtie_{\text{StudId}=\text{StudId}}$$
$$\text{TRANSCRIPT}[\text{StudId}, \text{CrsCode2}, \text{Semester2}, \text{Grade2}]$$
$$) \,)$$

Observe that we have joined the relation TRANSCRIPT with *itself.* To accomplish this in relational algebra, we have to apply the renaming operator to the second occurrence of TRANSCRIPT. In SQL, we must mention the TRANSCRIPT relation twice in the FROM clause and declare two different variables over this relation. Each variable is meant to represent a distinct occurrence of TRANSCRIPT in the join.

```
SELECT    T1.StudId
FROM      TRANSCRIPT T1, TRANSCRIPT T2                        5.11
WHERE     T1.CrsCode <> T2.CrsCode
              AND T1.StudId = T2.StudId
```

The symbol <> in this query is SQL's way of saying "not equal." Note that we do need *two distinct tuple variables* to range over TRANSCRIPT; if we were to use just one variable, T, the condition T.CrsCode <> T.CrsCode would never be satisfied, making the answer to the query the empty relation. Therefore, there is no obvious way to do this query without tuple variables.

Retrieving distinct answers. We already know from Chapter 3 that relations are sets, so no duplicate tuples are allowed. However, many relational operators can yield **multisets** (i.e., set-like objects that might contain multiple occurrences of identical elements) as an intermediate result of the computation. For instance, if we chop off the attribute Semester from the instance of the relation TEACHING depicted in Figure 3.5 (page 39), we get a list of tuples that contains duplicate occurrences of ⟨009406321, MGT123⟩ and of other tuples as well. As a consequence, in order for the SQL query

```
SELECT    T.ProfId, T.CrsCode
FROM      TEACHING   T                                       5.12
```

to return a relation (as required by the relational data model), the query processor must perform an additional scan of the query result in order to eliminate duplicates. In many cases, the application programmer is not willing to pay the price for duplicate elimination. Hence, the designers of SQL decided that, by default, duplicate tuples are not eliminated unless elimination is explicitly requested using the keyword DISTINCT.

```
SELECT    DISTINCT T.ProfId, T.CrsCode
FROM      TEACHING T                                        5.13
```

Note that this query is missing the WHERE clause, which is *optional* in SQL. When it is missing, the WHERE condition is assumed to be true regardless of the values of tuple variables in the FROM clause.

While the WHERE clause is optional, the SELECT and the FROM clauses are not.

Comments. As with every programming language, the programmer might wish to annotate queries with comments. In SQL, comments are strings that begin with the double minus sign, --, and end with a new line. For instance,

```
-- An example of  SELECT DISTINCT
SELECT    DISTINCT T.ProfId, T.CrsCode                      5.14
FROM      TEACHING T    --Look, no WHERE clause!
```

Expressions in the WHERE clause. So far, the conditions in the WHERE clause have been comparisons of attributes against constants or other attributes. For numeric values, SQL provides the following comparison operators: = (equal), <> (not equal), > (greater than), >= (greater than or equal to), < (less than), and <= (less than or equal to).

All of these operators can be applied to numerals and character strings as well. (Strings can also be compared against patterns using the LIKE operator, which we will describe later.) Strings are compared character-wise, from left to right. For the purposes of this text, we limit our attention to ASCII symbols and assume that the ordering of characters in making comparisons between two strings is determined by the ASCII codes assigned to these characters.

The operands of these comparison operators can be **expressions**, not just single attributes or constants. For numeric values, expressions are composed of the usual operators, $*$, $+$, and the like. For strings, the concatenation operator, $\|$, can be used. Assume, for instance, an appropriate EMPLOYEE relation with the attributes SSN, BossSSN, LastName, FirstName, and Salary. Then the query

```
SELECT    E.Id
FROM      EMPLOYEE  E, EMPLOYEE M
WHERE     E.BossSSN = M.SSN  AND  E.Salary > 2 * M.Salary
          AND E.LastName = 'Mc' || E.FirstName
```

returns all employees whose salary is more than twice that of their bosses' and whose last names are a concatenation of "Mc" and the first name (e.g., Donald McDonald).

Expressions and special features in the SELECT clause. The SELECT clause has a number of special features. In Section 2.2, we noted that the asterisk (*) represents the list of all attributes of all relations in the FROM clause. Note that when it is used and a relation appears twice (or more) in the FROM clause, its attributes appear twice (or more) as well. For instance, the query

```
SELECT    *
FROM      EMPLOYEE  E, EMPLOYEE M
```

is the same as

```
SELECT    E.SSN, E.BossSSN, E.FirstName, E.LastName, E.Salary,
          M.SSN, M.BossSSN, M.FirstName, M.LastName, M.Salary
FROM      EMPLOYEE E, EMPLOYEE M
```

SQL permits expressions in the target list, not only in the WHERE clause (which we have seen so far). This feature is illustrated using the following example.

Example 5.2.1 (Expressions in Target List). Suppose that an audit office needs a report on salary gaps between employees and their immediate bosses. This can be accomplished with the following query:

```
SELECT    E.SSN, M.SSN, M.Salary - E.Salary
FROM      EMPLOYEE  E,  EMPLOYEE M
WHERE     E.BossSSN = M.SSN
```

The noteworthy feature here is an arithmetic expression in the last member of the target list. ∎

If the above query is used interactively, most DBMSs would display a table where the first two columns are labeled SSN and the last column has no label at all. Obviously, this is not very satisfactory since it requires the user to remember the meaning of the items in the SELECT clause. To alleviate this problem, SQL allows the programmer to change attribute names and assign names where they do not exist. This is accomplished with the help of the keyword AS.

Example 5.2.2 (Naming Attributes in the Target List). For example, we can modify the previous query as follows.

```
SELECT    E.SSN AS EmplId,
          M.SSN AS MngrId,
          M.Salary - E.Salary AS SalaryGap
FROM      EMPLOYEE  E, EMPLOYEE M
WHERE     E.BossSSN = M.SSN
```

This query is identical to the previous one in all but the form of the output. While the result of the first query will have unnamed columns, the attributes of the last query will all be named and displayed as EmplId, MngrId, and SalaryGap. ∎

Negation. Any condition in the WHERE clause can be negated with NOT. For instance, instead of T1.CrsCode <> T2.CrsCode in query (5.11), we could have written NOT (T1.CrsCode = T2.CrsCode). The negated condition need not be atomic—it can consist of an arbitrary number of subconditions connected with AND or OR, and it can even have nested applications of NOT, as in the following example.

```
NOT (E.BossSSN = M.SSN AND E.Salary > 2 * M.Salary
     AND NOT (E.LastName = 'Mc'|| E.FirstName))
```

5.2.2 Set Operations

SQL uses the set-theoretic operators from the relational algebra. Here is a simple query where set-theoretic operators can be used: *Find all professors who are working for the* CS *or* EE *departments.*

```
(SELECT  P.Name
 FROM    PROFESSOR P
 WHERE   P.DeptId = 'CS' )
UNION                                          5.15
(SELECT  P.Name
 FROM    PROFESSOR P
 WHERE   P.DeptId = 'EE' )
```

The query is self-explanatory. It consists of two subqueries: one retrieving all CS professors and the other retrieving all EE professors. The results are collected into a single relation using the UNION operator of the algebra. Note that UNION removes duplicates from the result.

While this example illustrates the basic use of set-theoretic operators in SQL, the benefits of using UNION here are small, since this query can be rewritten without UNION and in a more efficient way:

```
SELECT DISTINCT  P.Name
FROM       PROFESSOR P                         5.16
WHERE      P.DeptId = 'CS' OR P.DeptId = 'EE'
```

Note that DISTINCT is used here because UNION removes duplicate tuples.

Our next example, the query *Find all computer science professors and also all professors who ever taught a computer science course,* is more involved, and the advantages of set-theoretic operators there are more substantial.

Let us assume that all course codes in computer science begin with CS. In designing the query, we need to match patterns against strings (course codes). To verify whether a string matches a pattern, SQL provides the LIKE predicate. For instance, T.CrsCode LIKE 'CS%' verifies that the value of T.CrsCode matches the pattern that starts with CS and can have *zero or more* additional characters. SQL patterns are similar to wildcards in UNIX or DOS, although SQL's arsenal for building patterns is somewhat limited: besides %, there is _, a symbol that matches an arbitrary *single* character.[6]

Without the UNION operator, CS professors or those who taught a CS course can be found as follows:

```
SELECT   P.Name
FROM     PROFESSOR P,  TEACHING T                        5.17
WHERE    (P.Id = T.ProfId AND T.CrsCode LIKE 'CS%')
         OR (P.DeptId = 'CS')
```

We see that, as the WHERE condition gets longer and more complicated, it becomes harder to read and understand. With the UNION operator, we can rewrite this query in the following way:

```
(SELECT  P.Name
 FROM    PROFESSOR P, TEACHING T
 WHERE   P.Id = T.ProfId AND T.CrsCode LIKE 'CS%')
 UNION                                                    5.18
(SELECT  P.Name
 FROM    PROFESSOR P
 WHERE   P.DeptId = 'CS')
```

Although this is no more succinct than (5.17), it is more modular and easier to understand.

If we want to change our query so that it retrieves all professors who taught a CS course without being a CS professor, we can easily modify (5.18) by replacing UNION with EXCEPT—the SQL counterpart of the MINUS operator in relational algebra.

---

[6] Suppose that you need to construct a pattern where the special characters % and _ stand for themselves. For instance, suppose you need to match all strings that start with _%. This is possible, albeit cumbersome. You have to declare an escape character and then prefix it to the special character to let SQL know that you want these characters to stand for themselves. For instance, C.Descr LIKE '_\%__$' ESCAPE '\' compares the value of C.Descr with a pattern that matches all strings that begin with _%, followed by a pair of arbitrary characters, and terminated with the symbol $. Here \ is declared as an escape character via the ESCAPE clause and then used to "escape" % and _.

Changing (5.17) to answer the new query is more complex. The WHERE clause of (5.17) would have to be rewritten as

```
P.Id = T.ProfId AND T.CrsCode LIKE 'CS%' AND P.DeptId <> 'CS'
```

This is not as modular a change as in the case of (5.18).

Example 5.2.3 (Set Operators Help Simplify Queries). Suppose that we need to find all students who took both the transaction processing course, CS315, and the database systems course, CS305. As a first try, we might write the following query:

```
SELECT    S.Name
FROM      STUDENT S, TRANSCRIPT  T                          5.19
WHERE     S.StudId = T.StudId AND T.CrsCode = 'CS305'
          AND T.CrsCode = 'CS315'
```

On closer examination, however, we discover that this SQL query is not what we need because it requires that there be a tuple in TRANSCRIPT such that T.CrsCode is equal to both CS305 and CS315—an unsatisfiable condition. Thus, the formulation (5.19) illustrates one very common mistake—failure to recognize the need for an additional tuple variable. The correct formulation is

```
SELECT    S.Name
FROM      STUDENT S, TRANSCRIPT  T1, TRANSCRIPT T2
WHERE     S.StudId = T1.StudId AND T1.CrsCode = 'CS305'      5.20
          AND S.StudId = T2.StudId AND T2.CrsCode = 'CS315'
```

Observe that we used two distinct tuple variables over the relation TRANSCRIPT to express the fact that student S has taken two different courses.

What does this have to do with the original subject of set-theoretic operators of the relational algebra? It turns out that the INTERSECT operator lets us rewrite (5.20) in a more modular and less error-prone way:

```
(SELECT  S.Name
 FROM     STUDENT S, TRANSCRIPT  T
 WHERE    S.StudId = T.StudId  AND T.CrsCode = 'CS305')
INTERSECT                                                    5.21
(SELECT  S.Name
 FROM     STUDENT S, TRANSCRIPT  T
 WHERE    S.StudId = T.StudId AND T.CrsCode = 'CS315')
```

Notice that here we do not need multiple variables to range over the same relation, which somewhat reduces the risk of error. Instead, we write two simple, essentially similar queries and take the intersection of their results. ∎

Set constructor.   Finally, we mention one related feature, the constructor for building finite sets within SQL queries. The syntax of the set constructor is simple: (set-$elem_1$, set-$elem_2$, . . . , set-$elem_n$). The operator IN lets us check if a particular element is within a set. For example, consider query (5.16), which, with the help of the set constructor, can be simplified to

```
SELECT   P.Name
FROM     PROFESSOR P                                    5.22
WHERE    P.DeptId  IN    ('CS','EE')
```

Note that if we take query (5.19) and replace its WHERE clause with

```
S.StudId = T.StudId  AND  T.CrsCode  IN ('CS305','CS315' )
```

we obtain a query with a meaning different from that of (5.19). This issue is further investigated in Exercise 5.13.

Negation and infix comparison operators.   Earlier we discussed the NOT operator. For some infix operators, such as LIKE and IN, SQL provides two forms of negation: NOT (X LIKE Y) and, equivalently, X NOT LIKE Y. Similarly, one can write X NOT IN Y instead of the more cumbersome NOT(X IN Y).

5.2.3 Nested Queries

SQL would be only half as much fun if it offered only one way to do each task. Consider the query *Select all professors who taught in fall 1994.* One way to say this in SQL was given in (5.6) on page 149, but there is (at least) one other, radically different way. First compute the set of all professors who taught in fall 1994 using a **nested subquery**; then collect their names and produce the result.

```
SELECT   P.Name
FROM     PROFESSOR P
WHERE    P.Id IN
         -- A nested subquery
         (SELECT T.ProfId
          FROM TEACHING T
          WHERE T.Semester = 'F1994')
```

Note that in this example the nested subquery is evaluated only once, and then each row of PROFESSOR can be tested in the WHERE clause against the result of that evaluation.

The above example illustrates one way in which nested subqueries can be of help—*increased readability*. However, readability alone is not a sufficient reason for using this facility as most query processors cannot optimize nested subqueries well enough, and thus indulging in subqueries has a performance penalty. A much more important reason for the existence of nested subqueries is that they increase the expressive power of SQL—some queries simply cannot be formulated in a natural way without them.

Consider the query *List all students who did not take any courses*. In English this query sounds deceptively simple, but in SQL it cannot be done without the nested subquery facility (or the EXCEPT operator—try this alternative on your own).

```
SELECT   S.Name
FROM     STUDENT  S
WHERE    S.Id NOT IN                          5.23
         -- Students who have taken a course
         (SELECT  T.StudId
          FROM    TRANSCRIPT T)
```

As a final example, a subquery can be used to extract a scalar value from a table. Suppose that you want to know which employees are paid a higher salary than you. Assuming that your Id is 111111111, you might use a subquery to return your salary from EMPLOYEE as follows:

```
SELECT   E.Id
FROM     EMPLOYEE  E
WHERE    E.Salary >                           5.24
         (SELECT  E1.Salary
          FROM    EMPLOYEE E1
          WHERE   E1.Id = '111111111')
```

The overall query then finds all employees that earn more.

Correlated nested subqueries. Although nested subqueries can sometimes improve readability, on the whole they are one of the most complex, expensive, and error-prone features of SQL. To a large extent, this complexity is due to **query correlation**—the ability to define variables in the outer query and use them in the inner subquery. Nesting and correlation are akin to the notion of begin/end blocks in programming languages and the associated idea of the scope of a variable.

To illustrate, suppose that we need to find student assistants for professors who are scheduled to teach in a forthcoming semester (for definiteness, let us say in fall 2004). For each professor, we compute the set of all courses she will be teaching during that semester and then find students who have taken one of these courses (and so are eligible to assist with them). The list of courses taught by professors can be computed in a nested subquery, and associating professors with students can be done in an outer query. Here is a realization of this plan in SQL:

```
SELECT    R.StudId,  P.Id,  R.CrsCode
FROM      TRANSCRIPT R,   PROFESSOR P
WHERE     R.CrsCode  IN                                          5.25
          -- Courses taught by P.Id in F2004
          (SELECT T1.CrsCode
           FROM   TEACHING T1
           WHERE T1.ProfId = P.Id AND T1.Semester = 'F2004' )
```

Here the scope of the variable T1 is limited to the subquery. In contrast, the variable P is visible in both the outer and inner queries. This variable parameterizes the inner query and correlates its result with the tuples of the outer query. For *each* value of P.Id, the inner query is computed independently *as if* P.Id *were a constant*. Each time an inner subquery is computed, the value of R.CrsCode is checked against the result returned. If this value belongs to the result, an output tuple is formed by the outer SELECT query.

Observe that, at a minimum, the inner query must be reevaluated for each row of PROFESSOR. This contrasts with uncorrelated nested queries and explains the expense associated with query correlation.

Even though nested queries are a challenge for query optimizers, inexperienced database programmers sometimes abuse them, substituting them for the much simpler ANDs, NOTs, and the like.

Example 5.2.4 (Abuse of Query Nesting).   Here is an example of how *not* to write the previous query (even though it is semantically correct):

```
SELECT    R.StudId,  T.ProfId,  R.CrsCode
FROM      TRANSCRIPT R,  TEACHING T
WHERE     R.CrsCode  IN
          -- Courses taught by T.ProfId in F2004
          (SELECT T1.CrsCode
           FROM   TEACHING T1
           WHERE T1.ProfId = T.ProfId AND
           -- Bad style: unreadable and slow!
           T1.ProfId IN   (SELECT T2.ProfId
                           FROM   TEACHING T2
                           WHERE T2.Semester = 'F2004' ) )
```

The third level of nesting can be avoided here. Not only is it a performance hit, but it is also much harder to understand compared to (5.25). ∎

The EXISTS operator.   It is often necessary to check if a nested subquery returns no answers. For instance, we might wish to *Find all students who never took a computer science course*. A way to approach this problem is to compute the set of all computer courses taken by a student and then list only those students for whom this set is empty. This can be done with the help of correlated nested subqueries and the EXISTS operator, which returns true if a set is non-empty.

Here is one SQL formulation of this query:

```
SELECT    S.Id
FROM      STUDENT S                                            5.26
WHERE     NOT EXISTS (
          -- All CS courses taken by S.Id
          SELECT    T.CrsCode
          FROM      TRANSCRIPT T
          WHERE     T.CrsCode LIKE 'CS%'
                    AND   T.StudId = S.Id )
```

Once again, the variable S is global with respect to the inner subquery; this subquery is evaluated for each value of S.Id, which is treated as a constant during the evaluation. All values of S.Id for which the inner query has no answers constitute the answer to the outer query.

Expressing the division operator. We now show that query nesting can help in expressing the relational division operator. For concreteness, consider the query *List the students who have taken all computer science courses*. We can solve the problem by first computing a single-attribute relation that has a row for each CS course (this is the denominator of the division operator). Then, for each student, we check if the student's transcript contains all of these courses.

To make the idea easier to understand, we first realize our plan assuming the availability of a predicate, CONTAINS, which does not actually exist in SQL. As its name suggests, CONTAINS tests if one set contains another. Then we will show how this predicate is expressed using the SQL operators that do exist.

```
SELECT    S.Id
FROM      STUDENT S
WHERE     -- All courses taken by S.Id
          (SELECT  R.CrsCode
           FROM    TRANSCRIPT R
           WHERE   R.StudId = S.Id )
          CONTAINS
          -- All CS courses
          (SELECT  C.CrsCode
           FROM    COURSE C
           WHERE   C.CrsCode  LIKE  'CS%' )
```

Now, observe that A **CONTAINS** B is equivalent to **NOT EXISTS** (B **EXCEPT** A). Therefore, we can rewrite the above query as follows using only the available SQL operators. Clearly, the result is much harder to understand and construct than the query that involves the (alas nonexistent) operator **CONTAINS**.

```
SELECT   S.Id
FROM     STUDENT S
WHERE    NOT EXISTS (
             (SELECT  C.CrsCode                          5.27
               FROM    COURSE C
               WHERE   C.CrsCode LIKE 'CS%' )
             EXCEPT
             (SELECT  R.CrsCode
               FROM    TRANSCRIPT R
               WHERE   R.StudId = S.Id ) )
```

The following is an example of an even harder query.

Example 5.2.5 (Complex Nested Query). Consider the query *Find the students who took a course from* every *professor in the* CS *department*. One possible SQL formulation of this query is

```
SELECT   S.Id
FROM     STUDENT S
WHERE
         NOT EXISTS (
         -- CS professors who did not teach S.Id
         (SELECT  P.Id -- All CS professors
           FROM    PROFESSOR P
           WHERE   P.Dept = 'CS')                        5.28
         EXCEPT
         (SELECT  T.ProfId -- Professors who have taught S.Id
           FROM    TEACHING T, TRANSCRIPT R
           WHERE   T.CrsCode = R.CrsCode
                   AND   T.Semester = R.Semester
                   AND   S.Id = R.StudId) )
```

The variable S is global, and the subquery is evaluated for each value of S. The variable R ranges over all tuples in TRANSCRIPT. It is local to the second subquery where it is related to S through a condition in the WHERE clause. Therefore, the values of R.Semester and R.CrsCode correspond to all recorded enrollments of student S.Id. Similarly T.ProfId gets successively bound to all professors who ever taught S.Id.

To understand why this SQL expression represents the query at hand, recall that the combination NOT EXISTS/EXCEPT is nothing but the aforesaid CONTAINS predicate over sets. ∎

Set comparison operators. Suppose that our STUDENT relation has one additional numeric attribute, GPA. We can ask the question *Is there a student in the university whose GPA is higher than that of* all *junior students?*

It turns out that nested queries are helpful here, too.

```
SELECT   S.Name, S.Id
FROM     STUDENT S
WHERE S.GPA >ALL  (SELECT  S.GPA                      5.29
                   FROM    STUDENT S
                   WHERE  S.Status ='junior')
```

Here > ALL is a comparison operator, which returns true whenever its left argument is greater than *every* element of the set to the right. If we replace > ALL with >=ANY, we obtain a query about students whose GPA is greater than or equal to the GPA of *some* junior student.

One other point is worth noting about this query. The variable S is declared in both the outer and the inner queries. So which one is referred to in the WHERE clause of the inner query? The answer, as with **begin/end** blocks, is that the inner declaration is valid within the inner query. (However, excessive reuse of existing variable names in inner queries can be confusing.)

Nested subqueries in the FROM clause. As if query (5.28) were not complex enough, SQL has more up its sleeve: you can have nested subqueries in the FROM clause! This works as follows: You write a nested subquery (it must not be correlated and hence cannot use global variables). This subquery can be used in the FROM clause as if it were a relation name. You can use the keyword AS to attach a tuple variable to it. (Actually, AS is optional here but is highly recommended for readability.)

To illustrate, consider a query similar to (5.28) but without NOT EXISTS (i.e., the required answer would consist of all students who were *not* taught by at least one CS professor). We can formulate an equivalent query by moving the first nested subquery of (5.28) to the FROM clause as shown below. (Note that we cannot move the second subquery, because it is correlated.)

```
SELECT   S.Id
FROM     STUDENT S,
         (SELECT  P.Id -- All CS professors
          FROM PROFESSOR P
          WHERE P.Dept = 'CS') AS C                   5.30
```

```
WHERE C.ProfId NOT IN
    (SELECT T.ProfId -- All S.Id's professors
     FROM Teaching T, Transcript R
     WHERE T.CrsCode = R.CrsCode
         AND T.Semester = R.Semester)
         AND S.Id = R.StudId )
```

The use of nested subqueries in the FROM clause should be avoided if at all possible as it tends to produce queries that are hard to understand and verify. A much better alternative is to use the view mechanism, which will be discussed in Section 5.2.8.

Apart from nested queries, SQL also permits explicit table joins in the FROM clause. However, we do not discuss this feature.

5.2.4 Quantified Predicates

Beginning with SQL:1999, the language supports a limited form of explicit universal and existential quantification. Although this new feature does not increase the expressive power of the language, it makes certain queries easier to understand. The basic idea is to include **quantified predicates** with the following general syntax:

```
FOR ALL table-name-or-query (condition)
FOR SOME table-name-or-query (condition)
```

A quantified predicate can be used in the WHERE clause like any other predicate. It is true if and only if every row (FOR ALL) or some rows (FOR SOME) in the set of tuples represented by *table-name-or-query* satisfy *condition*. The condition in a quantified predicate can be as complex as any WHERE-clause condition, and it can refer to the attributes of the tuples in *table-name-or-query*. To make this concrete, consider the following example of a quantified predicate:

```
FOR ALL Professor
        (Id IN (SELECT T.ProfId FROM Teaching))
```

When it appears in a WHERE clause (e.g., as a conjunct along with other predicates), it verifies that every professor (identified through the Id attribute) is teaching something. For a more complex example, we show how quantified predicates can make expression of the division operator easier to understand.

Example 5.2.6 (Expressing Division Using Universal Quantification). Consider the query *List the students who have taken all computer science courses*, which was earlier represented in SQL in quite a convoluted way (see query (5.27)). The preceding discussion on page 160 made it clear that part of the reason for this complexity is the absence of the CONTAINS predicate in SQL. Fortunately, CONTAINS can be expressed as a quantified predicate much more naturally than with the NOT EXISTS/EXCEPT combination used in (5.27):

```
SELECT   S.Id
FROM     STUDENT S
WHERE
      FOR ALL   (SELECT  C.CrsCode
                 FROM     COURSE C
                 WHERE    C.CrsCode LIKE 'CS%' )
                 (CrsCode IN
                       (SELECT  R.CrsCode
                        FROM     TRANSCRIPT R
                        WHERE    R.StudId = S.Id ) )
```

While this is not as simple as what would have been possible with CONTAINS, it comes close. ■

The explicit existential quantifier, **FOR SOME**, is less useful in SQL than the universal quantifier, but it is provided for symmetry. For instance, if we wanted to find out if any professor teaches CS305, we could use the following test in the WHERE clause:

```
FOR SOME  PROFESSOR
         (Id  IN   (SELECT T.ProfId FROM TEACHING
                    WHERE T.CrsCode = CS305 ))
```

5.2.5 Aggregation over Data

In many instances, it is necessary to compute average salary, maximum GPA, number of employees per department, total cost of a purchase, and so forth. These tasks are performed with the help of **aggregate functions**, which operate on sets of tuples. SQL uses five aggregate functions that are described in Figure 5.8.

Aggregate functions cannot be expressed in pure relational algebra. However, the algebra can be extended to allow their use (these extensions are beyond the scope of this text).

To illustrate the use of aggregate functions, we assume that both STUDENT and PROFESSOR relations have the attribute Age and that the STUDENT relation also has the attribute GPA. We start with a few simple examples.

```
-- Average age of the student body
SELECT   AVG(S.Age)
FROM     STUDENT  S

-- Minimum age among professors in the Management Department
SELECT   MIN(P.Age)
```

```
FROM      PROFESSOR P
WHERE     P.DeptId = 'MGT'
```

The above queries find only the average and the minimum ages, not the actual people who have them. If we need to find the youngest professor(s) within the Management Department, we can use a nested subquery.

```
-- Youngest professor(s) in the Management Department
SELECT    P.Name, P.Age
FROM      PROFESSOR P
WHERE     P.DeptId = 'MGT'  AND
          P.Age = (SELECT    MIN(P1.Age)
                   FROM      PROFESSOR P1
                   WHERE     P1.DeptId = 'MGT'   )
```

The query (5.29) that returns the names and Ids of juniors with the highest GPA (previously written without aggregates) can be equivalently written with the use of MAX:

```
SELECT    S.Name, S.StudId
FROM      STUDENT  S
WHERE     S.GPA >= (SELECT    MAX(S1.GPA)                        5.31
                    FROM      STUDENT  S1
                    WHERE     S1.Status = 'Junior')
```

COUNT([DISTINCT] Attr)	Count the number of values in column Attr of the query result. The optional keyword DISTINCT indicates that each value should be counted only once, even if it occurs multiple times in different answer tuples.
SUM([DISTINCT] Attr)	Sum up the values in column Attr. DISTINCT means that each value should contribute to the sum only once, regardless of how often it occurs in column Attr.
AVG([DISTINCT] Attr)	Compute the average of the values in column Attr. Again, DISTINCT means that each value should be used only once.
MAX(Attr)	Compute the maximum value in column Attr. DISTINCT is not used with this function, as it would have no effect.
MIN(Attr)	Compute the minimum value in column Attr. Again, DISTINCT is not used with this function.

FIGURE 5.8 SQL aggregate functions.

The use of DISTINCT in aggregate functions can sometimes make subtle differences in the query semantics. For instance,

```
SELECT   COUNT(P.Name)
FROM     PROFESSOR P                                    5.32
WHERE    P.DeptId = 'MGT'
```

returns the number of professors in the Management Department. On the other hand,

```
SELECT   COUNT(DISTINCT P.Name)
FROM     PROFESSOR P
WHERE    P.DeptId = 'MGT'
```

returns the number of distinct *names* of professors in that department, which can be different from the number of professors. Similarly,

```
SELECT   AVG(P.Age)
FROM     PROFESSOR P                                    5.33
WHERE    P.DeptId = 'MGT'
```

returns the average age of professors in the Management Department. However, if we write AVG (DISTINCT P.Age) in the above SELECT clause, the query result is the average value among *distinct* ages—a statistically meaningless number.

Now that you have seen the good things you can do with aggregates, you should also keep in mind the things you cannot do. It makes no sense to mix an aggregate and an attribute in the SELECT list, as in

```
SELECT   COUNT(*), S.Id
FROM     STUDENT S                                      5.34
WHERE    S.Name  = 'JohnDoe'
```

This is because the aggregate produces a single value that pertains to the entire set of rows corresponding to John Doe, while the attribute S.Id produces a distinct value for each row (in our case there can be several people named John Doe). In some cases, however, such associations can be made meaningful with the help of the GROUP BY construct, to be defined shortly.

While associating aggregates with attributes in the SELECT clause is not normally very useful, having multiple aggregates does make sense. For instance,

```
    SELECT    COUNT(*), AVG(P.Age)
    FROM      STUDENT S                                          5.35
    WHERE     S.Name = 'JohnDoe'
```

counts the number of John Does in the student relation and also computes their average age. Finally, one might be tempted to rewrite statement (5.31) as

```
    SELECT    S.Name, S.StudId
    FROM      STUDENT  S
    WHERE     S.GPA >= (MAX(SELECT  S1.GPA
                             FROM    STUDENT S1
                             WHERE   S1.Status = 'junior'))
```

but dare not—it is an invalid construct. Aggregates cannot be applied to the result of a query.

Aggregation and grouping. By now we know how to count professors in the Management Department. But what if we need this information for *each* department in the university? Of course, we could construct queries similar to (5.32) for each separate department. Each query would be the same, except that MGT in the WHERE condition would be replaced with other department codes. Clearly, this is not a practical solution, as even in a medium-sized enterprise the number of departments can reach several dozen. Furthermore, each time a new department is created, we have to construct a new query, and when departments change their name we have to do tedious maintenance.

A better solution is provided in the form of the GROUP BY clause, which can be included as a component of a SELECT statement. This clause lets the programmer partition a set of rows into groups whose membership is characterized by the fact that all of the rows in a single group agree on the values in some specified subset of columns. The aggregate function is then applied to each group and yields a single row for each such group, as shown in Figure 5.9. For example, if we group the instance of the relation TRANSCRIPT shown in Figure 3.5, page 39, based on the column StudId, five groups result. In any particular group, all rows have the same value in the StudId column but might differ in other columns.

For instance, the following query

```
    SELECT    T.StudId, COUNT(*) AS NumCrs,
              AVG(T.Grade) AS CrsAvg
    FROM      TRANSCRIPT T
    GROUP BY  T.StudId
```

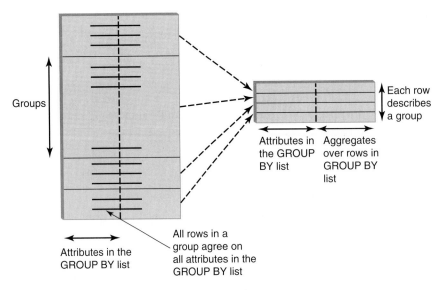

FIGURE 5.9 Effect of the GROUP BY clause.

produces the table

TRANSCRIPT	StudId	NumCrs	CrsAvg
	666666666	3	3.33
	987654321	2	2.5
	123454321	3	3.33
	023456789	2	3.5
	111111111	3	3.33

Here is how to determine the number of professors in each department and (why not?) their average age:

```
SELECT     P.DeptId, COUNT(P.Name) AS DeptSize,
           AVG(P.Age) AS AvgAge
FROM       PROFESSOR P
GROUP BY   P.DeptId
```

The important point to note in these two queries is that each column in the SELECT clause either must be named in the GROUP BY clause or must be the result of an aggregate function. Soon (on page 173) we will see why this is needed.

The HAVING clause. The HAVING clause is used in conjunction with GROUP BY. It lets the programmer specify a condition that restricts which groups (specified in the GROUP BY clause) are to be considered for the final query result. Groups that do not satisfy the condition are removed before the aggregates are applied. Suppose that we wish to know the number of professors and the average ages of professors by department, as in the previous query, but this time only if the department has more than 10 professors. This is accomplished as follows:

```
SELECT      P.DeptId, COUNT(*) AS DeptSize,
            AVG( P.Age) AS AvgAge
FROM        PROFESSOR P
GROUP BY    P.DeptId
HAVING      COUNT(*) > 10
```

The HAVING condition (unlike the WHERE condition) is applied to groups, *not* to individual tuples. So, for each group created by the GROUP BY clause, COUNT(*) counts the number of tuples. Only the groups where this count exceeds 10 are passed on for further processing. In the end, the aggregate functions are applied to each group to yield a single tuple per group.

Observe that the above queries use AS to give names to columns produced by aggregate functions. Furthermore, * is used with the COUNT function that appears in the HAVING clause. The * is often convenient in conjunction with aggregate functions, and it can be used in both the SELECT list and the HAVING clause. However, it should be noted that, in the above example, there are several alternatives. We can use P.Name and even P.DeptId instead of * because SQL will not eliminate duplicates without an explicit request (DISTINCT).

If we want to consider candidates for the dean's list on the basis of their grades for the 2003–2004 academic year, we might use

```
SELECT      T.StudId, AVG(T.Grade) AS CrsAvg
FROM        TRANSCRIPT T
WHERE       T.Semester IN ('F2003','S2004')
GROUP BY    T.StudId
HAVING      AVG(T.Grade) > 3.5
```

In general, the HAVING clause is just a syntactic convenience—the same result can always be achieved with the help of nested queries in the FROM clause. For example, the previous query can be replaced with the following query, which does not use HAVING:

```
SELECT  Stats.StudId, Stats.CrsAvg
FROM    (SELECT  T.StudId,
                 AVG(T.Grade) AS CrsAvg
         FROM    TRANSCRIPT T
         WHERE   T.Semester IN ('F2002', 'S2004')
         GROUP BY T.StudId) AS Stats
WHERE   Stats.CrsAvg > 3.5
```

However, the use of nested queries in the FROM clause should be avoided, as such queries are harder to understand and optimize.

The ORDER BY clause. Finally, the order of rows in the query result is generally not specified. If a particular ordering is desired, the ORDER BY clause can be used. For example, if we include the clause

```
ORDER BY CrsAvg
```

in the SELECT statement that produces the dean's list, rows of the query result will be in ascending order of the student's average grade. In general, the clause takes as an argument a list of column names of the query result. Rows are output in sorted order on the basis of the first column named in the list. In the case in which multiple rows have the same value in that column, the second column named in the list is used to decide the ordering, and so forth. For example, if we want to output the candidates for the dean's list ordered primarily by average grade and secondarily by student Id, we might use the following SELECT statement:

```
SELECT    T.StudId, AVG(T.Grade) AS CrsAvg
FROM      TRANSCRIPT T
WHERE     T.Semester IN ('F1997','S1998')
GROUP BY  T.StudId
HAVING    AVG(T.Grade) > 3.5
ORDER BY  CrsAvg, StudId
```

The attributes named in the ORDER BY clause must be the names of columns in the query result. Thus, we refer to the second element as StudId (not T.StudId) in this example since, by default, that is the column name in the query result. Similarly, we cannot order rows primarily by average grade without introducing the column alias CrsAvg in the SELECT clause because without the alias the column has no name.

Ascending order is used by default, but descending order can also be specified. If in the above example we had replaced the ORDER BY clause with

```
ORDER BY DESC CrsAvg, ASC StudId
```

the rows of the query result would have been presented in descending order of average grade and, for students with the same average grade, in ascending order of their Ids.

5.2.6 Join Expressions in the FROM Clause

In SQL terms, the objects that play the role of tables in the FROM clause are called **table expressions**. In most of the examples that we have seen so far, table expressions were simply table names. However, we have also seen that an entire SELECT query can be a table expression. But SQL does not stop there—it allows algebraic expressions to be table expressions as well. These expressions take the form of a join: natural, theta-join, and the three outer joins discussed on page 142. The syntax is as follows (we present only some of the options):

table1 [NATURAL] [INNER|FULL|LEFT|RIGHT] JOIN *table2* [ON *condition*]

The term INNER refers to the normal join, and FULL, LEFT, and RIGHT refer to the three types of the outer join. The options NATURAL and ON are alternatives. If NATURAL is specified, then the join is performed on the common attributes of both tables; otherwise, the ON *condition* option must be given, where *condition* can be any legal condition in the WHERE clause. More commonly, however, these conditions take the form

table1.col1_1 op1 table2.col2_1 AND *table1.col1_2 op2 table2.col2_2* AND...

where *op1*, *op2*, etc., are the usual comparisons =, >, and so on.

We illustrate this feature with an example of a left outer join, where the query computes the average grade for *every* student in the database. We assume that the grade attribute in the TRANSCRIPT relation is numeric.

```
SELECT    S.Name, AVG(S.Grade)
FROM      (STUDENT LEFT JOIN TRANSCRIPT          5.36
              ON STUDENT.Id = TRANSCRIPT.StudId) S
GROUP BY  S.Id
```

Here students who never took a course will have their tuples padded with NULLs over the Grade attribute. The AVG function ignores NULL values, so the average grade for such students will be 0. Note that a regular join query such as

```
SELECT    S.Name, AVG(T.Grade)
FROM      STUDENT S, TRANSCRIPT T
WHERE     S.Id = T.StudId
GROUP BY  S.Id
```

would be incorrect. In our database, the STUDENT relation has tuples that do not match any record in the TRANSCRIPT relation and, therefore, the above regular join query will miss students who never took any course.

5.2.7 A Simple Query Evaluation Algorithm

The overall query evaluation process in the presence of aggregates and grouping is illustrated in Figure 5.10.

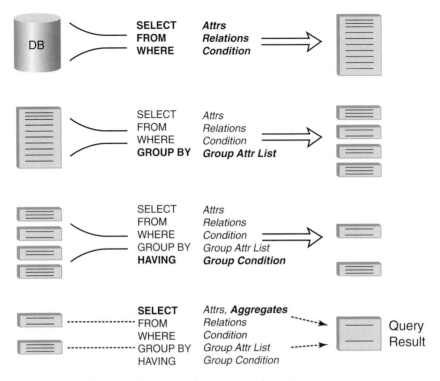

FIGURE 5.10 Query evaluation with aggregate functions.

Step 1. The FROM clause is evaluated. It produces a table that is the Cartesian product of the tables listed as its arguments.

Step 2. The WHERE clause is evaluated. It takes the table produced in step 1 and processes each row individually. Attribute values from the row are substituted for the attribute names in the condition, and the condition is evaluated. The table produced by the WHERE clause contains exactly those rows for which the condition evaluates to true. Steps 1 and 2 are shown in the top segment of Figure 5.10.

Step 3. The GROUP BY clause is evaluated. It takes the table produced in step 2 and splits it into groups of tuples, where each group consists precisely of those tuples that agree on all attributes of the group attribute list. This step is shown in the second segment of Figure 5.10.

Step 4. The HAVING clause is evaluated. It takes the groups produced in step 3 and eliminates those that fail the group condition. This step is shown in the third segment of Figure 5.10.

Step 5. The SELECT clause is evaluated. It takes the groups produced in step 4, evaluates the aggregate functions in the target list for each group, retains those columns that are listed as arguments of the SELECT clause, and produces a single row for each group. This step is illustrated by the bottom segment of Figure 5.10.

Step 6. The ORDER BY clause is evaluated. It orders the rows produced in step 5 using the specified column list. The resulting table is output by the SELECT statement. This step is not shown in Figure 5.10.

Restrictions on GROUP BY and HAVING. Like your apartment lease, grouping comes with several strings attached. The difference is, some of these restrictions actually make sense! Consider a general form of SQL queries with aggregates:

SELECT	*attributeList, aggregates*	
FROM	*relationList*	
WHERE	*whereCondition*	**5.37**
GROUP BY	*groupList*	
HAVING	*groupCondition*	

The purpose of the GROUP BY clause is to partition the result of the query into groups, with all tuples in the same group agreeing on each attribute in *groupList*. The aggregate functions in the SELECT clause are then applied to each group to produce a *single* tuple. Since a single value is output for each attribute in *attributeList* in the SELECT clause (and that value is not an aggregate), all tuples in any given group must agree on each attribute in the list. This property is achieved in SQL by requiring that *attributeList* be a subset of *groupList*, which is a sufficient condition to ensure that each group yields a single tuple. (The condition is not necessary but is good enough for most purposes.)

The second restriction concerns the HAVING condition. Intuitively, we need to ensure that *groupCondition* is either true or false for each group of tuples specified in GROUP BY. Generally, this condition consists of a number of comparisons of the form $expr_1$ op $expr_2$, which are tied together by the logical connectives AND, OR, and NOT. For an atomic comparison $expr_1$ op $expr_2$ to make sense, both $expr_1$ and $expr_2$ must evaluate to a single value for each group. In practice, this means that for every attribute mentioned in *groupCondition* either of the following must hold:

1. It is in *groupList* (and thus it has a single value per group).
2. It appears in *groupCondition* as an argument to an aggregate function (thus, the expression sees a single value when the aggregation is computed).

Most DBMSs enforce the above syntactic restrictions.

We should also note that the order of the clauses in (5.37) is important—for instance, the HAVING clause cannot precede the GROUP BY clause. However, the standard allows SQL statements that have the HAVING clause without the GROUP BY clause. In this case, the result of the SELECT-FROM-WHERE part of the query is treated as a single group and *groupCondition* in HAVING is applied to that group.

5.2.8 More on Views in SQL

The relations we have discussed up to this point are more technically referred to as **base relations**. They are the "normal" database relations. The contents of a base relation are physically stored on disk and are independent of the contents of other relations in the database.

As we already discussed in Chapter 3, a view is a relation whose contents are usually *not physically stored* in the database. Instead, it is defined as the query result of a SELECT statement. Each time the view is used, its contents are computed using the associated query. Hence, the *definition* of the view, that is, the query that determines the view's contents, is stored (in the system catalog) rather than the contents. Because each view is the result of executing a query, its contents depend on the contents of the base relations at the time the view is referenced.

The role of views in query languages is similar to that of *subroutines* in conventional programming languages. A view usually represents some meaningful query, which is used within several other, frequently asked queries, or it might have an independent interest. In either case, it makes sense to abstract the query and "pretend" that the database contains a relation whose contents precisely coincide with the query result.

Another important use of the view mechanism is to control user access to the data. Access control was discussed in Section 3.3.12; in the context of the views it is discussed later in this section.

Using views in queries.   Once a view is defined, it can be used in SQL queries in the same way as any other table. Whenever it is used in a query, its definition is automatically substituted in the FROM clause, as illustrated in Figure 5.11.

Suppose that the university needs to find the department(s) where the average age of professors is the lowest. The application designer might determine that, in addition to the above query, a number of other queries compute the average age. In query processing, as in programming languages, this is a good enough reason to build a view for computing the average age.

FIGURE 5.11 Process of query modification by views.

SELECT	... ...	*Query that uses*
FROM	VIEW1 V	*a view,* VIEW1
WHERE	... AND V.Attr = 'abc' AND ...	

becomes

SELECT	... ...	*Query modified by*
FROM	(*definition of* VIEW1) AS *V*	*the view definition*
WHERE	... AND V.Attr = 'abc' AND...	

```
CREATE VIEW AVGDEPTAGE(Dept,AvgAge) AS
    SELECT        P.DeptId, AVG(P.Age)
    FROM          PROFESSOR P
    GROUP BY      P.DeptId
```

Like a subroutine, this view allows us to solve part of a larger problem separately. For example, we can now find the departments with the minimum average age as follows:

```
SELECT   A.Dept
FROM     AVGDEPTAGE A                               5.38
WHERE    A.AvgAge =      (SELECT MIN(A.AvgAge)
                          FROM AVGDEPTAGE A )
```

Views can make a complex SQL query easier to understand (and debug!). Consider query (5.28), page 161, which finds all students who have taken a course from each professor in the Department of Computer Science. The query uses two nested subqueries, one of which is correlated with the outer query. Because the issues of nesting and correlation are subtly intertwined, it might be hard to construct the right query the first time.

We can simplify the task with the help of views. The view

```
CREATE VIEW ALLCSPROFIDS(ProfId) AS
    SELECT    P.Id
    FROM      PROFESSOR P
    WHERE     P.DeptId = 'CS'
```

constructs the set of Ids of all computer science professors. Next, we define a view to represent the second correlated subquery of (5.28). This subquery has a target list with only one attribute, ProfId, but it also uses a global variable, S, which parameterizes the sets of answers returned by the query. Each query execution returns the set of all professors who have taught a particular student. Since SQL does not allow the creation of views parameterized by a global variable, we improvise by including the appropriate attributes in the target list of the view. More precisely, we include those attributes that are actually used in the subquery in conjunction with the global variable. In our case, the global variable is S and the additional attribute is StudId. The result turns out to be the already familiar view, PROFSTUD, defined in (3.5), page 59.

Unfortunately, we cannot subtract PROFSTUD from ALLCSPROFIDS yet, as they are not UNION-compatible. Furthermore, SQL allows the EXCEPT operator to be applied only to the results of subqueries—we cannot simply subtract one table from another. Therefore, we still must use nested subqueries. However, the subqueries are now much more manageable than in (5.28) since the views enable us to decompose a complex problem into smaller tasks.

```
SELECT    S.Id
FROM      STUDENT S
WHERE

          NOT EXISTS  (
               (SELECT P.Id FROM ALLCSPROFIDS P)
               EXCEPT
               (SELECT P.Id FROM PROFSTUD P
                WHERE P.StudId = S.Id))
```

Although the CREATE VIEW statement is quite different from the CREATE TABLE statement used for base relations, the deletion of views and tables from the system catalog uses similar statements: DROP VIEW for views and DROP TABLE for base tables.

What if we want to drop a view or a base table but the database has other views that were defined through this view or this table? The problem here is that dropping such a view or table means that all of the views defined through them will become "abandoned" and there will be no way to use them. In such a case, SQL leaves the decision to the designer of the DROP statement. The general format of the statement is

DROP {TABLE | VIEW } *table-or-view* {RESTRICT | CASCADE}

If the RESTRICT option is used, the drop operation fails if some view is dependent on the table or view being dropped. With the CASCADE option, all dependent views are also dropped.

Access control and customization through views.   Database views are used not only as a subroutine mechanism but also as a flexible device for controlling access to the data. Thus, we might allow certain users to access a view but not some of the tables that underlie it. For instance, students might not be allowed to query the PROFESSOR relation because of the Social Security information stored there. However, there is nothing wrong with giving students access to the AVGDEPTAGE view defined earlier. Thus, while the access to PROFESSOR might be restricted to administrators, we might let students query the view AVGDEPTAGE:

GRANT SELECT ON AVGDEPTAGE TO ALL

Note that by using views we can repair a deficiency in the GRANT statement. In granting UPDATE (or INSERT) permission, we are allowed to (optionally) specify a list of columns that can be updated (or into which values can be inserted), but in granting SELECT permission SQL provides no way to specify such a list. We can get the same effect, however, by simply creating a view of accessible columns and granting access to that view instead of to the base table.

The creator (and thus the owner) of a view need not also be the owner of the underlying base relations. All that is required is that the view creator have SELECT privileges on all of the underlying relations. For instance, if the PROFESSOR relation is owned by *Administrator,* who in turn grants the SELECT privilege on PROFESSOR to *Personnel, Personnel* can create the view AVGDEPTAGE and later issue the above GRANT statement.

What happens if *Administrator* decides to revoke the SELECT privilege from *Personnel?* Notice that if *Administrator* revokes the privilege, the view becomes "abandoned" and nobody can query it. The actual result depends on how the REVOKE statement is issued. If the administrator uses the RESTRICT option in the REVOKE statement, revocation fails. If the CASCADE option is used, the revocation proceeds *and the view itself is dropped* from the system catalog.

Yet another use of views is customization, which goes hand in hand with access control. A real production database might contain hundreds of relations, each with dozens of attributes. However, most users (both "naive" users and application developers) need to deal with only a small portion of the database schema, the part that is relevant to the particular task performed by the user or the application. There is no benefit in subjecting all users to the tortuous process of learning large parts of the database schema. A better strategy is to create views customized to the various user categories so that, for instance, AVGDEPTAGE can be one of the views customized for the statisticians. The advantages of this approach are threefold:

1. *Ease of use and learning.* This speeds up application development and might prevent bugs that occur as a result of misunderstanding parts of the database schema.

2. *Security.* Various users and applications can be granted access to specific views, thereby reducing the possible damage from human errors and malicious behavior.

3. *Logical data independence* (as discussed in Chapter 3). This benefit can result in huge savings in maintenance costs if later there is a need to change the database schema. Provided that schema reorganization does not lead to loss of information, none of the applications written against the views have to be changed—the only required change is in the view definitions themselves.

5.2.9 Materialized Views

If a view becomes popular with many queries, its contents might be stored in a cache. Cached views are often referred to as **materialized views**. View caching can dramatically improve the response time of queries defined in terms of such views, but update transactions must pay the price. If a view depends on a base relation and a transaction updates the base relation, the view cache might need to be updated as well.

Consider the view PROFSTUD in (3.5), page 59, and suppose that a transaction adds tuple ⟨023456789, CS315, S1997, B⟩ to TRANSCRIPT. This tuple joins with tuple ⟨101202303, CS315, S1997⟩ in TEACHING to produce a view tuple, ⟨101202303, 023456789⟩. But this latter tuple is already in the view (see Figure 3.9, page 60), so this update does not change the view. Had we added ⟨023456789, MGT123, F1997, A⟩

to TRANSCRIPT, the view would have acquired new tuples, ⟨783432188, 023456789⟩ and ⟨009406321, 023456789⟩.

Consider now what might happen when tuples are deleted from the base relations underlying a materialized view. If a transaction deletes tuple ⟨123454321, CS305, S1996, A⟩ from TRANSCRIPT, one might think that tuple ⟨101202303, 123454321⟩ should also be deleted from the view cache. This is not the case, however, because ⟨101202303, 123454321⟩ can still be derived through a join between ⟨123454321, CS315, S1997, A⟩ and ⟨101202303, CS315, S1997⟩. Observe that Figure 3.9 indicates *two* reasons for tuple ⟨101202303, 123454321⟩ to be in the view, and the deletion of ⟨123454321, CS305,S1996, A⟩ removes only one of the reasons! However, if the transaction deleted ⟨123454321, MAT123, S1996, C⟩ from TRANSCRIPT, the tuple ⟨900120450, 123454321⟩ should be removed from the view cache as well.

View cache maintenance is an algorithmically nontrivial task. Of course, a view can be simply recomputed anew each time a base table is changed, but this can be unacceptably expensive, especially if base tables change frequently. A number of algorithms have been proposed, which make it possible to recompute views *incrementally*, that is, by recomputing only those parts of the view that are directly related to the changes in the base tables (refer back to the earlier discussion of the view PROFSTUD). These advanced methods include [Gupta et al. 1993; Mohania et al. 1997; Gupta et al. 1995; Blakeley and Martin 1990; Chaudhuri et al. 1995; Staudt and Jarke 1996; Gupta and Mumick 1995], and more research is still being conducted on the topic. The main difference between the various approaches is how to determine which parts of the view might need to be recomputed (which affects the amount of work involved in a view update) and what type of views a particular method can handle.

Materialized views are especially important in *data warehousing*. A **data warehouse** is an (infrequently updated) database that typically consist of complex materialized views of the data stored in a *separate* production database. Data warehouses are commonly used for online analytical processing (OLAP), which was briefly discussed in Chapter 1. In contrast to most production databases, data warehouses are optimized for querying, not transaction processing, and they are the primary beneficiaries of the advanced query capabilities of SQL discussed in this chapter. (In many transaction processing applications, rapid response time and high throughput requirements preclude the use of the complex queries.)

As materialized views are becoming more and more important, commercial DBMSs are beginning to provide support for such views. Unfortunately, the SQL standard has not yet caught up with the idea, so we will illustrate the SQL extensions for supporting these views using Oracle as an example. Other implementations differ in detail but not substance.

Maintenance of materialized views involves the following main considerations:

- **Build method**. This concerns the time when the view is actually materialized, that is, when its contents are first computed based on the base tables. The build method can be IMMEDIATE or DEFERRED. When the build method is immediate, the view is populated right after the view is created. With the deferred build method, the view is populated using a utility that Oracle specifically provides for this purpose. The user must execute this utility manually.

■ **Refresh mode**. This concerns the timing when the view is recomputed. Ideally, each materialized view should be refreshed each time a change is made to the underlying base tables. This refresh mode is known as ON COMMIT. However, if the changes happen frequently while the view access is infrequent, refreshing the view in this mode might consume computational resources for no apparent benefit. The ON DEMAND option allows the user to control when the refresh happens. In this case, the user must explicitly call a special routine to bring the view up to date. Yet another option is to refresh the view periodically (but automatically, without the user intervention). In this case, the user can tell when to perform the first refresh and how often to do it. This mode is especially useful in data warehousing applications where temporal discrepancy between views and the underlying base tables is not critical.

■ **Refresh method**. This option tells the system how to refresh the view. One obvious way is to recompute the view from scratch, a COMPLETE refresh. Another possibility is a FAST refresh. This means that the system will try to use one of the advanced methods mentioned earlier, which try to update the view incrementally without recomputing it from scratch. Still, some complex views cannot be refreshed incrementally. If the user has difficulties determining whether a particular view can be refreshed using the FAST method, she can always specify the FORCE method. In this case, the system will try to determine if FAST is possible, and if not, it will use COMPLETE.

■ **Query rewriting**. With a regular view, explicit references to the view cause the query to be rewritten to include the definition of the view, as explained in Figure 5.11. When a view is materialized, explicit references use the view cache instead. Using a cache instead of the view definition can have dramatic effects on performance. However, some queries might have been written without the mention of a materialized view even though the query can be equivalently rewritten into one that uses the view. This situation might occur for a number of reasons: the user might not have been aware of the view, the query could have been written before the view was added to the database, or the user might have failed to notice that the view can be used in a particular query. To illustrate the issue, consider the following query, which finds all students (just their Ids) who took a course from John Smyth.

```
SELECT R.StudId
FROM Transcript R, Teaching T, Professor P
WHERE T.ProfId = P.Id AND P.Name = 'John Smyth' AND
      R.CrsCode = T.CrsCode AND R.Semester = T.Semester
```

Notice that part of the WHERE clause, the condition R.CrsCode = T.CrsCode AND R.Semester = T.Semester, is equivalent to the one used to define the view

PROFSTUD in (3.5), page 59. Therefore, the above query can be rewritten in the following equivalent form:

```
SELECT S.Stud
FROM PROFSTUD S, PROFESSOR P
WHERE S.Prof = P.Id AND P.Name = 'John Smyth'
```

If the view PROFSTUD is materialized, such a rewriting might result in a significant performance gain. The option ENABLE QUERY REWRITE tells the query optimizer that it should try to rewrite queries using materialized views in a way similar to the above example.

Now we are ready to see examples of materialized views defined using Oracle's extensions of SQL.

```
CREATE MATERIALIZED VIEW PROFSTUD(Prof, Stud)
     BUILD IMMEDIATE
     REFRESH FAST ON COMMIT
     ENABLE QUERY REWRITE
AS
SELECT T.ProfId, R.StudId
FROM TRANSCRIPT R, TEACHING T
WHERE R.CrsCode = T.CrsCode AND R.Semester = T.Semester
```

This statement tells the system that the view should be filled in with data immediately and that it should be refreshed using an advanced algorithm for incremental view update. These refreshes should take place each time an update transaction commits changes to the underlying base tables. Finally, the query optimizer is told to attempt query rewriting using this view whenever possible. For the view AVGDEPTAGE, which was discussed in Section 5.2.8, we could choose different options:

```
CREATE MATERIALIZED VIEW AVGDEPTAGE(Dept, AvgAge)
     BUILD DEFERRED
     REFRESH COMPLETE
     START CURRENT_DATE + 1 NEXT CURRENT_DATE + 3
AS
  .
  .
  .
```

Here the view is said to be populated later on, when the user executes an appropriate system utility. View refreshing will be always done from scratch, and the first refresh should take place tomorrow. Subsequent refreshes should be done every other day regardless of the rate of changes to the base tables. No query rewriting should be attempted with this view.

5.2.10 The Null Value Quandary

In Chapter 3, we briefly discussed the concept of a *null value*. For instance, if we take the tuples in the TRANSCRIPT table to stand for courses taken in the past or those being taken in the current semester, some tuples might not have a valid value in the Grade attribute. NULL is a placeholder that SQL uses in such a case.

Null values are an unfortunately unavoidable headache in query processing. Indeed, what is the truth value of the condition T.Grade = 'A' if the value of T is a tuple that has NULL in the Grade attribute?

To account for this phenomenon, SQL uses so-called *3-valued logic*, where the truth values are *true*, *false*, and *unknown*, and where val_1 op val_2 (op being $<$, $>$, $<>$, $=$, etc.) is considered to be *unknown* whenever at least one of the values, val_1 or val_2, is NULL.

Nulls affect not only comparisons in the WHERE and CHECK clauses but also arithmetic expressions and aggregate functions. An arithmetic expression that encounters a NULL is itself evaluated to NULL. COUNT considers NULL to be a regular value (e.g., statement (5.32) on page 166 counts NULL as well as normal values in producing the number of professors in the Management Department). All other aggregates just throw NULLs away (e.g., statement (5.36) on page 171 ignores NULLs when computing the average). The following caveat holds, however: if such an aggregate function is applied to a column that has only NULLs, the result is a NULL.

If all this multitude of exceptions does not seem to be too bad—hang on: some vendors do not follow the standard and, for example, ignore NULL while counting.

Sadly, we have not reached the end of this confusing story. We also must decide what to do when a WHERE or a CHECK clause has the form $cond_1$ AND $cond_2$, $cond_1$ OR $cond_2$, or NOT $cond$, and one of the subconditions evaluates to *unknown* because of a pesky NULL hidden inside the subcondition. This issue is resolved by the truth tables in Figure 5.12, which shows the value of various Boolean functions depending on the values of subconditions.

$cond_1$	$cond_2$	$cond_1$ AND $cond_2$	$cond_1$ OR $cond_2$
true	true	true	true
true	false	false	true
true	unknown	unknown	true
false	true	false	true
false	false	false	false
false	unknown	false	unknown
unknown	true	unknown	true
unknown	false	false	unknown
unknown	unknown	unknown	unknown

cond	NOT *cond*
true	false
false	true
unknown	unknown

FIGURE 5.12 SQL's truth tables used to deal with the unknown.

If these tables seem bewildering, they should not be. The idea is very simple. Suppose that we need to compute the value of *true* AND *unknown*. Because *unknown* might turn out to be either *true* or *false*, the value of the entire expression can also be either *true* or *false* (that is, *unknown*). On the other hand, the expressions *false* AND *unknown* and *true* OR *unknown* evaluate to *false* and *true*, respectively, regardless of whether *unknown* turns out to be *true* or *false*. The table for NOT can be explained away similarly.

SQL introduces one additional predicate, IS NULL, which is specifically designed to test if some value is NULL. For instance, T.Grade IS NULL is true whenever the tuple assigned to T has a null value in the Grade attribute; it evaluates to false otherwise. Interestingly, this is the only true 2-valued predicate in SQL!

So what happens when the entire condition evaluates to *unknown*? The answer depends on whether this is a WHERE or a CHECK clause. If a WHERE clause evaluates to *unknown*, it is treated as *false* and the corresponding tuple is not added to the query answer. If a CHECK clause evaluates to *unknown*, the integrity constraint is considered to be observed (i.e., the result is treated as *true*). The difference in the way the unknown values are treated in queries and constraints can be given a rational explanation. It is assumed that the user expects the queries to return only the answers that are definitely *true*. On the other hand, a constraint of the form CHECK (*condition*) is viewed as a statement that the condition should *not* evaluate to *false*. Thus, the *unknown* truth value is considered acceptable.

We have presented only the general framework behind null values in SQL. Some details have been left out but can be found in most standard SQL references, such as [Date and Darwen 1997]. For instance, what is the impact of nulls on the LIKE condition, the IN condition, set comparisons (such as > ALL), the EXISTS feature, duplicate elimination (i.e., queries that use DISTINCT), and the like? Think of what might be reasonable in these cases and then compare your conclusions with those of [Date and Darwen 1997].

5.3 Modifying Relation Instances in SQL

So far we have been discussing the query sublanguage—by far the hardest part of SQL. However, databases exist not only for querying but also for entering and modifying the appropriate data. This section deals with the part of SQL that is used for data insertion, deletion, and modification.

5.3.1 Inserting Data

The INSERT statement has several forms, in the simplest of which the programmer specifies just the tuple to be inserted. The second version of this statement can insert multiple tuples and uses a query to tell which tuples to insert. To insert a single tuple, the programmer simply writes

```
INSERT INTO    PROFESSOR(DeptId,Id,Name)
VALUES ('MATH','100100100','Bob Parker')
```

The order of the attributes listed in the INTO clause need not correspond to the *default* order (i.e., the order in which they were listed in the CREATE TABLE statement). However, if you know the default attribute order, you can omit the attribute list in the INTO clause. Of course, the order of items in the VALUE clause must then correspond to the default attribute order. Despite the potential time-saving, omitting the attribute list in the INTO clause is error prone and is thus viewed as poor programming style (e.g., consider what might happen if the schema is later changed).

The second form of the INSERT statement enables bulk insertion of tuples into relations. The tuples to be inserted are the result of a query in the INSERT statement. Note that, even though a query is used to define the tuples to be inserted into a relation, this mechanism is fundamentally different from defining views via queries.

As an example, let us insert some tuples into a relation called HARDCLASS. A hard class[7] is one that is failed by more than 10% of the students. The attributes in HARDCLASS are course code, semester, and failure rate.

This query is actually quite complicated because expressing the failure rate in SQL requires some thought. We will tackle this query in steps and first define two views.

```
--Number of failures per class
CREATE VIEW CLASSFAILURES(CrsCode, Semester, Failed) AS
    SELECT    T.CrsCode, T.Semester, COUNT(*)
    FROM      TRANSCRIPT T
    WHERE     T.Grade = 'F'
    GROUP BY  T.CrsCode, T.Semester
```

Similarly, we can define the view CLASSENROLLMENT, which counts the number of students enrolled in each course.

```
--Number of enrolled students per class
CREATE VIEW CLASSENROLLMENT(CrsCode, Semester, Enrolled) AS
    SELECT    T.CrsCode, T.Semester, COUNT(*)
    FROM      TRANSCRIPT T
    GROUP BY  T.CrsCode, T.Semester
```

Now, HARDCLASS can be populated with tuples as follows:

```
INSERT INTO HARDCLASS(CrsCode, Semester, FailRate)
    SELECT    F.CrsCode, F.Semester, F.Failed/E.Enrolled          5.39
    FROM      CLASSFAILURES F, CLASSENROLLMENT E
    WHERE     F.CrsCode = E.CrsCode AND F.Semester = E.Semester
                AND (F.Failed/E.Enrolled) > 0.1
```

[7] By "class" we mean a particular course offering in a given semester.

The final query looks simple, but imagine how complex it would have been if not for the views!

There are a few more subtleties we must mention. First, if an INSERT statement inserts a tuple that violates some integrity constraint, the entire operation is aborted and no tuple is inserted (assuming that constraint checking has not been DEFERRED, as will be described in Section 8.3).

Second, it is possible to omit a value in the list of values in the VALUE clause (and the corresponding attribute in the attribute list) and an attribute in the SELECT clause if the CREATE TABLE statement does not specify NOT NULL. If the CREATE TABLE statement specifies a default for the missing attribute, that default value is used. Instead of omitting values, a better style is to use the more informative keywords DEFAULT or NULL (whichever is appropriate) in place of the missing values (e.g., (100100100, NULL, DEFAULT)).

5.3.2 Deleting Data

Deletion of tuples is analogous to the second form of INSERT, except that now the keyword DELETE is used. For example, to delete the hard classes taught in the fall and spring of 2003 we use

```
DELETE FROM HardClass
WHERE Semester IN ('S2003','F2003')
```

Note that the DELETE statement does not allow the use of tuple variables in the FROM clause.

Suppose that in order to improve teaching standards, the university decides to fire all professors with an excessively high failure rate in one of the courses. This turns out to be difficult (and not because of tenure!). The DELETE statement has a very limited form of the FROM clause. The programmer can specify just one relation, the one whose tuples are to be deleted. (What would it mean to delete rows from the Cartesian product of two relations?) However, in order to find out who to fire we need to look inside the HardClass relation, but there is no room for this relation in the FROM clause. So what are we to do? Use nested subqueries!

```
DELETE FROM Professor
WHERE IdIN
        (SELECT  T.ProfId
         FROM    Teaching T, HardClass H
         WHERE   T.CrsCode = H.CrsCode
                 AND T.Semester = H.Semester
                 AND H.FailRate > 0.5)
```

5.40

5.3.3 Updating Existing Data

Sometimes it is necessary to change the values of some attributes of existing tuples in a relation. For instance, the following statement changes the grade of student 666666666 for course EE101 from B to A:

```
UPDATE    TRANSCRIPT
SET       Grade ='A'
WHERE     StudId ='666666666' AND CrsCode = 'EE101'
```

Observe that, like DELETE, the UPDATE statement does not allow tuple variables and it uses only a limited form of the FROM clause (more precisely, UPDATE itself is a kind of FROM clause). As a result, some of the more complex updates require the use of nested subqueries. For instance, if instead of firing them we decide to transfer all poorly performing professors to administration, we use a subquery similar to the one in (5.40).

```
UPDATE    PROFESSOR
SET       DeptId = 'Adm'
WHERE     Id IN
              (SELECT T.ProfId
               FROM TEACHING T, HARDCLASS H                5.41
               WHERE T.CrsCode = H.CrsCode
                     AND T.Semester = H.Semester
                     AND  H.FailRate > 0.5)
```

And, yes, here is our favorite again: *Raise the salary of all administrators by 10%*:

```
UPDATE    EMPLOYEE
SET       Salary = Salary * 1.1
WHERE     Department = 'Adm'
```

5.3.4 Updates on Views

Because views are often used as a customization device that shields users and programmers from the complexities of the conceptual database schema, it is only natural to let programmers update their views. Unfortunately, this is easier said than done because of the following three problems:

1. Suppose that we have a simple view over TRANSCRIPT—a projection on the attributes CrsCode, StudId, and Semester. If the programmer wants to insert a new tuple in such a view, the value for the Grade attribute will be missing. This problem is not serious. We can pad the missing attributes with null values if the CREATE TABLE statement for the underlying base relation permits this; if it does not, the insertion command can be rejected.

2. Consider a view, CSPROF, over the PROFESSOR relation, which is obtained by a simple selection on DeptId = 'CS'. Suppose that the programmer inserts ⟨121232343, 'Paul Schmidt','EE'⟩. If we propagate this insertion to the underlying base relation (i.e., PROFESSOR), we can observe the anomaly that querying the view *after* the insertion does not show any traces of the tuple we just inserted! Indeed, Paul Schmidt is not a CS professor, so he does not appear in the view defined through the selection DeptId = 'CS'!

   By default, SQL does not forbid such anomalies, but a careful database designer might include the clause WITH CHECK OPTION to ensure that the newly inserted or updated tuples in a view do, indeed, satisfy the view definition. In our example, we can write

```
CREATE VIEW CSPROF(Id,Name,DeptId) AS
      SELECT   P.Id, P.Name, P.DeptId
      FROM     PROFESSOR P
      WHERE    P.DeptId = 'CS'
      WITH CHECK OPTION
```

3. The following problem is much more involved. It turns out that some view updates might have several possible translations into the updates of the underlying base relations. This is potentially a very serious problem because the possibilities arising from a single view update might have drastically different consequences with respect to the underlying stored data.

   To illustrate this problem, consider the view PROFSTUD, discussed earlier.

```
CREATE VIEW PROFSTUD(ProfId,StudId) AS
      SELECT   T.ProfId, R.StudId
      FROM     TEACHING T, TRANSCRIPT R
      WHERE    T.CrsCode = R.CrsCode
                  AND T.Semester = R.Semester
```

The contents of this view were depicted in Figure 3.9 on page 60. Suppose that we now decide to delete the tuple ⟨101202303, 123454321⟩ from that view. How should this update be propagated back to the base relations? There are four possibilities:

1. Delete ⟨101202303, CS315, S1997⟩ and ⟨101202303, CS305, S1996⟩ from the relation TEACHING.

2. Delete ⟨123454321, CS315, S1997, A⟩ and ⟨123454321, CS305, S1996, A⟩ from the relation TRANSCRIPT.

3. Delete ⟨101202303, CS315, S1997⟩ from TEACHING and ⟨123454321, CS305, S1996, A⟩ from TRANSCRIPT.

4. Delete ⟨101202303, CS305, S1996⟩ from TEACHING and ⟨123454321, CS315, S1997, A⟩ from TRANSCRIPT.

For each of these possibilities, the join implied by the view does not contain the tuple ⟨101202303, 123454321⟩. The only problem is, Which possibility should be used for the view update?

This example shows that, in the absence of additional information, it might not be possible to translate view updates into the updates of the underlying base relations uniquely. Much work has been done on defining heuristics aimed at disambiguating view updates, but none has emerged as an acceptable solution. SQL takes a simpleminded approach by defining only a very restricted class of views as updatable. The essence of these restrictions on the view definition is summarized here:

1. Exactly one table can be mentioned in the FROM clause (and only once). The FROM clause cannot have nested subqueries.

2. Aggregates, GROUP BY, or HAVING clauses and set operations, such as UNION and EXCEPT, are not allowed.

3. Nested subqueries in the WHERE clause of the view cannot refer to the (unique) table used in the FROM clause of the view definition. Moreover, a nested subquery cannot refer to this table, either explicitly, in the FROM clause, or implicitly, through a tuple variable defined in the outer query.

4. No expressions and no DISTINCT keyword in the SELECT clause are allowed.

Views satisfying these conditions (and some other rather obscure restrictions) are called **updatable** (in the SQL sense). Here is an example of an updatable view.

```
CREATE VIEW CANTEACH(Professor, Course)
    SELECT   T.ProfId, T.CrsCode
    FROM     TEACHING   T
```

Referring to the database of Figure 3.5, page 39, suppose that we delete ⟨09406321, MGT123⟩ from the view CANTEACH. There are two tuples in the underlying base relation (TEACHING) that give rise to the view tuple in question: ⟨09406321,MGT123, F1994⟩ and ⟨09406321, MGT123,F1997⟩. The translation of the view update into an update of TEACHING must therefore delete both of these tuples.

BIBLIOGRAPHIC NOTES

Relational algebra was introduced in Codd's seminal papers [Codd 1972, 1970]. SQL was developed by IBM's System R research group [Astrahan et al. 1981]. [Melton and Simon 1992; Date and Darwen 1997] are references to SQL-92, and [Gulutzan and Pelzer 1999] describe the extensions provided in SQL:1999.

The view update problem received considerable attention in the past. The following is a partial list of works that propose various solutions: [Bancilhon and Spyratos 1981; Masunaga 1984; Cosmadakis and Papadimitriou 1983; Gottlob et al. 1988; Keller 1985; Langerak 1990; Chen et al. 1995]. The maintenance problem for materialized views has also been an active research area [Gupta et al. 1993; Mohania et al. 1997; Gupta et al. 1995; Blakeley and Martin 1990; Chaudhuri et al. 1995; Staudt and Jarke 1996; Gupta and Mumick 1995]. More research is being conducted because of the importance of materialized views in data warehousing.

EXERCISES

5.1   Assume that **R** and **S** are relations containing n_R and n_S tuples, respectively. What is the maximum and minimum number of tuples that can possibly be in the result of each of the following expressions (assuming appropriate union compatibilities)?

   a. $R \cup S$
   b. $R \cap S$
   c. $R - S$
   d. $R \times S$
   e. $R \bowtie S$
   f. R / S
   g. $\sigma_{s=4}(R) \times \pi_{s,t}(S)$

5.2   Assume that **R** and **S** are tables representing the relations of the previous exercise. Design SQL queries that will return the results of each of the expressions of that exercise.

5.3   Verify that the Cartesian product is an associative operator—that is,

$$r \times (s \times t) = (r \times s) \times t$$

   for all relations **r**, **s**, and **t**.

5.4   Verify that selections commute—that is, for any relation **r** and any pair of selection conditions $cond_1$ and $cond_2$, $\sigma_{cond_1}(\sigma_{cond_2}(r)) = \sigma_{cond_2}(\sigma_{cond_1}(r))$.

5.5   Verify that, for any pair of relations **r** and **s**, $\sigma_{cond}(r \times s) = r \times \sigma_{cond}(s)$ if the selection condition *cond* involves *only* the attributes mentioned in the schema of relation **s**.

5.6   Prove that, if **r** and **s** are union-compatible, then $r \cap s = r \bowtie s$.

5.7   Using division, write a relational algebra expression that produces all students who have taken all courses offered in every semester (this implies that they might have taken the same course twice).

5.8   Using division, write a relational algebra expression that produces all students who have taken all courses that have been offered. (If a course has been offered more than once, they have to have taken it at least once.)

5.9   Construct a relational algebra query that produces the same result as the outer join $r \bowtie_{cond}^{outer} s$ using only these operators: union, difference, Cartesian product, projection, general join (not outer join). You can also use constant relations, that is, relations with fixed content (e.g., one that has tuples filled with nulls or other predefined constants).

5.10   Express each of the following queries in (*i*) relational algebra and (*ii*) SQL using the Student Registration System schema of Figure 3.4.

   a. List all courses that are taught by professors who belong to the EE or MGT departments.

b. List the names of all students who took courses *both* in spring 1997 and fall 1998.

c. List the names of all students who took courses from at least two professors in different departments.

d. List all courses that are offered by the MGT Department and that have been taken by all students.

*e. Find every department that has a professor who taught all courses ever offered by that department.

5.11 Use the relational algebra to find the list of all "problematic" classes (i.e., course-semester pairs) where the failure rate is higher than 20%. (Assume, for simplicity, that grades are numbers between 1 and 4, and that a failing grade is anything less than 2.)

Because the relational algebra does not have aggregate operators, we must add them to be able to solve the above problem. The additional operator you should use is $count_{A/B}(\mathbf{r})$.

The meaning of this operator is as follows: A and B must be lists of attributes in $\mathbf{r}$. The *schema* of $count_{A/B}(\mathbf{r})$ consists of all attributes in B plus one additional attribute, which represents the counted value. The *contents* of $count_{A/B}(\mathbf{r})$ are defined as follows: for each tuple, $t \in \pi_B(\mathbf{r})$ (the projection on B), take $\pi_A(\sigma_{B=t}(\mathbf{r}))$ and count the number of tuples in the resulting relation (where $\sigma_{B=t}(\mathbf{r})$ stands for the set of all tuples in $\mathbf{r}$ whose value on the attributes in B is t). Let us denote this number by $c(t)$. Then the relation $count_{A/B}(\mathbf{r})$ is defined as $\{< t, c(t) > | t \in \pi_B(\mathbf{r})\}$.

You should be able to recognize the above construction as a straightforward adaptation of GROUP BY of SQL to the relational algebra.

5.12 State the English meaning of the following algebraic expressions (some of these queries are likely to yield empty results in a typical university, but this is beside the point):

a. $\pi_{CrsCode,Semester}(\text{TRANSCRIPT})/ \pi_{CrsCode}(\text{TRANSCRIPT})$

b. $\pi_{CrsCode,Semester}(\text{TRANSCRIPT})/ \pi_{Semester}(\text{TRANSCRIPT})$

c. $\pi_{CrsCode,StudId}(\text{TRANSCRIPT})/ (\pi_{Id}(\text{STUDENT}))[\text{StudId}]$

d. $\pi_{CrsCode,Semester,StudId}(\text{TRANSCRIPT})/ (\pi_{Id}(\text{STUDENT}))[\text{StudId}]$

5.13 Consider the following query:

```
SELECT   S.Name
FROM     STUDENT S, TRANSCRIPT T
WHERE    S.Id = T.StudId
         AND T.CrsCode IN ('CS305','CS315')
```

What does this query mean (express the meaning in one short English sentence)? Write an equivalent SQL query without using the IN operator and the set construct.

5.14 Explain the conceptual difference between views and bulk insertion of tuples into base relations using the INSERT statement with an attached query.

5.15 Explain why a view is like a subroutine.

5.16 Write query (5.38) on page 175 without the use of the views.

5.17 Express the following queries using SQL. Assume that the STUDENT table is augmented with an additional attribute, Age, and that the PROFESSOR table has additional attributes, Age and Salary.

    a. Find the average age of students who received an A for *some* course.

    b. Find the minimum age among straight A students *per course*.

    c. Find the minimum age among straight A students per course among the students who have taken CS305 or MAT123. (Hint: a HAVING clause might help.)

    d. Raise by 10% the salary of every professor who is now younger than 40 and who taught MAT123 in the spring 1997 or fall 1997 semester. (*Hint*: Try a nested subquery in the WHERE clause of the UPDATE statement.)

    e. Find the professors whose salaries are at least 10% higher than the average salary of all professors. (*Hint*: Use views, as in the HARDCLASS example (5.39), page 183.)

    f. Find all professors whose salaries are at least 10% higher than the average salary of all professors *in their departments*. (*Hint*: Use views, as in (5.39).)

5.18 Express the following queries in relational algebra.

    a. (5.16), page 154

    b. (5.20), page 156

    c. (5.23), page 158

5.19 Write an equivalent expression in relational algebra for the following SQL query:

```
SELECT    P.Name, C.Name
FROM      PROFESSOR P, COURSE C, TAUGHT T
WHERE     P.Id = T.ProfId AND T.Semester = 'S2002'
              AND T.CrsCode = C.CrsCode
```

5.20 Consider the following schema:

```
TRANSCRIPT(StudId, CrsCode, Semester, Grade)
TEACHING(ProfId, CrsCode, Semester)
PROFESSOR(Id, ProfName, Dept)
```

Write the following query in relational algebra and in SQL: *Find all student Ids who have taken a course from* each *professor in the* MUS *Department.*

5.21 Define the above query as an SQL view and then use this view to answer the following query: *For each student who has taken a course from every professor in the* MUS *Department, show the number of courses taken, provided that this number is more than* 10.

5.22 Consider the following schema:

```
BROKER(Id, Name)    ACCOUNT(Acct#, BrokerId, Gain)
```

Write the following query in relational algebra and in SQL: *Find the names of all brokers who have made money in all accounts assigned to them (i.e.,* Gain > 0).

5.23 Write an SQL statement (for the database schema given in Exercise 5.22) to fire all brokers who lost money in at least 40% of their accounts. Assume that every broker has at least one account. (*Hint*: Define intermediate views to facilitate formulation of the query.)

5.24 Consider the following schema that represents houses for sale and customers who are looking to buy:

Customer(Id, Name, Address)
Preference(CustId, Feature)
Agent(Id, AgentName)
House(Address, OwnerId, AgentId)
Amenity(Address, Feature)

Preference is a relation that lists all features requested by the customers (one tuple per customer/feature; e.g., ⟨123, '5BR'⟩, ⟨123,'2BATH'⟩, ⟨432,'pool'⟩), and Amenity is a relation that lists all features of each house (one tuple per house/feature).

A customer is *interested* in buying a house if the set of all features specified by the customer is a subset of the amenities the house has. A tuple in the House relation states who is the owner and who is the real estate agent listing the house. Write the following queries in SQL:

a. Find all customers who are interested in every house listed with the agent with Id 007.

b. Using the previous query as a view, retrieve a set of tuples of the form ⟨*feature, number_of_customers*⟩, where each tuple in the result shows a feature and the number of customers who want this feature such that

  – Only the customers who are interested in every house listed with Agent 007 are considered.

  – The number of customers interested in *feature* is greater than three. (If this number is not greater than three, the corresponding tuple ⟨*feature, number_of_customers*⟩ is not added to the result.)

5.25 Consider the schema Person(Id, Name, Age). Write an SQL query that finds the 100th oldest person in the relation. A 100th oldest person is one such that there are 99 people who are strictly older. (There can be several such people who might have the same age, or there can be none.)

5.26 The last section of this chapter presented four main rules that characterize updatable views in SQL. The third rule states that if the WHERE clause contains a nested subquery, none of the tables mentioned in that subquery (explicitly or implicitly) can be the table used in the FROM clause of the view definition.

Construct a view that violates condition 3 but satisfies conditions 1, 2, and 4 for updatability, such that there is an update to this view that has two different translations into the updates on the underlying base relation.

5.27 Using the relations Teaching and Professor, create a view of Transcript containing only rows corresponding to classes taught by John Smyth. Can this view be used in a GRANT statement whose purpose is to allow Smyth to update student grades, but only those he has assigned? Explain.

6

Database Design with the Relational Normalization Theory

Conceptual modeling using the E-R or UML approach is a good way to start dealing with the complexity of modeling a real-world enterprise. However, conceptual modeling is only a set of guidelines that requires considerable expertise and intuition to use successfully, and it can lead to several alternative designs for the same enterprise. Unfortunately, E-R and UML do not provide the criteria or tools to help evaluate alternative designs and suggest improvements. In this chapter, we present the **relational normalization theory**, which includes a set of concepts and algorithms that can help with the evaluation and refinement of the designs obtained through conceptual modeling.

The main tool used in normalization theory is the notion of *functional dependency* (and, to a lesser degree, *join dependency*). Functional dependency is a generalization of the key dependencies in the E-R and UML approaches whereas join dependency does not have a counterpart. Both types of dependency are used by designers to spot situations in which conceptual modeling unnaturally places attributes of two distinct entity types into the same relation schema. These situations are characterized in terms of *normal forms*, from which comes the term "normalization theory." Normalization theory forces relations into an appropriate normal form using *decompositions*, which break up schemas involving unhappy unions of attributes of unrelated entity types. Because of the central role that decompositions play in relational design, the techniques that we are about to discuss are sometimes also called **relational decomposition theory**.

6.1 The Problem of Redundancy

The best way to understand the potential problems with relational designs based on the E-R or UML approach is through an example. Consider the CREATE TABLE PERSON statement (4.1) on page 87. Recall that this relation schema was obtained by direct translation from the E-R diagram in Figure 4.1. The first indication of something wrong with this translation was the realization that SSN is not a key of the resulting PERSON relation. Instead, the key is a combination (SSN, Hobby). In other words, the attribute SSN does not uniquely identify the tuples in the PERSON relation even though it does uniquely identify the entities in the PERSON entity set.

Not only is this counterintuitive, but it also has a number of undesirable effects on the instances of the PERSON relation schema.

To see this, we take a closer look at the relation instance shown in Figure 4.13, page 86. Notice that John Doe and Mary Doe are both represented by multiple tuples and that their addresses, names, and Ids occur multiple times as well. Redundant storage of the same information is apparent here. However, wasted space is the least of the problems. The real issue is that when database updates occur, we must keep all the redundant copies of the same data consistent with each other, and we must do it efficiently. Specifically, we can identify the following problems:

- **Update anomaly.** If John Doe moves to 1 Hill Top Drive, updating the relation in Figure 4.13 requires changing the address in both tuples that describe the John Doe entity.

- **Insertion anomaly.** Suppose that we decide to add Homer Simpson to the PERSON relation, but Homer's information sheet does not specify any hobbies. One way around this problem might be to add the tuple ⟨023456789, Homer Simpson, Fox 5 TV, NULL⟩—that is, to fill in the missing field with NULL. However, Hobby is part of the primary key, and SQL does not allow null values in primary keys. Why? For one thing, DBMSs generally maintain an index on the primary key, and it is not clear how the index should refer to the null value. Assuming that this problem can be solved, suppose that a request is made to insert ⟨023456789, Homer Simpson, Fox 5 TV, acting⟩. Should this new tuple just be added, or should it replace the existing tuple ⟨023456789, Homer Simpson, Fox 5 TV, NULL⟩? A human will most likely choose to replace it, because humans do not normally think of hobbies as a defining characteristic of a person. However, how does a computer know that the tuples with primary key ⟨111111111, NULL⟩ and ⟨111111111, acting⟩ refer to the same entity? (Recall that the information about which tuple came from which entity is lost in the translation!) Redundancy is at the root of this ambiguity. If Homer were described by at most one tuple, only one course of action would be possible.

- **Deletion anomaly.** Suppose that Homer Simpson is no longer interested in acting. How are we to delete this hobby? We can, of course, delete the tuple that talks about Homer's acting hobby. However, since there is only one tuple that refers to Homer (see Figure 4.13), this throws out perfectly good information about Homer's Id and address. To avoid this loss of information, we can try to replace acting with NULL. Unfortunately, this again raises the issue of nulls in primary key attributes. Once again, redundancy is the culprit. If only one tuple could possibly describe Homer, the attribute Hobby would not be part of the key.

For convenience, we sometimes use the term "update anomalies" to refer to all of the above anomaly types.

6.2 Decompositions

The problems caused by redundancy—wasted storage and anomalies—can be fixed using the following simple technique. Instead of having one relation describe all that is known about persons, we can use two separate relation schemas.

PERSON1(SSN, Name, Address)
HOBBY(SSN, Hobby)   **6.1**

Projecting the relation in Figure 4.13 on each of these schemas yields the result shown in Figure 6.1. The new design has the following important properties:

1. Assuming for the moment that everyone has hobbies, the original relation of Figure 4.13 is exactly the natural join of the two relations in Figure 6.1. In fact, one can prove that this property is not an artifact of our particular choice of relation instances—if SSN uniquely determines the name and address of a person, then *every* relation, **r**, over the schema of Figure 4.13 equals the natural join of the projections of **r** on PERSON1 and HOBBY. This property, called *losslessness,* will be discussed in Section 6.6.1. This means that our decomposition preserves the original information represented by the PERSON relation.

2. We no longer have to accept the unnatural result that the Hobby attribute is part of a key. SSN is now the key of both relations. Whereas we could not describe people with no hobbies in PERSON, it is now not even necessary to use nulls for this purpose: we simply do not include rows for such people in the relation HOBBY. Thus, the removal of Bart Simpson's hobbies from the database does not delete the information about his address. The natural join of PERSON1 and HOBBY is no longer PERSON, but then we should not expect this to be the case since we are now describing a more diverse group of people.

SSN	Name	Address
111111111	John Doe	123 Main St.
555666777	Mary Doe	7 Lake Dr.
987654321	Bart Simpson	Fox 5 TV

(a) PERSON1

SSN	Hobby
111111111	stamps
111111111	hiking
111111111	coins
555666777	hiking
555666777	skating
987654321	acting

(b) HOBBY

FIGURE 6.1 Decomposition of the PERSON relation shown in Figure 4.13.

SSN	Name	Address	Hobby
111111111	John Doe	123 Main St.	stamps
555666777	Mary Doe	7 Lake Dr.	hiking
987654321	Bart Simpson	Fox 5 TV	coins
			skating
			acting

FIGURE **6.2** The "ultimate" decomposition.

3. The redundancy present in the original relation of Figure 4.13 is gone and so are the update anomalies. The only items that are stored more than once are SSNs, which are identifiers of entities of type PERSON. Thus, changes to addresses, names, or hobbies now affect only a single tuple. The insertion anomaly is also gone because we can now add people and hobbies independently.

Observe that the new design still has a certain amount of redundancy and that we might still need to use null values in certain cases. First, since we use SSNs as tuple identifiers, each SSN can occur multiple times and all of these occurrences must be kept consistent across the database. So consistency maintenance has not been eliminated completely. However, if the identifiers are not dynamic (for instance, SSNs do not change frequently), consistency maintenance is considerably simplified. Second, imagine a situation in which we add a person to our PERSON1 relation and the address is not known. Clearly, even with the new design, we have to insert NULL in the Address field for the corresponding tuple. However, Address is not part of a primary key, so the use of NULL here is not that bad (we will still have difficulties joining PERSON1 on the Address attribute, though).

It is important to realize that not all decompositions are created equal. In fact, most of them do not make any sense even though they might be doing a good job at eliminating redundancy. The decomposition

SSN(SSN)
NAME(Name)
ADDRESS(Address)   6.2
HOBBY(Hobby)

is the ultimate "redundancy eliminator." Projecting of the relation of Figure 4.13 on these schemas yields a database where each value appears exactly once, as shown in Figure 6.2. Unfortunately, this new database is completely devoid of any useful information; for instance, it is no longer possible to tell where John Doe lives or who collects stamps as a hobby. This situation is in sharp contrast with the decomposition of Figure 6.1, where we were able to completely restore the information represented by the original relation using a natural join.

The need for schema refinement. Translation of the PERSON entity type into the relational model indicates that one cannot rely solely on conceptual modeling for designing database schemas. Furthermore, the problems exhibited by the PERSON example are by no means rare or unique. Consider the relationship HASACCOUNT of Figure 4.30. A typical translation of the relationship HASACCOUNT of Figure 4.30, page 108, into the relational model might be

```
CREATE TABLE HasAccount (
AccountNumber INTEGER NOT NULL,
ClientId       CHAR(20),                          6.3
OfficeId       INTEGER,
PRIMARY KEY (ClientId, OfficeId),
FOREIGN KEY (OfficeId) REFERENCES Office
... ... ... )
```

Recall that a client can have at most one account in an office, and hence (ClientId, OfficeId) is a key. Also, an account must be assigned to exactly one office. Careful analysis shows that this requirement leads to some of the same problems that we saw in the PERSON example. For example, a tuple that records the fact that a particular account is managed by a particular office cannot be added without also recording client information (since ClientId is part of the primary key), which is an insertion anomaly. This (and the dual deletion anomaly) is perhaps not a serious problem, because of the specifics of this particular application, but the update anomaly could present maintenance issues. Moving an account from one office to another involves changing OfficeId in every tuple corresponding to that account. If the account has multiple clients, this might be a problem.

We return to this example later in this chapter because HASACCOUNT exhibits certain interesting properties not found in the PERSON example. For instance, even though a decomposition of HASACCOUNT might still be desirable, it incurs additional maintenance overhead that the decomposition of PERSON does not.

The above discussion brings out two key points: (1) Decomposition of relation schemas can serve as a useful tool that complements the E-R approach by eliminating redundancy problems; (2) The criteria for choosing the right decomposition are not immediately obvious, especially when we have to deal with schemas that contain many attributes. For these reasons, the purpose of Sections 6.3 through 6.6 is to develop techniques and criteria for identifying relation schemas that are in need of decomposition as well as to understand what it means for a decomposition not to lose information.

The central tool in developing much of decomposition theory is **functional dependency**, which is a generalization of the idea of key constraints. Functional dependencies are used to define **normal forms**—a set of requirements on relational schemas that are desirable in update-intensive transaction systems. This is why the theory of decompositions is often also called **normalization theory**. Sections 6.7 through 6.9 develop algorithms for carrying out the normalization process.

6.3 Functional Dependencies

For the remainder of this chapter we use a special notation for representing attributes, which is common in relational normalization theory. Capital letters from the beginning of the alphabet (e.g., A, B, C, D) represent individual attributes; capital letters from the middle to the end of the alphabet with bars over them (e.g., $\overline{P}$, $\overline{V}$, $\overline{W}$, $\overline{X}$, $\overline{Y}$, $\overline{Z}$) represent *sets* of attributes. Also, strings of letters, such as $ABCD$, denote sets of the respective attributes ($\{A, B, C, D\}$ in our case); strings of letters with bars over them, (e.g., $\overline{X}\,\overline{Y}\,\overline{Z}$), stand for unions of these sets (i.e., $\overline{X} \cup \overline{Y} \cup \overline{Z}$). Although this notation requires some getting used to, it is very convenient and provides a succinct language, which we use in examples and definitions.

A **functional dependency** (FD) on a relation schema, $\mathbf{R}$, is a constraint of the form $\overline{X} \rightarrow \overline{Y}$, where $\overline{X}$ and $\overline{Y}$ are sets of attributes used in $\mathbf{R}$. If $\mathbf{r}$ is a relation instance of $\mathbf{R}$, it is said to **satisfy** this functional dependency if

> For every pair of tuples, t and s, in $\mathbf{r}$, if t and s agree on all attributes in $\overline{X}$, then t and s agree on all attributes in $\overline{Y}$.

Put another way, there must not be a pair of tuples in $\mathbf{r}$ such that they have the same values for every attribute in $\overline{X}$ but different values for some attribute in $\overline{Y}$.

Example 6.3.1 (Functional Dependencies).   Consider the relations PERSONI and HOBBY in Figure 6.1. The FD SSN → Name Address is satisfied by the relation PERSONI. On the other hand, the FD SSN → Hobby is *not* satisfied by the relation HOBBY. Indeed, there are tuples that have the same value 111111111 in the attribute SSN but different values in the attribute Hobby. Similarly, Hobby → SSN is violated by the relation HOBBY: the two tuples that have the value hiking in the Hobby attribute differ in their SSN attribute.   ∎

Note that the key constraint, introduced in Section 3.2.2, is a special kind of FD. Suppose that key($\overline{K}$) is a key constraint on the relational schema $\mathbf{R}$ and that $\mathbf{r}$ is a relational instance over $\mathbf{R}$. By definition, $\mathbf{r}$ satisfies key($\overline{K}$) if and only if there is no pair of distinct tuples, $t, s \in \mathbf{r}$, such that t and s agree on every attribute in key($\overline{K}$). Therefore, this key constraint is equivalent to the FD $\overline{K} \rightarrow \overline{R}$, where $\overline{K}$ is the set of attributes in the key constraint and $\overline{R}$ denotes the set of all attributes in the schema $\mathbf{R}$.

Keep in mind that functional dependencies are associated with relation schemas, but when we consider whether or not a functional dependency is satisfied we must consider relation instances over those schemas. This is because FDs are *integrity constraints* on the schema (much like key constraints), which restrict the set of allowable relation instances to those that satisfy the given FDs. It is quite common for some instances of the schema to satisfy the FDs that are not part of that schema. Such satisfaction is considered *accidental* because it not sanctioned in the schema and thus is not guaranteed to hold in the future.

Example 6.3.2 (Schema Constraints vs. Accidental FDs).   Consider again the relation PERSONI in Figure 6.1. In designing a real-life schema for a relation that is supposed to hold basic information about people, such as PERSON1, we will likely make the FD SSN → Name Address part of the schema but will leave out the FDs Name → Address and Address → SSN. Yet the relation in 6.1(a) *happens* to satisfy both of these FDs.

However, since we did not include these FDs into the schema for PERSON1, nothing precludes us from later adding another John Doe with a different SSN and a different address. Likewise, if we later find out that Mary Doe's child lives at 7 Lake Drive, we will be free to add this new person to the relation PERSON1 without the fear of violating a constraint. ■

To summarize, given a schema, $\mathbf{R} = (\bar{R};$ *Constraints*$)$, where $\bar{R}$ is a set of attributes and *Constraints* is a set of FDs, a **legal instance** of $\mathbf{R}$ is a relation with the attributes $\bar{R}$ that satisfies every FD in *Constraints*. We are interested in legal instances because only such relations can exist in a correct database state.

Brain Teaser: What does the FD $X \rightarrow Y$ mean, if X is an empty set of attributes?

Functional dependencies and update anomalies. Certain functional dependencies that exist in a relational schema can lead to redundancy in the corresponding relation instances. Consider the two examples discussed in Sections 6.1 and 6.2: the schemas PERSON and HASACCOUNT. Each has a primary key, as illustrated by the corresponding CREATE TABLE commands (4.1), page 87, and (6.3), page 197, respectively. Correspondingly, there are the following functional dependencies:

PERSON:	SSN,Hobby → SSN,Name,Address,Hobby	
HASACCOUNT:	ClientId,OfficeId → AccountNumber,	**6.4**
	ClientId,OfficeId	

These are not the only FDs implied by the original specifications, however. For instance, both Name and Address are defined as single-valued attributes in the E-R diagram of Figure 4.1. This clearly implies that one PERSON entity (identified by its attribute SSN) can have at most one name and one address. Similarly, the business rules of PSSC (the brokerage firm discussed in Section 4.7) require that every account be assigned to exactly one office, which means that the following FDs must also hold for the corresponding relation schemas:

PERSON:	SSN → Name, Address	
HASACCOUNT:	AccountNumber → OfficeId	**6.5**

It is easy to see that the syntactic structure of the dependencies in (6.4) closely corresponds to the update anomalies that we identified for the corresponding relations. For instance, the problem with PERSON is that for any given SSN we cannot change the values for the attributes Name and Address independently of whether the corresponding person has hobbies: if the person has multiple hobbies, the change has to occur in multiple rows. Likewise with HASACCOUNT we cannot change the value of OfficeId (i.e., transfer an account to a different office) without having to look for all clients associated with this account. Since a number of clients might share the same account, there can be multiple rows in HASACCOUNT that refer to the same account, hence, multiple rows in which OfficeId must be changed.

Note that in both cases, the attributes involved in the update anomalies appear on the left-hand sides of an FD. We can see that update anomalies are associated with certain kinds of functional dependencies. Which dependencies are the bad guys? At the risk of giving away the store, we draw your attention to one major difference between the dependencies in (6.4) and (6.5): the former specify key constraints for their corresponding relations whereas the latter do not.

However, simply knowing which dependencies cause the anomalies is not enough—we must do something about them. We cannot just abolish the offending FDs, because they are part of the semantics of the enterprise being modeled by the database. They are implicitly or explicitly part of the Requirements Document and cannot be changed without an agreement with the customer. On the other hand, we saw that schema decomposition can be a useful tool. Even though a decomposition cannot abolish a functional dependency, it can make it behave. For instance, the decomposition shown in (6.1) on page 195 yields schemas in which the offending FD, SSN → Name, Address, becomes a well-behaved key constraint.

6.4 Properties of Functional Dependencies

Before going any further, we need to learn some mathematical properties of functional dependencies and develop algorithms to test them. Since these properties and algorithms rely heavily on the notational conventions introduced at the beginning of Section 6.3, it might be a good idea to revisit these conventions.

The properties of FDs that we are going to study are based on *entailment*. Consider a set of attributes $\bar{R}$, a set, $\mathcal{F}$, of FDs over $\bar{R}$, and another FD, f, on $\bar{R}$. We say that $\mathcal{F}$ **entails** f if every relation **r** over the set of attributes $\bar{R}$ has the following property:

*If **r** satisfies every FD in $\mathcal{F}$, then **r** satisfies the FD f.*

Given a set of FDs, $\mathcal{F}$, the **closure** of $\mathcal{F}$, denoted $\mathcal{F}^+$, is the set of all FDs entailed by $\mathcal{F}$. Clearly, $\mathcal{F}^+$ contains $\mathcal{F}$ as a subset.[1]

If $\mathcal{F}$ and $\mathcal{G}$ are sets of FDs, we say that $\mathcal{F}$ **entails** $\mathcal{G}$ if $\mathcal{F}$ entails every individual FD in $\mathcal{G}$. $\mathcal{F}$ and $\mathcal{G}$ are said to be **equivalent** if $\mathcal{F}$ entails $\mathcal{G}$ and $\mathcal{G}$ entails $\mathcal{F}$.

Algorithm for computing a candidate key. Why should you care about entailment? For one, you will see that almost all design algorithms discussed in this section

---

[1] If $f \in \mathcal{F}$, then every relation that satisfies every FD in $\mathcal{F}$ obviously satisfies f. Therefore, by the definition of entailment, f is entailed by $\mathcal{F}$.

involve entailment in one way or another. Here is an immediate payoff, however—an algorithm for finding a candidate key in a relation schema. Let $\mathbf{R} = (\bar{R}, \mathcal{F})$ be a database schema with the set of attributes $\bar{R}$ and a set of FDs $\mathcal{F}$. Suppose that we know how to effectively check whether $\mathcal{F}$ entails an arbitrary FD (we will develop such an algorithm later). Then we can find a candidate key of $\mathbf{R}$ as follows: Pick up an arbitrary attribute, $A \in \bar{R}$, and check if $\mathcal{F}$ entails $(\bar{R} - A) \to \bar{R}$. If it does, we know that some candidate key hides inside $(\bar{R} - A)$. Remove another arbitrary attribute from what was left (let us denote the remaining set by X) and test that $X \to \bar{R}$ is still entailed by $\mathcal{F}$. If it does not, choose another attribute and test the same. Continue in this way trying to remove more and more attributes. The algorithm terminates when you cannot remove any attribute and still have $X \to \bar{R}$ entailed by $\mathcal{F}$. The remaining set of attributes must be a key.

The above algorithm works from the top down by eliminating attributes. There is also a bottom-up counterpart: start with an empty set of attributes and keep adding attributes until you find an X such that $X \to \bar{R}$ is entailed by $\mathcal{F}$. Can we find all keys in this way? The answer is yes, but not so quickly. There can be an exponential number of such keys, and insisting on finding all of them can cost you a lunch, dinner, and the next breakfast. One way, which is just slightly better than brute force, is to order all subsets of $\bar{R}$ by the amount of attributes in them and systematically apply the top-down algorithm or the bottom-up one until you cannot proceed any further. Each instance of the algorithm will discover some key. All the instances together will find all keys.

We now present several simple but important properties of entailment and later develop an algorithm for testing entailment.

Reflexivity. Some FDs are satisfied by every relation no matter what. These dependencies all have the form $\bar{X} \to \bar{Y}$, where $\bar{Y} \subseteq \bar{X}$, and are called **trivial** FDs.

- The reflexivity property states that, if $\bar{Y} \subseteq \bar{X}$, then $\bar{X} \to \bar{Y}$.

To see why trivial FDs are always satisfied, consider a relation, $\mathbf{r}$, whose set of attributes includes all of the attributes mentioned in $\bar{X}$. Suppose that $t, s \in \mathbf{r}$ are tuples that agree on $\bar{X}$. But, since $\bar{Y} \subseteq \bar{X}$, this means that t and s agree on $\bar{Y}$ as well. Thus, $\mathbf{r}$ satisfies $\bar{X} \to \bar{Y}$.

We can now relate trivial FDs and entailment. Because a trivial FD is satisfied by every relation, it is entailed by every set of FDs (even the empty set!). In particular, $\mathcal{F}^+$ contains every trivial FD.

Augmentation. Consider an FD, $\bar{X} \to \bar{Y}$, and another set of attributes, $\bar{Z}$. Let $\bar{R}$ contain $\bar{X} \cup \bar{Y} \cup \bar{Z}$. Then $\bar{X} \to \bar{Y}$ entails $\bar{X}\bar{Z} \to \bar{Y}\bar{Z}$. In other words, every relation $\mathbf{r}$ over $\bar{R}$ that satisfies $\bar{X} \to \bar{Y}$ must also satisfy the FD $\bar{X}\bar{Z} \to \bar{Y}\bar{Z}$.

- The augmentation property states that, if $\bar{X} \to \bar{Y}$, then $\bar{X}\bar{Z} \to \bar{Y}\bar{Z}$.

To see why this is true, observe that if tuples $t, s \in \mathbf{r}$ agree on every attribute of $\bar{X}\bar{Z}$ then in particular they agree on $\bar{X}$. Since $\mathbf{r}$ satisfies $\bar{X} \to \bar{Y}$, t and s must also agree on $\overline{Y}$. They also agree on $\overline{Z}$, since we have assumed that they agree on a bigger set of attributes, $\overline{X}\overline{Z}$. Thus, if s, t agree on every attribute in $\overline{X}\overline{Z}$, they must agree on $\overline{Y}\overline{Z}$. As this is an arbitrarily chosen pair of tuples in $\mathbf{r}$, it follows that $\mathbf{r}$ satisfies $\overline{X}\overline{Z} \to \overline{Y}\overline{Z}$.

Transitivity.   The set of FDs $\{\overline{X} \to \overline{Y},\ \overline{Y} \to \overline{Z}\}$ entails the FD $\overline{X} \to \overline{Z}$.

■   The transitivity property states that, if $\overline{X} \to \overline{Y}$ and $\overline{Y} \to \overline{Z}$, then $\overline{X} \to \overline{Z}$.

This property can be established similarly to the previous two (see the exercises at the end of the chapter).

These three properties of FDs are known as **Armstrong's axioms**; they are typically used as *inference rules* in the proofs of correctness of various database design algorithms. However, they are also a powerful tool used by (real, breathing, human) database designers because they can help spot problematic FDs in relational schemas. We now show how Armstrong's axioms are used to derive new FDs.

Union of FDs.   Any relation, $\mathbf{r}$, that satisfies $\overline{X} \to \overline{Y}$ and $\overline{X} \to \overline{Z}$ must also satisfy $\overline{X} \to \overline{Y}\overline{Z}$. To show this, we can derive $\overline{X} \to \overline{Y}\overline{Z}$ from $\overline{X} \to \overline{Y}$ and $\overline{X} \to \overline{Z}$ using simple syntactic manipulations defined by Armstrong's axioms. Such manipulations can be easily programmed on a computer, unlike the tuple-based considerations we used to establish the axioms themselves. Here is how it is done:

(a) $\overline{X} \to \overline{Y}$ Given

(b) $\overline{X} \to \overline{Z}$ Given

(c) $\overline{X} \to \overline{Y}\overline{X}$ Adding $\overline{X}$ to both sides of (a): Armstrong's augmentation rule

(d) $\overline{Y}\overline{X} \to \overline{Y}\overline{Z}$ Adding $\overline{Y}$ to both sides of (b): Armstrong's augmentation rule

(e) $\overline{X} \to \overline{Y}\overline{Z}$ By Armstrong's transitivity rule, applied to (c) and (d)

Decomposition of FDs.   In a similar way, we can prove the following rule: every relation that satisfies $\overline{X} \to \overline{Y}\overline{Z}$ must also satisfy the FDs $\overline{X} \to \overline{Y}$ and $\overline{X} \to \overline{Z}$. This is accomplished by the following simple steps:

(a) $\overline{X} \to \overline{Y}\overline{Z}$ Given

(b) $\overline{Y}\overline{Z} \to \overline{Y}$ By Armstrong's reflexivity rule, since $\overline{Y} \subseteq \overline{Y}\overline{Z}$

(c) $\overline{X} \to \overline{Y}$ By transitivity from (a) and (b)

Derivation of $\overline{X} \to \overline{Z}$ is similar.

Brain Teaser: What kind of FD is $X \to Y$, if Y is an empty set of attributes?

Armstrong's axioms are obviously *sound*. By **sound** we mean that any expression of the form $\overline{X} \to \overline{Y}$ derived using the axioms from a set of FDs $\mathcal{F}$ is actually a functional dependency that holds in any relation that satisfies every FD in $\mathcal{F}$. Soundness follows from the fact that we have proved that these inference rules are valid for every relation. It is much less obvious, however, that they are also **complete**—that is, if a set of FDs, $\mathcal{F}$, entails another FD, f, then f can be derived from $\mathcal{F}$ by a sequence of steps, similar to the ones above, that rely solely on Armstrong's axioms! For the curious, we provide a proof of this fact at the end of this section.

Note that the definition of entailment of FDs on page 200 does not even hint at an algorithm for checking entailment (i.e., for testing whether $f \in \mathcal{F}^+$). The definition is completely *semantic* in nature and, according to the definition, testing $f \in \mathcal{F}^+$ involves perusing an infinite number of relations. In contrast, Armstrong's axioms provide *syntactic* manipulations that can be carried out by a computer.

Of course, not all syntactic manipulations make sense. For instance, deleting attribute A from every FD does not. However, if the manipulations are sound and complete, then using them is *correct* and is *equivalent* to using the definition of entailment. Thus, soundness and completeness of Armstrong's axioms is not just a theoretical curiosity—this result has considerable practical value because it guarantees that entailment of FDs can be verified by a computer program. We are now going to develop one such algorithm (and a better one later).

Naive algorithm for checking entailment. An obvious way to verify entailment of an FD, f, by a set of FDs, $\mathcal{F}$, is to instruct the computer to apply Armstrong's axioms to $\mathcal{F}$ in all possible ways. Since the number of attributes mentioned in $\mathcal{F}$ and f is finite, this derivation process cannot go on forever. When we are satisfied that all possible derivations have been made, we can simply check whether f is among the FDs derived by this process. Completeness of Armstrong's axioms guarantees that $f \in \mathcal{F}^+$ if and only if f is one of the FDs thus derived.

Example 6.4.1 (Entailment Checking with Armstrong's Axioms). To see how this process works, consider the following sets of FDs: $\mathcal{F} = \{AC \rightarrow B, A \rightarrow C, D \rightarrow A\}$ and $\mathcal{G} = \{A \rightarrow B, A \rightarrow C, D \rightarrow A, D \rightarrow B\}$. We can use Armstrong's axioms to prove that these two sets are equivalent, that is, that every FD in $\mathcal{G}$ is entailed by $\mathcal{F}$, and vice versa. For instance, to prove that $A \rightarrow B$ is implied by $\mathcal{F}$, we can apply Armstrong's axioms in all possible ways. Most of these attempts will not lead anywhere, but a few will. For instance, the following derivation establishes the desired entailment:

(a) $A \rightarrow C$ An FD in $\mathcal{F}$

(b) $A \rightarrow AC$ From (a) and Armstrong's augmentation axiom

(c) $A \rightarrow B$ From (b), $AC \rightarrow B \in \mathcal{F}$, and Armstrong's transitivity axiom

The FDs $A \rightarrow C$ and $D \rightarrow A$ belong to both $\mathcal{F}$ and $\mathcal{G}$, so the derivation is trivial. For $D \rightarrow B$ in $\mathcal{G}$, the computer can try to apply Armstrong's axioms until this FD is derived. After awhile, it will stumble upon this valid derivation:

(a) $D \rightarrow A$ an FD in $\mathcal{F}$

(b) $A \rightarrow B$ derived previously

(c) $D \rightarrow B$ from (a), (b), and Armstrong's transitivity axiom

This shows that every FD in $\mathcal{F}$ entailed by $\mathcal{G}$ is done similarly. ∎

Although the simplicity of checking entailment by blindly applying Armstrong's axioms is attractive, it is not very efficient. In fact, the size of $\mathcal{F}^+$ can be exponential in the size of $\mathcal{F}$, so for large database schemas it can take a very long time before the designer ever sees the result. We are therefore going to develop a more efficient algorithm, which is also based on Armstrong's axioms but which applies them much more judiciously.

Checking entailment of FDs using attribute closure.   The idea of the new algorithm for verifying entailment is based on the concept of *attribute closure*.

Given a set of FDs, $\mathcal{F}$, and a set of attributes, $\overline{X}$, we define the **attribute closure** of $\overline{X}$ with respect to $\mathcal{F}$, denoted $\overline{X}_{\mathcal{F}}^+$, as follows:

$$\overline{X}_{\mathcal{F}}^+ = \{A \mid \overline{X} \to A \in \mathcal{F}^+\}$$

In other words, $\overline{X}_{\mathcal{F}}^+$ is a set of all those attributes, A, such that $\overline{X} \to A$ is entailed by $\mathcal{F}$. Note that $\overline{X} \subseteq \overline{X}_{\mathcal{F}}^+$ because, if $A \in \overline{X}$, then, by Armstrong's reflexivity axiom, $\overline{X} \to A$ is a trivial FD that is entailed by every set of FDs, including $\mathcal{F}$.

It is important to keep in mind that the closure of $\mathcal{F}$ (i.e., $\mathcal{F}^+$) and the closure of $\overline{X}$ (i.e., $\overline{X}_{\mathcal{F}}^+$) are related but *very different* notions: $\mathcal{F}^+$ is a set of functional dependencies, whereas $\overline{X}_{\mathcal{F}}^+$ is a set of attributes.

> Always true: $\overline{X} \subseteq \overline{X}_{\mathcal{F}}^+$ and $\mathcal{F} \subseteq \mathcal{F}^+$

Example 6.4.2 (Attribute Closure).   Let $\mathcal{F} = \{B \to E, C \to F, BD \to G\}$. Then the attribute closure of ABC with respect to $\mathcal{F}$ is $ABCEF$.

To see this, you can verify by direct inspection that $\mathcal{F}$ entails $ABCEF \to x$, where x is A, B, C, E, or F. You can also verify that $\mathcal{F}$ does *not* entail $ABCEF \to y$, where y is any other attribute. A standard method to prove such a negative result is to construct the following relation as a counterexample:

```
 A B C E F  D G ... y ...
-----------------------------
 0 0 0 0 0  0 0  ... 0 ... 0
 0 0 0 0 0  1 1  ... 1 ... 1
```

It obviously does not satisfy $ABCEF \to y$, but it does satisfy every FD in $\mathcal{F}$. Therefore $\mathcal{F}$ does not entail $ABCEF \to y$. ∎

If we knew how to compute attribute closure efficiently, we could check FD entailment using the following algorithm: Given a set of FDs, $\mathcal{F}$, and an FD, $\overline{X} \to \overline{Y}$, check whether $\overline{Y} \subseteq \overline{X}_{\mathcal{F}}^+$. If this is so, then $\mathcal{F}$ entails $\overline{X} \to \overline{Y}$. Otherwise, if $\overline{Y} \not\subseteq \overline{X}_{\mathcal{F}}^+$, then $\mathcal{F}$ does not entail $\overline{X} \to \overline{Y}$.

The correctness of this algorithm follows from Armstrong's axioms. If $\overline{Y} \subseteq \overline{X}_{\mathcal{F}}^+$, then $\overline{X} \to A \in \mathcal{F}^+$ for every $A \in \overline{Y}$ (by the definition of $\overline{X}_{\mathcal{F}}^+$). By the union rule for FDs,

FIGURE 6.3 Computation of attribute closure $\overline{X}_{\mathcal{F}}^+$.

$$
\begin{aligned}
&closure := \overline{X} \\
&\textbf{repeat} \\
&\qquad old := closure \\
&\qquad \textbf{if } \text{there is an FD } \overline{Z} \rightarrow \overline{V} \in \mathcal{F} \text{ such that } \overline{Z} \subseteq closure \text{ and } \overline{V} \not\subseteq closure \ \textbf{then} \\
&\qquad\qquad closure := closure \cup \overline{V} \\
&\textbf{until } \ old = closure \\
&\textbf{return } closure
\end{aligned}
$$

it follows that $\mathcal{F}$ entails $\overline{X} \rightarrow \overline{Y}$. Conversely, if $\overline{Y} \not\subseteq \overline{X}_{\mathcal{F}}^+$, then there is $B \in \overline{Y}$ such that $B \notin \overline{X}_{\mathcal{F}}^+$. Hence, $\overline{X} \rightarrow B$ is not entailed by $\mathcal{F}$. But then $\mathcal{F}$ cannot entail $\overline{X} \rightarrow \overline{Y}$. If it did, it would have to entail $\overline{X} \rightarrow B$ as well, by the decomposition rule for FDs.

The heart of the above algorithm is a check of whether a set of attributes belongs to $\overline{X}_{\mathcal{F}}^+$. Therefore, we are not done yet. We need an algorithm for computing the closure of $\overline{X}$, which we present in Figure 6.3. The idea behind the algorithm is to enlarge the set of attributes known to belong to $\overline{X}_{\mathcal{F}}^+$ by applying the FDs in $\mathcal{F}$. The closure is initialized to $\overline{X}$, since we know that $\overline{X}$ is always a subset of $\overline{X}_{\mathcal{F}}^+$.

The soundness of the algorithm can be proved by induction. Initially, *closure* is $\overline{X}$, so $\overline{X} \rightarrow closure$ is in $\mathcal{F}^+$. Then, assuming that $\overline{X} \rightarrow closure \in \mathcal{F}^+$ at some intermediate step in the **repeat** loop of Figure 6.3, and given an FD $\overline{Z} \rightarrow \overline{V} \in \mathcal{F}$ such that $\overline{Z} \subset closure$, we can use the *generalized transitivity rule* (see Exercise 6.10) to infer that $\mathcal{F}$ entails $\overline{X} \rightarrow closure \cup \overline{V}$. Thus, if $A \in closure$ at the end of the computation, then $A \in \overline{X}_{\mathcal{F}}^+$. The converse is also true: if $A \in \overline{X}_{\mathcal{F}}^+$, then at the end of the computation $A \in closure$ (see Exercise 6.11).

Unlike the simple-minded algorithm that uses Armstrong's axioms indiscriminately, the run-time complexity of the algorithm in Figure 6.3 is quadratic in the size of $\mathcal{F}$. In fact, an algorithm for computing $\overline{X}_{\mathcal{F}}^+$ that is *linear* in the size of $\mathcal{F}$ is given in [Beeri and Bernstein 1979]. This algorithm is better suited for a computer program, but its inner workings are more complex.

Example 6.4.3 (Checking Entailment). Consider a relational schema, $\mathbf{R} = (\overline{R};\ \mathcal{F})$, where $\overline{R} = ABCDEFGHIJ$, and the set of FDs, $\mathcal{F}$, which contains the following FDs: $AB \rightarrow C$, $D \rightarrow E$, $AE \rightarrow G$, $GD \rightarrow H$, $ID \rightarrow J$. We wish to check whether $\mathcal{F}$ entails $ABD \rightarrow GH$ and $ABD \rightarrow HJ$.

First, let us compute $ABD_{\mathcal{F}}^+$. We begin with *closure* = ABD. Two FDs can be used in the first iteration of the loop in Figure 6.3. For definiteness, let us use $AB \rightarrow C$, which makes *closure* = $ABDC$. In the second iteration, we can use $D \rightarrow E$, which makes *closure* = $ABDCE$. Now it becomes possible to use the FD $AE \rightarrow G$ in the third iteration, yielding *closure* = $ABDCEG$. This in turn allows $GD \rightarrow H$ to be applied in the fourth iteration, which results in *closure* = $ABDCEGH$. In the fifth iteration, we cannot apply any new FDs, so *closure* does not change and the loop terminates. Thus, $ABD_{\mathcal{F}}^+ = ABDCEGH$.

FIGURE **6.4** Testing equivalence of sets of FDs.

Input: $\mathcal{F}$, $\mathcal{G}$ – FD sets
Output: *true*, if $\mathcal{F}$ is equivalent to $\mathcal{G}$; *false* otherwise
for each $f \in \mathcal{F}$ do
    if $\mathcal{G}$ does not entail f then return *false*
for each $g \in \mathcal{G}$ do
    if $\mathcal{F}$ does not entail g then return *false*
return *true*

Since $GH \subseteq ABDCEGH$, we conclude that $\mathcal{F}$ entails $ABD \to GH$. On the other hand, $HJ \not\subseteq ABDCEGH$, so we conclude that $ABD \to HJ$ is not entailed by $\mathcal{F}$. Note, however, that $\mathcal{F}$ does entail $ABD \to H$. ∎

The above algorithm for testing entailment leads to a simple test for equivalence between a pair of sets of FDs. Let $\mathcal{F}$ and $\mathcal{G}$ be such sets. To check that they are equivalent, we must check that every FD in $\mathcal{G}$ is entailed by $\mathcal{F}$, and vice versa. The algorithm is depicted in Figure 6.4.

Proof of completeness of Armstrong's axioms. * Suppose that an FD $f : X \to A$ is entailed by a set of FDs $\mathcal{F}$, but there is no derivation of f from $\mathcal{F}$ based on Armstrong's axioms. We will show that then there must be a relation, **r**, that satisfies every FD in $\mathcal{F}$, but not f. This would be a contradiction since we assumed that f is entailed by $\mathcal{F}$.

Let the relation **r** consist of just two tuples, t_0 and t_1, where t_0 has 0 in every position and t_1 has 0 for every attribute in the set

$$\widehat{X} = \{B \mid X \to B \text{ can be derived from } \mathcal{F} \text{ using Armstrong's axioms}\}$$

and 1 everywhere else:

$\widehat{X}$	other attributes
t_0: 0 0 0 0 0	0 0 0 0 0 0 . . .
t_1: 0 0 0 0 0	1 1 1 1 1 1 . . .

Note that the set $\widehat{X}$ is similar to the attribute closure $\overline{X}_{\mathcal{F}}^+$ except that instead of using every $\overline{X} \to B$ that is *entailed* by $\mathcal{F}$ we consider only those that are *derivable* from $\mathcal{F}$. Because of the soundness of Armstrong's axioms, every derivable FD is entailed by $\mathcal{F}$, so $\widehat{X} \subseteq \overline{X}_{\mathcal{F}}^+$. In fact, the two sets are equal, but we do not know this yet because we have not proved the completeness of the axioms.

Let us note a few simple properties of $\widehat{X}$. First, $\overline{X} \subseteq \widehat{X}$, because $\overline{X} \to B$ is Armstrong's reflexivity axiom for every $B \in \overline{X}$. Second, since we assumed that $f : X \to A$ is not derivable from $\mathcal{F}$, the attribute A is not in $\widehat{X}$. Therefore, t_0 and t_1 have different values over A and so f is violated in **r**. Thus, if we show that every FD in $\mathcal{F}$ holds in **r**, then we will arrive at a contradiction with the assumption that $\mathcal{F}$ entails f.

So, let us prove that every $g : \overline{Y} \to C \in \mathcal{F}$ holds in **r**.

- If $\overline{Y} \subseteq \widehat{X}$ then C must be in $\widehat{X}$. Indeed, $\overline{Y} \subseteq \widehat{X}$ implies that the FD $\overline{X} \to \overline{Y}$ is derivable from $\mathcal{F}$ using Armstrong's axioms. (Proving this is left as a simple exercise.) Therefore, $\overline{X} \to C$ can be derived from $\overline{X} \to \overline{Y}$ and g by Armstrong's transitivity rule. By the definition of $\widehat{X}$, C must be in $\widehat{X}$; and since t_0 and t_1 have the same value 0 over all attributes of $\widehat{X}$, it follows that the FD g is satisfied in **r**.

- If $\overline{Y} \not\subseteq \widehat{X}$ then the tuples t_0 and t_1 have different values over some attributes in $\overline{Y}$, so they do not have to agree over C. In this case, g is satisfied in **r** in a trivial manner.

Since g was chosen arbitrarily, the above establishes that every FD in $\mathcal{F}$ is satisfied by **r**, which completes the proof.

6.5 Normal Forms

To eliminate redundancy and potential update anomalies, database theory identifies several *normal forms* for relational schemas such that, if a schema is in one of the normal forms, it has certain predictable properties. Each normal form is characterized by a set of restrictions. Thus, for a schema to be in a normal form it must satisfy the restrictions associated with that form. Originally, [Codd 1970] proposed three normal forms, each successively imposing more restrictions and eliminating more and more anomalies and redundancies than the previous one.

The **first normal form** (**1NF**), as introduced by Codd, is equivalent to the definition of the relational data model. In particular, the value of an attribute must be atomic. It cannot be anything that has structure, such as a record (with multiple fields) or a set. The **second normal form** (**2NF**) says that a schema must not have an FD, $X \to Y$, where X is a strict subset of that schema's key. This normal form is of no practical use, and we do not discuss it any further.

The **third normal form** (**3NF**) was initially thought to be the "ultimate" normal form. However, Boyce and Codd soon realized that 3NF can still harbor undesirable combinations of functional dependencies, so they introduced the **Boyce-Codd normal form** (**BCNF**). Unfortunately, there is rarely a free lunch in computational sciences. Even though BCNF is more desirable, it is not always achievable without paying a price elsewhere. In this section, we define both BCNF and 3NF. Subsequent sections in this chapter develop algorithms for automatically converting relational schemas that possess various bad properties into sets of schemas in 3NF and BCNF. We also study the trade-offs associated with such conversions.

In Section 6.9, we show that certain types of redundancy are caused by dependencies other than the FDs. To deal with this problem, we introduce the **fourth normal form** (**4NF**), which further extends BCNF.

FIGURE 6.5 Relationship among normal forms.

The relationship between the different normal forms is depicted in Figure 6.5. The higher normal forms (to the right) impose more restrictions on relational schemas, and this ensures that the corresponding relations have less redundant information. Note that as we go to the left, restrictions become weaker, and thus any relation schema that satisfies the conditions of a higher normal form also satisfies the conditions of the lower. The figure also shows that the lower normal forms can always be achieved, while the higher ones can be achieved only at a certain price. You will learn what all this means in the remainder of this chapter.

6.5.1 The Boyce-Codd Normal Form

A relational schema, $\mathbf{R} = (\overline{R};\ \mathcal{F})$, where $\overline{R}$ is the set of attributes of $\mathbf{R}$ and $\mathcal{F}$ is the set of functional dependencies associated with $\mathbf{R}$, is in Boyce-Codd normal form if, for every FD $\overline{X} \rightarrow \overline{Y} \in \mathcal{F}$, either of the following is true:

- $\overline{Y} \subseteq \overline{X}$ (i.e., this is a trivial FD).
- $\overline{X}$ is a superkey of $\mathbf{R}$.

In other words, the only nontrivial FDs are those in which a key functionally determines one or more attributes.

Examples. It is easy to see that PERSON1 and HOBBY, the relational schemas given in (6.1), are in BCNF, because the only nontrivial FD is SSN → Name, Address. It applies to PERSON1, which has SSN as a key.

On the other hand, consider the schema PERSON defined by the CREATE TABLE statement (4.1), page 87, and the schema HASACCOUNT defined by the SQL statement (6.3), page 197. As discussed earlier, these statements fail to capture some important relationships, which are represented by the FDs in (6.5), page 199. Each of these FDs is in violation of the requirement to be in BCNF. They are not trivial, and their left-hand sides—SSN and AccountNumber—are not keys of their respective schemas.

Properties of BCNF. Note that a BCNF schema can have more than one key. For instance, $\mathbf{R} = (ABCD;\ \mathcal{F})$, where $\mathcal{F} = \{AB \rightarrow CD,\ AC \rightarrow BD\}$ has two keys, AB and AC. And yet it is in BCNF because the left-hand side of each of the two FDs in $\mathcal{F}$ is a key.

Observe that we defined BCNF by looking only at the set of FDs in $\mathcal{F}$, not $\mathcal{F}^+$. One might wonder, therefore, whether $\mathcal{F}^+ - \mathcal{F}$ might have any FDs that violate BCNF, in which case this normal form will not make much sense. Fortunately, the above situation cannot occur. To see this, consider an arbitrary FD $\overline{X} \to A \in (\mathcal{F}^+ - \mathcal{F})$ such that $A \notin \overline{X}$. As we know, it must be the case that $A \in \overline{X}^+_{\mathcal{F}}$ and $\overline{X}^+_{\mathcal{F}}$ should be computable by the attribute closure algorithm in Figure 6.3. Recall that the main step in that algorithm hinges on being able to find an FD $\overline{Z} \to \overline{V} \in \mathcal{F}$ such that $\overline{Z} \subseteq closure$. Since initially $closure = \overline{X}$, there must be an FD in $\mathcal{F}$ whose left-hand side, $\overline{Z}$, is a subset of $\overline{X}$. But since the schema is in BCNF, $\overline{Z}$ must be a superkey. Hence, so must be $\overline{X}$, that is, the FD $\overline{X} \to A$ does not violate the BCNF conditions.

Nonredundancy of BCNF. An important property of BCNF schemas is that their instances do not contain redundant information that arises due to FDs. Since we have been illustrating redundancy problems only through concrete examples, the above statement might seem vague. Exactly what is redundant information? For instance, does the abstract relation

A	B	C	D
1	1	3	4
2	1	3	4

over the above-mentioned BCNF schema **R** store redundant information?

Superficially it might seem so because the two tuples agree on all but one at-tribute. However, having identical values in some attributes of different tuples does not necessarily imply that the tuples are storing redundant information. Redun-dancy arises when the values of some set of attributes, $\overline{X}$, necessarily implies the value that must exist in another attribute, A—a functional dependency. If two dis-tinct tuples have the same values in $\overline{X}$, they must have the same value of A. This means that an association between A and the attributes in $\overline{X}$ is stored multiple times. Redundancy is eliminated if we store such an association only once (in a separate relation) instead of repeating it in all tuples of an instance of the schema **R** that agree on $\overline{X}$. Since **R** does not have FDs over the attributes BCD, no redundant information is stored. The fact that the tuples in the relation coincide over BCD is coincidental. For instance, the value of attribute D in the first tuple can be changed from 4 to 5 without regard for the second tuple.

A DBMS automatically eliminates one type of redundancy. Two tuples with the same values in the key fields are prohibited in any instance of a schema. This is a special case. The key identifies an entity and so determines the values of all attributes describing that entity. As the definition of BCNF precludes associations that do not contain keys, the relations over BCNF schemas do not store redundant information. As a result, deletion and update anomalies do not arise in BCNF relations.

Relations with more than one key still can have insertion anomalies. To see this, suppose that associations over *ABD* and over *ACD* are added to our relation as shown:

A	B	C	D
1	1	3	4
2	1	3	4
3	4	NULL	5
3	NULL	2	5

Because the value over the attribute *C* in the first association and over *B* in the second is unknown, we fill in the missing information with NULL. However, now we cannot tell if the two newly added tuples are the same—it all depends on the real values for the nulls. A practical solution to this problem, as adopted by the SQL standard, is to designate one key as *primary* and to prohibit null values in its attributes. Under this restriction, every tuple is defined over the attributes of the primary key and, in particular, the above situation with newly added tuples is impossible.

6.5.2 The Third Normal Form

A relational schema, $\mathbf{R} = (\bar{R};\ \mathcal{F})$, where $\bar{R}$ is the set of attributes of **R** and $\mathcal{F}$ is the set of functional dependencies associated with **R**, is in **third normal form** if, for every FD $\bar{X} \to \bar{Y} \in \mathcal{F}$, any of the following conditions are true:

■ $\bar{Y} \subseteq \bar{X}$ (i.e., this is a trivial FD).

■ $\bar{X}$ is a superkey of **R**.

■   Each attribute in $A \in \bar{Y} - \bar{X}$ belongs to some candidate key, $\bar{K}$, of **R**.

Observe that the first two conditions in the definition of 3NF are identical to the conditions that define BCNF. Thus, 3NF is a relaxation of BCNF's requirements. Every schema that is in BCNF must also be in 3NF, but the converse is not true in general. For instance, the relation HASACCOUNT (6.3) on page 197 is in 3NF because the only FD that is not based on a key constraint is AccountNumber → OfficeId, and OfficeId is part of the key. However, this relation is not in BCNF, as shown previously.[2]

If you are wondering about the intrinsic merit of the third condition in the definition of 3NF, the answer is that there is none. In a way, 3NF was discovered by accident—in the search for what we now call BCNF! The reason for the remarkable survival of 3NF is that it was later found to have some very desirable algorithmic properties, which BCNF does not possess. We discuss these issues in subsequent sections.

---

[2] In fact, HASACCOUNT is the *smallest* possible example of a 3NF relation that is not in BCNF (see Exercise 6.5).

Brain Teaser: Find a 2NF relation that is not in 3NF.

Redundancy in 3NF.   Recall from Section 6.2 that relation instances over HAS-ACCOUNT might store redundant information. Now we can see that this redundancy arises because of the functional dependency that relates AccountNumber and OfficeId and that is not implied by key constraints.

For another example, consider the schema PERSON discussed earlier. This schema violates the 3NF requirements because, for example, the FD SSN → Name is not based on a key constraint (SSN is not a superkey) and Name does not belong to a key of PERSON. However, the decomposition of this schema into PERSON1 and HOBBY in (6.1), page 195, yields a pair of schemas that are in both 3NF and BCNF.

We can ask the same question as in the case of BCNF: is it possible that some FD in $\mathcal{F}^+ - \mathcal{F}$ violates the 3NF conditions, thereby making this normal form ill-defined? It is easy to guess that the answer is "no," for, otherwise, 3NF would not be worth including in a textbook. However, proving this is a notch harder than in the case of BCNF, so we leave it to Exercise 6.25.

6.6 Properties of Decompositions

Since there is no redundancy in BCNF schemas and redundancy in 3NF is limited, we are interested in decomposing a given schema into a collection of schemas, each of which is in one of these normal forms.

The main thrust of the discussion in the previous section was that 3NF does not completely solve the redundancy problem. Therefore, at first glance, there appears to be no justification to consider 3NF as a goal for database design. It turns out, however, that the maintenance problems associated with redundancy do not show the whole picture. As we will see, maintenance is also associated with integrity constraints,[3] and 3NF decompositions sometimes have better properties in this regard than do BCNF decompositions. Our first step is to define these properties.

Recall from Section 6.2 that not all decompositions are created equal. For instance, the decomposition of PERSON shown in (6.1) is considered good while the one in (6.2) makes no sense. Is there an objective way to tell which decompositions make sense and which do not, and can this objective way be explained to a computer? The answer to both questions is "yes." The decompositions that make sense are called *lossless*. Before tackling this notion, we need to be more precise about what we mean by a decomposition in the first place.

A **decomposition of a schema**, $\mathbf{R} = (\overline{R};\ \mathcal{F})$, where $\overline{R}$ is a set of attributes of the schema and $\mathcal{F}$ is its set of functional dependencies, is a collection of schemas

$$\mathbf{R}_1 = (\overline{R}_1; \mathcal{F}_1), \mathbf{R}_2 = (\overline{R}_2; \mathcal{F}_2), \ldots, \mathbf{R}_n = (\overline{R}_n; \mathcal{F}_n)$$

---

[3] For example, a particular integrity constraint in the original table might be checkable in the decomposed tables only by taking the join of these tables—which results in significant overhead at run time.

such that the following conditions hold:

1. $R_i \neq R_j$, if $i \neq j$
2. $\overline{R} = \cup_{i=1}^{n} \overline{R}_i$
3. $\mathcal{F}$ entails $\mathcal{F}_i$ for every $i = 1, \dots, n$.

The first part of the definition is clear: a decomposition should not introduce new attributes, and it should not drop attributes found in the original schema. The second part of the definition says that a decomposition should not introduce new functional dependencies (but may drop some). We discuss the second requirement in more detail later.

The decomposition of a schema naturally leads to decomposition of relations over it. A **decomposition of a relation**, $\mathbf{r}$, defined over schema $\mathbf{R}$, relative to a schema decomposition $\mathbf{R}_1 = (\overline{R}_1; \mathcal{F}_1), \dots, \mathbf{R}_n = (\overline{R}_n; \mathcal{F}_n)$ is a set of relations

$$\mathbf{r}_1 = \pi_{\overline{R}_1}(\mathbf{r}), \mathbf{r}_2 = \pi_{\overline{R}_2}(\mathbf{r}), \dots, \mathbf{r}_n = \pi_{\overline{R}_n}(\mathbf{r})$$

where π is the projection operator. It can be shown (see Exercise 6.12) that, if $\mathbf{r}$ is a valid instance of $\mathbf{R}$, then each $\mathbf{r}_i$ satisfies all FDs in $\mathcal{F}_i$ and thus each $\mathbf{r}_i$ is a valid relation instance over the schema $\mathbf{R}_i$. The purpose of a decomposition is to replace the original relation, $\mathbf{r}$, with a set of relations $\mathbf{r}_1, \dots, \mathbf{r}_n$ over the schemas that constitute the decomposed schema.

In view of the above definitions, it is important to realize that *schema decomposition* and *relation instance decomposition* are two different (but related) notions—the former is a set of relation schemas, while the latter is a set of relation instances.

Example 6.6.1 (Decomposition).   Applying the above definitions to our running example, we see that splitting PERSON into PERSON1 and HOBBY (see (6.1) and Figure 6.1 on page 195) yields a decomposition. Splitting PERSON as shown in (6.2) and Figure 6.2 is also a decomposition in the above sense. It clearly satisfies the first requirement for being a decomposition. It also satisfies the second since only trivial FDs hold in (6.2), and these are entailed by every set of dependencies.   ∎

This last example shows that the above definition of a decomposition does not capture all of the desirable properties of a decomposition because, as you may recall from Section 6.2, the decomposition in (6.2) makes no sense. In the following section, we introduce additional desirable properties of decompositions.

6.6.1 Lossless and Lossy Decompositions

Consider a relation, $\mathbf{r}$, and its decomposition, $\mathbf{r}_1, \dots, \mathbf{r}_n$, as defined above. Since after the decomposition the database no longer stores the relation $\mathbf{r}$ and instead maintains its projections $\mathbf{r}_1, \dots, \mathbf{r}_n$, the database must be able to reconstruct the original relation $\mathbf{r}$ from these projections. Not being able to reconstruct $\mathbf{r}$ means that the decomposition does not represent the same information as does the original database (imagine a bank losing the information about who owns which account or, worse, associating those accounts with the wrong owners!).

In principle, one can use any computational method that guarantees reconstruction of **r** from its projections. However, the natural and, in most cases, practical method is the natural join. We thus assume that **r** is reconstructible if and only if

$$\mathbf{r} = \mathbf{r}_1 \bowtie \mathbf{r}_2 \bowtie \cdots \bowtie \mathbf{r}_n$$

Reconstructibility must be a property of schema decomposition and not of a particular instance over this schema. At the database design stage, the designer manipulates schemas, not relations, and any transformation performed on a schema must guarantee that reconstructibility holds for all of its valid relation instances.

This discussion leads to the following notion. A decomposition of schema $\mathbf{R} = (\overline{R};\ \mathcal{F})$ into a collection of schemas

$$\mathbf{R}_1 = (\overline{R}_1;\ \mathcal{F}_1),\ \mathbf{R}_2 = (\overline{R}_2;\ \mathcal{F}_2),\ \ldots,\ \mathbf{R}_n = (\overline{R}_n;\ \mathcal{F}_n)$$

is **lossless** if, for *every* valid instance **r** of schema **R**,

$$\mathbf{r} \ = \ \mathbf{r}_1 \bowtie \mathbf{r}_2 \bowtie \cdots \bowtie \mathbf{r}_n$$

where

$$\mathbf{r}_1 = \pi_{\overline{R}_1}(\mathbf{r}),\ \mathbf{r}_2 = \pi_{\overline{R}_2}(\mathbf{r}),\ \ldots,\ \mathbf{r}_n = \pi_{\overline{R}_n}(\mathbf{r})$$

A decomposition is **lossy** otherwise.

In plain terms, a lossless schema decomposition is one that guarantees that any valid instance of the original schema can be reconstructed from its projections on the individual schemas of the decomposition. Note that

$$\mathbf{r} \subseteq \mathbf{r}_1 \bowtie \mathbf{r}_2 \bowtie \cdots \bowtie \mathbf{r}_n$$

holds for *any* decomposition whatsoever (Exercise 6.13), so losslessness really just asserts the opposite inclusion:

$$\mathbf{r} \supseteq \mathbf{r}_1 \bowtie \mathbf{r}_1 \bowtie \cdots \bowtie \mathbf{r}_n$$

The fact that

$$\mathbf{r} \subseteq \mathbf{r}_1 \bowtie \mathbf{r}_2 \bowtie \cdots \bowtie \mathbf{r}_n$$

holds, no matter what, may seem confusing at first. If we can get more tuples by joining the projections of **r**, why is such a decomposition called lossy? After all, we gained more tuples—not less! To clarify this issue, observe that what we might lose here are not tuples but rather information about *which tuples are the right ones*. Consider, for instance, the decomposition (6.2) of schema PERSON on page 196. Figure 6.2 presents the corresponding decomposition of a valid relation instance over PERSON shown in Figure 4.13. However, if we now compute a natural join of the relations in the decomposition (which becomes a Cartesian product since these relations do not share attributes), we will not be able to tell who lives where and who has what hobbies. The relationship among names and SSNs is also lost. In other words, when reconstructing the original relation, getting more tuples is as bad as getting fewer—we must get *exactly* the set of tuples in the original relation.

Now that we are convinced of the importance of losslessness, we need an algorithm that a computer can use to verify this property since the definition of lossless joins does not provide an effective test but only tells us to try every possible relation. This is neither feasible nor efficient.

A general test of whether a decomposition into n schemas is lossless exists but is somewhat complex. It can be found in [Beeri et al. 1981]. However, there is a much simpler test that works for binary decompositions, that is, decompositions into a pair of schemas. This test can establish losslessness of a decomposition into more than two schemas provided that this decomposition was obtained by a series of binary decompositions. Since most decompositions are obtained in this way, the simple binary test introduced below is sufficient for most practical purposes.

Testing the losslessness of a binary decomposition. Let $\mathbf{R} = (\bar{R};\ \mathcal{F})$ be a schema and $\mathbf{R}_1 = (\bar{R}_1;\ \mathcal{F}_1)$, $\mathbf{R}_2 = (\bar{R}_2;\ \mathcal{F}_2)$ be a binary decomposition of $\mathbf{R}$. This decomposition is lossless if and only if either of the following is true:

- $(\bar{R}_1 \cap \bar{R}_2) \to \bar{R}_1 \in \mathcal{F}^+$.
- $(\bar{R}_1 \cap \bar{R}_2) \to \bar{R}_2 \in \mathcal{F}^+$.

To see why this is so, suppose that $(\bar{R}_1 \cap \bar{R}_2) \to \bar{R}_2 \in \mathcal{F}^+$. Then $\bar{R}_1$ is a superkey of **R** since, by augmentation with $\bar{R}_1$, we can derive $\bar{R}_1 \to \bar{R}_1 \cup \bar{R}_2$, and $\bar{R} = \bar{R}_1 \cup \bar{R}_2$. Let **r** be a valid relation instance for **R**. Since $\bar{R}_1$ is a superkey of $\bar{R}$ every tuple in $\mathbf{r}_1 = \pi_{\bar{R}_1}(\mathbf{r})$ extends to exactly one tuple in **r**. Thus, as depicted in Figure 6.6, the cardinality (the number of tuples) in $\mathbf{r}_1$ equals the cardinality of **r**, and every tuple in $\mathbf{r}_1$ joins with exactly one tuple in $\mathbf{r}_2 = \pi_{\bar{R}_2}(\mathbf{r})$ (if more than one tuple in $\mathbf{r}_2$ joined with a tuple in $\mathbf{r}_1$, the FD $(\bar{R}_1 \cap \bar{R}_2) \to \bar{R}_2$ would not be satisfied in $\mathbf{r}_2$). Therefore, the cardinality of $\mathbf{r}_1 \bowtie \mathbf{r}_2$ equals the cardinality of $\mathbf{r}_1$, which in turn equals the cardinality of **r**. Since **r** must be a subset of $\mathbf{r}_1 \bowtie \mathbf{r}_2$, it follows that $\mathbf{r} = \mathbf{r}_1 \bowtie \mathbf{r}_2$. Conversely, if neither of the above FDs holds, it is easy to construct a relation **r** such that $\mathbf{r} \subset \mathbf{r}_1 \bowtie \mathbf{r}_2$. Details of this construction are left to Exercise 6.14.

The above test can now be used to substantiate our intuition that the decomposition (6.1) of PERSON into PERSON1 and HOBBY is a good one. The intersection of the attributes of HOBBY and PERSON1 is {SSN}, and SSN is a key of PERSON1. Thus, this decomposition is lossless.

Note that this test can be used to verify losslessness of certain decompositions into three or more schemas. Indeed, it is easy to verify that if we take a lossless decomposition and losslessly decompose one of its member schemas into a pair of subschemas, then the result is lossless as well (Exercise 6.15). Therefore, any decomposition that can be derived by a sequence of binary lossless decompositions is itself lossless.

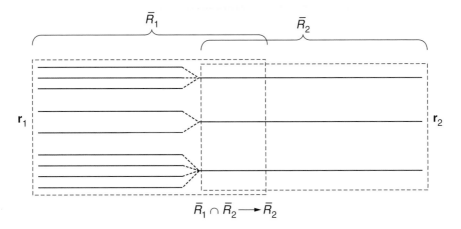

FIGURE 6.6 Tuple structure in a lossless binary decomposition: a row of $\mathbf{r}_1$ combines with exactly one row of $\mathbf{r}_2$.

A general algorithm for testing losslessness of an arbitrary *n*-ary decomposition exists but is outside of the scope of this book. A curious reader is referred to [Maier 1983].

6.6.2 Dependency-Preserving Decompositions

Consider the schema HASACCOUNT once again. Recall that it has attributes Account-Number, ClientId, OfficeId, and its FDs are

ClientId, OfficeId $\rightarrow$ AccountNumber	**6.6**
AccountNumber $\rightarrow$ OfficeId	**6.7**

According to the losslessness test, the following decomposition is lossless:

ACCTOFFICE = (AccountNumber, OfficeId;
                                {AccountNumber $\rightarrow$ OfficeId})   **6.8**
ACCTCLIENT = (AccountNumber, ClientId; { })

because AccountNumber (the intersection of the two attribute sets) is a key of the first schema, ACCTOFFICE.

Even though decomposition (6.8) is lossless, something seems to have fallen through the cracks. ACCTOFFICE hosts the FD (6.7), but ACCTCLIENT's associated set of FDs is empty. This leaves the FD (6.6), which exists in the original schema, homeless. Neither of the two schemas in the decomposition has all of the attributes needed to house this FD; furthermore, the FD cannot be derived from the FDs that belong to the schemas ACCTOFFICE and ACCTCLIENT.

In practical terms, this means that even though decomposing relations over the schema HASACCOUNT into relations over ACCTOFFICE and ACCTCLIENT does not lead to information loss, it might incur a cost for maintaining the integrity constraint that corresponds to the lost FD. Unlike the FD (6.7), which can be checked locally (in the relation ACCTOFFICE), verification of the FD (6.6) requires computing the join of ACCTOFFICE and ACCTCLIENT before checking of the FD can begin. In such cases, we say that the decomposition does not preserve the dependencies in the original schema. We now define what this means precisely.

Consider a schema, $\mathbf{R} = (\bar{R}; \mathcal{F})$, and suppose that

$$\mathbf{R}_1 = (\bar{R}_1; \mathcal{F}_1), \quad \mathbf{R}_2 = (\bar{R}_2; \mathcal{F}_2), \quad \ldots, \quad \mathbf{R}_n = (\bar{R}_n; \mathcal{F}_n)$$

is a decomposition. $\mathcal{F}$ entails each $\mathcal{F}_i$ by definition, so $\mathcal{F}$ entails $\cup_{i=1}^{n} \mathcal{F}_i$. However, this definition does not require that the two sets of dependencies be equivalent—that is, that $\cup_{i=1}^{n} \mathcal{F}_i$ must also entail $\mathcal{F}$. This reverse entailment is what is missing in the above example. The FD set of HASACCOUNT, which consists of dependencies (6.6) and (6.7), is not entailed by the union of the dependencies in decomposition (6.8), which consists of only a single dependency AccountNumber → OfficeId. Because of this, (6.8) is not a dependency-preserving decomposition.

Formally,

$$\mathbf{R}_1 = (\bar{R}_1; \mathcal{F}_1), \quad \mathbf{R}_2 = (\bar{R}_2; \mathcal{F}_2), \quad \ldots, \quad \mathbf{R}_n = (\bar{R}_n; \mathcal{F}_n)$$

is said to be a **dependency-preserving decomposition** of $\mathbf{R} = (\bar{R}; \mathcal{F})$ if and only if it is a decomposition of $\mathbf{R}$ and the sets of FDs $\mathcal{F}$ and $\cup_{i=1}^{n} \mathcal{F}_i$ are equivalent.

Example 6.6.2 (Dependency-Preserving Decomposition).   Consider a schema with the attributes SSN, EmplId, and DeptId, and the FDs $\mathcal{F} = \{f_1 : \text{SSN} \to \text{EmplId}, f_2 : \text{EmplId} \to \text{SSN}, f_3 : \text{SSN} \to \text{DeptId}\}$. Its decomposition into $\mathbf{R}_1 = (\text{SSN EmplId}; \mathcal{F}_1 = \{f_1, f_2\})$ and $\mathbf{R}_2 = (\text{EmplId DeptId}; \mathcal{F}_2 = \{f_4 : \text{EmplId} \to \text{DeptId}\})$ is dependency preserving.

Note that the FD $f_3 \in \mathcal{F}$ is not in $\mathcal{F}_1 \cup \mathcal{F}_2 = \{f_1, f_2, f_4\}$, but nonetheless $\mathcal{F}^+ = (\mathcal{F}_1 \cup \mathcal{F}_2)^+$ because f_3 can be derived from f_1 and f_4; and f_4 from f_2 and f_3. ∎

The above example shows that even if some FD, $f \in \mathcal{F}$, is not found in any of the $\mathcal{F}_i$s this does *not* mean that the decomposition is not dependency preserving, since f might be entailed by $\cup_{i=1}^{n} \mathcal{F}_i$. In this case, maintaining f as a functional dependency requires no extra effort. If the FDs in $\cup_{i=1}^{n} \mathcal{F}_i$ are maintained, f will be also. It is only when f is not entailed by $\cup_{i=1}^{n} \mathcal{F}_i$ that the decomposition is not dependency preserving and so maintenance of f requires a join.

Example 6.6.3 (Nonpreserving Decomposition).   The decomposition (6.8) of HAS-ACCOUNT is not dependency preserving, and this is precisely what is wrong. The dependencies that exist in the original schema but are lost in the decomposition become interrelational constraints that cannot be maintained locally. Each time a relation in the decomposition is changed, satisfaction of the interrelational con-

AccountNumber	ClientId	OfficeId
B123	111111111	SB01
A908	123456789	MN08

HASACCOUNT

AccountNumber	OfficeId
B123	SB01
A908	MN08

ACCTOFFICE

AccountNumber	ClientId
B123	111111111
A908	123456789

ACCTCLIENT

FIGURE 6.7 Decomposition of the HASACCOUNT relation.

straints can be checked only after the reconstruction of the original relation. To illustrate, consider the decomposition of HASACCOUNT in Figure 6.7.

If we now add the tuple ⟨B567, SB01⟩ to the relation ACCTOFFICE and the tuple ⟨B567, 111111111⟩ to ACCTCLIENT, the two relations will still satisfy their local FDs (in fact, we see from (6.8) that only ACCTOFFICE has a dependency to satisfy). In contrast, the interrelational FD (6.6) is not satisfied after these updates, but this is not immediately apparent. To verify this, we must join the two relations, as depicted in Figure 6.8. We now see that constraint (6.6) is violated by the first two tuples in the updated HASACCOUNT relation. ∎

AccountNumber	ClientId	OfficeId
B123	111111111	SB01
B567	111111111	SB01
A908	123456789	MN08

HASACCOUNT

AccountNumber	OfficeId
B123	SB01
B567	SB01
A908	MN08

ACCTOFFICE

AccountNumber	ClientId
B123	111111111
B567	111111111
A908	123456789

ACCTCLIENT

FIGURE 6.8 HASACCOUNT and its decomposition after the insertion of several rows.

The next question to ask is how hard it is to check whether a decomposition is dependency preserving. If we already have a decomposition complete with sets of functional dependencies attached to the local schemas, dependency preservation can be checked in polynomial time. We simply need to check that each FD in the original set is entailed by the union of FDs in the local schemas. For each such test, we can use the quadratic attribute closure algorithm discussed in Section 6.4.

In practice, the situation is more involved. Typically, we (and computer algorithms) must first decide how to split the attribute set in order to form the decomposition, and only then attach FDs to those attribute sets. We can attach the FD $\overline{X} \to \overline{Y}$ to an attribute set $\overline{S}$ if $\overline{X} \cup \overline{Y} \subseteq \overline{S}$. We state this more formally as follows.

Consider a schema, $\mathbf{R} = (\overline{R};\ \mathcal{F})$, a relation, $\mathbf{r}$, over $\mathbf{R}$, and a set of attributes, $\overline{S}$, such that $\overline{S} \subseteq \overline{R}$. If $\overline{S}$ is one of the schemas in a decomposition of $\mathbf{R}$, the only FDs that are guaranteed to hold over $\pi_{\overline{S}}(\mathbf{r})$ are $\overline{X} \to \overline{Y} \in \mathcal{F}^+$ such that $\overline{X}\,\overline{Y} \subseteq \overline{S}$. This leads us to the following notion:

$$\pi_{\overline{S}}(\mathcal{F}) \;=\; \{\overline{X} \to \overline{Y} \mid \overline{X} \to \overline{Y} \in \mathcal{F}^+ \text{ and } \overline{X} \cup \overline{Y} \subseteq \overline{S}\}$$

which is called the **projection of the set** $\mathcal{F}$ **of FDs** onto the set of attributes $\overline{S}$.

The notion of projection for FDs opens a way to construct decompositions knowing only how to split the attribute set of the original schema. If $\mathbf{R} = (\overline{R};\ \mathcal{F})$ is a schema and $\overline{R}_1, \ldots, \overline{R}_n$ are subsets of attributes such that $\overline{R} = \cup_{i=1}^{n} \overline{R}_i$, then the collection of schemas $(\overline{R}_1; \pi_{\overline{R}_1}(\mathcal{F})), \ldots, (\overline{R}_n; \pi_{\overline{R}_n}(\mathcal{F}))$ is a decomposition.

From now on we will consider only decompositions of this kind, that is, those where $\mathcal{F}_i$ is equivalent to $\pi_{\overline{R}_i}(\mathcal{F})$. Since, given an attribute set in a decomposition, it is now possible to uniquely determine the corresponding set of FDs by taking a projection, it is customary to omit the FDs when specifying schema decompositions.

Constructing decompositions thus requires computing projections of FDs. This computation involves calculating the closure of $\mathcal{F}$,[4] which, in the worst case, can take time exponential in the size of $\mathcal{F}$. If the cost of this computation is factored into the cost of checking for dependency preservation, this checking is exponential as well. In this regard, it is interesting that, in order to test a decomposition for losslessness, one does not need to compute the FDs that belong to the local schemas. The test presented earlier used the original set $\mathcal{F}$ of FDs and is polynomial in the size of $\mathcal{F}$.

To summarize, we considered two important properties of schema decomposition: losslessness and dependency preservation. We also saw an example of a relation (HASACCOUNT) that has a lossless but not dependency-preserving decomposition into BCNF (and which, as we shall see, does not have a BCNF decomposition that has both properties). Which of these two properties is more important? The answer is that losslessness is mandatory while dependency preservation, though very desirable, is optional. The reason is that lossy decompositions lose information contained in the original database, and this is not acceptable. In contrast, decompositions that

---

[4] There is a way to avoid computing the entire closure $\mathcal{F}^+$, but the worst-case complexity is the same.

do not preserve FDs only lead to computational overhead when the database is changed and interrelational constraints need to be checked.

6.7 An Algorithm for BCNF Decomposition

We are now ready to present our first decomposition algorithm. Let $\mathbf{R} = (\overline{R};\ \mathcal{F})$ be a relational schema that is not in BCNF. The algorithm in Figure 6.9 constructs a new decomposition by repeatedly splitting $\mathbf{R}$ into smaller subschemas so that at each step the new database schema has strictly fewer FDs that violate BCNF than does the schema in the previous iteration (see Exercise 6.16). Thus, the algorithm always terminates and all schemas in the result are in BCNF.

To see how the BCNF decomposition algorithm works, consider the HASAC-COUNT example once again. This schema is not in BCNF, because of the FD Ac-countNumber $\rightarrow$ OfficeId whose left-hand side is not a superkey. Therefore, we can use this FD to split HASACCOUNT in the **while** loop of Figure 6.9. The result is, not surprisingly, the decomposition we saw in (6.8).

The next example is more involved and also much more abstract.

Example 6.7.1 (BCNF Decomposition).   Consider a relation schema, $\mathbf{R} = (\overline{R};\ \mathcal{F})$, where $\overline{R} = ABCDEFGH$ (recall that A, B, etc., denote attribute names), and let the set $\mathcal{F}$ of FDs be

$$ABH \rightarrow C$$
$$A \rightarrow DE$$
$$BGH \rightarrow F$$
$$F \rightarrow ADH$$
$$BH \rightarrow GE$$

To apply the BCNF decomposition algorithm, we first need to identify the FDs that violate BCNF—those whose left-hand side is not a superkey. We can see that the first FD is *not* one of these because the attribute closure $(ABH)^+$ (computed with the algorithm in Figure 6.3) contains all schema attributes and so ABH is a superkey.

FIGURE **6.9** Lossless decomposition into BCNF.

Input: R $=\ (\overline{R};\ \mathcal{F})$
Output: A lossless decomposition of **R** where each local schema is in BCNF.

Decomposition := {**R**}
while there is a schema $\mathbf{S} = (\overline{S};\ \mathcal{F}')$ in *Decomposition* that is not in BCNF **do**
    /* Let $\overline{X} \rightarrow \overline{Y}$ be an FD in $\mathcal{F}^+$ such that $\overline{X}\,\overline{Y} \subseteq \overline{S}$ and
        it violates BCNF in **S**. Decompose using this FD   */
    Replace **S** in *Decomposition* with schemas $\mathbf{S}_1 = (\overline{X}\,\overline{Y};\ \mathcal{F}'_1)$ and
      $\mathbf{S}_2\ =\ ((\overline{S} - \overline{Y}) \cup \overline{X};\ \mathcal{F}'_2)$, where $\mathcal{F}'_1 = \pi_{\overline{X}\,\overline{Y}}(\mathcal{F}')$ and $\mathcal{F}'_2 = \pi_{(\overline{S} - \overline{Y}) \cup \overline{X}}(\mathcal{F}')$
end
return *Decomposition*

However, the second FD, $A \rightarrow DE$, does violate BCNF. The attribute closure of A is ADE, and so A is not a superkey. We can thus split **R** using this FD:

$$\mathbf{R}_1 = (ADE; \{A \rightarrow DE\})$$
$$\mathbf{R}_2 = (ABCFGH; \{ABH \rightarrow C, BGH \rightarrow F, F \rightarrow AH, BH \rightarrow G\})$$

Notice that we separated $F \rightarrow ADH$ into $\{F \rightarrow AH, F \rightarrow D\}$ and $BH \rightarrow GE$ into $\{BH \rightarrow G, BH \rightarrow E\}$ and that some FDs fell by the wayside: $F \rightarrow D$ and $BH \rightarrow E$ no longer have a home since none of the new schemas contains all the attributes used by these FDs. However, things are still looking bright since the FD $F \rightarrow D$ can be derived from other FDs embedded in the new schemas $\mathbf{R}_1$ and $\mathbf{R}_2$: $F \rightarrow AH$ and $A \rightarrow DE$. Similarly, $BH \rightarrow E$ can still be derived because the attribute closure of BH with respect to the FDs embedded in $\mathbf{R}_1$ and $\mathbf{R}_2$, contains E. (Verify this claim using the algorithm in Figure 6.3!) The above decomposition is therefore dependency preserving.

It is easy to see that $\mathbf{R}_1$ is in BCNF. Although $A \rightarrow DE$ violates BCNF in **R**, it does not violate BCNF in $\mathbf{R}_1$ since, by construction, A is a key of $\mathbf{R}_1$. Note that it will always be true that the offending FD, f, in **R** that is used as the basis for the decomposition is converted to a nonoffending FD in $\mathbf{R}_1$. In general, however, you cannot assume that $\mathbf{R}_1$ will always be in BCNF since there could be other FDs in $\mathbf{R}_1$ that violate BCNF.

What about $\mathbf{R}_2$? The FDs $ABH \rightarrow C$ and $BGH \rightarrow F$ did not violate BCNF in **R** since both ABH and BGH are superkeys. As a result, they do not violate BCNF in $\mathbf{R}_2$ (which has only a subset of the attributes of **R**). The FD that clearly violates BCNF here is $F \rightarrow AH$, so the algorithm might pick it up and split $\mathbf{R}_2$ accordingly.

$$\mathbf{R}_{21} = (FAH; \{F \rightarrow AH\})$$
$$\mathbf{R}_{22} = (FBCG; \{FB \rightarrow CG\})$$

(Note that the FD $FB \rightarrow CG$ is not in $\mathcal{F}$ but is derivable from it.)

Now both schemas, $\mathbf{R}_{21}$ and $\mathbf{R}_{22}$, are in BCNF. However, the price is that the FDs $ABH \rightarrow C$, $BGH \rightarrow F$, and $BH \rightarrow G$ that were present in $\mathbf{R}_2$ are now homeless. Furthermore, none of these FDs can be derived using the FDs that are still embedded in $\mathbf{R}_1$, $\mathbf{R}_{21}$, and $\mathbf{R}_{22}$. For instance, computing $(ABH)^+$ with respect to this set of FDs yields $ABHDE$, which does not contain C, so $ABH \rightarrow C$ is not derivable. Thus, we obtain a nondependency-preserving decomposition of **R** into three BCNF schemas: $\mathbf{R}_1$, $\mathbf{R}_{21}$, and $\mathbf{R}_{22}$.

This decomposition is by no means unique. For instance, if our algorithm had picked up $F \rightarrow ADH$ at the very first iteration, the first decomposition would have been

$$\mathbf{R}_1' = (FADH; \{F \rightarrow ADH, A \rightarrow D\})$$
$$\mathbf{R}_2' = (FBCEG; \{F \rightarrow E, FB \rightarrow CG\})$$

Observe that none of these schemas is in BCNF ($A \rightarrow D$ violates the BCNF requirements in the first schema and $F \rightarrow E$ in the second) and need to be decomposed further. This is not the end of the differences, however: some FDs that were present in the decomposition into $\mathbf{R}_1$, $\mathbf{R}_{21}$, $\mathbf{R}_{22}$ are no longer embedded in the new decomposition (e.g., $A \rightarrow E$). ∎

Properties of the BCNF decomposition algorithm. First and foremost, the BCNF decomposition algorithm in Figure 6.9 always yields a lossless decomposition. To see this, consider the two schemas involving attribute sets $\overline{X}\,\overline{Y}$ and $(\overline{S} - \overline{Y}) \cup \overline{X}$ that replace the schema $\mathbf{S} = (\overline{S}, \mathcal{F}')$ in the algorithm. Notice that $\overline{X}\,\overline{Y} \cap ((\overline{S} - \overline{Y}) \cup \overline{X}) = \overline{X}$ and thus $\overline{X}\,\overline{Y} \cap ((\overline{S} - \overline{Y}) \cup \overline{X}) \to \overline{X}\,\overline{Y}$ since $\overline{X} \to \overline{Y} \in \mathcal{F}$. Therefore, according to the losslessness test for binary decompositions on page 214, $\{\overline{X}\,\overline{Y},\ (\overline{S} - \overline{Y}) \cup \overline{X}\}$ is a lossless decomposition of $\mathbf{S}$. This means that at every step in our algorithm we replace one schema by its lossless decomposition. Thus, by Exercise 6.15, the final decomposition produced by this algorithm is also lossless.

Are the decompositions produced by the BCNF algorithm always dependency preserving? We have seen that this is not the case. Decomposition (6.8) of HasAccount is not dependency preserving. Moreover, it is easy to see that no BCNF decomposition of HasAccount (not only those produced by this particular algorithm) is both lossless and dependency preserving. Indeed, there are just three decompositions to try, and we can simply check them all.

> The BCNF decomposition algorithm is nondeterministic.

Finally, Example 6.7.1 shows that the BCNF decomposition algorithm is non-deterministic. The final result depends on the order in which FDs are selected in the **while** loop. The decomposition chosen by the database designer can be a matter of taste, or it can be based on objective criteria. For instance, some decompositions might be dependency preserving, others not; some might lead to fewer FDs left out as interrelational constraints (e.g., the decomposition $\mathbf{R}_1, \mathbf{R}_{21}, \mathbf{R}_{22}$ in Example 6.7.1 is better in this sense than the decomposition $\mathbf{R}'_1, \mathbf{R}'_2$). Some attribute sets might be more likely to be queried together so they better not be separated in the decomposition. The next section describes one common approach that can help in choosing one BCNF decomposition over another.

6.8 Synthesis of 3NF Schemas

We have seen that some schemas (such as HasAccount, in Figure 6.8) cannot be decomposed into BCNF so that the result is also dependency preserving. However, if we agree to settle for 3NF instead of BCNF, dependency-preserving decompositions are always possible (but recall that 3NF schemas might contain redundancies—see page 211).

Before we present a 3NF decomposition algorithm, we need to introduce the concept of *minimal cover*, which is really very simple. We know that sets of FDs might look completely different but nonetheless be logically equivalent. Figure 6.4 presented one fairly straightforward way of testing equivalence. Since there might be many sets of FDs equivalent to any given set, we question whether there is a set of FDs that can be viewed as canonical. It turns out that defining a unique canonical set is not an easy task, but the notion of minimal cover comes close.

6.8.1 Minimal Cover

Let $\mathcal{F}$ be a set of FDs. A **minimal cover** of $\mathcal{F}$ is a set of FDs, $\mathcal{G}$, that has the following properties:

1. $\mathcal{G}$ is equivalent to $\mathcal{F}$ (but, possibly, different from $\mathcal{F}$).
2. All FDs in $\mathcal{G}$ have the form $\overline{X} \to A$, where A is a single attribute.
3. It is not possible to make $\mathcal{G}$ "smaller" (and still satisfy the first two properties) by either of the following:
   (a) Deleting an FD
   (b) Deleting an attribute from an FD

An FD, f, that can be deleted from a set, $\mathcal{F}$, while preserving the equivalence (i.e., when $\mathcal{F} - f$ is equivalent to $\mathcal{F}$) is said to be a **redundant FD**. An attribute, A, in f that can be deleted while preserving the equivalence (i.e., if $\mathcal{F}$ and $\mathcal{F} - \{f\} \cup \{f'\}$ are equivalent, where f' is f with A deleted) is said to be a **redundant attribute**. Thus, a minimal cover has neither redundant FDs nor redundant attributes.

Clearly, because of Armstrong's rule of decomposition for functional dependencies, it is easy to convert $\mathcal{F}$ into an equivalent set of FDs where the right-hand sides are singleton attributes. However, property 3 is more subtle. Before presenting an algorithm for computing minimal covers, we illustrate it with a concrete example.

Example 6.8.1 (Minimal Cover).   Consider the attribute set $ABCDEFGH$ and the following set, $\mathcal{F}$, of FDs:

$$
\begin{array}{ll}
ABH \to C & F \to AD \\
A \to D & E \to F \\
C \to E & BH \to E \\
BGH \to F &
\end{array}
$$

Since not all right-hand sides are single attributes, we can use the decomposition rule to obtain an FD set that satisfies the first two properties of minimal covers.

$$
\begin{array}{ll}
ABH \to C & F \to A \\
A \to D & F \to D \\
C \to E & E \to F \\
BGH \to F & BH \to E
\end{array}
\tag{6.9}
$$

We can see that $BGH \to F$ is entailed by $BH \to E$ and $E \to F$, and that $F \to D$ is entailed by $F \to A$ and $A \to D$. Thus, we are left with

$$
\begin{array}{ll}
ABH \to C & F \to A \\
A \to D & E \to F \\
C \to E & BH \to E
\end{array}
\tag{6.10}
$$

It is easy to check by computing attribute closures that none of these FDs is redundant; that is, one cannot simply throw out an FD from this set without sacrificing equivalence to the original set $\mathcal{F}$. However, is the resulting set a minimal cover of $\mathcal{F}$? The answer turns out to be *no* because it is possible to delete the attribute A from the first FD, since $BH \rightarrow C$ is entailed by the set (6.10) (verify this by computing the attribute closure of BH) and $ABH \rightarrow C$ is obviously entailed by $BH \rightarrow C$. Thus, we get

$$
\begin{array}{lll}
BH \rightarrow C & \qquad F \rightarrow A & \\
A \rightarrow D & \qquad E \rightarrow F & \qquad \textbf{6.11} \\
C \rightarrow E & \qquad BH \rightarrow E &
\end{array}
$$

Interestingly, the latter set of FDs is still not minimal because the FD $BH \rightarrow E$ is redundant. Removing this FD yields a minimal cover at last. ∎

Nonuniqueness of minimal covers. Observe that the outcome of steps 2 and 3 in the algorithm in Figure 6.10 may depend on the particular order in which we test the candidates for removal (both attributes and FDs). This suggests that a set of FDs can have several minimal covers. For instance, $\{A \rightarrow B, B \rightarrow C, C \rightarrow A, A \rightarrow C, C \rightarrow B, B \rightarrow A\}$ has two minimal covers: $\{A \rightarrow B, B \rightarrow C, C \rightarrow A\}$ and $\{A \rightarrow C, C \rightarrow B, B \rightarrow A\}$.

Noninterchangeability of steps 2 and 3. The algorithm for computing minimal covers is presented in Figure 6.10. Step 1 is performed by a simple splitting of the FDs according to their right-hand sides. For instance, $\overline{X} \rightarrow AB$ turns into $\overline{X} \rightarrow A$ and $\overline{X} \rightarrow B$.

Step 2 is performed by checking every left-hand attribute in $\mathcal{G}$ for redundancy. That is, for every FD $\overline{X} \rightarrow A \in \mathcal{G}$ and every attribute $B \in \overline{X}$, we have to check if $(\overline{X} - B) \rightarrow A$ is entailed by $\mathcal{G}$—very tedious work if done manually. In the above example, we performed this step when we checked that $BH \rightarrow C$ is entailed by the FD set (6.10), which allowed us to get rid of the redundant attribute A in $ABH \rightarrow C$. Step 3 is accomplished by another tedious algorithm: for every $g \in \mathcal{G}$, check that the FD g is entailed by $\mathcal{G} - \{g\}$.

FIGURE 6.10 Computation of a minimal cover.

> **Input:** a set of FDs $\mathcal{F}$
> **Output:** $\mathcal{G}$, a minimal cover of $\mathcal{F}$
>
> *Step 1:* $\mathcal{G} := \mathcal{F}$, where all FDs are converted to use singleton attributes on the right-hand side.
> *Step 2:* Remove all redundant attributes from the left-hand sides of FDs in $\mathcal{G}$.
> *Step 3:* Remove all redundant FDs from $\mathcal{G}$.
>
> **return** $\mathcal{G}$

An important observation about the algorithm in Figure 6.10 is that steps 2 and 3 *cannot* be done in a different order. Performing step 3 before 2 will not always return a minimal cover. In fact, we have already seen this phenomenon in Example 6.8.1. We obtained set (6.10) by removing redundant FDs from (6.9); then we obtained set (6.11) by deleting redundant attributes. Nevertheless, the result still had a redundant FD, $BH \rightarrow E$. On the other hand, if we first remove the redundant attributes from (6.9), we get

$$
\begin{array}{ll}
BH \rightarrow C \qquad & F \rightarrow A \\
A \rightarrow D \qquad & F \rightarrow D \\
C \rightarrow E \qquad & E \rightarrow F \\
BH \rightarrow F \qquad & BH \rightarrow E
\end{array}
$$

Then removing the redundant FDs $BH \rightarrow F$, $F \rightarrow D$, and $BH \rightarrow E$ yields the following minimal cover:

$$
\begin{array}{lll}
BH \rightarrow C \qquad & F \rightarrow A & \\
A \rightarrow D \qquad & E \rightarrow F & \textbf{6.12} \\
C \rightarrow E & &
\end{array}
$$

6.8.2 3NF Decomposition through Schema Synthesis

The algorithm for constructing dependency-preserving 3NF decompositions works very differently from its BCNF counterpart. Instead of starting with one big schema and successively splitting it, the 3NF algorithm starts with individual attributes and groups them into schemas. For this reason, it is called **3NF synthesis**. Given a schema, $\mathbf{R} = (\bar{R};\ \mathcal{F})$, where $\bar{R}$ is a superset of attributes and $\mathcal{F}$ is a set of FDs, the algorithm carries out four steps:

1. Find a minimal cover, $\mathcal{G}$, for $\mathcal{F}$.
2. Partition $\mathcal{G}$ into FD sets $\mathcal{G}_1, \ldots, \mathcal{G}_n$, such that each $\mathcal{G}_i$ consists of all FDs in $\mathcal{G}$ that share the same left-hand side. (It is not necessary to assume that different $\mathcal{G}_i$s have different left-hand sides, but it is usually a good idea to merge sets whose left-hand sides are the same.)
3. For each $\mathcal{G}_i$, form a relation schema, $\mathbf{R}_i = (\bar{R}_i; \mathcal{G}_i)$, where $\bar{R}_i$ is the set of all attributes mentioned in $\mathcal{G}_i$.
4. If one of the $\bar{R}_i$s, is a superkey of $\mathbf{R}$ (i.e., $(\bar{R}_i)_{\mathcal{F}}^{+} = \bar{R}$), we are done—$\mathbf{R}_1, \ldots, \mathbf{R}_n$ is the desired decomposition. If no $\bar{R}_i$ is a superkey of $\mathbf{R}$, let $\bar{R}_0$ be some key of $\mathbf{R}$, and let $\mathbf{R}_0 = (\bar{R}_0;\ \{\})$ be a new schema. Then $\mathbf{R}_0, \mathbf{R}_1, \ldots, \mathbf{R}_n$ is the desired decomposition.

Note that the collection of schemas obtained after step 3 might not even be a decomposition because some attributes of $\mathbf{R}$ might be missing (see Example 6.8.2

below). However, any such missing attributes will be recaptured in step 4, because these attributes must be part of the key of **R** (Exercise 6.28).

Is it dependency preserving? This is easy to see: By construction, every FD in $\mathcal{G}$ has a home, so $\mathcal{G} = \cup \mathcal{G}_i$. By definition of minimal covers, $\mathcal{G}^+ = \mathcal{F}^+$, so $\mathcal{F}$ is preserved.

Checking for BCNF—pitfalls. It might seem that each $\mathbf{R}_i$ is in BCNF, because every FD in $\mathcal{G}_i$ is superkey-based. However, do not fall for this argument so easily. The FDs in $\mathcal{G}_i$ might not be the only ones that hold in $\mathbf{R}_i$, because $\mathcal{G}^+$ might have other FDs whose attribute set is entirely contained within $\overline{R}_i$. To see this, consider a slight modification of our tried-and-true schema HASACCOUNT. Here $\overline{R}$ consists of the attributes AccountNumber, ClientId, OfficeId, DateOpened, and $\mathcal{F}$ consists of the FDs ClientId, OfficeId $\rightarrow$ AccountNumber and AccountNumber $\rightarrow$ OfficeId, DateOpened. The above algorithm then produces two schemas:

$$\mathbf{R}_1 = (\{\text{ClientId,OfficeId,AccountNumber}\},$$
$$\{\text{ClientId,OfficeId} \rightarrow \text{AccountNumber}\})$$
$$\mathbf{R}_2 = (\{\text{AccountNumber,OfficeId,DateOpened}\},$$
$$\{\text{AccountNumber} \rightarrow \text{OfficeId,DateOpened}\})$$

A careful examination shows that, even though AccountNumber $\rightarrow$ OfficeId is not explicitly specified for $\mathbf{R}_1$, it must nonetheless hold over the attributes of that schema because this FD is implicitly imposed by $\mathbf{R}_2$.

To understand why the FDs specified for $\mathbf{R}_2$ must be taken into account when considering $\mathbf{R}_1$, observe that the pair of attributes AccountNumber, OfficeId represents the same real-world relationship in both $\mathbf{R}_1$ and $\mathbf{R}_2$, so it is an inconsistency if the tuples in $\mathbf{R}_2$ obey a constraint over this pair of attributes while the tuples in $\mathbf{R}_1$ do not.

Thus, in general, to check which of the schemas $\mathbf{R}_i$ obtained by the 3NF synthesis are in BCNF, it is not enough to look for violations of BCNF among the FDs in $\mathcal{G}_i$. Instead, it is necessary to compute the projections $\pi_{\overline{R}_i}(\mathcal{G})$ and look for the violations there. As explained earlier, this is rather tiresome to do manually (except for small examples) because computing projections of FDs is exponentially hard.

Is it really 3NF? It seems obvious that each $\mathbf{R}_i$ is a 3NF schema, because the only FDs associated with $\mathbf{R}_i$ are those in $\mathcal{G}_i$ and they all share the same left-hand side (which is thus a superkey of $\mathbf{R}_i$). However, the above argument regarding BCNF shows that schemas produced by the synthesis algorithm might have FDs with different left-hand sides and thus conformance to 3NF is not at all obvious. Nevertheless, it can be *proved* that the above algorithm always yields 3NF decompositions (see Exercise 6.17).

Is it lossless? The final question is whether the synthesis algorithm yields lossless decompositions of the input schema. The answer is yes, but proving this is more difficult than proving the 3NF property. Although it might not be obvious, achieving losslessness is in fact the only purpose of step 4 in that algorithm. This is illustrated in the following example.

> *Brain Teaser:* Does 3NF synthesis always produce a unique result?

Example 6.8.2 (3NF Synthesis Where Step 4 Is Essential). Consider the schema with FDs depicted in (6.9) on page 222. A minimal cover for this set is shown in (6.12). Since no two FDs here share the same left-hand side, we end up with the following schemas: $(BHC;\ BH \rightarrow C)\ (AD;\ A \rightarrow D)$, $(CE;\ C \rightarrow E)$, $(FA;\ F \rightarrow A)$, and $(EF;\ E \rightarrow F)$. Notice that none of these schemas forms the superkey for the entire set of attributes. For instance, the attribute closure of BHC does not contain G. In fact, the attribute G is not even included in any of the schemas! So, according to our remark about the purpose of step 4, this decomposition is not lossless (in fact, it is not even a decomposition!) To make it lossless, we perform step 4 and add the schema $(BGH;\ \{\ \})$. ∎

6.8.3 BCNF Decomposition through 3NF Synthesis

So, how can 3NF synthesis help design BCNF database schemas? The answer is simple. To decompose a schema into BCNF relations, do *not* use the BCNF algorithm first. Instead, use 3NF synthesis, which is lossless and guaranteed to preserve dependencies. If the resulting schemas are already in BCNF (as in Example 6.8.2), no further action is necessary. If, however, some schema in the result is not in BCNF, use the BCNF algorithm to split it until no violation of BCNF remains. Repeat this step for each non-BCNF schema produced by the 3NF synthesis.

The advantage of this approach is that, if a lossless and dependency-preserving decomposition exists, 3NF synthesis is likely to find it. If some schemas are not in BCNF after the first stage, loss of some FDs is inevitable (Exercise 6.34). But at least we tried hard. Here is a complete example that illustrates the above approach.

Example 6.8.3 (Combining Schema Synthesis and Decomposition). Let the attribute set be St (student), C (course), Sem (semester), P (professor), T (time), and R (room) with the following FDs:

$$St\ C\ Sem \rightarrow P \qquad P\ Sem\ T \rightarrow C\ R$$
$$P\ Sem \rightarrow C \qquad P\ Sem\ C\ T \rightarrow R$$
$$C\ Sem\ T \rightarrow P \qquad P\ Sem\ T \rightarrow C$$

These functional dependencies apply at a university in which multiple sections of the same course might be taught in the same semester (in which case providing the name of a course and a semester does not uniquely identify a professor) and a professor teaches only one course a semester (in which case providing the name of a professor and a semester uniquely identifies a course) and all the sections of a course are taught at different times.

We begin by finding a minimal cover for the above set. The first step is to split the right-hand sides of the set of FDs into singleton attributes.

St C Sem → P   P Sem T → C

P Sem → C   P Sem T → R

C Sem T → P   P Sem C T → R

                                P Sem T → C

Let $\mathcal{F}$ denote this set of FDs. The last FD is a duplicate, so we delete it from the set. Next we reduce the left-hand sides by eliminating redundant attributes. For instance, to check the left-hand side St C Sem, we must compute several attribute closures—(St Sem)$_{\mathcal{F}}^{+}$ = {St, Sem}; (St C)$_{\mathcal{F}}^{+}$ = {St, C}; (C Sem)$_{\mathcal{F}}^{+}$ = {C, Sem}—which show that there are no redundant attributes in the first FD. Similarly, P Sem, C Sem T, and P Sem T cannot be reduced. However, checking P Sem C T brings a reward: (P Sem T)$_{\mathcal{F}}^{+}$ = P Sem T C R, so C can be deleted.

The outcome from this stage is the following set of FDs, which we number for convenient reference.

FD1. St C Sem -> P
FD2. P Sem -> C
FD3. C Sem T -> P
FD4. P Sem T -> C
FD5. P Sem T -> R

The next step is to get rid of the redundant FDs, which are detected with the help of attribute closure, as usual. Since (St C Sem)$_{\{\mathcal{F}-\text{FD1}\}}^{+}$ = St C Sem, FD1 cannot be eliminated. Nor can FDs 2, 3, and 5. However, FD4 is redundant (because of FD2), so it can be eliminated. Thus, the minimal cover is

St C Sem -> P
P Sem -> C
C Sem T -> P
P Sem T -> R

This leads to the following dependency-preserving 3NF decomposition:

(St C Sem P; St C Sem -> P)
(P Sem C; P Sem -> C)
(C Sem T P; C Sem T -> P)
(P Sem T R; P Sem T -> R)

It is easy to verify that none of the above schemas forms a superkey for the original schema; therefore, to make the decomposition lossless we also need to add a schema whose attribute closure contains all the original attributes. The schema (St T Sem P; { }) is one possibility here.

If you trust that the 3NF synthesis algorithm is correct and that we did not make mistakes applying it, no checking for 3NF is necessary. However, a quick look reveals that the first and the third schemas are not in BCNF because of the FD P Sem → C embedded in the second schema.

Further decomposition of the first schema with respect to P Sem → C yields (P Sem C; P Sem → C) and (P Sem St; { })—a lossless decomposition but one in which the FD St C Sem → P is not preserved.

Decomposition of the third schema with respect to P Sem → C yields (P Sem C; P Sem → C) and (P Sem T; {})—another lossless decomposition, which, alas, does not preserve C Sem T → P.

So, the final BCNF decomposition is

(P Sem C; P Sem → C)
(P Sem St)
(P Sem T)
(P Sem T R; P Sem T → R)
(St T Sem P)

This decomposition is lossless because we first obtained a lossless 3NF decomposition and then applied the BCNF algorithm, which preserves losslessness. It is not dependency preserving, however, since St C Sem → P and C Sem T → P are not represented in the above schemas. ■

6.9 The Fourth Normal Form

Not all of the world's problems are due to bad FDs. Consider the following schema:

PERSON(SSN, PhoneN, ChildSSN)   **6.13**

---

where we assume that a person can have several phone numbers and several children. Here is one possible relation instance.

SSN	PhoneN	ChildSSN
111–22–3333	516–123–4567	222–33–4444
111–22–3333	516–345–6789	222–33–4444
111–22–3333	516–123–4567	333–44–5555
111–22–3333	516–345–6789	333–44–5555
222–33–4444	212–987–6543	444–55–6666
222–33–4444	212–987–1111	555–66–7777
222–33–4444	212–987–6543	555–66–7777
222–33–4444	212–987–1111	444–55–6666

6.14

As there are no nontrivial functional dependencies (we assume that most children in the database have two parents and so the FD ChildSSN → SSN does not hold), this schema is in 3NF and even BCNF. Nonetheless, it is clearly not a good design as it exhibits a great deal of redundancy. There is no particular association between phone numbers and children, except through the SSN, so every child item related to a given SSN must occur in one tuple with every PhoneN related to the same SSN. Thus, whenever a phone number is added or deleted, several tuples might need to be added or deleted as well. If a person gives up all phone numbers, the information about her children will be lost (or NULL values will have to be used).

It might seem that a compression technique can help here. For instance, we might decide to store only some tuples as long as there is a way to reconstruct the original information.

SSN	PhoneN	ChildSSN
111-22-3333	516-123-4567	222-33-4444
111-22-3333	516-345-6789	333-44-5555
222-33-4444	212-987-6543	444-55-6666
222-33-4444	212-987-1111	555-66-7777

Still, although this is more efficient, it solves none of the aforesaid anomalies. Also, it imposes an additional burden on the applications, which now must be aware of the compression schema.

In our discussion of BCNF, we concluded that redundancy arises when a particular semantic relationship among attribute values is stored more than once. In Figure 4.13 on page 86, the fact that the person with SSN 111111111 lives at 123 Main Street is an example of that—it is stored two times. In that case, the problem was traced back to the functional dependency that relates SSN and Address and the fact that SSN is not a key (and hence there can be several rows with the same SSN value). The redundant storage of a semantic relationship, however, is not limited to this situation. In the relation $\mathbf{r}$ shown in (6.14), the relationships SSN-PhoneN and SSN-ChildSSN are stored multiple times and there are no FDs involved. The problem arises here because there are several attributes—in this case PhoneN and ChildSSN—that have the property that their sets of values are associated with a single value of another attribute—in this case SSN. A relationship between a particular SSN value and a particular PhoneN value is stored as many times as there are children of the person with that SSN. Note that the relation satisfies the following property:

$$\mathbf{r} = \pi_{\texttt{SSN},\texttt{PhoneN}}(\mathbf{r}) \bowtie \pi_{\texttt{SSN},\texttt{ChildSSN}}(\mathbf{r}) \qquad \textbf{6.15}$$

Join dependencies. When (6.15) is required of all legal instances of a schema, this property is known as *join dependency*. A join dependency can arise when characteristics of an enterprise are described by sets of values. With the E-R approach to database design, we saw that such characteristics are represented as set-valued attributes and that translating them into attributes in the relational model is awkward. In particular, when an entity type or a relationship type has several set-valued attributes, a join dependency results.

Condition (6.15) should look familiar to you. It guarantees that a decomposition of $\mathbf{r}$ into the two tables $\pi_{\text{SSN,PhoneN}}(\mathbf{r})$ and $\pi_{\text{SSN,ChildSSN}}(\mathbf{r})$ will be lossless. That is certainly true in this case, but it is not our immediate concern. The condition also tells us something about $\mathbf{r}$: a join dependency indicates that semantic relationships can be stored redundantly in an instance of $\mathbf{r}$.

Formally, let $\overline{R}$ be a set of attributes. A **join dependency** (JD) is a constraint of the form

$$\overline{R} = \overline{R}_1 \bowtie \cdots \bowtie \overline{R}_n$$

where $\overline{R}_1, \ldots, \overline{R}_n$ are attribute sets that represent a decomposition of $\overline{R}$. Note that here the $\overline{R}_i$'s are sets of attributes and $\bowtie$ is just a symbol—we are not actually joining any relations. However, this expression *is* related to a join. Recall that earlier (on page 198) we defined the notion of satisfaction of FDs by relational instances. We now define the same notion for JDs: a relation instance, $\mathbf{r}$, over $\overline{R}$ **satisfies** the above join dependency if

$$\mathbf{r} = \pi_{\overline{R}_1}(\mathbf{r}) \bowtie \cdots \bowtie \pi_{\overline{R}_n}(\mathbf{r})$$

It is easy to see from the definition that the existence of a JD is really another way of saying that there is a lossless decomposition of the schema. Why are we defining the same thing twice? The answer is that previously we used FDs to state that such a decomposition exists, but now we find that a lossless decomposition cannot always be indicated by the presence of certain kinds of FDs. Therefore, we need a new kind of syntactic constraint—join dependencies—which we can attach to a database schema to indicate the presence of a lossless decomposition. In fact, as we will soon see, an FD always implies some sort of a JD, and this is precisely the reason why lossless decompositions are possible with respect to FDs. For instance, consider the schema PERSON2(SSN, Name, ChildSSN) with the FD SSN→Name. It is easy to see from the conditions for losslessness on page 214 that this FD implies the JD

$$(\text{SSN, Name, ChildSSN}) = (\text{SSN, Name}) \bowtie (\text{SSN, ChildSSN})$$

Moreover, due to the one-to-many relationship between SSN and ChildSSN, a typical relational instance over PERSON2 will have similar redundancy to that of relation (6.14) above.

Let $\mathbf{R} = (\overline{R};\ \textit{Constraints})$ be a relational schema, where $\overline{R}$ is a set of attributes and *Constraints* is a set of FDs and JDs. As in the case of FDs alone, a relation over the set of attributes $\overline{R}$ is a **legal instance** of $\mathbf{R}$ if and only if it satisfies all constraints in *Constraints*.

Multivalued dependencies and 4NF.   Of particular interest are **binary join dependencies**, also known as **multivalued dependencies** (*MVD*). These are JDs of the form

$\overline{R} = \overline{R}_1 \bowtie \overline{R}_2$. The redundancy exhibited by the relation schema PERSON (6.13) was caused by this particular type of join dependency. The *fourth normal form*, introduced in [Fagin 1977], is designed to prevent redundancies of this type.

MVDs constrain instances of a relation in the same way that FDs do, so a description of a relation schema must include both. As a result, we describe a relation schema, **R**, as $(\overline{R}; \mathcal{D})$, where $\mathcal{D}$ is now a set of FDs and MVDs. **Entailment** of JDs is defined in the same way as entailment of FDs. Let $\mathcal{S}$ be a set of JDs (and possibly FDs) and d be a JD (or an FD). Then $\mathcal{S}$ **entails** d if every relation instance **r** that satisfies all dependencies in $\mathcal{S}$ also satisfies d. In Section 6.10.1, we show how an MVD might be entailed by a set of MVDs. With this in mind, a relation schema, $\mathbf{R} = (\overline{R}; \mathcal{D})$, is said to be in **fourth normal form** (4NF) if, for every MVD $\overline{R} = \overline{X} \bowtie \overline{Y}$ that is entailed by $\mathcal{D}$, either of the following is true:

- $\overline{X} \subseteq \overline{Y}$ or $\overline{Y} \subseteq \overline{X}$ (i.e., the MVD is trivial).
- $\overline{X} \cap \overline{Y}$ is a superkey of $\overline{R}$ (i.e., $(\overline{X} \cap \overline{Y}) \to \overline{R}$ is entailed by $\mathcal{D}$).

It is easy to see that PERSON is *not* a 4NF schema, because the MVD PERSON = (SSN, PhoneN) $\bowtie$ (SSN, ChildSSN) holds whereas SSN = {SSN, PhoneN} $\cap$ {SSN, ChildSSN} is not a superkey. What is the intuition here? If SSN were a superkey, then for each value of SSN there would be at most one value of PhoneN and one value of ChildSSN and hence no redundancy. On the other hand, splitting PERSON into a relation over the attributes (SSN, PhoneN) and another one over the attributes (SSN, ChildSSN) yields a lossless decomposition where every relation is in 4NF and no redundant information is stored.

4NF and BCNF. As it turns out, 4NF schemas are also BCNF schemas (i.e., 4NF closes the loopholes that BCNF leaves behind). To see this, suppose that $\mathbf{R} = (\overline{R}; \mathcal{D})$ is a 4NF schema and $\overline{X} \to \overline{Y}$ is a nontrivial functional dependency that holds in **R**. To show that 4NF schemas are also BCNF schemas we must demonstrate that $\overline{X}$ is a superkey of **R**. For simplicity, assume that $\overline{X}$ and $\overline{Y}$ are disjoint. Then $\overline{R}_1 = \overline{X}\,\overline{Y}$, $\overline{R}_2 = \overline{R} - \overline{Y}$ is a lossless decomposition of **R**. This follows directly from the test for losslessness of binary schema decompositions presented in Section 6.6.1 on page 214. Thus, $\overline{R} = \overline{R}_1 \bowtie \overline{R}_2$ is a binary join dependency, that is, an MVD that holds in **R**. But by the definition of 4NF it follows that either $\overline{X}\,\overline{Y} = \overline{R}_1 \subseteq \overline{R}_2 = \overline{R} - \overline{Y}$ (an impossibility) or $\overline{R} - \overline{Y} = \overline{R}_2 \subseteq \overline{R}_1 = \overline{X}\,\overline{Y}$ (which implies that $\overline{R} = \overline{X}\,\overline{Y}$ and $\overline{X}$ is a superkey) or that $\overline{R}_1 \cap \overline{R}_2 \, (= \overline{X})$ is a superkey. This means that every nontrivial FD in **R** satisfies the BCNF requirements.

It can also be shown (but it is harder to do) that if $\mathbf{R} = (\overline{R};\ \mathcal{D})$ is such that $\mathcal{D}$ consists only of FDs, then **R** is in 4NF if and only if it is in BCNF (see [Fagin 1977]). In other words, 4NF is an extension of the requirements for BCNF to design environments where MVDs, in addition to FDs, must be specified.

Brain Teaser: Can a 4NF schema not be in BCNF if FDs are the only dependencies?

Designing 4NF schemas. Because 4NF implies BCNF, we cannot hope to find a general algorithm for constructing a dependency-preserving and lossless decomposition of an arbitrary relation into relations in 4NF. However, as with BCNF, a lossless decomposition into 4NF can always be achieved. Such an algorithm is very similar to that for BCNF. It is an iterative process that starts with the original schema and at each stage yields decompositions that have fewer MVDs that violate 4NF: if $\mathbf{R}_i = (\bar{R}_i; \mathcal{D}_i)$ is such an intermediate schema and $\mathcal{D}_i$ entails an MVD of the form $\bar{R}_i = \bar{X} \bowtie \bar{Y}$, which violates 4NF, then the algorithm replaces $\mathbf{R}_i$ with a pair of schemas $(\bar{X}; \mathcal{D}_{i,1})$ and $(\bar{Y}; \mathcal{D}_{i,2})$. The new schemas do not have the offending MVD. Eventually, there will be no MVDs left that violate the requirements for 4NF.

Two important points regarding this algorithm need to be emphasized. First, if $\mathbf{R}_i = (\bar{R}_i; \mathcal{D}_i)$ is a schema and $\bar{S} \to \bar{T} \in \mathcal{D}$ (for simplicity, assume that $\bar{S}$ and $\bar{T}$ are disjoint), then this FD implies the MVD $R_i = \bar{S}\bar{T} \bowtie (\bar{R}_i - \bar{T})$. Thus, the 4NF decomposition algorithm can treat FDs as MVDs. The other nonobvious issue in the 4NF decomposition algorithm has to do with determining the set of dependencies that hold in the decomposition. That is, if $\mathbf{R}_i = (\bar{R}_i; \mathcal{D}_i)$ is decomposed with respect to the MVD $\bar{R}_i = \bar{X} \bowtie \bar{Y}$, what is the set of dependencies that is expected to hold over the attributes $\bar{X}$ and $\bar{Y}$ in the resulting decomposition? The answer is $\pi_{\bar{X}}(\mathcal{D}_i^+)$ and $\pi_{\bar{Y}}(\mathcal{D}_i^+)$—the projections of $\mathcal{D}_i^+$ on $\bar{X}$ and $\bar{Y}$. Here $\mathcal{D}_i^+$ is the **closure** of $\mathcal{D}_i$, that is, the set of all FDs and MVDs entailed by $\mathcal{D}_i$ (the optional Section 6.10 provides a set of inference rules for MVD entailment).

Projection of an FD on a set of attributes has been defined in Section 6.6.2. **Projection of an MVD**, $\bar{R}_i = \bar{V} \bowtie \bar{W}$, denoted $\pi_{\bar{X}}(\bar{R}_i = \bar{V} \bowtie \bar{W})$, is defined as $\bar{X} = (\bar{X} \cap \bar{V}) \bowtie (\bar{X} \cap \bar{W})$, if $\bar{V} \cap \bar{W} \subseteq \bar{X}$, and it is undefined otherwise. It follows directly from the definitions that the projection rule for MVDs is sound, that is, if an MVD, m, holds in a relation $\mathbf{r}$ then $\pi_{\bar{X}}(m)$ holds in $\pi_{\bar{X}}(\mathbf{r})$ (see Exercise 6.31).

Example 6.9.1 (4NF Decomposition). Consider a schema with attributes $ABCD$ and the MVDs $ABCD = AB \bowtie BCD$, $ABCD = ACD \bowtie BD$, and $ABCD = ABC \bowtie BCD$. Applying the first MVD, we obtain the following decomposition: AB, BCD. Projection of the remaining MVDs on AB is undefined. Projection of the second MVD on BCD is $BCD = CD \bowtie BD$, and projection of the third MVD on BCD is $BCD = BC \bowtie BCD$, which is a trivial MVD. Thus, we can decompose BCD with respect to this last MVD, which yields the following final result: AB, BD, CD. Note that if we first decomposed $ABCD$ with respect to the third MVD, the final result would be different: AB, BC, BD, CD. ∎

The design theory for 4NF is not as well developed as that for 3NF and BCNF, and very few algorithms are known. The basic recommendation is to start with a decomposition into 3NF and then proceed with the above algorithm and further decompose the offending (non-4NF) schemas. On a more sophisticated level, the work reported in [Beeri and Kifer 1986a, 1986b, 1987], among others, develops a design theory and the corresponding algorithms that can rectify design problems by synthesizing *new*(!) attributes. These advanced issues are briefly surveyed in Section 6.10.

Example 6.9.2 (Combining 3NF Synthesis with 4NF Decomposition). Consider the schema **R** over the attributes ABCDEFG with the following functional dependencies:

$$AB \rightarrow C$$
$$C \rightarrow B$$
$$BC \rightarrow DE$$
$$E \rightarrow FG$$

and the following multivalued dependencies:

$$\mathbf{R} = BC \bowtie ABDEFG$$
$$\mathbf{R} = EF \bowtie FGABCD$$

We begin with 3NF synthesis using the FDs only. This step is already familiar to us, so we present only the final result:

$$\mathbf{R}_1 = (ABC; \{AB \rightarrow C, C \rightarrow B\})$$
$$\mathbf{R}_2 = (CBDE; \{C \rightarrow BDE\})$$
$$\mathbf{R}_3 = (EFG; \{E \rightarrow FG\})$$

The first schema, $\mathbf{R}_1$, is not in BCNF due to the FD $C \rightarrow B$ (this FD must hold in $\mathbf{R}_1$ because it is in the original set of FDs and its attributes are contained within $\mathbf{R}_1$). So, we follow the BCNF decomposition algorithm and decompose $\mathbf{R}_1$ further using $C \rightarrow B$: $\mathbf{R}_{11} = (AC; \{A \rightarrow C\})$ and $\mathbf{R}_{12} = (BC; \{C \rightarrow B\})$.

Now we still have two MVDs left. Note that $\mathbf{R} = BC \bowtie ABDEFG$ projects onto $\mathbf{R}_2$ as $\mathbf{R}_2 = BC \bowtie BDE$, and it violates 4NF there because $B = BC \cap BDE$ is not a superkey of $\mathbf{R}_2$. So, we can use this MVD to decompose $\mathbf{R}_2$ into $(BC; \{C \rightarrow B\})$ and $(BDE; \{ \})$. Similarly, $\mathbf{R} = EF \bowtie FGABCD$ projects onto $\mathbf{R}_3$ as $\mathbf{R}_3 = EF \bowtie FG$. This makes $\mathbf{R}_3$ violate 4NF, and we decompose it into $(EF; \{E \rightarrow F\})$ and $(FG; \{ \})$.

The resulting decomposition is not dependency preserving. For instance, the FD $A \rightarrow B$, which was present in the original schema, is now not derivable from the FDs that are attached to the schemas in the decomposition. ∎

The fifth normal form. We are not going to cover the fifth normal form in this book. Suffice it to say that it exists but that the database designer usually need not be concerned with it. 5NF is similar to 4NF in that it is based on join dependencies, but unlike 4NF it seeks to preclude all nontrivial JDs (not just the binary ones) that are not entailed by a superkey.

6.10 Advanced 4NF Design *

The 4NF design algorithm outlined in Section 6.9 was intended to familiarize you with MVDs and 4NF, but it only scratches the surface of the 4NF design process. In this section, we provide more in-depth information, explain the main difficulties in designing database schemas in the presence of both FDs and MVDs, and outline the solutions. In particular, we explain why the 4NF decomposition algorithm does

OPTIONAL

not truly solve the redundancy problem and why BCNF might be inadequate in the presence of MVDs. We refer you to the literature for more details.

6.10.1 MVDs and Their Properties

Multivalued dependencies are binary join dependencies. However, unlike general join dependencies they have a number of nice algebraic properties similar to those of FDs. In particular, a set of syntactic rules, analogous to Armstrong's axioms for FDs, exists for finding MVDs entailed by a given MVD set. These rules have a particularly simple form when we use a special notation for MVDs: It is customary to represent the multivalued dependency of the form $\overline{R} = \overline{V} \bowtie \overline{W}$ over a relation schema $\mathbf{R} = (\overline{R}, \mathcal{D})$ as $\overline{X} \twoheadrightarrow \overline{Y}$, where $\overline{X} = \overline{V} \cap \overline{W}$ and $\overline{X} \cup \overline{Y} = \overline{V}$ or $\overline{X} \cup \overline{Y} = \overline{W}$. Hence, $\overline{X} \twoheadrightarrow \overline{Y}$ is synonymous with $\overline{R} = \overline{X}\,\overline{Y} \bowtie \overline{X}(\overline{R} - \overline{Y})$.

Take a moment to understand the intuition behind this notation. An MVD arises when a single value of one attribute, for example, A, is related to a set of values of attribute B and a set of values of attribute C. Attribute A, contained in $\overline{X}$, can be thought of as an independent variable whose value determines (hence the symbol $\twoheadrightarrow$) the associated sets of values of both B and C, one of which is contained in $\overline{Y}$ and the other in the complement of $\overline{X}\,\overline{Y}$. For example, the MVD in the PERSON relation (6.13), SSN PhoneN $\bowtie$ SSN ChildSSN, can be expressed as SSN $\twoheadrightarrow$ PhoneN or SSN $\twoheadrightarrow$ ChildSSN.

In addition, it is often convenient to combine MVDs that share the same left-hand side. For example, $\overline{X} \twoheadrightarrow \overline{Y}$ and $\overline{X} \twoheadrightarrow \overline{Z}$ can be represented as $\overline{X} \twoheadrightarrow \overline{Y} \mid \overline{Z}$. It is simple to show that such a pair of MVDs is equivalent to a join dependency of the form $\overline{X}\,\overline{Y} \bowtie \overline{X}\,\overline{Z} \bowtie \overline{X}(\overline{R} - \overline{Y}\,\overline{Z})$. The representation $\overline{X} \twoheadrightarrow \overline{Y} \mid \overline{Z}$ is convenient not only for the inference system but also as a device that shows where the redundancy is: if the attributes of $\overline{X}$, $\overline{Y}$, and $\overline{Z}$ are contained within one relational schema, the associations between $\overline{Y}$ and $\overline{Z}$ are likely to be stored redundantly. We saw this problem in the context of the PERSON relation on page 228 and will come back to it later.

With this notation, we now present an inference system that can be used to decide entailment for *both* FDs and MVDs. The extended system contains Armstrong's axioms for FDs plus the following rules.

FD-MVD glue.　These rules mix FDs and MVDs.

- *Replication.*　$\overline{X} \to \overline{Y}$ entails $\overline{X} \twoheadrightarrow \overline{Y}$.
- *Coalescence.*　If $\overline{W} \subset \overline{Y}$ and $\overline{Y} \cap \overline{Z} = \emptyset$, then $\overline{X} \twoheadrightarrow \overline{Y}$ and $\overline{Z} \to \overline{W}$ entail $\overline{X} \to \overline{W}$.

MVD-only rules.　Some of these rules are similar to rules for FDs; some are new.

- *Reflexivity.*　$\overline{X} \twoheadrightarrow \overline{X}$ holds in every relation.
- *Augmentation.*　$\overline{X} \twoheadrightarrow \overline{Y}$ entails $\overline{X}\,\overline{Z} \twoheadrightarrow \overline{Y}$.
- *Additivity.*　$\overline{X} \twoheadrightarrow \overline{Y}$ and $\overline{X} \twoheadrightarrow \overline{Z}$ entail $\overline{X} \twoheadrightarrow \overline{Y}\,\overline{Z}$.
- *Projectivity.*　$\overline{X} \twoheadrightarrow \overline{Y}$ and $\overline{X} \twoheadrightarrow \overline{Z}$ entail $\overline{X} \twoheadrightarrow \overline{Y} \cap \overline{Z}$ and $\overline{X} \twoheadrightarrow \overline{Y} - \overline{Z}$.

■ *Transitivity.* $\overline{X} \twoheadrightarrow \overline{Y}$ and $\overline{Y} \twoheadrightarrow \overline{Z}$ entail $\overline{X} \twoheadrightarrow \overline{Z} - \overline{Y}$.

■ *Pseudotransitivity.* $\overline{X} \twoheadrightarrow \overline{Y}$ and $\overline{Y}\,\overline{W} \twoheadrightarrow \overline{Z}$ entail $\overline{X}\,\overline{W} \twoheadrightarrow \overline{Z} - (\overline{Y}\,\overline{W})$.

■ *Complementation.* $\overline{X} \twoheadrightarrow \overline{Y}$ entails $\overline{X} \twoheadrightarrow \overline{R} - \overline{X}\overline{Y}$, where $\overline{R}$ is the set of all attributes in the schema.

These rules first appeared in [Beeri et al. 1977], but [Maier 1983] provides a more systematic and accessible introduction to the subject. The rules are *sound* in the sense that in any relation where a rule premise holds, the consequent of the rule holds as well. For example, replication follows using the same reasoning that we used for losslessness: if $\overline{X} \rightarrow \overline{Y}$ then the decomposition of $\overline{R}$ into $\overline{R}_1 = \overline{X}\,\overline{Y}$ and $\overline{R}_2 = \overline{X}(\overline{R} - \overline{Y})$ is lossless; hence, $\overline{R} = \overline{X}\,\overline{Y} \bowtie \overline{X}(\overline{R} - \overline{Y})$ and so $\overline{X} \twoheadrightarrow \overline{Y}$.

A remarkable fact, however, is that given a set, $\mathcal{S}$, that consists of MVDs and FDs and a dependency, d (which can be either an FD or an MVD), $\mathcal{S}$ entails d if and only if d can be derived by a purely syntactic application of the above rules (plus Armstrong's axioms) to the dependencies in $\mathcal{S}$. A similar property for FDs alone was earlier called *completeness*. Proving the soundness of the above inference rules is a good exercise (see Exercise 6.24). Completeness is much harder to prove. The interested reader is referred to [Beeri et al. 1977; Maier 1983].

6.10.2 The Difficulty of Designing for 4NF

The inference rules for MVDs are useful because they can help eliminate redundant MVDs and FDs. Also, as in the case of FDs alone, using nonredundant dependency sets can improve the design produced by the 4NF decomposition algorithm described on page 232. However, even in the absence of redundant dependencies, things can go awry. We illustrate some of the problems on a number of examples. Three issues are considered: loss of dependencies, redundancy, and design using both FDs and MVDs.

A contracts example. Consider the schema

CONTRACTS(Buyer, Vendor, Product, Currency)

where a tuple of the form ⟨John Doe, Acme, Paper Clips, USD⟩ means that buyer John Doe has a contract to buy paper clips from Acme, Inc., using U.S. currency. Suppose that our relation represents contracts of an international network of buyers and companies. Although the contract was consummated in dollars, if Acme sells some of its products in Euros (perhaps it is a European company), it may be convenient to store the contract in two tuples: one with the financial information expressed in USD, the other with information expressed in Euros. In general, CONTRACTS satisfies the rule that, if a company accepts several currencies, each contract is described in each one. This can be expressed using the following combined MVD:

Buyer Vendor $\twoheadrightarrow$ Product | Currency   **6.16**

OPTIONAL

To be explicit, this MVD means

CONTRACTS = (Buyer Vendor Product) ⋈ (Buyer Vendor Currency)

The second rule of our international network example is that if two vendors supply a certain product, both accept a certain currency, and a buyer of that product has a contract to buy that product with one of the two vendors, then this buyer must have a contract for purchasing that product with the other vendor as well. For example, if, in addition to the above tuple, CONTRACTS contained ⟨Mary Smith, OfficeMin, Paper Clips, USD⟩, then it must also contain the tuples ⟨John Doe, OfficeMin, Paper Clips, USD⟩ and ⟨Mary Smith, Acme, Paper Clips, USD⟩. This type of constraint is expressed using the following MVD:

Product Currency ↠ Buyer | Vendor   **6.17**

Let us now attempt a design using the 4NF decomposition algorithm. If we first decompose using the dependency (6.16), we get the following lossless decomposition:

(Buyer, Vendor, Product)
(Buyer, Vendor, Currency)   **6.18**

Observe that once this decomposition is done, the second MVD can no longer be applied because no join dependency holds in either one of the above schemas.[5] The situation here is very similar to the problem we faced with the BCNF decomposition algorithm. Some dependencies might get lost in the process. In our case, it is the dependency (6.17). The same problem exists if we first decompose using the second dependency above, but in this case we lose (6.16).

Unlike losing FDs during BCNF decomposition, losing MVDs is potentially a more serious problem because the result might still harbor redundancy even if every relation in the decomposition is in 4NF! To see this, consider the following relation for the CONTRACTS schema:

Buyer	Vendor	Product	Currency
B_1	V_1	P	C
B_2	V_2	P	C
B_1	V_2	P	C
B_2	V_1	P	C

---

[5] This may not be obvious because we have not discussed the tools for verifying such facts. However, in this particular example, our claim can be checked directly using the definition of the natural join. We again recommend [Maier 1983] as a good reference for learning about such techniques.

It is easy to check that this relation satisfies MVDs (6.16) and (6.17). For instance, to verify (6.16) take the projections on decomposition schema (6.18).

Buyer	Vendor	Product
B_1	V_1	P
B_2	V_2	P
B_1	V_2	P
B_2	V_1	P

Buyer	Vendor	Currency
B_1	V_1	C
B_2	V_2	C
B_1	V_2	C
B_2	V_1	C

Joining these two relations (using the natural join) clearly yields the original relation for CONTRACTS. A closer look shows that the above relations still contain a great deal of redundancy. For instance, the first relation twice says that product P is supplied by vendors V_1 and V_2. Furthermore, it twice says that P is wanted by buyers B_1 and B_2. The first relation seems to beg for further decomposition into (Buyer, Vendor) and (Vendor, Product), and the second relation begs to be decomposed into (Buyer, Currency) and (Vendor, Currency). Alas, none of these wishes can be granted because none of these decompositions is lossless (for example, Vendor is not a key of the first relation). As a result, decomposition (6.18) suffers from the usual update anomalies even though each relation is in 4NF! Furthermore, since 4NF implies BCNF, even BCNF does not guarantee complete elimination of redundancy in the presence of MVDs!

A dictionary example. For another example, consider a multilingual dictionary relation, DICTIONARY(English, French, German), which provides translations from one language to another. As expected, every term has a translation (possibly more than one) into every language, and the translations are independent of each other. These constraints are easily captured using MVDs.

$$\text{English} \twoheadrightarrow \text{French} \mid \text{German}$$
$$\text{French} \twoheadrightarrow \text{English} \mid \text{German} \qquad \qquad \textbf{6.19}$$
$$\text{German} \twoheadrightarrow \text{English} \mid \text{French}$$

The problem, as before, is that applying any one of these MVDs in the 4NF decomposition algorithm loses the other two dependencies, and the resulting decomposition exhibits the usual update anomalies.

A multilingual thesaurus example. Let us enhance the previous example so that every term is now associated with a unique concept and each concept has an associated description. For the purpose of this example, ignore the language used for the

OPTIONAL

description. The corresponding schema becomes DICTIONARY(Concept, Description, English, French, German) and the dependencies are

```
English → Concept
French → Concept
German → Concept
Concept → Description
Concept ↠ English | French | German
```

6.20

An example of a concept is A5329 with description "homo sapiens" and translations {human, man}, {homme}, and {Mensch, Mann}.

The 4NF decomposition algorithm suggests that we start by picking up an MVD that violates 4NF and then use it in the decomposition process. Since every FD is also an MVD, we might choose English → Concept first, which yields the schema (English, Concept) and (English, French, German, Description). Using the transitivity rule for MVDs, we can derive the MVD English ↠ French | German | Description and further decompose the second relation into (English, French), (English, German), and (English, Description).

The resulting schema has two drawbacks. First, it is lopsided toward English whereas the original schema was completely symmetric. Second, every one of the bilingual relations, such as (English, French), redundantly lists all possible translations from English to French and back. For example, if a and b are English synonyms, c and d are French synonyms, and a translates into c, then the English-French dictionary (English, French) has all four tuples: $\langle a, c \rangle$, $\langle a, d \rangle$, $\langle b, c \rangle$, and $\langle b, d \rangle$.

A better way to use the 4NF decomposition algorithm is to compute the attribute closure (defined on page 204) of the left-hand side of the MVD in (6.20) with respect to functional dependencies in (6.20) and derive the following MVD by the augmentation rule:

```
Concept Description ↠ English | French | German
```

We can then apply the 4NF decomposition algorithm using this MVD, which yields the decomposition (Concept, Description, English), (Concept, Description, French), and (Concept, Description, German). We can further decompose each of these relations into BCNF using the FDs alone, splitting off (Concept Description). Not only do we end up with a decomposition into 4NF, but also all dependencies are preserved.

6.10.3 A 4NF Decomposition How-To

The above examples make it clear that designing for 4NF is not a straightforward process. In fact, this problem was an active area of research until the early 1980s [Beeri et al. 1978; Zaniolo and Melkanoff 1981; Sciore 1983]. Eventually, all of this work was integrated into a uniform framework in [Beeri and Kifer 1986b]. While we cannot go into the details of this approach, its highlights can be explained with our three examples: contracts, dictionary, and thesaurus.

1. *The anomaly of split left-hand sides*. It is indicative of a design problem when one MVD *splits the left-hand side* of another, as in our contracts example. We say that an MVD $X \twoheadrightarrow V \mid W$ **splits the left-hand side** of the MVD $Y \twoheadrightarrow K \mid L$ if $Y \cap V$, and $Y \cap W$ are both non-empty sets of attributes. For instance, the MVD (6.17) splits the left-hand side, (Buyer, Vendor), of (6.16), which indicates that Buyer and Vendor are unrelated attributes (every buyer is associated in some tuple with every vendor) and thus should not be in the same relation. This is precisely the reason for the redundancy that we observed in the decomposition of the CONTRACTS relation into (Buyer, Vendor, Product) and (Buyer, Vendor, Currency).

   One reason for the problem with this schema might be the incorrectly specified dependencies. Instead of the MVDs given in the CONTRACT schema, the join dependency

   ---

   Buyer Product ⋈ Vendor Product
          ⋈ Vendor Currency ⋈ Buyer Currency

   ---

   seems more appropriate. It simply says that each buyer needs certain products, each vendor sells certain products, a vendor can accept certain currencies, and a buyer can pay in certain currencies. As long as a buyer and a vendor can match on a product and a currency, a deal can be struck. This English-language description matches the requirements in the description of the contracts example, and the designer might simply have failed to recognize that the above JD is all that is needed.

2. *Intersection anomaly*. An **intersection anomaly** is one in which a schema has a pair of MVDs of the form $\overline{X} \twoheadrightarrow \overline{Z}$ and $\overline{Y} \twoheadrightarrow \overline{Z}$ but there is no MVD $\overline{X} \cap \overline{Y} \twoheadrightarrow \overline{Z}$. Notice that our dictionary example has precisely this sort of anomaly: there are MVDs English $\twoheadrightarrow$ French and German $\twoheadrightarrow$ French, but there is no dependency $\emptyset \twoheadrightarrow$ French. [Beeri and Kifer 1986b] argue that this is a design problem that can be rectified by inventing new attributes. In our case, the attribute Concept is missing. In fact, the thesaurus example was constructed out of the dictionary example by adding this very attribute[6] plus the dependencies that relate it to the old attributes. Perhaps somewhat unexpectedly, this type of anomaly can be corrected completely automatically—the new attribute and the associated dependencies can be invented by a well-defined algorithm [Beeri and Kifer 1986a, 1987].

3. *Design strategy*. Assuming that the anomaly of split left-hand sides does not arise,[7] a dependency-preserving decomposition of the schema $\mathbf{R} = (\overline{R}; \mathcal{D})$ into fourth normal form can be achieved in five steps:

   (a) Compute attribute closure, X^+, of the left-hand side of every MVD $X \twoheadrightarrow Y$ using the FDs entailed by $\mathcal{D}$. Replace every $X \twoheadrightarrow Y$ with $X^+ \twoheadrightarrow Y$.

---

[6] The other attribute, Description, was added to illustrate a different point. Ignore it for the moment.

[7] Any such anomaly means that the dependencies are incorrect or incomplete.

(b) Find the minimal cover of the resulting set of MVDs. It turns out that such a cover is unique if $\mathcal{D}$ does not exhibit the anomaly of split left-hand sides.

(c) Use the algorithm of [Beeri and Kifer 1986a, 1987] to eliminate intersection anomalies by adding new attributes.

(d) Apply the 4NF decomposition algorithm using MVDs only.

(e) Apply the BCNF design algorithm within each resulting schema using FDs only.

Every relation in the resulting decomposition is in 4NF and no MVD is lost on the way, which guarantees that no redundancy is present in the resulting schemas. Moreover, if the decompositions in the last stage are dependency preserving, so is the overall five-step process.

The transition from the dictionary example to the thesaurus example and then to the final decomposition of the thesaurus example is an illustration of this five-step process. Let us enhance the dictionary slightly by adding the Description attribute and the FDs English → Description, German → Description, and French → Description (so the dictionary example now contains four attributes). Then we can obtain a BCNF decomposition as follows:

- Apply steps (a) and (b). (Step (b) applies vacuously, as the set of MVDs is already minimal.) The resulting MVDs are English Description ↠ French | German, etc.

- Apply step (c). According to the algorithm in [Beeri and Kifer 1986a], this introduces a new attribute, Concept, with the exact set of dependencies depicted in the thesaurus example (6.20), except that the last MVD has a closed left-hand side: Concept Description ↠ English | French | German. (Of course, the algorithm does not propose the name for the newly invented attribute — this is a job for the database designer.)

- Apply step (d)—perform the 4NF decomposition with respect to the above MVD and then step (e)—apply the BCNF design process within each of the resulting schemas.

The result has four schemas, as explained in the thesaurus example: (Concept, English), (Concept, French), (Concept, German), and (Concept, Description), where English, French, and German are keys in the first three schemas and Concept in the last.

6.11 Summary of Normal Form Decomposition

We summarize some of the properties of the normal form decomposition algorithms discussed.

■ *Third normal form* schemas might have some redundancy. The decomposition algorithm that we discussed generates 3NF schemas that are lossless and dependency preserving. It does not take multivalued dependencies into account.

■ *Boyce-Codd* decompositions do not have redundancy if only FDs are considered. The decomposition algorithm we discussed generates BCNF schemas that are lossless but that might not be dependency preserving. (As we have shown, some schemas do not have Boyce-Codd decompositions that are both lossless and dependency preserving.) It does not take multivalued dependencies into account, so redundancy due to such dependencies is possible.

■ *Fourth normal form* decompositions do not have any nontrivial multivalued dependencies. The algorithm we sketched generates 4NF schemas that are lossless but that might not be dependency preserving. It attempts to eliminate redundancies associated with MVDs, but it does not guarantee that all such redundancies will go away.

Note that none of these decompositions produces schemas that have all of the properties we want.

6.12 Case Study: Schema Refinement for the Student Registration System

Having spent all that effort studying the relational normalization theory, we will now put the new knowledge to good use and verify our design for the Student Registration System as outlined in Section 4.8. The good news is that we did a pretty good job of converting the E-R diagram in Figure 4.33, page 114, into the relations in Figures 4.34 and 4.35, so most of the relations turn out to be in Boyce-Codd normal form. However, you did not struggle through this chapter in vain—read on!

To determine whether a schema is in a normal form we need to collect all FDs relevant to it. One source is the PRIMARY KEY and the UNIQUE constraints. However, there might be additional dependencies that are not captured by these constraints or the E-R diagram. They can be uncovered only by careful examination of the schema and of the specifications of the application, a process that requires much care and concentration. If no new dependencies are found, all FDs in the schema are the primary and the candidate keys (or the FDs entailed by them), so the schema is in BCNF. If additional FDs are uncovered, we must check if the schema is in a desirable normal form and, if not, make appropriate changes.

In our case, we can verify that all relation schemas in Figure 4.35, except CLASS, are in BCNF, as they have no FDs that are not entailed by the keys. This verification is not particularly hard because these schemas have six or fewer attributes. It is harder in the case of CLASS, which has ten.

We illustrate the process using the CLASS schema. Along the way, we uncover a missing functional dependency and then normalize CLASS. First, let us list the key constraints specified in the CREATE TABLE statement for that relation.

1. CrsCode SectionNo Semester Year → ClassTime
2. CrsCode SectionNo Semester Year → Textbook
3. CrsCode SectionNo Semester Year → Enrollment
4. CrsCode SectionNo Semester Year → MaxEnrollment
5. CrsCode SectionNo Semester Year → ClassroomId

6. CrsCode SectionNo Semester Year → InstructorId

7. Semester Year ClassTime InstructorId → CrsCode

8. Semester Year ClassTime InstructorId → Textbook

9. Semester Year ClassTime InstructorId → SectionNo

10. Semester Year ClassTime InstructorId → Enrollment

11. Semester Year ClassTime InstructorId → MaxEnrollment

12. Semester Year ClassTime InstructorId → ClassroomId

13. Semester Year ClassTime ClassroomId → CrsCode

14. Semester Year ClassTime ClassroomId → Textbook

15. Semester Year ClassTime ClassroomId → SectionNo

16. Semester Year ClassTime ClassroomId → Enrollment

17. Semester Year ClassTime ClassroomId → MaxEnrollment

18. Semester Year ClassTime ClassroomId → InstructorId

Verifying that additional dependencies hold in a large schema can be difficult: one has to consider every subset of the attributes of CLASS that is not a superkey and check if it functionally determines some other attribute. This "check" is not based on any concrete algorithm. The decision that a certain FD does or does not hold in a relation is strictly a matter of how the designer understands the semantics of the corresponding entity in the real-world enterprise that is being modeled by the database, and it is inherently error prone. However, research is being conducted to help with the problem. For instance, FDEXPERT [Ram 1995] is an expert system that helps database designers discover FDs using knowledge about typical enterprises and their design patterns.

Unfortunately, we do not have an expert system handy, so we do the analysis the hard way. Consider the following candidate FD:

    ClassTime ClassroomId InstructorId → CrsCode

It is easy to see why this FD does not apply: different courses can be taught by the same instructor in the same room at the same time—if all this happens in different semesters and years. Many other FDs can be rejected through a similar argument. However, since in Section 4.8 we assumed that at most one textbook can be used in any particular course, the following FD is an appropriate addition to the set of constraints previously specified for CLASS:

    CsrCode Semester Year → Textbook   **6.21**

Although the textbook used in a course can vary from semester to semester, if a certain course is offered in a particular semester and is split in several sections because of large enrollment, all sections use the same textbook.[8]

It is now easy to see the problem with the design of CLASS: the left-hand side of the above dependency is not a key, and Textbook does not belong to any key either. For these reasons, CLASS is not in 3NF. The 3NF synthesis algorithm on page 224 suggests that the situation can be rectified by splitting the original schema into the following pair:

- CLASS1, with all the attributes of CLASS, except Textbook, and FDs 1, 3–7, 9–13, 15–18 (these numbers refer to the numbered list of FDs on page 241.)

- TEXTBOOKS(CrsCode, Semester, Year, Textbook), with the single FD
  CrsCode Semester Year → Textbook

Both of these schemas are in BCNF—we can verify by direct inspection that all of their FDs are entailed by key constraints. The 3NF synthesis algorithm also guarantees that the above decomposition is lossless and dependency preserving.

Let us now consider a more realistic situation in which classes can have more than one recommended textbook and all sections of the class in a particular semester use the same set of textbooks. In this case, FD (6.21) does not hold, of course. Observe that the textbooks used in any particular class are independent of meeting time, instructor, enrollment, and so forth. This situation is similar to the one in Section 6.9 relative to the PERSON relation shown in (6.14): here, the independence of the attribute Textbook from the attributes ClassTime, InstructorId, and so forth, is formally represented through the following multivalued dependency:

(CrsCode Semester Year ClassTime SectionNo
    InstructorId Enrollment MaxEnrollment ClassroomId)
        ⋈ (CrsCode Semester Year Textbook)

Like the schema of the PERSON relation, CLASS is in BCNF; even so, it contains redundancy because of the above multivalued dependency. The solution to the problem is to try for a higher normal form—4NF—and, fortunately, this is easy using the algorithm in Section 6.9 on page 232. We simply need to decompose CLASS using the above dependency, which yields the following lossless decomposition (losslessness is guaranteed by the 4NF decomposition algorithm):

- CLASS1(CrsCode, Semester, Year, ClassTime, SectionNo, InstructorId, Enrollment, MaxEnrollment, ClassroomId) with the FDs 1, 3–7, 9–13, 15–18

- TEXTBOOKS(CrsCode, Semester, Year, Textbook) with no FDs

---

[8] This rule might not be true of all universities, but it is certainly true of many.

Note that the only difference between this schema and the one obtained earlier under the one-textbook-per-class assumption is the absence, in the second schema, of the FD

CrsCode Semester Year → Textbook

The result of applying relational normalization theory to the preliminary design for the Student Registration System developed in Section 4.8 is a lossless decomposition where every relation is in 4NF (and thus in BCNF as well). Luckily, this decomposition is dependency preserving, since every FD specified for the schema is embedded in one of the relations in the decomposition—something that is not always achievable with 4NF and BCNF design.

6.13 Tuning Issues: To Decompose or Not to Decompose?

In this chapter, we have learned a great deal about the schema decomposition theory. However, this theory was motivated by concerns that redundancy leads to consistency-maintenance problems in the presence of frequent database updates. What if most of the transactions are read-only queries? Schema decomposition seems to make query answering harder because associations that existed in one relation before the decomposition might be broken into separate relations afterward.

For instance, finding the average number of hobbies per address is more efficient using the monolithic relation of Figure 4.13 rather than the pair of relations of Figure 6.1 because the latter requires a join before the aggregates can be computed. This is an example of the classic time/space trade-off. Adding redundancy can improve query performance. Such a trade-off has to be evaluated in the context of a particular application if the performance of a frequently executed query is found wanting. The term **denormalization** describes situations in which achieving certain normal forms incurs a punishing performance penalty, and thus perhaps there should be no decomposition.

In general, no one recommendation works in all cases. Sometimes, simulation can help resolve the issue. Here is an incomplete list of conflicting guidelines that need to be evaluated against each particular mix of transactions:

1. Decomposition generally makes answering complex queries less efficient because additional joins must be performed during query evaluation.

2. Decomposition can make answering simple queries more efficient because such queries usually involve a small number of attributes that belong to the same relation. Since decomposed relations have fewer tuples, the tuples that need to be scanned during the evaluation of a simple query are likely to be fewer.

3. Decomposition generally makes simple update transactions more efficient. However, this may not be true for complex update transactions (such as *Raise the*

salary of all professors who taught every course required for computer science majors) since they might involve complex queries (and thus might require complex joins).

4. Decomposition can lower the demand for storage space since it usually eliminates redundant data.

5. Decomposition can increase storage requirements if the degree of redundancy is low. For instance, in the PERSON relation of (6.14), suppose that, with few exceptions, most people have just one phone number and one child. In this situation, schema decomposition can actually increase storage requirements without bringing tangible benefits. The same applies to the decomposition of HASACCOUNT in Figure 6.7, which can increase the overhead for update transactions. The reason is that verification of the FD

```
ClientId OfficeId → AccountNumber
```

after an update requires a join because the attributes `ClientId` and `OfficeId` belong to different relations in the decomposition.

BIBLIOGRAPHIC NOTES

Relational normal forms and functional dependencies were introduced in [Codd 1970]. Armstrong's axioms and the proof of their soundness and completeness first appeared in [Armstrong 1974], although more accessible exposition can be found in [Ullman 1988; Maier 1983]. An efficient algorithm for entailment of FDs first appeared in [Beeri and Bernstein 1979]. A general test for lossless decompositions was first developed in [Beeri et al. 1981]. The algorithm for synthesizing the third normal form is due to [Bernstein 1976].

The fourth normal form was introduced in [Fagin 1977], which also presents a naive decomposition algorithm and explores the relationship between 4NF and BCNF. The fifth normal form is discussed in [Beeri et al. 1977], but we recommend [Maier 1983] as a more systematic introduction to the subject. The survey in [Kanellakis 1990] is also a good starting point. Other papers on 4NF are [Beeri et al. 1978; Zaniolo and Melkanoff 1981; Sciore 1983]. Eventually, all of this work on designing 4NF schemas in the presence of FDs and MVDs was extended and integrated into a uniform framework in [Beeri and Kifer 1986a, 1986b, 1987]. More recent works on 4NF are [Vincent and Srinivasan 1993; Vincent 1999].

In-depth coverage of the relational design theory is provided in texts such as [Mannila and Raäihä 1992; Atzeni and Antonellis 1993].

As illustrated in Section 6.12, one of the most difficult obstacles to applying the results discussed in this chapter to database design is finding the right set of dependencies to use in the schema normalization process. We mentioned the FDEXPERT system [Ram 1995], which helps discover functional dependencies using knowledge about various types of enterprises. Extensive work has also been done on the algorithms for discovering FDs, MVDs, and inclusion dependencies using the techniques from *machine learning* and *data mining* [Huhtala et al. 1999; Kantola et al. 1992; Mannila and Raäihä 1994; Flach and Savnik 1999; Savnik and Flach 1993].

EXERCISES

6.1 The definition of functional dependencies does not preclude the case in which the left-hand side is empty—that is, it allows FDs of the form $\{\} \to A$. Explain the meaning of such dependencies.

6.2 Give an example of a schema that is not in 3NF and has just two attributes.

6.3 What is the smallest number of attributes a relation key can have?

6.4 A table, Abc, has attributes A, B, and C, and a functional dependency $A \to BC$. Write an SQL **CREATE ASSERTION** statement that prevents a violation of this functional dependency.

6.5 Prove that every 3NF relation schema with just two attributes is also in BCNF. Prove that every schema that has *at most* one nontrivial FD is in BCNF.

6.6 If the functional dependency $X \to Y$ is a key constraint, what are X and Y?

6.7 Can a key be the set of all attributes if there is at least one nontrivial FD in a schema?

6.8 The following is an instance of a relation schema. Can you tell whether the schema includes the functional dependencies $A \to B$ and $BC \to A$?

A	B	C
1	2	3
2	2	2
1	3	2
4	2	3

6.9 Prove that Armstrong's transitivity axiom is sound—that is, every relation that satisfies the FDs $\overline{X} \to \overline{Y}$ and $\overline{Y} \to \overline{Z}$ must also satisfy the FD $\overline{X} \to \overline{Z}$.

6.10 Prove the following *generalized transitivity rule*: If $\overline{Z} \subseteq \overline{Y}$, then $\overline{X} \to \overline{Y}$ and $\overline{Z} \to \overline{W}$ entail $\overline{X} \to \overline{W}$. Try to prove this rule in two ways:

- Using the argument that directly appeals to the definition of FDs, as in Section 6.4
- By deriving $\overline{X} \to \overline{W}$ from $\overline{X} \to \overline{Y}$ and $\overline{Z} \to \overline{W}$ via a series of steps using Armstrong's axioms

*6.11 We have shown the *soundness* of the algorithm in Figure 6.3—that if $A \in closure$ then $A \in \overline{X}_{\mathcal{F}}^{+}$. Prove the *completeness* of this algorithm; that is, if $A \in \overline{X}_{\mathcal{F}}^{+}$, then $A \in closure$ at the end of the computation. *Hint:* Use induction on the length of derivation of $X \to A$ by Armstrong's axioms.

6.12 Suppose that $\mathbf{R} = (\bar{R}, \mathcal{F})$ is a relation schema and $\mathbf{R}_1 = (\bar{R}_1; \mathcal{F}_1), \ldots, \mathbf{R}_n = (\bar{R}_n; \mathcal{F}_n)$ is its decomposition. Let $\mathbf{r}$ be a valid relation instance over $\mathbf{R}$ and $\mathbf{r}_i = \pi_{\bar{R}_i}(\mathbf{r})$. Show that $\mathbf{r}_i$ satisfies the set of FDs $\mathcal{F}_i$ and is therefore a valid relation instance over the schema $\mathbf{R}_i$.

6.13 Let $\bar{R}_1$ and $\bar{R}_2$ be sets of attributes and $\bar{R} = \bar{R}_1 \cup \bar{R}_2$. Let $\mathbf{r}$ be a relation on $\bar{R}$. Prove that $\mathbf{r} \subseteq \pi_{\bar{R}_1}(\mathbf{r}) \bowtie \pi_{\bar{R}_2}(\mathbf{r})$. Generalize this result to decompositions of $\bar{R}$ into $n > 2$ schemas.

6.14 Suppose that $\mathbf{R} = (\bar{R}; \mathcal{F})$ is a schema and that $\mathbf{R}_1 = (\bar{R}_1; \mathcal{F}_1)$, $\mathbf{R}_2 = (\bar{R}_2; \mathcal{F}_2)$ is a binary decomposition such that neither $(\bar{R}_1 \cap \bar{R}_2) \to \bar{R}_1$ nor $(\bar{R}_1 \cap \bar{R}_2) \to \bar{R}_2$ is implied by $\mathcal{F}$. Construct a relation, $\mathbf{r}$, such that $\mathbf{r} \subset \pi_{\bar{R}_1}(\mathbf{r}) \bowtie \pi_{\bar{R}_2}(\mathbf{r})$, where $\subset$ denotes strict subset. (This relation, therefore, shows that at least one of these FDs is necessary for the decomposition of $\mathbf{R}$ to be lossless.)

6.15 Suppose that $\mathbf{R}_1, \ldots, \mathbf{R}_n$ is a decomposition of schema $\mathbf{R}$ obtained by a sequence of binary lossless decompositions (beginning with a decomposition of $\mathbf{R}$). Prove that $\mathbf{R}_1, \ldots, \mathbf{R}_n$ is a lossless decomposition of $\mathbf{R}$.

6.16 Prove that the loop in the BCNF decomposition algorithm of Figure 6.9 has the property that the database schema at each subsequent iteration has strictly fewer FDs that violate BCNF than has the schema in the previous iteration.

*6.17 Prove that the algorithm for synthesizing 3NF decompositions in Section 6.8.2 yields schemas that satisfy the conditions of 3NF. (*Hint*: Use the proof-by-contradiction technique. Assume that some FD violates 3NF and then show that this contradicts the fact that the algorithm synthesized schemas out of a minimal cover.)

6.18 Consider a database schema with attributes A, B, C, D, and E and functional dependencies $B \to E$, $E \to A$, $A \to D$, and $D \to E$. Prove that the decomposition of this schema into AB, BCD, and ADE is lossless. Is it dependency preserving?

6.19 Consider a relation schema with attributes $ABCGWXYZ$ and the set of dependencies $\mathcal{F} = \{XZ \to ZYB, YA \to CG, C \to W, B \to G, XZ \to G\}$. Solve the following problems using the appropriate algorithms.

a. Find a minimal cover for $\mathcal{F}$.
b. Is the dependency $XZA \to YB$ implied by $\mathcal{F}$?
c. Is the decomposition into $XZYAB$ and $YABCGW$ lossless?
d. Is the above decomposition dependency preserving?

6.20 Consider the following functional dependencies over the attribute set $ABCDEFGH$:

$A \to E$	$BE \to D$
$AD \to BE$	$BDH \to E$
$AC \to E$	$F \to A$
$E \to B$	$D \to H$
$BG \to F$	$CD \to A$

Find a minimal cover, then decompose into lossless 3NF. After that, check if all the resulting relations are in BCNF. If you find a schema that is not, decompose it into a lossless BCNF. Explain all steps.

6.21 Find a projection of the following set of dependencies on the attributes *AFE*:

$$A \rightarrow BC \qquad\qquad E \rightarrow HG$$
$$C \rightarrow FG \qquad\qquad G \rightarrow A$$

6.22 Consider the schema with the attribute set *ABCDEFH* and the FDs depicted in (6.12), page 224. Prove that the decomposition (*AD*; $A \rightarrow D$), (*CE*; $C \rightarrow E$), (*FA*; $F \rightarrow A$), (*EF*; $E \rightarrow F$), (*BHE*; $BH \rightarrow E$) is not lossless by providing a concrete relation instance over *ABCDEFH* that exhibits the loss of information when projected on this schema.

6.23 Consider the schema *BCDFGH* with the following FDs: $BG \rightarrow CD$, $G \rightarrow F$, $CD \rightarrow GH$, $C \rightarrow FG$, $F \rightarrow D$. Use the 3NF synthesis algorithm to obtain a lossless, dependency-preserving decomposition into 3NF. If any of the resulting schemas is not in BCNF, proceed to decompose them into BCNF.

*6.24 Prove that all rules for inferring FDs and MVDs given in Section 6.10 are sound. In other words, for every relation, **r**, which satisfies the dependencies in the premise of any rule, *R*, the conclusion of *R* is also satisfied by **r** (e.g., for the augmentation rule, prove that if $\overline{X} \twoheadrightarrow \overline{Y}$ holds in **r** then $\overline{XZ} \twoheadrightarrow \overline{Y}$ also holds in **r**).

6.25 Prove that if a schema, $\mathbf{S} = (\overline{S}, \mathcal{F})$, is in 3NF, then every FD in $\mathcal{F}^+$ (not only those that are in $\mathcal{F}$) satisfies the 3NF requirements.

6.26 If $X = \{A, B\}$ and $F = \{A \rightarrow D, BC \rightarrow EJ, BD \rightarrow AE, EJ \rightarrow G, ADE \rightarrow H, HD \rightarrow J\}$, what is X_F^+? Are the FDs $AB \rightarrow C$ and $AE \rightarrow G$ entailed by *F*?

6.27 Using only Armstrong's axioms and the FDs

    (a) $AB \rightarrow C$
    (b) $A \rightarrow BE$
    (c) $C \rightarrow D$

give a complete derivation of the FD $A \rightarrow D$.

6.28 Consider a decomposition $\mathbf{R}_1, \ldots, \mathbf{R}_n$ of **R** obtained via steps 1, 2, and 3 (but not step 4) of the 3NF synthesis algorithm on page 224. Suppose there is an attribute *A* in **R** that does not belong to any of the $\mathbf{R}_i$, $i = 1, \ldots, n$. Prove that *A* must be part of every key of **R**.

6.29 Consider the schema $\mathbf{R} = (ABCDEFGH, \{BE \rightarrow GH, G \rightarrow FA, D \rightarrow C, F \rightarrow B\})$.

    a. Can there be a key that does not contain *D*? Explain.
    b. Is the schema in BCNF? Explain.
    c. Use one cycle of the BCNF algorithm to decompose **R** into two subrelations. Are the subrelations in BCNF?
    d. Show that your decomposition is lossless.
    e. Is your decomposition dependency preserving? Explain.

6.30 Find a minimal cover of the following set of FDs: $AB \rightarrow CD$, $BC \rightarrow FG$, $A \rightarrow G$, $G \rightarrow B$, $C \rightarrow G$. Is the decomposition of *ABCDFG* into *ABCD* and *ACFG* lossless? Explain.

6.31 Let $\overline{X}, \overline{Y}, \overline{S}, \overline{R}$ be sets of attributes such that $\overline{S} \subseteq \overline{R}$ and $\overline{X} \cup \overline{Y} = R$. Let **r** be a relation over $\overline{R}$ that satisfies the nontrivial MVD $\overline{R} = \overline{X} \bowtie \overline{Y}$ (i.e., neither set $\overline{X}$ or $\overline{Y}$ is a subset of the other).

　　a. Prove that if $\overline{X} \cap \overline{Y} \subseteq \overline{S}$, then the relation $\pi_{\overline{S}}(\mathbf{r})$ satisfies the MVD $\overline{S} = (\overline{S} \cap \overline{X}) \bowtie (\overline{S} \cap \overline{Y})$.

　　b. Suppose $\overline{X}, \overline{Y}, \overline{S}$, and $\overline{R}$ satisfy all the above conditions, except that $\overline{X} \cap \overline{Y} \not\subseteq \overline{S}$. Give an example of **r** that satisfies $\overline{R} = \overline{X} \bowtie \overline{Y}$ but does not satisfy $\overline{S} = (\overline{S} \cap \overline{X}) \bowtie (\overline{S} \cap \overline{Y})$.

6.32 Consider a relation schema over the attributes *ABCDEFG* and the following MVDs:

$$ABCD \bowtie DEFG$$
$$CD \bowtie ABCEFG$$
$$DFG \bowtie ABCDEG$$

Find a lossless decomposition into 4NF.

6.33 For the attribute set *ABCDEFG*, let the MVDs be:

$$ABCD \bowtie DEFG$$
$$ABCE \bowtie ABDFG$$
$$ABD \bowtie CDEFG$$

Find a lossless decomposition into 4NF. Is it unique?

6.34 Consider a decomposition $\mathbf{R}_1, \ldots, \mathbf{R}_n$ of **R** obtained through 3NF synthesis. Suppose that $\mathbf{R}_i$ is *not* in BCNF and let $X \rightarrow A$ be a violating FD in $\mathbf{R}_i$. Prove that $\mathbf{R}_i$ must have another FD, $Y \rightarrow B$, which will be lost if $\mathbf{R}_i$ is further decomposed with respect to $X \rightarrow A$.

＊6.35 This exercise relies on a technique explained in the optional Section 6.10. Consider a relation schema over the attributes *ABCDEFGHI* and the following MVDs and FDs:

$$D \rightarrow AH \qquad D \twoheadrightarrow BC$$
$$G \rightarrow I \qquad C \twoheadrightarrow B$$
$$\qquad\qquad G \twoheadrightarrow ABCE$$

Find a lossless and dependency-preserving decomposition into 4NF.

7

Triggers and Active Databases

In Chapter 3, we discussed triggers in the context of reactive constraints in databases. However, triggers have other uses as well. For example, they arise naturally in applications that require **active databases**—databases that must react to various external events. In these applications, the general classes of possible external events are known but their exact timings are not. This is what makes triggers a good paradigm for these applications.

Although triggers were not a part of the SQL-92 standard, a number of database vendors include (proprietary, nonstandard) support for triggers in their products. Triggers are a part of the SQL:1999 standard, and we discuss that part of the standard in this chapter. More information on triggers in SQL:1999 can be found in [Gulutzan and Pelzer 1999].

7.1 What Is a Trigger?

A **trigger** is an element of the database schema that has the following structure:

ON *event* IF *precondition* THEN *action*

where **event** is a request for the execution of a particular database operation (e.g., insert a row in a table whose rows represent students registered for a course), **precondition** is an expression that evaluates to true or false (e.g., the class is full), and **action** is a statement of what needs to be done when the trigger is **fired**, that is, when the event occurs and the precondition is true (e.g., delete something from the database or send e-mail to the administrator). Because triggers are built out of the above three ingredients, they are also called **event-condition-action**, or ECA, rules.

Triggers fill a number of roles in database processing, including

1. *Constraint maintenance.* In Section 3.3.8, we discussed triggers that are used to maintain the foreign-key and semantic constraints. The most common form of a trigger of this kind uses the ON DELETE and ON UPDATE clauses, which are attached to foreign keys. In the same section we saw an example of a

trigger intended to enforce a semantic constraint, which prevents dropping of a course after the grade is given. More generally, triggers can be used to maintain ASSERTION constraints of SQL.

2. *Business rules.* A business rule is a concise formal statement of a basic principle that underlies a business process in an enterprise. For instance, a business rule encoded as a database trigger could state that if an international money transfer is made into a client's account then an e-mail message should be sent to the client. Thus, insertion of a tuple of type "international money transfer" would trigger the action of insertion of an appropriate message into an e-mail queue (which might also be a relation in the same database).

3. *Monitoring.* Complex physical objects, such as power plants, spaceships, aircraft, etc., are monitored by sensor networks, which record their measurements in a database. Since insertion of each new record in the database is an event, triggers can be used, indirectly, to monitor the state of such physical objects. For instance, if a sensor records an elevated level of carbon monoxide, then the ventilation system should be turned on and the record of this secondary event inserted into the log.

4. *Maintenance of auxiliary cached data.* Materialized views, discussed in Section 5.2.9, is one example of such a use. A trigger can update a materialized view each time a change is made to the base tables on which the trigger depends.

5. *Simplified application design.* Separating core program logic from exception handling can drastically simplify certain applications. In cases where exceptions can be modeled as update operations on a database, triggers are an ideal vehicle for such separation.

7.2 Semantic Issues in Trigger Handling

Surprisingly, a number of complex issues lurk behind the conceptual simplicity of the notion of a trigger. First, several types of triggers are possible, each of which might be useful for different applications. Second, we will soon discover many nuances in how and when triggers are applied. Third, at any given point in time several triggers might be activated—how should a DBMS decide which to apply and in what order? Different choices can lead to different executions.

Finally, execution of a trigger might enable other triggers. Therefore, a single event can cause a chain reaction of trigger firing, and there is no guarantee that the process will ever stop. Chain reaction may be indicative of a design problem if it cannot be shown to always terminate. To prevent infinite executions, each DBMS has a limit on the depth of such chain reactions; for instance, if the depth exceeds 32, an exception is raised, the chain reaction stops, and all of the changes made by the original update statement and the triggers are rolled back. However, this limit is a safety valve, not a feature, and trigger systems should not be designed to rely on it. Some techniques for preventing chain reaction will be discussed in Section 7.4.

Trigger consideration. A trigger is **activated** when the triggering event is requested. The **consideration** of a trigger refers to when, after activation, the precondition specified in the trigger is checked. To see why consideration is an issue, assume that when the triggering event is requested, the triggering precondition is true and so the trigger can fire. However, moments later the precondition might become false (because of updates made by this or other transactions). If the precondition is not checked immediately, the trigger will not fire.

Consider the following trigger, whose purpose is to ensure that student registration does not exceed course capacity:

ON *inserting a row in course registration table*
IF *over course capacity*
THEN *abort registration transaction*

When a student attempts to insert her name in the course registration table, the course might be full. Thus, if the precondition is checked when the registration attempt is made, the student's request will be rejected. However, at about the same time another student might execute a transaction to drop the course (or the registrar might have increased the course capacity), and this second transaction might commit before the first one. Therefore, if the trigger precondition is checked at the time the registration transaction commits, rather than at the event time, our student will happily register for the course. In this example, deferring the consideration of trigger preconditions might be a suitable policy.

However, if our database is monitoring a nuclear power plant and the triggering event is a pressure increase while the precondition is that the pressure not exceed a certain limit, then in all likelihood the immediate consideration of the trigger precondition is a better idea.

In summary, there are at least two useful strategies: a trigger can be considered **immediately** when the triggering event is requested, or consideration can be **deferred** until the transaction commits.

Trigger consideration is actually a little more subtle. Suppose that a trigger, T, is activated by an event, e, that affects the relation R, and let C be the condition associated with T. Many systems (SQL:1999 included) make it possible for C to take into account the state of R immediately *before* e takes place and also immediately *after* e has been executed. Therefore, if C uses only these two states of R and does not refer to any other relation in the database, the immediate and the deferred considerations of T yield the same result. Moreover, if C refers only to the *before state* of R, we can say that C is evaluated before e takes place! But if C does take into account database relations other than R, the two consideration modes might yield different results.

Trigger execution. If trigger consideration is deferred, trigger execution is necessarily also deferred until the end of the triggering transaction. However, when triggers are considered immediately we have at least two options. We can execute the trigger immediately after its consideration, or we can defer execution until the end of the triggering transaction. Again, for a nuclear reactor database, immediate execution might be the way to go, but in less critical situations deferred execution might be a better option.

> *Brain Teaser:* What would immediate execution under deferred consideration mean?

With immediate execution, there are the following further possibilities. The trigger can be executed *after* the triggering event (an **after trigger**), *before* it (a **before trigger**), or *instead* of it (an **instead-of trigger**). At first glance, the last two possibilities seem quite strange. How can an action caused by a real-life event execute before or instead of that event? The answer lies in the fact that the event is a request to the DBMS issued by a transaction, so it is quite possible for the DBMS to ignore the request and execute the trigger instead. Or the system might execute the trigger first and then allow the requested action to occur.

SQL:1999 supports only before and after triggers, but some vendors (e.g., Oracle) support instead-of triggers as well. These triggers can be useful in a number of scenarios, the most common being maintenance of views. In this scenario, the events of insertion, deletion, and update on a view can be monitored by triggers. When, say, a tuple is inserted into a view, the trigger is activated and performs appropriate insertions into the base tables of the view *instead of* inserting the tuple directly into the view. (Recall from Section 5.3.4 that in most cases direct update of a view is not even feasible because such operation is ambiguous.) Example 7.3.5 illustrates this type of trigger.

> *Brain Teaser:* Do before triggers make any sense under deferred execution?

Trigger granularity.   The issue here is what constitutes an event. **Row-level granularity** assumes that a change to a single row is an event, and changes to different rows are viewed as separate events that might cause the trigger to be executed multiple times. In contrast, **statement-level granularity** assumes that events are statements, such as INSERT, DELETE, and UPDATE, *not* the individual tuple-level changes they make. Thus, for instance, an UPDATE statement that makes no changes (because the condition in its WHERE clause affects no tuples currently in the database) is an event that can cause a trigger to execute!

At row-level granularity, a trigger might need to know the old and the new values of the affected tuple so it can test the precondition properly. In the case of a salary increase, for example, the old tuple contains the old salary and the new one contains the new salary. If both values are available, the trigger can verify that the increase does not exceed 10% or can apply corrective actions as appropriate. Row-level triggers usually provide access to the old and the new values of the affected tuple through special variables.

At statement-level granularity, updates are collected in temporary structures, such as OLD TABLE and NEW TABLE. This allows the trigger to query both tables and act on the basis of the results.

Trigger conflicts. It is possible for an event to activate several triggers at once. For instance, when a student registers for a course, the following two triggers might be considered:

ON *inserting a row in course registration table*
IF *over course capacity*
THEN *notify registrar about unmet demands*

ON *inserting a row in course registration table*
IF *over course capacity*
THEN *put on waiting list*

In such situations, an important question is which trigger should be considered first. Two alternatives exist.

■ *Ordered conflict resolution.* Evaluate trigger preconditions in turn. When a condition is evaluated and found to be true, the corresponding trigger is executed; when that execution is complete, the next trigger is considered. In our case, the student might accept one of the alternative courses and abandon the request to add the course that is full. Therefore, by the time the second trigger is considered, its precondition is no longer true, and the trigger will not fire. One common way to order triggers is according to the times when their enabling events occur.

■ *Group conflict resolution.* Evaluate all trigger preconditions at once and then schedule for execution all those whose preconditions are true. In this case, all scheduled triggers will be executed (one after another or concurrently), even if the preconditions attached to some triggers might become false shortly after their evaluation.

With the first option, the system can decide on trigger ordering or it can pick triggers at random. With the second option, trigger ordering is not necessary since all triggers can be scheduled to run concurrently, although most DBMSs do order triggers anyway.

Triggers and integrity constraints. In Chapter 3, we discussed the possibility of updates to the database that might violate referential integrity constraints. We saw that SQL has a way of specifying compensating actions (such as ON DELETE CASCADE) that the DBMS should take to restore integrity. These actions can be viewed as special triggers with very strict semantics. At the end of the execution, the integrity of the database must be restored. The situation is complicated by the fact that a compensating action might activate other triggers that can cause violations of referential integrity. In this case, the scheduling of all of these triggers must have the goal of ultimately restoring the integrity constraint. The problem of trigger scheduling does not have an obvious solution. We will discuss how this issue is resolved in SQL:1999 in the next section.

7.3 Triggers in SQL:1999

Convergence of an agreeable syntax and semantics for triggers in the current SQL:1999 standard involved a rather long and painful process. First, the various database vendors already had triggers in their systems, so the standard had to offer sufficient benefits to convince the vendors to change their implementations. Second, as we have seen, the semantic issues associated with triggers are not trivial, and the standard would not have been accepted unless it offered reasonable solutions to the problems discussed earlier.

Armed with a new understanding of the issues associated with trigger handling, we can now approach the SQL:1999 standard systematically:

- *Triggering events.* An event can be the execution of an SQL INSERT, DELETE, and UPDATE statement as a whole or a change to individual rows made by such statements.

- *Trigger precondition.* Any condition allowed in the WHERE clause of SQL.

- *Trigger action.* An SQL query, a DELETE, INSERT, UPDATE, ROLLBACK, or SIGNAL statement, or a program written in the language of SQL's *persistent stored modules* (*SQL/PSM*), which smoothly integrates procedural control statements with SQL query and update statements. We discuss SQL/PSM in Chapter 8.

- *Trigger conflict resolution.* Ordered—SQL:1999 assumes that all triggers are ordered and executed in some implementation-specific way. Since the order is likely to be different from one database product to another, applications must be designed so that they do not rely on trigger ordering.

- *Trigger consideration.* Immediate—the preconditions of all triggers activated by an event are checked immediately when the event is requested.

- *Trigger execution.* Immediate—execution can be specified to be before or after the triggering event.

- *Trigger granularity.* Row-level and statement-level granularities are both available.

Here is the general syntax of SQL:1999 triggers. Constructs in square brackets are optional; clauses in curly brackets specify a choice of one of the constructs separated by vertical lines.

```
CREATE TRIGGER  trigger-name
        {BEFORE | AFTER}
            {INSERT | DELETE | UPDATE [ OF column-name-list ]}
        ON table-name
            [ REFERENCING [ OLD AS var-to-refer-to-old-tuple ]
                          [ NEW AS var-to-refer-to-new-tuple ] ]
```

                     [OLD TABLE AS *name-to-refer-to-old-table*]]
                     [NEW TABLE AS *name-to-refer-to-new-table*]]
    [FOR EACH { ROW | STATEMENT }]
    [WHEN (*precondition*)]
        statement-list

The syntax of SQL:1999 triggers closely follows the model discussed in Section 7.2. A trigger has a name; it is activated by certain events (specified by the INSERT-DELETE-UPDATE clause); it can be defined as a BEFORE or an AFTER trigger (indicating whether the precondition is to be checked in the state that exists before or after the event); and it can have a precondition (specified by the WHEN clause). The clauses FOR EACH ROW and FOR EACH STATEMENT specify the trigger granularity. If FOR EACH ROW is specified, the trigger is activated by the changes to every individual tuple in the table watched by that trigger. If FOR EACH STATEMENT is specified (which is the default), the trigger is activated once per execution of an INSERT, DELETE, or UPDATE statement on the table being monitored, regardless of the number of tuples changed by that execution (it will be activated even if no changes occurred).

The *statement list* following the WHEN clause defines the actions to be executed when the trigger is fired. Usually, these actions are SQL statements (that insert, delete, or modify tuples), but in general they can be statements written in SQL/PSM, which can include SQL statements intermixed with if-then-else statements, loops, local variables, and so forth. We discuss SQL/PSM in Chapter 8.

The REFERENCING *clause* is the means of referring to the pre-update and the post-update contents of the relation *table name*. This information can be used both in the WHEN condition and in the statement list that follows.

There are two types of references, depending on the granularity of the trigger. If the trigger has row-level granularity, we can use the clauses OLD AS and NEW AS, which define tuple variables to be used to refer to the old and the new value of the tuple that caused trigger activation. If the event is an INSERT, OLD is not applicable; if it is a DELETE, NEW is not applicable. If the trigger has statement-level granularity, SQL:1999 provides access to the old and the new values of the table affected by the triggering statement. Thus, the clause OLD TABLE names the table that contains the old state of the tuples affected by the update whereas the clause NEW TABLE defines the name under which the new state of these tuples can be accessed.

Note. NEW AS and OLD AS specify tuple variables that range *only over the tuples affected by the update*. That is, in tuple insertion, NEW AS refers to the inserted tuple. In tuple modification, it refers to the new state of the modified tuple. OLD AS refers to deleted tuples or to the old states of modified tuples.

      Likewise, OLD TABLE and NEW TABLE contain *only the tuples affected by the update*, not the entire old and new states of the table. If **r** was the state of a table before the update, the state after the update is (**r** − *old table*) ∪ *new table*.

Finally, SQL:1999 imposes certain restrictions on what BEFORE and AFTER triggers can do.

BEFORE triggers. All BEFORE triggers execute entirely before the triggering events. They are not allowed to modify the database, but can only test the pre-condition specified in the WHEN clause and either accept or abort the triggering transaction. Since BEFORE triggers cannot modify the database, they cannot activate other triggers.

A typical use of BEFORE triggers is to preserve application-specific data integrity. For instance, the following trigger makes sure that course enrollment limits are never exceeded.

Example 7.3.1 (Business Rule Enforced with a BEFORE Trigger). Let us assume that, in addition to the already familiar relation TRANSCRIPT, the database includes a relation CRSLIMITS with the attributes CrsCode, Semester, and Limit (with their usual meanings). The following is a trigger that enforces course enrollment limits by monitoring tuple insertions into the TRANSCRIPT relation.

```
CREATE TRIGGER RoomCapacityCheck
    BEFORE INSERT ON Transcript
      REFERENCING NEW AS N
    FOR EACH ROW
    WHEN
      ((SELECT COUNT(T.StudId) FROM Transcript T
        WHERE T.CrsCode = N.CrsCode AND T.Semester = N.Semester)
      >=
      (SELECT L.Limit FROM CrsLimits L
        WHERE L.CrsCode = N.CrsCode AND L.Semester = N.Semester))
    ROLLBACK
```

Observe that an INSERT statement can insert several tuples involving different courses. The trigger specifies row granularity, so each insertion is treated as a separate event. If the course is filled to capacity, the insertion is rejected. ▪

Note that the first SQL statement in the WHEN clause refers simultaneously to the new TRANSCRIPT tuples (through the tuple variable N) and to all tuples in the relation TRANSCRIPT (through the variable T). What state of the relation TRANSCRIPT is assumed while checking the validity of the WHEN condition? In the case of tuples referenced by N, the answer is clear. It must be the new state for each referenced tuple. However, it is less obvious what state is referenced by T. The answer is that BEFORE triggers assume that all referenced tables are in their old state while AFTER triggers assume the new state for each relation.

AFTER triggers. AFTER triggers execute entirely after the triggering event has applied its changes to the database. They are allowed to make changes to the database and thus can activate other triggers (which can cause a chain reaction, as explained earlier). In this way, AFTER triggers serve as an extension of the application logic. They can take care of various events automatically, thereby relieving application programmers of the need to code all of these event handlers in each application.

Example 7.3.2 (Business Rule Enforced with an AFTER Trigger).   The following
trigger enforces a dynamic constraint that caps any salary raises performed by a single
transaction at 5%. We assume that the database has a relation called EMPLOYEE with
an attribute named Salary.

```
CREATE TRIGGER LimitSalaryRaise
     AFTER UPDATE OF Salary ON Employee
     REFERENCING OLD AS O
                   NEW AS N
     FOR EACH ROW
     WHEN (N.Salary − O.Salary > 0.05 * O.Salary)
          UPDATE Employee
          SET Salary = 1.05 * O.Salary
          WHERE Id = O.Id
```

Whenever the Salary attribute in an EMPLOYEE tuple is updated, the trigger
causes the DBMS to compare its old and new values and, if the raise exceeds the cap,
to adjust the salary increase to just 5%. If the raise does not exceed the cap or if the
update is a salary decrease, the trigger does not fire. Note that the tuple variables O
and N in the above statement always *refer to the same tuple* that was affected by the
database update that activated the trigger. The difference is that O refers to the old
state of that tuple and N refers to the new state. ∎

Notice that when the trigger LIMITSALARYRAISE fires, its action overrides the
effect of the original event that triggered LIMITSALARYRAISE. Furthermore, execution
of the action is itself a triggering event for LIMITSALARYRAISE! However, the new
event does not lead to a chain reaction. When the trigger is checked the second
time, the salary actually decreases (to become exactly 5% above the original). Thus,
the WHEN condition is false, and the trigger does not fire a second time.

We have seen several examples of triggers that have the granularity of a single
row. However, some applications require that a trigger be fired only once per statement, after all updates specified in the statement have been processed. We illustrate
the use of statement-level triggers with the following examples.

Example 7.3.3 (Statement-Level Trigger).   Suppose that after each salary raise we
want to record the new average salary for all employees. We can achieve this with
the help of the following trigger:

```
CREATE TRIGGER  RecordNewAverage
     AFTER UPDATE OF  Salary ON Employee
     FOR EACH STATEMENT
          INSERT INTO Log
          VALUES (CURRENT_DATE,
                    (SELECT AVG(Salary) FROM Employee))
```

When the trigger is executed, it inserts a record into the table LOG that gives the new average salary. The record also indicates the date on which the average was calculated (CURRENT_DATE is a built-in SQL function that returns the current date). Since it does not make sense to compute a new average after every individual salary change, statement-level granularity is better suited here than is row-level granularity. ■

The next example illustrates the use of statement-level triggers for maintaining inclusion dependencies. We discussed inclusion dependencies in Chapter 3 as a useful generalization of foreign-key constraints, which occur frequently in practical settings. One such dependency, *No professor can be scheduled to teach a course that has no registered students*, was given in (3.1) on page 45. It is a referential integrity constraint that is *not* based on foreign keys, and its representation in SQL requires the use of assertions (see (3.4) on page 52). We now show how AFTER triggers can help maintain this constraint in the presence of updates.[1]

Example 7.3.4 (Maintenance of Inclusion Dependencies). The key idea is to construct an SQL view, IDLETEACHING, that includes precisely those tuples from the TEACHING relation that describe course offerings with no corresponding tuples in the TRANSCRIPT relation. In other words, the view contains precisely the tuples that violate the inclusion dependency. Designing such a view definition is left as an exercise.

The trigger works as follows: after one or more students drop a class (or several classes), the trigger deletes all tuples found in IDLETEACHING from TEACHING.

```
CREATE TRIGGER MaintainCoursesNonEmpty
     AFTER DELETE,UPDATE OF CrsCode,Semester ON Transcript
     FOR EACH STATEMENT
          DELETE FROM Teaching
               WHERE                                                    7.1
                    EXISTS (SELECT *
                               FROM IdleTeaching T
                               WHERE Semester = T.Semester
                                    AND CrsCode = T.CrsCode)
```

Similarly, we can construct a trigger to maintain the inclusion dependency when tuples are added to the TEACHING relation. This trigger should abort any transaction that tries to insert a tuple into TEACHING if there is no corresponding tuple in TRANSCRIPT. ■

Note that the above trigger might cause a chicken-and-egg problem. We cannot assign a course to a professor until somebody registers for it. However, in most schools the course schedule for the next semester is published before any student registers for any course, so some triggers might need to be created and then

---

[1] The same technique can be used to emulate the ON DELETE and ON UPDATE clauses of foreign-key constraints in systems that are not SQL-92 compliant.

destroyed. The above trigger, for instance, might need to be in effect *only* between the deadline for adding courses and the deadline for dropping them.

Example 7.3.5 (INSTEAD OF Triggers).   Although INSTEAD OF triggers are not part of the SQL standard, this advanced feature is included in a number of database products. In this example we illustrate the approach used in the Oracle DBMS. Consider the following view:

```
CREATE VIEW WORKSIN(ProfId,DeptName) AS
     SELECT   P.Id, D.Name
     FROM     PROFESSOR P, DEPARTMENT D
     WHERE    P.DeptId = D.DeptId
```

and suppose that the following operation is performed on the view:

```
DELETE FROM WORKSIN
WHERE Id = 111111111
```

Since the contents of a view is not stored in the database, such an operation must be translated into appropriate operations on the base tables of the view, PROFESSOR and DEPARTMENT. However, in general, there may be several translations: we could delete the department where the professor with Id 111111111 works; we can delete the professor; or we can set the DeptId field in the professor's tuple to NULL. There is no way to automatically decide which of these three possibilities is the right one. However, INSTEAD OF triggers offer a way for the application designer to specify the appropriate course of action. For instance,

```
CREATE TRIGGER WORKSINTRIG1
     INSTEAD OF DELETE ON WORKSIN
     REFERENCING OLD AS O
     FOR EACH ROW
           UPDATE PROFESSOR
           SET DeptId = NULL
           WHERE Id = O.ProfId
```

is a trigger that directs the DBMS to set the DeptId field to NULL whenever a deletion operation on the view WORKSIN is performed.   ∎

Summary of the trigger evaluation procedure.   Suppose that an event, **e**, occurs during the execution of a database update statement, S, and this event activates a set of triggers, $\mathbf{T} = \{T_1, \ldots, T_k\}$. Then we can summarize the procedure for trigger processing as follows:

1.   Put the newly activated triggers on the trigger queue, $\mathbf{Q}$.

2.   Suspend the execution of S.

3. Compute OLD and NEW if row-level granularity is used, or OLD TABLE and NEW TABLE if statement-level granularity is used.

4. Consider all BEFORE triggers in **T**. Execute those whose preconditions are true, and place all AFTER triggers whose preconditions are true on **Q**.

5. Apply the updates specified in S to the database.

6. Consider each AFTER trigger on **Q** according to the (implementation-dependent) priority, and execute it immediately if the triggering condition is true. If the execution of a trigger activates new triggers, execute this algorithm recursively, starting with step 1.

7. Resume the execution of statement S.

Triggers and foreign-key constraints. When the event that activates a trigger is invoked on a relation that has foreign-key constraints with ON DELETE and ON UPDATE clauses, the compensating actions specified in these clauses are likely to cause updates of their own. As a result, the exact semantics of the system becomes quite complicated. In fact, it took several iterations for the designers of the SQL:1999 standard to find a satisfactory solution.

One might ask why the actions attached to foreign-key constraints are not treated as regular triggers. The answer is that these constraints *are* triggers, but they have special semantics—they are intended to rectify states that violate foreign-key constraints, and it is desirable to capture this semantics in the trigger-evaluation procedure. To do so, we modify step 5:

5′. Apply the updates specified in S to the database (as before). For each FOREIGN KEY statement violated by the current (new) state, let **act** denote the associated compensating action (i.e., CASCADE, SET DEFAULT, SET NULL, or NO ACTION). Note that **act** is an event that can in turn activate other triggers, which we denote as $\mathbf{S} = \{S_1, \ldots, S_n\}$. Then

   (a) Consider all triggers in **S**. Execute the BEFORE triggers whose preconditions are true, and place on **Q** all AFTER triggers whose preconditions are true.

   (b) Apply the updates specified in **act**.

Note that in step 5′(b), we did not say whether the unprocessed triggers in **S** should be placed in front of **Q** or appended to it. The reason for this is that SQL processes triggers according to their implementation-dependent priority.

Observe that execution of AFTER triggers in step 6 can activate other triggers and also cause violation of foreign-key constraints. In this case, steps 1 through 6 are invoked recursively.

The above algorithm is designed to handle very complex interactions of triggers and foreign-key constraints—interactions that might involve dozens of triggers. We illustrate the algorithm on a simple example that involves just two triggers and one foreign-key constraint.

Example 7.3.6 (Interaction of Triggers and Foreign-Key Constraints). Let us assume that courses mentioned in the TRANSCRIPT relation must also be listed in the COURSE relation. Both of these relations are described in Figure 3.4 on page 38. The foreign-key constraint between these relations, which we call CHECKCOURSEVALIDITY, can be expressed as follows:

```
CREATE TABLE Transcript (
      StudId    INTEGER,
      CrsCode   CHAR(6),
      Semester  CHAR(6),
      Grade     grades,
      PRIMARY KEY (StudId, CrsCode, Semester),
      CONSTRAINT CheckCourseValidity
            FOREIGN KEY (CrsCode) REFERENCES Course (CrsCode)
               ON DELETE CASCADE
               ON UPDATE CASCADE )
```

CHECKCOURSEVALIDITY deletes or updates all TRANSCRIPT tuples if the corresponding COURSE tuple is deleted or updated.

Suppose, in addition, that there is an AFTER trigger, WATCHCOURSEHISTORY, that records all changes to the tuples in the COURSE relation. We leave it to Exercise 7.5 to define this trigger in SQL. Finally, the trigger MAINTAINCOURSES-NONEMPTY (7.1) is also part of the database scheme. Note that in this example we do not consider other foreign-key constraints (in particular, those associated with the TEACHING relation—including such constraints would make a much more complex example).

Suppose now that some course code is changed in the relation COURSE, specifically CS305 becomes CS405 beginning with fall 2000. This change activates the trigger WATCHCOURSEHISTORY and the CHECKCOURSEVALIDITY foreign-key constraint. Because WATCHCOURSEHISTORY is an AFTER trigger, it is placed on **Q**, and the trigger-processing algorithm handles the foreign-key constraint first as required in step 5'(b). Therefore, all tuples in the TRANSCRIPT relation that have CS305 in them are changed to refer to CS405.

This change activates the second trigger, MAINTAINCOURSESNONEMPTY. Since CS305 has been changed to CS405, the professor who is listed as teaching CS305 in fall 2000 is left without a class. In other words, CS305 is listed in TEACHING for the fall 2000 semester, but TRANSCRIPT does not have any corresponding tuples. Therefore, the WHEN condition in MAINTAINCOURSESNONEMPTY is true, and the trigger can be executed.

Because MAINTAINCOURSESNONEMPTY is an AFTER trigger, it is put on **Q** (step 5'(b)), which already contains WATCHCOURSEHISTORY. The order in which these two triggers in the queue are actually fired depends on the implementation of the particular DBMS being used and cannot be predicted.[2] When all triggers eventually

---

[2] Most vendors use scheduling strategies based on time stamps that reflect the time of trigger consideration. In our case, such time stamp ordering favors WATCHCOURSEHISTORY.

fire, the record about the course change goes into the history log and the teaching assignment for CS305 is deleted.

Note that the interaction of the two triggers and the foreign-key constraint described above might not yield the intended result in this example. For instance, it might be more reasonable to update the teaching assignment of CS305 to a teaching assignment of CS405. ■

7.4 Avoiding a Chain Reaction

The possibility of a never-ending chain reaction in trigger execution is a serious concern. As mentioned earlier, commercial DBMSs impose an a priori upper limit on the length of chain reactions. However, relying on this upper limit is not a good idea since it is hard to predict the final outcome.

Trigger systems in which chain firing terminates in all cases are called **safe**. Unfortunately, there is no algorithm that can tell whether any given set of triggers is safe. However, there are conditions that are sufficient to guarantee safety (i.e., if the conditions are satisfied, the triggers are safe), but they are not necessary (i.e., a set of triggers might be safe but not satisfy the conditions). The fact that there is no algorithm to test safety implies that there can be no verifiable necessary *and* sufficient condition for safety.

In view of this sorry state of affairs, we present one condition that is sufficient to guarantee safety but that rejects many perfectly safe trigger systems. A **triggering graph** is a graph whose nodes are triggers (or foreign-key constraints as a special case). An arc goes from trigger T to trigger T' if and only if execution of T is an event that can activate T'.

It is easy to see that one can use a simple syntactic analysis to determine whether one trigger might activate another trigger. Indeed, the events that enable a trigger are listed in the BEFORE/AFTER clause in the trigger definition (or in the ON DELETE/UPDATE clause in foreign-key constraint definitions); the events *caused* by the triggers can be determined from the statements in the trigger body. Figure 7.1 shows the triggering graph for some of the triggers discussed in this chapter.

Clearly, if the trigger graph is *acyclic*, it is not possible for the triggers to invoke each other in a nonterminating manner. By this criterion, the triggers WATCH-COURSEHISTORY, MAINTAINCOURSESNONEMPTY, and CHECKCOURSEVALIDITY cannot be involved in a chain reaction.

FIGURE 7.1 Cyclic trigger graph. The cycle does not cause a chain reaction.

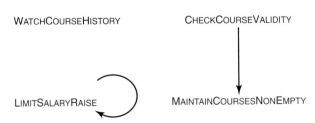

Even though this method can certify the safety of some systems, it fails in many cases. Indeed, the part of our triggering graph that involves LimitSalaryRaise is cyclic because syntactic analysis shows that its execution activates this very trigger again. However, this trigger will fire only once because its WHEN condition will be false on the second invocation. This analysis exposes a major weakness of the triggering graph method. It does not take into account the semantics of the triggering conditions associated with the triggers. For example, if one can verify that no cycle in the triggering graph can be traversed infinitely many times (as in our example), the trigger system is safe.

There are a number of enhancements to the triggering graph methods, but they are outside of the scope of this book.

BIBLIOGRAPHIC NOTES

The main concepts underlying triggers in databases are described in [Paton et al. 1993]. The algorithm for integration of triggers with foreign-key constraints originates in [Cochrane et al. 1996]. The syntax of SQL:1999 triggers is described in recent guides to SQL, such as [Gulutzan and Pelzer 1999].

There is a vast body of literature on active databases; the information on SQL:1999 triggers provided here is only the tip of an iceberg. The interested reader is referred to [Widom and Ceri 1996] for a comprehensive study.

EXERCISES

7.1   Explain the semantics of the triggers that are available in the DBMS that is used for your course project. Describe the syntax for defining these triggers.

7.2   Give the exact syntactic rules for constructing the triggering graphs from the sets of SQL triggers and foreign-key constraints.

7.3   Design a trigger that complements the trigger MaintainCoursesNonEmpty (see (7.1) on page 260) by precluding the insertion of tuples into the relation Teaching when there are no corresponding tuples in the Transcript relation.

7.4   Design a trigger that works like MaintainCoursesNonEmpty but is a row-level trigger.

7.5   Define the trigger WatchCourseHistory that uses a table Log to record all changes that transactions make to the various courses in the Course relation.

7.6   Define triggers that fire when a student drops a course, changes her major, or when her grade average drops below a certain threshold. (For simplicity, assume that there is a function, grade_avg(), which takes a student Id and returns the student average grade.)

7.7   Consider the IsA relationship between Student(Id,Major) and Person(Id, Name). Write the triggers appropriate for maintaining this relationship: when a tuple is deleted from Person, the tuple with the same Id must be deleted from Student;

when a tuple is inserted into STUDENT, check whether a corresponding tuple exists in PERSON and abort if not. (Do not use the ON DELETE and ON INSERT clauses provided by the FOREIGN KEY statement.)

7.8   Consider a brokerage firm database with relations HOLDINGS(AccountId, StockSymbol, CurrentPrice, Quantity) and BALANCE(AccountId, Balance). Write the triggers for maintaining the correctness of the account balance when stock is bought (a tuple is added to HOLDINGS or Quantity is incremented), sold (a tuple is deleted from HOLDINGS or Quantity is decremented), or a price change occurs.

Solve the problem using both row-level and statement-level triggers. Give an example of a situation when row-level triggers are more appropriate for the above problem and when statement-level triggers are more appropriate.

7.9   Consider an enterprise in which different projects use parts supplied by various suppliers. Define the appropriate tables along with the corresponding foreign-key constraints. Define triggers that fire when a project changes a supplier for a part; when a supplier discontinues a part; or when a project stops using a part.

7.10 Consider triggers with immediate consideration and deferred execution. What do OLD AS and NEW AS refer to during consideration and during execution?

7.11 Give an example of an application where SQL:1999 triggers could be used for a purpose other than just maintaining integrity constraints.

8

Using SQL in an Application

In the previous chapters, we discussed SQL as an interactive language. You type in a query, anxiously listen to your hard drive, and then see the results appear on your screen (or more likely scroll by on the screen too quickly to be read). This mode of execution, called **direct execution**, was part of the original vision of SQL.

In most transaction processing applications, however, SQL statements are part of an application program written in some conventional language, such as C, Cobol, Java, or Visual Basic, and the program executes on a computer different from the one on which the database server resides. In this chapter, we discuss some advanced features of SQL that address the issues involved in this type of execution. Our goal is to present the basic concepts involved, not to cover all the syntactic options.

8.1 What Are the Issues Involved?

We are interested in creating programs that involve a mixture of SQL statements and statements from a conventional language. The SQL statements enable the program to access a database. The conventional language, called the **host language**, supplies features that are unavailable in SQL. These features include control mechanisms, such as the **if** and **while** statements, assignment statements, and error handling.

In our discussion of how SQL statements can be included in a host language, we must deal with two issues, discussed here:

1. Prior to executing an SQL statement, a **preparation** step is performed. Preparation involves parsing the statement and then making a *query execution plan*, which determines the sequence of steps necessary for statement execution. In what order will tables be joined? Should the tables be sorted first? What indices will be used? What constraints will be checked? Because the execution of a single SQL statement can involve considerable computational and I/O resources, it is essential that it be carefully planned. The query execution plan is designed by the DBMS using the database schema and the structure of the statement: the statement type (e.g., SELECT, INSERT), the tables and columns accessed, and the column domains. Factors such as the number of rows in a table might also

be taken into account in query optimization. The SQL statement is executed according to the sequence of steps outlined in the plan.

2. SQL constructs can be included in an application program in two different ways:

(a) **Statement-level interface (SLI).** The SQL constructs appear as new statement types in the program. The program is then a mixture of statements in two languages: the host language and the new statement types. Before the program can be compiled by the host language compiler, the SQL constructs must be processed by a **precompiler**, which translates the constructs into calls to host language procedures. The entire program can then be compiled by the host language compiler. At run time, these procedures communicate with the DBMS, which takes the actions necessary to cause the SQL statements to be executed.

The SQL constructs can take two forms. In the first, referred to as **embedded SQL**, they are ordinary SQL statements (e.g., SELECT, INSERT). In the second, they are directives for preparing and executing SQL statements, but the SQL statements *appear in the program as the values of string variables that are constructed by the host language portion of the program at run time*. Since in this case the actual SQL statements to be executed might not be known at compile time, this form is referred to as **dynamic SQL**. This is in contrast to embedded SQL, where the SQL statements are known at compile time and are written directly into the program. Hence, embedded SQL is also referred to as **static SQL**. SQL-92 defines a standard for embedded SQL. We also discuss SQLJ—a version of SLI designed specifically for Java—which was standardized in SQL:2003.

(b) **Call-level interface (CLI).** Here, unlike static and dynamic SQL, the application program is written entirely in the host language. As with dynamic SQL, SQL statements are the values of string variables constructed at run time. These variables are passed as arguments to host language procedures provided by the CLI. Since no special syntax is used, no precompiler is needed.

We discuss two CLIs in this chapter: **JDBC** (Java DataBase Connectivity), which is specifically designed for the Java language, and **ODBC** (Open DataBase Connectivity), which can be used with many languages. JDBC was standardized in SQL:2003 and has an interface very similar to ODBC in SQL:1999.

8.2 Embedded SQL

Embedded SQL is a statement-level interface that allows SQL statements to be embedded in a host language program. The schema of the database to be accessed by the program must be known at the time the program is written so that the SQL statements can be constructed. For example, the programmer must know the names of tables and the names and domains of columns.

Before the compilation of the program by the host language compiler, a precompiler (usually supplied by the vendor of the DBMS) scans the application program and locates the embedded SQL statements. These statements are not part of the host language, so they cannot be processed by the host language compiler. Instead they are set off by a special syntax so that the precompiler can recognize them. The precompiler translates each statement into a sequence of subroutine calls in the host language to a run-time library, which can be processed by the host language compiler at the next stage. Later, when the program is run and the SQL statement is to be executed, the subroutines are called and they send the SQL statement (that was originally embedded in the application) to the DBMS, which prepares and executes it.

It would be reasonable for the precompiler to check the form of each SQL statement and prepare a query execution plan since that would eliminate a significant source of run-time overhead. However, most precompilers do not do this. Preparation requires the precompiler to communicate with the DBMS (to determine the schema of the database that the statement is accessing), and this communication might not be possible at compile time. Furthermore, since the query execution plan might depend on the size of tables, the closer in time the preparation is to the execution, the better.

In the best of all possible worlds, the embedded SQL constructs would be written in some standardized version of SQL (e.g., SQL-92 or SQL:1999), and the precompiler for each DBMS would perform any necessary translation to the dialect of SQL recognized by that DBMS. In the real world, however, most precompilers do not perform such translations, and the SQL constructs must be written in the exact dialect of the DBMS being accessed. In practice, then, the DBMS, as well as the database schema, must be known at the time the program is written.

Requiring the application program to use the exact dialect of the DBMS can be a disadvantage if, at some later time, it becomes necessary to change to a different DBMS with a different dialect. In some situations, however, using the dialect of the DBMS can be an advantage. Many DBMSs contain proprietary extensions to SQL. If the SQL embedded in the host language is exactly SQL-92, those extensions are not available to the programmer. Of course, if the proprietary extensions supported by a particular DBMS are used in an application, the difficulty of changing to a different DBMS at a later time increases.

The SQL standard requires that all implementations of embedded SQL provide precompilers for at least seven host languages: Ada, C, COBOL, Fortran, M (formerly known as MUMPS), Pascal, and PL/1. In practice, precompilers are available for other languages as well.

Figure 8.1 is a fragment of a C program with embedded SQL statements. Each embedded SQL statement is preceded by the words EXEC SQL, so it can be located by the precompiler. We use the syntax of SQL-92, but be aware that many database vendors use their own dialect of SQL.

All examples in this chapter come from the following two schemas:

CLASS(CrsCode:CHAR(6), Semester:CHAR(6),
   Enrollment:INTEGER, ProfId:CHAR(9), Room:CHAR(10))
The Key of CLASS: {CrsCode, Semester}
TRANSCRIPT(StudId:INTEGER, CrsCode:CHAR(6), Semester:CHAR(6),
    Grade:CHAR(1))
The Key of TRANSCRIPT: {StudId, CrsCode, Semester}

FIGURE 8.1 Fragment of an embedded SQL program written in C.

```
EXEC SQL BEGIN DECLARE SECTION;
         unsigned long num_enrolled;
         char *crs_code, *semester;
            .
            .
            .
EXEC SQL END DECLARE SECTION;
      .
      .    other host language declarations and statements
      .
      .
      .    statements to set the variables semester and crs_code
      .

EXEC SQL SELECT C.Enrollment
         INTO :num_enrolled
         FROM CLASS C
         WHERE C.CrsCode = :crs_code
               AND  C.Semester = :semester;
      .
      .    the rest of the host language program
      .
```

The domains of the attributes CrsCode, Semester, and Grade are the same as in Figure 3.5, page 39. That is, course codes are strings of the form MAT123 or CS305, semesters are strings of the form F1999 or S2000, and grades are letters, such as A or B.

For the application program as a whole to communicate with the database, host language statements and SQL statements must be able to access common variables. In that way, results computed by the host language portion of the program can be stored in the database, and data extracted from the database can be processed by host language statements.

The first group of statements in the fragment of Figure 8.1 declares variables of the host program, or **host variables**, that are used for that purpose. The declarations are included between EXEC SQL BEGIN DECLARE SECTION and EXEC SQL END DE-CLARE SECTION so that they can be easily found and processed by the precompiler. However, the declarations themselves are *not* preceded by EXEC SQL. In this way, the declarations can be processed by both the precompiler and the host language compiler.

Host variables are used in the SELECT statement shown in Figure 8.1. Note the colon that precedes each use of a host variable in the SELECT statement to differentiate it from the table and column names of the database schema. The value of Enrollment is returned in the host variable num_enrolled and can be accessed by host language statements in the normal way after the SELECT statement has been executed.

Since CrsCode and Semester together form the primary key of CLASS, the SELECT statement returns a *single* row. This is an important point. If the SELECT statement returned more than one row, which one would be used to provide the value for the variable `num_enrolled`? For this reason, it is an error for a SELECT INTO statement to return more than one row. We address the case in which the result consists of multiple rows in Section 8.2.4.

We can think of the host language variables as parameterizing the SQL statement. They are used to communicate scalar values, not table or column names or structured data. Host language variables that occur in WHERE clauses correspond to **in parameters**, while those used in INTO clauses correspond to **out parameters**. When the statement is executed, the values of the *in* parameters are used to form a complete SQL statement that can be executed by the database manager. Note, however, that the SQL statement can be prepared before the values of the in parameters are determined because, for example, table and column names are known (they cannot be parameters). Therefore, the query execution plan used when the statement is first executed can be saved for subsequent executions of the same statement (since only the parameter values differ on each execution). This is an important advantage of embedded SQL. One function of the precompiler is to select routines that, at run time, move values into and out of host language variables and to handle formatting for communication with the DBMS.

8.2.1 Status Processing

In the real world, things do not always proceed smoothly. For example, when you attempt to connect to a database on a distant server, the server might be down or it might reject the connection. Or an INSERT statement that you attempt to execute might be rejected by the DBMS because it would cause a constraint violation. You might categorize these as error situations since the requested action did not occur. In other situations, an SQL statement might execute correctly and return information describing the outcome of the execution. For example, the DELETE statement returns the number of rows deleted. SQL provides two mechanisms for returning information describing such situations to the host program: a five-character string SQLSTATE and a **diagnostics area**.

In Figure 8.2, we have added status processing to the fragment shown in Figure 8.1. SQLSTATE is declared within the declaration section since it is used for communication between the DBMS and the host language portion of the application. (It is declared as a six-character string when SQL is embedded in C, to account for the additional null character that terminates strings in C.) Note that SQLSTATE is not preceded by a colon when used in SQL statements because it is recognized by the preprocessor as a special keyword.

This declaration is required in all embedded SQL programs. (Earlier versions of SQL use a slightly different technique. Status is communicated through an integer variable, SQLCODE.) The DBMS sends information to be stored in that string after each SQL statement is executed. The statement can then be followed by a (host language) conditional statement that checks the value of SQLSTATE. If that value is 00000, the last SQL statement executed successfully. If not, the particular exception situation can be determined, and appropriate action can be taken. In Figure 8.2, a status message is printed.

FIGURE **8.2** Adding some status processing.

```
#define OK "00000"
EXEC SQL BEGIN DECLARE SECTION;
    char SQLSTATE[6];
    unsigned long num_enrolled;
    char *crs_code, *semester;
EXEC SQL END DECLARE SECTION;
        :
        :   other statements; get the values for crs_code, semester
        :
EXEC SQL SELECT C.Enrollment
    INTO :num_enrolled
    FROM CLASS C
    WHERE C.CrsCode = :crs_code
        AND C.Semester = :semester;
if (strcmp(SQLSTATE,OK) != 0)
    printf("SELECT statement failed\n");
```

Instead of checking status after each SQL statement, we can include a single WHENEVER statement anywhere before the first SQL statement is executed.

```
EXEC SQL WHENEVER SQLERROR GOTO label;
```

Then any nonzero status in a subsequently executed statement causes a transfer of control to `label`. The WHENEVER statement remains in effect until another WHENEVER statement is executed.

More detailed information on the outcome of the last executed SQL statement can be retrieved from the diagnostics area using a GET DIAGNOSTICS statement. A single SQL statement can raise several exceptions. The diagnostics area records information about all exceptions raised.

Before this becomes a problem, we should mention one confusing issue: the difference in string notation in SQL (including all of its components, such as embedded SQL) and many of the host languages, such as C and Java. In SQL, strings are set in single quotes, while in C and Java they are set in double quotes. Thus, a C program with embedded SQL can have both kinds of notation. For instance, in

```
semester = "F2000";
EXEC SQL SELECT C.Enrollment
    INTO :num_enrolled
    FROM CLASS C
    WHERE C.CrsCode = 'CS305'
        AND C.Semester = :semester;
```

the string F2000 appears in a regular assignment statement and is processed by the C compiler, while CS305 occurs in an SQL statement and is handled by the SQL preprocessor.

8.2.2 Sessions, Connections, and Transactions

We introduce some terminology from the SQL standard. Before an application program that includes SQL statements can perform any database operations, it must establish an **SQL connection** to an **SQL server**. That connection initiates an **SQL session** on the server. Once an SQL session has been established, the application program can execute any number of **SQL transactions**, until it disconnects from the server, breaking the SQL connection and ending the SQL session.

SQL connections are established by executing a CONNECT statement (possibly implicitly), the general form of which is

```
CONNECT TO  {DEFAULT  |  db-name-string}
     [AS  connection-name-string]   [USER  user-id-string]
```

Phrases in square brackets are optional. Phrases in curly brackets refer to alternatives: one of the enclosed phrases separated by a vertical line must be chosen.

The option *db-name-string* is the name of the data source, *connection-name-string* is the name that *you* give to the connection, and *user-id-string* is the name of a user account; it is used by the data source for authorization. The format used to specify a data source depends on the vendor. It can be a string that identifies the database by name on a local machine or something like

```
tcp:postgresql://db.xyz.edu:100/studregDB
```

on a remote machine.

A program can execute additional CONNECT statements to different servers, after which the new connection and the new session become current and the previous connection and session become dormant. The program can switch to a dormant connection and session by executing

```
SET CONNECTION TO {DEFAULT  |  connection-name-string}
```

SQL connections and SQL sessions are terminated by executing (possibly implicitly)

```
DISCONNECT  {DEFAULT  |  db-name-string}
```

8.2.3 Executing Transactions

There is no explicit SQL-92 statement that initiates a transaction. A transaction is initiated automatically when the first SQL statement that accesses the database is executed within a session.

In SQL:1999, transactions can also be initiated by using a START TRANSACTION statement that initiates a transaction and specifies certain of its characteristics similarly to the SET TRANSACTION statement, described below, in this section.

In SQL-92, transactions can be terminated with either COMMIT or ROLLBACK. The next SQL statement (after COMMIT or ROLLBACK) immediately starts a new transaction. This is referred to as **chaining**.

SQL:1999 also has COMMIT AND CHAIN and ROLLBACK AND CHAIN statements, which start a new transaction immediately after the commit or rollback completes without waiting until the start of the next SQL statement.

The default mode of execution for transactions is READ/WRITE, meaning that the transaction can both read and make changes to the database. Alternatively, it can be restricted to READ ONLY access to protect the database from unauthorized changes.

In Section 2.3, we pointed out that, although only serializable schedules guarantee correct execution for all applications, less demanding levels of isolation can often be used for a particular application to improve performance. Hence, the default isolation level is SERIALIZABLE, but other levels are offered as well. We discuss these levels at some length in Chapter 13.

If a mode of execution other than the default mode is wanted, the SET TRANSACTION statement can be used. For example,

```
SET TRANSACTION READ ONLY
        ISOLATION LEVEL READ COMMITTED
        DIAGNOSTICS SIZE 6;
```

sets the mode to READ ONLY and the isolation level to READ COMMITTED. The following isolation levels are defined:

```
READ UNCOMMITTED
READ COMMITTED
REPEATABLE READ
SERIALIZABLE
```

The DIAGNOSTICS SIZE clause determines the number of exception conditions (caused by the last executed SQL statement) that can be described at one time in the diagnostics area.

Figure 8.3 illustrates the use of connection and transaction statements as well as status processing. After the declarations, the next set of statements makes a connection to the server. The program does not use explicit statements for beginning

FIGURE 8.3 The use of connection and transaction statements in a C program with embedded SQL statements whose purpose is to deregister a student from a course.

```
#define OK  "00000"
EXEC SQL BEGIN DECLARE SECTION;
     unsigned long stud_id;
     char *crs_code, *semester;
     char SQLSTATE[6];
     char *dbName;
     char *connectName;
     char *userId;
EXEC SQL END DECLARE SECTION;

// Get values for dbName, connectName, userId
dbName = "studregDB";
connectName = "conn1";
userId = "ji21";

     ⋮  other statements

EXEC SQL CONNECT TO :dbName AS :connectName USER :userId;
if (strcmp(SQLSTATE,OK) != 0)
     exit(1);

   ⋮  get the values for stud_id, crs_code, etc.

EXEC SQL DELETE FROM TRANSCRIPT
     WHERE StudId = :stud_id
         AND Semester = :semester
         AND CrsCode = :crs_code;

if (strcmp(SQLSTATE,OK) != 0)
     EXEC SQL ROLLBACK;
else {
     EXEC SQL UPDATE CLASS
         SET Enrollment = (Enrollment - 1)
         WHERE CrsCode = :crs_code
               AND Semester = :semester;

     if (strcmp(SQLSTATE,OK) != 0)
         EXEC SQL ROLLBACK;
     else
         EXEC SQL COMMIT;
}
EXEC SQL DISCONNECT :connectName;
```

a transaction; instead, a transaction is implicitly started once the connection is established.

The figure shows a fragment of the program that deregisters a student from a course. We assume that the host language variable `semester` contains the current semester, which can be determined through a call to the operating system, such as `time()`. The program makes two modifications to the database state: deleting the row of TRANSCRIPT that indicates that the student is registered in the course, and decrementing the `Enrollment` attribute of the course's tuple in CLASS. If either the DELETE statement or the UPDATE statement fails (and hence the value of SQLSTATE is not "00000" when the statement completes), the ROLLBACK command is executed. Otherwise, the COMMIT command is executed. Then the transaction disconnects.

If the DELETE statement fails, no modification has been made to the database, which might lead us to think that the ROLLBACK command is not needed. However, the system must be notified that the transaction has completed so that, for example, an appropriate entry can be made in the system log and any locks acquired by the transaction can be released. The log is part of the mechanism the system uses to ensure transaction atomicity.

When an application executes either EXEC SQL COMMIT or EXEC SQL ROLL-BACK, it is requesting that the database server, S, to which the application has a current connection, commit or roll back any changes it has made to the database at S. However, the application program might be executing a transaction that does more than just access a single database server. For example, by establishing several connections and switching among them, it might be accessing several database servers, or it might be putting the results of its computation into a local file system. The COMMIT and ROLLBACK statements are sent over the connection to S and therefore do not apply to these tasks.

If the program is connected to more than one database, the transactions at each can be separately committed or rolled back. However, the global transaction consisting of all of the separate transactions might not be atomic (for example if the transaction at one database commits and the transaction at another database is rolled back).

8.2.4 Cursors

One of the advantages of SQL as a database language is that its statements can deal with entire tables. Thus, a SELECT statement might return a table, which we refer to as the **query result** or **result set**. When the statement is executed in direct or interactive mode rather than embedded in an application program, the result set scrolls out on the screen. The following SELECT statement, for example, returns the Ids and grades of all students enrolled in a particular course in a given semester.

```
EXEC SQL SELECT T.StudId, T.Grade
    FROM TRANSCRIPT T
    WHERE T.Semester = :semester
        AND T.CrsCode = :crs_code;
```

Suppose that we want to include such a statement in a host language program. The number of rows in the result set is not known until the statement is executed, so we face the problem of allocating storage within the program for an unknown number of rows. For example, if an array is to be used, how large should the array be?

This problem points up a fundamental difference between SQL and the host language. The fundamental unit dealt with by an SQL statement is a set of tuples, whereas the fundamental unit dealt with by a statement in the host language is a variable. This difference is often called an **impedance mismatch**.

The SQL mechanism for solving this problem is the **cursor**, which allows the application program to deal with one row in a result set at a time. Think of a cursor as a pointer to a row in the result set. A FETCH statement fetches the row pointed to by the cursor and assigns the attribute values in the row to host language variables in the program. In this way, variables need be allocated only for a single row. From the database schema, we know the types of the values in each row and so can declare variables of the appropriate type.

Figure 8.4 is a fragment of an embedded SQL program that uses cursors. The DECLARE CURSOR statement declares the name of the cursor as GETENROLLED, specifies it as INSENSITIVE (a qualification we discuss shortly), and associates it with a particular SELECT statement. It does not, however, cause that statement to be executed. The statement is executed when the OPEN statement is executed.

In the example, the associated SELECT statement is parameterized. Only tuples whose attributes CrsCode and Semester match the values stored in the host variables crs_code and semester are selected. When the OPEN statement is executed, parameter substitution takes place and then the SELECT statement is executed. Hence, changes to the values of the parameters made after the cursor is opened have no effect on the tuples that are retrieved through it. OPEN positions the cursor prior to the first row in the result set.

When the FETCH statement is executed, the cursor is advanced. Thus, the FETCH statement in Figure 8.4 points the cursor to the first row in the result set, and the values in that row are fetched and stored in the host language variables stud_id and grade. The CLOSE statement closes the cursor. (In this example, only the first row of the result set is retrieved—clearly an artificial situation. The next example is more realistic.)

Each of the SQL statements in the program has a number of options. The general form of the DECLARE CURSOR statement is

DECLARE *cursor-name* [INSENSITIVE] [SCROLL] CURSOR FOR
    table-expression
    [ORDER BY *order-item-comma-list*]
    [FOR { READ ONLY | UPDATE [OF *column-commalist*] }]

where *table-expression* is generally a table, view, or SELECT statement.

The option INSENSITIVE means that the execution of OPEN will effectively create a copy of the rows in the result set and all accesses through the cursor will be to that copy. The SQL standard uses the word "effectively" to mean that the standard

FIGURE **8.4** Using cursors.

```
#define OK  "00000"
EXEC SQL BEGIN DECLARE SECTION;
    unsigned long stud_id;
    char grade[1];
    char *crs_code, *semester;
    char SQLSTATE[6];
EXEC SQL END DECLARE SECTION;
    :
    :   input values for crs_code, semester, etc.
    :

EXEC SQL DECLARE GetEnrolled INSENSITIVE CURSOR FOR
    SELECT T.StudId, T.Grade
        FROM Transcript T
        WHERE T.CrsCode = :crs_code
            AND T.Semester = :semester;

EXEC SQL OPEN GetEnrolled;
if (strcmp(SQLSTATE,OK) != 0) {
    printf("Cannot open cursor\n");
    exit(1);
}
EXEC SQL FETCH GetEnrolled INTO :stud_id, :grade;
if (strcmp(SQLSTATE,OK) != 0){
    printf("Cannot fetch\n");
    exit(1);
}
EXEC SQL CLOSE GetEnrolled;
```

does not specify how the INSENSITIVE option must be implemented, but whatever implementation is used must have the same effect as if a separate copy had been made. This type of returned data is sometimes called a **snapshot**.

INSENSITIVE cursors have very intuitive semantics. The selection over the base tables implied by the SELECT statement is performed when OPEN is executed, and the result set is computed and stored. This copy can then be browsed at a later time using the cursor. The situation is shown in Figure 8.5 for the cursor of Figure 8.4, where semester = 'F1997' and crs_code = 'CS315'.

Because an INSENSITIVE cursor accesses a copy of the result set, any modifications to the base tables by other statements in the same transaction made (not through this cursor) after the cursor has been opened will not be seen through the cursor. For example, the transaction might execute

```
INSERT INTO Transcript
VALUES ('656565656', 'CS315', 'F1997', 'C');
```

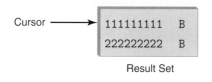

| Cursor ⟶ | 111111111 | B |
| | 222222222 | B |

Result Set

111111111	CS315	F1996	F
111111111	CS315	F1997	B
111111111	CS306	F1997	A
222222222	CS315	F1997	B
333333333	CS303	S1997	C

Transcript

FIGURE 8.5 With an insensitive cursor, the result set is effectively calculated when the cursor is opened and the underlying table is not accessed when rows are fetched.

after opening the cursor, thus inserting a new tuple directly (not through the cursor) into TRANSCRIPT. Although `crs_code = 'CS315'` and `semester = 'F1997'` at the time GETENROLLED is opened, the cursor will not retrieve values from the above newly inserted row. This is true even if the transaction executes an UPDATE statement that changes the attributes in one of the tuples in the result set after the cursor has been opened. Similarly, modifications of the base tables by concurrently executing transactions after the cursor has been opened will not be seen through the cursor.

The SQL standard does not specify what effects should be observed when changes are made to the base tables and the INSENSITIVE option has not been selected. Every database vendor is free to implement whatever it deems appropriate. Many vendors use the semantics called KEYSET_DRIVEN, which is part of ODBC and is described in Section 8.6.

If INSENSITIVE is not specified, the cursor has not been declared READ ONLY, and the SQL query in the cursor declaration satisfies the conditions for an updatable view (see Section 5.3), then the current row of the base table can be updated or deleted through the cursor, and the cursor is said to be "updatable." UPDATE or DELETE statements are used for this purpose, but the WHERE clause is replaced by WHERE CURRENT OF *cursor-name*. Thus, the general syntax is

UPDATE *table-name*
SET *assignment-comma-list*
WHERE CURRENT OF *cursor-name*

and

DELETE
FROM *table-name*
WHERE CURRENT OF *cursor-name*

Because an INSENSITIVE cursor points to a copy of the result set, UPDATE and DELETE statements would have no effect on tables from which the result set was calculated. Hence, to avoid confusion, these operations cannot be performed through an INSENSITIVE cursor.

If a particular ordering of rows in the result set is desired, the ORDER BY clause can be used. If, for example, we include the clause

```
ORDER BY Grade
```

in the declaration of GETENROLLED, rows of the result set will be in ascending order of Grade.

The general form of the FETCH statement is

```
FETCH  [  [ row-selector  ]  FROM  ]  cursor-name
INTO  target-commalist
```

where *target-commalist* is a list of host language variables that must match in number and type the list of attributes of the cursor's result set. The *row-selector* determines how the cursor is to be moved over the result set before the next row is fetched. The options are

```
FIRST
NEXT
PRIOR
LAST
ABSOLUTE  n
RELATIVE  n
```

If the row selector is NEXT, the cursor is moved to the next row of the result set and that row is fetched into the variables named in *target-commalist*. If the row selector is PRIOR, the cursor is moved to the preceding row and that row is fetched. Similarly, the FIRST row selector causes the cursor to be moved to the first row, and the LAST row selector causes the cursor to be moved to the last row. Finally, ABSOLUTE n refers to the nth row in the table, and RELATIVE n refers to the nth row before or after the row to which the cursor is pointing (as determined by a negative or positive n). If *row-selector* is omitted, NEXT is assumed. In that case, if the above ORDER BY clause is used in GETENROLLED, rows are fetched in ascending grade order.

The option SCROLL in the declaration of the cursor means that all forms of the FETCH statement are allowable. If SCROLL is not specified, only NEXT is allowable.

In Figure 8.6, we extend the example of Figure 8.4 so that all of the students enrolled in a particular course can be processed. The FETCH statement is now in a loop that terminates when the status returned indicates that execution was unsuccessful. The conditional statement following the loop checks for a "no data" condition (SQLSTATE has value "02000"), indicating that the result set has been completely scanned. It calls an error-handling routine if this is not the case.

FIGURE 8.6 Using a cursor to scan a table.

```
#define OK "00000"
#define EndOfScan "02000"
EXEC SQL BEGIN DECLARE SECTION;
    unsigned long stud_id;
    char grade[1];
    char *crs_code;
    char *semester;
    char SQLSTATE[6];
EXEC SQL END DECLARE SECTION;

EXEC SQL DECLARE GetEnrolled INSENSITIVE CURSOR FOR
    SELECT T.StudId, T.Grade
        FROM Transcript T
        WHERE T.CrsCode = :crs_code
            AND T.Semester = :semester
    FOR READ ONLY;

    :  get values for crs_code, semester
    :

EXEC SQL OPEN GetEnrolled;
if (strcmp(SQLSTATE,OK) != 0) {
    printf("Cannot open cursor\n");
    exit(1);
}

EXEC SQL FETCH GetEnrolled INTO :stud_id, :grade;
while (strcmp(SQLSTATE,OK) == 0) {
        :  process the values in stud_id and grade
        :
    EXEC SQL FETCH GetEnrolled INTO :stud_id, :grade;
}

if (strcmp(SQLSTATE,EndOfScan) != 0) {
    printf("Something fishy: error before end-of-scan\n");
    exit(1);
}

EXEC SQL CLOSE GetEnrolled;
```

8.2.5 Stored Procedures on the Server

Many DBMS vendors allow **stored procedures** to be included as elements of the database schema. These procedures can then be invoked by an application at a client site and executed at the server site. Among the advantages of stored procedures are the following:

- Since the procedure executes at the server, only its results need be transmitted from the server back to the application program. For example, a stored procedure might use a cursor to scan a large result set and analyze the rows to produce a single value that is returned to the application program. By contrast, if the cursor is used from within the application program, the entire result set must be returned to the application program for analysis, thereby increasing communication costs and response time.

- The SQL statements within a stored procedure can be prepared before the application is executed since the procedure is part of the schema stored at the server. By contrast, preparation of embedded SQL statements is generally done at run time. Hence, even if a stored procedure contains only a single SQL statement, that statement will execute more efficiently in the procedure than if it had been embedded directly in the application.

  This advantage can become a disadvantage because query plans tend to go stale when there are significant database changes after the preparation has been computed. Thus, "old" stored procedures might avoid the overhead of query preparation but incur run-time overhead due to out-of-date query plans. Some vendors (e.g., Sybase) provide an option, WITH RECOMPILE, that can be specified at the time of the procedure call. The application can thus periodically recompile stored procedures and keep query execution plans up to date.

- Authorization can be checked by the DBMS at the level of the stored procedure using the GRANT EXECUTE statement, which extends the GRANT statement introduced in Section 3.3. Thus, even the users who are not authorized to access particular relations in the database might be authorized to execute certain procedures that contain statements that access those relations. For example, both the registration and grade-changing transactions might invoke stored procedures that use a SELECT statement to access the same tuples in a particular table, but one stored procedure can be executed only by students and the other only by faculty.

  In addition, a stored procedure can control what the user can do beyond the capabilities of the SQL GRANT statement. For example, the code within the stored procedure can enforce the requirement that only the student can execute a transaction to register himself.

- The application programmer need not know the details of the database schema since all database accesses can be encapsulated within the procedure body. For example, the registrar's office might supply the procedure body for the registration transaction. The application programmer need only know how to call it.

■ Maintenance of the system is simplified since only one copy of the procedure, stored on the server, need be maintained and updated. By contrast, if the code contained in a procedure is part of a number of application programs, all of those copies have to be maintained and updated.

■ The physical security of the code for the procedure is enhanced because the code is stored on the server rather than with the application program.

The original SQL-92 standard did not support stored procedures, but this support was added retroactively in 1996. We illustrate the language of stored procedures through an example.

Figure 8.7 shows the DDL declaration of a stored procedure for the transaction that deregisters a student from a course. We assume that the application program will connect to the DBMS before calling the procedure and will disconnect after the procedure returns.

The procedure body is written in the **SQL Persistent Stored Modules** language (**SQL/PSM**), as specified by the expanded SQL-92 standard.[1] The standard also provides for stored procedures written in other languages, such as C. Note that in this context SQL/PSM is simply another host language in which SQL statements are embedded. The procedure in the example has three *in* parameters, indicated by the keyword IN, and two *out* parameters, indicated by the keyword OUT. The standard also allows parameters that can be used both ways (INOUT).

The body of the procedure is enclosed in a BEGIN/END block. The option ATOMIC ensures that the entire block executes as a single atomic unit (i.e., it either executes to completion or the partial results of the execution are rolled back). Next follows a series of variable declarations, which are given initial value using the DEFAULT statement (which is optional). Note that neither the parameters nor the host variables (i.e., PSM variables declared within the stored procedure) have the colon (:) prefix. This is because SQL/PSM is a unified language whose compiler understands the host variable declarations, the control statements, and the SQL query and update statements. Our example illustrates the use of the variables both within and outside of the query and update statements. In particular, their value can be changed with the SET clause, and they can be part of arithmetic and string expressions.

PSM is a powerful, full-blown programming language that is well integrated with the rest of SQL. In our brief discussion, we omit many features, such as the looping constructs, the case statement, and cursors. A detailed treatment of PSM and stored procedures appears in [Melton 1997]; here we only touch upon error handling in PSM, which is somewhat different from that in embedded SQL.

Rather than have the program check the variable SQLSTATE after each update statement (or using the WHENEVER statement), in SQL/PSM, **condition handlers** are declared for different values of SQLSTATE. A condition handler is a program that gets executed when an SQL statement terminates with a value for SQLSTATE that

---

[1] Other vendors provide similar languages that precede SQL/PSM and differ from it in various ways. Oracle has PL/SQL, Microsoft and Sybase offer Transact-SQL, and Informix has the SPL language.

FIGURE 8.7 A stored procedure that deregisters a student from a course.

```
CREATE PROCEDURE Deregister ( IN    crs_code CHAR(6),
                              IN    semester CHAR(6),
                              IN    student_id INTEGER,
                              OUT status INTEGER,
                              OUT statusMsg CHAR VARYING(100))
BEGIN ATOMIC
    DECLARE message CHAR VARYING(50)
        DEFAULT 'Houston, we have a problem: ';
    DECLARE Success INTEGER DEFAULT 0;
    DECLARE Failure INTEGER DEFAULT -1;

    IF 1 <> (SELECT COUNT(*) FROM CLASS C
             WHERE C.Semester = semester AND C.CrsCode = crs_code)
    THEN
        SET statusMsg = 'Course not offered';
        SET status = Failure;
    ELSE
        BEGIN    -- Block limits the scope of error handler
            DECLARE UNDO HANDLER FOR SQLEXCEPTION
                BEGIN
                    SET statusMsg = message || 'cannot delete';
                    SET status = Failure;
                END
            DELETE FROM TRANSCRIPT
                WHERE StudId = student_id
                    AND Semester = semester
                    AND CrsCode = crs_code;
        END
        BEGIN -- Block limits the scope of error handler
            DECLARE UNDO HANDLER FOR SQLEXCEPTION
                BEGIN
                    SET statusMsg = message || 'cannot update';
                    SET status = Failure;
                END
            UPDATE CLASS
                SET Enrollment = (Enrollment - 1)
                WHERE Semester = semester
                    AND CrsCode = crs_code;
        END
        -- Normal termination
        SET status = Success;
        SET statusMsg = 'OK';
    END IF;
END;
```

matches one of the values associated with that condition handler. In our case, we have two handlers associated with SQLEXCEPTION, which is a condition that matches any *error code* (an SQLSTATE value that does *not* begin with 00, 01, or 02). Each handler's scope is delimited by a BEGIN/END block, which allows us to associate different handlers with different SQL statements. Both handlers are UNDO handlers, which means that the DBMS will roll back the effects of the stored procedure and exit after the execution of the handler. UNDO handlers can occur only inside BEGIN ATOMIC blocks. If we specify CONTINUE handlers instead, the execution proceeds after the handler has been executed as if no error occurred. We can specify EXIT instead of UNDO, in which case the procedure will exit after the execution of the condition handler but the changes made by the procedure will *not* be rolled back.

In direct (interactive) SQL (and inside another stored procedure), a stored procedure can be executed using the SQL statement

---

CALL *procedure_name* (*argument-commalist*) ;

In a host program with embedded SQL, a CALL statement is preceded by EXEC SQL. In that case, the procedure arguments are host language variables preceded by a colon (:). For example, to execute the stored procedure Deregister(), we might use

---

EXEC SQL CALL Deregister(:crs_code,:semester,:stud_id);

---

where crs_code, semester, and stud_id are host variables.

8.3 More on Integrity Constraints

A consistent transaction moves the database from an initial to a final state, both of which satisfy all integrity constraints. However, a constraint might be false in an intermediate state during transaction execution; for example, in the case of referential integrity, if the reference to a row is added before the row itself. Similarly, the state produced by the DELETE statement in the procedure Deregister (Figure 8.7) violates the integrity constraint that the number of students listed as enrolled in a course in TRANSCRIPT be equal to the NumEnrolled attribute value for the course in CLASS. If the DBMS checks constraints immediately after each statement is executed, the DELETE would be rejected.

To deal with this situation, SQL allows the application to control the mode of each constraint. If a constraint is in **immediate mode**, it is checked immediately after the execution of any SQL statement in the transaction that might make it false. If it is in **deferred mode**, it is not checked until the transaction requests to commit.

■ If constraint checking for a particular constraint is immediate and an SQL statement causes the constraint to become false, the offending SQL statement is rolled back and an appropriate error code is returned through SQLSTATE. The transaction can retrieve the name of the violated constraint from the diagnostics area.

■ If constraint checking for a particular constraint is deferred, the constraint is not checked until the transaction requests to commit. If the constraint is found to be false at that time, the transaction is aborted and an appropriate error code returned. Deferred constraint checking is obviously preferable to immediate checking if integrity constraints are violated in intermediate transaction states.

When a constraint is initially defined, it can be specified with options. For example, a table constraint conforms to the rule

[CONSTRAINT *constraint-name*] CHECK *conditional-expression*
  [{ INITIALLY DEFERRED | INITIALLY IMMEDIATE }]
  [{ DEFERRABLE | NOT DEFERRABLE }]

The first option gives the initial mode of the constraint. Thus, if INITIALLY DEFERRED is specified, the constraint is checked in the deferred mode until the mode is changed by an explicit SET CONSTRAINTS statement. The second option tells whether or not the constraint can be deferred by a subsequent SET CONSTRAINTS statement. The options NOT DEFERRABLE and INITIALLY DEFERRED are considered contradictory and cannot be specified together.

A DEFERRABLE constraint can be in IMMEDIATE or DEFERRED mode at different times. The mode switch is performed with the following statement:

SET CONSTRAINTS { *constraint-list* | ALL } { DEFERRED | IMMEDIATE }

where *constraint-list* is a list of constraint names, given in CONSTRAINT statements.

8.4 Dynamic SQL

With static SQL, an SQL statement to be executed is designed and embedded in the application program at the time the program is written. All of the details of the statement (e.g., whether it is SELECT or INSERT), schema information (e.g., attribute and table names referred to in the statement), and host language variables used as *in* or *out* parameters are known at compile time.

In some applications, not all of this information is known when the program is written. To handle this situation, SQL defines a syntax for including **directives** in a host language program to construct, prepare, and execute an SQL statement. The statement is constructed by the host language portion of the program at run time. The directives are collectively referred to as *dynamic SQL* to distinguish them from static SQL and to indicate that SQL statements can be (dynamically) constructed at run time. Since, as with static SQL, the directives use a syntax that sets them apart from the host language, dynamic SQL is also a statement-level interface. Static and dynamic SQL use the same syntax, so they can be processed by the same precompiler. An application program can include both static and dynamic SQL constructs.

The constructed SQL statement appears in the program as the value of a host language variable of type string and is passed to the DBMS at run time as the argument of a dynamic SQL directive for preparation. Once prepared, the statement can be executed. As with static SQL, the statement must be constructed in the dialect understood by the target DBMS.

Suppose that, for example, your university has a single student registration system that allows a student to register for any course at any of its campuses. Assume that each campus has its own course database with its own table- and attribute-naming conventions. When a student executes the registration interaction, the application program might construct, at run time, the appropriate SQL statements to perform the registration at the specified campus. For example, it might have string representations of the appropriate SELECT statements for each campus stored in a file. The correct string is retrieved from the file at run time, assigned to a host language variable, and then prepared and executed. Or the program might use a skeleton of an appropriate SQL statement, which was prepared in advance, and then fill in appropriate table and attribute names at run time.

In the above example, there might be some commonality among the schemas and the SQL statements that must be executed to register a student at all campuses. Hence, the application program might know something about the SQL statements that it is executing. As another example, consider an application that monitors a terminal and allows the user to input an arbitrary SQL statement for execution at some database manager. The application now has no advance information about the SQL statements that it is sending to the database but must simply take the string that has been input to a variable and send it to the DBMS for processing. Similarly, consider an application in which a spreadsheet is connected to a database. At run time, the user might specify that the value of a particular entry in the spreadsheet is some expression involving database items that must be retrieved with queries. The queries might be expressed by the user in some graphical notation, but the application translates this notation into SELECT statements. Again, it has no advance information about the SQL statement to be executed and, possibly, none about the schema of the database the statement is accessing.

This lack of information can create a problem since the domains of the *in* and *out* parameters of the SQL statement must be known so that host language variables of the appropriate type can be used for parameter passing. For situations in which this information is not available to the application program at compile time, dynamic SQL provides directives that allow the program to query the DBMS at run time to obtain schema information.

8.4.1 Statement Preparation in Dynamic SQL

We illustrate the idea of dynamically constructed SQL statements with the following example:[2]

---

[2] For readers who need help with C, the function scanf() reads user input and puts the result in the variable column. The function sprintf() substitutes the value of the variable column for the format symbol %s and puts the result in the variable my_sql_stmt. The backslash in the SELECT clause indicates that the string continues on the following line.

```
printf("Which column of CLASS would you like to see?");
scanf("%s", column); // get user input (Enrollment or Room)
// Incorporate user input into SQL statement
sprintf(my_sql_stmt,
        "SELECT C.%s FROM CLASS C \
              WHERE C.CrsCode = ?  AND   C.Semester = ?",
        column);
EXEC SQL PREPARE st1 FROM :my_sql_stmt;
EXEC SQL EXECUTE st1
      INTO :some_string_var
      USING :crs_code, :semester;
```

Here, in addition to the fact that the values of CrsCode and Semester are not known at compile time, the exact form of the SELECT statement is also not known at that time since the column to be retrieved by the query depends on what the user inputs at run time. The PREPARE statement sends the query string (in the variable my_sql_stmt) to the database manager for preparation and assigns the name st1 to the prepared statement. Note that st1 here is an SQL variable (used only in SQL statements), not a host language variable, so it is not preceded with a colon (:).

The EXECUTE statement causes the statement named st1 to be executed. The string has two *in* parameters marked with ?. The host language variables whose values are to be substituted for these parameters are named in the USING clause. In addition, the host variable to receive the result is named in the INTO clause. The ? marker is called a **dynamic parameter**, or **placeholder**, and can be used in SELECT, INSERT, UPDATE, and DELETE statements. Once prepared, st1 can be executed many times with different host language variables as arguments. The query execution plan created by the PREPARE statement is used for all subsequent executions during the current session.

Note that, just like SELECT INTO, EXECUTE INTO requires that the query result be a single row. If the result has more than one row, a cursor must be used instead of EXECUTE INTO. We describe cursors over dynamic SQL statements in Section 8.4.3.

Parameter passing in dynamic SQL is different from that in static SQL. Placeholders, instead of the names of host language variables, are used in the string to be prepared, and the INTO clause is now attached to the EXECUTE statement instead of the SELECT statement. Why is parameter passing different in this case?

■ With static SQL, the names of the host language variables serving as parameters are provided to the precompiler in the WHERE and INTO clauses of the SQL statements. The precompiler parses these clauses at compile time. The variables are described in the compiler's symbol table that is used to translate variable names to addresses (recall that declarations in the DECLARE SECTION are processed by both the precompiler and the host language compiler). The symbol table entries contain the mapping between variable names and addresses plus the type information needed by the precompiler to generate the code for converting data items from the database representation to these variables and back. This code is executed in the host language program at the time the SQL statement is executed.

■ With dynamic SQL, as in the above example, the SQL statement might not be available to the precompiler. Thus, if host language variables to be used as parameters were embedded in the statement, they could not be processed using information contained in the symbol table. To make parameter information available at compile time, it is supplied in one of two ways: through the *SQLDA* mechanism, explained on page 291, and by supplying the input and output variables in the clauses USING and INTO, as in our example. In the latter case, the precompiler generates the code for fetching and storing the argument values from and to these variables for communication with the DBMS.

Applications should be designed using static SQL whenever possible since dynamic SQL is generally less efficient. The separation of preparation and execution implies added communication and processing costs—although, if the statement is executed multiple times, the added cost can be prorated over the executions because preparation need be done only once. Moreover, this cost can be eliminated in some cases. With certain SQL statement to be executed only once, we can combine preparation and execution using the EXECUTE IMMEDIATE directive:

```
EXEC SQL EXECUTE IMMEDIATE
    'INSERT INTO  TRANSCRIPT '
    || 'VALUES (''656565656'', ''CS315'', ''F1999'', ''C'') ';
```

Note the treatment of strings. INSERT INTO is part of the dynamic SQL statement, so we are using single quotes to denote strings. Since the statement is long, it is split into two strings, which are concatenated with the usual SQL concatenation operator, ||. To include a quote symbol in a string, it must be doubled, as in the case of ''656565656''. This enables the SQL parser to parse the string correctly. In the result, each occurrence of '' is replaced with a single quote, thus producing a valid SQL statement.

More generally, as with EXECUTE, the SQL statement can be constructed in a host language string variable, in which case the EXECUTE IMMEDIATE statement takes the form

```
EXEC SQL EXECUTE IMMEDIATE :my_sql_stmt;
```

Note the : prepended to the variable my_sql_stmt. As before, it indicates that my_sql_stmt is a host language variable rather than an SQL variable.

EXECUTE IMMEDIATE is merely a shortcut that combines the PREPARE and EXECUTE statements into one and does not preserve the execution plan after the statement has been executed. This shortcut imposes additional syntactic restrictions, some logical and some not. For instance, it does not allow an associated INTO clause.

Therefore, the statement to be executed cannot have any *out* parameters (i.e., it cannot retrieve any data) and so cannot be a SELECT statement.

EXECUTE IMMEDIATE also does not allow an associated USING clause, but this is not a serious limitation. The need for USING in the EXECUTE statement comes from the fact that the statement is prepared once, with dynamic *in* parameters marked as ?, and then is executed many times with different arguments. Since EXECUTE IMMEDIATE does preparation and execution in one step (and the prepared statement is not saved for posterity), the special dynamic parameters are not needed. We can simply *plug* the appropriate parameter values into the SQL statement (represented as a string in the host language) using the host language facilities and then pass the fully constructed statement to EXECUTE IMMEDIATE.

As in static SQL, SQLSTATE is used to return the status of PREPARE, EXECUTE, EXECUTE IMMEDIATE, and all other dynamic SQL statements.

8.4.2 Prepared Statements and the Descriptor Area*

Even though the query in the example of Section 8.4.1 on page 288 is constructed at run time and the name of the output column is not known at compile time, the example is still fairly simple because the application knows that the query target list contains exactly one attribute name and that the WHERE clause has exactly two dynamic parameters. Knowing the number of outputs and inputs thus allows us to use the EXECUTE statement and provide concrete variable names for the USING and INTO clauses. The precompiler can then supply such niceties as automatic format conversion. For example, if the user inputs `Enrollment`, which is an integer, conversion to the string format is automatic: the precompiler determines that the INTO variable is of type string. Since the DBMS provides, at run time, the type of the value returned by the SELECT statement, the nature of the conversion can be determined at that time.

Suppose now that, at run time, the application allows the user to specify the number of attributes in the target list and the condition in the WHERE clause. In this case we do not know the number of inputs and outputs at design time and will not be able to use the form of the EXECUTE statement described in Section 8.4.1 since we do not know how many variables to supply in the INTO and USING clauses at the time of writing the program.

To deal with this situation, dynamic SQL provides a run-time mechanism that the application program can use to request from the DBMS information describing the parameters of a statement. For example, suppose that an application allows the user to query any 1-tuple relation in the database:[3]

```
printf("Which table would you like to inspect?");
scanf("%s", table); // get user input (e.g., Class or Transcript)
// Incorporate user input into SQL statement
```

---

[3] Our example uses the EXECUTE statement, which can handle only 1-tuple queries. For the general case, a cursor and the FETCH statement are needed. We discuss the use of cursors in dynamic SQL in Section 8.4.3.

```
sprintf(my_sql_stmt,
        "SELECT * FROM %s WHERE COUNT(*)=1",
        table);
```

This statement has no input parameters but has an indeterminate number of output parameters because the table to be used in the FROM clause is not known in advance. Thus, it is not known how many table attributes (i.e., *out* parameters) are represented by the * in the SELECT clause. Although the application knows nothing about these parameters, once the statement has been prepared, the DBMS knows all there is to know about them and can provide this information to the application. It does this through a descriptor area. The application first requests that the DBMS allocate a **descriptor area**, sometimes called an **SQLDA**, in which parameter information can be stored. After the statement has been prepared, the application can then request that the DBMS populate the descriptor with the parameter information. For the above example, we populate the descriptor area as follows:

```
EXEC SQL PREPARE st FROM :my_sql_stmt;
EXEC SQL ALLOCATE DESCRIPTOR 'st_output' WITH MAX 21;
EXEC SQL DESCRIBE OUTPUT st
      USING SQL DESCRIPTOR 'st_output';
```

Here st_output is an SQL variable that references the descriptor area that has been allocated. The ALLOCATE DESCRIPTOR statement creates space in the database manager, which must be sufficient to describe at most 21 parameters of the statement (as specified by the WITH MAX clause). The descriptor can be thought of as a one-dimensional array with an entry for each parameter, together with a count of the *actual* number of parameters. Each entry has a fixed structure consisting of components that describe a particular parameter, such as its name, type, and value. All fields are initially undefined. The DESCRIBE statement causes the DBMS to populate the *i*th entry of the descriptor st_output with meta-information about the *i*th *out* parameter of the prepared statement st (which includes name, type, and length of the parameter). It also stores the number of these parameters in the descriptor.

Returning to our example, the application causes the prepared statement st to be executed using the directive

```
EXEC SQL EXECUTE st
      INTO SQL DESCRIPTOR 'st_output';
```

Execution causes the value of the ith attribute of the row returned to be stored in the *value field* of the ith entry in st_output. To retrieve the meta-information about the attributes as well as their values, the application can use the GET DESCRIPTOR statement. Typically this is done in a loop that inspects each column in the retrieved row, as illustrated in Figure 8.8. In the end, the program calls DEALLOCATE DESCRIPTOR to free the space occupied by the descriptor st_output.

FIGURE **8.8** Example of using GET DESCRIPTOR.

```
int collength, coltype, colcount;
char colname[255];
// Arrange variables for different types of data
char stringdata[1024];
int intdata;
float floatdata;
    :  variable declarations for other types
    .
// Store the number of columns in colcount
EXEC SQL GET DESCRIPTOR 'st_output' :colcount = COUNT;
for (i=0; i < colcount; i++) {
    // Get meta-information about the ith attribute
    // Note: type is represented by an integer constant, such as
    // SQL_CHAR, SQL_INTEGER, SQL_FLOAT, defined in a header file
    EXEC SQL GET DESCRIPTOR 'st_output' VALUE :i
        :coltype = TYPE,
        :collength = LENGTH,
        :colname = NAME;
    printf("Column %s has value: ", colname);
    switch (coltype) {
    case SQL_CHAR:
        EXEC SQL GET DESCRIPTOR 'st_output' VALUE :i :stringdata = DATA;
        printf("%s\n", stringdata); // print string value
        break;
    case SQL_INTEGER:
        EXEC SQL GET DESCRIPTOR 'st_output' VALUE :i :intdata = DATA;
        printf("%d\n", intdata); // print integer value
        break;
    case SQL_FLOAT:
        EXEC SQL GET DESCRIPTOR 'st_output' VALUE :i :floatdata = DATA;
        printf("%f\n", floatdata); // print floating point value
        break;
        :  other cases
        .
    } // switch
} // for loop
```

Situations in which the SQL statement to be executed contains an unknown number of input parameters are rare. When they do occur, the application can use ALLOCATE and DESCRIBE INPUT to set up a descriptor area for the *in* parameters specified as ? placeholders. As before, this descriptor is essentially an array with an entry for each placeholder. The application then uses the DESCRIBE INPUT statement to request that the DBMS populate the descriptor area with the information about each *in* parameter: for example, its type, length, and name. In this case the value has to be supplied by the application using the SET DESCRIPTOR statement. We do not discuss the details of this procedure and refer the reader to SQL manuals such as [Date and Darwen 1997; Melton and Simon 1992].

8.4.3 Cursors

Like SELECT INTO, EXECUTE INTO has the problem that the result of the query must be a single tuple. A more likely situation is that the result of a query is a relation and the cursor mechanism is needed to scan it. Fortunately, cursors can be defined for prepared statements in dynamic SQL as they are in static SQL, although the syntax is slightly different. For instance, the following is equivalent to the program in Figure 8.4 in static SQL (for brevity we have not shown the status checks in this case):

```
my_sql_stmt = "SELECT T.StudId, T.Grade \
                FROM Transcript T \
                WHERE T.CrsCode = ? \
                AND T.Semester = ?";
EXEC SQL PREPARE st2 FROM :my_sql_stmt;
EXEC SQL DECLARE GetEnroll INSENSITIVE CURSOR FOR st2;
EXEC SQL OPEN GetEnroll USING :crs_code, :semester;
EXEC SQL FETCH GetEnroll INTO :stud_id, :grade;
EXEC SQL CLOSE GetEnroll;
```

As with static SQL, the DECLARE CURSOR statement has the options INSENSITIVE and SCROLL, while the FETCH statement has the option that allows a row selector (FIRST, NEXT, PRIOR, etc.) to be specified for scrollable cursors. UPDATE and DELETE statements can also be performed through a dynamic cursor that is not insensitive.

8.4.4 Stored Procedures on the Server

Some DBMSs allow stored procedures to be called using dynamic SQL. To call the stored procedure of Figure 8.7, we might use

```
my_sql_stmt = "CALL Deregister(?,?,?)";
EXEC SQL PREPARE st3 FROM :my_sql_stmt;
EXEC SQL EXECUTE st3
    USING :crs_code, :semester, :stud_id;
```

The PREPARE statement prepares the call to the Deregister procedure. The EXEC SQL EXECUTE statement calls the procedure and supplies the values of host language variables as arguments.

8.5 JDBC and SQLJ

JDBC[4] is an API to the database manager that provides a call-level interface for the execution of SQL statements from a Java language program. As in dynamic SQL, an SQL statement can be constructed at run time as the value of a string variable. JDBC was developed by Sun Microsystems and is an integral part of the Java language.

In contrast, SQLJ is a statement-level interface to Java, analogous to static embedded SQL. Unlike JDBC, it was developed by a consortium of companies and has become a separate ANSI standard. In the end, both JDBC and SQLJ were included as part of SQL:2003.

Both JDBC and SQLJ are designed to access databases over the Internet and are much more portable than the various implementations of embedded and dynamic SQL. As part of SQL:2003, JDBC and SQLJ are described in the document titled *Object Language Bindings*.

8.5.1 JDBC Basics

Recall that, in dynamic and static SQL, the target DBMS must be known at compile time since the SQL statements must use the target's dialect. With dynamic SQL, the schema need not be known at compile time. By contrast, in JDBC neither the DBMS nor the schema need be known at compile time. Applications can use core SQL dialect that all JDBC drivers are required to support, and, as with dynamic SQL, JDBC supplies features that allow the application to request information about the schema from the DBMS at run time.

The mechanism that allows JDBC programs to deal with different DBMSs at run time is shown in Figure 8.9. The application communicates with a DBMS through a JDBC module called a **driver manager**. When the application first connects to a particular DBMS, the driver manager chooses another JDBC module, called a **driver**, to pass SQL statements specified in the JDBC calls to that DBMS. JDBC maintains a separate driver for most commonly used DBMSs. The manager chooses the one corresponding to the particular DBMS being accessed. When an SQL statement is to be executed, the application program sends a string representation of the statement to the appropriate driver, which performs any necessary reformatting and then sends the statement to the DBMS, where it is prepared and executed.

The software architecture of JDBC consists of a set of predefined object classes, such as `DriverManager` and `Statement`. The methods of these object classes provide the call-level interface to the database. A JDBC program must first load these predefined object classes, then create appropriate instances of the object types, and then use the appropriate methods to access the database. The general structure of JDBC calls within a Java program is shown in Figure 8.10. We explain each statement as it appears:

■   `import java.sql.*` imports all of the classes in the package `java.sql` and hence makes the JDBC API available within the Java program. The classes

---

[4] JDBC is a trademark of Sun Microsystems, which claims that it is not an acronym. Nevertheless, it is often assumed to stand for "Java DataBase Connectivity."

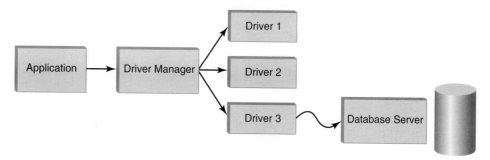

FIGURE 8.9 Connecting to a database through JDBC.

FIGURE 8.10 Skeleton of procedure calls needed for JDBC.

```
import java.sql.*;
    .
    .
    .
  String  url,userId,password;
  Connection  con1;
    .
    .
    .
  try {
     // Use the right driver for your database
     Class.forName("sun.jdbc.odbc.JdbcOdbcDriver"); // load the driver
     con1 = DriverManager.getConnection(url, userId, password);
  } catch (ClassNotFoundException e) {
     System.err.println("Cannot load driver\n");
     System.exit(1);
  } catch (SQLException e) {
     System.err.println("Cannot connect\n");
     System.exit(1);
  }
  Statement stat1 = con1.createStatement(); // create a statement object
  String myQuery = ... some SELECT statement ...
  ResultSet res1 = stat1.executeQuery(myQuery);
         .
         .   process results
         .
  stat1.close(); // free up the statement object
  con1.close();   // close connection
```

Connection, Statement, DriverManager, and ResultSet that occur in the figure are all in this package, as are PreparedStatement, CallableStatement, ResultSetMetadata, and SQLException. (CallableStatement is a subclass of PreparedStatement, which in turn is a subclass of Statement.)

■ `Class.forName()` loads the specified database driver and registers it with the driver manager. Although the naming convention might not be intuitive, there is a class in the `java.lang` package, called `Class`, with methods that allow a class to be loaded into a program at run time. One of its static methods, `forName()`, can be used to load and register the specified driver. If the application wants to connect to more than one database, `Class.forName()` is called separately for each.

This and the next statement are enveloped with the `try/catch` construct, which handles exceptions. We return to exception handling in Section 8.5.5.

■ `DriverManager.getConnection()` uses the static method `getConnection()` of the class `DriverManager` to connect to the DBMS at the given address. The method tests each of the database drivers that have been loaded to see if any are capable of establishing a connection to that DBMS. If so, it

1. Establishes the connection using the specified user Id and password
2. Creates a `Connection` object and assigns it to the variable `con1`, declared earlier

The parameter `url` contains the URL (uniform resource locator) of the target DBMS. This URL is obtained from the database administrator and looks something like

```
jdbc:odbc:http://server.xyz.edu/sturegDB:8000
```

The prefix `jdbc` specifies the main protocol for connecting to the database (JDBC, not surprisingly). The second component, `odbc`, specifies the subprotocol (which is vendor and driver specific). Next comes the address of the database server, followed by the communication port number on which the server is listening.

■ `con1.createStatement()` uses the `createStatement()` method of the `Connection` object `con1` to create a `Statement` object and assign it to the `Statement` variable `stat1`.

■ `stat1.executeQuery()` prepares and executes the SELECT statement provided as an argument, using the `Statement` object `stat1`. The SQL statement can have no *in* parameters, and the result set it returns is stored in the `ResultSet` object `res1`, which is created by the `executeQuery()` method. This method is analogous to the EXECUTE IMMEDIATE directive in dynamic SQL since it combines both preparation and execution. A major difference is that the JDBC method creates an object for returning data, which EXECUTE IMMEDIATE cannot do. We discuss the `ResultSet` class in Section 8.5.3.

To execute an UPDATE, DELETE, or INSERT statement (or a DDL statement), the appropriate form is

```
stat1.executeUpdate(... some SQL statement ...);
```

This function returns an integer denoting how many rows are affected (or 0 for a DDL statement, such as CREATE).

- `stat1.close()` and `con1.close()` deallocate the `Statement` object and close the connection (deallocating the `Connection` object), respectively. After a statement has been executed, the `Statement` object that supported it need not be closed but can be reused to support another statement.

8.5.2 Prepared Statements

The call to `executeQuery()` in Figure 8.10 both prepares and executes the specified statement. To prepare a statement and then execute it separately, the appropriate calls are

```
PreparedStatement ps1 =
        con1.prepareStatement(...  SQL preparable statement  ...);
```

which returns a `PreparedStatement` object that is assigned to `ps1`, followed by either

```
ResultSet res1 = ps1.executeQuery();
```

or in the case of an update statement,

```
int n = ps1.executeUpdate();
```

where `executeUpdate()` returns an integer denoting how many rows were updated.

`PreparedStatement` is a subclass of the class `Statement`. Note that both classes have methods with the names `executeQuery()` and `executeUpdate()`, but that the methods for `PreparedStatement` have no arguments (because a prepared statement knows which query it is).

As in dynamic SQL, the string argument of `prepareStatement()` can contain dynamic *in* parameters marked with the `?` placeholders. Also as with dynamic SQL, the placeholders must be given concrete values before execution. This is done using the `setXXX()` methods. For instance,

```
ps1.setInt(1, someIntVar);
```

replaces the first `?` placeholder with the value stored in the host language variable `someIntVar`. `PreparedStatement` has a number of `setXXX()` methods, where `XXX` specifies the type (e.g., `Int`, `Long`, `String`) to supply *in* arguments of different types.

8.5.3 Result Sets and Cursors

The execution of a query statement stores its result (the *out* arguments) in the specified `ResultSet` object. The rows in that result set are retrieved using a cursor.

FIGURE **8.11** Fragment of JDBC program using a cursor.

```java
import java.sql.*;
     .
     .
     .
     Connection con2;
     try {
        // Use appropriate URL and JDBC driver
        String url = "jdbc:odbc:http://server.xyz.edu/sturegDB:800";
        Class.forName("sun.jdbc.odbc.JdbcOdbcDriver");
        con2 = DriverManager.getConnection(url, "pml", "36.ty");
     } catch ...   // catch exceptions

     // Use the "+" operator, for readability
     String query2 = "SELECT T.StudId, T.Grade " +
                     "FROM TRANSCRIPT T " +
                     "WHERE T.CrsCode = ? " +
                       "AND T.Semester = ?";

     PreparedStatement ps2 = con2.prepareStatement(query2);
     ps2.setString(1, "CS308");
     ps2.setString(2, "F2000");
     ResultSet res2 = ps2.executeQuery();

     long studId;
     String grade;
     while (res2.next()) {
        studId = res2.getLong("StudId");
        grade = res2.getString("Grade");
        .
        .   process the values in studId and grade
        .
     }

ps2.close();
con2.close();
```

A JDBC cursor is implemented using the next() method of class ResultSet. When invoked on a ResultSet object, it scans the entire set tuple by tuple. In Figure 8.11, the result set object is stored in the variable res2, and res2.next() advances the cursor to the next row.

The program prepares the query, supplies arguments, and then executes the query. It then uses a while loop to retrieve all of the rows of the result set. The method next() moves the cursor and returns false when there are no more rows to return. In each iteration of the while loop, the result tuples are retrieved using calls to getLong() and getString(), which come in two forms: those that take attribute names as a parameter and those that take positional arguments. Thus, we can use getLong(1) to obtain the student Id (since StudId is the first attribute in the result set res2) and getString(2) to obtain the grade (since Grade is the second attribute). The class ResultSet has getXXX() methods for all primitive types supported by Java.

JDBC defines three result set types. They differ in their support of scrolling and sensitivity.

1. A *forward-only* result set, as its name implies, is not scrollable (the cursor can move only in the forward direction). It uses the default cursor type (INSENSITIVE or non-INSENSITIVE) of the underlying DBMS.

2. A *scroll-insensitive* result set is scrollable and uses an INSENSITIVE cursor of the specified DBMS so that changes made to the underlying tables after the result set is computed (either by the transaction that created the result set or by other transactions) are not seen in the result set.

3. A *scroll-sensitive* result set is scrollable and uses a non-INSENSITIVE cursor. As we discussed in Section 8.2.4, the SQL standard does not define any required behavior when the INSENSITIVE option has not been selected. Database vendors are free to implement whatever semantics they deem appropriate, and JDBC generally provides the semantics supported in the DBMS it is accessing. Many vendors have implemented the semantics called KEYSET_DRIVEN, which is part of the ODBC specification and is described in Section 8.6. In that semantics, row updates and deletes made after the result set is created are visible but inserts are not. JDBC provides a variety of methods for querying the driver to determine what to expect.

If the target DBMS does not support the scrolling or sensitivity properties requested by an application, a warning is issued.

A result set can be read-only or updatable. With an updatable result set, the SQL query on which the result set is based must satisfy the conditions for updatable views (see Section 5.3). For example, the following variant of createStatement() creates an instance s3 of the class Statement:

```
Statement s3 =
    con1.createStatement(ResultSet.TYPE_SCROLL_SENSITIVE,
                         ResultSet.CONCUR_UPDATABLE);
```

If the executeQuery() method of s3 is later invoked, the result set that will be created will be updatable and scroll-sensitive. Consult the description of classes ResultSet and Connection in your JDK documentation to see other options.

The current row of an updatable result set, res, produced by a SELECT statement that returns the value of a string attribute, Name, might be updated by assigning the value Smith to Name using

```
res.updateString("Name", "Smith");
```

As with the methods setXXX() and getXXX(), there is an updateXXX() method for every primitive type.

When the new value of the row has been completely constructed, the underlying table is updated by the execution of

```
res.updateRow();
```

Not only can rows in an updatable result set be updated and deleted but, in contrast to cursors in static and dynamic SQL, new rows can be inserted through the result set as well. The column values of the row to be inserted are first assembled in a buffer associated with the result set. The method res.insertRow() is then called to insert the buffered row in the result set res and in the database simultaneously.

8.5.4 Obtaining Information about a Result Set

As with dynamic SQL, information about a result set might not be known when the program is written. JDBC provides mechanisms for querying the DBMS to obtain such information. For example, JDBC provides a class ResultSetMetaData, whose methods can be used for this purpose. Thus

```
ResultSet rs3 = stmt3.executeQuery("SELECT * FROM TABLE3");
ResultSetMetaData rsm3 = rs3.getMetaData();
```

creates a ResultSetMetaData object, rsm3, and populates it with information about the result set rs3. This object can then be queried with such methods as

```
int numberOfColumns = rsm3.getColumnCount();
String columnName = rsm3.getColumnName(1);
String typeName = rsm3.getColumnTypeName(1);
```

The first method returns the number of columns in the result set, and the last two return the name and type of column 1. Using these methods, even without knowing the schema of a result set, one can iterate over the columns of each row in a loop, examine their types, and fetch the data. For instance, if rsm3.getColumnTypeName(2) returns "Integer", the program can call rs3.getInt(2) to obtain the value stored in the second column of the current row.

JDBC also has a class, DatabaseMetaData, which can be queried for information about the schema and other database information.

8.5.5 Status Processing

Status processing in JDBC uses the standard exception-handling mechanism of Java. The basic format is

```
try {
    :
    :    code that might cause an exception goes here
    :
}
```

```
catch (SQLException e) {
    System.err.println("Bad things have happened:\n");
    System.err.println("Message: " + e.getMessage());
    System.err.println("SQLState: " + e.getSQLState());
    System.err.println("ErrorCode: " + e.getErrorCode());
};
```

In fact, in our examples, all calls to executeQuery(), prepareStatement(), and the like should have been enveloped with such a try statement.

The system *tries* to execute the statements within the try clause. Each such statement can contain method calls for Java or JDBC objects, and the declaration of each method can specify that, if certain errors occur during method execution, one or more named exceptions are **thrown**, where the name of the exception denotes the type of error that occurred. For example, the JDBC method executeQuery() throws the exception SQLException if the DBMS returns an access error during query execution. An access error occurs whenever there is an unsuccessful or incomplete execution of an SQL statement—more precisely, an execution for which SQLSTATE has any value other than successful completion (of the form "00XXX"), warning (of the form "01XXX"), or no data ("02000").

If such an exception is thrown within the try clause, it is **caught** by the corresponding catch clause, which is then executed. In the example, an SQLException object, e, is created, whose methods can be used to print out an error message, return the value of SQLSTATE, or return any vendor-specific error code. When the catch clause completes, execution continues with the next statement following the clause.

8.5.6 Executing Transactions

By default, the database is in **autocommit mode** when a connection is created. Each SQL statement is treated as a separate transaction, which is committed when that statement is (successfully) completed. To allow two or more statements to be grouped into a transaction, autocommit mode is disabled using

```
con4.setAutoCommit(false);
```

where con4 is a Connection object.

Initially, each transaction uses the default isolation level of the database manager. The level can be changed with a call such as

```
con4.setTransactionIsolation(Connection.TRANSACTION_SERIALIZABLE);
```

Serialization levels TRANSACTION_SERIALIZABLE, TRANSACTION_REPEATABLE_READ, and the like are constants (static integers) defined in class Connection.

Transactions can be committed or aborted using the `commit()` or `rollback()` methods of class `Connection`.

```
con4.commit();
con4.rollback();
```

After a transaction is committed or rolled back, a new one starts when the next SQL statement is executed (or, in the case of the first SQL statement in the program, when that statement is executed). This way of structuring transactions is called *chaining*.

If the program is connected to more than one DBMS, the transactions at each can be separately committed or rolled back. JDBC does not support a commit protocol that ensures that the set of transactions will be globally atomic. However, a Java package, JTS (Java Transaction Service), includes a TP monitor (and an appropriate API, called JTA [Java Transaction API]), which does guarantee an atomic commit of distributed transactions using JDBC. Also J2EE (Java 2 Enterprise Edition) provides transaction services based on JDBC and JTS.

8.5.7 Stored Procedures on the Server

JDBC can be used to call a stored procedure if the DBMS supports this feature. For example, to call the stored procedure defined in Figure 8.7 on page 284 we might use the program fragment

```
CallableStatement cs5 =
        con5.prepareCall("{call Deregister(?,?,?,?,?)}");
cs5.setString(1, crs_code);
cs5.setString(2, semester);
cs5.setInt(3, stud_id);
cs5.getInt(4, status);
cs5.setString(5, message);
cs5.executeUpdate();
```

where con5 is a `Connection` object.

The first statement declares a `CallableStatement` object with the name cs5 and assigns to it the stored procedure `Deregister()`. The braces around the construct `{call Deregister(?,?,?,?,?)}` denote that the construct is part of the **SQL escape syntax** and signals the driver that the code within the braces should be handled in a special way. The values of the three *in* parameters of `Deregister()`, obtained from the Java variables `crs_code`, `semester`, and `stud_Id`, are specified with setXXX() method calls. (We omit the details of *out* parameters and return values, which are handled somewhat differently.) The final statement executes the call.

The DBMS might allow a stored procedure to return a result set, perhaps in addition to updating the database. A call to such a procedure is viewed as a query, in which case the last statement in the above program fragment is replaced by

```
ResultSet rs5 = cs5.executeQuery();
```

JDBC also has facilities for creating a stored procedure (as a string) and sending it to the DBMS.

8.5.8 An Example

Figure 8.12 is a fragment of a Java program containing calls to the JDBC API. The program performs roughly the same transaction as that of Figure 8.3, except that, for simplicity, it uses constants in the SQL statements instead of the ? placeholders.

8.5.9 SQLJ: Statement-Level Interface to Java

Although call-level interfaces, such as JDBC, can be used in static transaction processing applications (where the database schema and the format of the SQL statements are known at compile time), they are fundamentally less efficient at run time than statement-level interfaces, such as static SQL, because preparation and execution generally involve separate communication with the DBMS. For this reason, a consortium of companies developed a statement-level SQL interface to Java, called **SQLJ**, which is now an ANSI standard. An important goal of SQLJ is to obtain some of the run-time efficiency of embedded SQL for (static) Java applications while retaining the advantage of accessing DBMSs through JDBC.

SQLJ is analogous to embedded SQL but was designed specifically to be embedded in Java programs. Such programs are translated by a precompiler into standard Java, and the embedded SQLJ constructs are replaced by calls to an SQLJ run-time package, which accesses a database using calls to a JDBC driver. An SQLJ program can connect to multiple DBMSs using different JDBC drivers in this way. As with embedded SQL, the precompiler can also check SQL syntax and the number and types of arguments and results.

We do not discuss the syntax of SQLJ in detail but highlight some of the differences between SQLJ, embedded SQL, and JDBC:

- In contrast to embedded SQL, in which each DBMS vendor supports its own proprietary version of SQL, SQLJ supports a core sublanguage of SQL-92 and is much more portable across vendors. (DBMS vendors can provide proprietary extensions, however.)

- SQL statements appear in a Java program as part of an **SQLJ clause**, which begins with #SQL (instead of EXEC SQL, as in embedded SQL) and can contain an SQL

FIGURE **8.12** A fragment of a Java program using JDBC.

```java
import java.sql.*;
    .
    .
    .
    try {
        // Use the right JDBC driver here
        Class.forName("sun.jdbc.odbc.JdbcOdbcDriver");
    } catch (ClassNotFoundException e) {
        return(-1);   // Cannot load driver
    }
    Connection con6 = null;
    try {
        String url = "jdbc:odbc:http://server.xyz.edu/sturegDB:8000";
        con6 = DriverManager.getConnection(url,"john","ji21");
    } catch (SQLException e) {
        return(-2);   // Cannot connect
    }
    con6.setAutoCommit(false);
    Statement stat6 = con6.createStatement();
    try {
        stat6.executeUpdate("DELETE FROM TRANSCRIPT " +
                        "WHERE StudId = 123456789 " +
                            "AND Semester = 'F2000'   " +
                            "AND CrsCode = 'CS308'" );
    } catch (SQLException e) {
        con6.rollback();
        stat6.close();
        con6.close();
        return(-3);   // Cannot execute
    }
    try {
        stat6.executeUpdate("UPDATE CLASS " +
                        "SET Enrollment = (Enrollment - 1) " +
                            "AND Semester = 'F2000' " +
                            "WHERE CrsCode = 'CS308'");
    } catch (SQLException e) {
        con6.rollback();
        stat6.close();
        con6.close();
        return(-4);   // Cannot update
    }

    con6.commit();
    stat6.close();
    con6.close();
    return(0);   // Success!
```

FIGURE 8.13 Use of an iterator in SQLJ.

```
import java.sql.*
      ⋮

   #SQL iterator GetEnrolledIter(int studentId, String studGrade);
   GetEnrolledIter iter1;

   #SQL iter1 = { SELECT T.StudId AS "studentId",
                         T.Grade AS "studGrade"
                  FROM TRANSCRIPT T
                  WHERE T.CrsCode = :crsCode
                         AND T.Semester = :semester };
   int id;
   String grade;
   while (iter1.next()) {
        id = iter1.studentId();
        grade = iter1.studGrade();
        ⋮ process the values in id and grade
   }
   iter1.close();
```

statement inside curly braces. For example, the SELECT statement of Figure 8.1 becomes in SQLJ:

```
#SQL {SELECT C.Enrollment
        INTO :numEnrolled
        FROM CLASS C
        WHERE C.CrsCode = :crsCode
           AND C.Semester = :semester};
```

■ Any Java variable can be included as a parameter in an SQL statement prefixed with :, as in static SQL. This method of passing parameters into an SQL construct (which, you will recall, is done at compile time) is considerably more efficient during run time than the method used in JDBC, in which the value of each argument must be bound to a ? parameter at run time.

■ In SQLJ, a query returns an **SQLJ iterator** object instead of a ResultSet object. SQLJ iterators are similar to result sets in that they provide a cursor mechanism. In fact, both the SQLJ iterator object and the ResultSet object implement the same Java interface java.util.Iterator. (SQLJ iterators can be converted into result sets, and vice versa.) An iterator object stores an entire result set and provides methods, such as next(), to scan through the rows in the set. Figure 8.13 shows an SQLJ version of the program fragment in Figure 8.6.

The first statement in the figure tells the SQLJ preprocessor to generate Java statements that define a class, GetEnrolledIter, which implements the interface sqlj.runtime.NamedIterator. This is an interface that extends the standard Java interface, java.util.Iterator, and provides the venerable next() method. The class GetEnrolledIter can be used to store result sets in which each row has two columns: an integer and a string. The declaration gives a Java name to these columns, studentId and studGrade, and (implicitly) defines the **column accessor** methods, studentId() and studGrade(), which can be used to return data stored in the corresponding columns.

The second statement declares an object, iter1, in the class GetEnrolled-Iter.

The third statement executes SELECT and places the result set in iter1. Note that the AS clause is used to associate the SQL attribute names in the result set with the column names in the iterator. These names do not have to be the same, but the sequence of columns in the result set and the iterator must correspond in number and type.

The while statement fetches the results one at a time into the host variables id and grade and processes them.

■ SQLJ has its own mechanism, which we do not discuss, for defining connection objects and for connecting to a database. A program can have several such connections active at the same time. Unlike in embedded SQL, each individual SQLJ statement can optionally designate a specific database connection to which that clause is to be applied. For example, the SELECT statement on page 305 can be rewritten as

```
#SQL [db1] {SELECT C.Enrollment
            INTO :num_enrolled
            FROM CLASS C
            WHERE C.CrsCode = :crs_code
              AND C.Semester = :semester};
```

to specify that it is to be applied to the (previously defined) database connection named db1. If this option is not used, all SQL statements are applied to a default database connection, as in embedded SQL. Recall that, in JDBC, each SQL statement is always associated with a specific database connection *explicitly*, through its Statement object. In contrast, in embedded SQL, connection is set in a rather awkward and inflexible way via the SET CONNECTION statement.

■ Just as static and dynamic embedded SQL statements can be included in the same host language program, SQLJ statements and JDBC calls can be included in the same Java program.

8.6 ODBC *

ODBC (Open DataBase Connectivity) is an API to the DBMS that provides a call-level interface for SQL statement execution. Our presentation is based on the ODBC specification developed by Microsoft, but be aware that some vendors do not support all of the features.

It should also be noted that the SQL standardization body has for quite a long time been working on a specification for a call-level interface, known as **SQL/CLI**, to replace the bulky dynamic SQL. ODBC is a branch of an earlier version of this specification, and it has much in common with the recently finalized release of SQL/CLI, which is included in SQL:1999. Microsoft has pledged to align ODBC with this newly adopted standard.

The software architecture of an ODBC application is similar to that of JDBC in that it uses a driver manager and a separate driver for each DBMS to be accessed. ODBC is not object oriented, however, and its interface to the DBMS is at a much lower level. For example, in ODBC an application must specifically allocate and deallocate the storage it needs within the driver manager and the driver, whereas in JDBC that storage is automatically allocated when the appropriate objects are created, and deallocated when these objects are no longer needed. Thus, before an ODBC application calls the function SQLConnect() to request a connection to a database manager, it must first call the function SQLAllocConnect() to request that the driver manager allocate storage for that connection. Later, after the application calls SQLDisconnect() to disconnect from the database manager, it must call SQLFreeConnect() to deallocate this storage. As a result, ODBC applications are prone to **memory leaks**—an accumulation of garbage memory blocks that occurs when a program fails to free up ODBC structures that are no longer in use.

Figure 8.14 shows the structure of one version of the required function calls as they might appear in a C program.[5] Each function returns a value that denotes success or failure.

- SQLAllocEnv() allocates and initializes storage within the driver manager for use as ODBC's interface to the application. It returns an identifying *handle*, henv. A **handle** is simply a mechanism the application can use to refer to this data structure. In C, a handle is implemented as a pointer, but other host languages might implement it differently. The environment area is used internally by the ODBC driver manager to store run-time information.

- SQLAllocConnect() allocates memory within the driver manager for the connection and returns a connection handle, hdbc.

---

[5] We have simplified the syntax in this and subsequent examples to emphasize the semantics of the ODBC interaction. For example, in reality, string parameters, such as database_name, are passed with an accompanying length field.

FIGURE 8.14 Skeleton of procedure calls needed for ODBC in a C program.

```
SQLAllocEnv(&henv);
SQLAllocConnect(henv, &hdbc);
SQLConnect(hdbc,database_name,userId, password);
SQLAllocStmt(hdbc, &hstmt);
SQLExecDirect(hstmt, ... SQL statement ...);
    .
    : process results
    .
SQLFreeStmt(hstmt, fOption);
SQLDisconnect(hdbc);
SQLFreeConnect(hdbc);
SQLFreeEnv(henv);
```

OPTIONAL

- SQLConnect() loads the appropriate database driver and then connects to the DBMS server using previously allocated connection, hdbc, the database name, user Id, and password.

  If the application wants to connect to more than one database manager, SQLAllocConnect() and SQLConnect() are called separately for each manager. The drivers (there might be more than one in this case) maintain separate transactions for each such connection.

- SQLAllocStmt() allocates storage within the driver for an SQL statement and returns a handle, hstmt, for that statement.

- SQLExecDirect() takes a statement handle previously allocated using SQL-AllocStmt() and a string variable containing an SQL statement and asks the DBMS to prepare and execute the statement. The same handle can be used multiple times to execute different SQL statements.

  The SQL statement can be a data-manipulation statement, such as SELECT or UPDATE, as well as a DDL statement, such as CREATE or GRANT. It cannot contain an embedded reference to a host variable, since variable names can be translated to memory addresses only at compile time. Note that SQL-ExecDirect() is related to but is more versatile than EXECUTE IMMEDIATE in dynamic SQL. Whereas EXECUTE IMMEDIATE cannot return data to the application (see Section 8.4.1), SQLExecDirect() can produce a result set using a SE-LECT statement, and this set can then be accessed through a cursor (see Section 8.6.2).

- SQLDisconnect() disconnects from the server. This function takes the connection handle as an argument.

- SQLFreeStmt(), SQLFreeConnect(), and SQLFreeEnv() release the handles and free up the corresponding storage space allocated by the corresponding Alloc functions.

8.6.1 Prepared Statements

Instead of calling SQLExecDirect(), the application program can call

    SQLPrepare(hstmt, ... SQL statement ...);

to prepare the statement and then

    SQLExecute(hstmt);

to execute it.

As in dynamic SQL, the statement argument of SQLPrepare() can contain the ? placeholders. Arguments can be supplied to those parameters using the SQLBind-Parameters() function. For example, the call

    SQLBindParameters(hstmt, 1, SQL_PARAMETER_INPUT,
                      SQL_C_SSHORT, SQL_SMALLINT, &int1);

binds the first parameter of the statement hstmt, which is an *in* parameter, to the host language variable int1, where int1 is of type short in the C language. The parameter's value replaces the first ? placeholder in hstmt when SQLBindParameters() is executed. SQLBindParameters() performs the conversion from type short in C to type SMALLINT in SQL.[6] Since the procedure call is compiled by the host language compiler, references to host language variable int1 in the parameter list can be resolved at compile time. This contrasts with the use of SQLExecDirect(), where references to host variables are not allowed.

8.6.2 Cursors

The execution of a SELECT statement using SQLExecDirect() or SQLExecute() does not return any data to the application. Instead, data is returned through a cursor, which is maintained within the ODBC driver and referred to by the statement handle, hstmt, returned by SQLAllocStmt(). Additional ODBC functions must be called to bring the data into the application.

The program can optionally call SQLBindCol(), which binds a particular column of the result set to a specific host variable in the program. For example, we might use the following call to bind the first column to the integer variable int2.

    SQLBindCol(hstmt, 1, SQL_C_SSHORT, &int2);

---

[6] In a number of ODBC constructs, as in this one, the programmer must specify the desired conversion between the SQL data types used within the DBMS and the C language data types used within the application program.

When SQLFetch(hstmt) is then called, the cursor is advanced and the values in the columns of the current row that had been bound to host variables are stored in those variables. If a column has not been bound to a designated host variable, the program can call SQLGetData() to retrieve and store its value. For example, to store the value of the second column of the current row in the integer variable int3 we might use the call

```
SQLGetData(hstmt, 2, SQL_C_SSHORT, &int3);
```

Before executing the SELECT statement, the application can use SQLSet-StmtOption() to specify one of the following three types for the cursor:

1. STATIC. As with the INSENSITIVE option for cursors in embedded SQL, when the SELECT statement is executed, the driver effectively calculates the result set and stores it separately from the base table. A call to SQLFetch() fetches a row from the result set. The situation is shown in Figure 8.5, page 279. This type of returned data is called a *snapshot*.

2. KEYSET_DRIVEN. When the SELECT statement is executed, the driver effectively constructs a set of pointers to the rows in the base table that satisfy the WHERE clause. A call to SQLFetch() follows the pointer and fetches the row from the base table. The situation is shown in Figure 8.15. Note the difference between this figure and Figure 8.5, where the result set is calculated at the time the SELECT statement is executed and rows are fetched from the result set. This type of returned data is sometimes called a **dynaset**.

    Since rows are obtained from the base table, any change to the base table will be seen through the pointers. For example, if a statement in this or a concurrent transaction *modifies* or *deletes* a row that is the target of a pointer, the change will be seen in a subsequent call to SQLFetch(). Furthermore, if a statement in this or a concurrent transaction *inserts* a row that satisfies the WHERE clause, the new row will not be seen by subsequent calls to SQLFetch() (since a pointer to the row is not in the set). Unfortunately, that is not the only anomaly that can occur. A change of an attribute value in a row that previously satisfied the WHERE clause can cause the row to no longer satisfy the clause. However, the row will still be visible through the cursor.

3. DYNAMIC. The data in the result set is completely dynamic. A statement in this or some other concurrently executing transaction can change, delete, *and* insert a row into the result set after the SELECT statement is executed. Those changes will be seen in subsequent calls to SQLFetch().

The ODBC specification calls for the implementation of all of these cursor types. However, the mechanisms made available to ODBC by a particular DBMS might make the implementation of a particular cursor type difficult, so a driver for that DBMS might support only a subset of cursor types. Clearly, DYNAMIC cursors are the most difficult to implement, and many drivers do not implement them.

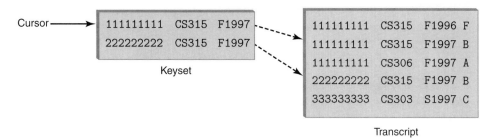

FIGURE 8.15 Effect of using a KEYSET_DRIVEN cursor to retrieve records from TRANSCRIPT.

The statement SQLSetStmtOption() is used to request a cursor type as follows:

```
SQLSetStmtOption(hstmt,SQL_CURSOR_TYPE, Option);
```

where *Option* is one of the constants SQL_CURSOR_STATIC, SQL_CURSOR_DYNAMIC, or SQL_CURSOR_KEYSET_DRIVEN.

ODBC also supports positioned updates through a non-STATIC cursor. For such an update, the SELECT statement must be defined with a FOR UPDATE clause. For example,

```
SQLExecDirect(hstmt1,  "SELECT * \
                       FROM EMPLOYEE \
                       FOR UPDATE OF Salary");
```

uses a previously allocated statement handle, hstmt1, to prepare a query whose cursor will allow updates to the EMPLOYEE relation through the Salary attribute.

Now, suppose we have executed a number of SQLFetch(hstmt1) statements and the cursor is now positioned at the employee named Joe Public. To raise Joe's salary by $1000, we might execute the following statement (where hstmt2 is a previously allocated statement handle):

```
SQLExecDirect(hstmt2,  "UPDATE EMPLOYEE \
                       SET Salary = Salary + 1000\
                       WHERE CURRENT OF employee_cursor");
```

The only problem with the above statement is that the cursor name, employee_cursor, required by the WHERE CURRENT OF clause, comes out of the blue. In particular, it is not connected in any way to the cursor associated with the hstmt1 handle that we used to execute the SELECT statement. Thus, before executing the above UPDATE statement we must first give a name to that cursor. ODBC provides a special call to do just this:

```
SQLSetCursorName(hstmt1, employee_cursor);
```

As with dynamic SQL, information about the result set of a query might not be known when the program is written. ODBC thus provides a number of functions to obtain this information. For example, after a statement has been prepared, the program can call the function SQLNumResultCols(), to obtain the number of columns in a result set, and the functions SQLColAttributes() and SQLDescribeCol(), to provide information about a specific column in a result set.

ODBC also has a number of functions, called **catalog functions**, which return information about the database schema. For example, SQLTables() returns, in a result set, the names of all tables, and SQLColumns() returns column names.

8.6.3 Status Processing

The ODBC procedures we have been discussing are actually functions, which return a value, of type RETCODE, indicating whether or not the specified action was successful. Thus, we might have

```
RETCODE retcode1;
  .
  .
  .
retcode1 = SQLConnect(...);
if (retcode1 != SQL_SUCCESS)   {
    .   do something
    .
}
```

Additional information about the error can be found by calling SQLError().

8.6.4 Executing Transactions

By default, the database is in autocommit mode when a connection is created. To allow two or more statements to be grouped into a transaction, autocommit mode is disabled using

```
SQLSetConnectionOption(hdbc,
                  SQL_AUTOCOMMIT,
                  SQL_AUTOCOMMIT_OFF);
```

where hdbc is a connection handle. Initially, each transaction uses the default isolation level of the database manager. This can be changed with a call such as

```
SQLSetConnectionOption(hdbc,
                         SQL_TXN_ISOLATION,
                         SQL_TXN_REPEATABLE_READ);
```

Transactions can be committed or rolled back using

```
SQLTransact(henv, hdbc, Action);
```

where `Action` is either `SQL_COMMIT` or `SQL_ABORT`.

After a transaction is committed or rolled back, a new transaction starts when the next SQL statement is executed (or, in the case of the first SQL statement in the program, when that statement is executed).

If the program is connected to more than one database, the transactions at each database can be separately committed or rolled back. ODBC does not support a commit protocol that ensures that the set of transactions will be globally atomic. However, Microsoft has introduced a new TP monitor, MTS (Microsoft Transaction Server), that includes a transaction manager (and an appropriate API) guaranteeing an atomic commit of distributed transactions using ODBC.

8.6.5 Stored Procedures on the Server

ODBC can be used to call a stored procedure if the DBMS supports this feature. For example, to call the stored procedure of Figure 8.7 on page 284 we might begin with the statement

```
SQLPrepare(hstmt, "{call Deregister(?,?,?,?,?)}");
```

which prepares the call statement. The braces around the call to `Deregister()` denote the SQL escape syntax discussed in Section 8.5.7. The parameters of `Deregister()` can be bound to host variables with `SQLBindParameter()` functions. Then the procedure call can be executed with

```
SQLExecute(hstmt);
```

As with embedded SQL, if the DBMS allows a stored procedure to return a result set, the application program can retrieve data from the result set using a cursor.

8.6.6 An Example

Figure 8.16 is a fragment of a C program containing ODBC procedure calls. It executes the same transaction as that in Figure 8.12. The constant `SQL_NTS`, when supplied as an argument to a procedure (`SQLConnect()` and `SQLExecDirect()` in this example) indicates that the preceding argument is a null-terminated string.

FIGURE 8.16 A fragment of an ODBC program written in C.

```
HENV henv;
HDBC hdbc;
HSTMT hstmt;
RETCODE retcode;
SQLAllocEnv(&henv);
SQLAllocConnect(henv, &hdbc);
retcode = SQLConnect(hdbc, dbName, SQL_NTS, "john", SQL_NTS, "j121",
                        SQL_NTS);
if (retcode != SQL_SUCCESS){
    SQLFreeEnv(henv);
    return(-1);
}
SQLSetConnectionOption(hdbc, SQL_AUTOCOMMIT, SQL_AUTOCOMMIT_OFF);
SQLAllocStmt(hdbc, &hstmt);
retcode = SQLExecDirect(hstmt,
                        "DELETE FROM TRANSCRIPT \
                            WHERE StudId = 123456789 \
                                AND Semester = 'F2000' \
                                AND CrsCode = 'CS308'",
                        SQL_NTS);
if (retcode != SQL_SUCCESS) {
    SQLTransact(henv, hdbc, SQL_ABORT);
    SQLFreeStmt(hstmt, SQL_DROP);
    SQLDisconnect(hdbc);
    SQLFreeConnect(hdbc);
    SQLFreeEnv(henv);
    return(-2);
}
retcode = SQLExecDirect(hstmt,
                        "UPDATE CLASS \
                            SET Enrollment = (Enrollment - 1) \
                            WHERE CrsCode = 'CS308'",
                        SQL_NTS);
if (retcode != SQL_SUCCESS)    {
    SQLTransact(henv, hdbc, SQL_ABORT);
    SQLFreeStmt(hstmt, SQL_DROP);
    SQLDisconnect(hdbc);
    SQLFreeConnect(hdbc);
    SQLFreeEnv(henv);
    return(-3);
}
SQLTransact(henv, hdbc, SQL_COMMIT);
SQLFreeStmt(hstmt, SQL_DROP);
SQLDisconnect(hdbc);
SQLFreeConnect(hdbc);
SQLFreeEnv(henv);
```

OPTIONAL

8.7 Comparison

We have discussed a variety of techniques for creating programs that can access a database—each has its own advantages and disadvantages. Here we summarize some of the issues involved:

- In some cases, the program contains SQL statements that use a special syntax (static SQL, SQLJ); in others, the statements are values of variables (dynamic SQL, JDBC, ODBC). An advantage of the former is its simplicity, but a disadvantage is that the interaction with the database is fixed at compile time. In some applications, the statement to be executed cannot be determined until run time; in such cases, it is important that the application be able to construct SQL statements dynamically.

- In some cases, the application must use the SQL dialect supported by the particular DBMS to which it is connected, making it difficult to port the application to a different vendor's product. In other cases (ODBC, JDBC), a single dialect or a common core is used in the application, and modules are provided to translate it to each vendor's dialect. Portability is thus enhanced, but the application might not have access to the proprietary features supported by a particular vendor's product.

- A number of factors are involved in assessing the run-time overhead incurred by each technique. These include the cost of communication, preparation, and parameter passing. In some cases, the cost depends on how a technique is implemented, but certain general observations can be made.

  With a statement-level interface, the SQL statement has embedded parameter names that can be processed at compile time to generate parameter-passing code. At run time, the statement can be passed to the server for both preparation and execution, so a single communication is sufficient. With a call-level interface and with dynamic SQL, parameter names are not included in the statement because the statement is not available at compile time when parameter names can be mapped to addresses using the symbol table. Instead, they are provided separately so that they can be dealt with at compile time. Except in special cases (e.g., EXECUTE IMMEDIATE), therefore, one communication is used to send the statement for preparation and one additional communication is needed for requesting execution. This issue is important, since communication is expensive and time consuming.

  Preparation must take place at run time if the SQL statement is constructed dynamically (dynamic SQL, JDBC, and ODBC). However, even with static SQL, preparation is generally done at run time when the statement is submitted for execution. In all of these cases, if the statement is executed many times, the preparation cost can be prorated over each execution and might not be a major factor. The most effective way to avoid run-time preparation is to use stored procedures, in which case the DBMS can be instructed to create and store a query execution plan prior to execution of the application. Often, this is simply a separate plan for each SQL statement in the procedure. More sophisticated systems create an optimized plan for the procedure as a whole, since the sequence of SQL statements is known. Data structures created for one statement might be preserved for use by the next.

BIBLIOGRAPHIC NOTES

Embedded and dynamic SQL date back to prehistoric times, and every SQL manual covers them to some degree. The following references are good places to look: [Date and Darwen 1997; Melton and Simon 1992; Gulutzan and Pelzer 1999].

There is vast literature on ODBC. Microsoft publishes an authoritative guide [Microsoft 1997], but there are more accessible books, such as [Signore et al. 1995]. The history and principles behind SQL/CLI, the new SQL standard analogous to (and designed to replace) ODBC, are discussed in [Venkatrao and Pizzo 1995]. SQL stored procedures are discussed in [Eisenberg 1996; Melton 1997]. Information on JDBC and SQLJ is readily available on the Web at [Sun 2000] and [SQLJ 2000], but published references, such as [Reese 2000; Melton et al. 2000], are better places to learn these technologies.

EXERCISES

8.1   Explain why a precompiler is needed for embedded SQL and SQLJ but not for ODBC and JDBC.

8.2   Since the precompiler for embedded SQL translates SQL statements into procedure calls, explain the difference between embedded SQL and call-level interfaces, such as ODBC and JDBC, where SQL statements are specified as the arguments of procedure calls.

8.3   Explain why constraint checking is usually deferred in transaction processing applications.

8.4   Give an example where immediate constraint checking is undesirable in a transaction processing application.

8.5   Explain the advantages and disadvantages of using stored procedures in transaction processing applications.

8.6   Write transaction programs in

a. Embedded SQL
b. JDBC
c. ODBC
d. SQLJ

that implement the registration transaction in the Student Registration System. Use the database schema from Figures 4.34 and 4.35.

8.7   Write transaction programs in

a. Embedded SQL
b. JDBC

    c. ODBC

    d. SQLJ

that use a cursor to print out a student's transcript in the Student Registration System. Use the database schema from Figures 4.34 and 4.35.

8.8   Explain the following:

    a. Why do embedded SQL and SQLJ use host language variables as parameters, whereas dynamic SQL, JDBC, and ODBC use the ? placeholders?

    b. What are the advantages of using host language variables as parameters in embedded SQL compared with ? placeholders?

8.9   Explain the advantages and disadvantages of using dynamic SQL compared with ODBC and JDBC.

8.10   Write a transaction program in

    a. Embedded SQL

    b. JDBC

    c. ODBC

    d. SQLJ

that transfers the rows of a table between two DBMSs. Is your transaction globally atomic?

8.11   Write a Java program that executes in your local browser, uses JDBC to connect to your local DBMS, and makes a simple query against a table you have created.

8.12   Suppose that, at compile time, the application programmer knows all of the details of the SQL statements to be executed, the DBMS to be used, and the database schema. Explain the advantages and disadvantages of using embedded SQL as compared with JDBC or ODBC as the basis for the implementation.

8.13   Section 8.6 discusses KEYSET_DRIVEN cursors.

    a. Explain the difference between STATIC and KEYSET_DRIVEN cursors.

    b. Give an example of a schedule in which these cursors give different results even when the transaction is executing in isolation.

    c. Explain why updates and deletes can be made through KEYSET_DRIVEN cursors.

8.14   Give an example of a transaction program that contains a cursor, such that the value returned by one of its FETCH statements depends on whether or not the cursor was defined to be INSENSITIVE. Assume that this transaction is the only one executing. We are not concerned about any effect that a concurrently executing transaction might have.

8.15   Compare the advantages and disadvantages of the exception handling mechanisms in embedded SQL, SQL/PSM, JDBC, SQLJ, and ODBC.

PART THREE

Optimizing DBMS Performance and Transaction Processing

In this part we will discuss various issues related to optimizing the performance of a database application. This subject is very important in the real world because it consumes a significant amount of the effort of database practitioners.

In Chapter 9 we will discuss the physical organization of databases, including various indexing mechanisms.

In Chapters 10 and 11 we will present the basic ideas of query processing and query optimization.

Chapter 12 discusses various aspects of database tuning, including the choice of indices, cache tuning, and methods for tuning the schema.

In conclusion, Chapter 13 provides an overview of transaction processing, which is one of the most important application areas for databases.

9

Physical Data Organization and Indexing

One important advantage of SQL is that it is declarative. An SQL statement describes a query about information stored in a database, but it does not specify the technique the system should use in executing it. The DBMS itself decides that.

Such techniques are intimately associated with **storage structures**, **indices**, and **access paths**. A table is stored in a file, and the term "storage structure" is used to describe the way the rows are organized in the file. An index is an auxiliary data structure, perhaps stored in a separate file, that supports fast access to the rows of a table. An access path refers to a particular technique for accessing a set of rows. It uses an algorithm based on the storage structure of the table and on a choice among the available indices for that table.

An important aspect of the relational model is that the result of executing a particular SQL statement (i.e., the statement's effect on the database and the information returned by it) is not affected by the storage structure used to store the table that is accessed, the indices that have been created for that table, or the access path that the DBMS chooses to use to access the table. Thus, when designing the query, the programmer does not have to be aware of these issues.

Although the choice of an access path does not affect the result produced by a statement, it does have a major impact on performance. Depending on the access path used, execution time might vary from seconds to hours, particularly when the statement refers to large tables involving thousands, and perhaps hundreds of thousands, of rows. Furthermore, different access paths are appropriate for different SQL statements used to query the same table.

Because execution time is sensitive to access paths, most database systems allow the database designer and system administrator to determine which access paths should be provided for each table. Generally, this decision is based on the nature of the SQL statements used to access the table and the frequency with which these statements are executed.

In this chapter, we describe a variety of access paths and compare their performance when used in the execution of different SQL statements. We continue this discussion in Chapter 12.

9.1 Disk Organization

For the following reasons, databases are generally stored on mass storage devices rather than in main memory:

- **Size.** Databases describing large enterprises frequently contain a huge amount of information. Databases in the gigabyte range are not uncommon, and those in the terabyte range already exist. Such databases cannot be accommodated in the main memory of current machines or of machines that are likely to be available in the near future.

- **Cost.** Even in situations in which the database can be accommodated in main memory (e.g., when its size is in the megabyte range), it is generally stored on mass storage.[1] The argument here is one of economy. The cost per byte of storage in main memory is on the order of one hundred times that of storage on disk.

- **Volatility.** We introduced the notion of durability in Chapter 2 in connection with the ACID properties of transactions. The argument for durability goes beyond transactions, however. It is an important property of any database system. The information describing an enterprise must be preserved in spite of system failures. Unfortunately, most implementations of main memory are **volatile**: the information stored in main memory can be lost during power failures and crashes. Hence, main memory does not naturally support database system requirements. Mass storage, on the other hand, is **nonvolatile** since the stored information survives failures. Hence, mass storage forms the basis of most database systems.

Since data on mass storage devices is not directly accessible to the system processors, accessing an item in the database involves first reading it from the mass storage device into a buffer in main memory—at which point a copy exists on both devices—and then accessing it from the buffer. If the access involves changing the item, the copy on mass storage becomes obsolete and the buffer copy must be used to overwrite it.

The most commonly used form of mass storage is a disk. Since the strategy used to enhance the performance of a database system is based on the physical characteristics of a disk, it is important to review how a disk works in order to understand performance issues.

A disk unit contains one or more circular **platters** attached to a rotating spindle, as shown in Figure 9.1. One, and sometimes both, surfaces of each platter are coated with magnetic material, and the direction of magnetism at a particular spot determines whether that spot records a one or a zero. Since information is stored magnetically, it is durable in spite of power failures.

Each platter (or surface) is accessed through an associated **read/write head** that is capable of either detecting or setting the direction of magnetism on the spot over which it is positioned. The head is attached to an arm, which is capable of moving

---

[1] In applications requiring very rapid response times, the database is often stored in main memory. Such systems are referred to as **main memory database systems**.

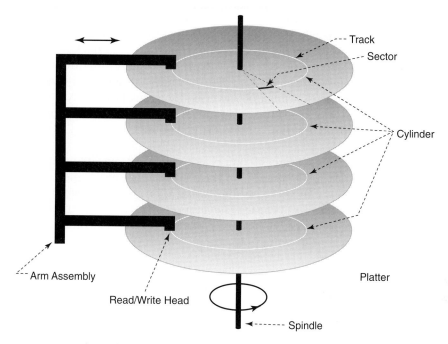

FIGURE 9.1 Physical organization of a disk storage unit.

radially toward either the center or the circumference of the platter. Since platters rotate, this movement enables the head to be positioned over an arbitrary spot on the platter's surface.

As a practical matter, data is stored in **tracks,** which are concentric circles on the surface of the platter. Each platter has the same fixed number, N, of tracks, and the storage area consisting of the ith track on all platters is called an ith **cylinder.** Since there is a head for each platter, the disk unit as a whole has an array of heads, and the arm assembly moves all heads in unison. Thus, at any given time all read/write heads are positioned over a particular cylinder. It would seem reasonable to be able to read or write all tracks on the current cylinder simultaneously, but engineering limitations generally allow only a single head to be active at a time. Finally, each track is divided into **sectors,** which are the smallest units of transfer allowed by the hardware.

Before a particular sector can be accessed, the head must be positioned over the beginning of the sector. Hence, the time to access a sector, S, can be divided into three components:

1. **Seek time.** The time to position the arm assembly over the cylinder containing S
2. **Rotational latency.** The additional time it takes, after the arm assembly is over the cylinder, for the platters to rotate to the angular position at which S is under the read/write head
3. **Transfer time.** The time it takes for the platter to rotate through the angle subtended by S

The seek time varies depending on the radial distance between the cylinder currently under the read/write heads and the cylinder containing the sector to be read. In the worst case, the heads must be moved from track 1 to track N; in the best case, no motion at all is required. If disk requests are uniformly distributed across the cylinders and are serviced in the order they arrive, it can be shown that the average number of tracks that must be traversed by a seek is about $N/3$.[2] Seek time is generally the largest of the three components because it involves not only mechanical motion but overcoming the inertia involved in starting and stopping the arm assembly.

Rotational latency is the next-largest component of access time and on average is about half the time of a complete rotation of the platters. Once again, mechanical motion is involved, although in this case inertia is not an issue. Transfer time is also limited by rotation time. The transfer rate supported by a disk is the rate at which data can be transferred once the head is in position; it depends on the speed of rotation and the density with which bits are recorded on the surface. We use the term **latency** to refer to the total time it takes to position the head and platter between disk accesses. Hence, latency is the sum of seek time and rotational latency.

A typical disk stores gigabytes of data. It might have a sector size of 512 bytes, an average seek time of 5 to 10 milliseconds, an average rotational latency of 2 to 5 milliseconds, and a transfer rate of several megabytes per second. Hence, a typical access time for a sector is on the order of 10 milliseconds.

The physical characteristics of a disk lead to the concept of the distance between two sectors, which is a measure of the latency between accesses to them. The distance is smallest if the sectors are adjacent on the same track since latency is zero if they are read in succession. After that, in order of increasing distance, sectors are closest if they are on the same track, on the same cylinder, or on different cylinders. In the last case, sectors on tracks n_1 and n_2 are closer than sectors on tracks n_3 and n_4 if $|n_1 - n_2| < |n_3 - n_4|$.

Several conclusions can be drawn from the physical characteristics of a disk unit:

- Most important, disks are extremely slow devices compared to CPUs. A CPU can execute hundreds of thousands of instructions in the time it takes to access a disk sector. Hence, in attempting to optimize the performance of a database system, it is necessary to optimize the flow of information between main memory and disk. While the database system should use efficient algorithms in processing data, the payoff in improved performance pales in comparison with that obtained from optimizing disk traffic. In recognition of this fact, in our discussion of access paths later in this chapter we estimate performance by counting I/O operations and ignoring processor time.

- In applications in which after accessing record A_1, the next access will, with high probability, be to record A_2, latency can be reduced if the distance between the

[2] The problem can be stated mathematically: suppose that we have an interval and we place two marks at random somewhere in the interval; how far apart are the marks on average?

sectors containing A_1 and A_2 is small. Thus the performance of the application is affected by the way the data is physically stored on the disk. For example, a sequential scan through a table can be performed efficiently if the table is stored on a single track or cylinder.

■ To simplify buffer management, database systems transfer the same number of bytes with each I/O operation. How many bytes should that be? Using the typical numbers quoted earlier, it is apparent that the transfer time for a sector is small compared with the average latency. This is true even if more than one sector is transferred with each I/O operation. Thus, even though from a physical standpoint the natural unit of transfer is the data in a single sector, it might be more efficient if the system transfers data in larger units.

The term **page** generally denotes the unit of data transferred with each I/O operation. A page is stored on the disk in a **disk block**, or simply a block, which is a sequence of adjacent sectors on a track such that the page size is equal to the block size. A page can be transferred in a single I/O operation, with a single latency to position the head at the start of the containing block since there is no need to reposition either the arm or the platter in moving from one sector of the block to the next.

A trade-off is involved in choosing the number of sectors in a block (i.e., the page size). If, when a particular application accesses a record, A, in a table, there is a reasonable probability that it will soon access another record, B, in the table that is close to A (this would be the case if the table was frequently scanned), the page size should be large enough so that A and B are stored in the same page. This avoids a subsequent I/O operation when B is actually accessed. On the other hand, transfer time grows with page size, and larger pages require larger buffers in main memory. Hence, too large a page size cannot be justified, since it is far from certain that B will actually be accessed. With considerations such as these in mind, a typical page size is 4096 bytes (4 kilobytes).

A checksum is generally computed each time the data in a page is modified and stored with the data in the block. Each time the page is read a checksum over the data is computed and compared with the stored checksum. If the page has been corrupted on the disk it is very unlikely that the two values will be equal, and hence storage failures can be readily detected.

The system keeps an array of page-size buffers, called a **cache**, in main memory. With page I/O, the following sequence of events occurs when an application requests access to a particular record, A, of a table. We assume that each table is stored in a **data file**. First, the database system determines which of the file's pages contains A. Then it initiates the transfer of the page from mass storage into one of the buffers in the cache (we modify this part of the description in a moment). At some later time (generally signaled by an interrupt from the mass storage device), the system recognizes that the transfer has completed and copies A from the page in the buffer to the application.

The system attempts to keep the cache filled with pages that are likely to be referenced in the future. Then, if an application refers to an item contained

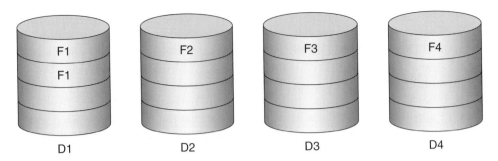

FIGURE **9.2** The striping of a file across four disks.

in a page in the cache, an I/O operation can be avoided and a **hit** is said to have occurred. Hence, proper cache management can greatly improve performance. Cache management is treated in more detail in Section 12.1.

9.1.1 RAID Systems

At various points in the book we will discuss a number of techniques that are made available to the application programmer or are provided within the DBMS to overcome the performance bottleneck caused by disk I/O: indices, query optimization, caches, and prefetching. A **RAID (Redundant Array of Independent Disks)** system is another, lower-level, approach to the problem. It consists of an array of disks configured to operate like a single disk. In particular, the RAID system responds to the usual operating system commands of read, write, and so on.

A RAID system has the potential for providing better throughput than a single disk of similar capacity since the individual disks of a RAID can function independently. There are two dimensions to this. If multiple requests access data on different disks of the RAID, they can be handled concurrently. Thus, a RAID involving n disks has the potential of improving throughput by a factor of n. The performance of a single request involving a large block of data can also be improved. If the data is spread over several disks, it can be transferred in parallel, reducing the transfer time. Thus, if it is spread over n disks, the transfer time can be reduced by a factor of n.

Data that is spread across an array of disks is said to be **striped**. The data is divided into **chunks** for this purpose, where the size of a chunk is configurable and might be a byte, a block, or some multiple of the block size. For example, if a file is striped over four disks, its first chunk, F1, would be stored on the first disk, D1, the second chunk, F2, on the second disk, D2, the third, F3, on D3, and the fourth, F4, on D4. The four chunks are referred to as a stripe. The fifth chunk, F5, is stored on D1 and successive chunks are laid out on the next stripe. The situation is shown in Figure 9.2. Then, if the entire file is to be read, data can be transferred from all four disks simultaneously.

In addition to increasing throughput, an important objective of RAID systems is to use redundant storage to increase the availability of the data by reducing downtime due to disk failure. Such failures are magnified when an array of disks is used since the mean time to failure of at least one disk in an array of n is (approximately) the mean time to failure of one disk divided by n. For example, if a single disk has a mean time to failure of 10 years, the mean time to failure of at least one disk in an array of 50 is about two months—an unacceptable failure rate for most applications. To address this issue, five RAID levels have been defined, with different types of redundancy.

Level 0. Level 0 uses striping to increase throughput but does not use any redundancy. The bad news is that if all files are striped, the failure of a single disk destroys them all. Some people would say that Level 0 is not really RAID at all since there is no redundancy—the R in RAID.

Level 1. Level 1 does not perform striping but involves **mirroring**. In this case the disks in the array are paired, and the data stored on both elements of a pair is identical. Hence, a write to one (automatically) results in a write to the other, and as long as one disk in each pair is operational, all the data stored in the RAID can be accessed. Note that, assuming both disks in a pair are operational, the pair has twice the read rate of a single disk since both disks can be independently read at the same time (perhaps by different transactions). Although it might seem that doubling the number of required disks would be too expensive for many applications, the sharply decreased prices of disks have made mirroring increasingly attractive. Many transaction processing systems use mirrored disks to store their log, which has a very high requirement for durability.

Level 3. The higher levels of RAID perform striping and, in addition, store various types of redundant information to increase availability. In Level 3, the chunks are bytes (the striping is at the byte level), and in addition to the n disks on which the data is stored, the stripe includes an $(n + 1)$st disk that stores the *exclusive or* (XOR) of the corresponding bytes on the other n disks. It follows that if $x_{i,j}$ is the jth bit on disk i then

$$x_{1,j} \text{ XOR } x_{2,j} \text{ XOR } \cdots \text{ XOR } x_{n+1,j} = 0$$

Thus, whenever a chunk is written on any one of the n disks, its XOR with the other $n - 1$ chunks in the stripe is computed and stored as a byte on the $(n + 1)$st disk. This disk is sometimes called the **parity disk** since taking the XOR of a set of bytes is called "computing their parity." In contrast to Level 1, instead of dedicating half of the capacity of the RAID to parity data, only $1/n + 1$ of the capacity is used in this way.

For example, consider a RAID containing six disks and assume that parity is stored on the sixth disk. If the first bit of each byte on the first five disks is 1 0 1 0 0, then the first bit of the corresponding byte on disk six is 0. Observe that setting the bit on the parity disk equal to the XOR of the bits on the others also makes the bit on *each* disk the XOR of the bits on the others. Thus, if any disk fails, its information can be reconstructed as the XOR of the bits on the other disks. (Note that this reconstruction method requires knowledge of which disk has failed, but this information can be supplied by the controller for that disk.)

With byte-level striping, a large data segment can be read at a very high transfer rate. This is important in a number of applications. For example, multimedia data must be transferred at a rate that is sufficient to keep up with real-time requirements. Level 3 is particularly useful for such single-user, high-transfer-rate applications.

Writes, however, can be a bottleneck since not only must new data be written to one of the n disks, but the new value of the parity must be computed and written to the parity disk. Its value is given by

$$new\_parity\_bit = (old\_data\_bit\ XOR\ new\_data\_bit)\ XOR\ old\_parity\_bit$$

Thus, four disk accesses are required to write a single byte: the old value of the byte to be overwritten and the old value of the parity byte must be read, and then the new data byte and the new parity byte must be written. Furthermore, since each write request to the RAID involves a write to the parity disk, that disk can become a bottleneck.

Level 5. Level 5 also involves striping and storing parity information, but it differs from Level 3 in two ways:

1. The chunks are disk blocks (or multiples of disk blocks), which is more efficient for some applications. For example, if there are many concurrent transactions, each of which wants to read a chunk of data, their requests can be satisfied in parallel. Thus, Level 5 can be viewed as an efficient way to distribute data over multiple disks to support parallel access.

2. The parity information is itself striped and is stored, in turn, on each of the disks, which eliminates the bottleneck caused by a single parity disk. Thus, in the above example, in the first stripe, the data blocks might be stored on the first five disks and the parity block on the sixth; in the second stripe, the data blocks might be stored on disks 1, 2, 3, 4, and 6 and the parity block on the fifth disk; in the third stripe, the parity block might be stored on the fourth disk, and so on.

Level 10. Many hardware vendors provide hybrid RAID levels combining some of the features of the basic RAID levels. One interesting hybrid is Level 10, which combines the disk striping of Level 0 with the mirroring of Level 1. It uses a striped array of n disks (as in Level 0), in which each of the n disks is mirrored (as in Level 1), making a total of $2n$ disks. In other words, it consists of a striped array of n mirrored disks. Level 10 has the performance benefits of disk striping with the disk redundancy of mirroring. It provides the best performance of all RAID levels, but, as with Level 1, it requires doubling the number of required disks.

Controller cache. To further improve the performance of a RAID system, a **controller cache** can be included. This is a buffer in the main memory of the disk controller that can speed up both reading and writing.

- When reading, the RAID system can transfer a larger portion of data than was requested into the cache. If the program that made the request subsequently requests the additional data, it is immediately available in the buffer—no I/O has to be performed. For example, if a transaction is scanning a table, it will access all the pages in sequence. If n successive pages are stored in a stripe, and the entire stripe is retrieved when the first page is requested, I/O operations for subsequent pages in the stripe are eliminated. This is an example of prefetching, to which we will return in Chapter 12.

- In a **write-back cache** the RAID reports back that the write is complete as soon as the data is in the cache, before it has actually been written to the disk. Thus, the effective write time appears to be very fast. To implement a write-back cache, there must be some means of protecting the data in case of failures in the cache system. Some write-back caches are mirrored and/or have battery backup in case of electrical failure.

- The overhead of writing to a Level 5 RAID can be alleviated with a cache if all the blocks in a stripe are to be updated. In that case the parity block can be computed in the cache, and then all the blocks can be written to the disks in parallel: no extra disk reads are required. When used in this way the cache is referred to as a **write-gathering cache**.

Of all the RAID levels, Level 5, with a controller cache, is the one most often recommended for high-performance transaction processing applications.

9.2 Heap Files

We assume that each table is stored in a separate file, in accordance with some storage structure. The simplest storage structure is a **heap file**. With a heap file, rows are effectively appended to the end of the file as they are created. Thus the ordering of rows in the file is arbitrary. No rule dictates where a particular row should be placed. Figure 9.3 shows table TRANSCRIPT stored as a heap file. Recall that the table has four columns: StudId, CrsCode, Semester, and Grade. We have modified the schema so that grades are stored as real numbers, and we have assumed that four rows fit in a single page.

The important characteristic of a heap file, as far as we are concerned, is the fact that its rows are unordered. We ignore a number of significant issues since they are internal to the workings of the database system and the programmer generally has no control over them. Still, you should be aware of what these issues are. For example, we have assumed in Figure 9.3 that all rows are of the same length, and hence exactly the same number of rows fit in each page. This is not always the case. If, for example, the domain associated with a column is VARCHAR (3000), the number of bytes necessary to store a particular column value varies from 1 to 3000. Thus, the number of rows that will fit in a page is not fixed. This significantly complicates storage allocation. Furthermore, whether rows are of fixed or variable length, each page must be formatted with a certain amount of header information that keeps

666666666	MGT123	F1994	4.0	
123454321	CS305	S1996	4.0	page 0
987654321	CS305	F1995	2.0	
111111111	MGT123	F1997	3.0	

123454321	CS315	S1997	4.0	
666666666	EE101	S1991	3.0	page 1
123454321	MAT123	S1996	2.0	
234567890	EE101	F1995	3.0	

234567890	CS305	S1996	4.0	
111111111	EE101	F1997	4.0	page 2
111111111	MAT123	F1997	3.0	
987654321	MGT123	F1994	3.0	

425360777	CS305	S1996	3.0	
666666666	MAT123	F1997	3.0	page 3

FIGURE 9.3 TRANSCRIPT table stored as a heap file. At most four rows can be fit in a page.

track of the starting point of each row in the page and that locates unused regions of the page. We assume that the logical address of a row in a data file is given by a **row Id** (*rid*) that consists of a **page number** within the file and a **slot number** identifying the row within the page. The actual location of the row is obtained by interpreting the slot number using the page's header information. The situation is further complicated if a row is too large to fit in a page.

The good thing about a heap file is its simplicity. Rows are inserted by appending them to the end of the file, and they are deleted by declaring the slot that they occupy as empty in the header information of the page in which they are stored. Figure 9.4 shows the file of Figure 9.3 after the records for the student with Id 111111111 were deleted and the student with Id 666666666 completed CS305 in the spring of 1998. Note that deletion leaves gaps in the file and eventually a significant amount of storage is wasted. These gaps cause searches through the file to take longer because more pages have to be examined. Eventually, the gaps become so extensive that the file must be compacted. Compaction can be a time-consuming process if the file is large since every page must be read and the pages of the compacted version written out.

Access cost. We can compare the efficiency of accessing a heap file with other storage structures, which we discuss later, by counting the number of I/O operations required to do various operations. Let *F* denote the number of pages in the file. First

666666666	MGT123	F1994	4.0	
123454321	CS305	S1996	4.0	page 0
987654321	CS305	F1995	2.0	

123454321	CS315	S1997	4.0	
666666666	EE101	S1991	3.0	page 1
123454321	MAT123	S1996	2.0	
234567890	EE101	F1995	3.0	

234567890	CS305	S1996	4.0	
				page 2
987654321	MGT123	F1994	3.0	

425360777	CS305	S1996	3.0	
666666666	MAT123	F1997	3.0	page 3
666666666	CS305	S1998	3.0	

FIGURE 9.4 TRANSCRIPT table of Figure 9.3 after insertion and deletion of some rows.

consider insertion. Before a row, A, can be inserted, we must ensure that A's key does not duplicate the key of a row already in the table. Hence, the file must be scanned. If a duplicate exists, it will be discovered in $F/2$ page reads on average, and at that point the insertion is abandoned. The entire file has to be read in order to conclude that no duplicate is present, and then the last page (with A inserted) has to be rewritten, yielding a total cost of $F + 1$ page transfers in this case.

A similar situation exists for deletion. If a tuple, A, with a specified key is present, it will be discovered in $F/2$ page reads on average, and then the page (with A deleted) will be rewritten, yielding a cost of $F/2 + 1$. If no such tuple is present, the cost is F. If the condition specifying the tuples to be deleted does not involve a key, the entire file must be scanned since an arbitrary number of rows satisfying the condition can exist in the table.

A heap file is an efficient storage structure if queries on the table involve accessing all rows and if the order in which the rows are accessed is not important. For example, the query

```
SELECT   *
FROM     TRANSCRIPT
```

returns the entire table. With a heap storage structure, the cost is F, which is clearly optimal. Of course, if we want the rows printed out in some specific order, the cost is much greater since the rows have to be sorted before being output. An example of such a query is

```
SELECT    *
FROM      TRANSCRIPT T
ORDER BY T.StudId
```

As another example, consider the query

```
SELECT    AVG(T.Grade)
FROM      TRANSCRIPT T
```

which returns the average grade assigned in all courses. All rows of the table must be read to extract the grades no matter how the table is stored, and the averaging computation is not sensitive to the order in which reading occurs. Again, the cost, F, is optimal.

Suppose, however, a query requests the grade received by the student with Id 234567890 in CS305 in the spring of 1996.

```
SELECT   T.Grade
FROM     TRANSCRIPT T                                              9.1
WHERE    T.StudId = '234567890' AND
         T.CrsCode = 'CS305' AND T.Semester = 'S1996'
```

Since {StudId, CrsCode, Semester} is the key of TRANSCRIPT, at most one grade will be returned. If TRANSCRIPT has the value shown in Figure 9.3, exactly one grade (namely, 4.0) will be returned. The database system must scan the file pages looking for a row with the specified key and return the corresponding grade. In this case, it must read three pages. Generally, an average of $F/2$ pages must be read, but if a row with the specified key is not in the table, all F pages must be read. In either case, the cost is high considering the small amount of information actually requested.

Finally, consider the following queries. The first returns the course, semester, and grade for all courses taken by the student with Id 234567890, and the second returns the Ids of all students who received grades between 2.0 and 4.0 in some course. Since, in both cases, the WHERE clause does not specify a candidate key, an arbitrary number of rows might be returned. Therefore, the entire table must be searched at a cost of F.

```
SELECT   T.Course, T.Semester, T.Grade
FROM     TRANSCRIPT T                                              9.2
WHERE    T.StudId = '234567890'
```

9.3

```
SELECT   T.StudId
FROM     TRANSCRIPT
WHERE    T.Grade BETWEEN '2.0' AND '4.0'
```

The conditions in the WHERE clauses of statements (9.1) and (9.2) are equality conditions since the tuples requested must have the specified attribute values. A search for a tuple satisfying an equality condition is referred to as an **equality search**. The condition in the WHERE clause of statement (9.3) is a **range condition**. It involves an attribute whose domain is ordered and requests that all rows with attribute values in the specified range be retrieved. The actual value of the attribute in a requested tuple is not specified in the range condition. A search for a tuple satisfying a range condition is referred to as a **range search**.

9.3 Sorted Files

The last examples ((9.1), (9.2), and (9.3)) illustrate the weakness of heap storage. Even though information is requested about only a subset of rows, the entire table (or half the table) must be searched since without scanning a page we cannot be sure that it does not contain a row in the subset. These examples motivate the need for more sophisticated storage structures, one of which we consider in this section.

Suppose that, instead of storing the rows of a table in arbitrary order, we sort them based on the value of some attribute(s) of the table. We refer to such a structure as a **sorted file**. For example, we might store TRANSCRIPT in a sorted file in which the rows of the table are ordered on StudId, as shown in Figure 9.5. An immediate advantage of this is that if we are using a scan to locate rows having a particular value of StudId, we can stop the scan at the point in the file at which those rows must be located. But beyond that, we can now use a binary search. We explore these possibilities next.

Access cost. A naive way to search for the data records satisfying (9.2) is to scan the records in order until the first record having the value 234567890 in the StudId column is encountered. All records having this value would be stored consecutively, and access to them requires a minimum of additional I/O. In particular, if successive pages are stored contiguously on the disk, seek time can be minimized. In the figure, the rows describing courses taken by student 234567890 are stored on a single page. Once the first of these rows is made available in the cache, all others satisfying query (9.2) can be quickly retrieved. If the data file consists of F pages, an average of $F/2$ page I/O operations is needed to locate the records—a significant improvement over the case in which TRANSCRIPT is stored in a heap file. Note that the same approach works for query (9.1).

In some cases, it is more efficient to locate the record with a **binary search** technique. The middle page is retrieved first, and its Id values are compared to 234567890. If the target value is found in the page, the record has been located; if the target value is less than (or greater than) the page values, the process is repeated

111111111	MGT123	F1997	3.0	
111111111	EE101	F1997	4.0	page 0
111111111	MAT123	F1997	3.0	
123454321	CS305	S1996	4.0	
123454321	CS315	S1997	4.0	page 1
123454321	MAT123	S1996	2.0	
234567890	EE101	F1995	3.0	
234567890	CS305	S1996	4.0	page 2
425360777	CS305	S1996	3.0	
666666666	MGT123	F1994	4.0	
666666666	MAT123	F1997	3.0	page 3
666666666	EE101	S1991	3.0	
987654321	MGT123	F1994	3.0	
987654321	CS305	F1995	2.0	page 4

FIGURE 9.5 TRANSCRIPT table stored as a sorted file. At most four rows fit in a page.

recursively on the first half (or last half) of the data file. With this approach, the worst-case number of page transfers needed to locate the record with a particular student Id is approximately log_2F.

Unfortunately, the number of page transfers is not always the most accurate way of measuring the cost of searching a sorted file since it does not take into account the seek latency incurred. While doing a binary search, we might have to visit pages located on different disk cylinders, and this might involve considerable seek-latency costs. In fact, under certain circumstances the seek latency might be more important than the number of page transfers. Consider a sorted file that occupies N consecutive cylinders and in which successive pages are stored in adjacent blocks. A binary search might cause the disk head to move across $N/2$, $N/4$, then $N/8$ cylinders, and so on. Hence, the total number of cylinders traversed by the disk head will be about N, and the total cost of binary search will be

$$N \times seek\ time + log_2F \times transfer\ time$$

On the other hand, if we do a simple sequential search through the file, the average number of cylinders canvassed by the disk head will be $N/2$ and the total cost

$$N/2 \times seek\ time + F/2 \times transfer\ time$$

Since seek time dominates transfer time, binary search is justified only if F is much larger than N.[3] In view of these results, neither sequential search nor binary search is considered a good option for equality searches in sorted files. A much more common approach is to augment sorted files with an index (see Section 9.4) and use binary search within the index. Since the index is designed to fit in main memory, a binary search over the index is very efficient and does not suffer from the disk-latency overhead described earlier.

Sorted files support range searches if the file is sorted on the same attribute as the requested range. Thus, the TRANSCRIPT file of Figure 9.5 supports a query requesting information about every student whose Id is between 100000000 and 199999999. An equality search for Id 100000000 locates the first tuple in the range (which might have Id 100000000 or, if such a tuple does not exist, will be the tuple with the smallest Id greater than this value). Subsequent tuples in the range occupy consecutive slots, and cache hits are likely to result as they are retrieved. If B is the number of rows stored in a page and R is the number of rows in a particular range, the number of I/O operations needed to retrieve all pages of the data file containing rows in the range (once the first row has been located) is roughly R/B.

Contrast these numbers with a heap file in which each row in the range can be on a different page and it is necessary to scan the entire file to ensure that all of them have been located. If the data file has F pages, the number of I/O operations is F. Similarly, a sorted file supports the retrieval of tuples that satisfy query (9.3), although in this case the table must be sorted on Grade instead. It cannot be sorted on both search keys at the same time.

Maintaining sorted order. In practice, it is difficult to maintain rows in sorted order if the table is dynamic. A heavy I/O price must be paid if, whenever a new row is inserted, all of the following rows have to be moved down one slot in the data file (that is, on average, half the pages have to be updated). One (partial) solution to this problem is to leave empty slots in each page when a data file is created to accommodate subsequent insertions between rows. The term **fillfactor** refers to the percentage of slots in a page that are initially filled. For example, the fillfactor for a heap file is 100%. In Figure 9.5 the fillfactor is 75% because three out of the four slots on a page are filled.

Empty slots do not provide a complete solution, however, since they can be exhausted as rows are inserted, and the problem then reappears for a subsequent insert. An **overflow page** might be used in this case, which Figure 9.6 illustrates using the TRANSCRIPT table. We have assumed that the initial state of the data file is as shown in Figure 9.5. Each page has a pointer field containing the page number of an overflow page (if it exists). In the figure, two new rows have been added to

---

[3] We have ignored the rotational delay, which strongly favors sequential over binary search.

111111111	MGT123	F1997	3.0	
111111111	EE101	F1997	4.0	page 0
111111111	MAT123	F1997	3.0	

123454321	CS305	S1996	4.0	
123454321	CS315	S1997	4.0	page 1
123454321	MAT123	S1996	2.0	

Overflow: 5				
234567890	EE101	F1995	3.0	
234567890	CS305	S1996	4.0	page 2
234567890	LIT203	F1997	3.0	
425360777	CS305	S1996	3.0	

666666666	MGT123	F1994	4.0	
666666666	EE101	S1991	3.0	page 3
666666666	MAT123	F1997	3.0	

987654321	MGT123	F1994	3.0	
987654321	CS305	F1995	2.0	page 4

313131313	CS306	F1997	4.0	page 5

FIGURE **9.6** The TRANSCRIPT table (augmented with overflow pointers) stored as a sorted file after the addition of several rows.

page 2 since the file was created. If an overflow page itself overflows, we can create an **overflow chain**: a linked list of overflow pages. Note that it is generally not the case that rows in the overflow chain are sorted. The problem of keeping the overflow chain sorted is the same as the problem of keeping the original file sorted.

While the use of overflow chains helps keep files **logically sorted**, we lose the advantage of the sorted files being stored in contiguous space on disk because an overflow page can be distant from the page that links to it. This causes additional latency during a sequential scan that reads records in order, and the number of I/O operations necessary to transfer records in a range is no longer R/B. If performance of sequential scan is an important issue (and it usually is), the data file must be reorganized periodically to ensure that all of its records are stored in contiguous disk space. The lesson here is that maintaining a data file in sorted order can be expensive if the file is dynamic.

9.4 Indices

Suppose that you have set up a database for an application and given it to a set of users. However, instead of receiving a check in the mail for your work, you start getting angry phone calls complaining that the system is too slow. Some users claim that they have to wait a long time to get a response to their queries. Others claim that throughput is unacceptable. Queries are being submitted to the system at a rate greater than that at which the system is capable of processing them.

Indices can be used to improve this situation. An index over a table is analogous to a book index or a library card catalog. In the case of a book, certain terms that are of interest to readers are selected and made into index entries. In this case, each **index entry** contains a term (e.g., "gas turbines") and a pointer (e.g., "p. 348") to the location(s) in the book where the term appears. The entries are then sorted on the term to construct a table, called an **index**, for easy reference. Instead of having to scan the entire book for the locations at which a particular term is discussed, we can access the index efficiently and go directly to those locations.

The analogy is even closer in the case of a card catalogue. In this case, there might be several indices based on different properties of books: author, title, and subject. In each index, the entries are sorted on that property's value and each entry points to a book in the collection. Thus, an entry in an author index contains an author's name and a pointer (e.g., section, shelf) to a book that she has written.

Similarly, an index on a database table provides a convenient mechanism for locating a row (data record) without scanning the entire table and thus greatly reduces the time it takes to process a query. The property to be located is a column (or columns) of the indexed table called a **search key**. Do not confuse a search key of an index on a table with a candidate key of the table. Remember that a candidate key is a set of one or more columns having the property that no two rows in any instance of the table can have the same values in these columns. A search key does not have this restriction, so, for example, TRANSCRIPT has more than one row for the student with Id 111111111, which means that the index on StudId will have several index entries with the search-key value 111111111.

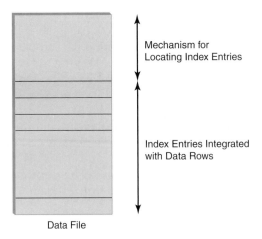

FIGURE **9.7** A storage structure in which an index is integrated with the data records.

As with a candidate key, a search key can involve several columns. For example, the search key might include both the student Id and the semester. However, in contrast to a candidate key, the order of columns in a search key makes a difference, so you should think of a search key as a sequence (as contrasted with a set) of columns of the indexed table. You will see a context in which the ordering is important when we discuss partial-key searches.

An index consists of a set of index entries together with a mechanism for locating a particular entry efficiently based on a search-key value. With some indices, such as an ISAM index or a B$^+$ tree, the location mechanism relies on the fact that the index entries are sorted on the search key. A hash index takes a different approach. In either case, the data structure that supports the location mechanism, together with the index entries, can be integrated into the data file containing the table itself, as shown in Figure 9.7. This integrated data file is regarded as a new storage structure and is called an **integrated index**. Later in this chapter we discuss ISAM, B$^+$ trees, and hash storage structures as alternatives to heap and sorted storage structures. With an integrated storage structure, each index entry actually *contains* a row of the table (no pointer is needed).

Alternatively, the index might not be integrated, but instead stored in a separate file, called an **index file**, in which each index entry contains a search-key value and a rid.[4] This organization is shown in Figure 9.8. For example, the table TRANSCRIPT of

---

[4] With some indices, only the page Id field of the rid is stored. Since the major cost of accessing the data file is the cost of transferring a page, storing only the page Id in the index entry makes it possible to locate the correct page. Once the page has been retrieved, the record within it with the target search-key value can be located using a linear search. The added computational time for this search is generally small compared to the time to transfer a page and might be justified by the saving of space in each index entry. With smaller index entries, the index can fit in fewer pages, and hence less page I/O is needed to access it. In some index organizations, a single index entry can contain several pointers. Since this feature only complicates the discussion without adding any new concepts, we do not consider it further.

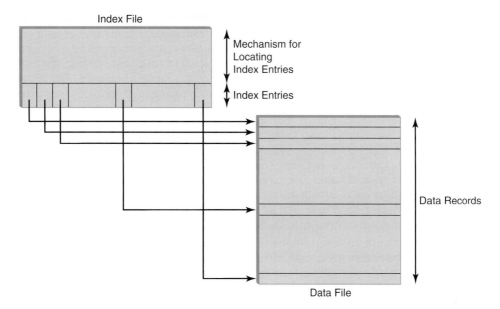

FIGURE 9.8 A clustered index that references a separate data file.

Figure 9.3 on page 330 might have an index on StudId. Each index entry contains a value that appears in the StudId column in some row of the table and the rid of that row in the data file. Thus, the entry (425360777, (3,1)) is present in the index.

Integration saves space since no pointer is needed and the search key does not have to be stored in both the index entry and the data record containing the corresponding row.

The SQL standard does not provide for the creation or deletion of indices. However, indices are an essential part of the database systems provided by most vendors. In some, for example, an index with a search key equal to the primary key is automatically created when a table is created. Such indices are often integrated storage structures that make it possible to efficiently guarantee that the primary key is unique when a row is added or modified (and to support the efficient execution of queries that involve the primary key). Heap storage structures result when no primary key is declared.

In addition to indices that are automatically created, database systems generally provide a statement (in their own dialect) that explicitly creates an index. For example,

CREATE INDEX TRANSGRD ON TRANSCRIPT (Grade)

creates an index named TRANSGRD on the table TRANSCRIPT with Grade as a search key. If CREATE INDEX does not provide an option to specify the type of index, a B^+ tree is generally the result. In any case, the index created might be stored in an index file, as shown in Figure 9.8. The index might reference a heap or sorted file, as shown in that figure, or the integrated storage structure shown in Figure 9.7 (in which case the table has two indices). A DBMS might automatically create such an index to enforce a UNIQUE constraint on a candidate key.

The use of an appropriate index can drastically reduce the number of data file pages that must be retrieved in a search, but accessing the index itself is a new form of overhead. If the index fits in main memory, this additional overhead is small. However, if the index is large, index pages must be retrieved from mass storage, and these I/O operations must be considered as part of the net cost of the search.

Because they require maintenance, indices must be added judiciously. If the indexed relation is dynamic, the index itself will have to be modified to accommodate changes in the relation as they occur. For example, a new row inserted into the relation requires a new index entry in the index. Thus, in addition to the cost of accessing the index used in a search, the index itself might have to be changed as a part of operations that modify the database. Because of this cost, it might be desirable to eliminate an index that does not support a sufficient number of the database queries. For this reason, an index is named in CREATE INDEX so that it can be referred to by a DROP INDEX statement, which causes it to be eliminated.

Before discussing particular index structures, we introduce several general properties for categorizing indices.

9.4.1 Clustered versus Unclustered Indices

In a *clustered* index, the physical proximity of index entries in the index implies some degree of proximity among the corresponding data records in the data file. Such indices enable certain queries to be executed more efficiently than with unclustered indices. Query optimizers can use the fact that an index is clustered to improve the execution strategy. (Chapters 10 and 11 explain how clustering information is used by the query optimizer.) Clustering takes different forms depending on whether index entries are sorted (as in ISAM and B^+ trees) or not (as in hash indices). A sorted index is **clustered** if the index entries and the data records are sorted on the same search key; otherwise, it is said to be **unclustered**. Clustered hash indices will be defined in Section 9.6.1. These definitions imply that, if the index is structured so that its entries are integrated with data records (the entries contain the records), it *must* be clustered. The index shown in Figure 9.8 is an example of a clustered index in which the index and the table are stored in separate files (and therefore the data records are not contained in the index entries). The regular pattern of the pointers from the index entries to the records in the data file is meant to reflect the fact that both index entries and data records are sorted on the same columns. The index shown in Figure 9.9 is unclustered.

A clustered index is often called a **main index**; an unclustered index is often called a **secondary index**.[5] There can be at most a single clustered index (since the

---

[5] Clustered indices are also sometimes called **primary indices**. We avoid this terminology because of a potential confusion regarding the connection between primary indices and the primary keys of relations. A primary index is *not* necessarily an index on the primary key of a relation. For instance, the PROFESSOR relation could be sorted on the Department attribute (which is not even a key) and

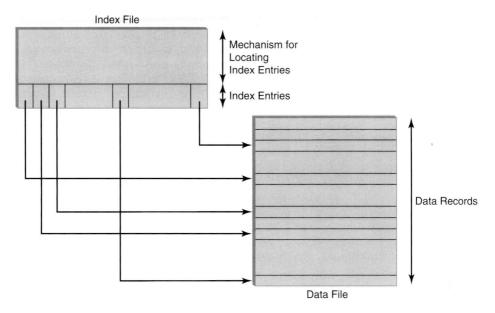

FIGURE 9.9 An unclustered index over a data file.

data file can be sorted on at most one search key), but there can be several secondary indices. An index created by a CREATE TABLE statement is often clustered. With some database systems, a clustered index is always integrated into the data file as a storage structure. In this case, index entries contain data records, as shown in Figure 9.7. An index created by CREATE INDEX is generally a secondary, unclustered index stored in a separate index file (although some database systems allow the programmer to request the creation of a clustered index, which involves reorganizing the storage structure). The search key of the main index might be the primary key of the table, but this is not necessarily so.

A file is said to be **inverted** on a column if a secondary index exists with that column as a search key. It is **fully inverted** if a secondary index exists on all columns that are not contained in the primary key.

A clustered index with a search key, *sk*, is particularly effective for range searches involving *sk*. Its location mechanism efficiently locates the index entry whose search-key value is at one end of the range, and, since entries are ordered on *sk*, subsequent entries in the range are in the same index page (or in successive pages—we discuss this situation in Section 9.5). The data records can be retrieved using these entries.

The beauty of a clustered index is that the data records are themselves grouped together (instead of scattered throughout the data file). They are either contained in

---

a clustered index could be built, while the index on the Id attribute of that relation (which is also its primary key) will be unclustered because rows will not be sorted on that attribute.

the index entries or ordered in the same way (see Figure 9.8). Hence, in retrieving a particular data record in the range, the probability of a cache hit is high since other records in the page containing that record are likely to have been accessed already. As described in Section 9.3, the number of I/O operations on the data file is roughly R/B, where R is the number of tuples in the range and B is the number of tuples in a page.

With a clustered index that is stored separately from the data, the data file does not have to be totally ordered to efficiently process range searches. For example, overflow pages might be used to accommodate dynamically inserted records. As each new row is inserted, a new index entry is constructed and placed in the index file in the proper place. The location mechanism of the index can then efficiently find all index entries in the range since they are ordered in one (or perhaps several successive) index pages. The cache-hit ratio for retrieving data pages is still high, although it might suffer somewhat from the scattering of the rows that were appended after the data file was sorted and are stored in overflow pages.

Although the data file does not have to be completely sorted, index entries cannot simply be appended to the index file—they must be integrated into the index's location mechanism. Hence, we seem to have replaced one difficult problem (keeping the data file sorted) with another (keeping the index file properly organized). However, the latter problem is not as difficult as it appears. For one thing, index entries are generally much smaller than data records, so the index file is much smaller than the data file and therefore index reorganization requires less I/O. Furthermore, as we will see, the algorithms associated with a B^+ tree index are designed to accommodate the efficient addition and deletion of index entries.

The algorithm for locating the index entries containing search-key values in a range is the same for clustered or unclustered indices. The problem with an unclustered index is that, instead of finding the corresponding data records in the index entries or grouped together in the data file, the records might be scattered throughout the data file. Thus, if there are R entries in the range, as many as R separate I/O operations might be necessary to retrieve the data records (we will discuss a technique for optimizing this number in a later section).

For example, a data file might contain 10,000 pages, but there might be only 100 records in the range of a particular query. If an unclustered index on the attributes of the WHERE clause of that query is available, at most 100 I/O operations will be needed to retrieve the pages of the data file (as compared with 10,000 I/O operations if the data is stored in a heap file with no index). If the index is clustered and each data file page contains an average of 20 data records, approximately five data pages will have to be retrieved. We have ignored the I/O operations on the index file in this comparison. We deal with index I/O in the individual discussions of different index structures later in this chapter.

9.4.2 Sparse versus Dense Indices

We have been assuming that indices are dense. A **dense index** is one whose entries are in a one-to-one correspondence with the records in the data file. A secondary,

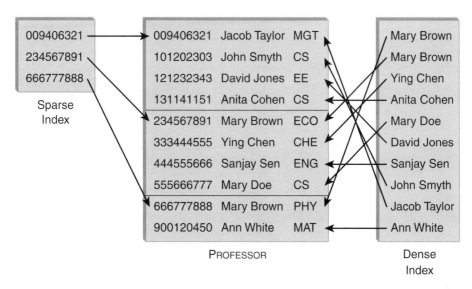

FIGURE 9.10 The index entries of (left) a sparse index with search key Id and (right) a dense index with search key Name. Both refer to the table Professor stored in a file sorted on Id.

unclustered index must be dense, but a clustered index need not be. A **sparse index** over a sorted file is one in which there is a one-to-one correspondence between index entries and pages of the data file. The entry contains a value that is less than or equal to all values in the page it refers to. The difference between a sparse and a dense index is illustrated using the table Professor in Figure 9.10. To simplify the figure we do not show overflow pages in the data file and assume that all slots are filled. The data file is indexed by two separate index files. Only the index entries are shown in the index files, not the location mechanisms. Once again, we assume four slots per page. The Id attribute is the primary key of this table and is also the search key for the sparse index shown at the left of the figure. The Name attribute is the search key for the dense index at the right.

To retrieve the record for the faculty member with Id 333444555, we can use the sparse index to locate the index entry containing the largest value that is smaller than the target Id. In our case, the entry contains the value 234567891 and points to the second page of the data file. Once that page has been retrieved, the target record can be found by searching forward in the page. With a sparse index, it is essential that the data file be ordered on the same key as the index since it is the ordering of the data file that allows us to locate a record not referenced by an index entry. Hence, the sparse index must be clustered.

An important point concerning sparse indices is that the search key should be a candidate key of the table since, if several records exist in the data file with the same search key value and they are spread over several pages, the records in the first of those pages might be missed. The problem is illustrated in Figure 9.11. The search key of the sparse index is the first column of the table, which is not a candidate key.

FIGURE 9.11 Sparse index with a problem: the search key is not a candidate key.

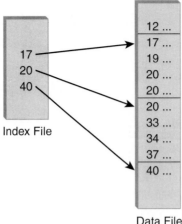

Index File

Data File

A search through the index for records having a search-key value of 20 follows the pointer in the index having a search-key value 20. Searching forward in the target page yields a single record with search-key value 20 and misses the records with that value in the previous page of the data file.

Several techniques can be used to correct this problem. The simplest is to start the search through the data file at the prior page when the target value is equal to the value in the sparse index. Another approach is to create an index entry for each *distinct search-key value* in the table (as opposed to one index entry per page). In that case, there might be several entries that point to the same page, but if there is considerable duplication of search-key values in the rows of the table, this index will still be considerably smaller than a dense index.

Unclustered indices are dense. The index on the right in Figure 9.10 is unclustered and, since an index entry exists for each record, the search key need not be a candidate key of the table. Therefore, several index entries can have the same search-key value (as shown in the figure).

9.4.3 Search Keys Containing Multiple Attributes

Search keys can contain multiple attributes. For example, we might construct an index on PROFESSOR by executing the statement

```
CREATE INDEX NameDept ON Professor (Name, DeptId)
```

Such an index is useful if clients of the supported application frequently request information about professors they identify by name and department Id. With such an index, the system can directly retrieve the required record. Not only is a scan of the entire table avoided, but records of professors with the same name in different departments are not retrieved (there might be two professors having the same name in a particular department, but this is unlikely).

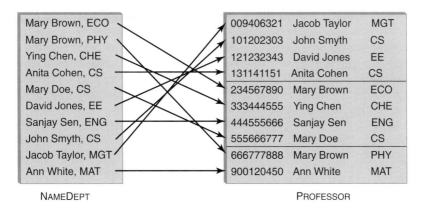

FIGURE 9.12 Dense index on PROFESSOR with search key `Name, DeptId`.

A dense, unclustered index that results from this statement is shown in Figure 9.12. The index entries are lexicographically ordered on `Name, DeptId` (notice that the order of the two entries for `Mary Brown` is now reversed from their position in the dense index of Figure 9.10).

One advantage of using multiple attributes in a search key is that the resulting index supports a finer granularity search. NAMEDEPT allows us to quickly retrieve the information about the professor named Mary Brown in the Economics Department; the dense index of Figure 9.10 requires that we examine two data records.

A second advantage of multiple attributes arises if the index entries are sorted (as with an ISAM or B$^+$ tree index but not a hash index) since then a variety of range searches can be supported. For example, we can not only retrieve the records of all professors named Mary Brown in a particular department (an equality search), but in addition we can retrieve the records of all professors named Mary Brown in any department with a name alphabetized between economics and sociology, or all professors named Mary Brown in all departments, or any professor whose name is alphabetized between Mary Brown and David Jones in all departments. All of these are examples of range searches. In each case, the search is supported because index entries are sorted first on `Name` and second on `DeptId`. Hence, the target index entries are (logically) consecutive in the index file, and we are able to limit the range of entries to be scanned. The last two searches are examples of **partial-key searches**—that is, the values for some of the attributes in the search key are not specified.

Note that a range search that is not supported by NAMEDEPT is one in which a value for `Name` is not supplied (e.g, retrieve the records of all professors in the Computer Science Department) since in that case the desired index entries are not consecutive in the index file. This is precisely the reason that, in distinguishing a search key from a candidate key, we said that the ordering of attributes in a search key is important whereas it is not important for a candidate key. With partial-key searches, values for a *prefix* of the search key can be used in the index search, while searching on a proper suffix of the key is not supported by the index.

Example 9.4.1 (Partial-Key Search).   In the design of the Student Registration System given in Section 4.8, the primary key for the table Transcript is (StudId, CrsCode, SectionNo, Semester, Year). A DBMS will generally automatically create an index whose search key consists of these attributes in the given order. The Student Grade interaction can use this index since, in assigning a grade to a student, all of this information must be supplied.

The Class Roster interaction performs a search on the attributes CrsCode, SectionNo, Semester, Year. It cannot use the index since a value of StudId is not provided, and this is the attribute on which index entries are primarily sorted.

However, the index is helpful for the Grade History interaction since StudId is supplied, but it is not optimal since the interaction uses a SELECT statement in which the WHERE clause specifies StudId, Semester, and Year. Unfortunately, the index does not support the use of Semester and Year unless CrsCode and SectionNo are also supplied. Reversing the order of the attributes in the primary key specification allows it to support the Grade History interaction optimally and also the Student Grade interacion. An additional index is needed for the Class Roster interaction. ■

In general, a tree index on table **R** with search key K supports a search of the form

$$\sigma_{attr_1 \mathrm{op}_1 val_1 \wedge \ldots \wedge attr_n \mathrm{op}_n val_n}(\mathbf{R}) \qquad \textbf{9.4}$$

if some prefix of K is a subset of $\{attr_1, attr_2, \ldots, attr_n\}$. For example, if s attributes of (9.4), $s \leq n$, are a prefix of K (assume for simplicity that these are the first s attributes), the search locates the smallest index entry satisfying $attr_1 = val_1 \wedge \ldots \wedge attr_s = val_s$ and scans forward from that point to locate all entries satisfying (9.4). Thus, a particular index can be used in different ways to support a variety of searches and can therefore be used in a variety of access paths to **R**.

Finally, since an index can have a search key with multiple attributes, it can contain an arbitrary fraction of the information in the indexed table. In particular, a dense unclustered index has an index entry for each row, r, and that entry contains r's values of the search-key attributes. The implication is that, for some queries, it is possible to find all the requested information in the index itself, *without accessing the table*. Thus, for example, the result of executing the query

```
SELECT   P.Name
FROM     PROFESSOR P
WHERE    P.DeptId = 'EE'
```

can be obtained from the index NameDept, without accessing Professor, by scanning the index entries. Such a scan is less costly than a scan of Professor, since the index is stored in fewer pages than is the table. The use of an index in this way is referred to as an *index-only strategy* and is discussed in Section 12.2.1.

9.5 **Multilevel Indexing**

In previous sections, we discussed the index entries but not the location mechanism used to find them. In this section we discuss the location mechanism used in tree indices and then describe its use more specifically in the *index-sequential access method (ISAM)* and in B^+ *trees*.

To understand how the location mechanism for a tree index works, consider the dense index on the table PROFESSOR shown in Figure 9.10. Since the search key is Name, the index entries are ordered on that field, and since the data records are ordered differently in the data file, the index is unclustered. We assume that the list of index entries is stored in a sequence of pages of the index file. A naive location mechanism for the index is a binary search over the entries. Thus, to locate the data record describing Sanjay Sen, we enter the list of index entries at its midpoint and compare the value Sanjay Sen with the search-key values found in that page. If the target value is found in the page, the index entry has been located; if it is less (or greater) than the values in the page, the process is repeated recursively on the first half (or, respectively, the last half) of the list. Once the index entry is located, the data page containing the record can be retrieved with one additional I/O operation.

It is important to note that a binary search on the list of index entries is a major improvement over a binary search on a sorted data file, as described in Section 9.3, since data records are generally much larger than index entries. Thus, if Q is the number of pages containing the index entries of a dense tree index and F is the number of pages in the data file, Q is much less than F. The number of I/O operations needed to locate a particular index entry using binary search can be no larger than approximately $log_2 Q$.

We can further reduce the cost of locating the index entry by indexing the list of index entries itself. We construct a sparse index, using the same search key, on the index entries (a sparse index is possible because the index entries are sorted on that key) and do a binary search on that index. The entries in this second-level index serve as separators that guide the search toward the index entries of the first-level index. We thus use **leaf entry** to refer to the index entries (the entries that reside in the lowest level of the tree) and **separator entry** to refer to the entries that reside at higher levels.

The technique is illustrated in Figure 9.13, which shows a two-level index. To keep the figure concise, we assume a table with a candidate key having an integer domain, and we use that key as a search key for the index. We assume that a page of the index file can accommodate four index entries. Of course, in real systems one index page accommodates many more (e.g., 100), and the size of the index is relatively insignificant compared to the size of the data file.

In this and subsequent figures, we do not explicitly show the data records. The figures can be interpreted in two ways: (1) the leaf entries contain pointers to the data records in a separate data file; (2) the leaf entries contain the data records (the index is clustered in this case), and the figure represents a storage structure. In interpretation 1, the index file contains both leaf entries and the second-level index, and one additional I/O operation is required to access the data record in the

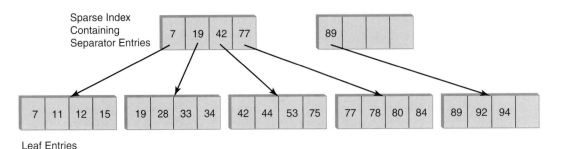

FIGURE 9.13 A two-level index. At most four entries fit in a page.

data file. In interpretation 2, retrieving a leaf entry also retrieves the corresponding data record, and no additional I/O is required. Our discussion of multilevel indices applies to both interpretations.

Finally, although in the figure the separators in the second-level index look identical to leaf entries, this is not always the case. In interpretation 2, only leaves, not separator entries, contain data records, and thus they are considerably larger than the separator entries. In interpretation 1, separators and leaf entries look identical, except that separators in the second level point to the nodes of the first level whereas leaf entries point to the records in the actual data file. The formats of these pointers will be different.

With a two-level index, we replace the binary search of the leaves by a two-step process. If we are looking for a data record with search-key value k, then we first do a binary search of the top-level sparse index to find the appropriate separator entry. The ith separator entry, with search-key value k_i, points to a page containing index entries with search-key values greater than or equal to k_i. It will be the appropriate entry if $k_i \leq k < k_{i+1}$. In this case we next retrieve that page to find the index entry (if it exists). Thus, if we are looking for a search-key value of 33, we first do a binary search of the upper index to locate the rightmost separator with a value less than or equal to 33, which in this case is the separator containing 19. We then follow the pointer to the second page of index leaves and do a linear search in that page to find the desired index entry. If the target search-key value were 32, we would perform the same steps and conclude that no row in the indexed table had value 32 in the candidate-key field.

What have we achieved by introducing the second-level index? Since the upper-level index is sparse, it has fewer separator entries than there are leaf entries at the first level. If we assume separate data and index files, separator and leaf entries in the index are roughly the same size. Moreover, if we assume 100 entries in an index page, the second-level index occupies $Q/100$ pages (where Q is the number of leaf pages) and the maximum cost of accessing a leaf entry using a binary search of the second-level index is roughly $log_2(Q/100)$ page I/Os plus 1 (for the page containing the index leaf). This compares to $log_2 Q$ for a binary search over the index's leaf entries and represents a major savings if Q is large.

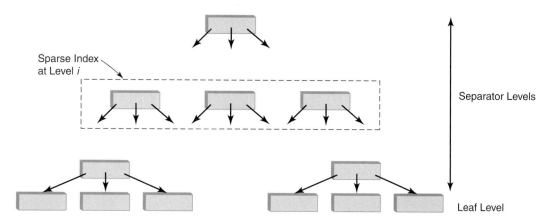

FIGURE 9.14 Schematic view of a multilevel index.

These considerations lead us to a multilevel index. If a two-level index is good, why not a multilevel index? Each index level is indexed by a higher-level sparse index of a smaller size, until we get to the point where the index is contained in a single page. The I/O cost of searching that index is 1, and so the total cost of locating the target leaf entry equals the number of index levels.

A multilevel index is shown schematically in Figure 9.14. Each shaded rectangular box represents a page. The lowest level of the tree contains the leaf entries and is referred to as the **leaf level**. If we concatenate all of the pages at this level in the order shown, the leaf entries form an ordered list. The upper levels contain separators and are referred to as **separator levels**. This is the location mechanism of a tree index. If we concatenate all of the pages at a particular separator level in the order shown, we get a sparse index on the level below. The root of the tree (the top separator level) is a sparse index contained in a single page of the index file. If the leaf entries contain data records, the figure shows the storage structure of a tree-indexed file.

We use the term **index level** to refer to any level of an index tree, leaf or separator. We use the term **fan-out** to refer to the number of index separators in a page. The fan-out controls the number of levels in the tree: the smaller it is, the more levels the tree has. The number of levels equals the number of I/O operations needed to fetch a leaf entry. If the fan-out is denoted by Φ, the number of I/O operations necessary to retrieve a leaf entry is $log_{\Phi}Q + 1$.

If, for example, there are 10,000 pages at the leaf level and the fan-out is 100 (10^6 rows in the data file assuming that leaf and separator entries are the same size), three page I/Os are necessary to retrieve a particular leaf. Thus, with a large fan-out, traversal of the index, even for a large data file, can be reduced to a few I/O operations. Since the root index occupies only a single page, it can often be kept in main memory, further reducing the cost. It might be practical to keep even the second-level index, which in this case occupies 100 pages, in main memory.

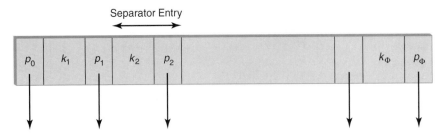

FIGURE 9.15 Page at a separator level in an ISAM index.

Multilevel indices form the basis for tree indices, which we discuss next, and these numbers indicate why tree indices are used so frequently. Not only do they provide efficient access to the data file, but, as we will see, they also support range queries.

9.5.1 Index-Sequential Access

The **index-sequential access method (ISAM)**[6] is based on the multilevel index. An ISAM index is a main index, and hence it is a clustered index over records that are ordered on the search key of the index. Generally, the records are contained in the leaf level, so ISAM is a storage structure for the data file.

The format of a page at a separator level is shown in Figure 9.15. Each separator level is effectively a sparse index over the next level below. Each separator entry consists of a search-key value, k_i, and a pointer, p_i, to another page in the storage structure. This page might be in the next, lower separator level, or it might be a page at the leaf levels. The separators are sorted in the page, and we assume that a page contains a maximum of Φ separators.

Each search-key value, k_i, separates the set of search-key values in the two subtrees pointed to by the adjacent pointers, p_{i-1} and p_i. If a search-key value, k, is found in the subtree referred to by p_{i-1}, it satisfies $k < k_i$; if it is found in the subtree referred to by p_i, it satisfies $k \geq k_i$ (hence the term "separator"). It appears as if an ISAM index page contains an extra pointer, p_0, if we compare it with a page of a sparse index in a multilevel index.[7] Actually, a better way to compare a page of an ISAM index to an index page at the separator level is that the latter contains an extra search-key value: the smallest search-key value in the page, k_0, is actually unnecessary.

Example 9.5.1 (ISAM Index).   Figure 9.16 is an example of an ISAM index. In it, the tree has two separator levels and a leaf level. Search-key values are the names

---

[6] The term "access method" is often used interchangeably with the term "access path." We prefer **access path** since it conforms more closely to the concept.
[7] Note that the fan-out is now $\Phi + 1$. Since Φ is generally much greater than 1, we ignore the difference between Φ and $\Phi + 1$ in cost calculations.

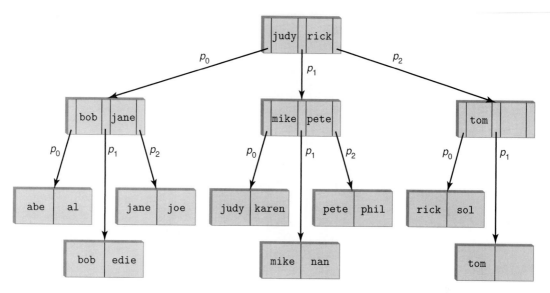

FIGURE 9.16 An example of an ISAM index.

of students, and the ordering is lexicographic. All search-key values in the leftmost subtree (the subtree referred to by p_0 in the root page) are less than judy, and all search-key values in the middle subtree (the subtree referred to by p_1 in the root page) are greater than or equal to judy.

A search for the data record containing the search-key value karen starts at the root, determines that the target value is between judy and rick, and follows p_1 to the middle page at the next index level. From that page, it determines that karen is less than mike and follows p_0 to the leaf page that must contain the index entry for karen (if it exists). If the goal were to retrieve all data records with search-key values between karen and pete, we would locate the index entry with the largest search-key value less than or equal to karen and then scan the leaf level until the first entry with search-key value greater than pete is encountered. Because pages at the leaf level are stored sequentially in sorted order, the desired entries are consecutive in the file. ∎

Example 9.5.1 illustrates the use of an ISAM index in supporting a range search. In addition the index supports keys with multiple attributes and partial-key searches.

An ISAM file is built by first allocating pages sequentially in the storage structure for the leaf pages (containing the data rows) and then constructing the separator levels from the bottom up: the root is the topmost index built. Therefore, the ISAM index initially has the property that all search-key values that appear at a separator level also appear at the leaf level.

The separator levels of an ISAM index never change once they have been constructed. It is for this reason that an ISAM index is referred to as a static index. Although the contents of leaf-level pages might change, the pages themselves are

FIGURE **9.17** Portion
of the ISAM index of
Figure 9.16 after an
insertion and a deletion.

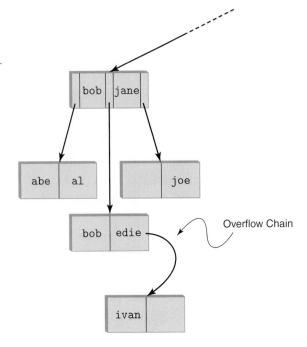

not allocated or deallocated and hence their position in the file is fixed. If a row
of the table is deleted, the corresponding leaf entry is deleted from the leaf-level
page but no changes are made to the separator levels. Such a deletion can create
a situation in which a search-key value in a separator entry has no corresponding
value in a leaf entry. This would happen, for example, if jane's row were deleted
from Figure 9.16: the entry for Jane at the leaf level would be removed, but the
entry at the separator level would remain. Such an index might seem strange, but
it still functions correctly and does not represent a serious problem (other than a
potential waste of space where the deallocated leaf entry resided).

Some systems take advantage of the static nature of an ISAM storage structure
by placing pages on the disk so that the access time for a scan of the leaf level is
minimized. The time to perform a range search can be minimized in this case.

A more serious problem arises when a new row is added since a new leaf entry
must be created and the appropriate leaf page might be full. This can be avoided
by using a fillfactor less than 1 (a fillfactor of .75 is reasonable for an ISAM file),
but overflow pages might ultimately be necessary. For example, if a row for ivan
were inserted (and the row for jane deleted), the leftmost subtree of the resulting
index would be as shown in Figure 9.17. Note that the new page is an overflow of a
leaf-level page, *not* a new level or even a new leaf-level page. If a table is dynamic,
with frequent insertions, overflow chains can become long and, as a result, the
index structure becomes less and less efficient because the overflow chains must be
searched to satisfy queries. The entries on the chains might not be ordered, and the

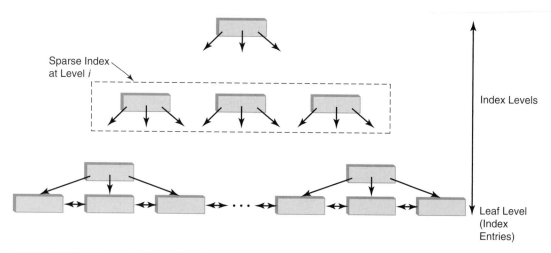

FIGURE 9.18 Schematic view of a B$^+$ tree.

overflow pages might not be physically close to one another on the mass storage device. The index can be reconstructed periodically to eliminate the chains, but this is expensive. For this reason, although an ISAM index can be effective for a relatively static table, it is generally not used when the table is dynamic.

9.5.2 B$^+$ Trees

A **B$^+$ tree** is the most commonly used index structure. Indeed, in some database systems it is the only one available. As with an ISAM index, the B$^+$ tree structure is based on the multilevel index and supports equality, range, and partial-key searches. Leaf pages might contain data records, in which case the B$^+$ tree acts not only as an index but as a storage structure that organizes the placement of records in the data file. Or the tree might be stored in an index file in which the leaf pages contain pointers to the data records. In the first case, the B$^+$ tree is a main index similar to an ISAM index since it is clustered. In the second case, it might be a main or a secondary index, and the data file need not be sorted on its search key.

Searching the tree. Figure 9.18 shows a schematic diagram of a B$^+$ tree in which each page contains a sorted set of entries. Each separator page has the form shown in Figure 9.14, and a search through the separator levels is conducted using the technique described for an ISAM index: if we are searching for a record with search-key value k, we choose the ith separator entry, where $k_i \leq k < k_{i+1}$.

The only difference between Figure 9.18 and Figure 9.14 is the addition of **sibling pointers**, which link pages at the leaf level in such a way that the linked list contains the search-key values of the data records of the table in sorted order. In contrast to an ISAM index, the B$^+$ tree itself changes dynamically. As records are added and deleted, leaf and separator pages have to be modified, added, and/or deleted, and hence leaf pages might not be consecutive in the file. However, the linked list enables the B$^+$ tree to support range searches. Once the leaf entry at one end of a range has been located using an equality search, the other leaf entries that contain search-key values in the range can be located by scanning the list. Note that this scheme works when the B$^+$ tree is used as either a main or a secondary index (in which case data records are not necessarily sorted in search-key order). With the addition of sibling pointers, Figure 9.16 becomes a B$^+$ tree (keep in mind that leaf-level pages might or might not contain data records).

Sibling pointers are not needed in an ISAM index because leaf pages (which generally contain data records) are stored in the file in sorted order when the file is constructed and, since the index is static, that ordering is maintained. Hence, a range search can be carried out by physically scanning the file. Dynamically inserted index entries are not stored in sorted order but can be located through overflow chains.

B$^+$ trees are descendants of **B trees**. The main difference is that B trees can have pointers to the records in the data file *at any level*—not just at the leaf level. Thus, each index page can have a mixture of separator and leaf entries. This implies that a particular search-key value appears exactly once in the tree. A B$^+$ tree does not possess this property. Therefore, a B tree can be smaller than the corresponding B$^+$ tree and searching in a B tree can be a little faster. However, it is harder to organize pointers to the data records in a sorted fashion in such a tree since not all such pointers are stored in the leaves (note that adding sibling pointers to a B tree will be of little help here). Therefore, performing range searches in a B tree is trickier.

Access cost. The second difference between a B$^+$ tree and an ISAM index is that a B$^+$ tree is a **balanced tree**. This means that, despite the insertion of new records and the deletion of old records, any path from the root to a leaf page has the same length as any other. This is an important property. If the tree is unbalanced, then it is possible that the path from the root to a leaf page becomes very long, the I/O cost of accessing index entries in that page is large, and the index becomes the problem rather than the solution.

With a balanced tree the I/O cost of retrieving a particular leaf page is the same for all leaves. We have seen that, for multilevel indices with a reasonable fan-out, this cost can be surprisingly small. Φ is the maximum number of separator entries that can be fit in an index page. If we assume that the algorithms for inserting and deleting entries (to be described shortly) ensure that the minimum number of separators stored in a page is $\Phi/2$ (i.e., $\Phi/2$ is the minimum fan-out),[8] then the maximum cost of a search through a B$^+$ tree having Q leaf pages is $log_{\Phi/2}Q + 1$. (In general, the root node can have fewer than $\Phi/2$ separators, which affects this formula slightly.) Contrast this with an ISAM index with overflow chains. Because the length of a chain is unbounded, the cost of retrieving a leaf page at the end of a chain is also unbounded.

---

[8] In case Φ is odd, the minimum number of separators should really be $\lceil \Phi/2 \rceil$—the smallest integer greater than $\Phi/2$.

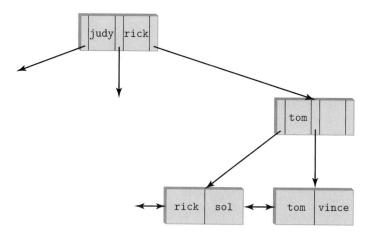

FIGURE 9.19 Portion of the index of Figure 9.16 after insertion of an entry for `vince`.

Inserting new entries.   A major advantage of the B$^+$ tree over an ISAM index is its adaptation to dynamically changing tables. Instead of creating an overflow chain when a new record is added, we modify the tree structure so that it remains balanced. As the structure changes, entries are added to and deleted from pages and the number of separators in a page varies between $\Phi/2$ and Φ.

Example 9.5.2 (B$^+$ Tree).   Let us trace a sequence of insertions into the index of Figure 9.16, viewing that index as a B$^+$ tree. In this case, $\Phi = 2$. Figure 9.19 shows the rightmost subtree after a record for `vince` has been added. Since `vince` follows `tom` in search-key order and there is room for an additional leaf entry in the rightmost leaf page, no modification to the B$^+$ tree structure is required.

Suppose that the next insertion is `vera`, which follows `tom`. Since the rightmost leaf page is now full, a new page is needed, but instead of creating an overflow page (as in an ISAM index), we create a new leaf page. This requires modifying the structure of the index, which sets the B$^+$ tree solution apart from the ISAM solution. Because the ordering of search-key values at the leaf level must be preserved, `vera` must be inserted between `tom` and `vince`. Hence, it is not sufficient simply to create a new rightmost leaf page containing `vera`. Instead, we must allocate a new leaf page and split the search-key values in sorted order between the existing leaf page and the new page so that roughly half are stored in each. The result is shown in Figure 9.20. The smallest entry in the new leaf page, labeled C in the figure, is `vince`, so `vince` becomes a new separator in index page D (all entries in leaf page B are less than `vince`), which fortunately has enough room for that entry. In general, when a (full) leaf page containing Φ entries is split to accommodate an insertion, we create two leaf pages—one containing $\Phi/2 + 1$ entries and the other containing $\Phi/2$ entries— and we insert a separator at the next index level up. We refer to this as Rule 1. Note that we have both a separator and a leaf entry for `vince`.

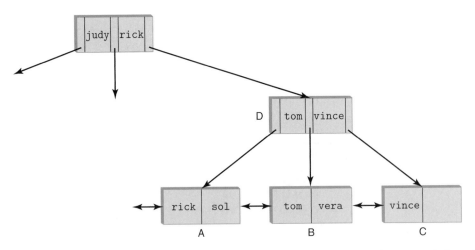

FIGURE 9.20 Index subtree of Figure 9.19 after the insertion of `vera` has caused the split of a leaf page.

If the next insertion is `rob`, the problem is more severe. The new index entry must lie between `rick` and `sol`, requiring a split of page A, and four pointers are needed at the separator level (to refer to the two pages that follow from the split as well as B and C) in page D. Unfortunately, a separator page can accommodate only three pointers, and therefore we must split D as well. Furthermore, following Rule 1, the new separator value is `sol` (since it will be the smallest search-key value in the new leaf page). In the general case, an index page is split when it has to store $\Phi + 1$ separators (in this case `sol`, `tom`, and `vince`) and thus $\Phi + 2$ pointers to index pages at the next lower level. Each page that results from the split contains $\Phi/2 + 1$ pointers and $\Phi/2$ separators. It might seem that we have misplaced a separator, but we are not done yet.

The situation after the split of page A into A1 and A2 and page D into D1 and D2 is shown in Figure 9.21. Note that the total number of separator entries in pages D1 and D2—two—is the same as in page D, although the values are different: `sol` has replaced `tom`. This number seems strange, since the number of separators required to separate the pages at the leaf level is three (`sol`, `tom`, and `vince`). The explanation is that `tom`, the separator that separates the values contained in the two subtrees rooted at D1 and D2, becomes a separator at a higher level. In general, in splitting a page at the separator level to accommodate $\Phi + 1$ separators, the middle separator in the separator sequence is not stored in either of the two separator pages resulting from the split, but instead is *pushed up* the tree. We refer to this pushing as Rule 2.

Hence, we are not finished. The separator has to be pushed and a reference has to be made to the new separator page (D2) at the next-higher index level. In other words, the process has to be repeated. In general, the process has to be repeated until an index level is reached that can accommodate a new separator without requiring a split. In our example, the next index level is the root page, and since it cannot

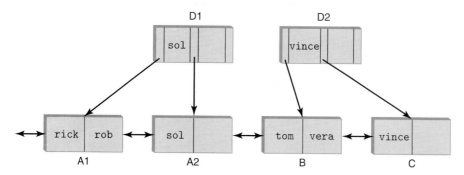

FIGURE 9.21 Index subtree of Figure 9.20 after the insertion of `rob` has caused the split of a leaf page and of a separator page.

accommodate another separator, it will have to be split. In this case, the sequence of separators that we are dealing with is `judy`, `rick`, and `tom`. Using Rule 2, `rick` must be pushed up to be stored in a new root page.

This completes the process and yields the B$^+$ tree shown in Figure 9.22. Note that the number of levels has increased by 1 but that the tree remains balanced. Four I/O operations are now required to access any leaf page. If the table is accessed frequently, the number of I/O operations might be reduced, keeping one or more of the upper levels of the tree in main memory. Also note that, in splitting A, the sibling pointer in B must be updated, which requires an additional I/O operation. ∎

A node split incurs overhead and should be avoided, if possible. One way to do this is to use a fillfactor that is less than 1 when the B$^+$ tree is created. A fillfactor of .75 is reasonable (however, if a table is read-only the fillfactor should be 1). Of course, this might increase the number of levels in the tree. One variation of the insertion algorithm that attempts to avoid a split involves redistributing index entries in the leaf-level pages. For example, if we insert a leaf entry for `tony`, in Figure 9.20 we might make room in page B by moving the entry for `vera` to page C (and replacing `vince` with `vera` as the separator in page D). Redistribution is generally done at the leaf level between neighboring pages that have the same immediate parent. Such pages are referred to as **siblings**.

The above discussion explains the main points of the process of inserting an entry into a B$^+$ tree. Exercise 9.12 asks you to formalize this process in an actual algorithm.

Deleting entries. Deletion presents a different problem. When pages become sparsely occupied, the tree can become deeper than necessary, increasing the cost of each search down the tree and each scan across the leaf level. To avoid such situations, pages can be compacted. A minimum occupancy requirement of Φ/2 entries per page is set for this purpose. When a deletion is made from a page, p, with Φ/2

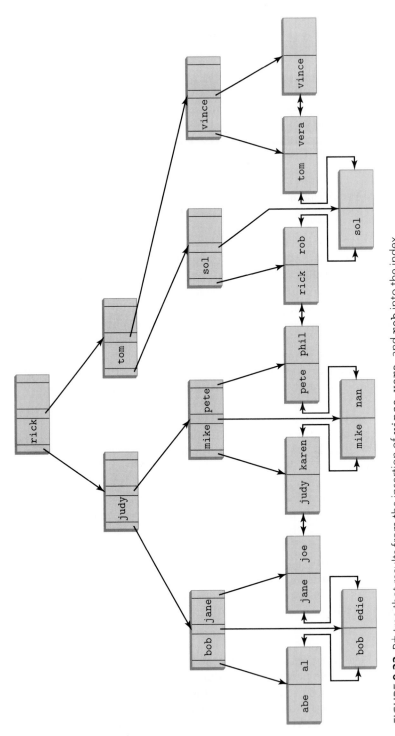

FIGURE 9.22 B$^+$ tree that results from the insertion of vince, vera, and rob into the index of Figure 9.16.

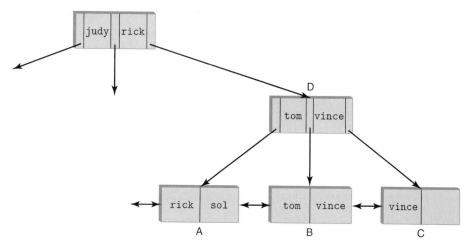

FIGURE 9.23 Index subtree of Figure 9.19 after the insertion of a duplicate entry for vince has caused the split of a leaf page.

entries, an attempt is first made to redistribute entries from one of p's siblings. This is not possible if both siblings also have $\Phi/2$ entries. In this case p is merged with a sibling: p and its sibling are deleted and replaced with a new page containing the $\Phi - 1$ entries previously stored in the deleted pages. Furthermore, a separator entry is deleted from the parent node in the next-higher level of the tree (recall that siblings have a common parent). Just as the effect of a split can propagate up the tree, so too can the effect of a merge. The deletion can cause the parent page to fall below the threshold level, requiring separators to be redistributed or pages to be merged. If the effect propagates up to the root and the last separator in the root is deleted, the depth of the tree is reduced by 1. In Exercise 9.13 you will formalize in an algorithm the process just described.

Since tables tend to grow over time, some database systems do not enforce the minimum occupancy requirement but simply delete pages when they become empty. If necessary, a tree can be completely reconstructed to eliminate pages that do not meet the minimum occupancy requirement.

Multiple identical search-key values.   Although we ignored this possibility in our previous discussion, when the search key is not a candidate key of the table, multiple rows might have the same search-key value. Suppose, for example, that a record for another student named vince is added to the B$^+$ tree of Figure 9.19. Using Rule 1, the rightmost leaf node must then be split to accommodate a second index entry with search-key value vince, and a new separator must be created, as shown in Figure 9.23. The first thing to note is that the search-key values in page B are no longer strictly less than the value vince in the separator entry in D. The second is that a search for vince terminates in leaf page C and therefore does not find the index entry for the other vince in B. Finally, if rows for additional students named vince are inserted, there will be several separators for vince at the lowest (and perhaps a higher) separator level. One way of handling duplicates is thus to modify the search algorithm to accommodate these differences. We leave the details of the modification to an exercise.

Another approach to handling the insertion of a duplicate is simply to create an overflow page if the leaf is full. In this way, the search algorithm does not have to be modified, although overflow chains can grow large and the cost estimates for using the tree described earlier will no longer apply.

9.6 Hash Indexing

Hashing is an important search algorithm in many computer applications. In this section, we discuss its use for indexing database relations, looking at both **static hashing**, where the size of the hash table stays constant, and **dynamic hashing**, where the table may grow or shrink. The first technique is superior when the contents of a relation are more or less stable; the second is superior when indexing relations that are subject to frequent inserts and deletes.

9.6.1 Static Hashing

A hash index divides the index entries corresponding to the data records of a table into disjoint subsets, called **buckets**, in accordance with some **hash function**, h. The particular bucket into which a new index entry is inserted is determined by applying h to the search-key value, v, in the entry. Thus, $h(v)$ is the address of the bucket. Since the number of distinct search-key values is generally much larger than the number of buckets, a particular bucket will contain entries with different search-key values. Each bucket is generally stored in a page (which might be extended with an overflow chain), identified by $h(v)$. The situation is shown in Figure 9.24.

As with a tree index, an index entry in a hash index might contain the data record or might store a pointer to the data record in the data file. If it contains the data record, the buckets serve as a storage structure for the data file itself: the data file is a sequence of buckets. If it contains a pointer to the record, the index entries are stored as a sequence of buckets in an index file and the records in the data file can be stored in arbitrary order. In this case, the hash index is secondary and unclustered. If the data records referred to by the index entries in a particular bucket are grouped together in the data file, the hash index is clustered. This implies that data records with the same value of the search key are physically close to each other on mass storage.

Hash search.   An equality search for index entries with search key v is carried out by computing $h(v)$, retrieving the bucket stored in the referenced page, and then scanning its contents to locate the index entries (if any) containing v. Since no other bucket can possibly contain entries with that key value, if the entry is not found in the bucket, it is not in the file. Thus, without having to maintain an index

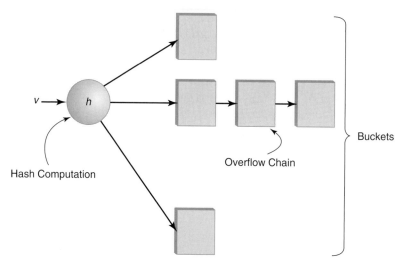

FIGURE 9.24 Schematic depiction of a hash index.

structure analogous to a tree, the target index entry of an equality search can be retrieved with a single I/O operation (assuming no overflow chain).

A properly designed hash index can perform an equality search more efficiently than a tree index can, since, with a tree index, several index-level pages must be retrieved before the leaf level is reached. If a succession of equality searches must be performed, however, a tree index might be preferable. Suppose, for example, that it is necessary to retrieve the records with search-key values $k_0, k_1, \ldots, k_l$, that the sequence is ordered on the search key (i.e., $k_i < k_{i+1}$), and that the sequence represents the order in which records are to be retrieved. Because the index leaves of a tree index are sorted on the key, the likelihood of cache hits when retrieving index entries is great. But with a hash index, each search-key value might hash to a different bucket, so the retrieval of successive index entries in the sequence might not generate cache hits. The example shows that, in evaluating which index might improve an application's performance, the entire application should be considered.

Despite the apparent advantage that hash indices have for equality searches, tree indices are generally preferable because they are more versatile: hash indices cannot support range or partial-key searches. A partial-key search is not supported because the hash function must be applied to the entire key. To understand why a range search cannot be supported efficiently, consider the student table discussed earlier. Suppose that we want to use a hash index to retrieve the records of all individuals in the file with names between paul and tom. Hashing can determine that there are no individuals with the name paul, and it can retrieve the index entry for tom, but it is of no help in locating index entries for individuals with names inside the range because we have no recourse but to apply the hash function to every *possible* value in the range—only a few of which are likely to appear in the database. Successive entries in the range are spread randomly through the buckets, so the cost of evaluating such a range query is proportional to the number of entries in the range. In the worst case (when the number of such entries exceeds the number of pages in the file), the cost associated with the use of the index might exceed the cost of simply scanning the entire file!

In contrast, with a clustered ISAM or B$^+$ tree index the data records in the range can be located by using the index to find the first record and then using a simple scan. A simple scan is possible because data records in the file are maintained in search-key order. The cost of this search is proportional to the number of pages in the range plus the cost of searching the index. The important difference is that the I/O cost of a B$^+$ tree search depends on the number of *leaf pages* in the range, while the cost of a hash index search depends on the number of *records* in the range, which is much larger.

Hash functions. Hash functions are chosen with the goal of randomizing the index entries over the buckets in such a way that, for an average instance of the indexed table, the number of index entries in each bucket is roughly the same. For example, h might be defined as

$$h(v) = (a * v + b) \bmod M$$

where a and b are constants chosen to optimize the way the function randomizes over the search-key values, M is the number of buckets, and v is a search-key value treated as a binary number in the calculation of the hash value. Note that, with some applications, no matter how clever the hash function, it might be impossible to keep the population of a bucket close to the average: if the search key is not a candidate key a large fraction of the rows might have the same search-key value and hence will necessarily reside in the same bucket. For simplicity, we assume M to be a power of 2 in all of the algorithms that follow (but in practice it is usually a large prime number).

The indexing scheme we have just described is referred to as a static hash because M is fixed when the index is created. With static hashing, the location mechanism is the hash function—no data structures are involved in this case. The efficiency of static hashing depends on the assumption that all entries in each bucket fit in a single page. The number of entries in a bucket is inversely proportional to M: if fewer buckets are used, the average bucket occupancy is larger. The larger the average occupancy, the more unlikely it is that a bucket will fit in a page and so overflow pages will be needed. The choice of M is thus crucial to the index's efficient operation.

If Φ is the maximum number of index entries that can fit in a page and L is the total number of index entries, choosing M to be L/Φ leads to buckets that overflow a single page. For one thing, h does not generally divide entries exactly evenly over the buckets, so we can expect that more than Φ entries will be assigned to some buckets. For another, bucket overflow results if the table grows over time. One way to deal with this growth is to use a fillfactor less than 1 and enlarge the number of buckets. The average bucket occupancy is chosen to be $\Phi * fillfactor$ so that buckets with larger than average populations can be accommodated in a single page. M then becomes

$L/(\Phi * fillfactor)$. Fillfactors as low as .5 are not unreasonable. The disadvantage of enlarging M is that space requirements increase because some buckets have few entries.

This technique reduces, but does not solve, the overflow problem, particularly since the growth of some tables cannot be predicted in advance. Therefore, bucket overflow must be dealt with, and this can be done with overflow chains as shown in Figure 9.24. Unfortunately, as with an ISAM index, overflow chains can be inefficient. Because an entire bucket must be scanned with each equality search, a search through a bucket stored in n pages costs n I/O operations. This multiplies the cost of a search by n over the ideal case. Fortunately, studies have shown that $n = 1.2$ for a good hash function.

9.6.2 Dynamic Hashing Algorithms

Just as B$^+$ trees are adapted from tree indices to deal with dynamic tables, dynamic hashing schemes are adapted from static hashing to deal with the same problem. The goal of dynamic hashing is to change the number of buckets dynamically in order to reduce or eliminate overflow chains as rows are added and deleted. Two dynamic hashing algorithms that have received the most attention are *extendable hashing* and *linear hashing*. We briefly discuss them here.

Static hashing uses a fixed hash function, h, to partition the set of all possible search-key values into subsets, S_i, $1 \le i \le M$, and maps each subset to a bucket, B_i. Each element, v, of S_i has the property that $h(v)$ identifies B_i. Dynamic hashing schemes allow S_i to be partitioned at run time into disjoint subsets, S_i' and S_i'', and B_i to be split into B_i' and B_i'', such that the elements of S_i' are mapped to B_i' and the elements of S_i'' are mapped to B_i''. By reducing the number of values that map to a bucket, a split has the potential of replacing one overflowing bucket with two that are not full. A change in the mapping implies a change in the hash function that takes into account the split of a single bucket (or the merge of two buckets). Extendable and linear hashing do this mapping in different ways.

Extendable hashing. **Extendable hashing** uses a sequence of hash functions, h_0, h_1, ..., h_b, based on a single hash function, h, which hashes a search-key value into a b-bit integer. For each k, $0 \le k \le b$, $h_k(v)$ is the integer formed by the last k bits of $h(v)$. Stated mathematically,

$$h_k(v) = h(v) \bmod 2^k$$

Thus, the number of elements in the range of each function, h_k, is twice that of its predecessor, h_{k-1}. At any given time, a particular function in the sequence, h_k, directs all searches.

Unlike static hashing, dynamic hashing uses a second stage of mapping to determine the bucket associated with some search-key value, v. This mapping uses a level of indirection implemented through a directory, as shown in Figure 9.25. The value produced by $h_k(v)$ serves as an index into the directory, and the pointer in the directory entry refers to the bucket associated with v. The key point is that distinct

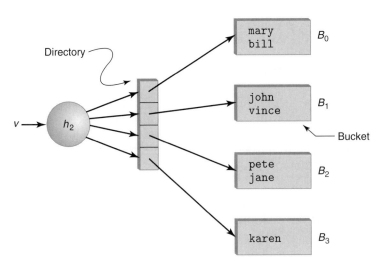

FIGURE 9.25 With extendable hashing, the hash result is mapped to a bucket through a directory.

entries in the directory might refer to the same bucket, so $v1$ and $v2$ might be mapped to the same bucket even though $h_k(v1)$ and $h_k(v2)$ are distinct. Example 9.6.1 shows how this situation might arise.

Example 9.6.1 (Extendable Hashing). Consider an extendable hash index of student names as shown in Figure 9.25, and suppose that the range of h is the set of integers between 0 and $2^{10} - 1$. We assume that a bucket page can hold two index entries. The figure depicts the algorithm at a point at which h_2 is used to hash search-key values (and, thus, the directory contains $2^2 = 4$ entries). Since h_2 uses only the last two bits of the values in the range of h, the figure could be produced by the following function h:

v	$h(v)$
pete	1001111010
mary	0100000000
jane	1100011110
bill	0100000000
john	0001101001
vince	1101110101
karen	0000110111

Thus, h hashes pete to 1001111010. Since h_2 uses only the last two bits (10), it indicates that the third directory entry refers to the bucket, B_2, that contains pete.

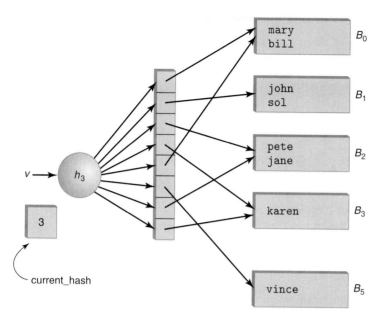

FIGURE 9.26 Bucket B_1 of Figure 9.25 has been split using extendable hashing.

Suppose that we now insert a record for sol into the table and that $h(\text{sol}) = 0001010001$. h_2 maps john, vince, and sol to B_1, causing an overflow. Rather than create an overflow chain, extendable hashing splits B_1 so that a new bucket, B_5, is created, as shown in Figure 9.26. To accommodate five buckets, it is necessary to use a hash function whose range contains more than four values, so the index replaces h_2 with h_3. Since the high-order bit of $h_3(\text{john})$, 0, and $h_3(\text{vince})$, 1, differ (whereas the two low-order bits, 01, are the same), h_3 avoids overflow by mapping john and vince to different buckets (h_2 does not do this). In Figure 9.26, note that if both $v1$ and $v2$ are elements of B_1 (or B_5), $h(v1)$ and $h(v2)$ agree in their last three bits.

The directory is needed to compensate for the fact that only B_1 has been split. Indeed, h_3 not only distinguishes between john and vince, but also produces different values for pete (010) and jane (110). Hence, without a directory it would be necessary to split B_2 as well when h_2 is replaced by h_3. By interposing a directory between the hash computation and the buckets, we can map both pete and jane to B_2, which we do by storing a pointer to B_2 in both the third (010) and seventh (110) directory entries. As a result, in contrast to B_1 and B_5, if $v1$ and $v2$ are elements of B_2, the values of the third bit of $h(v1)$ and $h(v2)$ might differ (but the values of the first two bits must be 10). ▪

The algorithm used in moving from Figure 9.25 to Figure 9.26 is quite simple.

1. A new bucket, B', is allocated and the contents of the overflowing bucket, B, are split between B and B' using the next hash function in the sequence.

2. A new directory is created by concatenating a copy of the old directory with itself.

3. The pointer to B in the copy is replaced by a pointer to B'.

Thus, the two halves of the directory in Figure 9.26 are identical except for the pointers in the second and sixth entry (which are the two halves of the bucket that has been split).

To give a complete description of the algorithm, we must deal with a few additional issues. First of all, how do we know which hash function in the sequence to use when a search has to be performed? That's easy. We simply store the index of the current hash function along with the directory. We assume a variable *current_hash* for this purpose, which is initialized to 0 (with only a single directory entry). In general, the number of directory entries is $2^{current\_hash}$. The value of *current_hash* is 2 in Figure 9.25 (not shown) and 3 in Figure 9.26.

A more subtle problem arises when an overflow occurs, but the current hash function can handle the new bucket that must be created. The situation is illustrated in Example 9.6.2, which extends Example 9.6.1.

Example 9.6.2 (Extendable Hashing, continued). Suppose a row for judy is inserted into the hash table shown in Figure 9.26 and $h(\text{judy}) = 1110000110$. judy is mapped to B_2 in Figure 9.26, causing the bucket to overflow and requiring it to be split. However, this situation is different from the one that caused us to replace h_2 with h_3, since h_3 itself is capable of distinguishing among index entries that are mapped to B_2 (recall that the hash values of the index entries in B_2 agree in only their last two bits). In the example, h_3 distinguishes judy and jane (110) from pete (010), so, instead of moving to a new hash function to deal with the overflow, we need only create a new bucket for judy and jane and update the appropriate pointer in the directory to refer to it. This is shown in Figure 9.27, in which the new bucket is labeled B_6. ■

There is a reason that the directory does not have to be enlarged this time. Each time it is enlarged, it becomes capable of storing pointers to accommodate the split of *every* bucket that exists at that time, whereas, in fact, only *one* bucket is actually split. Thus, when a directory is extended, all but one of the pointers in its new portion simply point back to an existing bucket. The directory in Figure 9.26 was created to accommodate the split of B_1, so only entry 101 in the new portion of that directory refers to a new bucket. Since entries 010 and 110 both point to B_2, the directory can accommodate a split of B_2 without further enlargement.

We can detect this case by storing, along with each bucket, the number of times it has been split. We refer to this value as the *bucket level* and associate a variable, *bucket_level*[i] to store it. Initially *bucket_level*[0] is 0 and, when B_i is split, we use *bucket_level*[i] + 1 as the bucket level of both B_i and the newly created bucket. Because each time the directory is enlarged without splitting B_i, we double the number of pointers in the directory that refer to B_i, $2^{current\_hash-(bucket\_level[i])}$ is the number of pointers that point to B_i in the directory. Furthermore, when a bucket is split, the index entries are divided between the two resulting buckets so that, if $v1$ and $v2$ are both elements of B_i, then $h(v1)$ and $h(v2)$ agree in their last *bucket_level*[i] bits.

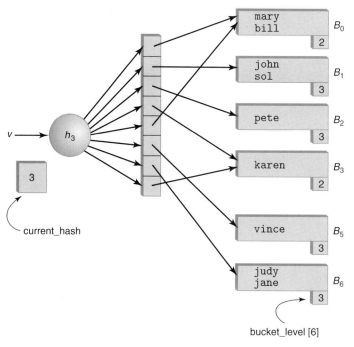

FIGURE 9.27 Bucket B_2 of Figure 9.26 is split, without enlargement of the directory.

bucket_level[1] is 3 in both Figure 9.26 (not shown) and Figure 9.27, whereas *bucket_level*[2] is 2 in Figure 9.26 and is incremented to 3 in Figure 9.27.

The merge of two buckets can be handled using the inverse of the split algorithm. If the deletion of an index entry causes a bucket, B', to become empty, and B' and B'' were created when B was split, B' can be released by redirecting the pointer to B' in the directory so that it points to B'' and decrementing the bucket level of B''. In addition, when merging creates a state in which the upper and lower halves of the directory are identical, one half can be released and *current_hash* decremented. Merging is often not implemented since it is assumed that, although a table might temporarily shrink, it is likely to grow in the long term, and therefore a merge will ultimately be followed by a split.

Extendable hashing eliminates most of the overflow chains that develop with static hashing when the number of index entries grows. Unfortunately, though, it has several deficiencies. One is that additional space is required to store the directory. The other is that the indirection through the directory to locate the buffer requires additional time. If the directory is small, it can be kept in main memory, so neither of these deficiencies is major. In that case, directory access does not impose the cost of an additional I/O operation. Nevertheless, a directory can grow quite large and, if it cannot be kept in main memory, the I/O cost of extendable hashing is twice that of static hashing. Finally, splitting a bucket does not necessarily divide its contents and eliminate the overflow. For example, when the overflow is caused by multiple entries with the same search-key value, splitting cannot remove the overflow.

OPTIONAL

Linear hashing. Because the deficiencies of extendable hashing are associated with the introduction of a directory, it is natural to search for a dynamic hashing scheme for which a directory is not required. A directory is needed with extendable hashing because, when a bucket is split, it might be necessary to switch to a hash function with a larger range: search keys stored in different buckets must hash to different values. Thus, the range of h_{i+1} contains twice as many elements as the range of h_i, and therefore $h_i(v)$ and $h_{i+1}(v)$ might not be the same. However, if v is an element of a bucket that is not being split, the index must direct the search to that bucket before and after the split. The directory overcomes this problem.

Can this problem be overcome in a way that does not involve a directory? One possible way uses the same sequence of hash functions, $h_0, h_1, \ldots, h_b$, as extendable hashing does, but differently. h_i and h_{i+1} are used concurrently: h_i for values belonging in buckets that have not been split and h_{i+1} for values belonging in buckets that have. This approach has the advantage of providing the same mapping before and after the split for search keys that belong in buckets not involved in the split. The trick is to be able to tell, when initiating a search through the index, which hash function to use.

With **linear hashing**, bucket splitting is divided into stages. The buckets that exist at the start of a stage are split consecutively during the stage so that there are twice as many buckets at the end of the stage as there were in the beginning. The situation is shown in Figure 9.28. Stages are numbered, and the number of the current stage is stored in the variable *current_stage*. Initially *current_stage* is 0 and there is a single bucket. The variable *next* indicates the next bucket in the sequence to be split during the current stage.

In Figure 9.28 *current_stage* has value i, indicating that it is in stage i. When stage i started there were 2^i buckets and *next* was initialized to 0, indicating that no buckets have yet been split in this stage. Since no buckets have yet been split, h_i, with range $\{0 \ldots 2^i - 1\}$, is used to hash search-key values for an index search. Once the algorithm starts splitting buckets during the stage, both h_i and h_{i+1} are used.

A decision is made periodically to split a bucket (we return to this point shortly), and the value of *next* is used to determine which bucket, among those that existed at the beginning of the stage, is to be split. *next* is incremented when the split occurs. Hence, buckets are split consecutively and *next* distinguishes those that have been split in the current stage from those that have not. Since *next* refers to the next bucket to be split, buckets with index less than *next* have been split in this stage. (Split buckets and their images are shaded in the figure.) Stage i is complete when the 2^i buckets that existed when the stage began have been split.

The new bucket created when B_{next} is split has index $next + 2^i$. Elements of B_{next} are divided using h_{i+1}: if v was an element of B_{next}, it remains in that bucket if $h_{i+1}(v) = h_i(v)$ and is moved to B_{next+2^i} otherwise. When the value of *next* reaches 2^i, a new stage is started by resetting *next* to 0 and incrementing *current_stage*.

When a search is to be performed on search key v, $h_i(v)$ is calculated. If $next \le h_i(v) < 2^i$, the bucket indicated by $h_i(v)$ is scanned for v. If $0 \le h_i(v) < next$, the bucket indicated by $h_i(v)$ has been split and $h_i(v)$ does not provide enough information to

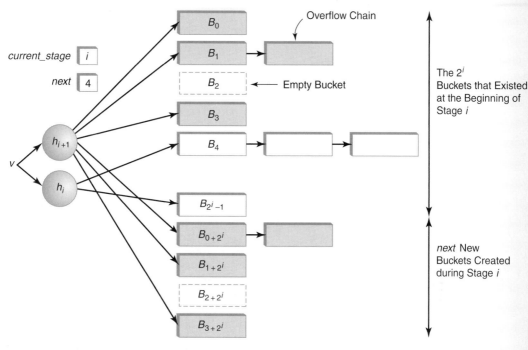

FIGURE 9.28 Linear hashing splits buckets consecutively. The shaded buckets are accessed through h_{i+1}.

determine whether $B_{h_i(v)}$ or $B_{h_i(v)+2^i}$ should be scanned for v. However, since h_{i+1} was used to divide the elements when the split was made, we can decide which bucket to search using $h_{i+1}(v)$. Hence, v is rehashed using h_{i+1}.

The important point to note about linear hashing is that the bucket that is split has not necessarily overflowed. We might decide to perform a split when a bucket, B_j, overflows, but the bucket that is split is B_{next}, and the value of $next$ might be different from j. Note that in Figure 9.28 $next = 4$, which means that B_0, B_1, B_2, and B_3 have been split. In particular, B_2 was split when it was empty and, hence, had certainly not overflowed. Thus, linear hashing does not eliminate overflow chains (in this case, an overflow page must be created for B_j). Ultimately, however, B_j will be split because every bucket that exists at the start of the current stage is split before the stage completes. So, although an overflow chain might be created for a bucket, B, it tends to be short and is normally eliminated the next time B is split. The average lifetime of an overflow page can be decreased by splitting more frequently, although the price for doing that is lower space utilization since buckets that have not overflowed are split during each stage.

Example 9.6.3 (Linear Hashing). Given the assumption that a split occurs each time an overflow page is created, Figure 9.29 shows the sequence of states that a linear index goes through when it starts in the same state as shown for extendable hashing

OPTIONAL

OPTIONAL

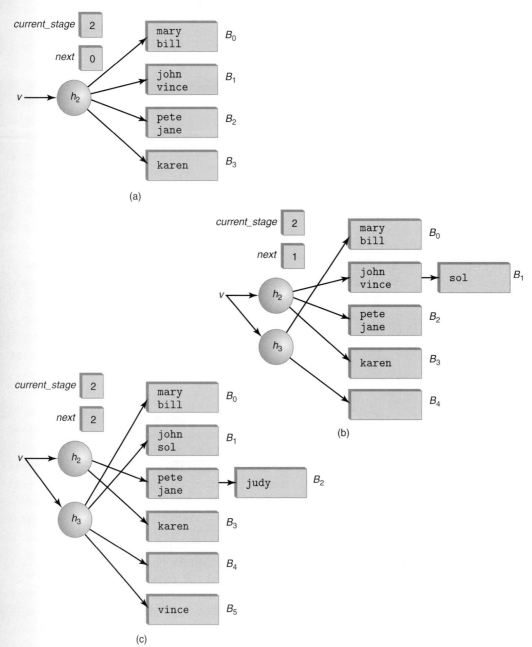

FIGURE 9.29 (a) State of a linear hash index at the beginning of a stage; (b) state after insertion of sol; (c) state after insertion of judy.

in Figure 9.25 and experiences the same subsequent insertions. In Figure 9.29(a) we have assumed that the index has just entered stage 2. Figure 9.29(b) shows the result of inserting sol into B_1. Although B_1 has overflowed, B_0 is split since *next* has value 0. Note that, since both mary and bill are hashed to B_0 by h_3, B_4 is empty. Figure 9.29(c) shows the result of inserting judy into B_2. B_1 is now split, eliminating its overflow chain, but a new overflow chain is created for B_2. ■

It might seem that linear hashing splits the wrong bucket, but this is the price that is paid for avoiding the directory. Splitting buckets in sequence makes it easy to distinguish the buckets that have been split from those that have not. Although overflow chains exist with linear hashing, there is no additional cost for fetching the directory.

9.7 Special-Purpose Indices

The index structures introduced so far can be used in a variety of situations. However, there are a number of index structures that are applicable in only very special cases but can yield large savings in storage space and processing time. We consider two such techniques: bitmap and join indices.

9.7.1 Bitmap Indices

A **bitmap index** [O'Neil 1987] is implemented as one or more bit vectors. It is particularly appropriate for attributes that can take on only a small number of values—for example, the Sex attribute of the PERSON relation, which can take only two values: Male and Female. Suppose that PERSON has a total of 40,000 rows. A bitmap index on PERSON contains two bit vectors, one for each possible value of Sex, and each bit vector contains 40,000 bits, one for each row in PERSON. Thus, the ith bit in the Male bit vector is 1 if, in the ith row of PERSON, the Sex attribute has value Male. As a result, we can identify the row numbers of males by scanning the Male bit vector. Given the row number, we can calculate the offset from the beginning of the data file and find the desired row on disk by direct access.

Note that the space to store the index in our example is just 80,000 bits, or 10K bytes, which can fit handily in main memory. Because searching such an index is done entirely in main memory, it can be carried out quickly using sequential scan.

You may have noticed that bitmap indices seem to waste more space than they need to. Indeed, to encode the Sex attribute we use *two* bits, while only one bit suffices to encode all of its possible values. The reason for this is that bitmap indices are designed to trade space for efficiency, especially the efficiency of selecting on two or more attributes. To illustrate, suppose that our PERSON relation represents the result of a health survey and that there is an attribute Smoker and an attribute HasHeartDisease, both accepting just two values, Yes and No. One query might request the number of males in a certain age group who smoke but do not have heart disease. As part of this query, we have a selection with the following condition:

```
Sex = 'Male' AND Smoker = 'Yes' AND HasHeartDisease = 'No'
```

If all three attributes have bit indices, we can easily find rids of all tuples that satisfy this condition: take the logical AND of the bit strings that correspond to the Male value of the Sex attribute, the Yes value of the Smoker attribute, and the No value of the HasHeartDisease attribute. The rids of the tuples that satisfy the condition correspond to the positions that have 1 in the resulting bit string.

More generally, bitmap indices can handle selection conditions that contain OR and NOT—all we have to do is compute an appropriate Boolean combination of the corresponding bit strings. For instance, suppose that the Age attribute has a bitmap index with 120 bit strings with a cost of 120 bits per PERSON record. This is quite acceptable, as a regular index will take at least 8 bytes (64 bits) per PERSON record anyway. Now we should be able to efficiently find all smoking males between the ages of 50 and 80 who never suffered from heart disease as follows: First compute the logical AND of the three bit strings as described above. Then compute the logical OR of the bit strings corresponding to ages 50 to 80 in the bitmap index for the Age attribute. Finally, compute the logical AND of the two results. Again, the 1s in the final bit string give us the Ids of the records we need to answer the query.

Bitmap indices play an important role in data mining and OLAP (online analytical processing) applications. The reason for their popularity is that such applications typically deal with queries that select on low-cardinality attributes, such as sex, age, company locations, financial periods, and the like. It also has to do with the fact that these applications operate on data that is fairly static, and bitmap indices are expensive to maintain if the underlying data changes frequently (think of what it takes to update a bitmap index if records are inserted or deleted in the data file).

In conclusion, we note that with a little more thought it is possible to devise a schema where only $n - 1$ bit vectors would be needed to index an attribute that can take n different values. In particular, for Boolean attributes, such as Sex, only one bit vector is needed. We leave the development of such a schema to Exercise 9.25.

9.7.2 Join Indices

Suppose we want to speed up an equi-join of two relations, such as $\mathbf{p} \bowtie_{A=B} \mathbf{q}$. A **join index** [Valduriez 1987] is a collection that consists of all pairs of the form $\langle p, q \rangle$, where p is a rid of a tuple, t, in $\mathbf{p}$ and q is a rid of a tuple, s, in $\mathbf{q}$, such that $t.A = s.B$ (i.e., the two tuples join).

A join index is typically sorted lexicographically in ascending order of rids. Thus, the pair $\langle 3, 3 \rangle$ precedes the pair $\langle 4, 2 \rangle$. Such an index can also be organized as a B$^+$ tree or as a hash table. The values of the search key in the entries of a B$^+$ tree are the rids of the rows in $\mathbf{p}$. To find the rids of all rows of $\mathbf{q}$ that join with a row of $\mathbf{p}$ having rid p, one searches the tree using p. The pointers in the leaf entries (if they exist) with search-key value p are the requested rids. Similarly, a hash index hashes on p to find the bucket containing the entries for that rid. Those entries contain the rids of the rows in **q** that join with the row in **p** at rid p.

A join index can be thought of as a precomputed join that is stored in compact form. Although its computation might require that a regular join be performed first, its advantage (apart from its compact size) is that it can be maintained incrementally: when new tuples are added to **p** or **q**, new index entries can be added to the join index without the entire join having to be recomputed from scratch (Exercise 9.24).

Given a join index, $\mathcal{J}$, the system can compute $\mathbf{p} \bowtie_{A=B} \mathbf{q}$ simply by scanning $\mathcal{J}$ and finding the rids of **p** and **q** that match. Note that, if $\mathcal{J}$ is sorted on its **p** field, the rids corresponding to the tuples in **p** appear in ascending order. Therefore, the join is computed in one scan of the index and of **p**. For each rid of a tuple in **q**, one access to **q** is also needed.

Worth mentioning is one other variation on the join index, called a **bitmapped join index** [O'Neil and Graefe 1995]. Recall that a join index is typically organized as a sorted file, a hash table, or a B$^+$ tree in a way that makes it easy to find the rids of all rows of **q** that join with the row of **p** at rid p. We can combine these rids in **q** in the following (at first, unusual) way: for each rid p in **p**, replace all tuples of the form $\langle p, q \rangle$ in $\mathcal{J}$ with a single tuple of the form

$$\langle p, \textit{ bitmap for matching tuples in } \mathbf{q} \rangle$$

The bitmap here has 1 in the ith position if and only if the ith tuple in **q** joins with the tuple in **p** at the rid p. Attaching a bitmap might seem like a huge waste of space, because each bitmap has as many bits as there are tuples in **q**. However, bitmaps are easily compressed, so this is not a major issue.

9.8 Tuning Issues: Choosing Indices for an Application

Each type of index is capable of improving the performance of a particular group of queries. Hence, in choosing the indices to support a particular application it is important to know the queries that are likely to be executed and their approximate frequency. Creating an index to improve the performance of a rarely executed query is probably not wise since each index carries with it added overhead, particularly for operations that update the database.

For example, if query (9.2) on page 332, with the value of StudId specified as a parameter, is executed frequently, an index to ensure fast response might be called for. The search key for such an index is chosen from among the columns named in the WHERE clause (*not* the SELECT clause) because these are the columns that direct the search. In this case, an index on TRANSCRIPT with search key StudId is useful. Instead of scanning the entire table for rows in which the value of StudId is 111111111, the location mechanism finds the index entries containing the search-key value. Each entry contains either the record or the rid of the record. Thus, while a scan requires that the system retrieve (on average) half the pages in the data file, access through the index requires only a single retrieval. On the other hand, an index on `StudId` is of no use in the execution of query (9.3) on page 333.

Suppose, however, that we need to support the query

```
SELECT   T.Grade
FROM     TRANSCRIPT T
WHERE    T.StudId = '111111111' AND T.Semester = 'F1997'
```

9.5

We might choose to create a multiattribute index on `StudId` and `Semester`. If, however, we choose to limit ourselves to an index on a single attribute (perhaps to support other queries and avoid too many indices), which attribute should be its search key? Generally, the attribute that is most selective is chosen. If an index on `StudId` is created, the database system uses it to fetch all rows for the target student and then scans the result, retaining those rows for the target semester. This is more efficient than fetching all rows for the target semester since there are likely to be many more rows for a given semester than for a given student. In general, columns that have only a few values in their domain (for example, `Sex`) are not likely to be very selective.

The following points provide some guidance in the choice of a search key:

1. A column used in a join condition might be indexed.

2. A clustered B$^+$ tree index on a column that is used in an **ORDER BY** clause makes it possible to retrieve rows in the specified order.

3. An index on a column that is a candidate key makes it possible to enforce the unique constraint efficiently.

4. A clustered B$^+$ tree index on a column used in a range search allows elements in a particular range to be quickly retrieved.

A more complete discussion of tuning can be found in Chapter 12.

BIBLIOGRAPHIC NOTES

B trees were introduced in [Bayer and McCreight 1972], and B$^+$ trees first appeared in [Knuth 1973]. The latest edition of that book, [Knuth 1998], contains much information on the material covered in this chapter. Hashing as a data structure was first discussed in [Peterson 1957]. Linear hashing was proposed in [Litwin 1980]; extendable hashing in [Fagin et al. 1979]. Index sequential files were analyzed in [Larson 1981].

Join indices were first proposed in [Valduriez 1987], and bitmap indices were first described in [O'Neil 1987]. Bitmapped join indices were introduced in [O'Neil and Graefe 1995].

EXERCISES

9.1   State the storage capacity, sector size, page size, seek time, rotational latency, and transfer time of the disk

a. On your local PC
b. On the server provided by your university

9.2   Explain the difference between an equality search and a range search.

9.3   a. Give an upper bound on the number of pages that must be fetched to perform a binary search for a particular name in the phone book for your city or town.
b. By how much is this number reduced if an index is prepared giving the name of the first entry on each page of the phone book? (Does that index fit on one page of the phone book?)
c. Conduct an experiment using your usual (informal) method to search for the name "John Lewis" in your local phone book, and compare the number of pages you look at with the number in Exercise 3(a).

9.4   Explain why a file can have only one clustered index.

9.5   Explain why a secondary, unclustered index must be dense.

9.6   Does the final structure of a B^+ tree depend on the order in which the items are added to it? Explain your answer and give an example.

9.7   Starting with an empty B^+ tree with up to two keys per node; show how the tree grows when the following keys are inserted one after another:

   18, 10, 7, 14, 8, 9, 21

9.8   Consider the partially specified B^+ tree in Figure 9.30.

a. Fill in the internal nodes without adding new keys.
b. Add the key bbb. Show how the tree changes.
c. Delete the key abc from the result of (b). Show how the tree changes.

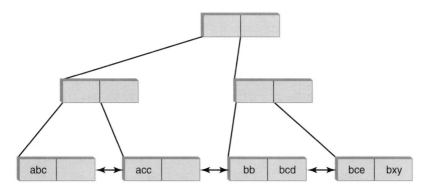

FIGURE 9.30 Partially specified B^+ tree.

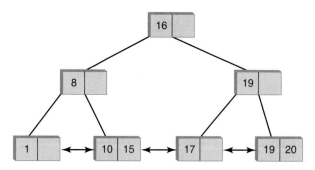

FIGURE 9.31 B$^+$ tree.

9.9   Consider the B$^+$ tree in Figure 9.31. Suppose that it was obtained by inserting a key into a leaf node of some other tree, *causing a node split*. What was the original tree and the inserted key? Is the solution unique? Explain your answer.

9.10   Describe a search algorithm for a B$^+$ tree in which the search key is not a candidate key. Assume that overflow pages are not used to handle duplicates.

9.11   Consider a hash function, h, that takes as an argument a value of a composite search key that is a sequence of r attributes, $a_1, a_2, \ldots, a_r$. If h has the form

$$h(a_1 \circ a_2 \circ \ldots \circ a_r) \; = \; h_1(a_1) \circ h_2(a_2) \circ \ldots \circ h_r(a_r)$$

where h_i is a hash of attribute a_i and $\circ$ is the concatenation operator, h is referred to as a **partitioned hash function**. Describe the advantages of such a function with respect to equality, partial-key, and range searches.

9.12   Express the algorithm for insertion into a B$^+$ tree using pseudocode.

9.13   Express the algorithm for deletion from a B$^+$ tree using pseudocode.

9.14   Express the algorithm for insertion and deletion of index entries in the extendable hashing schema using pseudocode.

9.15   Give examples of select statements that are

a. Speeded up due to the addition of the B$^+$ tree index shown in Figure 9.22 on page 358.
b. Slowed down due to the addition of the B$^+$ tree index shown in that figure.

9.16   Draw the B$^+$ tree that results from inserting `alice`, `betty`, `carol`, `debbie`, `edith`, and `zelda` into the index of Figure 9.22 on page 358.

9.17   A particular table in a relational database contains 100,000 rows, each of which requires 200 bytes of memory. A SELECT statement returns all rows in the table that satisfy an equality search on an attribute. Estimate the time in milliseconds to complete the query when each of the following indices on that attribute is used. Make realistic estimates for page size, disk access time, and so forth.

a. No index (heap file)
b. A static hash index (with no overflow pages)
c. A clustered, unintegrated B$^+$ tree index

9.18 Estimate the time in milliseconds to insert a new row into the table of Exercise 9.17 when each of the following indices is used:

a. No index (file sorted on the search key)
b. A static hash index (with no overflow pages)
c. A clustered, unintegrated B$^+$ tree index (with no node splitting required)

9.19 Estimate the time in milliseconds to update the search-key value of a row in the table of Exercise 9.17 when each of the following is used:

a. No index (file sorted on the search key)
b. A static hash index (where the updated row goes in a different bucket than the original row's page, but no overflow pages are required)
c. A clustered, unintegrated B$^+$ tree index (where the updated row goes on a different page than the original row's pages, but no node splitting is required)

9.20 Estimate the amount of space required to store the B$^+$ tree of Exercise 9.17 and compare that with the space required to store the table.

9.21 Explain what index types are supported by your local DBMS. Give the commands used to create each type.

9.22 Design the indices for the tables in the Student Registration System. Give the rationale for all design decisions (including those not to use indices in certain cases where they might be expected).

9.23 Explain the rationale for using fillfactors less than 1 in

a. Sorted files
b. ISAM indices
c. B$^+$ tree indices
d. Hash indices

9.24 Design an algorithm for maintaining join indices incrementally—that is, so that the addition of new tuples to the relations involved in the join do not require the entire join to be recomputed from scratch.

***9.25** Propose an improvement that permits bitmap indices to maintain only $n - 1$ bit vectors in order to represent attributes that can take n different values. Discuss the change that is needed to perform selection, especially in case of a multiattribute selection that requires a Boolean operation on multiple bit vectors.

10

The Basics of Query Processing

An application designer must understand the principles and methods of query processing in order to produce better systems. In this chapter, we examine the methods used to evaluate the basic relational operators and discuss their impact on physical database design. Chapter 11 will deal with a more advanced aspect of query processing: query optimization.

10.1 Overview of Query Processing

SQL queries submitted by the user are first parsed by the DBMS parser. The parser verifies the syntax of the query and, using the system catalogue, determines if the attribute references are correct. For instance, TRANSCRIPT.Student is not a correct reference because the relation TRANSCRIPT does not have Student as an attribute. Likewise, applying the AVG operator to the CrsCode attribute violates the type of that attribute.

Since an SQL query is declarative rather than procedural, it does not suggest any specific implementation. Thus, parsed queries must first be converted into relational algebra expressions. For instance, a query

```
SELECT S.Name
FROM TRANSCRIPT T, STUDENT S
WHERE T.Semester='F2004' AND S.Id=T.StudId AND S.Name='John Doe'
```

might be translated into the following expression:

$$\pi_{\text{Name}}(\sigma_{\text{Semester = 'F2004' AND StudId=Id AND Name = 'John Doe'}}(\text{TRANSCRIPT} \times \text{STUDENT}))$$

A naive way to evaluate this expression would be to compute the results of the relational operators directly as specified. If we did so on a large university database, we would quickly realize that it takes awhile to get an answer. The problem is that the expression involves the Cartesian product, and the intermediate result of the computation can become very large only to be reduced to a few bytes in the end.

To improve performance, a DBMS will play around with the above expression before trying to evaluate it. First, it might convert it to an equivalent expression of the following (or similar) form:

$$\pi_{\text{Name}}(\sigma_{\text{Semester='F2004'}}(\text{TRANSCRIPT} \bowtie_{\text{StudId=Id}} \sigma_{\text{Name = 'John Doe'}}(\text{STUDENT})))$$

This transformation is based on a heuristic that believes that joins are better than Cartesian products and that joining smaller relations is better than joining larger ones. Next, the system would choose the appropriate algorithms to compute each operator mentioned in the query. It will make these decisions based on a set of heuristics for estimating the cost of the different algorithms.

This complex series of transformations and estimates, which result in a **query execution plan**, are performed by a DBMS module called a **query optimizer**. A simplified view of query processing in a typical DBMS is depicted in Figure 5.1 on page 129.

We will study the workings of a query optimizer in the next chapter. But before we can do this, we need to familiarize ourselves with the repertoire of algorithms that a query optimizer has at its disposal, and we need to learn to estimate the cost of the alternative ways of computing the relational operators. These algorithms are the subject of this chapter.

10.2 External Sorting

Sorting is an important part of many algorithms used in computer programming and is at the very core of the algorithms that support relational operations. For instance, sorting is one of the most efficient ways to get rid of duplicate tuples and is also the basis of some join algorithms. The sorting algorithms used to process queries in relational DBMSs are not the ones you might have studied in a basic course on algorithms. The latter are designed to perform sorting when all data is stored in main memory, which usually cannot be assumed in the database context. When files are large and are kept in external storage, such as a disk, we use what is called **external sorting**.

The main idea behind external sorting is to bring portions of the file into main memory, sort them using one of the known in-memory algorithms (e.g., Quicksort), and then dump the result back to disk. This creates sorted file segments, which must be merged in order to create a single sorted file. Because the time to execute an I/O operation is several orders of magnitude greater than the time to execute an instruction, it is assumed that the cost of I/O dominates the cost of in-memory sorting. Hence, the computational complexity of external sorting is often measured only in the number of disk reads and writes. More specifically, we will measure the complexity in terms of the number of pages that need to be transfered between the main memory and the disk. A typical external sorting algorithm consists of two stages: *partial sorting* and *merging*.

Partial sorting.   The partial sorting stage is very simple. Suppose that we have a buffer in main memory that can accommodate M pages available for sorting and

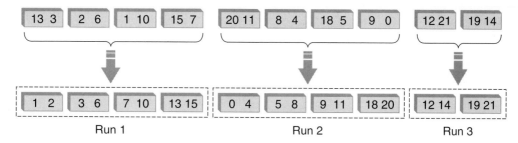

FIGURE 10.1 Partial sorting of a file, $M = 4$, $F = 10$.

that the file has F pages. F is typically much larger than M. The first stage of the algorithm is as follows:

---

do {
    read M pages from disk into main memory
    sort them in memory with one of the known methods.
        (Assume that, apart from the M-page buffer, additional memory
        is available to enable the in-memory sorting algorithm to run)
    dump the sorted file segment into a *new* file
} **until** (end-of-file)

We use the term **run** to refer to a sorted file segment produced by one iteration of the above loop. The size of a run is the number of pages in the segment. Thus, the first stage produces $\lceil F/M \rceil$ sorted runs at the cost of $2F$ disk I/O operations (for simplicity, we assume that each I/O operation transfers exactly one page to or from main memory). (The symbol $\lceil \ \rceil$ here denotes the operation of rounding up to the nearest integer that is greater than or equal to F/M.) The partial sorting stage is illustrated in Figure 10.1, in which we assume that each disk block contains two file records.

k-way merging. The next stage of the algorithm takes the sorted runs and merges them into larger sorted runs. This process can be repeated until we end up with just one sorted run, which is our final goal: the sorted version of the original file. A k-way merge algorithm takes k sorted runs of size R pages and produces one run of size kR, as illustrated in Figure 10.2. The actual algorithm works as follows:

---

while (there are nonempty input runs) {
    choose a smallest tuple (with respect to the sort key) in each
        run, and output the smallest among these
    delete the chosen tuple from the respective input run
}

Because each run is sorted, the choice step is simple since the smallest remaining element in a run is always its current head element. Figure 10.3 illustrates repeated

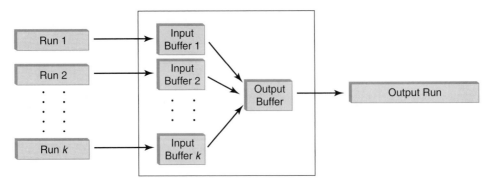

FIGURE 10.2 *k*-way merge.

application of the 2-way merge step; Figure 10.4 shows a 3-way merge. In each case we need to have a buffer with enough pages to perform the merge—three for the 2-way merge and four for the 3-way merge. The buffer size in the figures ($M = 4$) can accommodate both 2-way and 3-way merges.

What is the cost of a *k*-way merge of *k* runs of size *R* pages? Clearly, each run must be scanned once and then the entire output must be written back on disk. The cost is thus $2kR$. Since we might start with more than *k* runs, we divide them into groups of *k* and apply the *k*-way merge separately to each group. If we refer to this process as a step and if we start with *N* runs, we have $\lceil N/k \rceil$ groups, and the upper bound on the total cost of the merge step is $2RN$. Note that this value does not depend on *k*. Moreover, since at the next merge step we start with $\lceil N/k \rceil$ runs, each with a maximum size *kR*, the cost of the merge again does not exceed $2RN$, and we are left with $\lceil N/k^2 \rceil$ runs. In fact, it is easy to show by induction that this upper bound on the I/O cost holds for every step of the merge algorithm.

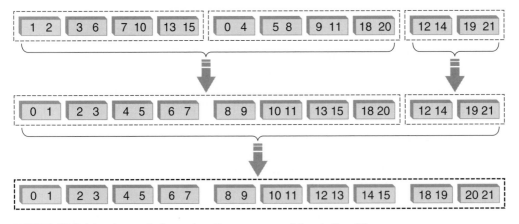

FIGURE 10.3 Merging sorted runs in a 2-way merge, $M = 4$, $F = 10$.

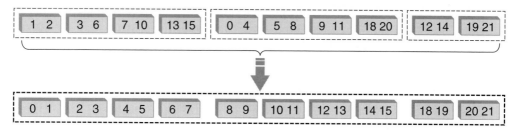

FIGURE 10.4 Merging sorted runs in a 3-way merge, $M = 4$, $F = 10$.

The next question is what the value of k should be at the merging stage in an external sort algorithm. If we start with N runs and perform a k-way merge at each step, the number of steps is $\lceil \log_k N \rceil$. Thus, the cost of the entire merging stage of the algorithm is bound by $2RN * \log_k N$, where R is the initial size of a sorted run. Since, in our case, $R = M$ (i.e., we can use the entire buffer to produce the largest possible initial runs) and consequently $N = \lceil F/M \rceil$, we conclude that the cost is bounded by $2F * \log_k \lceil F/M \rceil$.

Thus, it appears that the larger k is, the smaller is the cost of external sorting. Why, then, should we not take k to be the maximum possible—that is, the number of initial sorted runs? The answer is that we are limited by the size M of the main memory buffer allocated for the external sort procedure. This reasoning suggests that we should utilize this memory in such a way as to make k as large as possible. Since we must allocate at least one page to collect the output (which is periodically flushed to disk) during the merge, the maximum value of k is $M - 1$. By substituting this value into the earlier cost estimate, we obtain the following estimate:

$$2F \left(\log_{(M-1)}F - \log_{(M-1)}M\right) \approx 2F(\log_{(M-1)}F - 1)$$

Finally, by combining this cost with the cost of the partial sorting stage, we obtain an estimate for the entire procedure of external sorting:

$$2F * \log_{(M-1)}F \qquad\qquad \textbf{10.1}$$

In commercial DBMSs, the external sorting algorithms are highly optimized. They take into account not only the cost of in-memory sorting of the initial runs but also the fact that transferring multiple pages in one I/O operation might be more cost-effective than performing several I/O operations that transfer one page at a time. For instance, if we have a buffer that holds 12 pages, we can either perform an 11-way merge reading one page at a time or a 3-way merge reading three pages at a time. Since reading (and writing) three pages takes almost the same time as reading one, it is reasonable to consider such a 3-way merge as an alternative. Another consideration has to do with delays when the output buffer is being flushed to disk during the merge operation. Techniques such as double or triple buffering might be used to reduce such delays. Despite all of these simplifications, however, the algorithm and the cost estimate developed in this section provide a good approximation for what is happening in real systems. Our discussion of the algorithms in the remainder of this chapter relies on the understanding of the cost estimates and on the details of the sorting algorithm developed here.

Sorting and B$^+$ trees. The merge-based algorithm described above is the most commonly used sorting method in query processing because it works in all cases and does not require auxiliary data structures. However, when such structures are available, sorting can be performed at a lower cost.

For instance, suppose that a secondary B$^+$ tree index on the sort key is available. Traversal of the leaf entries of the tree produces a sorted list of the record Ids (rids) for the actual data file. In principle, then, we can simply follow the pointers and retrieve the records in the data file in the order of the search key. Surprisingly, this might not always beat the merge-based algorithm!

The main consideration in deciding whether a B$^+$ tree index is worth considering for sorting a file is whether the index is clustered or unclustered. The short answer is, if the index is clustered, using a B$^+$ tree index is a good idea; otherwise, it might be a bad idea. If the index is clustered, the data file must already be almost sorted (by definition), so there is nothing we need to do. However, if the index is unclustered, traversing the leaves of a B$^+$ tree and following the data record pointers retrieves pages of the main file in random order. In the worst case, this might mean that we must transfer one page for each *record* in the index leaf (recall that our previous analysis was based on the number of *pages* in the file—typically a much smaller number than the number of records). Exercise 10.1 deals with estimating the cost of using unclustered B$^+$ trees for external sorting.

10.3 Computing Projection, Union, and Set Difference

At first glance, computing the projection, union, and set difference operators is easy. With projection, for instance, we can just scan the relation and delete the unwanted columns. However, the situation is more complicated if the user query has the DISTINCT directive. The problem here is that duplicate tuples, which might arise as a result of the projection operation, must be eliminated. For instance, if we project out the attributes StudId and Grade of the relation TRANSCRIPT in Figure 3.5 on page 39, the tuple ⟨MGT123, F1994⟩ will appear twice in the result. Thus, we must find efficient ways of eliminating duplicate tuples.

The same problem with duplicates can arise in the computation of the union of two relations. In the case of the difference of two relations, **r** − **s**, duplicates cannot arise unless the relation **r** had them all along. Nevertheless, the problem we are facing is similar: to identify the tuples in **r** that are equal to tuples in **s**.

There are two techniques for finding identical tuples: sorting (which we discussed in Section 10.2) and hashing. We first apply these techniques to the projection operator and then discuss the modifications needed for union and set difference operators.

Sort-based projection. This technique scans the original relation, removes the tuple components that are to be projected out, and writes the result back on disk.

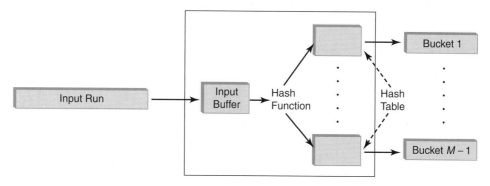

FIGURE 10.5 Hashing input relation into buckets.

(We assume that there is not enough memory to store the result.) The cost of this operation is of the order $2F$, where F is the number of pages in the relation. Then the result is sorted at the cost of $2F * log_{(M-1)} F$, where M is the number of main memory pages available for sorting. Finally, we scan the result again (at the cost of $2F$), and, since identical tuples are right next to each other (because the relation is sorted), we can easily delete the duplicates.

In fact, we can do better than that if we combine sorting and scanning. First, we delete the unwanted components from the tuples during the partial sorting stage of the sorting algorithm. At that stage, we have to scan the original relation anyway, so removal of the tuple components comes at no additional cost in terms of disk I/O. Second, we eliminate the final scan needed to remove the duplicates by combining duplicate elimination with the steps in which sorted runs are output to the disk. Since each such step writes out blocks of sorted tuples, duplicate elimination can be done in main memory, at no additional I/O cost.

Thus, the cost of the sort-based projection is $2F * log_{(M-1)} F$. Furthermore, if we take into account that the first scan is likely to produce a smaller relation (of size αF, where $\alpha < 1$ is the reduction factor), the cost of projection is even lower (see Exercise 10.2).

Hash-based projection.   Another way to quickly identify the duplicates is to use a hash function. Suppose that a hash function yields integers in the range of 1 to $M - 1$ and that there are M buffer pages in main memory, which includes an $(M - 1)$-page hash table and an input buffer. The algorithm works as follows. In the first phase, the original relation is scanned. During the scan, we chop off the tuple components that are to be projected out, and the rest of the tuple is hashed on the remaining attributes. Whenever a page of the hash table becomes full, it is flushed to the corresponding bucket on disk. This step is illustrated in Figure 10.5.

Clearly, duplicate tuples are always hashed into the same bucket, so we can eliminate duplicates in each bucket separately. This elimination is done in the second phase of the algorithm. Assuming that each bucket fits into the main memory, the second phase can be carried out by simply reading each bucket in its entirety, sorting it in main memory to eliminate the duplicates, and then flushing it to disk. The I/O complexity of the entire process is $4F$ (or $F + 3\alpha F$ if the size reduction factor due to projection, α ($\alpha < 1$), is taken into account). If the individual buckets do not fit in main memory, they must be sorted using external sorting, which incurs additional I/O overhead. Exercise 10.3 deals with the cost estimate in this case.

Comparison of sort-based and hash-based methods.   The assumption that every bucket can fit into main memory is realistic even for very large files. For instance, suppose that a 10,000-page buffer is available to the program to do the projection. Such a buffer requires only 40M of memory, which is well within the range of an inexpensive desktop computer. We can first use this buffer to store the hash table and then use it to read in the buckets. Let us assume that each hash bucket fits into our buffer and suppose we have a $10,000 \times 10,000 = 10^8$-page file (400G) to process. According to the above discussion, projection of such a file can be computed at the cost of just under 4×10^8 page transfers. Does the sort-based projection algorithm fare better? In this case, the sort-based algorithm costs a bit more: $2 \times 10^8 \log_{10^4 - 1} 10^8$ page transfers.

The possibility that we might have to externally sort an average-size hash bucket is fairly remote. A much bigger risk is that the hash function we use will not distribute tuples to the buckets evenly. In this case, although the average bucket might fit in main memory, other buckets will not. In the worst case (which is unlikely), all tuples might fall into the same buffer, which will require external sorting. The cost will then be $2F$ to scan the original relation and copy it into the single bucket plus $2F \log_{(M-1)} F$ to sort the bucket and eliminate the duplicates—a waste of $2F$ page transfers compared to sort-based projection.

Computing union and set difference.   Computing the union and set difference of two relations is similar to computing projection, except that we do not need to chop off unwanted attributes. For example, to compute a set difference, $\mathbf{r} - \mathbf{s}$, we sort both $\mathbf{r}$ and $\mathbf{s}$ and then scan them in parallel, similar to the merging process. However, instead of merging tuples, whenever we discover that a tuple, t, of $\mathbf{r}$ is also in $\mathbf{s}$, we do not add it to the result. Furthermore, we can combine this step with the final merges of the sorted runs of $\mathbf{r}$ and of $\mathbf{s}$, which are part of the sorting algorithm. Details of this combination are left to Exercise 10.9. Since the final scan of $\mathbf{r}$ and $\mathbf{s}$ comes for free, the cost of union and difference operations is the cost of sorting of these two relations.

In hash-based set difference computation, we can hash $\mathbf{r}$ and $\mathbf{s}$ into buckets as described earlier. However, in each bucket we must keep the distinction between tuples that came from $\mathbf{r}$ and those that came from $\mathbf{s}$. In the second stage, the set difference operation must be applied to each bucket separately.

10.4 Computing Selection

Computing the selection operator can be much more complex than computing projection and computing the set operations, and a wider variety of techniques can be used. The choice of a technique for a particular selection operator can depend on the type of the selection condition and on the physical organization of the relation in question. Typically, the DBMS decides automatically on the technique it will use based on the heuristics that we describe in the following subsections. However, understanding these heuristics gives the programmer an opportunity to request the physical organization that is most favorable to the selection types that occur most frequently in a particular application.

We first consider simple selection conditions of the form *attr* op *value* (where op is one of the comparisons $=$, $>$, $<$, and the like) and then generalize our techniques to complex conditions that involve Boolean operators.

Database queries usually lead to two distinct kinds of selection: those based on equality (*attr* $=$ *val*) and those based on inequality (such as *attr* $<$ *val*). The latter are called **range queries** because they usually come in pairs that specify a range of values, for example, $\sigma_{c_1 < attr \leq c_2}(\mathbf{r})$.

Our discussion of the techniques for implementing the selection operator focuses on the cost of retrieving the requisite tuples and ignores the cost of outputting the result. The reason is that the cost of the output is the same in all cases and thus is irrelevant for comparing the different techniques. Section 11.4 presents some heuristics for estimating this cost.

10.4.1 Selections with Simple Conditions

One obvious way of evaluating a selection, $\sigma_{attr\ op\ value}(\mathbf{r})$, is to scan the relation **r** and check the selection condition for each tuple, outputting those that satisfy it. However, if only a small number of tuples satisfies the condition, the price of scanning an entire relation seems too high. In situations where more information is available about the structure of **r**, a complete scan is not needed. We consider three cases: (1) when no index is available on *attr*; (2) when there is a B$^+$ tree index on *attr*; and (3) when there is a hash index on *attr*. In case 3, only the equality selections (where op is $=$) can be handled efficiently. In case 2, both equality selections and range queries can be handled efficiently, although case 3 is generally better for equality selection. In case 1, complete scan of **r** is the only option unless the relation **r** is already sorted on *attr*. In this case, both equality and range conditions can be handled, although not as efficiently as when a B$^+$ tree index is available.

No index. In general, we might have no choice but to scan the entire relation **r** at the cost of F page transfers (the number of disk blocks in **r**). However, if **r** is sorted on *attr*, we can use binary search to find the pages of **r** that house the first tuple where *attr* $=$ *value* holds. We can then scan the file in the appropriate direction to retrieve all of the tuples that satisfy *attr* op *value*.

The cost of such a binary search is proportional to $log_2 F$. To this, we must add the cost of scanning the blocks that contain the qualifying tuples. For instance, if **r** has 500 pages, the cost of the search is $\lceil log_2 500 \rceil$, that is, 9 page transfers (plus the number of disk blocks that contain the qualifying entries).

B$^+$ tree index. With a B$^+$ tree index on *attr*, the algorithm is similar to that for a sorted file. However, instead of the binary search, we use the index to find the first tuple of **r** where *attr = value*. More precisely, we find the leaf node of the B$^+$ tree that contains or points to the first row satisfying the condition. From there, we scan the leaves of the B$^+$ tree index to find all of the index entries that point to the pages that hold the tuples that satisfy *attr* op *value*.

The cost of finding the first qualifying leaf node of the index equals the depth of the B$^+$ tree. As before, we also have to add the cost of scanning the leaves of the index to identify all of the qualifying entries. Of course, this cost depends on the number of qualifying entries, which depends on the selection condition as well as on the actual data in the relation.

This is not the whole story, however. So far we have described only the process of getting the index entries. The cost of getting the actual tuples depends on whether or not the index is clustered. If the index is clustered, all of the tuples of interest are stored in one page or in several adjacent pages (this is true whether or not the index is integrated into the storage structure). For instance, if there are 1000 qualifying tuples and each disk block stores 100 tuples, getting all these tuples (assuming that we already had found the appropriate index nodes) requires 10 page transfers. On the other hand, if the index is unclustered, each qualifying tuple might be in a separate block, so retrieving all qualifying tuples might take 1000 page transfers!

This raises the unhappy prospect of having to perform as many page transfers as the number of qualifying tuples in the selection, which can handily beat the number of pages in the entire relation **r**. Fortunately, with a little thought, we can do better than that. Let us first sort the record Ids of the qualifying tuples that we obtained from the index. Then we can retrieve the data pages from the relation in the ascending order of qualifying record Ids, which guarantees that every data page will be retrieved at most once. Thus, even with an unclustered index, the cost is proportional to the number of pages that contain qualifying tuples (plus the cost of searching the index and sorting the record Ids). In the worst case, this cost can be as high as the number of pages in the original relation (but not as large as the number of tuples there!). This is because the qualifying tuples are not packed into the retrieved pages as they would be with a clustered index: a retrieved page might only contain a single qualifying tuple. Hence, a clustered index is still greatly preferred.

Hash index. In this case, we can use the hash function to find the bucket that has the tuples where *attr = value* holds. Since two tuples that differ only slightly in *value* can hash to different buckets, this method cannot be efficiently used with range conditions, such as *attr < value*.

Generally, the cost of finding the right bucket is constant (close to 1.2 for a good hash function). However, the actual cost of tuple retrieval depends on the number of qualifying tuples. If this number is larger than one, then, as in the case of B$^+$ tree indices, the actual cost depends on whether or not the index is clustered. In the clustered case, all qualifying tuples are packed into a few adjacent pages and the cost of retrieval is just the cost of scanning these pages. In the unclustered case, tuples are scattered through the data file and we face the same problem as with unclustered B$^+$ trees—sorting the record Ids results in a cost proportional to the number of pages that contain qualifying tuples.

10.4.2 Access Paths

The above algorithms for implementing the relational operators all assume that certain auxiliary data structures (indices) are available (or unavailable) for the relations being processed. These data structures, along with the algorithms that use them, are called **access paths**. So far, we have seen several examples of access paths that can be used to process a particular query: a *file scan* can always be used; a *binary search* can be used on files that are sorted on attributes specified in the query; a *hash index* or a B^+ tree can be used if the index has a search key that involves those attributes.

Example 10.4.1 (Access Paths). Consider the TRANSCRIPT relation of Figure 3.5, page 39, and suppose that we have a hash index on the search key ⟨StudId, Semester⟩. The index is useful in computing $\pi_{\text{StudId, Semester}}(\text{TRANSCRIPT})$, since we can be certain that any duplicates created as a result of the projection originate from tuples that were stored in the same bucket. This greatly simplifies duplicate elimination since the search for duplicates can be done one bucket at a time. If we compute $\pi_{\text{StudId, CrsCode}}(\text{TRANSCRIPT})$, on the other hand, the index is of no help in eliminating duplicates. Although the projections of tuples t_1 and t_2 on ⟨StudId, CrsCode⟩ might be identical, t_1 and t_2 might be hashed to different buckets since the values of their Semester attribute can differ. In order to use hashing for duplicate elimination, the entire search key of the hash index must be contained in the set of attributes that survive the projection (see Exercise 10.4).

At the same time, the above hash index can be very useful for computing the query $\sigma_{\text{StudId=666666666}\wedge\text{Grade='A'}\wedge\text{Semester='F1994'}}(\text{TRANSCRIPT})$. We can use the hash index to retrieve the tuples that satisfy the partial condition StudId=666666666 $\wedge$ Semester='F1994' and then scan the result (which presumably will be small) to find the tuples that additionally satisfy Grade='A'. On the other hand, the same index is of no help in evaluating the expression $\sigma_{\text{StudId=666666666}}(\text{TRANSCRIPT})$ since we cannot hash on a partial-search key and tuples satisfying this condition can be scattered over different buckets.

Finally, a hash index on ⟨Grade, StudId⟩ is not helpful for computing the query $\sigma_{\text{Grade>'C'}}(\text{TRANSCRIPT})$, but a B^+ tree index on the search key ⟨Grade, StudId⟩ can help (although a B^+ tree with search key ⟨StudId, Grade⟩ cannot). To use the hash function, we have to supply all possible values for StudId and all values for Grade above 'C', which is impractical. In contrast, since Grade is a *prefix* of the B^+ tree search key, we can use this tree to efficiently find all of the index entries with the search key ⟨g, id⟩, where g is higher than 'C'. ■

Example 10.4.1 leads to the notion of when an access path *covers* the use of a particular relational operator. We define this notion precisely only for a selection operator whose selection condition is a conjunction of terms of the form *attr* op *value*. Projection and set difference operators are left to Exercise 10.6.

Covering relates access paths to relational expressions that can be evaluated using those paths. Consider a relational expression of the form

$$\sigma_{attr_1 \text{ op}_1 \text{ } val_1 \wedge \ldots \wedge \text{ } attr_n \text{ op}_n \text{ } val_n}(\mathbf{R}) \qquad \textbf{10.2}$$

where **R** is a relation schema. This expression is **covered** by an access path if and only if one of the following conditions holds:

- The access path is a file scan. (A file scan can obviously be used to compute any expression.)

- The access path is a hash index whose search key is a subset of the attributes $attr_1, \ldots, attr_n$ *and* all op_i in this subset are equality operators. (We can use the hash index to identify the tuples that satisfy some of the conjuncts in the selection condition and then scan the result to verify the conjuncts that remain.)

- The access path is a B$^+$ tree index with the search key $sk_1, \ldots, sk_m$ such that some prefix $sk_1, \ldots, sk_i$ of that search key is a *subset* of $attr_1, \ldots, attr_n$. (Section 9.4.3 explained how to use B$^+$ trees for partial-key searches. This can help us find the tuples that satisfy some of the conjuncts in the selection. The rest of the conjuncts can be verified by a sequential scan of the result.)

- The access path is a binary search, and the relation instance corresponding to **R** is sorted on the attributes $sk_1, \ldots, sk_m$. The definition of covering in this case is the same as for B$^+$ tree indices.

Note that access paths based on hashing can be used only if all comparisons that correspond to the attributes in the search key are =. The other access paths can be used even if these comparisons involve inequalities, such as $\leq$, $<$, $>$, and $\geq$. If the comparison operator is $\neq$, the only applicable access path is a file scan since no index is effective in enumerating all the qualifying tuples in this case.

Example 10.4.2 (Covering Complex Selection).   Consider the expression $\sigma_{a_1 \geq 5 \wedge a_2 = 3.0 \wedge a_3 = 'a'}(\mathbf{R})$, and assume that there is a B$^+$ tree with search key a_2, a_1, a_4 on **R**. This access path covers the expression, which can be computed as follows. Use the index to find the leaf entry, e, in which a_2 has value 3.0 and a_1 has value 5 or, if such an entry is not present, the first entry in the index that would follow e. Then scan the leaf entries from that point on to find all those tuples in which, in addition, a_3 has value a.   ■

One more notion before we proceed: the **selectivity** of an access path is the number of pages that will be retrieved if we use the evaluation method corresponding to that path. The smaller the selectivity, the better the access path. Selectivity is closely related to the cost of evaluating a query, although the query cost might involve other factors. For example, multiple access paths might be used (see Section 10.4.3) or it might be necessary to sort the result before output (if an ORDER BY clause is used). Clearly, for any given relational expression, access path selectivity depends on the size of the result of that expression and is always greater than or equal to the number of pages that hold the tuples in that result. However, some access paths have selectivity that is closer to the theoretical minimum, while others are closer to the cost of the entire file scan. The notion of when an access path covers an expression helps in identifying access paths whose selectivity seems "reasonable" for the given type of expression.

10.4.3 Selections with Complex Conditions

We are now ready to discuss the methods used to evaluate arbitrary selection.

Selections with conjunctive conditions. These are the expressions of the form (10.2) considered on page 389. We have two choices:

1. *Use the most selective access path to retrieve the corresponding tuples.* Such an access path tries to form a prefix of the search key by using as many of the attributes mentioned in the selection condition as possible. In this way, it retrieves the smallest possible superset of the required tuples, and we can scan the result to find the tuples that satisfy the entire selection condition. For instance, suppose that we need to evaluate

$$\sigma_{\text{Grade}>'C' \wedge \text{Semester}='F1994'}(\text{TRANSCRIPT})$$

and there is a B^+ tree index with the search key $\langle$Grade, StudId$\rangle$. Since this access path covers the selection condition Grade>'C', we can use it to compute $\sigma_{\text{Grade}>'C'}(\text{TRANSCRIPT})$. Then we can scan the result to identify the transcript records that correspond to the fall 1994 semester. If we had a B^+ tree index with the search key $\langle$Semester, Grade$\rangle$, we could use *it* as an access path, because this path covers both selection conditions.

2. *Use several access paths that cover the expression.* For instance, we might have two secondary indices whose selectivity is less than that of the plain file scan. We can then use both access paths to find the rids of the tuples that might belong to the query result and then compute the intersection of those sets of rids. Finally, we can retrieve the selected tuples and test them for the remaining selection conditions. For instance, consider the expression

$$\sigma_{\text{StudId}=666666666 \wedge \text{Grade}='A' \wedge \text{Semester}='F1994'}(\text{TRANSCRIPT})$$

and suppose that there are two hash indices: on Semester and on Grade. Using the first access path, we can find the rids of the transcript records for the fall 1994 semester. Then we can use the second access path to find the rids for the records with grade 'A'. Finally, we can find the rids that belong to both sets and retrieve the corresponding pages. As we scan the tuples, we can further select those that correspond to the student Id 666666666.

Selections with disjunctive conditions. When selection conditions contain disjunctions, we must first convert them into *disjunctive normal form*. A condition is in **disjunctive normal form** if it has the form $C_1 \vee \ldots \vee C_n$, where each C_i is a conjunction of comparison terms (as in expression (10.2)).

It is known from elementary predicate calculus that every condition has an equivalent disjunctive normal form. For instance, for the condition

(Grade='A' ∨ Grade='B') ∧ (Semester='F1994' ∨ Semester='F1995')

the corresponding disjunctive normal form is

```
(Grade='A' ∧ Semester='F1994') ∨ (Grade='A' ∧ Semester='F1995')
  ∨ (Grade='B' ∧ Semester='F1994') ∨ (Grade='B' ∧ Semester='F1995')
```

For conditions in disjunctive normal form, the query processor must examine the available access paths for the individual disjuncts and choose the appropriate strategy. Here are some possibilities:

- *One of the disjuncts, C_i, must be evaluated using a file scan.* In this situation, we might as well evaluate the entire selection expression during that scan.
- *Each C_i has an access path that is better than the plain file scan.* We have two subcases here:
  1. The sum of the selectivities of all of these paths is close to the selectivity of the file scan. In this case, we should prefer the file scan because the overhead of the index search and other factors are likely to outweigh the small potential gain due to the use of more sophisticated access paths.
  2. The combined selectivity of the access paths for all disjuncts is much smaller than the selectivity of the file scan. In this case, we should compute $\sigma_{C_i}(\mathbf{R})$ separately, using the appropriate access paths, and then take the union of the results.

10.5 Computing Joins

The methods for computing projections, selections, and the like, are nothing but a prelude to a more difficult problem: evaluation of relational joins. With all of the attention given to the comparison of different access paths, the worst that can happen during the computation of a projection or selection is that we might have to scan or sort the entire relation. The result of such an expression is also well behaved: it cannot be larger than the original relation.

Compare this to relational joins, where both the number of pages to be scanned and the size of the result can be *quadratic* in the size of the input. While "quadratic" might not seem too bad in applications in which some algorithms have exponential complexity, it is prohibitive in database query evaluation because of the large amounts of data and the relative slowness of disk I/O. For example, joining two files that span a mere 1000 pages can require 10^6 I/O operations, which might be unacceptable even for batch jobs. And joining just three such relations would fetch 10^9 I/Os. For these reasons, joins are given special attention in database query processing.

Consider a join expression $\mathbf{r} \bowtie_{A=B} \mathbf{s}$, where A is an attribute of $\mathbf{r}$ and B is an attribute of $\mathbf{s}$. There are three main methods for computing joins: nested loops (with and without the help of indices), sort-merge, and hash-based joins. We consider them in this order.

10.5.1 Computing Joins Using Simple Nested Loops

One obvious way to evaluate the join $r \bowtie_{A=B} s$ is to use the following loop:

```
foreach t ∈ r do
    foreach t' ∈ s do
        if t.A = t'.B then output ⟨t, t'⟩
```

The cost of this procedure can be estimated as follows. Let F_r and F_s be the number of pages in **r** and **s**, and let τ_r and τ_s be the number of tuples in **r** and **s**, respectively. It is easy to see that the relation **s** must be scanned from start to end for each tuple in **r**, resulting in $\tau_r F_s$ page transfers. In addition, **r** must be scanned once in the outer loop. All in all, there are $F_r + \tau_r F_s$ page transfers. (In all cost estimates for the join operation, we ignore the cost of writing the final result to disk because this step is the same for all methods and also because the estimate at this stage depends on the actual size of the result. Trying to estimate this size takes us away from the main topic and is a distraction at this stage.)

The above cost estimate teaches us two lessons:

1. *It involves a lot of page transfers!* Let $F_r = 1000$, $F_s = 100$, and $\tau_r = 10,000$. Our cost estimate says that the computation might require $1000 + 10,000 \times 100 = 1,001,000$ page transfers—too much to join such relatively small tables (about 166 minutes if one page I/O takes 10 ms).

2. *The order of the loops matters.* Suppose that instead of scanning **r** in the outer loop, we scan **s** in the outer loop and **r** in the inner loop. Suppose that $\tau_s = 1000$. Switching **r** and **s** in the cost estimate yields: $100 + 1000 \times 1000 = 1,000,100$. Although, in this example, the reduction in operations is minimal (a whopping nine seconds!), it is clear that the order of scans matters.

Simple nested loops are actually never used for computing joins, because it is a hugely wasteful method. We will now consider a related, but much better technique.

Block-nested loops join. The complexity of the nested loops join can be reduced considerably if, instead of scanning **s** once per tuple of **r**, we scan it once per page of **r**. This will reduce the cost estimate to $F_r + F_r F_s$—a reduction of an order of magnitude from the above example. The way to achieve this feat is to output the result of the join for all tuples in the page of **r** that is currently in memory.

```
foreach page pr of r do
    foreach page ps of s do
        output pr ⋈A=B ps
```

If we can reduce the number of scans of **s** to one per page of **r**, can we further reduce this number to one per group of pages? The answer is yes—if we can use a little more memory. Suppose that the query processor has an M-page main memory buffer to do the join. We can allocate $M - 2$ of these pages for the outer loop relation

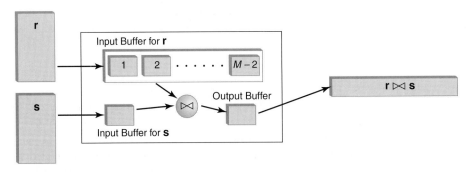

FIGURE 10.6 Block-nested loops join.

r and one page for the inner loop relation **s**, leaving the last page reserved for the output buffer. This process is depicted in Figure 10.6.

The cost of a block-nested loops join can be estimated similarly to our previous examples: the outer relation **r** is scanned once at the cost of F_r page transfers; the relation **s** is scanned once per group of $M - 2$ pages of **r**, that is, $\lceil \frac{F_r}{M-2} \rceil$. Thus, the cost (excluding the cost of writing the output to disk) is

$$F_r + F_s \lceil \tfrac{F_r}{M-2} \rceil \qquad\qquad \textbf{10.3}$$

Example 10.5.1 (An Estimate of a Block-Nested Loops Join). In our example, if $M = 102$, the cost will go down to $1000 + 100 \times 10 = 2000$. And, if the smaller relation, **s**, is scanned in the outer loop, the cost will be even lower: $100 + 100 \times 10 = 1100$ (or 11 seconds, assuming 10 ms per page I/O)—quite a reduction from 10^6, the cost of the original, naive implementation. ■

This example shows again that the order of the loops matters. Looking at the general formula (10.3) we can observe that $F_s \lceil \frac{F_r}{M-2} \rceil$ and $F_r \lceil \frac{F_s}{M-2} \rceil$ are approximately the same. Therefore, if $F_r > F_s$ then $F_r + F_s \lceil \frac{F_r}{M-2} \rceil > F_s + F_r \lceil \frac{F_s}{M-2} \rceil$.

> It is always cheaper to scan the smaller relation in the outer loop.

Index-nested loops join. The next idea is to use indices. This technique achieves particularly good results if the number of tuples in **r** and **s** that match on the attributes A and B is small compared to the size of the file.

Suppose that relation **s** has an index on attribute B. Then, instead of scanning **s** in the inner loop, we can use the index to find the matching tuples:

```
foreach t ∈ r do {
        Use the index on B to find all tuples t′ ∈ s such that t.A = t′.B
        Output ⟨t, t′⟩ for each such t′
}
```

To estimate the cost of this method, we have to take into account the type of index and whether it is clustered or not. The number of matching tuples in **s** also matters.

If the index is a B^+ tree, the cost of finding the first leaf node for the matching tuple in **s** is 2 to 4 I/O operations, depending on the size of the relation. In a hash-based index, it is about 1.2, if the hash function is well chosen. The next question is how many I/O operations are required to fetch the matching tuples in **s**, and the answer depends on the number of matching tuples and whether the index is clustered or unclustered.

If the index is unclustered, the number of I/Os needed to retrieve all matching tuples can be as high as the number of pages in **s** (this cost is bounded both by the number of pages in **s** and the number of patching tuples). So unclustered indices are not very useful for index-nested loops joins, *unless* the number of matching tuples is small (for instance, if B is a candidate key of **s**). For clustered indices, all matching tuples are likely to be in the same or adjacent disk blocks, so the number of I/Os needed to retrieve them is typically 1 or 2. Thus, in case of the clustered index the cost estimate is

$$F_{\mathbf{r}} + (\rho + 1) \times \tau_{\mathbf{r}}$$

where ρ is the number of I/Os needed to retrieve the leaf node of a B^+ tree index or to find the correct bucket of a hash index (we assume that the index is not integrated with the data file and that all matching tuples fit in one page, which is where the 1 comes from). In case of an unclustered index, the cost is

$$F_{\mathbf{r}} + (\rho + \mu) \times \tau_{\mathbf{r}}$$

where μ is the average number of matching tuples in **s** per tuple in **r**.[1]

Example 10.5.2 (An Estimate of an Index-Nested Loops Join).   Let us return to our example and compare this cost with the cost of block-nested loops joins. Assuming that ρ is 2 (our relations are fairly small), we obtain $1000 + 3 \times 10{,}000 = 31{,}000$ in the case of a clustered index—much higher than in the case of block-nested loops. However, if we switch **r** and **s** in the nested loop, the costs of index- and block-nested loops are much closer: $100 + 3 \times 1000 = 3100$ versus 1100.   ■

Still, in this example indices seem to be losing to block-nested loops by a large margin. Why consider indices at all? It turns out that indexed loops have one remarkable property: the cost is not significantly affected by the size of the inner relation, as can be seen from the above formulas. So, for example, if we use **s** in the inner loop and its size grows to 10,000 pages (100,000 tuples), the cost of block-nested loops joins grows to $1000 + 10{,}000 \times 10 = 101{,}000$ page transfers. In contrast, the cost of index-nested loops joins increases much more conservatively: $1000 + 3 \times 10{,}000 = 31{,}000$. Thus, indexed joins tend to work better when relations in the join are fairly large and one is much larger than the other.

---

[1] Assuming that the number of matching tuples in **s** per tuple in **r** is always less than the number of pages in **s**, which is typically the case.

FIGURE 10.7 The merge step of the sort-merge join algorithm.

Input: *relation* **r** *sorted on attribute A;*
　　　　relation **s** *sorted on attribute B*
Output: $\mathbf{r} \bowtie_{A=B} \mathbf{s}$

Result := {}　　　　　　　　　　　　　　// *initialize Result*
t_r := getFirst(**r**)　　　　　　　　　　// *get first tuple*
t_s := getFirst(**s**)
while !eof(**r**) **and** !eof(**s**) **do** {
　　while !eof(**r**) && $t_r.A < t_s.B$ **do**
　　　　t_r := getNext(**r**)　　　　　　// *get next tuple*
　　while !eof(**s**) **and** $t_r.A > t_s.B$ **do**
　　　　t_s := getNext(**s**)
　　if $t_r.A = t_s.B = c$ **then** {　　　　// *for some constant c*
　　　　Result := $(\sigma_{A=c}(\mathbf{r}) \times \sigma_{B=c}(\mathbf{s})) \cup$ *Result*;
　　　　t_r := the next tuple $t \in \mathbf{r}$ where $t.A > c$;
　　}
}
return *Result*;

10.5.2 Sort-Merge Join

The idea behind sort-merge is first to sort each relation on the join attributes and then to find matching tuples using a variation of the merge procedure, that is, scanning both relations simultaneously and comparing the join attributes. When a match is found, the joined tuple is added to the result.

The algorithm for this merge step is shown in Figure 10.7. The algorithm scans the relations **r** and **s** until a match on the attributes A and B is found. When this happens, all possible combinations (the Cartesian product) of the matching tuples are added to the result and the scan resumes.

Let us now estimate the cost of the sort-merge join in terms of the number of page transfers. Obviously, we must pay the usual price to sort the relations **r** and **s**: $2F_r\lceil log_{M-1}F_r\rceil + 2F_s\lceil log_{M-1}F_s\rceil$ (assuming that M buffers are available).

The cost of the merging step consists of the cost of scanning **r** and **s**, which is $F_r + F_s$ I/Os, plus the cost of computing $\sigma_{A=c}(\mathbf{r}) \times \sigma_{B=c}(\mathbf{s})$ for each match between **r** and **s**. At first, it seems that $\sigma_{A=c}(\mathbf{r}) \times \sigma_{B=c}(\mathbf{s})$ can be computed during the scan of **r** and **s** in Figure 10.7. However, if $\sigma_{A=c}(\mathbf{r})$ does not fit in main memory, computing the Cartesian product might require additional scans of $\sigma_{B=c}(\mathbf{s})$. The best way to compute this product would then be the block-nested loops join algorithm. The actual number of page transfers here depends on the sizes of $\sigma_{A=c}(\mathbf{r})$ and $\sigma_{B=c}(\mathbf{s})$, and on the amount of available memory. Typically, however, these subrelations are small and can fit in the available buffer, so the additional scans of $\sigma_{B=c}(\mathbf{s})$ can be avoided.

In this lucky case, the I/O cost of $\sigma_{A=c}(\mathbf{r}) \times \sigma_{B=c}(\mathbf{s})$ is zero and the entire sort-merge join takes $2F_\mathbf{r}\lceil log_{M-1}F_\mathbf{r}\rceil + 2F_\mathbf{s}\lceil log_{M-1}F_\mathbf{s}\rceil + F_\mathbf{r} + F_\mathbf{s} +$ cost of outputting the result.

> *Brain Teaser:* What is the maximum size of $\sigma_{A=c}(\mathbf{r}) \times \sigma_{B=c}(\mathbf{s})$ in terms of the sizes of $\mathbf{r}$ and $\mathbf{s}$?

An optimization. A more careful analysis of the sort-merge algorithm shows that one can save the cost of one scan of $\mathbf{r}$ and $\mathbf{s}$. The idea is to combine the scan needed for the merging step with the final stage of sorting $\mathbf{r}$ and $\mathbf{s}$—analogously to the optimization for the union and difference operators discussed earlier. This can be accomplished as follows.

First, $\mathbf{r}$ and $\mathbf{s}$ are sorted in parallel, each using $\frac{M}{2}$ buffer pages. (We could split the buffer into unequal chunks depending on the relative sizes of the files, but we will ignore this possible enhancement.) The final stage of sorting $\mathbf{r}$ consists of merging all the remaining sorted runs of $\mathbf{r}$ into one final sorted relation. Similarly, the final stage of sorting $\mathbf{s}$ merges the remaining sorted runs of $\mathbf{s}$. Instead of performing these final steps, we can modify the algorithm in Figure 10.7 to perform a generalized merge of the set of final sorted runs of $\mathbf{r}$ with the set of final sorted runs of $\mathbf{s}$. Since the number of runs in each file is $\leq (\frac{M}{2} - 1)$, we can use one buffer page for scanning each run of $\mathbf{r}$ and $\mathbf{s}$. One more page will be used for the output of the merge.

The new merge algorithm looks like the old one except that $\mathbf{r}$ is now understood as being a set of final runs of the first relation to be joined and $\mathbf{s}$ is viewed as a set of final runs of the second relation. The operation getNext is changed so that it will return the tuple with the lowest value of the join attributes in $\mathbf{r}$ and $\mathbf{s}$, respectively. Details are left to Exercise 10.10.

The overall cost of the optimized algorithm is: $2F_\mathbf{r}\lceil log_{\frac{M}{2}-1}F_\mathbf{r}\rceil + 2F_\mathbf{s}\lceil log_{\frac{M}{2}-1}F_\mathbf{s}\rceil$ (to sort and merge) plus the cost of outputting the final result (which is the same as before). Note that for large M and F, $log_{\frac{M}{2}-1}F = (log_{M-1}F) \times log_{\frac{M}{2}-1}(M - 1) \approx log_{M-1}F$, which means that we have eliminated the cost of one scan of $\mathbf{r}$ and $\mathbf{s}$.

Example 10.5.3 (An Estimate of a Sort-Merge). For our running example, we have the following relation sizes in blocks—$F_\mathbf{r} = 1000$, $F_\mathbf{s} = 100$—and the buffer dedicated to our join operation has 102 pages. This means $\mathbf{s}$ can be sorted in 200 page transfers and $\mathbf{r}$ in $2 \times 1000 \times \lceil log_{101}1000\rceil = 4000$ page transfers. Assuming that during the merge step of the join the matching tuples all fit in $M - 1$ pages, this step can be done without the need for an additional scan of $\mathbf{r}$ and $\mathbf{s}$ (by combining this step with the final merge performed while sorting $\mathbf{r}$ and $\mathbf{s}$, as explained earlier). Thus, the whole join will take 4200 page transfers. ∎

It may seem that the block-nested loops algorithm is better than sort-merge in this particular case. However, just as with the index-nested loops method, the asymptotic behavior of sort-merge is better than that of block-nested loops. When the sizes of $\mathbf{r}$ and $\mathbf{s}$ grow, the cost of block-nested loops grows quadratically— $O(F_\mathbf{r}F_\mathbf{s})$—while the cost of sort-merge join increases much more slowly (assuming that $\sigma_{A=c}(\mathbf{r})$ and $\sigma_{B=c}(\mathbf{s})$ are small, as discussed above)—$O(F_\mathbf{r}logF_\mathbf{r} + F_\mathbf{s}logF_\mathbf{s})$.

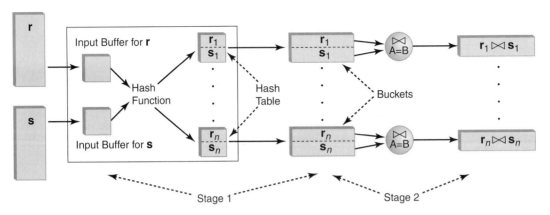

FIGURE 10.8 Hash join.

10.5.3 Hash Join

One way to compute a join, $r \bowtie_{A=B} s$, is to preprocess the relations r and s so that the tuples that possibly match will be placed on the same or adjacent pages. Such preprocessing eliminates the need for repeated scans of the inner-loop relation and is the basic idea behind the sort-merge technique described above. However, sorting is just one of the possible preprocessing techniques. Alternatively, we can use hashing to make sure that matching tuples are placed close to each other. We used this technique earlier, when we needed to place duplicates tuples (that arise due to projection or set-theoretic operations) close to each other. Clearly, the problem of identifying the duplicates is a special case of the problem we now face: identifying the tuples that have the same value for one or more attributes (e.g., A and B above). The idea is illustrated in Figure 10.8.

The hash-join method first hashes each input relation onto the hash table, where r is hashed on attribute A and s is hashed on attribute B. This has the effect that the tuples of r and s that can *possibly* match are put in the same bucket.

In the second stage, the r half and the s half of each bucket are joined to produce the final result. If both halves fit in main memory, all of these joins can be done at the cost of a single scan of r and s. If the buckets are too large for main memory, other join techniques can be tried. Typically in this case, the r portion of each bucket is further partitioned by hashing on the attribute A using a different hash function. Then the s portion of the corresponding bucket is scanned. In the process, each tuple of s is hashed on attribute B using the new hash function, and matching tuples in r are identified.

Assuming that each bucket fits in memory, we can join r and s at the cost of three I/Os per page of each relation: $3(F_r + F_s)$. First, r and s must be input and the resulting buckets output (2 I/Os per page). Then each bucket must be input to join the two parts of the bucket. This requires one additional scan for each relation (recall that we do not include the cost of dumping the final result of the join on disk). In our running example, the cost is 3300 page transfers, which is higher than the cost of block-nested loops but the asymptotic behavior of hash join is better. In fact, if each hash bucket produced at the first stage of the algorithm fits in main memory, the cost is linear in the size of **r** and **s**. This makes hash join the best among all of the methods considered so far. However, it is important to realize that hash-join heavily depends on the choice of hash function and can be easily subverted by an unfortunate data skew (what if all tuples are hashed into the same bucket?). In addition, hash joins can be used only for equi-joins and are inappropriate for more general join conditions, such as inequalities.

10.6 Multirelational Joins*

In Section 9.7, we discussed join indices and their use in computing joins. The algorithm for computing a join of the form $\mathbf{p} \bowtie_{A=B} \mathbf{q}$ works by scanning the join index and fetching the tuples whose rids are found in the index entries.

The actual computation is essentially similar to the indexed loop join, with **p** scanned in the outer loop, except that we use the join index to locate the tuples of **q** instead of a general-purpose index on attribute B of **q**. The advantage of the join index over other index types in this case is that it does not need to be searched: since all matching tuples are already associated with each other, the index can simply be scanned, the pairs or rids of the matching tuples fetched, and the tuples joined.

The idea underlying join indices can be extended to multirelational joins, where an index can be created to relate rids of more than two tuples. For instance, in a 3-way join, $\mathbf{p} \bowtie \mathbf{q} \bowtie \mathbf{r}$, a join index consists of triples of the form $\langle p, q, r \rangle$, where p is a rid of a tuple in relation **p**, q is a rid of a matching tuple in **q**, and r is a rid of a matching tuple in **r**. The triples are sorted in ascending order of rids beginning with the first column of the index, then the second, and then the third (the index can also be a B^+ tree).

With such an index, the join can be computed with a simple loop that scans the join index. For each triple $\langle p, q, r \rangle$ in the index, the tuples corresponding to the rids p, q, and r are fetched. Since the index is sorted on column 1 first, the join is performed in a single scan of the index and of the relation **p**. However, the relations **q** and **r** might have to be accessed many times. Indeed, if N is the average number of matching tuples in **q** per tuple in **p** and M is the average number of matching tuples in **r** per tuple in **p**, then, to compute the join, $|\mathbf{p}| \times N$ pages of **q** and $|\mathbf{p}| \times M$ pages of **r** might have to be retrieved.

Multiway join indices are especially popular for speeding up **star joins**—a common type of join used in online analytical processing.

A **star join** is a multiway join of the form $\mathbf{r} \bowtie_{cond_1} \mathbf{r}_1 \bowtie_{cond_2} \mathbf{r}_2 \bowtie_{cond_3} \cdots$, where each $cond_i$ is a join condition that involves the attributes of **r** and $\mathbf{r}_i$ only. In other words, there are no conditions that relate the tuples of $\mathbf{r}_i$ and $\mathbf{r}_j$ directly, and all matching is done through the tuples of **r**. An example of a star join is shown in

OPTIONAL

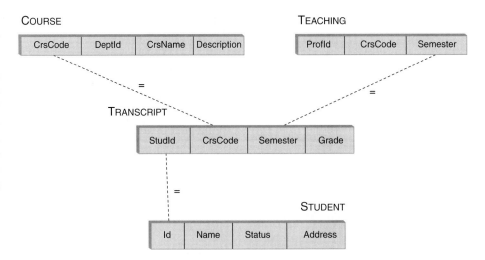

FIGURE 10.9 Star join.

Figure 10.9, where the "satellite" relations COURSE, TEACHING, and STUDENT are joined with the "star" relation TRANSCRIPT using equi-join conditions that match the attributes of the satellite relations only to the attributes of the star relation.

One reason that multiway join indices are good for computing star joins is that the join index of a star join is easier to maintain than the join index of a general multiway join (Exercise 10.14). Furthermore, computing a general multiway join using a join index can be expensive. Consider a join, $\mathbf{r} \bowtie \mathbf{r}_1 \bowtie \mathbf{r}_2 \bowtie \ldots \bowtie \mathbf{r}_n$, and suppose that N is the average number of matching tuples in $\mathbf{r}_i$ per tuple in $\mathbf{r}$. Then, using analysis similar to that for 3-way joins, a join index computation might need to access $|\mathbf{r}| \times N \times n$ pages.

Fortunately, star joins have more promising methods. One, described in [O'Neil and Graefe 1995], takes advantage of bitmapped join indices, introduced in Section 9.7.2. Instead of one join index that involves n relations, we can use one bitmapped join index, $\mathcal{I}_i$, for each partial join $\mathbf{r}_i \bowtie \mathbf{r}$. Each $\mathcal{I}_i$ is a collection of pairs $\langle v, bitmap \rangle$, where v is a rid of a tuple in $\mathbf{r}_i$ and $bitmap$ has 1 in the kth position if and only if the kth tuple in $\mathbf{r}$ joins with the $\mathbf{r}_i$'s tuple represented by v. We can then scan $\mathcal{I}_i$ and logically OR all of the bitmaps. This will give us the rids of all tuples in $\mathbf{r}$ that can join with *some* tuple in $\mathbf{r}_i$. After obtaining such an ORed bitmap for each satellite relation $\mathbf{r}_i$, where $i = 1, \ldots, n$, we can logically AND these bitmaps to obtain the rids of all tuples in $\mathbf{r}$ that join with some tuple in each $\mathbf{r}_i$. In other words, this procedure prunes away all tuples in $\mathbf{r}$ that *do not* participate in the star join. The rationale is that there will be only a small number of tuples left, so the join can be computed inexpensively by a brute-force technique like nested loops.

Join indices and star join optimization are supported by the recent versions of commercial DBMSs from the major vendors, such as IBM's DB/2, Oracle, and Microsoft's SQL Server.

10.7 Computing Aggregate Functions

Generally, computing aggregate functions (such as AVG or COUNT) in a query involves a complete scan of the query output. The only issue here is the computation of aggregates in the presence of the GROUP BY *attrs* statement. Once again, the problem reduces to finding efficient techniques for partitioning the tuples according to the values of certain attributes. We have identified three such techniques so far:

1. Sorting
2. Hashing
3. Indexing

All three techniques provide efficient ways to access the groups of tuples specified by the GROUP BY clause. All that remains is to apply the aggregate functions to the member tuples of these groups.

BIBLIOGRAPHIC NOTES

Sort-based evaluation techniques for relational operators are discussed in [Blasgen and Eswaran 1977]; hash-based techniques are covered in [DeWitt et al. 1984; Kitsuregawa et al. 1983]. Good surveys of techniques for evaluating relational operators and additional references can be found in [Graefe 1993; Chaudhuri 1998]. The use of join indices for computing multirelational joins is studied in [Valduriez 1987], and techniques for computing various relational operators with the help of bitmap indices are discussed in [O'Neil and Graefe 1995; O'Neil and Quass 1997].

EXERCISES

10.1 Consider the use of unclustered B^+ trees for external sorting. Let R denote the number of data records per disk block, and let F be the number of blocks in the data file. Estimate the cost of such a sorting procedure as a function of R and F. Compare this cost to merge-based external sorting. Consider the cases of $R = 1$, 10, and 100.

10.2 Estimate the cost of the sort-based projection assuming that, during the initial scan (where tuple components are deleted), the size of the original relation shrinks by the factor $\alpha < 1$.

10.3 Consider hash-based evaluation of the projection operator. Assume that all buckets are about the same size but do not fit in main memory. Let N be the size of the hash table measured in memory pages, F be the size of the original relation measured in pages, and $\alpha < 1$ be the reduction factor due to projection. Estimate the number of page transfers to and from the disk needed to compute the projection.

10.4 Give an example of an instance of the TRANSCRIPT relation (Figure 3.5) and a hash function on the attribute sequence ⟨StudId, Grade⟩ that sends two identical tuples in $\pi_{\text{StudId, Semester}}(\text{TRANSCRIPT})$ into *different* hash buckets. (This shows that such a hash-based access path cannot be used to compute the projection.)

10.5   Clearly, the theoretical minimum for the selectivity of an access path is the number of pages that hold the output of the relational operator involved. What is the best theoretical upper bound on the selectivity of an access path when selection or projection operators are involved?

10.6   Based on the discussion in Section 10.4.2, give a precise definition of when an access path covers the use of projection, union, and set-difference operators.

10.7   Consider the expression

$$\sigma_{\text{StudId}=666666666 \wedge \text{Semester}='F1995' \wedge \text{Grade}='A'}(\text{Transcript})$$

Suppose the following access paths are available:

- An unclustered hash index on StudId
- An unclustered hash index on Semester
- An unclustered hash index on Grade

Which of these access paths has the best selectivity, and which has the worst? Compare the selectivity of the worst access path (among the above three) to the selectivity of the file scan.

10.8   Compute the cost of $\mathbf{r} \bowtie_{A=B} \mathbf{s}$ using the following methods:

- Nested loops
- Block-nested loops
- Index-nested loops with a hash index on B in $\mathbf{s}$ (consider both clustered and unclustered index)

where $\mathbf{r}$ occupies 2000 pages, 20 tuples per page; $\mathbf{s}$ occupies 5000 pages, 5 tuples per page; and the amount of main memory available for a block-nested loops join is 402 pages. Assume that at most 5 tuples of $\mathbf{s}$ match each tuple in $\mathbf{r}$.

10.9   In sort-based union and difference algorithms, the final scan—where the actual union or difference is computed—can be performed at no cost in I/O because this step can be combined with the last merge step during sorting of the relations involved. Work out the details of this algorithm.

*10.10 In the sort-merge join of $\mathbf{r} \bowtie \mathbf{s}$, the scan in the algorithm of Figure 10.7 can be performed at no cost in I/O because it can be combined with the final merging step of sorting $\mathbf{r}$ and $\mathbf{s}$. Work out the details of such an algorithm.

10.11 Estimate the number of page transfers needed to compute $\mathbf{r} \bowtie_{A=B} \mathbf{s}$ using a sort-merge join, assuming the following:

- The size of $\mathbf{r}$ is 1000 pages, 10 tuples per page; the size of $\mathbf{s}$ is 500 pages, 20 tuples per page.
- The size of the main memory buffer for this join computation is 10 pages.
- The Cartesian product of matching tuples in $\mathbf{r}$ and $\mathbf{s}$ (see Figure 10.7) is computed using a block-nested loops join.
- r.A has 100 distinct values and s.B has 50 distinct values. These values are spread around the files more or less evenly, so the size of $\sigma_{A=c}(\mathbf{r})$, where $c \in$ r.A, does not vary much with c.

10.12 The methods for computing joins discussed in Section 10.5 all deal with equijoins. Discuss their applicability to the problem of computing inequality joins, such as $\mathbf{r} \bowtie_{A<B} \mathbf{s}$.

10.13 Consider a relation schema, $R(A, B)$, with the following characteristics:

- Total number of tuples: 1,000,000
- 10 tuples per page
- Attribute A is a candidate key; range is 1 to 1,000,000
- Clustered B^+ tree index of depth 4 on A
- Attribute B has 100,000 distinct values
- Hash index on B

Estimate the number of page transfers needed to evaluate each of the following queries for each of the proposed methods:

- $\sigma_{A<3000}$: sequential scan; index on A
- $\sigma_{A>3000 \wedge A<3200 \wedge B=5}$: index on A; index on B
- $\sigma_{A \neq 22 \wedge B \neq 66}$: sequential scan; index on A; index on B

10.14 Design an algorithm for incremental maintenance of a join index for a multiway star join.

10.15 Design a join algorithm that uses a join index. Define the notion of a *clustered* join index (there are three possibilities in the case of a binary join!) and consider the effect of clustering on the join algorithm.

11

An Overview of Query Optimization

This chapter is an overview of relational query optimization techniques typically used in database management systems. Our goal here is not to prepare you for a career as a DBMS implementor but rather to make you a better application designer or database administrator. Just as the knowledge of the evaluation techniques used in relational algebra can help you make better physical design, an understanding of the principles of query optimization can help you formulate SQL queries that stand a better chance of being efficiently implemented by the query processor.

Relational query optimization is a fascinating example of tackling a problem of immense computational complexity with relatively simple heuristic search algorithms. A more extensive treatment of the subject can be found in [Garcia-Molina et al. 2000].

11.1 Query Processing Architecture

When the user submits a query, it is first parsed by the DBMS, which verifies the syntax and type correctness of the query. Being a declarative language, SQL does not suggest concrete ways to evaluate its queries. Therefore, a parsed query has to be converted into a relational algebra expression, which can be evaluated directly using the algorithms presented in Chapter 10. A typical SQL query such as

SELECT	DISTINCT *TargetList*	
FROM	REL_1 $V_1, \ldots, REL_n$ V_n	**11.1**
WHERE	*Condition*	

is normally translated into the following relational algebraic expression:

$$\pi_{TargetList}(\sigma_{Condition'}(REL_1 \times \ldots \times REL_n))$$

where Condition' is Condition converted from SQL syntax to relational algebra form. Section 10.1 has an example of such a transformation from SQL to the relational algebra.

While the above algebraic expressions are straightforward and easy to produce, it might take ages to evaluate them. For one thing, they contain Cartesian products, so a join of four 100-block relations produces a 10^8-block intermediate relation, which, with a disk speed of 10 ms/page, takes about 50 hours just to write out. Even if we manage to convert the Cartesian product into equi-joins (as explained in Section 11.2), we might still have to grapple with the long turnaround time (dozens of minutes) for the above query. It is the job of the **query optimizer** to bring this time down to seconds (or, for very complex queries, a few minutes).

A typical **rule-based query optimizer** uses a set of rules (e.g., an access path based on an index is better than a table scan) to construct a **query execution plan**. A **cost-based query optimizer** estimates the cost of query plans based on statistics maintained by the DBMS and uses this information, in addition to the rules, to choose a plan. The two main components of a cost-based query optimizer are the **query execution plan generator** and the **plan cost estimator**. A query execution plan can be thought of as a relational expression with concrete evaluation methods (or *access paths*, as we called them in Chapter 10) attached to each occurrence of a relational operator in the expression. Thus, the main job of the optimizer is to propose a single plan that can evaluate the given relational expression at a "reasonably cheap" cost according to the cost estimator. This plan is then passed to the *query plan interpreter*, a software component directly responsible for query evaluation according to the given plan. The overall architecture of query processing is depicted in Figure 11.1.

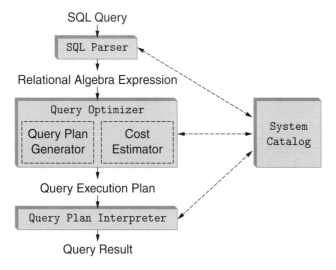

FIGURE 11.1 Typical architecture for DBMS query processing.

11.2 Heuristic Optimization Based on Algebraic Equivalences

The heuristics used in relational query evaluation are (for the most part) based on simple observations, such as that joining smaller relations is better than joining large ones, that performing an equi-join is better than computing a Cartesian product, and that computing several operations in just one relation scan is better than doing so in several scans. Most of these heuristics can be expressed in the form of relational algebra transformations, which take one expression and produce a different but equivalent expression. Not all transformations are optimizations by themselves. Sometimes they yield less efficient expressions. However, relational transformations are designed to work with other transformations to produce expressions that are better overall.

We now present a number of heuristic transformations used by the query optimizers.

Selection and projection-based transformations.

- $\sigma_{cond_1 \wedge cond_2}(\mathbf{R}) \equiv \sigma_{cond_1}(\sigma_{cond_2}(\mathbf{R}))$. This transformation is known as **cascading of selections**. It is not an optimization per se, but it is useful in conjunction with other transformations (see the discussion on page 408 of pushing selections and projections through joins).

- $\sigma_{cond_1}(\sigma_{cond_2}(\mathbf{R})) \equiv \sigma_{cond_2}(\sigma_{cond_1}(\mathbf{R}))$. This transformation is called **commutativity of selection**. Like cascading, it is useful in conjunction with other transformations.

- $\pi_{attr}(\mathbf{R}) \equiv \pi_{attr}(\pi_{attr'}(\mathbf{R}))$, if $attr \subseteq attr'$ and $attr'$ is a subset of the attributes of $\mathbf{R}$. This equivalence is known as **cascading of projections** and is used primarily with other transformations.

- $\pi_{attr}(\sigma_{cond}(\mathbf{R})) \equiv \sigma_{cond}(\pi_{attr}(\mathbf{R}))$, if $attr$ includes all attributes used in $cond$. This equivalence is known as the **commutativity of selection and projection**. It is usually used as a preparation step for pushing a selection or a projection through the join operator.

Cross product and join transformations. The transformations used for cross products and joins are the usual commutativity and associativity rules for these operators.

- $\mathbf{R} \bowtie \mathbf{S} \equiv \mathbf{S} \bowtie \mathbf{R}$
- $\mathbf{R} \bowtie (\mathbf{S} \bowtie \mathbf{T}) \equiv (\mathbf{R} \bowtie \mathbf{S}) \bowtie \mathbf{T}$
- $\mathbf{R} \times \mathbf{S} \equiv \mathbf{S} \times \mathbf{R}$
- $\mathbf{R} \times (\mathbf{S} \times \mathbf{T}) \equiv (\mathbf{R} \times \mathbf{S}) \times \mathbf{T}$

These rules can be useful in conjunction with the various nested loops evaluation strategies. As we saw in Chapter 10, it is generally better to scan the smaller relation in the outer loop, and the above rules can help maneuver the relations into the right positions. For instance, BIGGER $\bowtie$ SMALLER can be rewritten as SMALLER $\bowtie$ BIGGER, which intuitively corresponds to the query optimizer deciding to use SMALLER in the outer loop.

The commutativity and associativity rules (at least in the case of the join) can reduce the size of the intermediate relation in the computation of a multirelational join. For instance, $S \bowtie T$ can be much smaller than $R \bowtie S$, in which case the computation of $(S \bowtie T) \bowtie R$ might take fewer I/O operations than the computation of $(R \bowtie S) \bowtie T$. The associativity and commutativity rules can be used to transform the latter expression into the former.

In fact, the commutativity and associativity rules are largely responsible for the many alternative evaluation plans that might exist for the same query. A query that involves the join of N relations can have $T(N) \times N!$ query plans just to handle the join, where $T(N)$ is the number of different binary trees with N leaf nodes. ($N!$ is the number of permutations of N relations, and $T(N)$ is the number of ways a particular permutation can be parenthesized.) This number grows very rapidly and is huge even for very small N.[1] A similar result holds for other commutative and associative operations (e.g., union), but our main focus is on join because it is the most expensive operation to compute.

The job of the query optimizer is to estimate the cost of these plans (which can vary widely) and to choose one "good" plan. Because the number of plans is large, it can take longer to find a good plan than to evaluate the query by brute force. (It is faster to perform 10^6 I/Os than 15! in-memory operations.) To make query optimization practical, an optimizer typically looks at only a small subset of all possible plans, and its cost estimates are approximate at best. Therefore, query optimizers are very likely to miss the optimal plan and are actually designed only to find one that is "reasonable." In other words, the "optimization" in "query optimizer" should always be taken with a grain of salt since it does not adequately describe what is being done by that component of the DBMS architecture.

Pushing selections and projections through joins and Cartesian products.

- $\sigma_{cond}(R \times S) \equiv R \bowtie_{cond} S$. This rule is used when *cond* relates the attributes of both R and S. The basis for this heuristic is the belief that Cartesian products should never be materialized. Instead, selections must always be combined with Cartesian products and the techniques for computing joins should be used. By applying the selection condition as soon as a row of $R \times S$ is created, we can save one scan and avoid storing a large intermediate relation.

- $\sigma_{cond}(R \times S) \equiv \sigma_{cond}(R) \times S$, if the attributes used in *cond* all belong to R. This heuristic is based on the idea that if we absolutely must compute a Cartesian product, we should make the relations involved as small as possible. By pushing the selection down to R, we hope to reduce the size of R *before* it is used in the cross product.

---

[1] When $N = 4$, $T(4)$ is 5, and the number of all plans is 120. When $N = 5$, $T(5) = 14$, and the number of all plans is 1680.

- $\sigma_{cond}(\mathbf{R} \bowtie_{cond'} \mathbf{S}) \equiv \sigma_{cond}(\mathbf{R}) \bowtie_{cond'} \mathbf{S}$, if the attributes in *cond* all belong to $\mathbf{R}$. The rationale here is the same as for Cartesian products. Computing a join can be very expensive, and we must try to reduce the size of the relations involved. Note that if *cond* is a conjunction of comparison conditions, we can push each conjunct separately to either $\mathbf{R}$ or $\mathbf{S}$ as long as the attributes named in the conjunct belong to only one relation.

- $\pi_{attr}(\mathbf{R} \times \mathbf{S}) \equiv \pi_{attr}(\pi_{attr'}(\mathbf{R}) \times \mathbf{S})$, if $attributes(\mathbf{R}) \supseteq attr' \supseteq (attr \cap attributes(\mathbf{R}))$, where $attributes(\mathbf{R})$ denotes the set of all the attributes of $\mathbf{R}$. The rationale for this rule is that, by pushing the projection inside the Cartesian product, we reduce the size of one of its operands. In Chapter 10, we saw that the I/O complexity of the join operation (of which $\times$ is a special case) is proportional to the number of pages in the relations involved. Thus, by applying the projection early we might reduce the number of page transfers needed to evaluate the cross product.

- $\pi_{attr}(\mathbf{R} \bowtie_{cond} \mathbf{S}) \equiv \pi_{attr}(\pi_{attr'}(\mathbf{R}) \bowtie_{cond} \mathbf{S})$, if $attr' \subseteq attributes(\mathbf{R})$ is such that it contains all the attributes that $\mathbf{R}$ has in common with either *attr* or *cond*. The potential benefit here is the same as for the cross product. The important additional requirement is that *attr'* must include those attributes of $\mathbf{R}$ that are mentioned in *cond*. If some of these attributes are projected out, the expression $\pi_{attr'}(\mathbf{R}) \bowtie_{cond} \mathbf{S}$ will not be syntactically correct. This requirement is unnecessary in the case of the Cartesian product since no join condition is involved.

The rules for pushing selections and projections through joins and cross products are especially useful when combined with the rules for cascading σ and π. For instance, consider the expression $\sigma_{c_1 \wedge c_2 \wedge c_3}(\mathbf{R} \times \mathbf{S})$, where c_1 involves the attributes of both $\mathbf{R}$ and $\mathbf{S}$, c_2 involves only the attributes of $\mathbf{R}$, and c_3 involves only the attributes of $\mathbf{S}$. We can transform this expression into one that can be evaluated more efficiently by first cascading the selections, then pushing them down and finally eliminating the Cartesian product:

$$\sigma_{c_1 \wedge c_2 \wedge c_3}(\mathbf{R} \times \mathbf{S}) \equiv \sigma_{c_1}(\sigma_{c_2}(\sigma_{c_3}(\mathbf{R} \times \mathbf{S}))) \equiv \sigma_{c_1}(\sigma_{c_2}(\mathbf{R}) \times \sigma_{c_3}(\mathbf{S})) \equiv \sigma_{c_2}(\mathbf{R}) \bowtie_{c_1} \sigma_{c_3}(\mathbf{S})$$

We can optimize the expressions that involve projections in a similar way. Consider, for instance, $\pi_{attr}(\mathbf{R} \bowtie_{cond} \mathbf{S})$. Suppose that $attr_1$ is a subset of the attributes in $\mathbf{R}$ such that $attr_1 \supseteq attr \cap attributes(\mathbf{R})$ and such that $attr_1$ contains all the attributes in *cond*. Let $attr_2$ be a similar set for $\mathbf{S}$. Then

$$\pi_{attr}(\mathbf{R} \bowtie_{cond} \mathbf{S}) \equiv \pi_{attr}(\pi_{attr_1}(\mathbf{R} \bowtie_{cond} \mathbf{S})) \equiv \pi_{attr}(\pi_{attr_1}(\mathbf{R}) \bowtie_{cond} \mathbf{S})$$

$$\equiv \pi_{attr}(\pi_{attr_2}(\pi_{attr_1}(\mathbf{R}) \bowtie_{cond} \mathbf{S})) \equiv \pi_{attr}(\pi_{attr_1}(\mathbf{R}) \bowtie_{cond} \pi_{attr_2}(\mathbf{S}))$$

The resulting expression can be more efficient because it joins smaller relations.

Using the algebraic equivalence rules. Typically, the above algebraic rules are used to transform queries expressed in relational algebra into expressions that are believed to be better than the original. The word "better" here should not be understood literally because the criteria used to guide the transformation are heuristic. In fact, in the next section we will see that following through with all the suggested transformations might not yield the best result. Thus, the outcome of the algebraic transformation step should yield a set of candidate queries, which must then be further examined using cost-estimation techniques discussed in Section 11.3. Here is a typical heuristic algorithm for applying algebraic equivalences:

1. Use the cascading rule for selection to break up the conjunctions in selection conditions. The result is a single selection transformed into a sequence of selection operators, each of which can be applied separately.

2. The previous step leads to greater freedom in pushing selections through joins and Cartesian products. We can now use the rules for commutativity of selection and for pushing selections through joins to propagate the selections as far inside the query as possible.

3. Combine the Cartesian product operations with selections to form joins. As we saw in Chapter 10, there are efficient techniques for computing joins, but little can be done to improve the computation of a Cartesian product. Thus, converting these products into joins is a potential time and space saver.

4. Use the associativity rules for joins and Cartesian products to rearrange the order of join operations. The purpose here is to come up with the order that produces the smallest intermediate relations. (Note that the size of the intermediate relations directly contributes to overhead, so reducing these sizes speeds up query processing.) Techniques for the estimation of the size of intermediate relations are discussed in Section 11.3.

5. Use the rules for cascading projections and for pushing them into queries to propagate projections as far into the query as possible. This can potentially speed up the computation of joins by reducing the size of the operands.

6. Identify the operations that can be processed in the same pass to save time writing the intermediate results to disk. This technique is called *pipelining* and is illustrated in Section 11.3.

11.3 Estimating the Cost of a Query Execution Plan

As defined earlier, a query execution plan is more or less a relational expression with concrete evaluation methods (access paths) attached to each operation. In this section, we take a closer look at this concept and discuss ways to evaluate the cost of a plan to compute query results.

For discussion purposes, it is convenient to represent queries as trees. In a **query tree** each inner node is labeled with a relational operator and each leaf is labeled with a relation name. Unary relational operators have only one child; binary operators have two. Figure 11.2 presents four query trees corresponding to the following equivalent relational expressions, respectively:

$$\pi_{\text{Name}}(\sigma_{\text{DeptId='CS'} \wedge \text{Semester='F1994'}}(\text{PROFESSOR} \bowtie_{\text{Id=ProfId}} \text{TEACHING})) \quad \textbf{11.2}$$

$$\pi_{\text{Name}}(\sigma_{\text{DeptId='CS'}}(\text{PROFESSOR}) \bowtie_{\text{Id=ProfId}} \sigma_{\text{Semester='F1994'}}(\text{TEACHING})) \quad \textbf{11.3}$$

$$\pi_{\text{Name}}(\sigma_{\text{Semester='F1994'}}(\sigma_{\text{DeptId='CS'}}(\text{PROFESSOR}) \bowtie_{\text{Id=ProfId}} \text{TEACHING})) \quad \textbf{11.4}$$

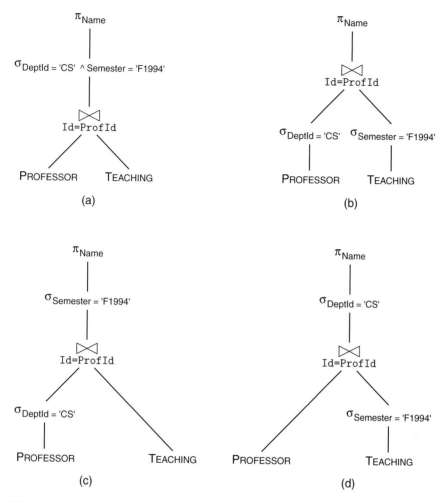

FIGURE 11.2 Query trees for relational expressions (11.2) through (11.5).

$$\pi_{\text{Name}}(\sigma_{\text{DeptId}='\text{CS}'}(\text{PROFESSOR} \bowtie_{\text{Id}=\text{ProfId}} \sigma_{\text{Semester}='\text{F1994}'}(\text{TEACHING}))) \quad \textbf{11.5}$$

The relations PROFESSOR and TEACHING were described in Figure 3.5, page 39.

Expression (11.2), corresponding to Figure 11.2(a), is what a query processor might initially generate from the SQL query (after combining the selection Id = ProfId with the cross product)

```
SELECT    P.Name
FROM      PROFESSOR P, TEACHING T
WHERE     P.Id = T.ProfId AND T.Semester = 'F1994'
          AND P.DeptId = 'CS'
```

11.6

The second expression, (11.3), corresponding to Figure 11.2(b), is obtained from the first by fully pushing the selections through the join, as suggested by the heuristic rules in the previous section. The third and fourth expressions, corresponding to Figure 11.2(c) and (d), are obtained from (11.2) by pushing only part of the selection condition down to the actual relations.

We are now going to augment these query trees with specific methods for computing joins, selections, and so on, and thus produce query execution plans. We will then estimate the cost of each plan and choose the best one.

Suppose that the following information is available on these relations in the system catalog:

PROFESSOR

> *Size*: 200 pages, 1000 records on professors in 50 departments (5 tuples/page).
>
> *Indices*: clustered 2-level B$^+$ tree on DeptId, hash index on Id.

TEACHING

> *Size*: 1000 pages, 10,000 teaching records for the period of 4 semesters (10 tuples/page).
>
> *Indices*: clustered 2-level B$^+$ tree index on Semester, hash index on ProfId

We need one additional piece of information before we can proceed: the weight of the attribute Id in the relation PROFESSOR and the weight of ProfId in the relation TEACHING. In general, the **weight** of an attribute, A, in a relation, **r**, is the average number of tuples that match the different values of attribute A. In other words, weight is the average number of tuples in $\sigma_{A=value}(\mathbf{r})$, where the average is taken over all values of A in **r**.

The weights for various attributes are typically derived from the statistical information stored in the system catalog and maintained by the DBMS. Recent query optimizers go as far as maintaining *histograms* for the distribution of values in a particular attribute. Histograms give more precise information about how many tuples are likely to be selected for a given value of the attribute. Attribute weights are needed to estimate the cost of computing the join using index-based techniques, as well as to estimate the size of the result of all of the operations in our examples. Since intermediate results of the various operations might later be used as input to other operators, knowing the sizes is important for estimating the cost of each concrete plan. Section 12.6 discusses statistics and size estimation in more detail.

Returning to our example, we first need to find realistic weights for the attributes Id and ProfId. For the Id attribute of PROFESSOR, the weight must be 1, since Id is a key. For the weight of ProfId in TEACHING, let us assume that each professor is likely to have been teaching the same number of courses. Since there are 1000 professors and 10,000 teaching records, the weight of ProfId must be about 10. Let us now consider the four cases in Figure 11.2. In all of them, we assume that a 52-page buffer is available for evaluating the join and that there is a small amount of additional memory to hold some index blocks and other auxiliary information (the exact amount will be specified when necessary).

Case a: selection not pushed. One possibility to evaluate the join is the index-nested loops method. For instance, we can use the smaller relation, PROFESSOR, in the outer loop. Since the indices on Id and ProfId are not clustered *and* because each tuple in PROFESSOR is likely to match some tuple in TEACHING (generally, every professor teaches something), the cost can be estimated as follows.

- *To scan the PROFESSOR relation*: 200 page transfers.

- *To find matching tuples in TEACHING*: We can use 50 pages of the buffer to hold the pages of the PROFESSOR relation. Since there are 5 PROFESSOR tuples in each such page, and since each tuple matches 10 TEACHING tuples, the 50-page chunk of the PROFESSOR relation can, on average, match $50 \times 5 \times 10 = 2500$ tuples of TEACHING. The index on the ProfId attribute of TEACHING is not clustered, so record Ids retrieved from it will not be sorted. As a result, the cost of fetching the matching rows of the data file (leaving aside for the moment the cost of fetching the Ids from the index), can be as much as 2500 page transfers. By sorting the record Ids of these matching tuples first, however (a technique described in Section 10.4.1), we can guarantee that the tuples will be fetched in no more than 1000 page transfers (the size of the TEACHING relation).[2] Since this trick must be performed four times (for each 50-page chunk of PROFESSOR), the total number of page transfers to fetch the matching tuples of TEACHING is 4000.

- *To search the index*: Since TEACHING has a hash index on ProfId, we can assume 1.2 I/Os per index search. For each ProfId, the search finds the bucket that contains the record Ids of all matching tuples (10 on average). These Ids can be retrieved in one I/O operation. Thus, the 10,000 matching record Ids of tuples in TEACHING can be retrieved 10 tuples per I/O—1000 I/Os in total. The total cost of the index search for all tuples is therefore 1200.

- *Combined cost*: $200 + 4000 + 1200 = 5400$ page transfers.

Alternatively, we can use a block-nested loops join or a sort-merge join. For a block-nested loops join that utilizes a 52-page buffer of main memory, the inner relation, TEACHING, must be scanned 4 times. This leads to a smaller number of page transfers: $200 + 4 \times 1000 = 4200$. Note, however, that if the weight of ProfId in TEACHING is lower, the comparison between the index-nested and block-nested techniques can be very different (Exercise 11.4) since the index may become more effective in reducing the number of I/Os.

The result of the join is going to have 10,000 tuples (because Id is a key for PROFESSOR and every PROFESSOR tuple matches roughly 10 TEACHING tuples). Since every PROFESSOR tuple is twice the size of a TEACHING tuple, the resulting file will be three times the size of TEACHING—3000 pages.

Next we need to apply the selection and the projection operators. As the result of the join does not have any indices, we choose the file scan access path. Moreover, we can apply selection and projection during the same scan. Examining each tuple

---

[2] Note that we need extra space for sorting the record Ids. Since we have rids for 2500 tuples and each rid is typically 8 bytes long, we need about five 4K pages to hold all these rids in main memory.

in turn, we discard it if it does not satisfy the selection condition; if it does, we discard the attributes not named in the SELECT clause and output the result.

We could treat the join phase and the select/project phase separately, outputting the result of the join to an intermediate file and then inputting the file to do the select/project, but there is a better way. By interleaving the two phases, we can eliminate the I/O operations associated with creating and accessing the intermediate file. With this technique, called **pipelining**, join and select/project operate as coroutines. The join phase is executed until the available buffers in memory are filled, and then select/project takes over, emptying the buffers and outputting the result. The join phase is then resumed, filling the buffers, and the process continues until select/project outputs the last tuple. In pipelining, the output of one relational operator is "piped" to the input of the next relational operator—without saving the intermediate result on disk.

The resulting query execution plan is depicted in Figure 11.3(a). All in all, using the block-nested loops strategy, evaluating this plan takes $4200 + \alpha \times 3000$ page I/Os, where 3000 is the size of the join (computed earlier) and α, a number between 0 and 1, is the reduction factor due to selection and projection. We study the techniques for estimating this reduction factor in Section 11.4. The last component, $\alpha \times 3000$, represents the cost of writing the query result out on disk. Since this cost is the same for all plans, (a) through (d), we will ignore it in our further analysis.

Case b: selection fully pushed. The query tree in Figure 11.2(b) suggests a number of alternative query execution plans. First, if we push selections down to the leaf nodes of the tree (the relations PROFESSOR and TEACHING), then we can compute the relations $\sigma_{\text{DeptId}='\text{CS}'}$ (PROFESSOR) and $\sigma_{\text{Semester}='\text{F1994}'}$ (TEACHING) using the existing B$^+$ tree indices on DeptId and Semester. However, the resulting relations will not have any indices (unless the DBMS decides that it is worth building them, which incurs additional cost). In particular, we cannot make use of the hash indices on PROFESSOR.Id and TEACHING.ProfId. Thus, we must use block-nested loops or sort-merge to compute the join. The projection is then applied to the result of the join on the fly, while it is being written out to disk. In other words, we again use pipelining to minimize the overhead of applying the projection operator.

We estimate the cost of the plan, depicted in Figure 11.3(b), where the join is performed using block-nested loops. Since there are 1000 professors in 50 departments, the weight of DeptId in the PROFESSOR relation is 20; hence, the size of $\sigma_{\text{DeptId}='\text{CS}'}$ (PROFESSOR) is about 20 tuples, or 4 pages. The weight of Semester in TEACHING is 10,000/4 = 2500 tuples, or 250 pages. Because the indices on DeptId and Semester are clustered, computing the selection will require the following I/Os: 4 (to access the two indices) + 4 (to access the qualifying tuples in PROFESSOR) + 250 (to access the qualifying tuples in TEACHING).

The results of the two selections do not need to be written out on disk. Instead, we can pipe $\sigma_{\text{DeptId}='\text{CS}'}$ (PROFESSOR) and $\sigma_{\text{Semester}='\text{F1994}'}$ (TEACHING) into the join operation, which is computed using block-nested loops. Since the first relation is only 4 pages long, we will keep it entirely in main memory. As we compute the second relation, we join the results with the 4-page $\sigma_{\text{DeptId}='\text{CS}'}$ (PROFESSOR) relation and pipe the result further into the operation π_{Name}. After the entire selection of

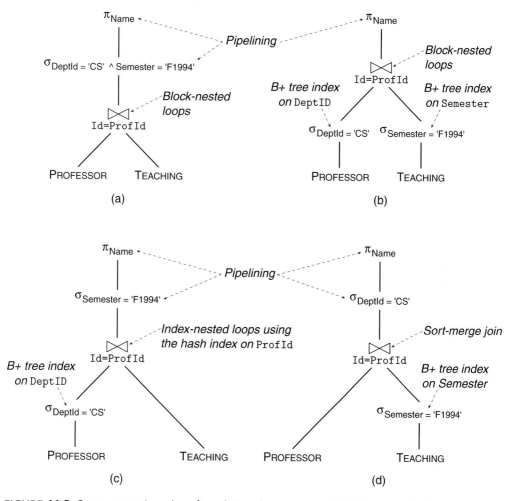

FIGURE 11.3 Query execution plans for relational expressions (11.2) through (11.5).

TEACHING is computed, the join will also be finished with no extra I/O. Thus, the total cost is $4 + 4 + 250 = 258$.

Note that if $\sigma_{\text{DeptId}='CS'}$ (PROFESSOR) were too big to fit in the buffer, then it would not be feasible to compute the join without writing $\sigma_{\text{Semester}='F1994'}$ (TEACHING) on disk. Indeed, scanning of $\sigma_{\text{DeptId}='CS'}$ (PROFESSOR) and the initial scan of $\sigma_{\text{Semester}='F1994'}$ (TEACHING) could still be done through pipelining but now $\sigma_{\text{Semester}='F1994'}$ (TEACHING) would have to be scanned multiple times, once for each chunk of $\sigma_{\text{DeptId}='CS'}$ (PROFESSOR). To enable this, $\sigma_{\text{Semester}='F1994'}$ (TEACHING) would have to be written out on disk after the first scan.

Case c: selection pushed to the PROFESSOR relation. For the query tree in Figure 11.2(c), a query execution plan can be constructed as follows. First, compute

$\sigma_{\text{DeptId}=\text{'CS'}}$ (PROFESSOR) using the B$^+$ tree index on PROFESSOR.DeptId. As in case b, this prevents us from further using the hash index on PROFESSOR.Id in the subsequent join computation. Unlike case b, however, the relation TEACHING remains untouched, so we can still use index-nested loops (utilizing the index on TEACHING.ProfId) to compute the join. Other possibilities are block-nested loops and sort-merge join. Finally, we can pipe the output of the join to the selection operator $\sigma_{\text{DeptId}=\text{'F1994'}}$ and apply the projection during the same scan.

The above query execution plan is depicted in Figure 11.3(c). We now estimate the cost of this plan.

- $\sigma_{\text{DeptId}=\text{'CS'}}$ (PROFESSOR). There are 50 departments and 1000 professors. Thus, the result of this selection will contain about 20 tuples, or 4 pages. Since the index on PROFESSOR.DeptId is clustered, retrieval of these tuples should take about 4 I/Os. Index search will take an additional 2 I/Os for a 2-level B$^+$ tree index. Because we intend to pipe the result of the selection into the join step that follows, there is no output cost.

- *Indexed-nested loops join.* We use the result of the previous selection and pipe it directly as input to the join. An important consideration here is that, because we chose index-nested loops utilizing the hash index on TEACHING.ProfId, the result of the selection does not need to be saved on disk even if this result is large. Once selection on PROFESSOR produces enough tuples to fill the buffers, we can immediately join these tuples with the matching TEACHING tuples, using the hash index, and output the joined rows. Then we can resume the selection and fill the buffers again.

  As before, each PROFESSOR tuple matches about 10 TEACHING tuples, which are going to be stored in one bucket. So, to find the matches for 20 tuples, we have to search the index 20 times at the cost of 1.2 I/Os per search. Another 200 I/Os are needed to actually fetch the matching tuples from disk since the index is unclustered. All in all, this should take $1.2 * 20 + 200 = 224$ I/Os.

- *Combined cost.* Since the result of the join is piped into the subsequent selection and projection, these latter operations do not cost anything in terms of I/O. Thus, the total cost is: $4 + 2 + 224 = 230$ I/Os.

Case d: selection pushed to the TEACHING relation. This case is similar to case c, except that selection is now applied to TEACHING rather than to PROFESSOR. Since the indices on TEACHING are lost after applying the selection, we cannot use this relation in the inner loop of the index-nested loops join. However, we can use it in the outer loop of the index-nested loops join that utilizes the hash index on PROFESSOR.Id in the inner loop. This join can also be computed using block-nested loops and sort-merge. For this example, we select sort-merge. The subsequent application of selection and projection to the result can be done using pipelining, as in earlier examples. The resulting query plan is depicted in Figure 11.3(d).

- *Join: the sorting stage.* The first step is to sort PROFESSOR on Id and $\sigma_{\text{Semester}=\text{'F1994'}}$ (TEACHING) on ProfId.

- To sort PROFESSOR, we must first scan it and create sorted runs. Since PROFESSOR fits in 200 blocks, there will be $\lceil 200/50 \rceil = 4$ sorted runs. Thus, creation of the 4 sorted runs and storing them back on disk takes $2 \times 200 = 400$ I/Os. These runs can then be merged in just one more pass, but we postpone this merge and combine it with the merging stage of the sort-merge join. (See below.)

- To sort $\sigma_{Semester='F1994'}$(TEACHING), we must first compute this relation. Since TEACHING holds information for about 4 semesters, the size of the selection is about $10{,}000/4 = 2500$ tuples. The index is clustered, so the tuples are stored consecutively in the file in 250 blocks. The cost of the selection is therefore about 252 I/O operations, which includes 2 I/O operations for searching the index.

   The result of the selection is not written to disk. Instead, each time the 50-page buffer in main memory is filled, it is immediately sorted to create a run and then written to disk. In this way we create $\lceil 250/50 \rceil = 5$ sorted runs. This takes 250 I/Os.

   The 5 sorted runs of $\sigma_{Semester='F1994'}$(TEACHING) can be merged in one pass. However, instead of doing this separately, we combine this step with the merging step of the join (and the merging step of sorting PROFESSOR, which was postponed earlier).

■ *Join: the merging stage.* Rather than merging the 4 sorted runs of PROFESSOR and the sorted runs of $\sigma_{Semester='F1994'}$(TEACHING) into two sorted relations, the runs are piped directly into the merge stage of the sort-merge join without writing the intermediate sorted results on disk. In this way, we combine the final merge steps in sorting these relations with the merge step of the join.

   The combined merge uses 4 input buffers for each of the sorted runs of PROFESSOR, 5 input buffers for each sorted run of $\sigma_{Semester='F1994'}$(TEACHING), and one output buffer for the result of the join. The tuple p with the lowest value of p.Id among the heads of the 4 PROFESSOR's runs is selected and matched against the tuple t with the lowest value of t.ProfId among the tuples in the head of the 5 runs corresponding to $\sigma_{Semester='F1994'}$(TEACHING). If p.Id=t.ProfId, t is removed from the corresponding run and the joined tuple is placed in the output buffer (we remove t and not p because the same PROFESSOR tuple can match several TEACHING tuples). If p.Id$<$ t.ProfId, p is discarded; otherwise, t is discarded. The process then repeats itself until all the input runs are exhausted.

   The combined merge can be done at a cost of reading the sorted runs of the two relations: 200 I/Os for the runs of PROFESSOR and 250 I/Os for $\sigma_{Semester='F1994'}$(TEACHING), respectively.

■ *The rest.* The result of the join is then piped directly to the subsequent selection (on DeptId) and projection (on Name) operators. Since no intermediate results are written to disk, the I/O cost of these stages is zero.

■ *Combined cost.* Summing up the costs of the individual operations, we get: $400 + 252 + 250 + 200 + 250 = 1352$.

And the winner is . . . . Tallying up the results, we can see that the best plan (among those considered—only a small portion of all possible plans) is plan (c) from Figure 11.3. The interesting observation here is that this plan is better than plan (b), even though plan (b) joins smaller relations (because the selections are fully pushed). The reason for this apparent paradox is the loss of an index when selection is pushed down to the TEACHING relation. This illustrates once again that the heuristic rules of Section 11.2 are just that—heuristics. While they are likely to lead to better query execution plans, they must be evaluated within a more general cost model.

11.4 Estimating the Size of the Output

The examples in Section 11.3 illustrate the importance of accurate estimates of the output size of various relational expressions. The result of one expression serves as input to the next, and the input size has a direct effect on the cost of the computation. To give a better idea of how such estimates can be done, we present a simple technique based on the assumption that all values have an equal chance of occurring in a relation.

The system catalog can contain the following set of statistics for each relation name **R**:

- *Blocks*(**R**). The number of blocks occupied by the instance of table **R**
- *Tuples*(**R**). The number of tuples in the instance of **R**
- *Values*(**R**.*A*). The number of distinct values of attribute *A* in the instance of **R**
- *MaxVal*(**R**.*A*). The maximum value of attribute *A* in the instance of **R**
- *MinVal*(**R**.*A*). The minimum value of attribute *A* in the instance of **R**.

Earlier we introduced the notion of attribute weight and used it to estimate sizes of selection and equi-join. We now define a more general notion, the *reduction factor*. Consider the following general query:

```
SELECT   TargetList
FROM     R₁ V₁, . . . , Rₙ Vₙ
WHERE    Condition
```

The **reduction factor** of this query is the ratio

$$\frac{Blocks(\text{the result set})}{Blocks(\mathbf{R}_1) \times \cdots \times Blocks(\mathbf{R}_n)}$$

At first, this definition seems cyclic: to find out the size of the result we need to know the reduction factor, but for this we need to know the size of the result set. However, the reduction factor can be *estimated* by induction on the query structure without knowing the size of the query result.

We assume that reduction factors associated with different parts of the query are independent of each other. Thus,

$$reduction(Query) = reduction(TargetList) \times reduction(Condition)$$

where *reduction(TargetList)* is the size reduction due to projection of rows on the attributes in the SELECT clause and *reduction(Condition)* is the size reduction due to the elimination of rows that do not satisfy *Condition*.

We also assume that if $Condition = Condition_1$ AND $Condition_2$ then

$$reduction(Condition) = reduction(Condition_1) \times reduction(Condition_2)$$

and if $Condition = Condition_1$ OR $Condition_2$, then

$$reduction(Condition) = min(1, \ reduction(Condition_1) + reduction(Condition_2))$$

Thus, the size reduction due to a complex condition can be estimated in terms of the size reduction due to the components of that condition.

It remains to estimate the reduction factors due to projection in the SELECT clause and due to atomic conditions in the WHERE clause. We ignore nested subqueries and aggregates in this discussion.

- $reduction(\mathbf{R}_i.A = value) = \frac{1}{Values(\mathbf{R}_i.A)}$, where $\mathbf{R}_i$ is a relation name and A is an attribute in $\mathbf{R}_i$. This estimate is based on the uniformity assumption—all values are equally probable.

- $reduction(\mathbf{R}_i.A = \mathbf{R}_j.B) = \frac{1}{\max(Values(\mathbf{R}_i.A), \ Values(\mathbf{R}_j.A))}$, where $\mathbf{R}_i$ and $\mathbf{R}_j$ are relations and A and B are attributes. Using the uniformity assumption, we can decompose $\mathbf{R}_i$ (respectively, $\mathbf{R}_j$) into subsets with the property that all elements of a subset have the same value of $\mathbf{R}_i.A$ (respectively, $\mathbf{R}_j.B$). If we assume that there are $N_{\mathbf{R}_i}$ tuples in $\mathbf{R}_i$ and $N_{\mathbf{R}_j}$ tuples in $\mathbf{R}_j$ and that every element of $\mathbf{R}_i$ matches an element of $\mathbf{R}_j$, then we can conclude that the number of tuples that satisfy the condition is $Values(\mathbf{R}_i.A) \times (N_{\mathbf{R}_i}/Values(\mathbf{R}_i.A)) \times (N_{\mathbf{R}_j}/Values(\mathbf{R}_j.B))$. In general, the reduction factor is calculated assuming (unrealistically) that each value in the smaller range always matches a value in the larger range. Assuming that $\mathbf{R}_i.A$ is the smaller range, and dividing this expression by $N_{\mathbf{R}_i} \times N_{\mathbf{R}_j}$, yields the above reduction factor.

- $reduction(\mathbf{R}_i.A > value) = \frac{MaxVal(\mathbf{R}_i.A) - value}{MaxVal(\mathbf{R}_i.A) - MinVal(\mathbf{R}_i.A)}$. The reduction factor for $\mathbf{R}_i.A < value$ is defined similarly. These estimates are also based on the assumption that all values are distributed uniformly.

- $reduction(TargetList) = \frac{\text{number-of-attributes}(TargetList)}{\Sigma_i \ \text{number-of-attributes}(\mathbf{R}_i)}$. Here, for simplicity, we assume that all attributes contribute equally to the tuple size.

The weight of an attribute, which we used in Section 11.3, can now be estimated using the notion of reduction factor:

$$weight(\mathbf{R}_i.A) \ = \ Tuples(\mathbf{R}_i) \times reduction(\mathbf{R}_i.A = value)$$

For instance, the reduction factor of the query PROFESSOR.DeptId = *value* is 1/50, since there are 50 departments. As the number of tuples in PROFESSOR is 1000, the weight of the attribute DeptId in PROFESSOR is 20.

11.5 Choosing a Plan

In Section 11.3 we looked at some query execution plans and showed how to estimate their cost. However, we did not discuss how to *produce* candidate plans. Unfortunately, the number of possible plans can be quite large, so we need an efficient way of choosing a relatively small, promising subset. We can then estimate the cost of each and choose the best. There are at least three major issues involved in this process:

1. Choosing a logical plan
2. Reducing the search space
3. Choosing a heuristic search algorithm

We discuss each of these issues in turn.

Choosing a logical plan.   We defined a query execution plan as a query tree with the relational implementation methods attached to each inner node. Thus, constructing such a plan involves two tasks: choosing a tree and choosing the implementation methods. Choosing the right tree is the more difficult job because of the number of trees involved, which, in turn, is caused by the fact that the binary associative and commutative operators, such as join, cross product, union, and the like, can be processed in so many different ways. We mentioned in Section 11.2 that the subtree of a query tree in which N relations are combined by such an operator can be formed in $T(N) \times N!$ ways. We want to deal with this kind of exponential complexity separately, so we first focus on **logical query execution plans**, which avoid the problem by grouping consecutive binary operators of the same kind into one node, as shown in Figure 11.4.

The different logical query execution plans are created from the "master plan" (as in Figure 11.2(a) on page 411) by pushing selections and projections down and by combining selections and Cartesian products into joins. Only a few of all possible logical plans are retained for further consideration. Typically, the ones selected are fully pushed trees (because they are expected to produce the smallest intermediate results) plus all the "nearly" fully pushed trees. The reason for the latter should be clear from the discussion and examples in Section 11.3: Pushing selection or projection down to a leaf node of a query tree might eliminate the option of using an index in the join computation.

According to this heuristic, the query tree in Figure 11.2(a) will not be selected since nothing has been pushed. The remaining trees include the one in Figure 11.3(c), which has the least estimated cost and which is superior to the fully pushed query plan in Figure 11.3(b). In this example, all joins are binary, so the transformation shown in Figure 11.4 does not pertain.

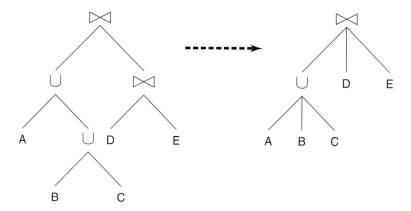

FIGURE 11.4 Transforming a query tree into a logical query execution plan.

Reducing the search space. Having selected candidate logical query execution plans, the query optimizer must decide how to evaluate the expressions that involve the commutative and associative operators. For instance, Figure 11.5 shows several alternative but equivalent ways of converting a commutative and associative node of a logical plan that combines multiple relations (a) into query trees (b), (c), and (d).

The space of all possible equivalent query (sub)trees that correspond to a node in a logical query plan is two-dimensional. First, we must choose the desired *shape* of the tree (by ignoring the labels on the nodes). For instance, the trees in Figure 11.5 have different shapes, with (d) being the simplest. Trees of such a shape are called **left-deep query trees**. A tree shape corresponds to a particular parenthesizing of a relational subexpression that involves an associative and commutative operator. Thus, the logical query execution plan in Figure 11.5(a) corresponds to the expression $A \bowtie B \bowtie C \bowtie D$, while the query trees (b), (c), and (d) correspond to the expressions $(A \bowtie B) \bowtie (C \bowtie D)$, $A \bowtie ((B \bowtie C) \bowtie D)$, and $((A \bowtie B) \bowtie C) \bowtie D$, respectively. A left-deep query tree always corresponds to an algebraic expression of the form $(\ldots ((E_{i_1} \bowtie E_{i_2}) \bowtie E_{i_3}) \bowtie \ldots) \bowtie E_{i_N}$.

Query optimizers usually settle on one particular shape for the query tree: left-deep. This is because, even with a fixed tree shape, query optimizers have plenty of work to do. Indeed, given the left-deep tree of Figure 11.5(d), there are still 4! possible ways to order the joins. For instance, $((B \bowtie D) \bowtie C) \bowtie A$ is another ordering of the join of Figure 11.5(d) that leads to a different left-deep query execution plan. So, if computing cost estimates for 4! query execution plans does not sound like a lot, think of what it would take to estimate the cost of 10! or 12! or 16! plans. Incidentally, all commercial query optimizers give up at around 16 joins.

Apart from the general need to reduce the search space, there is another good reason to choose left-deep trees over the trees of the form Figure 11.5(b): pipelining. For instance, in Figure 11.5(d) we can first compute $A \bowtie B$ and pipe the result to the next join with C. The result of this second join can also be piped up the tree

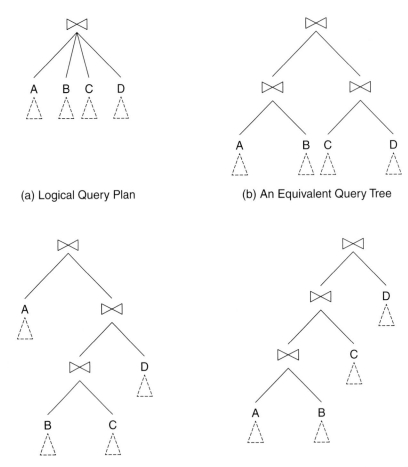

(a) Logical Query Plan   (b) An Equivalent Query Tree

(c) Another Equivalent Query Tree   (d) Yet Another Equivalent Tree: *Left-Deep Query Tree*

FIGURE 11.5 Logical plan and three equivalent query trees.

without materializing the intermediate relation on disk. The ability to do this is very important for large relations because the intermediate output from a join can be very large. For instance, if the size of the relations **A**, **B**, and **C** is 1000 pages, the intermediate relation can reach 10^9 pages just to shrink back to a few pages after joining with **D**. The overhead of storing such intermediate results on disk can be huge.

Note that the tree of Figure 11.5(b) does not lend itself to pipelining. For example, an attempt to pipe the result of $A \bowtie B$ and the result of $C \bowtie D$ to a module, M, that will join the two does not work. A row, t, of $A \bowtie B$ must be compared to every row of $C \bowtie D$ in order to compute the total join. That means that when t arrives, M must have received and stored all of $C \bowtie D$, which is exactly what we are trying to avoid. The alternative of storing one piece of $C \bowtie D$ at a time is unsatisfactory since

FIGURE 11.6 Heuristic search of the query execution plan space.

Input: *A logical plan $E_1 \bowtie \cdots \bowtie E_N$*
Output: *A "good" left-deep plan $(\ldots((E_{i_1} \bowtie E_{i_2}) \bowtie E_{i_3}) \bowtie \ldots) \bowtie E_{i_N}$*

1-Plans := all 1-relation plans
Best := all 1-relation plans with lowest cost
for $(i := 1; i < N; i++)$ **do**
    // *Below,* $\overset{\text{meth}}{\bowtie}$ *denotes join marked with an implementation method,* meth*
    Plans := { *best* $\overset{\text{meth}}{\bowtie}$ *1-plan* | *best* $\in$ Best; *1-plan* $\in$ 1-Plans, where
                                  1-plan is a plan for some E_j that has not
                                  been used so far in *best* }
        Best := { *plan* | *plan* $\in$ Plans, where *plan* has the lowest cost }
end
return Best;

---

it implies that t has to be re-sent to M each time a new piece arrives. Observe that the tree (c) in that figure is *equivalent* to a left-deep tree but is not one of them. This means that even though the query optimizer limits the search to left-deep trees, the search space actually covers a much larger domain, which includes all the trees that are equivalent to the left-deep ones.

A heuristic search algorithm. The choice of left-deep trees has reduced the size of the search space from immense to huge. Next we must assign relations to the leaf nodes of the left-deep tree. There are $N!$ such assignments, so estimating the cost of all is still a hopelessly intractable problem. Therefore, a heuristic search algorithm is needed to find a reasonable plan by looking at only a tiny portion of the overall search space. One such algorithm is based on *dynamic programming* and is used (with variations) in a number of commercial systems (e.g., DB2). We explain the main idea below; details are given in [Griffiths-Selinger et al. 1979]. A different heuristic search algorithm, described in [Wong and Youssefi 1976], is used in Ingres, another DBMS that was influential in the olden days.

A simplified version of the dynamic programming heuristic search algorithm is described in Figure 11.6. It builds a left-deep query tree by first evaluating the cost of all plans for computing each argument of an N-way join, $E_1 \bowtie \cdots \bowtie E_N$, where each E_j is a 1-relation expression. These are referred to as *1-relation plans*. Note that each E_j can have several such plans (due to different possible access paths; e.g., one might use a scan and another an index), so the number of 1-relation plans can be N or larger. The *best* among all these plans (i.e., those with lowest cost) are expanded into 2-relation plans, then 3-relation plans, etc., as follows. To expand a best 1-relation plan, p (for definiteness, assume that p is a plan for E_{i_1}) into a 2-relation plan, p is joined with every 1-relation plan, excluding the plans for E_{i_1} (because we already selected p as *the* plan for E_{i_1}). We then evaluate the cost of all such plans and retain the best 2-relation plans. Each best 2-relation plan, q (let us assume that it is a plan for $E_{i_1} \bowtie E_{i_2}$), is expanded into a set of 3-relation plans by joining q with every 1-relation plan, except the plans for E_{i_1} and E_{i_2} (since the latter are already accounted for in q). Again, only the lowest-cost plans are retained for the next stage. The process continues until a left-deep expression corresponding to the logical plan $E_1 \bowtie \cdots \bowtie E_N$ is fully constructed.

Example 11.5.1 (Choosing the Best Plan).   We illustrate the overall process using our running example, query (11.6). First, the query processor generates a number of plausible logical plans—in our case, most likely the fully pushed tree of Figure 11.2(b) on page 411 plus the two partially pushed trees (c) and (d).

The shape of the trees depicted in Figure 11.2 are left-deep, but there are two query execution plans corresponding to each such tree: they differ in the order of relations in the join. Let us consider the query execution plans generated using the algorithm of Figure 11.6 starting with the logical plan of Figure 11.2(c).

The 1-relation plans for $\sigma_{\text{DeptId}=\,'CS'}(\text{PROFESSOR})$ can use the following access paths: a scan, the clustered index on PROFESSOR.DeptId, or a binary search (because PROFESSOR is sorted on DeptId). The best plan uses the index, so it is retained. For the expression TEACHING, scan is all that can be done. We now have two 1-relation plans. In the next iteration, the algorithm expands the chosen 1-relation plans to 2-relation plans. This amounts to generating the two expressions $\sigma_{\text{DeptId}=\,'CS'}(\text{PROFESSOR}) \bowtie_{\text{Id}=\text{ProfId}} \text{TEACHING}$ and $\text{TEACHING} \bowtie_{\text{ProfId}=\text{Id}} \sigma_{\text{DeptId}=\,'CS'}(\text{PROFESSOR})$ and deciding on the evaluation strategy to use for the join in each. We estimated the different plans for the former expression in Section 11.3 and concluded that the index-nested loops join is the best. The second expression cannot be evaluated in the same way because the order of the arguments indicates that the relation TEACHING is scanned first. This expression can be evaluated using sort-merge or block-nested loops. Both methods are more expensive, so they are discarded.

Once the best plan for evaluating the join is selected, we can consider the result of the join as a 1-relation expression, E, and we now have to find a plan for $\pi_{\text{Name}}(\sigma_{\text{Semester}='F1994'}(E))$. Since the result of E is not sorted or indexed and since duplicate elimination is not requested, we choose a sequential scan access path to compute both selection and projection. Also, since E generates the result in main memory, we choose pipelining to avoid saving the intermediate result on disk. ∎

The dynamic programming algorithm is likely to miss some good plans because it focuses on what is best at the current moment without trying to look ahead. One improvement here is to retain not only the best plans but also certain "interesting" plans. A plan might be considered interesting if its output relation is sorted or if it has an index, even if the cost of the plan is not minimal. This heuristic recognizes the fact that a sorted relation can significantly reduce the cost of subsequent operations, such as sort-merge join, duplicate elimination, and grouping. Likewise, an indexed relation can reduce the cost of subsequent joins.

BIBLIOGRAPHIC NOTES

An extensive textbook treatment of query optimization can be found in [Garcia-Molina et al. 2000]. Heuristic search algorithms are described in [Griffiths-Selinger et al. 1979; Wong and Youssefi 1976].

For further reading on the latest query optimization techniques as well as additional references, see [Ioannidis 1996; Chaudhuri 1998].

EXERCISES

11.1   Is there a *commutativity* transformation for the projection operator? Explain.

11.2   Write down the sequence of steps needed to transform $\pi_A((\mathbf{R} \bowtie_{B=C} \mathbf{S}) \bowtie_{D=E} \mathbf{T})$ into $\pi_A((\pi_E(\mathbf{T}) \bowtie_{E=D} \pi_{ACD}(\mathbf{S})) \bowtie_{C=B} \mathbf{R})$. List the attributes that each of the schemas **R**, **S**, and **T** *must* have and the attributes that each (or some) of these schemas must *not* have in order for the above transformation to be correct.

11.3   Under what conditions can the expression $\pi_A((\mathbf{R} \bowtie_{cond_1} \mathbf{S}) \bowtie_{cond_2} \mathbf{T})$ be transformed into $\pi_A(\pi_B(\mathbf{R} \bowtie_{cond_1} \pi_C(\mathbf{S})) \bowtie_{cond_2} \pi_D(\mathbf{T}))$ using the heuristic rules given in Section 11.2?

11.4   Consider the join PROFESSOR $\bowtie_{Id=ProfId}$ TEACHING used in the running example of Section 11.3. Let us change the statistics slightly and assume that the number of distinct values for TEACHING.ProfId is 10,000 (which translates into lower weight for this attribute).

a. What is the cardinality of the PROFESSOR relation?

b. Let there be an unclustered hash index on ProfId and assume that, as before, 5 PROFESSOR tuples fit in one page, 10 TEACHING tuples fit in one page, and the cardinality of TEACHING is 10,000. Estimate the cost of computing the above join using index-nested loops and block-nested loops with a 51-page buffer.

11.5   Consider the following query:

```
SELECT DISTINCT E.Ename
FROM      EMPLOYEE E
WHERE     E.Title = 'Programmer' AND E.Dept = 'Production'
```

Assume that

- 10% of employees are programmers
- 5% of employees are programmers who work for the production department
- There are 10 departments
- The EMPLOYEE relation has 1000 pages with 10 tuples per page
- There is a 51-page buffer that can be used to process the query

Find the best query execution plan for each of the following cases:

a. The only index is on Title, and it is a clustered 2-level B$^+$ tree.

b. The only index is on the attribute sequence Dept, Title, Ename; it is clustered and has two levels.

c. The only index is on Dept, Ename, Title; it is a clustered 3-level B$^+$ tree.

d. There is an unclustered hash index on Dept and a 2-level clustered tree index on Ename.

11.6 Consider the following schema, where the keys are underlined:

> EMPLOYEE(SSN, Name, Dept)
> PROJECT(SSN, PID, Name, Budget)

The SSN attribute in PROJECT is the Id of the employee working on the project, and PID is the Id of the project. There can be several employees per project, but the functional dependency PID → Name, Budget holds (so the relation is not normalized). Consider the query

```
SELECT    P.Budget, P.Name, E.Name
FROM      EMPLOYEE E, PROJECT P
WHERE     E.SSN = P.SSN AND
          P.Budget > 99 AND
          E.Name = 'John'
ORDER BY P.Budget
```

Assume the following statistical information:

- 10,000 tuples in EMPLOYEE relation
- 20,000 tuples in PROJECT relation
- 40 tuples per page in each relation
- 10-page buffer
- 1000 different values for E.Name
- The domain of Budget consists of integers in the range of 1 to 100
- Indices
    - EMPLOYEE relation
        On Name: Unclustered, hash
        On SSN: Clustered, 3-level B$^+$ tree
    - PROJECT relation
        On SSN: Unclustered, hash
        On Budget: Clustered, 2-level B$^+$ tree

a. Draw the *fully pushed* query tree.

b. Find the "best" execution plan and the second-best plan. What is the cost of each? Explain how you arrived at your costs.

11.7 Consider the following schema, where the keys are underlined (different keys are underlined differently):

> PROFESSOR(Id, Name, Department)
> COURSE(CrsCode, Department, CrsName)
> TEACHING(ProfId, CrsCode, Semester)

Consider the following query:

```
SELECT   C.CrsName, P.Name
FROM     PROFESSOR P, TEACHING T, COURSE C
WHERE    T.Semester='F1995' AND P.Department='CS'
         AND P.Id = T.ProfId AND T.CrsCode=C.CrsCode
```

Assume the following statistical information:

- 1000 tuples with 10 tuples per page in PROFESSOR relation
- 20,000 tuples with 10 tuples per page in TEACHING relation
- 2000 tuples, 5 tuples per page, in COURSE
- 5-page buffer
- 50 different values for Department
- 200 different values for Semester
- Indices
    - PROFESSOR relation
        - On Department: Clustered, 2-level B$^+$ tree
        - On Id: Unclustered, hash
    - COURSE relation
        - On CrsCode: Sorted (no index)
        - On CrsName: Hash, unclustered
    - TEACHING relation
        - On ProfId: Clustered, 2-level B$^+$-tree
        - On Semester, CrsCode: Unclustered, 2-level B$^+$ tree

a. First, show the *unoptimized* relational algebra expression that corresponds to the above SQL query. Then *draw* the corresponding *fully pushed* query tree.

b. Find the best execution plan and its cost. Explain how you arrived at your costs.

11.8   Consider the following relations that represent part of a real estate database:

```
AGENT(Id, AgentName)
HOUSE(Address, OwnerId, AgentId)
AMENITY(Address, Feature)
```

The AGENT relation keeps information on real estate agents, the HOUSE relation has information on who is selling the house and the agent involved, and the AMENITY relation provides information on the features of each house. Each relation has its keys underlined. Consider the following query:

```
SELECT   H.OwnerId, A.AgentName
FROM     HOUSE H, AGENT A, AMENITY Y
WHERE    H.Address=Y.Address AND A.Id = H.AgentId
         AND Y.Feature = '5BR' AND H.AgentId = '007'
```

Assume that the buffer space available for this query has 5 pages and that the following statistics and indices are available:

- AMENITY
    10,000 records on 1000 houses, 5 records per page
    Clustered 2-level B$^+$ tree index on `Address`
    Unclustered hash index on `Feature`, 50 features
- AGENT
    200 agents with 10 tuples per page
    Unclustered hash index on `Id`
- HOUSE
    1000 houses with 4 records per page
    Unclustered hash index on `AgentId`
    Clustered 2-level B$^+$ tree index on `Address`

Answer the following questions (and explain how you arrived at your solutions).

a. Draw a fully pushed query tree corresponding to the above query.
b. Find the best query plan to evaluate the above query and estimate its cost.
c. Find the next-best plan and estimate its cost.

11.9 None of the query execution plans in Figure 11.3 for queries (11.2)–(11.5) does duplicate elimination. To account for this, let us add one more relational operator, δ, which denotes the operation of duplicate elimination. Modify the plans in Figure 11.3 by adding δ in appropriate places so as to minimize the cost of the computation. Estimate the cost of each new plan.

11.10 Build a database for the scenario in Exercise 11.5 using the DBMS of your choice. Use the EXPLAIN PLAN statement (or an equivalent provided by your DBMS) to compare the best plan that you found manually with the plan actually generated by the DBMS.

11.11 Follow Exercise 11.10, but use the scenario in Exercise 11.6.

11.12 Follow Exercise 11.10, but use the scenario in Exercise 11.7.

11.13 Consider the query execution plans in Figure 11.3. Show how each of these plans can be *enhanced* by pushing the projection operator past the join *without altering the strategies used for computing the join*.

11.14 Using the result of Exercise 11.13, show which of the enhanced plans can be further enhanced by adding the duplicate elimination operator δ introduced in Exercise 11.9.

12

Database Tuning

Tuning is the process of modifying an application and adjusting the parameters of the underlying DBMS to improve performance. Performance is measured in terms of the response time seen by a user (the time it takes to perform a task—for example, to execute an SQL statement) and throughput (the amount of work completed in a unit of time). It is important to realize that tuning does not affect the semantics of the system: the tuned and the original systems return the same information to the user and are left in the same final state when subjected to the same sequence of requests.

The first step in tuning a system is to determine where the bottlenecks are. If the system spends only 2% of its time executing a particular (hardware or software) module, then no matter how inefficient it is, revising or replacing it can improve performance by at most 2%.

An application and DBMS, taken together, form an exceedingly complicated system, and many different aspects of it are subject to tuning. The SQL code and schema are at the highest level. Tuning at this level is concerned with such issues as how queries should be expressed and what indices should be created. These are application-related questions and, since this is an "application-oriented" text, it is the level to which we pay the most attention. You might have wondered why the material in Chapters 10 and 11 was included in an application-oriented text since those chapters describe algorithms internal to the DBMS. The reason lies in this chapter. While Chapters 10 and 11 described a number of different techniques that a DBMS can use to process the SQL statements that your application submits, this chapter discusses methods that you can use to encourage the DBMS to use the technique that performs the best for the particular application you are implementing.

The DBMS occupies the next level. Examples of performance issues at this level are the physical placement of data on secondary storage and how the DBMS manages its buffers. Decisions in this area are largely under the control of the database administrator, and hence the application programmer can influence them indirectly. As a result we spend some time in this chapter discussing tuning at the DBMS level.

The lowest tuning level is the hardware level. In order to perform well the system must be supported by a sufficient amount of main memory, a sufficient number of

CPUs and secondary storage devices, and adequate communication facilities. The specification of these resources is generally beyond the control of the application programmer, and we do not discuss these issues.

12.1 Disk Caches

In Chapter 9 we discussed the huge difference between the speed of the CPU and the time to transfer a page between the CPU and mass store. In recognition of this, the cost of a query plan is measured as the estimated number of page transfers it incurs, and the job of the query optimizer is to find the plan that minimizes this number. While that plan is generally a good one, its cost is often still significant, and other measures are necessary to make query processing efficient. One of the most significant of these is the cache. A *cache* is a main memory buffer in the DBMS in which recently accessed database pages are stored. When a transaction accesses a database item, the DBMS brings the database page(s) on disk that contain that item into the cache and then copies the value of the item from the cache into the application's buffer. The page is generally retained in the cache under the assumption that there is a high probability that the application will either update the item or read another item in the same page at a later time. Or another application might concurrently reference an item in the page. In either case, a disk access will have been avoided since the page will be directly accessible in the cache. For example, an index page has a high probability of being accessed frequently.

Although it is natural to think of the database item as a page of a table or an index, it can also be the execution plan for an SQL statement or a stored procedure. In fact, some DBMSs maintain a separate **procedure cache** for this purpose. Although I/O cost is the major limitation on the performance of an application, the CPU cost of building an appropriate execution plan is also substantial. Hence, once an execution plan has been determined, it is saved since it might be possible to reuse it. Prior to preparing a new execution plan, existing plans are scanned to see if any are usable.

If a database item is to be updated, the database page containing the item must first be brought into the cache (if it is not already there), and it is the cache copy of the page that is modified (not the original copy in the database).

Eventually the cache becomes full, and any new page fetched from the database must overwrite a page, p, in the cache. If p has not been updated since arriving in the cache, its contents are identical to the corresponding page in the database, and hence it can simply be overwritten by the new page. However, if p has been updated since arriving in the cache, it must be written back to the database before the space it occupies in the cache can be freed. In order to distinguish between these two cases, the DBMS marks pages that have been updated as **dirty** and those that have not as **clean**.

Decisions concerning which pages should be kept in the cache and which can be overwritten when a new page is to be fetched are made by a **page replacement algorithm** whose goal is to maximize the number of database accesses that can be satisfied by pages in the cache. A least recently used (LRU) algorithm, for example, selects the least recently used page in the cache as the one to be replaced. It concludes that since no application has accessed the page recently it is no longer useful. Hence it tends to keep actively used pages in the cache.

A more sophisticated algorithm takes into account the circumstances under which a page was brought into the cache. For example, if the page was brought in as part of a table scan (which is typical, for example, when sorts are performed), once the rows in the page have been accessed it is not likely that the application will reference the page again. In this case a most recently used algorithm (MRU) is preferable. Hence a page replacement policy might use a combination of an LRU and an MRU algorithm depending on what information is contained in the page (index or data) and in what context the page is referenced.

If a transaction's access request can be satisfied from the cache, a **hit** is said to have taken place; if it cannot be satisfied, then a **miss** has occurred. To obtain a high throughput, many designers consider it mandatory to obtain a hit rate of over 90% (90% of the accesses can be satisfied from the cache). To achieve such a hit rate, the cache size must often be a significant percentage of the size of the database. Cache sizes in the megabyte range are normal. In some large applications, the cache size is measured in tens of gigabytes.

12.1.1 Tuning the Cache

Now that you have an understanding of how the cache works, the question is, "What can the application programmer or the database administrator do to optimize the way the DBMS uses the cache to improve the performance of her application?" DBMSs generally offer several mechanisms that can be invoked for this purpose.

■ Some DBMSs allow pieces to be carved out of the (default) cache to be managed as separate caches. The programmer can then bind a particular item (e.g., a table or an index) to a specific cache and in so doing cause all pages of that item to be buffered in that cache. For example, if tables T_1 and T_2 are bound to different caches, a page of T_1 can never overwrite a page of T_2. This approach might be useful if T_2 was not used very often but fast response time was required of the application that referenced it.

■ Some DBMSs allow a particular cache to be subdivided into several distinct pools of buffers of different sizes. For example, while by default all buffers in a cache might have 2K bytes, it might be possible to reallocate the cache storage area so that several buffer pools are created with sizes 2K, 4K, 8K, etc. If a table is bound to such a cache, the query optimizer then has the option of choosing the I/O size that best suits a query plan that accesses that table. For example, the page size on secondary storage might be 2K bytes, and the DBMS might allocate disk space to a table in contiguous blocks of eight pages. It then follows that the time to retrieve an eight-page block is not much larger than the time to retrieve a single page since the seek time is the same in both cases. If the query plan calls for a table scan, and the table is bound to a cache that has a 16K pool of buffers, the query optimizer can save time by retrieving eight pages with a single I/O operation.

Some query optimizers take this idea one step further by **prefetching** pages. Ordinarily, during the scan of a table or index, the next page is requested when the page fetched by the previous I/O operation has been scanned. The scan must then wait until the I/O operation for the next page completes. It is possible to improve on this in situations, such as scans, in which the optimizer can anticipate future requests. In such cases the optimizer can initiate the I/O operation for a page that has not yet been requested. Then, if the time to process a page is long enough, the next page will already be in the cache when it is requested.

By using both prefetching and a large I/O size, the time to do a table scan can be greatly reduced. This possible reduction has an impact on the query optimizer's choice between an access path that involves an index and an access path that uses a table scan for a particular query. It also raises the question of whether the application programmer should create an index for that query.

■ Some DBMSs provide commands that allow the page replacement policy for a cache to be specified. This is particularly useful when multiple caches are used. A policy appropriate to the items bound to the cache can then be chosen.

In addition to configuring a data cache to best suit the application, the programmer can design the application to make the best use possible of a procedure cache. For example, performance can be improved by not using explicit constants in SQL statements. The execution plan for the statement

```
SELECT   P.Name
FROM     PROFESSOR P
WHERE    P.DeptId = 'EE'
```

is essentially the same as the execution plan for the statement with the constant EE replaced by CS. But since the two statements are different, the DBMS might miss this fact when it scans the procedure cache looking for an execution plan, and as a result the DBMS might create a separate execution plan for each statement. It is possible to eliminate this overhead by instead using the statement

```
SELECT   P.Name
FROM     PROFESSOR P
WHERE    P.DeptId = :deptid
```

where deptid is a host variable (see Chapter 8), and successively assigning EE and CS to that variable. Since the same statement is now executed twice, the execution plan created when the statement is first executed will be reused when it is executed for the second time.

12.2 Tuning the Schema

The schema you design for your database is at the heart of the application. If the schema is well designed, it is possible to write SQL statements that perform efficiently. Your strategy in tuning at the application level is to first design a normalized database as described in Chapter 6 and then estimate the sizes of the tables, the distribution of column values, and the nature and frequency of the queries and updates that will be addressed to the database. Adjustments to the normalized schema to facilitate the most frequent operations follow from these estimates. Adding indices is the most important of these adjustments, and we discuss it first. Another technique is denormalization, which involves adding redundancy so that items of information that are generally associated with one another through frequently executed queries can be found in one place. Finally, we discuss partitioning, which is a rather specialized technique for dealing with very large tables.

12.2.1 Indices

In Chapter 11 we showed that different query plans for a particular query might have wildly different costs and that in many cases the differences were a function of the indices used in the plan. For better or worse, the choice of plan is made by the optimizer based on the indices available to it at the time the query is prepared. It is the role of the application programmer to "encourage" a good choice by making sure that appropriate indices have been created. In this section our goal is to expose the reasoning a programmer might use in deciding what indices to create.

Indices might seem like the ultimate database tuning device. However, free computational lunches are rare. Each index carries an associated storage overhead. More importantly, extra indices might significantly increase the processing time of statements that *modify* the database since every index must be updated whenever the table it references is changed. Thus, you should think twice before creating an index on a table where rows are frequently inserted or deleted. Similarly, you should think twice before creating an index with a search key involving a frequently updated column. Will the performance gain realized in processing queries be sufficient to compensate for the added cost of processing statements that modify the table? To illustrate some of the considerations involved in the tuning process, consider the following examples (which make use of the schema shown in Figure 3.4 on page 38).

1. Consider the query

   ```
   SELECT   P.DeptId
   FROM     PROFESSOR P
   WHERE    P.Name = :name
   ```

   Since the primary key of PROFESSOR is Id, we can expect that the DBMS has created a clustered index on that attribute. That index is no help for this query because we need a quick way to find all professors with a particular name. One possibility is to explicitly create an unclustered index on Name. Assuming that only a few professors have the same name, this index should speed things up. But suppose this is not the case: many professors have the same name. Then a better solution is to make the index on `Name` clustered and the index on `Id` unclustered. As a result, rows with the same name will be grouped together and can be retrieved in a single (or a few) I/O operations. The index could be a B^+ tree or a hash (since the condition on `Name` involves equality).

The lesson here is that since a table can have only one clustered index, it is pointless to waste it on an attribute that cannot take advantage of clustering. DBMSs generally create a clustered index on the primary key, but you should not be intimidated by this. An unclustered index on the primary-key attribute is sufficient to guarantee the key's uniqueness, and since at most one row can have a particular key value, clustering cannot be justified as a means of grouping rows with the same value of the attribute. So, if we are unlikely to want to order rows based on the primary key (as is the case with PROFESSOR), there is no reason to use a clustered index for this purpose.

Keep in mind that replacing one clustered index with another is a time-consuming operation since it implies a complete reorganization of the storage structure. You certainly do not want to create a new clustered index each time you execute a query. You should analyze your application in advance, considering the kinds of queries you expect and their frequency, create the clustered index that will do the most good, and stick with it until performance considerations indicate that the system needs a tune-up.

2. Consider the query

```
SELECT   T.Name, T.CrsCode
FROM     TRANSCRIPT T
WHERE    T.Grade = :grade
```

One is tempted to cluster the rows around `Grade` since we want to retrieve all rows with the same grade, but suppose that our first priority is to speed the response to a different query, a request for a class roster, and for that purpose we use a clustered index on the primary key ⟨`CrsCode`, `Semester`, `StudId`⟩. We could create an unclustered index on `Grade`, but using such an index might not be a good idea. In most cases the number of rows with a particular grade is a large fraction of the total number of rows (since the domain of `Grade` is small). In those cases we can expect that a large fraction of the table's pages will be fetched, one by one, in random order, through the unclustered index.[1] Unfortunately, the optimizer does not know what grade will be supplied at run time, and even if it did, it would not know which ones produced small result sets (we will correct this inadequacy shortly). Hence a table scan might be a better solution.

---

[1] If 10% of the rows are randomly fetched and each page contained 20 rows, then the probability that a particular page contains no rows in the result set is $(.9)^{20}$, which is approximately .12.

A number of lessons can be drawn from this example. First, an unclustered index is appropriate if only a few rows of a table are to be retrieved, and a full table scan is appropriate if a large fraction of the rows are to be retrieved. Determining a reasonable break-even point is not easy. One vendor states that a table scan is appropriate if more than 20% of the rows of the table are to be accessed. A more cautious approach would be to simulate the workload if more than a few rows are to be accessed to determine if building an index is a good idea. Second, do not create an index on a column with a small domain if attribute values tend to be evenly distributed over the domain. The query optimizer is *unlikely* to choose such an index since it will recognize that the selectivity of the access path through this index is large for any value of search key. Finally, do not create indices indiscriminately: they are costly to maintain, and, with the techniques described in Section 12.1, table scans can be quite fast.

3. Suppose that the most frequent access path to TRANSCRIPT selects rows based on a condition involving both StudId and CrsCode. A less frequently used path selects rows based on a condition on Semester. If we build one index on ⟨StudId,CrsCode⟩ (actually an index on the primary key ⟨StudId,CrsCode, Semester⟩ would work fine) and another on Semester, which should be clustered? At first glance, it might seem that the index on ⟨StudId,CrsCode⟩ should be clustered because it is the main access path. However, even though ⟨StudId, CrsCode⟩ is *not* a candidate key, the number of TRANSCRIPT rows that agree on both of these attributes will be one in almost all cases—only when a student retakes a course can this number be larger than one. Therefore, clustering around ⟨StudId, CrsCode⟩ will not yield significant benefits. Also, it is not likely that range queries will be asked against this pair of attributes, so the overhead of a B$^+$ tree index does not seem justified—a hash index is probably the best solution here. On the other hand, a clustered B$^+$ tree index on Semester can greatly improve the efficiency of selections and joins on that attribute and makes an excellent choice for a secondary access path.

   The lesson here is that clustering is useful to group together rows that might be output in a result set. These rows might be grouped because they all agree on the value of an attribute(s) or because they fall within a range of values of that attribute(s). In either case, when a choice has to be made as to what attribute to cluster on, you should make the choice based on the size of the result sets you expect in your application.

4. Assume the PROFESSOR table has the additional attribute Salary, and suppose we want to optimize the performance of the range query:

   ```
   SELECT   P.Name
   FROM     PROFESSOR P
   WHERE    P.Salary BETWEEN :lower AND :upper
   ```

   The analysis here is similar to that of example 1 with the exception that we now want a clustered index on Salary and it must be a B$^+$ tree.

5. If two different queries would benefit from two different clustered indices on the same table, we have a problem since only one clustered index is possible. One solution is to make it possible for the optimizer to use an **index-only strategy**. For example, suppose that TEACHING already has a clustered B$^+$ tree index on Semester, but another important query would benefit from a clustered index on ProfId in order to quickly access the course codes associated with a given professor. We can sidestep the problem by creating an *unclustered* B$^+$ tree index with search key ⟨ProfId, CrsCode⟩. Then all the information required by the query is contained in the index (and the index is often referred to as a **covering index**), and TEACHING does not have to be accessed at all! We simply search down the index using ProfId to the leaf level. Since the values of CrsCode at that level are clustered around ProfId, we can scan forward from that point at the leaf level of the index to get the required result set using only the index entries. This approach produces the same effect as that of a clustered index with search key ⟨ProfId, CrsCode⟩ on TEACHING (in fact, it is more efficient because the index is smaller and hence scanning a section of the leaf level requires fewer I/O operations than scanning a section of TEACHING).

    Index-only query processing comes in two varieties. In this example we searched the index using ProfId to quickly locate the associated course codes. Suppose, however, another query required that we find the ProfIds of all professors who had taught a particular course. Unfortunately, although all the information we need is in the index, it cannot be searched because CrsCode is not the first attribute of the search key. But all is not lost. Another way to produce the desired result set is to scan the entire leaf level of the index. This is not as efficient as a search, but it might be better than having to scan the entire data file (the index is smaller!) or create and use an unclustered index on CrsCode.

6. The ability to nest queries is one of the most powerful features of SQL. Unfortunately, however, nested queries are very difficult to optimize. Consider the query

```
SELECT   P.Name, C.CrsName
FROM     PROFESSOR P, COURSE C
WHERE    P.Department = 'CS' AND
         C.CrsCode IN
             (SELECT T.CrsCode
             FROM TEACHING T
             WHERE T.Semester = 'S2003' AND T.ProfId = P.Id)
```

that returns a set of rows in which the value of the first attribute is the name of a CS professor who has taught a course in the spring of 2003 and the value of the second is the name of one such course.

Typically, a query optimizer splits this query into two separate parts. The inner query is considered as an independently optimized unit. The outer query is also optimized independently (with the result set of the inner **SELECT** statement viewed as a database relation). In this case, the subquery is correlated, so it is crucial that it be executed efficiently since it will be executed many times. For example, a clustered index on TEACHING with search key ⟨ProfId, Semester⟩ would permit quick retrieval of all courses taught by a particular professor in a semester (and hopefully this is a small set). If possible (as in this example), the search key should involve all the attributes of the WHERE clause to avoid retrieving rows unnecessarily.

However, there is another point to note here. Because the two queries are optimized separately, certain alternatives might not be considered by the optimizer. For instance, the use of a clustered index on TEACHING with search key ⟨ProfId, CrsCode⟩ will not be considered since the correlated nested query simply produces a set of course codes for each value of P.Id that is supplied. On the other hand, it is easy to see that the above query is equivalent to

```
SELECT   C.CrsName, P.Name
FROM     PROFESSOR P, TEACHING T, COURSE C
WHERE    T.Semester='S2003' AND P.Department='CS'
         AND P.Id = T.ProfId AND T.CrsCode=C.CrsCode
```

and the use of that index *would be* considered in optimizing this query.

It should be remarked that some query optimizers do, in fact, try to eliminate nested subqueries and take other steps to reduce the cost of processing them. However, it is still a good idea to avoid query nesting whenever possible.

7. Consider the query

```
SELECT   T.Semester, COUNT(*)
FROM     TRANSCRIPT T
WHERE    T.Grade <= :grade
GROUP BY T.Semester
```

Our first inclination is to create a clustered B^+ tree on Grade since a range is indicated. Our intention is to influence the optimizer to first retrieve all rows satisfying the condition, sort them on Semester (which brings all the members of a group together), and then count the size of each group. But this is not necessarily a good idea. The condition is not selective, so we will have to sort a large intermediate table.

Suppose instead we reverse the order of operations: we do the sort before the selection. In fact, if we choose a clustered index on Semester, the table is sorted before the query is executed. Since the grouping is already done, all we have to do is scan the table and count all the qualifying rows in each group—clearly a better plan when the condition is not selective. Note that the index can be either a B$^+$ tree or a hash. In both cases the rows in a group will be together.

The lesson here is that an index is not simply an access path to data; it is a way of storing the data. In this example, the query plan does not actually use the index to find a particular row but simply takes advantage of the way the rows are stored.

8. Consider the query

```
SELECT   S.Name
FROM     STUDENT S, TRANSCRIPT T
WHERE    S.Id = T.StudId AND T.CrsCode = 'CS305'
```

If appropriate indices are not present, the optimizer might choose a block-nested loops join or a sort-merge join as the basis of a query plan. These choices are likely to be inefficient, since the size of the result set that we expect is considerably smaller than the size of the tables involved. As a general rule of thumb, you should investigate the possibility of an index-nested loops join when you expect a small result set, reserving other methods for large result sets.

So how can we encourage the optimizer to consider an index-nested approach? If we create a clustered index on TRANSCRIPT with search key CrsCode, the optimizer has a way of quickly finding, as part of the outer loop of the join, all students who have taken CS305. We can easily ensure that such an index exists since CrsCode is an attribute in the primary key of the table: all we have to do is make sure that it is declared as the first attribute of the key. The DBMS will generally oblige by creating a B$^+$ tree on the primary key.

For the inner loop of the join we need an index on STUDENT with search key Id. This is no problem at all since Id is the primary key. The DBMS will create an index, and we do not care whether it is clustered or unclustered, B$^+$ tree or hash, since Id is unique.

9. Consider the query

```
SELECT   Te.ProfId, Tr.StudId
FROM     TEACHING Te, TRANSCRIPT Tr
WHERE    Te.Semester = Tr.Semester AND Te.CrsCode = Tr.CrsCode
```

We expect the size of the result set to be much larger than the size of either table. Hence, a sort-merge algorithm is likely to be efficient in performing the join. We can make such an algorithm attractive to the optimizer by using clustered B$^+$ indices on the tables involved. For example, if such an index (with search key ⟨Semester, CrsCode⟩) is created on TRANSCRIPT, the relation will already be sorted on the join attributes and a significant part of the sorting step of the algorithm comes for free. Since these two attributes are a part of the primary key of the table, the DBMS has already created such an index—all we need to do is make sure that the ordering of primary-key attributes is ⟨Semester, CrsCode, StudId⟩.

10. Consider a database with two tables: PROJECTPART(ProjId, PartId), which relates a project to each part that it uses, and PARTSUPPLIER(PartId, SupplId), which relates a part to each supplier that sells that part. The query

---

```
SELECT   P.ProjId, S.SupplId
FROM     PROJECTPART P,  PARTSUPPLIER S
WHERE    P.PartId = S.PartId
```

---

produces a (ProjId, SupplId) pair for each project that uses a part that the supplier sells. An index-nested loops join could scan PROJECTPART and use an index with search key PartId on PARTSUPPLIER to find the rows of that table that match each scanned row. Encouraging the use of such an algorithm, however, is probably a bad idea since many rows of PARTSUPPLIER join with each row of PROJECTPART. Reversing the tables so that PARTSUPPLIER is scanned produces the same result. Hence a sort-merge or hash join might be less expensive. The lesson here is that it is not a good idea to create an index unless you are sure it is going to be of use. In this case it might lead to the wrong query plan and result in added overhead when the indexed table is updated.

Miscellaneous considerations. A foreign-key constraint can be essential in supporting the integrity of your database but introduces a hidden cost since it must be checked when certain modifications are made to the tables that it relates. Suppose such a constraint is declared on attribute $A1$ of table T1 referring to attribute $A2$ of table T2. When a row, $t1$, is inserted in T1, the DBMS must ensure that there is a row in T2 in which the value of $A2$ matches the value of $A1$ in $t1$. Fortunately, this is not a problem since $A2$ must be a key of T2 and hence there is an index with search key $A2$ that can be used to make the check quickly. Unfortunately, this approach does not work in reverse. If a row, $t2$, of T2 is deleted, the DBMS must check that there does not exist a row of T1 that refers to it. Since $A1$ is not a key of T1, T1 might not have an index with search key $A1$, and if not, a table scan will be required to check the foreign-key constraint. If T1 is large and rows of T2 are deleted or updated frequently, this table scan can be a significant source of overhead. In that case, an index on T1 with search key $A1$ should be created.

A common query is one that counts the rows in a table using COUNT. Such a query can result in a table scan if a proper index is not available. The table scan can be replaced by an index scan if the index is over a column that has a NOT NULL constraint because a row in which that attribute is null would not be indexed. The I/O cost of an index scan can be substantially less since the leaf level of the index can be packed into fewer pages than the table. Note that even if the DBMS has created statistics describing the table, the values will generally not be current and so cannot be used.

12.2.2 Denormalization

In Chapter 6, we learned a great deal about schema decomposition. That discussion was motivated by concerns that redundancy leads to consistency-maintenance problems in the presence of frequent database updates. What if most of the transactions are read-only queries? Schema decomposition seems to make query answering harder because associations between columns that existed in one relation before the decomposition might be broken into separate relations afterward.

For instance, finding the hobbies of the person with a particular SSN is more efficient using the monolithic relation of Figure 4.13 than the pair of relations of Figure 6.1 because the latter requires a join. This is an example of the classic time/space trade-off: the redundancy present in the monolithic relation improves query performance and argues against decomposing the relation. Such a trade-off has to be evaluated in a particular application if the performance of a frequently executed query is found wanting.

Denormalization refers to situations in which an attempt is made to improve performance of read-only queries by adding redundant information to a table. It reverses the normalization process and results in a violation of normal form conditions.

Denormalization often takes the form of adding a redundant column. For example, in order to print a class roster that lists student names, a join is required between the tables STUDENT and TRANSCRIPT. The join can be avoided by adding a Name column to TRANSCRIPT. In contrast to the previous example, STUDENT contains other information (e.g., Address), so denormalization does not eliminate the need to retain STUDENT.

As another example, a join involving the tables STUDENT and TRANSCRIPT is needed to produce a result set that associates a student's name with her cumulative grade point average. If the query is performed frequently, we might improve performance by adding a GPA column to the STUDENT table. Although prior to the modification the GPA was not stored in the database, redundancy has been added since the GPA can be computed from TRANSCRIPT. This is a particularly attractive example of denormalization because the additional storage requirements are nominal.

But do not get carried away with denormalization. In addition to the extra storage required, a price has to be paid to maintain consistency. In this case, every time a grade is changed or a new row added to TRANSCRIPT, GPA has to be updated. This might be done by the transaction doing the modification, adding to its complication and degrading its performance. A better alternative is to add a trigger that updates STUDENT when the modification takes place. Although the performance penalty is not avoided, complication is reduced and the possibility that transactions do not properly maintain consistency is avoided.

There is no general rule on when to denormalize. Here is an incomplete list of conflicting guidelines that need to be evaluated against each particular mix of transactions:

1. Normalization can lower the demand for storage space since it usually eliminates redundant data and null values. Tables and rows are smaller, reducing the

amount of I/O that must be performed and allowing more rows to fit into the cache.

2. Denormalization increases storage requirements since redundant data is added. When the degree of redundancy is low, however, normalization can also increase storage requirements. For instance, in the PERSON relation of (6.14) on page 228, suppose that most people have just one phone number and one child. In this case, schema decomposition actually increases storage requirements (since SSN must be repeated in each table) without bringing tangible benefits. The same applies to the decomposition of HASACCOUNT in Figure 6.7, which can increase the overhead for update transactions. The reason is that verification of the FD

```
ClientId OfficeId → AccountNumber
```

after an update requires a join because the attributes `ClientId` and `OfficeId` belong to different relations in the decomposition.

3. Normalization generally makes answering complex queries (for example, in OLAP systems) less efficient because joins must be performed during query evaluation.

4. Normalization can make answering simple queries (for example, in OLTP systems) more efficient because such queries often involve a small number of attributes that belong to the same relation. Since decomposed relations have fewer tuples, the tuples that need to be scanned during the evaluation of a simple query are likely to be fewer.

5. Normalization generally makes simple update transactions more efficient since it tends to reduce the number of indices per table.

6. Normalization might make complex update transactions (such as *Raise the salary of all professors who taught every course required for computer science majors*) less efficient since they might involve complex queries (and thus might require complex joins).

7. Normalization results in more tables, and hence more clustered indices, which translates into more flexibility when tuning queries.

12.2.3 Repeating Groups

In some situations the same information can be stored in either columns or rows, and the choice can be based on performance considerations. For example, suppose one wanted to store the total sales of each salesperson in each sales region of the country. One possible solution is to store the data for each salesperson in separate rows:

```
CREATE TABLE  SALES  (
     Id           INTEGER,
     Region       CHAR(6),
     TotalSales   DECIMAL )
```

The pair (Region, TotalSales) is referred to as a repeating group. Unfortunately, this requires retrieving multiple rows to access information about a single salesperson. Alternatively, the information describing a salesperson could be compacted into a single row. Assuming three regions, we could store the data using this table:

```
CREATE TABLE  SALES  (
     Id          INTEGER,
     Region1Sales  DECIMAL,
     Region2Sales  DECIMAL,
     Region3Sales  DECIMAL )
```

This schema has the limitation that only a fixed number of sales regions can be accommodated, but if it is generally the case that all of the information about a salesperson is retrieved at the same time, it might yield performance benefits.

12.2.4 Partitioning

The I/O cost of accessing a very large table can be reduced by explicitly splitting the table (in the schema) into partitions. One reason for doing this is to separate frequently accessed data in the table from data that is rarely referenced. By packing data that is frequently accessed into fewer pages, the number of I/O operations can be reduced and it is less likely that pages in the cache contain data that is not being referenced. A second reason is to make it possible to access different parts of the table concurrently, and we discuss this in Section 12.5.

With horizontal partitioning, all partitions have the same set of columns and each contains of a subset of the rows. The partitioning of the rows is based on a natural criterion that populates the partitions with disjoint subsets. For example, the table STUDENT might be partitioned into two partitions. Rows describing inactive students, those who have graduated, might be in a partition named ALUMNI. Rows describing active students, the current undergraduates, might be in a partition called CURRENT_STUDENTS. A page of CURRENT_STUDENTS in the cache is more likely to be referenced again than a page of ALUMNI since most references are to active students and a page of CURRENT_STUDENTS contains only those students. This reduces the number of I/O operations. Similarly, the cost of a scan to retrieve undergraduate information is greatly reduced.

With vertical partitioning, subsets of the columns of a table form the partitions. This can be useful when a table has many columns, and hence long rows, and some of the columns are infrequently referenced. Once again, without partitioning, performance is degraded by the need to transfer inactive data from the disk when active data is referenced. By storing the infrequently accessed columns in a separate partition, this problem can be alleviated. Oracle, for example, effectively separates infrequently accessed columns without requiring explicit partitioning. These columns are designated in the CREATE TABLE statement of a table that has an integrated, clustered index. In this case the infrequently accessed columns are not stored in the leaf level of the index but instead are stored in overflow pages linked to leaf pages. Scans involving only frequently accessed columns can skip the overflow pages.

An astute reader must have noticed that vertical partitioning is conceptually the same as schema decomposition, discussed in Chapter 6. In particular, partitions must form a lossless decomposition of the original relation, which can be ensured by, for example, including a key of the relation in all partitions. However, partitioning is typically driven not by the need to normalize the schema but by other considerations. For instance, if in a STUDENT table the attributes Address and Phone are accessed infrequently, they (and the student Id) might be separated into a different partition even though the STUDENT table is already in BCNF. With this secondary information split off, the main partition of the STUDENT table becomes smaller and thus queries involving this table run faster.

Partitioning involves a trade-off, and in this case the price that must be paid is the additional complexity of managing and accessing multiple tables. Hence, it should be used only when the performance benefits are clear.

12.3 Tuning the Data Manipulation Language

A modification of the schema of a particular table can have a global impact: it can affect (hopefully improve) the performance of all the SQL statements that access the table. A modification to a query or a statement of the DBMS has a local impact: it affects the performance of only that statement. There are many nuggets of wisdom that we could include here. We have chosen just a few based on what we think offers interesting insights into SQL and the way it is processed by a DBMS.

Avoid sorts.   Sorting is expensive and should be avoided if possible. You need to be aware of the kinds of queries that might cause an optimizer to introduce a sort into the query plan and avoid those queries if possible. In addition to the sort-merge join, duplicate elimination involves sorting. Hence, do not use DISTINCT unless it is important in the application. Set operators like UNION and EXCEPT also involve a sort to find duplicates, but their use may be unavoidable (however, some DBMSs provide the UNION ALL operator, which does not eliminate duplicates and hence does not involve a sort).

A sort is necessary to process an ORDER BY clause (so you should carefully consider whether an ordering on the output is necessary), and a GROUP BY clause will also frequently involve a sort. If sorting is unavoidable, consider presorting by using a clustered index (as in example 6 on page 436).

Do not scan unnecessarily.   Use of "not equals" in a WHERE condition is likely to result in a scan. For example, the optimizer might not use an index on CreditHours when evaluating the condition CreditHours ≠ 3. This is unfortunate since it is likely that the vast majority of courses carry three credits. Accessing the few that do not through an index would therefore be appropriate. If a histogram showing the distribution of values (see Section 12.6) were available to the optimizer, it might consider using the index if the condition were rewritten as CreditHours IN (1,2,4) or

```
CreditHours = 1 OR CreditHours = 2 OR CreditHours = 4
```

Similarly, a table scan will be used to resolve a condition of the form WHERE Name LIKE '%son' since a prefix of the search-key value is not provided.

An index on a column will not contain an entry for a row if the column value is null, so if you want to search for nulls you cannot use the index. A better way to handle the situation in that case is to use a default value (e.g., unknown) instead of null, and search for the default.

Minimize communication. Client/server communication is generally very expensive, so eliminate it where you can. A major culprit is the cursor, which invokes communication for every row fetched. Hence, if you are updating a table, try to use UPDATE statements instead of fetching the row, modifying it, and then writing it back. For example, an application might adjust the salary of employees based on the department in which they work. This might be done using a cursor in which the fetch is followed by a case statement with a branch for each department. The body of the branch for a particular department then makes the adjustment appropriate for that department. Alternatively, the application might use a sequence of UPDATE statements in which the WHERE clause of each statement in the sequence referred to a different department, and the SET clause performed the update appropriate to that department. The second approach involves far less communication, and this might compensate for any extra index searches or table scans.

If you are retrieving aggregate information, consider computing the aggregate in a stored procedure and then return only the result to the client. If you must analyze each row in the application code, see if your DBMS allows the fetch statement to retrieve multiple rows (some DBMSs support an array fetch).

Be careful with views. In Section 5.2.8 we discussed the fact that a query that names a view in its FROM clause is equivalent to a query with the view definition replacing the view name in the clause (and that it is the latter query that is analyzed by the DBMS). From this you can conclude that you are not going to get any performance gain by using a view since there is always an equivalent query that does not involve the view that will give exactly the same performance. This might seem like old news, but the really bad news is that the use of a view might actually impact performance negatively.

Consider the following view defined over the tables Course and Class of Section 4.8.

```
CREATE VIEW   Classes (C.CrsCode, C.DeptId, C.CrsName
                       CL.Enrollment, CL.MaxEnrollment) AS
```

```
SELECT    C.CrsCode, C.DeptId, C.CrsName,
                  CL.Enrollment, CL.MaxEnrollment
FROM      COURSE C, CLASS CL
WHERE     C.CrsCode = CL.CrsCode
```

The query

```
SELECT    C.CrsCode, C.CrsName
FROM      CLASSES
```

pays the price of a join, whereas the query

```
SELECT    C.CrsCode, C.CrsName
FROM      COURSE
```

achieves the same result without a join because the columns in the result set are all derived from the columns of a single base table.

Some optimizers, however, can recognize that a join is unnecessary and can eliminate the overhead.

Consider restructuring the query.   There are often several different ways to formulate a complex query. The cost of each formulation will depend on the state of the tables involved and the indices available, and there is no easy rule that you can use to decide which formulation is best. For example, we could express the query that returns the Ids of all professors who taught a course in the spring 2003 semester in the following three ways:

1.

```
SELECT    *
FROM      PROFESSOR P
WHERE EXISTS
              (SELECT *
               FROM TEACHING T
               WHERE T.Semester = 'S2003' AND T.ProfId = P.Id)
```

2.

```
SELECT    *
FROM      PROFESSOR P
WHERE     P.Id IN
              (SELECT T.ProfId
               FROM TEACHING T
               WHERE T.Semester = 'S2003')
```

3. _____

```
SELECT DISTINCT    P.Id, P.Name, P.DeptId
FROM      PROFESSOR P, TEACHING T
WHERE     P.Id = T.ProfId AND T.Semester = 'S2003'
```

The first formulation has a correlated subquery, so it looks bad. However, with an index on ⟨ProfId, Semester⟩, the subquery can be executed efficiently since only a few rows match the condition. In the second formulation, the subquery is only executed once so even if no usable index were available and a table scan were necessary, the cost might not be excessive. The cost of the third formulation is difficult to predict without knowing more about the state of the relations involved, and so would also have to be investigated.

Although a sort is generally unavoidable in the plan for a query with a GROUP BY clause, you should attempt to minimize its cost by making the relation to be sorted as small as possible. One way to do this is to strengthen the WHERE clause. For example, the query

```
SELECT    P.DeptId, MAX(P.Salary)
FROM      PROFESSOR P
GROUP BY P.DeptId
HAVING    P.DeptId IN('CS', 'EE', 'Math')
```

produces the same result as

```
SELECT    P.DeptId, MAX(P.Salary)
FROM      PROFESSOR P
WHERE     P.DeptId IN ('CS', 'EE', 'Math')
GROUP BY P.DeptId
```

but the second formulation has lower cost since nonparticipating rows are eliminated earlier.

12.4 Tools

DBMS vendors usually provide a variety of tools to help with tuning. The use of these tools normally requires creation of a mock-up database in which the different plans can be tried out. A typical tool in most DBMSs is the EXPLAIN PLAN statement, which lets the user see the query plans the DBMS generates. This statement is not part of the SQL standard, so the syntax varies among vendors. The basic idea is first to execute a statement of the form

```
EXPLAIN PLAN SET queryno=123 FOR
        SELECT    P.Name
```

```
FROM     PROFESSOR P, TEACHING T
WHERE    P.Id = T.ProfId AND T.Semester = 'F1994'
         AND T.Semester = 'CS'
```

which causes the DBMS to generate a query execution plan and store it as a set of tuples in a relation called PLAN_TABLE. queryno is one attribute of that table. Some DBMSs use a different attribute name, for example, id. The plan can then be retrieved by querying PLAN_TABLE as follows:

```
SELECT * FROM PLAN_TABLE WHERE queryno=123
```

Text-based facilities for examining query plans are extremely powerful, but these days they are used mostly by people who enjoy fixing their own cars. A busy database administrator uses text-based facilities only as a last resort because many vendors provide flashy graphical interfaces to their tuning tools. For instance, IBM has Visual Explain for DB/2, Oracle supplies Oracle Diagnostics Pack, and SQL Server from Microsoft has Query Analyzer. These tools not only show query plans, but they can also suggest indices that can speed up various queries.

By examining the query plan, you are in a position to determine whether or not the DBMS has chosen to ignore the hints you have provided (see page 450) and the indices you have so carefully created. If you are dissatisfied, you can try other strategies. More importantly, many DBMSs provide trace tools that allow you to trace the execution of a query as well as output the CPU and I/O resources used and the number of rows processed by each step. With a trace tool available, your strategy should be to coax the DBMS into using a variety of query plans and to evaluate the performance of each.

12.5 Managing Physical Resources

The physical resources—CPUs, I/O devices, etc.—available to the DBMS are an important factor in the performance of an application, but the application programmer is generally not in a position to control these resources. Some DBMSs, however, provide the programmer or database administrator, with mechanisms for controlling how the existing physical resources should be used.

A disk unit has a single doorway through which each read or write request for a table or index must pass in sequence. Hence, if many heavily used items are placed on the disk, a queue of waiting requests will form and response time will suffer. The lesson here is that many small disks can perform better than a single large disk because items can be spread across the disks and I/O can be performed concurrently on different disks. The discussion of RAID (Section 9.1.1) has already made this point. Since the assignment of items to disks can have a major impact on performance, DBMSs provide mechanisms that allow the user to specify the disk on which a particular item is placed.

In addition to spreading *different* tables across the available disks, concurrent access to a *single* table can be achieved by partitioning it and distributing the partitions on different disks. For example, the STUDENT table might be split into FRESH_STUDENT, SOPH_STUDENTS, JUN_STUDENTS, and SEN_STUDENTS. Note that in this case all partitions contain rows that are frequently referenced. If the partitions are placed on different disks, performance can be improved since multiple I/O requests for information about students can be performed concurrently.

Beyond distributing files across disks, the next point to note is that reading a file sequentially (e.g., a table scan) is generally more efficient than reading data randomly. This follows from the fact that DBMSs attempt to keep the pages of a file together, and as a result the seek time between the reads of two successive pages can be eliminated. But it is not so easy to take advantage of sequential I/O since, in general, a disk will store multiple files. Since requests for the files from different processes will be interleaved, the disk assembly will move from one cylinder to another. Thus, even though a process accesses a file sequentially, two successive requests from the process will pay a seek price since requests from other processes will be interleaved between them. Note that this is true even if *all* files on the disk are accessed sequentially. The lesson here is that if you want to take advantage of the fact that a file is accessed sequentially, place it on its own private disk. A good example of such a file is the log file maintained by a database system to implement atomicity.

In addition to influencing the way I/O devices are employed in an application, the programmer can influence the way CPUs are used. Generally, a single process (or thread) is assigned to execute the query plan for a particular SQL statement. Processes are sequential—they do one thing at a time. Either they require the services of a CPU to execute some code or they request an I/O transfer and wait until the operation completes. Hence, they make use of one physical device at a time. As a result, in an OLAP environment with only a few concurrent users, throughput may suffer because resource utilization is low. In an OLTP environment with many concurrent users, resource utilization will be high, but the response time possible when only a single process is assigned to execute a query plan can be unacceptable.

The response time of a query can often be improved using **parallel query processing** in which multiple concurrent processes are assigned to execute different components of the query plan. Improvement is likely when the system has multiple CPUs (so the processes can execute simultaneously), the query plan involves table scans, the query accesses very large tables (so considerable I/O is required), and the data is spread across multiple disks (so the processes can be using the disks simultaneously). DBMSs provide mechanisms, called *hints* (discussed on page 450), that the application programmer can use to request parallel query processing.

12.6 Influencing the Optimizer

In Chapters 10 and 11 we discussed algorithms used by the DBMS to create an efficient query execution plan. The plan selected depends on first identifying promising alternatives and then choosing from among those alternatives the plan that seems best. The application programmer is in a position to affect this process in two ways: he can modify the schema—primarily by creating appropriate indices—to create new alternatives that the DBMS might find promising, and he can influence the choice among the alternatives. We discussed schema modification earlier. In this section we will discuss mechanisms for influencing choice.

Statistics. In Section 11.1 we discussed the fact that cost-based query optimizers use statistics to predict the size of the output produced by various relational expressions in order to estimate the cost of a query plan. These statistics describe not only tables but the indices that can be used to access the tables (for example, the depth, number of leaf pages, number of distinct search-key values at the leaf level, etc.). Optimizers that use this information are referred to as **cost-based optimizers**. They contrast with **rule-based optimizers** that make decisions using rules based on the structure of the SQL statement and the availability of indices but do not attempt to evaluate the costs involved. The trend in DBMS design is toward cost-based optimization.

If some statistics are good, more statistics might be even better. Additional statistics take the form of histograms describing the distribution of values in particular columns. Advanced query optimizers can make use of such information in certain cases. For example, an employee table might have an integer-valued column Children that gives the number of children of each employee. Without a histogram the optimizer might be able to determine from the available statistics that the maximum value in the column is 9 and that there are 10,000 rows in the table. It can then conclude that on average, for each value between 0 and 9 there are 1000 employees with that many children. As a result, a query whose result set contains the rows satisfying the WHERE condition E.Children = 9 might use a table scan for the access path rather than an unclustered index on Children. (For example, if there were 500 pages in the table then it is likely that at least one row describing a fertile employee is contained in most pages.)

With a histogram the optimizer can do much better. Since the histogram contains the number of rows having each column value, the optimizer is in a position to determine that only two employees have nine children and, as a result, an access path that uses the index on Children is far superior to a table scan.

Maintaining a histogram is a time-consuming process. Hence, DBMSs that make use of histograms provide the programmer with a mechanism to specify the columns over which histograms are to be constructed.

If you have been reading carefully, you probably have noticed that we are describing an approach here that contradicts what was said in Section 12.1. There we argued that it was desirable to use host variables instead of literals so that query plans could be reused. Here we have made the point that literals are preferable since they allow the optimizer to use histograms. The choice of which to use has to be made for each specific application.

Care and feeding. Although a system might function efficiently when it is initially configured, you might discover that, over time, performance degrades even though the load is unchanged. This might be due to changes in the state of the database. Even though the size of tables might remain roughly the same, as rows are added and deleted the organization of the tables and indices might deteriorate. For example, although the pages of a B$^+$ tree might initially be full, the steady state situation might be one in which the occupancy of pages might be low. Although this might not cause the tree to be deeper, it might substantially increase the number of leaf pages, and hence the cost of scans at the leaf level. Similarly, the space created by deleted rows in a heap file is often not recovered since rows are added at the end. As a result, the cost of table scans is increased. Each DBMS has its own quirks in the way it stores information that may result in similar inefficiencies. Check your manual.

Maintaining statistics is time consuming, and hence statistics are not normally updated each time the value of a table changes. Instead, the DBMS supports a command that causes it to reevaluate statistics. It can be invoked by the programmer at a time when the state of the table has substantially changed since the last time the statistics were evaluated. The use of outdated statistics can lead to poor query plans. Furthermore, since the query plans of stored procedures might be saved, stored procedures that access dynamically changing tables should be recompiled frequently. Similarly, if indices of tables referred to by a stored procedure change, the procedure should be recompiled.

Hints. Some DBMSs allow the programmer to insert suggestions, called **hints**, into an SQL statement that the query optimizer can use in constructing a query plan. For example, we saw in Chapter 11 that there are $N!$ different orders in which N tables can be joined, and that the optimizer cannot explore all possibilities even when N is small. A major problem in joining tables is the I/O and storage costs of manipulating large intermediate tables. The wrong order can result in huge intermediate tables, which are reduced to just a few rows in the final step. Promising orders are those in which the first table to be joined is one in which the WHERE clause includes a selective condition that eliminates many rows that cannot possibly play a role in forming a row in the result set. Eliminating such rows early prevents them from producing useless rows at intermediate stages.

Unfortunately, it might be difficult for the optimizer to detect that a condition is selective. For example, although a condition such as T.Model = 'Rolls Royce' on a table containing the inventory of Slippery Joe's Used Cars might be very selective, the optimizer might have no way of knowing that. Even if a histogram were maintained on the attributes of the table, the optimizer would be stymied if 'Rolls Royce' were replaced by a host variable :model. Although the optimizer might not have enough information, the programmer probably does. He can list the tables in the FROM clause in the desired join order and provide a hint to the effect that the optimizer should use that order in the query plan.

Hints can cover many issues. For example, different databases allow you to specify the join methodology to use (hash, sort-merge, etc.), the index to use, whether parallel query execution should be considered, and whether to optimize a query plan so that it retrieves the first row of a result set quickly (for fast response time for an interactive query) or whether it should minimize the time for retrieving the entire result set (for batch queries).

BIBLIOGRAPHIC NOTES

A complete discussion of the principles and practices involved in tuning a DBMS (which is not specialized to any particular product) can be found in the book by [Shasha and Bonnet 2003]. The trade books and product manuals describing the measures taken in particular systems are also very informative: for SQL Server [Whalen et al 2001], for Oracle [Harrison 2001], for Sybase [Sybase 1999].

EXERCISES

12.1 Choose an index for each of the following SELECT statements. Specify whether your choice is clustered or unclustered and whether it is a hash index or a B+ tree.

a. _____

```
SELECT   S.Name
FROM     STUDENT S
WHERE    S.Id = '111111111'
```

b. _____

```
SELECT   S.Name
FROM     STUDENT S
WHERE    S.Status = 'Freshman'
```

c. _____

```
SELECT   T.StudId
FROM     TRANSCRIPT T
WHERE    T.Grade = 'B' AND T.CrsCode = 'CS305'
```

d. _____

```
SELECT   P.Name
FROM     PROFESSOR P
WHERE    P.Salary BETWEEN 20000 AND 150000
```

e. _____

```
SELECT   T.ProfId
FROM     TEACHING T
WHERE    T.CrsCode LIKE 'CS' AND T.Semester = 'F2000'
```

f. _____

```
SELECT   C.CrsName
FROM     COURSE C, TEACHING T
WHERE    C.CrsCode = T.CrsCode AND T.Semester = 'F2002'
```

12.2 Suppose both queries (e) and (f) from the previous exercise need to be supported. What indices should be chosen for TEACHING and COURSE?

12.3   The table FACULTY has 60,000 rows, each row occupies 100 bytes, and the database page size is 4^k bytes. Assuming pages in the index and data files are 100% occupied, estimate the number of page transfers required for the following SELECT statement in each of the cases listed below.

```
SELECT   F.DeptId
FROM     FACULTY F
WHERE    F.Id = '111111111'
```

a. The table has no index.
b. The table has a clustered B$^+$ tree index on Id. Assume a (nonleaf) index entry has 20 characters.
c. The table has an unclustered B$^+$ tree index on Id. Assume a (nonleaf) index entry has 20 characters.
d. The table has an unclustered B$^+$ tree index on (Id, DeptId). Assume that an index entry now has 25 characters.
e. The table has an unclustered B$^+$ tree index on (DeptId, Id). Assume that an index entry now has 25 characters.

12.4   The table FACULTY has 60,000 rows, each row occupies 100 bytes, and the database page size is 4^k bytes. The table contains an attribute City, indicating the city in which a professor lives, there are 50 cities with names city10 ... city50, and professors are randomly distributed over the cities. Assuming that pages in the index and data files are 100% occupied, estimate the number of page transfers required for the following SELECT statement in each of the cases listed below.

```
SELECT   F.Id
FROM     FACULTY F
WHERE    F.City > 'city10' AND F.City < 'city21'
```

a. The table has no index.
b. The table has a clustered B$^+$ tree index on City. Assume a (nonleaf) index entry has 25 characters.
c. The table has an unclustered B$^+$ tree index on City. Assume an index entry has 25 characters.
d. The table has an unclustered B$^+$ tree index on (City, Id). Assume an index entry has 40 characters.
e. The table has an unclustered B$^+$ tree index on (Id, City). Assume an index entry has 40 characters.

12.5   Choose indices for the following SELECT statement. Specify whether your choices are clustered or unclustered, hash index or B$^+$ tree.

```
SELECT   C.CrsName, COUNT(*)
FROM     COURSE C, TRANSCRIPT T
WHERE    T.CrsCode = C.CrsCode AND T.Semester = :sem
GROUP BY T.CrsCode, C.CrsName
HAVING COUNT(*) ≥ 100
```

12.6   Consider the following query:

```
SELECT    T.CrsCode, T.Grade
FROM      TRANSCRIPT T, STUDENT S
WHERE     T.StudId = S.Id AND S.Name = 'Joe'
```

Assume that Id is the primary key of STUDENT, (CrsCode, Semester, StudId) is the primary key of TRANSCRIPT, and that Name is not unique. Set up a database containing these two tables on the DBMS available to you. Initialize the tables with a large number of rows. Write a program that measures the query execution time by reading the clock before and after submitting the query. Be sure to flush the cache between successive measurements (perhaps by executing a query that randomly reads a sufficient number of rows of a large dummy table).

a. Test your understanding by making an educated guess of what query plan will be chosen by the DBMS assuming that there are no indices other than those for the primary keys. Run the query, output the query plan, and check your guess. Measure the response time.

b. Now assume that an unclustered index on StudId on TRANSCRIPT is added. What query plan would you expect? Run the query, check your answer, and measure the response time. Try the query under two conditions: Joe has taken very few courses; Joe has taken many courses.

c. In addition to the index added in (b), assume that an unclustered index on STUDENT on Name has been added and repeat the experiment.

12.7   Consider the table AUTHORS with attributes Name, Publ, Title, and YearPub. Assume that Name is the primary key (authors' names are unique) and hence one would expect that the DBMS would automatically create a clustered index on that attribute. Consider the statement

```
SELECT    A.Publ, COUNT(*)
FROM      AUTHORS A
WHERE     . . . range predicate on YearPub . . .
GROUP BY  A.Publ
```

a. Assume that the statement is generally executed with a very narrow range specified in the WHERE clause (the publication year of only a few books will fall within the range). What indices would you create for the table and what query plan would you hope the query optimizer would use (include any changes you might make to the index on Name).

b. Repeat (a) assuming that a very broad range is generally specified.

12.8   Give the trigger that maintains the consistency of the database when a GPA column is added to the table STUDENT, as described in Section 12.2.2.

12.9   In applications that cannot tolerate duplicates it may be necessary to use DISTINCT. However, the query plan needed to support DISTINCT requires a sort, which is expensive. Therefore you should only use DISTINCT when duplicates are possible in the result set. Using the schema of Section 4.8, check the following queries to see if duplicates are possible. Explain your answer in each case.

a. _____

```
SELECT   S.Name
FROM     STUDENT S
WHERE    S.Id LIKE '1'
```

b. _____

```
SELECT   S.Id
FROM     STUDENT S, FACULTY F
WHERE    S.Address = F.Address
```

c. _____

```
SELECT   C.CrsCode, COUNT(*)
FROM     TRANSCRIPT T
GROUP BY T.CrsCode
```

d. _____

```
SELECT   F.Name, F.DeptId, C.ClassTime, C.CrsCode,
         C.Semester, C.Year
FROM     FACULTY, CLASS C
WHERE F.Id = C.InstructorId
```

e. _____

```
SELECT   S.Name, F.Name, T.Semester, T.Year
FROM     FACULTY, CLASS C, TRANSCRIPT T, STUDENT S
WHERE F.Id = C.InstructorId AND S.Id = T.StudId AND
         C.CrsCode = T.CrsCode AND
         C.SectionNo = T.SectNo AND
         C.Year = T.Year AND C.Semester = T.Semester
```

12.10 A particular query can have several formulations, and a query optimizer may produce different query plans with different costs for each.

a. Assume that the Computer Science Department teaches only three 100-level courses: CS110, CS113, and CS114. Write an SQL statement whose result set contains the course codes of all courses that have these as prerequisites in three ways: using OR, UNION, and a nested subquery involving LIKE.

b. Write an SQL statement whose result set contains the names of all computer science courses that are prerequisites to other courses in three ways: using a join, a nested subquery involving EXISTS, and a nested subquery involving IN.

13

An Overview of Transaction Processing

The transactions of a transaction processing application should satisfy the ACID properties that we discussed in Chapter 2—atomic, consistent, isolated, and durable. As transaction designers, we are responsible for the consistency of the transactions in our system. We must ensure that, if each transaction is executed by itself (with no other transactions running concurrently), it performs correctly—that is, it maintains the database integrity constraints and performs the transformations listed in its specification. The remaining properties—atomicity, isolation, and durability—are the responsibility of the underlying transaction system. In this chapter we give an overview of how these remaining features are implemented.

13.1 Isolation

The transaction designer is responsible for designing each transaction so that, if it is executed by itself and the initial database correctly models the current state of the real-world enterprise, the transaction performs correctly and the final database correctly models the (new) state of the enterprise. However, if the transaction processing system executes a set of such transactions concurrently—in some interleaved fashion—the effect might be to transform the database to a state that does not correspond to the real-world enterprise it was modeling or to return incorrect results to the user.

The schedule of Figure 2.4 on page 23 is an example of an incorrect concurrent schedule. In that schedule, two registration transactions completed successfully, but the course became oversubscribed and the count of the total number of registrants was only incremented by one. The cause of the failure was the particular way the operations of the two transactions were interleaved. Both transactions read the same value of *cur_reg*, so neither took into account the effect of the other. We referred to this situation as a lack of isolation—the I in ACID.

One way for the system to achieve isolation is to run transactions one after the other in some serial order—each transaction is started only after the previous transaction completes, and no two transactions run concurrently. The resulting **serial schedule** will be correct since we assume that transactions that run by themselves perform correctly: each transaction is consistent. Thus, assuming that the database correctly models the real world when the schedule starts, and given that the first transaction is consistent, the database will correctly model the real world when that transaction completes. Hence the second transaction (which is also consistent) will run correctly and leave the database in a correct state for the third, and so forth.

Unfortunately, for many applications serial execution results in unacceptably small transaction throughput (measured in transactions per second) and unacceptably long response time for users. Although restricting transaction processing systems to run only serial schedules is impractical, serial schedules are important because they serve as the primary measure of correctness. Since serial schedules must be correct, a nonserial schedule is also correct if it has the same effect as a serial schedule.

Note that the implication goes in only one direction. Nonserial schedules that do not have the same effect as serial schedules are *not necessarily* incorrect. We will see that most DBMSs give the application designer the flexibility to run such nonserial schedules. First, however, we discuss serializable schedules—schedules that are equivalent to serial schedules.

13.1.1 Serializability

One way to improve performance over serial execution and yet achieve isolation is to allow interleaved schedules that are serializable. A **serializable schedule** is a schedule that is equivalent to a serial schedule. We discuss the meaning of equivalence below.

As a simple example, assume that in a banking system, transactions read and write database items $Balance_i$, where $Balance_i$ is the value of the balance in $Account_i$. Assume that T_1 reads and writes only $Balance_a$ and $Balance_b$ (perhaps it transfers money from one account to the other), and transaction T_2 reads and writes only $Balance_c$ (perhaps it makes a deposit in that account). Even if execution of the transactions is interleaved, as in the schedule

$$r_1(Balance_a)\ w_2(Balance_c)\ w_1(Balance_b)$$

T_2's write has no effect on T_1, and T_1's read and write have no effect on T_2. Hence the overall effect of the schedule is the same as if the transactions had executed serially in either the order $T_1\ T_2$ or the order $T_2\ T_1$—that is, in one of the following serial schedules:

$$r_1(Balance_a)\ w_1(Balance_b)\ w_2(Balance_c)$$

or

$$w_2(Balance_c)\ r_1(Balance_a)\ w_1(Balance_b)$$

Note that both of the equivalent serial schedules are obtained from the original schedule by interchanging operations that commute. In the first case, the two write operations have been interchanged. They commute because they operate on distinct items and hence leave the database in the same final state no matter in which order they execute. In the second case, we have interchanged $r_1(Balance_a)$ and $w_2(Balance_c)$. These operations also commute because they operate on distinct items, and hence, in both orders, the same value of $Balance_a$ is returned to T_1 and $Balance_c$ is left in the same final state.

Suppose that in addition both T_1 and T_2 read a common item, today's date, *date*. Again, the overall effect is the same as if the transactions had executed serially in either order. Thus, the schedule

$$r_1(Balance_a) \; r_2(date) \; w_2(Balance_c) \; r_1(date) \; w_1(Balance_b) \qquad \textbf{13.1}$$

has the same effect as does the serial schedule

$$r_1(Balance_a) \; r_1(date) \; w_1(Balance_b) \; r_2(date) \; w_2(Balance_c) \qquad \textbf{13.2}$$

in which all of T_1's operations precede those of T_2. The equivalence between the two schedules is again based on commutativity. The new feature illustrated by this example is that operations do not have to access distinct items in order to commute. In this case, $r_1(date)$ and $r_2(date)$ commute because they both return the same value to the transactions in either execution order.

In general, requests (from different transactions) commute if either of the following holds:

- They refer to different data items.
- They are both read requests.

In all of the above cases we say that the interleaved schedule is serializable since we can find at least one equivalent serial schedule. Furthermore, the equivalent serial schedule can be produced from the interleaved schedule by a sequence of interchanges of adjacent, commuting operations of different transactions. For example, the first interchange in going from schedule (13.1) to schedule (13.2) is to interchange $w_2(Balance_c)$ and $r_1(date)$.

In a serial schedule a transaction can affect the execution of a subsequent transaction (one that starts after that transaction commits) by causing a transition to a new database state. For example, the new balance established by executing a deposit transaction affects the balance reported by a subsequent read-balance transaction. However, the two transactions do not affect each other in any other way, and we say their execution is isolated. Because of the equivalence between serial and serializable schedules, we say that the transactions in a serializable schedule are also isolated.

In the schedule shown in Figure 2.4 on page 23 the two registration transactions have affected each other in a way that could not have happened in a serial schedule. Since they both increment the same value of *cur_reg*, the schedule produces an erroneous final state. The schedule is not serializable, and it is easy to see that we cannot obtain an equivalent serial schedule by a series of interchanges of adjacent commuting operations. A read and a write operation on the same data item do not commute: the value returned by the read depends on whether it precedes or follows the write. Similarly, two write operations on the same item do not commute: the final value of the item depends on which write came last.

In general, we are interested in specifying when a schedule, S, of some set of concurrently executing transactions is serializable: it is equivalent to (i.e., has the same effect as) some serial schedule, S_{ser}, of that set. Informally, what is required is that in both schedules

■ The values returned by the corresponding read operations in the two schedules are the same.

■ The write operations to each data item occur in the same order in both schedules.

To understand these conditions, note that the computation performed by a program depends on the values of the data items that it reads. Hence, if each read operation in a transaction returns the same value in schedules S and S_{ser}, the computations performed by the transaction will be identical in both schedules, and hence the transaction will write the same values back to the database. If the write operations occur in the same order in both schedules, they leave the database in the same final state. Thus, S has the same effect as (and hence is equivalent to) S_{ser}.

Database systems can guarantee that schedules are serializable. By allowing serializable, in addition to serial, schedules, they allow more concurrency, and hence performance is improved. In addition, database systems offer less stringent notions of isolation that do not guarantee that schedules will be serializable, and hence they support even more concurrency and better performance. Since nonserializable schedules are not necessarily equivalent to serial schedules, correctness is not guaranteed. Therefore, less stringent notions of isolation must be used with caution.

The part of the transaction processing system responsible for enforcing isolation is called the **concurrency control**. The concurrency control enforces isolation by controlling the schedule of database operations. When a transaction wishes to read or write a database item, it submits its request to the concurrency control. On the basis of the sequence of requests it has granted up to that point and given the fact that it does not know what requests might arrive in the future, the concurrency control decides whether isolation can be guaranteed if it grants the request at that time. If isolation cannot be guaranteed, the request is not granted. The transaction is either made to wait or is aborted. We describe one way a concurrency control might make these decisions in Section 13.1.2.

13.1.2 Two-Phase Locking

Most concurrency controls in commercial systems implement serializability using a **strict two-phase locking protocol** [Eswaran et al. 1976]. The protocol associates a lock with each item in the database and requires that a transaction hold the lock before it can access the item. When a transaction wishes to read (write) a database item, it submits a request to the concurrency control, which must grant to the transaction a **read lock** (**write lock**) on the item before passing the request on to the database system module that performs the access. The locks are requested, granted, and released according to the following rules:

	Granted Mode	
Requested Mode	read	write
read		X
write	X	X

FIGURE 13.1 Conflict table for a concurrency control. Conflicts between lock modes are denoted by X.

1. If a transaction, T, requests to read an item and no other transaction holds a write lock on that item, the control grants a read lock on that item to T and allows the operation to proceed. Note that since other transactions might be holding read locks that were granted at an earlier time, read locks are often referred to as **shared locks**. Note that the requested read operation commutes with the previously granted read operations.

2. If a transaction, T, requests to read an item and another transaction, T', holds a write lock on that item, T is made to wait until T' completes (and releases its lock). We say that the requested read operation **conflicts** (does not commute) with the previously granted write operation.

3. If a transaction, T, requests to write an item and no other transaction holds a read or write lock on that item, the control grants T a write lock on that item and allows the operation to proceed. Because a write lock excludes **all** other locks, it is often referred to as an **exclusive lock**.

4. If a transaction, T, requests to write an item and another transaction, T', holds a read or write lock on that item, T is made to wait until T' completes (and releases its lock). We say that the requested write operation **conflicts** (does not commute) with the previously granted read or write operation.

5. Once a lock has been granted to a transaction, the transaction retains the lock. A read lock on an item allows the transaction to do subsequent reads of that item. A write lock on an item allows the transaction to do subsequent reads or writes of that item. When the transaction completes, it releases all locks it has been granted.

Notice that the effect of the rules is that, if a request does not conflict with (that is, it commutes with) the previously granted requests of other active transactions, it can be granted. Figure 13.1 displays the conflict relation for an item in tabular form. An X indicates a conflict.

The concurrency control uses locks to remember the database operations previously performed by currently active transactions. It grants a lock to a transaction to perform an operation on an item only if the operation commutes with (that is, does not conflict with) all other operations on the item that have previously been performed by currently active transactions. For example, since two reads on an item commute, a read lock can be granted to a transaction even though a different transaction currently holds a read lock on that item. In this way, the control guarantees that the operations of active transactions commute, and hence the schedule of these operations is equivalent to a serial schedule. This result forms the basis of a proof that any schedule produced by the concurrency control is serializable.

The concurrency control has the property that once a transaction acquires a lock, it holds the lock until it completes. This is a special case of a more general class of concurrency controls referred to as **two-phase** controls. In general, with a two-phase control, each transaction goes through a locking phase in which it obtains locks on the items that it accesses, and then an unlocking phase in which it releases locks. Once it enters the second phase it is not permitted to acquire any additional locks. In our case the second phase is collapsed to a single point in time when the transaction completes. This makes the concurrency control **strict**.

In a **nonstrict** two-phase concurrency control, the unlocking phase starts after the transaction has obtained all of the locks it will ever need and continues until the transaction completes. During the second phase the transaction can release a lock at any time.

Note that since, in a strict control, locks are held until a transaction completes, the database system does not have to provide an explicit command that a transaction can use to release a lock. Such a mechanism (e.g., an unlock command) has to be provided, however, by a database system that supports a nonstrict control.

While the nonstrict two-phase protocol guarantees serializability, problems arise when transactions abort. If transaction T_1 modifies a data item, $Balance_a$, and then unlocks it in phase two, a second transaction, T_2, can read the new value and subsequently commit. Since T_1 unlocked $Balance_a$ before completing, it might subsequently abort. Atomicity requires that an aborted transaction have no effect on the database state, so if T_1 aborts, $Balance_a$ will be restored to its original value. These events are recorded in the following schedule:

$$w_1(Balance_a) \; r_2(Balance_a) \; w_2(CreditLimit) \; commit_2 \; abort_1 \qquad \textbf{13.3}$$

T_2 has written a new value to $CreditLimit$, and that value is based on the value of $Balance_a$ that it read. Since that value was produced by a transaction that subsequently aborted, a violation of atomicity has occurred. Even though T_1 aborted, it had an effect on the value T_2 wrote. T_1 might have deposited money into the account, and T_2 might have based its computation of $CreditLimit$ on the new balance. Since T_1 aborted, the value of $CreditLimit$ is in all probability incorrect.

For this reason, in a nonstrict two-phase concurrency control, although read locks can be released during phase two, write locks are not released early but are held until commit time.

Concurrency controls that use strict two-phase locking produce schedules that are serializable in commit order. By this we mean that a schedule, S, is equivalent to a serial schedule, S_{ser}, in which the order of transactions is the same as the order in which they commit in S. To understand why this is so, observe that write locks are not released until commit time, so a transaction is not allowed to read (or write) an item that has been written by a transaction that has not yet committed. Thus, each transaction "sees" the database produced by the sequence of transactions that committed prior to its completion. Nonstrict two-phase locking protocols produce schedules that are serializable, but not necessarily in commit order.

For many applications, users intuitively expect transactions to be serializable in commit order. For example, you expect that after your bank deposit transaction has committed, any transaction that commits later will see the effect of that deposit.

The idea behind a two-phase protocol is to hold locks until it is safe to release them. Early release of locks beyond what is allowed by a nonstrict two-phase control can result in an inconsistent database state or can cause transactions to return incorrect results to the user. Since performance considerations force database systems to provide mechanisms that support early release, the database community has developed special jargon to describe some of the problems, or **anomalies**, that can occur.

- *Dirty read.* Suppose that transaction T_2 reads an item, $Balance_a$, written by transaction T_1 before T_1 completes. This might happen if T_1 releases the write lock it has acquired on $Balance_a$ before it commits. Since the value of $Balance_a$ returned by the read was not written by a committed transaction it might never appear in the database. This is referred to as a **dirty read**. The problem in schedule (13.3) is caused by a dirty read.

- *Nonrepeatable read.* Suppose that transaction T_1 reads an item, $Balance_a$, and then releases the read lock it has acquired before it completes. Another transaction, T_2, might then write $Balance_a$ and commit. If T_1 reacquires a read lock on $Balance_a$ and reads it again, the value returned by the second read will not be the same as the value returned by the first. We refer to this as a **nonrepeatable read**. This situation is illustrated by the schedule

$$r_1(Balance_a) \; w_2(Balance_a) \; commit_2 \; r_1(Balance_a)$$

  Note that in this example T_2 has committed prior to the second read, and so the second read is not dirty. However, since T_1 releases the read lock and then reacquires it, it is not two-phase. While a nonrepeatable read might seem to be an unimportant issue (why would a transaction read the same item twice?), it is a symptom of a more serious problem. For example, suppose *List* is a list of passengers on an airline flight and *Count* is the count of passengers on the list. In the following schedule, T_2 reserves a seat on the flight and hence adds an entry to *List* and increments *Count*. T_1 reads both *List* and *Count*, thus sees the passenger list before the new passenger was added and the passenger count after it was incremented—an inconsistency.

$$r_1(List) \; r_2(List) \; w_2(List) \; r_2(Count) \; w_2(Count) \; commit_2 \; r_1(Count)$$

  This schedule is directly related to the previous one. In both cases, locking is not two-phase and T_2 overwrites an item that an active transaction, T_1, has read.

- *Lost update.* Suppose that a deposit transaction in a banking system reads the balance in an account, $Balance_a$, calculates a new value based on the amount deposited, and writes the new value back to $Balance_a$. If the transaction releases the read lock it has acquired on $Balance_a$ before acquiring a write lock, two deposit transactions on the same account can be interleaved, as illustrated in the following schedule:

$$r_1(Balance_a) \; r_2(Balance_a) \; w_2(Balance_a) \; commit_2 \; w_1(Balance_a) \; commit_1 \quad \textbf{13.4}$$

Unfortunately, the amount deposited by T_2 does not appear in the final value of $Balance_a$ and hence this problem is referred to as a **lost update**. The effect of T_2 is lost because the value written by T_1 is based on the original value of $Balance_a$ rather than the new value written by T_2.

These anomalies, as well as other as-yet-unnamed anomalies, can cause transactions to return incorrect results and the database to become inconsistent.

13.1.3 Deadlock

Suppose that transactions T_1 and T_2 both want to deposit money into the same account and hence they both want to execute the sequence

$$r(Balance_a)\ w(Balance_a)$$

In one possible partial schedule, T_1 read locks and reads $Balance_a$; T_2 read locks and reads $Balance_a$; T_1 requests to write $Balance_a$ but is made to wait because T_2 has a read lock on it; T_2 requests to write $Balance_a$ but is made to wait because T_1 has a read lock on it.

$$r_1(Balance_a)\ r_2(Balance_a)\ \text{Request\_}w_1(Balance_a)\ \text{Request\_}w_2(Balance_a)$$

At this point, T_1 is waiting for T_2 to complete, and T_2 is waiting for T_1 to complete. Both will wait forever because neither will ever complete.

This situation is called a **deadlock**. More generally, a deadlock occurs whenever there is a wait loop—that is, a sequence of transactions, T_1, T_2, ..., T_n, in which each transaction, T_i, is waiting to access an item locked by T_{i+1}, and T_n is waiting to access an item locked by T_1. Although two-phase locking is particularly prone to deadlock, deadlock can occur with any concurrency control that allows a transaction to hold a lock on one item when it requests a lock on another item. Such controls must have a mechanism for detecting a deadlock and then for aborting one of the transactions in the wait loop so that at least one of the remaining transactions can continue.

With one such mechanism, whenever a transaction is forced to wait, the control checks to see whether a loop of waiting transactions will be formed. Thus, if T_1 must wait for T_2, the control checks to see if T_2 is waiting and, if so, for what. As this process continues, a chain of waiting transactions is uncovered and a deadlock is detected if the chain loops back on itself. Another mechanism uses **timeout**. Whenever a transaction has been waiting for a "long" time (as defined by the system administrator), the control assumes that a deadlock exists and aborts the transaction.

Even with detection and abortion, deadlocks are undesirable because they waste resources (the computation performed by the aborted transaction must be redone) and slow down the system. Application designers should design tables and transactions so as to reduce the probability of deadlocks.

13.1.4 Locking in Relational Databases

Up to this point, our discussion of locking has assumed that a transaction requests access to some named item (for example, $Balance_a$). Locking takes a different form in a relational database, where transactions access tuples. Although tuples can be locked, a transaction describes the tuples it wants to access not by naming them (they do not have names), but by using a condition that the tuples must satisfy. For example, the set of tuples read by a transaction using a SELECT statement is specified by a selection condition in the WHERE clause.

For example, an ACCOUNTS table in a banking system might contain a tuple for each separate account, and a transaction T_1 might read all tuples that describe the accounts controlled by depositor Mary as follows:

```
SELECT *
FROM Accounts A
WHERE A.Name = 'Mary'
```

In this case, T_1 reads all tuples in ACCOUNTS that satisfy the condition that the value of their Name attribute is Mary. The condition A.Name = 'Mary' is called a **predicate**.

As with nonrelational databases, we can ensure serializability with a locking protocol. In designing such a protocol, we must decide what data items to lock. One approach is to always lock an entire table, even if only a few tuples in it are accessed. In contrast to tuples, tables are named in the statements that access them. Thus, the SELECT statement reads the data item(s)—tables—named in the FROM clause. Similarly, DELETE, INSERT, and UPDATE write the named tables. With this approach to locking, the concurrency control protocols described in the previous sections can be used and will yield serializable schedules. The problem is that table locks are coarse: a table might contain thousands of tuples, and locking an entire table because a small number of its tuples are being accessed might result in a serious loss of concurrency.

A second approach is to lock only the tuples returned by the SELECT statement. For example, in processing the above SELECT statement, only tuples describing Mary's accounts are locked. Unfortunately, this approach does not work. To understand the problem consider a database consisting of two tables: the ACCOUNTS table introduced earlier that has a tuple for every account in the bank, and a DEPOSITORS table that has a tuple for every depositor. One attribute of DEPOSITORS is TotalBalance, whose value is the sum of the balances in all the accounts owned by a particular depositor.

Two transactions access these tables. An audit transaction, T_1, for Mary might execute the SELECT statement

```
SELECT SUM(Balance)
FROM Accounts A
WHERE A.Name = 'Mary'
```

to compute the sum of the balances in all of Mary's accounts, and then it might compare the value returned with the result of executing

```
SELECT D.TotalBalance
FROM DEPOSITORS D
WHERE D.Name = 'Mary'
```

Concurrently, T_2, a new account transaction for Mary, might create a new account for Mary with an initial balance of $100 by inserting a tuple into ACCOUNTS using the statement

```
INSERT INTO ACCOUNTS
VALUES ('10021', 'Mary', 100)
```

and then updating TotalBalance by 100 in the appropriate tuple in DEPOSITORS using

```
UPDATE DEPOSITORS
SET TotalBalance = TotalBalance + 100
WHERE Name = 'Mary'
```

The operations on ACCOUNTS performed by T_1 and T_2 conflict since T_2's INSERT does not commute with T_1's SELECT. If INSERT is executed before SELECT, the inserted tuple will be returned by SELECT; otherwise, it will not be returned. In our earlier discussion we saw that a request to perform an operation should not be granted if it conflicts with an operation executed earlier by a still active transaction. Hence, we are justified in expecting that invalid results will be obtained if the execution of T_2 is interleaved between the time T_1 reads ACCOUNTS and the time it reads DEPOSITORS. In this case, the value of TotalBalance read by T_1 will not be equal to the sum of the Balances it read in its first statement, and the schedule is not serializable. (The operations on DEPOSITORS similarly conflict.)

The question is "Will tuple locking prevent this interleaving?" Unfortunately, the answer is "No." The locks that T_1 acquires on Mary's tuples in ACCOUNTS as a result of executing the first SELECT statement do not prevent T_2 from inserting an entirely new tuple into the table. We can conclude then that tuple locking does not guarantee serializable schedules. Table locking, on the other hand, would prevent the problem since it inhibits all accesses to the table.

The root cause of the problem is that T_2 has altered the contents of the set of tuples referred to by the predicate Name = 'Mary' by adding the new tuple. In this situation, the new tuple is referred to as a **phantom** because T_1 thinks it has locked all the tuples that satisfy the predicate but, unknown to T_1, a tuple satisfying the predicate has been inserted by a concurrent transaction. A phantom can lead to nonserializable schedules and hence invalid results. Hence, we have discovered a new anomaly.

13.1.5 Isolation Levels

Locks impede concurrency and hence performance. It is therefore desirable to minimize their use. Table locking used in a two-phase protocol produces serializable schedules but, because of the size of the item locked, has the greatest impact on concurrency. Tuple locking is more efficient but can result in nonserializable schedules even when used in a two-phase protocol (because of phantoms). Because locks are held until commit time, strict protocols inhibit concurrency more than nonstrict protocols.

For these reasons, most commercial DBMSs allow the application designer to choose among several locking protocols. The protocols differ in the items that they cause to be locked and in how long the locks are held. These options are often described in terms of the ANSI standard isolation levels. The application designer should choose a level that guarantees both that the application will execute correctly and that concurrency will be maximized. Levels other than the most stringent one permit nonserializable schedules. However, *for a particular application*, the nonserializable schedules permitted by a particular level might not lead to incorrect results or, for that application, all the schedules produced by the lower isolation level might be serializable and hence correct.

Each ANSI standard isolation level is specified in terms of the anomalies that it prevents. An anomaly that is prevented at one level is also prevented at each stronger (higher) level. The levels are (in the order of increasing strength):

- READ UNCOMMITTED. Dirty reads are possible.

- READ COMMITTED. Dirty reads are not permitted (but nonrepeatable reads and phantoms are possible).

- REPEATABLE READ. Nonrepeatable and dirty reads are not permitted (but phantoms are possible).

- SERIALIZABLE. Nonrepeatable reads, dirty reads, and phantoms are not permitted. Transaction execution must be serializable.

Describing isolation levels in terms of the anomalies they do or do not permit is a dangerous business. What about other anomalies that you might not have thought about? The standards organization must have had this in mind when they specified the SERIALIZABLE isolation level. *All* anomalies are ruled out if schedules are serializable, not just nonrepeatable reads, dirty reads, and phantoms. We will see an example of another anomaly shortly.

We need to discuss one other issue related to isolation. Recall that the query plan that implements a particular SQL statement is a complex program that generally involves a significant amount of computation and I/O and whose execution might take minutes or more. In order to provide reasonable throughput for demanding applications, many DBMSs support the concurrent execution of several SQL statements. This is a micro form of interleaving that we have not considered. It is interleaving at the instruction level rather than at the SQL statement level. Is the execution of the query plans for individual statements to be isolated? Clearly the answer must be "yes." Since a query plan involves access to data structures internal to the DBMS (e.g., buffers, tables for implementing locks) in addition to the database itself, internal locks—called **latches**—are used to provide this type of isolation. We do not discuss this aspect of isolation any further.

While a particular isolation level can be implemented in a variety of ways, locking is a common technique. It is instructive to propose a particular discipline for doing this. Each level uses locks in different ways. For most levels, locks are acquired by transactions on items they access when executing an SQL statement. Depending on how the item is accessed, the lock can be either a read lock or a write lock. Once acquired, it can be held until commit time—in which case it is referred to as a **long-duration lock**—or it can be held only as long as the statement is being executed—in which case it is referred to as a **short-duration lock**. In the implementation we describe, write locks at all isolation levels are long-duration locks on the entire table and read locks are handled differently at each level.

- READ UNCOMMITTED.   A read is performed without obtaining a read lock. Hence, a transaction executing at this level can read a tuple on which another transaction holds a write lock. As a result the transaction might read uncommitted (dirty) data.

- READ COMMITTED.   Short-duration read locks are obtained for each tuple before a read is permitted. Hence, conflicts with write locks will be detected, and the transaction will be made to wait until the write lock is released. Since write locks are of long duration, only committed data can be read. However, read locks are released when the read is completed, so two successive reads of the same tuple by a particular transaction might be separated by the execution of another transaction that updates the tuple and then commits. This means that reads might not be repeatable.

- REPEATABLE READ.   Long-duration read locks are obtained on each tuple returned by a SELECT.   Hence, a nonrepeatable read is not possible, although phantoms are.

- SERIALIZABLE.   Serializable schedules can be guaranteed if long-duration read locks are acquired on all tables read. This eliminates phantoms, although it reduces concurrency. A better implementation involves locking a table and/or portions of an index that is used to access a table. A description of that algorithm, however, is beyond the scope of this chapter.

Note that, while the standard does not explicitly speak of lost updates, this anomaly is allowed at READ COMMITTED but eliminated at REPEATABLE READ. Take a look at schedule (13.4) on page 461. The long-term read lock acquired on $Balance_a$ by T_1 would have prevented the request $w_2(Balance_a)$ from being executed. A closer examination of this situation shows that the two transactions would have become deadlocked—not a happy situation, but at least the lost update does not occur.

The SQL standard specifies that different transactions in the same application can execute at different isolation levels, and each such transaction sees or does not see the phenomena corresponding to its level. The locking implementation described above enforces this. For example, a transaction that executes at REPEATABLE

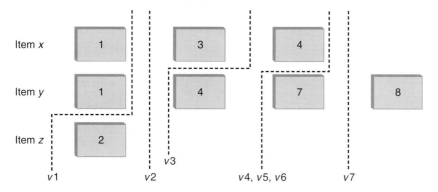

FIGURE 13.2 Multiversion database.

READ will see the same value if it reads a particular tuple several times, even though other transactions execute at other levels, since it gets a long-duration read lock on the tuple, while all other transactions must get long-duration write locks to update it. Similarly, a transaction that executes at SERIALIZABLE sees a view of the database that is serialized with respect to the changes made by all other transactions, regardless of their levels: it sees either all updates made by such a transaction or none. This follows from the same considerations.

One particularly troublesome type of nonrepeatable read occurs when a transaction accesses a tuple through a cursor. Since at READ COMMITTED read locks are short term, the tuple can be changed by a concurrent transaction while the cursor is pointing to it. Some commercial database systems support an isolation level called CURSOR STABILITY, which is essentially READ COMMITTED with the additional feature that a read lock is maintained on a tuple as long as a cursor is pointing at it. Thus, the read of the tuple is repeatable if the cursor is not moved. You can think of this as a medium-duration lock.

SNAPSHOT isolation. An isolation level that is not part of the ANSI standard, but is provided by at least one commonly used DBMS (Oracle), is called SNAPSHOT isolation. SNAPSHOT isolation uses a **multiversion** database: When a (committed) transaction updates a data item, the item's old value is not discarded. Instead, the old value (or version) is preserved and a new version is created. At any given time, therefore, multiple versions of the same item exist in the database. The system can construct, for any i, the value of each item that includes the effects of the ith transaction to commit and of all transactions that committed at a prior time.

Figure 13.2 illustrates this situation assuming that transactions are consecutively numbered in the order in which they commit and that each version of an item is tagged with the index of the transaction that produced it. The successive values of an item are aligned from left to right. A version of the database as a whole is indicated with a dashed line. Thus, in version $v4$—the version of the database at the time of the completion of the fourth transaction to commit, T_4—the values of x and y were written by T_4 and the value of z was written by T_2. Each database version is referred to as a **snapshot**.

With SNAPSHOT isolation, no read locks are used. *All* reads requested by transaction T are satisfied using the snapshot produced by the sequence of transactions that were committed when T's first request was made. Thus, if T's first read request was $r(z)$ and the request was made between the time T_4 and T_5 committed, the value returned would have been the value of z in $v4$, and that value would have been created by T_2. All of T's subsequent read requests would also have been satisfied from $v4$. Since a snapshot once produced is never changed, no read locks are necessary and read requests are never delayed.

The updates of each transaction are controlled by a protocol called **first-committer-wins**. A transaction, T, is allowed to commit if there is no other transaction that (1) committed between the time T made its first read request and the time it requested to commit and (2) updated a data item that T had also updated. Otherwise, T is aborted.

The first-committer-wins feature eliminates dirty reads since a transaction reads values from a snapshot that, by definition, contains values written by committed transactions. It eliminates lost updates, which occur when two concurrently active transactions write to the same data item. The problem encountered by the audit in Section 13.1.4 is also eliminated since all of its reads would be satisfied using the same snapshot.

However, SNAPSHOT isolation allows nonserializable—and hence possibly incorrect—schedules. For example, suppose a database integrity constraint asserts that the sum of x and y must be nonnegative. In the schedule

$$r_1(x)\ r_1(y)\ r_2(x)\ r_2(y)\ w_1(y)\ w_2(x)$$

T_1 and T_2 each read the values of x and y from the same snapshot. Assuming the sum is 5, T_1 might elect to subtract 5 from x and T_2 might elect to subtract 5 from y. Each transaction is consistent, but the schedule causes a violation of the constraint. The schedule is not serializable because it is not possible to produce an equivalent serial schedule by a series of interchanges of adjacent commuting operations. Unfortunately, it is allowed by SNAPSHOT isolation since the transactions write to different items in the database. This is an example of a new anomaly, called **write skew**.

The implementation of SNAPSHOT isolation is complicated by the fact that a multiversion database must be maintained. In practice, however, it is not possible to maintain all versions. Old versions eventually must be discarded. This can be a problem for long-running transactions since they must be aborted if they request access to a version that no longer exists.

13.1.6 Lock Granularity and Intention Locks

For performance reasons many commercial concurrency controls lock a unit larger than an individual data item. For example, instead of an item that might occupy only several bytes, the concurrency control might lock the entire disk page on which that item is stored. Since such a control locks *more* items than are actually necessary, it produces the same or a higher level of isolation than a concurrency control that locks only the item whose lock has been requested. For example, instead of locking a page containing some of the tuples in a table, the concurrency control might lock the entire table.

The size of the unit locked determines the lock **granularity**—it is **fine** if the unit locked is small and **coarse** otherwise. Granularity forms a hierarchy based on containment. Typically, a fine-granularity lock is a tuple lock. A medium-granularity lock is a lock on the page containing a desired tuple. A coarse-granularity lock is a table lock that covers all the pages of a table.

Fine-granularity locks have the advantage of allowing more concurrency than coarse-granularity locks since transactions lock only the data items they actually use. However, the overhead associated with fine-granularity locking is greater. Transactions using fine-granularity locks generally hold more locks since a single coarse-granularity lock might grant access to several items used by the transaction. (For example, the tuples on a disk page are generally elements of a single table, and there is a reasonable probability that a transaction accessing one such tuple will also access another. A single page lock grants permission to access both.) Therefore, more space is required in the concurrency control to retain information about fine-granularity locks. Also, more time is expended in requesting locks for each individual unit.

Because of these trade-offs, database systems frequently offer granularity at several different levels, and different levels can be used within the same application. Locking at multiple granularities introduces some new implementation problems. Suppose that transaction T_1 has obtained a write lock on a particular tuple in a table and transaction T_2 requests a read lock on the entire table (it wants to read all of the tuples in the table). The concurrency control should not grant the table lock because T_2 should not be allowed to read the tuple that was locked by T_1. The problem is how the concurrency control detects the conflict since the conflicting locks are on different items. The control needs a mechanism for recognizing that the locked tuple is contained within the table.

The solution is to organize locks hierarchically. Before obtaining a lock on a fine-granularity item (such as a tuple), a transaction must obtain a lock on all containing items (such as a page or table). But what kind of a lock? Clearly, it should not be a read or write lock since, in that case, there would be no point in acquiring the additional fine-granularity lock, and the effective lock granularity would be coarse.

For this reason, database systems provide a new lock mode, the **intention lock**. In a system supporting tuple and table locks, for example, before a transaction can obtain a read (shared) or write (exclusive) lock on a tuple, it must obtain an appropriate intention lock on the table containing that tuple. More generally, an intention lock must be acquired on all ancestors in the hierarchy.

Intention locks are weaker than read and write locks and come in three flavors:

1. If a transaction wants to obtain a shared lock on a tuple, it must first get an **intention shared**, or IS, lock on the table. The IS lock indicates that the transaction *intends* to obtain a shared lock on some tuple within that table.

Granted Mode

Requested Mode	IS	IX	SIX	S	X
IS					X
IX			X	X	X
SIX		X	X	X	X
S		X	X		X
X	X	X	X	X	X

FIGURE 13.3 Conflict table for intention locks. Conflicts between lock modes are denoted X.

2. If a transaction wants to obtain an exclusive lock on a tuple, it must first obtain an **intention exclusive**, or IX, lock on the table. The IX lock indicates that the transaction *intends* to obtain an exclusive lock on some tuple within the table.

3. If a transaction wants to update some tuples in the table but needs to read all of them to determine which ones to change (for example, it wants to change all tuples in which the value of a particular attribute is less than 100), it must first obtain a **shared intention exclusive**, or SIX, lock on the table. The SIX lock is a combination of a shared lock and an intention exclusive lock on the table. This allows it to read all the tuples in the table and subsequently to get exclusive locks on those it wants to update.

The conflict table for intention locks is given in Figure 13.3. It shows, for example, that after a transaction, T_1, has been granted an IX lock on a table, another transaction, T_2, will not be granted an S lock on that table (the entry in column IX and row S). To understand this, note that the shared lock allows T_2 to read all tuples in the table and that this conflicts with the fact that T_1 is updating one (or more) of them. On the other hand, T_2 can be granted an X lock on a different tuple in the table, but it must first acquire an IX lock on the table. This does not present a problem because, as shown in the figure, IX locks do not conflict. Note that if table locking were used, both transactions would need X locks on the table and one would have to wait. This is just one example of a situation in which intention locking outperforms table locking.

Lock escalation.   The space and time overhead of granular locking becomes excessive when a transaction accumulates too many fine-grain locks. When a transaction begins acquiring a large number of page or tuple locks on a table, it will likely continue to do so. Therefore, it is beneficial to trade in those locks for a single lock on the entire table.

This technique is known as **lock escalation**. A threshold (which the application can often control) is set in the concurrency control that limits the number of fine-grained locks a transaction, T, can obtain on a particular table. When T reaches the threshold, the concurrency control attempts to escalate the fine-grained locks for a single coarse-grained lock (in the same mode). Since the coarse-grained lock might conflict with locks that are currently held by concurrent transactions, T might have to wait. When the coarse-grained lock is granted, the fine-grained locks are released. Note the danger of deadlock in this scheme. For example, if two transactions are acquiring X locks on pages and both reach their threshold, a deadlock results since neither can escalate their locks to a table lock.

Serializable execution with granular locking. In Section 13.1.5 we discussed a simple implementation of the SERIALIZABLE isolation level that uses long-duration read and write locks on tables. We pointed out that a more efficient algorithm is often used when an index is used in the query plan. With granular locking, however, it is possible to improve on the table-locking protocol even when no index is available.

- If a transaction wants to read one or more tuples in a table, it gets an S lock on the entire table.

- If a transaction wants to write one or more tuples in a table, it gets a SIX lock on the table and write locks on the tuples it wants to write.

This protocol increases concurrency compared with the table-locking protocol. The table-locking protocol requires that transactions that want to update rows obtain a write lock on the entire table, which precludes *all* concurrent access to the table. With the granular protocol, after a transaction writes some tuples, the SIX lock it has obtained allows other transaction to read all the tuples in the table other than those that were written.

To see that this protocol guarantees serializable schedules note that since the updated tuples are write locked, the only issue is to show that phantoms cannot occur. But the SIX lock (which includes a shared lock on the entire table) prevents other transactions from updating or inserting any tuples in the table, and hence no phantoms can occur.

13.1.7 Summary

The question of how to choose an isolation level for a particular application is far from straightforward. Serializable schedules guarantee correctness for all applications but might not meet an application's performance requirements. However, some applications execute correctly at an isolation level lower than SERIALIZABLE. For example, a transaction that prints a mailing list of depositors might not need an up-to-date database view, but it might want to be sure that the addresses it reads are not partially updated. In that case, READ COMMITTED might be an appropriate isolation level.

Commercial DBMS vendors usually support a number of options (including, but not limited to, those discussed above), and they expect application designers to select the one appropriate for their particular application.

13.2 Atomicity and Durability

Atomicity requires that a transaction either successfully completes (and commits) or aborts (undoing any changes it made to the database). A transaction might be aborted by the user (perhaps using a cancel button), by the system (perhaps because of a deadlock or because some database update violated a constraint check), or by itself (when, for example, it finds unexpected data). Another way the transaction might not successfully complete is if the system crashes during its execution. Crashes are a bit more complicated than user- or system-initiated aborts because the information stored in main memory is assumed to be lost when the system crashes. Hence, the transaction must be aborted and its changes rolled back using only the information stored on mass storage. Furthermore, *all* transactions active at the time of the crash must be aborted.

Durability requires that, after a transaction commits, the changes it made to the database are not lost even if the mass storage device on which the database is stored fails.

While the application programmer must be involved in directing how isolation is to be performed (for example, by setting isolation levels and lock escalation thresholds), the implementation of atomicity and durability is generally hidden. Still it is important for you to be knowledgeable about a few of the important features in this area, so we introduce them here.

13.2.1 The Write-Ahead Log

We discuss atomicity and durability in the same section because they are frequently implemented using the same mechanism—the write-ahead log.

A log is a sequence of records that describes database updates made by transactions. Records are appended to the log as the transactions execute and are never changed. The log is consulted by the system to achieve both atomicity and durability. For durability, the log is used to restore the database after a failure of the mass storage device on which the database is stored. Therefore, it is generally stored on a different mass storage device than the database itself. Typically, a log is a sequential file on disk, and it is often duplexed (with the copies stored on different devices) so that it survives any single media failure.

A common technique for achieving atomicity and durability involves the use of **update** records. When a transaction updates a database item, an update record is appended to the log. No record needs to be appended if the operation merely reads the data item. The update record describes the change made and, in particular, contains enough information to permit the system to undo that change if the transaction is later aborted.

There are several ways to undo changes. In the most common, an update record contains the **before image** of the modified database item—a physical copy of the item before the change. If the transaction aborts, the update record is used to restore the item to its original value—which is why the update record is sometimes referred to as an **undo record**. In addition to the before image, the update record identifies the database item and the transaction that made the change—using a **transaction Id**.

If a transaction, T, is aborted, rollback using the log is straightforward. The log is scanned backwards, and, as T's update records are encountered, the before images are written to the item named in the record, undoing the change. Since the log might be exceedingly long, it is impractical to search back to the beginning to make sure that all of T's update records are processed. To avoid a complete backward scan, when T is initiated a **begin record** containing its transaction Id is appended to the log. The backward scan can be stopped when this record is encountered.

Rollback due to a crash is more complex than the abort of a single transaction since the system must abort all transactions that were active at the time of the crash. The hard part here is to identify these transactions using only the information contained in the log since the contents of main memory has been lost.

To do this we introduce two additional records. When a transaction commits, a **commit record** is written to the log. If it aborts, its updates are rolled back and an **abort record** is written to the log. Using these records, a backward scan can record the identity of transactions that completed prior to the crash and thus can ignore their update records as each is subsequently encountered during the backward scan. If, during the backward scan, the first record relating to T is an update record, T was active when the crash occurred and must be aborted.

Note the importance of writing a commit record to the log when T requests to commit. The commit request itself does not guarantee durability. If a crash occurs after the transaction has made the request but before the commit record is written to the log, the transaction will be aborted by the recovery procedure and will not be durable. Hence, a transaction is not actually committed until its commit record has been appended to the log on mass store.

One last issue has to be addressed. A mechanism must be provided to help the recovery process identify the transactions to be aborted. Without such a mechanism, the recovery process has no way of knowing when to stop the backward scan since a transaction that was active at the time of the crash might have logged an update record at an early point in the log and then have made no further updates. The recovery process will thus find no evidence of the transaction's existence unless it scans back to that record.

To deal with this situation, the system periodically appends a **checkpoint record** to the log that lists the currently active transactions. The recovery process must scan backward at least as far as the most recent checkpoint record. If T is named in that record and the backward scan prior to reaching the checkpoint record did not encounter a commit or abort record for T, then T was still active when the system crashed. The backward scan must continue past the checkpoint record until the begin record for T is reached. The scan terminates when all such transactions are accounted for.

An example of a log is shown in Figure 13.4. As the recovery process scans backward, it discovers that T_6 and T_1 were active at the time of the crash because the last records appended for them are update records. Since the first record it encounters for T_4 is a commit record, it learns that T_4 was not active at the time of the crash.

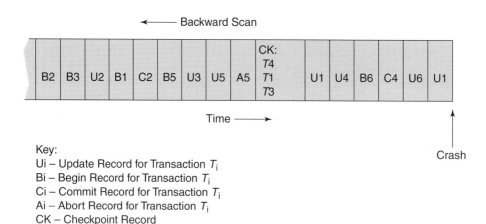

FIGURE **13.4** Log example.

When it reaches the checkpoint record, it learns that, at the time the record was written, T_1, T_3, and T_4 were active (T_6 is not mentioned in the checkpoint record since it began after the checkpoint was taken). Thus, it concludes that, in addition to T_1 and T_6, T_3 was active at the time of the crash (since it has seen no completion record for T_3). No other transaction could have been active, and hence these are the transactions that must be aborted. Recovery involves processing update records for T_1, T_3, and T_6 in a backward scan in the order they are encountered until their begin records have been reached.

We have assumed that an update record for a database item, x, is written to the mass storage device containing the log at the time the new value of x is written to the mass storage device containing the database. In fact, the transfer of the new value and the update record occur in some order. Does it make a difference which occurs first?

Consider the possibility of a crash occurring at the time the operations are performed. If neither operation has completed, there is no problem. The update record does not appear in the log, but there is nothing for the recovery process to undo since x has not been updated. If the crash occurs after both operations have completed, recovery proceeds correctly, as described above. Suppose, however, that x is updated on mass store first and the crash occurs between that time and the time the update record is appended to the log. Then the recovery process has no way of rolling the transaction back and returning the database to a consistent state since the original value of x appears nowhere on mass store—an unacceptable situation.

Suppose, on the other hand, the transfers are done in the opposite order: the update record is appended first, and, when that has completed, the new value of x is transferred to the database. If the crash occurs after the log has been updated, then, on restart, the recovery process will find the update record and use it to restore x. It makes no difference whether the crash occurred after x was updated or before the update could take place. If the crash occurred after both the log and x were updated, recovery proceeds as described earlier. If the crash occurred after the log was updated but before x could be updated, the value of x in the database and the before image in the update record are identical when the system is restarted. The recovery process uses the before image to overwrite x—which does not change its value—but the final state after recovery is correct.

Hence, the update record must always be appended to the log before the database is updated. When logging is done in this way, and it always is, the log is referred to as a **write-ahead log**.

Performance issues. Recovery from a crash is actually more complex than we have described. It would appear from what we have said so far that two I/O operations must be performed each time a data item is updated: one to update the database and another to append an update record to the log. Furthermore, the operations must be done in sequence. If this were the case, the performance of the system would be inadequate for all but the lightest loads. Two techniques are used to overcome this problem.

Most database systems maintain a cache—a set of page buffers in main memory used to store copies of database pages in active use (the cache is discussed in more detail in Section 12.1). Changes to the database are made in copies of database pages in the cache, and the copies need not be transferred to the database on mass store immediately. Instead, they might be kept in main memory for some time so that additional accesses to them (reads or writes) can be handled quickly. Since the probability is high that once an item in a page is accessed additional accesses to the page will follow, a considerable amount of I/O can be avoided.

Furthermore, and for similar reasons, log records are not immediately written to the log but are temporarily stored in a log buffer in main memory. To avoid a write to the log when each update record is appended, the entire buffer is written to the log when it is full. As a result, the amount of I/O to the log is reduced by a factor equal to the average number of records that fit in the buffer.

The fact that the most recent database and log information might be stored only in buffers in main memory at the time of a crash adds considerable complexity to recovery since the buffers are lost when a crash occurs. We will not describe the full recovery procedure here, except to discuss one problem. A page updated by a committed transaction, T, might still be in the cache at the time of the crash. Since durability requires that all of T's updates survive in the database, we need a mechanism for reconstructing them on recovery. The solution lies in the update records, but there are two issues that must be dealt with: do the update records contain the necessary information, and can we be sure that they were written to mass store before the crash occurred?

The second issue is easily dealt with. If T is committed, its commit record must have been written to mass store prior to the crash. Since its update records precede it in the log, they must also be on mass store and hence available to the recovery procedure.

The first issue is more problematic. The before image in an update record is of no use in restoring a data item written by T: it has the initial value of the item, not the new value. As a result, the update record is often augmented to include both an after image as well as a before image. The **after image** (or **redo record**) contains the new value of the item written by T. The recovery procedure can use the after image to roll the item forward and hence guarantee T's durability.

The management of the cache and log buffer and their use in updating the log and database on mass storage must be carefully coordinated to maintain the write-ahead feature in implementing atomicity and durability.

13.2.2 Recovery from Mass Storage Failure

Durability requires that no changes to the database made by a committed transaction be lost. Therefore, since mass storage devices can fail, the database must be stored on different devices redundantly.

One simple approach to achieving durability is to maintain separate copies of the database on different disks (perhaps supported by different power supplies). Since the simultaneous failure of both disks is unlikely, the probability is high that at least one copy of the database will always be available. Mirrored disks implement this approach. A **mirrored disk** is a mass storage system in which, transparently to the user, whenever an application requests a disk write operation, the system simultaneously writes the same information on two different disks. Thus one disk is an exact copy, or a mirror image, of the other.

In transaction processing applications, a mirrored-disk system can achieve increased system **availability** since, if one of the mirrored disks fails, the system can continue, without slowing or stopping, using the other one. When the failed disk is replaced, the system then must resynchronize the two. By contrast, when durability is achieved using only the log (as described next), the recovery after a disk failure might take a significant period of time, during which the system is unavailable to its users.

Keep in mind, however, that even when a transaction processing system uses mirrored disks, it must still use a write-ahead log to achieve atomicity—for example, to roll back transactions after a crash.

A second approach to achieving durability involves restoring the database from the log after a disk failure. Since update records contain after images, all we have to do is play the log forward from the beginning, writing the after images in each update record as it is encountered to the database item named in the record. The problem with this approach is the time it takes since the log can be quite long.

To overcome this problem, the entire database is periodically copied, or **dumped**, to mass storage. Then, to recover from a disk failure, the most recent dump is used to initialize a new copy of the database, and then the log records appended after that dump are used to roll the copy forward to the state the database was in at the time of the failure.

An important issue in this approach is how to produce the dump. For some applications, it can be produced offline after shutting down the system: no new transactions are admitted, and all existing transactions are allowed to complete. The dump then contains a snapshot of the database resulting from the execution of all transactions that committed prior to the start of the dump. Unfortunately, however, with many applications the system cannot be shut down, and the dump must be completed while the system is operating.

A **fuzzy dump** is a dump performed while the system is operating and transactions are executing. These transactions might later commit or abort. The algorithm for restoring the disk using a fuzzy dump must deal properly with the effects of these transactions.

13.3 Implementing Distributed Transactions

We have been assuming that the information accessed by a transaction is stored in a single DBMS. This is not always the case. The information supporting a large enterprise might be stored in multiple DBMSs at different sites in a network. For example, a manufacturing facility can have databases describing inventory, production, personnel, billing, and so forth. As these enterprises move to higher and higher levels of integration, transactions must access information at more than one DBMS. Thus, a single transaction initiating the assembly of a new component might allocate the parts by updating the inventory database, specify a particular employee for the job by accessing the personnel database, and create a record to describe the new activity in the production database. Systems of this type are referred to as **multidatabase** systems.

Transactions accessing multidatabase systems are often referred to as **global** transactions because they can access all the data of an enterprise. Since the databases often reside at different sites in a network, such transactions are also referred to as **distributed** transactions. Many of the considerations involved in designing global transactions do not depend on whether or not the data is distributed, and so the terms are frequently used interchangeably. Distribution across a network introduces new failure modes (e.g., lost messages, site crashes) and performance issues that do not exist when all databases are stored at the same site.

We assume that each individual database in a multidatabase exports a set of (local) transactions (perhaps as stored procedures) that can be used to access its data. For example, a bank branch might have deposit and withdraw transactions for accessing the accounts it maintains. Each such transaction can be invoked locally to reflect a purely local event (e.g., a deposit is made at the branch to a branch account) or remotely as part of a distributed transaction (e.g., money is transferred from an account at one branch to an account at another). When a transaction at a site is executed as a part of a distributed transaction, we refer to it as a **subtransaction**.

The database at each site has its own local integrity constraints relating data stored there. The multidatabase might, in addition, have global integrity constraints relating data at different sites. For example, the database at the bank's main office might contain a data item whose value is the sum of the balances of the accounts at all local branches. We assume that each distributed transaction is consistent and maintains all integrity constraints. Each subtransaction maintains the local integrity constraints at the site at which it executes, and all of the subtransactions of a distributed transaction taken together maintain the global integrity constraints.

A desirable goal in implementing distributed transactions over a multidatabase system is to ensure that they are globally atomic, isolated, and durable, as well as consistent. We have seen, however, that designers often choose to execute transactions at a single site at the weakest isolation level possible in the interest of enhancing system performance. With distributed transactions, it is sometimes necessary not only to reduce the isolation level, but also to sacrifice atomicity and isolation altogether. To better understand the underlying issues, we first present the techniques required to provide globally atomic and serializable distributed transactions.

13.3.1 Atomicity and Durability—The Two-Phase Commit Protocol

To make a distributed transaction, T, globally atomic, either all of T's subtransactions must commit or all must abort. Thus, even if some subtransaction completes successfully, it cannot immediately commit because another subtransaction of T might abort. If that happens, all of T's subtransactions must be aborted. For example, if T is a distributed transaction that transfers money between two accounts at different sites, we do not want the subtransaction that does the withdrawal at one site to commit if the subtransaction that does the deposit at the other site aborts.

The part of the transaction processing system responsible for making distributed transactions atomic is the **transaction manager**. One of its tasks is to keep track of which sites have participated in each distributed transaction. When all subtransactions of T have completed successfully, T sends a message to the transaction manager stating that it wants to commit. To ensure atomicity, the transaction manager and the database managers at which the subtransactions have executed then engage in a protocol, called a **two-phase commit protocol** [Gray 1978; Lampson and Sturgis 1979]. In describing this protocol, it is customary to call the transaction manager the **coordinator** and the database managers the **cohorts**.

The coordinator starts the first phase of the two-phase commit protocol by sending a *prepare message* to each cohort. The purpose of this message is to determine whether the cohort is willing to commit and, if so, to request that it prepare to commit by storing all of the subtransaction's update records on nonvolatile storage. If all update records are durable and the coordinator subsequently decides that the transaction should be committed, the cohort will be able to do so (since the update records contain after images), even if it subsequently crashes.

If the cohort is willing to commit, it appends a **prepared record** to the log buffer, writes the buffer to mass store, and waits until the I/O operation completes. This is referred to as a **force write** and guarantees that the prepared record, and hence all preceding records (including the transaction's update records), are durable when the cohort continues its participation in the protocol. The cohort is then said to be in the **prepared state** and can reply to the *prepare message* with a *vote message*.

The vote is **ready** if the cohort is willing to commit and **aborting** if not. Once a cohort votes ready, it cannot change its mind since the coordinator uses the vote to decide whether the transaction as a whole is to be committed. If the cohort votes **aborting**, it aborts the subtransaction immediately and exits the protocol. Phase 1 of the protocol is now complete.

The coordinator receives each cohort's vote. If all votes are ready, it decides that T can be committed globally and forces a commit record to its log. As with single-resource transactions, T is committed once its commit record is safely stored in mass storage. All update records for all cohorts are in mass storage at that time because each cohort forced a prepared record before voting. Note that we are assuming that the transaction manager and each of the local database managers have their own independent logs.

The coordinator then sends each cohort a *commit message* telling it to commit. When a cohort receives a *commit message* it forces a commit record to the database manager's log, releases locks, and sends a *done message* back to the coordinator indicating that it has completed the protocol.

It is now apparent why the coordinator's commit record must be forced. If a *commit message* were sent to a cohort before the commit record was durable, the coordinator might crash in a state in which the message had been sent, but the record was not durable. Since each cohort commits its subtransaction when the message is received, this would result in an inconsistent state: the distributed transaction is uncommitted, but the subtransaction is committed.

When the coordinator receives a *done message* from each cohort, it appends a **complete record** to the log. Phase 2 (and the complete protocol) is now complete. For a committed transaction, the coordinator makes two writes to its log, only one of which is forced. The cohort forces two records in the commit case: the prepared record and the commit record.

If the coordinator receives any aborting votes, it sends *abort messages* to each cohort that voted to commit (cohorts that voted to abort have already aborted and exited from the protocol). On receiving the message, the cohort aborts the subtransaction and writes an abort record in its log.

The sequence of messages exchanged between the application, the coordinator (transaction manager), and cohort (database manager) is shown in Figure 13.5.

For each cohort, the interval between sending a ready *vote message* to the coordinator and receiving the *commit* or *abort message* from the coordinator is called its **uncertain period** because the cohort is uncertain about the outcome of the protocol. The cohort is dependent on the coordinator during that period because it cannot commit or abort the subtransaction unilaterally since its decision might be different from the decision made by the coordinator. Locks held by the subtransaction cannot be released until the coordinator replies (since the coordinator might decide to abort and new values written by the subtransaction should not be visible in that case). This negatively impacts performance, and the cohort is said to be **blocked**. The uncertain period might be long because of communication delays.

There is also the possibility that the coordinator will crash or become unavailable because of communication failures during the uncertain period. Since the coordinator might have decided to commit or abort the transaction and then crashed before it could send *commit* or *abort messages* to all cohorts, a cohort has to remain blocked until it finds out what decision, if any, has been made. Again, this might take a long time. Because such long delays generally imply an unacceptable performance penalty, many systems abandon the protocol (and perhaps atomicity) when the uncertain period exceeds some predetermined time. They arbitrarily commit or abort

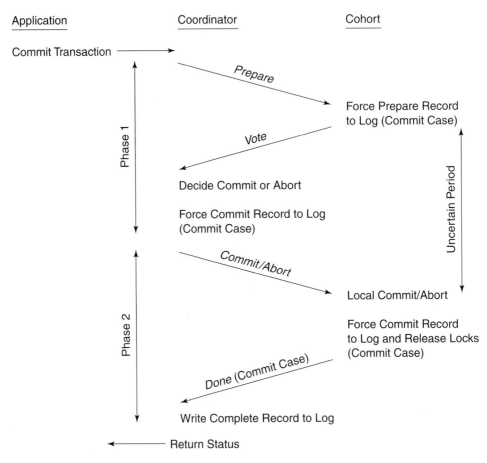

FIGURE 13.5 Exchange of messages in a two-phase commit protocol.

the local subtransaction (even though other subtransactions might have terminated in a different way) and let the system administrator clean up the mess.

In some situations, a site manager might refuse to allow the DBMS to participate in a two-phase commit protocol because of its possible negative effect on performance. In other situations, sites *cannot* participate because the DBMS is an older, **legacy**, system that does not support the protocol. Alternatively, client-side software (such as some versions of embedded SQL) might not support the protocol. In this circumstance, global atomicity is not realized.

13.3.2 Global Serializability and Deadlock

Each site in a multidatabase system might maintain its own, strict two-phase locking concurrency control, which schedules operations so that the subtransactions *at that site* are serializable. Furthermore, the control might ensure that deadlocks among subtransactions *at that site* are resolved. Unfortunately, this is not sufficient to guarantee that distributed transactions are serializable and deadlock free.

Global serializability. To guarantee the serializability of distributed transactions, we must ensure not only that the subtransactions are serializable at each site but that there is an equivalent serial order on which all sites can agree. For example, transactions T_1 and T_2 might have subtransactions at sites A and B. At site A, T_{1A} and T_{2A} might have conflicting operations and be serialized in the order T_{1A}, T_{2A}, while at site B conflicting subtransactions of the same two transactions might be serialized T_{2B}, T_{1B}. In that case, there is no equivalent serial schedule of T_1 and T_2 as a whole.

Surprisingly, global serializability can be achieved with no additional mechanisms beyond those we have already discussed:

> If the concurrency control at each site independently uses a strict two-phase locking protocol, and the system uses a two-phase commit protocol, every global schedule is serializable (in the order in which their coordinators have committed them). [Weihl 1984]

While we do not prove that result here, it is not hard to see the basic argument that can be generalized into a proof. Suppose that sites A and B use strict two-phase locking concurrency controls, that a two-phase commit algorithm is used to ensure global atomicity, and that transactions T_1 and T_2 are as described above. We argue by contradiction. Suppose that the conflicts described above occur (so that the transactions are not serializable) and that both transactions commit. T_{1A} and T_{2A} conflict on some data item at site A, so T_{2A} cannot complete until T_{1A} releases the lock on that item. Since the concurrency control is strict and a two-phase commit algorithm is used, T_{1A} does not release the lock until after T_1 has committed. Since, T_2 cannot commit until after T_{2A} completes, T_1 must commit before T_2. But if we use the same reasoning at site B, we conclude that T_2 must commit before T_1. Hence, we have derived a contradiction, and it follows that both transactions cannot have committed. In fact, the conflicts we have assumed at sites A and B yield a deadlock, and one of the transactions will have to be aborted.

We have discussed circumstances under which the two-phase commit protocol is not implemented. In such situations, global transactions are not guaranteed to be globally atomic or globally serializable.

Global deadlocks. Distributed systems are subject to a type of deadlock that involves subtransactions at different sites. For example, a subtransaction of T_1 at site A might be waiting for a lock held by a subtransaction of T_2 at A, while a subtransaction of T_2 at site B might be waiting for a lock held by a subtransaction of T_1 at B. Since all subtransactions of a global transaction must commit at the same time, T_1 and T_2 are in a distributed deadlock—they will both wait forever. Unfortunately, the deadlock cannot be detected at any single site: a distributed algorithm must be used. Fortunately, the techniques developed for deadlock detection at a single site can be generalized to detect a global deadlock.

13.3.3 Replication

In a distributed system, replicas of a data item can be stored at different sites in a network. This has two potential advantages. It can reduce the time it takes to access the item since the nearest (perhaps even local) replica can be used. It can also improve the availability of the item in case of failures since, if a site containing a replica crashes, the item can still be accessed using a different replica at another site.

The price that must be paid for these advantages, in addition to the added complexity and storage involved, is the cost of maintaining **mutual consistency**: all the replicas of an item should have the same value. Mutual consistency comes in two flavors. With **strong mutual consistency**, every committed replica of an item always has the same value as every other committed replica. Unfortunately, performance considerations often make this goal impractical to achieve, and so most replica controls maintain a more modest goal, **weak mutual consistency**: all committed replicas of an item *eventually* have the same value, although at any particular time some may have different values. A variety of algorithms are used to maintain these goals.

In most implementations of replication, the individual transactions are unaware that replicas exist. A transaction simply requests to access a data item, and the system performs the access on one or more replicas in accordance with the replication algorithm that it implements. The system knows which items are replicated and at what sites the replicas are stored. The portion of the system responsible for implementing replication is called the **replica control**.

The most common form of replication uses a **read-one/write-all** algorithm. When a transaction requests to read an item, the system fetches its value from the nearest replica; when a transaction requests to update an item, the system updates all replicas. Read-one/write-all replication has the potential for improving the speed with which a read request can be satisfied compared with nonreplicated systems since with no replication, a read request might require communication with a distant DBMS. The performance of write requests, however, might be worse since all replicas must be updated. Hence, read-one/write-all replication has a potential performance benefit in applications in which reading occurs substantially more frequently than writing.

Read-one/write-all systems can be characterized as synchronous update or asynchronous update.

■ *Synchronous-update systems.* When a transaction updates an item, all replicas are locked and updated before the transaction commits. Updates to replicas are thus treated in the same way as updates to any other data item, and strong mutual consistency is enforced since locks are not released until all replicas are mutually consistent. In addition to performance, availability is a problem for writes since if a replica site is down, a write operation on the item cannot be

FIGURE 13.6 Schedule illustrating the possibility of inconsistent views with asynchronous-update replication. T_1 updates x and y at sites A and B. T_{ru} propagates the updates after T_1 commits. Because propagation is asynchronous, T_2 sees the new value of y but the old value of x.

T_1: $w(x_A)$ $w(y_B)$ *commit*

T_2: $r(x_C)$ $r(y_B)$ *commit*

T_{ru}: $w(x_C)$ $w(x_B)$ $w(y_A)$ $w(y_C)$ *commit*

completed. However, synchronous-update systems based on two-phase locking and two-phase commit protocols produce globally serializable schedules.

- *Asynchronous-update systems.* Only one replica is updated before the transaction commits. The other replicas are updated after the transaction commits by another transaction that is triggered by the commit operation or that executes periodically at fixed intervals. Hence, even in systems based on two-phase locking and two-phase commit protocols, schedules might not be globally serializable. For example, transaction T_1 might write a new value to data items x and y. The replica control might choose to update the copy of x at site A and the copy of y at site B before T_1 commits. Transaction T_2 might be concurrently reading x and y, and the replica control might return the value of the replica of x at site C (an old value) and the value of y at site B (a new value). A transaction to propogate T_1's updates, T_{ru}, is executed when T_1 commits. The schedule is shown in Figure 13.6.

    Asynchronous-update systems come in two varieties.

- *Group replication.* A transaction can lock and update any replica (presumably the nearest one). After the transaction commits, the update is propagated asynchronously to the other replicas. Unfortunately, without further restrictions, even weak mutual consistency is not guaranteed by this protocol since transactions executing concurrently can update different replicas of the same item and although the new values produced by these transactions will ultimately arrive at all replicas, they might arrive at different replicas in different orders. If each replica site simply applies the updates in the order in which they arrive, the replicas might not converge to a common value. Weak mutual consistency can be enforced by attaching time stamps to each update and to each replica (the time stamp of a replica is the time stamp of the latest update that has been applied to it) and only apply an update if its time stamp is greater than the time stamp of the replica. With this scheme, some updates might be discarded.

    Situations such as these are called **conflicts**. Although the time stamp algorithm guarantees weak mutual consistency, it does not guarantee that anomalies are eliminated. Commercial replication systems offer a variety of ad hoc conflict resolution strategies, including: "oldest update wins," "youngest update wins," "update from the highest-priority site wins," and "user provides a procedure for conflict resolution." The application designer can select the strategy most suitable for the application.

■ ***Primary copy replication.*** A unique replica of each data item is designated the **primary copy**. All other replicas are designated **secondary copies**. Transactions requesting to update an item must lock and update its primary copy. When a transaction commits, the update it has made to the primary copy is propagated to the other replicas. By filtering all updates through the primary, write conflicts will be detected. Weak mutual consistency is ensured if propagation messages are delivered to all replicas in the order sent since all replicas will go through the same sequence of changes. Read requests are satisfied in the conventional way by accessing the nearest replica.

Since asynchronous update produces greater transaction throughput than does synchronous update, it is the most widely used form of replication. However, the designer should be aware that asynchronous-update systems (even primary copy systems) can produce nonserializable schedules and hence can produce incorrect results.

13.3.4 Summary

Many aspects of distributed transaction processing systems are surprisingly simple. If each site uses a strict two-phase locking concurrency control, a two-phase commit protocol is used to synchronize cohorts at commit time, and synchronous-update replication is used, then distributed transactions will be globally atomic and serializable. Global deadlocks can be resolved with algorithms that are generalizations of single-site deadlock detection and prevention algorithms.

Frequently these conditions do not hold. The application at some sites might use one of the lower isolation levels, sites might not participate in a two-phase commit protocol, and/or asynchronous replication might be used. In such situations, distributed transactions are not guaranteed to be serializable. Nevertheless, systems might have to be designed under these constraints, and the application designer must carefully assess the implications of nonserializable schedules on the correctness of the database and the ultimate utility of the application.

BIBLIOGRAPHIC NOTES

A comprehensive discussion of issues related to the implementation of distributed transactions can be found in [Gray and Reuter 1993]. [Ceri and Pelagatti 1984] is more theoretical in its orientation and describes the algorithms underlying the implementation. Two-phase locking was introduced in [Eswaran et al. 1976]. Isolation levels are discussed in [Gray et al. 1976]. The two-phase commit protocol was introduced in [Gray 1978; Lampson and Sturgis 1979]. See [Weihl 1984] for a proof that the two-phase commit protocol together with two-phase locking local concurrency controls guarantees global serializability. One of the first discussions on logging and recovery technology can be found in [Gray 1978]. Excellent summaries of the technology are in [Haerder and Reuter 1983; Bernstein and Newcomer 1997; Gray and Reuter 1993]. Primary copy replication was introduced in [Stonebraker 1979].

EXERCISES

13.1 State which of the following schedules are serializable.

a. $r_1(x)\ r_2(y)\ r_1(z)\ r_3(z)\ r_2(x)\ r_1(y)$
b. $r_1(x)\ w_2(y)\ r_1(z)\ r_3(z)\ w_2(x)\ r_1(y)$
c. $r_1(x)\ w_2(y)\ r_1(z)\ r_3(z)\ w_1(x)\ r_2(y)$
d. $r_1(x)\ r_2(y)\ r_1(z)\ r_3(z)\ w_1(x)\ w_2(y)$
e. $w_1(x)\ r_2(y)\ r_1(z)\ r_3(z)\ r_1(x)\ w_2(y)$

13.2 In the Student Registration System, give an example of a schedule in which a deadlock occurs.

13.3 Give an example of a schedule that might be produced by a nonstrict two-phase locking concurrency control that is serializable but not in commit order.

13.4 Give an example of a transaction processing system (other than a banking system) that you have interacted with, for which you had an intuitive expectation that the serial order was the commit order.

13.5 Suppose that the transaction processing system of your university contains a table in which there is one tuple for each current student.

a. Estimate how much disk storage is required to store this table.
b. Give examples of transactions in the student registration system that have to lock this entire table if a table locking concurrency control is used.

13.6 Give an example of a schedule at the READ COMMITTED isolation level in which a lost update occurs.

13.7 Give examples of schedules at the REPEATABLE READ isolation level in which a phantom is inserted after a SELECT statement is executed and

a. The resulting schedule is nonserializable and incorrect.
b. The resulting schedule is serializable and hence correct.

13.8 Give examples of schedules at the SNAPSHOT isolation that are

a. Serializable and hence correct.
b. Nonserializable and incorrect.

13.9 Give examples of schedules that would be accepted at

a. SNAPSHOT isolation but not REPEATABLE READ.
b. SERIALIZABLE but not SNAPSHOT isolation. (*Hint:* T_2 performs a write after T_1 has committed.)

13.10 Give an example of a schedule of two transactions in which a two-phase locking concurrency control

a. makes one of the transactions wait, but a control implementing SNAPSHOT isolation aborts one of the transactions.

      b. aborts one of the transactions (because of a deadlock), but a control imple-
menting SNAPSHOT isolation allows both transactions to commit.

13.11 A particular read-only transaction reads data entered into the database during the
previous month and uses it to prepare a report. What is the weakest isolation level
at which this transaction can execute? Explain.

13.12 What intention locks must be obtained by a read operation in a transaction
executing at REPEATABLE READ when the locking implementation given in
Section 13.1.5 is used?

13.13 Explain how the commit of a transaction is implemented within the logging
system.

13.14 Explain why the write-ahead feature of a write-ahead log is needed.

13.15 Explain why a cohort in the two-phase commit protocol cannot release locks
acquired by the subtransaction until its uncertain period terminates.

13.16 Two distributed transactions execute at the same two sites. Each site uses a strict
two-phase locking concurrency control, and the entire system uses a two-phase
commit protocol. Give a schedule for the execution of these transactions in which
the commit order is different at each site but the global schedule is serializable.

13.17 Give an example of an incorrect schedule that might be produced by an
asynchronous-update replication system.

13.18 Explain how to implement synchronous-update replication using triggers.

PART FOUR

Software Engineering Issues and Documentation

This part has two purposes:

1. To describe in some detail the Student Registration System, which is used as a case study throughout the book.
2. To describe the software engineering concepts that are needed to actually implement such a system. We illustrate how the Unified Modeling Language (UML) can be used in this process.

Chapter 14 presents a Requirements Document for the Student Registration System and describes how those requirements can be analyzed and expanded into a Specification Document.

Chapter 15 discusses design, coding, testing, and project management. It completes the design of the database schema for the Student Registration System (which was started in Section 4.8) and presents the design of one of the transactions.

14

Requirements and Specifications

The implementation of the Student Registration System is proceeding on schedule. A team consisting of faculty, students, and representatives of the registrar has met several times with an analyst and has refined the informal Statement of Objectives given in Section 2.1 into a formal Requirements Document, which we reproduce in Section 14.2. Now it is time to complete the remaining parts of the project. We have already jumped ahead and implemented the database design part of the project in Chapters 4 and 6. In this chapter and in Chapter 15 we review the entire software engineering process in more detail. Our main interest is in the software engineering issues involved in the design and implementation of transactions and databases.

14.1 Software Engineering Methodology

The implementation of a transaction processing system is a significant engineering endeavor. The project must complete on time and on budget, and, when operational, the system must meet its requirements and operate efficiently and reliably. The documentation and coding for the project must be such that the system can be maintained and enhanced over its lifetime. Most important, it must meet the needs of its users.

Many years' experience with both successful and unsuccessful software projects has given rise to a number of procedures and methodologies generally agreed to be "good engineering practice." Many books and entire courses are devoted to software engineering. Here we sketch one approach and apply it to the Student Registration System.

In particular we talk about what software engineers call the **Waterfall model**, in which the project is divided into separate phases: requirements, specification, design, code, and test. And after the system is delivered, there is a final phase: maintenance. Similar phases exist in the development of most large engineering systems—for example a commercial airliner. In this chapter we talk about the requirements and specification phases, and in Chapter 15 we discuss the remaining phases.

Requirements Document. Projects usually begin with an informal Statement of Objectives as given at the beginning of Section 2.1. The next step is for the customers and users of the system, perhaps with the help of a system analyst, to expand these objectives into a formal **Requirements Document** for the system as given in Section 14.2. The Requirements Document describes in some detail what the system is supposed to do, not how it will do it. In many contexts, the Requirements Document is a Request for Proposals (RFP) to the implementors, describing what the customer wants them to build.

Specification Document. The implementation group analyzes the Requirements Document in detail and produces a **Specification Document**, which is an expanded version of the Requirements Document that describes in still more detail what the system will do. In many contexts, the Specification Document is a contract proposal, describing exactly what the implementation group intends to build. The description is so precise that the User Manual and the Specification Document can be written and published at the same time. The following examples illustrate the different levels of detail in the requirements and specification documents.

- In the Requirements Document, the set of user interactions with the system is listed, together with what each interaction is intended to do. In the Specification Document, the forms associated with each interaction are specified, together with exactly what happens when each button is pressed and each menu item is accessed.

- The Requirements Document lists the information that must be contained in the system. The Specification Document includes the domains of all items of information.

14.1.1 UML Use Cases

The Requirements Document specifies what the system is supposed to do from the user's point of view. Specifically, it specifies the user interactions with the system.

A common way to describe user interactions with the system is as a set of *use cases*. A software engineering text might define a **use case** as a sequence of actions that are performed to produce an observable result of benefit to one or more users (called **actors**). For example, in the Requirements Document, we have a use case called *Registration* in which a student registers for a course. Analysts often develop use cases by asking potential users of the system, "How do you accomplish such and such?". Thus we might ask a student, "How do you register for a course?" and then ask the registrar, "What are some situations in which the registration should not succeed?". Their responses might be the basis for developing the Registration use case, in which a student is the actor. Such a use case might be described as follows:

Registration.
Purpose. Register a student in a course to be taught next semester.
Actor. A student.
Input. A course number.

Result. The student is registered for the course, and an appropriate message is displayed.

Exception. The registration shall not be successful for any of the following reasons, which shall be contained in the output.

A.   There exists a prerequisite course that the student is not currently enrolled in or has not completed with a grade of at least C.

B.   And so on. (The complete list of exceptions is in the Requirements Document.)

Different software engineering texts use different formats for describing use cases. We use a particular format that seems appropriate for this application. Other formats might include *Preconditions*—what must be true before the use case starts; for example a precondition for the Registration use case might be that the Authentication use case for that actor has been successful; or *Actions*—for example, the student first does this, then that happens, then the student does this, etc.

Note that we describe user interactions using use cases rather than transactions because at this stage we do not yet know how many transactions will be required to implement each use case—that is part of the design.

Use cases are part of the *Unified Modeling Language* (or UML). The UML is a graphical language for modeling the static and dynamic behavior of a system. It provides a standard set of diagrams, each of which models a different aspect of the system's behavior. Because these diagrams are graphical, they are particularly appropriate for communicating information between the customer and the implementation group and between different members of the implementation group. Also, because the UML has become a widely adopted standard, UML diagrams can be used to communicate with other people not directly involved in the project, perhaps consultants invited in for a project review.

UML diagrams are one of the sources on which the requirements, specification, and design documents are based. In particular they are used to capture and display certain key aspects of the system behavior needed for these documents. Use cases and, as we shall see, use case diagrams are a part of the UML that deals with formulating requirements. In Section 14.4, we discuss the use of UML sequence diagrams for formulating specifications. In Chapter 4 we discuss the use of UML class diagrams for database design, and in Section 15.1.2 we discuss the use of UML state diagrams for describing the dynamic behavior of objects as part of the design process.

Although use cases are not inherently graphic in nature, the UML provides a graphic way to display the use cases in an application: the **use case diagram**. Figure 14.1 shows a use case diagram for all the use cases in the Student Registration System (as described in Section 14.2). Each actor in the use case is represented as a labeled stick figure, and each use case is represented as a labeled oval. Arrows connect each actor with the use cases in which the actor participates. Such a use case diagram might be developed while interviewing various potential users of the system and then discussed with these users to ensure that the set of use cases is complete and that the final system will satisfy their needs and meet their goals

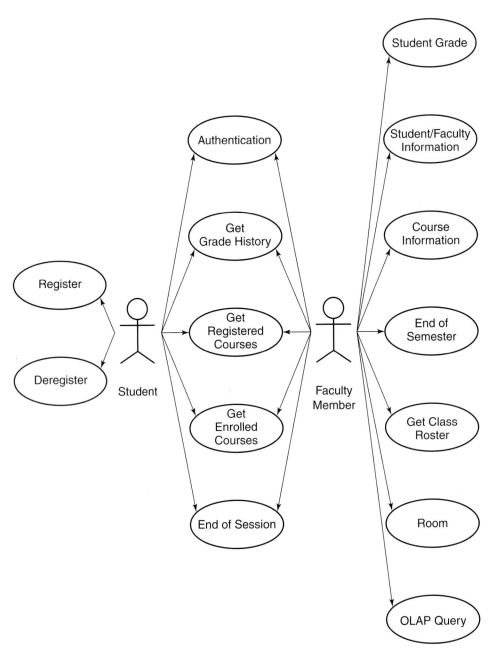

FIGURE 14.1 A use case diagram for the Student Registration System.

for the system. Use case diagrams provide a visually clear model for displaying the requirements of an application and might be included as part of the Requirements Document.

14.2 The Requirements Document for the Student Registration System

I. Introduction

The objectives of the Student Registration System are to allow students and faculty (as appropriate) to

A. Authenticate themselves as users of the system

B. Register and deregister for courses (offered for the next semester)

C. Obtain reports on a particular student's status

D. Maintain information about students and courses

E. Enter final grades for courses that a student has completed

In this document, the term "enrolled" refers to courses a student is currently taking and the terms "registered" and "deregistered" refer to courses to be taken or dropped by the student in the following semester.

II. Related Documents

A. *Statement of Objectives* of the Student Registration System (including date and version number)

B. This university's *Undergraduate Bulletin* (including date)

III. Information to Be Contained in the System

The information to be stored in the system includes four major categories of data: personal information about students and faculty members, academic records of students, teaching records of faculty members, and information about courses and course offerings. Information about classrooms and other auxiliary data is also stored in the system.

A. **Personal records**. The system shall contain a name, an Id number, and a password for each student and faculty member allowed to use the system.[1] The password and the Id authenticates users. Id numbers are unique. It is assumed

---

[1] Note that the requirements are numbered so that they can be referred to in later documents, such as the Test Plan, which must test that the system meets every one of its requirements. Also, requirements that are stated using words such as "shall" and "must" are mandatory. Words such as "should" and "can" do not connote a mandatory requirement and should be avoided unless the requirement is optional. For example, in one of the earliest recorded Requirements Documents (even then the requirements were numbered), the commandment is "Thou shalt not kill," not "Thou should not kill."

that at least one faculty member has been initialized as a valid user at startup time.

B. **Academic records**. The system shall contain the academic record of each student.

1. Each course the student has completed, the semester the student took the course, and the grade the student received (all grades are in the set {A, B, C, D, F, I})
2. Each course for which the student is enrolled this semester
3. Each course for which the student has registered for next semester

C. **Course information**. The system shall contain information about the courses offered, and for each course the system shall contain

1. The course name, the course number (must be unique), the department offering the course, the textbook, and the credit hours
2. Whether the course is offered in spring, fall, or both
3. The prerequisite courses (there can be an arbitrary number of prerequisites for each course)
4. The maximum allowed enrollment, the number of students who are enrolled (unspecified if the course is not offered this semester), and the number of students who have registered (unspecified if the course is not offered next semester)
5. If the course is offered this semester, the days and times at which it is offered; if the course is offered next semester, the days and times at which it will be offered. The possible values shall be selected from a fixed list of weekly slots (e.g., MWF10).
6. The Id of the instructor teaching the course this semester and next semester (the Id is unspecified if the course is not offered in the specified semester; it must be specified before the start of the semester in which the course is offered)
7. The classroom assignment of the course for this semester and next semester (the classroom assignment is unspecified if the course is not offered in the specified semester; it must be specified before the start of the semester in which the course is offered)

All course information shall be consistent with the *Undergraduate Bulletin*.

D. **Teaching information**. The system shall contain a record of all courses that have been taught, including the semester in which they were taught and the Id of the instructor.

E. **Classroom information**. The system shall contain a list of classroom identifiers and the corresponding number of seats. A classroom identifier is a unique three-digit integer.

F. **Auxiliary information**. The system shall contain the identity of the current semester (e.g., F2004).

IV. Integrity Constraints
The database shall satisfy the following integrity constraints.

A. Id numbers are unique.

B. If in item III.B.2 (or III.B.3) a student is listed as enrolled (or registered) for a course, that course must be indicated in item III.C.2 as offered this semester (or next semester).

C. In item III.C.4, the number of students registered or enrolled in a course cannot be larger than the maximum enrollment.

D. The count of students enrolled (or registered) in a course in item III.B.2 (or III.B.3) must equal the current enrollment (or registration) indicated in item III.C.4.

E. An instructor cannot be assigned to two courses taught at the same time in the same semester.

F. Two courses cannot be taught in the same room at the same time in a given semester.

G. If a student is enrolled in a course, the corresponding record must indicate that the student has completed all prerequisite courses with a grade of at least C.

H. A student cannot be registered (or enrolled) in two courses taught at the same hour.

I. A student cannot be registered for more than 20 credits in a given semester.

J. The room assigned to a course must have at least as many seats as the maximum allowed enrollment for the course.

K. Once a letter grade of A, B, C, D, or F has been assigned for a course, that grade cannot later be changed to an I.[2]

V. Use Cases
Use cases are performed during *sessions*. A session starts when a user executes an Authentication use case and ends when a user executes an End of Session use case. During a session, a user can execute one or more use cases. The use case diagram for these use cases is shown in Figure 14.1 (which is assumed to be part of the Requirements Document).

A. **Authentication**.
    Purpose. Identify the actor and determine whether she is a student or faculty member. Subsequent use cases in the same session depend on this distinction.
    Actor. A student or a faculty member.
    Input. The actor's Id number and password.

---

[2] This is an example of a *dynamic* integrity constraint, which limits the allowable changes to the state of a database, in contrast to a *static* integrity constraint, which limits the allowable states of the database. We discuss dynamic integrity constraints in Section 3.2.2.

Result. The actor is authenticated and can perform other use cases she is authorized to perform.

Exception. If the actor enters an incorrect Id or password, authentication does not occur and the actor is given another chance to enter an Id and password.

B. **Registration**.

Purpose. Register a student in a course to be taught next semester.

Actor. A student.

Input. A course number.

Result. The student is registered for the course, and an appropriate message is displayed.

Exception. The registration shall not be successful for any of the following reasons, which shall be contained in the output:

1. There exists a prerequisite course that the student is not currently enrolled in or has not completed with a grade of at least C.
2. The number of students registered for the course would exceed the allowed maximum.
3. The initiator of the use case is not a student.
4. The student has registered for another course scheduled at the same time.
5. The student is enrolled in the course or has taken the course and has received a grade of C or better.
6. The course is not offered next semester.
7. The student is already registered for the course.
8. The student would be taking more than 20 credits if the registration were to succeed.

C. **Deregistration**.

Purpose. Deregister the student from a course to be taught next semester for which that student previously registered.

Actor. A student.

Input. A course number.

Result. The student is no longer registered for the course, and an appropriate message is displayed.

Exception. If the student is not registered for the course, the deregistration shall be unsuccessful.

D. **Get Grade History**.

Purpose. Produce a report describing the grade history of a student for each semester in which he has completed courses.

Actor. A student or a faculty member.

Input. A student Id number. If a student is executing the use case, the number need not be entered because the student can request only his or her own report, and the Id of the invoker has been determined as part of authentication.

Result. The report shall include

1. Current semester
2. Student name and Id number

   3. List of courses completed with grade and instructor grouped by semester
   4. Semester GPA and total number of credits for each semester in which the
       student has completed courses
   5. Cumulative GPA and total number of credits of all courses completed so far

Exception. If a faculty member is executing the use case and an invalid student
Id is input, no report shall be produced.

E. **Get Registered Courses**.
    Purpose. Produce a report listing the courses for which a particular student has
    registered for the next semester.
    Actor. A student or a faculty member.
    Input. A student Id number. If a student is executing the use case, the number
    need not be entered because the student can request only his or her own report,
    and the Id of the invoker has been determined as part of authentication.
    Result. The report shall include

    1. Student's name and Id number
    2. Course number and credit hours
    3. Time schedule for every course
    4. Classroom assignment (if available)
    5. Instructor (if available)

    Exception. If a faculty member is executing the use case and an invalid student
    Id is input, no report shall be produced.

F. **Get Enrolled Courses**.
    Purpose. Produce a report listing the courses in which a particular student is
    enrolled this semester.
    Actor. A student or a faculty member.
    Input. A student Id number. If a student is executing the use case, the number
    need not be entered because the student can request only his or her own report,
    and the Id of the invoker has been determined as part of authentication.
    Result. The report shall include

    1. Student's name and Id number
    2. Course number and credit hours
    3. Time schedule for every course
    4. Classroom assignment
    5. Instructor

    Exception. If a faculty member is executing the use case and an invalid student
    Id is input, no report shall be produced.

G. **Student Grade**.
    Purpose. Assign or change a grade for a course a student has completed.
    Actor. The faculty member who taught the course.
    Input. A student Id number, a course number, a semester, and a grade.

Result.

1. The student shall no longer be shown as enrolled in that course, but shall be shown as having completed that course.
2. If the course is a prerequisite for some course in the following semester for which the student is currently registered and if the grade is less than C, the student shall be deregistered from that course.

Exception. The grade shall not be assigned or changed if

1. The invoker is not the faculty member who taught the course in the semester indicated.
2. The student Id number is invalid.
3. The student is not currently enrolled in the course or did not take the course in a previous semester.
4. The use case would change a grade (A, B, C, D, F) to an I.

H. **Student/Faculty Information**.
    Purpose. Add, delete, or edit an entry specified in item III.A.
    Actor. a faculty member.[3]
    Input. If an entry is to be added, the name, Id number, faculty/student status, and password must be supplied. If an entry is to be deleted or edited, the Id number must be provided as well as any fields to be changed.
    Result. The specified information is added, edited, or deleted.

I. **Course Information**.
    Purpose. Display or edit the information describing an existing course (item III.C) or enter information describing a new course.
    Actor. A student or a faculty member.
    Input. A course number.
    Result. The requested information is displayed and can be edited. A faculty member can change any characteristic of a course but cannot delete the course. Students shall be allowed only to display (not to enter or edit) information about a course.
    Exception. If the edited course information would violate any integrity constraint, no update shall take place.

J. **End of Semester**.
    Purpose. Update the database to reflect the end of the semester.
    Actor. A faculty member.
    Result.

1. The identity of the current semester, as specified in item III.F, shall be advanced.
2. For each student, an I grade shall be assigned for all courses in which that student is currently enrolled and for which no grade has yet been assigned.

---

[3] In a real system, this information would be controlled by a database administrator using a special set of transactions. In this project, we assume for simplicity that the database has been initialized with at least one faculty member's name, Id, and password.

3. Each student shall be indicated as enrolled in those courses for which the database previously indicated that the student was registered.

4. For each course listed in item III.C.4, the number of students enrolled shall be set equal to the number registered, and the number registered shall be set to 0.

Exception. If a course is scheduled to be taught next semester to which an instructor or classroom has not yet been assigned, the semester shall not be updated, no database changes shall be made, and an appropriate message shall be displayed.

K. **Get Class Roster**.
Purpose. Produce a list of the names and Id numbers of students currently enrolled in or registered for a course.
Actor. A faculty member.
Input. A course number and an indication of whether an enrollment or a registration list is requested.
Result. The requested class roster is displayed.
Exception. If an enrollment list for a course not currently being taught or a registration list for a course not to be taught next semester is requested, no display is returned.

L. **Room**.
Purpose. Display the size (i.e., number of seats) of an existing classroom (item III.E) or enter the identifier and size of a new classroom.
Actor. A faculty member.
Input. A classroom identifier and the number of seats (if a new classroom is to be entered) or just the identifier (if the size of an existing classroom is requested).
Result. The requested information is displayed or the identity and size of the new classroom is stored in the database.
Exception. If an existing classroom size is requested and the specified classroom identifier is incorrect, an appropriate error message is displayed.

M. **OLAP Query**.
Purpose. Allow the user to input an arbitrary query from the screen.
Actor. A faculty member (who, it is assumed, knows the database schema).
Input. A query in the form of a single SELECT statement.
Result. The table produced by the query is output on the screen with attribute names (where possible) heading each column.
Exception. If a statement other than a SELECT is input or if the statement is incorrect, an appropriate error message is returned.

N. **End of Session**.
Purpose. End the session.
Actor. A student or a faculty member.
Input. The actor clicks the logout button.
Result. Any subsequent use cases with the system require a new authentication.

VI. System Issues

A. The system shall be implemented as a client/server system. The client computer shall be a PC on which the application programs will execute.

B. The user interface shall be graphical and easy to use by students and faculty with little or no training.

C. The database can be any SQL database that executes on an available server computer and provides a transactional interface (in other words, it can perform the commit and abort operations).

VII. Deliverables

A. A Specification Document that describes in detail the sequence of events (input/output) that occurs for each use case, including
   1. The forms and controls to be used
   2. The effect of using each control on each form, including any new forms that are displayed as a result of each possible action
   3. The errors for which the system checks and the error messages that are output
   4. Integrity constraints

B. A Design Document that describes in detail
   1. An entity-relationship (E-R) diagram that describes the system
   2. The declaration of all database elements (including tables, domains, and assertions)
   3. The decomposition of each use case into transactions and procedures
   4. The behavior of each transaction and procedure

C. A Test Plan describing how the system will be tested, including how each of the numbered requirements and specifications will be tested

D. A demonstration of the completed system (including running the tests in the Test Plan)

E. Fully documented code for the system

F. A User Manual with separate sections for student and faculty

G. Version 2 of the Specification Document, the Design Document, and the Test Plan, describing the as-built system

14.3 Requirements Analysis—New Issues

The next phase of the project is to analyze the Requirements Document and produce a formal Specification Document. Experience has shown that, no matter how carefully the Requirements Document is written, when the implementation team analyzes the requirements in order to prepare the Specification Document, a number of new issues will be identified. Parts of the Requirements Document will be found to be inconsistent or incomplete, and questions will be raised about the desired behavior of the system in certain previously unforeseen situations. The implementation team customarily presents these issues to the customer, who resolves them in a written document. The resolved issues then become part of a revised version of the Requirements Document and part of the initial version of the Specification Document. This entire scenario underscores the difficulties in precisely specifying the desired behavior of a proposed system.

When the Requirements Document given in Section 14.2 was analyzed by our local implementation team, a number of issues were identified. Below we present some of these together with their resolution. Your local implementation team is likely to discover other issues.

Issue 1. What if, during the Course Information use case, an attempt is made to add a new prerequisite for a course such that the prerequisites form a cycle? For example, course A is a prerequisite for course B, B is a prerequisite for course C, and C is a prerequisite for A. In other words, course A is a prerequisite for itself.

Resolution. A new database integrity constraint must be added to deal with this situation: there must not be a cycle of prerequisites. Any transaction that implements the Course Information use case shall check for this condition, and, if it exists, the prerequisite shall not be added and an appropriate message shall be presented to the user. (The check for circularity in the general case is not simple. We might, however, require that the prerequisite for a course have a lower number than the course itself. Such a requirement eliminates the possibility of circularity.)

Issue 2. What if, during the Course Information use case, an attempt is made to add a new prerequisite for a course, and a student who does not have that prerequisite is already registered for that course?

Resolution. A new prerequisite for a course does not apply to the offering of the course (if any) in the following semester.

Issue 3. What if, during the Course Information use case, the maximum number of students allowed in a course is reduced to a value that is less than the number of students who have already registered for the course?

Resolution. Room rescheduling is a fact of academic life, so this use case must be allowed. However, the appropriate number of students must be deregistered from the course to bring the total number of registered students to the new maximum. The students shall be deregistered in the reverse order that they were registered. All deregistered students shall be notified in writing.

Issue 4. What if, during the Course Information use case, an attempt is made to change the day and/or time a course is offered?

Resolution. A change in day and/or time does not apply to the offering of the course (if any) in the following semester.

CASE STUDY

Issue 5. What if, during the Course Information use case, a course is canceled?

Resolution. Cancellation applies to the next semester. Students registered for the next semester shall be deregistered and notified in writing.

Issue 6. What if, during a Student/Faculty Information use case, an attempt is made to change a student's Id number?

Resolution. An Id number (in contrast to a name or password) is permanently associated with an individual, so an attempt to change it makes no sense, except if it was originally entered in error. As a result, a change in Id number is allowed only if there is no other information relevant to the student in the system.

Issue 7. Several of the use cases, such as Get Grade History, Get Registered Courses, and Get Enrolled Courses, produce reports that describe the state of the database at a particular instant. Should those reports include the date and time they were produced?

Resolution. Yes, all such reports shall include the date and time.

Issue 8. Should the information in items III.D and III.F contain the year as well as the semester?

Resolution. Yes, and the End of Semester use case shall appropriately update the year. This information shall be initialized at startup time.

Issue 9. How many digits should be used to indicate the year in the system?

Resolution. Four.

14.4 Specifying the Student Registration System

A Specification Document contains a complete description of what the system is supposed to do from the viewpoint of its end users—it is an expanded version of the Requirements Document. For a transaction processing system, the Specification Document should include

- The integrity constraints of the enterprise
- A complete description of the user interface
  - A picture of every form with every control specified
  - A description of what happens when each control is used, including
    - What application procedure is executed
    - What changes occur in the form or what new form is displayed
    - What error situations can occur and what happens in each such situation
- A description of each use case, including
  - The information input by the user and what events cause the use case to be executed

- A textual description of what the use case does (for example, "the student is registered for the course")
- A list of conditions under which the use case succeeds or fails, and what happens in each case

The Specification Document might also contain other information related to project planning (such as schedules, milestones, deliverables, cost information, etc.), information related to system issues (such as software and hardware on which the system must run), and any time or memory constraints. The Table of Contents for the Specification Document for the Student Registration System has the following sections:

I. Introduction

II. Related Documents

III. Forms and Use Cases

IV. Project Plans

A. **Milestones**

B. **Deliverables**

Note the relationship between the contents of the requirements and specification documents.

14.4.1 UML Sequence Diagrams

Part of the plan for developing a Specification Document from a Requirements Document might be to expand each use case into a UML sequence diagram. A **sequence diagram** is a graphic display of the temporal order of the interactions between the actors in a use case and the other modules in the system.

Figure 14.2 is a sequence diagram for the Authentication use case. The actors in the use case (in the figure, a student or a faculty member) and the pertinent modules in the system (in the figure, the Web server and the database) are labelled at the top of the diagram. Time moves downward through the diagram, and the vertical line descending from each actor and module show its lifetime during the use case. The boxes on the vertical line show when that actor (or module) is active in the use case. The horizontal lines show particular actions taken by an actor or module. Thus, the sequence diagram starts with the student or faculty member typing in the URL of the Student Registration System, after which the Web server displays the Welcome Form (Figure 14.3). Note the notation used for conditional actions: [*status = student*] *Display Student Options Form*. This means that if the status returned by the Authentication interaction is "student," the Web server displays the Student Options Form.

Note that Specification III.A in the Specification Document given in Section 14.5 is an English-language description of the sequence diagram in Figure 14.2.

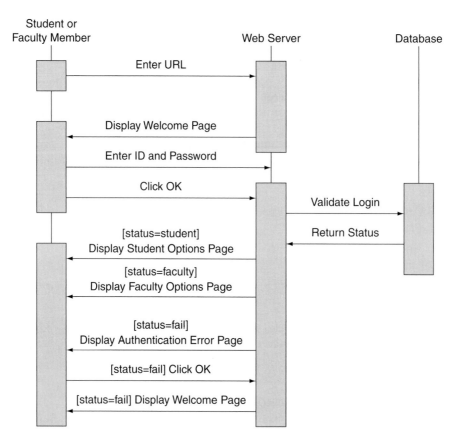

FIGURE 14.2 A sequence diagram for the Authentication use case.

In the following section, we present the initial part of Section III of the Specification Document. We give a design for the database in the the Student Registration System in Section 4.8 and the design and part of the code for the Registration Transaction in Section 15.7.

14.5 The Specification Document for the Student Registration System: Section III

Section III of the Specification Document—"Forms and Use Cases"—contains a detailed description of all interactions with users. Its initial part might look like this:

III. Forms and Use Cases

A. When the Student Registration System is entered, Form 1, the Welcome Form (Figure 14.3) is displayed. In Form 1

    1. The Id and Password text boxes are filled in.

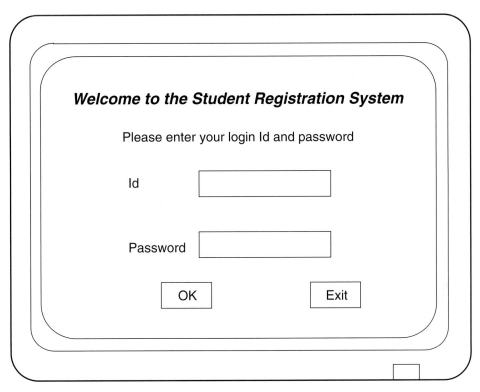

FIGURE 14.3 Introductory form for the Student Registration System.

2. The OK command button is clicked to run the *Authentication* use case.
   a. If the Authentication use case fails, Form 2, the Authentication Error Form, is displayed.[4] In Form 2, clicking the OK command button returns to Form 1.
   b. If the Authentication use case succeeds and the authenticated user is a student, Form 3, the Student Options Form, is displayed (as described in Specification III.B).
   c. If the Authentication use case succeeds and the authenticated user is a faculty member, Form 4, the Faculty Options Form, is displayed.
3. The Exit command button is clicked to display Form 5, the Do You Really Want To Exit Form. In Form 5
   a. The Yes command button is clicked to exit the Student Registration System.
   b. The No command button is clicked to return to Form 1.

---

[4] We omit the figures for the other forms; they would be included in the actual specification.

B.   In Form 3, the Student Options Form,

    1.   The Course description menu item is selected to run the *Get Course Names* use case, which displays Form 6, the Course Name Form. In Form 6

       a.   A course option box is selected.

       b.   The OK command button is clicked to run the *Get Course Description* use case, which displays Form 7, the Course Description Form.

       c.   The Cancel command button is clicked to return to Form 3.

The remainder of Section III of the Specification Document is similar and is therefore omitted.

14.6   The Next Step in the Software Engineering Process

After the implementation group has expanded the Requirements Document into the Specification Document and the customer has signed off on the Specification Document, the design portion of the project can begin. In contrast with specifications, which describe *what* the system is supposed to do, the design describes *how* the system is to do what it does. We discuss design in Chapter 15 and the specific issues involved in designing databases in Chapters 4 and 6. We gave a complete database design for the Student Registration System in Section 4.8 and the complete design and part of the code for the Registration Transaction in Section 15.7.

One reason so much time and effort is put into producing requirements and specification documents is that experience has shown it to be surprisingly difficult to build a system that actually satisfies the customer's needs. Often the system's requirements are quite complex, and the customer has difficulty articulating his needs in the precise manner needed for programming, or he leaves out important details (such as what is supposed to happen if a course is canceled after a number of students have registered for it) or specifies some feature and then is unhappy with that feature when it is implemented.

The U.S. Department of Defense, which is probably the largest customer for software systems in the world, says that over 56% of all the defects in software systems it contracts for are due to errors in the specifications. It is cheaper and more efficient to work with the customer at the beginning of the project to sharpen and refine the specifications than it is to reimplement the system at the end of the project if it does not meet the customer's needs.

BIBLIOGRAPHIC NOTES

There are many excellent books on software engineering—for example, [Summerville 2000]; [Pressman 2002]; [Schach 1999]. One of the very few books that address software engineering for database and transaction processing systems is [Blaha and Premerlani 1998].

EXERCISES

14.1 Prepare a Requirements Document for a simple calculator.

14.2 According to the Requirements Document for the Student Registration System, one session can include a number of use cases. Later, during the design, we will decompose each use case into one or more transactions. The ACID properties apply to all transactions, but a session that involves more than one transaction might not be isolated or atomic. For example, the transactions of several sessions might be interleaved. Explain why the decision was made not to require sessions to be isolated and atomic. Why is a session not one long transaction?

14.3 Suppose that the database in the Student Registration System satisfies all the integrity constraints given in Section IV of the Requirements Document Outline (Section 14.2). Is the database necessarily correct? Explain.

14.4 The Requirements Document for the Student Registration System does not address security issues. Prepare a section on security issues, which might be included in a more realistic Requirements Document.

14.5 In the resolution of issue 2 in Section 14.3, the statement was made that new prerequisites do not apply to courses offered in the next semester. How can a Registration Transaction know whether or not a prerequisite is "new"?

14.6 Suppose that the Student Registration System is to be expanded to include graduation clearance. Describe some additional items that must be stored in the database. Describe some additional integrity constraints.

14.7 Prepare a Specification Document for a simple calculator.

14.8 Prepare a Specification Document for the controls of a microwave oven.

14.9 Specify a use case for the Student Registration System that assigns a room to a course to be taught next semester.

15

Design, Coding, and Testing

Now that the Specification Document for the Student Registration System has been approved by the customer, we are ready to continue with the project. The next step is design.

15.1 The Design Process

In contrast to specifications, which describe *what* the system is supposed to do, the design describes *how* the system is to do what it does. Thus, the design of a transaction processing system includes

- The declaration of every global data structure used in the system, including the database schema and any data structures kept by application programs between transaction invocations

- The decomposition of each interaction described in the Specification Document into transactions and procedures

- Detailed description of the behavior of every module, object, procedure, and transaction contained in the system

The results of the design phase are presented in a Design Document, which, in a sense, is an extension of the Specification Document. The Specification Document describes in detail the capabilities of the system, whereas the Design Document describes in detail how each of these capabilities is to be implemented.

The design process itself is often viewed as the most creative part of the implementation project. Good designs are simple and elegant. The designer formulates and evaluates various design alternatives (for example, various table designs) to achieve the desired functionality and then, based on her judgment and experience, makes decisions that significantly influence the system implementation and its ultimate performance. Unfortunately, while making these decisions is the enjoyable part of the process, documenting the details in the Design Document is often one of the designer's more tedious (but nevertheless necessary) tasks.

The users of the Design Document include

- The coding group, who use it as their sole source of information in their coding

- The quality control group, who use it, together with the Specification Document, to design tests and to determine what went wrong when an error is discovered

- The maintenance group, who use it (at a later date) to implement enhancements to the system

An important part of the design process is to make all global decisions (i.e., those that affect multiple transactions and procedures) so that later, during the coding phase, each coder can implement each individual transaction or procedure with no knowledge of the overall system other than that provided in the Design Document. If the Design Document is incomplete to the extent that the coder of a particular transaction or procedure has to make a global decision, that decision is liable to be inconsistent with a decision made by the coder of another transaction or procedure about the same global issue—thus causing an error.

For example, suppose procedure P_1 calls procedure P_2 with certain arguments that must be in some specified range, and suppose the Design Document does not specify whether that range check is to be made in P_1 or P_2. Then if the programmer of P_1 expects it to be made in P_2 and the programmer of P_2 expects it to be made in P_1, that check will not be made at all, and a potentially serious error has occurred.

15.1.1 Database Design

The design document must contain a complete design of the database, including a set of executable statements that declare the database schema (such as SQL's CREATE statements).

A typical approach to database design, discussed in this book, includes several stages. First E-R or UML class diagrams are used to model the business objects involved in the enterprise. These diagrams are then converted into relational schema designs. This part of the process was discussed in Chapter 4, and a concrete case study for the Student Registration System was presented in Section 4.8. The next step is to normalize the schema and bring it into compliance with one of the desirable normal forms. This step was the subject of Chapter 6, and a case study was performed in Section 6.12. The last step in database design is tuning. Indexing, described in Chapter 9, is one important part of this step. The overall strategy for tuning databases was described in Chapter 12.

Database schema design is an integral part of the overall design document. Other parts of this document are described below.

15.1.2 Describing the Behavior of Objects with UML State Diagrams

UML class diagrams or E-R diagrams can be used to model the business objects stored in the database. However, these models are *static* in that they model only the data stored in the database, but not how that data changes when operations are performed on it. *UML state diagrams* are one way to model the *dynamic* behavior of these objects—how their internal state changes when their methods are invoked.

[Enrollment < MaxEnrollment − 1] Register / Enrollment = Enrollment + 1

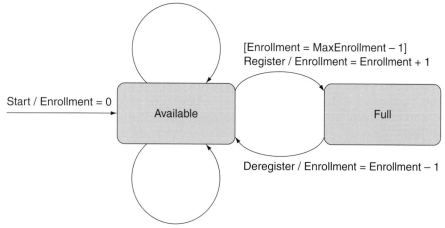

FIGURE **15.1** A UML state diagram for the CLASS object.

For example, in the Student Registration System, one part of the internal state of a CLASS object is its Enrollment attribute. One of the integrity constraints is that the value of Enrollment must be less than or equal to the value of the MaxEnrollment attribute. We might say that when Enrollment is equal to MaxEnrollment, the CLASS is *Full*; otherwise it is *Available*. Now we can describe the dynamic behavior of CLASS as follows:

1. When the CLASS is *Available*, a Register operation causes the value of Enrollment to be increased by one. If that increase causes Enrollment to equal MaxEnrollment, then CLASS becomes *Full*.
2. When the CLASS is *Full*, a Register operation cannot occur (is unsuccessful if attempted).
3. A Deregister operation causes the value of Enrollment to be decreased by one. If the CLASS is *Full*, it becomes *Available*.

We can model that behavior by the UML state diagram shown in Figure 15.1. CLASS has two *states*, *Available* and *Full*. The arrows between the states are *transitions*, which model the operations and denote when an operation causes the state of the object to change. Each transition is of the form

```
[guard] operation / action
```

for example,

```
[Enrollment < MaxEnrollment-1] Register / Enrollment = Enrollment+1
```

The *guard* is a Boolean expression, which states the condition under which the transition can take place. In the example, the transition can take place only if Enrollment is less than MaxEnrollment − 1. The *operation* specifies the method that causes the transition. The *action* then specifies how the attributes within the object change when the transition occurs.

Thus the state diagram provides a graphic model of the dynamic behavior of the object being modeled. That model can be used to communicate the design to the other designers, to the coders who must build the programs to implement the design, and to the test designers, who must design the test to demonstrate that the system works correctly.

UML state diagrams have many more options that are shown in this simple example. A more complete discussion, as well as more complex examples, can be found in any book on UML.

15.1.3 Structure of the Design Document

The sections of a design document for a transaction processing system might include

A. **Title, author(s), date, version number**.

B. **Introduction**. A brief description of the goals of the system

C. **Related documents**. References to the Requirements and Specification documents and to any other documents used in the design or implementation—for example, a Visual Basic user manual, an ODBC specification document, or a specification document for some object library used in the design

D. **High-level design**. An informal description of the design so the reader can more easily follow the detailed descriptions in later sections. Among the items that might be included:

   1. The decomposition of the system into modules or objects
   2. The decomposition of the interactions defined in the Specification Document into transactions and procedures
   3. A procedure calling tree
   4. A UML class diagram or an E-R diagram for the database design, including the rationale for any choices made in designing the diagram

Also included in this section can be the rationale for any design decisions that need to be documented. Examples might include:

   5. Why a session was decomposed into transactions in one way rather than in another, perhaps more intuitive, way
   6. Why a table was normalized, denormalized, or partitioned in a particular way, perhaps to meet some performance requirement
   7. Why certain indices were defined
   8. Why certain integrity constraints were to be checked by transactions rather than embedded in the database schema
   9. Why certain transactions were allowed to execute at lower isolation levels
  10. Why any other decisions were made to achieve performance requirements

E. **Declaration of the database schema and other global data structures**

   1. *Database schema.*

      a. The complete (compilable) set of statements that declare the database schema, including tables, indices, domain specifications, assertions, and access privileges—documented with the intended use of each table and column, and the rationale for each index

      b. A list of the integrity constraints, together with a description of where each constraint will be enforced: in the schema or by the individual transactions

   2. *Global data structures.* The complete (compilable) declaration of any other global data structures; for example, those kept by an application program for use by the transactions it initiates. Each item must be documented with its intended use and any constraints on its values.

F. **Graphical user interface.** Since a detailed description of the user interface appears in the Specification Document, only a reference to the appropriate document section is needed. However, any missing details of the user interface must be supplied here—including the specification of all events and objects (including their methods).

G. **Detailed description of transactions and procedures.** For each transaction and procedure,

   1. *Transaction or procedure name.*

   2. *Description.* An informal, one-sentence description of what the transaction or procedure does. For example: "This transaction registers a student in a specified course after checking that the prerequisites are satisfied." (The goal is to explain the general purpose of the transaction, not to give its detailed functional specification.)

   3. *Arguments. In* and *out* arguments of the transaction or procedure. Each argument must be documented, with its type and intended use.

   4. *Return values.* The values that can be returned by the transaction or procedure, together with their type and intended use.

   5. *Called from.* The procedures, or (GUI) events, that call this transaction. (For example, a transaction might be called when a particular mouse-click event occurs on some form object.)

   6. *Calls.* The procedures called by this transaction, including any events it causes and any exceptions it raises. (These last two items are useful when the design or code needs to be changed, and the designer or coder must propagate changes throughout the design.)

   7. *Preconditions.* Assumptions that the transaction or procedure can make (and does not have to check at run time) about the state of the database, the global data structure, and its arguments when it starts. For example, a transaction to register a student in a course might be able to assume that a previously executed transaction authenticated the student. As another example, a procedure invoked by a particular mouse-click event might be able to assume that an input value it needs was previously stored by the user

in a particular field of a particular form object. (Most of the global errors in large system implementations occur because of miscommunication about preconditions.)

8. *Isolation level*. The isolation level at which the transaction will execute.
9. *Actions*.
    a. Textual description of the actions taken by the transaction or procedure. (Perhaps one or two paragraphs, compared to the one-sentence description given earlier—the goal here is to help the coder write the code.)
    b. Database tables and global data structures accessed, together with the changes the transaction or procedure is supposed to make. For example, after a successful registration transaction, the student must be listed in the appropriate table(s) as being registered for the course, and the number of registrants for that course must be incremented.
    c. Error situations.
        i. Validity checks that the transaction or procedure must make about its arguments, the global data structure, or the database. For example, a transaction to register a student for a course might be required to check that the student has taken (or is taking) all the prerequisites for that course. Or a transaction accessing some field that is allowed to be null (for example, a registration transaction reading the course days and time) might be required to check that that field is not null at the time the transaction or procedure is executed. A description must be given of the actions to be taken when such a check fails.
        ii. Automatic constraint checks the system will make on the updates of this transaction and the actions to be taken if these updates fail.
        iii. Any other error or anomalous situations that might occur and the actions to be taken in each case. For example, what should happen if a database **CONNECT** statement fails? What exceptions should be raised and under what conditions?
    d. Forms to be displayed in various circumstances—perhaps on successful completion or if some specified error situation occurs.

15.1.4 Design Review

Near the end of the design process, a formal **design review** is often held in which all members of the design and quality assurance groups and perhaps some outside people participate. The participants are given the latest version of the specification and design documents before the review and are expected to have studied them before the meeting.

The designers make a formal presentation, and the participants are expected to gain an understanding of the design and to identify issues such as:

- Places where the Design Document is inconsistent with the Specification Document

- Places where the Design Document is incorrect, inconsistent, incomplete, or ambiguous

- Places where the efficiency of the design can be improved (perhaps by using a different table structure or a different indexing structure for a table)

- Any areas of risk to the project in meeting its goals. For example, does a particular search algorithm meet the response time specifications? Does the design require a new version of a database driver that might not be available in time to meet the schedule? Does some suspect assumption underlie a global decision?

- Any risks inherent in the execution of the delivered system. For example, is a person's life or health at risk if the system does not work according to its specifications. Does the design adequately address those risks?

The goal of the design review is to identify issues, not resolve them. Each issue identified is assigned to a member of the design team for resolution by some specified date and for inclusion in a later version of the Design Document.

Any errors found during the design review are much easier and cheaper to correct than those found later, during the coding or testing phases. Errors found after the system has been delivered to the customer are still more expensive to correct.

The design review meeting might also include a review of the Test Plan, as described in the next section.

15.2 Test Plan

Testing is an important part of all software projects, not an informal ad hoc activity that the testers begin to think about only when the coding is complete. It is carried out in accordance with a formal Test Plan document, which is prepared during the design and coding phases of the project. The Test Plan document specifies the tests to be performed, the test data to be used, and the design of any test driver or scripting software needed to perform the tests.

The complete Test Plan might involve **module tests** performed by the coder of each individual module before the module is submitted for integration into the system, **integration tests** performed by the group that is integrating the modules into the system, and finally the **QA test set** performed by the quality assurance group on the completely integrated system.

We focus our attention on the final QA test set, but we first note an important aspect of module testing—testing the individual SQL statements within the module. These tests might include **code checks**, in which a colleague examines each SQL statement to verify that it satisfies its English-language specifications, as well as more conventional tests in which the SQL statements are executed against actual or test databases.

The design of an appropriate QA test set for a commercial transaction processing system is a significant endeavor. The test set might include tests designed using two different approaches.

Black box tests are designed from the Specification Document, without looking at the Design Document or the code. These tests assume that the system is just a "black box," and they do not look inside. The goal is to verify that the system meets its specifications. Thus, there must be at least one test for every specification in the Specification Document (including error situations). Some specifications might have several tests. For example, to test that the number of students registered for a course does not exceed the specified maximum, the designer might include tests in which a registration transaction is executed when the number of previously registered students is both one less than the maximum and exactly the maximum. The test should also include cases in which the number is far from the maximum. (For example, what happens if the maximum is specified as 0 or 1?) Since it is impractical to include tests where the number of previously registered students and the maximum number of students both range over all possible integers (a completely exhaustive set of tests), the designer must use her experience to develop a test set that is representative of situations that might occur, meets the appropriate boundary conditions, and can be performed in the allotted testing time.

Because the user interface is specified in the Specification Document, the black box tests must test the user interface.

Glass box tests are designed using the Design Document and the code. They are called "glass box" because they look inside the system. The goal is to verify that the detailed coding is correct. Thus, glass box tests should visit every line of code, visit every branch of the code, check the boundary conditions of every loop, invoke every event, execute every integrity check, and exercise all aspects of every algorithm. For example, the code to check whether a student has all the prerequisites for a course might contain a while loop, and the test designer might include tests to verify that the exit condition of that loop is correct. Note that the existence of this while loop and its exit condition is not evident from the Specification Document, which is why we need glass box tests in addition to black box tests. However, we also need black box tests since the designers might have misunderstood some portion of the Specification Document, and any test set based only on the Design Document would not find such errors. For example, a glass box text might show that the exit condition of a while loop corresponds to the Design Document, but the Design Document might be an incorrect interpretation of the specification.

The Test Plan might also include **stress tests** in which a (possibly simulated) realistic load is placed on the system to verify that it meets its specifications for transaction throughput and response time. Such tests might uncover situations in which a large number of deadlocks occur or in which the database design needs tuning for other reasons to increase throughput or decrease response time.

If the application is built on a system that guarantees the ACID properties, we do not need additional tests to verify that the concurrent execution of transactions works correctly, assuming that we have already tested that each transaction works correctly when executed in isolation. However, if the application is being executed at some level of isolation less than SERIALIZABLE (see Section 8.2.3), additional tests might be necessary to ensure correctness under concurrent execution.

Often neglected in a Test Plan is testing of the User Manual (and other deliverable documentation) to ensure that it corresponds to the specifications and to the delivered system.

The Test Plan document contains a script of all tests that are to be performed and the correct result of each. Since the Test Plan contains a large number of tests and must be executed many times during the testing and maintenance phases (after fixing some error or adding some new feature), it is highly desirable to employ a test driver or scripting mechanism to automate the Test Plan execution. If such a mechanism is used, the Test Plan document contains the appropriate inputs to the test driver. If a test driver is to be implemented as part of the project, its design must also be included.

The Test Plan document also contains a description of the testing protocol that will be used by the testers when performing the tests (or a reference to the company's standard testing protocol document). That protocol should include an **Error Report Form**, which must be filled out when an error is found. The Error Report Form should include the tester's name, the date, the error description, and, most important, a detailed description of how to recreate the situation in which the error occurs. The Error Report Form is passed on to the person responsible for fixing the error, who fills in information about when and how the error was fixed and which version of the code contains the fix. The entire protocol must ensure that all errors that are found are eventually fixed and that some version of the code contains all of the fixes.

To design a Test Plan that is comprehensive (in the sense just described) and yet manageable takes a considerable amount of skill and experience. The actual size of the test set and the scope of the testing effort for any particular application are often marketing as well as technical decisions, dependent on a number of sometimes conflicting factors. For example,

- How critical is the correctness of the system? Are people's lives at stake?
- How important is time to market of the system? Is a competitive product about to be released or is there an upcoming trade show at which the system must be exhibited?

In some critical applications, half of the entire time allocated to the project is devoted to testing. Sometimes issues of professional ethics arise when management applies pressure to release an inadequately tested product.

In applications in which the system is being implemented by one group and delivered to another group, which will operate and maintain it, the test set (together with any drivers or scripting mechanisms) is often one of the deliverables, along with the code and the documentation.

Some customers might insist that a complete history of the testing process, including the dates and results of all tests, errors found, errors fixed, etc., be delivered with the software in order to demonstrate that the test plan had been successfully carried out. In some situations both the customer and the developers store this history permanently, together with the rest of the documentation for the system, in case they are needed in some future legal situation, which might involve alleged defects in the system. The company might need to demonstrate to a court that the system was developed and adequately tested according to standard software engineering practice.

Acceptance testing and beta testing. In addition to the Test Plan, which is prepared and carried out by the system implementors, the customer often prepares and carries out an **acceptance test** before accepting the system (and perhaps before making the final payment for it). An acceptance test is usually composed of realistic inputs and an actual database (in contrast with the implementor's Test Plan, which often involves boundary case inputs and test databases) and is intended to increase customer confidence that the system will fulfill its purpose. A savvy customer will spend considerable effort to design an acceptance test that comprehensively exercises the system in real-world situations.

If the system is a product with many customers, a small set of these customers is often selected to perform **beta testing**. In this context, the testing performed by the system implementors is called **alpha testing**. When the alpha testing is completed, the **beta test version** is supplied to customers, who use it on their actual applications and report any errors to the implementors. Because the beta test version might still contain serious errors, the customer might be at some risk in using it (especially since implementation groups have been known to minimize the amount of alpha testing and rely on beta testing to find many of the errors in their system), but the customer gets the benefits of receiving an early version and might receive some other financial or technical incentives as well. The beta testing continues for some period of time, perhaps weeks or months, after which the initial release of the system is made to all customers.

Even after all of this testing, customers with critical applications often run a new system in parallel with their existing system for some period of time until they gain sufficient confidence that it can do its job reliably and correctly.

15.3 Project Planning

Project planning is another important part of software engineering. While the Specification Document is being prepared, the project manager makes an initial version of the Project Plan. To make such a plan, the manager divides the project into a set of **tasks**, estimates the time required to complete each task, and then assigns each task to a specific person (or group) together with targeted start and completion dates.

A task might involve design, coding, testing, or documentation, but it must have the property that its completion can be precisely defined—for example, "The coding of module 3 is complete," not "Module 4 is 90% debugged." Estimating the time it will take to complete a given task is quite difficult and requires understanding the complexity of the task and relating that complexity to the skill of the person assigned to carry it out.

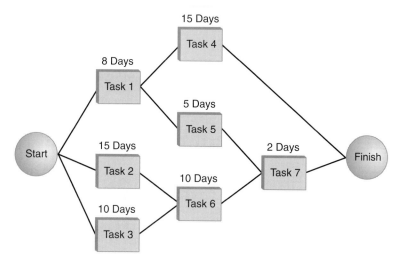

FIGURE 15.2 Dependency chart.

An essential aspect of task scheduling is **task dependency**: certain tasks cannot be started until certain others have been completed. For example, the testing of a module cannot begin until its coding is finished.

Given the dependencies and estimated duration of tasks, a **Dependency chart**, sometimes called a **PERT chart** (Program Evaluation and Review Technique), can be constructed, as shown in Figure 15.2. Activities are represented by rectangles with the duration written above each (sometimes maximal and minimal estimates of task duration are included) and dependencies represented by lines. In this way, the chart shows which tasks can be done in parallel and which must be done sequentially. The longest path through this chart from start to end is called the **critical path** and is an estimate of the minimum time required to complete the project.

Other charts used to document the Project Plan include the following:

- A **Gantt chart** (named after its developer, Henry Gantt)—a bar chart showing when tasks are scheduled to start and complete (see Figure 15.3)
- A **Staff Allocation chart**—a bar chart showing the assignments of individual staff members to specific tasks, together with the scheduled start and completion dates (see Figure 15.4)

As the project proceeds, the project manager schedules periodic (perhaps weekly) project meetings at which implementation team members report on the status and expected completion date of each assigned task, compared with its scheduled completion date in the Project Plan. The project manager should encourage an environment in which team members feel comfortable in honestly reporting when they are having trouble with their assigned task and might not be able to complete it on schedule. If necessary, the project manager then makes the appropriate decisions

FIGURE **15.3** Gantt chart.

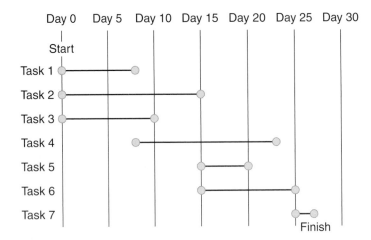

FIGURE **15.4** Staff allocation chart.

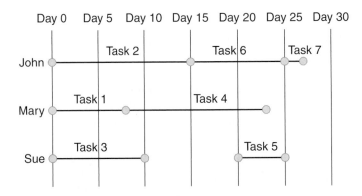

to ensure that the project completes on time. Tasks on the critical path must be monitored especially carefully. (Often the best people on the staff are assigned to them.) It is particularly important that minutes be kept of these meetings to document any decisions taken and assignments made.

When the project is completed, many project managers hold a windup meeting with the entire team to discuss what went right and wrong with the planning and other aspects of the project. The goal is to learn from any mistakes and to increase the software engineering skills of the manager and the team members.

Although project management software is available to automate the production of project planning charts, the preparation and monitoring of a Project Plan require a considerable amount of skill and experience. Indeed, the main reason many software projects fail or are late is the project manager's lack of skill in project planning and monitoring.

15.4 Coding

In most software projects, the time allocated for the coding phase is less than one-sixth of that allocated for the entire project. That fraction will become even smaller as reusable object libraries automate the production of code directly from the design.

A well-run IT department should have coding guidelines that every programmer follows. These guidelines vary from company to company, but there are many common rules. Some programming languages, such as Java, have their own coding styles, but this is usually only a small portion of what a typical set of coding standards mandates. One well-known example of such a set is known as the GNU Coding Guidelines [Stallman 2000]. Here we include some hints for producing professional-quality code:

- The two highest priorities in coding are *correctness* and *clarity*.[1] In addition to being correct, the code must be understandable to the large number of people (such as the quality assurance and maintenance groups) who will read it over its lifetime.

- All of the coders should use the same style of variable definitions, indentation, and the like. Good text editors and integrated development systems provide tools for automatically indenting programs according to certain rules. The program for the entire system should look as if it had been written by a single coder.

- Variables and procedures should have application-oriented names that make their use self-evident—for example, not S, or Stu, or even Student, but Student_Name or Student_ID_Number.

- Comments should be used effectively:
  - The code for each module, procedure, and transaction should begin with a **preamble**, which is the same as its detailed description in the Design Document and can also include the author, date, and revision number. Some guidelines require that a **revision history** be included in the program file, which can include entries such as

    ```
    1999-12-12: Mary Doe (md@company.com)
      foo.java (checkAll): added capability to check userids
    1998-03-22: John Public (jp@company.com)
      foo.java (checkCredentials): fixed bug in while loop
    ```

    However, keeping the revision history inside program files is becoming obsolete due to the development of sophisticated version control systems. A better approach is to keep the revision history for all files that are in the same directory in a separate file, often called ChangeLog. This allows

---

[1] The third "c," *cleverness*, has the lowest priority.

the developers to see the changes made to all files in one place and in chronological order. This style is superior when there are dependencies between the code in different files in the same directory. The history of individual files can typically be obtained from the version control system, which is a better place to keep it than inside the program file.

- Comments within a module, procedure, and transaction should be application oriented. For example, the following comment is useless

```
/* Increment number_registered */
number_registered = number_registered+1;
```

because it is self-evident from the code. If this line of code were part of the registration transaction and needed to be documented at all, a better comment might be

```
/* Another student has registered */
```

Not every statement needs to be commented. Some programming style books suggest that all loop and conditional statements be commented. For example, comments for a loop and conditional statement, respectively, might be

```
/* Give all employees making ≤ $10,000 a 5% raise. */
```

or

```
/* If the customer has exceeded the credit limit,
** then abort transaction. */
```

- When the program needs to be changed because of bug fixes or enhancements, the appropriate comments should be updated along with the code.

■ System-specific data structures and code should be clearly documented as such. For example, some vendors supply their own version of the embedded SQL CONNECT statement

```
EXEC SQL CONNECT student_database IDENTIFIED BY pml
    DBMS_PASSWORD = 'z9t.56';
    /* ***System Specific: Ingres version of CONNECT */
```

Then, if the system must be ported to a different DBMS at some future time, the system-specific statements can be easily found with a text editor. If the CONNECT statement appears several times in the system, it can be encapsulated within a procedure, which can be called at the appropriate points. Then if the system must be ported, only the body of that procedure need be changed.

Prototype coding. We have sharply differentiated the coding phase of the project from the requirements analysis and design phases. However, in practice, prototypes of parts of the system are often coded during the earlier phases in order to aid in decision making. For example, in a transaction processing system implementation, the following prototypes might be necessary:

■ *During the requirements analysis phase.*
  - Prototype of the user interface to evaluate its clarity and usability and to incorporate customer feedback
  - Prototype of the DBMS access code to compare the relative speeds of various design choices—for example, stored procedures compared with those stored within the application program. These experiments can also be used to validate the specification of the expected transaction throughput of the final system, or they might be used to evaluate (and perhaps reduce) the time required to perform these tasks in the coding and testing phases.

■ *During the design phase.*
  - Prototypes of possible designs for a specific table to evaluate the effect of various indexing schemes on the time required to execute particular SELECT or UPDATE statements
  - Prototypes of other parts of the design to evaluate and reduce the risk involved in certain design decisions

Sometimes this prototype code is later discarded. Sometimes it is used in the production version.

15.5 Incremental Development

Most large implementation projects take several years to complete. During that time, the goals and needs of the enterprise sponsoring the project might change considerably. Therefore, during the course of the project, the managers of the enterprise might request significant changes in the specifications of the system being built. An important issue is how the implementation team responds to such requests.

One approach is to continue building the system as originally specified. Unfortunately, even if the project is successfully completed, the resulting system might not completely satisfy the needs of the enterprise. Of course, implementation of the next version of the system, including some or all of the requested changes, can start as soon as the first version is completed and hopefully can be completed in a relatively short time.

Another approach is to try to keep up with the managers' requests, changing the specifications, design, and code many times during the project. Unfortunately, the project is often never successfully completed—the design is continuously being revised, the code is constantly being rewritten, and the project gets further and further behind schedule, with more and more money required to keep it going, until finally it is canceled. According to the Standish Group Report [Standish 2000], 31% of all information system projects are canceled before they are completed. Successful use of this approach requires discipline (in limiting the number and scope of changes that are allowed) and skill (in negotiating with management on budget increases and schedule extensions).

Still another approach, called **incremental development**, involves building the system in stages. First a **core version** of the system is built based on a subset of the initial specifications, perhaps some subset of the use cases, which can be implemented in a short period of time. Then successive versions are built, each including more of the specified functionality and some of the changes that the managers have requested, based on both the changed needs of the enterprise and the experience gained from running the previous versions. After several such incremental versions have been built, the system includes most of the requirements. Of course, it never includes all the requirements since the managers tend to continually revise them.

The incremental approach is often better than the other two approaches. Risk is minimized because an operational system is available in a relatively short period of time and any enhancements to it can be based on working experience. A potential disadvantage is that, unless the initial design is carefully done, design decisions made for early versions might be inappropriate for the increased functionality of later versions. However, good object-oriented design minimizes this disadvantage since the internal design of objects can be changed and new methods can be added without affecting any existing code.

Unfortunately, some designers use the incremental approach as an excuse to do no design at all and just hack together each version on top of the previous one. Needless to say, that approach can lead to disaster.

15.6 The Project Management Plan

Many organizations require that all of their software project managers prepare a Project Management Plan at the start of every project. In addition, if the project is to be built for some external customer organization, many such customers require that all prospective vendor organizations prepare and submit a Project Management Plan as a part of their project proposals, and then they use that plan to evaluate and compare the capabilities of the vendors.

The readers of a Project Management Plan include the management of the organization performing the project, the management of the customer organization, and the individual members of the implementation team. One of the goals in preparing the plan is to convince both managements that the project will be managed in a professional way and is likely to be completed on time and within the allocated budget. Another goal is to inform the team members of what will be happening during the course of the project. Perhaps the most important goal is to allow the project manager to organize and formalize her ideas as to how the project will be managed and to communicate those ideas to all concerned parties.

The sections of a Project Management Plan might include

A. **Title, author(s), date, version number.**

B. **Project scope.** A brief description of what the system is intended to accomplish, which features are and are not included in the system, what other systems it must interface with, etc.

C. **Deliverables.** Documentation, code, test results, testing software, etc.

D. **Schedule and cost estimates.** Milestones, project planning charts, rationale for cost estimates, etc.

E. **Personnel plan.** People (and their capabilities) assigned to the project, organization of teams to perform specified tasks, training plan if needed, etc.

F. **Quality assurance plan.** Scheduled reviews, test plan (including plan for designing tests, performing tests, and fixing error found during testing), QA plan for documentation, configuration management plan, standards to be used for documentation, coding, testing, etc.

G. **Project risk management plan.** Plan for identifying and dealing with risks involving project goals and schedules. For example, project managers might have identified a risk of a particular transaction not meeting its requirements for response time. The plan might be to assign a team to develop prototype code involving different transaction designs, database designs, indexing strategies, and assignments of space in the memory cache, and to perform experiments to evaluate the response times for each. Another risk might be not meeting the project schedule for the completion of a task involving interfacing two subsystems. The plan might be to assign a team to this task early in the project and to have that team consult with the developers of those subsystems.

H. **System risk management plan.** Plan for identifying and dealing with risks involving the execution of the delivered system. For example, in a system to control an X-ray machine, one risk might be that the patient would receive an excessive dose of X-rays. Again, the plan might be to assign a team to address that risk. The team might isolate the code that calculates the required dose and controls the dose delivered by the X-ray system, and then take special care in the design, coding, and testing of that code. In particular, the test plan for that segment of the system might be subject to special review by the customer and the entire team, including the manager.

15.7 Design and Code for the Student Registration System

In Section 4.8, we discussed the design of the tables and some simple constraints suitable for the Student Registration System. In this section, we complete the design by providing details of the more complex constraints and part of the code for the registration transaction.

15.7.1 Completing the Database Design: Integrity Constraints

An important part of database design is listing the database integrity constraints and deciding how each will be checked: automatically by the DBMS (in a CREATE TABLE, CREATE ASSERTION, or CREATE TRIGGER statement) or in one or more of the transactions. In the initial database design in Section 4.8, we did not fully discuss this issue because we had not yet introduced some needed SQL constructs.

The following is a list of the database integrity constraints, showing where each is enforced: in the schema (shown in Figures 4.34, 4.35, and 15.5 on pages 116, 117, and 527) or in the individual transactions. They are the same as those given in the Requirements Document in Section 14.2 except that they have been expanded to specify the attributes and tables involved in each constraint.

- *Uniqueness of Ids.* Each Id in the STUDENT table, each Id in the FACULTY table, and each CrsCode in the COURSE table must be unique. This is enforced by the primary-key constraints in the corresponding tables, as described in Section 4.8.

- *If a student is listed as registered for a course in some semester/year, that course must be offered at that time.* If a tuple exists in the TRANSCRIPT table with a particular CrsCode, Semester, and Year, there must be a tuple in the CLASS table with that CrsCode, Semester, and Year. This is enforced by the registration transaction, Register(), in Section 15.7.3.

- *Enforcement of the enrollment limit.* The value of the Enrollment attribute for a tuple in the CLASS table cannot be larger than the value of the MaxEnrollment attribute for that same tuple. This is enforced by a CHECK constraint in the CLASS table, Section 4.8.

- *Enrollment consistency.* The value of the Enrollment attribute for a class in the CLASS table must be equal to the number of tuples in the TRANSCRIPT table corresponding to students who have registered in that class for that semester and year. This is enforced by the ENROLLMENTCONSISTENCY assertion in Figure 15.5.

- *An instructor cannot be assigned to two courses taught at the same time in the same semester.* Two tuples in the CLASS table cannot have the same ClassTime, Semester, Year, and InstructorId. This is enforced by a UNIQUE constraint in the CLASS table in Section 4.8.

- *Two courses cannot be taught in the same room at the same time in the same semester.* Two tuples in the CLASS table cannot have the same ClassroomId, Semester, Year, and ClassTime. This is enforced by a UNIQUE constraint in the CLASS table in Section 4.8.

- *Students enrolled in a course must have completed all the prerequisites for it with a grade of C or higher.* For each tuple, t_i, in the TRANSCRIPT table with attributes StudId, CrsCode, Semester, and Year, if there are any tuples, t_r, in the REQUIRES table with that same CrsCode value and the value of EnforcedSince preceding the semester designated in t_i, then for each such t_r, there must be a tuple, t_n, in the TRANSCRIPT table with the same value of StudId, a CrsCode value equal to the value of the PrereqCrsCode attribute of t_r, an earlier value of Semester and

FIGURE **15.5** Some constraints for the Student Registration System.

```
CREATE ASSERTION  ROOMADEQUACY
    CHECK ( NOT EXISTS (SELECT *
                        FROM CLASS C, CLASSROOM R
                        WHERE C.MaxEnrollment > R.Seats
                            AND C.ClassroomId = R.ClassroomId ) )

CREATE ASSERTION  ENROLLMENTCONSISTENCY
    CHECK (
        NOT EXISTS (SELECT *
                    FROM CLASS C
                    WHERE C.Year = EXTRACT(YEAR FROM CURRENT_DATE)
                        -- current_semester() is a user-defined function
                        AND C.Semester = current_semester()
                        AND C.Enrollment <>
                            (SELECT COUNT( * )
                            FROM TRANSCRIPT T
                            WHERE T.CrsCode = C.CrsCode
                                AND T.Year = C.Year
                                AND T.Semester = C.Semester)

CREATE TRIGGER  CANTCHANGEGRADETOI
    AFTER UPDATE OF Grade ON TRANSCRIPT
    REFERENCING OLD AS O
                NEW AS N
    FOR EACH ROW
    WHEN  (O.Grade IN ('A','B','C','D','F') AND N.Grade = 'I')
        ROLLBACK
```

Year, and a Grade of at least C. This is enforced by a call to the checkPrerequisites() method in the registration transaction in Section 15.7.3.

- *A student cannot be registered for different courses taught at the same hour.* No pair of tuples in the TRANSCRIPT table with the same StudId can have values of CrsCode, SectionNo, Semester, and Year attributes, such that the tuples with the corresponding values of CrsCode, SectionNo, Semester, and Year attributes in the CLASS table have the same ClassTime. This constraint is not shown.

- *A student cannot be registered for more than 20 credits in any given semester.* Let S be a set of all tuples in TRANSCRIPT having the same values in attributes StudId, Semester, and Year. Then the sum of the values of the CreditHours attribute in the COURSE table corresponding to the CrsCode values in tuples in S must be less than or equal to 20. This is enforced by a call to the method checkRegisteredCredits() in the registration transaction in Section 15.7.3.

■ *The room assigned to a course must have at least as many seats as the maximum allowed enrollment for the course.* If *cl* and *cr* are tuples in tables CLASS and CLASSROOM, respectively, with the same value of ClassroomId, then the value of MaxEnrollment in *cl* is less than or equal to the value of Seats in *cr*. This is enforced by the ROOMADEQUACY assertion, in Figure 15.5.

■ *A valid letter grade cannot be changed to an Incomplete.* Once a value of A, B, C, D, or F has been assigned to a Grade attribute in a tuple in the TRANSCRIPT table, it cannot be changed later to an I. This is enforced by the CANTCHANGEGRADETOI trigger in Figure 15.5.

Figure 15.5 completes the database design by defining the assertions and trigger portion of the schema.

15.7.2 Design of the Registration Transaction

We now present a design for the registration transaction in the format given in part G of Section 15.1.3. When a student wants to register for a particular course, she starts an application, which presents a GUI with a choice of courses offered in the next semester. When a particular course is selected, the GUI creates an instance object of the Java class ClassTable on page 531 using the constructor ClassTable(). Then, when the student presses the registration button on the GUI, the registration transaction (whose code is in the body of the Register() method of that class) is invoked on the new object.

1. *Transaction name.*

   ```
   public int Register(Connection con, String sid)
   ```

   This transaction is implemented as a method of class ClassTable. It is invoked on concrete instances of that class. The variables courseId and sectionNo are set by the class constructor, ClassTable(), to correspond to a particular class offering.

2. *Description.* This transaction registers a student in a course, after making a number of checks on the validity of the registration.

3. *Arguments.*
   a. Connection con—the identifier of the database connection
   b. String sid—the Id of the student registering

4. *Return values.*
   a. If registration is successful, returns the constant OK.
   b. If any of the checks described in *Actions*, (item 9, below) fails, returns a string corresponding to the nature of the failure.
   c. If any database operation fails, returns the user-defined constant FAIL.

5. *Called from.* Not relevant here because we do not give the complete design with the names of the other classes and methods.

6. *Calls.*
    a. checkCourseOffering()
    b. checkCourseTaken()
    c. checkTimeConflict()
    d. checkRegisteredCredits()
    e. checkPrerequisites()
    f. addRegisterInfo()

    The first five of these procedures perform the checks described under *Actions*, (item 9, below). If all the checks succeed, the last procedure updates the database to complete the registration.

7. *Preconditions.*
    a. The student whose Id is contained in the argument sid has been authenticated.
    b. The database has been opened, and the connection con has been created.
    c. The JDBC method setAutoCommit(false) has been executed on the connection.

8. *Isolation level.* SERIALIZABLE: Set using the call to
    setTransactionIsolation(Connection.TRANSACTION_SERIALIZABLE)

9. *Actions.*
    a. *Textual description.*
        i. The transaction checks that
            a. The course is offered the following semester.
            b. The student is not already registered for the course, is not currently enrolled in the course, and has not completed the course with a grade of C or better.
            c. The student is not already registered for another course scheduled at the same time.
            d. The total number of credits taken by the student the following semester will not exceed 20.
            e. The student has completed all of the prerequisites for the course with a grade of C or better (or is currently enrolled in some prerequisites).
        ii. If the student satisfies all of the checks, the transaction completes the registration by adding a new tuple for that student and class to the TRANSCRIPT table and incrementing the Enrollment attribute for that class in the CLASS table. It then commits and returns with status OK.
    b. *Tables accessed.*
        i. For the checks: STUDENT, COURSE, REQUIRES, CLASS, TRANSCRIPT
        ii. For the updates: TRANSCRIPT, CLASS

c. *Error situations.*
  i. Validity checks
      If any of the checks described in *Actions* (item 9) fails, the transaction aborts and returns with a status that identifies the failure. For example, if the student has already taken the course with a grade of C or better, the method `checkCourseTaken()` returns the user-defined constant `CourseTaken` as a status, and the `Register()` transaction then returns with that status. Likewise, if a scheduling time conflict has been detected, the method `checkTimeConflict()` returns `TimeConflict`, and the transaction then returns with that status. The calling method is responsible for producing an appropriate error message.
  ii. Automatic constraint checks performed by the system
      The number of students registered must not exceed the maximum allowable enrollment, `MaxEnrollment`, for the course. (This is enforced by an assertion.) If this check fails, the transaction is aborted by the DBMS, and the calling procedure is responsible for producing an appropriate message.
  iii. Other anomalous situations
      If any database operation fails, the transaction aborts and returns `FAIL`. The calling procedure is responsible for producing an appropriate error message.

15.7.3 Partial Code for the Registration Transaction

The example that follows shows part of the Java program for the registration transaction. The program defines class `ClassTable` and, in particular, its key method `Register()`, which specifies the course registration transaction. In addition, the example provides the code for one consistency checking method, `checkCourse-Taken()`, but omits the others, which are similar.

The method has been structured to make it easy to code and understand. First the required checks are performed to see if the requested registration is allowed. Each check is made by a separate procedure. If all of the tests succeed, the tables are updated by the procedure `addRegisterInfo()`. If the updates succeed, the transaction commits. The bulk of the database actions performed by the check and update procedures can be implemented as stored procedures on the database server.

As the design specifies, all error and success messages are produced not by the registration transaction but by the GUI program that calls the registration transaction, based on the value the transaction returns. This design has advantages because it allows the system to be implemented in a two- or three-tiered architecture consisting of a presentation server, which contains programs that manage the displays on the screen, and an application server, which contains the application programs that do the actual work. Using a three-tiered architecture for the Student Registration System, the GUI program executes on the presentation server, the register method executes on the application server, and the procedures listed in item G.6 (page 513) of the Design Document are stored procedures executed at the database server.

```java
public class ClassTable
{
  private String courseId;       // The course Id of the class
  private String sectionNo;      // The section number of the class
  .
  .
  .
  // General return codes
  final public static int FAIL = -1;
  final public static int OK = 0;
  // Return codes for the various consistency checks
  final public static int CourseNotOffered = 1;
  final public static int CourseTaken = 2;
  final public static int TimeConflict = 3;
  final public static int TooManyCredits = 4;
  final public static int PrerequisiteFailure = 5;

  // The class constructor
  public ClassTable(String courseId, String sectionNo)
  {
    this.courseId = courseId;
    this.sectionNo = sectionNo;
  }

  // The registration transaction
  public int Register(Connection con, String sid)
  {
    int status = OK;           // return code of check*Status() methods
    int addResult = OK;        // return code of addRegisterInfo()

    try {
      // Make all the required consistency checks
      if ((status = checkCourseOffering(con,sid)) != OK) {
        con.rollback();        // Course not offered
        return status;
      } else if ((status = checkCourseTaken(con,sid)) != OK) {
        con.rollback();        // Course already taken
        return status;
      } else if ((status = checkTimeConflict(con,sid)) != OK) {
        con.rollback();        // Time conflict found
        return status;
      } else if ((status = checkRegisteredCredits(con,sid)) != OK) {
        con.rollback();        // Too many credits
        return status;
```

```
    } else if ((status = checkPrerequisites(con,sid)) != OK) {
        con.rollback();          // Lacks prerequisites
        return status;
    }
    // Consistency checks OK. Update tables now
    if ((addResult = addRegisterInfo(con,sid)) != OK) {
        // Failed to update tables—rollback
        con.rollback();
        return FAIL;
    }
    // Registration succeeded
    con.commit();
    return OK;
} catch (SQLException sqle) {
    // Catches exceptions raised during execution of commit or rollback
    return FAIL;
}        // try-catch

}        // Register()
```

The following program is an implementation of one of the checks performed in `Register()`—a check for whether the student has already taken the course and received a satisfactory grade.

```
// Another method of class ClassTable
private int checkCourseTaken (Connection con, String sid)
{
    // Construct the SQL command. Observe the use of single quotes
    // and spaces to produce a valid SQL statement
    // Also note: courseId is a variable defined in class ClassTable
    String SQLStatement = "select CrsCode from Transcript"
                + " where StudId ='" + sid
                + "' and CrsCode ='" + courseId
                + "' and Grade in ('A','B','C',NULL)";
    Statement stmt;
    try {
        stmt = con.createStatement();
        ResultSet rs = stmt.executeQuery(SQLStatement);
        // If the result set is non-empty, course has been taken
        if (rs.next()) {
            // course has been taken
            stmt.close();
            return CourseTaken;
        }
```

```
      // course has not been taken
      stmt.close();
      return OK;
   } catch(SQLException sqle) {
      // catches exceptions raised during execution of SELECT
      return FAIL;
   }    // try-catch
}      // end of checkCourseTaken()

   // Other methods of class ClassTable are defined here
      .
      .
      .
}      // end of class definition for ClassTable
```

BIBLIOGRAPHIC NOTES

Many of the issues in this chapter are discussed in greater detail in standard software engineering texts such as [Summerville 2000; Pressman 2002; Schach 1999]. The particular issues involved in modeling and designing databases and transaction processing applications are discussed in [Blaha and Premerlani 1998].

EXERCISES

15.1 Prepare a Design Document and Test Plan for a simple calculator.

15.2 Explain why

   a. Black box testing cannot usually test all aspects of the specifications.
   b. Glass box testing cannot usually test all execution paths through the code. (This does not mean that glass box testing cannot visit all lines and visit all branches of the code.)

15.3 Explain why concurrent systems (such as operating systems) are difficult to test. Explain why transaction processing applications, even though they are concurrent, do not have these same difficulties.

15.4 Explain the advantages of incremental system development from the viewpoint of

   a. The managers of the enterprise sponsoring the project
   b. The project manager
   c. The implementation team

15.5 In the design of the registration transaction given in Section 15.7.2, some of the required checks are performed in the schema and some in the transaction program.

   a. Which of the checks performed in the program can be performed in the schema?
   b. For each such check, change the schema to perform that check.

15.6 Rewrite the program for the registration transaction in Section 15.7.3

a. Using stored procedures for the procedures that perform the registration checks
b. Using one stored procedure that performs all of the checks that are performed by individual procedures in the figure
c. In C and embedded SQL
d. In C and ODBC

15.7 Evaluate the coding style used in the program for the registration transaction in Section 15.7.3.

15.8 Prepare a test plan for the registration transaction given in Section 15.7.2.

15.9 For the deregistration transaction in the Student Registration System

a. Prepare a design.
b. Write a program.
c. Prepare a test plan.

PART FIVE

Advanced Topics in Databases

In this part of the book we will discuss some of the more advanced topics: object-oriented databases, semistructured data, and XML databases.

Object databases are beginning to find their way into the mainstream both independently and as extensions to existing relational products. In Chapter 16, we will study the principles underlying the object data model and the corresponding SQL extensions.

XML databases represent an emerging field that is expected to become important once the underlying standards and tools are developed. In Chapter 17, we will discuss some of these emerging standards and their applications.

16

Introduction to Object Databases

In this chapter, we introduce the concept of a *database object* and define the *object data model*. As an application of these ideas, we present the recent object-oriented extensions to SQL, which appeared in the SQL:1999 and SQL:2003 standards. The full version of this book [Kifer et al. 2004] introduces other related standards, such as ODMG (from Object Database Management Group) and CORBA (from the Object Management Group).

16.1 Shortcomings of the Relational Data Model

Relational DBMSs swept the database market in the 1980s because of the simplicity of their underlying relational model and because tables turned out to be just the right representation for much of the data used in business applications. Encouraged by this success, attempts were made to use relational databases in other application domains for which the relational model was not specifically designed—for example, computer-aided design (CAD) and geographical data. It soon became obvious that relational databases are not appropriate for such "nontraditional" applications. Even in their core application area, relational databases have certain shortcomings. In this section, we use a series of simple examples to illustrate some of the problems with the relational data model.

Set-valued attributes. Consider the following relational schema that describes people by their Social Security number, name, phone numbers, and children:

PERSON (SSN: String, Name: String, PhoneN: String, Child: String)

We assume that a person can have several phone numbers and several children, and that Child is a foreign key to the relation PERSON. Thus, the key of this schema consists of the attributes SSN, PhoneN, and Child. Here is one possible relation instance of this schema:[1]

SSN	Name	PhoneN	Child
111-22-3333	Joe Public	516-123-4567	222-33-4444
111-22-3333	Joe Public	516-345-6789	222-33-4444
111-22-3333	Joe Public	516-123-4567	333-44-5555
111-22-3333	Joe Public	516-345-6789	333-44-5555
222-33-4444	Bob Public	212-987-6543	444-55-6666
222-33-4444	Bob Public	212-987-1111	555-66-7777
222-33-4444	Bob Public	212-987-6543	555-66-7777
222-33-4444	Bob Public	212-987-1111	444-55-6666

This schema is *not* in the third normal form because of the functional dependency

$$SSN \rightarrow Name$$

since SSN is not a key and Name is not one of the attributes in a key. Furthermore, it is easy to verify that, if we first decompose this relation into its projections onto SSN,Name,PhoneN and SSN,Name,Child and then join the projections, we get the original relation back. Thus, according to Section 6.9, this relation satisfies the following join dependency:

$$\text{PERSON} = (SSN\ Name\ PhoneN) \bowtie (SSN\ Name\ Child)$$

In Section 6.9, we argued that relations that satisfy nontrivial join dependencies might contain a great deal of redundant information (in fact, much more than the amount of redundancy caused by the FDs). Since information redundancy is a cause of update anomalies, the relational design theory suggests that we should decompose the original relation into the following three:

PERSON	SSN	Name
	111-22-3333	Joe Public
	222-33-4444	Bob Public

PHONE	SSN	PhoneN
	111-22-3333	516-345-6789
	111-22-3333	516-123-4567
	222-33-4444	212-987-6543
	222-33-4444	212-135-7924

[1] For brevity, we omit some tuples needed to satisfy the foreign-key constraint.

CHILDOF	SSN	Child
	111-22-3333	222-33-4444
	111-22-3333	333-44-5555
	222-33-4444	444-55-6666
	222-33-4444	555-66-7777

While this decomposition certainly removes update anomalies, there are still diffi-culties. Consider the query *Get the phone numbers of all of Joe's grandchildren.* The SQL statement

```
SELECT   G.PhoneN
FROM     PERSON P, PERSON C, PERSON G
WHERE    P.Name = 'Joe Public' AND              16.1
         P.Child = C.SSN AND
         C.Child = G.SSN
```

performs the query for the original schema, while the statement

```
SELECT   N.PhoneN
FROM     CHILDOF C, CHILDOF G,
         PERSON P, PHONE N
WHERE    P.Name = 'Joe Public' AND              16.2
         P.SSN = C.SSN AND
         C.Child = G.SSN AND
         G.SSN = N.SSN
```

does the same for the decomposed schema. Both of these SQL expressions seem rather cumbersome implementations of the simple query we just stated in English.

One problem is that the redundancy in the original schema for PERSON is solely due to the inability of the relational data model to handle set-valued attributes in a natural way. A much more appropriate schema for the original table would be

```
PERSON(SSN: String, Name: String,
       PhoneN: {String}, Child: {String})
```

where the braces {} represent set-valued attributes. For instance, Child: {String} says that the value of the attribute Child in a tuple is a *set* of elements of type String. The rows in such a table might look as follows (note the set-valued components):

```
(111-22-3333, Joe Public,
    {516-123-4567, 516-345-6789}, {222-33-4444, 333-44-5555})
(222-33-4444, Bob Public,
    {212-987-1111, 212-987-6543}, {444-55-6666, 555-66-7777})
```

The second problem with the example above is the awkwardness with which SQL handles queries (16.1) and (16.2).

Suppose that the type of the attribute Child were {PERSON} rather than {String} and that SQL could treat the value of the Child attribute as a set of PERSON tuples (rather than just a set of strings that represent SSNs). It would then be possible to formulate the query much more concisely and naturally because the expression P.Child.Child can be given precise meaning: the set of all tuples corresponding to the children of the children of P. This would allow us to write the above query in the following elegant way:

```
SELECT   P.Child.Child.PhoneN
FROM     PERSON P                                      16.3
WHERE    P.Name = 'Joe Public'
```

Expressions of the form P.Child.Child.PhoneN are called **path expressions**.

IsA hierarchies. Suppose that some but not all people in our database are students. Since a student is a person, we can represent this fact by drawing arrows in the corresponding E-R or UML diagrams. Since the relational model does not support the concept of IsA hierarchies, we would simulate it by factoring out the general information pertinent to all persons and have the schema for STUDENT contain only the information specific to students (see Section 4.5.3 for a discussion of the representation techniques for IsA):

```
STUDENT(SSN: String, Major: String)
```

Then we reason that, since a STUDENT is also a PERSON, every student has a Name attribute. Consider the query *Get the names of all computer science majors*, which we can *try* to write in SQL as follows:

```
SELECT   S.Name
FROM     STUDENT S
WHERE    S.Major = 'CS'
```

Unfortunately, SQL-92 would reject the above query because the attribute Name is not explicitly included in the schema of STUDENT. However, if the system *knew* about the IsA relationship between students and persons, it could infer that STUDENT inherits Name from PERSON.

Although IsA hierarchies exist in the E-R and UML models, these models do not come with their own query languages. We are thus compelled to use the relational model and standard SQL, which forces us to write the following, more complex query:

```
SELECT   P.Name
FROM     PERSON P, STUDENT S
WHERE    P.SSN = S.SSN AND S.Major = 'CS'
```

In essence, SQL-92 programmers must *explicitly* include an implementation of the IsA relationship with each query.

Blobs. The term "blob" means **binary large object**. Virtually all relational DBMSs allow relations to have attributes of type blob. For example, a database of movies can have this schema:

MOVIE (Name: String, Director: PERSON, Video: blob)   **16.4**

The attribute Video might hold a video stream, which can contain gigabytes of data. From the relational point of view, a video stream is a large, unstructured sequence of bits.

There are several problems with blobs. Consider the query

```
SELECT   M.Director
FROM     MOVIE M
WHERE    M.Name = 'The Simpsons'
```

Some systems might drag the entire tuple containing the blob from disk into main memory to evaluate the WHERE clause. This is a huge overhead. Even when a DBMS is optimized to handle blobs, its options are limited. Suppose that we need only the frames in the range 20,000 to 50,000. We cannot obtain this information if we stay within the traditional relational model. To handle such a query, we need a special routine, frameRange(from, to), perhaps implemented as a stored procedure, which, for a given video blob, returns frames in the specified range.

Would it make sense to add frameRange() as an operator to the relational data model? While this addition would enable anyone to play with video blobs, it would not help with blobs that store DNA sequences or VLSI chip designs. Thus, rather than burdening the data model with all kinds of specialized operations, a general mechanism is needed to let users define such operations separately for each type of blob.

Objects. The shortcomings of SQL, which we just discussed, led to the idea of databases that can store and retrieve objects. An object consists of a set of attributes and a set of methods that can access those attributes, together with an associated inheritance hierarchy.

Attribute values can be instances of complex data types or other objects. For example, the attributes of a person object might include a complex data type representing the person's address and an object representing her spouse.

Since the value of an attribute can be an instance of an object, the operations defined for the object can be used in queries. Thus, a video object might have a method, `frameRange()`, which can be used as follows:

```
SELECT   M.frameRange(20000,50000)
FROM     MOVIE M
WHERE    M.Name = 'The Simpsons'
```

Impedance mismatch in database languages.   It is impossible to write complete applications entirely in SQL, so database applications are typically written in a host language, such as C or Java, and they access databases by executing SQL queries embedded in a host program. Chapter 8 discussed a number of mechanisms for accessing databases from host languages.

One problem with this approach is that SQL is set oriented, meaning that its queries return sets of tuples. In contrast, C, Java, and other host languages do not understand relations and do not support high-level operations on them. Apart from this mismatch of types, there is a sharp difference between the declarative nature of SQL (which specifies *what* has to be done) and the procedural nature of host languages (in which the programmer must specify *how* things are to be done). This phenomenon has been dubbed the *impedance mismatch* between the data access language and the host language; the cursor mechanism (Section 8.2.4) was invented to serve as an adaptor between procedural host languages and SQL.

The problem of the impedance mismatch provided an important motivation for the development of the object-oriented data model, and one object database standard—the ODMG standard (developed by Object Database Management Group)—is designed to avoid this mismatch as much as possible. On the other hand, the impedance mismatch is inherent in the design of SQL, and its object-oriented *extensions* completely ignore this problem. We do not discuss ODMG further in this text, but it can be found in the full version of this book [Kifer et al. 2004].

Object Databases versus Relational Databases

From the previous examples, we can begin to see the broad outlines of the object model and how it relates to the relational model.

- A relational database consists of relations, which are sets of tuples, while an object database consists of classes, which are sets of objects. Thus, a relational database might contain a relation, called PERSON, with tuples containing information about each person, whereas an object database might contain a class, called PERSON, with objects containing information about each person. A particular relational database can be implemented within the object model by defining a class for each relation. The attributes of a particular class are the attributes of the corresponding relation, and each object instantiated from the class corresponds to a tuple.

- In a relational database, the components of a tuple must be primitive types (strings, integers, etc.); in an object database, the components of an object can, in addition, be complex types (sets, tuples, objects, etc.).

- Object databases have certain properties for which there is no analogy in relational databases:

  - Objects can be organized into an inheritance hierarchy, which allows objects of a lower type to inherit the attributes and methods from objects of a higher type. This helps reduce clutter in type specifications and leads to more concise queries.

  - Objects can have methods, which can be invoked from within queries. For instance, the specification of the class MOVIE mentioned earlier might contain a method, frameRange, with a declaration of the form

    ```
    list(VIDEOFRAME)    frameRange(Integer,Integer);
    ```

    which states that frameRange takes two integer arguments and returns a list of video frames. Such declarations are made using a special object definition language, which is similar to the data definition sublanguage of SQL.

  - Method implementations are written in advance using a standard host language (e.g., C++ or Java) and stored on the server. In this respect, methods are similar to stored procedures in SQL databases (Section 8.2.5). However, stored procedures are not associated with any particular relation, while a stored method is an integral part of the respective class and is inherited along the object type hierarchy in a manner similar to that for methods in object-oriented programming languages.

  - In some object database systems, the data manipulation language and the host language are the same.

16.2 The Conceptual Object Data Model

As in the case of the relational databases, we will first develop a conceptual view of a data model suitable for object databases. This model, the **Conceptual Object Data Model** (CODM), is derived from the work of the research team behind O_2 [Bancilhon et al. 1990]; it had significant influence on object-oriented database standards. In Section 16.2.4, we will introduce the object-relational extensions of SQL in terms of CODM.

In CODM, every object has a unique and immutable identity, called the **object Id** (**oid**), which is independent of the actual value of the object. The oid is assigned by the system when the object is created and does not change during the object's lifetime. Note the distinction between oids and the primary keys of relations. Like an oid, a primary key uniquely identifies the object. However, unlike an oid, the value of a primary key might change (a person might change her Social Security number). In addition, oids are normally hidden, while primary keys are visible and can be explicitly used in queries.

16.2.1 Objects and Values

An object that describes a person, Joe Public, might look as follows:

```
(#32, [ SSN: 111-22-3333,
        Name: Joe Public,
        PhoneN: {"516-123-4567", "516-345-6789"},                16.5
        Child: {#445, #73}] )
```

The symbol #32 is the oid of the data object that describes a real-world Joe Public. The rest specifies the *value* part of the object. The oid identifies this object among other objects, and the value provides the actual information about Joe. Observe that the value of the Child attribute is a set of oids that (presumably) describe Joe's children.

Formally, an **object** is a pair of the form (*oid*, *val*), where *oid* is an object Id and *val* is a value. The **value** part, *val*, can take one of the following forms:

- *Primitive value.* A member of an Integer, String, Float, or Boolean data type; example: "516-123-4567"

  Primitive values are not new to CODM—they also exist in the relational model.

- *Reference value.* An oid of an object; example: #445

  Reference values do not exist in the relational model, since it does not have a representation for complex objects.

- *Tuple value.* Of the form $[A_1 : v_1, \ldots, A_n : v_n]$, where the $A_1, \ldots, A_n$ are distinct attribute names and the $v_1, \ldots, v_n$ are values; example: the entire value part (inside the brackets) of object #32 in (16.5)

  Tuple values exist in the relational model also. However, they can occur only at the top level, as rows of relations. In CODM, tuple values can appear at any level. For instance, they can occur as components of top-level rows.

- *Set value.* Of the form $\{v_1, \ldots, v_n\}$, where the $v_1, \ldots, v_n$ are values; examples: {"516-123-4567", "516-345-6789"} or {#445,#73}

  Set values do not exist in the relational model except in the sense that relations are sets.

Thus, in addition to the objects of the form (16.5), other (perhaps less obvious) examples of objects are (#38, "Joe Average")—because "Joe Average" is a primitive value, (#77, #534)—because #534 is a reference value, and (#47, {#987,#34})—

because {#987,#34} is a set value. Reference, tuple, and set values are called **complex values** to distinguish them from primitive values.

   Note that the oid part of an object cannot change (if it did, it would indicate a different object). In contrast, the value part of an object can be replaced by another value as a result of an update. For example, if one of Joe Public's phone numbers should change, the value of the PhoneN attribute is replaced by a new value, but the object retains the same oid and is considered to be the same object.

> The oid of an object cannot change, but the value can.

16.2.2 Classes

In object-oriented systems, semantically similar objects are organized into **classes**. For instance, all objects representing persons are grouped into class PERSON.

   Classes play the same role in CODM that relations play in relational databases. Whereas in SQL-92 a database is a set of relations and each relation is a set of tuples, in CODM a database is a set of classes and each class is a set of objects. Thus, in SQL-92 we might have a relation called PERSON with tuples containing information about each person, and in CODM we might have a class called PERSON with objects containing information about each person. Note that we can always convert a relational database into an object database by attaching a unique oid to each tuple.

   Classes help organize objects into categories. A class has a **type**, which describes the common structure of all objects in the class (e.g., all objects in a class might be sets of tuples), and **method signatures**, which are declarations of the operations that can be applied to the class objects. We discuss these notions in more detail below. Only method signatures are part of CODM—method implementations are *not*. A method implementation is a procedure, written in a host language, that is stored on the database server. An ODBMS must provide a mechanism to invoke the appropriate implementation whenever the method is used in the program.

   In the relational data model, two tables can be related to each other by means of an interrelational constraint (e.g., a foreign-key constraint). In the object data model, one additional relationship—the *IsA relationship*—enjoys a special status. Suppose that, in addition to the PERSON class, which groups together all objects representing persons, we have a STUDENT class, which groups together all objects representing students. Naturally, every student is a person, so the set of objects that constitute class STUDENT must be a subset of the set of objects that constitute class PERSON. This is an example of the **subclass relationship**, in which STUDENT is a subclass of PERSON. The subclass relationship is also called the **IsA relationship**.

   The set of all objects assigned to a class is called the **extent** of the class. To adequately reflect our intuition about the subclass relationship, extents must satisfy the following property:

   If C_1 is a subclass of C_2, the extent of C_2 contains the extent of C_1.

For example, since STUDENT is a subclass of PERSON, the set of all students is a subset of the set of all persons.

The query language and the data manipulation languages are aware of the subclass relationship. For example, if a query is supposed to return all PERSON objects that have a certain property and if some STUDENT object has that property, the query will return the STUDENT object in the query result since every student is also a person.

To summarize, a class has a type (which describes the class structure), method signatures (which are often considered part of the type), and an extent (which lists all objects that belong to the class). Thus

> Class, type, and extent are related, but distinct, notions.

16.2.3 Types

An important requirement of any data model is that the data must be properly structured. Because of the simplicity of the structure of tuples in the relational model, typing is not a big issue in relational databases. It is more complex in object databases. Consider, for example, the object in (16.5). We can say that its type—let us call it PERSON—is represented by the following expression:

```
[SSN: String, Name: String, PhoneN: {String}, Child: {PERSON}]
```
16.6

This type definition states that the attributes SSN and Name draw their values from the primitive domain String; the attribute PhoneN must have values that are sets of strings; and the values of the attribute Child are sets of PERSON objects.

Intuitively, the type of an object is just the collection of the types of its components. More precisely, complex types suitable for structuring objects can be defined as follows:

■ *Basic types.* String, Float, Integer, and so forth

■ *Reference types.* User-defined class names, such as PERSON and STUDENT

■ *Tuple types.* Expressions of the form $[A_1 : T_1, \ldots, A_n : T_n]$, where each A_i is a distinct attribute name and T_i is a type. The type given in (16.6) is an example of a tuple type.

■ *Set types.* Expressions of the form $\{T\}$, where T is a type. For example, {String} is a set type.

Note that (16.6) describes a type in which complex structures are nested within other structures. For instance, the values of PhoneN are sets of primitive values, while the values of Child are sets of objects of type PERSON.

What does it mean for an object to conform to a type? Given the recursive structure of objects and the presence of the IsA hierarchy, the answer to this question is not straightforward. We develop this concept in the following paragraphs.

Subtyping. In addition to grouping objects structurally, the type system can tell which types have "more structure" than others. For instance, suppose the type of the PERSON objects is

```
[SSN: String, Name: String,
    Address: [StNumber: Integer, StName: String]]
```

This is a tuple type, in which the first two components have a basic type and the third has a tuple type.

Consider now the objects of type STUDENT. Clearly, students have names, addresses, and everything else that PERSON objects have. However, students have additional attributes, so an appropriate type might be

```
[SSN: String, Name: String,
  Address: [StNumber: Integer, StName: String],
  Majors: {String}, Enrolled: {COURSE}]
```

Our intuition suggests that type STUDENT has more structure than type PERSON because (1) it has all the attributes of PERSON, (2) the values of these attributes have at least as much structure as the corresponding attributes in PERSON, and (3) STUDENT has attributes not present in PERSON. This intuition leads to the notions of **subtype** and **supertype**: Type T is a *subtype* of (supertype) T' if $T \neq T'$ and one of the following conditions holds:

- T and T' are reference types, and T is a subclass of T'.
- $T = [A_1 : T_1, \ldots, A_n : T_n, A_{n+1} : T_{n+1}, \ldots, A_m : T_m]$ and $T' = [A_1 : T'_1, \ldots, A_n : T'_n]$ are tuple types (note that T includes all attributes of T', that is, $m \geq n$), and either $T_i = T'_i$ or T_i is a subtype of T'_i, for each $i = 1, \ldots, n$.
- $T = \{T_0\}$ and $T' = \{T'_0\}$ are set types, and T_0 is a subtype of T'_0.

According to this definition, STUDENT is a subtype of PERSON because it contains all of the structure defined for PERSON and has additional attributes of its own. Note, however, that having additional attributes is not necessary for a type to be a subtype. For instance,

```
[SSN: String, Name: String,
 Address: [StNumber: Integer, StName: String, POBox: String]     16.7
 ]
```

is still a subtype of PERSON even though it does not have attributes beyond those defined for PERSON. Instead, the attribute Address in (16.7) has more structure than the same attribute in PERSON.

Domain of a type.   The **domain** of a type is a set of all values that conform to that type. Intuitively the domain of a type, T, denoted $domain(T)$, is the appropriate combination of the domains of the components of T. More precisely,

- The domain of a basic type, such as `Integer` or `String`, is just what we would expect—the set of all integers or strings, respectively.

- The domain of a reference type, T, is the extent of T, that is, the set of all Ids of objects in class T. For instance, if T is PERSON, the domain is the set of all oids of PERSON objects.

- The domain of a tuple type, $[A_1 : T_1, \ldots, A_n : T_n]$, is

$$\{[A_1 : w_1, \ldots, A_n : w_n] \mid w_i \in domain(T_i)\}$$

that is, the set of all tuple values whose components conform to the corresponding types of attributes. Thus, the domain of type (16.6) is the set of all values of the form in (16.5).

- The domain of a set type, $\{T\}$, is

$$\{\{w_1, \ldots, w_k\} \mid w_i \in domain(T)\}$$

That is, it consists of *finite* sets of values that conform to the given type T. For instance, the domain of type {COURSE} is the set whose members are finite sets of oids for COURSE objects.

> *Brain Teaser:* Is it useful to allow infinite sets as elements of the domain for a set type?

It is easy to see that domains are defined in such a way that the domain of a subtype, S, is (in a sense) a subset of the domain of a supertype, S'. More precisely, for any given object, o, in S, either o is already in S' or we can use o to obtain another object, o', in S', by throwing out some components of o or of sub-objects included in o. For instance, a PERSON object can be obtained from a STUDENT object by throwing out the components corresponding to the `Majors` and `Enrolled` attributes. Similarly, a PERSON object can be obtained from an object of type (16.7) by throwing out the `POBox` component from the nested address.

> *Brain Teaser:* What is the domain of the tuple type [ ], which has no attributes?

Database schema and instance.   In object databases, the **schema** contains the specification for each class of objects that can be stored in the database. For each class, C, it includes

- The *type* associated with C. This type determines the structure of each object of C.

- The *method signatures* of C. A **method signature** specifies the method name, the type and order for the allowed method arguments, and the type of the result produced by the method. For instance, the method `enroll()` in class COURSE might have the following signature:

```
Boolean enroll (STUDENT);
```

and the method `enrolled()` in class STUDENT might have the signature

```
{COURSE} enrolled ();
```

The signature of `enroll()` says that in order to enroll a student in a course, one must invoke the method `enroll()` on the COURSE-object and supply the STUDENT-object as a parameter. The method returns a Boolean value that indicates the outcome of the operation. The signature of `enrolled()` says that, to check the enrollment of a student, one can invoke the method `enrolled()` in the context of the STUDENT-object corresponding to that student, and the result will be a set of COURSE-objects corresponding to courses in which the student is enrolled.

- The *subclass-of* relationship, which identifies the superclasses of C
- The *integrity constraints*, such as key constraints, referential constraints, or more general assertions, which are similar to constraints in relational databases

An **instance** of the database is a set of objects for the classes specified in the schema. The objects must satisfy all of the constraints implied by the schema, which includes type constraints. Thus, the value of each object must belong to the domain of the type associated with the object's class. Each object must also have a unique oid.

> *Brain Teaser:* What domains must an object belong to if it is a member of several classes?

This completes the definition of the conceptual object model. As you can see, most of the notions used in CODM are extensions of familiar concepts from the relational model, but they require considerably more care because of the richness of the underlying data model.

16.2.4 Object-Relational Databases

This breed of DBMS arrived in the early 1990s, when a number of vendors began advocating object-relational DBMS (instead of full-blown object databases) as a safer migration path from relational DBMS. The main selling point was that such databases could be implemented as conservative extensions to the existing relational DBMSs. After long deliberation, the SQL:1999 working group finally adopted a subset of the object-relational data model. SQL:2003 gave support for the full object-relational submodel of CODM.

An **object-relational database** consists of a set of top-level classes, which are populated by *tuple objects*. A **tuple object** is of the form (*oid*, *val*), where *oid* is an object Id and *val* is a tuple value whose components can be *arbitrary* values (i.e., primitive values, sets, tuples, and references to other objects).

Since the top-level structure of the top-level classes is a tuple, these classes are called *relations,* which explains the term "object-relational."

The main difference between the object-relational and CODM models is that in the former, the top-level structure of each object instance is always a tuple while in the latter, the top-level structure can be an arbitrary value. However, this restriction on object-relational DBMSs does not significantly decrease the ability to model real-world enterprises.

What differentiates object-relational and traditional relational models is that the tuple components must be primitive values in the relational model whereas they can be arbitrary values in the object-relational model. Thus, the relational model can be viewed as a subset of the object-relational model (and hence of CODM).

We discuss the object-relational model underlying SQL:1999/2003 in the next section.

16.3 Objects in SQL:1999 and SQL:2003

Object-oriented extensions in SQL have gone through many revisions. The final result is a reasonably clean version of the object-relational model. It was a difficult standardization process, given the requirement to preserve backward compatibility with SQL-92—a language *not* designed with objects in mind.

The goals of this backward compatibility were that SQL:1999/2003 could be used in any of the following ways:

- To work with standard SQL-92 relations
- To work with relations that are similar to those in SQL-92 except that attributes can have values of complex user-defined types (such as sets or tuples)

In this section, we survey the new object-relational extensions of SQL:1999 and 2003. SQL:1999 is described in [Gulutzan and Pelzer 1999]. SQL:2003 is available through the standards organizations, such as ISO (*http://www.iso.org/*).

An SQL:1999/2003 database consists of a set of relations. Each relation is either a set of tuples or a set of objects. An **SQL object** is a pair of the form (*o*, *v*), where *o* is an oid and *v* is an SQL tuple value. An SQL **tuple value** has the form $[A_1 : v_1, \ldots, A_n : v_n]$, where $A_1, \ldots, A_n$ are distinct attribute names and each v_j takes one of the following values (using the terms introduced in Section 16.2.1):

- *Primitive value.* Constants of the usual SQL primitive types, such as CHAR(18), INTEGER, DECIMAL, and BOOLEAN
- *Reference value.* Object Ids

- *Tuple value.* Of the form $[A_1 : v_1, \ldots, A_n : v_n]$, where each A_i is a distinct attribute name and each v_i is a value

- *Collection value.* Created using the MULTISET construct. It is the only major object-oriented addition introduced by SQL:2003. (SQL:1999 also provides the ARRAY construct, but it is only of marginal interest and will not be discussed in this book.)

As expected of a data model in the object-relational mold, the top-level value of every object in SQL:1999/2003 is a tuple. Tuples and sets can be nested, however.

16.3.1 Row Types

The simplest way to construct a tuple type is with the ROW **type constructor**. For instance, we can define the relation PERSON as follows:

```
CREATE TABLE Person (
    Name CHAR(20),
    Address ROW(Number INTEGER, Street CHAR(20), ZIP CHAR(5)) )
```

We reference the components of a row type using the usual mechanism of path expressions.

```
SELECT P.Name
FROM Person P
WHERE P.Address.ZIP = '11794'
```

A table with row types can be populated with the help of the ROW **value constructor** as follows:

```
INSERT INTO Person(Name, Address)
VALUES ('John Doe', ROW(666, 'Hollow Rd.', '66666'))
```

Updating tables that have attributes of type ROW is also straightforward.

```
UPDATE Person
SET Address.ZIP = '12345'
WHERE Address.ZIP = '66666'
```

When John Doe moves, we can change the entire address as follows:

```
UPDATE Person
SET Address = ROW(21, 'Main St.', '12345')
WHERE Address = ROW(666, 'Hollow Rd.', '66666')
      AND Name = 'John Doe'
```

16.3.2 User-Defined Types

Recall from Section 16.2.3 that a type (in CODM) is a set of rules for structuring data. The set of objects that conform to these rules is the type's domain. A class consists of a schema (which includes the type and method signatures) and an extent—a subset of the domain of the type. When we add method bodies to the signatures associated with a type, we get an **abstract data type**. In SQL:1999/2003, abstract data types are called **user-defined types** (or UDT). The following are examples of UDT definitions:

```
CREATE TYPE PersonType AS (
    Name CHAR(20),
    Address ROW(Number INTEGER, Street CHAR(20), ZIP CHAR(5)));
CREATE TYPE StudentType UNDER PersonType AS (
    Id INTEGER,
    Status CHAR(2) )
METHOD award_degree() RETURNS BOOLEAN;
CREATE METHOD award_degree() FOR StudentType
LANGUAGE C
EXTERNAL NAME 'file:/home/admin/award_degree';
```

The first **CREATE TYPE** statement is syntactically similar to the earlier definition of table PERSON, except that now we define a type rather than a table. This type does not have any explicitly defined methods, but we will soon see that the DBMS automatically creates a number of methods for us.

The second statement is more interesting. It defines STUDENTTYPE as a subtype of PERSONTYPE, which is indicated with the clause UNDER. As such, it inherits the attributes of PERSONTYPE. In addition, STUDENTTYPE is defined to have attributes of its own plus a method, award_degree(). The type definition includes only the signature of the method. The actual definition is done using the **CREATE METHOD** statement (which is associated with STUDENTTYPE through the FOR clause). The statement says that the method body is written in the C language (so that the DBMS knows how to link with this procedure) and tells where its executable can be found. If we specified LANGUAGE SQL instead, we could have defined the method code inside an attached BEGIN/END block using SQL/PSM, the language of stored procedures (see Chapter 8).

User-defined types can appear in two main contexts. First, they can be used to specify the domain of an attribute in a table, just like the primitive types of integers or character strings:

```
CREATE TABLE Transcript (
    Student StudentType,  -- a previously defined UDT
    CrsCode CHAR(6),
    Semester CHAR(6),
    Grade CHAR(1) )
```

16.8

Here we are using the CREATE TABLE statement with the only difference that some attributes (Student) have complex types (STUDENTTYPE).

Second, a UDT can be used to specify the type of an entire table. This is done through a new kind of CREATE TABLE statement, which, instead of enumerating the columns of a table, simply provides a UDT. This means that all rows of the table must have the structure specified by the UDT. For instance, we can define the following table based on the previously defined UDT STUDENTTYPE:

CREATE TABLE STUDENT OF STUDENTTYPE;   **16.9**

Tables constructed via the CREATE TABLE ... OF statement, as in (16.9), are called **typed tables**. The rows of a typed table are considered to be **objects**. Thus the rows of the table in (16.9) are objects, while the values of the Student attribute in (16.8) are *not*—even though the same UDT is used in both cases. These two distinct uses of UDTs are discussed next.

16.3.3 Objects

The only way to create an object in SQL is to insert a row into a typed table. In other words, every row in such a table is treated as an object with its own oid. The table itself is then viewed as a class (as defined in CODM), and its set of rows corresponds to the extent of the class.

It is instructive to compare (16.9) with the following declaration:

```
CREATE TABLE STUDENT1 (
      Name CHAR(20),
      Address ROW(Number INTEGER, Street CHAR(20), ZIP CHAR(5)),
      Id INTEGER,
      Status CHAR(2) )
```

Note that STUDENT1 contains exactly the same attributes as STUDENT—both names and types. However, STUDENT is a typed table whereas STUDENT1 is not, which means that SQL considers the tuples of STUDENT—but not the tuples of STUDENT1—to be objects. This disparity (one may even say inconsistency) between the two ways of constructing tables is solely due to the need to stay backward-compatible with SQL-92. Note also the difference in the use of STUDENTTYPE in (16.8) and (16.9). Instances of STUDENTTYPE in (16.8) are *not* objects, while they *are* objects in (16.9).

The next question concerns how we refer to an object. To understand the issue, let us come back to the TRANSCRIPT table in (16.8) and consider the attribute Student. Since the same student is likely to have taken several courses, he has several tuples in TRANSCRIPT. The trouble is that the declaration

```
Student STUDENTTYPE
```

means that the value of this attribute in a row of TRANSCRIPT is *not* a reference to a STUDENTTYPE object. Thus, information about every student (name, address, etc.) must be duplicated in each transcript record for that student. Clearly, this is the same redundancy we tried to eliminate in Chapter 6 using the relational normalization theory. SQL solves the problem by introducing the explicit **reference type**, denoted REF(STUDENTTYPE), which we will discuss further in Section 16.3.6. For now, we have to remember that the domain of a reference type is a set of oids. To reference an object in SQL, we need to obtain its oid, and so we have to look at the mechanism provided for this purpose.

The SQL:1999/2003 standard says that every typed table, such as (16.9), has a **self-referencing column**. For each tuple, this column holds the oids of that tuple (hence the name "self-referencing"). The oid is generated automatically when the tuple is created. However, to gain access to the oids stored in the self-referencing column, we have to give the column a name explicitly. The declaration of STUDENT-TYPE above does not name the self-referencing column, thus there is no way to refer to the oids of the objects in that table.

Here is a way to take care of the self-referencing column:

```
CREATE TABLE STUDENT2 OF STUDENTTYPE                            16.10
REF IS stud_oid;
```

The REF IS clause gives an explicit name, stud_oid, to the self-referencing column. (Note that this column also exists in (16.9) but is unnamed and hence cannot be referenced.) For most purposes, stud_oid is an attribute like any other. In particular, we can use it in queries (in both SELECT and WHERE clauses), but we cannot change its value because oids are assigned by the system and are immutable.

The distinction between objects and their references, as manifested by the reference types and self-referencing columns, is one of the muddier aspects of the object-relational extensions of SQL. This complication exists thanks to the undue influence of the C and C++ languages and also because the object extensions were tacked onto SQL as an afterthought. Note that such a distinction does not exist in Java, which is a true object-oriented language, or in the ODMG standard, which is discussed in the full version of this book [Kifer et al. 2004].

16.3.4 Querying User-Defined Types

Querying UDTs does not present any new problems. We can simply use path expressions to descend into the objects and extract the needed information. For instance,

```
SELECT T.Student.Name, T.Grade
FROM TRANSCRIPT T                                              16.11
WHERE T.Student.Address.Street = 'Hollow Rd.'
```

queries the TRANSCRIPT relation and returns the names and grades of the students who live on Hollow Road. Note that T.Student returns complex values of type

STUDENTTYPE, and inheritance from PERSONTYPE allows us to access the Name and Address attributes defined for it.

Note also that although STUDENT and STUDENT1 are defined differently, queries concerning students look identical in both cases. Thus,

```
SELECT S.Address.Street
FROM X S
WHERE S.Id = '111111111'
```

returns the street name of a student with Id 111111111 regardless of whether X is STUDENT or STUDENT1.

16.3.5 Updating User-Defined Types

Having discussed the data definition aspects of UDTs, we turn to the issue of populating relations based on these UDTs. We have already seen in Section 16.3.1 how to insert tuples into the PERSON table. By analogy, we can use the same method to insert tuples into the tables STUDENT and STUDENT2. The fact that these relations contain objects (and the extra self-referencing attribute) does not matter because the oids are generated by the system. We have to worry about only the actual attributes. We might try a similar INSERT statement to populate the relation TRANSCRIPT:

```
INSERT INTO TRANSCRIPT(Student, Course, Semester, Grade)
VALUES (????, 'CS308', '2000', 'A')
```

But what should appear as the first component of the VALUES clause? There are two answers to this question. One is discussed later in this section, and the other in Section 16.3.6.

Insertion is further complicated by the fact that a UDT is considered to be **encapsulated**, that is, its components can be accessed only through the methods provided by the type. Although we did not define any methods for STUDENTTYPE, the DBMS did it for us. Namely, for each attribute the system provides an **observer method**, which can be used to query the attribute value, and a **mutator method**, which is used to change that value. Both the observer and the mutator have the same name as the attribute. In the case of STUDENTTYPE, the system provides the following observer methods:

- Id: () $\longrightarrow$ INTEGER. This method returns an integer and, like all observers, it does not take any arguments.[2]
- Name and Status: These methods have the types () $\longrightarrow$ CHAR(20) and () $\longrightarrow$ CHAR(2), respectively.
- Address: () $\longrightarrow$ ROW(INTEGER, CHAR(20), CHAR(5)).

---

[2] The notation () indicates that the method takes no arguments.

Looking back at query (16.11) we can now say that it uses the observer methods Name and Address. On the other hand, the Grade attribute of the table TRANSCRIPT used in that same query is not part of a UDT, so it does not use an observer method. However, the difference is conceptual and not syntactic—syntactically we reference Grade in the same way we do Name.

The mutator methods are called in the context of a STUDENTTYPE object and return this same object. For instance, the mutator for an attribute, say, Id, takes a value for Id and returns the original object with the changed value of the Id attribute.

- Id: INTEGER $\longrightarrow$ STUDENTTYPE. This method takes an integer and replaces the value of Id of the object with that integer. In other words, this mutator method changes the student Id and returns the modified object.

- Name: CHAR(20) $\longrightarrow$ STUDENTTYPE. This method takes a string and replaces the value of the Name attribute in the student object. It returns the updated student object. The mutator for Status is similar.

- Address: ROW(INTEGER, CHAR(20), CHAR(5)) $\longrightarrow$ STUDENTTYPE. This method takes a row that represents an address and replaces the student address with it.

> *Brain Teaser:* Why does a mutator, such as Id(), return the entire object rather than just the new value for the Id attribute?

Note that SQL does not have the public and private specifiers of C++ and Java to control access to methods. Instead, access is controlled through the EXECUTE privilege and the usual GRANT/REVOKE mechanism introduced in Section 3.3.

We are now ready for our first insertion into a UDT:

```
INSERT INTO TRANSCRIPT(Student, Course, Semester, Grade)
VALUES (NEW StudentType()
        .Id(666666666)
        .Status('G5')
        .Name('Vlad Dracula')
        .Address(ROW(666,'Transylvania Ave.','66666')),
       'HIS666',
       'F1462',
       'D')
```

16.12

Two things should be noted here. A blank student object in the first component of the inserted tuple is created by a call to StudentType()—a default constructor that the DBMS creates for every UDT. Then the mutator methods are invoked one by one on the newly created object to fill it in with data.[3]

---

[3] Note that the syntax above is just an indented and more readable form of
NEW StudentType().Id(...).Status(...).Name(...).Address(...).

If the student's address, name, and grade are to be changed, we can use the following update statement:

```
UPDATE Transcript
SET Student = Student
                  .Address(ROW(21,'Main St.','12345'))
                  .Name('John Smith'),
      Grade = 'A'
WHERE Student.Id = 666666666
          AND CrsCode = 'HIS666' AND Semester = 'F1462'
```

To change the value of the student object, we use the mutator methods for STUDENTTYPE, which are generated for us by the DBMS. First, we apply the Address() mutator to change the address and then the Name() mutator. In contrast, since the type of the Grade attribute is primitive, the grade is changed by a direct assignment.

You have certainly noticed that inserting new tuples into relations that involve UDTs is rather cumbersome. However, the ability to associate methods with complex data types can simplify this to some extent. Namely, we can define a special constructor method that takes only scalar values. In this way, a complex object can be created in one call to the constructor.

We illustrate the idea using the language of SQL stored procedures. First, we need to add the following declaration to our earlier definition of STUDENTTYPE:

```
ALTER TYPE StudentType
ADD METHOD StudentConstr(name CHAR(20), id INTEGER,
                           streetNumber INTEGER,
                           streetName CHAR(20),
                           zip CHAR(5), status CHAR(2))
RETURNS StudentType;
```

Then we define the body of the method as follows:

```
CREATE METHOD StudentConstr(name CHAR(20), id INTEGER,
                             streetNumber INTEGER,
                             streetName CHAR(20),
                             zip CHAR(5), status CHAR(2))
FOR StudentType
RETURNS StudentType
LANGUAGE SQL
    BEGIN
          RETURN NEW StudentType()
                   .Name(name)
                   .Id(id)
```

```
                              .Status(status)
                              .Address(ROW(streetNumber,streetName,zip));
           END;
```

With this new constructor, the insertion of a new tuple into the TRANSCRIPT relation corresponding to (16.12) becomes less of a chore:

```
    INSERT INTO TRANSCRIPT(Student, Course, Semester, Grade)
    VALUES (StudentConstr('Vlad Dracula', 666666666, 666,
                          'Transylvania Ave.', '66666', 'G5'),
              'HIS666',
              'F1462',
              'D')
```

16.3.6 Reference Types

In schema (16.8) for the TRANSCRIPT relation, the attribute Student has the type STUDENTTYPE. As explained in Section 16.3.3, this prevents sharing of student objects because every student object is physically stored inside the corresponding transcript tuple. To enable object sharing, SQL uses **reference data types**. A reference is an oid, and the domain of a type of the form REF(*SomeUDT*) consists of all of the oids of objects of type *SomeUDT*. With this feature, we can rewrite our definition of TRANSCRIPT in (16.8) as follows:

```
    CREATE TABLE TRANSCRIPT1 (
            Student REF(STUDENTTYPE) SCOPE STUDENT2,
            CrsCode CHAR(6),                                    16.13
            Semester CHAR(6),
            Grade CHAR(1) )
```

The type of the Student attribute needs more explanation. First, the type REF(STUDENTTYPE) means that the value of Student must be an oid of an object of type STUDENTTYPE. However, we can create many different tables and associate them with STUDENTTYPE. Each such table can contain all kinds of students. We might not want Student to refer to just *any* student. Instead, we want some kind of referential integrity that ensures that this attribute refers to students described by a *particular* table. The clause SCOPE achieves just that by requiring that the value of Student be not just any oid of type STUDENTTYPE but one that belongs to an existing object in the table STUDENT2. To be consistent, the scope, such as the STUDENT2 relation, must have the type mentioned in REF. In our example, STUDENT2 is of type STUDENTTYPE, which is consistent with the type REF(STUDENTTYPE) of the attribute Student.

Stay tuned: the use of STUDENT2 rather than STUDENT in (16.10) is not accidental. We will come back to discuss this issue later in this section.

Querying reference types. "Misfeatures" often come on the heels of new features. Here is how query (16.11) looks when applied to the table TRANSCRIPT1, defined in (16.13):

```
SELECT T.Student->Name, T.Grade
FROM TRANSCRIPT1 T
WHERE T.Student->Address.Street = 'Hollow Rd.'
```

Recall that T.Student returns the Id of an object of type STUDENTTYPE. Observe the use of the symbol -> to refer to the attributes of that type. This means that the syntax for accessing the attributes of an object depends on whether the object is given by its oid or its value. The unfortunate distinction between references by . and -> is the disease that SQL contracted from C and C++. Such a distinction is not necessary in an object-oriented language, and it does not exist in Java or in ODMG databases.

The rule for deciding whether to use . or -> is the same as in C and C++. If an attribute has a reference type, then -> is used in path expressions; if it has an object type, then . is used. In our case, T.Student has a reference type, REF(STUDENTTYPE), so we use T.Student -> Address to access the attributes of the student object. In contrast, the earlier query (16.11) uses T.Student.Address because there T.Student has the type STUDENTTYPE, which is not a reference type.

Creating tuples that contain reference types. The next important question is how to populate the table TRANSCRIPT1. In Section 16.3.5, we saw examples of tuple insertion into complex types. However, in those cases we did not deal with object references. In order to insert a tuple into TRANSCRIPT1, we must find a way to access oids of student objects and assign them to the attribute Student. This is where the self-referencing column, introduced in Section 16.3.3, comes in handy. Recall that table STUDENT2 defined in that section has a self-referencing column, called stud_oid.[4] Recall also that the table STUDENT in (16.9) has the same type as STUDENT2, except that its self-referencing column is unnamed. Thus, we cannot obtain oids of the tuples in STUDENT and assign them as values of the Student attribute in the table TRANSCRIPT1. Because of this handicap, we have to use STUDENT2 instead of STUDENT in the definition of TRANSCRIPT1.

Assuming that the Id attribute in STUDENT2 is a key, we can now insert a student into TRANSCRIPT1 as follows:

```
INSERT INTO TRANSCRIPT1(Student, Course, Semester, Grade)
SELECT S.stud_oid, 'HIS666', 'F1462', 'D'
FROM STUDENT2 S
WHERE S.Id = '666666666'
```

---

[4] Note that the self-referencing attribute stud_oid has nothing to do with the attribute Id. The latter is a regular attribute of STUDENTTYPE whose value is set explicitly by the programmer.

Observe that we use the SELECT statement to retrieve the oid of the desired student object (S.stud_oid). This oid becomes the value for the Student attribute. The values for the attributes Course, Semester, and Grade are simply tacked on to the target list of the SELECT statement.

16.3.7 Inheritance

Recall that STUDENTTYPE was defined in Section 16.3.2 as being UNDER (i.e., as a subtype) of PERSONTYPE. This means that although the attributes of PERSONTYPE, Name and Address, are not explicitly defined in STUDENTTYPE, they are nevertheless applicable to the rows of the tables that have the type STUDENTTYPE.

Let STUDENT be a table of type STUDENTTYPE and PERSON a table of type PERSONTYPE. Suppose we insert a tuple into the STUDENT table as follows:

```
INSERT INTO STUDENT(Name, Address, Id, Status)
VALUES ('John Jones', ROW(123,'Main St.',11733), 111222333, 'G2')
```

Will this tuple automatically show up in the relation PERSON? The answer is *no*. The reason is actually quite logical: one can define several tables using the same UDT PERSONTYPE. Should the above STUDENT tuple show up in all such tables or only in some? The designers of SQL decided that it should show up in only some tables—those that the user explicitly marked as **supertables** (by analogy with superclasses) of the table STUDENT. Supertables are specified with the same keyword, UNDER, but this time it applies to tables rather than types:

```
CREATE TABLE STUDENT OF STUDENTTYPE UNDER PERSON
```

With this declaration, PERSON becomes a supertable of the table STUDENT, and all tuples inserted into STUDENT will automatically show up in PERSON (with the attributes that do not belong to PERSONTYPE removed).

To summarize, in order for a table, *T1*, to be a subtable of another table, *T2*, the following must hold:

1. The UDT of *T1* must be a subtype of (defined as being UNDER) the UDT of *T2*; and
2. The table *T1* must be defined as being UNDER the table *T2*.

Brain Teaser: What will the value of the attributes Name and Address be if we insert a tuple into STUDENT using only the proper attributes of the STUDENTTYPE data type: INSERT INTO STUDENT(Id, Status) VALUES (111222333, 'G2')?

16.3.8 Collection Types

SQL:2003 introduced the MULTISET collection type, thereby making the SQL data model fully object-relational. A **multiset** collection type is like a set except that the same element can occur in the collection more than once. This is in accordance with the default SQL strategy of retaining duplicate tuples, which makes query results into multisets (see Section 5.2). To illustrate the new collection type, we will add a new set-valued attribute, Enrolled, to STUDENTTYPE:

```
CREATE TYPE StudentType UNDER PersonType AS (
    Id INTEGER,
    Status CHAR(2),
    Enrolled REF(CourseType) MULTISET
)
```

In this example, the value of the attribute Enrolled must be a (multi)set of oids of tuples of the type COURSETYPE. We assume that COURSETYPE is a new data type that has attributes CrsCode, Name, and Description.

With multiset collection types, a new kind of query becomes possible in which multiset-valued path expressions can act as table expressions in the FROM clause. This is analogous to SELECT statements in the FROM clause, which is permitted in SQL-92. We illustrate the use of multisets with a query that returns all tuples of the form $\langle i, n \rangle$, where the student with Id i took the course with name n.

```
SELECT S.Id, C.Name
FROM Student S, Course C
WHERE C.CrsCode IN
          ( SELECT E ->TmpCrsCode
            FROM UNNEST(S.Enrolled) AS TmpCourse(TmpCrsCode) E)
```

We assume that the relation STUDENT is of type STUDENTTYPE and COURSES of type COURSETYPE. The WHERE clause tests each course object for whether student S is enrolled in it. The condition uses a nested SELECT statement to produce the set of course codes of the courses taken by student S.

The new feature here appears in the FROM clause of the nested SELECT statement. The range of the variable E is the set of references to courses specified by a path expression, S.Enrolled. It lists the courses in which S is enrolled. This set is not a table, however, since the elements of this set are object Ids, not tuples. The UNNEST function converts multisets into one-column tables. This conversion is shown in Figure 16.1.

The UNNEST function can also specify a temporary relation name and its attributes, which can be used to refer to the table produced by unnesting. In our example, this relation is TMPCOURSES(TmpCrsCode).

FIGURE 16.1 Conversion between multisets and one-column tables.

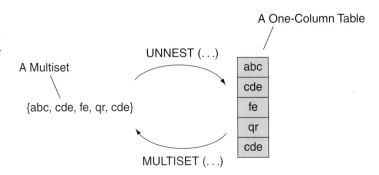

Note that since E ranges over object references, we must access the attributes of the individual objects using the -> operator.

SQL:2003 also supports conversion in the opposite direction, from one-column tables to multisets. This is done with the help of the MULTISET function. In the following example, we use this function to add a new tuple to the STUDENT table. To create such a tuple, we need to construct a multiset of type COURSETYPE and assign it to the attribute Enrolled. Let us assume that transcripts reside in the following relation:

```
CREATE TABLE TRANSCRIPTI (
     Student REF(STUDENTTYPE),
     Course REF(COURSETYPE),
     Semester CHAR(6),
     Grade CHAR(1) )
```

We can now insert a new record into STUDENT as follows:

```
INSERT INTO STUDENT(Id, Status, Enrolled)
VALUES(123987564, 'G2', MULTISET(SELECT T.Course
                        FROM TRANSCRIPTI T
                        WHERE TRANSCRIPTI->Id=123987564)
      )
```

The last component of the inserted tuple corresponds to the attribute Enrolled and thus must be a multiset of references to objects of type COURSETYPE. The nested query returns a one-column table that includes the desired references; the MULTISET function converts this column into a multiset.

SQL:2003 introduces a number of additional functions and predicates to facilitate working with multisets:

- SET(*multiset*)—function. Eliminates duplicates from *multiset*
- CARDINALITY(*multiset*)—function. Returns the cardinality of *multiset*

- *multiset1* INTERSECT *multiset2*, *multiset1* EXCEPT *multiset2*, etc.—functions. Return the results of the corresponding set-theoretic operations on multisets

- *multiset* IS [NOT] A SET—predicate. Tests if *multiset* is (or is not) a set

- *multiset1* [NOT] SUBMULTISET OF *multiset2*—predicate. Tests if *multiset1* is (or is not) a submultiset of *multiset2*

- *element* [NOT] MEMBER OF *multiset*—predicate. Tests if *element* is (or is not) a member of *multiset*

Here is a modification of a previous query that uses some of these functions and predicates:

```
SELECT S.Id, C.Name
FROM STUDENT S, COURSE C
WHERE C.CrsCode IN
        ( SELECT E -> Code
          FROM UNNEST(S.Enrolled) AS TEMPCOURSES(Code) E
          WHERE CARDINALITY(SET(S.Enrolled)) < 3
                  AND S.Enrolled IS NOT A SET  )
```

This query will return student-course name pairs for only those students who are enrolled in fewer than three distinct courses (CARDINALITY(SET(S.Enrolled)) < 3) and in at least one course, two or more times (S.Enrolled IS NOT A SET). (This situation is possible if a student is enrolled in different sections of the same course, such as Independent Study, which permit this kind of enrollment).

BIBLIOGRAPHIC NOTES

The emergence of object-oriented databases was preceded by many developments—in particular, the growing popularity of object-oriented languages and the realization of the limitations of the relational data model. The idea of using an existing object-oriented language as a data manipulation language first appeared in [Copeland and Maier 1984]. Nested relations, which represent early attempts to enrich the relational data model, are discussed in [Makinouchi 1977; Arisawa et al. 1983; Roth and Korth 1987; Jaeschke and Schek 1982; Ozsoyoglu and Yuan 1985; Mok et al. 1996].

POSTGRES [Stonebreaker and Kemnitz 1991] was an early proposal for enriching relational databases with abstract data types. Now known as PostgreSQL, this system is a powerful open-source object-relational DBMS that is freely available at [PostgreSQL 2000]. The object database O_2, which strongly influenced the ODMG data model and its query language, is described in [Bancilhon et al. 1990]. The latest version of the ODMG standard can be found in [Cattell and Barry 2000].

The conceptual object data model, presented in Section 16.2, and related issues, are discussed more fully in [Abiteboul et al. 1995]. Logical foundations of object-oriented database query languages have been developed in [Kifer et al. 1995].

The use of path expressions for querying object-like structures first appeared in the GEM system [Zaniolo 1983]. Path expressions were later incorporated in all major proposals for querying objects, including the various object-oriented extensions of SQL, such as XSQL, discussed in [Kifer et al. 1992].

The early databases that supported the object-relational data model were UniSQL, POSTGRES, and O_2. Currently, most major relational database vendors (such as Oracle, Informix, and IBM) provide object-relational extensions to their products. Many ideas underlying the design of these systems found their way into the SQL:1999 and SQL:2003 standards. Further details on the SQL:1999 object-relational extensions can be found in [Gulutzan and Pelzer 1999], while at the time of this writing SQL:2003 is available only through the standards organizations, such as ISO (*http://www.iso.org/*).

Since SQL:1999/2003 object extensions are rather new, there are no products that fully conform to this standard. However, IBM's DB/2 and Oracle 9i come close in terms of syntax and supported features.

This chapter omitted discussion of the database design issues associated with object-oriented databases, which would correspond to the material developed in Chapters 4 and 6 for relational databases. For further discussion see [Biskup et al. 1996a; Biskup et al. 1996b; Gogola et al. 1993; Missaoui et al. 1995]. The approach to object-oriented database design that is growing in popularity is the **Unified Modeling Language** (UML) [Booch et al. 1999; Fowler and Scott 2003]. We described the basics of conceptual database design using UML (and applied it to the relational model) in Chapter 4.

While object-oriented E-R style modeling is currently well developed, the corresponding normalization theory has turned out to be much harder than in the relational case. Beginnings of such a theory can be found in [Weddell 1992; Ito and Weddell 1994; Biskup and Polle 2000a; Biskup and Polle 2000b].

EXERCISES

16.1   Give examples from the Student Registration System where

a. It would be convenient to use a set-valued attribute

b. It would be convenient to use inheritance

16.2   Specify an appropriate set of UDTs for the Student Registration System.

16.3   Explain the difference between the object id in an object database and the primary key of a tuple in a relational database.

16.4   Explain the different senses in which the objects in an object database can be considered equal.

16.5   A relational database might have a table called ACCOUNTS with tuples for each account and might support stored procedures deposit() and withdraw(). An object database might have a class (a UDT) called ACCOUNTS with an object for each account and methods deposit() and withdraw(). Explain the advantages and disadvantages of each approach.

16.6 Consider the following type in CODM: [Name: STRING, Members: {PERSON}, Address: [Building: INTEGER, Room: INTEGER]]. Give three examples of subtype for this type. In one example, add more structure to the attribute Members; in another, add structure to the attribute Address; and in the third, add structure by introducing new attributes.

16.7 Give an example of an object that belongs to the domain of the type [Name: STRING, Children: {PERSON}, Cars: {[Make: STRING, Model: STRING, Year: STRING]}]. Consider a supertype [Name: STRING, Cars: {[Make: STRING, Model: STRING]}] of that type. Show how one can obtain an object of the second type from the object of the first type, which you constructed earlier.

16.8 Consider the following type, which describes projects: [Name: STRING, Members: {PERSON}, Address: [Building: INTEGER, Room: INTEGER]]. Use SQL:1999/2003 to specify the UDT corresponding to this type.

16.9 Use the UDT constructed in Exercise 16.8 to answer the following query: *List the names of all projects that have more than five members.*

16.10 Suppose that the Accounts class in the object database of the previous example has child classes SavingsAccounts and CheckingAccounts and that CheckingAccounts has a child class EconomyCheckingAccounts. Explain how the semantics of inheritance affects the retrieval of objects in each class. (For example, what classes need to be accessed to retrieve all checking account objects that satisfy a particular predicate?)

16.11 Use SQL:2003 (with the MULTISET construct, if necessary) to complete the schema partially defined in Section 16.3. Include the following UDTs: Student, Course, Professor, Teaching, and Transcript. Your solution should follow the object-oriented design methodology. Repeating the statements from Chapters 3 and 4, which use SQL-92, is *not* acceptable.

16.12 Use the schema defined for the previous problem to answer the following queries:
a. Find all students who have taken more than five classes in the Mathematics Department.
b. Represent grades as a UDT, called GradeType, with a method, value(), that returns the grade's numeric value.
c. Write a method that, for each student, computes the average grade. This method requires the value() method that you constructed for the previous problem.

16.13 Use SQL:2003 and its MULTISET construct to represent a bank database with UDTs for accounts, customers, and transactions.

16.14 Use SQL:1999/2003 and the schema constructed for the previous exercise to answer the following queries:
a. Find all accounts of customers living at the postal ZIP code 12345.
b. Find the set of all customers satisfying the property that for each the total value of his or her accounts is at least $1,000,000.

16.15 E-R diagrams can be used in designing the class definitions of object databases. Design SQL:1999/2003 definitions for the E-R diagrams in Figure 4.1, Figure 4.6, and Figure 4.36.

17

Introduction to XML and Web Data

The Web opens a new frontier in information technology and presents new challenges to the existing database framework. Unlike traditional databases, data sources on the Web do not typically conform to any well-known structure, such as a relation or object schema. Thus, traditional database storage and manipulation techniques are inadequate to deal with such data sources. This creates a need to extend existing database technologies to support new Web-based applications in electronic information delivery and exchange.

17.1 Semistructured Data

At first sight, the information on the Web bears no resemblance to the information stored in traditional databases. However, certain of its characteristics make it possible to apply many of the techniques developed in databases and information retrieval. First note that much of the Web data is presented in a somewhat structured form. For example, Figure 17.1 shows a student list as a tree encoded in Hypertext Markup Language (HTML), in which different data elements are set out using HTML tags.

To the human eye—albeit not quite so to the machine—the information on this HTML page appears to be a completely structured list of students, which, as shown in Figure 17.2, can be represented using the conceptual object data model (CODM) of Section 16.2. The actual object appears at the top of the figure. (We represent this object as an oid-value pair, as in Chapter 16.) The schema corresponding to the student list appears at the bottom of the figure.

How did we get from Figure 17.1, where the structure is implicit and intermixed with the data, to Figure 17.2, where the structure is represented separately from the data? Fortunately, the designer of the Web page was conscious of the need to make the structure easily understandable to a human and so made the data **self-describing** by including the names of the attributes (e.g., Name) along with the values (e.g., John Doe) within the data fields (e.g., Name: John Doe). In contrast, the object contains only the values and the schema contains only the attributes and their types. The label PERSONLIST has been added as the name of the type described by the schema.

Suppose now that the same information is delivered over the Web to a machine (rather than a human) for processing. Unlike the human reader, the machine is less

FIGURE 17.1 A student list in HTML.

```
<html>
  <head><Title>Student List</Title></head>
  <body>
      <h1>ListName: Students</h1>
      <b>Contents:</b>
      <dl>
        <dt>Name: John Doe
          <dd>Id: 111111111
          <dd>Address:
              <ul>
              <li>Number: 123
              <li>Street: Main St
              </ul>
        <dt>Name: Joe Public
          <dd>Id: 666666666
          <dd>Address:
              <ul>
              <li>Number: 666
              <li>Street: Hollow Rd
              </ul>
      </dl>
  </body>
</html>
```

FIGURE 17.2 Student list in object form.

Object :
```
    (#12345, ["Students",
              { ["John Doe", "111111111", [123,"Main St"]],
                ["Joe Public", "666666666", [666,"Hollow Rd"]] }
    ])
```

Schema :
```
    PERSONLIST [ ListName: STRING,
                 Contents: {
                     [ Name: STRING,
                       Id: STRING,
                       Address: [Number: INTEGER, Street: STRING] ] }
              ]
```

likely to make an intelligent guess about the intended structure of the data received, since it cannot distinguish attributes from values in Figure 17.1. Furthermore, the schema might not even be well defined, as some students on the list might have additional attributes, such as a phone number, or some addresses might have a variable structure (e.g., post office box instead of street address). Therefore, to facilitate machine-to-machine exchange of information, it is advantageous to agree on a format that makes the data self-describing by distinguishing the attribute names from values within the data.

In sum, Web data *created for machine consumption* is likely to have the following characteristics:

- It is *object-like*; that is, it can be represented as a collection of objects of the form described by the conceptual data model introduced in Section 16.2.
- It is *schemaless*; that is, it is not guaranteed to conform to any type structure, unlike the objects discussed in Section 16.2.
- It is *self-describing*.

Data with the above characteristics has been dubbed **semistructured**. The "self-describing" property may be somewhat misleading, since it can imply that the meaning of the data is carried along with the data itself. In reality, semistructured data carries only the names of the attributes and has a lower degree of organization than the data in databases. In particular, since the schema is absent, there is no guarantee that all objects have the same attributes and that the same attribute in different objects has the same meaning.

In view of our observations, Figure 17.2 is not a completely adequate representation of the original data depicted in Figure 17.1 because neither the object notation nor the schema notation of CODM was designed for self-describing data representation. However, an appropriate notation can be developed by combining elements from both the object and the schema notation of CODM. With the new notation, our student list can be represented as schemaless but self-describing as follows:

```
(#12345,
  [ListName:"Students",
   Contents:{ [Name:"John Doe",
              Id: "111111111",
              Address:[Number:123, Street:"Main St"]],
             [Name:"Joe Public",
              Id: "666666666",
              Address:[Number:666, Street:"Hollow Rd"]] }
  ])
```
                                                                              17.1

Like the specification in Figure 17.2 (and unlike that in Figure 17.1), this syntax for self-describing objects is precise, machine-understandable, and conforms to the best of database practices. However, this is not the format chosen for data exchange on the Web. The winner is called the **extensible markup language** (XML)—a standard adopted in 1998 by the World Wide Web Consortium (W3C).

Since its introduction, XML has been steadily gaining momentum and is on the way to becoming the main format for the information intended for both human and machine consumption. Section 17.2 introduces the various components of the language and provides examples of its use.

Although at its core, XML data is schemaless, schema-compliant data is always more useful. In particular, the needs of electronic data exchange require stricter enforcement of the formats for transmission than that provided by semistructured data. To help, XML has *optional* mechanisms for specifying document structure. We discuss two such mechanisms: the **document type definition** language (**DTD**), which is part of the XML standard itself, and the **XML Schema**, which is a more recent specification built on top of XML. In the last part of the chapter, we introduce two query languages for XML: a lightweight language called **XPath** and an extension of SQL, called SQL/XML, which is designed to provide interoperability between the relational world and the world of XML. The full version of this book [Kifer et al. 2004] includes a study of two other important XML query languages: **XSLT** [XSLT 1999] and **XQuery** [XQuery 2004].

17.2 Overview of XML

XML is not a solution to all of the world's problems. It is not a revolutionary or even a new idea. Why, then, is it causing a revolution? In a nutshell, XML is a human- and machine-readable data format that can be easily parsed by an application and thus considerably simplifies data exchange. Formats for data exchange were proposed in the past, but either they were nonopen, proprietary standards or they did not have enough momentum. XML happened to be in the right place at the right time. People saw what the Web and open standards were doing for communication, education, publishing, and commerce, and they recognized the need to simplify data exchange among software agents. It also helped that a trusted standards body, the W3C, was in place and not affiliated with any particular industry group or government. For the first time a simple, open, and widely accepted data standard emerged, and this gave a boost to a wide range of Web applications.

XML is an HTML-like language with an arbitrary number of user-defined tags and no a priori tag semantics. To better understand what this means, consider HTML, a document format in which various pieces of text are marked with tags that affect the rendering of that text by a Web browser. An important point is that the number of tags in HTML is *fixed* by the HTML definition and each tag has its own well-defined semantics. The browser displays an HTML document by implementing the semantics of each tag. For instance, any text between the tags `<table>` and `</table>` is supposed to be rendered by the browser as a table, and the tag `<p>` tells the browser to start a new paragraph. In contrast, the repertoire of tags in XML is not set in advance, and the user is free to introduce new tag names. Furthermore, there is no set semantics for any XML tag.

The lack of semantics in XML might seem like a step backward. How does the receiver of an XML document know what to do with the documents it receives? The answer is that each category of applications will supply its own semantic layer on top of XML. Browser rendering is just one type of application. A browser renders an XML document using a **stylesheet**—a transformation that converts the XML document into an HTML document (which the browser already knows how to present). In this way, a stylesheet supplies a "visualization semantics" to XML documents. Most XML documents, however, are not intended for visual display. Instead, they are exchanged by applications and are processed without human intervention (for example, invoices, payments, purchase orders). As with browsers, the application infers the semantics by interpreting XML tags appropriate to the application domain. For example, a retail application might interpret the tag `<price>` to be the price of a product. At this time, whole industries are developing semantic layers for representing information in application domains such as catalogs, commerce, engineering, and other fields. All these efforts have the same common need: the ability to define schema. We discuss the structuring mechanisms available in XML in Sections 17.2.4 and 17.3, although it should be noted that, despite the schema, XML data remains semistructured. Compliance with the schema remains optional, and applications are free to ignore part or all of it.

For concreteness, consider the document in Figure 17.3, which is one possible XML representation of the student list from Figure 17.1. The first line is a mandatory statement that tells the program receiving the document (any such program is called **XML processor**) that it is dealing with XML version 1.0. The rest is structured like an HTML document except for the following important points:

- The document contains a large assortment of tags chosen by the document author. In contrast, the only valid tags in HTML are those sanctioned by the official specification of the language; other tags are ignored by the browser.

- Every opening tag *must* have a matching closing tag, and the tags must be properly nested (i.e., sequences such as `<a><b></a></b>` are not allowed). In contrast, some HTML tags are not required to be closed (e.g., `<p>`), and browsers are forgiving even when closing tags are missing.

- The document has a **root element**—the element that contains all other elements. In Figure 17.3, the root element is `PersonList`.

Any properly nested piece of text of the form `<sometag>...</sometag>` is called an **XML element**, and `sometag` is the **name** of that element. The text between the opening and closing tag is called the **content** of the element. Elements directly nested within other elements are called **children**. For instance, in our example `Name`, `Id`, and `Address` are children of `Person`, which is a child of `Contents`, which is a child of the top-level element, `PersonList`. Conversely, `PersonList` is said to be the **parent** of the elements `Contents` and `Title`, and `Contents` is a parent of `Person`.

XML also defines the **ancestor/descendant** relationships among elements, which are important for querying XML documents and will be revisited in Section 17.4. These relationships have their natural meaning: an ancestor is a parent,

FIGURE **17.3** XML representation of the student list.

```
<?xml version="1.0" ?>
<PersonList Type="Student" Date="2000-12-12">
    <Title Value="Student List"/>
    <Contents>
        <Person>
            <Name>John Doe</Name>
            <Id>111111111</Id>
            <Address>
                <Number>123</Number>
                <Street>Main St</Street>
            </Address>
        </Person>
        <Person>
            <Name>Joe Public</Name>
            <Id>666666666</Id>
            <Address>
                <Number>666</Number>
                <Street>Hollow Rd</Street>
            </Address>
        </Person>
    </Contents>
</PersonList>
```

a grandparent, and so on, and a descendant is a child, a grandchild, and so on. For instance, PersonList is an ancestor of Person and Address, and Address is a descendent of PersonList.

An opening tag can have **attributes**. In the tag <PersonList Type="Student"> of Figure 17.3, Type is the name of an attribute that belongs to the element PersonList, and Student is the attribute value. Unlike HTML, all attribute values must be quoted, as shown in the figure, but text strings between tags are not. Also note the element <Title Value="Student List"/>, which contains an attribute. This element does not have a closing tag, but instead is enclosed in <.../> and is called an **empty element** because it has no content. In XML, this notation is a shorthand for the combination <Title Value="Student List"> </Title>.

Apart from elements and attributes, XML allows **processing instructions** and **comments**. A processing instruction is a statement of the form

```
<?my-command go bring coffee?>
```

and can contain pretty much anything the document author might want to communicate to the XML processor (in the hope that the processor knows what to do with this information). Processing instructions are used fairly rarely.

A comment takes the following form:

```
<!-- A comment -->
```

It is allowed to occur everywhere except inside the **markups**, that is, between the symbols < and >, which open or close tags. Perhaps surprisingly, a comment is an integral part of the document—the sender is *not* supposed to delete comments prior to transmission, and the receiver is permitted to look inside the comments and use what it finds. Although such treatment of comments goes against prevailing practice in programming and database languages, it is not unheard of in document processing. For instance, JavaScript programs are often placed as comments in HTML documents, and an HTML browser is not supposed to ignore them. Instead, it executes JavaScript programs found inside the comments, unless the JavaScript feature is turned off.

Another feature of XML that is worth a brief mention is the CDATA construct, which serves as a quotation mechanism. Suppose we use XML to write a structured guide to Web publishing. We might want to include the following text:

> Web browsers attempt to correct publisher's errors, such as improperly nested tags. For instance, `<b><i>Attention!</b></i>` would be displayed properly by most browsers.

Because of the XML tags included in this text, its inclusion would result in an ill-formed document rejected by every XML-compliant processor. Fortunately, *any* text can be included inside `<![CDATA[...]]>` brackets. For instance, the following is correct XML:

```
<![CDATA[<b><i>Attention!</b></i>]]>
```

Finally, a document can have an optional **document type definition** (or DTD), which determines document structure. We discuss DTDs in Section 17.2.4.

17.2.1 XML Elements and Database Objects

Let us now evaluate the XML document of Figure 17.3 as a format for sending semistructured data over the Web. It is easy to see that the element names effectively serve as attribute names for the object (XML attribute names can serve the same purpose), so this document is essentially yet another, equivalent textual representation for the self-describing object depicted in (17.1).

Conversion of XML elements into objects. A moment's reflection should convince us that the nested tag structure of XML is well suited to represent tree-structured self-describing objects. Each element in an XML document can be viewed as an object. The tag names of the children elements then correspond to the object's attributes, and the child elements themselves are the attribute values. For instance, the first `Person` element in Figure 17.3 can be partially mapped back to an object as follows (where #6543 is some object Id):

```
{#6543, [Name: "John Doe",
         Id: "111111111",
         Address: <Address>
                       <Number>123</Number>
                       <Street>Main St</Street>
                  </Address>
         ]
}
```

The conversion process is recursive. Simple elements such as `Name` and `Id` are converted immediately by directly extracting their contents. The element `Address` is left unchanged because it has a complex internal structure, which can be broken further by applying the same conversion procedure recursively. This results in a creation of a new address object:

```
{#098686, [Number: "123",
           Street: "Main St" ]
}
```

Differences between XML elements and objects. Despite the apparent close correspondence between XML elements and structured database objects, there are several fundamental differences. First, XML evolved from and was greatly influenced by SGML [SGML 1986], which is a *document* markup language rather than a *database* language. For instance, XML allows documents of the form

```
<Address>
     Sally lives on
     <Street>Main St</Street>
     house number
     <Number>123</Number>
     in the beautiful Anytown, USA.
</Address>
```

This mixture of text and child elements, allowed in XML, is a hindrance when it comes to automated data processing since the mixture complicates the document.

Second, XML elements are *ordered*, while the attributes of an object in a database are not. Thus, the following two objects are considered the same:

```
{#098686, [Number: "123",          {#098686, [Street: "Main St",
           Street: "Main St" ]                 Number: "123" ]
}                                  }
```

whereas the following two XML documents are different:

```
<Address>                          <Address>
    <Number>123</Number>               <Street>Main St</Street>
    <Street>Main St</Street>           <Number>123</Number>
</Address>                          </Address>
```

Third, XML has only one primitive type, a string, and very weak facilities for specifying constraints. Fortunately, many of these weaknesses are addressed by the XML Schema specification in Section 17.3.

17.2.2 XML Attributes

We saw the use of XML attributes such as Type and Value in Figure 17.3. An element can have any number of user-defined attributes. However, considering the expressive power of XML elements illustrated earlier, we are left to wonder about the role of XML attributes as a tool for data representation. That is, are they useful in data representation, and do they offer anything beyond what elements can offer?

The answer is that XML attributes are sometimes convenient for representing data, but almost everything they can do can also be done with elements. Still, attributes are widely used in XML-based specifications, such as XML Schema, which we introduce in Section 17.3. We also use attributes extensively in the examples to illustrate the various features of XML and because this often leads to more concise representation.

In document processing, attributes are used to annotate pieces of text enclosed between a pair of tags with values that are *not* part of that text but are related to it. In the following dialog,

```
<Act Number="5">
    <Scene Number="1" Place="Mantua. A street.">
        .
        .
        .
        <Apothecary Voice="scared">
            Such mortal drugs I have; but Mantua's law
            Is death to any he that utters them.
        </Apothecary>
        <Romeo Voice="persistent">
            Art thou so bare and full of wretchedness,
            And fear'st to die?
```

```
                      .
                      .
                      .
            </Romeo>
                 .
                 .
                 .
         </Scene>
      </Act>
```

we use attributes to annotate the text with meta-information that is not part of the dialog per se but is still relevant. They are convenient to use here because they do not disrupt the dialog flow. In data processing, on the other hand, text flow is a minor concern since computers are unlikely to start appreciating this type of prose in the near future. The concern here is that XML attributes represent yet another, unnecessary dimension in data representation that database programmers have to worry about.

In addition, attribute values can only be strings, which severely limits their usefulness, while XML elements can have children elements, which makes them much more versatile.

Having made these unflattering remarks, we should mention some advantages of attributes. First, the order of attributes in an element does not matter. Thus, the documents

```
<thing price="2" color="yellow">foobar</thing>
```

and

```
<thing color="yellow" price="2">foobar</thing>
```

are considered the same—much as they are in databases. Second, an attribute can occur at most once (i.e., `<thing price="2" price="2">` is not allowed), while elements with the same tag can be repeated, as in Figure 17.3. This constraint can be handy in the right circumstances. Third, attributes can lead to more succinct representation. For instance, `<thing price="2" color="yellow"/>` is much shorter than `<thing><price>2</price><color>yellow</color></thing>`.

Useful features of an XML attribute are that it can be declared to have a unique value and it can also be used to enforce a limited kind of referential integrity. This cannot be done with elements alone in plain XML. (However, this and much more can be done with the help of XML Schema, discussed in Section 17.3.) After we discuss document type definitions (DTDs) in Section 17.2.4, we will see that an attribute can be declared to be of type ID, IDREF, or IDREFS.

An attribute of type ID must have a unique value throughout the document. This means that if attr1 and attr2 are of type ID, it is illegal for both `<elt1 attr1="abc">` and `<elt2 attr2="abc">` to occur in the same document (regardless of whether elt1 and elt2 are the same tag, or whether attr1 and attr2 are the same attribute). In a sense, ID is a poor cousin of a *key* in relational databases. An attribute of type IDREF must refer to a valid Id declared in the same document. That is, its value must occur somewhere in the document as a value of another attribute of type ID. Thus, IDREF is a poor cousin of a *foreign key*.

To illustrate, we consider the report document in Figure 17.4. An attribute of type IDREFS represents a space-separated list of strings, which are references to valid Ids. In our document, we can declare the attribute StudId of the element Student and the attribute CrsCode of the element Course to be of type ID; the attribute CrsCode of the element CrsTaken to be of type IDREF; and the attribute Members of the element ClassRoster of type IDREFS. As a result, any compliant XML processor will verify that no student or course is declared twice and that referential integrity holds—that is, that a course referenced in a CrsTaken element does exist and that all students mentioned in the Members lists are also present in the document.

You might be wondering why we have changed the Ids of students in Figure 17.4 from purely numerical to Ids that start with a letter. The answer is that XML requires that the values of attributes of type ID (and thus of IDREF as well) start with a letter.

We can now define an important correctness requirement. An XML document is **well formed** if the following conditions hold:

- It has a root element.

- Every opening tag is followed by a matching closing tag, and the elements are properly nested inside each other.

- Any attribute can occur at most once in a given opening tag; its value must be provided, as discussed above; and this value must be quoted.

Note that the restrictions on ID, IDREF, and IDREFS are not part of the definition of "well formed" because these attribute types are specified using DTDs, which well-formedness completely ignores.

17.2.3 Namespaces

Namespaces were not part of the original XML specification and were added as an afterthought. However, they have become central to many important standards built on top of XML, so we consider them to be an integral XML feature for all practical purposes.

The driving force behind the introduction of namespaces was the realization that different communities will be building vocabularies of terms appropriate for the various domains (e.g., education, finance, electronics) and will use them as XML tags. In this situation, naming conflicts between different vocabularies are inevitable, and the integration of information obtained from different sources becomes very hard. For instance, the term Name might have different meanings and structure depending on whether we are talking about people or companies, as we see in these two document fragments:

```
<Name><First>John</First>  <Last>Doe</Last></Name>
<Name>IBM</Name>
```

FIGURE **17.4** A report document with cross-references.

```xml
<?xml version="1.0" ?>
<Report Date="2000-12-12">
  <Students>
    <Student StudId="s111111111">
      <Name><First>John</First><Last>Doe</Last></Name>
      <Status>U2</Status>
      <CrsTaken CrsCode="CS308" Semester="F1997"/>
      <CrsTaken CrsCode="MAT123" Semester="F1997"/>
    </Student>
    <Student StudId="s666666666">
      <Name><First>Joe</First><Last>Public</Last></Name>
      <Status>U3</Status>
      <CrsTaken CrsCode="CS308" Semester="F1994"/>
      <CrsTaken CrsCode="MAT123" Semester="F1997"/>
    </Student>
    <Student StudId="s987654321">
      <Name><First>Bart</First><Last>Simpson</Last></Name>
      <Status>U4</Status>
      <CrsTaken CrsCode="CS308" Semester="F1994"/>
    </Student>
  </Students>
  <Classes>
    <Class>
      <CrsCode>CS308</CrsCode><Semester>F1994</Semester>
      <ClassRoster Members="s666666666 s987654321"/>
    </Class>
    <Class>
      <CrsCode>CS308</CrsCode><Semester>F1997</Semester>
      <ClassRoster Members="s111111111"/>
    </Class>
    <Class>
      <CrsCode>MAT123</CrsCode><Semester>F1997</Semester>
      <ClassRoster Members="s111111111 s666666666"/>
    </Class>
  </Classes>
  <Courses>
    <Course CrsCode="CS308">
      <CrsName>Software Engineering</CrsName>
    </Course>
    <Course CrsCode="MAT123">
      <CrsName>Algebra</CrsName>
    </Course>
  </Courses>
</Report>
```

So it will become harder for an application to process documents that are built out of the vocabularies that contain conflicting tag names.

To overcome this problem, it has been decided that the name of every XML tag must have two parts: the **namespace** and the **local name**, with the general structure *namespace:local-name*. Local names have the same form as regular XML tags except that they cannot have a : in them. A namespace is represented by a string in the form of a **uniform resource identifier** (**URI**), which can be an abstract identifier (a general string of characters serving as a unique identifier) or a **uniform resource locator** (**URL**) (a Web page address).

The overall idea seems simple enough: different authors use different name-space identifiers for different domains, and thus terminological clashes are avoided. The strategy generally followed since the introduction of namespaces is that authors choose as namespace identifiers the URLs that are under their control. For instance, if Joe Public authors a vocabulary for the school supplies marketed by Acme, Inc., he uses a namespace such as

```
http://www.acmeinc.com/jp#supplies
```

and for toys the namespace could be

```
http://www.acmeinc.com/jp#toys
```

Note that these URLs need not refer to actual documents.

Namespace declarations. The W3C recommendation[1] for incorporating name-spaces into XML [Bray 1999] goes beyond a simple two-part naming schema—it also fixes a particular syntax for declaring namespaces, their use, and scoping rules. Here is an example:

```
<item xmlns="http://www.acmeinc.com/jp#supplies"
      xmlns:toy="http://www.acmeinc.com/jp#toys">
   <name>backpack</name>
   <feature>
       <toy:item>
           <toy:name>cyberpet</toy:name>
       </toy:item>
   </feature>
</item>
```

Namespaces are defined using the attribute xmlns, which is a reserved word. In fact, W3C has advised that all names starting with xml be considered as reserved

---

[1] The final documents produced by W3C are inconspicuously called "recommendations," but in reality they are as good as standards.

for the W3C's use. In our example, we declare two namespaces in the scope of the element `item`. The first one is declared using the syntax `xmlns=` and is called the **default namespace**. Naturally, there can be only one default namespace declaration per opening tag (this follows not only because of the semantics but also because XML does not permit multiple occurrences of the same attribute within the same opening tag). The second namespace is defined with the `xmlns:toy=` declaration. The **prefix** `toy` serves as a shorthand for the full namespace string `http://www.acmeinc.com/jp#toys`. One can declare several prefixed namespaces as long as the prefixes are distinct.[2]

Tags belonging to the namespace `http://www.acmeinc.com/jp#toys` should be prefixed with `toy:`. In our example, they are the inner tags `toy:item` and `toy:name`. Tags without any prefix (the outer `item`, `name`, and `feature`) are assumed to belong to the default namespace.

Namespace declarations have scope, which can be nested like a program block. To illustrate, we consider the following example:

```
<item xmlns="http://www.acmeinc.com/jp#supplies"
      xmlns:toy="http://www.acmeinc.com/jp#toys">
    <name>backpack</name>
    <feature>
        <toy:item>
            <toy:name>cyberpet</toy:name>
        </toy:item>
    </feature>
    <item xmlns="http://www.acmeinc.com/jp#supplies2"
          xmlns:toy="http://www.acmeinc.com/jp#toys2">
        <name>notebook</name>
        <toy:name>sticker</toy:name>
    </item>
</item>
```

Here we added one more child element to the outermost `item` element. The child is also called `item`, but it has its own default namespace and a redeclared namespace prefix, `toy`. Thus, the outermost `item` tag belongs to the default namespace

```
http://www.acmeinc.com/jp#supplies
```

The inner unprefixed `item` tag and its unprefixed child tag, `name`, are both in the scope of the default namespace

---

[2] Nevertheless, two tags are assumed to belong to the same namespace, even if they have different prefixes, if and only if their prefixes refer to the same URI ("same" meaning that the URIs are equal as character strings).

```
http://www.acmeinc.com/jp#supplies2
```

Similarly, the tags `toy:item` and `toy:name` inside the `feature` element belong to the namespace

```
http://www.acmeinc.com/jp#toys
```

The occurrence of `toy:name` at the end of the document belongs to the namespace

```
http://www.acmeinc.com/jp#toys2
```

Observe that, just as the innermost declaration of the default namespace overshadows the outermost declaration, the innermost declaration of the prefix `toy` overshadows the outermost declaration for the same prefix. A namespace-aware XML processor is supposed to understand these subtleties and, in particular, to recognize that the two unprefixed occurrences of `item` are *different tags* since they belong to different namespaces. Similarly, the unprefixed occurrences of `name` are different tags, and so are the prefixed versions of `name`. An XML processor that is *unaware* of namespaces will still be able to parse the above document. However, it will think that all unprefixed versions of `item` and `name` are the same and that all occurrences of the prefixed tag `toy:name` are the same. It will just wonder why the name has that weird : inside.

Even though the idea of a namespace seems like motherhood and apple pie—who could possibly be against it—it has been one of the least understood recommendations coming out of W3C [Bourret 2000]. Everyone agrees that tag names should come in two parts, but people have been trying to read between the lines of the recommendation and find things that are not there. One of the most confusing issues is the use of URLs as namespace identifiers. In our everyday experience, a URL points to some Web resource, and if a URL is used for a namespace, one tends to assume that it is a real address that contains some kind of schema describing the corresponding set of names. In reality, the name of a namespace is just a string that happens to be a URL, and it can be a big disappointment when pointing the browser toward such a URL brings up an unattractive error message.

The idea behind namespaces is nothing more than a mechanism for disambiguating tag names. An XML processor that reads a document encoded with namespaces should "know" how to parse it—that is, how to find its schema (represented as a DTD or an XML Schema—the specification languages described later). The information on the schema location can be provided in a special attribute, or it can be part of the convention used in a particular enterprise or community. For example, the toy industry might agree that all toy-related documents should be parsed using the DTD at a particular URL. One convention taking hold right now is that certain vocabularies (such as those used in the XML Schema specification—see Section 17.3) be identified using certain "well-known" namespaces, which prescribe the document schema uniquely.

17.2.4 Document Type Definitions

There are fixed rules that an author must follow in order to create an HTML document that can be properly rendered by the browser. For instance, the `table` element cannot occur inside the `form` element. XML, on the other hand, is intended for a variety of application domains (e.g., retail, healthcare, education), and each has its own idea of a properly structured document. Therefore, XML includes a language for specifying the document structure.

A set of rules for structuring an XML document is called a **document type definition** (DTD). A DTD can be specified as part of the document itself, or the document can give a URL where its DTD can be found. A document that conforms to its DTD is said to be **valid**. The XML specification does not require processors to check each document for conformance to its DTD because some applications might not care if the document is valid. In some cases, the processor does not check validity, instead relying on the guarantee of the sender for this (e.g., in electronic billing, where both sides use software guaranteed to produce valid documents). XML does not even require that the document have a DTD, but it does require that all documents be well formed. (The conditions for well-formedness—proper element nesting and restrictions on the attributes—have been discussed in Section 17.2.2.)

These two notions of correctness can lead to significant simplification and speedup for XML processors. An HTML browser usually tries to correct bugs in the HTML documents and to display as much of a buggy document as possible. In contrast, an XML processor is expected to simply reject documents that are not well formed. A processor that expects valid documents would reject invalid ones (those that do not comply with the DTD) even if they are well formed.

For those who are familiar with formal languages, a DTD is a *grammar* that specifies a valid XML document, based on the tags used in the document and their attributes. For instance, the following DTD is consistent with the document in Figure 17.3 on page 572:

```
<!DOCTYPE PersonList [
    <!ELEMENT PersonList (Title,Contents)>
    <!ELEMENT Title EMPTY>
    <!ELEMENT Contents (Person*)>
    <!ELEMENT Person (Name,Id,Address)>
    <!ELEMENT Name (#PCDATA)>
    <!ELEMENT Id (#PCDATA)>
    <!ELEMENT Address (Number,Street)>
    <!ELEMENT Number (#PCDATA)>
    <!ELEMENT Street (#PCDATA)>
    <!ATTLIST PersonList Type CDATA #IMPLIED
                         Date CDATA #IMPLIED>
    <!ATTLIST Title Value CDATA #REQUIRED>
]>
```

This example illustrates the most common DTD components: a **name** (Person-List in the example) and a set of ELEMENT and ATTLIST statements. The name of a DTD must coincide with the tag name of the root element of the document that conforms to that DTD. One ELEMENT statement exists for each allowed tag, including the root tag. Furthermore, for each tag that can have attributes, the ATTLIST statement specifies the allowed attributes and their type.

In our example, the first ELEMENT statement says that the element PersonList consists of a Title element followed by a Contents element. A Title element (the second ELEMENT statement) does not contain any elements (it is an empty element). The * in the definition of the Contents element indicates that there are zero or more elements of type Person. If we use + instead of "*", it would mean that at least one Person element must be present. The elements Name, Number, and Street are declared to be of type #PCDATA, that is, a character string.[3]

Following the element list, a DTD contains the description of allowed element attributes. In our case, PersonList is permitted to have the attributes Type and Date, while Title can only have the attribute Value. Other elements are not allowed to have attributes. Moreover, both attributes of PersonList are *optional*, as specified by the keyword #IMPLIED, while the Value attribute of Title is mandatory. All three attributes have the type CDATA, which is, again, a character string. (Note that different syntax is used to declare character string types for elements and attributes.)

Observe that our document in Figure 17.3 is valid with respect to the above DTD, but if, for example, we delete some Address elements from it, it will become invalid because the DTD says that each person must have an address. On the other hand, if the DTD has

```
<!ELEMENT Person (Name,Id,Address?)>
```

the address field becomes optional since ? indicates zero or one occurrences of the Address element.

It is also possible to state that the order of elements in a person's description does not matter, using the connective |, which represents alternatives:

```
<!ELEMENT Person
    ((Name,Id,Address)|(Name,Address,Id)|(Id,Address,Name)
    |(Id,Name,Address)|(Address,Id,Name)|(Address,Name,Id))>
```

You can see that it becomes rather awkward, however.

DTDs allow the author to specify several types for an attribute. We have seen CDATA. The other frequently used types are ID, IDREF, and IDREFS, mentioned on page 576 in connection with the report document in Figure 17.4. We pointed out that a document of this type needs a mechanism for enforcing referential integrity—much as in the database examples of Chapter 3.

---

[3] PCDATA stands for *parsed character data*.

FIGURE 17.5 A DTD for the report document in Figure 17.4.

```
<!DOCTYPE Report [
    <!ELEMENT Report (Students,Classes,Courses)>
    <!ELEMENT Students (Student*)>
    <!ELEMENT Classes (Class*)>
    <!ELEMENT Courses (Course*)>
    <!ELEMENT Student (Name,Status,CrsTaken*)>
    <!ELEMENT Name (First,Last)>
    <!ELEMENT First (#PCDATA)>
    .
    .
    .
    <!ELEMENT CrsTaken EMPTY>
    <!ELEMENT Class (CrsCode,Semester,ClassRoster)>
    <!ELEMENT Course (CrsName)>
    .
    .
    .
    <!ELEMENT ClassRoster EMPTY>
    <!ATTLIST Report Date CDATA #IMPLIED>
    <!ATTLIST Student StudId ID #REQUIRED>
    <!ATTLIST Course CrsCode ID #REQUIRED>
    <!ATTLIST CrsTaken CrsCode IDREF #REQUIRED
                       Semester CDATA #REQUIRED>
    <!ATTLIST ClassRoster Members IDREFS #IMPLIED>
]>
```

Specifically, we want to make sure that the values of the attributes StudId in Student and CrsCode in Course are distinct throughout the document, that the attribute CrsCode in CrsTaken represents a reference to a course mentioned in this document (that there is a Course element with a matching value in its CrsCode attribute), and that the members in a list indicated by Members in ClassRoster refer to student records mentioned in the document (for each such member there is a Student element with the matching value of its StudId attribute). This can be enforced with the DTD shown in Figure 17.5, in which we omit some easily reconstructible parts.

A compliant XML processor that insists on document validity is obliged by this DTD to make sure that no two Student elements have the same value in their StudId attribute (similarly for Course elements). This is because StudId is declared to have the type ID. In fact, no pair of attributes of type ID (with the same or different names) can have the same value in a valid XML document.

Referential integrity is maintained using the IDREF and IDREFS declarations. Because the attribute CrsCode of the element CrsTaken is declared as IDREF, referential integrity for course codes is preserved. The attribute Members in ClassRoster is declared as IDREFS, which represents *lists* of values of type IDREF. This secures the integrity of references to student Ids.

There are also constraints in the document that beg to be noticed, but they cannot be enforced using DTDs. We discuss these issues in the next section.

17.2.5 Inadequacy of DTDs as a Data Definition Language

XML was conceived as a simplified, streamlined version of SGML [SGML 1986], which was standardized years before the work on XML began. SGML was created for specifying documents that can be exchanged and automatically processed by software agents, and this was the original goal of XML as well. DTDs and the rationale behind their use were borrowed from SGML. Their technical underpinnings come from the theory of formal languages, and general-purpose parsers that can validate any document against any DTD are well known. Such validation has important implications for document-processing software. For instance, if an XML processor can expect that the documents it receives have been validated and will conform to the DTD Report shown in Figure 17.5, it does not need to take care of special cases and exceptions, such as the possibility that a student might have taken a nonexisting course or that a street address is missing.

During the development of XML, new ideas started to emerge. In particular, XML introduced the possibility of treating Web documents as data sources that can be queried (similarly to database relations) and that can be related to each other through semantically meaningful links (similar to foreign-key constraints). It was at this point that XML began to outgrow its SGML heritage. One of the first enhancements, which came too late to be included in XML 1.0, was namespaces, discussed earlier. A much more significant enhancement is the development of the XML Schema specification (Section 17.3), which is designed to rectify many of the limitations of DTD as a data definition language. These limitations include the following:

- DTDs are not designed with namespaces in mind. A DTD views xmlns as just another attribute with no special meaning. It is not hard to extend them to include namespaces, but there is a problem of backward compatibility and, in view of other limitations of DTDs, such enhancement is probably a futile exercise.

- DTDs use syntax that is quite different from that of XML documents. While this is not a fatal drawback, it is not the most elegant feature of XML 1.0 either.

- DTDs have a very limited repertoire of basic types (essentially just glorified strings).

- DTDs provide only limited means for expressing data-consistency constraints. They do not have keys (except for the very limited ID type), and the mechanism for specifying referential integrity is very weak. The only way to reference something is through the IDREF and IDREFS attributes, and even these are based on only one primitive type, a string. In particular, it is not possible to type the references. One cannot require that the attribute CrsCode of the element

CrsTaken in the report document of Figure 17.4 reference only Course elements. Thus, it is possible for John Doe to have a child element

```
<CrsTaken CrsCode="s666666666" Semester="F1999"/>
```

which refers to the student Id of Joe Public instead of to a course, and no XML 1.0 compliant processor can detect this problem. DTDs have ways of enforcing referential integrity for attributes but no corresponding feature for elements. For example, the contents of the element Class include the elements CrsCode and Semester (not to be confused with similarly named attributes of the tag CrsTaken). Clearly, we want the content of the element CrsCode to refer to a valid course and match a value of the attribute CrsCode in some Course element. Furthermore, for each pair of values of the attributes in the element CrsTaken, there must be a corresponding pair of values of CrsCode/Semester tags in some Class element. These constraints cannot be enforced using DTDs.

- XML data is ordered; database data is unordered (e.g., the order of tuples does not matter). Also, the order of the attributes in a database relation or an object does not matter; the order of elements in XML matters. We already saw that DTDs allow us to specify alternatives, and through them we can state that the order of elements is immaterial (as in the earlier example of the Name, Address, and Id children of the element Person). However, this becomes extremely awkward as the number of attributes grows. For instance, to state that the order among *N* children elements is immaterial, a DTD must specify *N*! alternatives.

- Element definitions are global to the entire document. If a DTD specifies that, for example, Name consists of children elements First and Last, then it is not possible to have a *differently structured* Name element anywhere else in the document. This happens because a DTD can have only one ELEMENT clause per element name. There is no way to localize it with respect to a parent element so that different definitions would apply to different occurrences of Name, depending on where it is nested.

17.3 XML Schema

XML Schema, a data definition language for XML documents, became a recommendation of W3C in 2001. It was developed in response to the aforesaid limitations of the DTD mechanism and has the following main features:

- It uses the same syntax as that used for ordinary XML documents.
- It is integrated with the namespace mechanism. In particular, different schemas can be imported from different namespaces and integrated into one schema.
- It provides a number of built-in types, such as string, integer, and time—similar to SQL.
- It provides the means to define complex types based on simpler ones.

- It allows the same element name to be defined as having different types depending on where the element is nested.

- It supports key and referential integrity constraints.

- It provides a better mechanism for specifying documents where the order of element types does not matter.

The downside is that XML Schema is an order of magnitude more complex than the DTDs, and the DTDs are still widely used for simpler kinds of XML processing, those where the advanced features just described are not required.

An XML document that conforms to a given schema is said to be **schema valid** and is called an **instance** document of the schema. As with DTDs, the XML Schema specification does not require an XML processor to actually use the document schema. It is free to ignore the schema or to use a different one. For instance, the XML processor might want to consider only the documents that satisfy stricter integrity constraints than those given in the schema, or it might decide to enforce only part of the schema. This liberal attitude should be contrasted with databases, where *all* data must comply with the schema. In this sense, XML data as a whole should be considered semistructured (Section 17.1) despite the fact that a schema might partially describe it.

17.3.1 XML Schema and Namespaces

An XML Schema document (like a DTD) describes the structure of other (instance) XML documents. It begins with a declaration of the namespaces to be used in the schema, three of which are particularly important:

- `http://www.w3.org/2001/XMLSchema`—The namespace that identifies names of tags and attributes used *in the schema*. These names are not related to, nor do they appear in, any particular instance document. Instead, they are used in schema documents to describe structural properties of instance documents. Hence, this namespace is part of schema documents but is not used in instance documents. Among the names associated with this namespace are `schema`, `attribute`, and `element`.

- `http://www.w3.org/2001/XMLSchema-instance`—Another namespace used in conjunction with `http://www.w3.org/2001/XMLSchema`. It identifies a small number of special names, which are also defined in the XML Schema specification but are used in the instance documents rather than in their schema (whence the name `XMLSchema-instance`). One such name, `schemaLocation`, specifies the location of the schema for the document. Another defines the special null value when it appears in a document. We will discuss these features in due time. This namespace is part of the specification of instance documents since it defines tags used in those documents.

- The **target namespace**—Identifies the set of names *defined* by a particular schema document, in other words, the user-defined names that are to be used in the instance documents of that particular schema. For instance, in the schema document for Figure 17.4, the names CrsTaken, Student, Status, and so forth, would be associated with the target namespace. (We will soon start developing the various parts of that schema.) The target namespace is declared using the attribute targetNameSpace of the opening tag of the schema element—the root tag of every schema document.

The integration with namespaces is one of the important items missing in DTDs: a DTD can define any number of tags, but there is no way to associate those tags with a namespace.

We now begin to develop a schema for the report document of Figure 17.4. Our first example simply declares the namespaces to be used in the schema we are creating.

```
<schema xmlns="http://www.w3.org/2001/XMLSchema"
        targetNameSpace="http://xyz.edu/Admin">


        <!-- Nothing here yet -->
</schema>
```

The first namespace declared in this example makes the standard XMLSchema namespace the default. This is handy because in creating the schema, we are likely to use many special tags defined by the XML Schema specification, and making XMLSchema the default namespace will obviate the need for namespace prefixes for them. If, however, we want a different namespace to be the default, we can use

```
xmlns:xsd="http://www.w3.org/2001/XMLSchema"
```

By convention, xsd is the prefix for names in the standard XMLSchema namespace. In this case, we have to use xsd whenever a name associated with the XML Schema's namespace is used:

```
<xsd:schema xmlns:xsd="http://www.w3.org/2001/XMLSchema"
            xsd:targetNameSpace="http://xyz.edu/Admin">


        <!-- Nothing here yet -->
</xsd:schema>
```

The first attribute here says that xsd is the prefix for names associated with the XMLSchema namespace. The second attribute says that the new tags and attributes defined by the above schema document are considered to be part of the http://xyz.edu/Admin namespace. Note that, since targetNameSpace is a name defined by the XML Schema specification, its use is prefixed with xsd.

Suppose now that we have filled in all the blanks in the above schema. How does the fact that we now have a schema for the instance document in Figure 17.4 change this document? We need to add three things to the instance: the declaration of the

FIGURE **17.6** Schema and an instance document.

```
<!-- An XML schema document; located at http://xyz.edu/Admin.xsd -->
<schema xmlns="http://www.w3.org/2001/XMLSchema"
        targetNameSpace="http://xyz.edu/Admin">

        <!-- Nothing here yet -->
</schema>

<!-- An instance document conforming to the above schema;
     it uses the target namespace defined in that schema -->
<?xml version="1.0" ?>
<Report xmlns="http://xyz.edu/Admin">
        xmlns:xsi="http://www.w3.org/2001/XMLSchema-instance"
        xsi:schemaLocation="http://xyz.edu/Admin
        http://xyz.edu/Admin.xsd">

<!-- Same contents as in the report document of Figure 17.4 -->
</Report>
```

default namespace it uses (in our case, `http://xyz.edu/Admin`), the location of its schema, and the `XMLSchema-instance` namespace. The latter is needed because the attribute `schemaLocation`, which specifies the schema location, occurs in instance documents and is part of the `XMLSchema-instance` namespace. To better understand the relationship among the schema, the actual instance document, and the various namespaces, we show the report document and its schema together in Figure 17.6.

Note in the figure that the default namespace in the instance document is `http://xyz.edu/Admin`—the namespace defined in the `targetNameSpace` attribute of the schema document.[4] There need not be anything at this URL because a namespace is just an identifier that is used to disambiguate the names of document tags and attributes. This namespace is chosen as a default in order to minimize the number of namespace prefixes that need to be used in the document. Because the document in Figure 17.6 is supposed to have the same contents as in the report in Figure 17.4, most of the tag and attribute names belong to this default namespace.

The attribute `xsi:schemaLocation` is part of the XML Schema specification and belongs to the namespace

```
http://www.w3.org/2001/XMLSchema-instance
```

The value of the attribute is a namespace-URL pair, and it says that the schema for the namespace `http://xyz.edu/Admin` can be found in an XML Schema document

---

[4] Most namespaces and document locations used in the examples have been changed to protect the innocent. However, the XMLSchema and XMLSchema-instance namespaces are real.

at the URL `http://xyz.edu/Admin.xsd`. However, as mentioned earlier, XML processors are not bound by these hints. They can choose to ignore the schema or to use a different one.

Before plunging into the specifics of defining the actual schema, we mention one other important detail, the `include` statement. It is easy to see from Figure 17.4 that our report has three distinct components: a student list, a class list, and a course list. Since these components have very different structures, it is reasonable to assume that they might well occur separately in other contexts and that they might have their own schemas. Given this, it is unreasonable for us to copy those schemas over in order to create the schema for the report document. Instead, we can use the `include` statement in the schema document as follows:

```
<schema xmlns="http://www.w3.org/2001/XMLSchema"
        targetNameSpace="http://xyz.edu/Admin">

    <include schemaLocation="http://xyz.edu/StudentTypes.xsd"/>
    <include schemaLocation="http://xyz.edu/ClassTypes.xsd"/>
    <include schemaLocation="http://xyz.edu/CourseTypes.xsd"/>

    <!-- Nothing here yet -->
</schema>
```

The effect of the `include` statement is to include the schemas at the specified address in the given document. This technique allows for greater flexibility and modularity of XML schemas. Included schemas must have the same target namespace as the including schema since the include statement effectively integrates them into the including schema document. Observe one possibly confusing detail in the above example. We have used the attribute `schemaLocation` without prefixing it with `xsi`, and, unlike the previous example, we did not include the `XMLSchema-instance` namespace. This discrepancy has a rational explanation. The `schemaLocation` attribute of the tag `include` belongs to the standard `XMLSchema` namespace (like the `include` tag itself); that is, this attribute is different from the similarly named attribute in the report document above. Since, unlike the report document, our schema does not use any names from the `XMLSchema-instance` namespace, this namespace was not declared.

17.3.2 Simple Types

Primitive types. The dearth of primitive types was one of the criticisms leveled against DTDs. The XML Schema specification rectifies the problem by adding many useful primitive types, such as `decimal`, `integer`, `float`, `boolean`, and `date`, in addition to `string`, `ID`, `IDREF`, and `IDREFS`. More important, it provides type constructors, such as *list* and *union*, and a mechanism to derive new primitive types from the basic ones. This mechanism is similar to the CREATE DOMAIN statement of SQL (see Section 3.3.6).

Deriving simple types using the `list` **and** union **constructors.** As in DTDs, IDREFS is one of the primitive types in the XML Schema specification. However, it can also be derived using the list constructor:[5]

```
<simpleType name="myIdrefs">
    <list itemType="IDREF"/>
</simpleType>
```

Here the `name` attribute is used to give a name, `myIdrefs`, to the newly defined type. This and any other name introduced by the `name` attribute in a schema document belongs to the target namespace of that document.

The `union` type can be useful when there is a need for two or more ways to enter data. For instance, in the United States a telephone number can be 7 or 10 digits long, which can be expressed as follows:

```
<simpleType name="phoneNumber">
    <union memberTypes="phone7digits phone10digits"/>
</simpleType>
```

We will see the definitions of the types `phone7digits` and `phone10digits` shortly.

Deriving simple types by restriction. A more interesting way of deriving new types is via the **restriction** mechanism, which allows us to constrain a basic type using one or more constraints from a fixed repertoire defined by the XML Schema specification. This is how we are going to define the type `phone7digits`:

```
<simpleType name="phone7digits">
    <restriction base="integer">
        <minInclusive value="1000000"/>
        <maxInclusive value="9999999"/>
    </restriction>
</simpleType>
```

The 10-digit number type is defined similarly. In the definition of `phone7digits`, we used the tags `maxInclusive` and `minInclusive` to define the range of acceptable numbers. XML Schema provides a large number of built-in constraints to play with, such as `minInclusive/maxInclusive` [XMLSchema 2000a, XMLSchema 2000b].

---

[5] Unless stated otherwise, all examples of XML schemas assume the standard `http://www.w3.org/2000/10/XMLSchema` namespace as a default.

Here we mention just a few of the more interesting ones. Suppose that, in addition, we let the user specify phone numbers in the XXX-YYYY format. This can be done in several ways, one being

```
<simpleType name="phone7digitsAndDash">
    <restriction base="string">
        <pattern value="[0-9]{3}-[0-9]{4}"/>
    </restriction>
</simpleType>
```

Here we use the `pattern` tag to restrict the set of all strings to those that match the given pattern. The language for constructing patterns is similar to that used in the Perl programming language, but the basics should be familiar to anyone with a working knowledge of text editors such as Vi or Emacs. In the above example, [0-9] means "any digit between 0 and 9" and {3} is a pattern modifier that says that only a sequence of exactly three digits is allowed.

Other ways to derive simple types from the basic `string` type include the following:

- `<length value="7"/>`—Restricts the domain to strings of length 7.

- `<minLength value="7"/>`—Restricts the domain to strings of length *at least* 7.

- `<maxLength value="14"/>`—Restricts the domain to strings of length *at most* 14.

- `<enumeration value="ABC"/>`—Specifies one value in an enumerated set.

The above constraints are not limited to strings, and `enumeration` is applicable to virtually any base type. Here is an example:

```
<simpleType name="emergencyNumbers">
    <restriction base="integer">
        <enumeration value="911"/>
        <enumeration value="333"/>
        <enumeration value="5431234"/>
    </restriction>
</simpleType>
```

Simple types for the report document.   We now define some simple types for our report document of Figure 17.4 on page 578. We will later attach these types to the appropriate attributes in the document schema. For easy reference, we summarize all student-related types in Figure 17.9 on page 605 and all course-related types in Figure 17.10 on page 606.

```
<simpleType name="studentId">
    <restriction base="ID">
        <pattern value="s[0-9]{9}"/>
```

```
        </restriction>
    </simpleType>
    <simpleType name="studentRef">
        <restriction base="IDREF"
            <pattern value="s[0-9]{9}"/>
        </restriction>
    </simpleType>
    <simpleType name="studentIds">
        <list itemType="adm:studentRef"/>
    </simpleType>
    <simpleType name="courseCode">
        <restriction base="ID">
            <pattern value="[A-Z]{3}[0-9]{3}"/>
        </restriction>
    </simpleType>
    <simpleType name="courseRef">
        <restriction base="IDREF">
            <pattern value="[A-Z]{3}[0-9]{3}"/>
        </restriction>
    </simpleType>
```

The first type, studentId, defines student Ids as digit strings of length 9; it will be used to specify the domain of values for studId in the report. The second defines the type of *references* to student Ids, the third defines *lists* of references to student Ids, the fourth defines course codes as strings of three uppercase letters followed by three digits, and the fifth is the type for course references. Note also that we have used ID and IDREF as base types. They have the same semantics as they do in DTDs, so uniqueness and referential integrity are guaranteed. The definition of the type studentIds uses a previously defined type studentRef. Note that the reference to that type is tagged with a namespace prefix adm, which is here assumed to be associated with the target namespace of the schema document. The need for this prefix will be explained shortly.

Observe that we are already doing better than in the case of the Report DTD shown in Figure 17.5 on page 584. It is impossible for a DTD to say that the attribute Members returns a list of references to students rather than to courses or to impose a similar restriction on the attribute CrsCode of the tag CrsTaken. In contrast, the above simple types prevent such meaningless references because the type courseRef is disjoint from the domain of studentId and the domain of studentRef is disjoint from that of courseCode.

Type declarations for simple elements and attributes. So far, we have been talking about types without attaching them to elements and attributes. Here are some simple cases of type declaration for tags in our report document, which will later become part of the schema document for this report.

```
<element name="CrsName" type="string"/>
<element name="Status" type="adm:studentStatus"/>
```

The first declaration states that the element CrsName has a simple content of type string. The last declaration is fancier: it associates the Status tag with a derived type, studentStatus, defined as an enumeration of strings U1, U2, U3, U4, G1, G2, G3, G4, and G5, which represent the various status codes for undergraduate and graduate students.

```
<simpleType name="studentStatus">
    <restriction base="string">
        <enumeration value="U1"/>
        <enumeration value="U2"/>
            .
            .
            .
        <enumeration value="G5"/>
    </restriction>
</simpleType>
```

A subtle but very important point in this example is the prefix adm attached to studentStatus in (17.2)—a consequence of the namespace consideration. To understand this better, let us consider the context in which the above statements appear:

```
<schema xmlns="http://www.w3.org/2001/XMLSchema"
        xmlns:adm="http://xyz.edu/Admin"
        targetNameSpace="http://xyz.edu/Admin">
        .
        .
        .
    <element name="CrsName" type="string"/>
    <!-- reference to StudentStatus -->
    <element name="Status" type="adm:studentStatus"/>
        .
        .
        .
    <!-- definition of StudentStatus -->
    <simpleType name="studentStatus">
            .
            .
            .
    </simpleType>
        .
        .
        .
</schema>
```

In a schema document the default is typically the standard XMLSchema namespace. This enables us to use frequently occurring symbols, such as element, simpleType, name, and type, without a prefix. In addition, a schema document defines a number of types (e.g., studentStatus), elements (e.g., Status), and attributes (see Section 17.3.3) that belong to a target namespace (http://xyz.edu/Admin in our case). When we define a new element or type, we use it without a prefix (for example, name="Status" and name="studentStatus") because these names are newly defined and hence cannot be part of the default namespace. They are automatically placed in the target namespace. However, how do we *refer* to the names defined within the same schema (for example, our reference to studentStatus in the type attribute)? If we do not use any prefix, the XML processor is supposed to assume that the name belongs to the default namespace. This is precisely what happens with the string type of the element CrsName. Since string is not prefixed, it is assumed to be taken out of the standard XMLSchema namespace, which is correct. In contrast, using studentStatus without a prefix causes the XML processor to assume that this symbol also comes from the default namespace, which is an error since XML Schema does not define studentStatus. Therefore, we need to define a namespace prefix for the target namespace and use it with every reference to a component of the target schema. The purpose of the second occurrence of the xmlns attribute of the schema element in the above example is thus to associate the prefix adm to the target namespace. From now on, we assume that the target namespace has the prefix adm, and we will use it with defined types without mention.

Next, consider how one specifies the types of some attributes in our document:

```
<attribute name="Date" type="date"/>
<attribute name="StudId" type="adm:studentId"/>
<attribute name="Members" type="adm:studentIds"/>
<attribute name="CrsCode" type="adm:courseCode"/>
```

Notice that these declarations do not associate attributes with elements, so they are not very meaningful at this point. We cannot make the association here because elements that have attributes are considered to have *complex types* (even if they have empty content, such as CrsTaken), so we need to familiarize ourselves with such types first.

17.3.3 Complex Types

Basic example. So far we have seen how to define *simple types*—the only types allowed in attributes and the types of elements that do not have attributes or children. The fragment of a schema in Figure 17.7 defines a complex type suitable for the Student element in the report document.

This example contains two type declarations and many new features. First, the tag complexType is used instead of simpleType to warn the XML processor of things to come. Second, the sequence tag is used to specify that the elements Name, Status, and CrsTaken must occur in the given order. Third, the CrsTaken element (whose

FIGURE 17.7 Definition of the complex type `studentType`.

```
<complexType name="studentType">
    <sequence>
        <element name="Name" type="adm:personNameType"/>
        <element name="Status" type="adm:studentStatus"/>
        <element name="CrsTaken" type="adm:courseTakenType"
            minOccurs="0" maxOccurs="unbounded"/>
    </sequence>
    <attribute name="StudId" type="adm:studentId"/>
</complexType>
<complexType name="personNameType">
    <sequence>
        <element name="First" type="string"/>
        <element name="Last" type="string"/>
    </sequence>
</complexType>
```

type will be defined shortly) is said to occur zero, one, or more times. In general, we can specify any number as a value of `minOccurs` and `maxOccurs`. Doing the same with DTDs is possible but extremely awkward since one must use alternatives (specified using |), which leads to unwieldy schemas. For other elements, we did not specify `minOccurs` and `maxOccurs` because they both default to 1 (which we want anyway). Finally, the attribute declaration at the end of the complex type definition associates `StudId` with the type `studentId` (Figure 17.9 on page 605), and, because it occurs in the scope of the definition of `studentType`, it means that every element of type `studentType` must have this attribute (and no other).

The second type declaration in Figure 17.7 supplies the type for the `Name` element used in the definition of `studentType`. This declaration does not introduce new features.

Associating a complex type with an element is no different from associating a simple type with an element. The following statement associates the `Student` element with the complex type `studentType`:

```
<element name="Student" type="adm:studentType"/>
```

Special cases. The simple picture just described is complicated by two special cases: how do we define the type of an element that has both a simple content (just text with no children elements) *and* attributes, and how can we define the type of an element that has attributes but *no* content (defined as EMPTY in the DTD)? We have seen the first kind of element in the dialog between Romeo and Apothecary on page 575; the second kind is represented by the element `CrsTaken` of Figure 17.4, page 578.

Defining the first type of element is a little awkward, and we skip this topic since it rarely occurs in data representation using XML.[6] On the other hand, defining the type for elements such as CrsTaken is easy:

```
<complexType name="courseTakenType">
    <attribute name="CrsCode" type="adm:courseRef"/>
    <attribute name="Semester" type="string"/>
</complexType>
```

Combining elements into groups. The example of studentType in Figure 17.7 shows how to combine elements into an ordered group using sequence. Tags such as sequence, which describe how elements can be combined into groups, are called **compositors**; they are required when an element has **complex content**, that is, when the element has at least one child element. XML Schema defines several compositors; one provides a way to combine elements into *unordered* sets. Note that the lack of a practical way to specify unordered collections of elements was one of the criticisms of DTDs in Section 17.2.5.

Suppose that we want to allow the street name, number, and the city name to appear in any order in an address. We can specify this using the compositor all:

```
<complexType name="addressType">
    <all>
        <element name="StreetName" type="string"/>
        <element name="StreetNumber" type="string"/>
        <element name="City" type="string"/>
    </all>
</complexType>
```

Unfortunately, there are a number of restrictions on all that make it hard to use in many cases. First, all must appear directly below complexType, so the following is illegal:

```
<complexType name="studentType2">
    <sequence>
        <all>
            <element name="Name" type="adm:personNameType"/>
            <element name="Status" type="adm:studentStatus"/>
        </all>
        <element name="CrsTaken" type="adm:courseTakenType"
                 minOccurs="0" maxOccurs="unbounded"/>
```

---

[6] Defining an element whose content is just text (no children elements) and which has attributes is done with the help of the simpleContent tag defined by XML Schema; see, for example, the XML Schema Primer [XMLSchema 2000a].

```
        </sequence>
        <attribute name="StudId" type="adm:studentId"/>
    </complexType>
```

Second, no element within it can be repeated. In other words, maxOccurs must be 1 for every child of all, so the following is also not allowed:

```
<complexType name="studentType3">
    <all>
        <element name="Name" type="adm:personNameType"/>
        <element name="Status" type="adm:studentStatus"/>
        <element name="CrsTaken" type="adm:courseTakenType"
                minOccurs="0" maxOccurs="unbounded"/>
    </all>
    <attribute name="StudId" type="adm:studentId"/>
</complexType>
```

The third grouping construct of XML Schema is the choice compositor, which plays the same role for complex types as union does for simple types. For instance, in the following example,

```
<complexType name="addressType">
    <sequence>
        <choice>
            <element name="POBox" type="string"/>
            <sequence>
                <element name="Name" type="string"/>
                <element name="Number" type="string"/>
            </sequence>
        </choice>
        <element name="City" type="string"/>
    </sequence>
</complexType>
```

choice lets us substitute the post office box for the street address. That is, a valid address must have precisely one of the two possibilities: a post office box or a street address.

Note that a content descriptor, such as a compositor, is required even if the type contains only one child element. For instance,

```
<complexType name="foo">
    <element name="bar" type="integer"/>
</complexType>
```

is illegal, but

```
<complexType name="foo">
    <sequence>
        <element name="bar" type="integer"/>
    </sequence>
</complexType>
```

is correct.

Local element names. In DTDs, all element declarations are global because only one ELEMENT statement per element name is allowed. Thus, it is not possible to define a valid report document (with respect to *any* DTD) where both Student and Course have a Name child element with different types. Indeed, this is the case in Figure 17.4 on page 578, where a course name is a string while a student name has complex type personNameType. Since the types are different, we could not use Name as the element name for both. Instead, we had to use CrsName to identify course names. For the same reason, DTDs do not let us use the element name Course instead of the name CrsCode for the child element of Class: the Course child inside the element Courses has a different structure than the CrsCode element inside Class. Thus, if we replace the tag name CrsCode with Course, the DTD must have two different ELEMENT statements for Course, which is impossible.

The XML Schema specification corrects this problem by providing local scope to element declarations. This is done as in any programming language. A declaration of an element type is considered local to the nearest containing <complexType ... > ... </complexType> block. In the report document, this local scoping allows us to rename the CrsName tag to Name and define the following schema:

```
<complexType name="studentType">
    <sequence>
        <element name="Name" type="adm:personNameType"/>
        <element name="Status" type="adm:studentStatus"/>
        <element name="CrsTaken" type="adm:courseTakenType"
            minOccurs="0" maxOccurs="unbounded"/>
    </sequence>
    <attribute name="StudId" type="adm:studentId"/>
</complexType>
<complexType name="courseType">
    <sequence>
        <element name="Name" type="string"/>
    </sequence>
    <attribute name="CrsCode" type="adm:courseCode"/>
</complexType>
```

Here both studentType and courseType include a child element, Name. In the first case, this element has a complex type personNameType, which includes two elements: First and Last. In the second case, it has a simple type, string. However, unlike in a DTD, the two declarations have a different scope and thus their definitions do not clash.

Importing schemas.   In Section 17.3.1, we illustrated the use of the include instruction for constructing a schema out of separate components that reside in different files. This facility supports modular construction of complex XML Schemas by small teams of collaborating programmers. Therefore, it requires that the target namespace of an included schema be the same as the target namespace of the containing schema.

At the same time, the designers of the XML Schema specification understood that the true potential of the Web can be realized only if people can pull together schemas constructed by different groups or organizations. This is the goal of the import statement. As with the include statement, the schemaLocation attribute is provided, but it is optional for import. The only required attribute is namespace because it is possible to import a schema whose target namespace is different from the target namespace of the importing schema. In the absence of schemaLocation, the XML processor is supposed to find the schema on its own, possibly deriving it from the namespace using some convention. Even when schemaLocation is provided, the processor is allowed to ignore it or to use a different schema. The only thing that the processor must not ignore is the namespace. Thus, the namespace attribute of the import statement determines the target namespace of the imported schema.

In the following example, we use import instead of include:

```
<schema xmlns="http://www.w3.org/2001/XMLSchema"
        targetNameSpace="http://xyz.edu/Admin"
        xmlns:reg = "http://xyz.edu/Registrar"
        xmlns:crs = "http://xyz.edu/Courses">
    <import namespace="http://xyz.edu/Registrar"
        schemaLocation="http://xyz.edu/Registrar/StudentTypes.xsd"/>
    <import namespace="http://xyz.edu/Courses"/>
    .
    .
    .
</schema>
```

Here we assume that the schemas describing students and courses use different target namespaces and that the report processing software knows where to find the schema that describes courses. Therefore, the schemaLocation attribute is not provided in the second import statement (but it is in the first). The first import statement imports a schema with target namespace http://xyz.edu/Registrar. This namespace is assigned the prefix reg so that any part of the imported schema, for example, x, could be referred to as reg:x.

Deriving new complex types by extension and restriction. In some cases, the user might need to modify parts of the included or imported schema. This is easy with inclusion because all documents are assumed to be under the author's control. With importing, however, the control is usually with an external entity and the importer might not be allowed to copy the schema, or this might not be desirable. For example, in many cases, the importer just wants to have a "view" of the original schema so that the importer's schema would change along with that original.

XML Schema provides two mechanisms for modifying imported schema: **extension** and **restriction**. Both are special cases of the notion of *subtype* defined in Section 16.2.3. **Extending** a schema means adding new elements or attributes to it. **Restricting** a schema means tightening its definition in order to exclude some instance documents.

Suppose that foo.edu decides to follow the example of xyz.edu and "XML-ize" their registration system. Overall they like the schema of xyz.edu but want to add a short course syllabus to every course record. Because xyz.edu is constantly improving its XML student registration tools, foo.edu decides that it can take advantage of these improvements by importing and *extending* the schema rather than copying it over. Specifically, foo.edu wants to extend the type courseType (Figure 17.10, page 606) with an additional element, syllabus. To this end, they create the following schema document:

```
<schema xmlns="http://www.w3.org/2001/XMLSchema"
        xmlns:xyzCrs="http://xyz.edu/Admin"
        xmlns:fooAdm="http://foo.edu/Admin"
        targetNameSpace="http://foo.edu/Admin">
    <!-- fooAdm is the prefix to be used for references
         to the target namespace within this schema -->
    <import namespace="http://xyz.edu/Admin"/>

    <complexType name="courseType">
        <complexContent>
            <extension base="xyzCrs:courseType">
                <element name="syllabus" type="string"/>
            </extension>
        </complexContent>
    </complexType>
    <!-- Now define a Course element for the target namespace
         and associate it with the derived type -->
    <element name="Course" type="fooAdm:courseType"/>
    .
    .
    .
</schema>
```

Notice that the target namespace is now `http://foo.edu/Admin`—that of the client university—and we associate the prefix `fooAdm` with it. The document uses the import statement to obtain the schema of `xyz.edu` to use as a basis for constructing a new schema. We assume that the important schema has the namespace `http://xyz.edu/Admin`. Since the new schema refers to the names defined in `xyz.edu`'s namespace (such as `courseType`), we need to associate a prefix with the imported namespace of `xyz.edu`. We choose `xyzCrs`.

After defining the namespaces, we define a new type, `courseType`, using a similar type in the imported schema. The newly defined type is not prefixed because we want it to belong to the target namespace. However, the base type imported from `xyz.edu` is prefixed and is referred to as `xyzCrs:courseType`. To signal the XML processor that a complex type is to be defined by modifying another type, the XML Schema specification requires the `<complexContent> ... </complexContent>` tag pair. Inside this pair, either an `extension` or a `restriction` clause is specified. We use `extension` in the above example, which means that the specified element, `syllabus`, is to be added to the contents of the type `xyzCrs:courseType` to form the new type `courseType` (in the target namespace `http://foo.edu/Admin`).

`foo.edu` might need to make other changes to the schema. For instance, they might generally like the type `studentType` defined in the namespace `http://xyz.edu/Admin` (Figure 17.9, page 605), but not that it allows students to take any number of courses (because of `maxOccurs="unbounded"`). Thus, `foo.edu` decides to limit this number to 63 by *restricting* the original schema:

```
<schema xmlns="http://www.w3.org/2001/XMLSchema"
    xmlns:xyzCrs="http://xyz.edu/Admin"
    xmlns:fooAdm="http://foo.edu/Admin">
    targetNameSpace="http://foo.edu/Admin">

  <import namespace="http://xyz.edu/Admin"/>
    .
    .
    .
  <complexType name="studentType">
    <complexContent>
      <restriction base="xyzCrs:studentType">
        <sequence>
          <element name="Name" type="xyzCrs:personNameType"/>
          <element name="Status" type="xyzCrs:studentStatus"/>
          <element name="CrsTaken" type="xyzCrs:courseTakenType"
                   minOccurs="0" maxOccurs="63"/>
        </sequence>
        <attribute name="StudId" type="xyzCrs:studentId"/>
      </restriction>
    </complexContent>
  </complexType>
```

```
<!-- Now define a Student element for the target namespace
        and associate it with the derived type -->
<element name="Student" type="fooAdm:studentType"/>
    .
    .
    .

</schema>
```

Analogously to the type extension mechanism, we use the tag `restriction` inside the `complexContent` block. The important difference, however, is that, when restricting a complex type, we must repeat all the element and attribute declarations from the base type. At the same time, we can impose restrictions on the components of the base type, for instance, by replacing `maxOccurs="unbounded"` with the more restrictive `maxOccurs="63"`. Thus, a restriction of a complex base type has exactly the same overall structure as the base type except that some elements and attributes comprising the restriction may be subsets of the corresponding ranges of the base type.

17.3.4 Putting It Together

We have now defined a large number of simple and complex types, and we are ready to put them together to form a complete schema, which can describe document instances such as the report in Figure 17.4 on page 578. Such a schema requires a number of type definitions and at least one declaration of a **global element**. One of these global elements typically serves as the root element of the document instances described by the schema (e.g., the `Report` element in Figure 17.8). The others can be elements that are used in the definition of the type of the root. We will discuss global elements more fully on page 607. In our example, a single global declaration associates the root element, called `Report`, with its type, `adm:reportType`. This complex type contains declarations of other elements and attributes together with their types. Starting with the root element, then, we can descend into its type and find all of its elements and attributes. Repeating this recursively, we can find the elements and attributes at any depth in the document structure. A complete schema for our example (whose parts are defined elsewhere and inserted using the `include` statement) is shown in Figure 17.8.

We omit the definition of the lower-level types `classOfferings` and `course-Catalog`, which are defined similarly to `studentList`. Like `studentList`, these types are defined in terms of the types shown in Figures 17.9 and 17.10, which are the targets of the `include` statement in Figure 17.8.

As before, we must be careful about the namespaces, so we define `adm` as a prefix for the target namespace and use it in all references to the names defined in this schema (except in the statements that define these names using the attribute `name`). Recall that the including and included schemas are required to have the same namespace, so one prefix, `adm`, suffices to refer both to the names defined by the including schema (e.g., `adm:courseCatalog`) and the names defined in the included schemas (e.g., `adm:studentType`).

FIGURE **17.8** A complete schema.

```
<schema xmlns="http://www.w3.org/2001/XMLSchema"
    xmlns:adm="http://xyz.edu/Admin"
    targetNameSpace="http://xyz.edu/Admin">

<!-- The following schemas are shown in Figures 17.9, 17.10, and 17.11 -->
<include schemaLocation="http://xyz.edu/StudentTypes.xsd"/>
<include schemaLocation="http://xyz.edu/ClassTypes.xsd"/>
<include schemaLocation="http://xyz.edu/CourseTypes.xsd"/>

<element name="Report" type="adm:reportType"/>

<complexType name="reportType">
  <sequence>
    <element name="Students" type="adm:studentList"/>
    <element name="Classes" type="adm:classOfferings"/>
    <element name="Courses" type="adm:courseCatalog"/>
  </sequence>
</complexType>
<complexType name="studentList">
  <sequence>
    <element name="Student" type="adm:studentType"
            minOccurs="0" maxOccurs="unbounded"/>
  </sequence>
</complexType>

<!-- Plus the definition of classOfferings, courseCatalog -->
<!-- The definition of studentType is in the included schema
     http://xyz.edu/studentTypes.xsd -->
</schema>
```

FIGURE **17.9** Student types at http://xyz.edu/StudentTypes.xsd.

```
<schema xmlns="http://www.w3.org/2001/XMLSchema"
          xmlns:adm="http://xyz.edu/Admin"
          targetNameSpace="http://xyz.edu/Admin">

    <complexType name="studentType">
        <sequence>
            <element name="Name" type="adm:personNameType"/>
            <element name="Status" type="adm:studentStatus"/>
            <!-- courseTakenType is defined in Figure 17.10 -->
            <element name="CrsTaken" type="adm:courseTakenType"
                      minOccurs="0" maxOccurs="unbounded"/>
        </sequence>
        <attribute name="StudId" type="adm:studentId"/>
    </complexType>
    <complexType name="personNameType">
        <sequence>
            <element name="First" type="string"/>
            <element name="Last" type="string"/>
        </sequence>
    </complexType>
    <simpleType name="studentStatus">
        <restriction base="string">
            <enumeration value="U1"/>
            <enumeration value="U2"/>
                .
                .
                .
            <enumeration value="G5"/>
        </restriction>
    </simpleType>

    <simpleType name="studentId">
        <restriction base="ID">
            <pattern value="[0-9]{9}"/>
        </restriction>
    </simpleType>
    <simpleType name="studentIds">
        <list itemType="adm:studentRef"/>
    </simpleType>
    <simpleType name="studentRef">
        <restriction base="IDREF">
            <pattern value="[0-9]{9}"/>
        </restriction>
    </simpleType>
</schema>
```

FIGURE **17.10** Course types at `http://xyz.edu/CourseTypes.xsd`.

```
<schema xmlns="http://www.w3.org/2001/XMLSchema"
                xmlns:adm="http://xyz.edu/Admin"
                targetNameSpace="http://xyz.edu/Admin">

    <complexType name="courseTakenType">
        <attribute name="CrsCode" type="adm:courseRef"/>
        <attribute name="Semester" type="string"/>
    </complexType>
    <complexType name="courseType">
        <sequence>
            <element name="Name" type="string"/>
        </sequence>
        <attribute name="CrsCode" type="adm:courseCode"/>
    </complexType>

    <simpleType name="courseCode">
        <restriction base="ID">
            <pattern value="[A-Z]{3}[0-9]{3}"/>
        </restriction>
    </simpleType>
    <simpleType name="courseRef">
        <restriction base="IDREF">
            <pattern value="[A-Z]{3}[0-9]{3}"/>
        </restriction>
    </simpleType>
</schema>
```

17.3.5 Shortcuts: Anonymous Types and Element References

We will now present two constructs that can help reduce the size and complexity of a schema document.

Anonymous types. All types defined so far were **named types** because each type definition had an associated name, and every element was explicitly associated with a named type. Naming is useful when we expect to share the same type among several definitions of elements or attributes. In many cases, however, a type might be one of a kind and not expected to be reused. For instance, in the above combined schema for the report document, the type `reportType` (as well as several other types such as `studentList` and `classOfferings`) is not shared. In this case, **anonymous types** can be a convenient shortcut.

Anonymous types are defined similarly to named types, except that the name attribute is not used and the type definition must be attached to the appropriate element or attribute definition that uses it. These definitions with attached anonymous types are also slightly different from definitions of named types. First, they do not use the type attribute to introduce the anonymous type. Second, instead of the empty tags <element ... /> and <attribute ... />, they use tag pairs, and the definition of the anonymous type is physically enclosed by the opening and closing tag. Thus, we can change the definition of the element Report in our schema to use an anonymous type as follows:

```
<element name="Report">
  <complexType>
    <sequence>
      <element name="Students" type="adm:studentList"/>
      <element name="Classes" type="adm:classOfferings"/>
      <element name="Courses" type="adm:courseCatalog"/>
    </sequence>
  </complexType>
</element>
```

Similarly, we can change the definitions of the elements Students, Classes, and Courses to use anonymous types. In this case, the contents of the corresponding type definitions would be physically included in the above schema.

Referencing global elements.   We conclude the discussion of the facilities for type definition in XML Schema with a mention of yet another shortcut, **global element referencing**, which is frequently used in schema definitions.

The overall scenario in which element referencing is used is as follows. First, a global element is defined as usual. A **global element** definition is one that appears as a direct child of the schema tag (not inside of any type definition). For instance, the element Report in Figure 17.8 is global. The ref attribute of an element tag allows us to include any global element in any type definition.

To illustrate, suppose that we want to use the element Comment, defined as

```
<element name="Comment" type="string"/>                      17.3
```

in several parts of the schema in Figure 17.8 (for instance, both in reportType and studentList types). To do so, we would place (17.3) as a child of schema (for example, right after the definition of the element Report) and then place

```
<element ref="Comment"/>                                     17.4
```

in each place where a comment element is to appear. For instance, the following modification of our previous definition includes Comment as part of reportType:

```
<complexType name="reportType">
  <sequence>
    <element ref="Comment"/>
    <element name="Students" type="adm:studentList"/>
    <element name="Classes" type="adm:classOfferings"/>
    <element name="Courses" type="adm:courseCatalog"/>
  </sequence>
</complexType>
```

One can say that we have not achieved a great deal of savings through the use of the reference facility since (17.4) is not much shorter than the full definition (17.3). Nevertheless, if the Comment element needs to be inserted in many places, the referencing facility can provide a degree of consistency.

17.3.6 Integrity Constraints

In Section 17.3.2 we touched upon the issue of referential integrity in XML documents and showed how the XML Schema specification improves upon DTDs in this regard. Even in XML Schema, however, we still used the special types ID and IDREF that are inherited from DTDs. In XML Schema, the types ID and IDREF can be given to elements as well as attributes, which is already an improvement over DTDs. Still, these types are inadequate for representing integrity constraints. First, ID values must be globally unique. More importantly, the ID type cannot represent multiattribute keys. To illustrate, consider Figure 17.11, which shows a definition for the type classType.

If a student claims to have taken a course using a CrsTaken element (of the type declared in Figure 17.10), the corresponding course should have been offered in the

FIGURE 17.11 `http://xyz.edu/ClassTypes.xsd`: type for the element Class in Figure 17.4, page 578.

```
<element name="Class" type="adm:classType"/>
<complexType name="classType">
  <sequence>
    <!-- courseCode type is defined in Figure 17.10 -->
    <element name="CrsCode" type="adm:courseCode"/>
    <element name="Semester" type="string"/>
    <element name="ClassRoster" type="adm:classListType"/>
  </sequence>
</complexType>
<complexType name="classListType">
  <!-- studentIds is defined in Figure 17.9 -->
  <attribute name="Members" type="adm:studentIds"/>
</complexType>
```

specified semester. Such offerings are described by `Class` elements in the instance document. Given an element such as

```
<CrsTaken CrsCode="CS308" Semester="F1997"/>
```

there must exist an element of the form

```
<Class>
   <CrsCode>CS308</CrsCode><Semester>F1997</Semester>
   .
   .
   .
</Class>
```

The problem is that neither `CrsCode` nor `Semester` alone uniquely determines the `Class` element, so the `ID/IDREF` mechanism is inapplicable.

XML keys. To address the above problems, the XML Schema specification allows general multiattribute keys and foreign-key constraints in a way that resembles SQL. There is a slight complication, however. SQL deals with flat relations, so to specify a key we simply list the attributes that belong to that key. Similarly, to specify a foreign-key constraint in SQL we simply specify a sequence of attributes in both the referencing and the referenced relation. In XML, we are dealing with complex structures, and the notion of a key is more involved. Indeed, a key might be composed of a sequence of values located at different depths inside an element.

Assuming that the frame of reference is the parent element of the `Class` elements, we can say that the key of the collection of `Class` elements is composed of values reachable using the pair of path expressions `Class/CrsCode` and `Class/Semester`. The idea of path expressions is familiar to us from Chapter 16, but in XML they take a more elaborate form. In fact, XML path expressions are part of another specification, called **XPath**, which we study in Section 17.4.1.

To see how complicated a key specification can be, let us expand the definition of `Class` in the schema by adding sections and splitting the season from the year in semester names. Then, in an instance document we might have the following class:

```
<Class>
   <CrsCode Section="2" Number="CS308"/>
   <Semester><Term>Fall</Term><Year>1997</Year></Semester>
   .
   .
   .
</Class>
```

Here the set of values that uniquely determines the class is scattered in different places (in attributes and in element content) and at different levels (in the attributes of the tag `CrsCode` and in the `Term` and `Year` children of the `Semester` element). The path expressions needed to reach each of these components are specified in XPath as follows:

```
CrsCode/@Section
CrsCode/@Number
Semester/Term
Semester/Year
```

All of these path expressions are relative to Class elements in the report document. The first selects the value of the attribute Section of the tag CrsCode, which must be a child of the current element (assumed to be Class). The second selects the value of the attribute Number of the CrsCode element. The third and fourth select the contents of the elements Term and Year, respectively, which must be children of the element Semester, which in turn must be a child of the current element.

XML Schema provides two ways to specify a key. One uses the tag unique and is similar to the UNIQUE constraint in SQL; it specifies *candidate keys*, in the terminology of Chapter 3. The other uses the tag key and corresponds to the PRIMARY KEY constraint in SQL. The only difference between unique and key is that keys cannot have *null values*. (In XML, the value of an element of the form <footag></footag> is an empty string and not necessarily a null.) For footag to have a null value (called a **nil** in XMLSchema) the following is used:

```
<footag xsi:nil="true"></footag>
```

Here nil is a symbol defined in the namespace

```
http://www.w3.org/2001/XMLSchema-instance
```

(and we assume that xsi is a prefix that has been defined to refer to that namespace).

Next is an example of a primary-key declaration for the report document. Declaring candidate keys is similar, except that the tag unique is used instead of the tag key. Referring to the type classType of Figure 17.11 (not the more elaborate type with section numbers that we just discussed), we want to specify that the pair of values of tags CrsCode and Semester uniquely identifies the Class element within the document. To show how this is done we elaborate on the earlier schema in Figure 17.8 on page 604.

```
<schema xmlns="http://www.w3.org/2001/XMLSchema"
        xmlns:adm="http://xyz.edu/Admin">
        targetNameSpace="http://xyz.edu/Admin">

    <include schemaLocation="http://xyz.edu/StudentTypes.xsd"/>
    <include schemaLocation="http://xyz.edu/ClassTypes.xsd"/>
    <include schemaLocation="http://xyz.edu/CourseTypes.xsd"/>
```

```
<element name="Report" type="adm:reportType"/>

<complexType name="reportType">
  <sequence>
    <element name="Students" type="adm:studentList"/>
    <element name="Classes">
      <!-- Replacing adm:classOfferings with anonymous type -->
      <complexType>
        <sequence>
          <!-- adm:classType is defined in Figure 17.11 and
                  included with http://xyz.edu/ClassTypes.xsd -->
          <element name="Class" type="adm:classType"
                    minOccurs="0" maxOccurs="unbounded"/>
        </sequence>
      </complexType>

      <key name="PrimaryKeyForClass">
        <selector xpath="Class"/>
        <field xpath="CrsCode"/>
        <field xpath="Semester"/>
      </key>
    </element>
    <element name="Courses" type="adm:courseCatalog"/>
  </sequence>
</complexType>
    .
    .
    .
</schema>
```

The above schema lists the relevant type definitions for our report document. The namespace declarations and the include statements have already been discussed. The type reportType is used for the root element, Report. It is a sequence of three elements: Students, Classes, and Courses. Their types were defined in Figures 17.9, 17.11, and 17.10 on pages 605, 608, and 606, respectively. The definition of course-Catalog, the type for the element Courses, is an easy exercise.

The most interesting feature here is the key declaration specified with a key tag; it is named PrimaryKeyForClass using the attribute name. Declaration of a key is always part of an element specification. However, observe that PrimaryKeyForClass appears in the definition of the element Classes rather than of Class, even though the key involves only the components of type classType and refers to Class elements only. This is intentional, to illustrate the point that XML key declarations are associated with collections of objects (which typically are sets of elements), and these objects can be identified using XPath expressions regardless of where the key definition occurs. The xpath attribute of the selector tag specifies a path expression (relative to the element that contains the key declaration), which identifies the collection of objects to which the key declaration applies. In our case, the selecting path expression is Class; it is relative to the element Classes because the key declaration appears as a child of this element declaration. The collection identified by the selector is simply the set of all Class elements in the document.

Having identified the appropriate collection of objects, we use the subsequent field elements to specify the fields that constitute the key. As explained earlier, these fields can come from different places in an object and can be nested in complex ways. In our case, however, things are simple: the first field in the key is the contents of the child element CrsCode of the element Class, and the second field is the contents of the child element Semester. (Path expressions specified in the xpath attribute of the field clause are relative to the collection of the objects determined by the selector. This is why, for example, the first path expression is simply CrsCode rather than Class/CrsCode.) Note that, for a path expression to make sense as a specification of a field in a key, it must return precisely one value for each object to which it applies. For instance, the path expression CrsCode returns precisely one value for any given Class element, so the field specification

```
<selector xpath="Class"/>
<field xpath="CrsCode"/>
    .
    .
    .
```

is allowed. In contrast, the path expression CrsTaken/@CrsCode within the scope of a Student element can return a set of courses taken by the student (refer to studentType defined in Figure 17.9 on page 605), so the field specification

```
<selector xpath="Student"/>
<field xpath="CrsTaken/@CrsCode"/>
    .
    .
    .
```

is not allowed within the scope of the element Students.

Foreign-key constraints in XML. Next, we want to be able to state that every element CrsTaken in a student record refers to an actual class element in the same report. This is akin to a foreign-key constraint and is defined using the keyref element, as depicted in Figure 17.12.

A foreign-key constraint has a name, a reference identifier, a selector, and a list of fields. The name of a foreign key is of little importance. The reference is defined using the attribute refer, and its value must match the name of a key or unique constraint. In our case, it matches the key constraint, PrimaryKeyForClass, defined within the scope of the element Classes. In SQL, this corresponds to the REFERENCES *relation-name* part of a foreign-key constraint. Next comes the selector.

FIGURE **17.12** Part of a schema with a key and a foreign-key constraint.

```
<schema xmlns="http://www.w3.org/2001/XMLSchema"
    xmlns:adm="http://xyz.edu/Admin">
    targetNameSpace="http://xyz.edu/Admin">

  <complexType name="courseTakenType">
    <attribute name="CrsCode" type="adm:courseRef"/>
    <attribute name="Semester" type="string"/>
  </complexType>
  <complexType name="classType">
    <sequence>
      <element name="CrsCode" type="adm:courseCode"/>
      <element name="Semester" type="string"/>
      <element name="ClassRoster" type="adm:classListType"/>
    </sequence>
  </complexType>

  <complexType name="reportType">
    <sequence>
      <element name="Students" type="adm:studentList"/>
        <keyref name="NoEmptyClasses" refer="adm:PrimaryKeyForClass">
          <selector xpath="Student/CrsTaken"/>
          <field xpath="@CrsCode"/>
          <field xpath="@Semester"/>
        </keyref>
      </element>
      <element name="Classes" type="adm:classOfferings"/>
        <key name="PrimaryKeyForClass">
          <selector xpath="Class"/>
          <field xpath="CrsCode"/>
          <field xpath="Semester"/>
        </key>
      </element>
      <element name="Courses" type="adm:courseCatalog"/>
    </sequence>
  </complexType>
</schema>
```

As in the case of the key constraint, it identifies a **source collection** of elements through its xpath attribute. In our case, the collection in question consists of all CrsTaken elements. Each of these is supposed to reference the key of an object from the **target collection** specified in the key constraint PrimaryKeyForClass.

Finally, we have to specify the foreign key itself, that is, the fields inside the CrsTaken elements (the source collection) that actually reference the fields in the target collection (specified in the key constraint). We do this using the already familiar field tag. As before, this tag provides a path expression (relative to the selected collection of objects) that leads to a value. We want the attributes CrsCode and Semester of the source collection of CrsTaken elements to refer to the fields that constitute the key of the target collection of Class elements. In XPath, we use the path expressions @CrsCode and @Semester to identify these attributes (Figure 17.10). As with the fields that form a key, each path expression in a foreign key (@CrsCode and @Semester in our case) must yield a single value when applied to an object in the source collection.

In a similar way, we can specify other key and foreign-key constraints in the report document and replace the constraints previously specified using the ID and IDREF data types (see Exercises 17.5 and 17.7).

We should note that it is not clear how to specify IDREFS-style referential integrity with the help of the key and keyref tags. For instance, the attribute Members in ClassRoster (Figure 17.11) has the type studentIds, which is a list of values of type studentRef. Since studentRef is derived by restriction from the base type IDREF (see Figure 17.9 on page 605), studentIds can be seen as a specialized version of IDREFS. We can *try* to specify the desired referential integrity using something like this:

```
<keyref name="RosterToStudIdRef" refer="adm:studentKey">
  <selector xpath="Class"/>
  <field xpath="ClassRoster/@Members"/>
</keyref>
```

where studentKey is an appropriately defined key constraint for Student elements:

```
<key name="studentKey">
  <selector xpath="Student"/>
  <field xpath="@StudId"/>
</key>
```

The problem here is that the value of the attribute Members is a *list* while the value of the key attribute StudId in the Student tag is a *single* item. Unfortunately, it is not possible in XPath to create a reference from the individual components of a list data type (represented by the Members attribute) to other entities in the document (i.e., student Ids defined in the Student elements). The only solution is to use a representation where student Ids are not in a list but occur as individual elements (Exercise 17.9).

17.4 XML Query Languages

Why would you want to query an XML document? Will databases soon begin storing XML and speak it fluently?

Storing XML documents in a database specifically designed for this kind of data is one possibility—methods exist for efficient storage and retrieval of tree-structured objects, including XML documents [Deutsch et al. 1999; Zhao and Joseph 2000]—and major relational database vendors are beginning to offer an option for native storage for XML documents. Native storage is also supported by SQL/XML, a forthcoming standard for interoperability between SQL databases and XML (see Section 17.4.2). In this capacity, SQL/XML can be seen as an alternative way of storing objects in a database (the other alternative being the SQL object-relational extensions).

XML documents can also be stored by mapping them to the relational or object-oriented format. Utilities that perform such mapping automatically are widely available and are part of most major database products. Such databases can receive XML documents and convert them into relations or objects; they also provide tools for generating XML from the data already stored in the database. Once generated, an XML document is transmitted to another machine, which either presents it to the user or processes it automatically. To help with this task, the W3C has developed the **document object model** (**DOM**) for XML [DOM 2000], which standardizes the API by which a client application can access various parts of an XML document and thereby simplifies the task of writing such applications.

What does a query language have to do with all this? First, if XML is stored natively in a database, one needs a way to query it. The second possibility is even more intriguing. Imagine that you are preparing your next semester's schedule and need to find all courses offered in that semester between 3 PM and 7 PM. If the university database server lets you pose such a query, you are in good shape, but more likely it provides a fixed interface that supports only a limited set of queries. In this case, finding what you want might require a tedious process of filling out a series of forms and eyeballing the results, and you might also have to use low-tech instruments, such as pen and paper, to record the needed information.

An alternative is to ask the server for an XML document containing the list of all courses offered this semester and have a client application find the desired information. As mentioned, DOM simplifies this task considerably. Still, it provides only a low-level interface to XML. If your query requires joining information stored in different parts of the document or in separate documents, you might end up writing a fairly large program (and the semester will be over by the time you debug it). An analogy here is using nested loops and IF-statements to replace a complex SQL query. We will see how a powerful, high-level query language can simplify this task, enabling a new class of client applications capable of processing information in an intelligent and custom-tailored way.

In the remainder of Section 17.4, we discuss two query languages for XML: **XPath** [XPath 1999] and **SQL/XML**. The first is an official W3C recommendation, and the last is going to be part of the forthcoming SQL:2003 standard.

XPath is intended to be simple and efficient. It is based on the idea of path expressions, with which we became familiar in Chapter 16, and is designed so that queries are compact and can be incorporated into URLs. SQL/XML is an extension of SQL designed to provide interoperability between data stored in relational databases and XML documents.

17.4.1 XPath: A Lightweight XML Query Language

In an object-oriented language, such as SQL:1999, a path expression is a sequence of object attributes that provides the exact route to a data element nested deep within the object structure. The requirement to provide an exact route is not a problem when the schema of the database is known to the programmer and is not likely to change. However, when the schema is not known and the structure of data needs to be explored (which is often the case in Web applications), merely adopting path expressions from object-oriented languages is not enough.

XPath extends path expressions with query facilities by allowing the programmer to replace parts of the route to data elements with search conditions. By then examining the data, the XPath interpreter is supposed to find the missing parts of the route at run time. The idea of augmenting path expressions with queries is not new. It appeared in [Kifer and Lausen 1989; Kifer et al. 1992; Frohn et al. 1994] in the context of object-oriented databases and was further developed in works on semistructured data, such as [Buneman et al. 1996; Abiteboul et al. 1997; Deutsch et al. 1998; Abiteboul et al. 2000]. XPath was built on these ideas and became an important basis for many XML extensions.

The XPath data model. XPath views XML documents as trees and views elements, attributes, comments, and text as nodes of those trees. There is a special **root node** in the tree, which should not be confused with the root element of an XML document. This is illustrated in Figures 17.13 and 17.14. The XML instance document in Figure 17.13 (itself a fragment of the report document in Figure 17.4, page 578) is the basis for the XPath document tree in Figure 17.14.

Note that the root node of the XPath tree is different from the node that corresponds to Students, which is the root element of the document. The need for the special root node is apparent from Figure 17.14: it serves as a gathering point for all of the document components, including the comments that are allowed to occur outside the scope of the root element.

As usual in a tree, every node except the root node has a parent. A node, P, immediately above another node, C, is the **parent** of that node, and C is a **child** of P. However, the XPath specification has an important and sometimes confusing exception: an attribute is *not considered a child of its parent node*. That is, if C corresponds to an attribute of P, then P is a parent of C, but C is not a child of P. Because of the potential confusion due to the peculiar XPath terminology, we use the standard terminology for tree data structures and do regard attributes as children of their parents. To avoid ambiguity, we sometimes talk about *e-children*,

FIGURE **17.13** Fragment of the report document in Figure 17.4, page 578.

```
<?xml version="1.0" ?>
<!-- Some comment -->
<Students>
    <Student StudId="s111111111">
        <Name><First>John</First><Last>Doe</Last></Name>
        <Status>U4</Status>
        <CrsTaken CrsCode="CS308" Semester="F1997"/>
        <CrsTaken CrsCode="MAT123" Semester="F1997"/>
    </Student>
    <Student StudId="s987654321">
        <Name><First>Bart</First><Last>Simpson</Last></Name>
        <Status>U4</Status>
        <CrsTaken CrsCode="CS308" Semester="F1994"/>
    </Student>
</Students>
<!-- Some other comment -->
```

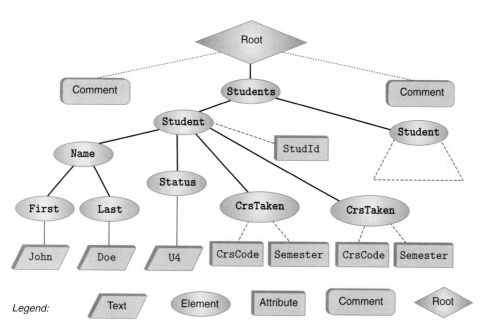

FIGURE **17.14** XPath document tree corresponding to document in Figure 17.13.

a-children, and *t*-children when we want to restrict attention to the particular type of children: elements, attributes, or text. For example, Name is an *e*-child of Student, StudId is an *a*-child of Student, and John is a *t*-child of First. When we want to include both element children and text children, we refer to *et*-children. Similarly, *ta*-children refers to text and attribute children, and so on.

Another peculiarity of the XPath data model is that text that occurs inside XML elements (e.g., John, U4) is represented by a node in the tree. However, text that represents attribute values (e.g., the value s987654321 of the attribute StudId) is not deemed to be worthy of a tree node of its own.

The XPath data model provides operators for navigating the document and accessing its various components. These operators include accessing the root of the XPath tree, the parent of a node, its children, the contents of an element, the value of an attribute, and the like.

We saw some of these operators when we discussed constraints in XML Schemas. The basic syntax is that of the UNIX file naming schema: The symbol "/" represents the root of the XPath tree, "." represents the current node, and ".." represents the parent node of the current node. An XPath expression takes a document tree and returns a list of nodes in the tree. The path expression /Students/Student/CrsTaken is **absolute**; it returns the set of nodes that correspond to the elements CrsTaken, which are reachable from the root through a Students child and a Student grandchild. Our tree has three such CrsTaken nodes (one is not shown in the figure). If the current node corresponds to the element Name, then First and ./First both refer to the same child element. If the current node corresponds to the element First, then ../Last is the sibling node corresponding to the element Last. These are **relative path expressions** since their departure point for navigation is the *current node* rather than the root.

Many uses of XPath provide some notion of a context in which one of the nodes in the document tree is the **current node**. We have already seen this in the way XPath is used in XML Schema. For instance, in Figure 17.12 on page 613 we used relative path expressions in the definition of the primary key PrimaryKeyForClass and of the foreign key NoEmptyClasses. The primary key is defined as part of the XML type reportType, and in this context the current node corresponds to the Report element. A relative XPath expression Classes/Class is applied to that node to yield the set of all Class nodes that are grandchildren of Report. The two relative XPath expressions CrsCode and Semester are applied in the context of the Class nodes returned by the aforesaid expression Classes/Class. Here the current node can be any of these Class nodes, and the CrsCode expression returns the CrsCode child of that node; similarly the Semester expression returns the Semester child.

To access an attribute, the symbol @ is used. For instance, the list of attribute nodes that correspond to CrsCode in the document of Figure 17.13 is obtained using the path expression /Students/Student/CrsTaken/@CrsCode. In our case, this list consists of three nodes because the CrsCode attribute occurs three times: with the values CS308, MAT123, and CS308 (note the repetition due to the fact that the same value occurs more than once in different attribute nodes). Text nodes are accessed using the text() function. For instance, /Students/Student/Name/First/text()

represents the collection of nodes, each representing the text content of an element of type First. We have two such nodes in our document; one corresponds to John and the other to Bart. If you were wondering, the two comment nodes in Figure 17.13 can be selected using the expression /comment().

Advanced navigation in XPath. The more advanced features of XPath navigation include facilities to select specific nodes of an XML document as well as facilities to jump through an indeterminate number of children. For instance, to select the second course taken by John Doe, we use the expression /Students/ Student[1]/CrsTaken[2]. Here, /Students/Student[1] selects the first of the two Student nodes in the document tree. The expression CrsTaken[2] then selects the second CrsTaken *e*-child in that first Student node. Another example of selection of a particular node is /Students/Student/CrsTaken[last()]. This is similar to the above except that the prefix /Students/Student selects all nodes that correspond to Student and CrsTaken[last()] then chooses the last CrsTaken node under each selected Student node. In our case, the above expression returns

```
<CrsTaken CrsCode="MAT123" Semester="F1997"/>
<CrsTaken CrsCode="CS308" Semester="F1994"/>
```

At times, we might not know the exact structure of the document, or specifying the exact navigation path might be cumbersome, so XPath provides several wildcard facilities. One is the *descendant-or-self* operation, //, illustrated by the expression //CrsTaken, which is an absolute path expression that starts at the root and selects all CrsTaken elements in the entire tree. In our particular case, the effect is the same as that produced by /Students/Student/CrsTaken. However, if the document contains elements CrsTaken nested under different types of elements and at different depths, then selecting all such elements without a wildcard is hard and unwieldy. Similarly, /Students//CrsTaken selects all CrsTaken elements that are descendants of Students nodes regardless of the nesting level.

The descendant operation can be used in relative expressions as well. For instance, .//CrsTaken searches through all descendants (or self) of the current node to find the CrsTaken elements. Observe that ./CrsTaken and CrsTaken are the same. However, .//CrsTaken, CrsTaken, and //CrsTaken are all different: the first expression returns all CrsTaken descendants at the current node (or the current node itself, if it is a CrsTaken element); the second expression returns only the CrsTaken children at the current node; and the third, all CrsTaken elements found anywhere in the document.

XPath also allows searching through all ancestors (parent, grandparent, etc.) of any given node, but we omit this wildcard.

The third wildcard, *, lets us collect all *e*-children of a node irrespective of type. For instance, Student/* selects all *e*-children of the Student children of the current node. (If the current node is the (only) Students node, the wildcard selects the two Name nodes, the two Status nodes, and the three CrsTaken nodes.) The

expression /*//* selects all *e*-children of the root and their *e*-descendants (since //
is descendant-or-self, the set of nodes /*//* includes the set of children nodes of
the root, /*).

The * wildcard can also be applied to attributes. For instance, CrsTaken/@*
selects all attribute values of the CrsTaken nodes that sit below the current node.
Note that * does not include the text nodes that could possibly exist among the
children of the Student element. To select those, the expression Student/text()
is used.

XPath semantics. The general form of an XPath query is

locationStep$_1$/locationStep$_2$/... or /locationStep$_1$/locationStep$_2$/...

where each location step is of the form *axis*::*nodeSelector* [*selectionCondition*]. The
term *axis* refers to the **navigation axis**, which indicates the direction along which
navigation is taking place in the corresponding location step. The available axes
are *child* (i.e., go to a child node), *parent*, *descendant* (i.e., child, grandchild, etc.),
descendant-or-self, etc. The node selector is either the name of the node (e.g., the
name of an element or attribute; a selector for an unnamed node, such as text()
or comment(); or a wildcard, such as * or @*). For instance, child::Student is a
simple location step that directs navigation from the current node down to a child
element named Student, and descendant-or-self::@Semester directs navigation from the current node to a Semester attribute in either the current node or
in a descendant of that node. Because the full syntax of XPath is so verbose, most
axes have convenient abbreviations, and this is what we have been using up until now (and will continue using). For instance, child::Student abbreviates as
Student, the relative expression descendant-or-self::@Semester abbreviates
as .//@Semester, and the absolute expression /descendant-or-self::@Semester
as //@Semester. The optional selectionCondition in a location step selects a subset of nodes reachable by the location step. We will see examples of such conditions
shortly.

The value of a location step axis::nodeSelector[selectionCondition] on
an instance document is the set of all nodes of the form nodeSelector that are
reachable by the navigation axis and that satisfy selectionCondition. For instance, .//@Semester specifies the set of attribute nodes called Semester, which
are reachable from the current node by the axis descendant-or-self. In plain English: the set of all Semester attributes that appear in either the current node or in
one of its descendants.

For a path expression locationStep$_1$/locationStep$_2$/..., the value on a source
document is the set of all document nodes computed as follows: From the current
node, find all nodes reachable by locationStep$_1$. For each such node, *N*, find the
set of all nodes that are reachable from *N* via locationStep$_2$. Take the union of all
node sets reachable by locationStep$_2$. Apply locationStep$_3$ to each node in the

union, etc., until the last location step is reached. The value of the path expression is the set of nodes obtained at this last step.

XPath queries. We are particularly interested in the features of XPath that give it the ability to select nodes using a query facility. XPath queries can include selection conditions at any step in the navigation process. To give meaningful examples of XPath expressions with queries, we go back to our report document in Figure 17.4, page 578.

Here is a simple example of a path expression that selects all student nodes where the student has taken a course in fall 1994:

```
//Student[CrsTaken/@Semester = "F1994"]
```

Here we have a wildcard expression, //Student, that selects all Student nodes under the root node. The expression inside the square brackets is a **selection condition** that eliminates the nodes that do not satisfy the condition by selecting a Student node only if the path expression CrsTaken/@Semester can be applied at this node and if it returns a set that *includes* F1994.[7] To select elements based on the content of an element rather than of an attribute, we use the following expression:

```
//Student[Status = "U3" and starts-with(.//Last, "P")
          and not(.//Last = .//First)]
```

This example introduces several important features:

1. Selection conditions can be combined using and, or, and not.
2. To select an element based on the content of one of its children or descendants, we simply equate the appropriate path expression with another such expression or a constant. Strictly speaking, we should have written Status/text() = "U3" instead of Status = "U3", but since Status does not have subelements, XPath allows us to be less pedantic in this case. This is possible because, in order to evaluate a comparison such as the one above, XPath converts every node returned by the path expression into its **string value** and then compares strings. For simple element nodes such as those returned by //Student/Status or //Student//Last, the string value is simply the text inside the element. For attribute nodes, such as those returned by //Student/CrsTaken/@Semester the string value is the value of the attribute. A full set of rules that defines string values for the various nodes in an XPath tree is given in [XPath 1999].
3. XPath has a rich repertoire of functions that greatly increase its expressive power. For the full list of these functions, we refer you to the XPath specification [XPath 1999].

---

[7] Note that if a Student node has several CrsTaken children, then the path expression CrsTaken/@Semester returns a *set* of nodes.

In the above example, we use the built-in predicate starts-with() to select only those students whose last names start with P. To summarize the above query, it selects all students who have the status U3, whose last names start with P, and whose last and first names are different. The other string manipulation functions allow us to check for containment, perform concatenation, determine length, and so forth. For instance, the following query can be used to search for students who have "van" as part of their name:

```
//Student[contains(concat(Name//text()), "van")]
```

Here Name//text() returns the set of all text nodes that are descendants of the Name element, and the concatenation function makes one string out of those nodes—in this case the student's first and last names. Then we check if the result contains van as a substring.

Aggregate functions available in XPath include sum() and count(). For example, the following selects the students who have taken at least five courses:

```
//Student[count(CrsTaken) &gt;= 5]
```

In this expression, CrsTaken returns the set of all *e*-children of type CrsTaken for the current node (which must be a Student node). Thus, Count(CrsTaken) returns the number of these children, which is compared with "5". The obscure >= contraption, stands for >=. This complication is due to the fact that the symbols < and > must be encoded as < and > because < and > are reserved for tag delimiters.

It should be noted that selection conditions can be applied at different levels and multiple times in a path expression. Thus, the following is legal:

```
//Student[Status="U4"]/CrsTaken[@CrsCode="CS305"]
```

This expression selects all the CrsTaken elements in the document that occur in Student elements with status U4 and whose CrsCode attribute has the value CS305.

Multiple selection conditions can also be applied at the same level in a path expression, as shown in the following expression that selects all Student elements having the property that the student took (among other courses) MAT123 in fall 1994:

```
//Student/CrsTaken[@CrsCode="MAT123"][@Semester="F1994"]
```

The same expression can be written as

```
//Student/CrsTaken[@CrsCode="MAT123" and @Semester="F1994"]
```

Note that this expression is different from

```
//Student[CrsTaken/@CrsCode="MAT123" and CrsTaken/Semester="F1994"]
```

which selects students who either took MAT123 or took a course in the fall of 1994. The reason for this difference in the interpretation is that nothing in the latter expression tells us that the two occurrences of the CrsTaken expression select the same element node. The "or" connective—for example, CrsTaken/@CrsCode="MAT123" or CrsTaken/@Semester="F1994"—is also allowed.

There is one other interesting form of selection condition, one where a path expression is used as a predicate rather than as an argument to a predicate. Suppose that Grade is an optional attribute of CrsTaken. Then

```
//Student[CrsTaken/@Grade]
```

selects all student elements that have a CrsTaken child element with an explicitly specified Grade attribute (regardless of its value). Likewise,

```
//Student[Name/First or CrsTaken]
```

selects all Student elements that have either the element First as a grandchild or the element CrsTaken as a child.

Finally, recall that SQL allows the use of algebraic query operators, such as UNION and EXCEPT. XPath, being a frugal language, allows only the union operator, which is denoted by the symbol |, as in the expression

```
//CrsTaken[@Semester="F1994"] | //Class[Semester="F1994"]
```

The set of nodes selected by this query is a union of elements of different types: the CrsTaken elements that pertain to the fall 1994 semester and the Class elements that describe fall 1994 course offerings. This illustrates how a path expression can return a set containing elements of different types.

17.4.2 SQL/XML

SQL is not called Intergalactic Dataspeak for nothing. When OQL-speaking aliens (see Chapter 16) descended on our galaxy, SQL was extended with object-relational constructs. SQL is now being extended with a new dialect, called SQL/XML. This extension can be viewed as yet another way to introduce object-relational data into SQL—see Section 16.3 for an earlier proposal, which became part of SQL:1999. The major vendors have implemented most of the proposed extensions. When complete, it is expected that SQL/XML will become part of the SQL:2003 standard.

SQL/XML addresses the following practical needs:

- To publish the contents of SQL tables and even the contents of entire databases as XML documents. This requires the development of conventions for translation of the primitive SQL data types, such as CHAR(4), into XML Schema data types and back.

- More generally, to create XML documents out of SQL query results. This requires the addition of primitives to allow the creation of XML elements by SQL queries.

- To store XML documents in relational databases and to query them effectively using SQL. Since SQL is unable to deal with tree-like structures directly, XPath is used for that purpose.

In the remainder of this section, we review the current state of SQL/XML. Keep in mind, however, that the work on this standard is still ongoing, that some details will definitely change by the time this text is published, and that vendor implementations (e.g., from Oracle, IBM, and Microsoft) may vary slightly from the SQL/XML proposal.

Encoding Relations as XML Documents

This part of the SQL/XML specification defines the conventions for converting relations into XML documents (and relation schemas into XML schemas). The main purpose is to provide a standard way of exchanging relations on the Internet. The current proposal does not include a built-in function that would take a table and return an XML document. However, it provides more general functions that make it possible to create arbitrary XML documents using the SELECT clause. We discuss these functions in the next subsection, on page 627.

There are many ways to encode relational data in XML (see Exercise 17.1). SQL/XML does this as follows:

- The entire relation is enclosed in a pair of tags named after the relation.

- Each row is enclosed within the row tag pair.

- Each attribute value is enclosed within a pair of tags named after that attribute.

For instance, the PROFESSOR relation in Figure 3.5 on page 39 will be represented as

```
<Professor>
  <row>
    <Id>101202303</Id>
    <Name>John Smyth</Name><DeptId>CS</DeptId>
  </row>
  <row>
    <Id>783432188</Id>
    <Name>Adrian Jones</Name><DeptId>MGT</DeptId>
  </row>
  <row>
```

17.5

```
      <Id>121232343</Id>
      <Name>David Jones</Name><DeptId>EE</DeptId>
    </row>
     .
     .
     .
  </Professor>
```

Suppose the type of the Id attribute in the PROFESSOR relation is INTEGER and the types for Name and DeptId are CHAR(50) and CHAR(3), respectively. Defining an XML Schema document corresponding to the relational schema of the PROFESSOR relation is not hard. The only question is the representation of SQL types in XML Schema. In our particular case, this representation is easy:

```
<schema xmlns="http://www.w3.org/2001/XMLSchema"
        xmlns:tnc="http://xyz.edu/Admin"
        targetNameSpace="http://xyz.edu/Admin">
  <element name="Professor">
    <complexType>
      <sequence>
        <element name="row" minOccurs="0" maxOccurs="unbounded">
          <complexType>
            <sequence>
              <element name="Id"  type="integer"/>
              <element name="Name" type="CHAR_50"/>
              <element name="DeptId" type="CHAR_3"/>
            </sequence>
          </complexType>
        </element>
      </sequence>
    </complexType>
  </element>
</schema>
```

The types CHAR_50 and CHAR_3 are standard conventions within SQL/XML for the corresponding SQL CHAR(...) types. For example, CHAR_50 is defined by restricting the base XML Schema type string as follows:

```
<simpleType name="CHAR_50">
   <restriction base="string">
      <length value="50"/>
   </restriction>
</simpleType>
```

The real problem is that SQL has a large number of built-in types, such as INTERVAL, TIMESTAMP, MULTISET, etc., as well as user-defined types, which are created using the CREATE DOMAIN statement. All of these need to be painstakingly defined in XML, and much of the XML/SQL specification deals with this issue. We omit the gory details in this text.

Storing and Manipulating XML in Relational Databases

The XML data type. Although an XML document could be stored inside a table as an attribute of type string, doing so would make querying the document extremely inefficient. For example, XPath would have to scan the entire string and parse it before an expression could be evaluated. Hence, SQL/XML envisions support for *native storage* of an XML document as a hierarchical tree structure, which facilitates navigation within the document. For example, the structure would make it easy to locate the children of each node. Fortunately, efficient storage and indexing techniques exist to support native storage of XML documents [Deutsch et al. 1999; Zhao and Joseph 2000], and a new data type, XML, was added to SQL for this purpose. For instance, we might decide to store transcripts in the native XML format along with the student information, as follows:

```
CREATE TABLE  STUDENTXML (
   Id         INTEGER,                              17.6
   Details    XML )
```

The Details attribute is supposed to contain XML documents of the form

```
<Student>
    <Name><First>John</First><Last>Doe</Last></Name>
    <Status>U2</Status>                            17.7
    <CrsTaken CrsCode="CS308" Semester="F1997"/>
    <CrsTaken CrsCode="MAT123" Semester="F1997"/>
</Student>
```

However, since we indicated that the type of Details is XML, such a document will be stored not as a string, but in a special data structure, which supports efficient navigation and querying.

Using a CHECK constraint, we can even tell the DBMS to validate the above Student XML document against a suitable schema before allowing the document to be inserted:

```
CREATE TABLE  STUDENTXML (
   Id         INTEGER,
   Details    XML,
   CHECK(Details IS VALID INSTANCE OF 'http://xyz.edu/student.xsd'))
```

Here we have assumed that the schema is stored at the URL `http://xyz.edu /student.xsd`.

The XMLELEMENT and XMLATTRIBUTES functions. Since SQL is a relational language, an SQL query does not produce an XML document directly. Instead, a query result can contain tuples in which the value in a particular column is an XML document. We already know that XML documents can be stored as values of an attribute. What is new here is the ability to construct such documents on the fly from data stored in tables. The simplest way to do this is to use the XMLELEMENT function, which takes as parameters the name to be given to the element's tag and (optionally) the element's attributes and content. For instance, the following query produces a relation with a column that contains XML documents:

```
SELECT P.Id, XMLELEMENT(
               Name "Prof",                        -- The tag name
               XMLATTRIBUTES(P.DeptId AS "Dept"),  -- The attribute(s)
               P.Name                              -- The content
             ) AS Info
FROM    PROFESSOR P
```

The parameter that provides the element's tag is identified by the keyword `Name`, which in this case is `Prof`. The XMLATTRIBUTES function produces the element's attributes. In this case the element has the single attribute `Dept`. The remaining parameters specify the element's content. In this case the element has no *e*-children and the content is simply the value of `P.Name` associated with `P.Id`. Using the PROFESSOR relation depicted in Figure 3.5, page 39, the query would produce the following tuples:

```
( 101202303, <Prof Dept="CS">John Smyth</Prof> )
( 783432188, <Prof Dept="MGT">Adrian Jones</Prof> )
   .
   .
   .
```

The query maps each row of PROFESSOR into a row of the query result. The second component in each row is an XML element, and the column name is `Info`.

The XMLELEMENT constructs can be nested. This feature can be used to create arbitrarily complex XML elements. For instance, we could publish the PROFESSOR relation in the standard form defined by SQL/XML (see the document (17.5)) as follows:

```
SELECT  XMLELEMENT( Name "Professor",              -- The tag name
                  XMLELEMENT(Name "Id", P.Id),    -- Child elements
                  XMLELEMENT(Name "Name", P.Name),
```

```
                        XMLELEMENT(Name "DeptId", P.DeptId)
                   ) AS ProfElement
      FROM      PROFESSOR P
```

The result of this query is not a set of XML elements, but a table containing a single column with name ProfElement. Each row contains an XML element. The absence of an XMLATTRIBUTES parameter indicates that the element has no attributes. The remaining parameters of the outer XMLELEMENT define the content. In this case each element has exactly three child elements.

The XMLGEN function. XMLGEN provides similar functionality to XMLELEMENT in that it produces a table whose rows contain XML documents. It has, however, a more convenient format and is thus simpler to use. Its first argument is an XML template, which can contain *placeholder variables* of the form {$foo}. The remaining arguments to XMLGEN are named expressions whose values are substituted for the placeholders with the same name. For instance, the above query can be rewritten with the help of XMLGEN as follows:

```
SELECT XMLGEN( '<Professor>
                   <Id>{$I}</Id><Name>{$N}</Name>
                   <DeptId>{$D}</DeptId>
                </Professor>',
                P.Id AS I,
                P.Name AS N,
                P.DeptId AS D,
              ) AS ProfElement
      FROM    PROFESSOR P
```

Placeholder variables can occur in the position of XML elements and attributes, which provides great flexibility in the way XML documents can be constructed from relational data.

The expressions to be substituted for the placeholders in XMLGEN are not limited to SQL variables, such as P.Id in the above example—they can be XML-generating expressions or even SELECT statements. For instance, we could rewrite the above query in the following way, where the expression to be substituted for $I generates an XML element of the form <Id>...</Id>:

```
SELECT XMLGEN( '<Professor>
                   {$I}<Name>{$N}</Name><DeptId>{$D}</DeptId>
                </Professor>',
                XMLELEMENT(Name "Id", P.Id) AS I,
                P.Name AS N,
                P.DeptId AS D,
              ) AS ProfElement
      FROM    PROFESSOR P
```

Grouping and XMLAGG. In SQL/XML, SELECT statements can be embedded inside XML constructors (such as XMLELEMENT) that appear in the SELECT clause of a parent query. As a result, it is possible to group elements as children of another element. The following example illustrates this facility with a query that returns student transcripts grouped inside Student elements, as shown in (17.7). For brevity, we omit student name and status from the output.

```
SELECT XMLELEMENT( Name "Student",
                   XMLATTRIBUTES(S.Id AS "Id"),
                   ( SELECT
                        XMLELEMENT(Name "CrsTaken",
                           XMLATTRIBUTES(T.CrsCode AS "CrsCode",
                                         T.Semester AS "Semester"))
                     FROM TRANSCRIPT T
                     WHERE S.Id = T.StudId ) )
FROM    STUDENT S
```

In this example, we assume that information is stored inside the relations STUDENT and TRANSCRIPT, as in Figures 3.2 and 3.5 on pages 36 and 39. The statement produces a table with a single column and a row corresponding to each row of STUDENT. The content of each row is an XML element describing a particular student. The element is produced by the outer XMLELEMENT function with tag Student and attribute Id. The nested SELECT clause creates the content of the Student element, which in this case is a list of CrsTaken child elements corresponding to that student. Each of these *e*-children has two attributes defined by the XMLATTRIBUTES function, but no other content. The result of this query will thus be a set of XML elements that look like Student elements at the top of Figure 17.4 on page 578 (with student name and status information omitted).

Note that, strictly speaking, the nested SELECT clause produces not a list of CrsTaken elements (despite what we said earlier), but a set of 1-tuples, each containing a CrsTaken element. At the time of this writing it is unclear whether such a set of tuples will be converted into a list of XML elements automatically or if a special function will be provided for this purpose.

Alternatively, we could express the same query using aggregation with the help of the XMLAGG function of SQL/XML. To understand how it works, consider the following example, which reformulates the previous query using XMLAGG.

```
SELECT   XMLELEMENT( Name "Student",
                     XMLATTRIBUTES(S.Id AS "Id"),
                     XMLAGG(
                        XMLELEMENT(Name "CrsTaken",
                           XMLATTRIBUTES(T.CrsCode AS "CrsCode",
                                         T.Semester AS "Semester"))
                        ORDER BY T.CrsCode )  )
```

```
FROM       STUDENT S,  TRANSCRIPT T
WHERE      S.Id = T.StudId
GROUP BY S.Id
```

XMLAGG provides the content of a Student element created by the outer XML-ELEMENT function. Each Student element corresponds to a particular group produced by the GROUP BY clause, and each row in that group (selected from the set of tuples in the join of STUDENT and TRANSCRIPT, which have the same student Id) describes a course taken by a particular student. XMLAGG refers to that group through its use of the tuple variable T.

XMLAGG takes as an argument an XML construct, such as the nested XMLELE-MENT invocation in the example, in which an SQL variable is a parameter—T in this case. The invocation of XMLAGG produces a *list* of elements—one for each legal value of the variable. Here the legal values are the rows of TRANSCRIPT that are joined with the particular row of STUDENT used to form the group. The list is nested within the Student element and is ordered by course codes using the optional ORDER BY clause of XMLAGG.

For instance, if a student, Bart Simpson, with Id 987654321 took CS305 in the fall of 1995 and MGT123 in the fall of 1994, then when S.Id is bound to 987654321, the GROUP BY clause will produce a group of two bindings for the variables S and T: one where S = ⟨987654321,Bart Simpson,...⟩ and T = ⟨987654321,CS305,F1995,C⟩, and another where S = ⟨987654321,Bart Simpson,...⟩ and T = ⟨987654321, MGT123,F1994,B⟩. For each binding of T, the XMLAGG operator will produce one CrsTaken element. Thus, for this particular group of tuples the above query will construct the following element:

```
<Student Id="987654321">
    <CrsTaken CrsCode="CS305" Semester="F1995"/>
    <CrsTaken CrsCode="MGT123" Semester="F1994"/>
</Student>
```

You may find the reference to the word "aggregate" in the function name XML-AGG confusing. The aggregate here is the list—think of the above list of CrsTaken elements as a "sum" of the courses the student has taken.

Querying XML Documents Stored inside Relations

Once XML documents are stored as instances of the new XML data type (see (17.6) and (17.7)), it becomes necessary to provide a mechanism to query them in order to extract their contents. This is done using a pair of new functions, XMLEXTRACT and XMLEXISTS, which are discussed below.

The XMLEXTRACT function. The XMLEXTRACT function applies an XPath expression to XML documents stored as XML data type. To illustrate this, we use the relation STUDENTXML defined in (17.6), which stores documents of the form (17.7). The query returns the names and Ids of all students who have status U3 and who have taken MAT123.

```
SELECT   S.Id, XMLEXTRACT(S.Details, '//Name')
FROM     StudentXML S
WHERE    XMLEXTRACT(S.Details, '//Status/text()') = 'U3'  AND
         XMLEXTRACT(S.Details, '//CrsTaken/@CrsCode') = 'MAT123'
```

The first parameter of XMLEXTRACT names an attribute of type XML, which contains a document. The second parameter is an XPath expression. XMLEXTRACT returns the result of an application of the expression to the document.

In this query, application of the path expression, //Name, to any document in S.Details yields a single Name element, so the result of the query is a set of regular tuples (modulo the fact that the second tuple component is an XML element). In general, however, a path expression can yield a set. Will the result still be legal? The answer is yes—in SQL:2003, which introduced the MULTISET type to allow the components of a tuple to be sets. The MULTISET data type is described in Section 16.3.8.

The predicate XMLEXISTS. The function XMLEXTRACT makes it possible to query XML documents that are stored inside SQL databases. When the set of nodes returned by the associated XPath expression is empty, XMLEXTRACT returns an empty document. Sometimes, however, it is necessary to just test if this set is empty and act based on the result. In SQL/XML, this purpose is served by the predicate XMLEXISTS. The following example, which lists all students who have at least one course in their transcript, illustrates the use of this feature.

```
SELECT   S.Id, XMLEXTRACT(S.Details, '//Name')
FROM     StudentXML S
WHERE    XMLEXISTS(S.Details, '//CrsTaken')
```

17.8

Modifying Data in SQL/XML

So far we have been focusing on schema and query-related issues pertaining to XML data stored in SQL databases. In this section we briefly review the support for updating such data. The material in this section is somewhat more tentative than the other parts of SQL/XML, and the details are more likely to change.

Functions XMLPARSE and XMLVALIDATE. We have seen some queries involving StudentXML (17.6), a relation that stores XML documents of the form (17.7) in the Details column. But how do you put XML documents into such a table in the first place?

Since an XML document can be viewed as a string of characters, we could, in principle, store it as a string data type. However, this misses an important point behind SQL/XML—the XML data type. XML documents are stored in columns of type XML, not as strings but rather using special tree structures. To produce such a structure, SQL/XML provides a special function, XMLPARSE, that converts an XML document represented as a string into the tree structures appropriate for the XML data type prior to storing it. This makes it possible to insert tuples into a relation that contains XML documents, as shown in the following example.

```
INSERT INTO StudentXML(Id, Details)
VALUES ( 123987456,
         XMLPARSE(
            '<Student>
               <Name><First>John</First><Last>Doe</Last></Name>
                  <Status>U2</Status>
                  <CrsTaken CrsCode="CS310" Semester="F2003"/>
                  <CrsTaken CrsCode="CS305" Semester="F2003"/>
            </Student>' )
         )
```

The XMLPARSE function parses documents (to put them into the format appropriate to the XML data type) and checks for correctness, but it is not supposed to validate them—this is reserved for the XMLVALIDATE function. At present there is only a preliminary proposal, which indicates that the function should work as in the following modification of the above example:

```
INSERT INTO StudentXML(Id, Details)
VALUES ( 123987456,
         XMLVALIDATE(XMLPARSE(
            '<Student>
               <Name><First>John</First><Last>Doe</Last></Name>
                  <Status>U2</Status>
                  <CrsTaken CrsCode="CS310" Semester="F2003"/>
                  <CrsTaken CrsCode="CS305" Semester="F2003"/>
            </Student>' ) )
         )
```

The result is the same as in the previous case, except that the XML document will be stored in the database only if it is validated against an appropriate schema document. If the XML document includes the mention of the corresponding schema document, the above scenario would be adequate. This is not the case, however, in our example. In the future, presumably there will be an option to provide the location of an XML Schema document to validate against.

It is also expected that a future release of SQL/XML will include primitives for direct modification of documents stored using the XML data type.

The function XMLSERIALIZE.   This function is less relevant to update operations, but it is appropriate to mention it here since it is the reverse of XMLPARSE. It takes a document of the XML data type and returns a string representation of that document.

One scenario in which this might be useful is when you want (for some reason) to store a copy of an XML document as a string. A more common case, however, is when SQL is embedded in a host language, such as C or C++, that does not understand XML. In this case, the embedded SQL query might need to convert the XML output into a string before the host program can deal with it. In the following example, we declare a cursor for query (17.8), which previously returned tuples with native XML documents in them. The only difference now is the use of the XMLSERIALIZE function.

```
EXEC SQL DECLARE GetEnrolled CURSOR FOR
    SELECT   S.Id, XMLSERIALIZE(XMLEXTRACT(S.Details, '//Name'))
    FROM     StudentXML S
    WHERE    XMLEXISTS(S.Details, '//CrsTaken')
```

Since the XML documents, which are returned by the XPath expression '//Name', are now converted to strings, we can process each tuple in the result one by one using the following statement:

```
EXEC SQL FETCH GetEnrolled INTO :studId, :details;
```

BIBLIOGRAPHIC NOTES

The semistructured data model had an important influence on a number of developments in the XML arena, especially on XML query languages. A more in-depth study of semistructured data can be found in [Abiteboul et al. 2000].

XML came as a result of an effort to bring some order to Web information processing. Conceptually, it is a rewrite and a simplification of the well-established SGML standard [SGML 1986]. Version 1 was approved in 1998 and became a widely accepted standard [XML 1998]. As with every new hot topic, many publications appeared in a short period of time. There are too many to list here, so we mention just two recent ones, [Ray 2001; Bradley 2000a].

XML Schema is covered in a number of books, but, because it was a moving target until recently, we recommend the authoritative sources [XMLSchema 2000a; XMLSchema 2000b].

XPath, the XML path expression language, is described in most recent publications on XML. The official W3C recommendation can be found in [XPath 1999]. The original idea of path expressions comes from [Zaniolo 1983]. The idea of enhancing path expressions with query capability was developed by [Kifer and Lausen 1989; Kifer et al. 1992; Frohn et al. 1994; Abiteboul et al. 1997; Deutsch et al. 1998] and others.

SQL/XML is a standard in the making, which will eventually be incorporated into SQL:2003. A number of relational vendors already support parts of this specification. Details on the SQL/XML standardization activity and the current document drafts can be found at *http://www.sqlx.org/*.

Two other important XML query languages, which have not been discussed here but are found in the full version of this book [Kifer et al. 2004], are XSLT [XSLT 1999] and XQuery [XQuery 2004].

EXERCISES

17.1 Use XML to represent the contents of the STUDENT relation in Figure 3.2, page 36. Specify a DTD appropriate for this document. Do *not* use the representation proposed by the SQL/XML specification discussed in Section 17.4.2.

17.2 Specify a DTD appropriate for a document that contains data from both the COURSE table in Figure 4.34, page 116, and the REQUIRES table in Figure 4.35, page 117. Try to reflect as many constraints as the DTDs allow. Give an example of a document that conforms to your DTD.

17.3 Restructure the document in Figure 17.4, page 578, so as to completely replace the elements Name, Status, CrsCode, Semester, and CrsName with attributes in the appropriate tags. Provide a DTD suitable for this document. Specify all applicable ID and IDREF constraints.

17.4 Define the following simple types:
 a. A type whose domain consists of lists of strings, where each list consists of 7 elements
 b. A type whose domain consists of lists of strings, where each string is of length 7
 c. A type whose domain is a set of lists of strings, where each string has between 7 and 10 characters and each list has between 7 and 10 elements
 d. A type appropriate for the letter grades that students receive on completion of a course—A, A−, B+, B, B−, C+, C, C−, D, and F. Express this type in two different ways: as an enumeration and using the pattern tag of XML Schema.

17.5 Use the key statement of XML Schema to define the following key constraints for the document in Figure 17.4:
 a. The key for the collection of all Student elements
 b. The key for the collection of all Course elements
 c. The key for the collection of all Class elements

17.6 Assume that any student in the document of Figure 17.4 on page 578 is uniquely identified by the last name and the status. Define this key constraint.

17.7 Use the keyref statement of XML Schema to define the following referential integrity for the document in Figure 17.4:

 a. Every course code in a CourseTaken element must refer to a valid course.
 b. Every course code in a Class element must refer to a valid course.

17.8 Express the following constraint on the document of Figure 17.4: no pair of CourseTaken elements within the same Student element can have identical values of the CrsCode attribute.

17.9   Rearrange the structure of the Class element in Figure 17.4 so that it becomes possible to define the following referential integrity: every student Id mentioned in a Class element references a student from the same document.

17.10 Write a unified XML schema that covers both documents in Figures 17.15 and 17.16. Provide the appropriate key and foreign-key constraints.

17.11 Use XML Schema to represent the fragment of the relational schema in Figure 3.6, page 43. Include all key and foreign-key constraints.

17.12 Use XPath to express the following queries to the document in Figure 17.15:

　　a. Find all Student elements whose Ids end with 987 and who have taken MAT123.
　　b. Find all Student elements whose first names are Joe and who have taken fewer than three courses.
　　c. Find all CrsTaken elements that correspond to semester S1996 and that belong to students whose names begin with P.

FIGURE 17.15 Transcripts at `http://xyz.edu/transcripts.xml`.

```
<?xml version="1.0" ?>
<Transcripts>
    <Transcript>
        <Student StudId="s111111111" Name="John Doe"/>
        <CrsTaken CrsCode="CS308" Semester="F1997" Grade="B"/>
        <CrsTaken CrsCode="MAT123" Semester="F1997" Grade="B"/>
        <CrsTaken CrsCode="EE101" Semester"F1997" Grade="A"/>
        <CrsTaken CrsCode="CS305" Semester="F1995" Grade="A"/>
    </Transcript>
    <Transcript>
        <Student StudId="s987654321" Name="Bart Simpson"/>
        <CrsTaken CrsCode="CS305" Semester="F1995" Grade="C"/>
        <CrsTaken CrsCode="CS308" Semester="F1994" Grade="B"/>
    </Transcript>
    <Transcript>
        <Student StudId="s123454321" Name="Joe Blow"/>
        <CrsTaken CrsCode="CS315" Semester="S1997" Grade="A"/>
        <CrsTaken CrsCode="CS305" Semester="S1996" Grade="A"/>
        <CrsTaken CrsCode="MAT123" Semester="S1996" Grade="C"/>
    </Transcript>
    <Transcript>
        <Student StudId="s023456789" Name="Homer Simpson"/>
        <CrsTaken CrsCode="EE101" Semester="F1995" Grade="B"/>
        <CrsTaken CrsCode="CS305" Semester="S1996" Grade="A"/>
    </Transcript>
</Transcripts>
```

FIGURE 17.16 Classes at `http://xyz.edu/classes.xml`.

```
<?xml version="1.0" ?>
<Classes>
    <Class CrsCode="CS308" Semester="F1997">
        <CrsName>Software Engineering</CrsName>
        <Instructor>Adrian Jones</Instructor>
    </Class>
    <Class CrsCode="EE101" Semester="F1995">
        <CrsName>Electronic Circuits</CrsName>
        <Instructor>David Jones</Instructor>
    </Class>
    <Class CrsCode="CS305" Semester="F1995">
        <CrsName>Database Systems</CrsName>
        <Instructor>Mary Doe</Instructor>
    </Class>
    <Class CrsCode="CS315" Semester="S1997">
        <CrsName>Transaction Processing</CrsName>
        <Instructor>John Smyth</Instructor>
    </Class>
    <Class CrsCode="MAT123" Semester="F1997">
        <CrsName>Algebra</CrsName>
        <Instructor>Ann White</Instructor>
    </Class>
</Classes>
```

17.13 Formulate the following XPath queries for the document in Figure 17.16:

a. Find the names of all courses taught by Mary Doe in fall 1995.
b. Find the set of all document nodes that correspond to the course names taught in fall 1996 or all instructors who taught MAT123.
c. Find the set of all course codes taught by John Smyth in spring 1997.

17.14 Write an XML Schema specification for a simple document that lists stockbrokers with the accounts that they handle and lists client accounts separately. The information about the accounts includes the account Id, ownership information, and the account positions (i.e., stocks held in that account). To simplify matters, it suffices to list the stock symbol and quantity for each account position. Use ID, IDREF, and IDREFS to specify referential integrity.

17.15 Write a sample XML document, which contains

- A list of parts (part name and Id)
- A list of suppliers (supplier name and Id)
- A list of projects; for each project element, a nested list of subelements that represent the parts used in that project. Include the information on who supplies that part and in what quantity.

Write a DTD for this document and an XML Schema. Express all key and referential constraints.

Choose your representation in such a way as to maximize the number of possible key and referential constraints representable using DTDs.

17.16 Consider the relational schema in Figure 3.6, page 43. Assume that the contents of these relations are stored in a single XML column of a relation using the following XML format: the name of the relation is the top-level element, each tuple is represented as a `tuple` element, and each relation attribute is represented as an empty element that has a `value` attribute. For instance, the STUDENT relation would be represented as follows:

```
<Student>
    <tuple>
        <Id value="s111111111"/> <Name value="John Doe"/>
        <Address value="123 Main St."/> <Status value="U1"/>
    </tuple>
        .
        .
        .
</Student>
```

Formulate the following queries in SQL/XML:

(a) Create the list of all professors who ever taught MAT123. The information must include all attributes available from the PROFESSOR relation.

(b) Create the list of all courses in which Joe Public received an A.

(c) Create the list of all students (include student Id and name) who have taken a course from John Smyth and received an A.

17.17 Consider an SQL/XML database schema that consists of two relations:

- The SUPPLIER relation has the following attributes:
  - Id, an integer
  - Name, a string
  - Address, an XML type appropriate for addresses
  - Parts, an XML type that represents the parts supplied by the supplier. Each part has Id, Name, and Price.
- The PROJECT relation has the following attributes:
  - Project Name, a string
  - Project Members, an appropriate XML type
  - Project Parts, an XML type. This attribute represents the list of parts used by the project and supplied by a supplier. Each part has an Id, a Name, and a SupplierId.

Use SQL/XML to define the database schema. Make sure that a CHECK constraint validates the XML documents inserted into the database using appropriate XML Schema document. Then answer the following queries:

(a) Find all projects that are supplied by Acme Inc. and that have Joe Public as a member.

(b) Find all projects that are *not* supplied by Acme Inc., that is, none of the parts used by the project comes from Acme Inc.

(c) Find all project members who participate in every project.

(d) Find the projects with the highest number of members.

17.18 Consider the database depicted in Figure 3.5 on page 39. Use SQL/XML to answer the following queries:

(a) Based on the relation TRANSCRIPT, output the same information in a different format. The output should have two attributes: StudId and Courses, where Courses should have XML type similar to the one used throughout this chapter for the CourseTaken element (e.g., as in Figure 17.4).

(b) Repeat the previous query, but use TEACHING instead. The output should have the attributes ProfId and Courses. The latter should have XML type and should describe the courses that the professor with the given ProfId has even taught.

(c) Produce a list of professors (Id and Name) along with the list of courses that professor teaches in spring 2004. The list of courses should have the XML type and should include CrsCode and DeptId as attributes of an element and CrsName as a text node.

(d) For each course, produce a list of the professors who have ever taught it. The professor list should have the XML type. Choose your own schema.

(e) Repeat the previous query, but output only the courses that have the greatest number of professors who have taught it.

Bibliography

Abiteboul, S., Buneman, P., and Suciu, D. (2000). *Data on the Web*. Morgan Kaufmann, San Francisco.

Abiteboul, S., Hull, R., and Vianu, V. (1995). *Foundations of Databases*. Addison-Wesley, Boston, MA.

Abiteboul, S., Quass, D., McHugh, J., Widom, J., and Wiener, J. (1997). The Lorel query language for semistructured data. *International Journal on Digital Libraries* **1**(1): 68–88.

Arisawa, H., Moriya, K., and Miura, T. (1983). Operations and the properties of non-first-normal-form relational databases. *Proceedings of the International Conference on Very Large Data Bases (VLDB)*, Florence, 197–204.

Armstrong, W. (1974). Dependency structures of database relations. *IFIP Congress*, Stockholm, 580–583.

Astrahan, M., Blasgen, M., Gray, J., King, W., Lindsay, B., Lorie, R., Mehl, J., Price, T., Selinger, P., Schkolnick, M., Traiger, D. S. I., and Yost, R. (1981). A history and evaluation of System R. *Communications of the ACM* **24**(10): 632–646.

Atzeni, P., and Antonellis, V. D. (1993). *Relational Database Theory*. Benjamin-Cummings, San Francisco.

Bancilhon, F., Delobel, C., and Kanellakis, P. (eds.) (1990). *Building an Object-Oriented Database System: The Story of O2*. Morgan Kaufmann, San Francisco.

Bancilhon, F., and Spyratos, N. (1981). Update semantics of relational views. *ACM Transactions on Database Systems* **6**(4): 557–575.

Batini, C., Ceri, S., and Navathe, S. (1992). *Database Design: An Entity Relationship Approach*. Benjamin-Cummings, San Francisco.

Bayer, R., and McCreight, E. (1972). Organization and maintenance of large ordered indices. *Acta Informatica* **1**(3): 173–189.

Beeri, C., and Bernstein, P. (1979). Computational problems related to the design of normal form relational schemes. *ACM Transactions on Database Systems* **4**(1): 30–59.

Beeri, C., Bernstein, P., and Goodman, N. (1978). A sophisticate's introduction to database normalization theory. *Proceedings of the International Conference on Very Large Data Bases (VLDB)*, San Mateo, CA, 113–124.

Beeri, C., Fagin, R., and Howard, J. (1977). A complete axiomatization for functional and multivalued dependencies in database relations. *Proceedings of the ACM SIGMOD International Conference on Management of Data*, Toronto, Canada, 47–61.

Beeri, C., and Kifer, M. (1986a). Elimination of intersection anomalies from database schemes. *Journal of the ACM* **33**(3): 423–450.

Beeri, C., and Kifer, M. (1986b). An integrated approach to logical design of relational database schemes. *ACM Transactions on Database Systems* **11**(2): 134–158.

Beeri, C., and Kifer, M. (1987). A theory of intersection anomalies in relational database schemes. *Journal of the ACM* **34**(3): 544–577.

Beeri, C., Mendelson, A., Sagiv, Y., and Ullman, J. (1981). Equivalence of relational database schemes. *SIAM Journal of Computing* **10**(2): 352–370.

Bernstein, P. (1976). Synthesizing third normal form from functional dependencies. *ACM Transactions on Database Systems* **1**(4): 277–298.

Bernstein, P., and Newcomer, E. (1997). *Principles of Transaction Processing*. Morgan Kaufmann, San Francisco.

Biskup, J., Menzel, R., and Polle, T. (1996). Transforming an entity-relationship schema into object-oriented database schemas. In J. Eder and L. Kalinichenko (eds.), *Advances in Databases and Information Systems*, Workshops in Computing. Springer-Verlag, Moscow, Russia, 109–136.

Biskup, J., Menzel, R., Polle, T., and Sagiv, Y. (1996). Decomposition of relationships through pivoting. *Proceedings of the 15th International Conference on Conceptual Modeling*. In Vol. 1157 of *Lecture Notes in Computer Science*. Springer-Verlag, Heidelberg, Germany, 28–41.

Biskup, J., and Polle, T. (2000a). *Constraints in Object-Oriented Databases* (manuscript).

Biskup, J., and Polle, T. (2000b). Decomposition of database classes under path functional dependencies and onto constraints. *Proceedings of the Foundations of Information and Knowledge-Base Systems*. In Vol. 1762 of *Lecture Notes in Computer Science*. Springer-Verlag, Heidelberg, Germany, 31–49.

Blaha, M., and Premerlani, W. (1998). *Object-Oriented Modeling and Design for Database Applications*. Prentice Hall, Englewood Cliffs, NJ.

Blakeley, J., and Martin, N. (1990). Join index, materialized view, and hybrid-hash join: A performance analysis. *Proceedings of the International Conference on Data Engineering (ICDE)*, Los Angeles, 256–263.

Blasgen, M., and Eswaran, K. (1977). Storage access in relational databases. *IBM Systems Journal* **16**(4): 363–378.

Booch, G. (1994). *Object-oriented Analysis and Design with Applications*. Addison-Wesley, Boston, MA.

Booch, G., Rumbaugh, J., and Jacobson, I. (1999). *The Unified Modeling Language User Guide*. Addison-Wesley, Boston, MA.

Bourret, R. (2000). Namespace myths exploded. *http://www.xml.com/pub/a/2000/03/08/namespaces/index.html*.

Bradley, N. (2000a). *The XML Companion*. Addison-Wesley, Boston, MA.

Bray, T., Hollander, D., and Layman A. (1999). *http://www.w3.org/TR/1999/REC-xml-names-19990114/*.

Buneman, P., Davidson, S., Hillebrand, G., and Suciu, D. (1996). A query language and optimization techniques for unstructured data. *Proceedings of the ACM SIGMOD International Conference on Management of Data*, Montreal, Canada, 505–516.

Cattell, R., and Barry, D. (eds.) (2000). *The Object Database Standard: ODMG 3.0*. Morgan Kaufmann, San Francisco.

Ceri, S., Negri, M., and Pelagatti, G. (1982). Horizontal partitioning in database design. *Proceedings of the International ACM SIGMOD Conference on Management of Data*, Orlando, FL, 128–136.

Ceri, S., and Pelagatti, G. (1984). *Distributed Databases: Principles and Systems*. McGraw-Hill, New York.

Chaudhuri, S. (1998). An overview of query optimization in relational databases. *ACM SIGACT-SIGMOD-SIGART Symposium on Principles of Database Systems (PODS)*, Seattle, 34–43.

Chaudhuri, S., Krishnamurthy, R., Potamianos, S., and Shim, K. (1995). Optimizing queries with materialized views. *Proceedings of the International Conference on Data Engineering (ICDE)*, Taipei, Taiwan, 190–200.

Chen, I.-M., Hull, R., and McLeod, D. (1995). An execution model for limited ambiguity rules and its application to derived data update. *ACM Transactions on Database Systems* **20**(4): 365–413.

Chen, P. (1976). The Entity-Relationship Model—Towards a unified view of data. *ACM Transactions on Database Systems* **1**(1): 9–36.

Cochrane, R., Pirahesh, H., and Mattos, N. (1996). Integrating triggers and declarative constraints in SQL database systems. *Proceedings of the International Conference on Very Large Data Bases (VLDB)*, Bombay, India, 567–578.

Codd, E. (1970). A relational model of data for large shared data banks. *Communications of the ACM* **13**(6): 377–387.

Codd, E. (1972). Relational completeness of data base sublanguages. *Data Base Systems*. In Vol. 6 of *Courant Computer Science Symposia Series*. Prentice Hall, Englewood Cliffs, NJ.

Codd, E. (1979). Extending the database relational model to capture more meaning. *ACM Transactions on Database Systems* **4**(4): 397–434.

Codd, E. (1990). *The Relational Model for Database Management, Version 2*. Addison-Wesley, Boston, MA.

Copeland, G., and Maier, D. (1984). Making Smalltalk a database system. *Proceedings of the ACM SIGMOD International Conference on Management of Data*, Boston, 316–325.

Cosmadakis, S., and Papadimitriou, C. (1983). Updates of relational views. *ACM SIGACT-SIGMOD-SIGART Symposium on Principles of Database Systems (PODS)*, Atlanta, 317–331.

Date, C., and Darwen, H. (1997). *A Guide to the SQL Standard*. (4th ed.). Addison-Wesley, Boston, MA.

Deutsch, A., Fernandez, M., Florescu, D., Levy, A., and Suciu, D. (1998). XML-QL: A query language for XML. *Technical Report W3C. http://www.w3.org/TR/1998/NOTE-xml-ql-19980819/.*

Deutsch, A., Fernandez, M., and Suciu, D. (1999). Storing semistructured data with stored. *Proceedings of the ACM SIGMOD International Conference on Management of Data*, Philadelphia, 431–442.

DeWitt, D., Katz, R., Olken, F., Shapiro, L., Stonebraker, M., and Wood, D. (1984). Implementation techniques for main-memory database systems. *Proceedings of the ACM SIGMOD International Conference on Management of Data*, Boston, 1–8.

DOM (2000). Document Object Model (DOM). *http://www.w3.org/DOM/.*

Eisenberg, A. (1996). New standard for stored procedures in SQL. *SIGMOD Record* **25**(4): 81–88.

Eswaran, K., Gray, J., Lorie, R., and Traiger, I. (1976). The notions of consistency and predicate locks in a database system. *Communications of the ACM* **19**(11): 624–633.

Fagin, R. (1977). Multivalued dependencies and a new normal form for relational databases. *ACM Transactions on Database Systems* **2**(3): 262–278.

Fagin, R., Nievergelt, J., Pippenger, N., and Strong, H. (1979). Extendible hashing—A fast access method for dynamic files. *ACM Transactions on Database Systems* **4**(3): 315–344.

Flach, P. A., and Savnik, I. (1999). Database dependency discovery: A machine learning approach. *AI Communications* **12**(3): 139–160.

Fowler, M., and Scott, K. (2003). *UML Distilled,* 3rd ed. Addison-Wesley, Boston, MA.

Frohn, J., Lausen, G., and Uphoff, H. (1994). Access to objects by path expressions and rules. *Proceedings of the International Conference on Very Large Data Bases (VLDB)*, Santiago, Chile, 273–284.

Garcia-Molina, H., Ullman, J., and Widom, J. (2000). *Database System Implementation,* Prentice Hall, Englewood Cliffs, NJ.

Gogola, M., Herzig, R., Conrad, S., Denker, G., and Vlachantonis, N. (1993). Integrating the E-R approach in an object-oriented environment. *Proceedings of the 12th International Conference on the Entity-Relationship Approach*, Arlington, TX, 376–389.

Gottlob, G., Paolini, P., and Zicari, R. (1988). Properties and update semantics of consistent views. *ACM Transactions on Database Systems* **13**(4): 486–524.

Graefe, G. (1993). Query evaluation techniques for large databases. *ACM Computing Surveys* **25**(2): 73–170.

Gray, J. (1978). Notes on database operating systems. *Operating Systems: An Advanced Course*. In Vol. 60 of *Lecture Notes in Computer Science*, Springer-Verlag, Berlin, 393–481.

Gray, J., Laurie, R., Putzolu, G., and Traiger, I. (1976). Granularity of locks and degrees of consistency in a shared database. *Modeling in Data Base Management Systems*, Elsevier, North Holland.

Gray, J., and Reuter, A. (1993). *Transaction Processing: Concepts and Techniques*. Morgan Kaufmann, San Francisco.

Griffiths-Selinger, P., Astrahan, M., Chamberlin, D., Lorie, R., and Price, T. (1979). Access path selection in a relational database system. *Proceedings of the ACM SIGMOD International Conference on Management of Data*, Boston, 23–34.

Gulutzan, P., and Pelzer, T. (1999). *SQL-99 Complete, Really*. R&D Books, Gilroy, CA.

Gupta, A., and Mumick, I. (1995). Maintenance of materialized views: Problems, techniques, and applications. *Data Engineering Bulletin* **18**(2): 3–18.

Gupta, A., Mumick, I., and Ross, K. (1995). Adapting materialized views after redefinitions. *Proceedings of the ACM SIGMOD International Conference on Management of Data*, San Jose, CA, 211–222.

Gupta, A., Mumick, I., and Subrahmanian, V. (1993). Maintaining views incrementally. *Proceedings of the ACM SIGMOD International Conference on Management of Data*, Washington, DC, 157–166.

Haerder, T., and Reuter, A. (1983). Principles of transaction-oriented database recovery. *ACM Computing Surveys* **15**(4): 287–317.

Harrison, G. (2001) *Oracle SQL: High-Performance Tuning* (2nd ed.). Prentice Hall, Upper Saddle River, New Jersey

Huhtala, Y., Karkkainen, J., Porkka, P., and Toivonen, H. (1999). TANE: An efficient algorithm for discovery of functional and approximate dependencies. *The Computer Journal* **42**(2): 100–111.

Ioannidis, Y. (1996). Query optimization. *ACM Computing Surveys* **28**(1): 121–123.

Ito, M., and Weddell, G. (1994). Implication problems for functional constraints on databases supporting complex objects. *Journal of Computer and System Sciences* **49**(3): 726–768.

Jacobson, I., Christerson, M., Jonsson, P., and Övergaard, G. (1992). *Object-Oriented Software Engineering: A Use Case Driven Approach*. Addison-Wesley, Boston, MA.

Jaeschke, G., and Schek, H.-J. (1982). Remarks on the algebra of non-first-normal-form-relations. *ACM SIGACT-SIGMOD-SIGART Symposium on Principles of Database Systems (PODS)*, Los Angeles, 124–138.

Kanellakis, P. (1990). Elements of relational database theory. In J. V. Leeuwen (ed.), *Handbook of Theoretical Computer Science*, Vol. B, *Formal Models and Semantics*. Elsevier, Amsterdam, 1073–1156.

Kantola, M., Mannila, H., Raäihä, K.-J., and Siirtola, H. (1992). Discovering functional and inclusion dependencies in relational databases. *International Journal of Intelligent Systems* **7**(7): 591–607.

Keller, A. (1985). Algorithms for translating view updates to database updates for views involving selections, projections, and joins. *ACM SIGACT-SIGMOD-SIGART Symposium on Principles of Database Systems (PODS)*, Portland, OR, 154–163.

Kifer, M., Kim, W., and Sagiv, Y. (1992). Querying object-oriented databases. *Proceedings of the ACM SIGMOD International Conference on Management of Data*, Washington, DC, 393–402.

Kifer, M., Bernstein, A. J., and Lewis, P. M. (2004). *Databases and Transaction Processing: An Application-Oriented Approach*. Addison-Wesley, Boston, MA.

Kifer, M., and Lausen, G. (1989). F-Logic: A higher-order language for reasoning about objects, inheritance and schema. *Proceedings of the ACM SIGMOD International Conference on Management of Data*, Portland, OR, 134–146.

Kifer, M., Lausen, G., and Wu, J. (1995). Logical foundations of object-oriented and frame-based languages. *Journal of the ACM* **42**(4): 741–843.

Kitsuregawa, M., Tanaka, H., and Moto-oka, T. (1983). Application of hash to database machine and its architecture. *New Generation Computing* **1**(1): 66–74.

Knuth, D. (1973). *The Art of Computer Programming: Vol III, Sorting and Searching,* (1st ed.), Addison-Wesley, Boston, MA.

Knuth, D. (1998). *The Art of Computer Programming: Vol III, Sorting and Searching*, (3rd ed.), Addison-Wesley, Boston, MA.

Lampson, B., Paul, M., and Seigert, H. (1981). *Distributed Systems: Architecture and Implementation (An Advanced Course)*. Springer-Verlag, Heidelberg, Germany.

Lampson, B., and Sturgis, H. (1979). Crash recovery in a distributed data storage system. *Technical Report*. Xerox Palo Alto Research Center, Palo Alto, CA.

Langerak, R. (1990). View updates in relational databases with an independent scheme. *ACM Transactions on Database Systems* **15**(1): 40–66.

Larson, P. (1981). Analysis of index sequential files with overflow chaining. *ACM Transactions on Database Systems* **6**(4): 671–680.

Litwin, W. (1980). Linear hashing: A new tool for file and table addressing. *Proceedings of the International Conference on Very Large Databases (VLDB)*, Montreal, Canada, 212–223.

Maier, D. (1983). *The Theory of Relational Databases*. Computer Science Press. Rockville, MD. (Available through Books on Demand: *http://www.umi.com/hp/Support/BOD /index.html.*)

Makinouchi, A. (1977). A consideration on normal form of not-necessarily-normalized relations in the relational data model. *Proceedings of the International Conference on Very Large Data Bases (VLDB)*, Tokyo, Japan, 447–453.

Mannila, H., and Raäihä, K.-J. (1992). *The Design of Relational Databases*. Addison-Wesley, Workingham, U.K.

Mannila, H., and Raäihä, K.-J. (1994). Algorithms for inferring functional dependencies. *Knowledge Engineering* **12**(1): 83–99.

Maslak, B., Showalter, J., and Szczygielski, T. (1991). Coordinated resource recovery in VM/ESA. *IBM Systems Journal* **30**(1): 72–89.

Masunaga, Y. (1984). A relational database view update translation mechanism. *Proceedings of the International Conference on Very Large Data Bases (VLDB)*, Singapore, 309–320.

Melton, J. (1997). *Understanding SQL's Persistent Stored Modules*. Morgan Kaufmann, San Francisco.

Melton, J., Eisenberg, A., and Cattell, R. (2000). *Understanding SQL and Java Together: A Guide to SQLJ, JDBC, and Related Technologies*. Morgan Kaufmann, San Francisco.

Melton, J., and Simon, A. (1992). *Understanding the New SQL: A Complete Guide*. Morgan Kaufmann, San Francisco.

Microsoft (1997). *Microsoft ODBC 3.0 Software Development Kit and Programmer's Reference*. Microsoft Press, Seattle.

Missaoui, R., Gagnon, J.-M., and Godin, R. (1995). Mapping an extended entity-relationship schema into a schema of complex objects. *Proceedings of the 14th International Conference on Object-Oriented and Entity Relationship Modeling*, Brisbane, Australia, 205–215.

Mohania, M., Konomi, S., and Kambayashi, Y. (1997). Incremental maintenance of materialized views. *Database and Expert Systems Applications (DEXA)*. Springer-Verlag, Heidelberg, Germany.

Mok, W., Ng, Y.-K., and Embley, D. (1996). A normal form for precisely characterizing redundancy in nested relations. *ACM Transactions on Database Systems* **21**(1): 77–106.

O'Neil, P. (1987). Model 204: Architecture and performance. *Proceedings of the International Workshop on High Performance Transaction Systems*. In Vol. 359 of *Lecture Notes in Computer Science*. Springer-Verlag, Heidelberg, Germany, 40–59.

O'Neil, P., and Graefe, G. (1995). Multi-table joins through bitmapped join indices. *SIGMOD Record* **24**(3): 8–11.

O'Neil, P., and Quass, D. (1997). Improved query performance with variant indexes. *Proceedings of the ACM SIGMOD International Conference on Management of Data*, Tucson, 38–49.

Ozsoyoglu, Z., and Yuan, L.-Y. (1985). A normal form for nested relations. *ACM SIGACT-SIGMOD-SIGART Symposium on Principles of Database Systems (PODS)*, Portland, OR, 251–260.

Paton, N., Diaz, O., Williams, M., Campin, J., Dinn, A., and Jaime, A. (1993). Dimensions of active behavior. *Proceedings of the Workshop on Rules in Database Systems*, Heidelberg, Germany, 40–57.

Peterson, W. (1957). Addressing for random access storage. *IBM Journal of Research and Development* **1**(2): 130–146.

PostgreSQL (2000). PostgreSQL. *http://www.postgresql.org*.

Pressman, R. (2002). *Software Engineering: A Practitioner's Approach,* 5th ed. McGraw-Hill, New York.

Ram, S. (1995). Deriving functional dependencies from the entity-relationship model. *Communications of the ACM* **38**(9): 95–107.

Ray, E. (2001). *Learning XML*. O'Reilly and Associates, Sebastopol, CA.

Reese, G. (2000). *Database Programming with JDBC and Java*. O'Reilly and Associates, Sebastopol, CA.

Roth, M., and Korth, H. (1987). The design of non-1nf relational databases into nested normal form. *Proceedings of the ACM SIGMOD International Conference on Management of Data*, San Francisco, 143–159.

Rumbaugh, J., Blaha, M., Premerlani, W., Eddy, F., and Lorenzen, W. (1991). *Object-Oriented Modeling and Design*. Prentice Hall, Englewood Cliffs, NJ.

Savnik, I., and Flach, P. (1993). Bottom-up induction of functional dependencies from relations. *Proceedings of the AAAI Knowledge Discovery in Databases Workshop (KDD)*, Ljubliana, Slovenija, 174–185.

Schach, S. (1999). *Software Engineering,* 5th ed. Aksen Associates, Homewood, IL.

Sciore, E. (1983). Improving database schemes by adding attributes. *ACM SIGACT-SIGMOD-SIGART Symposium on Principles of Database Systems (PODS)*, New York, 379–383.

SGML (1986). Information processing—text and office systems—Standard Generalized Markup Language (SGML). *ISO Standard 8879*. International Standards Organization, Geneva, Switzerland.

Shasha, D., and Bonnet, P. (2003). *Database Tuning: Principles, Experiments and Troubleshooting Techniques*. Morgan Kaufman, San Francisco.

Signore, R., Creamer, J., and Stegman, M. (1995). *The ODBC Solution: Open Database Connectivity in Distributed Environments*. McGraw-Hill, New York.

Spaccapietra, S. (ed.) (1987). *Entity-Relationship Approach: Ten Years of Experience in Information Modeling, Proceedings of the Entity-Relationship Conference*, Elsevier, North Holland.

SQL (1992). ANSI X3.135-1992, *American National Standard for Information Systems—Database Language—SQL*. American National Standards Institute, Washington, DC.

SQLJ (2000). SQLJ. *http://www.sqlj.org*.

Stallman, R. (2000). GNU coding standards. *http://www.gnu.org/prep/standards.html*.

Standish (2000). Chaos. *http://standishgroup.com/visitor/chaos.htm*.

Staudt, M., and Jarke, M. (1996). Incremental maintenance of externally materialized views. *Proceedings of the International Conference on Very Large Data Bases (VLDB)*, Bombay, India, 75–86.

Stonebraker, M. (1979). Concurrency control and consistency of multiple copies of data in INGRES. *IEEE Transactions on Software Engineering* **5**(3): 188–194.

Stonebraker, M. (1986). *The INGRES Papers: Anatomy of a Relational Database System*. Addison-Wesley, Boston, MA.

Stonebreaker, M., and Kemnitz, G. (1991). The POSTGRES next generation database management system. *Communications of the ACM* **10**(34): 78–92.

Summerville, I. (2000). *Software Engineering,* 5th ed. Addison-Wesley, Boston, MA.

Sun (2000). JDBC data access API. *http://java.sun.com/products/jdbc/*.

Sybase (1999). Sybase Adaptive Server Enterprise Performance and Tuning Guide. *http://sybooks.sybase.com/onlinebooks/group-as/asg1200e/aseperf*.

Teorey, T. (1999). *Database Modeling and Design: The E-R Approach*. Morgan Kaufmann, San Francisco.

Thalheim, B. (1992). *Fundamentals of Entity-Relationship Modeling*. Springer-Verlag, Berlin.

Ullman, J. (1988). *Principles of Database and Knowledge-Base Systems,* Volumes 1 and 2. Computer Science Press, Rockville, MD.

Valduriez, P. (1987). Join indices. *ACM Transactions on Database Systems* **12**(2): 218–246.

Venkatrao, M., and Pizzo, M. (1995). SQL/CLI—A new binding style for SQL. *SIGMOD Record* **24**(4): 72–77.

Vincent, M. (1999). Semantic foundations of 4nf in relational database design. *Acta Informatica* **36**(3): 173–213.

Vincent, M., and Srinivasan, B. (1993). Redundancy and the justification for fourth normal form in relational databases. *International Journal of Foundations of Computer Science* **4**(4): 355–365.

Weddell, G. (1992). Reasoning about functional dependencies generalized for semantic data models. *ACM Transactions on Database Systems* **17**(1): 32–64.

Weihl, W. (1984). *Specification and Implementation of Atomic Data Types*. Ph.D. thesis, Department of Computer Science, Massachusetts Institute of Technology, Cambridge, MA.

Whalen, G., Garcia, M., DeLuca, S., and Thompson, D. (2001). *Microsoft SQL Server 2000 Performance Tuning Technical Reference*. Microsoft Press, Redmond, Washington.

Widom, J., and Ceri, S. (1996). *Active Database Systems*. Morgan Kaufmann, San Francisco.

Wong, E., and Youssefi, K. (1976). Decomposition—A strategy for query processing. *ACM Transactions on Database Systems* **1**(3): 223–241.

XML (1998). Extensible Markup Language (XML) 1.0. *http://www.w3.org/TR/REC-xml*.

XMLSchema (2000a). XML Schema, part 0: Primer. *http://www.w3.org/TR/xmlschema-0/*.

XMLSchema (2000b). XML Schema, parts 1 and 2. *http://www.w3.org/XML/Schema*.

XPath (1999). XML path language (XPath), version 1.0. *http://www.w3.org/TR/xpath/*.

XQuery (2004). XQuery 1.0: An XML query language. Eds: S. Boag, D. Chamberlin, M. F. Fenrandez, D. Florescu, T. Robie, and T. Simeon. *http://www.w3.org/TR/xquery*.

XSLT (1999). XSL transformations (XSLT), version 1.0. *http://www.w3.org/TR/xslt/*.

Zaniolo, C. (1983). The database language GEM. *Proceedings of the ACM SIGMOD International Conference on Management of Data*, San Jose, CA, 423–434.

Zaniolo, C., and Melkanoff, M. (1981). On the design of relational database schemata. *ACM Transactions on Database Systems* **6**(1): 1–47.

Zhao, B., and Joseph, A. (2000). XSet: A lightweight XML search engine for Internet applications. *http://www.cs.berkeley.edu/~ravenben/xset/*.

Index